# The Aims of Argument

**FOURTH EDITION**

# The Aims of Argument

## A TEXT AND READER

**Timothy W. Crusius**
*Southern Methodist University*

**Carolyn E. Channell**
*Southern Methodist University*

Boston   Burr Ridge, IL   Dubuque, IA   Madison, WI   New York
San Francisco   St. Louis   Bangkok   Bogotá   Caracas   Kuala Lumpur
Lisbon   London   Madrid   Mexico City   Milan   Montreal   New Delhi
Santiago   Seoul   Singapore   Sydney   Taipei   Toronto

# McGraw-Hill Higher Education

## A Division of The McGraw-Hill Companies

*The Aims of Argument: A Text and Reader*

Published by McGraw-Hill, an imprint of The McGraw-Hill Companies, Inc., 1221 Avenue of the Americas, New York, NY 10020. Copyright © 2003, 2000, 1998, 1995 by The McGraw-Hill Companies, Inc. All rights reserved. No part of this publication may be reproduced or distributed in any form or by any means, or stored in a database or retrieval system, without the prior written consent of The McGraw-Hill Companies, Inc., including, but not limited to, in any network or other electronic storage or transmission, or broadcast for distance learning.

This book is printed on acid-free paper.

1 2 3 4 5 6 7 8 9 0 FGR/FGR 0 9 8 7 6 5 4 3

ISBN 0-07-294835-3

Vice president and Editor-in-chief: *Thalia Dorwick*
Senior developmental editor: *Renée Deljon*
Senior marketing manager: *David S. Patterson*
Senior production editor: *David M. Staloch*
Senior production supervisor: *Richard DeVitto*
Design manager: *Violeta Díaz*
Interior and cover designer: *Ellen Pettengell*
Photo researcher: *Holly Rudelitsch*
Art editor: *Cristin Yancey*
Compositor: *G & S Typesetters, Inc.*
Typeface: *10.25 / 12 Giovanni Book*
Paper: *45# New Era Matte*
Printer and binder: *Quebecor Printing, Fairfield*

*Text and photo credits begin on page C1 and constitute an extension of the copyright page.*

LIBRARY OF CONGRESS CATALOGING-IN-PUBLICATION DATA

Crusius, Timothy W., 1950–
    The aims of argument: a text and reader / Timothy W. Crusius,
Carolyn E. Channell.— 4th ed.
        p. cm.
    Includes index.
    ISBN 0-07-294835-3
    1. English language—Rhetoric.   2. Persuasion (Rhetoric)   3. College readers.
    4. Report writing.   I. Channell, Carolyn E.   II. Title.

PE1431.C78 2002
808'.0427—dc21                                                          2002023041

www.mhhe.com

*For W. Ross Winterowd*

# Preface

As its first three editions were, the fourth edition of *The Aims of Argument* is different from other argumentation texts because it remains the only one that focuses on the aims, or purposes, of argument. That this book's popularity increases from edition to edition tells us that our approach does in fact satisfy the previously unmet need that moved us to become textbook authors. We're gratified that our approach has proven useful — and seemingly more effective than others available.

## NOTES ON THIS TEXT'S ORIGINS

With over thirty years of teaching experience between us, we had tried most of the available argument books. Many of them were quite good, and we learned from them. However, we found ourselves adopting a text not so much out of genuine enthusiasm but rather because it had fewer liabilities than any of the others we were considering. True, all textbook selection involves comparisons of the "lesser evil" sort. But we wondered why we were so lukewarm about even the best argumentation textbooks. We found many problems, both major and minor, that explained our dissatisfaction, and we boiled them down to a few major criticisms:

- Most treatments were too formalistic and prescriptive.
- Most failed to integrate class discussion and individual inquiry with written argumentation.
- Apart from moving from simple concepts and assignments to more complicated ones, no book offered a learning sequence.
- Despite the fact that argument, like narrative, is clearly a mode or means of development, not an end in itself, no book offered a well-developed view of the aims or purposes of argument.

We thought that these shortcomings had many undesirable results in the classroom, including the following:

- The overemphasis on form confused students with too much terminology, made them doubt their best instincts, and drained away energy and interest from the process of inventing and discovering good arguments. Informal argumentation is not cut-and-dried but open-ended and creative.
- The separation of class discussion from the process of composition created a hiatus (rather than a useful distinction) between oral and written argument so that students had difficulty seeing the relation between the two and using the insights learned from each to improve the other.
- The lack of a learning sequence—of assignments that begin by refining and extending what students can do without help and that then build on these capacities with each subsequent assignment—meant that courses in argumentation were less coherent and less meaningful than they could be. Students did not understand why they were doing what they were doing and could not envision what might reasonably come next.
- Finally, inattention to what people actually use argument to accomplish resulted in too narrow a view of the functions of argument and thus in unclear purposes for writing. Because instruction was mainly limited to what we call arguing to convince, too often students saw argument only as a monologue of advocacy. Even when their viewpoint was flexible, too often they assumed a pose of dogmatism and ignored any true spirit of inquiry.

We set out consciously to solve these problems—or at least to render them less problematical—when we wrote the first edition of this book. The result was a book different in notable respects from any other argument text available because it focuses on the four aims of argument:

*Arguing to inquire,* the process of questioning opinions
*Arguing to convince,* the process of making cases
*Arguing to persuade,* the process of appealing to the whole person
*Arguing to negotiate,* the process of mediating between or among conflicting positions

## COMMON QUESTIONS ABOUT THE AIMS OF ARGUMENT

We have found that instructors have certain questions about these aims, especially in terms of how they relate to one another. No doubt we have yet to hear all the questions that will be asked, but we hope that by answering the ones we have heard, we can clarify some of the implications of our approach.

1. *What is the relative value of the four aims? Because mediation comes last, is it the best or most valued?* Our answer is that no aim is "better" than any other aim. Given certain needs or demands for writing and certain audiences, one aim can be more appropriate than an-

other for the task at hand. We treat mediation last because it involves inquiry, convincing, and persuading and thus comes last in the learning sequence.

2. *Must inquiry be taught as a separate aim?* Not at all. We have designed the text so that it may be taught as a separate aim (the use of argument Plato and Aristotle called *dialectic*), but we certainly do not intend this "may" to be interpreted as a "must." We do think that teaching inquiry as a distinct aim has certain advantages. Students need to learn how to engage in constructive dialogue, which is more disciplined and more focused than class discussion usually is. Once they see how it is done, students seem to enjoy dialogue with one another and with texts. Dialogue helps students think through their arguments and imagine reader reaction to what they say, both of which are crucial to convincing and persuading. Finally, as with the option of teaching negotiation, teaching inquiry offers instructors another avenue for assignments other than the standard argumentative essay.

3. *Should inquiry come first?* For a number of reasons, inquiry has a certain priority over the other aims. Most teachers are likely to approach inquiry as a prewriting task, preparatory to convincing or persuading. And very commonly, we return to inquiry when we find something wrong with a case we are trying to construct, so the relationship between inquiry and the other aims is as much recursive as it is a matter of before and after.

    However, we think inquiry also has psychological, moral, and practical claims to priority. When we are unfamiliar with an issue, inquiry comes first psychologically, often as a felt need to explore existing opinion. Regardless of what happens in the "real world," convincing or persuading without an open, honest, and earnest search for the truth is, in our view, immoral. Finally, inquiry goes hand-in-hand with research, which, of course, normally precedes writing in the other aims of argument.

    In sum, we would not defend Plato's concept of the truth. Truth is not simply "out there" in some wordless realm waiting to be discovered; rather, our opinion is that we discover or uncover truth as we grapple with a controversial issue and that it results largely from how we interpret ourselves and our world. We agree, therefore, with Wayne Booth that truth claims ought to be provisional and subject to revision, held for good reasons until better ones change our minds. Moreover, we agree with Plato that rhetoric divorced from inquiry is dangerous and morally suspect. The truth (if always provisional — some person's, some group's, or some culture's version of the truth) must count for more than sheer technical skill in argumentation.

4. *Isn't the difference between convincing and persuading more a matter of degree than of kind?* Fairly sharp distinctions can be drawn between inquiry and negotiation and between either of these two aims and the

monologues of advocacy: convincing and persuading. But convincing and persuading do shade into one another so that the difference is only clear at the extremes, with carefully chosen examples. Furthermore, the "purest" appeal to reason—a legal brief, a philosophical or scientific argument—appeals in ways beyond the sheer cogency of the case being made. Persuasive techniques are typically submerged but not absent in arguing to convince.

Our motivation for separating convincing from persuading is not so much theoretical as pedagogical. Students usually have so much difficulty with case-making that individual attention to the logical appeal by itself is justified. Making students focally conscious of the appeals of character, emotion, and style while they are struggling to cope with case-making is too much to ask and can overburden them to the point of paralysis.

Regardless, then, of how sound the traditional distinction between convincing and persuading may be, we think it best to take up convincing first and then persuasion, especially because what students learn in the former can be carried over more or less intact into the latter. And, of course, it is not only case-making that carries over from convincing into persuading. Because one cannot make a case without unconscious appeal to character, emotional commitments (such as values), and style, teaching persuasion is really a matter of exposing and developing what is already there in arguing to convince.

The central tenets of an approach based on aims of argument may be summarized as follows:

- *Argumentation is a mode or means of discourse, not an aim or purpose of discourse;* consequently, our task is to teach the aims of argument.
- *The aims of argument are linked in a learning sequence so that convincing builds on inquiry, persuasion on convincing, and all three contribute to mediation;* consequently, we offer this learning sequence as an aid to conceiving a course or courses in argumentation.

We believe in the learning sequence as much as we do in the aims of argument. We think that anyone giving it an honest chance will come to prefer this way of teaching argument over any other ordering currently available.

At the same time, we recognize that textbooks are used selectively, as teachers and programs need them for help in achieving their own goals. As with any other text, this one can be used selectively, ignoring some parts, playing up others, designing other sequences, and so on. If you want to work with our learning sequence, it is there for creative adaptation. If not, the text certainly does not have to be taught as a whole and in sequence to be useful and effective.

## A NOTE ABOUT THE READINGS

You will discover that many of the issues around which this text's essays are organized unavoidably involve students in issues of race, class, and gender difference. This slant is not intended to be political, nor does it reflect a hidden agenda on our part. Rather, we think students can come to feel more deeply about issues of this sort than they do about others we have tried. Class debates are livelier, maybe because such issues hit closer to home—the home and community they came from, the campus they live on now. Whatever the case, we have found that the issues work, both for students and for us.

They work, we think, because such issues help expose something obvious and basic about argumentation: People differ because they are different, and not just on the basis of race, class, and gender. Without some confrontation with difference, students may miss the deep social and cultural roots of argument and fail to understand why people think in such varied ways about homosexuality, education, welfare, abortion, and other issues that turn on difference, as well as issues such as the news, which may seem at first to have nothing to do with difference.

We have consciously avoided the "great authors, classic essays" approach (with the exception of Martin Luther King, Jr.'s "Letter from Birmingham Jail," which we include and discuss in depth). Otherwise, we tried instead to find bright, contemporary people arguing well from diverse viewpoints—articles and chapters similar to those that can be found in our better journals and trade books, the sort of publications students will read most in doing research on the issues. We have also tried to bring students into the argument as it currently stands, recognizing that the terms of the debate are necessarily always changing. Finally, we have not presented any issue in a simple proand-con fashion, as if there were only two sides to a question. We want the readings to provide models for writing not too far removed from what students can reasonably aspire to, as well as stimulation toward thinking through and rethinking positions on the issues in question.

Included in this range of perspectives are arguments made not only with words but also with images. Therefore, attentive to the predominance, power, and appeal of visuals today, we include (in a full instructional chapter) examples of arguments made in visuals such as editorial cartoons, advertisements, public sculpture, and photographs.

## A FINAL WORD ABOUT THE APPROACH

Some reviewers and users have called our approach innovative. But is it better? Will students learn more? Will instructors find the book more satisfying and more helpful than what they currently use? Our experience—both in using the book ourselves and in listening to the responses of those who have read it or tested it in the classroom or used it for years—is that they will. Students complain less about having to read this book than about having to read others used in our program. They do seem to learn more. Teachers claim to enjoy the text and find it stimulating, something to work with rather than around. We hope your experience is as positive as ours has been. We invite your comments and will use them in the process of perpetual revision that constitutes the life of a text and of our lives as writing teachers.

## NEW TO THE FOURTH EDITION

On the whole, we think this revision has made *Aims* more user-friendly and more diverse in its appeal while maintaining its attempt not to dodge or gloss over the genuine complexities and special challenges of argumentation. As always, we invite your comments and suggestions, as we continue to learn a great deal from the students and teachers who use this book.

The major changes from the third edition are as follows:

### New Organization

In an effort to make materials easier to locate and more accessible, we've reorganized the book into four parts and changed the format, including the addition of a much-needed second color. We now have up front, in Part One, all the materials we think of as "basic training": understanding rhetoric and argumentation, reading arguments, analyzing them, doing research. The popular chapter on visual rhetoric is here as well because visuals are especially useful for teaching reading and analysis and because they are often used as an aid for making arguments, regardless of aim.

Among other important topics, Chapter 1, Understanding Argument, confronts the popular notions of rhetoric and argument and moves students immediately into working with both. Reading an Argument, Chapter 2, addresses the problems students have in reading arguments and provides detailed strategies for overcoming those challenges. Because many contemporary students are not used to processing uninterrupted blocks of prose that advance sustained arguments, we see this greatly enhanced coverage as part of our continuing effort to develop still better ways to help students become critical readers. This chapter includes an analytical writing assignment and a student example of the completed assignment.

### Entirely Rewritten Inquiry Chapter

Part Two groups together what has been and will always be the foundation of the book: the sequence of four aims. The only significant change in this part is an extensive overhaul of the inquiry chapter. Most composition texts focus on helping students find sources rather than showing them what to do once sources are located. Making useful note cards is important but only a small part of the problem students face in analyzing and assessing sources. Therefore, the fourth edition of *The Aims of Argument* now offers more detailed guidance, with illustrations, in thinking critically about sources and relating them to the issues connected with controversial topics. Included is a section on how to assess sources defending opposing theses on the same issue, a challenge students typically encounter in research but which is rarely addressed sufficiently in composition textbooks. We also show students, complete with examples and exercises, the difference between conversation and dialogue and especially how to move from merely asserting opinions to questioning them. Finally, we've designed a new assignment for this chapter, one we think will contribute significantly to making the exploratory essay a more rewarding experience for both students and instructors.

## New Boxes

In response to reviewers' suggestions, we added numerous boxes throughout Parts One and Two, and to help students get the most out of them, we identify the majority of the boxes as one of two types: Concept Close-Up or Best Practices. We intend each type to achieve a different purpose. The contents of Concept Close-Up boxes provide, as the boxes' name suggests, a summary or an expanded discussion of a covered concept or topic. Best Practices boxes offer guidelines for successfully completing reading, writing, and thinking tasks; employing the full range of argumentation strategies; and writing effective arguments.

## Two New Casebooks

Part Three, Two Casebooks for Argument, is entirely new to *Aims*'s fourth edition. Comprising Chapters 10 and 11, the two casebooks realize an ambition we've had for some time — to offer more extensive and varied texts on selected topics. The idea was not just to offer more of what we usually encounter in argumentation rhetoric readers. We especially wanted to include background information, knowledge students usually lack and surely need to argue well. Terrorism, unfortunately, is now a topic none of us can ignore, and Chapter 10 primarily offers materials published after the September 11 attack. This section is the only entirely new group of readings for this edition, as Chapter 11, the casebook on marriage and family, includes among its many texts selections carried over from the third edition's chapter on this topic. We chose to expand our treatment of the issues surrounding marriage and family because our students are drawn to them more than to any of the other issues we've offered in readings in past editions. No selection of readings can obviate the need for outside research, but at least these two casebooks take students deeper into the subject matters and open up more avenues for pursuing them. We only wish space would permit us to treat all controversial subjects this way.

Part Four preserves, with few changes, the most-used readings chapters from the third edition: Feminism (Chapter 12), Gay and Lesbian Rights (Chapter 13); The News and Ethics (Chapter 14); and Liberal Education and Contemporary Culture (Chapter 15). We're sorry if the space we needed for the casebooks meant eliminating a readings chapter you especially liked. We hope the casebooks will compensate for your loss.

## New Web Site

In addition to the many changes the fourth edition offers in the text itself, and in addition to the text's print instructor resources manual, this edition of *Aims* is also accompanied by a new Web site that provides not only a wealth of links to relevant sites but also interactive activities to help students develop skills such as evaluating online sources. The Web site's address is <www.mhhe.com/crusius>.

## Online Course Delivery and Distance Learning

In addition to the supplements described previously (the print *Instructor's Resources to Accompany The Aims of Argument*, Fourth Edition and the book's new Web site), McGraw-Hill also offers the following technology products for composition classes. The online content of *The Aims of Argument* is supported by WebCT, Blackboard, eCollege.com, and most other course systems. Additionally, McGraw-Hill's PageOut service is available to get you and your course up and running online in a matter of hours — at no cost! To find out more, contact your local McGraw-Hill representative or visit <http://www.pageout.net>.

### PageOut

McGraw-Hill's widely used click-and-build Web site program offers a series of templates and many design options, requires no knowledge of HTML, and is intuitive and easy to use. With PageOut, anyone can produce a professionally designed course Web site in very little time.

### AllWrite!

Available online or on CD-ROM, *AllWrite!* offers over 3,000 exercises for practice in basic grammar, usage, punctuation, context spelling, and techniques for effective writing. The popular program is richly illustrated with graphics, animations, video, and Help screens.

### Webwrite

This online product, available through our partner company Meta Text, makes it possible for writing teachers and students to, among other things, comment on and share papers online.

*Teaching Composition Faculty Listserv at <www.mhhe.com/tcomp>*

Moderated by Chris Anson at North Carolina State University and offered by McGraw-Hill as a service to the composition community, this listserv brings together senior members of the college composition community with newer members—junior faculty, adjuncts, and teaching assistants—in an online newsletter and accompanying discussion group to address issues of pedagogy, in both theory and in practice.

## ACKNOWLEDGMENTS

We have learned a great deal from the comments of both teachers and students who have used this book, so please continue to share your thoughts with us.

We wish to acknowledge the work of the following reviewers who guided our work on the first, second, and third editions: Linda Bensel-Meyers, University of Tennessee, Knoxville; Lisa Canella, DePaul University; Mary F. Chen-Johnson, Tacoma Community College; Matilda Cox, University of Maryland—College Park; Margaret Cullen, Ohio Northern University; Richard Fulkerson, Texas A&M University—Commerce; Judith Gold Stitzel, West Virginia University; Matthew Hearn, Valdosta State University; Elizabeth Howard Borczon, University of Kansas; Peggy B. Jolly, University of Alabama at Birmingham; James L. Kastely, University of Houston; William Keith, Oregon State University; Dr. Charles Watterson Davis, Kansas State University; Anne Williams, Indiana University-Purdue University Indianapolis.

We are grateful to the reviewers whose helpful comments guided our work on this edition: Joel R. Brouwer, Montcalm Community College; Amy Cashulette Flagg, Colorado State University; Lynee Lewis Gaillet, Georgia State University; Cynthia Haynes, University of Texas at Dallas; Lisa J. McClure, Southern Illinois University, Carbondale; Rolf Norgaard, University of Colorado at Boulder; Julie Robinson, Colorado State University; Gardner Rogers, University of Illinois, Urbana-Champaign; Cara-Lynn Ungar, Portland Community College; N. Renuka Uthappa, Eastern Michigan University.

The work of David Staloch, our production editor, and April Wells-Hayes, our copyeditor, went far beyond the call of duty in helping us refine and complete the revised manuscript. At McGraw-Hill, Marty Granahan's work with permissions and Holly Rudelitsch's photo research also deserve special recognition and our deepest gratitude. Finally, Renée Deljon, our editor, showed her usual brilliance and lent her unflagging energy throughout the process that led to this new edition of *Aims*.

Timothy Crusius
Carolyn Channell
Dallas, Texas

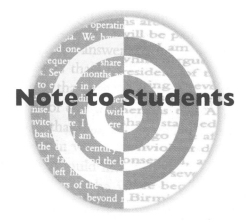

# Note to Students

Our goal in this book is not just to show you how to construct an argument but also to make you more aware of why people argue and what purposes that argument serves in our society. Consequently, Part Two of this book introduces four specific aims that people may have in mind when they make arguments: to inquire, to convince, to persuade, and to negotiate. Part One precedes the chapters on the aims of argument and consists of relatively short chapters that focus on understanding argumentation in general, reading and analyzing arguments, doing research, and working with forms of visual persuasion such as advertising.

As examples of the aims of argument, the selections in Parts One and Two offer something for you to emulate. All writers learn from studying the strategies of other writers. The object is not so much to imitate what a more experienced writer does as it is to understand the range of approaches and strategies you might use in your own way and for your own purposes.

Included in this range of approaches are arguments made not only with words but also with images. Part One therefore includes some examples of editorial cartoons, advertisements, and photographs.

The additional readings in Parts Three and Four serve another function as well. To learn about argument, we have to argue; to argue, we must have something to argue about. So we have grouped essays and images around central issues of current public discussion. Parts Three and Four consist of readings and visuals in various controversial topics. Part Three's two casebooks offer expanded treatment of two subjects we think you'll find especially interesting, terrorism and marriage and family. Part Four's chapters provide less extensive selections on issues students have favored from past editions of this book. We selected these particular issues rather than other widely debated ones for two main reasons. One is that they have worked well in our own classes, better than others we tried and rejected. The other reason is that most of these issues deal centrally with society and more or less require us to think about difference, about what leads people to disagree with one another in the first place.

Basically, people argue with one another because they do not see the world the same way, and they do not see the world the same way because of their different backgrounds. Therefore, in dealing with how people differ, a book about argument must deal with what makes people different, with the sources of disagreement itself—including gender, race/ethnicity, class, sexual orientation, and religion. Rather than ignoring or glossing over difference, the readings in Parts Three and Four will help you better understand difference—as well as provide interesting and significant subjects to argue about.

This book concludes with an appendix that focuses on editing, the art of polishing and refining prose, and on proofreading for some common errors. We suggest that you consult this reference repeatedly as you work through the text's assignments.

Arguing well is difficult for anyone. For many college students it is especially challenging because they have had little experience writing arguments. We have tried to write a text that is no more complicated than it has to be, and we welcome your comments so that we may improve future editions. Please write us at the following address:

The Rhetoric Program
Dallas Hall
Southern Methodist University
Dallas, Texas 75275

You may also e-mail your comments to the following address:

cchannel@mail.smu.edu

# About the Authors

Timothy W. Crusius is professor of English at Southern Methodist University, where he teaches beginning and advanced composition. He's also the author of books on discourse theory, philosophical hermeneutics, and Kenneth Burke. He resides in Dallas with his wife, Elizabeth, and their children, Micah and Rachel.

Carolyn E. Channell taught high school and community college students before coming to Southern Methodist University, where she is now a senior lecturer and a specialist in first-year writing courses. She resides in Richardson, Texas, with her husband, David, and her "child"—a boxer named Heidi.

# Contents

**Part Four**   Readings: Issues and Arguments

## BOXES BY TYPE

### Concept Close-Up Boxes

### Best Practices Boxes

# Part One Resources for Reading and Writing Arguments

**Part One** # Resources for Reading and Writing Arguments

# Chapter 1

# Understanding Argument

The *Aims of Argument* is based on two key concepts: argument and rhetoric. These days, unfortunately, the terms *argument* and *rhetoric* have acquired bad reputations. The popular meaning of *argument* is *disagreement;* we think of raised voices, hurt feelings, winners and losers. Most people think of *rhetoric,* too, in a negative sense — as language that sounds good but evades or hides the truth. In this sense, rhetoric is the language we hear from the politician who says whatever will win votes, the public relations person who puts "positive spin" on dishonest business practices, the buck-passing bureaucrat who blames the foul-up on someone else, the clever lawyer who counterfeits passion to plead for the acquittal of a guilty client.

The words *argument* and *rhetoric,* then, are commonly applied to the darker side of human acts and motives. This darker side is real — arguments are often pointless and silly, ugly and destructive; all too often, rhetoric is empty words contrived to mislead or to disguise the desire to exert power. But this book is not about that kind of argument or that kind of rhetoric. Here we develop the meanings of *argument* and *rhetoric* in an older, fuller, and far more positive sense — as the language and art of mature reasoning.

## WHAT IS ARGUMENT?

In this book, **argument** means *mature reasoning.* By *mature,* we mean an attitude and approach to argument, not an age group. Some older adults are incapable of mature reasoning, whereas some young people reason very well. And all of us, regardless of age, sometimes fall short of mature reasoning — when we are tired, bored, on edge, or when a situation pushes all the wrong buttons. What is "mature" about the kind of argument we have in mind? One meaning of *mature* is "worked out fully by the mind" or "considered" (*American Heritage Dictionary*). Mature decisions, for example, are thoughtful ones, reached slowly after full consideration of all the consequences. And this is true also of mature reasoning.

We also consider the second term in this definition of argument: *reasoning*. If we study logic in depth, we find many definitions of reasoning, but for practical purposes, *reasoning* here means *an opinion plus a reason (or reasons) for holding that opinion*. As we will see in detail later in this chapter, good arguments require more than this; to be convincing, reasons must be developed with evidence like specific facts and examples. However, understanding the basic form of opinion-plus-a-reason is the place to begin when considering your own and other people's arguments.

One way to understand argument as mature reasoning is to contrast it with *debate*. In debate, opponents take a predetermined, usually assigned, side and attempt to defend it, in much the same way that an army or a football team must hold its ground. The point is to win, to best one's opponent. In contrast, rather than starting with a position to defend, mature reasoners work toward a position. If they have an opinion to start with, mature reasoners think it through and evaluate it rather than rush to its defense. To win is not to defeat an opponent but rather to gain insight into the topic at hand. The struggle is with the problem, question, or issue we confront. Rather than seeking the favorable decision of the judges, as in debate, we are after a sound opinion in which we can believe—an opinion consistent with the facts and that other people will respect and take seriously.

Of course, having arrived at an opinion that seems sound to us, we still must *make our case*—argue in the sense of providing good reasons and adequate evidence in support of them. But whereas debaters must hold their positions at all costs, mature reasoners may not. The very process of making a case will often show us that what we thought was sound really isn't. We try to defend our opinion and find that we can't—or at least, not very well. And so we rethink our position until we arrive at one for which we *can* make a good case. From beginning to end, therefore, mature reasoning is a process of discovery. We find out what we really think about something and whether what we think holds water. It's a learning process. It's what makes argument worthwhile, not merely a test of our cleverness.

One other important difference from debate is this: Once we have arrived at a position we want to defend, the goal of mature reasoning is not to score points to impress an outside observer or judge. Our goal is to convince or persuade a real-life opponent to see the issue as we do. Mature reasoning takes into consideration those who disagree and their reasons for disagreeing. We must offer them reasons and evidence they can accept, and we must argue in a way that shows respect and charity, not aggression and anger. (See page 5.)

## WHAT IS RHETORIC?

Over time, the meanings of most words in most languages change—sometimes only a little, sometimes a lot. The word *rhetoric* is a good example of a big change. As indicated already, the popular meaning of *rhetoric* is empty verbiage—the art of sounding impressive while saying little—or the art of

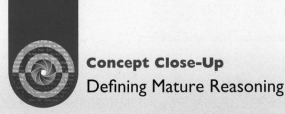

Argument as mature reasoning means:

- Defending *not the first position* you might take on an issue *but the best position*, determined through open-minded inquiry
- Providing reasons for holding that position that can earn the respect of an opposing audience

verbal deception. This meaning of *rhetoric* confers a judgment, and not a positive one.

In contrast, in ancient Greece, where rhetoric was invented about 2,500 years ago, *rhetoric* referred to the art of public speaking. The Greeks recognized that rhetoric could be abused, but, for their culture in general, it was not a negative term. They had a goddess of persuasion (see Figure 1.1), and they respected the power of the spoken word to move people. It dominated their law courts, their governments, and their public ceremonies and events. As an art, the spoken word was an object of study. People enrolled in schools of rhetoric to become effective public speakers. Further, the ancient rhetoricians put a high value on good character. Not just sounding ethical but being known as an ethical person contributed to a speaker's persuasive power.

This old, highly valued meaning of rhetoric as oratory survived well into the nineteenth century. In Abraham Lincoln's day, Americans assembled by the thousands to hear speeches that went on for hours. For them, a good speech held the same level of interest as a big sporting event does for people today.

In this book, we are interested primarily in various ways of using *written* argument, but the rhetorical tradition informs our understanding of mature reasoning. Mature reasoning has nothing to do with the current definition of rhetoric as speech that merely sounds good or deceives people. The ancient meaning of *rhetoric* is more relevant, but we update it here to connect it directly with mature reasoning.

If argument is mature reasoning, then rhetoric is its *art*—that is, how we go about arguing with some degree of success. Just as there is an art of painting or sculpture, so is there an art of mature reasoning. Since the time of Aristotle, teachers of rhetoric have taught their students *self-conscious* ways of reasoning well and arguing successfully. The study of rhetoric, therefore, includes both what we have already defined as reasoning *and* ways of appealing to an audience. These include self-conscious efforts to project oneself as a good and intelligent person as well as efforts to connect with the audience through humor, passion, and image.

Note the emphasis on self-consciousness, which means awareness of what we are doing. Rhetoric teaches us how to make the best conscious choices when we put together an argument.

*Figure 1.1    Peitho, the goddess of Persuasion, was often involved in seductions and love affairs. On this piece (a detail from a terracota kylix, c. 410 B.C.), Peitho, the figure on the left, gives advice to a dejected-looking woman, identified as Demonassa. To the right, Eros, the god of Love, stands with his hands on Demonassa's shoulder, suggesting the nature of this advice.*

There's a sense in which no one has to teach anyone else how to argue; it's human nature. From the time they can talk, kids argue with other kids and with their parents. But the fact that we know how to argue doesn't mean that we do it well, as you probably know from looking at the daily letters to the editor in your local newspaper. To master the rhetorical arts, we need good models, much as we do when we work with conscious awareness on our serve in tennis or on our batting in baseball. And we must develop the habits and skills of good rhetoric, just as we do to gain proficiency in any art, whether it's singing, drawing, or cooking.

## AN EXAMPLE OF ARGUMENT

So far, we've been talking about argument in the abstract—definitions and explanations. To really understand argument, especially as we define it here, we need a concrete example. One thing mature reasoning does is to challenge unexamined belief, the stances people take out of habit without much thought. The following argument by a syndicated columnist would have us consider more carefully our notion of "free speech."

## Defining Rhetoric

**Rhetoric** is the art of argument as mature reasoning. The study of rhetoric develops self-conscious awareness of the principles and practices of mature reasoning and effective arguing.

---

## You Also Have the Right to Tell a Bigot What You Think

### Leonard Pitts

For the record, I have no idea who let the dogs out. I didn't even know the gate was open.

We Americans get hooked on saying some pretty silly things, you know? "Where's the beef?" "Make my day."

Generally, it is pretty harmless stuff. Granted, after the fifteenth time someone avows that he feels your pain, you probably are ready to inflict some of your own. But overall, yeah — pretty harmless.

There is, however, one expression that never fails to make me nuts. Truth be told, it is less a catchphrase than a cop-out, a meaningless thing people say — usually when accusations of racism, sexism, anti-Semitism or homophobia have been leveled and they are being asked to defend the indefensible.

"Entitled to my opinion," they say. Or "entitled to his opinion," as the    5
case may be. The sense of it is the same even when the words vary: People clamber atop the First Amendment and remind us that it allows them or someone they decline to criticize to say or believe whatever they wish.

It happened again just the other day, on the eve of the Grammys. One of the entertainment news programs did an informal poll of musicians, asking them to comment on the rapper Eminem's violently homophobic and misogynistic music. You would have sworn they all were reading from the same script: "He is entitled to say what he feels," they said.

In that, they echoed the folks who thought John Rocker was unfairly maligned for his bigotry: "He is entitled to his opinion," the ballplayer's defenders told us. And that, in turn, was an echo of what happened in 1993 when a reporter asked a student at City University of New York about Dr. Leonard Jeffries' claim of a Jewish conspiracy against black people. "He had a right to say whatever he chooses to say," the student replied.

As I said, it makes me crazy — not because the observation isn't correct, but because it is beside the point.

Anybody who is a more ardent supporter of the First Amendment than I probably ought to be on medication. I believe the liberties it grants are meaningless unless extended as far as possible into the ideological hinterlands. Only in this way can you preserve and defend those liberties for the rest of us. So, as far as I am concerned, every sexist, homophobe, communist, flag burner, Jew baiter, Arab hater and racist must be protected in the peaceful expression of his or her beliefs.

But after acknowledging the right of the hateful to be hateful and the vile to be vile, it seems to me that the least I can do is use my own right of free speech to call those people what they are. It seems to me, in fact, that I have a moral obligation to do so. But many people embrace moral cowardice instead and blame it on the First Amendment.    10

It is a specious claim. The First Amendment is violated when the government seeks to censor expression. That didn't happen to Eminem. That didn't happen to John Rocker, either. What did happen was that the media and private citizens criticized them and demanded that some price—public condemnation or professional demotion—be extracted as a penalty for the stupid things they said.

Friends and neighbors, that isn't a violation of free speech. That *is* free speech. And if some folks confuse the issue, well, that is because too many of us believe freedom of speech means freedom from censure, the unfettered right to say whatever you please without anyone being allowed to complain. Worse, many of us accept that stricture for fear of seeming "judgmental." These days, of course, "judgmental" is a four-letter word.

I make no argument for being closed-minded. People ought to open themselves to the widest possible variety of ideas and expressions. But that doesn't mean losing your ability to discern or abdicating your responsibility to question, criticize . . . *think*. All ideas aren't created equal. To pretend otherwise is to create a rush from judgment—to free a bigot from taking responsibility for his beliefs and allow him a facade of moral validity to hide behind.

So I could happily live the rest of my life without being reminded that this fool or that has the right to say what he thinks. Sure, he does. But you know what? We all do.

---

## Discussion of "You Also Have the Right . . ."

Leonard Pitts's argument is an example of a certain type or *genre* of written argument, the opinion column we find in the editorial section of newspapers. Arguments of this genre are usually brief and about some issue of general public concern, often an issue prominent in recent news stories. Most arguments written for college assignments are longer and deal with academic topics, but if we want to grasp the basics of mature reasoning, it's good to begin with the concise and readable arguments of professional columnists. Let's consider both the argument Pitts makes and his rhetoric—the art he uses to make his argument appealing to readers.

*Pitts's Reasoning*

In defining argument as mature reasoning, we stressed the process of arriving at an opinion as much as defending it. Arriving at an opinion is part of the aim of argument we call *inquiry*, and it's clearly very important for college writers who must deal with complex subjects and digest much information. Unfortunately, we can't see how authors arrived at their opinions by reading their finished work. As readers, we "come in" at the point where the writer states and argues for a position; we can't "go behind" it to appreciate how he or she got there. Consequently, all we can do with a published essay is discover how it works. That is, we can study its reasoning, its author's appeal to the readers' need for logical thinking.

Let's ask the first question we must ask of any argument we're analyzing: What is Pitts's opinion, or claim? If a piece of writing is indeed an argument, we should be able to see that the author has a clear position or opinion. We can call this the **claim** of the argument. It is what the author wants the audience to believe or to do.

*All statements of opinion are answers to questions,* usually **implied questions** because the question itself is too obvious to need spelling out. But when we study an argument, we must be willing to be obvious and spell it out anyway to see precisely what's going on. The question behind Pitts's argument is: What should we do when we hear someone making clearly bigoted remarks? His answer to the question is this: We have the right and even the moral obligation to "call those people what they are." That is his claim.

What reasons does he give his readers to convince them of his claim? He tells them that the common definition of freedom of speech is mistaken. Freedom of speech does not give everyone the right to say whatever he or she wants without fear of consequences, without even the expectation of being criticized. He thinks people use this definition as an excuse not to speak up when they hear or read bigotry.

In developing his reason, Pitts explains that this common definition is beside the point because no one is suggesting that people aren't entitled to their opinions. Of course they are, even if they are uninformed and full of hatred for some person or group of people. But freedom of speech is not the right to say anything without suffering consequences; rather, as Pitts says, it's a protection against government censorship, what's known in law as *prior restraint*. In other words, if a government authority prevents you from saying or printing something, that is censorship and a violation of the First Amendment in most cases. Nor should we feel that someone's rights have been taken away if a high price—for instance, "public condemnation or professional demotion" (paragraph 11)—must be paid for saying stupid things. The First Amendment does not protect us from the social or economic consequences of what we say or write. "All ideas aren't created equal," as Pitts maintains. Some deserve the condemnation they receive.

Now that we understand what Pitts is arguing, we can ask another question: What makes Pitts's argument mature, an example of the kind of reasoning worth learning how to do? First, it's mature in contrast to the opinion about free speech he criticizes, which clearly does not result from a close examination of what free speech means. Second, it's mature because it assumes civic responsibility. It's not a cop-out. It argues for doing the difficult thing because it is right and good for our society. It shows mature reasoning when it says: "People ought to open themselves to the widest possible variety of ideas and expressions. But that doesn't mean losing your responsibility to question, criticize . . . *think.*" Finally, it's mature in contrast to another common response to bigotry that Pitts doesn't discuss — the view that "someone ought to shut that guy up" followed by violence or the threat of violence directed at the offending person. Such an attitude is neither different from nor better than the attitude of a playground bully, and the mature mind does not accept it.

In recognizing the maturity of Pitts's argument, we should not be too respectful of it. Ultimately, the point of laying out an argument is to respond to it maturely ourselves, and that means asking our own questions. For instance, we might ask:

> When we say, "He's entitled to his opinion," are we *always* copping out, or is such a response justified in some circumstances?
>
> Does it do any good to call a bigot a bigot? Is it wiser sometimes to just ignore hate speech?
>
> How big a price is too big for stating a foolish opinion? Does it matter if a bigot later retracts his opinion, admits he was wrong, and apologizes?

One of the good things about mature arguments is that we can pursue them at length and learn a lot from discussing them.

## Following Through

Select an opinion column on a topic of interest to your class from your local city or campus newspaper. Choose an argument that you think exemplifies mature reasoning. Discuss its reasoning as we have here with Pitts's essay. Can you identify the claim or statement of the author's opinion? The claim or opinion is what the author wants his or her readers to believe or to do. If you can find no exact sentence to quote, can you nevertheless agree on what it is he or she wants the readers to believe or to do? Can you find in the argument one or more reasons for doing so?

### Other Appeals in Pitts's Argument

Finally, we ask, what makes Pitts's argument effective? That is, what makes it succeed with his readers? We have said that reasoning isn't enough when it comes to making a good argument. A writer, like a public speaker, must employ more than reason and make a conscious effort to project personality, to connect with his or her readers. Most readers seem to like Leonard Pitts because of his T-shirt-and-shorts informality and his conversational style, which includes remarks like "it makes me crazy" and sentence fragments like "But overall, yeah — pretty harmless."

We can't help forming impressions of people from reading what they write, and often these impressions correspond closely to how authors want us to perceive them anyway. Projecting good character goes all the way back to the advice of the ancient rhetoric teachers. Showing intelligence, fairness, and other signs of maturity will help you make an argument effectively, at least to an intelligent audience.

Pitts also makes a conscious effort to appeal to his readers (that is, to gain their support) by appealing to their feelings and acknowledging their attitudes. Appreciating Pitts's efforts here requires first that we think for a moment about who these people probably are. Pitts writes for the *Miami Herald*, but his column appears in many local papers across the United States. It's safe to say that the general public — those with time to read the newspaper and an interest in reactions to events in the news — are his readers. Because he is writing an argument, we assume he envisions them as not already seeing the situation as he sees it. They might be "guilty" of saying, "Everyone's entitled to an opinion." But he is not angry with them. He just wants to correct their misperception. Note that he addresses them as "friends and neighbors" in paragraph 12.

He does speak as a friend and neighbor, opening with some small talk, alluding to a popular song that made "Who let the dogs out" into a catch phrase. Humor done well is subtle, as here, and it tells the readers he knows they are as tired of this phrase as he is. Pitts is getting ready to announce his serious objection to one particular catch phrase, and he wants to project himself as a man with a life, an ordinary guy with common sense, not some neurotic member of the language police about to get worked up over nothing. Even though he shifts to a serious tone in the fourth paragraph, he doesn't completely abandon this casual and humorous personality — for example, in paragraph 9, where he jokes about his "ardent" support of the First Amendment.

But Pitts also projects a dead serious tone in making his point and in presenting his perspective as morally superior. One choice that conveys this attitude is his comment about people in the "ideological hinterlands": "every sexist, homophobe, communist, flag burner, Jew baiter, Arab hater and racist must be protected in the peaceful expression of his or her beliefs."

## Following Through

For class discussion: What else in Pitts's argument strikes you as particularly good, conscious choices? What choices convey his seriousness of purpose? Pay special attention to paragraphs 9 and 13. Why are they

(continues)

## Following Through (continued)

there? How do they show audience awareness? Which of Pitts's strategies or choices seem particularly appropriate for op-ed writing? Which might not be appropriate in an academic essay? One reason for noticing the choices professional writers make in their arguments is to learn some of their strategies, which you can use when writing your own arguments.

## FOUR CRITERIA OF MATURE REASONING

Students often ask, "What does my professor want?" Although you will be writing many different kinds of papers in response to the assignments in this textbook, your professor will most likely look for evidence of mature reasoning. When we evaluate student work, we look for four criteria that we consider marks of mature reasoning. They will give you a better idea of what instructors have in mind when they talk about "good writing" in argumentation.

### Mature Reasoners Are Well Informed

Your opinions must develop from knowledge and be supported by reliable and current evidence. If the reader feels that the writer "doesn't know his or her stuff," the argument loses all weight and force.

You may have noticed that people have opinions about all sorts of things, including subjects they know little or nothing about. The general human tendency is to have the strongest opinions on matters about which we know the least. Ignorance and inflexibility go together because it's easy to form an opinion when few or none of the facts get in the way and we can just assert our prejudices. Conversely, the more we know about most topics, the harder it is to be dogmatic. We find ourselves changing or at least refining our opinions more or less continuously as we gain more knowledge.

Of course, being well informed is not an absolute. We can be relatively knowledgeable about something and still not know that much compared to someone who has studied it for years. We can't be experts on everything we argue about. We should, however, recognize and admit the limitations of our knowledge. We should listen to those who know more. When the situation calls for more than tossing out a casual opinion—and college writing assignments always call for much more—you need to be sufficiently informed to respond appropriately.

### Mature Reasoners Are Self-Critical and Open to Constructive Criticism from Others

We have opinions about all sorts of things that don't matter much to us, casual opinions we've picked up somehow and may not even bother to defend if challenged. But we also have opinions in which we are heavily invested, sometimes to the point that our whole sense of reality, right and wrong, good and bad—our very sense of ourselves—is tied up in them. These opinions we defend passionately.

On this count, popular argumentation and mature reasoning are alike. Mature reasoners are often passionate about their convictions, as committed to them as the fanatic on the street corner is to his or her cause. A crucial difference, however, separates the fanatic from the mature reasoner. The fanatic is all passion; the mature reasoner is able and willing to step back and examine even deeply held convictions. "I may have believed this for as long as I can remember," the mature reasoner says to him- or herself, "but is this conviction really justified? Do the facts support it? When I think it through, does it really make sense? Can I make a coherent and consistent argument for it?" These are questions that don't concern the fanatic and are seldom posed in the popular argumentation we hear on talk radio.

In practical terms, being self-critical and open to well-intended criticism boils down to this: Mature reasoners can and do change their minds when they have good reasons to do so. In popular argumentation, changing one's mind can be taken as a weakness, as "wishy-washy," and so people tend to go on advocating what they believe, regardless of what anyone else says. But there's nothing wishy-washy about, for example, confronting the facts, about realizing that what we thought is not supported by the available evidence. In such a case, far from being a weakness, changing one's mind is a sign of intelligence and the very maturity mature reason values. Nor is it a weakness to recognize a good point made against one's own argument. If we don't listen and take seriously what others say, they won't listen to us.

You may agree with all this and yet still feel uncomfortable. Perhaps you think that being critical is a fault. Perhaps, when you've been criticized in the past, you felt "picked on" or embarrassed. But there is such a thing as *constructive* and *friendly* criticism. The hostile sort is as out of place in mature reasoning as refusal to listen to any criticism, no matter how well intentioned. Let's look at it this way: We all have blind spots and prejudices. We all argue badly sometimes. We need others to help us see and correct our shortcomings. The golden rule certainly applies to mature reasoning.

## Mature Reasoners Argue with Their Audience or Readers in Mind

Nothing drains energy from argument more than the feeling that it will accomplish nothing. As one student put it, "Why bother? People just go on thinking what they want to." This attitude is understandable. Popular, undisciplined argument often does seem futile: minds aren't changed; no progress is made; it's doubtful that anyone learned anything. Sometimes the opposing positions only harden, and the people involved are more at odds than before.

Why does this happen so often? One reason we've already mentioned— nobody's really listening to anyone else. We tend to hear only our own voices

·and see only from our own points of view. But there's another reason: The people making the arguments have made no effort to reach their audience. This is the other side of the coin of not listening—when we don't take other points of view seriously, we can't make our points of view appealing to those who don't already share them.

To have a chance of working, arguments must be *other-directed*, attuned to the people they want to reach. This may seem obvious, but it's also commonly ignored and not easy to do. We have to imagine the other guy. We have to care about other points of view, not just see them as obstacles to our own. We have to present and develop our arguments in ways that won't turn off the very people for whom we're writing. In many ways, *adapting to the audience* is the biggest challenge of argument.

Note that the challenge is *adapting to*, not manipulating. Mature reasoning is not a bag of tricks or a slick way to fool people into agreeing with us. Rather, *adapting to* means that we want a fair hearing, and so we "talk the talk," making a sincere effort to understand and connect with other people, other points of view.

## Mature Reasoners Know Their Arguments' Contexts

All arguments are part of an ongoing conversation. We think of arguments as something individuals make. We think of our opinions as *ours*, almost like private property. But arguments and opinions have pasts: Other people argued about more or less the same issues and problems before—often long before—we came on the scene. They have a present: Who's arguing what now, the current state of the argument. And they have a future: What people will be arguing about tomorrow, in different circumstances, with knowledge we don't have now.

So most arguments are not the isolated events they seem to be. Part of being well informed is knowing something about the history of an argument. By understanding an argument's past, we learn about patterns that will help us develop our own position. To some extent, we must know what's going on now and what other people are saying to make our own reasoning relevant. And although we can't know the future, we can imagine the drift of the argument, where it might be heading. In other words, there's a larger context we need to join—a big conversation of many voices to which our few belong.

Throughout this book, we'll emphasize the backgrounds or contexts of arguments and try to heighten your awareness of them. For now, remember this: Arguments are living things, and like all living things, they evolve. When we argue, we are part of a flow of life, part of a conversation going on in many places and among many people. The more aware we are of the big conversation, the better we'll argue in our smaller ones.

## Concept Close-Up
## Four Criteria of Mature Reasoning

**Mature Reasoners Are Well Informed**
Their opinions develop out of knowledge and are supported by reliable and current evidence.

**Mature Reasoners Are Self-Critical and Open to Constructive Criticism**
They balance their passionate attachment to their opinions with willingness to evaluate and test them against differing opinions, acknowledge when good points are made against their opinions, and even, when presented with good reasons for doing so, change their minds.

**Mature Reasoners Argue with Their Audiences in Mind**
They make a sincere effort to understand and connect with other people and other points of view because they do not see differences of opinion as obstacles to their own points of view.

**Mature Reasoners Know Their Arguments' Contexts**
They recognize that what we argue about now was argued about in the past and will be argued about in the future, that our contributions to these ongoing conversations are influenced by who we are, what made us who we are, where we are, what's going on around us—just as those arguing about the topic before and after us were and will be subject to similar influences.

---

### Following Through

Look again at the article by Leonard Pitts on pages 7–8. Do you see mature reasoning in his essay? Cite passages you think are especially indicative of our criteria.

## WHAT ARE THE AIMS OF ARGUMENT?

The heart of this book is the section entitled "The Aims of Argument." In conceiving this book, we worked from one basic premise: Mature reasoners do not argue just to argue; rather, they use argument to accomplish something: *to inquire* into a question, problem, or issue (commonly part of the research process); *to convince* their readers to assent to an opinion, or claim; *to persuade* readers to take action, such as buying a product or voting for a candidate; and *to mediate* conflict, as in labor disputes, divorce proceedings, and so on.

Let's look at each of these aims in more detail.

## Arguing to Inquire

Arguing to **inquire** is using reasoning to determine the best position on an issue. We open the "Aims" section with inquiry because mature reasoning is not a matter of defending what we already believe but of questioning it. Arguing to inquire helps us form opinions, question opinions we already have, and reason our way through conflicts or contradictions in other people's arguments on a topic. Inquiry is open minded, and it requires that we make an effort to find out what people who disagree think and why.

The ancient Greeks called argument as inquiry **dialectic;** today we might think of it as dialogue or serious conversation. There is nothing confrontational about such conversations; they are friendly. We have them with friends, family, and colleagues, even with ourselves. We have these conversations in writing, too, as we make notations in the margins of the arguments we read. Listserv groups engage in inquiry about subjects of mutual interest.

Inquiry centers on questions and involves some intellectual legwork to answer them—finding the facts, doing research. This is true whether you are inquiring into what car to buy, what major to choose in college, what candidate to vote for, or what policy our government should pursue on any given issue. A research scientist may devote years, even a lifetime, to formulating, testing, and reformulating hypotheses that explore a single set of phenomena, like black holes. Businesspeople must find solutions to practical problems, such as how to increase sales in a region of the country or how to anticipate changes in societal attitudes. Inquiry takes work, but without it the world would stall. What kind of world would we live in if no one questioned what they already knew or believed? Through inquiry, we don't just take a position—we earn it.

## Arguing to Convince

We've seen that the goal of inquiry is to reach some kind of conclusion on an issue. This conclusion can go by many names, but we'll call it a **conviction** and define it as "an earned opinion, achieved through careful thought, research, and discussion." Once we arrive at a conviction, we usually want others to share it. The aim of further argument is to secure the assent of people who do not share our conviction (or who do not share it fully). Such assent is an agreement of minds secured by reason rather than by force.

Argument to **convince** centers on making a case, which means offering reasons and evidence in support of our opinion. Arguments to convince are all around us. In college, we find them in scholarly and professional writing. For example, one historian has just concluded that the dancer known during World War I as Mata Hari was not a dangerous spy and should not have been executed by the French. His book presents his case for this conclusion. In everyday life, we find arguments to convince in editorials, in the courtrooms, and in political speeches. Whenever we encounter an opinion supported by reasons and asking us to agree, we are dealing with argument to convince. Whenever we as writers intend to gain the intellectual agreement of our readers, to get them to say, "You're right," we are arguing to convince.

## Arguing to Persuade

Like convincing, persuasion attempts to earn agreement, but it aims further. **Persuasion** attempts to influence not just thinking but also behavior. It motivates. An advertisement for Mercedes-Benz aims to convince us not only that the company makes a high-quality car but also that we should go out and buy one. A Sunday sermon asks for more than agreement with some interpretation of a biblical passage; the minister wants the congregation to live according to its message. Persuasion asks us to do something—spend money, give money, join a demonstration, recycle, vote, enlist, acquit. Because we don't always act on our convictions, persuasion cannot rely on reasoning alone. It must appeal in broader, deeper ways.

Persuasion appeals to readers' emotions. It tells stories about individual cases of hardship that move us to pity. It often uses photographs, as when charities confront us with pictures of poverty or suffering. Visual persuasion plays a role in architecture, from cathedrals to shopping malls. Persuasion uses many of the devices of poetry, such as patterns of sound, repetitions, metaphors, and similes to arouse a desired emotion in the audience.

Persuasion also relies on the personality of the writer to an even greater degree than does convincing. The persuasive writer attempts to represent something "higher" or "larger" than him- or herself—some ideal with which the reader would like to be associated. For example, a war veteran and hero like John McCain naturally brings patriotism to the table when he makes a speech.

Persuasion is one form of argument that some people distrust, and with good reason. It's important to note the difference between ethical persuasion and manipulation or even propaganda. We believe persuasion's role in the world cannot be denied. We need to study it so that we can make intelligent responses to it wherever it occurs—in the marketplace, the political arena, or the jury room. But we also need to study it to use it effectively in our work and public lives.

## Arguing to Negotiate

By the time we find ourselves in a situation where our aim is to **negotiate,** we will have already attempted to convince an opponent of our case and to persuade that opponent to settle a conflict or dispute to our satisfaction. Our opponent will no doubt also have used convincing and persuading in an attempt to move us similarly. Yet neither side will have been able to secure the assent of the other, and "agreeing to disagree" is not a practical solution because the participants must come to some agreement in order to pursue a necessary course of action.

In most instances of negotiation, the parties involved try to work out the conflict themselves because they have some relationship they wish to preserve—as employer and employee, business partners, family members, neighbors, even coauthors of an argument textbook. Common differences requiring negotiation include the amount of a raise or the terms of a contract, the wording of a bill in a congressional committee, and trade agreements among nations. In private life, negotiation helps roommates live together and families decide on everything from budgets to vacation destinations.

Just like other aims of argument, arguing to negotiate requires sound logic and the clear presentation of positions and reasons. However, negotiation challenges our interpersonal skills more than do the other aims. Each side must listen closely to understand not just the other side's case but also the other side's emotional commitments and underlying values. Initiating such a conversation and keeping it going sometimes can be so difficult that an outside party, a mediator, must assist in the process. With or without a mediator, when negotiation works, the opposing sides begin to converge. Exchanging viewpoints and information and building empathy enable all parties to make concessions, to loosen their hold on their original positions, and finally to reach consensus—or at least a resolution that all participants find satisfactory.

As Chapter 6 makes clear, this final aim of argument brings us full circle, back to *dialogue*, to the processes involved in arguing to inquire. The major difference is that in negotiation we are less concerned with our own claims to truth than we are with overcoming conflict, with finding some common ground that will allow us to live and work together.

## WHERE ARE THE AIMS OF ARGUMENT USED?

Although most college writing assignments in other courses will ask you to argue to convince, we think it's important to learn to argue with a full range of aims. In the future, you will need to argue well not just for academic purposes but also about public issues and problems you'll encounter "out there," in public meetings, in business settings, and so on. The first two aims are therefore most appropriate for college argumentation; the last two are for public or civic argumentation. (See the Concept Close-Up box on page 19.) By structuring the book in this way, we intend to offer specific guidance toward arguing well as both a student and a citizen.

## A GOOD TOOL FOR UNDERSTANDING AND WRITING ARGUMENTS: THE WRITER'S NOTEBOOK

As you've probably already noticed, argumentation places unique demands on readers and writers. One of the most helpful tools that you can use to meet these demands is a writer's notebook.

## Concept Close-Up
## Comparing the Aims of Argument

The aims of argument have much in common. For example, besides sharing argument, they all tend to draw on sources of knowledge (research) and to deal with controversial issues. But the aims also differ from one another, mainly in terms of purpose, audience, situation, and method, as summarized here and on the inside front cover.

|  | Purpose | Audience | Situation | Method |
|---|---|---|---|---|
| **Inquiry** | Seeks truth | Oneself, friends, and colleagues | Informal; a dialogue | Questions |
| **Convincing** | Seeks assent to a thesis | Less intimate; wants careful reasoning | More formal; a monologue | Case-making |
| **Persuading** | Seeks action | More broadly public, less academic | Pressing need for a decision | Appeals to reason and emotions |
| **Negotiating** | Seeks consensus | Polarized by differences | Need to cooperate, preserve relations | "Give-and-take" |

We offer this chart as a general guide to the aims of argument. Think of it as the "big picture" you can always return to as you work your way through Part Two, which deals with each of the aims in detail.

We hope you will explore on your own how the aims converge and diverge and how they overlap and interact in specific cases.

The main function of a writer's notebook is to help you sort out what you read, learn, accomplish, and think as you go through the stages of creating a finished piece of writing. A writer's notebook contains the writing you do before you write; it's a place to sketch out ideas, assess research, order what you have to say, and determine strategies and goals for writing.

### Why Keep a Notebook?

Some projects require extensive research and consultation, which involve compiling and assessing large amounts of data and working through complex chains of reasoning. Under such conditions, even the best memory will fail without the aid of a notebook. Given life's distractions, we often forget too much and imprecisely recall what we do manage to remember. With a writer's notebook, we can preserve the idea that come to us as we walk across campus or stare into space over our morning coffee. Often, a writer's notebook even provides sections of writing that can be incorporated into your papers and so can help you save time.

Any entry that helps or that you may want to use for future reference is appropriate to make in your writer's notebook. It's for private exploration, for your eyes only—so don't worry about organization, spelling, or grammar. Following are some specific possibilities.

### To Explore Issues You Encounter in and out of Class

Bring your notebook to class each day. Use it to respond to ideas presented in class and in every reading assignment. When you're assigned a topic, write down your first impressions and opinions about it. When you're to choose your own topic, use the notebook to respond to controversial issues in the news or on campus. Your notebook then becomes a source of ideas for your essays.

### To Record and Analyze Assignments

Staple your instructors' handouts to a notebook page, or write the assignment down word for word. Take notes as your instructor explains the assignment. Later, look it over more carefully, circling and checking key words, underlining due dates and other requirements. Record your questions, ask your instructor as soon as possible, and jot down the answers.

### To Work Out Timetables for Completing Assignments

To avoid procrastination, schedule. Divide the task into blocks—preparing and researching, writing a first draft, revising, editing, final typing and proofreading— and work out how many days you can devote to each. Your schedule may change as you complete the assignment, but making a schedule and attempting to stick to it should help you avoid last-minute scrambling.

### To Make Notes As You Research

Record ideas, questions, and preliminary conclusions that occur to you as you read, discuss your ideas with others, conduct experiments, compile surveys and questionnaires, consult with experts, and pursue information on your topic. Keep your notebook handy at all times; write down ideas as soon as possible and assess their value later.

### To Respond to Arguments You Hear or Read

To augment the notes you make in the margins of books, jot down more extended responses in your notebook. Evaluate the strengths and weaknesses of texts, compare an argument with other arguments; make notes on how to use what you read to build your own arguments. Note page numbers to make it easier to use this information later.

### To Write a Rhetorical Prospectus

A *prospectus* details a plan for proposed work. A **rhetorical prospectus** will start you thinking about *what, to whom, how,* and *why* you are writing. In your notebook, explore and then briefly outline:

*Your thesis:* What are you claiming?

*Your aim:* What do you want to accomplish?

*Your audience:* Who should read this? Why? What are these people like?

*Your persona:* What is your relationship to the audience? How do you want them to perceive you?

*Your subject matter:* What does your thesis obligate you to discuss? What do you need to learn more about? How do you plan to get the information?

*Your organizational plan:* What should you talk about first? Where might that lead? What might you end with?

### To Record Useful Feedback

Points in the writing process when it is useful to seek feedback from other students and the instructor include:

When your *initial ideas* have taken shape, to discover how well you can explain your ideas to others and how they respond

After you and other students have *completed research* on similar topics, to share information and compare evaluations of sources

Upon completion of a *first draft,* to uncover what you need to do in a second draft to accommodate readers' needs, objections, and questions

At the end of the *revising process,* to correct surface problems such as awkward sentences, usage errors, misspellings, and typos

Prepare specific questions to ask others, and use your notebook to jot them down; leave room to sum up the comments you receive.

### To Assess a Graded Paper

Look over your instructor's comments carefully, and write down anything useful for future reference. For example, what did you do well? What might you carry over to the next assignment? Is there a pattern in the shortcomings your instructor has pointed out? If so, list the types of problems you discover. Refer to these notes when you compose the next essay.

In the chapters that follow, we refer frequently to your writer's notebook. Whether or not you keep one may depend on your instructor's requirements, but we hope you'll try out this excellent tool.

### Following Through

What issues do you currently have strong opinions about? Although you can look to today's newspaper or the evening news for inspiration, also think about events you've noticed on campus, at your job, or around your town — a change in course requirements for your planned major, a conflict over some aspect of your work environment, or a proposed land development near your house. Write a notebook entry in which you list several possible topics for written arguments. Then pick one or two, and create the briefest of arguments — a statement of your position followed by a statement of your best reason for holding that position. Think about who the audience for such an argument could be. Think also about your aim: Would you be arguing to inquire, convince, persuade, or negotiate?

# Chapter 2

# Reading an Argument

In a course in argumentation, you will read many arguments. Our book contains a wide range of argumentative essays, some by students, some by established professionals. In addition, you may find arguments on your own in books, newspapers, and magazines, or on the Internet. You'll read them to develop your understanding of argument. That means you will analyze and evaluate these texts—known as **critical reading.** Critical reading involves special skills and habits that are not essential when you read a book for information or entertainment. This chapter discusses skills and habits that are essential when an assignment involves writing an analysis of an argument or researching an argument of your own.

By the time most students get to high school, reading as a subject has dropped out of the curriculum. While there's plenty to read in high school and college, any advice on *how to read* is usually about increasing vocabulary or reading speed, not reading critically. This is too bad, because in high school and college you are called upon to read more critically than ever, and doing it well is not just a matter of time or intuition.

So have patience with yourself and with the texts you work with in this course. Reading each text will involve much more than reading it through once, no matter how careful that single reading may be. You will go back and look at the text again and again, asking new questions each time. That takes patience; but we ourselves read and reread a text, analyzing it thoroughly, when we prepare to teach it in class. Just as when one sees a film a second time, one notices new details, so it is with critical reading, whether one is a student or a teacher. We suggest three different encounters to have with a text in the process of reading it critically—not three linear, line-by-line readings, but three visits to the text in which you practice different critical-reading skills and habits.

Before we start, a bit of advice: Attempt critical reading only when your mind is fresh. Some experts on reading half-jokingly have suggested "rules" for reading when your purpose is to put yourself to sleep: "Get into bed in a comfortable position, make sure the light is inadequate. . . ." Conversely, when your purpose is to stay alert, find a time and place conducive to that goal—such as a table in the library. As you will see, critical reading is about being an active reader, not a passive one.

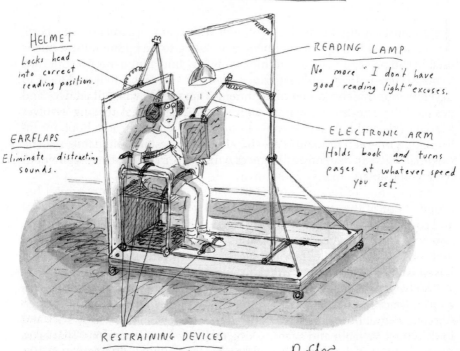

NORDIC TRAK
READING MACHINE

HELMET
Locks head into correct reading position.

READING LAMP
No more "I don't have good reading light" excuses.

EARFLAPS
Eliminate distracting sounds.

ELECTRONIC ARM
Holds book and turns pages at whatever speed you set.

RESTRAINING DEVICES
Prevent reader from leaving machine for snacks, phone calls, quick channel flip-throughs, etc.

# THE FIRST ENCOUNTER: SEEING THE TEXT IN CONTEXT

Critical reading begins not with a line-by-line reading but with a fast over-view of the whole text, followed by some thinking about how the text fits into a bigger picture, or *context*, which we describe shortly.

We like to use the word *sampling* to explain the first critical encounter with a text. Sampling can be fast, superficial, and not even sequential. Look at how long the text is. Look at the headings and subdivisions, if such exist. Get a sense of how the text is organized. Note what parts look interesting and which ones look boring or hard to understand. Note any information about the author appearing before or after the text itself, as well as any publication information (where and when the piece was originally published). Most im-portant, look at the opening and closing paragraphs to discern the author's main point or view.

Experts have found that reading comprehension depends less on a large vocabulary than on the ability to see how the text fits into contexts. Sampling will help you consider the text in light of two contexts that are particularly important:

1. *The general climate of opinion* surrounding the topic of the text. This includes debate on the topic both before and since the text's publication.
2. *The rhetorical context* of the text. This includes facts about the au-thor, the intended audience, and the setting in which the argument takes place.

## Considering the Climate of Opinion

Your familiarity with the topic of an argument and the climate of opinion surrounding it naturally will help you read critically. Imagine trying to cri-tique an argument written over two hundred years ago protesting the condi-tion of the poor in Ireland if you had no knowledge of social conditions in Ireland at the time or of the politics of English rule over Ireland. Yet many high school students are asked to analyze Jonathan Swift's "A Modest Pro-posal" without the knowledge of history—the context—that would enable them to understand it. The arguments reproduced in this text are more recent than Swift's essay; their topics are likely to have caught your attention already through TV, reading, or personal experience. But thinking about the climate of opinion surrounding them, including your own preconceptions, is still necessary.

Familiarity with the climate of opinion will help you view any argu-ment critically, recognize a writer's biases and assumptions, and spot gaps or errors in the information. Your own perspective, too, will affect your interpretation of the text. So think about what you know, how you know it, what your opinion is, and what might have led to its formation. The text is not just "out there"—you will interact with it, so be aware of yourself as a participant.

We suggest that before reading an assigned argument, you and your classmates discuss the topic and the climate of opinion surrounding it so that all can learn what others know about the context of the essay. More formally, your instructor may ask you to write in your writer's notebook a summary of your prior knowledge of topic and the climate of opinion surrounding it.

## Following Through

An argument on the topic of body decoration (tattoos and piercing) appears later in this chapter. More specifically, "On Teenagers and Tattoos" is about motives for decorating the body. Imagine that you are about to read this argument, and practice identifying the climate of opinion surrounding this topic. Think about what people say about motives for tattooing and piercing. Have you heard people argue that it is "low-class"? a rebellion against middle-class conformity? immoral? an artistic expression? a fad? an affront to school or parental authority? an expression of individuality? If you would not want a tattoo, why not? If you have a tattoo or a piercing, why did you get it? In your writer's notebook, jot down some positions you have heard debated, and state your own viewpoint. Why do you feel as you do? If you have no opinions on the topic, why hasn't it become an issue for you?

## Considering the Rhetorical Context

Critical readers also are aware of the **rhetorical context** of an argument. They do not see the text merely as words on a page but as a contribution to some debate among interested people. When you look at rhetorical context, you are considering the text as communication and identifying its elements: the author, to whom he or she was writing and why, as well as where and when the argument was written (its date and place of publication). The reader who knows in advance something about the author's politics or affiliations will have an advantage over the reader who does not. For example, knowing if the periodical that printed it was liberal, like *The Nation*, or conservative, like *National Review*, will also enable you to read more intelligently.

An understanding of rhetorical context comes from both external and internal clues—information outside the text and information you gather as you read and reread it. You can gather a lot of information about rhetorical

*Dr.... with declaration*

To determine an argument's rhetorical context, answer the following questions:

**Who** wrote this argument, and what are his or her occupation, personal background, and political leanings?

**To whom** do you think the author is writing? Arguments are rarely aimed at "the general public" but rather at a definite target audience, such as "entertainment industry moguls," "drivers in Dallas," or "parents of teenagers."

**Where** does the article appear? If it is reprinted, where did it appear originally? What do you know about the publication?

**When** was the argument written? If not recently, what do you know about the time during which it appeared?

**Why** was the article written? What prompted its creation, and what purpose does the author have for writing? (In order to answer this last question, you will probably have to read the argument.)

context from external evidence such as publishers' notes about the author or about a magazine's editorial board or sponsoring foundation. You can usually find this information in a column in the first few pages or by following an information link on the homepage of an online publication. On the Internet, though, check out the homepage for this kind of background before you waste time reading something because much material on the Internet is propaganda rather than serious argument.

You may also have prior knowledge of rhetorical context — for example, you may have heard of the author. Or you can look in a database such as *InfoTrac* (see pages 110, 117–118) to see what else the author has written. Later, when you read the argument more thoroughly, you will enlarge your understanding of rhetorical context as you discover what the text itself reveals about the author's bias, character, and purpose for writing.

One of the biggest differences between high school research and college research is knowledge of rhetorical context. This awareness deepens with repeated encounters with the text, but as you sample an argument, you should begin to see it as an act of communication, taking place at a certain time, for a reason, between an author and an audience.

In sum, the first encounter with a text is preliminary to a careful, close reading. It prepares you to get the most out of the second encounter. If you are researching a topic and looking for good sources of information and viewpoints about it, the first encounter with any text will help you decide whether you want to read it at all. A first encounter can be a time-saving last encounter if the text does not seem appropriate or credible.

### Following Through

Read the following information about "On Teenagers and Tattoos."

*When* published: First published in 1997, reprinted in fall 2000.

*Where* published: First in the *Journal of Child and Adolescent Psychiatry,* which is published by the American Academy of Child and Adolescent Psychiatry, then reprinted in a journal entitled *Reclaiming Children and Youth.*

Written by *whom:* Andres Martin, MD. Martin is identified as an assistant professor of child psychiatry at the Yale Child Study Center in New Haven, CT.

Then do a fast sampling of the text itself, which appears on pages 28– 32. In your writer's notebook, make some notes about what you expect to find in this argument. What do you expect the author's perspective to be on the topic, and why? How might it differ from that of a teen, a parent, or a teacher? Do the subheadings give you any idea of the main point? Do you notice at the opening or closing any repeated ideas that might give a clue to the author's claim? To whom do you imagine the author was writing, and what might be the purpose of an essay in a journal such as the one that published his argument?

---

## On Teenagers and Tattoos
### Andres Martin

*The skeleton dimensions I shall now proceed to set down are copied verbatim from my right arm, where I had them tattooed: as in my wild wanderings at that period, there was no other secure way of preserving such valuable statistics.*

—MELVILLE, *Moby Dick*

Tattoos and piercing have become a part of our everyday landscape. They are ubiquitous, having entered the circles of glamour and the mainstream of fashion, and they have even become an increasingly common feature of our urban youth. Legislation in most states restricts professional tattooing to adults older than 18 years of age, so "high end" tattooing is rare in children and adolescents, but such tattoos are occasionally seen in older teenagers. Piercings, by comparison, as well as self-made or "jailhouse" type tattoos, are not at all rare among adolescents or even among school-age children. Like hairdo, makeup, or baggy jeans, tattoos and piercings can be subject to fad influence or peer pressure in an effort toward group affiliation. As with any other fashion statement, they can be construed as bodily aids in the inner struggle toward identity consolidation, serving as adjuncts

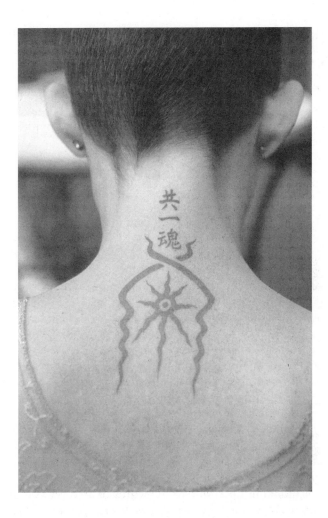

to the defining and sculpting of the self by means of external manipulations. But unlike most other body decorations, tattoos and piercings are set apart by their irreversible and permanent nature, a quality at the core of their magnetic appeal to adolescents.

Adolescents and their parents are often at odds over the acquisition of bodily decorations. For the adolescent, piercing or tattoos may be seen as personal and beautifying statements, while parents may construe them as oppositional and enraging affronts to their authority. Distinguishing bodily adornment from self-mutilation may indeed prove challenging, particularly when a family is in disagreement over a teenager's motivations and a clinician is summoned as the final arbiter. At such times it may be most important to realize jointly that the skin can all too readily become but another battleground for the tensions of the age, arguments having less to do with tattoos and piercings than with core issues such as separation from the family matrix. Exploring the motivations and significance [underlying] tattoos (Grumet, 1983) and piercings can go a long way toward resolving such differences and can become a novel and additional way of getting to know teenagers. An interested and nonjudgmental appreciation of teenagers' surface presentations may become a way of making contact not only in their terms but on their turfs: quite literally on the territory of their skins.

The following three sections exemplify some of the complex psychological underpinnings of youth tattooing.

### Identity and the Adolescent's Body

Tattoos and piercing can offer a concrete and readily available solution for many of the identity crises and conflicts normative to adolescent development. In using such decorations, and by marking out their bodily territories, adolescents can support their efforts at autonomy, privacy, and insulation. Seeking individuation, tattooed adolescents can become unambiguously demarcated from others and singled out as unique. The intense and often disturbing reactions that are mobilized in viewers can help to effectively keep them at bay, becoming tantamount to the proverbial "Keep Out" sign hanging from a teenager's door.

Alternatively, feeling prey to a rapidly evolving body over which they have no say, self-made and openly visible decorations may restore adolescents' sense of normalcy and control, a way of turning a passive experience into an active identity. By indelibly marking their bodies, adolescents can strive to reclaim their bearings within an environment experienced as alien, estranged, or suffocating or to lay claim over their evolving and increasingly unrecognizable bodies. In either case, the net outcome can be a resolution to unwelcome impositions: external, familial, or societal in one case; internal and hormonal in the other. In the words of a 16-year-old girl with several facial piercings, and who could have been referring to her body just as well as to the position within her family: "If I don't fit in, it is because I say so."

### Incorporation and Ownership

Imagery of a religious, deathly, or skeletal nature, the likenesses of fierce animals or imagined creatures, and the simple inscription of names are some of the time-tested favorite contents for tattoos. In all instances, marks become not only memorials or recipients for dearly held persons or concepts: they strive for incorporation, with images and abstract symbols gaining substance on becoming a permanent part of the individual's skin. Thickly embedded in personally meaningful representations and object relations, tattoos can become not only the ongoing memento of a relationship, but at times even the only evidence that there ever was such a bond. They can quite literally become the relationship itself. The turbulence and impulsivity of early attachments and infatuations may become grounded, effectively bridging oblivion through the visible reality to tattoos.

Case Vignette: "A," a 13-year-old boy, proudly showed me his tattooed deltoid. The coarsely depicted roll of the dice marked the day and month of his birth. Rather disappointed, he then uncovered an immaculate back, going on to draw for me the great "piece" he envisioned for it. A menacing figure held a hand of cards: two aces, two eights, and a card with two sets of dates. "A's" father had belonged to Dead Man's Hand, a motorcycle gang named after the set of cards (aces and eights) that the legendary Wild Bill Hickock had held in the 1890s when shot dead over a poker table in Deadwood, South Dakota. "A" had only the vaguest memory of and sketchiest information about his father, but he knew he had died in a motorcycle accident: The fifth card marked the dates of his birth and death.

The case vignette also serves to illustrate how tattoos are often the culmination of a long process of imagination, fantasy, and planning that can start at an early age. Limited markings, or relatively reversible ones such as piercings, can at a later time scaffold toward the more radical commitment of a permanent tattoo.

## The Quest of Permanence

The popularity of the anchor as a tattoo motif may historically have had to do less with guild identification among sailors than with an intense longing for rootedness and stability. In a similar vein, the recent increase in the popularity and acceptance of tattoos may be understood as an antidote or counterpoint to our urban and nomadic lifestyles. Within an increasingly mobile society, in which relationships are so often transient — as attested by the frequencies of divorce, abandonment, foster placement, and repeated moves, for example — tattoos can be a readily available source of grounding. Tattoos, unlike many relationships, can promise permanence and stability. A sense of constancy can be derived from unchanging marks that can be carried along no matter what the physical, temporal, or geographical vicissitudes at hand. Tattoos stay, while all else may change.

Case Vignette: A proud father at 17, "B" had had the smiling face of his 4-month-old baby girl tattooed on his chest. As we talked at a tattoo convention, he proudly introduced her to me, explaining how he would "always know how beautiful she is today" when years from then he saw her semblance etched on himself.   10

The quest for permanence may at other times prove misleading and offer premature closure to unresolved conflicts. At a time of normative uncertainties, adolescents may maladaptively and all too readily commit to a tattoo and its indefinite presence. A wish to hold on to a current certainty may lead the adolescent to lay down in ink what is valued and cherished one day but may not necessarily be in the future. The frequency of self-made tattoos among hospitalized, incarcerated, or gang-affiliated youths suggests such motivations: A sense of stability may be a particularly dire need under temporary, turbulent, or volatile conditions. In addition, through their designs teenagers may assert a sense of bonding and allegiance to a group larger than themselves. Tattoos may attest to powerful experiences, such as adolescence itself, lived and even survived together. As with Moby Dick's protagonist, Ishmael, they may bear witness to the "valuable statistics" of one's "wild wandering(s)": those of adolescent exhilaration and excitement on the one hand; of growing pains, shared misfortune, or even incarceration on the other.

Adolescents' bodily decorations, at times radical and dramatic in their presentation, can be seen in terms of figuration rather than disfigurement, of the natural body being through them transformed into a personalized body (Brain, 1979). They can often be understood as self-constructive and adorning efforts, rather than prematurely subsumed as mutilatory and destructive acts. If we bear all of this in mind, we may not only arrive at a position to pass more reasoned clinical judgment, but become sensitized through our patients' skins to another level of their internal reality.

References [1]

Brain, R. (1979). *The decorated body*. New York: Harper & Row.
Grumet, G. W. (1983). Psychodynamic implications of tattoos. *American Journal of Orthopsychiatry, 53*, 482–92.

## THE SECOND ENCOUNTER: READING AND ANALYZING THE TEXT

We turn now to suggestions for reading and analyzing. These are our own "best practices," what we writing instructors ourselves do when we prepare to discuss or write about a written text. Remember, when you read critically, your purpose goes beyond reading merely to find out what an argument says and to agree or disagree. The critical reader is different from the target audience. As a critical reader, you are more like the food critic who dines not merely to eat but to evaluate the chef's efforts.

In the second encounter, you will read the text through carefully, rereading difficult passages and attempting to clarify in your own mind not only what the text says but also how it works as an argument. Here again, we emphasize the difference between reading and critical reading.

---

[1] These references are formatted in the style recommended by the American Psychological Association, the style used by many scholarly journals in the social sciences.

To see the difference, consider the different perspectives that an ant and a bird would have when looking at the same suburban lawn. The ant is down among the blades of grass, climbing one and then the next. It's a close look, but the view is limited. The bird in the sky above looks down, noticing the size and shape of the yard, the brown patches, the difference between the grass in this yard and the grass in the surrounding yards. The bird has the big picture, the ant the close-up. Critical readers move back and forth between the perspective of the ant and the perspective of the bird, each perspective enriching the other. The big picture helps one notice the larger details, even as the details offer clues to the big picture.

Because critical reading means interacting with the text, be ready with pencil or pen to mark up the text to help yourself understand what it says and how it works. Highlighting or underlining are not the most helpful marks you can make; all they tell you later is that you read those lines and for some reason thought that passage was important. Later, we suggest more useful ways to mark up an argument. Finally, the observations you made in your first encounter with the text are not just so many facts to file away. As you read, keep in mind what you know about the topic, its climate of opinion, and the rhetorical context for this specific argument. All of this information will aid you in comprehending the text.

## Wrestling with Difficult Passages

Because one goal of the second encounter is to understand the argument fully, you will need to figure out the meanings of unfamiliar words and difficult passages. In most college-level texts, you will find some difficult passages, especially if you are not part of the original audience, the one you identified as part of the rhetorical context. You may encounter new words. You may find allusions or references to other books or authors that you have not read. You may find that an author speaks figuratively rather than directly, using metaphors. The author may speak ironically or for another person. The author may assume that readers have lived through all that he or she has or that readers share the same political viewpoint. All of this can make reading harder. Following are some features that often make reading difficult.

### Unfamiliar Contexts

If the author and his or her intended audience are removed from your own experiences, perspectives, and store of knowledge about the world, you will find the text difficult. Texts from a distant culture or period in history will necessarily include concepts familiar to the original writer and readers but not to you. This is true also of contemporary writing intended for a group of specialists. Even a general newspaper such as the *New York Times* publishes articles and editorials aimed at audiences familiar with certain scholarly theories, such as postmodernism in literature, art, and philosophy. And if you have lived a life removed from much discussion of politics or ideologies, you may miss the political agenda in a piece of writing. The role of college is to increase your store of such concepts and introduce you to new (and ancient) perspectives on the world. Accepting the challenge of difficult texts is part of that education. Seek help when you are confused. Your instructors are there to help you bridge the gaps between your world and that of your texts.

### Contrasting Voices and Views

Authors often put into their texts viewpoints that contradict their own. They may concede that part of an opposing argument is true, or they may put in an opposing view in order to refute it. These voices and viewpoints may be in the form of direct quotations or paraphrases. In order to avoid misreading these views as the author's, be alert to words that signal contrast. The most common are *but* and *however*. Much confusion can result from failure to note these turning points in a text.

### Allusions

Allusions are brief references to things outside the text—to people, works of art, songs, events in the news—anything in the culture that the author assumes he or she shares knowledge of with the readers. Allusions are one way for an author to form a bond with readers—provided the readers' and authors' opinions are the same about what is alluded to. Allusions influence readers. They are persuasive devices that can provide positive associations with the author's viewpoint.

In "On Teenagers and Tattoos," the epigraph (the quotation that appears under the title of the essay) is an allusion to the classic novel *Moby Dick*. Martin alludes to the novel again in paragraph 11 (we might say that here he alludes to his own earlier allusion). Martin assumes that his readers know the work—not just its title but also its characters, in particular, the narrator, Ishmael. And he assumes his readers would know that the "skeleton dimensions" of a great whale were important and that readers would therefore understand the value of preserving these statistics. The allusion predisposes readers to see that there are valid reasons for permanently marking the body.

### Specialized Vocabulary

If an argument is aimed at an audience of specialists, it will undoubtedly contain vocabulary peculiar to that group or profession. Martin's essay contains social science terminology: "family matrix" and "surface presentations" (paragraph 2), "individuation" (paragraph 4), "grounded" (paragraph 6), "sense of constancy" (paragraph 9) and "normative uncertainties" (paragraph 11).

The text surrounding these terms provides enough help for most lay readers to get a fair understanding. For example, the text surrounding *individuation* suggests that the person would stand out as a separate physical presence; this is not quite the same meaning as *individuality*, which refers more to one's character. Likewise, the text around *family matrix* points to something the single word *family* does not; it emphasizes the family as the surroundings in which one develops.

If you need to look up a term and a dictionary does not seem to offer an appropriate definition, go to one of the specialized dictionaries available on the library reference shelves. (See pages 113–119 for more on these.)

If you encounter an argument with more jargon than you can handle, you may have to accept that you are not an appropriate reader for it. Some readings are aimed at people with highly specialized graduate degrees or training. Without advanced courses, no one could read these articles with full comprehension, much less critique their arguments.

## Following Through

Find other words in Martin's essay that sound specific to the field of psychology. Use the surrounding text to come up with laymen's terms for these concepts.

*Missing Persons*

A common difficulty with scientific writing is that it can sound disembodied and abstract. You won't find a lot of people doing things in it. Generally, a sentence is clearer if the subject is a person or thing that performs the action of the verb. Sentences are easiest to read when they take a "who-does-what" form. A technical term for this kind of sentence is **agent-action.** ("*Agent:* one who has the power or authority to act," *American Heritage Dictionary.*) But in many of Martin's sentences, we have a hard time seeing exactly who does what. His subjects tend to be abstractions, like the long phrase italicized below, and he uses many nonaction verbs like *to be* and *to become:*

> *An interested and nonjudgmental appreciation of teenagers' surface presentations* may become a way of making contact not only in their terms but on their turfs . . .

In this sentence, Martin is being indirect rather than saying, "Psychiatrists who take an interest in teenagers' tattoos can make contact with their patients." In at least one other sentence, Martin goes so far in leaving people out that his sentence is grammatically incorrect, as in this example of a dangling modifier, which we have italicized:

> Alternatively, *feeling prey to a rapidly evolving body over which they have no say,* self-made and openly visible decorations may restore adolescents' sense of normalcy and control, a way of turning passive experience into active identity.

The italicized phrase describes adolescents, not decorations. We wonder, "Where was Martin's editor?" If you have trouble reading passages like this, take comfort in the fact that the difficulty is not your fault. But recasting the idea into who-does-what form can clear things up. We offer the following paraphrase:

> Teens may feel like helpless victims of the changes taking place in their bodies. They may mark themselves with highly visible tattoos and piercings to regain a sense of control over their lives.

### Passive Voice

Passive voice is another common form of the missing-person problem. In an active-voice sentence, we see our predictable who-does-what pattern:

*Active voice:* The rat ate the cheese.

In passive-voice sentences, the subject of the verb is not an agent; it does not act. Here, the cheese is the subject but not the agent (actor).

*Passive voice:* The cheese was eaten by the rat.

At least in this sentence, we know who the agent is — it's the rat. But scientists often leave out any mention of agents. Thus, in Martin's essay we have sentences like this one, in which we have italicized the passive verb:

> Adolescents' bodily decorations . . . *can be seen* in terms of figuration rather than disfigurement. . . .

Who can see them? Martin really means that *psychiatrists should see tattoos* as figuration rather than disfigurement. But that would sound too committed, not scientific. Passive-voice sentences are common in the sciences and social sciences as part of an effort to sound objective. However, Martin is nowhere near as objective as he attempts to sound, as we note in our third encounter with this text.

You might note other places in the essay where a switch to active voice would heat up the rhetoric. However, our point here is that passive voice generally makes sentences abstract, disembodied, and harder to read for those not accustomed to scientific writing. Rhetorically, however, passive voice may be effective with the target audience, who might think active voice sounds unprofessional.

If you learn to recognize passive voice, you can often mentally convert the troublesome passage into active voice, making it clearer. Passive voice is explained in more detail on pages A3–A4, but it always takes this pattern:

> A helping verb in some form of the verb *to be: Is, was, were, has been, will be, will have been, could have been,* and so forth.

Followed by a main verb, a past participle: Past participles end in *ed,
en, g, k,* or *t.*

Some examples:

The car *was being driven* by my roommate when we had the wreck.

Infections *are spread* by bacteria.

The refrain *is sung* three times.

## Following Through

Convert the following sentences into active voice. We have put the
passive-voice verbs in bold type, but you may need to look at the surrounding text to figure out who the agents are.

A sense of constancy *can be derived* from unchanging marks that
*can be carried* along no matter what the physical, temporal, or geographical vicissitudes at hand. (paragraph 9) To edit this one,
ask *who* can derive what and *who* can carry what.

The intense and often disturbing reactions that *are mobilized* in
viewers can help to effectively keep them at bay, becoming tantamount to the proverbial "Keep Out" sign hanging from a teenager's door. (paragraph 4) To edit, ask *what* mobilizes the reactions in other people.

*Using Paraphrase to Aid Comprehension*

As we all know, explaining something to someone else is the best way to
make it clear to ourselves. Putting an author's ideas into your own words,
that is, **paraphrasing** them, is like explaining the author to yourself — or to a
classmate who is having trouble understanding a passage in an argument.
(Because paraphrasing is an important skill in writing a researched essay, we
cover it in more detail in Chapter 5. See pages 128–131.)

Unlike summary (see pages 131–132 in Chapter 5), paraphrase makes
no effort to shorten. In fact, a paraphrase is often longer than the original, as
it tends to loosen up what is dense. Try to make both the language and the
syntax (word order) simpler. This could mean making two sentences where
there was one. It often means finding plainer, more everyday language, con-
verting passive voice to active voice, breaking a complicated sentence into
several shorter sentences, and making the subjects concrete rather than abstract. It is hard to write a good paraphrase of a difficult passage if you read it
out of context. Paraphrasing a passage is something you do after reading the
whole argument through twice — or more.

- Use your own words, but don't strain to find a different word for every single one in the original. Some of the author's plain words are clearer than what you might find as substitutes.
- If you take a phrase from the original, enclose the phrase in quotation marks.
- Don't use the sentence pattern of the original. Make a simpler pattern, even if it means making several short sentences. You are aiming for clarity.
- Check the surrounding sentences to make sure you understand the passage in its context. You may want to add an idea from the context.
- Aim for who-does-what sentences.

Wrestling with difficult passages means noting and checking allusions, writing out definitions, and writing paraphrases either in the margins or in your writer's notebook. All of these are better aids to comprehension than simply underlining a passage.

## Following Through

Pair up with another member of your class. Together, select a passage of one or two sentences from Martin's essay that you both agree is not obvious or easy to say in your own words. Each work out a paraphrase of the passage, then compare your attempts, and combine what is best in each to make a good paraphrase. Discuss what makes the passage easier to read.

## Analyzing the Reasoning of an Argument

As part of your second encounter with the text, you should be able to pick out its reasoning. The reasoning is the author's case, which consists of the *claim* (what the author wants the readers to believe or do) and the *reasons* and evidence offered in support of it. In the second reading, we want to be able to state the case, preferably in our own words, and also describe what else is going on the argument, such as the inclusion of opposing views or background information.

If a text is an argument, we ought to be able to find a sentence in the text (or create such a sentence ourselves) stating what the author wants the readers to believe or do. And we should be able to find another statement (or more) that tells us *why* they should believe it or do it. This is the essential structure of argument. A claim and a reason — or two, or more. (Don't expect to find many reasons. In a good argument, much space and effort may go toward developing and supporting only one reason.) Of course, we should also look for evidence presented to make the reasons seem good and believable. Marking claims and reasons in the margin is something we always do when preparing to teach an argument. We advise that you do it too (unless you are reading a library book).

For people not experienced at analyzing arguments, picking out a case can be challenging, unless the author has explicitly laid out the case with direct statements such as "My first reason for claiming . . . is. . . ." Not many mature writers make arguments so explicitly or arrange them in as simple a form as the five-paragraph essay pattern that teachers may have imposed on you. Although it's good to be clear and organized, most readers are likely to find such a heavy-handed approach insulting rather than persuasive. Then there is always the possibility that an author has failed to make a case — has written his or her opinions but failed to provide good reasoning to support them.

Therefore, most complex arguments require critical reading. Two critical-reading skills will help you rise to the challenge. Both ask you to take the perspective of the bird, who sees the big picture and its patterns, rather than the ant. One is **subdividing the text.** The other, already discussed, is **considering contexts.** Critical readers use these in combination simultaneously, but here we describe them one at a time.

## Finding Parts

Critical readers develop the habit of breaking a text down into parts instead of seeing it as a monolith. By *parts of the text,* we mean groups of paragraphs that work together to perform some role in the essay. Examples of such roles are to introduce the essay, to provide background material, to give an opposing view, to conclude the piece, and so on. When we talk about the parts of the text, we mean how the essay itself is arranged.

Discovering the parts of a text can be simple. Authors often make them obvious with subheadings and blank space. Even without these, transitional expressions and clear statements of intention make subdividing a text almost as easy as breaking a Hershey bar into its already well-defined segments. However, other arguments are more loosely constructed, their subdivisions less readily discernible. But even with these, close inspection will usually reveal some fault lines that indicate subdivisions, and you should be able to see the roles played by the various chunks.

We have placed numbers next to every fifth paragraph in the essays reprinted in our text. Numbering makes it easier to refer to specific passages and to discuss parts. You too should number the paragraphs of essays you find, considering every single indention a new paragraph, no matter how short. (Block quotations, such as the epigraph at the beginning of Martin's essay, however, are part of the paragraphs that contain them.)

Martin helps us see the parts of his essay by announcing early on, in paragraph 3, that it will have three sections, each "[exemplifying] some of the complex psychological underpinnings of youth tattooing." Martin's essay can thus be subdivided into the following six parts:

1. Epigraph
2. Paragraphs 1, 2, and 3: the introduction
3. Paragraphs 4 and 5: an example
4. Paragaphs 6, 7, and 8: another example
5. Paragraphs 9, 10, and 11: a third example
6. Paragraph 12: the conclusion

When preparing to teach an argument, we write numbers next to each paragraph and draw lines across the page to mark the major subdivisions of the argument. Looking for transitional expressions as well as changes in topic or focus will help you mark a text this way. Again, this kind of marking up of the text is superior to underlining if your intention is to think analytically about the essay.

## Using Context

Taking the bird's-eye view again, we can use surroundings or contexts to help pick out the reasoning. While a quick reading might suggest that Martin is arguing that teens have good reasons for decorating their bodies, we need to recall that the essay appeared in a journal for psychiatrists—doctors, not parents or teachers. Martin is writing to other psychiatrists and psychologists, clinicians who work with families. Reading carefully, we learn that his audience is an even smaller portion of this group: clinicians who have been "summoned as the final arbiter" in family disputes involving tattoos and other body decoration (paragraph 2). Because journals such as the *Journal of Child and Adolescent Psychiatry* are aimed at improving the practice of medicine, we can assume that Martin is trying to help his readers in their own practices. We want to look for sentences that tell these readers what they ought to do and how it will make them better doctors.

## Identifying the Claim and Reasons

*The claim:* Martin is very clear about his claim, repeating it three times, using just slightly different wording:

His readers should "[explore] the motivations and significance [underlying] tattoos and piercings. . . ." (paragraph 2)

His readers should have "[a]n interested and nonjudgmental appreciation of teenagers' surface presentations. . . ." (paragraph 2)

His readers should see "[a]dolescents' bodily decorations . . . in terms of
figuration rather than disfigurement. . . ." (paragraph 12)

Asked to identify Martin's claim, you could choose any one of these statements or write a paraphrase of the idea. Why might an author repeat the
claim, or any key idea, as often as Martin does here? By using slightly different language in each version, he moves from a neutral claim to a more biased
one—from just exploring the motives to seeing them in positive terms.

*The reason:* The reason is the "because" part of the argument. Why should
the readers believe or do as he suggests? We can find the answer in paragraph 2, in the same sentences with his claim:

Because doing so **"can go a long way toward resolving . . . differences and
can become a novel and additional way of getting to know teenagers."**

Because doing so **"may become a way of making contact not only in their
terms but on their turfs. . . ."**

And the final sentence of Martin's essay offers a third version of the same
reason:

Because **"we may not only arrive at a position to pass more reasoned clinical judgment, but become sensitized through our patients' skins to another
level of their internal reality."**

Again, we could choose any one of these sentences or paraphrase his reason. Using paraphrase, we can begin to outline the case structure of Martin's
argument:

**Claim:** Rather than dismissing tattoos as disfigurement, mental health professionals should take a serious interest in the meaning of and motivation behind
the tattoos.

**Reason:** Exploring their patients' body decorations can help them gain insight
and make contact with teenagers on teenagers' own terms.

What about the rest of the essay? Where is Martin's evidence? Martin tells us
that the three subsections will "exemplify some of the complex psychological underpinnings of youth tattooing." In each, he offers a case, or vignette,
as evidence.

**Example and Evidence** (paragraphs 4 and 5): Tattoos are a way of working out
identity problems when teens need either to mark themselves off from others
or to regain a sense of control of a changing body or an imposing environment.
The sixteen-year-old-girl who chose not to fit in.

**Example and Evidence** (paragraphs 6, 7, and 8): Tattoos can be an attempt to
make the intangible a tangible part of one's body. The thirteen-year-old boy remembering his father.

**Example and Evidence** (paragraphs 9, 10, and 11): Tattoos are an "antidote" to a society that is on the run. The seventeen-year-old father.

## THE THIRD ENCOUNTER: RESPONDING CRITICALLY TO AN ARGUMENT

Once you feel confident that you have the argument figured out, you are ready to respond to it, which means evaluating it and comparing it with other perspectives, including your own. You already should have marked the text with lines, numbers, and highlighting or underlining, but only by *writing words* can you respond critically. As the reading expert Mortimer Adler says in his book entitled *How to Read a Book*,

> Reading, if it is active, is thinking, and thinking tends to express itself in words, spoken or written. The person who says he knows what he thinks but cannot express it in words usually does not know what he thinks. (49)

### Annotation Is Key

So we suggest that you annotate heavily. *Annotation* simply means to make a note. You may use the margins for these notes of critical response, but you may also find you need to move to your writer's notebook. Many writers keep reading journals just for this purpose, to practice active interaction with what they read and to preserve the experience of reading a text they want to remember.

What should you write about? Think of questions you would ask the author if he or she were in the room with you. Think of your own experience with the subject. Note similarities and contrasts with other arguments you have read or experiences of your own that confirm or contradict what the author is saying. Write about anything you notice that seems interesting, unusual, brilliant, or wrong. Comment, question—the more you actually write on the page, the more the essay becomes your own. And you will write more confidently (that is, better) about a text you own than one you are just borrowing.

The list on the next page will give you ideas for annotations, but don't be limited by these suggestions.

- Paraphrase the claim and reasons next to where you find them stated.
- Does the author support his or her reasons with evidence? Is the evidence sufficient in terms of both quantity and quality?
- Circle the key terms. Note how the author defines or fails to define them.
- What does the author assume? Behind every argument, there are assumptions. For example, a baseball fan wrote to our local paper arguing that the policy of fouls after the second strike needs to be changed. His reason was that the fans would not be subjected to such a long game. The author assumed that a fast game of hits and outs is more interesting than a slow game of strategy between batters and hitters. Not every baseball fan would share that assumption.
- Do you see any contradictions, either within the text itself or with anything else you've read or learned?
- What are the implications of the argument? If we believe and/or do what the author argues, what is likely to happen?
- Think of someone who would disagree with this argument, and say what that person might object to.
- If you see any opposing views in the argument, has the author been fair in presenting them? Consider whether the author has represented opposing views fairly or has set them up to be easily knocked down.
- What is the author overlooking or leaving out, in your opinion?
- Where does the argument connect with anything else you have read?
- Does the argument exemplify mature reasoning as explained in Chapter 1, "Understanding Argument"?
- What aim does the argument seem to pursue? One of the four in the box on page 19, or some other aim?
- What about the character or projected personality of the author? What kind of person does he or she sound like? Mark places where you hear the author's voice. Describe the tone. How does the author establish credibility—or fail to?
- What about the author's values and biases? Note places where the author sounds liberal or conservative, religious or materialistic, and so on.
- Note places where you see clues about the intended audience of the argument and where the author has made an effort to appeal to their interests, values, tastes, and so on. Maybe you see manipulation or pandering—note it!

There are no margins wide enough to let you write about all the points we raise here, but pick out what is salient to the argument before you, and if you run out of space, you can always turn to your notebook to do more free-writing in response to the argument.

A concluding comment about responses: Even if you agree with an argument, think about who might oppose it and what their objections might be. It may be easier (and more fun) to challenge arguments you disagree with, but if you are studying arguments as claims to truth, it is even more important to challenge the views you find most sympathetic.

As an example of annotation, we offer here our annotations of some paragraphs from Martin's argument.

## Sample Annotations

*How is he defining "solution"? Do tattoos solve a problem or just indicate one?*

Tattoos and piercing can offer a concrete and readily available solution for many of the identity crises and conflicts normative to adolescent development. In using such decorations, and by marking out their bodily territories, adolescents can support their efforts at autonomy, privacy, and insulation. Seeking individuation, tattooed adolescents can

*It seems like there are more mature ways to do this.*

become unambiguously demarcated from others and singled out as unique. The intense and often disturbing reactions that are mobilized in viewers can help to effectively

*Or would it cause parents to pay attention to them rather than leave them alone?*

keep them at bay, becoming tantamount to the proverbial "Keep Out" sign hanging from a teenager's door.

Alternatively, feeling prey to a rapidly evolving body over which they have no say, self-made and openly visible decorations may restore adolescents' sense of normalcy and control, a way of turning a passive experience into an active identity. By indelibly marking their bodies, adolescents can strive to reclaim their bearings within an environment experienced as alien, estranged, or suffocating or to lay claim over their evolving and increasingly unrecognizable bodies. In either case, the net outcome can be a resolution to unwelcome impositions: external, familial, or societal in one case, internal and hormonal in the other. In the words of a 16-year-old girl with several facial piercings, and who could have been referring to her body just as well as to the position within her family: "If I don't fit in, it is because I say so."

*What is norma[l]*

*Would he say the same abou[t] anorexia?*

*Is he implying that the indelible mark is one they will not outgrow? What if they do?*

*Does he assume this family needs counseling — or will not need it? He says the problem is "resolved."*

5

# WRITING ASSIGNMENT: A CRITICAL RESPONSE TO A SINGLE ARGUMENT

This assignment asks you to write an essay about your critical reading of an argument. Writing about your encounters with the text will make you self-conscious about your critical thinking, bringing to your own attention the habits and practices of critical reading. However, we think you should have your classmates in mind as an audience for this paper. The goal of your paper can be twofold: to help your classmates better comprehend and criticize an essay you have all read and to demonstrate the steps involved in giving any argument a thorough critical reading.

## In Part One

The project will have two parts. In Part One (2–4 paragraphs), explain the rhetorical context, including who the author is and where he or she is coming from, as well as the intended audience for the argument as you infer it from clues both outside and inside the text. Describe the reasoning, explaining what you see as the claim and reasons. You should comment on the organization of the argument, referring to sections or groups of paragraphs, and on how well the argument is organized. Also in Part One, tell about your experience of reading the essay—whether you found it easy, difficult, confusing in parts, and why. Be specific, and refer to actual passages from the argument when you talk about what made the difficult parts difficult or what made the ideas accessible.

## In Part Two

In Part Two (3–4 paragraphs), evaluate the argument. Say how effective it may have been for its target audience and also whether you think it is a good example of mature reasoning. Remember to focus on the text of the argument. Don't make an argument of your own, but talk about the strengths and weaknesses of the argument about which you have chosen to write. Your point is not to agree or disagree with the author; instead, show your understanding of the qualities of good argumentation based on what you have learned so far from *The Aims of Argument*. In developing Part Two, use the suggestions for annotation on pages 42–44 as well as the criteria for mature reasoning on pages 11–15. Although your responses may be critical in the sense of negative criticisms of the text, we use the term *critical* here in the broader sense of film or literary criticism, "a careful and exact evaluation and judgment" (*American Heritage Dictionary*). So support your judgments.

This can be a very informal paper. Many scholars keep journals about the things they read, both as a way of preserving what they learned about a text and as a way to do some thinking of their own about it. Think of this paper as a cleaned-up journal entry, but use first person to describe your experiences of reading and responding.

### Other Advice for Both Parts

Be specific. Refer to paragraphs in the text by number.

If you use direct quotations, make sure they are exact, and enclose them in quotation marks. Indicate in parentheses what paragraph they come from.

Use paraphrase when talking about key ideas in the essay, and cite the paragraph in which the original passage appeared. It is important to demonstrate that you can state these key ideas in your own words.

Use first person. This will help keep your writing clear.

Refer to the author by full name on first mention and by last name only from there on.

## STUDENT SAMPLE ESSAY: CRITICAL RESPONSE TO A SINGLE ARGUMENT

Here we have reproduced another argument on the topic of tattoos and body decorations. Following it is one student's critical response to this essay.

### The Single Argument

---

## The Decorated Body
### France Borel

*Nothing goes as deep as dress nor as far as the skin; ornaments have the dimensions of the world.*

—Michel Serres, *The Five Senses*

Human nakedness, according to social custom, is unacceptable, unbearable, and dangerous. From the moment of birth, society takes charge, managing, dressing, forming, and deforming the child—sometimes even with a certain degree of violence. Aside from the most elementary caretaking concerns—the very diversity of which shows how subjective the motivation is—an unfathomably deep and universal tendency pushes families, clans, and tribes to rapidly modify a person's physical appearance.

One's genuine physical makeup, one's given anatomy, is always felt to be unacceptable. Flesh, in its raw state, seems both intolerable and threatening. In its naked state, body and skin have no possible existence. The organism is acceptable only when it is transformed, covered with signs. The body only speaks if it is dressed in artifice.

For millennia, in the four quarters of the globe, mothers have molded the shape of their newborn babies' skulls to give them silhouettes conforming to prevalent criteria of beauty. In the nineteenth century, western children were tightly swaddled to keep their limbs straight. In the so-called primitive world, children were scarred or tattooed at a very early age in rituals which were repeated at all the most important steps of their lives. At a very young age, children were fitted with belts, necklaces, or bracelets; their lips, ears, or noses were pierced or stretched.

Some cultures have designed sophisticated appliances to alter physical structure and appearance. American Indian cradleboards crushed the skull to flatten it; the Mangbetus of Africa wrapped knotted rope made of bark around the child's head to elongate it into a sugar-loaf shape, which was considered to be aesthetically pleasing. The feet of very young Chinese girls were bound and spliced, intentionally and irreversibly deforming them, because this was seen to guarantee the girls' eventual amorous and matrimonial success.[1]

Claude Lévi-Strauss said about the Caduveo of Brazil: "In order to be a man, one had to be painted; whoever remained in a natural state was no different from the beasts."[2] In Polynesia, unless a girl was tattooed, she would not find a husband. An unornamented hand could not cook, nor dip into the communal food bowl. Pink lips were despicable and ugly. Anyone who refused the test of the tattoo was seen to be marginal and suspect.

Among the Tivs of Nigeria, women called attention to their legs by means of elaborate scarification and the use of pearl leg bands; the best decorated calves were known for miles around. Tribal incisions behind the ears of Chad men rendered the skin "as smooth and stretched as that of a drum." The women would laugh at any man lacking these incisions, and they would never accept him as a husband. Men would subject themselves willingly to this custom, hoping for scars deep enough to leave marks on their skulls after death.

At the beginning of the eighteenth century, Father Laurent de Lucques noted that any young girl of the Congo who was not able to bear the pain of scarification and who cried so loudly that the operation had to be stopped was considered "good for nothing."[3] That is why, before marriage, men would check to see if the pattern traced on the belly of their intended bride was beautiful and well-detailed.

The fact that such motivations and pretexts depend on aesthetic, erotic, hygienic, or even medical considerations has no influence on the result, which is always in the direction of transforming the appearance of the body. Such a transformation is wished for, whether or not it is effective.

The body is a supple, malleable, and transformable prime material, a kind of modeling clay, easily molded by social will and wish. Human skin is an ideal subject for inscription, a surface for all sorts of marks which make it possible to differentiate the human from the animal. The physical body offers itself willingly for tattooing or scarring so that, visibly and recognizably, it becomes a social entity.

The absolutely naked body is considered as brutish, reduced to the level 10 of nature where no distinction is made between man and beast. The decorated body, on the other hand, dressed (if even only in a belt), tattooed, or mutilated, publicly exhibits humanity and membership in an established group. As Theophile Gautier said, "The ideal disturbs even the roughest nature, and the taste for ornamentation distinguishes the intelligent being from the beast more exactly than anything else. Indeed, dogs have never dreamed of putting on earrings."

So, it is by their categorical refusal of nakedness that human beings are distinguished from nature. The "mark makes unremarkable"—it creates an interval between what is biologically and brutally given in the animal realm and what is won in the cultural realm. The body is tamed continuously; social custom demands, at any price—including pain, constraint, or discomfort—that wildness be abandoned.

Each civilization chooses—through a network of elective relationships which are difficult to determine—which areas of the body deserve transformation. These areas are as difficult to define and as shifting as those of eroticism or modesty. An individual alone eludes bodily modifications; they are the expression of a homogeneous collectivity which, at a chosen moment, comes to a tacit agreement to attack one or another part of the anatomy.

Whatever the choices, options, or differences may be, that which remains constant is the transformation of appearance. In spite of our contemporary western belief that the body is perfect as it is, we are constantly changing it: clothing it in musculature, suntan, or makeup; dying its head hair or pulling out its bodily hair. The seemingly most innocent gestures for taking care of the body very often hide a persistent and disguised tendency to make it adhere to the strictest of norms, reclothing it in a veil of civilization. The total nudity offered at birth does not exist in any region of the world. Man puts his stamp on man. The body is not a product of nature, but of culture.

### Notes

1. Of course, there are also many different sexual mutilations, including excisions and circumcisions, which we will not go into at this time as they constitute a whole study in themselves.
2. C. Lévi-Strauss, Tristes Tropiques (Paris: Plon, 1955), p. 214.
3. J. Cuvelier, Relations sur le Congo du Père Laurent de Lucques (Brussels: Institut royal colonial belge, 1953), p. 144.

From France Borel, *Le Vêtement incarné: Les Métamorphoses du corps* (Paris: Calmann-Lévy, 1992), pp. 15–18. Copyright © Calmann-Lévy, 1992. Translated by Ellen Dooling Draper with the permission of the publisher.

## A SAMPLE STUDENT RESPONSE

ANALYSIS OF "THE DECORATED BODY"

Katie Lahey

**Part One**

"The Decorated Body" by France Borel addresses the idea of external body manipulation not only as an issue prevalent to our own culture and time but also as a timeless concept that exists beyond cultural boundaries. It was published in *Parabola,* a magazine supported by the Society for the Study of Myth and Tradition. Borel discusses the ways in which various cultures both ancient and modern modify the natural body. Borel, who has written books on clothing and on art, writes with a style that is less a critique than an observation of his populations. This style suggests an anthropological approach rather than a psychological one, focusing on the motivations of people as a whole and less on the specific individuals within the societies. It seems, therefore, that he may be targeting an academic audience of professional anthropologists or other readers who are interested in the similarities of both "primitive" and "modern" cultures and the whole idea of what it means to be human.

Borel makes the claim that "social custom" dictates that all humans manipulate their bodies to brand themselves as humans. He says in the first paragraph that "an unfathomably deep and universal tendency pushes families, clans, and tribes to rapidly modify a person's physical appearance." He restates the idea in paragraph 2: The body "is acceptable only when it is transformed, covered with signs." He believes that in all cultures this type of branding or decorating is essential to distinguish oneself as legitimate within a civilization. Man has evolved from his original body; he has defied nature. We are no longer subject to what we are born with; rather, we create our bodies and identities as we see fit.

Borel reasons that this claim is true simply because all cultures conform to this idea and do so in such diverse ways. As he says, "the very diversity . . . shows how subjective the motivation is . . ." (paragraph 1). He provides ample evidence to support this reasoning in paragraphs 3 through 7, citing various cultures and examples of how they choose to decorate the body.

**Part Two**

However, Borel does not provide a solid explanation as to why the human race finds these bodily changes necessary to distinguish itself as human. It serves his argument to state that the various specific motivations behind these changes are irrelevant. All he is interested in proving is that humans must change their bodies, and he repeats this concept continually throughout the essay, first saying that a man remaining "in a natural state was no different from the beasts" in paragraph 5 and again in paragraphs 9 and 10. Maybe some readers would think this reiteration makes his point stronger, but I was unsatisfied.

I found myself trying to provide my own reasons why humans have this need to change their bodies. What makes this essay so unsatisfying to me is that, once I thought about it, it does in fact matter why cultures participate in body decoration. For example, why did the Chinese find it necessary to bind the feet of their young girls, a tradition so painful and unhealthy and yet so enduring? In such traditions, it becomes obvious that ulterior motives lie beneath the surface. The binding of the feet is not simply a tradition that follows the idea of making oneself human. In fact, it methodically attempts to put women below men. By binding the feet, a culture disables the young women not only physically but emotionally as well. It teaches them that they do not deserve the same everyday comforts as men and belittles them far beyond simply having smaller feet. Borel, however, fails to discuss any of these deeper motives. He avoids supplying his own opinion because he does not want to get into the politics of the practices he describes. He wants to speak in generalizations about body modification as a mark of being human, even though people in modern Western culture might see some of these activities as violations of human rights.

Borel barely touches on modern Western civilization. He really only addresses our culture in the final paragraph, where he alleges that everyday things we do to change ourselves, whether it be shaving, tanning, toning, dying, or even applying makeup, are evidence that we have the same need to mark ourselves as human. He challenges our belief that "the body is perfect as it is" by showing that "we are constantly changing it" (paragraph 13). But many people today, especially women, *do* doubt that their individual bodies are perfect and would concede that they are constantly trying to "improve" them. What does Borel mean by "perfect as it is?" Is he talking about an ideal we would like to achieve?

His placement of this paragraph is interesting. I wondered why he leaves this discussion of our own culture until the very end of the essay so that his ideas of European and American culture appear as an afterthought. He spends the majority of the essay discussing other, more "primitive cultures" that yield many more examples of customs, such as the American Indian cradleboards, that clearly mark one as a member of a tribe. Perhaps Borel tends to discuss primitive cultures as opposed to our modern Western culture because primitive cultures generally back up his thesis, whereas American culture, in particular, veers from his claim that people decorate themselves in order to demonstrate what they have in common.

Borel ignores any controversy over tattoos and piercing, which people in Western culture might do to mark themselves as different from other

people in their culture. In America, we value individualism, where everyone tries to be unique, even if in some small way. Other authors like Andres Martin, who wrote "On Teenagers and Tattoos," look at American
culture and claim that we use body decoration as a means to show and
celebrate our individuality. Martin says one good reason for teens to tattoo themselves is for "individuation"—to mark themselves as distinct
from their peers and their families. This goes completely opposite from
Borel's claim that "[a]n individual alone eludes bodily modifications; they
are the expression of a homogeneous collectivity . . ." (paragraph 12).

　　Borel makes a sound argument for his claim that human existence is
something more complex or more unnatural than simply being alive. But
we know this already through humans' use of speech, social organization,
and technology. Before I read his argument and even after the first time
I read it, I wasn't swayed by Borel. I was looking for something more
specific than what he is saying. In fact, all he is showing is that we decorate to symbolize our humanity. He does support this claim with good evidence. In this sense, the argument holds. But I cannot help but prefer to
think about the other, more specific things we symbolize through our body
decorations.

# Chapter 3

# Analyzing Arguments: A Simplified Toulmin Method

In Chapter 2, we discussed the importance of reading arguments critically: breaking them down into their parts to see how they are put together, noting in the margins key terms that are not defined, and raising questions about the writer's claims or evidence. Although these general techniques are sufficient for analyzing many arguments, sometimes—especially with intricate arguments and with arguments we sense are faulty but whose weaknesses we are unable to specify—we need a more systematic technique.

In this chapter, we explain and illustrate such a technique based on the work of Stephen Toulmin, a contemporary philosopher who has contributed a great deal to our understanding of argumentation. This method will allow you to analyze the logic of any argument, whether written or spoken; you will also find it useful in examining the logic of your own arguments as you draft and revise them. Keep in mind, however, that because it is limited to the analysis of logic, the Toulmin method is not sufficient by itself. It is also important to question an argument through dialogue (see Chapter 6) and to look at the appeals of character, emotion, and style (see Chapter 8).

## A PRELIMINARY CRITICAL READING

Before we consider Toulmin, let's first explore the following argument carefully, using the general process for critical reading we described in Chapter 2.

---

## Rising to the Occasion of Our Death
### William F. May

*William F. May (b. 1927) is a distinguished professor of ethics at Southern Methodist University. The following essay appeared originally in* The Christian Century *(1990).*

For many parents, a Volkswagen van is associated with putting children to sleep on a camping trip. Jack Kevorkian, a Detroit pathologist, has now linked the van with the veterinarian's meaning of "putting to sleep." Kevorkian conducted a dinner interview with Janet Elaine Adkins, a 54-year-old Alzheimer's patient, and her husband and then agreed to help her commit suicide in his VW van. Kevorkian pressed beyond the more generally accepted practice of passive euthanasia (allowing a patient to die by withholding or withdrawing treatment) to active euthanasia (killing for mercy).

Kevorkian, moreover, did not comply with the strict regulations that govern active euthanasia in, for example, the Netherlands. Holland requires that death be imminent (Adkins had beaten her son in tennis just a few days earlier); it demands a more professional review of the medical evidence and the patient's resolution than a dinner interview with a physician (who is a stranger and who does not treat patients) permits; and it calls for the final, endorsing signatures of two doctors.

So Kevorkian-bashing is easy. But the question remains: Should we develop a judicious, regulated social policy permitting voluntary euthanasia for the terminally ill? Some moralists argue that the distinction between allowing to die and killing for mercy is petty quibbling over technique. Since the patient in any event dies—whether by acts of omission or commission—the route to death doesn't really matter. The way modern procedures have made dying at the hands of the experts and their machines such a prolonged and painful business has further fueled the euthanasia movement, which asserts not simply the right to die but the right to be killed.

But other moralists believe that there is an important moral distinction between allowing to die and mercy killing. The euthanasia movement, these critics contend, wants to engineer death rather than face dying. Euthanasia would bypass dying to make one dead as quickly as possible. It aims to relieve suffering by knocking out the interval between life and death. It solves the problem of suffering by eliminating the sufferer.

The impulse behind the euthanasia movement is understandable in an age when dying has become such an inhumanly endless business. But the movement may fail to appreciate our human capacity to rise to the occasion of our death. The best death is not always the sudden death. Those forewarned of death and given time to prepare for it have time to engage in acts of reconciliation. Also, advanced grieving by those about to be bereaved may ease some of their pain. Psychiatrists have observed that those who lose a loved one accidentally have a more difficult time recovering from the loss than those who have suffered through an extended period of illness before the death. Those who have lost a close relative by accident are more likely to experience what Geoffrey Gorer has called limitless grief. The community, moreover, may need its aged and dependent, its sick and its dying, and the virtues which they sometimes evince—the virtues of humil-

5

ity, courage, and patience—just as much as the community needs the
virtues of justice and love manifest in the agents of care.

*claim*

On the whole, our social policy should allow terminal patients to die,
but it should not regularize killing for mercy. Such a policy would recognize and respect that moment in illness when it no longer makes sense to
bend every effort to cure or to prolong life and when one must allow patients to do their own dying. This policy seems most consonant with the
obligations of the community to care and of the patient to finish his or her
course.

Advocates of active euthanasia appeal to the principle of patient autonomy—as the use of the phrase "voluntary euthanasia" indicates. But emphasis on the patient's right to determine his or her destiny often harbors
an extremely naïve view of the uncoerced nature of the decision. Patients

*rebuttal*

who plead to be put to death hardly make unforced decisions if the terms
and conditions under which they receive care already nudge them in the direction of the exit. If the elderly have stumbled around in their apartments,
alone and frightened for years, or if they have spent years warehoused in
geriatrics barracks, then the decision to be killed for mercy hardly reflects
an uncoerced decision. The alternative may be so wretched as to push patients toward this escape. It is a huge irony and, in some cases, hypocrisy to
talk suddenly about a compassionate killing when the aging and dying may
have been starved for compassion for many years. To put it bluntly, a country has not earned the moral right to kill for mercy unless it has already sustained and supported life mercifully. Otherwise we kill for compassion only
to reduce the demands on our compassion. This statement does not charge
a given doctor or family member with impure motives. I am concerned
here not with the individual case but with the cumulative impact of a social policy.

*coun-
should
work on
providing
better
care*

I can, to be sure, imagine rare circumstances in which I hope I would
have the courage to kill for mercy—when the patient is utterly beyond
human care, terminal, and in excruciating pain. A neurosurgeon once
showed a group of physicians and an ethicist the picture of a Vietnam
casualty who had lost all four limbs in a landmine explosion. The catastrophe had reduced the soldier to a trunk with his face transfixed in horror.
On the battlefield I would hope that I would have the courage to kill the
sufferer with mercy.

But hard cases do not always make good laws or wise social policies.
Regularized mercy killings would too quickly relieve the community of its
obligation to provide good care. Further, we should not always expect the
law to provide us with full protection and coverage for what, in rare circumstances, we may morally need to do. Sometimes the moral life calls us out
into a no-man's-land where we cannot expect total security and protection
under the law. But no one said that the moral life is easy.

# A STEP-BY-STEP DEMONSTRATION OF THE TOULMIN METHOD

The Toulmin method requires an analysis of the claim, the reasons offered to support the claim, and the evidence offered to support the reasons, along with an analysis of any refutations offered.

## Analyzing the Claim

Logical analysis begins with identifying the *claim*, the thesis or central contention, along with any specific qualifications or exceptions.

### Identify the Claim

First ask yourself, *What statement is the author defending?* In "Rising to the Occasion of Our Death," for example, William May spells out his claim in paragraph 6:

> [O]ur social policy should allow terminal patients to die, but it should not regularize killing for mercy.

In his claim, May supports passive euthanasia (letting someone die by withholding or discontinuing treatment) but opposes "regularizing" (making legal or customary) active euthanasia (administering, say, an overdose of morphine to cause a patient's death).

Much popular argumentation is sometimes careless about what exactly is being claimed: Untrained arguers too often content themselves with merely taking sides ("Euthanasia is wrong"). Note that May, a student of ethics trained in philosophical argumentation, makes a claim that is both specific and detailed. Whenever an argument does not include an explicit statement of its claim, you should begin your analysis by stating the writer's claim yourself. Try to state all claims fully and carefully in sentence form, as May's claim is stated.

### Look for Qualifiers

Next, ask, *How is the claim qualified?* Is it absolute, or does it include words or phrases to indicate that it may not hold true in every situation or set of circumstances?

May qualifies his claim in paragraph 6 with the phrase "on the whole," indicating that he recognizes possible exceptions to the application of his claim. Other possible qualifiers include "typically," "usually," and "most of the time." Careful arguers are generally wary of making absolute claims. Although unqualified claims are not necessarily faulty, they do insist that there are no cases or circumstances in which the claim might legitimately be contradicted. Qualifying words or phrases are often used to restrict a claim and improve its defensibility.

## Find the Exceptions

Finally, ask, *In what cases or circumstances would the writer not press his or her claim?* Look for any explicit exceptions the writer offers to qualify the claim.

May, for example, is quite clear in paragraph 8 about when he would not press his claim:

> I hope I would have the courage to kill for mercy—when the patient is utterly beyond human care, terminal, and in excruciating pain.

Once he has specified these conditions in abstract terms, he goes further and offers a chilling example of a case in which he believes mercy killing would be appropriate. Nevertheless, he insists that such exceptions are rare and thus do not justify making active euthanasia legal or allowing it to become common policy.

Critical readers respond to unqualified claims skeptically—by hunting for exceptions. With qualified claims, they look to see what specific exceptions the writer will admit and what considerations make restrictions necessary or desirable.

## Summarize the Claim

At this point it is a good idea to write out in your writer's notebook the claim, its qualifiers, and its exceptions so that you can see all of them clearly. For May, they look like this:

> (qualifier)  "On the whole"
>
> (claim)  "our social policy should allow terminal patients to die, but it should not regularize killing for mercy"
>
> (exception)  "when the patient is utterly beyond human care, terminal, and in excruciating pain"

Record the claim and its qualifiers and exceptions in whatever way that helps you see them best, but do not skip this step. Not only will it help you remember the results of your initial claim analysis, but you will also be building on this summary when you analyze the argument in more detail.

# Analyzing the Reasons

Once you have analyzed the claim, you should next identify and evaluate the reasons offered for the claim.

## List the Reasons

Begin by asking yourself, *Why is the writer advancing this claim?* Look for any statement or statements that are used to justify the thesis. May groups all of his reasons in paragraph 5:

> The dying should have time to prepare for death and to reconcile with relatives and friends.

Those close to the dying should have time to come to terms with the impending loss of a loved one.

The community needs examples of dependent but patient and courageous people who sometimes do die with dignity.

The community needs the virtues ("justice and love") of those who care for the sick and dying.

When you list reasons, you need not preserve the exact words of the arguer; often doing so is impossible because reasons are not always explicit but may have to be inferred. Be very careful, however, to adhere as closely as possible to the writer's language. Otherwise, your analysis can easily go astray, imposing a reason of your own that the writer did not have in mind.

Note that reasons, like claims, can be qualified. May does not say, for instance, that "the aged and dependent" *always* show "the virtues of humility, courage, and patience." He implicitly admits that they can be ornery and cowardly as well. But for May's purposes it is enough that they sometimes manifest the virtues he admires.

Use your writer's notebook to list the reasons following your summary of the claim, qualifiers, and exceptions. One possibility is to list them beneath the summary of the claim in the form of a tree diagram (see the model diagram in the Concept Close-Up box on page 60).

### Examine the Reasons

There are two questions to ask as you examine the reasons. First ask, *Are they really good reasons?* A reason is only as good as the values it invokes or implies. A value is something we think is good—that is, worth pursuing for its own sake or because it leads to attaining other goods. For each reason, you should specify the values involved and then determine whether you accept those values as generally binding.

Second, ask, *Is the reason relevant to the thesis?* In other words, does the relationship between the claim and the reason hold up to examination? For example, the claim "You should buy a new car from Fred Freed" cannot be supported by the reason "Fred is a family man with three cute kids" unless you accept a relationship between an auto dealer's having cute children and his or her reliability in dealing with customers.

Be careful and deliberate as you examine whether reasons are good and whether they are relevant. No other step is as important in assessing the logic of an argument, and no other can be quite as tricky.

To illustrate, consider May's first reason: Those who know they are about to die should have time to prepare for death and to seek reconciliation with people from whom they have become estranged. Is this a good reason? Most of us would probably think so, valuing the chance to prepare for death and to reconcile ourselves with estranged friends or family members. Not to do so would seem immature, irresponsible, unforgiving.

But is the reason relevant? May seems to rule out the possibility that a dying person seeking active euthanasia would be able to prepare for death and reconcile with others. But this is obviously not the case. Terminally ill people who decide to arrange for their own deaths may make any number of preparations beforehand, so the connection between this reason and May's claim is really quite weak. To accept a connection, we would have to assume that active euthanasia necessarily amounts to a sudden death without adequate preparation. Because we cannot do so, we are entitled to question the relevance of the reason, no matter how good it might be in itself.

### Following Through

Now examine May's second, third, and fourth reasons on your own, as we have just examined the first one. Make notes about each reason, evaluating how good each is in itself and how relevant it is to the thesis. In your writer's notebook, create your own diagram based on the model on page 60.

## Analyzing the Evidence

Once you have finished your analysis of the reasons, the next step is to consider the evidence offered to support any of those reasons.

### List the Evidence

Ask, *What kinds of evidence (data, anecdotes, case studies, citations from authority, and so forth) are offered as support for each reason?* Some arguments advance little in the way of evidence. May's argument is a good example of a moral argument from and about principles; such an argument does not require much evidence to be effective. Lack of evidence, then, is not always a fault. For one of his reasons, however, May does offer some evidence: After stating his second reason in paragraph 5 — the chance to grieve before a loved one dies can be helpful for those who must go on living after the patient's death — he invokes authorities who agree with him about the value of advanced grieving.

### Examine the Evidence

Two questions apply. First, ask, *Is the evidence good?* That is, is it sufficient, accurate, and credible? Second, ask, *Is it relevant to the reason it supports?* Clearly, the evidence May offers in paragraph 5 is sufficient; any more would probably be too much. We assume his citations are accurate and credible as well.

**Concept Close-Up**

# Model Toulmin Diagram for Analyzing Arguments

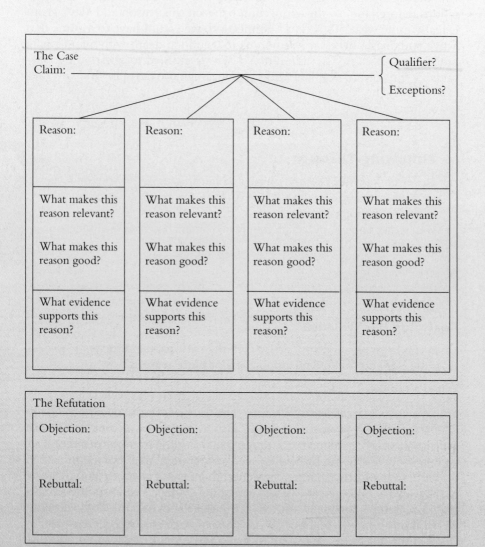

The Case
Claim: _____ ⎰ Qualifier?
⎱ Exceptions?

| Reason: | Reason: | Reason: | Reason: |
|---|---|---|---|
| What makes this reason relevant? | What makes this reason relevant? | What makes this reason relevant? | What makes this reason relevant? |
| What makes this reason good? | What makes this reason good? | What makes this reason good? | What makes this reason good? |
| What evidence supports this reason? | What evidence supports this reason? | What evidence supports this reason? | What evidence supports this reason? |

The Refutation

| Objection: | Objection: | Objection: | Objection: |
|---|---|---|---|
| Rebuttal: | Rebuttal: | Rebuttal: | Rebuttal: |

We would generally also accept them as relevant because apart from our own experience with grieving, we have to rely on expert opinion. (See Chapter 5 for a fuller discussion of estimating the adequacy and relevance of evidence.)

## Noting Refutations

A final — and optional — step is to assess an arguer's refutations. In a refutation, a writer anticipates potential objections to his or her position and tries to show why they do not undermine the basic argument. Refutations do not relate directly to claims, reasons, and evidence. A skilled arguer typically uses them not as part of the main logic of an argument but as a separate step to deal with any obvious objections a reader is likely to have.

First, ask, *What refutations does the writer offer?* Summarize all refutations and list them on your tree diagram of claims, reasons, and evidence. Then, ask, *How does the writer approach each objection?* May's refutation occupies paragraph 7. He recognizes that the value of free choice lends weight to the pro-euthanasia position, and so he relates this value to the question of "voluntary euthanasia." Because in our culture individual freedom is so strong a value, May doesn't question the value itself; rather, he leads us to question whether voluntary euthanasia is actually a matter of free choice. He suggests that unwanted people may be subtly coerced into "choosing" death or may be so isolated and neglected that death becomes preferable to life. Thus, he responds to the objection that dying people should have freedom of choice where death is concerned.

## Summarizing Your Analysis

Once you have completed your analysis, it is a good idea to summarize the results in a paragraph or two. Be sure to set aside your own position on the issue, confining your summary to the argument the writer makes. In other words, whether or not you agree with the author, attempt to assess his or her logic fairly.

Although May's logic is strong, it doesn't seem fully compelling. He qualifies his argument and uses exceptions effectively, and his single use of refutation is skillful. However, he fails to acknowledge that active euthanasia need not be a sudden decision leading to sudden death. Consequently, his reasons for supporting passive euthanasia can be used to support at least some cases of active euthanasia as well. It is here — in the linkage between reasons and claim — that May's argument falls short. Furthermore, we may question whether the circumstances under which May would permit active euthanasia are in fact as rare as he suggests. Experience tells us that many people are beyond human care, terminal, and in pain, and many others suffer acute anguish for which they might legitimately seek the relief of death.

## A. Analyze the Claim

1. **Find the claim.** In many arguments, the claim is never explicitly stated. When it isn't, try to make the implied claim explicit by stating it in your own words. (Note: If, after careful analysis, you aren't sure *exactly* what the writer is claiming, you've found a serious fault in the argument.)
2. **Look for qualifiers.** Is the claim absolute? Or is it qualified by some word or phrase like *usually* or *all things being equal*? If the claim is absolute, can you think of circumstances in which it might not apply? If the claim is qualified, why is it not absolute? That is, is there any real thought or content in the qualifier—good reasons for qualifying the claim?
3. **Look for explicit exceptions to the claim.** If the writer has pointed out conditions in which he or she would *not* assert the claim, note them carefully.

Summarize steps 1–3. See the diagram on page 60.

## B. Analyze the Reasons

1. **Find the reason or reasons advanced to justify the claim.** All statements of reason will answer the question, "Why are you claiming what you've claimed?" They can be linked to the claim with *because*. As with claims, reasons may be implied. Dig them out and state them in your own words. (Note: If, after careful analysis, you discover that the reasons aren't clear or relevant to the claim, you should conclude that the argument is either defective and in need of revision or invalid and therefore unacceptable.)
2. **Ponder each reason advanced.** Is the reason good in itself? Is the reason relevant to the thesis? Note any problems.

List the reasons underneath the claim. See the diagram on page 60.

## C. Analyze the Evidence

1. **For each reason, locate all evidence offered to back it up.** Evidence is not limited to hard data. Anecdotes, case studies, and citations from authorities also count as evidence. (Note: Not all reasons require extensive evidence. But we should be suspicious of reasons without evidence, especially when it seems that evidence ought to be available. Unsupported reasons are often a sign of bad reasoning.)
2. **Ponder each piece of evidence.** Is it good? That is, is it sufficient, accurate, believable? Is it relevant to the reason it supports? Note any problems.

List the evidence underneath the claim. See the diagram on page 60.

## D. Examine the Refutations

If there are refutations—efforts to refute objections to the case—examine them. If not, consider what objections you think the writer should have addressed.

## Following Through

Following is a student-written argument on capital punishment. Read it through once, and then use the Toulmin method as described in this chapter to analyze its logic systematically.

**STUDENT SAMPLE:** *An Argument for Analysis*

CAPITAL PUNISHMENT: SOCIETY'S SELF-DEFENSE

Amber Young

Just after 1:00 A.M. on a warm night in early June, Georgeann, a pretty college student, left through the back door of a fraternity house to walk the ninety feet down a well-lighted alley to the back door of her sorority house. Lively and vivacious, Georgeann had been an honor student, a cheerleader, and Daffodil Princess in high school, and now she was in the middle of finals week, trying to maintain her straight A record in college. That evening, several people saw Georgeann walk to within about forty feet of the door of her sorority house. However, she never arrived. Somewhere in that last forty feet, she met a tall, handsome young man on crutches, his leg in a cast, struggling with a brief case. The young man asked Georgeann if she could help him get to his car, which was parked nearby. Georgeann consented. Meanwhile, a housemother sleeping by an open window in a nearby fraternity house was awakened by a high-pitched, terrified scream that suddenly stopped. That was the last anyone ever heard or saw of Georgeann Hawkins. Her bashed skull and broken body were dumped on a hillside many miles away, along with the bodies of several other young female victims who had also been lured to their deaths by the good looking, clean-cut, courteous, intelligent, and charming Ted Bundy.

By the time Ted Bundy was caught in Utah with his bashing bar and other homemade tools of torture, he had bludgeoned and strangled to death at least thirty-two young women, raping and savaging many of them in the process. His "hunting" trips had extended into at least five Western states, including Washington, Oregon, Idaho, Utah, and Colorado, where he randomly selected and killed his unsuspecting victims.

Bundy was ultimately convicted of the attempted kidnapping of Carol DeRonche and imprisoned. For this charge he probably would have been paroled within eighteen months. However, before parole could be approved, Bundy was transferred to a jail in Colorado to stand trial for the murder of Caryn Campbell. With Bundy in jail, no one died at his hands or at the end of his savagely swung club. Young women could go about their lives normally, "safe" and separated from Ted Bundy by prison walls. Yet any number of things could have occurred to set Bundy free—an acquittal, some sympathetic judge or parole board, a psychiatrist pronouncing him rehabilitated and safe, a state legislature passing shorter sentencing or earlier parole laws, inadequate prison space, a federal court ruling abolishing life in prison without any possibility for parole, or an escape.

In Bundy's case, it was escape—twice—from Colorado jails. The first time, he was immediately caught and brought back. The second time, Bundy made it to Florida, where fifteen days after his escape he bludgeoned and strangled Margaret Bowman, Lisa Levy, Karen Chandler, and Kathy Kleiner in their Tallahassee sorority house, tearing chunks out of Lisa Levy's breast and buttock with his teeth. Ann Rule, a noted crime writer who became Bundy's confidant while writing her book *The Stranger Beside Me,* described Bundy's attack on Lisa Levy as like that of a rabid animal. On the same night at a different location, Bundy sneaked through an open window and so savagely attacked Cheryl Thomas in her bed that a woman in the apartment next door described the clubbing as seeming to reverberate through the whole house for about ten seconds. Then, three weeks later, less than forty days after his escape from the Colorado jail, Bundy went hunting again. He missed his chance at one quarry, junior high school student Leslie Ann Parmenter, when her brother showed up and thwarted her abduction. But Bundy succeeded the next day in Lake City, where he abducted and killed twelve-year-old Kimberly Diane Leach and dumped her strangled, broken body in an abandoned pig barn.

The criminal justice system and jails in Utah and Colorado did not keep Margaret Bowman, Lisa Levy, Karen Chandler, Kathy Kleiner, Cheryl Thomas, Leslie Ann Parmenter, or little Kimberly Leach safe from Ted Bundy. The state of Florida, however, with its death penalty, has made every other young woman safe from Ted Bundy forever. Capital punishment is society's means of self-defense. Just as a person is justified in using deadly force in defending herself or himself against a would-be killer, so society also has a right to use deadly force to defend itself and its citizens from those who exhibit a strong propensity to kill whenever the opportunity and the urge arise.

However, while everyone wants a safe society, some people would say that capital punishment is too strong a means of ensuring it. Contemporary social critic Hendrick Hertzberg often attacks the death penalty, using arguments that are familiar, but not compelling, to those who do not share his absolute value-of-life position. For example, in one article he tries to paint a graphic picture of how horrible and painful even the most modern execution methods, such as lethal injection, are to the prisoner ("Premeditated"). Elsewhere he dismisses the deterrence argument as "specious," since "[n]o one has ever been able to show that capital punishment lowers the murder rate" ("Burning" 4). But the Florida death penalty has, in fact, made certain that Ted Bundy will never again go on one of his hunt-

5

*Refuting*

ing trips to look for another young woman's skull to bash or body to ravage. A needle prick in the arm hardly conjures up images of excruciating pain so great as to be cruel and unusual. Thousands of good people with cancer and other diseases or injuries endure much greater pain every day until death. Therefore, waiting for death, even in pain, is more a part of a common life experience than a cruel or unusual punishment.

Of course, the possibility of mistakenly executing an innocent person is a serious concern. However, our entire criminal justice system is tilted heavily toward the accused, who is protected from the start to the end of the criminal justice procedure by strong individual-rights guarantees in the Fourth, Fifth, Sixth, and Seventh Amendments of the U.S. Constitution. The burden of proof in a criminal case is on the government, and guilt must be proved beyond a reasonable doubt. The chances of a guilty person going free in our system are many times greater than those of an innocent person being convicted. Those opposed may ask, "How do we know that the number of innocent people found guilty is really that low?" The number must be low because when the scandal of an innocent person being convicted comes to light, the media covers it from all angles. The movie *The Thin Blue Line* is an example of such media attention. In addition, the story of *The Thin Blue Line* is illustrative in that the U.S. Supreme Court caught the error and remanded the case, and Randall Adams is no longer subject to the death penalty.

*[handwritten margin note: Why does this follow?]*

If, however, such a mistake should occur in spite of all the protections guaranteed to the accused, such an innocent death would certainly be tragic, just as each of the nearly 50,000 deaths of innocent people each year on our highways are tragic. As much as we value human life, we inevitably weigh and balance that value against social costs and benefits, whether we like to admit it or not. If the rare, almost nonexistent, chance that an innocent person might be executed is such a terrible evil as to require abolition of capital punishment, then why don't we also demand the abolition of automobiles as well? Because we balance the value of those lives lost in traffic accidents against the importance of automobiles in society. In doing so, we choose to accept the thousands of automobile deaths per year in order to keep our cars. It is interesting to note that even opponents of capital punishment like Hertzberg do not demand abolition of the automobile, which leads to the observation that even they may not be at the extreme, absolute end of the life-value scale, where preservation of life takes precedence over *all* other social concerns.

*[handwritten margin note: most of these are accidental. Is it the same?]*

Just as we as a society have decided that the need for automobiles outweighs their threat to innocent life, we can decide that capital punishment is necessary for the safety and well-being of the general populace. The most legitimate and strongest reason for capital punishment is not punishment, retribution, or deterrence, but simply society's right to self-defense. Society has a right to expect and demand that its government remove forever those persons who have shown they cannot be trusted to circulate in society, even on a limited basis, without committing mayhem. First degree murderers, like Bundy, who hunt and kill their victims with premeditation and malice aforethought must be removed from society permanently as a matter of self-defense.

Having made that decision, there are only two alternatives available—life in prison or death. We base our approval or disapproval of capital punishment as an option on fundamental values and ideals relating to life itself, rather than on statistics or factual evidence. Most of us are a long way from the extreme that considers life to have no value; instead, we crowd more closely to the other side, where life is viewed as inviolable. However, few in our society go so far as to believe that life is sacrosanct, that its preservation is required above all else. Our founding fathers wrote in the Declaration of Independence that all men are endowed by their Creator with unalienable rights, including "life, liberty, and the pursuit of happiness." However, there is no indication that life was more sacred to them than liberty. In fact, Patrick Henry, who would later be instrumental in the adoption of the Bill of Rights to the U.S. Constitution, is most famous for his defiant American Revolutionary declaration, "I know not what course others may take, but as for me, give me liberty or give me death!"

The sentiment that some things are worse than death remains pervasive in this country where millions of soldiers and others have put themselves in harm's way and even sacrificed their lives to preserve and defend freedom for themselves or for the people they leave behind. Many people will readily or reluctantly admit to their willingness to use deadly force to protect themselves or their families from a murderer. The preservation of life, any life, regardless of everything else, is not an absolute value that most people in this country hold.

In fact, many prisoners would prefer to die than to languish in prison. While some might still want to read and expand their minds even while their bodies are confined, for those who are not intellectually or spiritually oriented, life in prison would be a fate worse than death. Bundy himself, in his letters from prison to Ann Rule, declared, "My world is a cage," as he tried to describe "the cruel metamorphosis that occurs in captivity" (qtd. in Rule 148). After his sentencing in Utah, Bundy described his attempts to prepare mentally for the "living hell of prison" (qtd. in Rule 191). Thus, some condemned prisoners, including Gary Gilmore, the first person to be executed after the U.S. Supreme Court found that Utah's death penalty law met Constitutional requirements, refused to participate in the appeals attempting to convert his death sentence to life in prison because he preferred death over such a life. In our society, which was literally founded and sustained on the principle that liberty is more important than life, the argument that it is somehow less cruel and more civilized to deprive someone of liberty for the rest of his or her life than just to end the life sounds hollow. The Fifth Amendment of the U.S. Constitution prohibits the taking of either life or liberty without due process of law, but it does not place one at a higher value than the other.

The overriding concerns of the Constitution, however, are safety and self-defense. The chance of a future court ruling, a release on parole, a pardon, a commutation of sentence, or an escape—any of which could turn the murderer loose to prey again on society—creates a risk that society should not have to bear. Lisa Levy, Margaret Bowman, Karen Chandler, Kathy Kleiner, Cheryl Thomas, and Kimberly Leach were not protected from Bundy by the courts and jails in Utah and Colorado, but other young women who were potential victims are now absolutely protected from Bundy by the Florida death penalty.

The resolutions of most great controversies are, in fact, balancing acts, and capital punishment is no exception. There is no perfect solution; rather, the best answer lies on the side with the greatest advantages. It comes down to choosing, and choosing has a price. Capital punishment carries with it the slight risk that an innocent person will be executed; however, it is more important to protect innocent, would-be victims of already convicted murderers. On balance, society was not demeaned by the execution of Bundy in Florida, as claimed by Hertzberg ("Burning" 49). On the contrary, society is, in fact, better off with Ted Bundy and others like him gone.

Works Cited

Hertzberg, Hendrick. "Burning Question." The New Republic 20 Feb.
    1989: 4+.
---. "Premeditated Execution." Time 18 May 1992: 49.
Rule, Ann. The Stranger Beside Me. New York: Penguin, 1989.
The Thin Blue Line. Dir. Errol Morris. HBO Video, 1988.

## A FINAL NOTE ABOUT LOGICAL ANALYSIS

No method for analyzing arguments is perfect, and no method can guarantee that everyone using it will assess an argument the same way. Uniform results are not especially desirable anyway. What would be left to talk about? The point of argumentative analysis is to step back and examine an argument carefully, to detect how it is structured, to assess the cogency and power of its logic. The Toulmin method helps us move beyond a hit-or-miss approach to logical analysis, but it cannot yield a conclusion as compelling as mathematical proof.

Convincing and persuading always involve more than logic, and, therefore, logical analysis alone is never enough to assess the strength of an argument. For example, William May's argument attempts to discredit those like Dr. Jack Kevorkian who assist patients wishing to take their own lives. May depicts Kevorkian as offering assistance without sufficient consultation with the patient. Is his depiction accurate? Clearly, we can answer this question only by finding out more about how Kevorkian and others like him work. Because such questions are not a part of logical analysis, they have not been of concern to us in this chapter. But any adequate and thorough analysis of an argument must also address questions of fact and the interpretation of data.

# Chapter 4

# Reading and Writing about Visual Arguments

We live in a world awash in pictures. We turn on the TV and see not just performers, advertisers, and talking heads but dramatic footage of events from around the world, commercials as visually creative as works of art, and video images to accompany our popular music. We boot up our computers and surf the Net; many of the waves we ride are visual swells, enticing images created or enhanced by the very machines that take us out to sea. We drive our cars through a gallery of street art — on billboards and buildings and on the sides of buses and trucks. We go to movies, video stores, arcades, and malls and window-shop, entertained by the images of fantasy fulfillment each retailer offers. Print media are full of images; in our newspapers, for instance, photos, drawings, and computer graphics appear in color and vie with print for space. Even college textbooks, once mostly blocks of uninterrupted prose with an occasional black-and-white drawing or photo, now often have colorful graphics and elaborate transparency overlays.

If a picture is indeed worth a thousand words, then perhaps our image-saturated world is all to the good. Or perhaps, as some argue, all this rapid-fire, reality-manipulating technology yields jaded people with short attention spans who haven't the patience for the slower thought needed to understand words in print. But no matter how we assess it, the technology rolls on, continually extending its range and reach, filling our minds and, more importantly, *forming* them. Visual images are not just "out there" clamoring for our attention but also "in here," part of how we attend to and judge experience. Like language, visual images are rhetorical. They persuade us in obvious and not-so-obvious ways. And so we need some perspective on visual rhetoric; we need to learn how to recognize its power and how to use it effectively and responsibly.

## UNDERSTANDING VISUAL ARGUMENTS

**Visual rhetoric** is *the use of images, sometimes coupled with sound or appeals to the other senses, to make an argument or persuade us to act as the image-maker would have us act.* Probably the clearest examples are advertisements and political cartoons, a few of which we will examine shortly. But visual rhetoric is as ubiquitous and as old as human civilization. We do not ordinarily think, say, of a car's body style as "rhetoric," but clearly it is, because people are persuaded to pay tens of thousands of dollars for the sleekest new body style when they could spend a few thousand for an older car that would get them from home to work or school just as well. Consider also the billions of dollars we spend on clothes, hairstyles, cosmetics, diets, and exercise programs—all part of the rhetoric of making the right "visual statement" in a world that too often judges us solely by how we look. We spend so much because our self-images depend in part on others' responses to our cars, bodies, offices, homes—to whatever appears to represent "us." No doubt we all want to be liked and loved for our true selves, but distinguishing this "inside" from the "outside" we show the world has never been easy. Because we tend to become the image we cultivate, the claim that "image is everything" may not be as superficial as it sounds. Even if it isn't everything, image certainly is important enough to preoccupy us, and we would be hard pressed to name a significant human activity that is not entangled in visual rhetoric.

We might imagine that visual rhetoric is something peculiarly modern—that without photography, computers, and Madison Avenue it wouldn't amount to much. But we would be mistaken. The pharaohs of ancient Egypt didn't build the pyramids merely to have a place to be buried; these immense structures "proclaim" the power and status of the rulers who had them built, as well as the civilization and empire they symbolize, and they "argue" against a view of human existence as merely transitory. Even now, millennia after ancient Egypt's decline, we can only stand before the pyramids in awe and wonder. The impact of visual rhetoric is not always as fleeting as the clever new commercial on television.

As old as the pyramids are, visual rhetoric is still older. We will never find its origins, for it began with natural places that prehistoric people invested with sacred power, with the earliest drawings and paintings, with natural and sculpted objects used in religious rites and festivals. When a culture disappears, most visual rhetoric is lost, leaving only a few fragments that archaeologists dig up and speculate about thousands of years later. There is no way to know exactly what these artifacts meant and no way to even estimate what remains undiscovered or lost beyond any possibility of recovery.

Although there is much that we cannot know about visual rhetoric—where and why it began, or what it might be like hundreds or thousands of years in the future, in cultures we cannot imagine, using technologies we cannot envision—we can still study how it works now, in our culture and time. We can learn to appreciate the art that goes into making potent images. We can learn how to interpret and evaluate images. We can reflect on the ethics of visual argumentation and persuasion. We can create visual rhetoric ourselves, in images that stand alone or in visuals combined with text. This chapter analyzes some common forms of visual rhetoric. The assignments will give you practice in analyzing images and creating visual rhetoric of your own.

## "READING" IMAGES

Rhetorical analysis of visual rhetoric involves examining images to see how they attempt to convince or persuade an audience. We must first recognize that "reading" an image demands interpretive skills no less than does reading a written text. Pictures, even photographs, do not merely reflect reality, as many people assume. Pictures are symbols that must be read, just as language is read; this becomes clear when we look at art from different cultures. The bodies in Egyptian paintings seem distorted to us, flattened onto a geometrical plane in a combination of full frontal and profile views, but the Egyptians understood these figures as representing the human form as timeless and ideal. Also, visual symbols operate within a culture—the color white, for example, suggests purity in one culture, death in another. To read an argument made through images, a critic must be able to recognize visual allusions to other aspects of the culture. For example, initially Americans knew that the white mustaches on the celebrities in the milk commercials alluded to children's milk-drinking style; but more recently, the milk mustache has become an allusion to the ad campaign itself, which has become part of our culture.

As with inquiry into any argument, we ought to begin with questions about rhetorical context: When was the visual argument created and by whom? To what audience was it originally aimed and with what purpose? Then we can ask what claim a visual argument makes and what reasons it offers in support of that claim. "Reading" the claims and reasons of purely visual arguments requires greater interpretive skills than does reading verbal arguments, simply because pictures are even more ambiguous than words— they mean different things to different people. Then, as with verbal texts that make a case, we can examine the visual argument for evidence, assumptions, and bias, and we can ask what values it favors and what will be the implications of accepting the argument—for instance, if we buy the Jaguar, what kind of debt will we incur?

Although it is possible to make a claim and support it with no words at all, most arguments that use images do not rest their cases entirely on the images. If the visual argument includes some verbal text, some of the reasoning usually appears in the words. Either way, if we see that an argument is offered, we can inquire into it as we have done with verbal texts: What is the claim?

the reason(s)? the evidence? the assumptions? the bias? the implications? What values are being promoted? We cannot, however, expect a visual argument to make a fully developed argument to convince.

Many visual arguments do not even attempt to persuade through reasoning; they rely instead on ethical and emotional appeals. Appeals to emotions and character are frequent and powerful in visual arguments. They are most obvious in advertising, where the aim is to move a target audience to buy a service or product. In many advertisements, especially for products like beer, cigarettes, and perfume, where the differences are subjective or virtually non-existent, emotional appeal and character identification are all there is. Although some images make us fear what will happen if we don't buy the product, vote for the candidate, or at least believe the argument's claim, most emotional appeals work by promising to reward our desires for love, status, peace of mind, or escape from everyday responsibilities.

Advertisements and other forms of visual argument use ethical appeals as well, associating their claim with values the audience approves of and wants to identify with—such as images that show nature being preserved, races living in harmony, families staying in touch, and people attaining the American dream of upward mobility. However, some advertisements appeal to counterculture values through images of rebellion against conventional respectability. Such ads project an ethos of "attitude" and rule-breaking.

In evaluating the ethics of visual rhetoric, we need to consider whether the argument appeals to logic and, if so, whether the case is at least reasonable: Does the image encourage good reasoning, or does it oversimplify and even mislead? Most likely, we will want to look for the emotional and ethical appeals as well and decide if the argument panders to the audience by playing to their weaknesses and prejudices or manipulates them by playing to their fantasies and fears. We can ask what values the image seems to endorse or wants the audience to identify with, and we can question the implications of widespread acceptance of such values and behavior.

## ANALYSIS: FIVE COMMON TYPES OF VISUAL ARGUMENT

In the next pages, we analyze some specific visual arguments in various genres: advertisements, editorial cartoons, public sculpture, and news photographs. We show how "reading" visual texts requires interpretive skills and how interpretive skills, in turn, depend on the critic's knowledge of the context in which the image appears. Practice in analyzing visual rhetoric helps us appreciate the role of culture and context in all communication.

### Advertisements

In the arguments made by advertisements, the claims, if not the reasons, are usually clear. And because advertisers aim carefully at target audiences, we can readily see how strategy comes into play in making a persuasive case and in choosing ethical and emotional appeals. Here we examine some advertisements to see how visual images and verbal texts combine to sell products and services to specific audiences.

An advertisement for Pentax (see Figure C-1 in the color section) appeared originally in *Sierra* magazine, published by the environmentalist Sierra Club. *Sierra's* readership is primarily middle-class adults who love nature and are concerned about preserving the environment. It is not a radical environmental group, however, and most of the ads and articles are of interest to parents planning family trips and wanting to ensure that wilderness will be around for their children and grandchildren to enjoy.

The logical appeal of the ad is obvious. The ad argues that readers should buy a Pentax IQZoom 140M because it is a convenient, light camera with many features that will help them take great pictures. The features of the camera are the reasons for buying it, and these are clearly indicated by the large photo of the camera itself and the text in red print. The small, tacked-on snapshot of the boys is evidence in support of the reasons. Readers who want a user-friendly camera would find the argument persuasive. They want good pictures with minimal fussing. However, rather than letting the argument rest on the technological features of the camera, the advertisers depend heavily on ethical and emotional appeals to sell it to the *Sierra* readers.

The ad features the image of a stock character in mainstream American culture: the soccer mom—although in this case she is the Badger den mother. The choice of this figure shows the strategy of ethical appeal targeted at parents: a wholesome, friendly, young mother reaches out—literally—and "testifies" to how successfully she uses the camera. The advertiser expects *Sierra* readers would trust such a character and admire her values. Her affectionate descriptions of the "scrappy champions" and her reference to the "box of bandages" show that she is loving and nurturing. The Band-Aid on her right knee shows that she is a participant in the action. She is energetic and cheerful in her bright yellow uniform as she smiles up at the readers. They would find nothing in this ad to intimidate them or challenge their ideas about traditional gender roles for women and boys. In short, she confirms middle-American values.

None of what we have said so far addresses the real appeal of the ad, however. The advertisers wanted to get the audience laughing, and the eye-catching image of the woman does just that as it plays with photographic effects. The knowledge of how to "read" a two-dimensional photograph as a realistic image of three-dimensional space is nearly universal, but this image distorts even that "reality," providing some ridiculous relationships in size, such as between the woman's head and the cap that should fit it. The camera and the woman's hand seem grossly out of proportion as they float above her tiny hiking boots. These distortions of reality are funny, not threatening or disorienting, as images in serious art photography can be. Most Americans know that such distorted effects occur when a wide-angle lens is used for a close-up or when the dog decides to sniff the wide-angle lens. Like the ex-aggeratedly childish uniform on the woman, the wide-angle distortions are merely for fun.

The direct, friendly relationship between the viewer and the woman in the ad is supported by the angle of the camera that took her photograph. The camera angle puts the viewers above her in the position of power. There is nothing intimidating or pretentious about this ad, which suggests through both visual images and verbal text that the Pentax IQZoom 140M is a way for ordinary people to capture fun on film.

You may not think of postage as a form of advertising, but the stamp that appears as Figure C-2 in the color section has raised over $22.3 million for breast cancer research since it was first issued on July 29, 1998. Its fundrais-ing success makes it a compelling example of visual rhetoric, despite the tiny dimensions of its actual size. Called a "semi-postal" stamp, because a per-centage of its sale price is donated to fund the cause it represents, it and other stamps in the postal service's "social awareness" stamp category rely on all of the appeals—logical, ethical, emotional, and stylistic.

That you need to buy stamps anyway, and for just a few cents more can get an attractive stamp *and* contribute to a good cause, is a logical reason to buy such a stamp. But the breast cancer stamp persuades people to buy it be-cause all postage stamps confer honor on the subjects they represent. "Get-ting your face on a stamp" is a highly desirable form of social validation, as not just stamp collectors notice who, or what, has "gotten a stamp": Mal-colm X got a stamp; the Sonoran Desert got a stamp. That they did confirms their importance and credibility—their worthiness of our consideration and respect. Furthermore, every time we buy a stamp because of its subject, we re-confirm the subject's value, and, in a sense, participate in our country's shared values as well as reinforce the federal government's inherent authority, since it decides who or what gets a stamp.

Is it, however, just federal validation that has sold more than 377.2 mil-lion copies of this stamp? No, its success as a product and rhetorical appeal also has a lot to do with how its image works visually. Designed by breast cancer survivor Ethel Kessler of Bethesda, Maryland, and illustrated by Whit-ney Sherman of Baltimore, the stamp depicts a goddess. While we may not consciously recognize the female figure as a goddess, we do recognize the im-age's combination of femaleness and strength: Non-angular lines dominate, suggesting softness, traditionally considered a female attribute; however, the stamp's colors are bold—suggesting vitality and even triumph—and exclude the traditionally feminine color pink. The stamp's minimal main text, "Fund the Fight. Find a Cure," furthers its rhetorical effectiveness by beginning at the left edge of the image, moving in a straight line, and then curving down sharply and encircling the area where the figure's right breast would be. The visual effect is that of highlighting, or circling, an important point.

We may not have noticed the feelings the US postal service evokes or how those feelings contribute to the credibility and appeal of the postal service's products. Nor may we have thought about what an effective advertisement its tiniest product can be, even if it's not specifically helping to raise money for a social cause. That organizations like the Human Genome Project are aggressively competing to get their "faces" on a stamp, however, is evidence that it is.

As the postage stamp shows, visual images with little or no accompanying text can be powerfully persuasive by implying an argument rather than stating it explicitly. Consider the poster reproduced as Figure C-3 of the color section, created by an advertising agency for the Southampton Anti-Bias Task Force. It shows a line of five sharp new crayons, each labeled "flesh." On one level, a viewer may see the poster as an eye-catching message for racial tolerance. However, anyone old enough to recall a now-discontinued Crayola crayon called "flesh" that was the color of the center crayon will see a more complicated argument. This prior knowledge allows viewers to read the image as an argument against the cultural bias that allowed millions of children to grow up thinking that "flesh" was the color skin was supposed to be—and all other skin colors were deviations from the norm. While white people might remember thinking that this "flesh" didn't quite match their own, they knew it approximated the color of white people's skin. Children of other races or mixed races knew that "flesh" was not their flesh.

Because an image invites interpretation rather than blatantly stating a message, it opens a space for contemplation, just as we may contemplate the implied message of any work of art—fiction, film, poetry, painting. Our own reading of this poster led us to wonder if other examples of bias, invisible to all except the victims, exist in American culture. As we noted earlier in this chapter, studying visual rhetoric reminds us of the reader's contribution to the meaning of any text, visual or verbal.

## Following Through

1. Although the advertisement for the Volkswagen Beetle shown in Figure C-4 of the color section features an image of the product, as is customary with car ads, the lack of background, the size of the image relative to the white space surrounding it, and the unusual wording of the text all contribute to making this an unconventional piece of visual rhetoric. Consider these elements and any other aspect of the ad as you discuss how it might appeal to a specific audience of car buyers.

2. An advertisement for Comstock, Inc., a company that rents out photographs for commercial purposes, promotes its service with a striking example of its own product. The company wishes to persuade potential clients that it can supply a visual image for any idea. Discuss how the image of the goldfish bowl, (Figure C-5 of the color section) conveys the feeling of being "stuck." Do you find the image and accompanying text persuasive?

(continues)

**Following Through (continued)**

3. The Adidas advertisement shown as Figure C-7 of the color section is an example of the creative effects possible with photographic techniques. How do you "read" the image of the man in relation to the image of the shadow? How does the entire picture convey the idea of speed? Why do you think the advertisers chose to identify the celebrity athlete in such fine print?

## Editorial Cartoons

Editorial cartoons comment on events and issues in the news. At times they can be riotously funny, but more often they offer serious arguments in a concise and witty form. Many political cartoons rely on captions and on dialogue spoken by characters in the picture to make their argument, so they combine visual and verbal argument. Like advertisements, editorial cartoons are not ambiguous in their purpose; their arguments are clearly stated or at least easily inferred. However, as they age, editorial cartoons may become harder to "read" because they usually allude to current events. But some cartoons have longer lifespans, like the one by Mike Keefe (Figure 4.1. See page 77.) that comments on a general condition of contemporary culture—how computers are affecting people's ideas of knowledge.

This cartoon illustrates how "reading" a visual argument depends on a shared knowledge of symbols and visual metaphors within a culture. The image of a thirsty man crawling on hands and knees through a desert is a common visual metaphor suggesting any environment that denies humans something they need to sustain themselves. Other treatments of this metaphor suggest that sustenance could be anything from love to religion to the music of Mozart. In Keefe's cartoon, a highway labeled "information" runs through the desert. The cartoon takes our common metaphor for the Internet, as "information superhighway," and depicts it in a graphic way. The man is literally on the Internet, and he is desperate for wisdom. To read the argument of the cartoon and appreciate its humor, the viewer has to know something about what can be found on the Internet—the advertising, the data, the opinions, and especially the overwhelming glut of information, as suggested by the size of the letters on the road. The cartoon argues that relying on the Internet for knowledge will deprive a civilization of the wisdom it needs to sustain itself.

We might question how convincing political cartoons can be. Can they change people's views on an issue? A picture may indeed be worth a thousand words, but visual arguments must present a concise argument, not a fully reasoned case. Anthony Blair, one critic of visual arguments, has written that "visual arguments tend to be one-dimensional; they present the case for one side only, without including arguments against it. . . . Visual arguments,

*Figure 4.1*

then, must always be suspect in this respect and their power countered by a degree of skepticism and a range of critical questions: 'Is that the whole story?' 'Are there other points of view?' 'Is the real picture so black and white?' "

Cartoons also may fail to change people's minds because their humor comes at the expense of the side they oppose — they satirize and often exaggerate the opposition's view. In fact, political cartoons are usually arguments that "preach to the choir." Believers will applaud having their position cleverly portrayed, while nonbelievers will be more annoyed or offended than persuaded by cartoons that ridicule their position. Consider the two cartoons in Figure 4.2 (page 78), which use both language and visual images to make cases about what the cartoonists see as misplaced priorities in the pro-life and the pro-choice movements.

The McCloskey cartoon (top) argues that the pro-choice demonstrators are hypocritical in their protests about murdered doctors, for they ignore the death of the fetus. The lower half of the drawing emphasizes the fetus by putting it in a black background and giving it wings to symbolize its human soul. This half of the cartoon stands in stark contrast to the "noisy" upper half, in which the protesters look deranged. In the Luckovich cartoon (bottom), the contrast is between the shapeless fetus and the more fully depicted corpse of the doctor, both preserved in specimen bottles. One is a person; the other clearly is not. Viewers on either side of this issue would argue that these portraits misrepresent their positions through oversimplification.

## Public Sculpture

Public sculptures, such as war memorials, aim to teach an audience about a nation's past and to honor the values for which its citizens were willing to die.

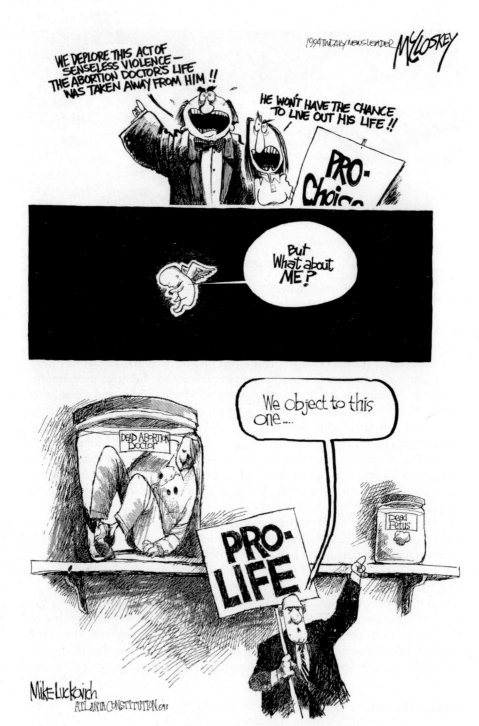

Figure 4.2

*Figure C-1*

_Figure C-2_

Source: AP Photo/U.S. Postal Service

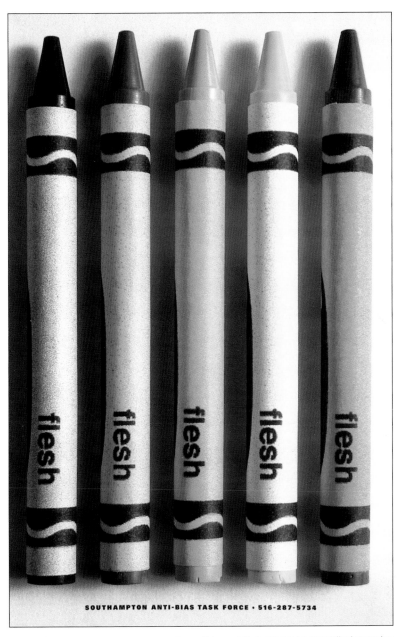

SOUTHAMPTON ANTI-BIAS TASK FORCE · 516-287-5734

*Figure C-3*    Source: Holzman & Kaplan Worldwide, Bret Wills-Photographer.

Hug it? Drive it? Hug it? Drive it?

Drivers wanted.

*Figure C-4*

Source: By permission of Volkswagen of America, Inc.

*Figure C-5*

Source: Reuters/Gregg Newton Archive Photos

*Figure C-6*

The World's Fastest Man, Donovan Bailey, wears the adiStar Sprint. See our complete new line of track & field spikes at www.adidas.com.

*Figure C-7*

*Figure 4.3*

## Following Through

1. The above cartoon by Gary Varvel (Figure 4.3) comments on attempts in Oregon to legalize doctor-assisted suicide. This is not
   a funny topic, but Varvel makes a humorous comment on it by exploiting a stock situation in American comedy—that of the ledge-
   jumper and the would-be rescuer. How does the humor work here
   to poke fun at the idea of doctor-assisted suicide? What aspects of
   the larger issue does the cartoon leave out?
2. Find a recent editorial cartoon on an issue of interest to you. Bring
   it to class, and be prepared to elaborate on its argument and explain
   its persuasive tactics. Do you agree or disagree with the cartoonist's
   perspective? Discuss the fairness of the cartoon. Does it minimize
   the complexity of the issue it addresses?

An example of a public sculpture that can be read as an argument is the Marine Corps Memorial (better known as the Iwo Jima Memorial), which was
erected in 1954 on the Mall in Washington, DC (see Figure 4.4, the photograph on page 80). The memorial honors all Marines who gave their lives for
their country through a literal depiction of one specific act of bravery, the
planting of the American flag on Iwo Jima, a Pacific island that the United
States captured from the Japanese in 1945. The claim that the sculpture makes

*Figure 4.4*

to American audiences is clear: Honor your country. The image of the soldiers straining every muscle to raise the American flag gives the reason: "These men made extreme sacrifices to preserve the values symbolized by this flag." Interpreting the memorial is not difficult for Americans who associate the flag with freedom and who know not only the military custom of raising flags in victory but also the history of the fierce Iwo Jima battle. But the sculpture has more to say. It communicates an emotional appeal to patriotism through details like the wind-whipped flag and the angles of the men's arms and legs, which suggest their supreme struggle.

The Iwo Jima sculpture is indeed a classic war memorial, glorifying a victory on enemy soil. We might therefore compare its argument with the argument of a very different memorial, the Vietnam War Memorial, which was dedicated in Washington in November 1982. Maya Lin designed what has come to be known simply as "the Wall" while she was an undergraduate architecture student at Yale. Her design was controversial because the monument was so untraditional in its design (see Figures 4.5 and 4.6, page 81) and in its argument, which is ambiguous and more difficult to interpret than most public sculpture. With its low, black granite slates into which are etched the names of the war casualties, the Wall conveys a somber feeling; it honors not a victory but the individuals who died in a war that tore the nation apart.

## News Photographs

While some news photographs seem merely to record an event, the camera is not an objective machine. The photographer makes many "editorial"

Figure 4.5

Figure 4.6

decisions—whether to snap a picture, when to snap it, what to include and exclude from the image—and artistic decisions about light, depth of field, and so on. Figure 4.7 (see page 83), a photograph that appeared in the *New York Times*, shows one scene photographer Bruce Young encountered when covering a snowstorm that hit Washington, DC, in January 1994. The storm was severe enough to shut down the city and all government operations. Without the caption supplied by the *New York Times*, readers might not have recognized the objects in the foreground as human beings, homeless people huddled on benches, covered by undisturbed snow.

The picture argues that homelessness in America is a national disgrace, a problem that must be solved. The composition of the picture supports this claim. The White House in the background is our nation's "home," a grand and lavishly decorated residence symbolic of our national wealth. In juxtaposition in the foreground, the homeless people look like bags of garbage; they mar the beautiful picture of the snow-covered landscape. Viewers are unlikely to find in this picture evidence to blame the homeless for their condition: they are simply too pathetic, freezing under their blankets of snow. True, there is no in-depth argument here taking into account causes of the problem such as unemployment or mental illness, or solutions such as shelters. The picture simply shows that homelessness is a fact of life in our cities, tarnishing the idealized image of our nation.

## Following Through

1. The Vietnam War Memorial invites interpretation and analysis. Because it does not portray a realistic scene or soldiers as does the Iwo Jima Memorial, readings of it may vary considerably—and this was the source of the controversy surrounding it. Look at the two photographs on page 82, and if you have visited the Wall, try to recall your reaction to it. What specific details—the low black wall, its shape, its surfaces—lead to your interpretation? Could you characterize the Wall as having logical, ethical, and emotional appeals?

2. Even if you do not live in Washington, DC, or New York City, where the Statue of Liberty serves as another outstanding example of visual rhetoric, you can probably find public sculpture or monuments to visit and analyze. Alone or with some classmates, take notes and photographs. Then develop your interpretation of the sculpture's argument, specifying how visual details contribute to the case, and present your analysis to the class. Compare your interpretation with those of your classmates.

## Graphics

Visual supplements to a longer text such as an essay, article, or manual are known as *graphics*. Given the ubiquity of visual appeals in almost everything

(continues on page 84)

*Figure 4.7*

## Following Through

1. A color news photograph of the October 1998 launch of the space shuttle *Discovery* is reproduced as Figure C-6 of the color section. This was the flight that carried John Glenn into space for the second time. Photographer Gregg Newton captured this image well into the launch, when the plume of smoke was all that was visible. Although some Americans were skeptical that Glenn's flight was merely a clever public relations ploy by NASA, most people celebrated Glenn's accomplishment. Media images such as this contributed to Americans' perspective on the launch. How do you "read" the photo's argument?

2. In a recent newspaper or news magazine, find a photograph related to an issue in the news, something people may have differing opinions about. What perspective or point of view does the photograph offer? Explain your "reading" of the photograph through an analysis of the content, composition, and any other details that contribute to your interpretation.

we read and the widespread use of them in business and industry, it is odd how few school writing assignments require graphics or multimedia support. When students want to use photos, drawings, graphs, and the like in a paper, they tend to ask permission, as if they fear violating some unspoken rule. We believe that the pictorial should not be out of bounds in English papers or other undergraduate writing. Many texts could be more rhetorically effective with visual supplements, and we encourage you to use them whenever they are appropriate and helpful.

Most graphics fall into one of the following categories:

Tables and charts (typically an arrangement of data in columns and
    rows that summarizes the results of research)
Graphs (including bar, line, and pie graphs)
Photographs
Drawings (including maps and cartoons)

Although charts and tables are not technically images or figures, they present data in the form of visual arrangement rather than linear prose. Tables are used to display data economically in one place so that readers can find the information easily, both as they read and afterward if they want to refer to the table again. Consider Figure 4.8, which combines a table with bar graphs. It comes from a study of poverty in the United States. Note how much information is packed into this single visual. Note also how easy it is to read, moving from top to bottom and left to right through the categories. Finally, consider how many long and boring paragraphs it would take to say the same thing in prose.

Graphs are usually no more than tables transformed into visuals we can "read" and interpret more easily. Bar graphs are one example. They allow us to compare subcategories within the major categories almost at a glance. Making the comparisons would be much more difficult if we had only the percentages listed in a table. Bar graphs are best at showing comparisons at some single point in time. In contrast, line graphs allow us to see trends—for example, the performance of the stock market. Pie graphs highlight relative proportions well. When newspapers or news magazines want to show us how the federal budget is spent, for example, they typically use pie graphs with the pieces labeled in some way to represent categories such as national defense, welfare, entitlement programs, and the like. Who gets the biggest pieces of the pie becomes instantly clear and easier to remember—the two major purposes all graphs try to achieve. Graphs in themselves may not make arguments, but they are powerful deliverers of evidence and in that sense fall into the category of visual rhetoric.

As graphics, photographs represent people, objects, and scenes realistically and concretely. They give us a "human's eye" view of something as nothing else can. Thus, for instance, owner's manuals for cars often have a shot of the engine compartment that shows where fluid reservoirs are located. Clearly,

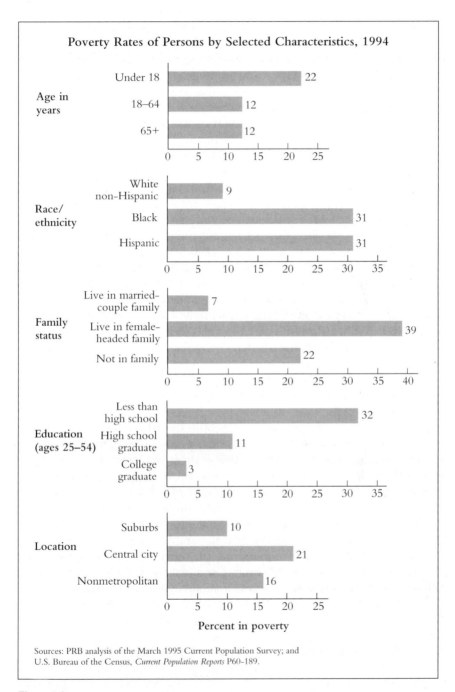

Poverty Rates of Persons by Selected Characteristics, 1994

Sources: PRB analysis of the March 1995 Current Population Survey; and
U.S. Bureau of the Census, *Current Population Reports* P60-189.

*Figure 4.8*

such photos serve highly practical purposes, such as helping us locate the dipstick. But they're also used, for example, in biographies; we get a better sense of, say, Abraham Lincoln's life and times when pictures of him, his family, his home, and so on are included. But photographs can do much more than merely inform. They can also be highly dramatic and powerfully emotional in ways that only the best writers can manage with prose—hence their inclusion to generate interest and excitement or to communicate an overall impression of a subject matter or theme. Photos are powerful persuaders.

But photogaphs are not very analytical—by their nature, they give us the surface of things, only what the camera can "see." A different type of graphic, drawings, are preferable when we want to depict how something is put together or structured. For instance, instructions for assembling and installing a ceiling fan or a light fixture usually have many diagrams—a large one showing how all the parts fit together and smaller ones that depict steps in the process in more detail. Corporate publications often include diagrams of the company's organizational hierarchy or chain of command. Scientific articles and textbooks are often full of drawings or illustrations created with computer graphics; these publications use drawings because science writers want us to understand structures, particularly internal structures, that often are difficult to capture on film and difficult to interpret when they are so captured. For example, our sense of what DNA looks like and our understanding of its double helix structure comes almost entirely from diagrams.

The following article illustrates how a variety of graphics can contribute to the effectiveness of a written text that informs readers about a complicated and often misunderstood subject, attention-deficit hyperactivity disorder (ADHD). ADHD afflicts millions of people the world over, most in their youth, during the years of formal education. We have taught many college students diagnosed with ADHD, and you probably have friends whose intense struggle for self-control and focus makes coping with college especially difficult. This article both informs us about ADHD and argues two theses about it: (1) that self-control is the primary problem and (2) that the disorder is genetic, related to smaller-than-usual structures in the brain that regulate attention. As you read, notice how the graphics support the author's informative and argumentative purposes. (In our textbook's reproduction of the article, the original page layout has been changed. You may wish to consult a copy of the magazine or access it via the Net at <www.sciam.com>.)

---

# Attention-Deficit Hyperactivity Disorder
## Russell A. Barkley

*This article appeared in the September 1998 issue of* Scientific American; *its author, Russell Barkley, is a professor of psychiatry and neurology at the University of Massachusetts Medical Center in Worcester and an internationally recognized expert on ADHD.*

*Children with ADHD cannot control their responses to their environment. This lack of control makes them hyperactive, inattentive, and impulsive.*

As I watched five-year-old Keith in the waiting room of my office, I could see why his parents said he was having such a tough time in kindergarten. He hopped from chair to chair, swinging his arms and legs restlessly, and then began to fiddle with the light switches, turning the lights on and off again to everyone's annoyance — all the while talking nonstop. When his mother encouraged him to join a group of other children busy in the play-room, Keith butted into a game that was already in progress and took over, causing the other children to complain of his bossiness and drift away to other activities. Even when Keith had the toys to himself, he fidgeted aim-lessly with them and seemed unable to entertain himself quietly. Once I examined him more fully, my initial suspicions were confirmed: Keith had attention-deficit hyperactivity disorder (ADHD).

Since the 1940s, psychiatrists have applied various labels to children who are hyperactive and inordinately inattentive and impulsive. Such youngsters have been considered to have "minimal brain dysfunction," "brain-injured child syndrome," "hyperkinetic reaction of childhood," "hyperactive child syndrome" and, most recently, "attention-deficit disorder." The frequent name changes reflect how uncertain researchers have been about the underlying causes of, and even the precise diagnostic criteria for, the disorder.

Within the past several years, however, those of us who study ADHD have begun to clarify its symptoms and causes and have found that it may have a genetic underpinning. Today's view of the basis of the condition is strikingly different from that of just a few years ago. We are finding that ADHD is not a disorder of attention per se, as had long been assumed. Rather it arises as a developmental failure in the brain circuitry that underlies inhibition and self-control. This loss of self-control in turn impairs other important brain functions crucial for maintaining attention, including the ability to defer immediate rewards for later, greater gain.

ADHD involves two sets of symptoms: inattention and a combination of hyperactive and impulsive behaviors (see table on page 89). Most children are more active, distractible and impulsive than adults. And they are more inconsistent, affected by momentary events and dominated by objects in their immediate environment. The younger the children, the less able they are to be aware of time or to give priority to future events over more immediate wants. Such behaviors are signs of a problem, however, when children display them significantly more than their peers do.

Boys are at least three times as likely as girls to develop the disorder; indeed, some studies have found that boys with ADHD outnumber girls with the condition by nine to one, possibly because boys are genetically more prone to disorders of the nervous system. The behavior patterns that typify ADHD usually arise between the ages of three and five. Even so, the age of onset can vary widely: some children do not develop symptoms until late childhood or even early adolescence. Why their symptoms are delayed remains unclear.

Huge numbers of people are affected. Many studies estimate that between 2 and 9.5 percent of all school-age children worldwide have ADHD; researchers have identified it in every nation and culture they have studied. What is more, the condition, which was once thought to ease with age, can persist into adulthood. For example, roughly two thirds of 158 children with ADHD my colleagues and I evaluated in the 1970s still had the disorder in their twenties. And many of those who no longer fit the clinical description of ADHD were still having significant adjustment problems at work, in school or in other social settings.

To help children (and adults) with ADHD, psychiatrists and psychologists must better understand the causes of the disorder. Because researchers have traditionally viewed ADHD as a problem in the realm of attention,

## Diagnosing ADHD

Psychiatrists diagnose attention-deficit hyperactivity disorder (ADHD) if the individual displays six or more of the following symptoms of inattention or six or more symptoms of hyperactivity and impulsivity. The signs must occur often and be present for at least six months to a degree that is maladaptive and inconsistent with the person's developmental level. In addition, some of the symptoms must have caused impairment before the age of seven and must now be causing impairment in two or more settings. Some must also be leading to significant impairment in social, academic or occupational functioning; none should occur exclusively as part of another disorder.

| Inattention | Hyperactivity and Impulsivity |
| --- | --- |
| Fails to give close attention to details or makes careless mistakes in schoolwork, work or other activities | Fidgets with hands or feet or squirms in seat |
| Has difficulty sustaining attention in tasks or play activities | Leaves seat in classroom or in other situations in which remaining seated is expected |
| Does not seem to listen when spoken to directly | Runs about or climbs excessively in situations in which it is inappropriate (in adolescents or adults, subjective feelings of restlessness) |
| Does not follow through on instructions and fails to finish schoolwork, chores or duties in the workplace | |
| Has difficulty organizing tasks and activities | Has difficulty playing or engaging in leisure activities quietly |
| Avoids, dislikes or is reluctant to engage in tasks that require sustained mental effort (such as schoolwork) | Is "on the go" or acts as if "driven by a motor" |
| Loses things necessary for tasks or activities (such as toys, school assignments, pencils, books or tools) | Talks excessively |
| | Blurts out answers before questions have been completed |
| Is easily distracted by extraneous stimuli | Has difficulty awaiting turns |
| Is forgetful in daily activities | Interrupts or intrudes on others |

*Source:* Reprinted with permission from the *Diagnostic and Statistical Manual of Mental Disorders,* Fourth Edition, Text Revision. © 2000, American Psychiatric Association.

some have suggested that it stems from an inability of the brain to filter competing sensory inputs, such as sights and sounds. But recently scientists led by Joseph A. Sergeant of the University of Amsterdam have shown that children with ADHD do not have difficulty in that area; instead they cannot inhibit their impulsive motor responses to such input. Other researchers have found that children with ADHD are less capable of preparing motor responses in anticipation of events and are insensitive to feedback about

errors made in those responses. For example, in a commonly used test of reaction time, children with ADHD are less able than other children to ready
themselves to press one of several keys when they see a warning light. They
also do not slow down after making mistakes in such tests in order to improve their accuracy.

### The Search for a Cause

No one knows the direct and immediate causes of the difficulties experienced by children with ADHD, although advances in neurological imaging
techniques and genetics promise to clarify this issue over the next five years.
Already they have yielded clues, albeit ones that do not yet fit together into
a coherent picture.

Imaging studies over the past decade have indicated which brain regions might malfunction in patients with ADHD and thus account for
the symptoms of the condition. That work suggests the involvement of
the prefrontal cortex, part of the cerebellum, and at least two of the clusters of nerve cells deep in the brain that are collectively known as the
basal ganglia (see illustration on page 91). In a 1996 study F. Xavier
Castellanos, Judith L. Rapoport and their colleagues at the National Institute of Mental Health found that the right prefrontal cortex and two basal
ganglia called the caudate nucleus and the globus pallidus are significantly
smaller than normal in children with ADHD. Earlier this year Castellanos's
group found that the vermis region of the cerebellum is also smaller in
ADHD children.

The imaging findings make sense because the brain areas that are re-       10
duced in size in children with ADHD are the very ones that regulate attention. The right prefrontal cortex, for example, is involved in "editing" one's
behavior, resisting distractions and developing an awareness of self and
time. The caudate nucleus and the globus pallidus help to switch off automatic responses to allow more careful deliberation by the cortex and to coordinate neurological input among various regions of the cortex. The exact
role of the cerebellar vermis is unclear, but early studies suggest it may play
a role in regulating motivation.

What causes the structures to shrink in the brains of those with ADHD?
No one knows, but many studies have suggested that mutations in several
genes that are normally very active in the prefrontal cortex and basal ganglia
might play a role. Most researchers now believe that ADHD is a polygenic
disorder—that is, that more than one gene contributes to it.

Early tips that faulty genetics underlie ADHD came from studies of the
relatives of children with the disorder. For instance, the siblings of children
with ADHD are between five and seven times more likely to develop the

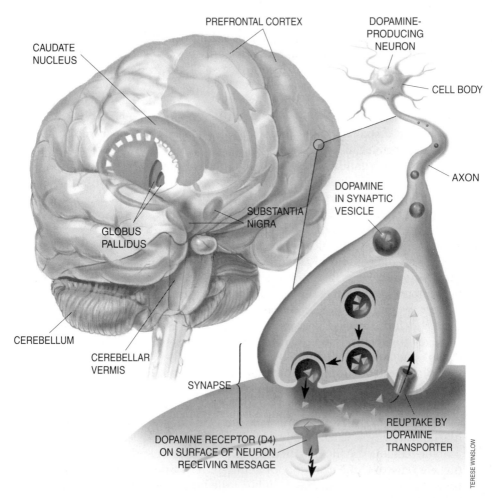

*Brain structures affected in ADHD use dopamine to communicate with one another. Genetic studies suggest that people with ADHD might have alterations in genes encoding either the D4 dopamine receptor, which receives incoming signals, or the dopamine transporter, which scavenges released dopamine for reuse. The substantia nigra, where the death of dopamine-producing neurons causes Parkinson's disease, is not affected in ADHD.*

syndrome than children from unaffected families. And the children of a parent who has ADHD have up to a 50 percent chance of experiencing the same difficulties.

The most conclusive evidence that genetics can contribute to ADHD, however, comes from studies of twins. Jacquelyn J. Gillis, then at the University of Colorado, and her colleagues reported in 1992 that the ADHD risk of a child whose identical twin has the disorder is between 11 and 18 times greater than that of a nontwin sibling of a child with ADHD; between 55 and 92 percent of the identical twins of children with ADHD eventually develop the condition.

One of the largest twin studies of ADHD was conducted by Helene Gjone and Jon M. Sundet of the University of Oslo with Jim Stevenson of the University of Southampton in England. It involved 526 identical twins, who inherit exactly the same genes, and 389 fraternal twins, who are no more alike genetically than siblings born years apart. The team found that ADHD has a heritability approaching 80 percent, meaning that up to 80 percent of the differences in attention, hyperactivity and impulsivity between people with ADHD and those without the disorder can be explained by genetic factors.

Nongenetic factors that have been linked to ADHD include premature birth, maternal alcohol and tobacco use, exposure to high levels of lead in early childhood and brain injuries—especially those that involve the prefrontal cortex. But even together, these factors can account for only between 20 and 30 percent of ADHD cases among boys; among girls, they account for an even smaller percentage. (Contrary to popular belief, neither dietary factors, such as the amount of sugar a child consumes, nor poor child-rearing methods have been consistently shown to contribute to ADHD.)

15

Which genes are defective? Perhaps those that dictate the way in which the brain uses dopamine, one of the chemicals known as neurotransmitters that convey messages from one nerve cell, or neuron, to another. Dopamine is secreted by neurons in specific parts of the brain to inhibit or modulate the activity of other neurons, particularly those involved in emotion and movement. The movement disorders of Parkinson's disease, for example, are caused by the death of dopamine-secreting neurons in a region of the brain underneath the basal ganglia called the substantia nigra.

Some impressive studies specifically implicate genes that encode, or serve as the blueprint for, dopamine receptors and transporters; these genes are very active in the prefrontal cortex and basal ganglia. Dopamine receptors sit on the surface of certain neurons. Dopamine delivers its message to those neurons by binding to the receptors. Dopamine transporters protrude from neurons that secrete the neurotransmitter; they take up unused dopamine so that it can be used again. Mutations in the dopamine receptor gene can render receptors less sensitive to dopamine. Conversely, mutations in the dopamine transporter gene can yield overly effective transporters that scavenge secreted dopamine before it has a chance to bind to dopamine receptors on a neighboring neuron.

In 1995 Edwin H. Cook and his colleagues at the University of Chicago reported that children with ADHD were more likely than others to have a particular variation in the dopamine transporter gene DAT1. Similarly, in 1996 Gerald J. LaHoste of the University of California at Irvine and his co-workers found that a variant of the dopamine receptor gene *D4* is more common among children with ADHD. But each of these studies involved 40 or 50 children—a relatively small number—so their findings are now being confirmed in larger studies.

### From Genes to Behavior

How do the brain-structure and genetic defects observed in children with ADHD lead to the characteristic behaviors of the disorder? Ultimately, they might be found to underlie impaired behavioral inhibition and self-control, which I have concluded are the central deficits in ADHD.

Self-control—or the capacity to inhibit or delay one's initial motor (and perhaps emotional) responses to an event—is a critical foundation for the performance of any task. As most children grow up, they gain the ability to engage in mental activities, known as executive functions, that help them deflect distractions, recall goals and take the steps needed to reach them. To achieve a goal in work or play, for instance, people need to be able to remember their aim (use hindsight), prompt themselves about what they need to do to reach that goal (use forethought), keep their emotions reined in and motivate themselves. Unless a person can inhibit interfering thoughts and impulses, none of these functions can be carried out successfully. 20

In the early years, the executive functions are performed externally: children might talk out loud to themselves while remembering a task or puzzling out a problem. As children mature, they internalize, or make private, such executive functions, which prevents others from knowing their thoughts. Children with ADHD, in contrast, seem to lack the restraint needed to inhibit the public performance of these executive functions.

The executive functions can be grouped into four mental activities. One is the operation of working memory—holding information in the mind while working on a task, even if the original stimulus that provided the information is gone. Such remembering is crucial to timeliness and goal-directed behavior: it provides the means for hindsight, forethought, preparation and the ability to imitate the complex, novel behavior of others—all of which are impaired in people with ADHD.

The internalization of self-directed speech is another executive function. Before the age of six, most children speak out loud to themselves frequently, reminding themselves how to perform a particular task or trying to cope with a problem, for example. ("Where did I put that book? Oh, I left it under the desk.") In elementary school, such private speech evolves into inaudible muttering; it usually disappears by age 10 [see "Why Children Talk to Themselves," by Laura E. Berk; *Scientific American*, November 1994]. Internalized, self-directed speech allows one to reflect to oneself, to follow

## A Psychological Model of ADHD

A loss of behavioral inhibition and self-control leads to the following disruptions in brain functioning:

| Impaired Function | Consequence | Example |
|---|---|---|
| Nonverbal working memory | Diminished sense of time<br>Inability to hold events in mind<br>Defective hindsight<br>Defective forethought | Nine-year-old Jeff routinely forgets important responsibilities, such as deadlines for book reports or an after-school appointment with the principal |
| Internalization of self-directed speech | Deficient rule-governed behavior<br>Poor self-guidance and self-questioning | Five-year-old Audrey talks too much and cannot give herself useful directions silently on how to perform a task |
| Self-regulation of mood, motivation and level of arousal | Displays all emotions publicly; cannot censor them<br>Diminished self-regulation of drive and motivation | Eight-year-old Adam cannot maintain the persistent effort required to read a story appropriate for his age level and is quick to display his anger when frustrated by assigned schoolwork |
| Reconstitution (ability to break down observed behaviors into component parts that can be recombined into new behaviors in pursuit of a goal) | Limited ability to analyze behaviors and synthesize new behaviors<br>Inability to solve problems | Fourteen-year-old Ben stops doing a homework assignment when he realizes that he has only two of the five assigned questions; he does not think of a way to solve the problem, such as calling a friend to get the other three questions |

*Source:* Lisa Burnett

rules and instructions, to use self-questioning as a form of problem solving and to construct "meta-rules," the basis for understanding the rules for using rules—all quickly and without tipping one's hand to others. Laura E. Berk and her colleagues at Illinois State University reported in 1991 that the internalization of self-directed speech is delayed in boys with ADHD.

A third executive mental function consists of controlling emotions, motivation and state of arousal. Such control helps individuals achieve goals by enabling them to delay or alter potentially distracting emotional reactions to a particular event and to generate private emotions and motiva-

*Psychological tests used in ADHD research include the four depicted here. The tower-building test (upper left), in which the subject is asked to assemble balls into a tower to mimic an illustration, measures forethought, planning and persistence. The math test (upper right) assesses working memory and problem-solving ability. In the auditory attention test (lower left), the subject must select the appropriate colored tile according to taped instructions, despite distracting words. The time estimation test (lower right) measures visual attention and subjective sense of time intervals. The subject is asked to hold down a key to illuminate a lightbulb on a computer screen for the same length of time that another bulb was illuminated previously.*

tion. Those who rein in their immediate passions can also behave in more socially acceptable ways.

The final executive function, reconstitution, actually encompasses two 25 separate processes: breaking down observed behaviors and combining the parts into new actions not previously learned from experience. The capacity for reconstitution gives humans a great degree of fluency, flexibility and creativity; it allows individuals to propel themselves toward a goal without having to learn all the needed steps by rote. It permits children as they mature to direct their behavior across increasingly longer intervals by combining behaviors into ever longer chains to attain a goal. Initial studies imply that children with ADHD are less capable of reconstitution than are other children.

I suggest that like self-directed speech, the other three executive functions become internalized during typical neural development in early childhood. Such privatization is essential for creating visual imagery and verbal thought. As children grow up, they develop the capacity to behave covertly, to mask some of their behaviors or feelings from others. Perhaps because of faulty genetics or embryonic development, children with ADHD have not attained this ability and therefore display too much public behavior and speech. It is my assertion that the inattention, hyperactivity and impulsivity of children with ADHD are caused by their failure to be guided by internal instructions and by their inability to curb their own inappropriate behaviors.

### Prescribing Self-Control

If, as I have outlined, ADHD is a failure of behavioral inhibition that delays the ability to privatize and execute the four executive mental functions I have described, the finding supports the theory that children with ADHD might be helped by a more structured environment. Greater structure can be an important complement to any drug therapy the children might receive. Currently children (and adults) with ADHD often receive drugs such as Ritalin that boost their capacity to inhibit and regulate impulsive behaviors. These drugs act by inhibiting the dopamine transporter, increasing the time that dopamine has to bind to its receptors on other neurons.

Such compounds (which, despite their inhibitory effects, are known as psychostimulants) have been found to improve the behavior of between 70 and 90 percent of children with ADHD older than five years. Children with ADHD who take such medication not only are less impulsive, restless and distractible but are also better able to hold important information in mind, to be more productive academically, and to have more internalized speech and better self-control. As a result, they tend to be liked better by other children and to experience less punishment for their actions, which improves their self-image.

My model suggests that in addition to psychostimulants—and perhaps antidepressants, for some children—treatment for ADHD should include training parents and teachers in specific and more effective methods for managing the behavioral problems of children with the disorder. Such methods involve making the consequences of a child's actions more frequent and immediate and increasing the external use of prompts and cues about rules and time intervals. Parents and teachers must aid children with ADHD by anticipating events for them, breaking future tasks down into smaller and more immediate steps, and using artificial immediate rewards. All these steps serve to externalize time, rules and consequences as a replacement for the weak internal forms of information, rules and motivation of children with ADHD.

In some instances, the problems of ADHD children may be severe        30
enough to warrant their placement in special education programs. Although
such programs are not intended as a cure for the child's difficulties, they
typically do provide a smaller, less competitive and more supportive environment in which the child can receive individual instruction. The hope
is that once children learn techniques to overcome their deficits in self-
control, they will be able to function outside such programs.

There is no cure for ADHD, but much more is now known about
effectively coping with and managing this persistent and troubling developmental disorder. The day is not far off when genetic testing for
ADHD may become available and more specialized medications may be
designed to counter the specific genetic deficits of the children who suffer
from it.

---

## Analyzing Barkley's Graphics

Barkley's article contains the following graphics, listed in order of
appearance:

A cartoon depicting the whirling, chaotic world of the ADHD sufferer
A chart of the symptoms of the disorder entitled "Diagnosing ADHD"
A computer-generated, three-dimensional graphic depicting the brain
    and processes having to do with neural activity
Another chart entitled "A Psychological Model of ADHD"
A set of photographs showing tests used in ADHD research

Thus, in a relatively short article, we have a wide range of graphics, each one
of which we could comment on at far greater length than we do here. The following comments are designed to stimulate thinking about how graphics
function rhetorically in a text, not to exhaust what could be said about any
of the graphics.

Turning to the first graphic on page 87, we should notice what it "says"
about the intended audience. *Scientific American*'s readership is mixed; it is
not limited to scientists, but it includes scientists who enjoy reading about
the work of other scientists in other fields. Thus, the articles must be "real science" but also must have broad appeal. The cartoonlike image we first encounter would almost certainly not appear in a "hard-core" science journal
written by specialists for specialists. We might also consider how well the
graphic works to "predict" the content of the article and to represent the
problem of ADHD.

We might compare the opening graphic with the drawing of the brain on
page 91. Clearly, the cartoon is intended for the more "pop" side of *Scientific
American*'s readership, whereas the drawing targets those who want a more detailed understanding of the "hard science" involved in ADHD research. The

article itself moves from knowledge that can be widely shared to information more specialized and harder to grasp, returning at the end to its broader audience's interests. The movement from the cartoon to the drawing mirrors the text's development from the relatively accessible to the more specialized. The drawing assists Barkley in presenting essential information about the disorder itself.

The four photos near the end of the article (page 95) reflect a turning from brain structures and neural processes to a humanistic concern for the welfare of ADHD children. The role of these photographs is less informative than it is persuasive. Because this article from *Scientific American* seems more informative than argumentative, we need to consider how it fits into the general context of debate about ADHD. Although less controversial than it once was, when even its existence was in dispute, ADHD remains a disputed topic. Some contend that the syndrome is diagnosed too often and too easily, perhaps in part at the urging of parents who know that laws mandate special treatment for ADHD cases in schools, such as more time to complete tests. Others argue that the disorder is more environmental than genetic and trace its source to a chaotic family life, too much TV, bad eating habits, and factors other than (or in addition to) brain abnormalities. Finally, among other doubts and criticism are questions often raised by teachers: When a child is properly treated for ADHD, just how impaired is he or she? Is special treatment really warranted? up to what age?

Barkley's article hardly alludes to the controversies surrounding ADHD, probably because the view he develops represents an emerging consensus among researchers. But if we read the article with its unspoken context in mind, we see much in it intended to refute dissenters and skeptics. Clearly, the genetic hypothesis is advanced by both text and graphics, and the concluding four photos claim, in effect, that actual and reliable testing is part of the diagnostic process.

We turn now to another graphic, the charts. Surely the chart entitled "Diagnosing ADHD" on page 89 is included to confirm the existence of definite criteria for diagnosis and to insist that, once made, diagnosis should be neither hasty nor uncertain. Note especially the sentence "The signs must occur often and be present for at least six months to a degree that is maladaptive and inconsistent with the person's developmental level." A similar implicit argument can be found in the second chart, "A Psychological Model of ADHD." It "says" that the disorder is thoroughly conceived, that we know much about it, and that we can be concrete about how the symptoms manifest themselves. These charts, then, although they may appear to be merely information to a casual reader, are actually arguments—claims about the solid, objective reality of the syndrome we call ADHD. They are definitely not merely decorative throw-ins but rather serve complex rhetorical purposes that become especially clear in the larger context of debate about ADHD.

## Following Through

1. Discuss the first graphic in the article as an introduction to the article's topic and argument. What function does this graphic serve? What message is conveyed by the assortment of items swirling around the child? Into what categories do the items fall? Why is the child male? How would you characterize his expression? What attitude about his plight does this image suggest that readers will find in the article?

2. Consider these questions as you examine the drawing of the brain on page 91 and the enlarged drawing of the connections between nerve cells, or neurons. What purposes do these visuals serve? For what part of the audience are they intended? Do they help you understand the physiology of the disorder? Can you explain how perspective comes into play in the drawing of the two neurons? Without these graphics, how much would you understand about the complex brain and neural processes discussed?

3. Discuss the four concluding photographs in the article as persuasion. How much information about psychological testing is conveyed by the photos themselves? Why are the adult figures women? How are they dressed? (Suppose they were men in white lab coats. What different impression would this create?) How would you characterize the office or clinical environment in which the child performs the tests? What messages are sent by the child's gender, age, race, clothes, hair, and cast on his left arm? by his body language and facial expressions? What might the persuasive intent be? If there is an implicit argument, what would it be, and why is it necessary?

4. Discuss why Barkley decided to present the material in the two charts in this tabulated form rather than incorporating it into the body of the article.

5. As an exercise in considering the role of graphics, bring to class a paper you have written recently for a college or high school assignment. If you didn't use graphics, ask yourself the following questions: Could the paper be improved with graphic support? If so, given your audience and purpose(s), what graphic types would you use and why? How would you go about securing or creating the graphics? If you did use graphics, be prepared to discuss them — what you did and why, how you went about creating the visuals, and so on. If you now see ways to improve the graphics, discuss your revision strategies as well.

# WRITING ASSIGNMENTS

## Assignment 1: Analyzing an Advertisement or Editorial Cartoon

Choose an ad or cartoon from a current magazine or newspaper. First, inquire into its rhetorical context: What situation prompted its creation? What purpose does it aim to achieve? Where did it originally appear? Who is its intended audience? What would they know or believe about the product or issue? Then inquire into the argument being made. To do this, you should consult the questions for inquiry on pages 177–178 to the extent that they apply to visual rhetoric. You should also consider some of the points we have made in this chapter that pertain to visual images in particular: What visual metaphors or allusions appear in the ad or cartoon? What prior cultural knowledge and experiences would the audience have to have to "read" the image? Consider how the visual argument might limit the scope of the issue or how it might play to the audience's biases, stereotypes, or fears. After thorough inquiry, reach some conclusion about the effectiveness or ethics of this particular visual argument. Write up your conclusion as a thesis or claim. Write up your analysis as an argument to convince, using the evidence gathered during the inquiry as material to support and develop your claim. Be sure to be specific about the visual details of the ad or cartoon.

**STUDENT SAMPLE:** *Analysis of Visual Rhetoric*

The following student essay by Kelly Williams serves as an example of the foregoing assignment. Before you begin your own essay, you might want to read the essay and discuss the conclusions Kelly reached about an advertisement for Eagle Brand condensed milk. Unfortunately, we were unable to obtain permission to reprint the advertisement itself, but the descriptions of the ad's text and visual images should make Kelly's analysis easy to follow.

A MOTHER'S TREAT

Kelly Williams

Advertisements are effective only if they connect with their audiences. Advertisers must therefore study the group of people they hope to reach and know what such groups value and what images they like to have of themselves. Often these images come from societal expectations that tell businessmen, mothers, fathers, teens that they should look or act a certain way. Most people have a hard time deviating from these images or stereotypes because adhering to them gives social status. Advertisers tend to look to these stereotypes as a way to sell their products. For example, an ad depicts a man in an expensive suit driving a luxury car, and readers assume he is a lawyer, physician, or business executive. Therefore, doctors, lawyers, and businessmen will buy this car because they associate it with the image of status that they would like to project. Likewise, some advertisements try to manipulate women with children by associating a product with the ideal maternal image that society places on mothers.

An advertisement for Eagle Brand condensed milk typifies the effort to persuade mothers to buy a product to perform the ideal maternal role. The advertisement appeared in magazines aimed at homemakers and in *People* magazine's "Best and Worst Dressed" issue of September 1998. The readers of this issue are predominantly young females; those with children are probably second-income producers or maybe even single mothers. These readers are struggling to raise a family, and they have many demands on their time. They may feel enormous pressure to fulfill ideal corporate and domestic roles. These readers may be susceptible to pressure to invest in an image that is expected of them.

The advertisement itself creates a strong connection with a maternal audience. The black-and-white photograph depicts a young girl about kindergarten age. The little girl's facial expression connotes hesitation and sadness. In the background is a school yard. Other children are walking toward the school, their heads facing down, creating a feeling of gloom. All readers will recognize the situation taking place. The little girl is about to attend her first day of school. One could easily guess that she is looking back to her mother with a sense of abandonment, pleading for support. Without a mother pictured, the audience assumes the maternal perspective. The girl's eyes stare at the reader. Her expression evokes protectiveness, especially in an audience of young mothers.

The wording of the text adds some comic relief to the situation. The ad is not intended to make the readers sad. The words seem to come from the mind of the child's mother: "For not insisting on bunny slippers for shoes, for leaving Blankie behind, for actually getting out of the car. . . ." These words also show that the mother is a good mother, very empathetic to her daughter's situation. Even the type of print for these words is part of an effective marketing strategy. The font mimics a "proper" mother's handwriting. The calligraphy contains no sharp edges, which reinforces the generalization that mothers are soft, feminine, and gentle.

The intent of the advertisement is to persuade mothers that if they 5 buy Eagle Brand milk and make the chocolate bar treat, they will be good mothers like the speaker in the ad. It tells women that cooking such treats helps alleviate stressful situations that occur in everyday family life. The little girl in the ad is especially effective in reminding maternal figures of their duty to care for and comfort their kids. She evokes the ideal maternal qualities of compassion, empathy, and protectiveness. Indirectly, the girl is testing her mother's maternal qualities. The expectations for her mother (and the reader) to deliver on all of these needs are intense. Happily, there is an easy way to do it. By making these treats, she can fulfill the role of a genuine mother figure.

The ad also suggests that good mothers reward good behavior. The statements listing the girl's good behavior suggest that it would be heartless not to reward her for her willingness to relinquish her childhood bonds. As the ad says, "It's time for a treat." But good mothers would also know that "Welcome Home Chocolate Bars" are very sweet and rich, so this mother has to say, "I'll risk spoiling your dinner." The invisible mother in the ad is still ideal because she does care about her child's nutrition, but in this case she will make an exception out of her concern for the emotional state of her child. The ad succeeds in selling the product by triggering mothers' maternal instincts to respond to their children's needs.

In many ways this ad is unethical. It pressures women to fit certain ideals so that Eagle Brand can sell more condensed milk. The ideal "mommy" makes the home a warm, safe, comforting place, and the ad suggests that using Eagle Brand is the way to do it. While the ad looks harmless and cute, it actually reinforces social pressures on women to make baked goods as part of their maternal duties. If you don't bake a treat to welcome your child back to the home after school, you are failing as a mother. The recipe includes preparation time, showing that the treat can be made with minimal effort. It gives mothers no excuse for not making it. Moreover, the advertisement exploits children to sell their product. All children have anxieties about new situations, but putting this into the ad just makes women feel guilty about unavoidable stresses their children have to deal with. The ad works by manipulating negative emotions in the readers.

Desserts do not have much nutritional value. It would be hard to make a logical case for making the Welcome Home Bars, so Eagle Brand used an emotional approach and an appeal to the image of the nurturing mother. There is nothing wrong with spoiling a child with a treat once in a while, but it is wrong to use guilt and social pressures to persuade mothers to buy a product.

## Assignment 2: Using Visual Rhetoric to Promote Your School

Colleges and universities compete fiercely for students and are therefore as concerned about their image as any corporation or politician. As a class project, collect all the images your school uses to promote itself, including brochures for prospective students, catalogs, class lists, and Web homepages. Choose three or four of the best ones, and in class discussions subject them to careful scrutiny as we did in the previous section with ads and cartoons. Then, working in groups of three or four students or individually, do one or all of the following:

1. Find an aspect of your college or university that has been overlooked in the publications put out by the admissions office but that you believe is a strong selling point. Employing photographs, drawings,

paintings, or some other visual medium, create an image appropriate for one of the school publications you have collected to write an appropriate and appealing short text to go with the image. Then, in a page or two, explain why you think your promotional image would work as well as or better than some of the ones presently in circulation.

2. If someone in the class has the computer knowledge to do so, create an alternative to your school's homepage, or make changes that would make it more appealing to prospective students, their parents, and other people who might use the Web.

3. Imagine that for fun or for purposes of parody or protest you wanted to call attention to aspects of your school that the official images deliberately omit. Proceed as in item 1. In a one- or two-page statement, explain why you chose the image you did and what purpose(s) you want it to serve.

4. Select a school organization (a fraternity or sorority, a club, etc.) whose image you think could be improved. Create a promotional image for it either for the Web or for some other existing or desirable publication.

5. As in item 3, create a visual parody of the official image of a school organization, perhaps as an inside joke intended for other participants in the organization.

No matter which of the preceding you or your group chooses, be sure to consult with other class members as you create and discuss the final results, including how revision or editing might enhance the impact. Remember that visual rhetoric can be altered in many ways; photos, for instance, can be taken from different angles and in different lighting conditions, processed in different ways, enlarged, reduced, trimmed, and so on.

### Assignment 3: Analyzing Your Own Visual Rhetoric

Study all the images your class created as argument and/or persuasion in the previous assignment. Select an image to analyze in depth. Write an essay that addresses the following questions:

What audience does the image intend to reach?
What goal did the creator of the image seek to accomplish?

If something is being argued, ask:

What thesis is advanced by the image or its accompanying text?
Are there aspects of the image or text functioning as reasons for holding the thesis?

If an image persuades more than it argues, attempt to discover and understand its major source or sources of appeal. Persuasion appeals to the whole person in an effort to create **identification,** a strong linking of the reader's interests and values with the image that represents something desired or potentially desirable. Hence, we can ask:

How do the images your class created appeal to the audience's interests and values?
Do the images embody emotional appeals? How?

## Assignment 4: Writing to Convince

Newspapers have been criticized for printing pictures that used to be considered too personal or gruesome for publication. The famous picture of the firefighter carrying the baby killed in the Oklahoma City bombing is an example, as are pictures of victims of war atrocities in Kosovo and elsewhere. Highly respected newspapers like the *New York Times* have offered defenses for their decisions on this issue. Look into what publishers, readers, and critics have to say on this topic. What issues and questions come up in these debates? Draw a conclusion of your own on this topic, and write an essay supporting it.

## Assignment 5: Using Graphics to Supplement Your Own Writing or Other Texts

Select an essay from the preceding assignment that could be improved either by adding graphics or by revising the graphics used. (If none of the papers seems appropriate for visual supplementation or revision, you may want to use one provided by your instructor.) Working alone or collaboratively with a writing group, rewrite/revise one of the papers. Pay attention to purpose and audience. Graphics should be efficient and memorable, designed to achieve a definite purpose and to have impact on a definite audience. For help with using graphics effectively in your writing, see the Best Practices box on page 105, "Guidelines For Using Visuals."

Recall that the best way to learn how to use graphics is by studying how others use them in respected publications. After reading and analyzing the graphics in the article from *Scientific American,* you may want to examine other examples of graphics in news magazines, scholarly books and articles, technical journals, institutional or business reports, and so on. You have many options: Besides adding visuals, you can cut unneeded ones, redesign existing ones, change media (for example, from a photo to a drawing), change types (for example, from a table to a graph), and so on. Working with graphics always means reworking the text as well. Expect changes in one to require changes in the other.

If more than one group works with the same paper, do not consult until rewriting or revising is complete. Then compare the results and discuss the strategies used. Which changes seem to improve the paper most? Why?

Graphics come in a variety of useful forms: as tables to display numerical data economically, as graphs to depict data in a way that permits easy comparison of proportions or trends, as photographs to convey realism and drama, and as drawings to depict structures. Whatever graphics you use, be sure to do the following:

- Make sure every graphic has a definite function. Graphics are not decorative and should never be "thrown" into an essay.
- Choose the kind or form best suited to convey the point you are trying to make.
- Design graphics so that they are easy to "read" and interpret. That is, keep them simple, make them large enough to be read without strain, and use clear labeling.
- Place graphics as close as possible to the text they explain or illustrate. Remember, graphics should be easier to understand than the text they supplement.
- Refer to all your graphics in the text. Readers usually need both the graphic and a text discussion for full understanding.
- Acknowledge the creator or source of each graphic next to the graphic itself. As long as you acknowledge the source or creator, you can borrow freely, just as you can with quotations from texts. Of course, if you wish to publish an essay that includes borrowed graphics, you must obtain written permission.

# Chapter 5

# Writing Research-Based Arguments

This chapter is intended to help you with any argument you write. Research, which simply means "careful study," is essential to serious inquiry and most well-constructed cases. Before you write, you need to investigate the ongoing conversation about your issue. As you construct your argument, you will need specific evidence and the support of authorities to make a convincing case to a skeptical audience.

Your high school experience may have led you to regard the research paper as different from other papers, but this distinction between researched and nonresearched writing does not usually apply to argumentation. An argument with no research behind it is generally a weak one. Many of the arguments you read may not appear to have been researched because the writers have not cited their sources—most likely because they were writing for the general public rather than for an academic or professional audience. In college writing, however, students are usually required to document all sources of ideas. Although documentation is important for many reasons, perhaps the two most important are these: (1) It allows readers to look up source material for themselves, should they wish to, and (2) it protects both the source and the writer of the paper from **plagiarism,** the presenting of another's words as one's own. (See the Concept Close-Up box on page 108.)

Research for argumentation usually begins not as a search for evidence but as inquiry into an issue you have chosen or been assigned. Your task in inquiry is to discover information about the issue and, what is more important, to find arguments that address the issue and to familiarize yourself with the range of positions and the cases people make for them. You should inquire into these arguments, using your critical-reading skills and entering into dialogues with the authors until you feel satisfied with and confident about the position you take.

Sometimes, however, research must begin at an even earlier stage—for example, when your instructor asks you to select an issue to write about. So we begin with suggestions for finding an issue.

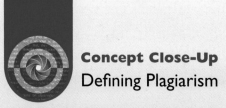

## Concept Close-Up
## Defining Plagiarism

**Plagiarism:** From the Latin *plagiarius*, a plunderer, kidnapper, literary thief.

> The appropriating and putting forth as one's own the ideas, language, or designs of another.—*New Grolier Webster International Dictionary*

> Act or instance of taking and passing off as one's own someone else's work or ideas.—*Scribner Dictionary*

Plagiarism is not limited to copying a source or having someone else write a paper for you. These are just the worst cases. It also includes taking an idea from a source without acknowledgment or using a source's actual words without quotation marks. All are serious violations of academic honesty.

## FINDING AN ISSUE

Let's say you have been assigned to write an essay on any issue of current public concern, ranging from one debated on your campus to one rooted in international affairs. If you have no idea what to write about, or if you want to follow up on an idea from your writer's notebook, what should you do?

### Understand that an Issue Is More Than Just a Topic

You must look for a subject about which people genuinely disagree. For example, homelessness is a **topic:** you could report on many different aspects of it—from the number of homeless people in our country to profiles of individual homeless people. But homelessness in itself is not really an issue, because virtually everyone agrees that the problem exists. However, once you start considering solutions to the problem of homelessness, you are dealing with an **issue,** because people will disagree about how to solve the problem.

### Keep Abreast of Current Events and Research the News

Develop the habit of regularly reading newspapers and magazines in print or online to keep informed of debates on current issues. It has become easy to browse the day's news stories when you first turn on your computer. Many newspapers are available online. Major daily newspapers, such as the *New York Times* and the *Wall Street Journal*, maintain commercial Web sites. Here are several:

*Chicago Tribune* <http://www.chicagotribune.com>
*Los Angeles Times* <http://www.latimes.com>
*New York Times* <http://www.nytimes.com>

*Wall Street Journal* <http://www.wsj.com>
*Washington Post* <http://www.washingtonpost.com>

Another site, *Newslibrary,* <http://www.newslibrary.com>, allows you to search approximately thirty-five different newspapers. It is best to write on issues of genuine concern to you rather than to manufacture concern at the last minute because a paper is due. In your writer's notebook, record your responses to your reading so that you have a readily available source of ideas.

Visit the current periodicals shelves of your library or local newsstand. Consult the front pages and the editorial/opinion columns of your city's daily papers. In addition, most newsstands and libraries carry the *New York Times* and other large-city dailies that offer thorough coverage of national and international events. Remember that you are looking for an issue, not just a topic, so if you find an article on the front page that interests you, think about how people might disagree over some question it raises. For example, an article announcing that health care costs rose a record fourteen percent in the past year might suggest the issue of government control over the medical profession; a campus newspaper article about a traditionally African-American fraternity could raise the issue of colleges tolerating racial segregation in the Greek system. In addition to newspapers, such magazines as *Time, Newsweek,* and *U.S. News & World Report* cover current events; and others, such as *Harper's, Atlantic Monthly, New Republic, National Review,* and *Utne Reader,* offer essays, articles, and arguments on important current issues. With the growth of the Internet, new resources are now available online that allow quick and easy access to a broad range of information sources.

## Research Your Library's Periodicals Indexes

Indexes are lists of articles in specific publications or groups of publications. Your school's library probably has a number of periodicals indexes in print, online, or in other electronic formats. You may be familiar with one index, the *Readers' Guide to Periodical Literature.* (For names of other indexes, see the section "Finding Sources," which begins on page 110.) If you have a vague subject in mind, such as gender discrimination, consulting an index for articles and arguments on the topic can help you narrow your focus. However, if you don't have an issue in mind, looking through the *Readers' Guide* won't be very helpful, so we offer some suggestions for using indexes more efficiently.

You can look, for example, in a newspaper index (some are printed and bound; others are computerized) under "editorial" for a list of topics on which the editors have stated positions, or you can look under the name of a columnist—such as William F. Buckley, Anna Quindlen, or A. M. Rosenthal—whose views on current issues regularly appear in that paper. The bonus for using a newspaper index in this way is that it will lead you directly to arguments on an issue.

Another resource for finding arguments on an issue when you have a topic in mind is *InfoTrac,* a computerized index to magazines, journals, and selected current articles in the *New York Times.* After you type in an appropriate subject word or key word, *InfoTrac* allows you to narrow your search further. If you type in the key word of your subject followed by "and editorial" or "and opinion," only argumentative columns and editorials will appear on your screen. *InfoTrac* now also includes online many full texts of articles.

A further possibility is to browse through an index dedicated solely to periodicals that specialize in social issues topics, such as the *Journal of Social Issues* and *Vital Speeches of the Day.* Finally, *Speech Index* will help you find speeches that have been printed in books.

### Inquire into the Issue

Once you have chosen an issue, you can begin your inquiry into positions already articulated in the public conversation. You may already hold a position of your own, but during inquiry you should be open to the full range of viewpoints on the issue; you should look for informative articles and arguments about the issue. This attitude of inquiry is central to the mature reasoning discussed in Chapter 1 (see pages 11–15).

Inquiring into an issue also involves evaluating sources. Remember that research means "careful study," and being careful as you perform these initial steps will make all the difference in the quality of the argument you eventually write. And, the more care you take now, the more time you'll save in the overall preparation of your paper.

Before you read further, take a moment to read the Concept Close-Up box, "Understanding the Ethics of Plagiarism," on page 111. In all writing— but especially in research writing, where you examine, evaluate, and record views and ideas from many different sources—a grasp of the full importance of plagiarism is crucial.

## FINDING SOURCES

Sources for developing an argument can be found through several kinds of research. Library and Internet research will lead you to abundant sources, but don't overlook what social scientists call *field research.* All research requires time and patience as well as a knowledge of tools and techniques.

### Field Research

Research "in the field" means studying the world directly through observations, questionnaires, and interviews.

## Concept Close-Up
## Understanding the Ethics of Plagiarism

A student who plagiarizes faces severe penalties: a failing grade on a paper, perhaps failure in a course, even expulsion from the university and an ethics violation recorded on his or her permanent record. Outside of academe, in the professional world, someone who plagiarizes may face public humiliation, loss of a degree, rank, or job, perhaps even a lawsuit. Why is plagiarism such a serious offense?

**Plagiarism is theft.** If someone takes our money or our car, we rightly think that person should be punished. Stealing ideas or the words used to express them is no less an act of theft. That's why we have laws that protect *intellectual property* such as books and essays.

**Plagiarism is a breach of ethics.** In our writing, we are *morally obligated* to distinguish between our ideas, information, and language and somebody else's ideas, information, and language. If we don't, it's like taking someone else's identity, pretending to be what we're not. Human society cannot function without trust and integrity—hence the strong condemnation of plagiarism.

**Plagiarism amounts to taking an unearned and unfair advantage.** You worked hard to get that "B" on the big paper in your political science class. How would you feel if you knew that another student had simply purchased an "A" paper, thereby avoiding the same effort? At the very least, you'd resent it. We hope you would go beyond resentment to actually report the plagiarism. For plagiarism is not just a moral failure with potentially devastating consequences for an individual. *Plagiarism, like any form of dishonesty intended to gain an unfair advantage, damages human society and hurts us.*

### Observations

Do not discount the value of your own personal experiences as evidence in making a case. You will notice that many writers of arguments offer as evidence what they themselves have seen, heard, and done. Such experiences may be from the past.

Alternatively, you may seek out a specific personal experience as you inquire into your topic. For example, one student writing about the homeless in Dallas decided to visit a shelter. She called ahead to get permission and schedule the visit. Her paper was memorable because she was able to include the stories and physical descriptions of several homeless women, with details of their conversations.

### Questionnaires and Surveys

You may be able to get information on some topics, especially if they are campus related, by doing surveys or questionnaires. This can be done very efficiently in electronic versions (Web-based or e-mail). Be forewarned, however, that it is very difficult to conduct a reliable survey.

First, there is the problem of designing a clear and unbiased instrument. If you have ever filled out an evaluation form for an instructor or a course, you will know what we mean about the problem of clarity. For example, one evaluation might ask whether an instructor returns papers "in a reasonable length of time"; however, what is "reasonable" to some students may be far too long for others. As for bias, consider the question, "Have you ever had trouble getting assistance from the library's reference desk?" To get a fair response, this questionnaire had better also ask how many requests for help were handled promptly and well. If you do decide to draft a questionnaire, we suggest you do it as a class project so that students on all sides of the issue can contribute and troubleshoot for ambiguity.

Second, there is the problem of getting a representative response. For the same reasons we doubt the results of certain magazine-sponsored surveys of people's sex lives, we should be skeptical about the statistical accuracy of surveys targeting a group that may not be representative of the whole. For example, it might be difficult to generalize about all first-year college students in the United States based on a survey of only your English class—or even the entire first-year class at your college. Consider, too, that those who respond to a survey often have an ax to grind on the topic.

We don't rule out the value of surveys here, but we caution you to consider the difficulties of designing, administering, and interpreting such research tools.

## Interviews

You can get a great deal of current information about an issue, as well as informed opinions, by talking to experts. As with any kind of research, the first step in conducting an interview is to decide exactly what you want to find out. Write down your questions, whether you plan to conduct the interview over the telephone, in person, or through e-mail.

The next step, which can take some effort and imagination, is to find the right person to interview. As you read about an issue, note the names (and the possible biases) of any organizations mentioned; these may have local offices, the telephone numbers of which you could find in the directory. In addition, institutions such as hospitals, universities, and large corporations have information and public relations offices whose staffs are responsible for providing information. An excellent source of over 30,000 names and phone numbers of experts in almost any field is a book by Matthew Lesko, *Lesko's Info-Power*. Finally, do not overlook the expertise available from faculty members at your own school.

Once you have determined possible sources for interviews, you must begin a patient and courteous round of telephone calls, continuing until you are connected with the right person; according to Lesko, this can take as many as seven calls. Remain cheerful and clear in your pursuit. If you have a subject's e-mail address, you might write to introduce yourself and schedule an appointment for a telephone interview.

Whether your interview is face to face or over the telephone, begin by being sociable but also by acknowledging that the interviewee's time is valuable. Tell the person something about the project you are working on, but withhold your own position on any controversial matters. Try to sound neutral, and be specific about what you want to know. Take notes, and include the title and background of the person being interviewed and the date of the interview, which you will need when citing this source in the finished paper. If you want to tape the interview, be sure to ask permission first. Finally, if you have the individual's mailing address, it is thoughtful to send a follow-up note thanking him or her for the assistance.

If everyone in your class is researching the same topic and it is likely that more than one person will contact a particular expert on campus or in your community, avoid flooding that person with requests. Perhaps one or two students could be designated to interview the subject and report to the class, or, if convenient, the expert could be invited to visit the class.

## Library and Online Research

University libraries are vast repositories of information in print and electronic form. To use them most efficiently, consult with professional librarians. Do not hesitate to ask for help. Even college faculty can discover new sources of information by talking with librarians about current research projects.

The Internet and its most popular component element, the World Wide Web, offer immediate access to millions of documents on almost any subject. The Internet provides currency and convenience, but it does not offer the reliability of most print sources. Do not overrely on the Internet; it is not a shortcut to the research process. We begin with a discussion of the resources available in your library or through its online network.

### Library of Congress Subject Headings

Finding library sources will involve using the card or computerized catalog, reference books, and indexes to periodicals. Before using these, however, it makes sense first to look through a set of books every library locates near its catalog—the *Library of Congress Subject Headings*. This multivolume set will help you know what terms to look under when you move on to catalogs and indexes. The Library of Congress catalog is also available on the Internet at <http://catalog.loc.gov>. (See Figure 5.1.) Consulting these subject headings first will save you time in the long run: It will help you narrow your search and keep you from overlooking potentially good sources, because it also suggests related terms under which to look. For example, if you look under the

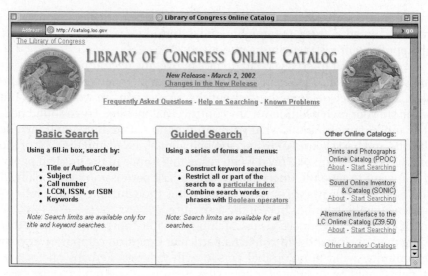

Figure 5.1

term "mercy killing," you will be directed to "euthanasia," where you can find the following helpful information:

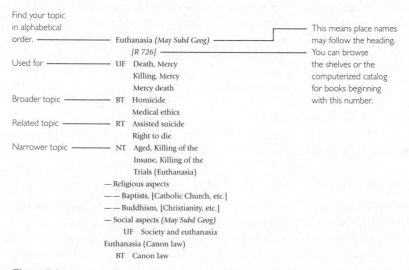

Figure 5.2

## Your Library's Catalog

Use your library's catalog primarily to find books or government documents. (For arguments and information on very current issues, however, keep in mind that the card or computer catalog is not the best source; because books

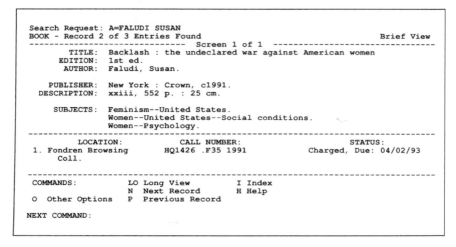

```
Search Request: A=FALUDI SUSAN
BOOK - Record 2 of 3 Entries Found                              Brief View
----------------------------- Screen 1 of 1 -----------------------------
        TITLE:   Backlash : the undeclared war against American women
       EDITION:  1st ed.
        AUTHOR:  Faludi, Susan.

     PUBLISHER:  New York : Crown, c1991.
   DESCRIPTION:  xxiii, 552 p. : 25 cm.

      SUBJECTS:  Feminism--United States.
                 Women--United States--Social conditions.
                 Women--Psychology.
-------------------------------------------------------------------------
         LOCATION:          CALL NUMBER:                     STATUS:
 1. Fondren Browsing       HQ1426 .F35 1991         Charged, Due: 04/02/93
    Coll.

-------------------------------------------------------------------------
 COMMANDS:           LO  Long View        I  Index
                     N   Next Record       H  Help
 O  Other Options    P   Previous Record

 NEXT COMMAND:
```

*Figure 5.3*

take years to write and publish, they quickly become outdated.) Library cata-logs list all holdings and are referenced according to author, title, and sub-ject. With a computerized catalog, it is also possible to find works according to key words and by Library of Congress number. Look under the subject head-ings you find in the *Library of Congress Subject Headings*. Moreover, because the Library of Congress system groups books according to subject matter, you may want to browse in the catalog (or on the shelves) for other books in the same range of call numbers.

Typically, the library's catalog card or screen will appear as illus-trated in Figure 5.3.

### Indexes to Periodicals

Good libraries contain many indexes that list articles in newspapers, maga-zines, and journals. Some of these are printed and bound; others are online and on CD-ROM. Once again, the *Library of Congress Subject Headings* can help you determine the best words to search in these indexes.

*Newspaper Indexes*  The *New York Times Index* is printed and bound in vol-umes. Each volume indexes articles for one year, grouped according to sub-ject and listed according to the month and day of publication. The subject headings in the *New York Times Index* tend to be very general. For example, we could not find the heading "euthanasia," the term for mercy killing used in the *Library of Congress Subject Headings*. We had to think of a more general term, so we tried "medicine." There we found the information in Figure 5.4.

MEDICINE AND HEALTH. See also
Abortion
Accidents and Safety
Acupuncture
Aged
Anatomy and Physiology
Anesthesia and Anesthetics
Antibiotics
Autopsies
Bacteria
Birth Control and Family Planning
Birth Defects
Blood
Death ————————————————————— The subject
Environment                                                        heading most
Epidemics                                                          likely to lead
Exercise                                                           to articles on
Faith Healers                                                      euthanasia
First Aid
Food Contamination and Poisoning
Handicapped
Hormones
Immunization and Immunity
Implants
Industrial and Occupational Hazards
Malpractice Insurance
Mental Health and Disorders
Nursing Homes
Pesticides and Pests
Population
Radiation
Smoking
Spas
Surgery and Surgeons
Teeth and Dentistry
Transplants
Vaccination and Vaccines
Veterinary Medicine
Viruses
Vitamins
Water Pollution
Workmen's Compensation Insurance
X-Rays

*Figure 5.4*

We decided the entry "death" on this list seemed most likely to lead us to articles on euthanasia, and we were correct. Figure 5.5 on page 117 shows a small selection of what we found.

You will also find a limited number of *New York Times* articles listed in the computerized periodicals index known as *InfoTrac*. Better yet, search the major newspapers' online archives. *The New York Times on the Web*, for example, provides access to all *NYT* articles published after 1996. Another excellent source of online articles from magazines and newspapers is *Lexis-Nexis*.

Other printed and bound newspaper indexes carried by most libraries are the *Christian Science Monitor Index*, the *Times Index* (to the London *Times*, a good source for international issues), the *Wall Street Journal Index*, and the *Washington Post Index* (good for federal government issues).

Topic headings are listed in alphabetical order.

Each entry contains an abstract.

(S), (M), or (L) before the date indicates whether an article is short, medium, or long.

**DEATH. See also**
Deaths

Several laws enacted in New York State in 1990 are set to take effect, including measure that will allow New Yorkers to designate another person to make health-care decisions on their behalf if they become unable to do so (M). Ja 1.1.32:1

Another right-to-die case emerges in Missouri, where Christine Busalacchi had been in persistent vegetative state as result of auto accident on May 29, 1987, when she was 17-year-old high school junior: her father, Pete Busalacchi, who has been seeking unsuccessfully to have his daughter transferred to Minnesota, where feeding tube may possibly be removed, says that Christine never discussed matters of life or death; Nancy Cruzan case recalled; photo (M). Ja 2.A.12:1

Missouri state court dismisses order preventing Pete Busalacchi from moving his comatose daughter Christine to another state where less strict rules might allow removal of feeding tube (S). Ja S.A.16:1

In a case that medical ethicists and legal experts say is apparently a first, Minneapolis-based Hennapin County Medical Center plans to go to court for permission to turn off 37-year-old Helga Wanglie's life support system against her family's wishes; photos (L). Ja 10.A.1:1

Probate Judge Louis Kohn of St. Louis County rules that Pete Busalacchi may move his daughter, Christine, from Missouri hospital where she has lain for more than three years with severe brain damage and take her to Minnesota where law might allow removal of her feeding tube (S). Ja 17.3.5:1

People wishing to avoid heroic medical treatment in event they become hopelessly ill and unable to speak for themselves are often poorly served by so-called "living wills" to achieve that end: many health care experts recommend a newer document, health care proxy, in which patients designate surrogate who has legal authority to make medical decisions if they are too sick to offer an opinion; others recommend combining living will with health care proxy; drawing (M). Ja 17.3.9:1

Missouri Judge Louis Kohn rules Pete Busalacchi had right to determine medical care of his daughter Christine, who has been severely brain-damaged for more than three years; gives him authority to have feeding tube removed (S). Ja 18.A.16:4

Missouri appeals court bars Pete Busalacchi from moving his comatose 20-year-old daughter Christine to Minnesota where laws governing removal of life-support systems are less restrictive (S). Ja 19.1.17:2

Editorial Notebook commentary by Fred M. Hechinger says his 94-year-old mother's last days were fiilled with needless suffering and fear because doctors ignored her, and her family's wish that no heroic efforts be taken to prolong her life; says inhumane legal restrictions have made doctors accomplices in torture, and medical profession has shown little courage in fighting them (M). Ja 24.A.22:1

Articles are listed in chronological order.

Each entry concludes with the month, day, section, page, and column.

*Figure 5.5*

*Newsbank* offers computerized indexes of hundreds of local and state newspapers. Your library is likely to subscribe to *Newsbank* for indexes of only one or two regional papers in your area. *Newsbank*'s CD-ROMs contain the entire text of each article indexed.

***Indexes to Magazines, Journals, and Other Materials***   Many libraries have CD-ROM databases indexing journals in business and academic fields. *Info-Trac,* one such database, indexes current articles from the *New York Times* and many other periodicals, so you may want to begin your search here rather than with the printed and bound indexes discussed previously. Be aware, however, that *InfoTrac* is a very selective index, far less comprehensive than the printed and bound indexes, which also go back much further in time. In addition, *InfoTrac* will not include many articles that can be found in the specialized indexes that follow. However, *InfoTrac* is constantly being upgraded, so check with your reference librarian to see how this database can help you research your issue.

1. General interest indexes:

   *Readers' Guide to Periodical Literature*
   *Public Affairs Information Service (PAIS)*
   *Essay and General Literature Index*
   *Speech Index*

2. Arts and humanities indexes:

   *Art Index*
   *Film Literature Index*
   *Humanities Index*
   *Music Index*
   *Philosopher's Index*
   *Popular Music Periodical Index*

3. Social science, business, and law indexes:

   *Business Periodicals Index*
   *Criminology Index*
   *Education Index*
   *Index to Legal Periodicals*
   *Psychological Abstracts*
   *Social Sciences Index*
   *Sociological Abstracts*
   *Women's Studies Abstracts*

4. Science and engineering indexes:

   *Applied Science and Technology Index*
   *Biological and Agricultural Index*
   *Current Contents*
   *Environmental Index*
   *General Science Index*

### Reference Books

Students tend to overlook many helpful reference books, often because they are unaware of their existence. You may find reference books useful early in the process of inquiring into your issue, but they are also useful for locating supporting evidence as you develop your own argument. The following are some reference books you might find helpful:

> *First Stop: The Master Index to Subject Encyclopedias* (a subject index to 430 specialized encyclopedias—a good source of general background information)
> *Demographic Yearbook*
> *Facts on File*
> *Guide to American Law* (a reference work that explains legal principles and concepts in plain English)
> *Statistical Abstract of the United States*
> *World Almanac and Book of Facts*

### Bibliographies

Books and articles sometimes include works-cited lists or bibliographies, which can reveal numerous additional sources. Library catalog entries and many indexes indicate whether a book or article contains a bibliography.

## Internet Research

The *Internet* is a global network that links computers, and the files stored on them, to one another. It is a valuable research tool because it provides access to information in the computers of educational institutions, businesses, government bureaus, and nonprofit organizations all over the world. Most people now use the World Wide Web for access to the Internet. The Web is that portion of the Internet that uses HTML (hypertext mark-up language) to present information in the form of Web sites that contain individual Web pages.

The Internet also provides the connections for e-mail and real-time communications, such as ongoing discussions among groups with common areas of interest; the communication functions of the Internet can also be useful for researching a topic. Because nearly all college computer networks are linked to the Internet, as a student you will have access to it (even if you do not own a computer). Most schools have a department of computer and educational technology that can tell you where and how to get connected.

Just as we advise you to seek help from a librarian when beginning your library research, so we also suggest that you begin electronic or online research by consulting one of the librarians at your school who has specialized training in navigating the information superhighway. Because the Internet is so large and complex and—like most real highways—is perpetually "under construction," we will offer only general advice about what Internet resources would be most useful for undergraduate research on comtemporary public issues. One of the best online sources for help with the Internet is the Library of Congress Resource Page, at <http://lcweb.loc.gov/global/search.html>. Once you are connected to this page, you can link to any number of the following resources.

## The World Wide Web

Of all the networks on the Internet, the *World Wide Web* is the friendliest and the most fun because it links files from various "host" computers around the world; from one site on the Web, you can click on highlighted words known as *hypertext links* that will take you to other sites on the Web where related information is stored. For example, an online article on euthanasia may highlight the words "Hippocratic oath"; clicking on the highlighted words will allow you to see a copy of the oath and learn a little more about it.

Although the Web continues to expand, finding useful sites is not always as easy as finding books and articles in the library because there is no system that neatly catalogs all the information as material is posted. However, technology to help users navigate the Internet is constantly improving. The Web does support a number of *search engines*, which index existing and newly posted information, usually through the use of key words. Once you connect to your school's Internet browser (such as Netscape or Microsoft Internet Explorer), you can type in the address of one of these engines, or you may be able to load the engine by simply clicking on an icon. Addresses on the Internet are known as *uniform resource locators (URLs)*. The following lists the names and URLs of search engines and metasearch engines that are recommended by the Librarians' Index to the Internet <http://www.lii.org>. World Wide Web URLs begin with "http," which stands for "hypertext transfer protocol."

Search Engines Recommended by Librarians

Google <http://www.google.com>
AllTheWeb <http://www.alltheweb.com>
AltaVista <http://www.altavista.com>
Excite <http://www.excite.com>
HotBot <http://www.hotbot.lycos.com>
NorthernLight <http://www.northernlight.com>

Recommended Metasearch Engines

Ixquick <http://www.ixquick.com>
MetaCrawler <http://www.metacrawler.com>

Once you access the search engine, enter key words describing the information you want. For example, by typing in "search engine," you can find the addresses of other search engines. We recommend that you try this because new search engines are being created all the time.

Surfing the Web, however, is not always a quick and easy way to do research. Be prepared to spend some time and to try a variety of search engines and metasearch engines, which, as their name suggests, search multiple search engine databases at once. Web searches can often take more time than library research because you will encounter so much irrelevant information. You will also find much information that is not suitable for use in academic writing.

Because anyone can post a document on the Web, you need to check the author's credentials carefully. (See "Evaluating Sources," pages 122–127.) The Internet is a tool that can provide new avenues for your research, but it will not replace the library as your primary research venue.

## GopherSpace

Gopher, a program for accessing Internet information through hierarchical menus, is named for the Golden Gopher mascot at the University of Minnesota, where this software was developed. Gopher is an older system than the World Wide Web. Like other protocols such as FTP and telnet, Gopher looks different because it lacks a hypertext format. However, many documents are stored in *GopherSpace*. Once Gopher has retrieved a document for you, you can read it on your screen, save it to a disk, or even print out a copy of it. Instead of hypertext links, Gopher organizes hierarchical menus based on topic areas. For example, you may open a menu that lists major subject areas such as "government and politics." If you select this category, you will get another menu that may have the item "Supreme Court cases." Selecting that, you will find another list, and so on. Many of the Web search engines previously described include GopherSpace in their searches, so you may happen to find Gopher documents while you are searching the World Wide Web.

## Listservs and Usenet Newsgroups

The Internet allows groups of people to communicate with one another on topics of common interest; observing and participating in such groups is another way to learn about a topic and find out what issues are being debated. *Listservs* are like electronic bulletin boards or discussion groups, where people with a shared interest can post or ask for information and simply converse about a topic. Listservs are supported by e-mail, so if you have an e-mail account, it will cost you nothing to join a group. You may find an appropriate listserv group by e-mailing <listserv@listserve.net> with a message specifying your area of interest, such as "list environmentalism" or "list euthanasia." You can also find listserv groups on the World Wide Web at <http://tile.net/lists>. *Usenet newsgroups* also act like electronic bulletin boards, which your college's system administrator may or may not make available on your school's server. To find lists of active newsgroups, type in "newsgroups" as a search term in one of the Web search engines, such as Yahoo! Newsgroups and listservs are often composed of highly specialized professionals who expect other participants to have followed their discussions for weeks and months before participating. They even post lists of *frequently asked questions (FAQs)* to avoid having to cover the same topics repeatedly. Finding the exact information you need in the transcripts of their discussions is like looking for the proverbial needle in a haystack, so Usenet is not likely to be as useful as the Web as a general research tool. However, while searching the Web, you may encounter links to some discussions relevant to your topic that have been archived on the Web. You may want to cite information gathered from these groups, but you need to be very careful about what you choose to use as a source because anyone can join in, regardless of his or her credentials and expertise. Most correspondents who have professional affiliations list them along with their name and "snail mail" (U.S. postal service) address. In addition to credentials, be sure to note the name of the group, the name of the individual posting the message, the date and time it was posted, and the URL if you have found it on the Web. (See the section "Creating Works-Cited and Reference Lists" on pages 144–157 for more information on citing electronic sources.)

## EVALUATING SOURCES

Before you begin to read and evaluate your sources, you may need to reevaluate your issue. If you have been unable to find many sources that address the question you are raising, step back and consider changing the focus of your argument or at least expanding its focus.

For example, one student had the choice of any issue under the broad category of the relationship between humans and other animals. Michelle decided to focus on the mistreatment of circus animals, based on claims made in leaflets handed out at the circus by animal rights protestors. Even with a librarian's help, however, Michelle could find no subject headings that led to even one source in her university's library. She then called and visited animal rights activists in her city, who provided her with more materials written and published by the animal rights movement. She realized, however, that researching the truth of their claims was more than she could undertake, so she had to acknowledge that her entire argument was based on inadequate inquiry and heavily biased sources.

Once you have reevaluated your topic, use the following method to record and evaluate sources.

### Eliminate Inappropriate Sources

If you are a first-year college student, you may find that some books and articles are intended for audiences with more specialized knowledge of the subject than you have. If you have trouble using a source — if it confuses you or shakes your confidence in your reading comprehension — put it aside, at least temporarily.

Also, carefully review any electronic sources you are using. While search engines make it easy to find source material on the Web, online documents often have met no professional standards for scholarship. Material can be "published" electronically without the rigorous review by experts, scholars, and editors that must occur in traditional publishing. Nevertheless, you will find legitimate scholarship on the Internet — many news reports, encyclopedias, government documents, and even scholarly journals appear online.

While the freedom of electronic publishing creates an exciting and democratic arena for discussion, it also puts a much heavier burden on students to ensure that the sources they use are worthy of readers' respect. You must exercise caution whenever you use a Web source as part of your research paper.

## Carefully Record Complete Bibliographic Information

For every source you are even considering using, be sure to record full bibliographic information. You should take this information from the source itself, not from an index, which may be incomplete or even inaccurate. If you make a record of this information immediately, you will not have to go back later to fill in careless omissions. We recommend that you use a separate index card for each source, but whatever you write on, you must record the following:

1. For a book:

   > Author's full name (or names)
   > Title of book
   > City where published
   > Name of publisher
   > Year published

For an article or essay in a book, record all of the information for the book, including the names of the book's author or editor and the title and the author(s) of the article; also record the inclusive page numbers of the article or chapter (for example, "pp. 100–150").

2. For a periodical:

   > Author's full name (or names)
   > Title of the article
   > Title of the periodical
   > Date of the issue
   > Volume number, if given
   > Inclusive page numbers

3. For a document found on the World Wide Web:

   > Author's full name (or names)
   > Title of the work
   > Original print publication data, if applicable
   > Title of the database or Web site
   > Full URL
   > Date you accessed the document

4. For a document found through Gopher:

   > Author's full name (or names)
   > Title of the work

Original print publication data, if applicable
Title of the database
Full Gopher search path that accessed the document
Date you accessed the document

5. For material found through listservs and Usenet newsgroups:

Author's full name (or names)
Author's e-mail address
Subject line from the posting
Date of the posting
Address of the listserv or newsgroups
Date you accessed the document

## Read the Source Critically

As discussed in Chapter 2, critical reading depends on having some prior knowledge of the subject and the ability to see a text in its rhetorical context. As you research a topic, your knowledge naturally becomes deeper with each article you read. But your sources are not simply windows onto your topic, giving you a clear view; whether argumentative or informative, they present a bias. Before looking through them, you must look *at* your sources. Therefore, it is essential that you devote conscious attention to the rhetorical context of the sources you find. As you read, keep these questions in mind.

### Who Is the Writer, and What Is His or Her Bias?

Is there a note that tells you anything about the writer's professional title or university or institutional affiliation? If not, a quick look in the *Dictionary of American Biographies* might help; or you can consult the *Biography and Genealogy Master Index,* which will send you to numerous specialized biographical sketches. If you are going to cite the writer as an authority in your argument, you need to be able to convince your audience of his or her credibility.

### How Reliable Is the Source?

Again, checking for credibility is particularly important when you are working with electronic sources. For example, one student found two sites on the Web, both through a key word search on "euthanasia." One, entitled "Stop the Epidemic of Assisted Suicide," was posted by a person identified only by name, the letters MD, and the affiliation "Association for Control of Assisted Suicide." There was no biographical information, and the "snail mail" address was a post office box. The other Web site, entitled "Ethics Update: Euthanasia," was posted by a professor of philosophy at the University of San Diego whose homepage included a complete professional biography detailing his educational background and the titles and publishers of his many other books and articles. The author gave his address at USD in the Department of Philosophy. The student decided that although the first source had some interesting information—including examples of individual patients who were living with pain rather than choosing suicide—it was not a source that skeptical readers would find credible. Search engines often land you deep within a Web site, and you have to visit the site's homepage to get any background information about the source and its author. Be suspicious of sites that do not contain adequate source information; they may not be reliable.

### When Was This Source Written?

If you are researching a very current issue, you need to decide what sources may be too old. Keep in mind, though, that arguments on current issues often benefit from earlier perspectives.

### Where Did This Source Appear?

If you are using an article from a periodical, be aware of the periodical's readership and any editorial bias. For example, *National Review* has a conservative bent, whereas *The Nation* is liberal; an article in the *Journal of the American Medical Association* will usually defend the medical profession. Looking at the table of contents and scanning any editorial statements will help give you a feel for the periodical's political leanings. Also look at the page that lists the publisher and the editorial board. You would find, for example, that *New American* is published by the ultra-right-wing John Birch Society. If you need help determining political bias, ask a librarian. A reference book that lists periodicals by subject matter and explains their bias is *Magazines for Libraries*.

### Why Was the Book or Article Written?

Although some articles are occasioned by events in the news, most books and arguments are written as part of an ongoing debate or conversation among scholars or journalists. Being aware of the issues and the participants in this conversation is essential, as you will be joining it with your own researched argument. You can check *Book Review Index* to find where a book has been reviewed, and then consult some reviews to see how the book was received.

### What Is the Author's Aim?

First, be aware of whether the source is intended to inform or whether it is an argument with a claim to support. Both informative and argumentative sources are useful, and even informative works will have some bias. When your source is an argument, note whether it aims primarily to inquire, to convince, to persuade, or to mediate.

### How Is the Source Organized?

If the writer does not employ subheadings or chapter titles, try to break the text into its various parts, and note what function each part plays in the whole.

1. Look at the last segment of the domain name, which will tell you who developed the site. The most reliable sites are those developed by colleges and universities (*.edu*) or by the government (*.gov*). Remember that commercial sites (*.com, .biz*) are usually profit-minded.
2. Check whether the name of the creator of the Web page or its Webmaster appears, complete with an e-mail address and the date of the last update, near either the top or the bottom of the page.
3. Check whether the source includes a bibliography; such inclusion indicates a scholarly page.
4. Ask yourself if the links are credible.
5. Remember that a tilde (˜) indicates a personal page; these pages must be evaluated carefully.

## Inquire into the Source

Because we devote so much attention to inquiry in Chapters 3 and 6, we will not go into detail about this process here. However, you should identify any author's claim and evaluate the support offered for it. Look especially closely at arguments that support your own position; seeing weaknesses in such "friendly" arguments has caused many students to experience an epiphany, or moment of enlightenment, in which they change their whole stance on an issue. The box "Additional Guidelines for Evaluating Internet Sources," above, will help you evaluate Web sources for reliability.

## Consider How You Might Use the Source

If you are fortunate, your research will uncover many authoritative and well-crafted arguments on your issue. The challenge you now face is to work out a way to use them in an argument of your own, built on your own structure and strategy and suited to your own aim and audience.

A good argument results from synthesizing, or blending, the results of your research. Your sources should help you come up with strong reasons and evidence as well as ideas about opposing views. But it is unlikely that all your reasons will come from one source or that each part of your argument will draw primarily upon a single source, and you don't want to create an argument that reads like a patchwork of other people's ideas. Thus, you must organize your sources according to your own argumentative strategy and integrate material from a variety of sources into each part of your argument.

We suggest that you review Chapter 7, where we discuss developing and refining a thesis (or claim) and constructing a brief of your argument. As you make your brief, identify those sources that will help you offer reasons or support, such as expert opinion or specific data.

Avoid plagiarism by being conscious of whether you are quoting or paraphrasing. Anytime you take exact words from a source, even if it is only a phrase or a significant word that expresses an author's opinion, you are quoting. You must use quotation marks in addition to documenting your source. If you make any change at all in the wording of a quotation, you must indicate the change with ellipses and/or brackets. Even if you use your own words to summarize or paraphrase portions of a source, you must still name that source in your text and document it fully. Be careful about using your own words when paraphrasing and summarizing.

1. At the very least, use an attributive tag such as "According to . . ." to introduce quotations both direct and indirect. Don't just drop them in to stand on their own.
2. Name the person whose words or idea you are using. Give the person's full name on first mention.
3. Identify the author(s) of your source by profession or affiliation so readers will understand the significance of what he or she has to say. Omit this if the speaker is someone readers would recognize without your help.
4. Use transitions into and out of quotations to link the ideas they express to whatever point you are making—that is, to the context of your essay.
5. If your lead-in to a quotation is a simple phrase, follow it with a comma. But if your lead-in can stand alone as a sentence, follow it with a colon.
6. Place the period at the end of a quotation or paraphrase after the parenthetical citation, except with block quotations. (See pages 141–142 for treatment of block quotations.)

## USING SOURCES

How you use a source depends on what you need it for. After you have drafted an argument, you may simply need to consult an almanac for some additional evidence or, say, look up John F. Kennedy's inaugural address to find a stirring quotation. But at earlier stages of the writing process, you may be unsure of your own position and even in need of general background information on the issue. What follows is some advice for those early stages, in which you will encounter a great deal of information and opposing viewpoints. As you research, remember to write down all of the bibliographical information for every source you might use.

### Taking Notes

Just as you can check out books from the library for your own use at home or in your dormitory, so you can photocopy entire articles for your personal

1. Note your source. Use the author's last name or an abbreviated title, or devise a code, such as "A," "B," "C," and so forth.
2. Note the exact page or pages where the information or quotation appears.
3. When you quote, be exact, and put quotation marks around the writer's words to avoid plagiarism if you use them later in your paper.
4. Paraphrase and summarize whenever possible; reserve quotations for passages in which the writer's words are strongly opinionated or especially memorable.

use away from the library. Likewise, if you are working with electronic sources, you can print out the entire text of many online documents. These various methods of gathering materials are helpful for doing research, but when it is time to use the sources in a paper of your own, the traditional writing skills of note-taking, paraphrasing, and summarizing will help you work efficiently and avoid plagiarism.

Whether you are working with a book, a photocopied article, or a document retrieved from the Internet, you will save time if you write down—preferably on a large notecard—anything that strikes you as important or useful. By taking notes, you will avoid having to sort through the entire text of your research materials to find the idea you thought would work in your paper two weeks ago. The box "Guidelines for Taking Notes," above, summarizes the process.

## Paraphrasing

**Paraphrasing,** which means restating a passage in your own words, improves reading comprehension. When you put an idea, especially a complex one, into your own words, you are actually explaining the idea to yourself. When you have a firm grasp of an idea, you can write more confidently, with a sense of owning the idea rather than simply borrowing it. The box "Guidelines for Paraphrasing" on page 129 summarizes the technique.

We illustrate paraphrasing with an excerpt from a source selected by one student, Patrick Pugh, who was researching the topic of euthanasia and planning to defend active euthanasia, or assisted suicide. In the university library, Patrick found a book entitled *Suicide and Euthanasia: The Rights of Personhood,* a collection of essays written by doctors, philosophers, theologians, and legal experts. Published in 1981, the book was somewhat dated in 1991, when Patrick was doing his research, but he felt that the question of whether suicide is moral or immoral was a timeless one. He read an essay entitled "In Defense of Suicide" by Joseph Fletcher, a former professor at the Episcopal

1. Use a dictionary if any words in the original are not completely familiar to you.
2. Work with whole ideas—that is, remember that paraphrasing involves more than keeping the original word order and just plugging in synonyms. Don't be afraid to make your paraphrase longer than the original. Try to break a complex sentence into several simpler ones of your own; take apart a difficult idea and rebuild it, step by step. Don't just echo the original passage thoughtlessly.
3. Don't be a slave to the original—or to the thesaurus. Read the passage until you think you understand it, or a part of it. Then write your version without looking back at the original. Rearrange the order of ideas if doing so makes the passage more accessible.
4. Don't strain to find substitutes for words that are essential to the meaning of a passage.

Divinity School and president of the Society for the Right to Die. Before taking notes on Fletcher's essay, Patrick made a bibliography card recording all the necessary information about this source, like this:

Fletcher, Joseph. "In Defense of Suicide."
In _Suicide and Euthanasia : The_
_Rights of Personhood_. Eds. Samuel E.
Wallace and Albin Eser. Knoxville : U of
Tennessee P 1981

Fletcher's article : pp. 38—50.

The following passage from Fletcher's essay offers a crucial definition; it is the kind of passage that a researcher should paraphrase on a notecard rather than quote so that the idea becomes part of one's own store of knowledge.

> We must begin with the postulate that no action is intrinsically right or wrong, that nothing is inherently good or evil. Right and wrong, good and evil, desirable and undesirable—all are ethical terms and all are predicates, not properties. The moral "value" of any human act is always contingent, depending on the shape of the action in the situation. . . . The variables and factors in each set of circumstances are the determinants of what ought to be done—not prefabricated generalizations or prescriptive rules. . . . No "law" of conduct is always obliging; what we ought to do is whatever maximizes human well-being.
>
> —JOSEPH FLETCHER, "In Defense of Suicide"

Patrick paraphrased this passage on the following notecard. Note that he names the author of the essay, the editors of the book, and the exact pages on which the idea was found.

---

*Fletcher's definition of ethical action:*

*The ethical value of any human action is not a quality inherent in the act itself. It is a judgment that we make about the act after examining the entire situation in which it takes place. Rather than relying on general rules about what is moral and immoral, we should make our decision on the basis of what is best for human well-being in any given set of circumstances.*

*Fletcher, pp. 38-39, in Wallace/Eser.*

## Following Through

From your own research, select a passage of approximately one paragraph that presents a complicated idea. Write a paraphrase of the passage.

Alternatively, write a paraphrase of the following paragraph, also from Joseph Fletcher's "In Defense of Suicide":

> What is called positive euthanasia — doing something to shorten or end life deliberately — is the form [of euthanasia] in which suicide is the question, as a voluntary, direct choice of death. For a long time the Christian moralists have distinguished between negative or indirectly willed suicide, like not taking a place in one of the *Titanic's* lifeboats, and positive or directly willed suicide, like jumping out of a lifeboat to make room for a fellow victim of a shipwreck. The moralists mean that we may choose to allow an evil by acts of omission but not to do an evil by acts of comission. The moralists contend that since all suicide is evil, we may only "allow" it; we may not "do" it. (47)

Your instructor may ask you to compare your paraphrase with that of a classmate's before revising it and handing it in.

## Summarizing

Whereas a paraphrase may be longer or shorter than the original passage, a summary is always considerably shorter. It ought to be at least one-third of the length of the original and is often considerably less: you may, for example, reduce an entire article to one or two paragraphs.

A summary of an argument must contain the main idea or claim and the main points of support or development. The amount of evidence and detail you include depends on your purpose for summarizing: If you merely want to give your audience (or remind yourself of) the gist of the original, a bare-bones summary is enough; but if you plan to use the summary as part of making your case, you had better include the original's evidence as well. The box "Guidelines for Summarizing" on page 132 outlines the process.

For an example of using a summary as part of an argument, we return to Patrick Pugh's investigation of euthanasia. In another book, *The End of Life: Euthanasia and Morality* by James Rachels, Patrick found what Rachels describes as the chief religious objections to euthanasia, with Rachels' rebuttals for each. Patrick decided to include this material, in summary, in his paper. First read the passage from Rachels's book, then read Patrick's summarized version that follows immediately after.

1. Read and reread the original text until you have identified the claim and the main supporting points. You ought to be able to write a brief or outline of the case, using your own words. Depending on your purpose for summarizing and the amount of space you can devote to the summary, decide how much, if any, of the evidence you will need to include.
2. Make it clear at the start whose ideas you are summarizing.
3. If you are summarizing a long passage, break it down into subsections and work on summarizing each one at a time.
4. As with paraphrasing, work as independently as you can — from memory — as you attack each part. Then go back to the text to check your version for accuracy.
5. Try to maintain the original order of points, with this exception: If the author delayed presenting the thesis, you may want to refer to it earlier in your summary.
6. Use your own words as much as possible.
7. Avoid quoting entire sentences. If you want to quote key words and phrases, try to incorporate them into sentences of your own, using quotation marks around the borrowed words.
8. Write a draft summary, then summarize your draft.
9. Revise for conciseness and coherence; look for ways to combine sentences, using connecting words to show how ideas relate. (See the section in the appendix entitled "Use Transitions to Show Relationships between Ideas," pages A12–A13.)

## The End of Life*

### James Rachels

**RELIGIOUS ARGUMENTS**

Social observers are fond of remarking that we live in a secular age, and there is surely something in this. The power of religious conceptions was due, in some considerable measure, to their usefulness in explaining things. In earlier times, religious ideas were used to explain everything from the origins of the universe to the nature of human beings. So long as we had no other way of understanding the world, the hold of religion on us was powerful indeed. Now, however, these explanatory functions have largely been

---

* "The End of Life" by James Rachels. Copyright © 1986 James Rachels. Reprinted from *The End of Life: Euthanasia and Morality* by James Rachels, 1986, by permission of Oxford University Press.

taken over by the sciences: physics, chemistry, and their allies explain physical nature, while evolutionary biology and psychology combine to tell us about ourselves. As there is less and less work for religious hypotheses to do, the grip of religious ideas on us weakens, and appeals to theological conceptions are heard only on Sunday mornings. Hence, the "secular age."

However, most people continue to hold religious beliefs, and they especially appeal to those beliefs when morality is at issue. Any discussion of mercy killing quickly leads to objections based on theological grounds, and "secular" arguments for euthanasia are rejected because they leave out the crucial element of God's directions on the matter.

Considering the traditional religious opposition to euthanasia, it is tempting to say: If one is not a Christian (or if one does not have some similar religious orientation), then perhaps euthanasia is an option; but for people who do have such a religious orientation, euthanasia cannot be acceptable. And the discussion might be ended there. But this is too quick a conclusion; for it is possible that the religious arguments against euthanasia are not valid *even for religious people.* Perhaps a religious perspective, even a conventional Christian one, does *not* lead automatically to the rejection of mercy killing. With this possibility in mind, let us examine three variations of the religious objection.

## What God Commands

It is sometimes said that euthanasia is not permissible simply because God forbids it, and we know that God forbids it by the authority of either scripture or Church tradition. Thus, one eighteenth-century minister, Humphrey Primatt, wrote ironically that, in the case of aged and infirm animals,

> God, the Father of Mercies, hath ordained Beasts and Birds of Prey to do that distressed creature the kindness to relieve him his misery, by putting him to death. A kindness which *We* dare not show to our own species. If thy father, thy brother, or thy child should suffer the utmost pains of a long and agonizing sickness, though his groans should pierce through thy heart, and with strong crying and tears he should beg thy relief, yet thou must be deaf unto him; he must wait his appointed time till his charge cometh, till he sinks and is crushed with the weight of his own misery.

When this argument is advanced, it is usually advanced with great confidence, as though it were *obvious* what God requires. Yet we may well wonder whether such confidence is justified. The sixth commandment does not say, literally, "Thou shalt not *kill*"—that is a bad translation. A better translation is "Thou shalt not commit *murder,*" which is different, and which does not obviously prohibit mercy killing. Murder is by definition *wrongful* killing; so, if you do not think that a given kind of killing is wrong, you will not call it murder. That is why the sixth commandment is not normally taken to forbid killing in a just war; since such killing is (allegedly) justified,

5

it is not called murder. Similarly, if euthanasia is justified, it is not murder, and so it is not prohibited by the commandment. At the very least, it is clear that we cannot infer that euthanasia is wrong *because* it is prohibited by the commandment.

If we look elsewhere in the Christian Bible for a condemnation of euthanasia, we cannot find it. These scriptures are silent on the question. We do find numerous affirmations of the sanctity of human life and the fatherhood of God, and some theologians have tried to infer a prohibition on euthanasia from these general precepts. (The persistence of the attempts, in the face of logical difficulties, is a reminder that people insist on reading their moral prejudices *into* religious texts much more often than they derive their moral views *from* the texts.) But we also find exhortations to kindness and mercy, and the Golden Rule proclaimed as the sum of all morality; and these principles, as we have seen, support euthanasia rather than condemn it.

We *do* find a clear condemnation of euthanasia in Church tradition. Regardless of whether there is scriptural authority for it, the Church has historically opposed mercy killing. It should be emphasized, however, that this is a matter of history. Today, many religious leaders favour euthanasia and think the historical position of the Church has been mistaken. It was an Episcopal minister, Joseph Fletcher, who in his book *Morals and Medicine* formulated the classic modern defence of euthanasia. Fletcher does not stand alone among his fellow churchmen. The Euthanasia Society of America, which he heads, includes many other religious leaders; and the recent "Plea for Beneficent Euthanasia," sponsored by the American Humanist Association, was signed by more religious leaders than people in any other category. So it certainly cannot be claimed that *contemporary* religious forces stand uniformly opposed to euthanasia.

It is noteworthy that even Roman Catholic thinkers are today reassessing the Church's traditional ban on mercy killing. The Catholic philosopher Daniel Maguire has written one of the best books on the subject, *Death by Choice*. Maguire maintains that "it may be moral and should be legal to accelerate the death process by taking direct action, such as overdosing with morphine or injecting potassium"; and moreover, he proposes to demonstrate that this view is "*compatible with historical Catholic ethical theory*," contrary to what most opponents of euthanasia assume. Historical Catholic ethical theory, he says, grants individuals permission to act on views that are supported by "good and serious reasons," even when a different view is supported by a majority of authorities. Since the morality of euthanasia *is* supported by "good and serious reasons," Maguire concludes that Catholics are permitted to accept that morality and act on it.

Thus, the positions of both scripture and Church authorities are (at least) ambiguous enough so that the believer is not bound, on these grounds, to reject mercy killing. The argument from "what God commands" should be inconclusive, even for the staunchest believer.

### The Idea of God's Dominion

Our second theological argument starts from the principle that "The life   10
of man is solely under the dominion of God." It is for God alone to decide when a person shall live and when he shall die; we have no right to
"play God" and arrogate this decision unto ourselves. So euthanasia is
forbidden.

This is perhaps the most familiar of all the theological objections to euthanasia; one hears it constantly when the matter is discussed. However, it
is remarkable that people still advance this argument today, considering that
it was decisively refuted over 200 years ago, when Hume made the simple
but devastating point that *if it is for God alone to decide when we shall live and
when we shall die, then we "play God" just as much when we cure people as when
we kill them.* Suppose a person is sick and we have the means to cure him or
her. If we do so, then we are interfering with God's "right to decide" how
long the life shall last! Hume put it this way:

> Were the disposal of human life so much reserved as the peculiar providence
> of the Almighty that it were an encroachment on his right, for men to dispose
> of their own lives; it would be equally criminal to act for the preservation of
> life as for its destruction. If I turn aside a stone which is falling upon my head,
> I disturb this course of nature, and I invade the peculiar providence of the
> Almighty by lengthening out my life beyond the period which by the general
> laws of matter and motion he had assigned it.

We alter the length of a person's life when we save it just as much as when
we take it. Therefore, if the taking of life is to be forbidden on the grounds
that only God has the right to determine how long a person shall live, then
the saving of life should be prohibited on the same grounds. We would
then have to abolish the practice of medicine. But everyone (except, perhaps, Christian Scientists) concedes that this would be absurd. Therefore,
we may *not* prohibit euthanasia on the grounds that only God has the right
to determine how long a life shall last. This seems to be a complete refutation of this argument, and if refuted arguments were decently discarded, as
they should be, we would hear no more of it.

### Suffering and God's Plan

The last religious argument we shall consider is based on the idea that suffering is a part of God's plan for us. God has ordained that people should
suffer; he never intended that life should be continually pleasurable. (If
he had intended this, presumably he would have created a very different
world.) Therefore, if we were to kill people to "put them out of their misery," we would be interfering with God's plan. Bishop Joseph Sullivan, a
prominent Catholic opponent of euthanasia, expresses the argument in
a passage from his essay "The Immorality of Euthanasia":

If the suffering patient is of sound mind and capable of making an act of divine resignation, then his sufferings become a great means of merit whereby he can gain reward for himself and also win great favors for the souls in Purgatory, perhaps even release them from their suffering. Likewise the sufferer may give good example to his family and friends and teach them how to bear a heavy cross in a Christlike manner.

As regard those that must live in the same house with the incurable sufferer, they have a great opportunity to practice Christian charity. They can learn to see Christ in the sufferer and win the reward promised in the Beatitudes. This opportunity for charity would hold true even when the incurable sufferer is deprived of the use of reason. It may well be that the incurable sufferer in a particular case may be of greater value to society than when he was of some material value to himself and his community.

This argument may strike some readers as simply grotesque. Can we imagine this being said, seriously, in the presence of suffering such as that experienced by Stewart Alsop's roommate? "We know it hurts, Jack, and that your wife is being torn apart just having to watch it, but think what a good opportunity this is for you to set an example. You can give us a lesson in how to bear it." In addition, some might think that euthanasia is exactly what *is* required by the "charity" that bystanders have the opportunity to practice.

But, these reactions aside, there is a more fundamental difficulty with      15
the argument. For if the argument were sound, it would lead not only to the condemnation of euthanasia but of *any* measures to reduce suffering. If God decrees that we suffer, why aren't we obstructing God's plan when we give drugs to relieve pain? A girl breaks her arm; if only God knows how much pain is right for her, who are we to mend it? The point is similar to Hume's refutation of the previous argument. This argument, like the previous one, cannot be right because it leads to consequences that no one, not even the most conservative religious thinker, is willing to accept.

We have now looked at three arguments that depend on religious assumptions. They are all unsound, but I have *not* criticized them simply by rejecting their religious presuppositions. Instead, I have criticized them on their own terms, showing that these arguments should not be accepted even by religious people. As Daniel Maguire emphasizes, the ethics of theists, like the ethics of all responsible people, should be determined by "good and serious reasons," and these arguments are not good no matter what world-view one has.

The upshot is that religious people are in the same position as everyone else. There is nothing in religious belief in general, or in Christian belief in particular, to preclude the acceptance of mercy killing as a humane response to some awful situations. So, as far as these arguments are concerned, it appears that Christians may be free, after all, to accept the Golden Rule.

**STUDENT SAMPLE:** *A Summary*

In the following paper, the numbers in parentheses indicate the original pages where material appeared. We explain this method of documentation later in this chapter.

SUMMARY OF EXCERPT FROM *THE END OF LIFE*

Patrick Pugh

According to James Rachels, in spite of the fact that we live in a secular age, many objections to active euthanasia focus on religion, and particularly Christianity. However, even religious people ought to be able to see that these arguments may not be valid. For example, one of the most often-stated objections is that in the Ten Commandments God forbids killing. Rachels counters by pointing out that the Sixth Commandment is more accurately translated as "Thou shalt not commit murder." Because we define murder as "wrongful killing," we will not call some killing murder if we do not see it as wrong. Thus, the Sixth Commandment "is not normally taken to forbid killing in a just war; since such killing is (allegedly) justified" (161–62). Rachels points out that although the scriptures do not mention euthanasia and in fact affirm the "sanctity of human life," one also finds "exhortations to kindness and mercy" for fellow humans, principles that "support active euthanasia rather than condemn it" (162).

To those who claim that "[i]t is for God alone to decide when a person shall live and when he shall die," Rachels responds that "if it is for God alone to decide when we shall live and when we shall die, then we 'play God' just as much when we cure people as when we kill them" (163). He notes that philosopher David Hume made this argument more than two hundred years ago.

A third common Christian argument is that because suffering is a part of God's plan for humans, we should not interrupt it by euthanasia. Rachels responds to this with the question, How can we then justify the use of any pain-relieving drugs and procedures? (165). He concludes that "[t]here is nothing in religious belief in general, or in Christian belief in particular, to preclude the acceptance of mercy killing as a humane response to some awful situations" (165).

## Following Through

Write a summary of the argument opposing euthanasia entitled "Rising to the Occasion of Our Death" by William F. May, on pages 53–55. Or summarize any other argument that you are considering using as a source for a project you are currently working on.

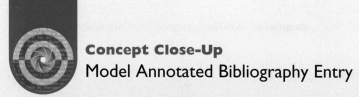

Ames, Katrine. "Last Rights." *Newsweek* 26 Aug. 1991: 40–41.

> This is a news article for the general public about the popularity of a book called *Final Exit,* on how to commit suicide. Ames explains the interest in the book as resulting from people's perception that doctors, technology, and hospital bureaucrats are making it harder and harder to die with dignity in this country. The article documents with statistics the direction of public opinion on this topic and also outlines some options, besides suicide, that are becoming available to ensure people of the right to die. Ames shows a bias against prolonging life through technology, but she includes quotations from authorities on both sides. This is a good source of evidence about public and professional opinion.

## Creating an Annotated Bibliography

To get an overview of the sources they have compiled, many writers find it useful to create an annotated bibliography. A **bibliography** is simply a list of works on a particular topic; it can include any kind of source — from newspaper articles to books to government documents. The basic information of a bibliography is identical to that of a works-cited list: author, title, publisher, date, and, in the case of articles, periodical name, volume, and page numbers. (See the section "Creating Works-Cited and Reference Lists" for examples.) Like a works-cited list, a bibliography is arranged in alphabetical order, based on each author's last name.

To **annotate** a bibliography means to include critical commentary about each work on the list, usually in one or two short paragraphs. Each annotation should contain the following:

- A sentence or two about the rhetorical context of the source. Is it an informative news article? an opinion column? a scholarly essay? Is it intended for lawyers? the public? students? the elderly? What is the bias?
- A capsule summary of the content.
- A note about why this source seems valuable and how you might use it.

**Following Through**

Write an annotated bibliography of the sources you are using for a re-searched argument of your own. Use the model above as a guide.

## INCORPORATING AND DOCUMENTING SOURCE MATERIAL IN THE TEXT OF YOUR ARGUMENT

We turn now to the more technical matter of how to incorporate source material into your own writing and how to document the material you include. You incorporate material through direct quotation or through summary or paraphrase; you document material by naming the writer and providing full publication details of the source—a two-step process. In academic writing, documenting sources is essential, even for indirect references, with one exception: You do not need to document your source for factual information that could easily be found in many readily available sources, such as a Supreme Court decision or the number of women currently in the U.S. Senate.

### Different Styles of Documentation

Different disciplines have specific formal conventions for documenting sources in scholarly writing. In the humanities, the most common style is that of the Modern Language Association (MLA). In the physical, natural, and social sciences, the American Psychological Association (APA) style is most often used. We will illustrate both in the examples that follow. Unlike the footnote style of documentation, MLA and APA use parenthetical citations in the text and simple, alphabetical bibliographies at the end of the text, making revision and typing much easier. (For a detailed explanation of these two styles, refer to the following manuals: *MLA Handbook for Writers of Research Papers.* 5th ed. New York: MLA, 1999; and the *Publication Manual of the American Psychological Association.* 5th ed. Washington, DC: APA, 2001. You may also visit Web sites for the MLA at <http://www.mla.org> and the APA at <http://apa.org>.)

In both MLA and APA formats, you provide some information in the body of your paper and the rest of the information under the heading "Works Cited" (MLA) or "References" (APA) at the end of your paper. The following summarizes the essentials of both systems.

### Instructions for Using MLA and APA Styles

*MLA Style*

1.  In parentheses at the end of both direct and indirect quotations, supply the last name of the author of the source and the exact page

number(s) where the quoted or paraphrased words appear. If the name of the author appears in your sentence that leads into the quotation, you can omit it in the parentheses.

> A San Jose State University professor who is black argues that affirmative action "does not teach skills, or educate, or instill motivation" (Steele 121).

> Shelby Steele, a black professor of English at San Jose State University, argues that the disadvantages of affirmative action for blacks are greater than the advantages (117).

2. In a works-cited list at the end of the paper, provide complete bibliographical information in MLA style, as explained and illustrated later in this chapter.

*APA Style*

1. In parentheses at the end of the directly or indirectly quoted material, place the author's last name, the date of the cited source, and the exact page number(s) where the material appears. If the author's name appears in the sentence, the date of publication should follow the name directly, in parentheses; the page number still comes in parentheses at the end of the sentence. Unlike MLA, the APA style uses commas between the parts of the citation and "p." or "pp." before the page numbers.

> A San Jose State University professor who is black argues that affirmative action "does not teach skills, or educate, or instill motivation" (Steele, 1990, p. 121).

> Shelby Steele (1990), a black professor of English at San Jose State University, argues that the disadvantages of affirmative action for blacks are greater than the advantages (p. 117).

2. In a reference list at the end of the paper, provide complete bibliographical information in APA style, as explained and illustrated later in this chapter.

## Direct Quotations

Direct quotations are exact words taken from a source. The simplest direct quotations are whole sentences worked into your text, as illustrated in the following excerpt from a student essay.

*MLA Style*

> In a passage that echos Seneca, <u>Newsweek</u> writer Katrine Ames describes the modern viewpoint: "Most of us have some choices in how we live, certainly in how we conduct our lives" (40).

This source is listed in the works-cited list as follows:

> Ames, Katrine. "Last Rights." <u>Newsweek</u> 26 Aug. 1991: 40–41.

*APA Style*

> In a passage that echos Seneca, *Newsweek* writer Katrine Ames (1991) describes the modern viewpoint: "Most of us have some choices in how we live, certainly in how we conduct our lives" (p. 40).

This source is listed in the reference list as follows:

> Ames, K. (1991, August 26). Last rights. *Newsweek*, pp. 40–41.

*Altering Direct Quotations with Ellipses and Brackets*

Although there is nothing wrong with quoting whole sentences, it is often more economical to quote selectively, working some words or parts of sentences from the original into sentences of your own. When you do this, use *ellipses* (three evenly spaced periods) to signify the omission of words from the original; use brackets to substitute words, to add words for purposes of clarification, and to change the wording of a quotation so that it fits gracefully into your own sentence. (If ellipses already appear in the material you are quoting and you are omitting additional material, it is necessary to place your ellipses in brackets to distinguish them.)

The following passage from a student paper illustrates quoted words integrated into the student's own sentence, using ellipses and brackets. The citation is in MLA style.

> Robert Wennberg, a philosopher and Presbyterian minister, explains that "euthanasia is not an exclusively modern development, for it was widely endorsed in the ancient world. [It was] approved by such respected ancients as . . . Plato, Sophocles, . . . and Cicero" (1).

The source appears in the works-cited list as follows:

> Wennberg, Robert N. <u>Terminal Choices: Euthanasia, Suicide, and the Right to Die</u>. Grand Rapids: Eerdmans, 1989.

*Using Block Quotations*

If a quoted passage runs to four lines of text in your essay, indent it one inch (or ten spaces if typewritten) from the left margin, double-space it as with the rest of your text, and omit quotation marks. In block quotations, a period is placed at the end of the final sentence, followed by one space and the parenthetical citation.

> The idea of death as release from suffering was expressed by Seneca, a Stoic philosopher of Rome, who lived during the first century C.E.:
>
> > Against all the injuries of life, I have the refuge of death. If I can choose between a death of torture and one that is simple and easy, why should I not select the latter? As I chose the ship in which I sail and the house which I inhabit, so will I choose the death by which I leave life. . . . Why should I endure the agonies of disease . . . when I can emancipate myself from all my torments? (qtd. in Wennberg 42–43)

Note that the source of the Seneca quotation is the book by Wennberg. In the parenthetical citation, "qtd." is an abbreviation for "quoted." The entry on the works-cited page would be the same as for the previous example.

## Indirect Quotations

Indirect quotations are paraphrases or summaries of material, either fact or opinion, taken from a source. The Concept Close-Up box on page 143 gives an example of a direct quotation on a student notecard.

Here is how this quotation might be incorporated into a paper as an indirect quotation. Note that the author of the book is the same as the person indirectly quoted, so it is not necessary to repeat his name in parentheses.

*MLA Style*

> One cannot help but agree with pioneer heart-transplant surgeon Christiaan Barnard that death should involve dignity and that society may have to accept the practice of euthanasia as a means to death with dignity (8).

The entry on the works-cited list would appear as follows:

> Barnard, Christiaan. <u>Good Life, Good Death</u>. Englewood Cliffs: Prentice, 1980.

*APA Style*

> One cannot help but agree with pioneer heart-transplant surgeon Christiaan Barnard (1980) that death should involve dignity and that

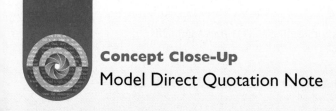
> *Expert's opinion — pro:*
>
> *"It is time to rethink many of our attitudes toward death and dying. [...] I feel that society is ready to take a giant step toward a better understanding of the dignity of death, and in the attainment of that dignity, if necessary, through the acceptance of euthanasia."*
>
> — *Barnard in Barnard, p. 8*

society may have to accept the practice of euthanasia as a means to death with dignity (p. 8).

The entry in the reference list would appear as follows.

Barnard, C. (1980). *Good life, good death.* Englewood Cliffs, NJ: Prentice-Hall.

### In-Text References to Electronic Sources

Obviously, the conventions just described apply to print sources, but you should adapt the examples given, being as specific as you can, when you are using sources drawn from the Internet and other electronic communications. Because you will be including the electronic sources in your works-cited or reference list at the end of your paper, your in-text citations should help your readers make the connection between the material you are quoting or paraphrasing in your text and the matching citation on the list. Therefore, your in-text citation, whether parenthetical or not, should begin with the author's name or, in the absence of an author, the title of the work or posting. The APA format requires that you also include the date of the posting.

## CREATING WORKS-CITED AND REFERENCE LISTS

At the end of your paper, include a bibliography of all sources that you quoted, paraphrased, or summarized. If you are using MLA style, your heading for this list will be *Works Cited;* if you are using APA style, your heading will be *References*. In either case, the list is in alphabetical order based on either the author's (or editor's) last name or — in the case of anonymously written works — the first word of the title, not counting the articles *a, an, the*. The entire list is double-spaced both within and between entries. See the works-cited page of the sample student paper at the end of this chapter for the correct indentation and spacing. Note that MLA format requires that the first line of each entry be typed flush with the left margin; subsequent lines of each entry are indented half an inch (or five spaces on a typewriter). The APA recommends that papers submitted in final form, such as student papers, use the same indentation.

The following examples illustrate the correct form for the types of sources you will most commonly use.

### Books

*Book by One Author*

MLA:   Crusius, Timothy W. <u>Discourse: A Critique & Synthesis of Major Theories</u>. New York: MLA, 1989.

APA:   Crusius, T. W. (1989). *Discourse: A critique & synthesis of major theories.* New York: Modern Language Association.

(Note that APA uses initials rather than the author's first name and capitalizes only the first word and proper nouns in the titles and subtitles of books and articles.)

*Two or More Works by the Same Author*

MLA:   Crusius, Timothy W. <u>Discourse: A Critique & Synthesis of Major Theories</u>. New York: MLA, 1989.

   ---. <u>A Teacher's Introduction to Philosophical Hermeneutics</u>. Urbana: NCTE, 1991.

(Note that MLA arranges works alphabetically by title and uses three hyphens to show that the name is the same as the one directly above.)

APA:   Crusius, T. W. (1989). *Discourse: A critique & synthesis of major theories.* New York: Modern Language Association.

Crusius, T. W. (1991). *A teacher's introduction to philosophical hermeneutics.* Urbana, IL: National Council of Teachers of English.

(Note that APA repeats the author's name and arranges works in chronological order.)

## Book by Two or Three Authors

**MLA:**  Deleuze, Gilles, and Felix Guattari. <u>Anti-Oedipus: Capitalism and Schizophrenia</u>. New York: Viking, 1977.

**APA:**  Deleuze, G., & Guattari, F. (1977). *Anti-Oedipus: Capitalism and schizophrenia.* New York: Viking.

(Note that MLA style inverts only the first author's name. APA style, however, inverts both authors' names and uses an ampersand (&) between authors instead of the word "and.")

## Book by Four or More Authors

**MLA:**  Bellah, Robert N., et al. <u>Habits of the Heart: Individualism and Commitment in American Life</u>. New York: Harper, 1985.

(Note that the Latin abbreviation *et al.,* meaning "and others," stands in for all subsequent authors' names. MLA style also accepts spelling out all authors' names instead of using *et al.*)

**APA:**  Bellah, R., Madsen, R., Sullivan, W., Swidler, A., & Tipton, S. (1985). *Habits of the heart: Individualism and commitment in American life.* New York: Harper & Row.

(Note that APA uses *et al.* only for more than six authors.)

## Book Prepared by an Editor or Editors

**MLA:**  Connors, Robert J., ed. <u>Selected Essays of Edward P. J. Corbett</u>. Dallas: Southern Methodist UP, 1989.

**APA:**  Connors, R. J. (Ed.). (1989). *Selected essays of Edward P. J. Corbett.* Dallas: Southern Methodist University Press.

## Work in an Edited Collection

**MLA:**  Jackson, Jesse. "Common Ground: Speech to the Democratic National Convention." <u>The American Reader</u>. Ed. Diane Ravitch. New York: Harper, 1991. 367–71.

APA:    Jackson, J. (1991). Common ground: Speech to the Democratic National Convention. In D. Ravitch (Ed.), *The American reader* (pp. 367–371). New York: HarperCollins.

### Translated Book

MLA:    Vattimo, Gianni. <u>The End of Modernity: Nihilism and Hermeneutics in Postmodern Culture</u>. Trans. Jon R. Snyder. Baltimore: Johns Hopkins UP, 1988.

APA:    Vattimo, G. (1988). *The end of modernity: Nihilism and hermeneutics in postmodern culture*. (J. R. Snyder, Trans.). Baltimore: Johns Hopkins University Press.

## Periodicals

### Article in a Journal with Continuous Pagination

MLA:    Herron, Jerry. "Writing for My Father." <u>College English</u> 54 (1992): 928–37.

APA:    Herron, J. (1992). Writing for my father. *College English, 54,* 928–937.

(Note that in APA style the article title is not fully capitalized, but the journal title is. Note also that the volume number is italicized in APA style.)

### Article in a Journal Paginated by Issue

MLA:    McConnell, Margaret Liu. "Living with *Roe v. Wade*." <u>Commentary</u> 90.5 (1990): 34–38.

APA:    McConnell, M. L. (1990). Living with *Roe v. Wade. Commentary, 90*(5), 34–38.

(In both these examples, "90" is the volume number and "5" is the number of the issue.)

### Article in a Magazine

MLA:    D'Souza, Dinesh. "Illiberal Education." <u>Atlantic</u> Mar. 1990: 51+.

(Note that the plus sign indicates that the article runs on nonconsecutive pages.)

APA:   D'Souza, D. (1990, March). Illiberal education. *Atlantic,* pp. 51–58,
       62–65, 67, 70–74, 76, 78–79.

(Note that APA requires all page numbers to be listed.)

*Anonymous Article in a Newspaper*

MLA:   "Clinton Warns of Sacrifice." <u>Dallas Morning News</u> 7 Feb.
       1993: A4.

APA:   Clinton warns of sacrifice. (1993, February 7). *The Dallas Morning
       News,* p. A4.

(In both these examples, the "A" refers to the newspaper section in which
the article appeared.)

*Editorial in a Newspaper*

MLA:   Lewis, Flora. "Civil Society, the Police and Abortion." Editorial.
       <u>New York Times</u> 12 Sept. 1992, late ed.: A14.

APA:   Lewis, F. (1992, September 12). Civil society, the police and abor-
       tion [Editorial]. *The New York Times,* p. A14.

(Note that in MLA style the edition of the newspaper must be specified.)

## Nonprint Sources

*Interview*

MLA:   May, William. Personal interview. 24 Apr. 1990.

(Note that APA style documents personal interviews only parenthetically
within the text: "According to W. May (personal interview, April 24, 1990), ..."
Personal interviews are not included on the reference list.)

*Sound Recording*

MLA:   Glass, Philip. <u>Glassworks</u>. CBS Sony, MK 37265, 1982.

APA:   Glass, P. (1982). *Glassworks* [CD Recording No. MK 37265].
       Tokyo: CBS Sony.

*Film (on video—for DVD, substitute "DVD" for "videocassette")*

MLA:   Scott, Ridley, dir. <u>Thelma and Louise</u>. Perf. Susan Sarandon,
       Geena Davis, and Harvey Keitel. 1991. Videocassette.
       MGM/UA Home Video, 1996.

APA:    Scott, R. (Director). (1991). *Thelma and Louise* [motion picture].
Culver City, CA: MGM/UA Home Video.

(Note that with nonprint media, APA asks you to identify the medium —
CD, cassette, film, and so forth. MLA includes the principal actors, but APA
does not. APA specifies the place of production, but MLA does not.)

## Electronic Sources

Although the documentation requirements for MLA and APA citations contain much of the same information, there are subtle format differences between the two styles. Use the following lists as general guides when you cite
Internet sources.

*MLA Style: Citing Internet Sources*

1. Author or editor name, followed by a period
2. The title of the article or short work (such as a short story or poem)
   followed by a period and enclosed by quotation marks
3. The name of the book, journal, or other longer work underlined
4. Publication information, followed by a period:

   > City, publisher, and date for books
   > Volume and year for journals
   > Date for magazines
   > Date for and description of government documents

5. The date on which you accessed the information (no period)
6. The URL, placed inside angle brackets, followed by a period

*APA Style: Citing Internet Sources*

1. Author or editor last name, followed by a comma and the initials
2. The year of publication, followed by a comma, with the month and
   day for magazine and newspaper articles, within parentheses and
   followed by a period
3. The title of the article, book, or journal (follow APA conventions for
   titles of works)
4. The volume number
5. Page numbers
6. The words "Retrieved from," followed by the date of access, followed
   by the source (such as the World Wide Web) and a colon
7. The URL, without a period

*An Online Book*

MLA:    Strunk, William. <u>The Elements of Style</u>. 1st ed. Geneva:
Humphrey, 1918. May 1995. Columbia U Academic
Information Systems, Bartleby Lib. 12 Apr. 1999.

<http://www.Columbia.edu/acis/bartleby/strunk/
strunk100.html>.

APA:    Strunk, W. (1918). *The elements of style* (1st ed.). [Online].
Retrieved April 12, 1999, from the World Wide Web:
http://www.Columbia.edu/acis/bartleby/strunk/
strunk100.html

(Note that MLA requires that the original publication data be included if
it is available for works that originally appeared in print. The APA, however,
requires only an online availability statement.)

## World Wide Web Site

MLA:    Victorian Women Writers Project. Ed. Perry Willett. Apr. 1999.
Indiana U. 12 Apr. 1999 <http://www.indiana.edu/
~letrs/vwwp>.

APA:    Willett, P. (1999, April). *Victorian women writers project* [Web
page]. Retrieved April 12, 1999, from http://www.indiana.
edu/~letrs/vwwp

## Article in an Electronic Journal

MLA:    Harnack, Andrew, and Gene Kleppinger. "Beyond the MLA
Handbook: Documenting Sources on the Internet." Kairos
1.2 (Summer 1996). 7 Jan. 1997 <http://english.ttu.edu/
Kairos/1.2/index.html>.

APA:    Harnack, A., & Kleppinger, G. (1996). Beyond the *MLA Handbook:*
Documenting sources on the Internet. *Kairos* [Online], *1*(2).
Retrieved January 7, 1997, from http://english.ttu.edu/
Kairos/1.2/index.html

## Encyclopedia Article on CD-ROM

MLA:    Duckworth, George. "Rhetoric." Microsoft Encarta '95. CD-ROM.
Redmond: Microsoft, 1995.

APA:    Duckworth. G. (1995). Rhetoric. In *Microsoft encarta '95* [CD-ROM].
Redmond, WA: Microsoft.

## Encyclopedia Article Online

MLA:    "Toni Morrison." Encyclopaedia Britannica Online. 1994–1999. Encyclopaedia Britannica. 4 Mar. 1999

&lt;http://members.eb.com/bol/
topic?eu=55183&sctn=#s_top&gt;.

**APA:**    (1994–1999). Toni Morrison. In *Encyclopaedia Britannica
Online* [Online]. Retrieved March 4, 1999, from http://
members.eb.com/bol/topic?eu=55183&sctn=#s_top

### E-Mail, Listserv, and Newsgroup Citations

For **MLA**, give in this order the author's name, the title of the document (in
quotation marks), followed by the description *Online posting,* the date when
the material was posted, the name of the forum (if known), the date of access, and in angle brackets the online address of the list's Internet site or, if
unknown, the e-mail address of the list's moderator.

**MLA:**    Stockwell, Stephen. "Rhetoric and Democracy." Online posting.
13 Jan. 1997. 22 Jan. 1997 &lt;H-Rhetor@msu.edu&gt;.

For **APA**, the custom is to not include e-mail, listservs, and newsgroups
in a reference list but rather to give a detailed in-text citation as follows:
(S. Stockwell, posting to H-Rhetor@msu.edu, January 13, 1997).

However, if the content of the message is scholarly, many researchers do
include messages in the references:

**APA:**    Stockwell, S. (1997, January 13). Rhetoric and democracy.
Retrieved January 22, 1997, from e-mail: H-Rhetor@msu.edu

## STUDENT SAMPLE: *A Research Paper (MLA Style)*

Following is student Patrick Pugh's research paper in MLA style.

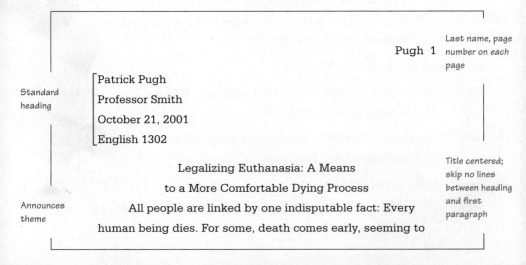

Pugh 1    Last name, page
number on each
page

Standard    Patrick Pugh
heading      Professor Smith
October 21, 2001
English 1302

Legalizing Euthanasia: A Means       Title centered;
to a More Comfortable Dying Process    skip no lines
between heading
Announces    All people are linked by one indisputable fact: Every    and first
theme       human being dies. For some, death comes early, seeming to    paragraph

Pugh 2

cut off life before many of its mysteries have even begun to
unfold. For others, death is the conclusion to a lengthy and
experience-filled existence. Death is life's one absolute
certainty.

*Paragraphs indented 5 character spaces or 1/2"*

At issue, however, is the desire by some men and
women, many of the most vocal of whom are in the medical
profession, to intervene in what they describe as a heartless
extension of the dying process. The term *euthanasia*, a Greek
word whose literal translation is "good death," has been
adopted by those who advocate legalizing certain measures to
ensure a transition from life to death that is as comfortable and

*No word breaks at ends of lines*

*Poses issue*

dignified as possible. One cannot help but agree with pioneer
heart-transplant surgeon Dr. Christiaan Barnard that death
should involve dignity and that society may have to accept the
practice of euthanasia as a means to death with dignity (8).

*Takes stance*

*Parenthetical page number only because author's name mentioned in text. Note: Page number goes before period.*

To me, having watched both my grandfather and
my aunt spend months dying slow, torturous deaths
from incurable lung cancer, there can be little doubt that
euthanasia would have provided a far more humane close
to their lives than the painful and prolonged dying that the
ultimately futile regimens of chemotherapy and radiation
caused them to suffer. My family members' experiences
were far too common, for "80 percent of Americans who
die in hospitals are likely to meet their end . . . in a
sedated or comatose state; betubed nasally, abdominally,
and intravenously, far more like manipulated objects than
moral subjects" (Minow 124).

*Ties stance to personal experience*

*"Run in" quotation; use for shorter citations. Note brackets used with ellipses.*

*Both author and page number used because author not mentioned in sentence*

Advocates of euthanasia can turn to history for support
of their arguments. Robert Wennberg, a philosopher and
Presbyterian minister, explains that "euthanasia is not an

Pugh 3

exclusively modern development, for it was widely endorsed
in the ancient world. [It was] approved by such respected
ancients as . . . Plato, Sophocles, . . . and Cicero" (1). The
idea that we have a right to choose death was expressed by
Seneca, a Stoic philosopher of Rome, who lived in the first
century C.E.:

> Against all the injuries of life, I have the refuge of
> death. If I can choose between a death of torture and
> one that is simple and easy, why should I not select
> the latter? As I chose the ship in which I sail and the
> house which I inhabit, so will I choose the death by
> which I leave life. In no matter more than death
> should we act according to our desire. . . . Why
> should I endure the agonies of disease . . . when I
> can emancipate myself from all my torments? (qtd. in
> Wennberg 42–43)

In a passage that echos Seneca, <u>Newsweek</u> writer Katrine
Ames describes the modern viewpoint: "Most of us have
some choices in how we live, certainly in how we conduct
our lives. How we die is an equally profound choice, and,
in the exhilarating and terrifying new world of medical
technology, perhaps almost as important" (40).

Regardless of historical precedents and humane
implications, euthanasia in both of its forms remains a
controversial issue for many. In the first kind, known as
passive or indirect euthanasia, death results from such
measures as withholding or withdrawing life-support
systems or life-sustaining medications. Passive euthanasia is
often equated with simply "letting someone die," in contrast
to the far more controversial active or direct euthanasia, in
which life is ended by direct intervention, such as giving a

---

*Marginal annotations:*

Identifies source unknown to audience; establishes authority of source

Block quotation; use for longer citations. Note: No quotation marks; indented 10 character spaces or 1".

Note parenthetical citation. No end punctuation after block quote; contrast with "run in" quotation.

Makes important distinction

Pugh 4

patient a lethal dose of a drug or assisting a patient in his or her suicide.

During the past two decades, the so-called Right to Die movement has made great strides in the promotion of passive euthanasia as an acceptable alternative to the extension of impending death.

> There seems to be a clear consensus that the competent adult has the right to refuse treatments. . . . This legal recognition of the right to reject medical treatment is grounded in a respect for the bodily integrity of the individual, for the right of each person to determine when bodily invasions will take place. (Wennberg 116)

*End of sentence plus omission from text; A period plus three spaced periods used.*

Passive euthanasia, as an extension of the stated wishes of the dying patient, has become a widely accepted practice, a fact confirmed by medical ethicist and theologian Joseph Fletcher:

*Three periods; omission from cited text*

> What is called passive euthanasia, letting the patient die . . . is a daily event in hospitals. Hundreds of thousands of Living Wills have been recorded, appealing to doctors, families, pastors, and lawyers to stop treatment at some balance point of the pro-life, pro-death assessment. (47)

The case for passive euthanasia has withstood, for the most part, the arguments of those who claim that life must be preserved and extended at all costs.

The euthanasia debate that is currently being waged focuses on active or direct euthanasia, where another person, notably a physician, assists a terminally ill patient in dying by lethal injection or provides the dying patient with the means to commit suicide. The case for active euthanasia is strong. For example, active euthanasia is preferable to passive

Pugh 5

euthanasia in cases of chronic and incurable diseases that promise the patient pain and suffering for the duration of his or her life. As Robert K. Landers explains, with the advance of AIDS and diseases such as Alzheimer's affecting our aging population, Americans are paying more attention to the idea of "giving death a hand" (555). Surely, many terminally ill patients whose only hope for release from agonizing pain or humiliating helplessness is death would welcome the more comfortable and dignified death that physician-assisted suicide can bring.

*Restates stance, now focused on active euthanasia only*

Still, there are those who argue that although passive euthanasia is moral, the active type is not. Ethically, is there a difference between passive and active euthanasia? Christiaan Barnard thinks not:

> Passive euthanasia is accepted in general by
> the medical profession, the major religions, and
> society at large. Therefore, when it is permissible
> for treatment to be stopped or not instituted in order
> to allow the patient to die, it makes for small mercy
> and less sense when the logical step of actively
> terminating life, and hence suffering, is not taken.
> Why, at that point, can life not be brought to an end,
> instead of extending the suffering of the patient by
> hours or days, or even weeks? . . . Procedurally,
> there is a difference between direct and indirect
> euthanasia, but ethically, they are the same. (68–69)

*Argues that active euthanasia is ethical*

Barnard's ethics are supported by Joseph Fletcher's definition of ethical action, which holds that the ethical value of any human action is not a quality inherent in the act itself but rather a judgment that we make about the act after examining the entire situation in which it takes place. We should decide what is moral and immoral on the basis of

*Defines ethics in situational terms*

Pugh 6

what is best for human well-being in any given set of circumstances (38–39).

Although Fletcher is an Episcopal theologian, many other Christians do make arguments against active euthanasia on religious grounds. However, according to ethicist James Rachels, even religious people ought to be able to see that these arguments may not be valid. For example, one of the most often-stated objections is that in the Ten Commandments God forbids killing. Rachels counters by pointing out that the Sixth Commandment is more accurately translated as "Thou shalt not commit murder." Because we define murder as "wrongful killing," we will not call some killing murder if we do not see it as wrong. Thus, the Sixth Commandment "is not normally taken to forbid killing in a just war; since such killing is (allegedly) justified" (161–62). Rachels points out that although the scriptures do not mention euthanasia and in fact affirm the "sanctity of human life," one also finds "exhortations to kindness and mercy" for fellow humans, principles that "support active euthanasia rather than condemn it" (162).

*Takes up major objection; refutes the notion that mercy killing is murder*

To those who claim that "[i]t is for God alone to decide when a person shall live and when he shall die," Rachels responds that "if it is for God alone to decide when we shall live and when we shall die, then we 'play God' just as much when we cure people as when we kill them" (163). He notes that philosopher David Hume made this argument over two hundred years ago.

*Transitional sentences signal change of focus, allow smooth movement from paragraph to paragraph*

A third common Christian argument is that because suffering is a part of God's plan for humans, we should not interrupt it by euthanasia. Rachels responds to this with the question, How can we then justify the use of any pain-relieving drugs and procedures? (165). He concludes that "[t]here is nothing in religious belief in general, or in Christian belief in particular, to preclude the acceptance of mercy killing as a humane response to some awful situations" (165).

In fact, the American public supports active euthanasia, specifically physician-assisted euthanasia, as an alternative to a lingering death for terminal patients. Polls show support running as high as 70 percent (ERGO). Support for assisted suicide may have leveled off recently, but polls still indicate that more Americans favor assisted suicide than oppose it (American Life League). Fifty percent of doctors also support it, with about 15 percent actually practicing it when a patient's dire situation warrants (ERGO).

Public support, however, has not translated into significant changes in the law. Only Oregon permits assisted suicides (ERGO). Maine rejected a measure similar to the Oregon law in the 2000 election ("Assisted Suicide"), and Attorney General John Ashcroft, reversing the stance of his predecessor, Janet Reno, has recently taken action to block implementation of Oregon's law (Vicini). Furthermore, the Supreme Court has ruled in two cases that the Constitution does not provide a right to die and therefore has upheld state laws against assisted suicide ("Physician"; Vacco v. Quill).

At this point, then, the law seems unresponsive to public opinion. There is no way to predict whether active euthanasia will be legalized in the near future. One thing is reasonably certain, however: Any compassionate person who has sat by helplessly as a fellow human being has spent his or her final days thrashing around on a sweat-soaked bed or who has observed a once-alert mind that has become darkened by the agony of inescapable pain will consider the eventual fate that awaits him or her. In times like these,

*Forceful conclusion; avoids saying "in conclusion"*

Pugh 8

frightened humans are united in the universal prayer, "God, spare me from this when my time comes," and even the most stubborn anti-euthanasia minds are opened to the option of an easier journey between life and death, an option that can be made a reality by the legalization of physician-assisted euthanasia.

Works Cited

American Life League, Inc. <u>Legislative Guide to End-of-Life Issues</u>. 11 Dec. 2001 <http://www.all.org/legislat/guide01.htm>.

Ames, Katrine. "Last Rights." <u>Newsweek</u> 26 Aug. 1991: 40–41.

"Assisted Suicide, Gay Rights, Lose in Maine." <u>USA Today Network</u>. 8 Nov. 2000. 11 Dec 2001 <http://www.usatoday.com/news/vote2000/me/main.htm>.

Barnard, Christiaan. <u>Good Life, Good Death</u>. Englewood Cliffs: Prentice, 1980.

ERGO (Euthanasia Research & Guidance Organization). "Frequently Asked Questions." <u>Euthanasia World Directory</u>. 11 Dec. 2001 <http://www.finalexit.org>.

Fletcher, Joseph. "In Defense of Suicide." <u>Suicide and Euthanasia: The Rights of Personhood</u>. Ed. Samuel E. Wallace and Albin Eser. Knoxville: U of Tennessee P, 1981. 38–50.

Landers, Robert. "Right to Die: Medical, Legal, and Moral Issues." <u>Editorial Research Reports</u> 1.36 (1990): 554–64.

Minow, Newton. "Communications in Medicine." <u>Vital Speeches of the Day</u>. 1 Dec. 1990: 121–25.

"Physician-Assisted Suicide: Vacco v. Quill; Washington v. Glucksberg." <u>Supreme Court—Key Cases 1996–1997</u>. <u>Washington Post</u> database. 11 Dec. 2001

*Sources listed in alphabetical order*

*Author's last name first*

Pugh 9

<http://www.washingtonpost.com/wp-dyn/
    politics>.

Rachels, James. <u>The End of Life</u>. Oxford: Oxford UP, 1987.

Vacco v. Quill. 95-1858. U.S. Supreme Ct. 1997. FindLaw
    Resources legal database. 11 Dec. 2001
    <http://caselaw.lp.findlaw.com/us/000/95-1858.html>.

Vicini, James. "Doctor-Assisted Suicide Policy Reversed."
    <u>Excite Canada</u>. 6 Nov. 2001. 11 December 2001
    <http://www.excite.com>.

Wennberg, Robert N. <u>Terminal Choices: Euthanasia,
    Suicide, and the Right to Die</u>. Grand Rapids:
    Eerdmans, 1989.

**Part Two** The Aims of
Argument

**Part Two** The Aims of Argument

# Chapter 6

# Looking for Some Truth: Arguing to Inquire

To inquire is to look into something. Inquiry can be a police investigation or a doctor's attempt to diagnose a patient's illness, a scientist's experiment or an artist's attempt to see the world differently. According to singer and songwriter Lucinda Williams, one of the joys of life in this "sweet old world" is "looking for some truth."

It is satisfying to be able to say, "This is true." If we are religious, we find truth in the doctrines of our faith. But in our daily lives, we often must discern for ourselves what is true. We look for truth in messages from family and friends and lovers, in the study of nature, and in good art, music, and literature. Often, though, we have to work to decide what to believe, for even newspapers and textbooks sometimes offer differing versions of fact. The search for truth, then, is closely allied to the question, "What is knowledge?" The pursuit of both is inquiry.

## INQUIRY AND INTERPRETATION IN ACADEMIC WRITING

Inquiry is an important part of college learning because college is where we learn that one "true" body of knowledge or set of objective facts about the world simply does not exist. Take, for example, something usually considered to be fact:

> Columbus discovered America in 1492.

If this statement were on a true/false test, would your answer be "true," "false," or "that depends"? With hardly any inquiry at all, we see that this "fact" depends upon:

- the calendar you use to mark time on this earth
- your definition of the word "discover"
- your definition of "America"

- whether your ancestors were here before Columbus
- whether you know anything about Vikings and other early explorers

So what we accept as fact, as truth, really is *an interpretation*. Most significant claims to truth are *efforts to understand and/or explain;* as such, they are interpretations that need defending. In college, we realize that knowledge is contested, as we read scholars' attempts to make the best cases for their interpretations. Later in this chapter, you will read several arguments, each claiming to know the truth about whether violence on television causes children to act out violently. The arguments offer data to prove their claims, but data itself is meaningless without interpretation. And interpretations are open to inquiry.

The current state of knowledge on any given topic depends on who is doing the interpreting, whether anyone pays attention to that person, and whether the observed data are of interest to people in a particular culture. Some facts remain unknown for centuries because for some reason no one thought they mattered. What one considers knowledge or truth, then, depends on the perspective of the interpreters, which in turn depends on the interpreters' social class, politics, religion, and a host of other factors that make up who they are and how they see the world. What you learn from research about a topic will depend on the perspectives of your sources.

Like the high school research paper, college writing requires research. Unlike the high school paper, which might have required only that you obtain some information, organize it, and restate in your own words the accepted knowledge about a topic, most college assignments will require that you *inquire* into your sources.

It's important to gather information and viewpoints. But research itself is not the goal of inquiry. The most important part of inquiry is the thinking you do before and after gathering sources. The quality of your paper will depend on the quality of your initial thinking as well as upon the quality of your sources and your understanding of them. Nothing is more vital to writing well than learning how to inquire well.

As we begin to inquire, it is important not to try to prove anything. Argument as inquiry is not confrontational; rather, it is conversational. It is part of our conversation with friends, family, and colleagues. We can have these kinds of conversations with ourselves, and we can ask and answer questions about the arguments we read.

To inquire well, we must question our initial viewpoints instead of holding onto them. We need to ask hard questions, even if the answers threaten our preconceptions and beliefs. Before Copernicus, "common sense" told people that the Earth was stationary, and religious beliefs reinforced this "truth." To question our truths makes us uncomfortable, to say the least. But for knowledge to advance, the willingness to hold a question open is essential. The scientist whose theory wins respect from other scientists must continue to test its truth rather than try to protect the idea from further inquiry.

Likewise, a college student needs to test the received wisdom from his or her past in order to grow intellectually. After inquiry, you may still hold the same belief, but because you have tested it, your belief will be a claim to truth that you have earned, not just received wisdom.

This chapter offers guidelines for inquiring and shows how writing plays a part in arguing to inquire. The writing project for inquiry is the exploratory essay, through which the following pages will guide you.

## THE WRITING PROJECT: EXPLORATORY ESSAY, PART 1

The exploratory essay is a written account of your own inquiry. Your goal is to share with your readers the experience of questioning your opinions and the arguments of others on your chosen topic. The paper will be an intellectual journey; it will have a starting point, a tour of viewpoints on the issue, and a destination, some truth you feel you can defend. The essay will have three parts, one written before inquiry and the other two written after you have thoroughly explored the topic. In this informal paper, you will refer to yourself and your own thoughts and experiences. Feel free to write in first person.

In this chapter, we give specific, step-by-step advice about writing the paper; for now, though, here is an overview.

In Part 1, you will tell what question or issue interests you most about a given topic and express your initial opinion about or answer to this question.

Part 2 will be the exploration itself. The point of Part 2 is to open the question and keep it open, testing your opinions and exploring the issue through conversations and research that introduce you to a range of expert opinions. You are not trying to support your initial opinions but to test them. In Part 2, you will write about readings that confirm and contradict your thinking, and you'll evaluate these arguments with an open mind. You will use your critical-reading skills to discuss the strengths and weaknesses of the arguments you encounter.

Part 3, the conclusion of your paper, will be a statement of your thinking after the process of inquiry, an explanation of the truth you have found as a result of your conversations and readings. Think of exploration as the process of *arriving* at a claim. Ideally, in the conclusion of your exploratory essay, you will state a claim whose truth you have tested and earned.

Your instructor may follow up on this paper by asking you to read Chapter 7, "Making Your Case: Arguing to Convince," and to write an argument convincing others to assent to your claim. But in this paper, for the moment, you will explore an issue, not make a case for an opinion.

We illustrate the process of inquiry and the steps of writing the exploratory essay by exploring the topic of violence in the media and its relation to violence in our society. We show some students' initial thinking about this issue and take you through their exploration of it through dialogues and readings. For your own paper, you may continue to explore this topic or choose a different topic that interests you or your class.

## Step 1: Choosing a Topic for Inquiry

If your instructor has not assigned a topic for inquiry, you might begin by looking at the newspapers. In a writing class focused on argumentation, current events are often topics, and they need interpretation. If you are familiar with some topic in the news, you probably already have an opinion about it, and that is a good place to begin inquiry. Because you are learning to write in an academic setting, it would make sense to pick a topic that is related to some part of the curriculum. The topic we've selected for illustration—violence in the media—is relevant to psychology, sociology, law, political science, courses in popular culture and film, and so on. We came upon our topic by noticing an op-ed column on the subject in the *New York Times*, but yours could come from a front-page story or an item on television.

Once you have selected a topic, consider what you already know about it and toward what smaller aspect of the topic your knowledge points. For example, violence in the media is a huge subject. There's violence in the sense of staged or *pretend violence*—the quarrels, muggings, rapes, fistfights, knifings, shootings, battlefield scenes, and so on of television and movie dramas. There's *virtual violence*—some computer games and Internet sites. There's also *actual violence*, the staple of broadcast news. "If it bleeds, it leads": Local TV news programs often start with an account of a brutal murder or a big traffic accident with injuries and fatalities.

You can find more needles in a small haystack than in a big one; the more you narrow your topic, the easier it will be to find issues to argue about and sources that converse with each other on these issues. For example, narrowing the topic of media violence to violence in video games or music lyrics will yield more perspectives and specific evidence that might be lost if you cast a wider net.

## Step 2: Finding an Issue

An issue is a question the answer to which people disagree about. With our topic, we can begin to list such questions: Why do people find violence so engrossing, so entertaining? Why do we like to see violence in sports like football, hockey, and auto racing? Why do we go to movies that feature violence? Is it something in our nature or in our culture? Is it related to hormones, to gender roles?

These are worthwhile questions, but for purposes of systematic inquiry, most topics have one central or primary issue. In this instance, that issue is whether pretend violence can be connected to aggressive acts. This issue is central because most articles about the topic address it. It's also central because our answer largely determines what the other issues are.

Systematic inquiry recognizes order or hierarchy among issues; that is, the answer to one question leads to another question. *If* there is a link between fantasy violence and actual violence, *then* the next question is, How significant is the connection? We can't ask the second question until we answer the first. *If* we decide that pretend violence is a major contributor to actual aggression, *then* we must decide what action should be taken, if any—and this leads to issues of censorship, the First Amendment, and the freedom to create and consume violent entertainment. For our topic, then, we can list this hierarchy of issues:

- Is there a link between fantasy violence and real-world violence? If so, what is the nature of the link?
- How serious are the effects? Does media violence make people more aggressive and less sensitive to the suffering of others? Does it contribute to crimes such as murders and assaults?
- If the contribution is significant, can/should we consider censorship, or does Constitutional protection of free expression prohibit taking this kind of action?
- If censorship is out of the question, what other action(s) can we suggest to mitigate the negative effect?

Fortunately, locating the issues usually is not difficult. Often we can supply them from our own general knowledge and experience. We need only ask, What have we heard people arguing about when this topic came up? What have we ourselves argued about it? If we can't identify the issues before starting our research, the research will reveal them. In fact, once you begin reading what others have said about your topic, you may discover an issue you would not have considered but find more interesting than your initial question.

It is important to be conscious of issues, not just topics. A thorough exploration involves more than one issue, but the point is to inquire more deeply into one or two related questions rather than to broadly survey all issues surrounding a topic. And when you do research, be sure to select readings that address the same issues.

## Following Through    *the American family*

In preparation for writing your exploratory paper, select a topic of current interest. What do you see as the main issue that people debate? With some answers to that question, draw up a chain of questions that follow one from another. Which are most interesting to you?

### Following Through

Read an argument on a topic of current interest, perhaps on the topic you intend to explore. You can find such an argument in the newspaper, on the Internet, or elsewhere in this textbook. What issue does this argument primarily address? What is the central question it attempts to answer? What is the author's answer to this question—in other words, what is the author's claim? Try to restate it in your own words. What other issues are raised in the argument? Besides these, what *other* issues are raised in discussion of this topic?

## Step 3: Stating Your Initial Opinions

In this step, you will write Part 1 of your exploratory essay, the part in which you state your initial ideas on the topic before inquiry. You may have read one or two articles about your topic or had a discussion with someone, but you should write this part of your paper before doing any serious research. Begin by introducing your topic and the issue or issues you have decided are most interesting. State your opinions on those issues, and explain your reasoning. Include some explanation of what, in your own experiences or observations, has contributed to your opinions.

Below is Part 1 of the essay of a student who is about to explore the connection between media violence and real-life violence.

**STUDENT SAMPLE:** *Exploratory Essay, Part 1*

*Lauren's Initial Opinions*

I have to admit that I am somewhat biased when it comes to the topic of the correlation between the entertainment industry and violence in children. Unfortunately, I have been involved in several life-altering experiences that even before this assignment made me feel very strongly that virtual violence and aggressive behavior in children are causally related. When I was in high school, a group of kids that I grew up with started getting mixed up in the whole "gangster" era. They listened to rap music that preached about murder, drugs, and human destruction. Ultimately, these boys decided to take the life of a fellow student at the McDonald's down the street from my school. They used an illegally purchased shotgun to murder him in a drug deal gone bad. Because I knew these kids when they were younger, I can say that when they were in the seventh grade, I would not have imagined they were capable of committing such a horrid act of violence. Did the rap music influence them to commit this heinous crime? We will never really know the truth, but they had to get the idea from somewhere, and I personally cannot think of another reasonable explanation.

Even though music cannot be the culprit that implants evil in the mind of a child, it can be the root of some problems. Throughout my senior year, I did a great deal of volunteer work at the Salvation Army recreation center. This rec center is located in the so-called "ghetto" of Lincoln, Nebraska. It is intended for children to walk to after school when their parents are working. It is like a daycare center, only it's free. Working here really opened up my eyes to how the future of America is growing up.

My first encounter was with a six-year-old boy who started calling me such profane names that I honestly couldn't imagine anyone ever using language like that. Not only was I verbally abused on several occasions, but I was also pushed, shoved, and kicked. Later, after discussing the situation with the young boy in time out, I found out that he had heard these names in an Eminem song that bashes women. Because of these experiences, I am interested in exploring this topic, but I am skeptical about whether my opinion will change.

*For past time*

## Following Through

Draft Part 1 of your paper. In the opening paragraph or two, state what your opinions were before you researched the topic. In the case of violence in the media or entertainment, for instance, you might discuss the impact of violent entertainment on you or a younger sister or brother. If you seek out or avoid such entertainment, say so and explain why. Be specific. Describe and explain experiences that influenced your outlook. Refer to specific films or music or news broadcasts. If you've read or heard about the topic before or discussed it in school or elsewhere, try to recall both context and content and share them with your readers. Edit for clarity and correctness.

*Explain Writer's Notebook*

## Step 4: Exploring an Issue

Once you have written Part 1 of your paper, turn to the task of exploring—reading and talking about your topic. Because you will eventually write about these experiences in Part 2 of your paper, use your writer's notebook and other writing, such as good annotations in the margins of what you read, to record your thoughts. These notes are the raw material from which you will eventually write the account of your exploration.

## CONVERSATION AND DIALOGUE IN INQUIRY

A good way to begin inquiry is to talk through your position on an issue in serious conversation with a friend, family member, classmate, or teacher. More often than we might think, inquiry takes the form of discussion or conversation. Unsurprisingly, conversation is a big part of higher education. Many college classes are devoted to discussion rather than lectures; even lecturers break on occasion to allow the class to discuss controversial questions. Out of class, students often have the opportunity to talk with professors one-on-one as well as with each other.

As you know from watching talk shows, conversation is not always a search for truth. There is an art to productive conversation. In Chapter 2, we noted that critical reading depends on developing certain practices and habits of mind. Conversation aimed at finding some truth also depends on good practices and habits. The key to good conversation is this: Participants need to move beyond ordinary conversation, which is often just an exchange of opinions, to *dialogue*, which is a *questioning* of opinions.

Let's begin by looking at a conversation about the topic of violence in entertainment.

### An Example Conversation

The conversation that follows took place shortly after the Columbine High School killings. It was recorded and transcribed, and an excerpt of it appeared in the May 17, 1999, issue of *Newsweek*. The conversation is neither especially good nor especially bad but rather typical, the sort of thing we encounter routinely in media-arranged talk. Just read it carefully. The comments that follow explain what we can learn from it.

---

## Moving beyond the Blame Game
### Jonathan Alter, Moderator

A month after the Littleton tragedy, the conversation continues — in schools, in homes and at this week's White House conference on youth violence. The theories of why Eric Harris and Dylan Klebold went on their rampage have given way to a broader discussion of the deeper sources of the problem and where to go from here. Obviously, there are no quick fixes; everything from more values [in] education to better supervision of antidepressant medication has been introduced into the debate. But Americans have singled out a few issues for special attention. According to the new *Newsweek* Poll, about half of all Americans want to see the movie industry, the TV industry, computer-game makers, Internet services and gun manufacturers and the NRA make major policy changes to help reduce teen violence. Slightly fewer want the music industry to change fundamentally. Younger Americans are less concerned about media violence than their elders are. On guns, there's a racial gap, with 72 percent of nonwhites and 41 percent of whites seeking major changes.

To further the conversation, *Newsweek* assembled a panel last week to explore the complexities. One after another, the people who actually make heavily violent movies, records and games declined to participate, just as they did when the White House called. This could be a sign that they are feeling the heat — or perhaps just avoiding it. Those who did take part in the *Newsweek* forum include Wayne LaPierre, executive director of the NRA; Jack Valenti, president of the Motion Picture Association of America; Hillary Rosen, president of the Recording Industry Association of America; Doug Lowenstein, president of the Interactive Digital Software Association; Marshall Herskovitz, TV and movie producer and director; and Jonah Green, a 15-year-old New York high-school student. *Newsweek*'s Jonathan Alter moderated the discussion.

Excerpts:

**Alter:** Youth shall be served, so I want to start with Jonah. You seem to think that there's [a] lot of scapegoating going on.

**Green:** Well, I have to say that America is very confused and scared. There's no one simple answer to teen violence. It's understandable because we're seeking answers, but right now people are focusing too much on putting the blame somewhere. We should be focusing on solutions.

**Alter:** Ok, Wayne, wouldn't making guns less easily accessible be at least a partial solution?                                                                                       5

**LaPierre:** You can't talk about easy access to guns by people we all don't want to have guns without talking about the shameful secret that really hasn't been reported. Which is the complete collapse of enforcement of the existing firearm laws on the books by the Department of Justice [in] the last six years. The proof is in the statistics. Six thousand kids illegally brought guns to school the last two years. We've only had 13 [federal] prosecutions. And only 11 prosecutions for illegally transferring guns to juveniles.

**Alter:** Do you think that if an 11-year-old brings his father's gun to school, the child should be prosecuted?

**LaPierre:** Yes, I do. They did not prosecute Kip Kinkel out in Oregon after he was blowing up cats, threatening people. He walks into school with a gun. They do nothing to him except send him home. And he comes back to the school two days later with a gun and shoots those kids. I mean, the fact is we're either serious about this situation or we're not.

**Alter:** How about Clinton's gun-limit proposal? Why does anyone need to buy more than one gun a month?

**LaPierre:** That's just a sound bite.                                                    10

**Alter:** Doug, some of your industry's games are a long way from Pac-Man, right?

**Lowenstein:** Oh, absolutely. There are some very violent videogames, although they represent only a small fraction of the market. There's a critical parental role here: It costs over $1,000 to own a computer. A hundred dollars plus to own a videogame machine. There's a very conscious choice involved in bringing this kind of entertainment into your home. And the parent needs the tools to make an informed choice.

**Alter:** You don't think it desensitizes kids to violence to play games over and over?

**Green:** Personally, I think some kids use videogames, especially the violent ones, just as some violent movies, as a vent. You know, they like to live vicariously and vent their anger through that. And Doug was right that we can't really map out everything a kid has and how they use it and what makes them able to kill somebody.

**Alter:** Hillary, MTV is doing a stop-the-violence campaign, but then they                15
air—and you supported—something like Eminem's song about stuffing a woman into the trunk of a car. Don't you see a contradiction here?

**Rosen:** Young people are so much smarter than anybody—the media or politicians or most adults, in fact—may give them credit for being. They understand the difference between fantasy and reality, and that's why giving them concrete steps to take when they face personal conflict or when they face a gang conflict or school bullying, or those sorts of things, are much more productive means for giving them tools to be nonviolent in their lives than taking away their culture.

**Alter:** Do you think that a music-rating system just makes it forbidden fruit and makes kids want to play or see it more?

**Rosen:** We've done surveys that show it doesn't encourage young people to buy artists. People buy music that they connect with, that they like, that has a good beat, that sounds good. The label is there for parents and for retailers.

**Green:** I actually think artists like Eminem are very sarcastic. It is more playful than hard core. I find rap being a little more human than it used to be. Gangsta rap isn't as big anymore, and now sampling is.

**Rosen:** It's true.                                                                      20

**Green:** Edgar Allan Poe talked about death—he was dark, but he was a celebrated poet. It's about having an edge, a hook. That can be violence.

**Alter:** You don't have any problem with Marilyn Manson naming himself after a serial killer?

**Green:** I think it's in bad taste. It was just stupid and controversial.

**Alter:** Hillary, how about you?

**Rosen:** Well, I agree with Jonah that it's bad taste, but that's the point. Marilyn Manson in an act. It's an act that's sort of designed to create a persona of empowering the geek. Unfortunately, Charles Manson was a real person. People don't have to make up horrible tragedies in this world.

25

**Green:** Entertainment and the media were never really for getting across good, moral messages like "I love my school and my mother." People rarely feel they need to express bland feelings like that.

**Rosen:** But it is on some level, because Britney Spears sells more records than Marilyn Manson. You know there's been a resurgence of young pop music. B*Witched and the Dixie Chicks and Britney Spears and 'N Sync. I mean, these artists are selling a hell of a lot more records than Marilyn Manson.

**Alter:** Do you think that kids have kind of gotten that message and are less interested in gratuitously violent lyrics than they used to be? Because they've seen so much death, either in their own neighborhoods or on TV?

**Rosen:** Well, there's no question that what used to be known as gangsta rap is definitely played out. Rap is much more light-hearted. It's about getting money and getting women. The music has evolved.

**Alter:** Why is that?

30

**Rosen:** Well, this might be controversial, but I'm actually one of those people who believes that young people are a lot more positive about the world today than most of the media is giving them credit for in the last couple of weeks. Surveys have shown that young people are more optimistic about their future, they're more positive, they're more connected to their parents than they have been in generations. And these all speak to really good, positive things.

**Alter:** Marshall, what do you think are some of Hollywood's responsibilities in this area?

**Herskovitz:** I think we now have virtual reality available to people that is nihilistic, anarchic and violent. And it is possible for a person to so completely live in that virtual reality that they come to confuse it for the real world around them.

**Alter:** But you know from firsthand experience that violence sells.

**Herskovitz:** "Legends of the Fall" was a very violent movie. I think violence has a potentially strong part in any artistic venture. It's not something I would ever want to talk about legislatively. I would like to talk about it in terms of individual responsibility, yes.

35

**Alter:** So where should the thoughtful consumer of all of this draw the line between gratuitous violence and necessary violence for dramatic purposes?

**Herskovitz:** Oh, I think that's the point. The thoughtful consumers feel it in their gut. I think the problem in this culture is that thoughtful consumers are not particularly influencing their children.

**Alter:** But isn't it a little too easy to just say it's all the parent's responsibility?

**Valenti:** Well, I don't think the movie industry can stand *in loco parentis.* Over 30 years ago I put in place a movie-rating system, voluntary, which gives advanced cautionary warnings to parents so that parents can make their own judgments about what movies they want their children to see.

**Alter:** I think what a lot of parents wonder is, why is it that NC-17 is not       40
applied to gratuitously violent movies?

**Valenti:** Well, it's because the definition of "gratuitous" is shrouded in subjectivity. There is no way to write down rules. I think Marshall can tell you that creative people can shoot a violent scene a hundred different ways. Sex and language are different, because there are few ways that you can couple on the screen that—there's only a few. And language is language. It's there or it isn't. But violence is far more difficult to pin down. It's like picking up mercury with a fork.

**Alter:** A movie director told me recently that he went to see "The Matrix," and there was a 5-year-old at the film with his mother. Isn't that a form of child abuse?

**Valenti:** If a parent says he wants his 5-year-old to be with him, who is to tell this parent he can't do it? Who is to tell him?

**Alter:** But if it was NC-17, that 5-year-old wouldn't be allowed to go, right?

**Valenti:** Well, that's right.       45

**Alter:** So why allow them in when it's R?

**Valenti:** Because the way our system is defined, we think there's a dividing line.

**Alter:** When parents aren't doing their job properly, where does the responsibility of everybody else begin?

**LaPierre:** I was talking with John Douglas, the FBI's criminal profiler. And he said, "Wayne, never underestimate the fact that there are some people that are just evil." And that includes young people. We go searching for solutions, and yet some people are just plain bad apples. You look around the country—the cities that are making progress across the board are really combining prevention and working with young people when you get the first warning signs. And making sure they find mentors. Making sure they're put into programs. And they're combining that with very, very tough enforcement of things like the gun laws.

**Herskovitz:** I have a fear that modern society, and in particular television,       50
may be beyond the ability of parents to really control. I think movies are different, because the kid has to go out of the house and go there. TV is a particular problem because it's in the house.

**Alter:** But Marshall, maybe that's because the values that are being propagated by the media, broadly speaking, are so much more powerful that parents can't compete as easily as they used to.

**Herskovitz:** I don't believe that. I accept a lot of responsibility for the picture the media create of the world. But I don't think there's a conflict between that and the responsibility of parents to simply sit down and talk with their children. Most violent crime is committed by males. Young men are not being educated in the values of masculinity by their fathers.

**Alter:** So why then let all of these boys see scenes of gratuitous violence that don't convey human values to them?

**Valenti:** There are only three places where a child learns what Marshall was talking about, values. You learn them in the church. You learn them in school. And you learn them at home. And if you don't have these moral shields built in you by the time you're 10 or 12 years old, forget it.

**Alter:** I'm not sure that people in Hollywood are thinking, "Is what we do part of the solution on this values question, or does it just contribute to the problem?"                                                                               55

**Herskovitz:** The answer is the people who aren't contributing to the problem are thinking about it a lot, and the people who are contributing to the problem are not thinking about it.

**Valenti:** Well, how does *Newsweek* then condone its putting on the cover of your magazine Monica Lewinsky? What kind of a value system does that convey?

**Alter:** Well, that's a separate discussion.

**Valenti:** Oh, I don't think it is.

**Alter:** Well, let me say this. We very explicitly did not put Dylan Klebold and Eric Harris on our cover the first week. We're wrong in these judgments     60
sometimes, but we do at least try to think about the consequences of what we put out there, instead of just saying it's up to the parents. That seems to me a cop-out.

**Lowenstein:** What you're looking for is an elimination of any problematic content.

**Alter:** No, I'm not. I'm looking for a sense of shame and a sense of responsibility. I'm wondering where it is in all of the industries that we have represented here today.

**Herskovitz:** Most people, especially in electronic journalism, don't think at all about this, and their role is incredibly destructive, just like most people in the movie and television business don't think at all about this. And their role is destructive. I think there's a great need for shame. Most people I know and speak to are very ashamed, but unfortunately they're not the people who make violent movies.

*Analysis of "Moving beyond the Blame Game"*

It's obvious that the *Newsweek* excerpts are not part of a natural, spontaneous conversation, the sort of thing we might have with friends around a campfire, at a campus mixer, or at a bar or café after work. This conversation has been *arranged*. The participants didn't just happen to come together some place and start talking; they were invited. Furthermore, they knew why they were invited—each represents a group or industry implicated in teen violence. Even Jonah Green, the fifteen-year-old, is cast (that's the right word) as "youth," as if one young person could stand for all young people. Each participant knew his or her role in advance, then, and what was at stake. Except perhaps for Jonah Green, each had an agenda and an interest in protecting their reputations and the public image of their businesses and organizations. Therefore, unlike the conversations in which we ask you to engage, theirs from the start was something less than an open-minded search for truth. Even the moderator, Alter, takes a hit for his own magazine's covers. In a genuine dialogue for inquiry, people question each other in a friendly way and do not attack each other or become defensive.

In addition to its adversarial tone, this discussion falls short of good inquiry because it lacks depth. It is an extreme example of what tends to go wrong with *all* discussions, including many class discussions. In the classroom, the teacher plays Alter's role, trying, sometimes with more than a hint of desperation, to get students to talk. When a question from the podium is greeted by silence from the class, sometimes even teachers do what Alter does: solicit opinions by addressing questions to individuals who then have no choice but to answer. Often the instructor is happy to get any opinion, no matter how unconsidered, just to get things going. Once the ice is broken, students usually join in and opinions come forth. It can be stimulating just to hear what everybody else is thinking. Before long, we're caught up in the discussion and don't perceive what is happening: a superficial exchange of opinions, more or less like the *Newsweek* example. Much is said, but almost nothing is really discussed, that is, *examined, pursued, genuinely explored.*

Exactly what do we mean? Look at the first few exchanges in the *Newsweek* example. Alter addresses Jonah Green, the fifteen-year-old high school student, who had apparently talked enough previously to reveal an opinion. Alter summarizes that opinion: "There's a lot of scapegoating going on." Green himself immediately offers two more intelligent observations, better than anything we get from the adult participants: "There's no one simple answer to teen violence" and "we should be focusing on solutions" rather than on blame.

These statements merit our attention. But what happens? Alter must get the others into the discussion, so he turns to LaPierre and asks if better gun control might be part of the solution. *The secret of a good discussion is not to allow intelligent comments to go unquestioned.* Imagine, for example, what the following line of questioning might lead to. ("Q" stands for "questioner," who could be anyone involved in the discussion.)

Green: There's a lot of scapegoating going on.

Q: What do you mean by "scapegoating"?

Green: A scapegoat is someone who gets blamed or punished for doing something everyone is guilty of or responsible for.

Q: So you're saying that youth violence is a collective problem that everyone contributes to in one way or another. Is that right?

Green: Yes.

Now that we know what Green's assertion actually means or implies, we can really discuss it, look for whatever truth it may convey. Are we *all* really implicated in youth violence? How exactly? If we are, what can each of us do?

We handle Green's comment about looking for solutions the same way. All we need to ask is, What might be part of the solution? It would be interesting to hear Jonathan's ideas. Maybe he has an idea how high schools could build more community or how parents could get involved. But no — the conversation moves away in a new direction.

Our intent is not to put down conversation. Exchanging opinions is one of the great pleasures of social life. For inquiry, however, we need genuine dialogue.

To help your conversations become dialogue, we offer "Questions for Inquiry" later in the chapter on pages 177–178. These same questions will help you inquire into written texts, such as the sources you might encounter in researching your topic. Most of the questions on this list can be traced back to the origins of dialogue in ancient Greece and have demonstrated their value in opening up arguments for about 2,500 years. Commit the list to memory, and practice asking these questions until they become second nature. There's no guarantee that this list will give you the best questions to ask of any given text, but you'll never be wholly at a loss when it's time to test the views you hear or read.

## Following Through

Mark up the *Newsweek* dialogue. Use the "Questions for Inquiry" to probe the participants' comments. For example, one question suggests that you inquire about analogies and comparisons. We might ask Jonah if Edgar Allen Poe's "darkness" is truly comparable to the creations of Marilyn Manson. Aren't there some significant differences in the context in which these art forms present violence? Be ready to point out places where the discussants failed to answer questions directly or where you would have posed a good question if you had been there. Note places where the discussion moved toward dialogue and where it moved toward mere venting of opinion. Does Alter do a good job as moderator, or is he mainly concerned with moving on — going broader rather than deeper? Be ready to discuss your annotations in class.

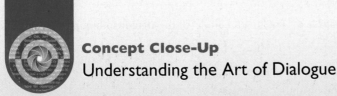

## Concept Close-Up
## Understanding the Art of Dialogue

To be useful for inquiry, conversations must become dialogues. They become dialogues when someone questions, in a nonhostile way, what someone else has said. Only then are we really discussing something, not just stating our opinion and talking for talking's sake.

### Step 5: Engaging in a Dialogue about Your Initial Opinions

Earlier, you wrote Part 1 of your exploratory essay, a statement of your initial opinions on the topic you will explore. A good way to begin exploration is with what you said in Part 1. Exchanging these initial statements with a classmate and then asking each other questions will get you thinking more deeply about what you already know and believe. This exercise should be not just a conversation but also a true dialogue about each other's opinions.

Read the example below, which shows one student's first thoughts and the dialogue that he and another student had about his thoughts. These students used a software program that allowed them to record their conversation, and what follows is a transcript of a real-time chat on the subject of media violence and violence in society. They had hard-copy printouts of each other's initial opinions in front of them as they took turns being each other's friendly questioner. First, we read Matt's initial thoughts and then the dialogue he had with Lauren, whose own first thoughts we reproduced earlier. Note where the dialogue seems to be a conversation and where Lauren attempts to make it an inquiry. Where does it succeed as inquiry, and where does it not?

**STUDENT SAMPLE:** *Example Dialogue for Analysis—Matt's Initial Opinions*

I think the issue of violence in the media is way overdone. I believe that violence is a conscious act by people who are evil, not people who are motivated by what they have seen or heard in the media. There are simply some people who are violent, and they cannot be stopped from committing their crimes simply by depriving the media of their freedom to create false violence. Violence is an act of nature; it is an instinct all humans are born with, yet the majority of society is able to restrain themselves from acting on their impulse to be violent. Though I have seen and heard my share of violence in the media, I am not a violent person. Sure, sometimes after watching a violent movie, I think about what it would be like to do some of that stuff, but I am not stupid enough to act on my curiosity.

*Review*

1. *Ask if you have understood the arguer's position on the issue.* The best way to do this is to restate, paraphrase, or summarize the thesis. (Face-to-face, you might say, "I believe that you are saying . . . Am I understanding you?") Be sure to note how strongly the claim is made. If you are inquiring into your own argument, ask if you have stated your own position clearly. Do you need to qualify it in any way?

2. *Ask about the meaning of any words that seem central to the argument.* You can do this at any point in a conversation and as often as it seems necessary. When dealing with a written text, try to discern the meaning from the context. For instance, if an author's case depends on the fairness of a proposed solution, you'll need to ask what "fair" means, because the word has a range of possible applications. You might ask, "Fair to whom?"

3. *Ask what reasons support the thesis.* Paraphrasing reasons is a good way to open up a conversation to further questions about assumptions, values, and definitions.

4. *Ask about the assumptions on which the thesis and reasons are based.* Most arguments are based on one or more unstated assumptions. For example, if a college recruiter argues that the school he or she represents is superior to most others (thesis) because its ratio of students to teachers is low (reason), the unstated assumptions are (1) that students there will get more attention and (2) that more attention results in a better education. As you inquire into an argument, note the assumptions, and ask if they are reasonable.

5. *Ask about the values expressed or implied by the argument.* For example, if you argue that closing a forest to logging operations is essential even at the cost of dozens of jobs, you are valuing environmental preservation over the livelihoods of the workers who must search for other jobs.

6. *Ask how well the reasons are supported.* Are they offered as opinions only, or are they supported with evidence? Is the evidence recent? sufficient? What kind of testimony is offered? Who are the authorities cited? What are their credentials and biases?

7. *Consider analogies and comparisons.* If the author makes an argument by analogy, does the comparison hold up? For example, advocates of animal rights draw an analogy with civil rights when they claim that just as we have come to recognize the immorality of exploiting human beings, so we should recognize the immorality of exploiting other species. But is this analogy sound?

8. *Ask about the arguer's biases and background.* What past experiences might have led the arguer to take this position? What does the holder

(continues)

of this position stand to gain? What might someone gain by challenging it?

9. *Ask about implications.* Where would the argument ultimately lead if we accept what the speaker advocates? For example, if someone contends that abortion is murder, asking about implications would lead to the question, Are you willing to put women who get abortions on trial for murder and, if they are convicted, to punish them as murderers are usually punished?

10. *Ask whether the argument takes opposing views into account.* If it does, are they presented fairly and clearly or with mockery and distortion? Does the author take them seriously or dismiss them? Are they effectively refuted?

**STUDENT SAMPLE:** *Example*

*Dialogue between Matt and Lauren*

**Lauren:** You don't think there is any correlation between violence and the entertainment industry?

**Matt:** Not really. I don't see how music could influence someone to the point of violence.

**Lauren:** I kind of agree with you, but I don't know. I think that sometimes it gives a person the mentality to do that kind of stuff when their friends are—when people are impressionable like that, they will do a lot of stupid things. When I was in high school, a group of kids I grew up with started getting into the whole "gangster" era. They listened to rap talking about murder, drugs, and destruction. They murdered a fellow student at the McDonalds down the street from the school. Did the music make them do this? We'll never know, but they had to get the idea from somewhere.

**Matt:** What happened to the guys that killed that person?

**Lauren:** They are all in jail now. Only one has gone to trial.

**Matt:** That's crazy. I listened to all kinds of music, and I am not violent.

**Lauren:** You can't assume everyone is like you. How do you explain kids doing the kind of stuff they are doing?

**Matt:** There are just some violent, evil people. They just aren't right, if you know what I mean.

**Lauren:** Do you mean they are crazy?

**Matt:** Yes, they're crazy.

**Lauren:** I think you said violence is an act of nature. Does that mean we are born violent? Is it normal to be violent?

**Matt:** I think everyone has a violent side, but they act on it in different ways. I go play sports or work out to get rid of the aggression.

**Lauren:** But is violence the same thing as evil? Or aggression? Those kids at my school were evil, not natural. I think you need to think more about what you mean by violent when you say it's natural. Maybe it's natural for animals to have aggression and to attack and kill to stay alive, but is that evil? When you say people are "just not right," do you mean that they are natural or not natural?

**Matt:** OK, I think we are born violent, but some of us are also born evil.

**Lauren:** So are you saying that nothing good could change these people for the better, like having a good family or going to church? Are they just how they were born?

**Matt:** I'd have to think about that. They could maybe be taught.

**Lauren:** Well, I'm just saying, if they can be influenced for the better, why not for the worse? That the media could influence them to be worse.

**Matt:** I don't know.

**Lauren:** What about real life? When the media pays too much attention to one issue, like the school shooting in Columbine, do you think it makes other people want to do the same thing?

**Matt:** I don't know. I had a good friend of mine get kicked out of school for calling in a bomb threat. He probably wouldn't have done that if all that hadn't been on the news.

## Following Through

Look at Lauren's initial opinion statement on pages 166–167. Use the "Questions for Inquiry" to suggest questions you would have asked her if you had been her partner.

## Following Through

Writing should be a rhythm between "drawing in"—the solo act of composing—and "reaching out" through dialogues during every phase of the composing process.

Exchange initial opinion statements with a classmate. Take turns asking each other questions based on the "Questions for Inquiry" in the box on pages 177–178. Explore one person's thinking at a time. After twenty minutes, trade roles. If you do not have a software program that

(continues)

**Following Through (continued)**

allows you to record a transcript of the discussion, tape it, or simply take notes after each questioning session. Be ready to report on how the dialogue caused you to clarify or modify your thinking. What did the dialogue make you realize you need to think and read more about?

We should never think of dialogue as something distinct and unrelated to writing. We should think instead about how dialogue can help us write better, especially how it can reveal some truth. The notes and written records of these purposeful exchanges will provide material for your paper, so save them now as we turn to the next step, which is to read about the topic.

## Step 6: Engaging in Dialogue with a Reading

Inquiry requires us to look into arguments that more knowledgeable people have written. Inquiry into a written text begins with a critical reading of the text, including attention to its rhetorical context, as we discussed in Chapter 2, "Reading an Argument" (pages 23–52). Sample the text quickly to see if it is worth your attention. If it is, read the text thoroughly and mark it up, noting its subdivisions and the structure of its argument. Mark claims and note evidence.

What we have just discussed about turning conversation into dialogue — posing questions about opinions — also applies to reading, but conversations and written arguments can't be approached the same way.

In conversations that don't reach the level of dialogue, we mostly encounter simple statements of opinion. People say what they think without much explanation or support unless someone asks for it. In sharp contrast, writers *argue* their opinions. That is, a written piece typically contains an opinion, sometimes called a *thesis* or *claim*. Then the claim is usually *explained*, and the claim is justified or defended with reasons and supported with evidence, because a text must stand on its own — the writer is not present to supply reasons and evidence in response to individual reader's questions. Instead, the writer must anticipate the questions an alert, critical reader will have and answer them in advance.

Consequently, whereas in conversation we can question simple statements of opinion as they occur, with written arguments we must question *entire cases* — claims, reasons, evidence, whatever the author uses to explain, justify, and defend his or her opinion. We need to look carefully at the "Questions for Inquiry" with special attention to recognizing the claim and its key terms, the reasons, and the evidence. We should note as well whether opposing views appear in the argument and how the author handles them. We can't know in advance all the questions to ask of any particular text; the best occur to us as we read the text thoughtfully or discuss it with others.

## Example Dialogue with a Reading

As an example of how to engage in dialogue with a written text, we first look at the newspaper argument that got us thinking in the first place about violence in the entertainment industry. "Hollow Claims about Fantasy Violence," by Richard Rhodes, appeared September 17, 2000, in the *New York Times.* Rhodes is a nonfiction writer who has won awards for his books on the making of the atomic and hydrogen bombs. This essay appeared after the publication of his most recent book, *Why They Kill,* which is based on interviews with convicted murderers.

---

## Hollow Claims about Fantasy Violence
### Richard Rhodes

The moral entrepreneurs are at it again, pounding the entertainment industry for advertising its Grand Guignolesque confections to children. If exposure to this mock violence contributes to the development of violent behavior, then our political leadership is justified in its indignation at what the Federal Trade Commission has reported about the marketing of violent fare to children. Senators John McCain and Joseph Lieberman have been especially quick to fasten on the F.T.C. report as they make an issue of violent offerings to children.

But is there really a link between entertainment and violent behavior?

The American Medical Association, the American Psychological Association, the American Academy of Pediatrics and the National Institute of Mental Health all say yes. They base their claims on social science research that has been sharply criticized and disputed within the social science profession, especially outside the United States. In fact, no direct, causal link between exposure to mock violence in the media and subsequent violent behavior has ever been demonstrated, and the few claims of modest correlation have been contradicted by other findings, sometimes in the same studies.

History alone should call such a link into question. Private violence has been declining in the West since the media-barren late Middle Ages, when homicide rates are estimated to have been 10 times what they are in Western nations today. Historians attribute the decline to improving social controls over violence—police forces and common access to courts of law—and to a shift away from brutal physical punishment in child-rearing (a practice that still appears as a common factor in the background of violent criminals today).

The American Medical Association has based its endorsement of the media violence theory in major part on the studies of Brandon Centerwall, a psychiatrist in Seattle. Dr. Centerwall compared the murder rates for whites in three countries from 1945 to 1974 with numbers for television set ownership. Until 1975, television broadcasting was banned in South Africa, and "white homicide rates remained stable" there, Dr. Centerwall found, while corresponding rates in Canada and the United States doubled after television was introduced.

A spectacular finding, but it is meaningless. As Franklin E. Zimring and Gordon Hawkins of the University of California at Berkeley subsequently pointed out, homicide rates in France, Germany, Italy and Japan either failed to change with increasing television ownership in the same period or actually declined, and American homicide rates have more recently been sharply declining despite a proliferation of popular media outlets—not only movies and television, but also video games and the Internet.

Other social science that supposedly undergirds the theory, too, is marginal and problematic. Laboratory studies that expose children to selected incidents of televised mock violence and then assess changes in the children's behavior have sometimes found more "aggressive" behavior after the exposure—usually verbal, occasionally physical.

But sometimes the control group, shown incidents judged not to be violent, behaves more aggressively afterward than the test group; sometimes comedy produces the more aggressive behavior; and sometimes there's no change. The only obvious conclusion is that sitting and watching television stimulates subsequent physical activity. Any kid could tell you that.

As for those who claim that entertainment promotes violent behavior by desensitizing people to violence, the British scholar Martin Barker offers this critique: "Their claim is that the materials they judge to be harmful can only influence us by trying to make us be the same as them. So horrible things will make us horrible—not horrified. Terrifying things will make us terrifying—not terrified. To see something aggressive makes us feel aggressive—not aggressed against. This idea is so odd, it is hard to know where to begin in challenging it."

Even more influential on national policy has been a 22-year study by two University of Michigan psychologists, Leonard D. Eron and L. Rowell Huesmann, of boys exposed to so-called violent media. The Telecommunications Act of 1996, which mandated the television V-chip, allowing parents to screen out unwanted programming, invoked these findings, asserting, "Studies have shown that children exposed to violent video programming at a young age have a higher tendency for violent and aggressive behavior later in life than children not so exposed."

Well, not exactly. Following 875 children in upstate New York from third grade through high school, the psychologists found a correlation between a preference for violent television at age 8 and aggressiveness at age 18. The correlation—0.31—would mean television accounted for about 10 percent of the influences that led to this behavior. But the correlation only turned up in one of three measures of aggression: the assessment of students by their peers. It didn't show up in students' reports about themselves or in psychological testing. And for girls, there was no correlation at all.

Despite the lack of evidence, politicians can't resist blaming the media for violence. They can stake out the moral high ground confident that the First Amendment will protect them from having to actually write legislation that would be likely to alienate the entertainment industry. Some use the issue as a smokescreen to avoid having to confront gun control.

But violence isn't learned from mock violence. There is good evidence—causal evidence, not correlational—that it's learned in personal violent encounters, beginning with the brutalization of children by their parents or their peers.

The money spent on all the social science research I've described was diverted from the National Institute of Mental Health budget by reducing support for the construction of community mental health centers. To this day there is no standardized reporting system for emergency-room findings of physical child abuse. Violence is on the decline in America, but if we want to reduce it even further, protecting children from real violence in their real lives—not the pale shadow of mock violence—is the place to begin.

*[handwritten margin note: How can families do this?]*

Inquiring into sources presents a special challenge: to overcome the authority the source projects. When ideas are in print, we tend to accept them too uncritically, especially when they support our own opinion. If the argument appears in a leading newspaper like the *New York Times*, as it does in this case, the piece can seem to have such authority that people just quote it and don't bother to assess it critically, especially when the author is as respected as Rhodes. We think, Who am I to question what he says? After all, I've gone to him to find out about fantasy violence. Shouldn't I just accept what he says, at least until I read other sources that oppose his view?

Our earlier chapters on reading and analyzing an argument show how we can overcome this natural tendency to be passive when we encounter an authoritative text. It's true that we are only inquirers, not experts, and so we cannot question Rhodes as another expert might. But we are hardly powerless. We can put into practice the critical-reading habits and skills discussed in Chapter 2. And we can use the "Questions for Inquiry" on pages 177–178 to open an argument to scrutiny.

### A Dialogue with Rhodes

Looking at the "Questions for Inquiry," we noticed that some seemed like perfect entry points into Rhodes's argument. We have no problems

### Following Through

After sampling Rhodes's essay and reading it through thoroughly, mark it up. What do you consider the introduction and the conclusion? Are there any other subsections besides the presentation of the reasoning? Do you see the claim, reasons, and evidence? (You might want to review Chapter 3, "Analyzing Arguments," pages 53–68.) Mark them with annotations. How does he present opposing views? Finally, use the "Questions for Inquiry" in the Best Practices box on pages 177–178 to open up the argument to inquiry. Make marginal annotations in response to Rhodes, and compare them with our discussion of the argument's strengths and weaknesses, following (pages 183–185).

### Following Through

If you are working on a different topic, find an argument that addresses one of the topic's central issues. Read that argument critically (see the explanation and cross-references in the previous Following Through).

understanding his claim, but we might ask him about the second item on our list, "the meaning of any words that seem central to the argument." We wonder how he defines "violence." In this fourth, fifth, and sixth paragraphs, he refers to homicide rates having declined despite the proliferation of media violence. But when we think of violence today, we think of a lot of behavior that does not fall into the narrow category of homicide: date rape, child abuse and other domestic violence, bullying, and even aggressive driving and road rage.

Looking again at definitions, we could question the thinking of one of Rhodes's sources, Martin Barker, who says it is "odd" to assume that watching "horrible things will make us horrible—not horrified," that "terrifying things will make us terrifying—not terrified." What can he mean by "horrible" and "terrifying"? The terrorist attack on the World Trade Center made most of us terrified, not terrible, but there are many types of terrifying acts shown in the media, and some of them glorify models of terrible behavior or even make it seem funny. So Barker's nice-sounding language oversimplifies the problem.

We might also ask the sixth question for inquiry, which concerns evidence. In the third paragraph, Rhodes acknowledges that the American Medical Association, the American Psychological Association, the American Academy of Pediatrics, and the National Institute of Mental Health all affirm "a link between entertainment and violent behavior." Much of the rest of the article is an effort to undermine the science that claims to establish such a link. Is it likely that the AMA, APA, and the other institutions mentioned are *all* wrong? Is it likely that the AMA based its opinion "in major part" on only *one* study of fantasy violence, as Rhodes claims in paragraph five? Neither seems very likely, and so we should be suspicious. We could visit one of the Web sites for these organizations to find out more about the basis of their endorsements.

And we might question an assumption Rhodes makes, using question 4 as our inspiration. When he says that the rates of television ownership rose in France, Germany, Italy, and Japan while homicide rates did not change, is he assuming that the same shows were broadcast as in America and Canada, where homicide rates doubled in the same period? He seems to assume that the technology itself, rather than the programs, is an appropriate basis for comparison.

Finally, we might question his assumption that if one thing is not necessary for another thing to happen, it therefore cannot be a factor at all. For example, cell phone use is not necessary for a car wreck to occur; people are perfectly capable of having accidents without using cell phones while driving. So cell phone use alone is not a sufficient cause. However, cell phone use could—and does—*contribute* to automobile accidents. Rhodes claims that "violence isn't learned from mock violence. There is good evidence—causal evidence, not correlational—that it's learned in personal violent encounters, beginning with the brutalization of children by their parents or their peers." Does anyone doubt that real violence in children's lives contributes more than fantasy violence to aggressive behavior? Probably not. But that doesn't mean that fantasy violence contributes *nothing*. We can't dismiss something that might contribute to violent behavior just because other factors obviously contribute more. There may be no "proof" that fantasy violence is a necessary or sufficient cause of real-life violence, but it would not be logical to dismiss it as a factor. We could find examples of people abused as children who have not become violent, but would that make Rhode's own argument invalid?

## Following Through

If you are inquiring into a topic of your own, use the "Questions for Inquiry" to open it up, as we have illustrated with Rhodes's essay. Do not try to pose every possible question; find questions that point to the areas of weakness in the argument.

## Another Example of Dialogue with a Reading

We next inquired into a recent book on violent entertainment, Sissela Bok's *Mayhem* (1998). Following is one chapter from a section entitled "Opportunities," in which Bok assesses various ways to resist the destructive effects of media violence. The chapter reprinted here is especially interesting because it focuses on what children can do, guided by teachers and supported by parents, "to think for themselves and to become discriminating viewers."

Sissela Bok is professor of philosophy at Brandeis University and the author of numerous books and articles.

---

# Media Literacy
## Sissela Bok

How can children learn to take a more active and self-protective part in evaluating what they see? For an example of such learning, consider a class of second-graders in Oregon that Peter Jennings introduced on ABC's evening news in March 1995. With the help of their teacher, these children had arranged to study the role that television violence played in their lives: now they were presenting their "Declaration of Independence from Violence" to the rest of the student body. Their assignment had been to watch half an hour of television at home for several days running and to count the incidents of violence in each one—kicking, shooting, bombarding, killing. To their amazement, they had found nearly one such incident a minute in the programs they watched. The media mayhem they had taken for granted as part of their daily lives was suddenly put in question. One girl acknowledged that "before, I didn't even know what violence was."

The children then discussed the role of media violence in their own lives and concluded that what they saw on TV did affect them. Together, they considered different types of responses, often also discussing these choices in their homes. In their "Declaration of Independence from Violence," they addressed not only their school but the county board of education and community service organizations. Some pledged to limit their intake of violent programming and to refuse to watch certain shows; others wrote letters to television stations; a few organized a boycott of the products advertised on the programs they considered most violent.

These children were learning the rudiments of critical judgment and experiencing the pleasure of thinking for themselves about the messages beamed at them by advertisers and programmers. They were beginning to draw distinctions with respect to types of violence and their effects and to consider what might lie in their power to do in response. Throughout, they were learning to make active use of the media, including having their own initiative beamed to millions via the Jennings broadcast.

In so doing, the second-graders were participating in what has come to be called "media literacy education."[1] The media literacy movement, begun in Australia in the 1980s, views all media as offering scope for participants to learn not to submit passively to whatever comes along, but instead to examine offerings critically while recognizing the financial stakes of programmers and sponsors, to make informed personal and group choices, and to balance their own TV intake with participation in other activities. The hope is that children who become able to take such an approach will be more self-reliant, more informed, and correspondingly less fearful and passive, when it comes to their use of modern media. And since few adults have acquired critical viewing skills, such education is important at all ages.

Maturing, learning how to understand and deal with violence, coping better with its presence on the screen as in the world, knowing its effects, and countering them to the extent possible involves exploring distinctions such as the following:

- between physical violence and psychological and other forms of violence
- between actual and threatened violence
- between direct and indirect violence
- between active violence and violence made possible by neglect or inaction
- between unwanted violence and, say, surgery, performed with consent
- between violence done to oneself and that done to others
- between seeing real violence and witnessing it on the screen
- between portrayals of "real" and fictional violence
- between violence conveyed as information and as entertainment
- between levels of violence in the media and in real life
- between oneself as viewer and as advertising or programming target
- between gratuitous portrayals of violence and others
- between violence glamorized or not

Learning to deal with violence involves sorting out such distinctions and categories and seeking to perceive when they overlap and interact and shade into one another. It is as inaccurate to view all these distinctions as utterly blurred as to imagine each category in a watertight compartment. Exploring these distinctions and their interactions is facilitated by talking them over with others and by seeing them illuminated, first in the simplest stories and pictures, later in literature and works of art.

Because the approach must be gradual and attuned to children's developmental stage, a film such as Steven Spielberg's *Schindler's List*, which offers searing insight into most of the distinctions listed above, is inappropriate for small children, who have not learned to make the necessary distinctions.[2] If they are exposed to such a film before they have learned to draw even rudimentary distinctions with respect to violence, they can respond with terror, numbing, sometimes even misplaced glee. As far as they are concerned, it is beside the point whether the horrors the film conveys are gratuitous or not, real or fictional, or meant as entertainment or not. They cannot tell the difference and should not be exposed to such material before they can do so. The film can be misunderstood, too, by those who would ordinarily be old enough to perceive such distinctions but whose capacity to respond to them has been thwarted or numbed, through personal experience, perhaps from violence in the home, or through overexposure to entertainment violence. The half-embarrassed, half-riotous laughter with which some high school audiences greeted the film troubled many: it was as if these students had lost their ability to make even the most basic distinctions.

A number of these distinctions are hard even for the most experienced media critics to pin down. Take the concept of "gratuitous" violence, violence not needed for purposes of the story being told but added for its shock or entertainment value. Some regard it as a characterization primarily in the eye of the beholder, while others insist that it can be clearly identified in particular films and television programs. Whatever the answer, there are borderline cases of violence where it is hard for anyone to be sure whether it is gratuitous or not. Works such as Spielberg's *Schindler's List* show instances of extreme cruelty that are necessary to convey the horror and inhumanity of the work's subject, and are thus not gratuitous in their own right; yet that film also explores how gratuitous violence is inflicted, even enjoyed, by its perpetrators. The film is about gratuitous violence, then, without in any sense exploiting it or representing an instance of it; and it is emphatically not meant as entertainment violence. Perhaps this is part of what Spielberg meant in saying that he made the film "thinking that if it did entertain, then I would have failed. It was important to me not to set out to please. Because I always had."[3]

Long before callous or uncomprehending ways of responding become ingrained, children can learn, much as the second-graders in the Jennings program were learning, to play a greater part in sorting out the distinctions regarding violence and media violence and to consider how they wish to respond. They can learn to think for themselves and to become discriminating viewers and active participants, rather than passive consumers of the entertainment violence beamed at them daily. Such learning helps, in turn, with the larger goal of achieving resilience—the ability to bounce back, to resist and overcome adversity.

Just as "Buyer beware" is an indispensable motto in today's media environment but far from sufficient, so is a fuller understanding of the role of violence in public entertainment. Individuals, families, and schools can do a great deal; but unless they can join in broader endeavors devoted to enhancing collective resilience, the many admirable personal efforts now under way will not begin to suffice. When neither families nor schools, churches, and neighborhoods can cope alone, what is the larger social responsibility?

10

### Notes

1. See Neil Anderson, *Media Works* (Oxford: Oxford University Press, 1989); and Madeline Levine, *Viewing Violence* (New York: Doubleday, 1996).

2. When *Schindler's List* was about to be broadcast on television, Spielberg was quoted as saying that the film was not, in his opinion, one that should be shown to the very young. His own children, of elementary school age, had not seen it in 1997; but he would want them to once they were of high school age. See Caryn James, "Bringing Home the Horror of the Holocaust," *New York Times,* February 23, 1997, p. 36 H.

3. Steven Spielberg, quoted by Stephen Schiff in "Seriously Spielberg," *New Yorker,* March 21, 1994, p. 101.

*Possibilities for Dialogue with "Media Literacy"*

There is no one right way to have a dialogue, just as there is no magic question that will always unlock the text in front of us. But it's a good idea to begin with the first question on our "Questions for Inquiry" list, *What exactly is the arguer's position?* It's clear that Bok favors "media literacy education." She advocates it, but as only part of the solution to children's exposure to media violence. Her last paragraph implies that we will need other measures as well. And so we might ask, "Why is media education not the only solution?" or "Why isn't media education enough?" Can we tell what she thinks the limitations are?

Having begun with the first question, where we go from there *depends on the nature of the text.* In this case, we need to ask question 2, *What do certain key terms mean?* Paragraph 5 is about the kind of distinctions necessary to a mature understanding of violence. But are we ourselves sure about these distinctions? What is "psychological violence"? Bok doesn't say. How would we answer? If there are both physical and psychological forms of violence, what other forms are there? Again, Bok provides no explanation or examples. Can we? It's far from clear what she means. We must figure this out ourselves or work through these distinctions in class discussion.

We should also ask about assumptions and implications, questions 4 and 9 on our list. Bok admits that "a number of these distinctions are hard even for the most experienced media critics to pin down" (paragraph 8). As adults and college students, we're certainly having our troubles with them; how can we assume that the second-graders referred to in the first paragraph can make even the most rudimentary distinctions? Do they really understand whatever distinctions their teacher is helping them to make?

Once we question what the argument assumes—that young children (about seven or eight years old) can make meaningful distinctions and understand them—we begin to wonder about implications as well. For instance, the students present what they call a "Declaration of Independence from Violence" to "the rest of the student body." Does the declaration imply that violence is *not* part of the human condition? Are we ignoring reality or learning how to cope with it? More broadly, Bok's discussion implies that media education must continue as students grow up. Is this practical? realistic? Is it something our schools can or should undertake?

**Following Through**

In class discussion, continue the dialogue with "Media Literacy." What other questions are relevant from our list of "Questions for Inquiry"? What questions can we ask that do not appear on the list? Be sure to consider the rather unusual case of *Schindler's List*. Why might high school students laugh at it? Is the *only* explanation the one that Bok offers, that the students didn't understand the horror of Nazi violence against the Jews? Does a movie like *Schindler's List*, when audiences understand and react appropriately to it, help us in "achieving resilience—the ability to bounce back, to resist and overcome adversity"?

**Following Through**

As prewriting for Part 2 of your exploratory essay, read one substantial argument on the topic. The argument may or may not agree with your initial opinions. Write a brief summary of the argument, noting its claim and reasons. Then write a few paragraphs of response to it, as we have done with Rhodes's essay and Bok's chapter, showing how the "Questions for Inquiry" opened up that argument to closer inspection. How did the argument compare with your own initial opinions? Was your thinking changed in any way? Why or why not?

## INQUIRY AGAIN: DIGGING DEEPER

Inquiry always leads to more inquiry. For example, if, after reading Bok, we doubt that media literacy can work, we can find out more about it, including what went on in Australia in the 1980s. If we question what second-graders can understand about media violence, we can research the cognitive development of young children. If we aren't sure about the impact of *Schindler's List*, we can watch it ourselves and/or read about Spielberg's making of the film and the popular and critical reception of it. There's nothing important in "Media Literacy" that can't be researched and explored further. Digging deeper means getting more information about the issue into which you are inquiring. But mere quantity is not your goal. Moving deeper into an issue means finding out what experts are saying. For example, Richard Rhodes is a journalist, not a social scientist. He consulted experts, social scientists, to write his argument. To evaluate Rhodes's claim to truth, we need to do the same. Digging deeper should take us closer to people who ought to know most.

Digging deeper also means sharpening the focus of inquiry. As we said earlier, the narrow but deep inquiry will produce a better argument than a broad survey of the topic. Be on the lookout for arguments and other informative sources that address exactly the same aspects of a topic. Ideally, you might find two or more arguments that directly debate each other.

What kinds of readings make good sources for a project like this, one for which you don't have an entire semester to do research? Your sources may be articles and arguments from periodicals, chapters from books, chapters or sections in reference books, newspaper reports, and newspaper columns, as long as they are substantial (more than 500 words) and reliable. Use sources from the Web only if you have checked their reliability and credibility.

To find good sources, read the discussion of finding and evaluating sources on pages 110–125. There are always resources for digging deeper into a question. Reference librarians are an excellent first stop once you have focused your line of inquiry. They can help you find the answers to your questions. They are experts at finding the experts.

When should you stop digging deeper? One answer is, when you have run out of allotted time for inquiring and have to start composing an argument. But suppose you had no deadline. You'll know when you're near the end of inquiry on a topic. You will be reading a lot but not finding much you haven't seen already. That's the time to stop—or, if you still aren't satisfied with what you know, to find another avenue for further research.

Most important, *seek out some sources with points of view that differ from your own*—sources that tell you things you didn't know and challenge your point of view. The whole point of inquiry is to seek out the new and different. *Remember: We are trying not to defend what we already think but to put it to the test.*

---

### Following Through

Read pages 110–125 on finding and evaluating sources. Using the library and electronic indexes available, find at least five good articles and arguments about your chosen issue. Be sure to find sources that contain a variety of opinions but that all address the same issues. Read each carefully, and write notes and annotations based on the "Questions for Inquiry."

---

## When the Experts Disagree

One of our own professors once advised his classes, "If you want to think you know something about a subject, read one book, because reading a second will just confuse you." The fact is, confusion is an unavoidable part of the process of exploring an issue. If you are digging deeply in the true spirit of inquiry, you will find sources that conflict. If you don't become confused, you are probably not looking hard enough into your issue. Instead of avoiding conflicting sources (our professor was mocking the "one-book expert"), seek out conflict and deal with it. Decide which sources to accept and which to reject. We illustrate some strategies for dealing with conflict in the following exploration of two articles by social scientists who assess in opposite ways the research linking fantasy violence to actual violence.

## An Example of Experts Disagreeing

When we left Richard Rhodes, we still wondered how to answer the question, Does violent entertainment contribute to violence in our society? He made a good case against such a link, but we can't ignore all the experts he mentions who do take it seriously. Nor can we put aside the results of our own inquiry into the article, which gave us good reason to doubt his position. So we've decided to go to the social scientists themselves to see how they interpret the research. We've located the following exchange from the *Harvard Mental Health Letter* (1996). In the May issue, Jonathan L. Freedman, a professor of psychology at the University of Toronto, argues much as Rhodes did—that there's no proof linking fantasy violence to actual violence. In the June issue, L. Rowell Huesmann, a professor of psychology at the University of Michigan, and his graduate assistant, Jessica Moise, defend the link, based in part on their own research.

Now we have arguments on both sides of the question. Read the following articles and assess them on your own. Ask yourself, Who makes the better case? We should accept the position we think is the stronger.

---

## Violence in the Mass Media and Violence in Society: The Link Is Unproven*

### Jonathan L. Freedman

Imagine that the Food and Drug Administration (FDA) is presented with a series of studies testing the effectiveness of a new drug. There are some laboratory tests that produce fairly consistent positive effects, but the drug does not always work as expected and no attempt has been made to discover why. Most of the clinical tests are negative; there are also a few weak positive results and a few results suggesting that the drug is less effective than a placebo. Obviously the FDA would reject this application, yet the widely accepted evidence that watching television violence causes aggression is no more adequate.

In laboratory tests of this thesis, some children are shown violent programs, others are shown nonviolent programs, and their aggressiveness is measured immediately afterward. The results, although far from consistent,

*"Violence in the Mass Media and Violence in Society: The Link is Unproven." Excerpted from the May 1996 issue of the *Harvard Mental Health Letter.* Copyright © 1996, President and Fellows of Harvard College. Reprinted by permission.

generally show some increase in aggression after a child watches a violent program. Like most laboratory studies of real-world conditions, however, these findings have limited value. In the first place, most of the studies have used dubious measures of aggression. In one experiment, for example, children were asked, "If I had a balloon, would you want me to prick it?" Other measures have been more plausible, but none is unimpeachable. Second, there is the problem of distinguishing effects of violence from effects of interest and excitement. In general, the violent films in these experiments are more arousing than the neutral films. Anyone who is aroused will display more of almost any behavior; there is nothing special about aggression in this respect. Finally and most important, these experiments are seriously contaminated by what psychologists call demand characteristics of the situation: the familiar fact that people try to do what the experimenter wants. Since the children know the experimenter has chosen the violent film, they may assume that they are being given permission to be aggressive.

**Putting It to the Test**

The simplest way to conduct a real-world study is to find out whether children who watch more violent television are also more aggressive. They are, but the correlations are small, accounting for only 1% to 10% of individual differences in children's aggressiveness. In any case, correlations do not prove causality. Boys watch more TV football than girls, and they play more football than girls, but no one, so far as I know, believes that television is what makes boys more interested in football. Probably personality characteristics that make children more aggressive also make them prefer violent television programs.

To control for the child's initial aggressiveness, some studies have measured children's TV viewing and their aggression at intervals of several years, using statistical techniques to judge the effect of early television viewing on later aggression. One such study found evidence of an effect, but most have found none.

For practical reasons, there have been only a few truly controlled experiments in which some children in a real-world environment are assigned to watch violent programs for a certain period of time and others are assigned to watch nonviolent programs. Two or three of these experiments indicated slight, short-lived effects of TV violence on aggression; one found a strong effect in the opposite of the expected direction, and most found no effect. All the positive results were obtained by a single research group, which conducted studies with very small numbers of children and used inappropriate statistics.

**Scrutinizing the Evidence**

An account of two studies will give some idea of how weak the research results are and how seriously they have been misinterpreted.

A study published by Lynette Friedrichs and Aletha Stein is often described (for example, in reports by the National Institute of Mental Health and the American Psychological Association) as having found that children who watched violent programs became more aggressive. What the study actually showed was quite different. In a first analysis the authors found that TV violence had no effect on physical aggression, verbal aggression, aggressive fantasy, or object aggression (competition for a toy or other object). Next they computed indexes statistically combining various kinds of aggression, a technique that greatly increases the likelihood of connections appearing purely by chance. Still they found nothing.

They then divided the children into two groups—those who were already aggressive and those who were not. They found that children originally lower in aggression seemed to become more aggressive and children originally higher in aggression seemed to become less aggressive no matter which type of program they watched. This is a well-known statistical artifact called regression toward the mean, and it has no substantive significance. Furthermore, the less aggressive children actually became more aggressive after watching the neutral program than after watching the violent program. The only comfort for the experimenters was that the level of aggression in highly aggressive children fell more when they watched a neutral program than when they watched a violent program. Somehow that was sufficient for the study to be widely cited as strong evidence that TV violence causes aggression.

An ambitious cross-national study was conducted by a team led by Rowell Huesmann and Leonard Eron and reported in 1986. In this widely cited research the effect of watching violent television on aggressiveness at a later age was observed in seven groups of boys and seven groups of girls in six countries. After controlling for initial aggressiveness, the researchers found no statistically significant effect for either sex in Australia, Finland, the Netherlands, Poland, or kibbutz children in Israel. The effect sought by the investigators was found only in the United States and among urban Israeli children, and the latter effect was so large, so far beyond the normal range for this kind of research and so incongruous with the results in other countries, that it must be regarded with suspicion. Nevertheless, the senior authors concluded that the pattern of results supported their position. The Netherlands researchers disagreed; they acknowledged that they had not been able to link TV violence to aggression, and they criticized the methods used by some of the other groups. The senior authors refused to include their chapter in the book that came out of the study, and they had to publish a separate report.

**A Second Look**

If the evidence is so inadequate, why have so many committees evaluating it concluded that the link exists? In the first place, these committees have     10 been composed largely of people chosen with the expectation of reaching that conclusion. Furthermore, committee members who were not already familiar with the research could not possibly have read it all themselves, and must have relied on what they were told by experts who were often biased. The reports of these committees are often seriously inadequate. The National Institute of Mental Health, for example, conducted a huge study but solicited only one review of the literature, from a strong advocate of the view that television violence causes aggression. The review was sketchy — it left out many important studies — and deeply flawed.

The belief that TV violence causes aggression has seemed plausible because it is intuitively obvious that this powerful medium has effects on children. After all, children imitate and learn from what they see. The question, however, is what they see on television and what they learn. We know that children tend to imitate actions that are rewarded and avoid actions that are punished. In most violent television programs villains start the fight and are punished. The programs also show heroes using violence to fight violence, but the heroes almost always have special legal or moral authority; they are police, other government agents, or protectors of society like Batman and the Power Rangers. If children are learning anything from these programs, it is that the forces of good will overcome evil assailants who are the first to use violence. That may be overoptimistic, but it hardly encourages the children themselves to initiate aggression.    — *It does show them, though, that aggression is the way to solve conflict.*

### Telling the Difference

Furthermore, these programs are fiction, and children know it as early as the age of five. Children watching Power Rangers do not think they can beam up to the command center, and children watching "Aladdin" do not believe in flying carpets. Similarly, children watching the retaliatory violence of the heroes in these programs do not come to believe they themselves could successfully act in the same way. (Researchers concerned about mass media violence should be more interested in the fights that occur during hockey and football games, which are real and therefore may be imitated by children who play those sports.)

Recently I testified before a Senate committee, and one Senator told me he knew TV made children aggressive because his own son had met him at the door with a karate kick after watching the Power Rangers. The Senator was confusing aggression with rough play, and imitation of specific actions with learning to be aggressive. Children do imitate what they see on television; this has strong effects on the way they play, and it may also influence the forms their real-life aggression takes. Children who watch the Ninja Turtles or Power Rangers may practice martial arts, just as years ago they might have been wielding toy guns, and long before that, wrestling or dueling with wooden swords. If there had been no television, the Senator's son might have butted him in the stomach or poked him in the ribs with a gun. The question is not whether the boy learned his karate kick from TV, but whether TV has made him more aggressive than he would have been otherwise.

Television is an easy target for the concern about violence in our society but a misleading one. We should no longer waste time worrying about this subject. Instead let us turn our attention to the obvious major causes of violence, which include poverty, racial conflict, drug abuse, and poor parenting.

---

## Media Violence: A Demonstrated Public Health Threat to Children*

### L. Rowell Huesmann and Jessica Moise

Imagine that the Surgeon General is presented with a series of studies on a widely distributed product. For 30 years well-controlled experiments have been showing that use of the product causes symptoms of a particular affliction. Many field surveys have shown that this affliction is always more common among people who use the product regularly. A smaller number of studies have examined the long-term effects of the product in different environments, and most have shown at least some evidence of harm, although it is difficult to disentangle effects of the product itself from the effects of factors that lead people to use it. Over all, the studies suggest that if a person with a 50% risk for the affliction uses the product, the risk rises to 60% or 70%. Furthermore, we have a fairly good understanding of how use of the product contributes to the affliction, which is persistent, difficult to cure, and sometimes lethal. The product is economically important, and its manufacturers spend large sums trying to disparage the scientific research. A few scientists who have never done any empirical work in the field regularly point out supposed flaws in the research and belittle its conclusions. The incidence of the affliction has increased dramatically since the product was first introduced. What should the Surgeon General do?

This description applies to the relationship between lung cancer and cigarettes. It also applies to the relationship between aggression and children's viewing of mass media violence. The Surgeon General has rightly come to the same conclusion in both cases and has issued similar warnings.

### Cause and Effect

Dr. Freedman's highly selective reading of the research minimizes overwhelming evidence. First, there are the carefully controlled laboratory studies in which children are exposed to violent film clips and short-term changes in their behavior are observed. More than 100 such studies over the last 40 years have shown that at least some children exposed to visual depictions of dramatic violence behave more aggressively afterward both toward inanimate objects and toward other children. These results have been found in many countries among boys and girls of all social classes, races, ages, and levels of intelligence.

Freedman claims that these studies use "dubious measures of aggression." He cites only one example: asking children whether they would want the researcher to prick a balloon. But this measure is not at all representative. Most studies have used such evidence as physical attacks on other children and dolls. In one typical study Kaj Bjorkqvist exposed five- and six-year-old Finnish children to either violent or non-violent films. Observers who did not know which kind of film each child had seen then watched them play together. Children who had just seen a violent film were more likely to hit other children, scream at them, threaten them, and intentionally destroy their toys.

Freedman claims that these experiments confuse the effects of arousal with the effects of violence. He argues that "anyone who is aroused will display more of almost any behavior." But most studies have shown that prosocial behavior decreases after children view an aggressive film. Finally, Freedman says the experiments are contaminated by demand characteristics. In other words, the children are only doing what they think the researchers want them to do. That conclusion is extremely implausible, considering the wide variety of experiments conducted in different countries by researchers with different points of view.

### Large Body of Evidence

More than 50 field studies over the last 20 years have also shown that children who habitually watch more media violence behave more aggressively and accept aggression more readily as a way to solve problems. The relationship usually persists when researchers control for age, sex, social class, and previous level of aggression. Disbelievers often suggest that the correlation is statistically small. According to Freedman, it accounts for "only 1% to 10% of individual differences in children's aggressiveness." But an increase of that size (a more accurate figure would be 2% to 16%) has real social significance. No single factor has been found to explain more than 16% of individual differences in aggression.

Of course, correlations do not prove causality. That is the purpose of laboratory experiments. The two approaches are complementary. Experiments establish causal relationship, and field studies show that the relationship holds in a wide variety of real-world situations. The causal relationship is further confirmed by the finding that children who view TV violence at an early age are more likely to commit aggressive acts at a later age. In 1982 Eron and Huesmann found that boys who spent the most time viewing violent television shows at age eight were most likely to have criminal convictions at age 30. Most other long-term studies have come to similar conclusions, even after controlling for children's initial aggressiveness, social class, and education. A few studies have found no effect on some measures of violence, but almost all have found a significant effect on some measures.

Freedman singles out for criticism a study by Huesmann and his colleagues that was concluded in the late 1970s. He says we found "no statistically significant effect for either sex in Australia, Finland, the Netherlands, Poland, or kibbutz children in Israel." That is not true. We found that the television viewing habits of children [as] young as six or seven predicted subsequent increases in childhood aggression among boys in Finland and among both sexes in the United States, in Poland, and in Israeli cities. In Australia and on Israeli kibbutzim, television viewing habits were correlated with simultaneous aggression. Freedman also suggests that another study conducted in the Netherlands came to conclusions so different from ours that we banned it from a book we were writing. In fact, the results of that study were remarkably similar to our own, and we did not refuse to publish it. The Dutch researchers themselves chose to publish separately in a different format.

### Cultural Differences

Freedman argues that the strongest results reported in the study, such as those for Israeli city children, are so incongruous that they arouse suspicion. He is wrong. Given the influence of culture and social learning on aggressive behavior, different results in different cultures are to be expected. In fact, the similarity of the findings in different countries is remarkable here. One reason we found no connection between television violence viewing and aggression among children on [kib]butzim is the strong cultural prohibition against intra-group aggression in those communities. Another reason is that kibbutz children usually watched television in a group and discussed the shows with an adult caretaker afterward.

Two recently published meta-analyses summarize the findings of many studies conducted over the past 30 years. In an analysis of 217 experiments and field studies, Paik and Comstock concluded that the association between exposure to television violence and aggressive behavior is extremely strong, especially in the data accumulated over the last 15 years. In the other meta-analysis, Wood, Wong, and Chachere came to the same conclusion after combined analysis of 23 studies of unstructured social interaction.

We now have well-validated theoretical explanations of these results. Exposure to media violence leads to aggression in at least five ways. The first is imitation, or observational learning. Children imitate the actions of their parents, other children, and media heroes, especially when the action is rewarded and the child admires and identifies with the model. When generalized, this process creates what are sometimes called cognitive scripts for

10

complex social problem-solving: internalized programs that guide everyday
social behavior in an automatic way and are highly resistant to change.

**Turning Off**

Second, media violence stimulates aggression by desensitizing children
to the effects of violence. The more televised violence a child watches, the
more acceptable aggressive behavior becomes for that child. Furthermore,
children who watch violent television become suspicious and expect others
to act violently—an attributional bias that promotes aggressive behavior.

Justification is a third process by which media violence stimulates aggression. A child who has behaved aggressively watches violent television
shows to relieve guilt and justify the aggression. The child then feels less
inhibited about aggressing again.

A fourth process is cognitive priming or cueing—the activation of existing aggressive thoughts, feelings, and behavior. This explains why children
observe one kind of aggression on television and commit another kind
of aggressive act afterward. Even an innocuous object that has been associated with aggression may later stimulate violence. Josephson demonstrated
this . . . in a study of schoolboy hockey players. She subjected the boys to
frustration and then showed them either a violent or a non-violent television program. The aggressor in the violent program carried a walkie-talkie.
Later, when the referee in a hockey game carried a similar walkie-talkie, the
boys who had seen the violent film were more likely to start fights during
the game.

**A Numbing Effect**

The fifth process by which media violence induces aggression is physio-    15
logical arousal and desensitization. Boys who are heavy television watchers
show lower than average physiological arousal in response to new scenes
of violence. Similar short-term effects are found in laboratory studies. The
arousal stimulated by viewing violence is unpleasant at first, but children
who constantly watch violent television become habituated, and their emotional and physiological responses decline. Meanwhile the propensity to
aggression is heightened by any pleasurable arousal, such as sexual feeling,
that is associated with media violence.

Freedman argues that in violent TV shows, villains start the fight and
are punished and the heroes "almost always have special legal or moral authority." Therefore, he concludes, children are learning from these programs
that "the forces of good will overcome evil assailants." On the contrary, it is
precisely because media heroes are admired and have special authority that
children are likely to imitate their behavior and learn that aggression is an

acceptable solution to conflict. Freedman also claims that media violence has little effect because children can distinguish real life from fiction. But children under 11 do not make this distinction very well. Studies have shown that many of them think cartoons and other fantasy shows depict life as it really is.

The studies are conclusive. The evidence leaves no room for doubt that exposure to media violence stimulates aggression. It is time to move on and consider how best to inoculate our children against this insidious threat.

## Commentary on the Experts' Disagreement

When experts disagree, the rest of us can respond in only a few ways. We can throw up our hands and say, "Who knows?" But this response doesn't work very well because expert disagreement is so common. We'd have to give up on most issues. Another response is to take seriously only those experts who endorse the opinion we favor, using them to make our case and ignoring the rest, a common tactic in debate, legal pleadings, business, and politics whenever the search for truth gives way to self-interest. We can also "go with our gut," opting for the opinion that "feels right" to us. But often these gut feelings amount to no more than our prejudices talking; in addition, such an approach to resolving conflict is not rational enough for inquiry. And so we are left with the only response appropriate to inquiry: rational assessment of the competing arguments. We should take as true the better or best case — at least until we encounter another more convincing. This is the way of genuine, honest inquiry.

We know, then, what we need to do, but how do we go about doing it? How can we decide which of two or several arguments is better or best?

In this instance, let's recognize that Huesmann and Moise have an advantage simply because they wrote second, after Freedman, who has no opportunity to respond to what they've said. Huesmann and Moise can *both* refute Freedman *and* make their own case without the possibility of rebuttal. Granting this, however, it's still hard to find Freedman's case more convincing. Why?

We'll offer only a few reasons for thinking that we must assent to the Huesmann–Moise argument. You and your class can carry out the analysis further — it's a good opportunity to practice critical reading and thinking.

Both articles begin with an analogy. Freedman compares the research on violent TV programs with the research required to approve a drug. Huesmann and Moise compare the research linking cigarettes to lung cancer with the research linking violent TV to aggressive behavior in children. The second comparison is better because the two instances of research compared are more nearly alike. Furthermore, the fact that the Surgeon General has issued warnings both for cigarettes and for violent entertainment's effect on children shows how seriously research on the latter is taken by qualified authorities. In fact, one of the more convincing aspects of the Huesmann–Moise case is the amount of support they claim for their position. They are specific about the numbers: "50 field studies over the last 20 years" (paragraph 6); "an analysis of 217 experiments and field studies" (paragraph 10)—all confirm their conclusion. If Freedman has evidence to rival this, he does not cite it. We must assume he doesn't because he doesn't have it.

Another strength of the Huesmann–Moise article is that they go beyond a review of the research linking TV violence to aggression; they offer five *explanations* for the negative impact of fantasy violence (paragraphs 11–15). We come away not only convinced that the link has been established but also with an understanding of why it exists. Freedman has no well-developed theoretical explanation to support his position. What he offers, such as the assertion that children know the difference between pretend and real violence, is refuted by Huesmann and Moise.

If you are thinking that the better or best case won't always be so easy to discern, you're right. Our point is certainly not that comparative assessment will always yield a clearly superior case. Often, we will argue with ourselves and others over whose case merits our support. Our point is this: When we encounter opposing positions in our sources, we should set aside our own prejudices and study the arguments they've made. We should resolve the conflict by taking the better or best case as the truth or the closest thing we have to the truth. We cannot just accept the argument that sides with our initial position. We must accept the better argument.

We think that, in most cases, the better or best argument will emerge as you think your way through the arguments and compare their strengths and weaknesses. What's hard is to let go of a position we're attracted to when another position has a better case. The real challenge of inquiry is to change or revise our own opinions as we encounter good arguments for positions different from our own.

---

## Following Through

Even if they do not speak directly to each other, as our examples here do, find two sources that present conflicting data or information or conflicting interpretations of the same information. Write an evaluation of these arguments, telling which one seemed to present the best case. Explain why you think so. Did you find that comparing these arguments influenced your own thinking in any way? If so, how?

---

## THE WRITING PROJECT: PART 2

By now, you have many notes that you can use as raw material for writing Part 2 of your essay. You have had a serious dialogue with at least one other person about your ideas. You should have notes about this dialogue and maybe even a recording or transcript of it. Look over this material, and make some more notes about how this conversation modified your ideas—by clarifying them, by presenting you with an idea you had not thought of, or by solidifying a belief you already held. If the conversations revealed conflicting opinions, to what would you attribute those differences?

You have also read several printed arguments and done some research. You have written some evaluations of these arguments and marked them up. Continue to do so, noting places where they touch upon the same points, whether in agreement or contrast. We suggest using highlighters to color-code passages that connect across the readings. Make some notes or draft paragraphs about what different experts have to say on the same question, and include an estimate of the effectiveness of their points and support in increasing your own knowledge about the issue. In which viewpoints did you feel you had found some truth, and why?

You are ready to draft the body of your paper. It should contain at least four well-developed paragraphs in which you describe your inquiry. Discuss the conversations you had and the materials you read, and show how these lines of inquiry influenced your thinking on the issue you explored. Assess the arguments you read, consider their rhetorical context, include the names of the authors and the biases they might have. Talk about why an author's argument was sound or not sound, why it influenced your initial opinion or why it did not.

Part 2 could be organized around a discussion of ideas that were strengthened by your research versus those that you have reconsidered because of it. Did a source offer new information that has caused you to reconsider part or all of what you thought? Tell what the information was, and explain why it's changed your outlook. Did you encounter a well-developed argument defending a position different from your own? How did you react? What aspects of the argument do you take seriously enough to consider modifying or changing your own opinion? Be sure to explain why. If you found sources or individual people who disagreed, which side did you find more convincing, and why?

Although some paragraphs could be devoted to a single source, others could compare an idea across two or three sources, and you could point out the ways in which they concur or disagree, showing how each contributed to the change in your opinion.

No matter how you organize your paper, be specific about what you have read. You will need to quote and paraphrase the ideas in your sources; when you refer to sources, do so very specifically. See our advice about using sources on pages 110–127. Paraphrase clearly and quote exactly. Use Modern Language Association (MLA) style for in-text citations (pages 139–143).

Be careful not to merely summarize your sources or use them in the conventional way of supporting and illustrating your own discussion or argument. You are evaluating the thinking expressed in the sources, so it is important not just to cite an author's name but also to include some information about that person's professional affiliation and point of view.

In other words, rhetorical context is vital here, and it should be part of your consideration of each source. Also, in the body of your paper, *be selective.* Select what struck you as particularly important in confirming or challenging your view. Explain what most strongly impressed you as strong or weak thinking and why. Obviously, your readers don't want to get bogged down in needless detail; they want the information that altered your understanding of the topic and the arguments that opened up new considerations. *The point is to show how your research-inquiry refined, modified, or changed your initial opinions and to explain why.* Anything that doesn't contribute significantly and directly to this end should not be in the final draft of your paper.

## THE WRITING PROJECT: PART 3

In preparation for writing the conclusion of your essay, reread Part 1, the overview of your exploration. Decide whether you have found "some truth" about the issues you have explored. Can you arrive at a claim you want to defend in an essay to convince or persuade an audience to think differently? If so, what is it? Perhaps you're still unsure; what then? One option is to conclude your paper by explaining what you are unsure of and why, and what you'd like to learn from further research. An inconclusive but honest ending is better than a forced closing for the sake of making a claim.

Your goal, then, is to draft a conclusion for your paper in which you honestly discuss the results of your exploration, whatever they were. This section is about where you stand now, but it needn't be final or conclusive. If you have doubts, state them honestly, and indicate how you might resolve them through further research and inquiry.

## AFTER DRAFTING YOUR ESSAY

*Revise* your draft to make sure each paragraph is unified around one point and to remove any unnecessary summarizing. You will quote and paraphrase from your sources, so check your work against the guidelines for incorporating source material in your own writing (pages 110–127).

*Edit* your paper for wordiness, repetition, and excessive passive voice. See the suggestions for editing in the appendix.

*Proofread* your paper. Read it aloud to catch omissions and errors of grammar and punctuation. You can ask for help with common errors such as comma splices or apostrophe problems. (But make sure your helper helps you see the problems and correct them yourself and doesn't do the job for you.)

**STUDENT SAMPLE:** *An Exploratory Essay*

EXPLORATORY ESSAY

Sydney Owens

*Part 1*

I think that the relationship between violence and the media is hard to define. There is definitely some correlation between them, but to what extent it is hard to say. Media itself is only one word, but it includes television, radio, CDs, video games, papers, books, the Internet, and more. It is complicated, when you group them all together, to say that they cause violence. Also you have to look at what kind of violence you are talking about. Do media influence more aggressive behavior, such as killing? And lastly, a child's environment, personality, parents, and media all have to be considered. It is difficult to say why people do anything, let alone why they commit acts of violence.

Each human is so unique that it seems too general to say that media violence makes people more violent. One person could watch gruesome violence every day and remain a very caring and loving person, whereas another individual might see minimal violent media and then go out and kill someone. Where do you draw the line? I guess you have to start taking averages and define a norm. But then that norm only defines "normal" people's reactions to violence seen or heard in the media. You might control the masses in this way, but this will not keep a person outside of the norm from committing acts of violence.

When I see or hear violence in the media, I know that I am not inclined to do anything noticeably more violent than if I had not. Then again, I do know that a high-action movie thriller has given me that feeling of kick-ass satisfaction and that exposure to rap songs has caused me to more readily use somewhat inappropriate language. Feelings and slang are not acts of violence, but these examples do show that there is a connection between the media and undesirable effects on people.

*Part 2*

When I read "Violence in the Mass Media and Violence in Society: The Link Is Unproven," I began to think that there really is not strong enough evidence to say that media violence leads to violent behavior. The author, Jonathan Freedman, argued that you could not prove the link because the "studies . . . used dubious measures of aggression," they could not "distinguish effects of violence from effects of interest and excitement," and the studies were "seriously contaminated by . . . demand characteristics of the situation." All of this made sense to me. I especially agreed with the contamination of the demand characteristics because I had just learned about this term in my psychology class. I was taught that experimenters have to take into account the fact that many subjects alter

their own behavior to mirror what they think the experimenter is looking for.

Freedman also gave an example that really stuck out in my mind as
proof that there is not a strong enough link to prove anything. He said to
imagine that the FDA was testing out the effectiveness of a new drug.
The results came out negative, weakly positive, and even less effective
than a placebo. He said that obviously the FDA would reject this drug as
having no effect and that, likewise, media should be rejected as having no
effect on violence. This seemed to make perfect sense until I compared it
to "Media Violence: A Demonstrated Public Health Threat to Children," an
article by L. Rowell Huesmann and Jessica Moise that counters Freedman's
position. The FDA analogy that had sounded so good now looked faulty
compared with Huesmann's Surgeon General analogy. In Huesmann's
analogy, he points out that if something has shown even the slightest
negative effect, it is justifiable to put out a warning because it is always
better to be safe than sorry. I agree with this reasoning. Freedman was
right to say that we cannot prove for certain that media violence leads to
violent behavior, but what he failed to acknowledge is that we should still
put out the warning if any effects are negative. After contrasting these
two articles, I had changed my mind and decided that media violence
does induce violent behavior.

With this new state of mind, I read several other articles that
reinforced the claim that media violence promotes more violent behavior.
In the article "We Are Training Our Kids to Kill," Dave Grossman claims
that "the desensitizing techniques used for training soldiers are being
replicated in contemporary mass media movies, television, and video
games, giving rise to the alarming rate of homicide and violence in our
schools and communities." Not only was this article interesting, but it
also made sense. Grossmann, who travels the world training medical, law
enforcement, and U.S. military personnel about the realities of warfare,
supported his claim by showing how classical and operant conditioning
used in the military parallel the effects of violent media on young children. Grossman's article was simple and straightforward. I followed his
argument and agreed that the desensitizing effects of media train our
kids to kill.

To be sure that his argument was true, I tried looking for some evidence that would prove that desensitizing did not have an effect. The only
text I could find that even attempted to counter that desensitizing techniques influence violent behavior was the article by Richard Rhodes, "Hollow Claims about Fantasy Violence." In this article, there is one short and
very confusing paragraph (paragraph 9) in which Rhodes offers "a British
scholar's" critique of the desensitization argument:

> [T]heir claim is that the materials they judge to be harmful can only
> influence us by trying to makes us be the same as them. So horrible

things will make us horrible—not horrified. . . . This idea is so odd, it is hard to know where to begin in challenging it.

After reading this, I felt like saying the same thing to Rhodes. His paragraph was so confusing I had a hard time knowing where to begin in challenging it. This was a very poor argument. In reality, it is not really an argument at all because Rhodes offers only a quote without any explanation. The quote lumps all forms of violence into one heap and ignores the fact that some violent entertainment is made to make us laugh. After realizing that this was a very poor argument, I stuck with my initial viewpoint that desensitization does promote violent behavior.

*Part 3*

After reading all of these articles and deciding that I definitely do think that media contributes to violent behavior, I began thinking about my own personal experiences again. I thought about that "kick-ass feeling" I get when I watch certain action movies, and I began feeling somewhat ashamed. As film producers Edward Zwick and Marshall Herskovitz pointed out in their *New York Times* column "When the Bodies Are Real" after the tragedies surrounding September 11, "perhaps what this event has revealed, with its real bodies blown to bits and real explosions bringing down buildings, is the true darkness behind so much of the product coming out of Hollywood today."

Annotated Bibliography

Freedman, Jonathan. "Violence in the Mass Media and Violence in Society: The Link Is Unproven." Harvard Mental Health Letter May 1996: 4–6.

This is an article for the general public that claims that there is not solid proof that mass media leads to violence. The author, Jonathan Freedman, proves his claim by showing that the studies have used dubious measures of aggression, by showing that it is hard to distinguish effects of violence from effects of excitement, and to separate either from the effects of demand characteristics. This would be a good article to use to prove that media does not influence aggressive behavior; however, I used the article's weak points to prove that media does lead to aggressive behavior.

Grossman, Dave. "We Are Training Our Kids to Kill." Saturday Evening Post July/Aug 1999: 64–70.

This is an article for the general public explaining the killings committed by America's youth as a result of media violence. First the author discusses how killing is unnatural. He then goes on to show how several military techniques for training soldiers mirror the ways in which the media interact with our children. This article gives logical support to the claim that media influences violent behavior.

Herskovitz, Marshall, and Edward Zwick. "When the Bodies Are Real." Editorial. New York Times.

This is a short article written in response to the horrible tragedies that befell the people of the United States on September 11. It is written for the general public, but it focuses specifically on how the media community will respond to this tragedy. The authors, Marshall Herskovitz and Edward Zwick, are producers, directors, and writers. Their most recent film was *Traffic*. They point out how this tragedy has shamed Hollywood, along with all of us, to turn our eyes back to ourselves and examine what is there.

Huesmann, L. Rowell, and Jessica Moise. "A Demonstrated Public Health Threat to Children." Harvard Mental Health Letter June 1996: 5–7.

This is an article written in response to Jonathan Freedman's article, "Violence in the Mass Media and Violence in Society: The Link Is Unproven." The authors refute most of Freedman's article with research. The article offers good support for the link between media and real violence.

Rhodes, Richard. "Hollow Claims about Fantasy Violence." Editorial. New York Times 17 Sept. 2000.

This is an article that attempts to prove that there is not enough evidence to claim that media violence leads to real violence. The author, Richard Rhodes, implies that people (in particular, politicians) use media as a scapegoat for not looking to the real problems behind violence. I used this source to prove that the media does induce violence because it contained a paragraph that made a very weak attempt at proving that desensitization does not make people more violent.

*Note:* For a discussion of how to create an annotated bibliography, see Chapter 5, page 138.

## INQUIRY: SUMMING UP THE AIM

In this chapter, we've introduced you to college-level inquiry. Here are the key points:

- In college, we don't just ransack sources for information and quotes. *We interact with them.* "Interact" means both to be critical of sources and to allow them to influence, even change, our point of view.
- Informal conversation is a valuable medium of inquiry. But it becomes more valuable when we turn conversation into dialogue. *Assert opinions less, and question opinions more.* When a good question elicits a good response, follow it up with more questions.

- The best and most stimulating sources need dialogue. *Think of texts as something to "talk with."* Such dialogues will uncover more potential research possibilities. Pursue these, and you'll approach the depth of inquiry valued in college work and beyond, in graduate school and in the workplace.

Inquiry is learning. Inquiry is finding what we really think and therefore what we have to say. It's the most creative part of the writing process. Invest in it. It will repay your best efforts.

# Chapter 7

# Making Your Case: Arguing to Convince

The last chapter ended where inquiry ends—with the attempt to formulate a position, an opinion that we can assert with some confidence. Once our aim shifts from inquiring to convincing, everything changes.

The most significant change is in audience. In inquiry, our audience consists of our fellow inquirers—generally, friends, classmates, and teachers we can talk with face to face. We seek assurance that our position is at least plausible and defensible, a claim to truth that can be respected whether or not the audience agrees with it. In convincing, however, our audience consists of readers whose positions differ from our own or who have no position at all. The audience changes from a small, inside group that helps us develop our argument to a larger, public audience who will either accept or reject it.

As the audience changes, so does the situation or need for argument. Inquiry is a cooperative use of argument; it cannot take place unless people are willing to work together. Conversely, convincing is competitive. We pit our case against the case(s) of others in an effort to win the assent of readers who will compare the various arguments and ask, Who makes the best case? With whom should I agree? Our arguments now compete for "best or better" status, just as do the disagreeing arguments of experts.

Because of the change in audience and situation, our thinking also changes, becoming more strategic and calculated to influence the readers. In inquiry, we try to make a case we can believe in; in convincing, we must make a case that readers can believe in. What we find compelling in inquiry will sometimes also convince our readers, but in convincing we must adapt our reasoning to appeal to their beliefs, values, and self-interest. We will also likely offer reasons that did not occur to us at all in inquiry but that come as we attempt to imagine the people we hope to convince. Convincing, however, does not mean abandoning the work of inquiry. Our version of the truth, our convictions, must first be earned through inquiry before we seek to convince others.

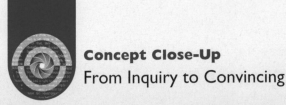

## Concept Close-Up
## From Inquiry to Convincing

| Inquiry | ⟶ Convincing |
|---|---|
| Intimate audience | Public readership |
| Cooperative | Competitive |
| Earns a conviction | Argues a thesis |
| Seeks a case convincing *to us* | Makes a case convincing *to them*, the readers |

Essentially, we take the position we discovered through inquiry and turn it into a thesis supported by a case designed to gain the assent of a specific group of readers.

In this chapter, we look first at the structure and strategy of complete essays that aim to convince. Then we provide a step-by-step analysis of the kind of thinking necessary to produce such an essay.

## THE NATURE OF CONVINCING: STRUCTURE AND STRATEGY

An argument is an assertion supported by a reason. To convince an audience, writers need to expand on this structure. They usually must offer more than one reason and support all reasons with evidence. In this chapter, we use the term **case structure** to describe a flexible plan for making *any argument to any audience* who expects sound reasoning. We use the term **case strategy** to describe the moves writers make *to shape a particular argument*—selecting reasons, ordering them, developing evidence, and linking the sections of the argument for maximum impact.

### Case Structure

All cases have at least three levels of assertion. The first level is the thesis, or central claim, which everything else in the case supports. The second level is the reason or reasons the arguer advances for holding the thesis. The third level is the evidence offered to support each reason, typically drawn from some authoritative source.

In the abstract, then, cases look like this:

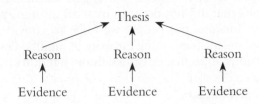

*Figure 7.1*

210

## Concept Close-Up
## Key Questions for Case-Making

1. Who is your **target audience**?
2. What **preconceptions** and **biases** might they hold about your topic?
3. What **claim** do you want your readers to accept?
4. What **reasons** are likely to appeal to this audience?
5. How should you **arrange** these reasons for **maximum impact** on your target audience?
6. How might you **introduce** your case?
7. How might you **conclude** it?
8. How can you gain the **trust** and **respect** of your audience?

Essentially, convincing is audience centered. Every choice we make must be made with the target audience in mind.

Our diagram shows three reasons, but good cases can be built with only one reason or with more than three.

### Case Strategy

In Chapter 2, we explain that you can read an argument with greater comprehension if you begin with a sense of the rhetorical context in which the writer worked. Likewise, in preparing to write an argument, consider the "Key Questions for Case-Making" above.

By working out answers to these questions in your writer's notebook, you will create a rhetorical prospectus that will help you envision a context within which to write and a tentative plan to follow.

To demonstrate case strategy, we will look at "Arrested Development: The Conservative Case against Racial Profiling." The author, James Forman, Jr., is an educator and fellow at the New American Foundation in Washington, D.C. His article was published in *The New Republic*, September 10, 2001.

### Thinking about Audience

To make an effective case for his position, Forman envisions an audience who favors racial profiling, and his strategy is to use reasons and evidence to convince readers who disagree with him. Therefore, he had to consider their likely responses. To develop a strategy, he posed questions like these:

- Who will my readers be?
- How will they be predisposed to view racial profiling?
- What will they have on their minds as soon as they see that my argument is against it?

Based on these questions, Forman assumes something like the following about the intended audience:

My conservative audience supports the police and approves or at least tolerates racial profiling as a tactic for apprehending criminals. I want to show them not only that profiling doesn't work but also, more important, that it violates fundamental conservative principles.

Strategy, then, must begin with thoughts about the audience, its values and preconceptions. Next, we examine how Forman shapes the elements of case structure—thesis, reasons, and evidence—to appeal to his readers.

## Formulating the Thesis

Your thesis may not be explicitly stated in the text of your argument, but it must be *strongly implied* and clear to you and your reader. It must be clear to you because you must build a case around it. It must be clear to your readers so they know what you're claiming and what to expect from your case. Forman's thesis is implied and can be stated as follows: *Political conservatives, most of whom now support racial profiling, ought to oppose it.*

## Choosing Reasons

Forman constructs his case around four reasons, all designed to appeal to his audience and undercut their support of racial profiling.

> *Thesis:* Political conservatives, most of whom now support racial profiling, ought to oppose it.
>
> *Reason 1:* Racial profiling is ineffective—it doesn't reliably identify criminals. (Strategy: Forman wants to take away the major justification for profiling, that it helps the police catch lawbreakers.)
>
> *Reason 2:* Racial profiling harasses law-abiding blacks just because they are black. (Strategy: Forman wants his readers, most of whom have not been stopped and frisked by the police, to appreciate how discriminatory profiling is and the damage it does to people's respect for authority.)
>
> *Reason 3:* Racial profiling violates the conservative principle that equates equal rights with equal responsibilities. (Strategy: Forman wants his readers to see that racial profiling contradicts his audience's values—in this instance, the relationship of individual achievement to full, equal participation in the community.)
>
> *Reason 4:* Racial profiling violates the conservative ideal of a color-blind society. (Strategy: Forman wants his audience to see that their reasons for opposing affirmative action apply with equal force to racial profiling.)

As you read Forman's argument, note how he arranges his reasons; the order of presentation matters. We have more to say later about his strategies for developing his reasons, especially his use of evidence.

*Figure 7.2   Hulbert Waldroup, the artist who painted the controversial mural of Amadou Diallo in the Bronx near where Diallo was shot, signs his initials to his latest work, a painting on racial profiling, after unveiling it in Times Square, Tuesday, July 24, 2001, in New York. Waldroup says his work portrays racial profiling "through the eyes of a cop—what he sees, what he thinks, the stereotypes we are all responsible for." (AP Photo/Kathy Willens)*

## Arrested Development:
## The Conservative Case against Racial Profiling
### James Forman, Jr.

The Maya Angelou Public Charter School in Washington, D.C., is the kind of institution conservatives love—a place that offers opportunity but demands responsibility. Students are in school ten and a half hours per day, all year long, mostly studying core subjects like reading, writing, math, and history. When not in class, they work in student-run businesses, where they earn money and learn job skills. Those who achieve academically are held in high esteem not only by their teachers but by their peers. Those who disrupt class or otherwise violate the rules are subject to punishment, including expulsion, as determined by a panel of students and teachers.

The results have been impressive. Most Maya Angelou students had academic difficulty at their previous schools. In fact, more than one-half had stopped even attending school on a regular basis before they came to Maya

Angelou, while more than one-third had been in the juvenile court system. Yet more than 90 percent of its graduates go on to college, compared with a citywide rate of just 50 percent. This success stems in part from the school's small classes, innovative curriculum, and dedicated staff. But it is also due to its fundamentally conservative ethos: If you work hard and don't make excuses, society will give you a chance, no matter what your background is.

I can speak to this with some authority because I helped establish the school four years ago and still teach an elective there today. But, for all the school's accomplishments, we keep running up against one particularly debilitating problem. It's awfully hard to convince poor, African American kids that discrimination isn't an obstacle, that authority must be respected, and that individual identity matters more than racial identity when experiences beyond school walls repeatedly contradict it. And that's precisely what's happening today, thanks to a policy many conservatives condone: Racial profiling by the police.

The prevalence of racial profiling is no secret. Numerous statistical studies have shown that being black substantially raises the odds of a person being stopped and searched by the police—even though blacks who are stopped are no more likely than whites to be carrying drugs. As David Cole and John Lamberth recently pointed out in *The New York Times*, in Maryland "73 percent of those stopped and searched on a section of Interstate 95 were black, yet state police reported that equal percentages of the whites and blacks who were searched, statewide, had drugs or other contraband." Blacks were actually far less likely than whites to be found carrying drugs in New Jersey, a state whose police force has acknowledged the use of racial profiling. According to Cole and Lamberth, consensual searches "yielded contraband, mostly drugs, on 25 percent of whites, 13 percent of blacks and only 5 percent of Latinos."

Behind these statistics are hundreds if not thousands of well-chronicled anecdotes, some from America's most prominent black citizens. Erroll McDonald, vice president and executive editor of Pantheon publishing, was driving a rented Jaguar in New Orleans when he was stopped—simply "to show cause why I shouldn't be deemed a problematic Negro in a possibly stolen car." . . .

Even off-duty black police frequently tell of being harassed by their unsuspecting white colleagues. Consider the case of Robert Byrd, an eleven-year veteran of the D.C. police, who was off duty and out of uniform when he tried to stop a carjacking and robbery in Southeast Washington last March. After witnessing the crime, Byrd used his police radio to alert a police dispatcher, then followed the stolen van in his own. Byrd got out of his van as marked police vehicles arrived. According to Byrd, white officers then began beating him in the belief that he was the African American suspect. The real perpetrators were caught later that night.

None of these stories would surprise the students at Maya Angelou. Almost weekly this past spring, officers arrived at the corner of 9th and

5

T Streets NW (in front of our school), threw our students against the wall, and searched them. As you might imagine, these are not polite encounters. They are an aggressive show of force in which children are required to "assume the position": legs spread, face against the wall or squad car, hands behind the head. Police officers then search them, feeling every area of their bodies. Last spring, a police officer chased one male student into the school, wrestled him to the ground, then drew his gun. Another time, when a student refused a police request to leave the corner in front of our school (where the student was taking a short break between classes, in complete compliance with school rules and D.C. law), the officer grabbed him, cuffed him, and started putting him into a police van, before a school official intervened. These students committed no crime other than standing outside a school in a high-drug-use neighborhood. Indeed, despite the numerous searches, no drugs have ever been discovered, and no student has ever been found in violation of the law.

Liberals generally decry such incidents; conservatives generally deny that they take place. "[T]he racial profiling we're all supposed to be outraged about doesn't actually happen very much," explained Jonah Goldberg in his *National Review Online* column last spring. And even those conservatives who admit the practice's frequency often still insist it does more good than harm. "The evidence suggests," William Tucker wrote in a recent issue of *The Weekly Standard*, "that racial profiling is an effective law enforcement tool, though it undeniably visits indignity on the innocent."

In other words, liberals—who are generally more concerned about individual rights and institutionalized racism—believe racial profiling contradicts their principles. Conservatives, on the other hand—who tolerate greater invasions of privacy in the name of law and order—consider racial profiling to be generally consistent with theirs. But conservatives are wrong—racial profiling profoundly violates core conservative principles.

It is conservatives, after all, who remind us that government policy    10
doesn't affect only resources; it affects values, which in turn affect people's behavior. This argument was at the heart of the conservative critique of welfare policy. For years, conservatives (along with some liberals) argued that welfare policies—like subsidizing unmarried, unemployed women with children—fostered a culture of dependency. Only by demanding that citizens take responsibility for their own fates, the argument went, could government effectively combat poverty.

But if sending out welfare checks with no strings attached sends the wrong message, so does racial profiling. For the conservative ethos about work and responsibility to resonate, black citizens must believe they are treated the same way as white citizens—that with equal responsibilities go equal rights. In *The Dream and the Nightmare*, which President Bush cites as one of the most influential books he has ever read, the conservative theorist Myron Magnet writes: "[W]hat underclass kids need most . . . is an authoritative link to traditional values of work, study, and self-improvement, and the assurance that these values can permit them to claim full membership in the larger community." Magnet quotes Eugene Lange, a businessman who promised scholarships to inner-city kids who graduated from high school: "It's important that [inner-city kids] grow up to recognize that they are not perpetuating a life of the pariah, but that the resources of the community are legitimately theirs to take advantage of and contribute to and be a part of."

Magnet is right. But random and degrading police searches radically undermine this message. They tell black kids that they are indeed pariahs—that, no matter how hard they study, they remain suspects. As one Maya Angelou first-year student explained to me: "We can be perfect, perfect, doing everything right, and they still treat us like dogs. No, worse than dogs, because criminals are treated worse than dogs." Or, as a junior asked me, noting the discrepancy between the message delivered by the school and the message delivered by the police: "How can you tell us we can be anything if they treat us like we're nothing?"

Indeed, people like myself—teachers, counselors, parents—try desperately to convince these often jaded kids that hard work really will pay off. In so doing, we are quite consciously pursuing an educational approach that conservatives have long advocated. We are addressing what conservative criminologist James Q. Wilson calls "intangible problems—problems of 'values,'" the problems that sometimes make "blacks less likely to take advantage of opportunities." But we are constantly fighting other people in the neighborhood who tell kids that bourgeois norms of work, family, and sexuality are irrelevant and impossible. Since the state will forever treat you as an outlaw, they say, you might as well act like one. Every time police single out a young black man for harassment, those other people sound more credible—and we sound like dupes.

Then there's that other vaunted conservative ideal: color-blindness. In recent years, conservatives have argued relentlessly for placing less emphasis on race. Since discrimination is on the wane, they suggest, government itself must stop making race an issue—i.e., no more affirmative action in admissions, no more set-asides in contracting, no more tailoring of government programs to favor particular racial or ethnic groups. In the words of affirmative action critics Abigail and Stephen Thernstrom, it's essential to fight the "politics of racial grievance" and counter the "suspicion that nothing fundamental [has] changed." Society, says Magnet, "needs to tell [blacks] that they can do it—not that, because of past victimization, they cannot."

But it's hard to tell young black men that they are not victims because of their race when police routinely make them victims because of their race. Students at Maya Angelou are acutely aware that the police do not treat young people the same way at Sidwell Friends and St. Albans, schools for Washington's overwhelmingly white elite. As another Maya Angelou first-year told me, "You think they would try that stuff with white kids? Never." Such knowledge makes them highly suspicious of the conservative asser-

15

tion that blacks should forego certain benefits—such as racial preferences in admissions—because of the moral value of color-blindness. Why, they wonder, aren't white people concerned about that principle when it hurts blacks as well as when it benefits them? And racial profiling makes them cynical about the conservative demand that blacks not see the world in racialized, group-identity terms. Why, they wonder, don't white people demand the same of the police?

Most conservatives who support racial profiling are not racist; they simply consider the practice an essential ingredient of effective law enforcement. But it isn't. Indeed, the great irony of conservative support for racial profiling is that conservative principles themselves explain why racial profiling actually makes law enforcement less effective.

. . . [D]iscriminatory police practices create unnecessary and unproductive hostility between police and the communities they serve. Imagine that you are 17, standing outside your school during a break from class, talking to friends, laughing, playing, and just relaxing. Imagine that squad cars pull up; officers jump out, shouting, guns drawn; and you are thrown against the wall, elbowed in the back, legs kicked apart, and violently searched. Your books are strewn on the ground. You ask what's going on, and you are told to "shut the fuck up" or you will be taken downtown. When it finally ends, the officers leave, giving no apology, no explanation, and you are left to fix your clothes, pick up your books, and gather your pride. Imagine that this is not the first time this has happened to you, that it has happened repeatedly, in one form or another, throughout your adolescence. Now imagine that, the day after the search, there is a crime in your neighborhood about which you hear a rumor. You know the police are looking for information, and you see one of the officers who searched you yesterday (or indeed any officer) asking questions about the crime. How likely are you to help? . . .

---

### Arranging Reasons

Conservative support for racial profiling depends upon belief in its effectiveness, especially in combating the traffic in illegal drugs. Forman therefore challenges this belief first. If he can show that profiling doesn't produce the results claimed for it, his readers should then be more receptive to his other reasons, all of which establish its negative impact.

His second reason has force because no law-abiding citizen wants to be treated as if she or he were suspected of criminal activity. No matter who you are, however, and no matter what you are doing, you can be so treated if you fit the profile. Such harassment would not be tolerated by the conservative, mostly white audience Forman is trying to reach and so should not be condoned by that audience when directed toward other racial and ethnic groups. It's a matter of fairness.

Forman's first two reasons engage relatively concrete and easily grasped issues: Does racial profiling work? Are innocent people harassed when it's used? His third and fourth reasons are more abstract and depend on the reader's recognition of contradiction and desire to be consistent. If we oppose welfare because it encourages dependency and lack of personal responsibility, shouldn't we oppose racial profiling because it "tell[s] black kids that they are indeed pariahs—that, no matter how hard they study, they remain suspects"? Similarly, if we oppose affirmative action because it favors people because of their race, shouldn't we also oppose profiling because it, too, singles out race? Rational people want to be consistent; Forman shows his readers that they haven't been consistent—a powerful strategy after he's argued that profiling doesn't work and harasses innocent people.

## Using Evidence

How well does Forman use the third level of case structure, the supporting evidence for each reason?

Note that he uses different *kinds* of evidence appropriately. To support his contention that racial profiling doesn't work, he cites *data*—in this case, statistical evidence—showing that blacks are no more likely, or even less so, than whites or Latinos to be caught with contraband (paragraph 4). Profiling blacks, therefore, makes no sense. Next, he uses *individual examples* to confirm that innocent people, including police officers, are treated as suspects simply because their skin is black. These individual examples may have more impact than statistics because they personalize the problem. Used together, individual examples and statistics complement each other.

Then, in paragraph 7, Forman draws on *personal experience*, what he himself has observed as evidence. He's seen police shake down students at the school where he teaches. He wants his readers to *feel* the sense of violation involved and so offers a graphic description. Clearly, personal experience can be a powerful source of evidence.

Finally, to back up his last two reasons, Forman cites *well-known authorities*, prominent conservatives such as Myron Magnet and Abigail and Stephen Thernstrom (paragraphs 11 and 14). He cites these sources, obviously, because his audience considers them representative of their own viewpoint and therefore voices meriting respect. Forman combines these authorities with the voices of his own students, who gain additional credibility simply by being cited along with the experts.

Forman's essay merits close attention for its use of evidence alone. He employs different kinds of evidence, combines different types well, and never forgets that evidence must appeal to his audience.

## Introducing and Concluding the Argument

We have analyzed Forman's strategic use of the three levels of case structure—thesis, reasons, and evidence—to build an argument that should convince his audience not to support racial profiling. Arguing to convince also requires a writer to think strategically about ways to open and close the case.

*The Introduction*   When you read Forman's essay the first time, you may have thought that somehow we had attached the wrong title to an essay about school reform. Not until the end of the third paragraph does the author announce his actual subject, racial profiling. Why this long introduction about the Maya Angelou Public Charter School?

The introduction accomplishes at least the following key purposes. Conservatives are strong supporters of alternatives to public schools. One of these is the charter school, and the author uses his story about a highly successful one to confirm conservative policy about educational reform. Note how he emphasizes the seriousness of the curriculum and other school activities. He also points to the strict rules and discipline and how the Maya Angelou school has turned around standard public school failures, including kids headed for serious trouble with the law. All of this is likely to sound good to conservatives.

The story also establishes the author's authority as someone who makes conservative ideas and values work. Later on, when he cites his students' words to confirm his points, we do not doubt their authenticity or his trustworthiness in representing black reactions to racial profiling. We can see, then, how crucial the introduction is to setting up the case.

Finally, the introduction anticipates the contradictions he'll address later, especially in reasons 3 and 4. The Maya Angelou school has succeeded in educating the kind of student that other schools often don't reach. Kids who could be a public danger now and adult criminals later are apparently becoming good citizens instead. But everything the school has accomplished can be undone by racial profiling. Thus, conservative educational reform clashes with conservative law enforcement policy. They don't fit together, and clearly the former is more important than the latter because the school is creating students who will stay on the right side of the law. Forman is already implying that racial profiling must go, which is the whole point of his essay.

The point for us is that introductions shouldn't be dashed off carelessly, thrown together just because we know we need one. Our introductions must prepare the way for our case.

*The Conclusion*   Paragraphs 16 and 17 conclude his argument. What do they achieve?

Paragraph 16 states that most conservatives are not racists, that they just have been misled into thinking profiling works. In effect, these assertions release conservatives from the common accusation that they don't care about blacks and support policies that discriminate against them. Forman also reminds his readers that he has used *conservative principles* to explain why racial profiling diminishes police effectiveness.

Paragraph 17 explains in a concrete and memorable way how police tactics like profiling can interfere with law enforcement. He wants his readers to remember the harshness of the procedures and that the experience makes minorities suspicious of and uncooperative with police officers. We see the damage profiling does from the inside so to speak, and we cannot help but appreciate its negative consequences for law enforcement itself. The implied message is: If you value law and order, be against racial profiling. In this way, Forman advances his major point again but this time from another conservative vantage point — support for the police.

Like introductions, conclusions are not throwaways, not merely hasty summaries. Like introductions, they should do something, not just repeat what we've said already. The conclusion must clinch our case by ending it forcefully and memorably.

### Following Through

A successful essay has smooth transitions between its opening and its first reason and between its last reason and its conclusion, as well as between each reason in the body of the essay. In your writer's notebook, describe how Forman (1) announces that he is moving from his introduction to the first reason, from the first reason to the second, and so on and (2) at the same time links each section to what has come before.

## WRITING A CONVINCING ARGUMENT

Few people draft an essay sequentially, beginning with the first sentence of the first paragraph and ending with the last sentence of the last paragraph. But the final version of any essay must read as if it had been written sequentially with the writer fully in control throughout the process.

A well-written essay is like a series of moves in a chess game, in which each move is made to achieve some end or ends, to gain a strategic advantage, as part of an overall plan to win. In the case of convincing, the overall plan is to win the agreement of the reader.

Although readers may not be fully aware of the "moves" that make up a convincing argument, the writer probably created most of them more or less consciously. As we have seen in this chapter, we can learn much about how to convince by studying finished essays — polished arguments that convince. However, it is one thing to understand how something works and quite another to produce it ourselves. In part, the difficulty is that we cannot see from someone else's final product everything that went into making it work so well. Just as a movie audience typically cannot imagine all the rehearsals, the many takes, and the editing that make a scene powerful, so it is hard for us to imagine all the research and thinking, the many drafts, and the process of editing and proofreading that Forman must have gone through to make "Arrested Development" worth printing. Yet it is precisely this process you must understand and immerse yourself in if you are to go beyond appreciating the structure and strategies of someone else's writing to actually produce convincing arguments of your own.

1. Your thesis can be stated or implied, but **you and your readers must have no doubt about what you're contending.**
2. **Begin with your most important reason.** (For example, if your audience supports racial profiling because they think it works, begin your case against profiling by showing them that it doesn't.)
3. In general, **provide the kind of evidence each reason requires.** (For example, if you contend that helmet laws will reduce head injuries in motorcycle accidents, such a reason requires *data* for support. In contrast, if you contend that helmet laws do not seriously intrude upon personal freedom, data won't help—you must show that helmet laws are no more restrictive than other laws we accept as justified, such as seat belt or maximum speed laws.)
4. Use the **full range** of evidence available (data, individual examples, personal experience, expert opinion, etc.). When possible and appropriate, **mix different kinds of evidence to support a single reason.**
5. **Devote serious effort to introductions and conclusions.** They should accomplish definite tasks, such as generating interest at the beginning and leaving your reader with something memorable at the end. Avoid "throw-away," high school introductions that begin with "In this essay, I will discuss . . ." or "In conclusion . . ." conclusions.

The following discussion of the composing process assumes that the work of research (Chapter 5) and inquiry (Chapter 6) has already been done. It also assumes that you have worked out a rhetorical prospectus (see Chapter 1, page 21) to guide you in combining structure with strategy.

## Preparing a Brief

Before you begin to draft, it is a good idea to prepare a brief. Recall that we defined *case structure* as the basic components of any case. In a brief, you adapt case structure to make a particular argument. The brief shows the thesis and reasons you plan to use and gives some indication of how you will support each reason with evidence. The brief ought to indicate a tentative plan for arranging the reasons, but that plan may change as you draft and revise.

### Working toward a Position

First, we need to distinguish a position from a thesis. A **position** (or a stance or opinion) amounts to an overall, summarizing attitude or judgment about some issue. "Universities often exploit student athletes" is an example of a position. A **thesis** is not only more specific and precise but also more strategic, designed to appeal to readers and to be consistent with available evidence. For example, "Student athletes in revenue-generating sports ought to be paid for their services" is one possible thesis representing the preceding position, perhaps for an audience of college students. Because a case is nothing more than the reasons and evidence that support a thesis, we cannot construct a case without a thesis. But without a position, we do not know where we stand in general on an issue and so cannot experiment with various thesis formulations. So a position typically precedes a thesis.

The goal of inquiry is to earn an opinion, to find a stance that holds up in dialogue with other inquirers. What often happens in inquiry, however, is that we begin with a strong opinion, usually unearned, find it failing under scrutiny, discover other positions that do not fully satisfy us, and so emerge from inquiry uncertain about what we do think. Another common path in inquiry is to start out with no opinion at all, find ourselves attracted to several conflicting positions, and so wind up in much the same condition as the person whose strong initial position collapses under scrutiny—unsure, confused, even vexed because we can't decide what to think.

In such situations, resolve first to be patient with yourself. Certainty is often cheap and easy; the best, most mature positions typically come to us only after a struggle. Second, take out your writer's notebook and start making lists. Look over your research materials, especially the notecards on which you have recorded positions and evidence from your sources. Make lists in response to these questions:

> What positions have you encountered in research and class discussion?
> What seems strongest and weakest in each stance? What modifications might be made to eliminate or minimize the weak points? Are there other possible positions? What are their strong and weak points?
> What evidence impressed you? What does each piece of evidence imply or suggest? What connections can you draw among the pieces of evidence given in various sources? If there is conflict in the implications of the evidence, what is that conflict?

While all this list-making at times may seem to be only doodling, you can often begin to see convergences as you begin to sort things out.

Bear in mind that although emotional commitment to ideas and values is important to a healthy life, it is often an impediment to clear thought and effective convincing. Sometimes we find our stance by relinquishing a strongly held opinion for which a case proves hard to make—perhaps for lack of compelling reasons or evidence that appeals to readers outside the group who already agrees with us. The more emotional the issue—abortion, pornography, affirmative action, among others—the more likely we are to cling to a position that is difficult to defend. When we sense deep conflict, when we want to argue a position even in the face of strong contradictory evidence and counter-arguments to which we cannot respond, it is time to reconsider our emotional commitments and perhaps even to change our minds.

Finally, if you find yourself holding out for the "perfect" position, the one that is all strength and no weakness, the best advice is to give up. Controversial issues are controversial precisely because no single stance convinces everyone, because there is always room for counterargument and for other positions that have their own power to convince.

*Student Sample: Working toward a Position*   Justin Spidel's class began by reading many arguments about homosexuality and discussing issues related to gay rights. Justin decided to investigate whether same-sex marriage should be legal. His initial perspective on the issue was that same-sex marriage ought to be legal because he thought that gays and lesbians should be treated as equals and that no harm would result. As he did research, he learned that a majority of Americans strongly oppose same-sex marriage, mainly because they believe its legalization would change a long-standing definition of marriage and alter its sacred bond. Justin read articles opposing gay marriage by such well-known public figures as William Bennett, but he also read many in favor. He found especially convincing the arguments by gays and lesbians who were in long-standing, loving, monogamous relationships but who were barred from marrying their partners. Justin's initial round of research led him to the position "Gays and lesbians should be able to marry."

During the inquiry stage, Justin discussed his position with his classmates and instructor. Knowing that gays and lesbians do sometimes get married in churches, Justin's classmates asked him to clarify the phrase "able to marry." Justin explained that he meant legal recognition of same-sex marriages by individual state governments and therefore all states, as marriage in any one state is usually recognized by the rest. When asked if other countries recognize same-sex marriage, Justin admitted that only Denmark does. He decided to argue for his position anyway on the grounds that the United States should take the lead in valuing equality and individual rights. He was asked about the implications of his position: Would granting legal status to same-sex marriage devalue the institution? Justin responded that the people who are fighting for legalization have the deepest respect for marriage and that marriage is about love and commitment rather than sexual orientation.

## Following Through

Formulate a tentative position on a topic that you have researched and into which you have inquired. Write it up with a brief explanation of why you support this stand. Be prepared to defend your position in class or with a peer in a one-on-one exchange of position statements.

### Analyzing the Audience

Before you decide on a thesis, give some thought to the rhetorical context of your argument. Who needs to hear it? What are their values? What common ground might you share with them? How might you have to qualify your position to influence their opinions?

To provoke thought, people occasionally make cases for theses that they know have little chance of winning significant assent. One example is the argument for legalizing all drug use; although reasonably good cases have been made for this position, most Americans find it too radical to be convincing. If you want to convince rather than provoke, you must formulate a thesis that both represents your position and creates as little resistance in your readers as possible. Instead of arguing for legalizing drugs, for example, you might argue that much of the staggering amount of money spent on enforcement, prosecution, and imprisonment should be diverted to rehabilitation and social problems connected with drug abuse. Because most positions allow for many possible theses, a writer should analyze the audience before settling on one.

*Student Sample: Analyzing the Audience* Justin knew that many people would view same-sex marriage as a very radical idea. Some possible audiences, such as conservative Christians, would never assent to it. So Justin targeted an audience he had some chance of convincing—people who opposed same-sex marriage but were not intolerant of homosexuals. Justin wrote the following audience profile:

> My audience would be heterosexual adults who accept that some people are homosexual or lesbian; they may know people who are. They would be among the nearly 47 percent of Americans who do not object to same-sex relationships between consenting adults. They may be fairly well educated and could belong to any age group, from college students to grandparents. They are not likely to have strong religious objections, so my argument will not have to go deeply into the debate about whether homosexuality is a sin. However, these readers oppose legalizing marriage between gays and lesbians because they think it would threaten the traditional role of marriage as the basis of family life. They think that marriage has come into enough trouble lately through divorce, and they want to preserve its meaning as much as possible. Their practical position would be that if same-sex couples want to live together and act like they're married, there is nothing to stop them, so they are really not being hurt by leaving things as they are. They believe in the value of heterosexual marriage for the individual and society, so I can appeal to that. They also hold to basic American principles of equal rights and the right to the "pursuit of happiness." But mainly I want to show my readers that gays and lesbians are missing out on some basic civil rights and that letting them marry would have benefits for everyone.

### Following Through

Write a profile of the audience you hope to reach through an argument you are currently planning. Be as specific as possible; include any information—age, gender, economic status, and so forth—that may con-

(continues)

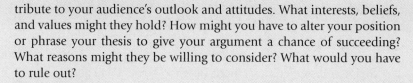

**Following Through (continued)**

tribute to your audience's outlook and attitudes. What interests, beliefs, and values might they hold? How might you have to alter your position or phrase your thesis to give your argument a chance of succeeding? What reasons might they be willing to consider? What would you have to rule out?

## Developing a Thesis

A good thesis grows out of a combination of things: your position, your research, your exploration of reasons to support your position, and your understanding of the audience. During the process of drafting, you may refine the thesis by phrasing it more precisely, but for now you should concentrate only on stating a thesis that represents your position clearly and directly.

We advise against trying to make your thesis do more than simply present the claim. Naturally, your mind runs to reasons in support, but it makes more sense to save the reasons until you can present them thoroughly as the body of the paper unfolds.

*Student Sample: Developing a Thesis*    Justin's original statement, "Gays and lesbians should be able to marry," expresses a position, but it could be more precise and better directed toward the readers Justin defined in his audience profile. He already had some reasons to support his argument, and he wanted the thesis to represent his current position accurately without locking him into some rigid plan. He refined his position to the following:

A couple's right to marry should not be restricted because of sexual orientation.

This version emphasized that marriage is a right everyone should enjoy, but it did not go far enough in suggesting why the readers should care or recognize it as a right. Justin tried again:

Every couple who wishes to commit to each other in marriage should have the right to do so, regardless of sexual preference.

Justin was fairly satisfied with this version because it appealed to a basic family value—commitment.

He then started thinking about how committed relationships benefit society in general, an argument that would appeal to his readers. He wondered if he could point the thesis not just in the direction of rights for homosexuals and lesbians but also in the direction of benefits for everyone, which would broaden his appeal. It would also allow him to develop his essay further by using some good arguments he had encountered in his reading. He tried one more time and settled on the following thesis:

Everyone, gay and straight, will benefit from extending the basic human right of marriage to all couples, regardless of sexual preference.

### Following Through

1. Write at least three versions of a tentative thesis for the essay on which you are currently working. For each version, write an evaluation of its strengths and weaknesses. Why is the best version the best?
2. As we saw in analyzing William May's case against assisted suicide (Chapter 3), sometimes a thesis needs to be qualified and exceptions to the thesis stated and clarified. Now is a good time to think about qualifications and exceptions.

You can handle qualifications and exceptions in two ways. First, you can add a phrase to your thesis that limits it, as William May did in his argument on assisted suicide: "*On the whole,* our social policy . . . should not regularize killing for mercy." May admits that a few extreme cases of suffering justify helping someone die. The other method is to word the thesis in such a way that exceptions or qualifications are implied rather than spelled out. As an example, consider the following thesis: "Life sentences with no parole are justifiable for all sane people found guilty of first-degree murder." Here the exceptions would be "those who are found insane" and "those tried on lesser charges."

Using your best thesis statement from the previous exercise, decide whether qualifications and exceptions are needed. If they are, determine how best to handle them.

*Analyzing the Thesis*

Once you have a thesis, your next task is to *unpack* it to determine what you must argue. To do this, put yourself in the place of your readers. To be won over, what must they find in your argument? Answering that question requires looking very closely at both what the thesis says and what it implies. It also requires thinking about the position and attitudes of your readers as you described them earlier in your audience profile.

Although many thesis sentences appear simple, analysis shows that they are quite complex. Let's consider a thesis on the issue of whether Mark Twain's *Huckleberry Finn* should be taught in the public schools. Some have argued that Twain's classic novel should be removed from required reading lists because a number of readers, especially African Americans, find its subject matter and language offensive. In fact, in some schools the novel is not assigned at all, whereas in others it may be assigned, but students have the option of choosing to study another novel of the same period instead. In our example thesis, the writer supports the teaching of the novel: "Mark Twain's *Huckleberry Finn* should be required reading for all high school students in the United States."

Unpacking this thesis, we see that the writer must first argue for *Huckleberry Finn* as *required* reading—not merely as a good book but also as one that is indispensable to an education in American literature. The writer must also argue that the book should be required at the high school level rather than in middle school or college. Finally, knowing that some people find certain passages offensive, the author must defend the novel from charges of racism, even though the thesis does not explicitly state, "*Huckleberry Finn* is not a racist book." Otherwise, these charges stand by default; to ignore them is to ignore the context of the issue.

*Student Sample: Analyzing the Thesis*   By analyzing his thesis—"Everyone, gay and straight, will benefit from extending the basic human right of marriage to all couples, regardless of sexual preference"—Justin realized that his main task was to explain specific benefits that would follow from allowing gays to marry. He knew that he would have to cite ways in which society, as well as those in same-sex relationships who want to marry, will be better off. He knew that his readers would agree that marriage is a "basic human right" for heterosexual adults, but he could not assume that they would see it that way for homosexual couples. Therefore, he had to make them see that same-sex couples have the same needs as other couples. He also wanted to make certain that his readers understood that he was arguing only that the law of the land should recognize such marriages, not that all churches and denominations should sanctify them.

## Following Through

Unpack a tentative thesis of your own or one that your instructor gives you to see what key words and phrases an argument based on that thesis must address. Also consider what an audience would expect you to argue given a general knowledge about the topic and the current context of the dispute.

### Finding Reasons

For the most part, no special effort goes into finding reasons to support a thesis. They come to us as we attempt to justify our opinions, as we listen to the arguments of our classmates, as we encounter written arguments in research, and as we think about how to reach the readers we hope to convince. Given good writing preparation, we seldom formulate a thesis without already having some idea of the reasons we will use to defend it. Our problem, rather, is usually selection—picking out the best reasons and shaping and stating them in a way that appeals to our readers. When we do find ourselves searching for reasons, however, it helps to be aware of their common sources.

*The Audience's Belief System*   Ask yourself, What notions of the real, the good, and the possible will my readers entertain? Readers will find any reason unconvincing if it is not consistent with their understanding of reality. For example, based on their particular culture's notions about disease, people will accept or reject arguments about how to treat illness. Likewise, people have differing notions of what is good. Some people think it is good to exploit natural resources so that we can live with more conveniences; those who place less value on conveniences see more good in preserving the environment. Finally, people disagree about what is possible. Those who believe it is not possible to change human nature will not accept arguments that certain types of criminals can be rehabilitated.

*Special Rules or Principles*   Good reasons can also be found in a community's accepted rules and principles. For example, in the United States, citizens accept the principle that a person is innocent until proven guilty. The Fourteenth Amendment states that no one may be "deprived of life, liberty, or property, without due process of law." We apply this principle in all sorts of nonlegal situations whenever we argue that someone should be given the benefit of the doubt.

The law is only one source of special rules or principles. We also find them in politics ("one person, one vote"), in business (the principle of seniority, which gives preference to employees who have been on a job longest), and even in the home, where each family formulates its own house rules. In other words, all human settings and activities have their own norms, and in any search for reasons we must ask ourselves what norms may apply to our particular topic or thesis.

*Expert Opinion and Hard Evidence*   Probably the next most common source of reasons is expert opinion, on which we must rely when we lack direct experience with a particular subject. Most readers respect the opinion of a trained professional with advanced degrees and prestige in his or her field. And when you can show that experts are in agreement, you have an even better reason.

Hard evidence can also provide good reasons. Readers generally respect the scientific method of gathering objective data upon which conclusions can be drawn. Research shows, for example, that wearing a bicycle helmet significantly reduces the incidence of head injuries from accidents. Therefore, we can support the thesis "Laws should require bicycle riders to wear helmets" with the reason "because statistics show that fewer serious head injuries occurred in bicycle accidents when the riders were wearing helmets than when no helmets were worn."

When you argue about any topic, you will be at a disadvantage if you don't have detailed, current information about it in the form of expert opinion and hard evidence.

*Tradition*   We can sometimes strengthen a position by citing or alluding to well-known sources that are part of our audience's cultural tradition — for example, the Bible, the Constitution, and the sayings or writings of people our readers recognize and respect. Although reasons drawn from tradition may lose their force if many audience members identify with different cultures or are suspicious of tradition itself, they will almost always be effective when readers revere the source.

*Comparison*  A reason based on similarity argues that what is true in one instance should be true in another. For example, we could make a case for legalizing marijuana by showing that it is similar in effect to alcohol, which is legal — and also a drug. The argument might look like this:

> *Thesis:* Marijuana use should be decriminalized.
>
> *Reason:* Marijuana is no more harmful than alcohol.

Many comparison arguments attempt to show that present situations are similar to past ones. For example, many who argue for the civil rights of gays and lesbians say that discrimination based on sexual preference should not be tolerated today just as discrimination based on race, common thirty years ago, is no longer tolerated.

A special kind of argument based on similarity is an *analogy*, which attempts to explain one thing, usually abstract, in terms of something else, usually more concrete. For example, in an argument opposing sharing the world's limited resources, philosopher Garrett Hardin reasons that requiring the wealthy nations of the world to feed the starving nations is analogous to requiring the occupants of a lifeboat filled to a safe capacity to take on board those still in the water until the lifeboat sinks and everyone perishes.

Arguments of comparison can also point to difference, showing how two things are not the same, not analogous. For example, many Americans supported participation in the 1992 Persian Gulf War by arguing that, unlike the disastrous conflict in Vietnam, this war was winnable. The argument went as follows:

> *Thesis:* America can defeat Iraq's military.
>
> *Reason:* Warfare in the deserts of Kuwait and Iraq is very different from warfare in the jungles of Vietnam.

*The Probable or Likely*  Of course, all reasoning about controversial issues relies on making a viewpoint seem probable or likely, but specific reasons drawn from the probable or likely may often come into play when we want to defend one account of events over another or when we want to attack or support a proposed policy. For example, defenders of Supreme Court nominee Clarence Thomas attempted to discredit Anita Hill's accusations of sexual harassment in a number of ways, all related to probability: Is it likely, they asked, that she would remember so clearly and in such detail events that happened as long as ten years ago? Is it probable that a woman who had been harassed would follow Thomas from one job to another, as Hill did?

Because a proposed policy may have no specific precedent, particularly if it is designed to deal with a new situation, sometimes all a writer can do who is arguing for or against the new policy is to speculate about its probable success or failure. For example, the collapse of communism in eastern Europe and the former Soviet Union has left the United States in the unusual position of having no serious military threat to its own or its allies' security. What, then, should we do—drastically reduce our armed forces, especially the nuclear arsenal? redirect part of what we once spent on defense into dealing with pressing domestic problems? Any proposal for confronting this new situation is defended and attacked based on what we are likely to face in the foreseeable future.

*Cause and Effect*    People generally agree that most circumstances result from some cause or causes, and they also agree that most changes in circumstances will result in some new effects. This human tendency to believe in cause-and-effect relationships can provide reasons for certain arguments. For example, environmentalists have successfully argued for reductions in the world's output of hydrofluorocarbons by showing that the chemicals damage the earth's ozone layer.

Cause-and-effect arguments are difficult to prove; witness the fact that cigarette manufacturers have argued for years that the connection between smoking and lung disease cannot be demonstrated. Responsible arguments from cause and effect depend on credible and adequate hard evidence and expert opinion. And they must always acknowledge the possible existence of hidden factors; smoking and lung disease, for example, may be influenced by genetic predisposition.

*Definition*    All arguments require definitions for clarification. However, a definition can often provide a reason in support of the thesis as well. If we define a term by placing it in a category, we are saying that whatever is true for the category is true for the term we are defining. For example, Elizabeth Cady Stanton's landmark 1892 argument for women's rights ("The Solitude of Self") was based on the definition "women are individuals":

> *Thesis:* Women must have suffrage, access to higher education, and sovereignty over their own minds and bodies.
>
> *Reason:* Women are individuals.

If Stanton's audience, the American Congress, accepted that all individuals are endowed with certain inalienable rights, Stanton's definition reminded them that women belong in the category of "individual" just as much as men do and so deserve the same rights.

Almost all good reasons come from one or some combination of these eight sources. However, simply knowing the sources will not automatically provide you with good reasons for your argument. Nothing can substitute for thoughtful research and determined inquiry. Approach each of these sources as an angle from which to think about your thesis statement and the results of your research and inquiry. They can help you generate reasons initially or find better reasons when the ones you have seem inadequate.

Finally, do not feel that quantity is crucial in finding good reasons. While it is good to brainstorm as many reasons as you can, focus on those that you think will appeal most to your audience and that you can develop thoroughly. A good argument is often based on just one or two good reasons.

*Student Sample: Finding Reasons*  Justin used the eight sources listed in this section to help find some of his reasons. He also considered his audience and the beliefs they would likely hold. Here are the possible reasons he found; note that each reason is stated as a complete sentence.

*From the audience's belief system:*
Marriage is primarily about love and commitment, not sex.
Marriage is a stabilizing influence in society.

*From rules or principles the audience would likely subscribe to:*
Everyone has an equal right to life, liberty, and the pursuit of happiness.

*From expert opinion (in this case, a lawyer and some noted authors on gay rights):*
Denying gays and lesbians the right to marry is an incredible act of discrimination.
Allowing gays and lesbians to marry will promote family values such as monogamy and the two-parent family.

*From comparison or analogy:*
Just as we once thought marriage between blacks and whites should be illegal, we now think same-sex marriage should be illegal.
Gay and lesbian couples can love each other just as devotedly as can heterosexual couples.

*From cause and effect:*
Marriage is a way for people to take care of each other rather than being a burden on society should they become ill or unemployed.

Justin now had far more ideas for his case than he needed. He now had to evaluate his list to check the fit between his thesis sentence and the reasons he thought were best.

## Following Through

Here is one way to brainstorm for reasons. First, list the eight sources for finding reasons discussed on pages 227–230 in your writer's notebook, perhaps on the inside front cover or on the first or last page — someplace where you can easily find them. Practice using these sources by writing your current thesis at the top of another page and then going through the list, writing down reasons as they occur to you.

## Selecting and Ordering Reasons

Selecting reasons from a number of possibilities depends primarily on two considerations: your thesis and your readers. Any thesis demands a certain line of reasoning. For example, the writer contending that *Huckleberry Finn* should be required reading in high school must offer a compelling reason for accepting no substitute — not even another novel by Mark Twain. Such a reason might be, "Because many critics and novelists see *Huckleberry Finn* as the inspiration for much subsequent American fiction, we cannot understand the American novel if we are not familiar with *Huckleberry Finn*." A reason of this kind — one that focuses on the essential influence of the book — is likely to appeal to teachers or school administrators.

It is often difficult to see how to order reasons prior to drafting. Because we can easily reorder reasons as we write and rewrite, in developing our case we need only attempt to discover an order that seems right and satisfies us as an overall sequence. The writer advocating *Huckleberry Finn*, for example, should probably first defend the novel from the charge that it is racist. Readers unaware of the controversy will want to know why the book needs defending, and well-informed readers will expect an immediate response to the book's critics because it is these critics' efforts to remove the book from classrooms that has created the controversy. Once the charge of racism has been disposed of, readers will be prepared to hear the reasons for keeping the book on required-reading lists.

Besides thinking about what your readers need and expect and how one reason may gain force by following another one, keep in mind a simple fact about memory: We recall best what we read last; next best, what we read first. A good rule of thumb, therefore, is to begin and end your defense of a thesis with your strongest reasons, the ones you want to emphasize. A strong beginning also helps keep the reader reading; a strong conclusion avoids a sense of anticlimax.

***Student Sample: Selecting and Ordering Reasons***    Justin generated eight possible reasons to support his position on gay and lesbian marriage. To help decide which ones to use, he looked again at his audience profile. What had he said about the concerns of people who oppose same-sex marriage? Which of his potential reasons would best address these concerns?

Because his audience did not believe that the ban on same-sex marriage was a great loss to gays and lesbians, Justin decided to use the lawyer's point that the ban is discriminatory. The audience's other main concern was with the potential effect of gay marriage on the rest of society, particularly traditional marriage and family. Therefore, Justin decided to use the reasons about the benefits of same-sex marriage to society: that family values would be reinforced and that marriage keeps people from burdening society if they become unable to support themselves.

Justin noticed that some of his reasons overlapped one another. For example, the point that marriage is a stabilizing influence was merely a general statement that was better expressed in combination with his more specific reasons about economic benefits and family values. And his reason that mentioned discrimination overlapped his point that it is wrong to deny "life, liberty, and the pursuit of happiness." Overlapping is common because there are many ways of saying the same idea.

What is the best strategy for arranging these reasons? Initially, Justin wanted to begin with the point about discrimination, but then he decided to appeal to his audience's interests by listing the advantages first. Saving the argument about discrimination until the second half of his essay would let him end more strongly with an appeal to the readers' sympathy and sense of fairness.

Then Justin rechecked his thesis to confirm that the reasons really supported it. He decided that his readers might not accept that marriage is a "basic human right" for those of the same sex, so he decided to add one more reason in support of the similarities between heterosexuals and homosexuals.

Justin wrote up the following brief version of his argument:

> *Thesis:* Everyone, gay and straight, will benefit from extending the basic human right of marriage to all couples, regardless of sexual preference.
>
> *Reason:* It would reinforce family values such as monogamy and the two-parent family.
>
> *Reason:* It would help keep people from burdening society.
>
> *Reason:* Denying people the right to marry is discrimination.
>
> *Reason:* The love homosexuals have for each other is no different from love between heterosexuals.

## Following Through

We call the case structure a flexible plan because as long as you maintain the three-level structure of thesis, reasons, and evidence, you can change everything else at will: throw out one thesis for another or alter its wording, add or take away reasons or evidence, or reorder both to achieve the desired impact. Therefore, when writing your brief, don't feel that the order in which you have found your reasons and evidence should determine their order in your essay. Rather, make your decisions based on the following questions:

What will my audience need or expect to read first?

Will one reason help set up another?

Which of my reasons are strongest? Can I begin and conclude my argument with the strongest reasons I have?

To a thesis you have already refined, now add the second level of your brief, the reason or reasons. Be ready to explain your decisions about selection and arrangement. Final decisions about ordering will often be made quite late in the drafting process—in a second or third writing. Spending a little time now, however, to think through possible orderings can save time later and make composing less difficult.

## Using Evidence

The skillful use of evidence involves many complex judgments. Let's begin with some basic questions.

**What Counts as Evidence?**   Because science and technology rely on the hard data of quantified evidence — especially statistics — some people assume that hard data are the only really good source of evidence. Such a view, however, is far too narrow for our purposes. Besides hard data, evidence includes the following:

- Quotation from authorities: expert opinion, statements from people with special knowledge about an issue, and traditional or institutional authorities such as respected political leaders, philosophers, well-known authors, and people who hold positions of power and influence. Besides books and other printed sources, you can gather both data and quotations from interviews with experts or leaders on campus and in the local community.
- Constitutions, statutes, court rulings, organizational bylaws, company policy statements, and the like.
- Examples and case histories (that is, extended narratives about an individual's or an organization's experience).
- The results of questionnaires that you devise and administer.
- Personal experience.

In short, evidence includes anything that confirms a good reason or that might increase your readers' acceptance of a reason advanced to justify your thesis.

**What Kind of Evidence Is Best?**   What evidence is best depends on what particular reasons call for. To argue for bicycle helmet legislation, we need to cite facts and figures — hard data — to back up our claim that wearing helmets reduces the number of serious head injuries caused by bicycling accidents. To defend *Huckleberry Finn* by saying that it is an indictment of racism will require evidence of a different kind: quoted passages from the novel itself, statements from respected interpreters, and so forth.

When you have many pieces of evidence to choose from, what is best depends on the quality of the evidence itself and its likely impact on readers. In general — especially for hard data — the best evidence is the most recent. Also, the more trusted and prestigious the source, the more authority it will have for readers. Arguments about the AIDS epidemic in the United States, for example, often draw on data from the Centers for Disease Control in Atlanta, a respected research facility that specializes in the study of epidemics. And because the nature of the AIDS crisis changes relatively quickly, the most recent information is the most authoritative.

Finally, always look for evidence that will give you an edge in winning reader assent. For example, given the charge that *Huckleberry Finn* is offensive to blacks, its vigorous defense by an African-American literary scholar would ordinarily carry more weight than its defense by a white scholar.

***How Much Evidence Is Needed?*** The amount of evidence required depends on two judgments: (1) the more crucial a reason is to your case and (2) the more resistant readers are likely to be to a reason. Most cases have at least one pivotal reason, one point upon which the whole case is built and upon which, therefore, the whole case stands or falls. Forman's case against racial profiling turns on our accepting its unreliability for detecting criminals. Such a pivotal reason needs to be supported at length, regardless of the degree of reader resistance to it; about one-fourth of Forman's essay supports his contention that racial profiling is unreliable.

Of course, a pivotal reason may also be the reason to which readers will be most resistant. For instance, many arguments supporting women's right to abortion depend on the point that a fetus cannot be considered a human being until it reaches a certain stage of development and, therefore, does not qualify for protection under the law. This reason is obviously both pivotal and likely to be contested by many readers, so devoting much space to evidence for the reason would be a justified strategy.

***Student Sample: Using Evidence*** Justin took the brief showing his case so far and on a large table laid out all of his notecards and the material he had photocopied and marked up during his research. He needed to find the expert opinions, quotations, statistics, dates, and other hard evidence that would support the reasons he intended to use. Doing this before starting to draft is a good idea because it reveals where evidence is lacking or thin and what further research is necessary. If you have a lot of sources, it may help to use different-colored markers to indicate which passages will work with which of your reasons. Justin was now able to add the third level—evidence—to his case structure, including the sources from which he took it. For articles longer than one page, he included page numbers to turn to as he drafted his paper.

> *Thesis:* Everyone, gay and straight, will benefit from extending the basic human right of marriage to all couples, regardless of sexual preference.
>
>> *Reason:* It would reinforce family values such as monogamy and the two-parent family.
>>
>>> *Evidence:* Marriage stabilizes relationships. (Sources: Rauch 23; Dean 114)
>>> *Evidence:* Children of gays and lesbians should not be denied having two parents. (Sources: Dean 114; Sullivan; Salholz)
>>> *Evidence:* If gays can have and adopt children, they should be able to marry. (Source: Salholz)

*Reason:* It would provide a means of keeping people from burdening society.
   *Evidence:* Spouses take care of each other. (Source: Rauch)

*Reason:* Denying gays and lesbians the right to marry is discriminatory.
   *Evidence:* Marriage includes rights to legal benefits. (Source: Dean 112)
   *Evidence:* Domestic partnerships fail to provide these rights. (Sources: Dean 112; Salholz)
   *Evidence:* Barring these marriages violates many democratic principles. (Sources: "Declaration"; Dean 113; Salholz)

*Reason:* The love homosexuals have for each other is no different from love between heterosexuals.
   *Evidence:* Many gays and lesbians are in monogamous relationships. (Source: Ayers 5)
   *Evidence:* They have the same need to make a public, legal commitment. (Source: Sullivan)

## Following Through

Prepare a complete brief for an argument. Include both reasons and some indication of the evidence you will use to support each one, along with a note about sources. Remember that a brief is a flexible plan, not an outline engraved in stone. The plan can change as you begin drafting.

## From Brief to Draft

Turning a rough outline or brief of your argument into a piece of prose is never easy. Even if you know what points to bring up and in what order, you will have to (1) determine how much space to devote to each reason, (2) work in your evidence from sources, and (3) smoothly incorporate and correctly cite all quotations, summaries, and paraphrases. Furthermore, you will have to create parts of the essay that are not represented in the brief, such as an introduction that appeals to your audience and a conclusion that does not simply rehash all that you have said before. As you draft, you may also see a need for paragraphs that provide background on your topic, clarify or define an important term, or present and rebut an opposing argument. Following are some suggestions and examples that you may find helpful as you begin to draft.

1. A position or general outlook on a topic is not a thesis. A thesis is a carefully worded **claim** that your entire essay backs up with reasons and evidence. **Experiment with various ways of stating your thesis** until it says *exactly* what you want it to say and at the same time creates the least resistance in your readers.

2. Be willing to give up or modify significantly a thesis you find you cannot support with good reasons and strong evidence that appeal *to your readers*. **We must argue a thesis that fits the available evidence,** which may differ a little or a lot from what we really believe.

3. Take the time to create a specific **audience profile.** What is the age, gender, and economic status of your target audience? What interests, beliefs, and values might they bring to your topic and thesis? Remember: There is no such thing as a "general audience." **We are always trying to convince some definite group of possible readers.**

4. **Unpack your thesis** in an effort to discover what you must argue to uphold it adequately. If you say, for instance, that *Huckleberry Finn* should be *required* reading in high school, you must show why *this particular novel* should be an experience shared by all American high school students. It won't be enough just to argue that it's a good book.

5. Select your reasons based on what you must argue to defend your thesis combined with what you think you should say **given your audience's prior knowledge, preconceptions, prejudices, and interests.**

6. Be prepared to **try out different ways of ordering your reasons.** The order that seemed best in your brief might not work best as you draft and redraft your essay.

## The Introduction

Some writers must work through a draft from start to finish, beginning every piece of writing with the introductory paragraph. They ask, How can you possibly write the middle unless you know what the beginning is like? Other writers feel they can't write the introduction until they have written the body of the argument. They ask, How can you introduce something until you know what it is you are introducing? Either approach will eventually get the job done, as long as the writer takes the rhetorical context and strategy into account when drafting the introduction and goes back to revise it when the draft is completed.

Introductions are among the hardest things to write well. Remember that an introduction need not be one paragraph; it is often two or even three short ones. A good introduction (1) meets the needs of the audience by setting up the topic with just enough background information and (2) goes right to the heart of the issue as it relates to the audience's concerns.

Should the introduction end with the thesis statement? This strategy works well in offering the easiest transition from brief to draft in that it immediately sets the stage for the reasons. However, the thesis need not be the last sentence in the introduction, and it need not appear explicitly until much later in the draft — or at all, provided that readers can tell what it is from the title or from reading the essay.

*Student Sample: The Introduction*   Our student writer Justin had to consider whether he needed to provide his readers with a detailed history of the institution of marriage and even whether people feel strongly about the value of marriage. Because they oppose same-sex marriage, he assumed that his readers were familiar with the traditions underpinning the institution. What would these readers need to be told in the introduction? Essentially that the gay and lesbian rights movement calls for extending to same-sex couples the legal right to marry and that Justin's argument supported its position.

For example, if Justin had opened with, "Americans' intolerant attitudes toward homosexuality are preventing a whole class of our citizens from exercising the right to marry," he would have been assuming that there are no valid reasons for denying same-sex marriage. Such a statement would offend his target audience members, who are not homophobic and might resent the implication that their arguments are based only on prejudice. Rather than confronting his readers, Justin's introduction attempts to establish some common ground with them:

> When two people fall deeply in love, they want to share every part of their lives with each other. For some, that could mean making a commitment, living together, and maybe having children together. But most people in love want more than that; they want to make their commitment public and legal through the ceremony of marriage, a tradition thousands of years old that has been part of almost every culture.
>
> But not everyone has the right to make that commitment. In this country and in most others, gays and lesbians are denied the right to marry. According to many Americans, allowing them to marry would destroy the institution and threaten traditional family values. Nevertheless, "advances in gay and lesbian civil rights [are] bringing awareness and newfound determination to many," and hundreds of same-sex couples are celebrating their commitment to each other in religious ceremonies (Ayers 6). These couples would like to make their unions legal, and we should not prohibit them. Everyone, gay and straight, will benefit from extending the basic human right of marriage to all couples, regardless of sexual orientation.

Justin's first paragraph builds common ground by offering an overview of marriage that his readers are likely to share. In the second paragraph, he goes on to introduce the conflict, showing his own awareness of the main objections offered by thoughtful critics of same-sex marriage. Notice the even tone with which he presents these views; this sort of care is what we define in Chapter 1 as paying attention to character—presenting yourself as fair and responsible. Finally, Justin builds common ground by showing the gay and lesbian community in a very positive light, as people who love and commit to each other just as heterosexuals do.

A good introduction attracts the reader's interest. To do this, writers use a number of techniques, some more dramatic than others. They may open with the story of a particular person whose experience illustrates some aspect of the topic. Or they may attempt to startle the reader with a surprising fact or opinion, as Jonathan Rauch, one of Justin's sources, did when he began his essay this way: "Whatever else marriage may or may not be, it is certainly falling apart." Generally, dictionary definitions are dull openers, but a *Newsweek* writer used one effectively to start her article on gay marriage: "Marry. 1 a) to join as husband and wife; unite in wedlock, b) to join (a man) to a woman as her husband, or (a woman) to a man as his wife." The technique works partly because the writer chose to use the definition not in an opening sentence but rather as an *epigraph*—words set off at the beginning of a piece of writing to introduce its theme. Pithy quotations work especially well as epigraphs. All of these are fairly dramatic techniques, but the best and most common bit of advice about openings is that specifics work better than generalizations at catching a reader's notice; this same *Newsweek* article had as its first sentence, "Say marriage and the mind turns to three-tiered cakes, bridal gowns, baby carriages."

How you choose to open depends on your audience. Popular periodicals like *Newsweek* are a more appropriate setting for high drama than are academic journals and college term papers, but every reader appreciates a writer's efforts to spark attention.

### The Body: Presenting Reasons and Evidence

We now turn to drafting the body paragraphs of the argument. Although it is possible in a short argument for one paragraph to fully develop one reason, avoid thinking in terms of writing only one paragraph per reason. Multiple paragraphs are generally required to develop and support a reason.

The key thing to remember about paragraphs is that each one is a unit that performs some function in presenting the case. You ought to be able to say what the function of a given paragraph is—and your readers ought to be able to sense it. Does it introduce a reason? Does it define a term? Does it support a reason by setting up an analogy? Does another paragraph support the same reason by offering examples or some hard data or an illustrative case?

Not all paragraphs need topic sentences to announce their main point. Try instead to open each paragraph with some hints that allow readers to recognize the function of the paragraph. For example, some transitional word or phrase could announce to readers that you are turning from one reason to a new one. When you introduce a new reason, be sure that readers can see how it relates to the thesis. Repeating a key word or offering a synonym for one of the words in the thesis is a good idea.

*Student Sample: Presenting Reasons and Evidence*   As an example, let's look at how Justin developed the first reason in his case. Recall that he decided to put the two reasons about benefits to society ahead of his reasons about discrimination. Of the two benefits he planned to cite, strengthening family values seemed the stronger reason, so he decided to lead off with that one. Notice how Justin uses a transitional phrase to connect his first reason to the introductory material (printed earlier), which had mentioned opposing views. Observe how Justin develops his reason over a number of paragraphs, by drawing upon multiple sources, using both paraphrase and direct quotation. (Justin uses the Modern Language Association style for citing his sources. See Chapter 5 for guidelines on quoting and citing sources.)

In contrast to many critics' arguments, allowing gays and lesbians to marry actually promotes family values because it encourages monogamy and gives children a two-parent home. As Jonathan Rauch, a gay writer, explains, marriage stabilizes relationships:

> One of the main benefits of publicly recognized marriage is that it binds couples together not only in their own eyes but also in the eyes of society at large. Around the partners is woven a web of expectations that they will spend nights together, go to parties together, take out mortgages together, buy furniture at Ikea together, and so on—all of which helps tie them together and keep them off the streets and at home. (23)

Some people would say that gays and lesbians can have these things without marriage simply by living together, but if you argue that marriage is not necessary for commitment, you are saying marriage is not necessary for heterosexuals either. Many people think it is immoral to live together and not have the legal bond of marriage. If gays and lesbians could marry, they would be "morally correct" according to this viewpoint. Craig Dean, a Washington, D.C., lawyer and activist for gay marriage, says that it is "paradoxical that mainstream America stereotypes Gays and Lesbians as unable to maintain long-term relationships, while at the same time denying them the very institutions to stabilize such relationships" (114).

Furthermore, many homosexual couples have children from previous marriages or by adoption. According to a study by the American Bar Association, gay and lesbian families with children make up six percent of the population in the United States (Dean 114). A secure environment is very important for raising children, and allowing same-sex couples to marry would promote these children having two parents, not just one. It would also send these children the positive message that marriage is the foundation for family life. As Andrew Sullivan, a senior editor of *The New Republic*, asks, why should gays be denied the very same family values that many politicians are arguing everyone else should have? Why should their children be denied these values? *Newsweek* writer Eloise Salholz describes a paradox: If "more and more homosexual pairs are becoming parents . . . but cannot marry, what kind of bastardized definition of family is society imposing on their offspring?"

At this point, Justin is ready to take up his next reason: Marriage provides a system by which people take care of each other, lessening the burden on society. Justin's entire essay appears on pages 246–249. You may wish to look it over carefully before you begin to draft your own essay. Note which paragraphs bring in the remaining reasons and which paragraphs smoothly present and rebut some opposing views.

## The Conclusion

Once you have presented your case, what else is there to say? You probably do not need to sum up your case; going over your reasons one more time is not generally a good strategy and will likely bore your readers. And yet you know that the conclusion is no place to introduce new issues.

Strategically, you want to end by saying, "Case made!" Here are some suggestions for doing so:

1. Look back at your introduction. Perhaps some idea you used there to attract your readers' attention could come into play again to frame the argument—a question you posed has an answer, or a problem you raised has a solution.
2. Think about the larger context into which your argument fits. For example, an argument that *Huckleberry Finn* should be taught in public high schools, even if some students are offended by its language, could end by pointing out that education becomes diluted and artificial when teachers and administrators design a curriculum that avoids all controversy.
3. If you end with a well-worded quotation, try to follow it up with some words of your own, as you normally would whenever you quote.
4. Be aware that too many conclusions run on after their natural endings. If you are dissatisfied with your conclusion, try lopping off the last one, two, or three sentences. You may uncover the real ending.
5. Pay attention to style, especially in the last sentence. An awkwardly worded sentence will not have a sound of finality, but one with some rhythmic punch or consciously repeated sounds can wrap up an essay neatly.

***Student Sample: The Conclusion***   Following is Justin's conclusion to his argument for same-sex marriage.

It's only natural for people in love to want to commit to each other; this desire is the same for homosexuals and lesbians as it is for heterosexuals. One recent survey showed that "over half of all lesbians and almost 40% of gay men" live in committed relationships and share a house together (Ayers 5). As Sullivan, who is gay, explains, "At some point in our lives, some of us are lucky enough to meet the person we truly love. And we want to commit to that person in front of family and country for the rest of our lives. It's the most simple, the most natural, the most human instinct in the world. How could anyone seek to oppose that?" And what does anyone gain when that right is denied? That's a question that everyone needs to ask themselves.

Justin's conclusion is unusual because although reasons usually appear in the body paragraphs of a written argument, Justin offers his fourth reason in the last paragraph: Gay and lesbian couples can love each other with the same devotion and commitment as can heterosexual couples. This reason and its development as a paragraph make an effective conclusion because they enable Justin to place the topic of same-sex marriage into the larger context of what marriage means and why anyone wishes to enter into it. Also, Justin was able to find a particularly moving quotation to convince his audience that this meaning is the same for homosexuals. The quotation could have ended the essay, but Justin wanted to conclude with words of his own that would make the readers think about their own positions.

### Following Through

Using your brief as a guide, write a draft version of your argument to convince. In addition to the advice in this chapter, refer to Chapter 5, which covers paraphrasing, summarizing, quoting, incorporating, and documenting source material.

## Revising the Draft

Too often, revising is confused with editing. Revising, however, implies making large changes in content and organization, not simply sentence-level corrections or even stylistic changes, which fall into the category of editing.

To get a sense of what is involved in revising, you should know that the brief of Justin Spidel's essay on pages 235–236 is actually a revised version. Justin had originally written a draft with his reasons presented in a different order and without three of the sources that now appear in his paper. When Justin exchanged drafts with another classmate who was writing on the same topic, he discovered that some of her sources would also help him develop more solidly his own case. The following paragraph was the original third paragraph of Justin's draft, immediately following the thesis. Read this draft version, and then note how in the revised essay, printed on pages 246–249, Justin improved this part of his argument by developing the point more thoroughly in two paragraphs and by placing them toward the end of the paper.

> Not to allow same-sex marriage is clearly discriminatory. The Human Rights Act of 1977 in the District of Columbia "prohibits discrimination based on sexual orientation. According to the Act, 'every individual shall have an equal opportunity to participate in the economic, cultural, and intellectual life of the District and have an *equal opportunity to participate in all aspects of life*'" (Dean 112). If politicians are going to make such laws, they need to recognize all their implications and follow them. Not allowing homosexuals to marry is denying the right to "participate" in an aspect of life that is important to every couple that has found love in each other. Also, the Constitution guarantees equality to every man and woman; that means nondiscrimination, something that is not happening for gays and lesbians in the present.

## Reading Your Own Writing Critically

As we explained in Chapter 2, to be a critical reader of arguments means to be an analytical reader. In that chapter, we made suggestions for reading any argument; here we focus on what to look for in reading your own writing critically.

*Read with an Eye to Structure* Remember, different parts of an argument perform different jobs. Read to see if you can divide your draft easily into its strategic parts, and be sure you can identify what role each group of paragraphs plays in the overall picture. The draft should reflect your brief, or you should be able to create a new brief from what you have written. If you have trouble identifying the working parts and the way they fit together, you need to see where points overlap, where you repeat yourself, or what distant parts actually belong together. This may be the time for scissors and tape, or electronic cutting and pasting if you are working at a computer.

*Read with an Eye to Rhetorical Context* You may need to revise to make the rhetorical context clearer: Why are you writing, with what aim, and to whom? You establish this reader awareness in the introduction, and so you need to think about your readers' values and beliefs as well as any obvious personal data that might help explain their position on the issue—age, gender, race, occupation, economic status, and so on. You may need to revise your introduction now, finding a way to interest your readers in what you have to say. The more specific you can make your opening, the more likely you are to succeed.

*Inquire into Your Own Writing*    Have a dialogue with yourself about your own writing. Some of the questions that we listed on pages 177–178 will be useful here:

1. Ask what you mean by the words that are central to the argument. Have you provided definitions when they are needed?
2. Find the reasons, and note their relation to the thesis. Be able to state the connection, ideally, with the word "because": *thesis* because *reason*.
3. Be able to state what assumptions lie behind your thesis and any of your reasons. Ask yourself, What else would someone have to be-lieve to accept this as valid? If your audience is unlikely to share the assumption, then you must add an argument for it — or change your thesis.
4. Look at your comparisons and analogies. Are they persuasive?
5. Look at your evidence. Have you offered facts, expert opinion, illus-trations, and so on? Have you presented these in a way that would not raise doubts but eliminate them?
6. Consider your own bias. What do you stand to gain from advocating the position you take? Is your argument self-serving or truth-serving?

### Getting Feedback from Other Readers

Because it is hard to be objective about your own work, getting a reading from a friend, classmate, teacher, or family member is a good way to see where revision would help. An unfocused reading, however, usually isn't crit-ical enough; casual readers may applaud the draft too readily if they agree with the thesis and condemn it if they disagree. Therefore, ask your readers to use a revision checklist, such as the one outlined in the "Reader's Check-list for Revision" on page 245.

### Following Through

1. After you have written a draft of your own argument, revise it using the suggestions in the preceding section. Then exchange your re-vised draft for a classmate's, and use the "Reader's Checklist for Re-vision" to guide you in making suggestions for each other's drafts.
2. Read the final version of Justin Spidel's argument on pages 246–249. Then apply the questions for inquiry listed on pages 177–178 to inquire into the case presented in his argument.
3. You may or may not agree with Justin Spidel's views on same-sex marriage; however, if you were assigned to suggest ways to improve his written argument, what would you advise him to do? Reread his audience profile (page 224), and use the "Reader's Checklist for Revision" to help you decide how his presentation could be improved.

1. Be sure you understand the writer's intended audience, by either discussing it with the writer or reading any notes the writer has provided. Then read through the entire draft. It is helpful to number the paragraphs so you can refer to them by number later.

2. If you can find an explicit statement of the author's thesis, underline or highlight it. If you cannot find one, ask yourself whether it is necessary that the thesis be stated explicitly, or could any reader infer it easily? If the thesis is easily inferred, restate it in your own words at the top of the first page of the draft.

3. Think about how the thesis could be improved. Is it offensive, vague, too general? Does it have a single focus? Is it clearly stated? Suggest more concrete diction, if possible.

4. Circle the key terms of the thesis—that is, the words most central to the point. Could there be disagreement about the meaning of any of these terms? If so, has the author clarified what he or she means by these terms?

5. Look for the structure and strategy of the argument. Underline or highlight the sentences that most clearly present the reasons, and write "Reason 1," Reason 2," and so forth in the margin. If identifying the reasons is not easy, indicate this problem to the author. Also think about whether the author has arranged the reasons in the best order. Make suggestions for improvement.

6. Identify the author's best reason. Why would it appeal to the audience? Has the author placed it strategically in the best position for making his or her case?

7. Look for any weak parts in the argument. What reasons need more or better support? Next to any weakly supported reasons, write questions to let the author know what factual information seems lacking, what sources don't seem solid or credible, what statements sound too general, or what reasoning—such as analogies—seems shaky. Are there any reasons for which more research is in order?

8. Ask whether the author shows an awareness of opposing arguments. Where? If not, should this be added? Even if you agree with the argument, take the viewpoint of a member of the opposition: What are the best challenges you can make to anything the author has said?

9. Evaluate the introduction and conclusion.

## Editing and Proofreading

The final steps of writing any argument are editing and proofreading, which we discuss in the appendix.

**STUDENT SAMPLE:** *An Essay Arguing to Convince*

WHO SHOULD HAVE THE RIGHT TO MARRY?

Justin Spidel

When two people fall deeply in love, they want to share every part of their lives with each other. For some, that could mean making a commitment, living together, and maybe having children together. But most people in love want more than that; they want to make their commitment public and legal through the ceremony of marriage, a tradition thousands of years old that has been part of almost every culture.

But not everyone has the right to make that commitment. In this country and in most others, gays and lesbians are denied the right to marry. According to many citizens and politicians, allowing them the right to marry would destroy the institution and threaten traditional family values. Nevertheless, "advances in gay and lesbian civil rights [are] bringing awareness and newfound determination to many," and hundreds of same-sex couples are celebrating their commitment to each other in religious ceremonies (Ayers 6). These couples would like to make their unions legal, and we should not prohibit them. Everyone, gay and straight, will benefit from extending the basic human right of marriage to all couples, regardless of sexual orientation.

In contrast to many critics' arguments, allowing gays and lesbians to marry actually promotes family values because it encourages monogamy and gives children a two-parent home. As Jonathan Rauch, a gay writer, explains, marriage stabilizes relationships:

> One of the main benefits of publicly recognized marriage is that it binds couples together not only in their own eyes but also in the eyes of society at large. Around the partners is woven a web of expectations that they will spend nights together, go to parties together, take out mortgages together, buy furniture at Ikea together, and so on—all of which helps tie them together and keep them off the streets and at home. (23)

Some people would say that gays and lesbians can have these things without marriage simply by living together, but if you argue that marriage is not necessary for commitment, you are saying marriage is not necessary for heterosexuals either. Many people think it is immoral to live together and not have the legal bond of marriage. If gays and lesbians could marry, they would be "morally correct" according to this viewpoint. Craig Dean, a Washington, D.C., lawyer and activist for gay marriage, says that it is "paradoxical that mainstream America stereotypes Gays and Lesbians as unable to maintain long-term relationships, while at the same time denying them the very institutions to stabilize such relationships" (114).

Furthermore, many homosexual couples have children from previous marriages or by adoption. According to a study by the American Bar Association, gay and lesbian families with children make up six percent of the population in the United States (Dean 114). A secure environment is very important for raising children, and allowing same-sex couples to marry would promote these children having two parents, not just one. It would also send these children the positive message that marriage is the foundation for family life. As Andrew Sullivan, a senior editor of *The New Republic,* asks, why should gays be denied the very same family values that many politicians are arguing everyone else should have? Why should their children be denied these values? *Newsweek* writer Eloise Salholz describes a paradox: If "more and more homosexual pairs are becoming parents . . . but cannot marry, what kind of bastardized definition of family is society imposing on their offspring?"

Also, binding people together in marriage benefits society because marriage provides a system for people to take care of each other. Marriage means that individuals are not a complete burden on society when they become sick, injured, old, or unemployed. Jonathan Rauch argues, "If marriage has any meaning at all, it is that when you collapse from a stroke, there will be at least one other person whose 'job' it is to drop everything and come to your aid" (22). Rauch's point is that this benefit of marriage would result from gay marriages as well as straight and in fact may be even more important for homosexuals and lesbians because their relationships with parents and other relatives may be strained, and they are also less likely than heterosexuals to have children to take care of them in their old age. Same-sex couples already show such devotion to each other; it's just that the public recognition of legal marriage helps keep all spouses together through hard times.

In spite of these benefits, many people say that same-sex marriage should not be allowed because it would upset our society's conventional definition of marriage as a bond between people of opposite sexes. As William Bennett has written, letting people of the same sex marry "would obscure marriage's enormously consequential function—procreation and childrearing." Procreation may be a consequence of marriage, but it is not the main reason anymore that people get married. Today "even for heterosexuals, marriage is becoming an emotional union and commitment rather than an arrangement to produce and protect children" ("Marriage" 770). And what about heterosexual couples who are sterile? No one would say that they should not be allowed to marry. If the right to marry is based on the possibility of having children, "then a post-menopausal woman who applies for a marriage license should be turned away at the courthouse door" (Rauch 22). No one would seriously expect every couple who gets married to prove that they are capable of having children and intend to do so. That would be a clear violation of their individual rights.

In the same way, to outlaw same-sex marriage is clearly discriminatory. According to Craig Dean, "Marriage is an important civil right because it gives societal recognition and legal protection to a relationship and confers numerous benefits to spouses" (112). Denying same-sex marriage means that gays and lesbians cannot enjoy material benefits such as health insurance through a spouse's employer, life insurance benefits, tax preferences, leaves for bereavement, and inheritance. In some states, laws about domestic partnership give same-sex couples some of these rights, but they are never guaranteed as they would be if the couple were legally next of kin. Thomas Stoddard, a lawyer, says that domestic partnership is the equivalent of "second-class citizenship" (qtd. in Salholz).

Aside from these concrete types of discrimination, denying same-sex marriage keeps gay and lesbian citizens from enjoying the basic human right to "life, liberty, and the pursuit of happiness." The Human Rights Act of 1977 in the District of Columbia makes one of the strongest stands against discrimination based on sexual orientation. According to the Act, "every individual shall have an equal opportunity to participate in the economic, cultural, and intellectual life of the District and have an equal opportunity to participate in all aspects of life" (qtd. in Dean 113). Not allowing homosexuals to marry does deny them the right to "participate" in an aspect of life that is important to almost every couple that has found love in each other. The Hawaii Supreme Court ruled in 1993 that the ban on gay marriage is probably in violation of the Constitution (Salholz).

Of course, many churches will never agree to perform these marriages because they believe that homosexuality is a sin. It is possible to debate the interpretations of the Bible passages that these people cite as evidence, and many religious leaders do. The separation of church and state allows all churches to follow their own doctrines, and many things that are legal in this country are disapproved of by some churches. My point is that the government should not deny the *legal* right to marry in relationships where couples want to express their love toward each other.

It's only natural for people in love to want to commit to each other; this desire is the same for homosexuals and lesbians as it is for heterosexuals. One recent survey showed that "over half of all lesbians and almost 40% of gay men" live in committed relationships and share a house together (Ayers 5). As Sullivan, who is gay, explains, "At some point in our lives, some of us are lucky enough to meet the person we truly love. And we want to commit to that person in front of family and country for the rest of our lives. It's the most simple, the most natural, the most human instinct in the world. How could anyone seek to oppose that?" And what does anyone gain when that right is denied? That's a question that everyone needs to ask themselves.

## Works Cited

Ayers, Tess, and Paul Brown. The Essential Guide to Lesbian and Gay Weddings. San Francisco: Harper, 1994.

Bennett, William, "Leave Marriage Alone." Newsweek 3 June 1996: 27.

Dean, Craig R. "Gay Marriage: A Civil Right." The Journal of Homosexuality 27.3–4 (1994): 111–15.

"Marriage." The Encyclopedia of Homosexuality. Ed. Wayne R. Dynes. New York: Garland, 1990.

Rauch, Jonathan. "For Better or Worse?" The New Republic 6 May 1996: 18–23.

Salholz, Eloise. "For Better or For Worse." Newsweek 24 May 1993: 69.

Sullivan, Andrew. "Let Gays Marry." Newsweek 3 June 1996: 26.

# Chapter 8

# Motivating Action: Arguing to Persuade

In Chapter 1, we defined persuasion as "convincing *plus*" because, in addition to reason, three forms of appeal are required for persuasion: (1) appeal to the writer's character, (2) appeal to the emotions of the audience, and (3) appeal to style, the artful use of language itself. Building on what you learned about making cases in Chapter 7, this chapter's goal is to help you understand and control this wider range of appeals.

But shouldn't reason be enough? Perhaps it would be if human beings were completely rational creatures. But human beings are only sometimes rational—and even then imperfectly. We often agree with an argument but lack the courage or motivation to translate our assent into action.

Persuasion, then, aims to close the gap between assent and action. Because persuasion seeks a deeper and stronger commitment from readers, it appeals to the whole person, to our full humanity, not just to the mind. It offers reasons, of course, because people respond to good reasons. But it also encourages the reader to identify with the writer, to respond not only to the quality of an argument but also to the quality of the arguer. In addition, the persuader wants to stir the reader's emotions because strong feelings prompt the will to act; persuasion works on the heart as much as on the mind. Finally, style matters in persuasion because the response to what is said depends on how well it is said. (See the Concept Close-Up box on page 252.)

## WHEN TO CONVINCE AND WHEN TO PERSUADE: A MATTER OF EMPHASIS

When should you aim to persuade rather than to convince? Always notice what an academic assignment calls for because the full range of persuasive appeal is not always appropriate for written arguments in college. In general, the more academic the audience or the more purely intellectual the issue, the

## Concept Close-Up
## The Four Forms of Appeal

| Form | Function | Presence in Text |
|------|----------|------------------|
| **Reason** | Logical cogency | Your case; any supported contention |
| **Character** | Personal appeal | Indications of author's status and values |
| **Emotion** | Appeals to feelings | Concrete descriptions, moving images |
| **Style** | Appeals through language | Word choice, sentence structure, metaphor |

Essentially, persuasion differs from convincing in that it wants action, not just agreement; it seeks to integrate rational appeal with the full range of resources for influencing people.

less appropriate it is to appeal to the whole person. Often, philosophy or science papers require you to convince, but rarely will they require you to persuade. For those papers, you should confine yourself primarily to thesis, reasons, and evidence.

But when you are working with public issues, with matters of policy or questions of right and wrong, persuasion's fuller range of appeal is usually appropriate because such topics address a broader readership and involve a more inclusive community. Arguments in these areas affect not just how we think but also how we act, and the heightened urgency of persuasion goes further to spark action or change.

Convincing primarily requires that we control case making. But persuasion asks us to make conscious decisions about three other appeals as well: (1) We must gain our readers' confidence and respect through the deliberate projection of our good character; (2) We must touch our readers' emotions; and (3) We must focus on language itself as a means of affecting people's thoughts and behavior. The writer who aims to persuade integrates these other forms of appeal with a well-made case, deliberately crafting the essay so that they all work together.

As with convincing, writing a persuasive argument begins with inquiry and research—a patient search for the truth as preparation for earning a claim to truth. However, before you can move from a general idea of your own position to a specific thesis, you must think about the audience you seek to persuade.

## ANALYZING YOUR READERS

Persuasion begins with difference and, when it works, ends with identity. That is, we expect that before reading our argument, our readers will differ from us not only in beliefs but also in attitudes and desires. A successful persuasive argument brings readers and writer together; it creates a sense of connection between parties who were previously separate in viewpoint. But what means can we use to overcome difference and create a sense of identity? First, we need to focus on our readers and attempt to understand their frames of mind by asking certain key questions.

## Who Is the Audience, and How Do They View the Topic?

The first step is to identify possible appeals to your readership. Keep in mind that good persuaders are able to empathize and sympathize with other people, building bridges of commonality and solidarity. To aid your audience analysis, ask these questions:

- Who are my readers? How do I define them in terms of age, economic and social class, gender, education, and so forth?
- What typical attitudes or stances toward my topic do they have?
- What in their background or daily experiences helps explain their point of view?
- What are they likely to know about my topic?
- How might they be uninformed or misinformed about it?
- How would they like to see the problem, question, or issue resolved, answered, or handled? Why? That is, what personal stake do they have in the topic?
- In what larger framework—religious, ethical, political, economic— do they place my topic? That is, what general beliefs and values are involved?

## What Are Our Differences?

Audience analysis is not complete until you can specify exactly what divides you from your readers. Sometimes specifying difference is difficult to do before formulating a detailed case; understanding exactly what divides you from your readers comes later, at the point of the first draft. But as soon as you can, you must clarify differences; knowing exactly what separates you from your readers tells you what to emphasize in making your case and in choosing other strategies of appeal. These questions can help:

- Is the difference a matter of assumptions? If so, how can I shake my readers' confidence in their assumptions and offer another set of assumptions favorable to my position?
- Is the difference a matter of principle, the application of general rules to specific cases? If so, should I dispute the principle itself and offer a competing one the audience will also value? Or should I show why the principle should not apply in some specific instance relevant to my case?
- Is the difference a matter of a hierarchy of values—that is, do we value the same things but to different degrees? If so, how might I restructure my readers' values?
- Is the difference a matter of ends or of means? If ends, how can I show that my vision of what ought to be is better or that realizing

my ends will also secure the ends my readers value? If a difference of means, how can I show that my methods are justified and effective, more likely to bear fruit than others?

- Is the difference a matter of interpretation? If so, how can I shake my readers' confidence in the traditional or common interpretation of something and show them that my interpretation is better, that it accounts more adequately for the facts?
- Is the difference a matter of implications or consequences? If so, how can I convince my readers that what they fear may happen will not happen, or that it will not be as bad as they think, or that other implications or consequences outweigh any negatives?

## What Do We Have in Common?

In seeking to define the common ground you and your readers share, the key point to remember is that no matter how sharp the disagreements that divide you from those you hope to persuade, resources for identification always exist. Ask these sorts of questions:

- Do we have a shared local identity—as members of the same organization, for example, or as students at the same university?
- Do we share a more abstract, collective identity—as citizens of the same region or nation, as worshippers in the same religion, and so forth?
- Do we share a common cause—such as promoting the good of the community, preventing child abuse, or overcoming racial prejudice?
- Is there a shared experience or human activity—raising children, caring for aging parents, helping a friend in distress, struggling to make ends meet?
- Can we connect through a well-known event or cultural happening—a popular movie, a best-selling book, something in the news that would interest both you and your readers?
- Is there a historical event, person, or document that we both respect?

## READING A PERSUASIVE ESSAY

To illustrate the importance of audience analysis, we turn to a classic essay of the twentieth century, Martin Luther King's "Letter from Birmingham Jail," a brilliant example of the art of persuasion. As we will see, King masterfully analyzed his audience and used the full range of appeals to suit that particular readership.

### Background

To appreciate King's persuasive powers, we must first understand the events that led up to the "Letter" and also the actions King wanted to move his readers to take. In 1963, as president of the Southern Christian Leadership Con-

## Concept Close-Up
## Audience Analysis

To understand any audience we hope to persuade, we must know *both* what separates us from them *and* what common ground we share.

We may **differ** from our audience in:

| Kind of Difference | Example |
| --- | --- |
| Assumptions | Western writers assume that separation of church and state is normal; some Muslim audiences do not make the distinction. |
| Principles | Most conservative writers believe in the principle of the open market; labor audiences often believe in protecting American jobs from foreign competition. |
| Value rankings | Some writers value personal freedom over duty and obligation; some audiences place duty and obligation above personal freedom. |
| Ends and means | Writer and audience may agree about purpose (for example, making America safe from terrorism) but disagree about what policies will best accomplish this end. |
| Interpretation | Some writers understood the September 11, 2001, attack as an act of war; some audiences saw it as a criminal act that demanded legal rather than military measures. |
| Consequences | Some writers think making divorce harder would keep more couples together; some audiences think it would only promote individual unhappiness. |

We may **share** with our audience:

| Kind of Identification | Example |
| --- | --- |
| Local identity | Students and teachers at the same university |
| Collective identity | Citizens of the same state or the same nation |
| Common cause | Improving the environment |
| Common experience | Pride in the success of American Olympic athletes |
| Common history | Respect for soldiers that have died defending the United States |

Essentially, we must understand differences to discover how we need to argue; we must use the resources of identification to overcome differences separating us from our readers.

ference, a civil rights organization dedicated to nonviolent social change, King had been organizing and participating in demonstrations in Birmingham, Alabama. He was arrested, and while he was in jail, eight white Alabama clergymen of various denominations issued a public statement reacting to his activities. Published in a local newspaper, the statement deplored the illegal demonstrations of King and his organization as "unwise and untimely":

> We the undersigned clergymen are among those who, in January, issued "An Appeal for Law and Order and Common Sense," in dealing with racial problems in Alabama. We expressed understanding that honest convictions in racial

*Figure 8.1    Rosa Parks, whose refusal to move to the back of a bus touched off the Montgomery bus boycott and the beginning of the civil rights movement, is fingerprinted by Deputy Sheriff D. H. Lackey in Montgomery, Alabama, February 22, 1956. She was among some 100 people charged with violating segregation laws. (AP Photo/Gene Herrick)*

matters could properly be pursued in the courts, but urged that decisions of those courts should in the meantime be peacefully obeyed.

Since that time there had been some evidence of increased forbearance and a willingness to face facts. Responsible citizens have undertaken to work on various problems which cause racial friction and unrest. In Birmingham, recent public events have given indication that we all have opportunity for a new constructive and realistic approach to racial problems.

However, we are now confronted by a series of demonstrations by some of our Negro citizens, directed and led in part by outsiders. We recognize the natural impatience of people who feel that their hopes are slow in being realized. But we are convinced that these demonstrations are unwise and untimely.

We agree rather with certain local Negro leadership which has called for honest and open negotiation of racial issues in our area. And we believe this kind of facing of issues can best be accomplished by citizens of our own metropolitan area, white and Negro, meeting with their knowledge and experience of the local situation. All of us need to face that responsibility and find proper channels for its accomplishment.

Just as we formerly pointed out that "hatred and violence have no sanction in our religious and political traditions," we also point out that such actions as incite to hatred and violence, however technically peaceful those actions may be, have not contributed to the resolution of our local problems. We do not believe that these days of new hope are days when extreme measures are justified in Birmingham.

We commend the community as a whole, and the local news media and law enforcement officials in particular, on the calm manner in which these demonstrations have been handled. We urge the public to continue to show restraint should the demonstrations continue, and the law enforcement officials to remain calm and continue to protect our city from violence.

We further strongly urge our own Negro community to withdraw support from these demonstrations, and to unite locally in working peacefully for a better Birmingham. When rights are consistently denied, a cause should be pressed in the courts and in negotiations among local leaders, and not in the streets. We appeal to both our white and Negro citizenry to observe the principles of law and order and common sense.

Signed by:
C. C. J. Carpenter, D.D., LL.D., *Bishop of Alabama*
Joseph A. Durick, D.D., *Auxiliary Bishop, Diocese of Mobile, Birmingham*
Rabbi Milton L. Grafman, *Temple Emanu-El, Birmingham, Alabama*
Bishop Paul Hardin, *Bishop of the Alabama-West Florida Conference of the Methodist Church*
Bishop Nolan B. Harmon, *Bishop of the North Alabama Conference of the Methodist Church*
George M. Murray, D.D., LL.D., *Bishop Coadjutor, Episcopal Diocese of Alabama*
Edward V. Ramage, *Moderator, Synod of the Alabama Presbyterian Church in the United States*
Earl Stallings, *Pastor, First Baptist Church, Birmingham, Alabama*

In his cell, King began his letter on the margins of that newspaper page, addressing it specifically to the eight clergymen in the hope that he could move them from disapproval to support, from inaction to a recognition of the necessity of the demonstrations. As a public figure, King knew that his letter would reach a larger audience, including the demonstrators themselves, who were galvanized by its message when 50,000 copies were later distributed by his supporters. In the years since, King's letter has often been published, reaching a global audience with its argument for civil disobedience in the service of a higher moral law.

## The Basic Message

King's letter is long; he even apologizes to his readers for having written so much. Its length is not due to its basic message, however, but to its persuasive appeals—to the way the main points are made. Before turning to King's "Letter from Birmingham Jail," read the following summary, which differs as greatly from King's prose as a nursery song differs from a Beethoven symphony.

> Because I am the leader of an organization that fights injustice, it is most appropriate for me to be in Birmingham, where human rights are being violated. Our campaign of nonviolent civil disobedience was not rash and unpremeditated but the result of a history of failed negotiations and broken promises. We aim to increase tensions here until the city leaders realize that dialogue must occur. Our actions are not untimely but long overdue, given that blacks have been denied their civil rights in this country for over 340 years.
>
> While we advocate breaking some laws, we distinguish between moral laws and immoral laws that degrade the human personality. The former must be obeyed, the latter disobeyed openly and lovingly. We may be extremists, but people who accomplish great things are often so labeled, and our nonviolent protests are preferable to inaction.
>
> In failing to support us, white Southern religious leaders such as yourselves fail to meet the challenges of social injustice. You should not praise the police for their work at breaking up the demonstrations but rather praise the demonstrators for standing up for their human dignity.

---

## Letter from Birmingham Jail
### Martin Luther King, Jr.

*April 16, 1963*

My Dear Fellow Clergymen:

   While confined here in the Birmingham city jail, I came across your recent statement calling my present activities "unwise and untimely." Seldom do I pause to answer criticism of my work and ideas. If I sought to answer all the criticisms that cross my desk, my secretaries would have little time for anything other than such correspondence in the course of the day, and I would have no time for constructive work. But since I feel that you are men of genuine good will and that your criticisms are sincerely set forth, I want to try to answer your statement in what I hope will be patient and reasonable terms.

   I think I should indicate why I am here in Birmingham, since you have been influenced by the view which argues against "outsiders coming in." I have the honor of serving as president of the Southern Christian Leadership

Conference, an organization operating in every southern state, with headquarters in Atlanta, Georgia. We have some eighty-five affiliated organizations across the South, and one of them is the Alabama Christian Movement for Human Rights. Frequently we share staff, educational, and financial resources with our affiliates. Several months ago the affiliate here in Birmingham asked us to be on call to engage in a nonviolent direct-action program if such were deemed necessary. We readily consented, and when the hour came we lived up to our promise. So I, along with several members of my staff, am here because I was invited here. I am here because I have organizational ties here.

But more basically, I am in Birmingham because injustice is here. Just as the prophets of the eighth century B.C. left their villages and carried their "thus saith the Lord" far beyond the boundaries of their home towns, and just as the Apostle Paul left his village of Tarsus and carried the gospel of Jesus Christ to the far corners of the Greco-Roman world, so am I compelled to carry the gospel of freedom beyond my own home town. Like Paul, I must constantly respond to the Macedonian call for aid.

Moreover, I am cognizant of the interrelatedness of all communities and states. I cannot sit idly by in Atlanta and not be concerned about what happens in Birmingham. Injustice anywhere is a threat to justice everywhere. We are caught in an inescapable network of mutuality, tied in a single garment of destiny. Whatever affects one directly, affects all indirectly. Never again can we afford to live with the narrow, provincial "outside agitator" idea. Anyone who lives inside the United States can never be considered an outsider anywhere within its bounds.

You deplore the demonstrations taking place in Birmingham. But your   5
statement, I am sorry to say, fails to express a similar concern for the conditions that brought about the demonstrations. I am sure that none of you would want to rest content with the superficial kind of social analysis that deals merely with effects and does not grapple with underlying causes. It is unfortunate that demonstrations are taking place in Birmingham, but it is even more unfortunate that the city's white power structure left the Negro community with no alternative.

In any nonviolent campaign there are four basic steps: collection of the facts to determine whether injustices exist; negotiation; self-purification; and direct action. We have gone through all these steps in Birmingham. There can be no gainsaying the fact that racial injustice engulfs this community. Birmingham is probably the most thoroughly segregated city in the United States. Its ugly record of brutality is widely known. Negroes have experienced grossly unjust treatment in the courts. There have been more unsolved bombings of Negro homes and churches in Birmingham than in any other city in the nation. These are the hard, brutal facts of the case. On the basis of these conditions, Negro leaders sought to negotiate with the city fathers. But the latter consistently refused to engage in good-faith negotiation.

Then, last September, came the opportunity to talk with leaders of Birmingham's economic community. In the course of the negotiations, certain promises were made by the merchants—for example, to remove the stores' humiliating racial signs. On the basis of these promises, the Reverend Fred Shuttlesworth and the leaders of the Alabama Christian Movement for Human Rights agreed to a moratorium on all demonstrations. As the weeks and months went by, we realized that we were the victims of a broken promise. A few signs, briefly removed, returned; the others remained.

As in so many past experiences, our hopes had been blasted, and the shadow of deep disappointment settled upon us. We had no alternative except to prepare for direct action, whereby we would present our very bodies as a means of laying our case before the conscience of the local and the national community. Mindful of the difficulties involved, we decided to undertake a process of self-purification. We began a series of workshops on nonviolence, and we repeatedly asked ourselves: "Are you able to accept blows without retaliating?" "Are you able to endure the ordeal of jail?" We decided to schedule our direct-action program for the Easter season, realizing that except for Christmas, this is the main shopping period of the year. Knowing that a strong economic-withdrawal program would be the byproduct of direct action, we felt that this would be the best time to bring pressure to bear on the merchants for the needed change.

Then it occurred to us that Birmingham's mayoral election was coming up in March, and we speedily decided to postpone action until after election day. When we discovered that the Commissioner of Public Safety, Eugene "Bull" Connor, had piled up enough votes to be in the run-off, we decided again to postpone action until the day after the run-off so that the demonstrations could not be used to cloud the issues. Like many others, we waited to see Mr. Connor defeated, and to this end we endured postponement after postponement. Having aided in this community need, we felt that our direct-action program could be delayed no longer.

You may well ask: "Why direct action? Why sit-ins, marches and so   10
forth? Isn't negotiation a better path?" You are quite right in calling for negotiation. Indeed, this is the very purpose of direct action. Nonviolent direct action seeks to create such a crisis and foster such a tension that a community which has constantly refused to negotiate is forced to confront the issue. It seeks so to dramatize the issue that it can no longer be ignored. My citing the creation of tension as part of the work of the nonviolent-resister may sound rather shocking. But I must confess that I am not afraid of the word "tension." I have earnestly opposed violent tension, but there is a type of constructive, nonviolent tension which is necessary for growth. Just as Socrates felt that it was necessary to create a tension in the mind so that individuals could rise from the bondage of myths and half-truths to the unfettered realm of creative analysis and objective appraisal, so must we see the need for nonviolent gadflies to create the kind of tension in society that will help men rise from the dark depths of prejudice and racism to the majestic heights of understanding and brotherhood.

The purpose of our direct-action program is to create a situation so crisis-packed that it will inevitably open the door to negotiation. I therefore concur with you in your call for negotiation. Too long has our beloved Southland been bogged down in a tragic effort to live in monologue rather than dialogue.

One of the basic points in your statement is that the action that I and my associates have taken in Birmingham is untimely. Some have asked: "Why didn't you give the new city administration time to act?" The only answer that I can give to this query is that the new Birmingham administration must be prodded about as much as the outgoing one, before it will act. We are sadly mistaken if we feel that the election of Albert Boutwell as mayor will bring the millennium to Birmingham. While Mr. Boutwell is a much more gentle person than Mr. Connor, they are both segregationists, dedicated to maintenance of the status quo. I have hope that Mr. Boutwell will be reasonable enough to see the futility of massive resistance to desegregation. But he will not see this without pressure from devotees of civil rights. My friends, I must say to you that we have not made a single gain in civil rights without determined legal and nonviolent pressure. Lamentably, it is an historical fact that privileged groups seldom give up their privileges voluntarily. Individuals may see the moral light and voluntarily give up their unjust posture; but, as Reinhold Niebuhr has reminded us, groups tend to be more immoral than individuals.

We know through painful experience that freedom is never voluntarily given by the oppressor; it must be demanded by the oppressed. Frankly, I have yet to engage in a direct-action campaign that was "well timed" in the view of those who have not suffered unduly from the disease of segregation. For years now I have heard the word "Wait!" It rings in the ear of every Negro with piercing familiarity. This "Wait" has almost always meant "Never." We must come to see, with one of our distinguished jurists, that "justice too long delayed is justice denied."

We have waited for more than 340 years for our constitutional God-given rights. The nations of Asia and Africa are moving with jetlike speed toward gaining political independence, but we still creep at horse-and-buggy pace toward gaining a cup of coffee at a lunch counter. Perhaps it is easy for those who have never felt the stinging darts of segregation to say, "Wait." But when you have seen vicious mobs lynch your mothers and fathers at will and drown your sisters and brothers at whim; when you have seen hate-filled policemen curse, kick, and even kill your black brothers and sisters; when you see the vast majority of your twenty million Negro brothers smothering in an airtight cage of poverty in the midst of an affluent society; when you suddenly find your tongue twisted and your speech stammering as you seek to explain to your six-year-old daughter why she can't go to the public amusement park that has just been advertised on television, and see tears welling up in her eyes when she is told that Funtown is closed to colored children, and see ominous clouds of inferiority beginning to form in her little mental sky, and see her beginning to distort her personality by developing an unconscious bitterness toward white people; when you have to concoct an answer for a five-year-old son who is asking: "Daddy, why do white people treat colored people so mean?"; when you take a cross-country drive and find it necessary to sleep night after night in the uncomfortable corners of your automobile because no motel will accept you; when you are humiliated day in and day out by nagging signs reading "white" and "colored"; when your first name becomes "nigger," your middle name becomes "boy" (however old you are), and your last name becomes "John," and your wife and mother are never given the respected title "Mrs."; when you are harried by day and haunted by night by the fact that you are a Negro, living constantly at tiptoe stance, never quite knowing what to expect next, and are plagued with inner fears and outer resentments; when you are forever fighting a degenerating sense of "nobodiness"—then you will understand why we find it difficult to wait. There comes a time when the cup of endurance runs over, and men are no longer willing to be plunged into the abyss of despair. I hope, sirs, you can understand our legitimate and unavoidable impatience.

You express a great deal of anxiety over our willingness to break laws. 15 This is certainly a legitimate concern. Since we so diligently urge people to obey the Supreme Court's decision of 1954 outlawing segregation in the public schools, at first glance it may seem rather paradoxical for us consciously to break laws. One may well ask: "How can you advocate breaking some laws and obeying others?" The answer lies in the fact that there are two types of laws: just and unjust. I would be the first to advocate obeying just laws. One has not only a legal but a moral responsibility to obey just laws. Conversely, one has a moral responsibility to disobey unjust laws. I would agree with St. Augustine that "an unjust law is no law at all."

Now, what is the difference between the two? How does one determine whether a law is just or unjust? A just law is a man-made code that squares with the moral law or the law of God. An unjust law is a code that is out of harmony with the moral law. To put it in the terms of St. Thomas Aquinas: An unjust law is a human law that is not rooted in eternal law and natural law. Any law that uplifts human personality is just. Any law that degrades human personality is unjust. All segregation statutes are unjust because segregation distorts the soul and damages the personality. It gives the segregator a false sense of superiority and the segregated a false sense of inferiority. Segregation, to use the terminology of the Jewish philosopher Martin Buber, substitutes an "I–it" relationship for an "I–thou" relationship and ends up relegating persons to the status of things. Hence, segregation is not only politically, economically, and sociologically unsound, it is morally wrong and sinful. Paul Tillich has said that sin is separation. Is not segregation an existential expression of man's tragic separation, his awful estrangement, his terrible sinfulness? Thus it is that I can urge men to obey the 1954 decision of the Supreme Court, for it is morally right; and I can urge them to disobey segregation ordinances, for they are morally wrong.

Let us consider a more concrete example of just and unjust laws. An unjust law is a code that a numerical or power majority group compels a minority group to obey but does not make binding on itself. This is *difference* made legal. By the same token, a just law is a code that a majority compels a minority to follow and that it is willing to follow itself. This is *sameness* made legal.

Let me give another explanation. A law is unjust if it is inflicted on a minority that, as a result of being denied the right to vote, had no part in enacting or devising the law. Who can say that the legislature of Alabama which set up that state's segregation laws was democratically elected? Throughout Alabama all sorts of devious methods are used to prevent Negroes from becoming registered voters, and there are some counties in which, even though Negroes constitute a majority of the population, not a single Negro is registered. Can any law enacted under such circumstances be considered democratically structured?

Sometimes a law is just on its face and unjust in its application. For instance, I have been arrested on a charge of parading without a permit. Now, there is nothing wrong in having an ordinance which requires a permit for a parade. But such an ordinance becomes unjust when it is used to maintain segregation and to deny citizens the First-Amendment privilege of peaceful assembly and protest.

I hope you are able to see the distinction I am trying to point out. In no sense do I advocate evading or defying the law, as would the rabid segregationist. That would lead to anarchy. One who breaks an unjust law must do so openly, lovingly, and with a willingness to accept the penalty. I submit that an individual who breaks a law that conscience tells him is unjust, and who willingly accepts the penalty of imprisonment in order to arouse the conscience of the community over its injustice, is in reality expressing the highest respect for law.

Of course, there is nothing new about this kind of civil disobedience. It was evidenced sublimely in the refusal of Shadrach, Meshach, and Abednego to obey the laws of Nebuchadnezzar, on the ground that a higher moral law was at stake. It was practiced superbly by the early Christians, who were willing to face hungry lions and the excruciating pain of chopping blocks rather than submit to certain unjust laws of the Roman Empire. To a degree, academic freedom is a reality today because Socrates practiced civil disobedience. In our own nation, the Boston Tea Party represented a massive act of civil disobedience.

We should never forget that everything Adolf Hitler did in Germany was "legal" and everything the Hungarian freedom fighters did in Hungary was "illegal." It was "illegal" to aid and comfort a Jew in Hitler's Germany. Even so, I am sure that, had I lived in Germany at the time, I would have aided and comforted my Jewish brothers. If today I lived in a Communist country where certain principles dear to the Christian faith are suppressed, I would openly advocate disobeying that country's antireligious laws.

I must make two honest confessions to you, my Christian and Jewish brothers. First, I must confess that over the past few years I have been gravely disappointed with the white moderate. I have almost reached the regrettable conclusion that the Negro's great stumbling block in his stride toward freedom is not the White Citizen's Counciler or the Ku Klux Klanner, but the white moderate, who is more devoted to "order" than to justice; who prefers a negative peace which is the presence of tension to a positive peace which is the presence of justice; who constantly says: "I agree with you in the goal you seek, but I cannot agree with your methods of direct action"; who paternalistically believes he can set the timetable for another man's freedom; who lives by a mythical concept of time and who constantly advises the Negro to wait for a "more convenient season." Shallow understanding from people of good will is more frustrating than absolute misunderstanding from people of ill will. Lukewarm acceptance is much more bewildering than outright rejection.

I had hoped that the white moderate would understand that law and order exist for the purpose of establishing justice and that when they fail in this purpose they become the dangerously structured dams that block the flow of social progress. I had hoped that the white moderate would understand that the present tension in the South is a necessary phase of the transition from an obnoxious negative peace, in which the Negro passively accepted his unjust plight, to a substantive and positive peace, in which all men will respect the dignity and worth of human personality. Actually, we who engage in nonviolent direct action are not the creators of tension. We merely bring to the surface the hidden tension that is already alive. We bring it out in the open, where it can be seen and dealt with. Like a boil that can never be cured so long as it is covered up but must be opened with all its ugliness to the natural medicines of air and light, injustice must be exposed, with all the tension its exposure creates, to the light of human conscience and the air of national opinion before it can be cured.

In your statement you assert that our actions, even though peaceful, 25 must be condemned because they precipitate violence. But is this a logical assertion? Isn't this like condemning a robbed man because his possession of money precipitated the evil act of robbery? Isn't this like condemning Socrates because his unswerving commitment to truth and his philosophical inquiries precipitated the act by the misguided populace in which they made him drink hemlock? Isn't this like condemning Jesus because his unique God-consciousness and never-ceasing devotion to God's will precipitated the evil act of crucifixion? We must come to see that, as the federal courts have consistently affirmed, it is wrong to urge an individual to cease his efforts to gain his basic constitutional rights because the quest may precipitate violence. Society must protect the robbed and punish the robber.

I had also hoped that the white moderate would reject the myth concerning time in relation to the struggle for freedom. I have just received a letter from a white brother in Texas. He writes: "All Christians know that the colored people will receive equal rights eventually, but it is possible that you are in too great a religious hurry. It has taken Christianity almost two thousand years to accomplish what it has. The teachings of Christ take time to come to earth." Such an attitude stems from a tragic misconception of time, from the strangely irrational notion that there is something in the very flow of time that will inevitably cure all ills. Actually, time itself is neutral; it can be used either destructively or constructively. More and more I feel that the people of ill will have used time much more effectively than have the people of good will. We will have to repent in this generation not merely for the hateful words and actions of the bad people but for the appalling silence of the good people. Human progress never rolls in on wheels of inevitability; it comes through the tireless efforts of men willing to be co-workers with God, and without this hard work, time itself becomes an ally of the forces of social stagnation. We must use time creatively, in the knowledge that the time is always ripe to do right. Now is the time to make real the promise of democracy and transform our pending national elegy into a creative psalm of brotherhood. Now is the time to lift our national policy from the quicksand of racial injustice to the solid rock of human dignity.

You speak of our activity in Birmingham as extreme. At first I was rather disappointed that fellow clergymen would see my nonviolent efforts as those of an extremist. I began thinking about the fact that I stand in the middle of two opposing forces in the Negro community. One is a force of complacency, made up in part of Negroes who, as a result of long years of oppression, are so drained of self-respect and a sense of "somebodiness" that they have adjusted to segregation; and in part of a few middle-class Negroes who, because of a degree of academic and economic security and because in some ways they profit by segregation, have become insensitive to the problems of the masses. The other force is one of bitterness and hatred, and it comes perilously close to advocating violence. It is expressed in the various black nationalist groups that are springing up across the nation, the largest and best-known being Elijah Muhammad's Muslim movement. Nourished by the Negro's frustration over the continued existence of racial discrimination, this movement is made up of people who have lost faith in America, who have absolutely repudiated Christianity, and who have concluded that the white man is an incorrigible "devil."

I have tried to stand between these two forces, saying that we need emulate neither the "do-nothingism" of the complacent nor the hatred and despair of the black nationalist. For there is the more excellent way of love and nonviolent protest. I am grateful to God that, through the influence of the Negro church, the way of nonviolence became an integral part of our struggle.

If this philosophy had not emerged, by now many streets of the South would, I am convinced, be flowing with blood. And I am further convinced that if our white brothers dismiss as "rabble-rousers" and "outside agitators" those of us who employ nonviolent direct action, and if they refuse to support our nonviolent efforts, millions of the Negroes will, out of frustration and despair, seek solace and security in black-nationalist ideologies—a development that would inevitably lead to a frightening racial nightmare.

Oppressed people cannot remain oppressed forever. The yearning for freedom eventually manifests itself, and that is what has happened to the American Negro. Something within has reminded him of his birthright of freedom, and something without has reminded him that it can be gained. Consciously or unconsciously, he has been caught up by the *Zeitgeist*, and with his black brothers of Africa and his brown and yellow brothers of Asia, South America, and the Caribbean, the United States Negro is moving with a sense of great urgency toward the promised land of racial justice. If one recognizes this vital urge that has engulfed the Negro community, one should readily understand why public demonstrations are taking place. The Negro has many pent-up resentments and latent frustrations, and he must release them. So let him march; let him make prayer pilgrimages to the city hall; let him go on freedom rides—and try to understand why he must do so. If his repressed emotions are not released in nonviolent ways, they will seek expression through violence; this is not a threat but a fact of history. So I have not said to my people: "Get rid of your discontent." Rather, I have tried to say that this normal and healthy discontent can be channeled into the creative outlet of nonviolent direct action. And now this approach is being termed extremist.

But though I was initially disappointed at being categorized as an extremist, as I continued to think about the matter I gradually gained a measure of satisfaction from the label. Was not Jesus an extremist for love: "Love your enemies, bless them that curse you, do good to them that hate you, and pray for them which despitefully use you, and persecute you." Was not Amos an extremist for justice: "Let justice roll down like waters and righteousness like an ever-flowing stream." Was not Paul an extremist for the Christian gospel: "I bear in my body the marks of the Lord Jesus." Was not Martin Luther an extremist: "Here I stand; I cannot do otherwise, so help me God." And John Bunyan: "I will stay in jail to the end of my days before I make a butchery of my conscience." And Abraham Lincoln: "This nation cannot survive half slave and half free." And Thomas Jefferson: "We hold these truths to be self-evident, that all men are created equal. . . ." So the question is not whether we will be extremists, but what kind of extremists we will be. Will we be extremists for hate or for love? Will we be extremists for the preservation of injustice or for the extension of justice? In that dramatic scene on Calvary's hill three men were crucified. We must never forget that all three were crucified for the same crime—the crime of extremism. Two were extremists for immorality, and thus fell below their environment. The other, Jesus Christ, was an extremist for love, truth and goodness, and thereby rose above his environment. Perhaps the South, the nation and the world are in dire need of creative extremists.

I had hoped that the white moderate would see this need. Perhaps I was too optimistic; perhaps I expected too much. I suppose I should have realized that few members of the oppressor race can understand the deep groans and passionate yearnings of the oppressed race, and still fewer have the vision to see that injustice must be rooted out by strong, persistent, and determined action. I am thankful, however, that some of our white brothers in the South have grasped the meaning of this social revolution and committed themselves to it. They are still all too few in quantity, but they are big in quality. Some—such as Ralph McGill, Lillian Smith, Harry Golden, James McBride Dabbs, Ann Braden, and Sarah Patton Boyle—have written about our struggle in eloquent and prophetic terms. Others have marched with us down nameless streets of the South. They have languished in filthy, roach-infested jails, suffering the abuse and brutality of policemen who view them as "dirty nigger-lovers." Unlike so many of their moderate brothers and sisters, they have recognized the urgency of the moment and sensed the need for powerful "action" antidotes to combat the disease of segregation.

Let me take note of my other major disappointment. I have been so greatly disappointed with the white church and its leadership. Of course, there are some notable exceptions. I am not unmindful of the fact that each of you has taken some significant stands on this issue. I commend you, Reverend Stallings, for your Christian stand on this past Sunday, in welcoming Negroes to your worship service on a nonsegregated basis. I commend the Catholic leaders of this state for integrating Spring Hill College several years ago.

But despite these notable exceptions, I must honestly reiterate that I have been disappointed with the church. I do not say this as one of those negative critics who can always find something wrong with the church. I say this as a minister of the gospel, who loves the church; who was nurtured in its bosom; who has been sustained by its spiritual blessings and who will remain true to it as long as the cord of life shall lengthen.

When I was suddenly catapulted into the leadership of the bus protest   35
in Montgomery, Alabama, a few years ago, I felt we would be supported by the white church. I felt that the white ministers, priests, and rabbis of the South would be among our strongest allies. Instead, some have been outright opponents, refusing to understand the freedom movement and misrepresenting its leaders; all too many others have been more cautious than courageous and have remained silent behind the anesthetizing security of stained-glass windows.

In spite of my shattered dreams, I came to Birmingham with the hope that the white religious leadership of this community would see the justice of our cause and, with deep moral concern, would serve as the channel through which our just grievances could reach the power structure. I had hoped that each of you would understand. But again I have been disappointed.

I have heard numerous southern religious leaders admonish their worshipers to comply with a desegregation decision because it is the law, but I have longed to hear white ministers declare: "Follow this decree because integration is morally right and because the Negro is your brother." In the midst of blatant injustices inflicted upon the Negro, I have watched white churchmen stand on the sideline and mouth pious irrelevancies and sanctimonious trivialities. In the midst of a mighty struggle to rid our nation of racial and economic injustice, I have heard many ministers say: "Those are social issues, with which the gospel has no real concern." And I have watched many churches commit themselves to a completely otherworldly religion which makes a strange, un-Biblical distinction between body and soul, between the sacred and the secular.

I have traveled the length and breadth of Alabama, Mississippi, and all the other southern states. On sweltering summer days and crisp autumn mornings I have looked at the South's beautiful churches with their lofty spires pointing heavenward. I have beheld the impressive outlines of her massive religious-education buildings. Over and over I have found myself asking: "What kind of people worship here? Who is their God? Where were their voices when the lips of Governor Barnett dripped with words of interposition and nullification? Where were they when Governor Wallace gave a clarion call for defiance and hatred? Where were their voices of support when bruised and weary Negro men and women decided to rise from the dark dungeons of complacency to the bright hills of creative protest?"

Yes, these questions are still in my mind. In deep disappointment I have wept over the laxity of the church. But be assured that my tears have been tears of love. There can be no deep disappointment where there is not deep love. Yes, I love the church. How could I do otherwise? I am in the rather unique position of being the son, the grandson, and the great-grandson of preachers. Yes, I see the church as the body of Christ. But, oh! How we have blemished and scarred that body through social neglect and through fear of being nonconformists.

There was a time when the church was very powerful—in the time when the early Christians rejoiced at being deemed worthy to suffer for what they believed. In those days the church was not merely a thermometer that recorded the ideas and principles of popular opinion; it was a thermostat that transformed the mores of society. Whenever the early Christians entered a town, the people in power became disturbed and immediately sought to convict the Christians for being "disturbers of the peace" and "outside agitators." But the Christians pressed on, in the conviction that they were "a colony of heaven," called to obey God rather than man. Small in number, they were big in commitment. They were too God-intoxicated to be "astronomically intimidated." By their effort and example they brought an end to such ancient evils as infanticide and gladiatorial contests.

Things are different now. So often the contemporary church is a weak, ineffectual voice with an uncertain sound. So often it is an archdefender of

40

the status quo. Far from being disturbed by the presence of the church, the power structure of the average community is consoled by the church's silent—and often even vocal—sanction of things as they are.

But the judgment of God is upon the church as never before. If today's church does not recapture the sacrificial spirit of the early church, it will lose its authenticity, forfeit the loyalty of millions, and be dismissed as an irrelevant social club with no meaning for the twentieth century. Every day I meet young people whose disappointment with the church has turned into outright disgust.

Perhaps I have once again been too optimistic. Is organized religion too inextricably bound to the status quo to save our nation and the world? Perhaps I must turn my faith to the inner spiritual church, the church within the church, as the true *ekklesia* and the hope of the world. But again I am thankful to God that some noble souls from the ranks of organized religion have broken loose from the paralyzing chains of conformity and joined us as active partners in the struggle for freedom. They have left their secure congregations and walked the streets of Albany, Georgia, with us. They have gone down the highways of the South on tortuous rides for freedom. Yes, they have gone to jail with us. Some have been dismissed from their churches, have lost the support of their bishops and fellow ministers. But they have acted in the faith that right defeated is stronger than evil triumphant. Their witness has been the spiritual salt that has preserved the true meaning of the gospel in these troubled times. They have carved a tunnel of hope through the dark mountain of disappointment.

I hope the church as a whole will meet the challenge of this decisive hour. But even if the church does not come to the aid of justice, I have no despair about the future. I have no fear about the outcome of our struggle in Birmingham, even if our motives are at present misunderstood. We will reach the goal of freedom in Birmingham and all over the nation, because the goal of America is freedom. Abused and scorned though we may be, our destiny is tied up with America's destiny. Before the pilgrims landed at Plymouth, we were here. Before the pen of Jefferson etched the majestic words of the Declaration of Independence across the pages of history, we were here. For more than two centuries our forebears labored in this country without wages; they made cotton king; they built the homes of their masters while suffering gross injustice and shameful humiliation—and yet out of a bottomless vitality they continued to thrive and develop. If the inexpressible cruelties of slavery could not stop us, the opposition we now face will surely fail. We will win our freedom because the sacred heritage of our nation and the eternal will of God are embodied in our echoing demands.

Before closing I feel impelled to mention one other point in your statement that has troubled me profoundly. You warmly commended the Birmingham police force for keeping "order" and "preventing violence." I doubt that you would have so warmly commended the police force if you had seen its dogs sinking their teeth into unarmed, nonviolent Negroes. I doubt that you would so quickly commend the policemen if you were to observe their ugly and inhumane treatment of Negroes here in the city jail; if you were to watch them push and curse old Negro women and young Negro girls; if you were to see them slap and kick old Negro men and young boys; if you were to observe them, as they did on two occasions, refuse to give us food because we wanted to sing our grace together. I cannot join you in your praise of the Birmingham police department.

It is true that police have exercised a degree of discipline in handling the demonstrators. In this sense they have conducted themselves rather "nonviolently" in public. But for what purpose? To preserve the evil system of segregation. Over the past few years I have consistently preached that nonviolence demands that the means we use must be as pure as the ends we seek. I have tried to make clear that it is wrong to use immoral means to attain moral ends. But now I must affirm that it is just as wrong, or perhaps even more so, to use moral means to preserve immoral ends. Perhaps Mr. Connor and his policemen have been rather nonviolent in public, as was Chief Pritchett in Albany, Georgia, but they have used the moral means of nonviolence to maintain the immoral end of racial injustice. As T. S. Eliot has said: "The last temptation is the greatest treason: To do the right deed for the wrong reason."

I wish you had commended the Negro sit-inners and demonstrators of Birmingham for their sublime courage, their willingness to suffer and their amazing discipline in the midst of great provocation. One day the South will recognize its real heroes. They will be the James Merediths, with the noble sense of purpose that enables them to face jeering and hostile mobs, and with the agonizing loneliness that characterizes the life of the pioneer. They will be old, oppressed, battered Negro women, symbolized in a seventy-two-year-old woman in Montgomery, Alabama, who rose up with a sense of dignity and with her people decided not to ride segregated buses, and who responded with ungrammatical profundity to one who inquired about her weariness: "My feets is tired, but my soul is at rest." They will be the young high school and college students, the young ministers of the gospel and a host of their elders, courageously and nonviolently sitting in at lunch counters and willingly going to jail for conscience's sake. One day the South will know that when these disinherited children of God sat down at lunch counters, they were in reality standing up for what is best in the American dream and for the most sacred values in our Judaeo-Christian heritage, thereby bringing our nation back to those great wells of democracy which were dug deep by the founding fathers in their formulation of the Constitution and the Declaration of Independence.

Never before have I written so long a letter. I'm afraid it is much too long to take your precious time. I can assure you that it would have been much shorter if I had been writing from a comfortable desk, but what else can one do when he is alone in a narrow jail cell, other than write long letters, think long thoughts, and pray long prayers?

If I have said anything in this letter that overstates the truth and indicates an unreasonable impatience, I beg you to forgive me. If I have said anything that understates the truth and indicates my having a patience that allows me to settle for anything less than brotherhood, I beg God to forgive me.

I hope this letter finds you strong in faith. I also hope that circumstances will soon make it possible for me to meet each of you, not as an integrationist or a civil-rights leader but as a fellow clergyman and a Christian brother. Let us all hope that the dark clouds of racial prejudice will soon pass away and the deep fog of misunderstanding will be lifted from our fear-drenched communities, and in some not too distant tomorrow the radiant stars of love and brotherhood will shine over our great nation with all their scintillating beauty.

Yours for the cause of Peace and Brotherhood<br>Martin Luther King, Jr.

50

## King's Analysis of His Audience: Identification and Overcoming Difference

King's letter is worth studying for his use of the resources of identification alone. For example, he appeals in his salutation to "My Dear Fellow Clergymen," which emphasizes at the outset that he and his readers share a similar role. Elsewhere he calls them "my friends" (paragraph 12) and "my Christian and Jewish brothers" (paragraph 23). In many other places, King alludes to the Bible and to other religious figures; these references put him on common ground with his readers.

King's letter also successfully deals with various kinds of difference between his readers and himself.

### Assumptions

King's readers assumed that if black people waited long enough, their situation would naturally grow better. Therefore, they argued for patience. King, in paragraph 26, questions "the strangely irrational notion that . . . the very flow of time . . . will inevitably cure all ills." Against this common assumption that "time heals," King offers the view that "time itself is neutral," something that "can be used either destructively or constructively."

### Principles

King's readers believed in the principle of always obeying the law, a principle blind to both intent and application. King substitutes another principle: Obey just laws, but disobey, openly and lovingly, unjust laws (paragraphs 15–22).

## Hierarchy of Values

King's readers elevated the value of reducing racial tension over the value of securing racial justice. In paragraph 10, King's strategy is to talk about "constructive, nonviolent tension," clearly an effort to get his readers to see tension as not necessarily a bad thing but a condition for achieving social progress.

## Ends and Means

King's audience seems to disagree with him not about the ends for which he was working but about the means. King, therefore, focuses not on justifying civil rights but on justifying civil disobedience.

## Interpretation

King's audience interpreted extremism as always negative, never justifiable. King counters by showing, first, that he is actually a moderate, neither a "do-nothing" nor a militant (paragraph 28). But then he redefines their interpretation of extremism, arguing that extremism for good causes is justified and citing examples from history to support his point (paragraph 31).

## Implications or Consequences

King's readers doubtless feared the consequences of supporting the struggle for civil rights too strongly—losing the support of more conservative members of their congregations. But as King warns, "If today's church does not recapture the sacrificial spirit of the early church, it will . . . be dismissed as an irrelevant social club" (paragraph 42). King's strategy is to turn his readers' attention away from short-term consequences and toward long-term consequences—the loss of the vitality and relevance of the church itself.

### Following Through

As a class, look closely at one of the essays from an earlier chapter, and consider it in terms of audience analysis. What audience did the writer attempt to reach? How did the writer connect or fail to connect with the audience's experience, knowledge, and concerns? What exactly divides the author from his or her audience, and how did the writer attempt to overcome the division? How effective were the writer's strategies for achieving identification? What can you suggest that might have worked better?

## USING THE FORMS OF APPEAL

We turn now to the forms of appeal in persuasion, noting how Martin Luther King, Jr., used them in his letter.

### The Appeal to Reason

Persuasion, we have said, uses the same appeal to reason that we find in convincing; that is, the foundation of a persuasive argument is the case structure of thesis, reasons, and evidence. King, however, seems to have realized that an argument organized like a case would seem too formal and public for his purposes, so he chose instead to respond to the clergymen's statement with a personal letter, organized around their criticisms of him. In fact, most of King's letter amounts to self-defense and belongs to the rhetorical form known as *apologia*, from which our word "apology" derives. An **apologia** is an effort to explain and justify what one has done, or chosen not to do, in the face of condemnation or at least widespread disapproval or misunderstanding.

Although, strictly speaking, he does not present a case, King still relies heavily on reason. He uses a series of short arguments, occupying from one to as many as eight paragraphs, in responding to his readers' criticisms. These are the more important ones, in order of appearance:

Refutation of the "outside agitator" concept (paragraphs 2–4)
Defense of nonviolent civil disobedience (paragraphs 5–11)
Definitions of "just" versus "unjust" laws (paragraphs 15–22)
Refutation and defense of the label "extremist" (paragraphs 27–31)
Rejection of the ministers' praise for the conduct of the police during
   the Birmingham demonstration (paragraphs 45–47)

In addition to defending himself and his cause, King pursues an offensive strategy, advancing his own criticisms, most notably of the "white moderate" (paragraphs 23–26) and the "white church and its leadership" (paragraphs 33–44). This concentration on rational appeal is both effective and appropriate: It confirms King's character as a man of reason, and it appeals to an audience of well-educated professionals.

King also cites evidence that his readers must respect. In paragraph 16, for example, he cites the words of St. Thomas Aquinas, Martin Buber, and Paul Tillich—who represent, respectively, the Catholic, Jewish, and Protestant traditions—to defend his position on the nature of just and unjust laws. He has chosen these authorities carefully so that each of his eight accusers has someone from his own tradition with whom to identify. The implication, of course, is that King's distinction between just and unjust laws and the course of action that follows from this distinction is consistent with Judeo-Christian thought as a whole.

---

## Following Through

1. Look at paragraphs 2–4 of King's letter. What reasons does King give to justify his presence in Birmingham? How well does he support each reason? How do his reasons and evidence reflect a strategy aimed at his clergy audience?

(continues)

**Following Through (continued)**

2. King's argument for civil disobedience (paragraphs 15–22) is based on one main reason. What is it, and how does he support it?

3. What are the two reasons King gives to refute his audience's charge that he is an extremist (paragraphs 27–31)?

4. Think about a time in your life when you did (or did not do) something for which you were unfairly criticized. Choose one or two of the criticisms, and attempt to defend yourself in a short case of your own. Remember that your argument must be persuasive to your accusers, not just to you. Ask yourself, as King did, How can I appeal to my readers? What will they find reasonable?

## The Appeal to Character

In Chapter 7, our concern was how to make a good case. We did not discuss self-presentation explicitly there; but the fact is, when you formulate a clear and plausible thesis and defend it with good reasons and sufficient evidence, you are at the same time creating a positive impression of your own character. A good argument will always reveal the writer's values, intelligence, knowledge of the subject, grasp of the reader's needs and concerns, and so on. We tend to respect and trust a person who reasons well, even when we do not assent to his or her particular case.

In terms of the appeal to character, the difference between convincing and persuading is a matter of degree. In convincing, this appeal is implicit, indirect, and diffused throughout the argument; in persuading, the appeal to character is often quite explicit, direct, and concentrated in a specific section of the essay. The effect on readers is consequently rather different: In convincing, we are seldom consciously aware of the writer's character as such; in persuading, the writer's character assumes a major role in determining how we respond to the argument.

The perception of his character was a special problem for King when he wrote his letter. He was not a national hero in 1963 but rather a controversial civil rights leader whom many viewed as a troublemaker. Furthermore, of course, he wrote this now celebrated document while in jail—hardly a condition that inspires respect and trust in readers. Self-presentation, then, was very significant for King, something he concentrated on throughout his letter and especially at the beginning and end.

In his opening paragraph, King acknowledges the worst smirch on his character—that he is currently in jail. But he goes on to establish himself as a professional person like his readers, with secretaries, correspondence, and important work to do.

Just prior to his conclusion (paragraphs 48–50), King offers a strongly worded critique of the white moderate and the mainstream white church, taking the offensive in a way that his readers are certain to perceive as an attack.

In paragraph 48, however, he suddenly becomes self-deprecating and almost apologetic: "Never before have I written so long a letter." As unexpected as it is, this sudden shift of tone disarms the reader. Then, with gentle irony (the letter, he says, would have been shorter "if I had been writing from a comfortable desk"), King explains the length of his letter as the result of his having no other outlet for action. What can one do in jail but "write long letters, think long thoughts, and pray long prayers?" King paradoxically turns the negative of being in jail into a positive, an opportunity rather than a limitation on his freedom.

His next move is equally surprising, especially after the confident tone of his critique of the church. He begs forgiveness—from his readers if he has overstated his case and from God if he has understated his case or shown too much patience with injustice. This daring, dramatic penultimate paragraph is just the right touch, the perfect gesture of reconciliation. Because he asks so humbly, his readers must forgive him. What else can they do? The further subordination of his own will to God's is the stance of the sufferer and martyr in both the Jewish and Christian traditions.

Finally, King sets aside that which divides him from his readers—the issue of integration and his role as a civil rights leader—in favor of that which unifies him with his audience: All are men of God and brothers in faith. Like an Old Testament prophet, he envisions a time when the current conflicts will be over, when "the radiant stars of love and brotherhood will shine over our great nation." In other words, King holds out the possibility for transcendence, for rising above racial prejudice to a new age, a new America. In the end, his readers are encouraged to soar with him, to hope for the future.

Here King enlists the power of identification to overcome the differences separating writer and reader, invoking his status as a "fellow clergyman and a Christian brother" as a symbol of commonality. The key to identification is to reach beyond the individual self, associating one's character with something larger—the Christian community, the history of the struggle for freedom, national values, "spaceship Earth," or any appropriate cause or movement in which readers can also participate.

## Following Through

We have already seen how King associates himself with the Christian community in the essay's final paragraph. Look at the list of questions for creating audience identification on pages 253–254. Find some examples in King's letter in which he employs some of these resources of identification. Which parts of the letter are most effective in creating a positive impression of character? Why? What methods does King use that any persuader might use?

## The Appeal to Emotion

Educated people aware of the techniques of persuasion are often deeply suspicious of emotional appeal. Among college professors—those who will read and grade your work—this prejudice can be especially strong because all fields of academic study claim to value reason, dispassionate inquiry, and the critical analysis of data and conclusions. Many think of emotional appeal as an impediment to sound thinking and associate it with politicians who prey on our fears, with dictators and demagogues who exploit our prejudices, and with advertisers and televangelists who claim they will satisfy our dreams and prayers.

Of course, we can all cite examples of the destructive power of emotional appeal. But to condemn it wholesale, without qualification, is to exhibit a lack of self-awareness. Most scientists will concede, for instance, that they are passionately committed to the methods of their field, and mathematicians will confess that they are moved by the elegance of certain formulas and proofs. In fact, all human activity has some emotional dimension, a strongly felt adherence to a common set of values.

Moreover, we ought to have strong feelings about certain things: revulsion at the horrors of the Holocaust, pity and anger over the abuse of children, happiness when a war is concluded or when those kidnapped by terrorists are released, and so on. We cease to be human if we are not responsive to emotional appeal.

Clearly, however, we must distinguish between legitimate and illegitimate emotional appeals, condemning the latter and learning to use the former when appropriate. Distinguishing between the two is not always easy, but answering certain questions can help us do so:

> Do the emotional appeals substitute for knowledge and reason?
> Do they employ stereotypes and pit one group against another?
> Do they offer a simple, unthinking reaction to a complex situation?

Whenever the answer is yes, our suspicions should be aroused.

Perhaps an even better test is to ask yourself, If I act on the basis of how I feel, who will benefit, and who will suffer? You may be saddened, for example, to see animals used in medical experiments, but an appeal showing only these animals and ignoring the benefits of experimentation for human life is pandering to the emotions.

In contrast, legitimate emotional appeal supplements argument rather than substituting for it, drawing on knowledge and often on first-hand experience. At its best, it can bring alienated groups together and create empathy or sympathy where these are lacking. Many examples could be cited from Martin Luther King's letter, but the most effective passage is surely paragraph 14:

> We have waited for more than 340 years for our constitutional God-given rights. The nations of Asia and Africa are moving with jetlike speed toward gaining political independence, but we still creep at horse-and-buggy pace toward gaining a cup of coffee at a lunch counter. Perhaps it is easy for those who have

never felt the stinging darts of segregation to say, "Wait." But when you have seen vicious mobs lynch your mothers and fathers at will and drown your sisters and brothers at whim; when you have seen hate-filled policemen curse, kick, and even kill your black brothers and sisters; when you see the vast majority of your twenty million Negro brothers smothering in an airtight cage of poverty in the midst of an affluent society; when you suddenly find your tongue twisted and your speech stammering as you seek to explain to your six-year-old daughter why she can't go to the public amusement park that has just been advertised on television, and see tears welling up in her eyes when she is told that Funtown is closed to colored children, and see ominous clouds of inferiority beginning to form in her little mental sky, and see her beginning to distort her personality by developing an unconscious bitterness toward white people; when you have to concoct an answer for a five-year-old son who is asking: "Daddy, why do white people treat colored people so mean?"; when you take a cross-country drive and find it necessary to sleep night after night in the uncomfortable corners of your automobile because no motel will accept you; when you are humiliated day in and day out by nagging signs reading "white" and "colored"; when your first name becomes "nigger," your middle name becomes "boy" (however old you are), and your last name becomes "John," and your wife and mother are never given the respected title "Mrs."; when you are harried by day and haunted by night by the fact that you are a Negro, living constantly at tiptoe stance, never quite knowing what to expect next, and are plagued with inner fears and outer resentments; when you are forever fighting a degenerating sense of "nobodiness"—then you will understand why we find it difficult to wait. There comes a time when the cup of endurance runs over, and men are no longer willing to be plunged into the abyss of despair. I hope, sirs, you can understand our legitimate and unavoidable impatience.

Just prior to this paragraph, King has concluded an argument justifying the use of direct action to dramatize social inequities and to demand the rights and justice denied to oppressed people. Direct-action programs are necessary, he says, because "freedom is never voluntarily given by the oppressor; it must be demanded by the oppressed." It is easy for those not oppressed to urge an underclass to wait. But "[t]his 'Wait' has almost always meant 'Never.'"

At this point King deliberately sets out to create in his readers a feeling of outrage. Having ended paragraph 13 by equating "wait" with "never," King next refers to a tragic historical fact: For 340 years, since the beginning of slavery in the American colonies, black people have been waiting for their freedom. He sharply contrasts the "jetlike speed" with which Africa is overcoming colonialism with the "horse-and-buggy pace" of integration in the United States. In African homelands, black people are gaining their political independence; but here, in the land of the free, they are denied even "a cup of coffee at a lunch counter." Clearly, this is legitimate emotional appeal, based on fact and reinforcing reason.

In the long and rhythmical sentence that takes up most of the rest of the paragraph, King unleashes the full force of emotional appeal in a series of concrete images designed to make his privileged white readers feel the anger, frustration, and humiliation of the oppressed. In rapid succession, King alludes to mob violence, police brutality, and economic discrimination—the more public evils of racial discrimination—and then moves to the personal, everyday experience of segregation, concentrating especially on what it does to the self-respect of innocent children. For any reader with even the least capacity for sympathy, these images must strike home, creating identification with the suffering of the oppressed and fueling impatience with the evil system that perpetuates this suffering. In short, through the use of telling detail drawn from his own experience, King succeeds in getting his audience to feel what he feels—feelings, in fact, that they ought to share, that are wholly appropriate to the problem of racial prejudice.

What have we learned from King about the available means of emotional appeal? Instead of telling his audience they should feel a particular emotion, he has brought forth that emotion using five specific rhetorical techniques:

Concrete examples
Personal experiences
Metaphors and similes
Sharp contrasts and comparisons
Sentence rhythm, particularly the use of intentional repetition

We next consider how style contributes to a persuasive argument.

## Following Through

1. We have said that emotional appeals need to be both legitimate and appropriate—that is, honest and suitable for the subject matter, the audience, and the kind of discourse being written. Find examples of arguments from various publications—books, newspapers, magazines, and professional journals—and discuss the use or avoidance of emotional appeal in each. On the basis of this study, try to generalize about what kinds of subjects, audiences, and discourse allow direct emotional appeal and what kinds do not.

2. Write an essay analyzing the tactics of emotional appeal in the editorial columns of your campus or local newspaper. Compare the strategies with those used by King. Then evaluate the appeals. How effective are they in arousing your emotions? How well do they reinforce the reasoning offered? Be sure to discuss the way the appeals work and their legitimacy and appropriateness.

## The Appeal through Style

By *style*, we mean the choices a writer makes at the level of words, phrases, and sentences. It would be a mistake to think of style as merely a final touch, something to "dress up" an argument. Style actually involves all of a writer's choices about what words to use and how to arrange them. Ideas and arguments do not develop apart from style, and all of the appeals discussed so far involve stylistic choices. For example, you are concerned with style when you consider what words will state a thesis most precisely or make yourself sound knowledgeable or provide your reader with a compelling image. The appeal of style works hand in hand with the appeals of reason, character, and emotion.

Furthermore, style makes what we say memorable. George Bush may wish he had never said it, but his statement, "Read my lips: No new taxes" was a message that generated high enthusiasm and, to the former president's dismay, remained in people's minds long after he had compromised himself on that issue. Because the persuasive effect we have on readers depends largely on what they remember, the appeal through style matters as much as the appeal to reason, character, and emotion.

Writers with effective style make conscious choices on many levels. One choice involves the degree of formality or familiarity they want to convey. You will notice that King strikes a fairly formal and professional tone throughout most of his letter, choosing words like *cognizant* (paragraph 4) rather than the more common *aware*. Writers also consider the **connotation** of words (what a word implies or what we associate it with) as much as their **denotation** (a word's literal meaning). For example, King opens his letter with the phrase "While confined here in the Birmingham city jail." The word *confined* denotes the same condition as *incarcerated* but has less unfavorable connotations, because people can also be *confined* in ways that evoke our sympathy.

Memorable writing often appeals to the senses of sight and sound. Concrete words can paint a picture; in paragraph 45, for example, King tells about "dogs sinking their teeth" into the nonviolent demonstrators. Writers may also evoke images through implied and explicit comparisons (respectively, metaphor and simile). King's "the stinging darts of segregation" (paragraph 14) is an example of metaphor. In this same paragraph King refers to the "airtight cage of poverty," the "clouds of inferiority" forming in his young daughter's "mental sky," and the "cup of endurance" that has run over for his people—each a metaphor with a powerful emotional effect.

Even when read silently, language has sound. Therefore, style includes the variation of sentence length and the use of rhythmic patterns as well. For example, a writer may emphasize a short, simple sentence by placing it at the end of a series of long sentences or a single long sentence, as King does in paragraph 14. One common rhythmic pattern is the repetition of certain phrases to emphasize a point or to play up a similarity or contrast; in the fourth sentence of paragraph 14, King repeats the phrase "when you" a number of times, piling up examples of racial discrimination and creating a powerful rhythm that carries readers through this unusually long sentence. Another common rhythmic pattern is parallelism. Note the following phrases, again from the fourth sentence of paragraph 14:

"lynch your mothers and fathers at will"

"drown your sisters and brothers at whim"

Here King uses similar words in the same places, even paralleling the number of syllables in each phrase. The parallelism here is further emphasized by King's choice of another stylistic device known as *alliteration,* the repetition of consonant sounds. In another passage from paragraph 14, King achieves a sound pattern that suggests violence when he describes the actions of police who "curse, kick, and even kill" black citizens. The repetition of the hard *k* sound, especially in words of one syllable, suggests the violence of the acts themselves.

Beyond the level of words, phrases, and sentences, the overall arrangement of an essay's main points or topics can also be considered a matter of style, for such arrangement determines how one point contrasts with another, how the tone changes, how the force of the argument builds. When we discuss style, we usually look at smaller units of an essay, but actually all the choices a writer makes contribute in some way to the essay's style.

### Following Through

1. Analyze King's style in paragraphs 6, 8, 23, 24, 31, and 47. Compare what King does in these paragraphs with paragraph 14. How are they similar? How are they different? Why?
2. To some extent, style is a gift or talent that some people have more of than others. But it is also learned, acquired by imitating authors we admire. Use your writer's notebook to increase your stylistic options; whenever you hear or read something stated effectively, copy it down and analyze why it is effective. Try to make up a sentence of your own using the same techniques but with a different subject matter. In this way, you can begin to use analogy, metaphor, repetition, alliteration, parallelism, and other stylistic devices. Begin by imitating six or so sentences or phrases that you especially liked in King's letter.
3. Write an essay analyzing your own style in a previous essay. What would you do differently now? Why?

## DRAFTING A PERSUASIVE ESSAY

Outside the classroom, persuasion begins, as Martin Luther King's letter did, with a real need to move people to action. In a writing course, you may have to create the circumstances for your argument. You should begin by thinking

The following list summarizes pages 280-288, "Drafting a Persuasive Essay."

1. Choose a **specific** audience whose characteristics you **know well** and who have some capacity for **taking action** or **influencing events.** Avoid writing to a "general audience" or seeking to persuade audiences whose opinions are unalterably opposed to yours.
2. Identify your audience **early** in the process.
3. In your case, show a **need** for action and emphasize **urgency.** Connect your proposal for action **directly and clearly** with the need you've established.
4. Your readers must feel that you are **well-informed, confident, fair, honest,** and have their **interests** and **values** in mind. **Avoid ridicule** of other positions. **Recognize** and **respond** to the **main** objections your readers are likely to have to your proposal.
5. Seek to arouse emotions that you **genuinely feel.** Concentrate on those feelings your audience may **lack** or not feel **strongly enough.** Use emotional appeal **sparingly,** and favor **middle to conclusion** locations in your essay for it.
6. Favor a **middle style** for persuasion, conversational without being too familiar or informal.

Essentially, you are making a case, just as you do when arguing to convince. To this, add careful attention to the impression you make on your audience, especially at the beginning of the essay. Add also descriptive and narrative detail designed to arouse emotions favorable to your case. Finally, work hard on style, especially in second and third drafts.

of an issue that calls for persuasion. Your argument must go beyond merely convincing your readers to believe as you do; now you must decide what action you want them to take and move them to take it.

## Conceiving a Readership

Assuming that the task you have chosen or been assigned calls for persuasion, finding and analyzing your readership is your first concern. Because instructors evaluate the writing of their students, it is probably unavoidable that college writers, to some extent, tend to write for their instructors. However, real persuasion has a genuine readership, some definite group of people with a stake in the question or issue being addressed. Whatever you say must be adapted for this audience because moving the reader is the whole point of persuasion.

How can you go about conceiving a readership? First, you should throw out the whole notion of writing to the "general public." Such a "group" is a nearly meaningless abstraction, not defined enough to give you much guidance. Suppose, for example, you are arguing that sex education in public schools must include a moral dimension as well as the clinical facts of reproduction and venereal disease. You need to decide if you are addressing students, who may not want the moral lectures; school administrators, who may not want the added responsibility and curriculum changes; or parents, who may not want the schools to take over what they see as the responsibility of family or church.

Second, given the issue and the position you will probably take, you should ask who you would want to persuade. On the one hand, you do not need to persuade those who already agree with you; on the other, it would be futile to try to persuade those so committed to an opposing position that nothing you could say would make any difference. An argument against logging in old-growth forests, for example, would probably be aimed neither at staunch environmentalists nor at workers employed in the timber industry but rather at some readership between these extremes—say, people concerned in general about the environment but not focused specifically on the threat to mature forests.

Third, when you have a degree of choice among possible readerships, you should select your target audience based on two primary criteria. First, because persuasion is directly concerned with making decisions and taking action, seek above all to influence those readers best able to influence events. Second, when this group includes a range of readers (and it often will), also

## Following Through

For a persuasive argument you are about to write, determine your audience; that is, decide who can make a difference with respect to this issue and what they can do to make a difference. Be sure that you go beyond the requirements of convincing when you make these decisions. For example, you may be able to make a good case that just as heterosexuals do not "choose" their attraction to the opposite sex, so homosexuality is also not voluntary. Based on this point, you could argue to a local readership of moderate-to-liberal voters that they should press state legislators to support a bill extending full citizens' rights to homosexuals. But with such a desire for action in mind, you would have to think even more about who your audience is and why they might resist such a measure or not care enough to support it strongly.

In your writer's notebook respond to the questions "Who is my audience?" and "What are our differences?" (refer to the lists of questions on pages 253–254 to help formulate answers). Use your responses to write an audience profile that is more detailed than the one you wrote for an argument to convince.

consider which of these readers you know the most about and can therefore appeal to best.

Because all appeals in persuasion are addressed to an audience, try to identify your reader early in the process. You can, of course, change your mind later on, but doing so will require considerable rethinking and rewriting. Devoting time at the outset to thinking carefully about your intended audience can save much time and effort in the long run.

## Discovering the Resources of Appeal

With an audience firmly in mind, you are ready to begin thinking about how to appeal to them. Before and during the drafting stage, you will be making choices about the following:

How to formulate a case and support it with research, as needed
How to present yourself
How to arouse your readers' emotions
How to make the style of your writing contribute to the argument's effectiveness

All of these decisions will be influenced by your understanding of your readers' needs and interests.

### Appealing through Reason

In both convincing and persuading, rational appeal amounts to making a case or cases—advancing a thesis or theses and providing supporting reasons and evidence. What you learned in Chapter 7 about case-making applies here as well, so you may want to review that chapter as you work on rational appeal for a persuasive paper. Of course, research (Chapter 5) and inquiry into the truth (Chapter 6) are as relevant to persuasion as they are to convincing.

One difference between convincing and persuading, however, is that in persuasion you will devote much of your argument to defending a course of action. The steps here are basically a matter of common sense:

1. Show that there is a need for action.
2. If your audience, like that for Martin Luther King's letter, is inclined to inactivity, show urgency as well as need—we must act and act now.
3. Satisfy the need, showing that your proposal for action meets the need or will solve the problem. One way to do this is to compare your course of action with other proposals or solutions, indicating why yours is better than the others.

Sometimes your goal will be to persuade your audience *not* to act because what they want to do is wrong or inappropriate or because the time is not right. Need is still the main issue. The difference, obviously, is the goal of showing that no need exists or that it is better to await other developments before a proposed action will be appropriate or effective.

### Following Through

Prepare a brief of your argument (see Chapter 7). Be ready to present an overview of your audience and to defend your brief, either before the class or in small groups. Pay special attention to how well the argument establishes a need for your defined audience or motivation to act (or shows that there is no need for action). If some action is called for, assess the solution in the context of other, common proposals: Will the proposed action meet the need? Is it realistic—that is, can it be done?

*Appealing through Character*

A reader who finishes your essay should have the following impressions:

The author is well-informed about the topic.
The author is confident about his or her own position and sincere in advocating it.
The author has been fair and balanced in dealing with other positions.
The author understands my concerns and objections and has dealt with them.
The author is honest.
The author values what I value; his or her heart is in the right place.

What can you do to communicate these impressions? Basically, you must earn these impressions, just as you must earn a conviction and a good argument. There are no shortcuts, and educated readers are seldom fooled.

To *seem* well informed, you must *be* well informed. This requires that you dig into the topic, thinking about it carefully, researching it thoroughly and taking good notes, discussing the topic and your research with other students, consulting campus experts, and so on. This work will provide you with the following hallmarks of being well informed:

The ability to make passing references to relevant events and people connected with the issue now or recently
The ability to create a context or provide background information, which may include comments on the history of the question or issue
The ability to produce sufficient high-quality evidence to back up contentions

Just as digging in will make you well informed, so inquiry (struggling to find the truth) and convincing (making a case for your conviction about the truth) will lend your argument sincerity and confidence. Draw upon personal experience when it has played a role in determining your position, and don't be reluctant to reveal your own stake in the issue. Make your case boldly, qualifying it as little as possible. If you have prepared yourself with good research, genuine inquiry, and careful case-making, you have earned authority; what remains is to claim your authority, which is essential in arguing to persuade.

Represent other positions accurately and fairly; then present evidence that refutes those positions, or show that the reasoning is inadequate or inconsistent. Don't be afraid to agree with parts of other opinions when they are consistent with your own. Such partial agreements can play a major role in overcoming reader resistance to your own position.

It is generally not a good idea to subject other positions to ridicule. Some of your readers may sympathize with all or part of the position you are attacking and take offense. Even readers gratified by your attack may feel that you have gone too far. Concentrate on the merits of your own case rather than the faults of others.

Coping with your readers' concerns and objections should present no special problems, assuming that you have found an appropriate audience and thought seriously about both the common ground you share and the way their outlook differs from yours. You can ultimately handle concerns and objections in one of two ways: (1) by adjusting your case—your thesis and supporting reasons—so that the concerns or objections do not arise or (2) by taking up the more significant objections one by one and responding to them in a way that reduces reader resistance. Of course, doing one does not preclude doing the other: You can adjust your case and also raise and answer whatever objections remain. What matters is that you never ignore any likely and weighty objection to what you are advocating.

Responding to objections patiently and reasonably will also help with the last and perhaps most important impression that readers have of you—that you value what they value. Sensitivity to the reasoning and moral and emotional commitments of others is one of those values you can and must share with your readers.

If you are to have any chance of persuading at all, your readers must feel that you would not deceive them, so you must conform to the standards of honesty readers will expect. Leaving readers with the impression of your honesty requires much more than simply not lying. Rather, honesty requires (1) reporting evidence accurately and with regard for the original context; (2) acknowledging significant counterevidence for your case, pointing to its existence and explaining why it does not change your argument; and (3) pointing out areas of doubt and uncertainty that must await future events or study.

## Following Through

The "Following Through" assignment on page 284 asked you to prepare an audience profile and explore your key areas of difference. Now use the results of that work to help you think through how you could appeal to these readers. Use the questions on page 254 to help establish commonality with your audience and formulate strategies for bringing you and your readers closer together.

## *Appealing to Emotion*

In both convincing and persuading, your case determines largely what you have to say and how you order your presentation. As in King's essay, argument is the center, the framework, while emotional appeal plays a supporting role to rational appeal, taking center stage only occasionally. Consequently, your decisions must take the following into account:

What emotions to arouse and by what means
How frequent and intense the emotional appeals should be
Where to introduce emotional appeals

The first of these decisions is usually the easiest. Try to arouse emotions that you yourself have genuinely felt; whatever moved you will probably also move your readers. If your emotions come from direct experience, draw upon that experience for concrete descriptive detail, as King did. Study whatever you heard or read that moved you; you can probably adapt your sources' tactics for your own purposes. (The best strategy for arousing emotions is often to avoid emotionalism yourself. Let the facts, the descriptive detail, the concrete examples do the work, just as King did.)

Deciding how often, at what length, and how intensely to make emotional appeals presents a more difficult challenge. Much depends on the topic, the audience, and your own range and intensity of feeling. In every case, you must estimate as best you can what will be appropriate, but the following suggestions may help.

As always in persuasion, your primary consideration is your audience. What attitudes and feelings do they have already? Which of these lend emotional support to your case? Which work against your purposes? Emphasize those feelings that are consistent with your position, and show why any others are understandable but inappropriate.

Then ask a further question: What does my audience not feel or not feel strongly enough that they must feel or feel more strongly if I am to succeed in persuading them? King, for example, decided that his readers' greatest emotional deficit was their inability to feel what victims of racial discrimination feel—hence paragraph 14, the most intense emotional appeal in his letter. Simply put, devote space and intensity to arousing emotions central to your case that are lacking or only weakly felt by your readers.

The questions of how often and where to include emotional appeals are both worth careful consideration. Regarding frequency, the best principle is to take your shots sparingly, getting as much as you can out of each effort. Positioning emotional appeals depends on pacing: Use them to lead into or to clinch a key point. So positioned, they temporarily relieve the audience of the intellectual effort required to follow your argument.

It is generally not a good idea to begin an essay with your most involved and most intense emotional appeal; you don't want to peak too early. Besides that, in your introduction you need to concentrate on establishing your tone and authority, providing needed background information, and clearly and forcefully stating your thesis. The conclusion can be an effective position for emotional appeals because your audience is left with something memorable to carry away from the reading. In most cases, however, it is best to concentrate emotional appeals in the middle or near the end of an essay.

## Following Through

After you have a first draft of your essay, reread it with an eye to emotional appeal. Highlight the places where you have deliberately sought to arouse the audience's emotions. (You might also ask a friend to read the draft or exchange drafts with another student in your class.)

Decide if you need to devote more attention to your emotional appeal through additional concrete examples, direct quotations, or something else. Consider also how you could make each appeal more effective and intense and whether each appeal is in the best possible location in the essay.

### *Appealing through Style*

As we have seen, the style of your argument evolves with every choice you make, even in the prewriting stages. As you draft, think consciously about how stylistic choices can work for you, but don't agonize over them. In successive revisions, you will be able to make refinements and experiment for different effects.

In the first draft, however, set an appropriate level of formality. Most persuasive writing is neither chatty and familiar nor stiff and distant. Rather, persuasive prose is like dignified conversation — the way people talk when they care about and respect one another but do not know each other well. We can see some of the hallmarks of persuasive prose in King's letter:

- It uses *I, you,* and *we.*
- It avoids both technical jargon and slang.
- It inclines toward strong action verbs.
- It chooses examples and images familiar to the reader.
- It connects sentence to sentence and paragraph to paragraph with transitional words and phrases like *however, moreover,* and *for instance.*

All of these and many other features characterize the **middle style** of most persuasive writing.

As we discovered in King's letter, this middle style can cover quite a range of choices. King varies his style from section to section, depending on his purpose. Notice how King sounds highly formal in his introduction (paragraphs 1–5), where he wants to establish authority, but more plainspoken when he narrates the difficulties he and other black leaders had in their efforts to negotiate with the city's leaders (paragraphs 6–9). Notice as well how his sentences and paragraphs shorten, on average, in the passage comparing just and unjust laws (paragraphs 15–22). And we have already noted the use of sound and imagery in the passages of highest emotional appeal, such as paragraphs 14 and 47.

Just as King matches style with function, so you need to vary your style based on what each part of your essay is doing. This variation creates *pacing,* or the sense of overall rhythm in your essay. Readers need places where they can relax a bit between points of higher intensity such as lengthy arguments and passionate pleas.

As you prepare to write your first draft, then, concern yourself with matching your style to your purpose from section to section, depending on whether you are providing background information, telling a story, developing a reason in your case, mounting an emotional appeal, or doing something else. Save detailed attention to style (as explained in the appendix) for later in the process while editing a second or third draft.

### Following Through

Once you have completed the first draft of an argument to persuade, select one paragraph in which you have consciously made stylistic choices to create images, connotations, sound patterns, and so on. It may be the introduction, the conclusion, or a body paragraph where you are striving for emotional effect. Be ready to share the paragraph with your class, describing your choices as we have done with many passages from Martin Luther King's letter.

### Following Through

Read the following argument, and be ready to discuss its effectiveness as persuasion. You might build your evaluation around the suggestions listed in the "Reader's Checklist for Revising a Persuasive Essay" on page 289.

**STUDENT SAMPLE:** *An Essay Arguing to Persuade*

The following essay was written in response to an assignment for a first-year rhetoric course. The intended readers were other students, eighteen to twenty-two years old and for the most part middle-class, who attended the same large, private university as the writer. Within this group, Shanks was trying to reach those who might sit in class and disagree with the opinions of more

The following list will direct you to specific features of a good persuasive essay. You and a peer may want to exchange drafts; having someone else give your paper a critical reading often helps identify weaknesses you may have overlooked. After you have revised your draft, use the suggestions in the appendix to edit for style and check for errors at the sentence level.

☐ Read the audience profile for this essay. Then read the draft all the way through, projecting yourself as much as possible into the role of the target audience. After reading the draft, find and mark the essay's natural divisions. You may also want to number the paragraph so that you can refer to them easily.

☐ Recall that persuasive arguments must be based on careful inquiry and strategic case making. Inspect the case first. Begin by underlining the thesis and marking the main reasons in support. You might write "Reason 1," "Reason 2," and so forth in the margins. Circle any words that need clearer definition. Also note any reasons that need more evidence or other support, such as illustrations or analogies.

☐ Evaluate the plan for organizing the case. Are the reasons presented in a compelling and logical order? Does the argument build to a strong conclusion? Can you envision an alternative arrangement? Make suggestions for improvement, referring to paragraphs by number.

☐ Remember that persuasion requires the writer to make an effort to present him- or herself as worthy of the reader's trust and respect. Reread the draft with a highlighter or pen in hand, marking specific places where the writer has sought identification with the target audience. Has the writer made an effort to find common ground with readers by using any of the ideas listed on page 254? Make suggestions for improvement.

☐ Be aware that persuasion also requires the writer to make a conscious effort to gain the audience's emotional support through concrete examples and imagery, analogies and metaphors, first-person reporting, quotations, and so on. How many instances of conscious emotional appeal are there? Are the efforts at emotional appeal uniformly successful? What improvements can you suggest? Has the writer gone too far with emotional appeal? Or should more be done?

☐ Add conscious stylistic appeals later, in the editing stage, because style involves refinements in word choice and sentence patterns. However, look now to see if the draft exhibits a middle style appropriate to the targeted audience. Mark any instances of the following:

    Poor transitions between sentences or paragraphs
    Wordy passages, especially those containing the passive voice (see the section "Editing for Clarity and Conciseness" in the appendix)

(continues)

    Awkward sentences

    Poor diction—that is, the use of incorrect or inappropriate words

☐ Note any examples of effective style—good use of metaphor, repetition, or parallelism, for example.

☐ Describe the general tone. Does it change from section to section? How appropriate and effective is the tone in general and in specific sections of the essay?

☐ After studying the argument, ask whether you are sure what the writer wants or expects of the audience. Has the writer succeeded in persuading the audience? Why or why not?

outspoken students but, for whatever reasons, refrain from expressing their own dissenting viewpoints.

## AN UNCOMFORTABLE POSITION

### Joey Shanks

I sat quietly in my uncomfortable chair. Perhaps it was my position, I thought, and not the poly-wood seat that tormented me; so I sat upright, realizing then that both the chair and my position were probably responsible for my disposition. But I could do nothing to correct the problem.

Or maybe it was the conversation. I sat quietly, only for a lack of words. Usually I rambled on any subject, even if I knew nothing about it. No one in my rhetoric class would ever accuse me of lacking words, but today I was silent. The opinions of my classmates flew steadily across the room with occasional "I agree's" and "that's the truth's." My teacher shook her head in frustration.

She mediated the debate, if it was a debate. I could not imagine that a group of white college students angrily confessing that we all were constantly victims of reverse racism could provide much of a debate. For our generalizations to have formed a legitimate debate, there should have been two opposing sides, but the power of the majority had triumphed again. I sat quietly, knowing that what I heard was wrong. The little I said only fueled the ignorance and the guarded, David Duke–like articulations.

Did everyone in the class really think America had achieved equal opportunity? I could only hope that someone else in the classroom felt the same intimidation that I felt. I feared the majority. If I spoke my mind, I would only give the majority a minority to screw with.

But what about the young woman who sat next to me? She was Hispanic, with glasses and no name or voice that I knew of. She was the visible minority in a class full of Greek letters and blond hair. She must have been more uncomfortable than I was. She sat quietly every day.

The individual in society must possess the courage and the confidence to challenge and oppose the majority if he or she feels it necessary. In the classroom, I had not seen this individualism. My classmates may have had different backgrounds and interests, but eventually, in every discussion, a majority opinion dominated the debate and all personalities were lost in a mob mentality. In rhetoric class, we read and discussed material designed to stimulate a debate with many sides; however, the debate was rendered useless because the power of the majority stifled open discussion and bullied the individual to submit or stay quiet.

Tocqueville wrote of the dangerous power of the majority in his book *Democracy in America:* "The moral authority of the majority is partly based upon the notion that there is more intelligence and wisdom in a number of men united than in a single individual" (113). Tocqueville illustrated a point that I witnessed in class and that history has witnessed for ages. The majority rules through the power of numbers. No matter how wrong, an opinion with many advocates becomes the majority opinion and is difficult to oppose. The majority makes the rules; therefore, we accept that "might makes right."

The true moral authority, however, lies in the fundamental acceptance that right and wrong are universal and not relative to time and place. Thomas Nagel, a contemporary philosopher, states, "Many things that you probably think are wrong have been accepted as morally correct by large groups of people in the past" (71). The majority is not right simply because it is a large group. An individual is responsible for knowing right from wrong, no matter how large the group appears. Ancient philosophers such as Aristotle and Socrates have defied generations of majorities. They preached that morality is universal and that the majority is not always right.

In our classroom, after the first week all the students chose their chairs in particular areas. Certain mentalities aligned, acknowledging similar philosophies on politics, hunting, sports, African Americans, welfare, and women. Debate on *The Awakening* awoke the beefcake majority with confused exclamations: "She's crazy! Why did the chick kill herself?" The majority either misunderstood the book or was not willing to accept another opinion.

Mark Twain, a pioneer of American literature, fought an empire of slavery with his book *The Adventures of Huckleberry Finn.* Twain saw through the cruelty of racism and spoke against a nation that treated men and women like animals because of the color of their skin. Twain possessed the confidence and individualism to fight the majority, despite its power. Mark Twain protected individualism when he opposed racism and the institution of slavery. He proved that the single individual is sometimes more intelligent than men united.

Ramsey Clark, a former attorney general and now a political activist, expressed a great deal of distress over the Persian Gulf war. He spoke for the minority, a position of peace. In an interview in *The Progressive,* Clark stated, "We really believe that might makes right, and that leads us to perpetual war" (qtd. in Dreifus 32). Clark was referring to the United States' foreign policy of peace through intimidation, but his words can be taken on a universal level. We will never accomplish anything if might makes right and humanity is in a perpetual war of opinions. Clark is an example of individualism against the majority, though he will never be considered an American hero; few may remember his words, but like Mark Twain, he fought the majority's "moral authority."

In the classroom, or in the post-slavery South, or in the deserts of the Middle East, the majority has the power, and whoever has the power controls the world and may even seem to control all the opinions in it. As a country, we abuse the power of the majority. America, the spokesperson for the world majority, manipulates its position while flexing and growling, "Might makes right!" This situation is a large-scale version of a rhetoric seminar in which students too frequently align with or submit to the majority opinion. In rhetoric seminar, we lack champions, individuals who see wrong and cry, "Foul!" Maybe the young Hispanic woman who quietly sits is just waiting for the right moment. Perhaps I had my chance and lost it, or maybe the majority has scared all the individuals into sitting quietly in their uncomfortable chairs.

Works Cited

Dreifus, Claudia. "An Interview with Ramsey Clark." The Progressive Apr. 1991: 32–35.

Nagel, Thomas. What Does It All Mean? Oxford: Oxford UP, 1987.

Tocqueville, Alexis de. Democracy in America. 1835. New York: Penguin, 1956.

# Chapter 9

# Resolving Conflict: Arguing to Negotiate and Mediate

A rgument to convince and persuade is a healthy force within a community. Whatever the issue, people hold a range of positions, and debate among advocates of these various positions serves to inform the public and draw attention to problems that need solution. Yet, although some issues seem to be debated endlessly—the death penalty, abortion, gun control, the U.S. role in the affairs of other nations—a time comes when the conflict must be resolved and a particular course of action pursued.

But what happens after each side has made its best effort to convince and persuade, yet no one position has won general assent? If the conflicting parties have equal power, the result can be an impasse, a stalemate. More often, however, one party has greater authority and is able to impose its will, as, for example, when a university dean or president imposes a policy decision on students or faculty. But imposing power can be costly—especially in terms of the worsened relationships—and it is often temporary. Foes of abortion, for example, have been able to influence policy significantly under conservative administrations, only to see their policy gains eroded when more liberal politicians gain power. If conflicts are going to be resolved—and stay resolved—each side needs to move beyond advocating its own position and argue with a new aim in mind: negotiation.

Arguing to negotiate aims to resolve, or at least reduce, conflict to the mutual satisfaction of all parties involved. But negotiation involves more than simply making a deal in which each side offers a few concessions while retaining a few of its initial demands. As this chapter shows, through the process of negotiating, opposing sides come to a greater understanding of their differing interests, backgrounds, and values; ideally, negotiation builds consensus and repairs strained relationships.

## CONFLICT RESOLUTION AND
## THE OTHER AIMS OF ARGUMENT

You may find it difficult to think of negotiation and mediation as argument if you see argument only as presenting a case for a particular position or as persuading an audience to act in accordance with that position. Both of these aims clearly involve advocating one position and addressing the argument to those with different viewpoints. But recall that one definition of *argue* is "to make clear." As we discussed in Chapter 6, sometimes we argue in order to learn what we should think; that is, we argue to inquire, trying out an argument, examining it critically and with as little bias as possible with an audience of nonthreatening partners in conversation such as friends or family.

Arguing to mediate or negotiate shares many of the characteristics of arguing to inquire. Like inquiry, negotiation most often takes the form of dialogue, although writing plays an important role in the process. Also, whether the negotiator is a party in the conflict or an outside mediator among the various parties, he or she must inquire into the positions of all sides. Furthermore, someone who agrees to enter into negotiation, especially someone who is a party to the conflict, must acknowledge his or her bias and remain open to the positions and interests of others, just as the inquirer does. Negotiation differs from inquiry, however, in that negotiation must find a mediating position that accommodates at least some of the interests of all sides. The best position in negotiation is the one all sides will accept.

As we will see in more detail, argument as mediation draws upon the strategies of the other aims of argument as well. Like convincing, negotiation requires an understanding of case structure, as negotiators must analyze the cases each side puts forth, and mediators often need to build a case of their own for a position acceptable to all. And like persuasion, negotiation recognizes the role of human character and emotions both in the creation of conflict and in its resolution.

To illustrate the benefits to be gained through the process of negotiation, in this chapter we concentrate on one of the most heated conflicts in the United States today: the debate over abortion. A wide range of positions exists on this issue. Extremists for fetal rights, who sometimes engage in violent acts of civil disobedience, and extremists for the absolute rights of women, who argue that a woman should be able to terminate a pregnancy at any time and for any reason, may not be amenable to negotiation. However, between these poles lie the viewpoints of most Americans, whose differences possibly can be resolved.

Negotiation has a chance only among people who have reasoned through their own positions through inquiry and who have attempted to defend their positions not through force but through convincing and persuasive argumentation. And mediation has a chance only when people see that the divisions caused by their conflict are counterproductive. They must be ready to listen to each other. They must be willing to negotiate.

**Concept Close-Up**

## Characteristics of Negotiation

1. Aims to **resolve conflict** between opposing and usually **hardened** positions, often because action of some kind must be taken.
2. Aims to reduce hostility and promote understanding between or among conflicting parties; **preserving human relationships and promoting communication** are paramount.
3. Like inquiry, negotiation **involves dialogue** and requires that one understand all positions and strive for an **open mind.**
4. Like convincing, negotiation involves taking stances and making cases, but negotiation involves making a case that **appeals to all parties in the controversy.**
5. Like persuasion, negotiation depends on the **good character** of the negotiator and on sharing **values and feelings.**
6. Negotiation depends on conflicting parties' desire to **find solutions to overcome counterproductive stalemates.**

Essentially, negotiation comes into play when convincing and persuading have resulted in sharply differing viewpoints. The task is first to understand the positions of all parties involved and second to uncover a mediating position capable of producing consensus and a reduction in hostility.

## THE PROCESS OF NEGOTIATION AND MEDIATION

As a student in a writing class, you can practice the process of negotiation in at least two ways. You and several other students who have written conflicting arguments on a common topic may negotiate among yourselves to find a resolution acceptable to all, perhaps bringing in a disinterested student to serve as a mediator. Or your class as a whole may mediate a dispute among writers whose printed arguments offer conflicting viewpoints on the same issue. Here we illustrate the mediator approach, which can be adapted easily to the more direct experience of face-to-face negotiation.

### Understanding the Spirit of Negotiation and Mediation

In arguing issues of public concern, it is a mistake to think of negotiation as the same thing as negotiating the price of a car or a house or even a collective bargaining agreement. In a dialogue between buyer and seller, both sides typically begin by asking for much more than they seriously hope to get, and the process involves displays of will and power as each side tries to force the other to back down on its demands. Negotiation as rhetorical argument, however, is less adversarial; in fact, it is more like collaborative problem solving in which various opposing parties work together not to rebut one another's arguments but to understand them. Negotiation leads to the most permanent resolution of conflict when it is based on an increased understanding of difference rather than on a mere exchange of concessions. Negotiators must let go of the whole notion of proving one side right and other sides wrong. Rather, the negotiator says, "I see what you are demanding, and you see what I am demanding. Now let's sit down and find out *why* we hold these positions. What are our interests in this issue? Maybe together we can work out a solution that will address these interests." Unlike negotiators, mediators are impartial, and if they have a personal viewpoint on the issue, they must suppress it and be careful not to favor either side.

## Understanding the Opposing Positions

Resolving conflict begins with a close look at opposing views. As in inquiry, the first stage of the process is an analysis of the positions, the thesis statements, and the supporting reasons and evidence offered on all sides. It is a good idea for each party to write a brief of his or her case, as described on pages 221–236 and 312–313. These briefs should indicate how the reasons are supported so that disputants can see where they agree or disagree about data.

The mediator also must begin by inquiring into the arguments presented by the parties in dispute. To illustrate, we look at two reasoned arguments representing opposing views on the value of the Supreme Court's *Roe v. Wade* decision. In that decision, which was handed down in 1973, the Court ruled that the Constitution does grant to citizens a zone of personal privacy, which for women includes the decision regarding whether to terminate a pregnancy. The Court stipulated, however, that the right to abortion was not unqualified and that states could regulate abortions to protect the fetus after viability.

The first argument, "Living with *Roe v. Wade*," is by Margaret Liu McConnell, a writer and mother of three, who herself had an abortion while she was in college. This experience led McConnell to decide that abortion on demand should not have become a constitutional right. To those who applaud abortion rights, McConnell argues that *Roe v. Wade* has had serious social and moral consequences for our nation. She does not call for the decision to be overturned, but she does want abortion rights supporters to take a closer look at the issue and recognize that abortion is fundamentally an immoral choice, one that should result in a sense of guilt. This essay originally appeared in 1990 in *Commentary,* a journal published by the American Jewish Committee.

The second argument is by Ellen Willis, also a mother who once had an abortion. For Willis, abortion is very much a right; in fact, it is the foundation of women's equality with men. Willis defends *Roe v. Wade* as the "cutting edge of feminism." Her audience consists of liberals who oppose abortion — "the left wing of the right-to-life movement" — specifically, the editors of *Com-*

*Figure 9.1   In a familiar scene, angry pro-choice and pro-life activists confront each other at a pro-choice demonstration. Although abortion remains one of the most contentious issues of our time, some of its proponents and opponents remain committed to working toward reconciling their differences.*

*monweal*, a liberal Catholic journal. Her audience could also include people like Margaret Liu McConnell, who see abortion as a moral question rather than as a political question framed in terms of equal rights. Willis' "Putting Women Back into the Abortion Debate" originally appeared in the left-leaning *Village Voice* in 1985.

## Living with *Roe v. Wade*
### Margaret Liu McConnell

There is something decidedly unappealing to me about the pro-life activists seen on the evening news as they are dragged away from the entrances to abortion clinics across the country. Perhaps it is that their poses remind me of sulky two-year-olds, sinking to their knees as their frazzled mothers try to haul them from the playground. Or perhaps it is because I am a little hard put to believe, when one of them cries out, often with a Southern twang, "Ma'am, don't keel your baby," that he or she could really care that deeply about a stranger's fetus. After all, there are limits to compassion and such concern seems excessive, suspect.

Besides, as pro-choice adherents like to point out, the fact that abortion is legal does not mean that someone who is against abortion will be forced to have one against her wishes. It is a private matter, so they say, between a woman and her doctor. From this it would follow that those opposed to abortion are no more than obnoxious busybodies animated by their own inner pathologies to interfere in the private lives of strangers.

Certainly this is the impression conveyed by those news clips of anti-abortion blockades being broken up by the police. We pity the woman, head sunk and afraid, humiliated in the ancient shame that all around her know she is carrying an unwanted child. Precisely because she is pregnant, our hearts go out to her in her vulnerability. It would seem that those workers from the abortion clinic, shielding arms around her shoulders, their identification vests giving them the benign look of school-crossing guards, are her protectors. They are guiding her through a hostile, irrational crowd to the cool and orderly safety of the clinic and the medical attention she needs.

But is it possible that this impression is mistaken? Is it possible that those who guide the woman along the path to the abortionist's table are not truly her protectors, shoring her up on the road to a dignified life in which she will best be able to exercise her intellectual and physical faculties free from any kind of oppression? Is it possible that they are serving, albeit often unwittingly, to keep her and millions of other women on a demeaning and rather lonely treadmill—a treadmill on which these women trudge through cycles of sex without commitment, unwanted pregnancy, and abortion, all in the name of equal opportunity and free choice?

Consider yet again the woman on the path to an abortion. She is already     5 a victim of many forces. She is living in a social climate in which she is expected to view sex as practically a form of recreation that all healthy women should pursue eagerly. She has been conditioned to fear having a child, particularly in her younger years, as an unthinkable threat to her standard of living and to the career through which she defines herself as a "real" person. Finally, since 1973, when the Supreme Court in *Roe v. Wade* declared access to abortion a constitutional right, she has been invited, in the event that she does become pregnant, not only to have an abortion, but to do so without sorrow and with no moral misgivings. As the highly vocal proabortion movement cheers her on with rallying cries of "Freedom of Choice," she may find herself wondering: "Is this the great freedom we've been fighting for? The freedom to sleep with men who don't care for us, the freedom to scorn the chance to raise a child? The freedom to let doctors siphon from our bodies that most precious gift which women alone are made to receive: a life to nurture?"

My goal here is not to persuade militant pro-choicers that abortion is wrong. Instead, it is to establish that abortion cannot and should not be seen as strictly a matter between a woman and her doctor. For the knowledge that the law allows free access to abortion affects all of us directly and indirectly by the way it shapes the social climate. Most directly and most easy to illustrate, the realization that any pregnancy, intended or accidental, may be aborted at will affects women in their so-called childbearing years. The indirect effects are more difficult to pinpoint. I would like tentatively to suggest that *Roe v. Wade* gives approval, at the highest level of judgment in this country, to certain attitudes which, when manifest at the lowest economic levels, have extremely destructive consequences.

But to begin with the simpler task of examining *Roe*'s questionable effect on the world women inhabit: I—who at thirty-two am of the age to have "benefited" from *Roe*'s protections for all my adult years— offer here some examples of those "benefits."

It was my first year at college, my first year away from my rather strict, first-generation American home. I had a boyfriend from high school whom I liked and admired but was not in love with, and I was perfectly satisfied with the stage of heavy-duty necking we had managed, skillfully avoiding the suspicious eyes of my mother. But once I got to college I could think of no good reason not to go farther. For far from perceiving any constraints around me, I encountered all manner of encouragement to become "sexually active"—from the health center, from newspapers, books, and magazines, from the behavior of other students, even from the approval of other students' parents of their children's "liberated" sexual conduct.

Yet the truth is that I longed for the days I knew only from old movies and novels, those pre-60's days when boyfriends visiting from other colleges stayed in hotels (!) and dates ended with a lingering kiss at the door. I lived in an apartment-style dormitory, six women sharing three bedrooms and a kitchen. Needless to say, visiting boyfriends did not stay in hotels. By the end of my freshman year three out of the six of us would have had abortions.

How did it come to pass that so many of us got pregnant? How has it come to pass that more than one-and-one-half million women each year get pregnant in this country, only to have abortions? Nowadays it is impossible to go into a drugstore without bumping into the condoms on display above the checkout counters. And even when I was in college, contraception was freely available, and everyone knew that the health center, open from nine to four, was ready to equip us with the contraceptive armament we were sure to need.

Nevertheless, thanks to *Roe v. Wade*, we all understood as well that if anything went wrong, there would be no threat of a shotgun marriage, or of being sent away in shame to bear a child, or of a dangerous back-alley abortion. Perhaps the incredible number of "accidental" pregnancies, both at college and throughout the country, finds its explanation in just that understanding. Analogies are difficult to construct in arguments about abortion, for there is nothing quite analogous to terminating a pregnancy. That said, consider this one anyway. If children are sent out to play ball in a yard near a house, a responsible adult, knowing that every once in a while a window will get broken, will still tell them to be very careful not to break any. But what if the children are sent into the yard and told something like this: "Go out and play, and don't worry about breaking any windows. It's bound to happen, and when it does, no problem: it will be taken care of." How many more windows will be shattered?

There were, here and there, some women who seemed able to live outside these pressures. Within my apartment one was an Orthodox Jewish freshman from Queens, another a junior from Brooklyn, also Jewish, who was in the process of becoming Orthodox. They kept kosher as far as was possible in our common kitchen, and on Friday afternoons would cook supper for a group of friends, both men and women. As darkness fell they would light candles and sing and eat and laugh in a circle of light. I remember looking in at their evenings from the doorway to the kitchen, wishing vainly that I could belong to such a group, a group with a code of behavior that would provide shelter from the free-for-all I saw elsewhere. But the only group I felt I belonged to was, generically, "young American woman," and as far as I could see, the norm of behavior for a young American woman was to enjoy a healthy sex life, with or without commitment.

A few months later, again thanks to *Roe v. Wade*, I discovered that the logistics of having an abortion were, as promised, extremely simple. The school health center was again at my service. After a few perfunctory questions and sympathetic nods of the head I was given directions to the nearest abortion clinic.

A strange thing has happened since that great freedom-of-choice victory in 1973. Abortion has become the only viable alternative many women feel they have open to them when they become pregnant by accident. Young men no longer feel obligated to offer to "do the right thing." Pregnancy is most often confirmed in a medical setting. Even though it is a perfectly normal and healthy state, in an unwanted pregnancy a woman feels distressed. The situation thus becomes that of a distressed woman looking to trusted medical personnel for relief. Abortion presents itself as the simple, legal, medical solution to her distress. A woman may have private reservations, but she gets the distinct impression that if she does not take advantage of her right to an abortion she is of her own accord refusing a simple solution to her troubles.

That is certainly how it was for me, sitting across from the counselor at    15
the health center, clutching a wad of damp tissues, my heart in my throat. The feeling was exactly parallel to the feeling I had had at the beginning of the school year: I could be defiantly old-fashioned and refuse to behave like a normal American woman, or I could exercise my sexual liberation. Here, six weeks pregnant, I could be troublesome, perverse, and somehow manage to keep the baby, causing tremendous inconvenience to everyone, or I could take the simple route of having an abortion and not even miss a single class. The choice was already made.

Physically, also, abortion has become quite a routine procedure. As one of my grosser roommates put it, comforting me with talk of her own experiences, it was about as bad as going to the dentist. My only memory of the

operation is of coming out of the general anesthesia to the sound of sobbing all around. I, too, was sobbing, without thought, hard and uncontrol-
lably, as though somehow, deep below the conscious level, below whatever
superficial concerns had layered themselves in the day-to-day mind of a
busy young woman, I had come to realize what I had done, and what
could never be undone.

I have since had three children, and at the beginning of each pregnancy
I was presented with the opportunity to have an abortion without even
having to ask. For professional reasons my husband and I have moved several times, and each of our children was born in a different city with a different set of obstetrical personnel. In every case I was offered the unsolic-
ited luxury of "keeping my options open": of choosing whether to continue
the pregnancy or end it. The polite way of posing the question, after a positive pregnancy test, seems to be for the doctor to ask noncommittally, "And
how are we treating this pregnancy?"

Each one of those pregnancies, each one of those expendable bunches
of tissue, has grown into a child, each one different from the other. I cannot
escape the haunting fact that if I had had an abortion, one of my children
would be missing. Not just a generic little bundle in swaddling clothes interchangeable with any other, but a specific child.

I still carry in my mind a picture of that other child who was never born,
a picture which changes as the years go by, and I imagine him growing up.
For some reason I usually do imagine a boy, tall and with dark hair and
eyes. This is speculation, of course, based on my coloring and build and on
that of the young man involved. Such speculation seems maudlin and mor-
bid and I do not engage in it on purpose. But whether I like it or not, every
now and then my mind returns to that ghost of a child and to the certainty
that for seven weeks I carried the beginnings of a being whose coloring and
build and, to a large extent, personality were already determined. Buoyant
green-eyed girl or shy, dark-haired boy, I wonder. Whoever, a child would
have been twelve this spring.

I am not in the habit of exposing this innermost regret, this endless re- [20]
morse to which I woke too late. I do so only to show that in the wake of
*Roe v. Wade* abortion has become casual, commonplace, and very hard to
resist as an easy way out of an unintended pregnancy, and that more unintended pregnancies are likely to occur when everyone knows there is an
easy way out of them. Abortion has become an option offered to women,
married as well as unmarried, including those who are financially, physically, and emotionally able to care for a child. This is what *Roe v. Wade*
guarantees. For all the pro-choice lobby's talk of abortion as a deep personal moral decision, casting abortion as a right takes the weight of morality out of the balance. For, by definition, a right is something one need not
feel guilty exercising.

I do not wish a return to the days when a truly desperate woman unable to get a safe legal abortion would risk her life at the hands of an illegal

abortionist. Neither could I ever condemn a woman whose own grip on life is so fragile as to render her incapable of taking on the full responsibility for another life, helpless and demanding. But raising abortion to the plane of a constitutional right in order to ensure its accessibility to any woman for any reason makes abortion too easy a solution to an age-old problem.

Human beings have always coupled outside the bounds deemed proper by the societies in which they lived. But the inevitable unexpected pregnancies often served a social purpose. There was a time when many young couples found in the startling new life they had created an undeniable reason to settle down seriously to the tasks of earning a living and making a home. That might have meant taking on a nine-to-five job and assuming a mortgage, a prospect which sounds like death to many baby boomers intent on prolonging adolescence well into middle age. But everyone knows anecdotally if not from straight statistics that many of these same baby boomers owe their own lives to such happy (for them) accidents.

When I became pregnant in college, I never seriously considered getting married and trying to raise a child, although it certainly would have been possible to do so. Why should I have, when the road to an abortion was so free and unencumbered, and when the very operation itself had been presented as a step on the march to women's equality?

I know that no one forced me to do anything, that I was perfectly free to step back at any time and live by my own moral code if I chose to, much as my Orthodox Jewish acquaintances did. But this is awfully hard when the society you consider yourself part of presents abortion as a legal, morally acceptable solution. And what kind of a world would it be if all those in need of a moral structure stepped back to insulate themselves, alone or in groups — ethnic, religious, or economic — each with its own exclusive moral code, leaving behind a chaos at the center? It sounds like New York City on a bad day.

This is not, of course, to ascribe the chaos reigning in our cities directly    25
to *Roe v. Wade.* That chaos is caused by a growing and tenacious underclass defined by incredibly high rates of drug abuse, and dependence on either crime or welfare for financial support. But sometimes it does seem as though the same attitude behind abortion on demand lies behind the abandonment of parental responsibility which is the most pervasive feature of life in the underclass and the most determinative of its terrible condition.

Parental responsibility can be defined as providing one's offspring at every level of development with that which they need to grow eventually into independent beings capable of supporting themselves emotionally and financially. Different parents will, of course, have different ideas about what is best for a child, and different parents will have different resources to draw upon to provide for their children. But whatever the differences may be, responsible parents will try, to the best of their ability and in accordance with their own rights, to raise their children properly. It is tedious, expensive, and takes a long, long time. For it is not a question of fetal weeks before a human being reaches any meaningful stage of "viability" (how "viable" is a two-year-old left to his own devices? A five-year-old?). It is a question of years, somewhere in the neighborhood of eighteen.

Why does any parent take on such a long, hard task? Because life is a miracle that cannot be denied? Because it is the right thing to do? Because there is a certain kind of love a parent bears a child that does not require a calculated return on investment? Because we would hate ourselves otherwise? All these factors enter into the powerful force that compels parents to give up years of their free time and much of their money to bring up their children. Yet the cool, clinical approach *Roe v. Wade* allows all of us—men no less than women—in deciding whether or not we are "ready" to accept the responsibility of an established pregnancy seems to undermine an already weakening cultural expectation that parents simply have a duty to take care of their children.

A middle- or upper-class woman may have high expectations of what she will achieve so long as she is not saddled with a baby. When she finds herself pregnant she is guaranteed the right under *Roe v. Wade* to opt out of that long and tedious responsibility, and does so by the hundreds of thousands each year. By contrast, a woman in the underclass who finds herself pregnant is not likely to have great expectations of what life would be like were she free of the burden of her child; abortion would not broaden her horizons and is not usually her choice. Yet she often lacks the maternal will and the resources to take full responsibility for the well-being of her child until adulthood.

To be sure, these two forms of refusing parental responsibility have vastly different effects. But how can the government hope to devise policies that will encourage parental responsibility in the underclass when at the highest level of judgment, that of the Supreme Court, the freedom to opt out of parental responsibility is protected as a right? Or, to put the point another way, perhaps the weakening of the sense of duty toward one's own offspring is a systemic problem in America, present in all classes, with only its most visible manifestation in the underclass.

The federal Family Support Act of 1988 was the result of much study and debate on how to reform the welfare system to correct policies which have tended to make it easier for poor families to qualify for aid if the father is not part of the household. Among other provisions intended to help keep families from breaking up, states are now required to pay cash benefits to two-parent families and to step up child-support payments from absent fathers. New York City, for example, has this year begun to provide its Department of Health with information, including Social Security numbers, on the parents of every child born in the city. Should the mother ever apply for aid, the father can be tracked down and child-support payments can be deducted from his paycheck. Such a strict enforcement of child-support obligations is a powerful and exciting legal method for society to show that it will not tolerate the willful abandonment of children by their fathers.

30

It is evident that there is a compelling state interest in promoting the responsibility of both parents toward their child. The compelling interest is that it takes a great deal of money to care for a child whose parents do not undertake the responsibility themselves. For whatever else we may have lost of our humanity over the last several decades, however hardened we have been by violence and by the degradation witnessed daily in the lost lives on the street, we still retain a basic decent instinct to care for innocent babies and children in need.

It is also evident that parental responsibility begins well before the child is born. Thus, the Appellate Division of the State Supreme Court of New York in May of this year ruled that a woman who uses drugs during pregnancy and whose newborn has drugs in its system may be brought before Family Court for a hearing on neglect. Yet how can we condemn a woman under law for harming her unborn child while at the same time protecting her right to destroy that child absolutely, for any reason, through abortion? Is the only difference that the first instance entails a monetary cost to society while the second does not?

There is another kind of behavior implicitly condoned by *Roe v. Wade*, which involves the value of life itself, and which also has its most frightening and threatening manifestation in the underclass. Consensus on when human life begins has yet to be established and perhaps never will be. What is clear, however, is that abortion cuts short the development of a specific human life; it wipes out the future years of a human being, years we can know nothing about. Generally we have no trouble conceiving of lost future years as real loss. Lawsuits routinely place value on lost future income and lost future enjoyment, and we consider the death of a child or a young person to be particularly tragic in lost potential, in the waste of idealized years to come. Yet under *Roe v. Wade* the value of the future years of life of the fetus is determined by an individual taking into account only her own well-being.

Back in 1965, justifying his discovery of a constitutional right to privacy which is nowhere mentioned in the Constitution itself, and which helped lay the groundwork for *Roe v. Wade*, Justice William O. Douglas invoked the concept of "penumbras, formed by emanations" of constitutional amendments. Is it far-fetched to say that there are "penumbras, formed by emanations" of *Roe v. Wade* that grant the right to consider life in relative terms and to place one's own interest above any others? This same "right" when exercised by criminals is a terrifying phenomenon: these are people who feel no guilt in taking a victim's life, who value the future years of that life as nothing compared with their own interest in the victim's property. Of course, one might argue that a fetus is not yet cognizant of its own beingness and that, further, it feels no pain. Yet if a killer creeps up behind you and blows your head off with a semi-automatic, you will feel no pain either, nor will you be cognizant of your death.

*Roe v. Wade* was a great victory for the women's movement. It seemed to promote equality of opportunity for women in all their endeavors by free-    35 ing them from the burden of years of caring for children conceived unintentionally. But perhaps support for *Roe v. Wade* should be reconsidered in light of the damage wrought by the kind of behavior that has become common in a world in which pregnancy is no longer seen as the momentous beginning of a new life, and life, by extension, is no longer held as sacred.

At any rate, even if one rejects my speculation that *Roe v. Wade* has at least some indirect connection with the degree to which life on our streets has become so cheap, surely there can be no denying the direct connection between *Roe v. Wade* and the degree to which sex has become so casual. Surely, for example, *Roe v. Wade* will make it harder for my two daughters to grow gracefully into womanhood without being encouraged to think of sex as a kind of sport played with a partner who need feel no further responsibility toward them once the game is over.

For me, that is reason enough not to support this elevation of abortion to the status of a constitutional right.

---

## Putting Women Back into the Abortion Debate
### Ellen Willis

Some years ago I attended a New York Institute for the Humanities seminar on the new right. We were a fairly heterogeneous group of liberals and lefties, feminists and gay activists, but on one point nearly all of us agreed: The right-to-life movement was a dangerous antifeminist crusade. At one session I argued that the attack on abortion had significance far beyond itself, that it was the linchpin of the right's social agenda. I got a lot of supporting comments and approving nods. It was too much for Peter Steinfels, a liberal Catholic, author of *The Neoconservatives,* and executive editor of *Commonweal.* Right-to-lifers were not all right-wing fanatics, he protested. "You have to understand," he said plaintively, "that many of us see abortion as a *human life issue.*" What I remember best was his air of frustrated isolation. I don't think he came back to the seminar after that.

Things are different now. I often feel isolated when I insist that abortion is, above all, a *feminist issue.* Once people took for granted that abortion was an issue of sexual politics and morality. Now, abortion is most often discussed as a question of "life" in the abstract. Public concern over abortion centers almost exclusively on fetuses; women and their bodies are merely the stage on which the drama of fetal life and death takes place. Debate about abortion—if not its reality—has become sexlessly scholastic. And the people most responsible for this turn of events are, like Peter Steinfels, on the left.

The left wing of the right-to-life movement is a small, seemingly eccentric minority in both "progressive" and antiabortion camps. Yet it has played a critical role in the movement: By arguing that opposition to abortion can be separated from the right's antifeminist program, it has given antiabortion sentiment legitimacy in left-symp[1] and (putatively) profeminist circles. While left antiabortionists are hardly alone in emphasizing fetal life, their innovation has been to claim that a consistent "pro-life" stand involves opposing capital punishment, supporting disarmament, demanding government programs to end poverty, and so on. This is of course a leap the right is neither able nor willing to make. It's been liberals—from Garry Wills to the Catholic bishops—who have supplied the mass media with the idea that prohibiting abortion is part of a "seamless garment" of respect for human life.

Having invented this countercontext for the abortion controversy, left antiabortionists are trying to impose it as the only legitimate context for debate. Those of us who won't accept their terms and persist in seeing opposition to abortion, antifeminism, sexual repression, and religious sectarianism as the real seamless garment have been accused of obscuring the issue with demagoguery. Last year *Commonweal*—perhaps the most important current forum for left antiabortion opinion—ran an editorial demanding that we shape up: "Those who hold that abortion is immoral believe that the biological dividing lines of birth or viability should no more determine whether a developing member of the species is denied or accorded essential rights than should the biological dividing lines of sex or race or disability or old age. This argument is open to challenge. Perhaps the dividing lines are sufficiently different. Pro-choice advocates should state their reasons for believing so. They should meet the argument on its own grounds. . . ."

In other words, the only question we're allowed to debate—or the only 5 one *Commonweal* is willing to entertain—is "Are fetuses the moral equivalent of born human beings?" And I can't meet the argument on its own grounds because I don't agree that this is the key question, whose answer determines whether one supports abortion or opposes it. I don't doubt that fetuses are alive, or that they're biologically human—what else would they be? I do consider the life of a fertilized egg less precious than the well-being of a woman with feelings, self-consciousness, a history, social ties; and I think fetuses get closer to being human in a moral sense as they come closer to birth. But to me these propositions are intuitively self-evident. I wouldn't know how to justify them to a "nonbeliever," nor do I see the point of trying.

I believe the debate has to start in a different place—with the recognition that fertilized eggs develop into infants inside the bodies of women. Pregnancy and birth are active processes in which a woman's body shelters, nourishes, and expels a new life; for nine months she is immersed in the most intimate possible relationship with another being. The growing fetus makes considerable demands on her physical and emotional resources, cul-

[1] *Left-symp:* sympathetic to the left.

minating in the cataclysmic experience of birth. And child-bearing has unpredictable consequences; it always entails some risk of injury or death.

For me all this has a new concreteness: I had a baby last year. My much-
desired and relatively easy pregnancy was full of what antiabortionists like
to call "inconveniences." I was always tired, short of breath; my digestion
was never right; for three months I endured a state of hormonal siege; later
I had pains in my fingers, swelling feet, numb spots on my legs, the dread
hemorrhoids. I had to think about everything I ate. I developed borderline
glucose intolerance. I gained fifty pounds and am still overweight; my shape
has changed in other ways that may well be permanent. Psychologically,
my pregnancy consumed me—though I'd happily bought the seat on the
roller coaster, I was still terrified to be so out of control of my normally
tractable body. It was all bearable, even interesting—even, at times, transcendent—because I wanted a baby. Birth was painful, exhausting, and
wonderful. If I hadn't wanted a baby it would only have been painful and
exhausting—or worse. I can hardly imagine what it's like to have your body
and mind taken over in this way when you not only don't look forward to
the result, but positively dread it. The thought appalls me. So as I see it,
the key question is "Can it be moral, under any circumstances, to make
a woman bear a child against her will?"

From this vantage point, *Commonweal*'s argument is irrelevant, for in a
society that respects the individual, no "member of the species" in *any* stage
of development has an "essential right" to make use of someone else's body,
let alone in such all-encompassing fashion, without that person's consent.
You can't make a case against abortion by applying a general principle
about everybody's human rights; you have to show exactly the opposite—
that the relationship between fetus and pregnant woman is an exception,
one that justifies depriving women of their right to bodily integrity. And in
fact all antiabortion ideology rests on the premise—acknowledged or simply assumed—that women's unique capacity to bring life into the world
carries with it a unique obligation that women cannot be allowed to "play
God" and launch only the lives they welcome.

Yet the alternative to allowing women this power is to make them impotent. Criminalizing abortion doesn't just harm individual women with
unwanted pregnancies, it affects all women's sense of themselves. Without
control of our fertility we can never envision ourselves as free, for our biology makes us constantly vulnerable. Simply because we are female our
physical integrity can be violated, our lives disrupted and transformed, at
any time. Our ability to act in the world is hopelessly compromised by our
sexual being.

Ah, sex—it does have a way of coming up in these discussions, despite   10
all. When pressed, right-to-lifers of whatever political persuasion invariably
point out that pregnancy doesn't happen by itself. The leftists often give
patronizing lectures on contraception (though some find only "natural
birth control" acceptable), but remain unmoved when reminded that

contraceptives fail. Openly or implicitly they argue that people shouldn't have sex unless they're prepared to procreate. (They are quick to profess a single standard—men as well as women should be sexually "responsible." Yes, and the rich as well as the poor should be allowed to sleep under bridges.) Which amounts to saying that if women want to lead heterosexual lives they must give up any claim to self-determination, and that they have no right to sexual pleasure without fear.

Opposing abortion, then, means accepting that women must suffer sexual disempowerment and a radical loss of autonomy relative to men: If fetal life is sacred, the self-denial basic to women's oppression is also basic to the moral order. Opposing abortion means embracing a conservative sexual morality, one that subordinates pleasure to reproduction: If fetal life is sacred, there is no room for the view that sexual passion—or even sexual love—for its own sake is a human need and a human right. Opposing abortion means tolerating the inevitable double standard, by which men may accept or reject sexual restrictions in accordance with their beliefs, while women must bow to them out of fear . . . or defy them at great risk. However much *Commonweal*'s editors and those of like mind want to believe their opposition to abortion is simply about saving lives, the truth is that in the real world they are shoring up a particular sexual culture, whose rules are stacked against women. I have yet to hear any left right-to-lifers take full responsibility for that fact or deal seriously with its political implications.

Unfortunately, their fuzziness has not lessened their appeal—if anything it's done the opposite. In increasing numbers liberals and leftists, while opposing antiabortion laws, have come to view abortion as an "agonizing moral issue" with some justice on both sides, rather than an issue—however emotionally complex—of freedom versus repression, or equality versus hierarchy, that affects their political self-definition. This above-the-battle stance is attractive to leftists who want to be feminist good guys but are uneasy or ambivalent about sexual issues, not to mention those who want to ally with "progressive" factions of the Catholic church on Central America, nuclear disarmament, or populist economics without that sticky abortion question getting in the way.

Such neutrality is a way of avoiding the painful conflict over cultural issues that continually smolders on the left. It can also be a way of coping with the contradictions of personal life at a time when liberation is a dream deferred. To me the fight for abortion has always been the cutting edge of feminism, precisely because it denies that anatomy is destiny, that female biology dictates women's subordinate status. Yet recently I've found it hard to focus on the issue, let alone summon up the militance needed to stop the antiabortion tanks. In part that has to do with second-round weariness—do we really have to go through all these things twice?—in part with my life now.

Since my daughter's birth my feelings about abortion—not as a political demand but as a personal choice—have changed. In this society, the difference between the situation of a childless woman and of a mother is immense; the fear that having a child will dislodge one's tenuous hold on a nontraditional life is excruciating. This terror of being forced into the seachange of motherhood gave a special edge to my convictions about abortion. Since I've made that plunge voluntarily, with consequences still unfolding, the terror is gone; I might not want another child, for all sorts of reasons, but I will never again feel that my identity is at stake. Different battles with the culture absorb my energy now. Besides, since I've experienced the primal, sensual passion of caring for an infant, there will always be part of me that does want another. If I had an abortion today, it would be with conflict and sadness unknown to me when I had an abortion a decade ago. And the antiabortionists' imagery of dead babies hits me with new force. Do many women—left, feminist women—have such feelings? Is this the sort of "ambivalence about abortion" that in the present atmosphere slides so easily into self-flagellating guilt?

Some left antiabortionists, mainly pacifists—Juli Loesch, Mary Meehan, and other "feminists for life"; Jim Wallis and various writers for Wallis's radical evangelical journal *Sojourners*—have tried to square their position with concern for women. They blame the prevalence of abortion on oppressive conditions—economic injustice, lack of child care and other social supports for mothers, the devaluation of childrearing, men's exploitative sexual behavior and refusal to take equal responsibility for children. They disagree on whether to criminalize abortion now (since murder is intolerable no matter what the cause) or to build a long-term moral consensus (since stopping abortion requires a general social transformation), but they all regard abortion as a desperate solution to desperate problems, and the women who resort to it as more sinned against than sinning.

This analysis grasps an essential feminist truth: that in a male-supremacist society no choice a woman makes is genuinely free or entirely in her interest. Certainly many women have had abortions they didn't want or wouldn't have wanted if they had any plausible means of caring for a child; and countless others wouldn't have gotten pregnant in the first place were it not for inadequate contraception, sexual confusion and guilt, male pressure, and other stigmata of female powerlessness. Yet forcing a woman to bear a child she doesn't want can only add injury to insult, while refusing to go through with such a pregnancy can be a woman's first step toward taking hold of her life. And many women who have abortions are "victims" only of ordinary human miscalculation, technological failure, or the vagaries of passion, all bound to exist in any society, however utopian. There will always be women who, at any given moment, want sex but don't want a child; some of these women will get pregnant; some of them will have abortions. Behind the victim theory of abortion is the implicit belief that women are always ready to be mothers, if only conditions are right, and that sex for pleasure rather than procreation is not only "irresponsible" (i.e., bad) but something men impose on women, never something women

15

actively seek. Ironically, left right-to-lifers see abortion as always coerced (it's "exploitation" and "violence against women"), yet regard mother-hood—which for most women throughout history has been inescapable, and is still our most socially approved role—as a positive choice. The anal-ogy to the feminist antipornography movement goes beyond borrowed rhetoric: the antiporners, too, see active female lust as surrender to male domination and traditionally feminine sexual attitudes as expressions of women's true nature.

This Orwellian version of feminism, which glorifies "female values" and dismisses women's struggles for freedom—particularly sexual free-dom—as a male plot, has become all too familiar in recent years. But its use in the abortion debate has been especially muddleheaded. Somehow we're supposed to leap from an oppressive patriarchal society to the egali-tarian one that will supposedly make abortion obsolete without ever allow-ing women to see themselves as people entitled to control their reproduc-tive function rather than be controlled by it. How women who have no power in this most personal of areas can effectively fight for power in the larger society is left to our imagination. A "New Zealand feminist" quoted by Mary Meehan in a 1980 article in *The Progressive* says, "Accepting short-term solutions like abortion only delays the implementation of real re-forms like decent maternity and paternity leaves, job protection, high-quality child care, community responsibility for dependent people of all ages, and recognition of the economic contribution of childminders"—as if these causes were progressing nicely before legal abortion came along. On the contrary, the fight for reproductive freedom is the foundation of all the others, which is why antifeminists resist it so fiercely.

As "pro-life" pacifists have been particularly concerned with refuting charges of misogyny, the liberal Catholics at *Commonweal* are most exer-cised by the claim that antiabortion laws violate religious freedom. The edi-torial quoted above hurled another challenge at the proabortion forces:

> It is time, finally, for the pro-choice advocates and editorial writers to aban-don, once and for all, the argument that abortion is a religious "doctrine" of a single or several churches being imposed on those of other persuasions in vio-lation of the First Amendment. . . . Catholics and their bishops are accused of imposing their "doctrine" on abortion, but not their "doctrine" on the needs of the poor, or their "doctrine" on the arms race, or their "doctrine" on human rights in Central America. . . .
>
> The briefest investigation into Catholic teaching would show that the church's case against abortion is utterly unlike, say, its belief in the Real Presence, known with the eyes of faith alone, or its insistence on a Sunday obligation, applicable only to the faithful. The church's moral teaching on abortion . . . is for the most part like its teaching on racism, warfare, and capital punishment, based on ordinary reasoning common to believers and nonbelievers. . . .

This is one more example of right-to-lifers' tendency to ignore the sexual ideology underlying their stand. Interesting, isn't it, how the editorial neglects to mention that the church's moral teaching on abortion jibes neatly with its teaching on birth control, sex, divorce, and the role of women. The traditional, patriarchal sexual morality common to these teachings is explicitly religious, and its chief defenders in modern times have been the more conservative churches. The Catholic and evangelical Christian churches are the backbone of the organized right-to-life movement and—a few Nathansons and Hentoffs notwithstanding—have provided most of the movement's activists and spokespeople.

Furthermore, the Catholic hierarchy has made opposition to abortion   20
a litmus test of loyalty to the church in a way it has done with no other political issue—witness Archbishop O'Connor's harassment of Geraldine Ferraro during her vice-presidential campaign. It's unthinkable that a Catholic bishop would publicly excoriate a Catholic officeholder or candidate for taking a hawkish position on the arms race or Central America or capital punishment. Nor do I notice anyone trying to read William F. Buckley out of the church for his views on welfare. The fact is there is no accepted Catholic "doctrine" on these matters comparable to the church's absolutist condemnation of abortion. While differing attitudes toward war, racism, and poverty cut across religious and secular lines, the sexual values that mandate opposition to abortion are the bedrock of the traditional religious world view, and the source of the most bitter conflict with secular and religious modernists. When churches devote their considerable political power, organizational resources, and money to translating those values into law, I call that imposing their religious beliefs on me—whether or not they're technically violating the First Amendment.

Statistical studies have repeatedly shown that people's views on abortion are best predicted by their opinions on sex and "family" issues, not on "life" issues like nuclear weapons or the death penalty. That's not because we're inconsistent but because we comprehend what's really at stake in the abortion fight. It's the antiabortion left that refuses to face the contradiction in its own position: you can't be wholeheartedly for "life"—or for such progressive aspirations as freedom, democracy, equality—and condone the subjugation of women. The seamless garment is full of holes.

---

## Analysis of the Writers' Positions

These essays by McConnell and Willis represent the two sides on which most Americans fall regarding the issue of legalized abortion. Because abortion is likely to stay legal, what is the point of trying to reconcile these positions? One benefit is that doing so might help put to rest the controversy surrounding abortion—a controversy that rages at abortion clinics and in the media, distracting Americans from other issues of importance and causing divisiveness and distrust, and that also rages within millions of Americans who want abortion to remain legal but at the same time disapprove of it. In addition, reaching some consensus on abortion might resolve the contradiction of its being legal but unavailable to many women, as extremist opponents have caused many doctors to refuse to perform abortions and restrictions on public funding for abortion have limited the access of poor women. Finally, some consensus on abortion will be necessary to formulate decisions of public policy: What restrictions, if any, are appropriate? Should parental notification or consent be required for women under eighteen? Should public funds be available for an abortion when a woman cannot otherwise afford one?

We have said that the first step in resolving conflict is to understand what the parties in conflict are claiming and why. Using the following outline form, or brief, we can describe the positions of each side:

*McConnell's position:* She is against unrestricted abortion as a woman's right.

*Claim (or thesis):* The right to abortion has hurt the moral and social climate of our nation.

   *Reason:* It has put pressure on young single women to adopt a "liberated" lifestyle of sex without commitment.
      *Evidence:* Her own college experiences.

   *Reason:* It has caused an increase in unintended pregnancies.
      *Evidence:* The analogy of children playing ball.

   *Reason:* It has taken questions about morality out of the decision to end a pregnancy.
      *Evidence:* Her own experiences with doctors and clinics.

   *Reason:* It has allowed middle- and upper-class men and women to avoid the consequences of their sex lives and to evade the responsibilities of parenthood.
      *Evidence:* None offered.

   *Reason:* It has reduced people's sense of duty toward their offspring, most noticeably in the lower classes.
      *Evidence:* Legislation has become necessary to make fathers provide financial support for their children and to hold women legally culpable for harming their fetuses through drug use.

*Willis's position:* She is for unrestricted abortion as a woman's right.

*Claim (or thesis):* The right to abortion is an essential part of feminism.

   *Reason:* Without control of their reproductive lives, women constantly fear having their lives disrupted.
      *Evidence:* A fetus makes immense demands on a woman's physical and mental resources. Her own pregnancy is an example.

*Reason:* Without abortion, women must live according to a sexual double standard.

*Evidence:* Sex always carries the risk of pregnancy. The fear of pregnancy puts restrictions on women's ability to enjoy sex for pleasure or passion rather than procreation.

## Following Through

If you and some of your classmates have written arguments taking opposing views on the same issue, prepare briefs of your respective positions to share with one another. (You might also create briefs of your opponents' positions to see how well you have understood one another's written arguments.)

Alternatively, write briefs summarizing the opposing positions offered in several published arguments as a first step toward mediating these viewpoints.

## Locating the Areas of Disagreement

Areas of disagreement generally involve differences over facts and differences in interests.

### Differences over Facts

Any parties involved in negotiation, as well as any mediator in a dispute, should consider both the reasons and evidence offered on all sides in order to locate areas of factual agreement and particularly disagreement. Parties genuinely interested in finding the best solution to a conflict rather than in advocating their own positions ought to be able to recognize when more evidence is needed, no matter the side. Negotiators and mediators should also consider the currency and the authority of any sources. If new or better research could help resolve factual disparities, the parties should do it collaboratively rather than independently.

## Following Through

In the preceding arguments on abortion, the writers do not present much factual evidence, as their arguments are relatively abstract. Are there any facts on which they agree? Would more facts make a difference in getting either side to reconsider her position? How could you gather more solid evidence or hard data?

## Differences in Interests

Experts in negotiation have found that conflicts most often result from interpretive differences rather than from factual differences; that is, people in conflict look at the same situation differently depending on their values, their beliefs, and their interests. McConnell opens her argument with this very point
by showing how most women's rights advocates would interpret the scene at
a typical antiabortion protest and then by offering a second perspective, affected by her view that legalized abortion has victimized women.

What kinds of subjective differences cause people to draw conflicting
conclusions from the same evidence? To identify these differences, we can ask
the same questions that are useful in persuasion to identify what divides us
from our audience (see the box "Questions for Understanding Difference,"
page 317). In negotiation and mediation, these questions can help uncover
the real interests that any resolution must address. It is in identifying these
interests that the dialogue of negotiation begins, because only when the interests that underlie opposing positions are identified can creative solutions
be formulated. Often, uncovering each party's real interests leads to the discovery of previously ignored common ground. Finding these interests should
be a collaborative project, one that negotiation experts compare to problem
solving through teamwork.

Here we apply the questions about difference to McConnell's and Willis's
positions on abortion rights.

*Is the Difference a Matter of Assumptions?*   Both arguments make the assumption that legalizing abortion removed constraints on women's sexuality. McConnell blames abortion for this presumed effect, but Willis credits
abortion with enabling women to enjoy sex as men have traditionally been
able to do. A mediator might begin by pointing out that this assumption itself could be wrong, that it is possible, for example, that the introduction of
birth control pills and the political liberalism of the 1970s contributed more
to the increased sexual activity of women. McConnell wants young women
not to feel pressured to have sex, while Willis's interest is in freeing women
from a sexual double standard.

McConnell also assumes that abortion becomes guilt free for most
women because it is legal. Willis insists that women should not feel guilty. A
mediator might ask what interest McConnell has in making women feel
guilty and what Willis means when she says she would now feel "conflict and
sadness" (paragraph 14) over choosing an abortion. What is the difference
between "conflict and sadness" and "guilt"?

The main assumption these writers do not share concerns the motives of
those who cast abortion as a moral issue. Willis assumes that any question
about the morality of abortion is part of an effort to repress and subordinate
women. This assumption makes Willis see those who disagree with her as a
threat to her chief interest—women's rights. McConnell, on the other hand,
challenges the feminist assumption that abortion has liberated women. To

her, the legalization of abortion, rather than protecting women's rights, has actually contributed to the further exploitation of women sexually, which she sees as immoral.

*Is the Difference a Matter of Principle?*   The principle of equal rights for all individuals is featured in both arguments but in different ways. Willis is interested in equal rights among men and women. McConnell is concerned with the equal rights of the fetus as a potential human being.

*Is the Difference a Matter of Values or Priorities?*   The question of priorities brings us to a key difference underlying the positions of McConnell and Willis. Willis puts the value of a woman's well-being above the value of a fetus's life (paragraph 5). In paragraph 8, she states, "in a society that respects the individual, no [fetus] in *any* stage of development has an 'essential right' to make use of someone else's body . . . without that person's consent." For Willis, it is immoral to force any woman to bear a child against her will. For McConnell, however, the fetus counts too. Denying rights to the unborn is denying life itself (paragraph 33).

In addition, these two writers have very different values regarding sex. For McConnell, sex for pleasure, without commitment, is demeaning to women, something to which they acquiesce only because they have been told that it is normal and healthy. For Willis, sexual passion "for its own sake is a human need and a human right" (paragraph 11); she seems to be responding directly to McConnell in paragraph 16: "Behind the victim theory of abortion is the implicit belief . . . that sex for pleasure is not only 'irresponsible' (i.e., bad) but something men impose on women, never something women actively seek."

*Is the Difference a Matter of Ends or Means?*   McConnell and Willis both claim to have the same end in mind—a society in which women are truly free and equal, able to live dignified and uncompromised lives. However, they differ over legalized abortion as a means to this end. McConnell does not argue that *Roe v. Wade* should be overturned; rather, she wants her audience to recognize that abortion has cheapened both sex and life, allowing women to be victimized by men who want sex without commitment and encouraging a society that wants rights without responsibilities. Her ultimate goal is higher moral standards for the community. Willis, on the other hand, wants to make sure that freedom and equality for women stay in the forefront of the abortion debate. She resists any compromise on the abortion issue—even the concession that women should feel guilt about having abortions—because she sees the issue of morality as a slope down which women could slide back into a subordinate societal role.

*Is the Difference a Matter of Interpretation?*   These two writers interpret abortion from polar extremes. McConnell sees it as totally negative; to her, abortion is a convenience, a way of avoiding responsibility after an act of sexual carelessness. Willis's definition of abortion stresses its positive political value; it is the "cutting edge of feminism" because it guarantees to women absolute reproductive freedom. Furthermore, as we have seen, they interpret individualism differently: for Willis, individualism is positive, the autonomy and freedom to reach one's goals; for McConnell it is more negative, with connotations of selfishness and immaturity.

*Is the Difference a Matter of Implications or Consequences?*   Both writers are concerned with consequences, but neither entertains the other's concerns. Willis sees the result of legalized abortion as a more just society. McConnell argues that the positive consequences Willis claims for women are illusory and that women have been harmed by the easy availability of abortion.

*Is the Difference a Result of Personal Background, Basic Human Needs, or Emotions?*   In their arguments about abortion, both writers are fairly open about some of their emotions. McConnell is quite frank about her "remorse" over her abortion in her first year of college. In her description of that experience, she suggests that she was coerced by the university's health counselors. Notice, too, that she describes herself as the child of "first-generation" Americans with strict moral standards, a fact that surely influenced her perception of liberated sexual morals.

Willis expresses anger that the arena of debate over abortion has moved from its original focus on women's rights to a new focus on the rights of the fetus. She fears that hard-won ground for women's rights could be slipping. Yet, in discussing her own child, she reveals an emotional vulnerability that could possibly make her rethink her position on the morality of abortion. Note, for example, that she mentions her own abortion only once, in paragraph 14.

In face-to-face negotiation and mediation, having a conversation about underlying differences can go a long way toward helping opposing parties understand each other. Each side must "try on" the position of those who see the issue from a different perspective. They may still not agree or change their positions, but at this point each side ought to be able to say to the other, "I see what your concerns are." Progress toward resolution begins when people start talking about their underlying concerns or interests rather than their positions.

As a student mediating among written texts, you must decide what you could say to help each side see other viewpoints and to loosen the commitment each side has to its own position. (See the Best Practices box on page 317.)

## Defining the Problem in Terms of the Real Interests

As we have said, although it is important in negotiating to see clearly what each side is demanding, successful negotiation looks for a solution that addresses the interests that underlie the positions of each side. Uncovering

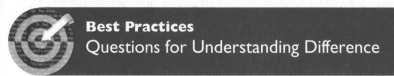
1. Is the difference a matter of *assumptions*? As we discussed in Chapter 3 on the Toulmin method of analysis and in Chapter 6 on inquiry, all arguments are based on some assumptions.
2. Is the difference a matter of *principle*? Are some parties to the dispute following different principles, or general rules, from others?
3. Is the difference a matter of *values* or a matter of having the same values but giving them different *priorities*?
4. Is the difference a matter of *ends* or *means*? That is, do people want to achieve different goals, or do they have the same goals in mind but disagree on the means to achieve them?
5. Is the difference a matter of *interpretation*?
6. Is the difference a matter of *implications* or *consequences*?
7. Is the difference a result of *personal background, basic human needs,* or *emotions*?

To our list of questions about difference in persuasive writing, we add this last question because negotiation requires the parties involved to look not just at one another's arguments but also at one another as people with histories and feelings. It is not realistic to think that human problems can be solved without taking human factors into consideration. Negotiators must be open about their emotions and such basic human needs as personal security, economic well-being, and a sense of belonging, recognition, and control over their own lives. They can be open with one another about such matters only if their dialogue up to this point has established trust between them. If you are mediating among printed texts, you must use the texts themselves as evidence of these human factors.

## Following Through

If you are negotiating between your own position and the arguments of classmates, form groups and use the questions in the Best Practices box above to identify the interests of each party. You may ask a student outside the group to mediate the discussion. As a group, prepare a report on your conversation: What are the main interests of each party?

If you are mediating among printed arguments, write an analysis based on applying the questions to two or more arguments. You could write out your analysis in list form, as we did in analyzing the differences between McConnell and Willis, or you could treat it as an exploratory essay.

As a creative variation for your analysis, write a dialogue with yourself as mediator, posing questions to each of the opposing parties. Have each side respond to your questions just as we demonstrated in our sample dialogue on pages 178–179.

those interests is the first step. The next is summing them up, recognizing the most important ones a solution must address. Meeting these underlying interests is the task that negotiators undertake collaboratively.

To illustrate, let's look at the two arguments about legalized abortion. Although McConnell criticizes abortion and those who choose it, she admits that she would keep it legal. Her real interest is in reducing what she sees as the consequences of legalized abortion: irresponsible sex and a disregard for life.

Willis is not totally unwilling to consider the moral value of the fetus as human life, admitting that it begins to acquire moral value as it comes to term; her problem with the moral question is the possibility that considering it at all will endanger women's right to choose for—or against—having an abortion. Her real interest is in equality of the sexes.

A mediator between these two positions would have to help resolve the conflict in a way that guarantees women's autonomy and control over their reproductive lives and that promotes responsibility and respect for the value of life. Any resolution here must ensure both the rights of the individual and the good of the community.

## Following Through

For the conflict among classmates' positions that you have been negotiating or the conflict among written texts that you have been mediating, write a description of the problem that a resolution must solve: What are the key interests that must be addressed? If you are negotiating, write a statement collaboratively.

## Inventing Creative Options

Parties can work toward solutions to a problem in collaboration, each party can brainstorm solutions alone, or an individual mediator can take on this task. Collaboration can help or hinder the invention process, depending on the relationship of the negotiators. Because coming up with possible solutions means making some concessions, you might want to do so privately rather than state publicly what you would be willing to give up. Whether you are a mediator or a negotiator, this is the stage for exploring options, for entertaining wild ideas, for experimenting without making judgments.

With respect to the abortion issue, Willis might be willing to consider counseling for women contemplating abortion and admit that the issue inevitably involves some ethical concerns. McConnell might be willing to take a less judgmental position and concede that it is not really fair to impose either motherhood or guilt on every woman who has an unwanted pregnancy.

### Following Through

1. Think about a possible compromise on the issue of legalized abortion. Your ideas should address the interests of both Willis and McConnell. How likely is it that they would accept your compromise?
2. For a class assignment on negotiating or mediating a dispute, brainstorm possible solutions either independently or collaboratively. Try to make your list of options as long as you can.

## Gathering More Data

Once a mediator has proposed a solution or negotiators have created a tentative resolution, some or all of the parties might think they could accept it if only they had a little more information. For example, one side in the abortion issue might want to know not only that there are approximately 1.5 million abortions performed each year in the United States but also that many of them are second or third abortions for the same women. If Willis learned that many women have abortions repeatedly, she might agree that the right is being abused — and that some counseling might help. If McConnell were to find out that most women have only a single abortion, she might decide that women do not interpret the right to abortion as nonchalantly as she had imagined. Professional negotiators suggest that information gathering at this point be done collaboratively. However, the trust and spirit of collaboration built so far can be damaged if each side tries to gather data favorable to its own original position.

### Following Through

1. If you have an idea for a compromise that would address the interests of Willis and McConnell, what additional data do you think either or both of these authors would want to have before accepting your solution?
2. If you have come up with a proposal for resolving a conflict that you and some classmates have been negotiating or that you have been mediating, decide together if additional information could help you reach consensus. What questions need to be answered? Try to answer these questions collaboratively with a joint visit to the library.

## Reaching a Solution Based on Agreed-Upon Principles

The kind of negotiation we have been discussing in this chapter is not the "I give a little, you give a little" sort that occurs between a buyer and seller or in a hostage situation when terrorists offer to trade a number of hostages for an equal number of released prisoners. Such a resolution involves no real principle other than that concessions ought to be of equal value. It brings the opposing sides no closer to understanding why they differed in the first place.

Instead, negotiated settlements on matters of public policy such as abortion or sexual harassment or gun control ought to involve some principles that both sides agree are fair. For example, Willis might agree that abortion ought to be a real choice, not something a woman is railroaded into as McConnell feels she was at age eighteen. Based on this principle, Willis might agree that professional counseling about ethics and options at least ought to be available to women considering abortion.

## Following Through

If you have been mediating or negotiating a conflict with classmates, formalize your resolution if possible. Be ready to explain what principles you have agreed on as the basis for the compromise.

## THE MEDIATORY ESSAY

Arguments that appear in newspapers and popular magazines usually seek to convince or persuade an audience to accept the author's position. Sometimes, however, the writer assumes the role of mediator and attempts to negotiate a solution acceptable to the opposing sides. This writer moves beyond the stated positions and the facts of the dispute to expose the underlying interests, values, and beliefs of those in opposition. The goal is to show what interests they may have in common, to increase each side's understanding of the other, and to propose a solution to the dispute, a new position based on interests and values that will be acceptable to both sides. The following essay by Roger Rosenblatt aims to mediate one of the most deeply entrenched conflicts of our day—the issue of legalized abortion. As you read it, keep in mind the arguments of Margaret Liu McConnell and Ellen Willis. Do you think that reading this mediatory essay might bring them closer to some consensus on the question of how to live with legalized abortion?

---

## How to End the Abortion War
### Roger Rosenblatt

*Roger Rosenblatt is a writer who regularly contributes to the* New York Times Maga-zine, *in which this essay originally appeared.*

The veins in his forehead bulged so prominently they might have been blue worms that had worked their way under the surface of his skin. His eyes bulged, too, capillaries zigzagging from the pupils in all directions. His face was pulled tight about the jaw, which thrust forward like a snowplow attachment on the grille of a truck. From the flattened O of his mouth, the word "murderer" erupted in a regular rhythm, the repetition of the r's giving the word the sound of an outboard motor that failed to catch.

She, for her part, paced up and down directly in front of him, saying nothing. Instead, she held high a large cardboard sign on a stick, showing the cartoonish drawing of a bloody coat hanger over the caption, "Never again." Like his, her face was taut with fury, her lips pressed together so tightly they folded under and vanished. Whenever she drew close to him, she would deliberately lower the sign and turn it toward him, so that he would be yelling his "murderer" at the picture of the coat hanger.

For nearly twenty years these two have been at each other with all the hatred they can unearth. Sometimes the man is a woman, sometimes the woman a man. They are black, white, Hispanic, Asian; they make their homes in Missouri or New Jersey; they are teenagers and pharmacists and college professors; Catholic, Baptist, Jew. They have exploded at each other on the steps of the Capitol in Washington, in front of abortion clinics, hospitals, and politicians' homes, on village greens and the avenues of cities. Their rage is tireless; at every decision of the United States Supreme Court or of the President or of the state legislatures, it rises like a missile seeking only the heat of its counterpart.

This is where America is these days on the matter of abortion, or where it seems to be. In fact, it is very hard to tell how the country really feels about abortion, because those feelings are almost always displayed in political arenas. Most ordinary people do not speak of abortion. Friends who gladly debate other volatile issues—political philosophy, war, race—shy away from the subject. It is too private, too personal, too bound up with one's faith or spiritual identity. Give abortion five seconds of thought, and it quickly spirals down in the mind to the most basic questions about human life, to the mysteries of birth and our relationship with our souls.

We simply will not talk about it. We will march in demonstrations, shout and carry placards, but we will not talk about it. In the Presidential election of 1992, we will cast votes for a national leader based in part on his or her position on abortion. Still, we will not talk about it.

The oddity in this unnatural silence is that most of us actually know what we feel about abortion. But because those feelings are mixed and complicated, we have decided that they are intractable. I believe the opposite is true: that we are more prepared than we realize to reach a common, reasonable understanding on this subject, and if we were to vent our mixed feelings and begin to make use of them, a resolution would be at hand.

Seventy-three percent of Americans polled in 1990 were in favor of abortion rights. Seventy-seven percent polled also regard abortion as a kind

5

of killing. (Forty-nine percent see abortion as outright murder, 28 percent solely as the taking of human life.) These figures represent the findings of the Harris and Gallup polls, respectively, and contain certain nuances of opinion within both attitudes. But the general conclusions are widely considered valid. In other words, most Americans are both for the choice of abortion as a principle and against abortion for themselves. One has to know nothing else to realize how conflicted a problem we have before and within us.

The fact that abortion entails conflict, however, does not mean that the country is bound to be locked in combat forever. In other contexts, living with conflict is not only normal to America, it is often the only way to function honestly. We are for both Federal assistance and states' autonomy; we are for both the First Amendment and normal standards of propriety; we are for both the rights of privacy and the needs of public health. Our most productive thinking usually contains an inner confession of mixed feelings. Our least productive thinking, a nebulous irritation resulting from a refusal to come to terms with disturbing and patently irreconcilable ideas.

Yet acknowledging and living with ambivalence is, in a way, what America was invented to do. To create a society in which abortion is permitted and its gravity appreciated is to create but another of the many useful frictions of a democratic society. Such a society does not devalue life by allowing abortion; it takes life with utmost seriousness and is, by the depth of its conflicts and by the richness of its difficulties, a reflection of life itself.

Why, then, are we stuck in political warfare on this issue? Why can we not make use of our ambivalence and move on?    10

The answer has to do with America's peculiar place in the history of abortion, and also with the country's special defining characteristics, both ancient and modern, with which abortion has collided. In the 4,000-year-old history extending from the Greeks and Romans through the Middle Ages and into the present, every civilization has taken abortion with utmost seriousness. Yet ours seems to be the only civilization to have engaged in an emotional and intellectual civil war over the issue.

There are several reasons for this. The more obvious include the general lack of consensus in the country since the mid-60's, which has promoted bitter divisions over many social issues—race, crime, war, and abortion, too. The sexual revolution of the 60's resulted in the heightened activity of people who declared themselves "pro-choice" *and* "pro-life"—misleading terms used here principally for convenience. The pro-life movement began in 1967, six years before *Roe v. Wade*. The women's movement, also revitalized during the 60's, gave an impetus for self-assertion to women on both sides of the abortion issue.

But there are less obvious reasons, central to America's special character, which have helped to make abortion an explosive issue in this country.

**Religiosity.** America is, and always has been, a religious country, even though it spreads its religiosity among many different religions. Perry Miller, the great historian of American religious thought, established that the New England colonists arrived with a ready-made religious mission, which they cultivated and sustained through all its manifestations, from charity to intolerance. The Virginia settlement, too, was energized by God's glory. Nothing changed in this attitude by the time the nation was invented. If anything, the creation of the United States of America made the desire to receive redemption in the New World more intense.

Yet individuals sought something in American religion that was different, more emotional than the religion practiced in England. One member of an early congregation explained that the reason he made the long journey to America was "I thought I should find feelings." This personalized sense of religion, which has endured to the present, has an odd but telling relationship with the national attitude toward religion. Officially, America is an a-religious country; the separation of church and state is so rooted in the democracy it has become a cliché. Yet that same separation has created and intensified a hidden national feeling about faith and God, a sort of secret, undercurrent religion, which, perhaps because of its subterranean nature, is often more deeply felt and volatile than that of countries with official or state religions.

The Catholic Church seems more steadily impassioned about abortion in America than anywhere else, even in a country like Poland—so agitated, in fact, that it has entered into an unlikely, if not unholy, alliance with evangelical churches in the pro-life camp. In Catholic countries like Italy, France, and Ireland, religion is often so fluidly mixed with social life that rules are bent more quietly, without our personal sort of moral upheaval.

Americans are moral worriers. We tend to treat every political dispute that arises as a test of our national soul. The smallest incident, like the burning of the flag, can bring our hidden religion to the surface. The largest and most complex moral problem, like abortion, can confound it for decades.

**Individualism.** Two basic and antithetical views of individualism have grown up with the country. Emerson, the evangelist of self-reliance and nonconformity, had a quasi-mystical sense of the value of the individual self.[1] He described man as a self-sufficient microcosm: "The lightning which explodes and fashions planets, maker of planets and suns, is in him." Tocqueville had a more prosaic and practical view.[2] He worried about the tendency of Americans to withdraw into themselves at the expense of the public good, confusing self-assertion with self-absorption.

Abortion hits both of these views of the individual head on, of course; but both views are open to antipodal interpretations. The Emersonian

---

[1] Ralph Waldo Emerson (1803–1882) was an essayist and leader of New England transcendentalism.

[2] Alexis de Tocqueville (1805–1859) was a French aristocrat and magistrate who toured the United States in 1831 to study the effects of democracy. His classic work *Democracy in America* was first published in 1835.

celebration of the individual may be shared by the pro-choice advocate who sees in individualism one's right to privacy. It may be seen equally by a pro-life advocate as a justification for taking an individual stance—an anti-liberal stance to boot—on a matter of conscience.

The idea of the independent individual may also be embraced by the    20
pro-life position as the condition of life on which the unborn have a claim immediately after conception. Pro-life advocates see the pregnant woman as two individuals, each with an equal claim to the riches that American individualism offers.

Tocqueville's concern with individualism as selfishness is also available for adoption by both camps. The pro-life people claim that the pro-choice advocates are placing their individual rights above those of society, and one of the fundamental rights of American society is the right to life. Even the Supreme Court, when it passed *Roe v. Wade,* concluded that abortion "is not unqualified and must be considered against important state interests in regulation."

To those who believe in abortion rights, the "public good" consists of a society in which people, collectively, have the right to privacy and individual choice. Their vision of an unselfish, unself-centered America is one in which the collective sustains its strength by encouraging the independence of those who comprise it. Logically, both camps rail against the individual imposing his or her individual views on society at large, each feeling the same, if opposite, passion about both what society and the individual ought to be. Passion on this subject has led to rage.

**Optimism.** The American characteristic of optimism, like that of individualism, is affected by abortion in contradictory ways. People favoring the pro-life position see optimism exactly as they read individual rights: Every American, born or unborn, is entitled to look forward to a state of infinite hope and progress. The process of birth is itself an optimistic activity.

Taking the opposite view, those favoring abortion rights interpret the ideas of hope and progress as a consequence of one's entitlement to free choice in all things, abortion definitely included. If the individual woman wishes to pursue her manifest destiny unencumbered by children she does not want, that is not only her business but her glory. The issue is national as well as personal. The pro-choice reasoning goes: The country may only reach its ideal goals if women, along with men, are allowed to achieve their highest potential as citizens, unburdened by limitations that are not of their own choosing.

Even the element of American "can-do" ingenuity applies. The invention    25
of abortion, like other instruments of American optimism, supports both the pro-life and pro-choice stands. Hail the procedure for allowing women to realize full control over their invented selves. Or damn the procedure for destroying forever the possibility of a new life inventing itself. As with all else pertaining to this issue, one's moral position depends on the direction

in which one is looking. Yet both directions are heaving with optimism, and both see life in America as the best of choices.

**Sexuality.** The connection of abortion with American attitudes toward sexuality is both economic and social. The American way with sex is directly related to the country's original desire to become a society of the middle class, and thus to cast off the extremes of luxury and poverty that characterized Europe and the Old World. The structure of English society, in particular, was something the new nation sought to avoid. Not for Puritan America was the rigid English class system, which not only fixed people into economically immobile slots but allowed and encouraged free-wheeling sexual behavior at both the highest and lowest strata.

At the top of the English classes was a self-indulgent minority rich enough to ignore middle-class moral codes and idle enough to spend their time seducing servants. At the opposite end of the system, the poor also felt free to do whatever they wished with their bodies, since the world offered them so little. The masses of urban poor, created by the Industrial Revolution, had little or no hope of bettering their lot. Many of them wallowed in a kind of sexual Pandemonium,[1] producing babies wantonly and routinely engaging in rape and incest. Between the two class extremes stood the staunch English middle class, with its hands on its hips, outraged at the behavior both above and below them, but powerless to insist on, much less enforce, bourgeois values.

This was not to be the case in America, where bourgeois values were to become the standards and the moral engine of the country. Puritanism, a mere aberrant religion to the English, who were able to get rid of it in 1660 after a brief eighteen years, was the force that dominated American social life for a century and a half. Since there has been a natural progression from Puritanism to Victorianism and from Victorianism to modern forms of fundamentalism in terms of social values, it may be said that the Puritans have really never loosened their headlock on American thinking. The Puritans offered a perfect context for America's desire to create a ruling middle class, which was to be known equally for infinite mobility (geographic, social, economic) and the severest forms of repression.

Abortion fits into such thinking more by what the issue implies than by what it is. In the 1800's and the early 1900's, Americans were able to live with abortion, even during periods of intense national prudery, as long as the practice was considered the exception that proved the rule. The rule was that abortion was legally and morally discouraged. Indeed, most every modern civilization has adopted that attitude, which, put simply, is an attitude of looking the other way in a difficult human situation, which often cannot and should not be avoided. For all its adamant middle-classedness,

---

[1] In *Paradise Lost*, John Milton's name for the capital of Hell. From Greek *para* ("all") and *daimon* ("demon")—hence, a place of wild disorder.

it was not uncomfortable for Americans to look the other way, either—at least until recently.

When abortion was no longer allowed to be a private, albeit danger-    30
ous, business, however, especially during the sexual revolution of the 60's, America's basic middle-classedness asserted itself loudly. Who was having all these abortions? The upper classes, who were behaving irresponsibly, and the lower orders, who had nothing to lose. Abortion, in other words, was a sign of careless sexuality and was thus an offense to the bourgeois dream.

The complaint was, and is, that abortion contradicts middle-class values, which dictate the rules of sexual conduct. Abortion, it is assumed, is the practice of the socially irresponsible, those who defy the solid norms that keep America intact. When *Roe v. Wade* was ruled upon, it sent the harshest message to the American middle class, including those who did not oppose abortion themselves but did oppose the disruption of conformity and stability. If they—certainly the middle-class majority—did not object to *Roe v. Wade* specifically, they did very much object to the atmosphere of lawlessness or unruliness that they felt the law encouraged. Thus the outcry; thus the warfare.

There may be one other reason for abortion's traumatic effect on the country in recent years. Since the end of the Second World War, American society, not unlike modern Western societies in general, has shifted intellectually from a humanistic to a social science culture; that is, from a culture used to dealing with contrarieties to one that demands definite, provable answers. The nature of social science is that it tends not only to identify, but to create issues that must be solved. Often these issues are the most significant to the country's future—civil rights, for example.

What social science thinking does not encourage is human sympathy. By that I do not mean the sentimental feeling that acknowledges another's pain or discomfort; I mean the intellectual sympathy that accepts another's views as both interesting and potentially valid, that deliberately goes to the heart of the thinking of the opposition and spends some time there. That sort of humanistic thinking may or may not be humane, but it does offer the opportunity to arrive at a humane understanding outside the realm and rules of politics. In a way, it is a literary sort of thinking, gone now from a post-literary age, a "reading" of events to determine layers of depth, complication, and confusion and to learn to live with them.

Everything that has happened in the abortion debate has been within the polarities that social science thinking creates. The quest to determine when life begins is a typical exercise of social science—the attempt to impose objective precision on a subjective area of speculation. Arguments over the mother's rights versus the rights of the unborn child are social science arguments, too. The social sciences are far more interested in rights than in how one arrives at what is right—that is, both their strength and weakness. Thus the abortion debate has been political from the start.

A good many pro-choice advocates, in fact, came to lament the political 35 character of the abortion debate when it first began in the 60's. At that time, political thinking in America was largely and conventionally liberal. The liberals had the numbers; therefore, they felt that they could set the national agenda without taking into account the valid feelings or objections of the conservative opposition. When, in the Presidential election of 1980, it became glaringly apparent that the feelings of the conservative opposition were not only valid but were politically ascendant, many liberals reconsidered the idea that abortion was purely a rights issue. They expressed appreciation of a more emotionally complicated attitude, one they realized that they shared themselves, however they might vote.

If the abortion debate had risen in a humanistic environment, it might never have achieved the definition and clarity of the *Roe v. Wade* decision, yet it might have moved toward a greater public consensus. One has to guess at such things through hindsight, of course. But in a world in which humanistic thought predominated, abortion might have been taken up more in its human terms and the debate might have focused more on such unscientific and apolitical components as human guilt, human choice and human mystery.

If we could find the way to retrieve this kind of conflicted thinking, and find a way to apply it to the country's needs, we might be on our way toward a common understanding on abortion, and perhaps toward a common good. Abortion requires us to think one way and another way simultaneously. Americans these days could make very good use of this bifurcated way of thinking.

This brings me back to the concern I voiced at the beginning: Americans are not speaking their true minds about abortion because their minds are in conflict. Yet living with conflict is normal in America, and our reluctance to do so openly in this matter, while understandable in an atmosphere of easy polarities, may help create a false image of our country in which we do not recognize ourselves. An America that declares abortion legal and says nothing more about it would be just as distorted as one that prohibited the practice. The ideal situation, in my view, would consist of a combination of laws, attitudes, and actions that would go toward satisfying both the rights of citizens and the doubts held by most of them.

Achieving this goal is, I believe, within reach. I know how odd that must sound when one considers the violent explosions that have occurred in places like Wichita as recently as August of last year,[1] or when one sees the pro-life and pro-choice camps amassing ammunition for this year's Presidential campaign. But for the ordinary private citizen, the elements of a reasonably satisfying resolution are already in place. I return to the fact that the great majority of Americans both favor abortion rights and disapprove of abortion. Were that conflict of thought to be openly expressed,

[1] That is, 1991.

and were certain social remedies to come from it, we would not find a middle of the road on this issue — logically there is no middle of the road. But we might well establish a wider road, which would accommodate a broad range of beliefs and opinions and allow us to move on to more important social concerns.

What most Americans want to do with abortion is to permit but discourage it. Even those with the most pronounced political stands on the subject reveal this duality in the things they say; while making strong defenses of their positions, they nonetheless, if given time to work out their thoughts, allow for opposing views. I discovered this in a great many interviews over the past three years.

40

Pro-choice advocates are often surprised to hear themselves speak of the immorality of taking a life. Pro-life people are surprised to hear themselves defend individual rights, especially women's rights. And both sides might be surprised to learn how similar are their visions of a society that makes abortion less necessary through sex education, help for unwanted babies, programs to shore up disintegrating families and moral values, and other forms of constructive community action. Such visions may appear Panglossian,[1] but they have been realized before, and the effort is itself salutary.

If one combines that sense of social responsibility with the advocacy of individual rights, the permit-but-discourage formula could work. By "discourage," I mean the implementation of social programs that help to create an atmosphere of discouragement. I do not mean ideas like parental consent or notification, already the law in some states, which, however well-intentioned, only whittle away at individual freedoms. The "discourage" part is the easier to find agreement on, of course, but when one places the "permit" question in the realm of respect for private values, even that may become more palatable.

Already 73 percent of America finds abortion acceptable. Even more may find it so if they can tolerate living in a country in which they may exercise the individual right not to have an abortion themselves or to argue against others having one, yet still go along with the majority who want the practice continued. The key element for all is to create social conditions in which abortion will be increasingly unnecessary. It is right that we have the choice, but it would be better if we did not have to make it.

Were this balance of thought and attitude to be expressed publicly, it might serve some of the country's wider purposes as well, especially these days when there is so much anguish over how we have lost our national identity and character. The character we lost, it seems to me, was one that exalted the individual for what the individual did for the community. It honored and embodied both privacy and selflessness. A balanced attitude on abortion would also do both. It would make a splendid irony if this

---

[1] Ideal, utopian. A reference to Dr. Pangloss is Voltaire's *Candide;* as Candide's tutor, he taught that "all is for the best in this best of possible worlds."

most painful and troublesome issue could be converted into a building block for a renewed national pride based on good will.

For that to happen, the country's leaders—Presidential candidates come to mind—have to express themselves as well. As for Congress, it hardly seems too much to expect our representatives to say something representative about the issue. Should *Roe v. Wade* be overturned, as may well happen, the country could be blown apart. To leave the matter to the states would lead to mayhem, a balkanization of what ought to be standard American rights. Congress used to pass laws, remember? I think it is time for Congress to make a law like *Roe v. Wade* that fully protects abortion rights, but legislates the kind of community help, like sex education, that would diminish the practice. 45

Taking a stand against abortion while allowing for its existence can turn out to be a progressive philosophy. It both speaks for moral seriousness and moves in the direction of ameliorating conditions of ignorance, poverty, the social self-destruction of fragmented families, and the loss of spiritual values in general. What started as a debate as to when life begins might lead to making life better.

The effort to reduce the necessity of abortion, then, is to choose life as wholeheartedly as it is to be "pro-life." By such an effort, one is choosing life for millions who do not want to be, who do not deserve to be, forever hobbled by an accident, a mistake or by miseducation. By such an effort, one is also choosing a different sort of life for the country as a whole—a more sympathetic life in which we acknowledge, privileged and unprivileged alike, that we have the same doubts and mysteries and hopes for one another.

Earlier, I noted America's obsessive moral character, our tendency to treat every question that comes before us as a test of our national soul. The permit-but-discourage formula on abortion offers the chance to test our national soul by appealing to its basic egalitarian impulse. Were we once again to work actively toward creating a country where everyone had the same health care, the same sex education, the same opportunity for economic survival, the same sense of personal dignity and worth, we would see both fewer abortions and a more respectable America.

---

## Analyzing a Mediatory Essay

Rosenblatt's argument poses a possible resolution of the abortion controversy and in so doing analyzes the opposing positions and interests, as all mediation must. The following analysis shows how Rosenblatt takes his readers through the process of mediation.

### Understanding the Spirit of Negotiation

A mediator has to be concerned with his or her own ethos, as well as with helping the opposing parties achieve an attitude that will enable negotiation to begin. The mediator must sound fair and evenhanded; the opposing parties must be open-minded.

Rosenblatt, interestingly, opens his essay in a way that invites commentary. In his first two paragraphs, he portrays both sides at their worst, as extremists in no frame of mind to negotiate—and, in fact, in no frame of mind even to speak to each other. In his third paragraph he relates the history of their debate, describing their emotions with words like *hatred* and *rage* and their behavior with metaphors of war and destruction. Readers who see themselves as reasonable will disassociate themselves from the people in these portraits.

### Following Through

Do you think Rosenblatt's introduction is a good mediation strategy? In your writer's notebook, describe your initial response to Rosenblatt's opening. Having read the whole essay, do you think it is an effective opening? Once he has presented these warriors on both sides, do you think he goes on to discuss the opposing positions and their values in an evenhanded, neutral way? Can you cite some passages where you see either fairness or bias on his part?

## Understanding the Opposing Positions

Rosenblatt establishes the opposing positions, already well known, in the first two paragraphs: the "pro-life" position that abortion is murder, the "pro-choice" position that outlawing abortion violates women's rights. Interestingly, Rosenblatt does not wait until the close of the essay to suggest his compromise position. Rather, he presents it in paragraph 9, although he goes into more detail about the solution later in the essay.

### Following Through

In your writer's notebook, paraphrase Rosenblatt's compromise position on abortion. Do you think this essay would have been more effective if Rosenblatt had postponed presenting his solution?

## Locating Areas of Disagreement over Facts

Rosenblatt points out that both sides' focus on the facts alone is what has made the issue intractable. As he points out in paragraph 34, the opposing sides have adopted the "objective precision" of the social sciences: The pro-life side has focused on establishing the precise moment of the beginning of life; the pro-choice side has focused on the absolute rights of women, ignoring the emotions of their conservative opponents.

### Following Through

Reread paragraph 33. In your writer's notebook, paraphrase Rosenblatt's point about humanistic thinking as opposed to social science thinking. If you have taken social science courses, what is your opinion?

### *Locating Areas of Disagreement in Interests*

Rosenblatt perceives that the disagreement over abortion may in fact be a disagreement over certain underlying interests and emotions held by each side, involving their perceptions about what life should be like in America. His aim is to help the two sides understand how these "less obvious reasons" have kept them from reaching any agreement. At the same time, he points out that many of the differences that seem to put them at odds are tied to common values deeply rooted in American culture. Thus, Rosenblatt attempts to show each side that the other is not a threat to its interests and perceptions of the American way of life.

Rosenblatt notes that both sides share an assumption that is keeping them apart: They both assume that there is one answer to the question of abortion rights rather than a solution that accepts ambivalence. He locates the source of this assumption in what he calls "social science thinking," which leads both sides to think that problems can be objectively studied and solved apart from human subjectivity. Thus, both sides are ignoring the very thing that is so vital to the process of negotiation and mediation.

Rosenblatt further shows how different principles underlie the arguments of each side. One side bases its argument on the right to privacy and free choice, whereas the other bases its argument on the right to life. Both principles are fundamental to American society — and neither is completely unqualified.

In addition, Rosenblatt shows how each side values the rights of the individual but interprets these rights differently. For example, antiabortion advocates see the fetus as an individual with the right to life, whereas pro-choice advocates argue for the individual right of the mother to privacy. In paragraphs 18–22, Rosenblatt shows how two perceptions or interpretations of individualism, one positive (emphasizing self-reliance) and one more critical (emphasizing selfishness), are traceable throughout American culture. In fact, he shows how both sides embrace individualism as an element of their arguments.

In addressing the main difference between the opposing parties over values, Rosenblatt shows how legalized abortion could be perceived as a threat to traditional middle-class economic and social values, and he traces middle-class sexual repression back to the Puritans. Rosenblatt may be stepping outside of the neutral stance of a mediator here, as he suggests that antiabortionists are somewhat prudish. He makes no corresponding remarks about the sexual values of the pro-choice side.

Rosenblatt points out that both sides see different consequences of legalizing abortion. Antiabortion advocates see abortion as destabilizing society and undermining the middle-class American way of life. These people worry not merely about abortion but about an "unruly" society. Pro-choice advocates, on the other hand, see abortion as the route to a better society; as Rosenblatt paraphrases their vision, "The country may only reach its ideal goals if women, along with men, are allowed to achieve their highest potential as citizens . . ." (paragraph 24).

In addressing the emotional characteristics of those involved in the dispute over abortion, Rosenblatt points to the role of religion in America. He explains that Americans historically have been more emotional about religion and morality than people of other nations, even ones where Catholicism is a state religion.

## Following Through

Recall the chief areas of difference between Ellen Willis and Margaret Liu McConnell in their respective arguments on the value of abortion rights. In your writer's notebook, indicate which of their stated concerns correspond to points in Rosenblatt's analysis of the differences that fuel the abortion war. Does Rosenblatt say anything that might help bring Willis and McConnell closer together?

### Defining the Problem in Terms of the Real Interests

Rosenblatt finds the real issue in the abortion controversy to be not whether abortion should be legal or illegal but rather how fundamental, conflicting interests in American society can be addressed. In other words, how can we create laws and institutions that reflect the ambivalence most Americans feel on the topic of abortion? How do we permit abortion legally, in order to satisfy our traditional values for privacy and individual rights, but also discourage it morally, in order to satisfy the American religious tradition that values life, respects fetal rights, and disapproves of casual and promiscuous sex?

### Following Through

In your writer's notebook, give your opinion of whether Rosenblatt has defined the abortion debate in terms of the opposing sides' real interests. Would his definition of the problem affect related issues, such as making the "abortion pill," or RU 486, available in the United States?

## *Inventing Creative Options*

Rosenblatt's solution is based on what he calls humanistic thinking, that is, thinking that permits conflict and rejects simple solutions to complicated human problems. He shows that many Americans think that abortion is both right and wrong but cannot even talk about their feelings because they are so contradictory. His creative option is for us to accept this ambivalence as a society and pass legislation that would satisfy both "the rights of citizens and the doubts held by most of them" (paragraph 38). In paragraph 45, Rosenblatt suggests that Congress pass a law legalizing abortion but at the same time requiring various activities, such as sex education, that over time promote respect for life and strengthen community moral standards.

### Following Through

Reread paragraphs 39–48, and explore in your writer's notebook your opinion of Rosenblatt's proposed solution. Should he have made it more specific?

## *Gathering More Data*

Before opposing sides can reach an agreement based on the real issues, they often need to get more information. Rosenblatt's mediatory argument is short on actual data. In response to his proposed solution, the antiabortion side might have severe doubts that the social programs proposed could in fact reduce the number of abortions performed.

### Following Through

In your writer's notebook, suggest what kinds of evidence Rosenblatt might have to offer to convince the antiabortion side that sex education and other social programs could reduce the number of abortions performed.

*Reaching a Solution Based on Agreed-Upon Principles*

Rosenblatt attempts to get those who support abortion rights and those who oppose them to reduce their differences by accepting the "permit but discourage" principle. This is a principle that American society applies to other areas, such as marital infidelity, which is legal but certainly discouraged through social institutions and customs.

### Following Through

1. Reread, if necessary, the two arguments on abortion by McConnell and Willis. Would each writer accept the principle of "permit but discourage"?
2. Draft a letter to the editor of the *New York Times Magazine,* in which Rosenblatt's argument originally appeared. In no more than three paragraphs, evaluate the argument as an attempt at mediation. Then read the following letters to the magazine, written in response to Rosenblatt's essay.

   Alternatively, write a letter or letters to the editor of the *New York Times,* playing the role of either Willis or McConnell, or both, responding as you think each would.

*Three Readers' Responses to Rosenblatt*

Roger Rosenblatt's essay on abortion is timely and welcome ("How to End the Abortion War," Jan. 19). However, his belief that Americans can coalesce on a policy that "discourages" abortion without making it illegal is probably too optimistic. The polarization of Americans on this issue results from some pretty deep differences. Differences in life style, for one thing, can dictate profound political polarization. Many American women derive their most fundamental sense of self-worth from child-rearing and care of the family; many others find theirs in lives that include participation in the larger society, particularly the work place. For women in "traditional" families (and their husbands), untrammeled access to abortion constitutes a form of permissiveness that threatens the things they hold most dear. For women whose identities are tied to work outside the home, the right to control reproductive lives is essential.

So I'm afraid these wars will continue. Rosenblatt and others should not tire in their efforts to find middle ground, but it would be unrealistic to think that we will be able to occupy it together anytime soon.

—PHILIP D. HARVEY, Cabin John, MD

I don't want to "permit but discourage" abortion. I want to stop abortion the way the abolitionists wanted to stop slavery. I believe slavery is wrong: that no one has the right to assure his or her quality of life by owning another. In the same way, and for the same reasons, I believe abortion is wrong: that no one has the right to assure her quality of life by aborting another.

—ANITA JANDA, Kew Gardens, Queens

Your article states that "most of us actually know what we feel about abortion." It is true that most people have a position on abortion, but that position is seldom an informed one in this era of the 10-second sound bite and the oversimplification of issues.

Few people understand that *Roe v. Wade* gives the interests of the woman precedence over those of the embryo early in the pregnancy, but allows Government to favor the fetus once it has attained viability.

Were a poll to propose full freedom of choice for women during the early stages of pregnancy, and prohibition of abortion during the later stages, except in cases of fetal deformity or a threat to a woman's life, I believe that the response of the American public would be overwhelmingly positive. Rosenblatt is right on the mark in saying that the public "simply will not talk about abortion." With thoughtful and dispassionate discussion, we might lay aside the all-or-nothing attitude that currently prevails.

—RICHARD A. KELLEY, Rumson, NJ

## Following Through

Analyze the three letters to the *New York Times Magazine* critiquing Rosenblatt's article. What values does each contribute to the debate? How might Rosenblatt respond to each?

## Writing a Mediatory Essay

### Prewriting

If you have been mediating the positions of two or more groups of classmates or two or more authors of published arguments, you may be assigned to write a mediatory essay in which you argue for a compromise position, appealing to an audience of people on all sides. In preparing to write such an essay, you should work through the steps of negotiation and mediation as described on pages 295–320. In your writer's notebook, prepare briefs of the various conflicting positions, and note areas of disagreement; think hard about the differing interests of the conflicting parties, and respond to the questions about difference on page 317.

If possible, give some thought to each party's background—age, race, gender, and so forth—and how it might contribute to his or her viewpoint on the issue. For example, in a debate about whether *Huckleberry Finn* should be taught and read aloud in U.S. high schools, an African-American parent whose child is the only minority student in her English class might well have a different perspective from that of a white teacher. Can the white teacher be made to understand the embarrassment that a sole black child might feel when the white characters speak with derision about "niggers"?

In your writer's notebook, also describe the conflict in terms of the opposing sides' real interests rather than the superficial demands each side might be stating. For example, considering the controversy over *Huckleberry Finn*, you might find some arguments in favor of teaching it anytime, others opposed to teaching it at all, others suggesting that it be an optional text for reading outside of class, and still others proposing that it be taught only in twelfth grade, when students are mature enough to understand Twain's satire. However, none of these suggestions addresses the problem in terms of the real interests involved: a desire to teach the classics of American literature for what they tell us about the human condition and our country's history and values; a desire to promote respect for African-American students; a desire to ensure a comfortable learning climate for all students; and so on. You may be able to see that people's real interests are not as far apart as they might seem. For example, those who advocate teaching *Huckleberry Finn* and those who are opposed may both have in mind the goal of eliminating racial prejudice.

At this point in the prewriting process, think of some solutions that would satisfy at least some of the real interests on all sides. It might be necessary for you to do some additional research. What do you think any of the opposing parties might want to know more about in order to accept your solution?

Finally, write up a clear statement of your compromise. Can you explain what principles it is based on? In the *Huckleberry Finn* debate, we might propose that the novel be taught at any grade level provided that it is presented as part of a curriculum to educate students about the African-American experience with the involvement of African-American faculty or visiting lecturers.

## Drafting

There is no set form for the mediatory essay. In fact, it is an unusual, even somewhat experimental, form of writing. As with any argument, the important thing is to have a plan for arranging your points and to provide clear signals to your readers. One logical way to organize a mediatory essay is in three parts:

*Overview of the conflict.* Describe the conflict and the opposing positions in the introductory paragraphs.

*Discussion of differences underlying the conflict.* Here your goal is to make all sides more sympathetic to one another and to sort out the important real interests that must be addressed by the solution.

*Proposed solution.* Here you make a case for your compromise position, giving reasons why it should be acceptable to all—that is, showing that it does serve at least some of their interests.

## Revising

When revising a mediatory essay, you should look for the usual problems of organization and development that you would be looking for in any essay to convince or persuade. Be sure that you have inquired carefully and fairly into the conflict and that you have clearly presented the cases for all sides, including your proposed solution. At this point, you also need to consider how well you have used the persuasive appeals:

*The appeal to character.* Think about what kind of character you have projected as a mediator. Have you maintained neutrality? Do you model open-mindedness and genuine concern for the sensitivities of all sides?

*The appeal to emotions.* To arouse sympathy and empathy, which are needed in negotiation, you should take into account the emotional appeals discussed on pages 276–278. Your mediatory essay should be a moving argument for understanding and overcoming difference.

*The appeal through style.* As in persuasion, you should put the power of language to work. Pay attention to concrete word choice, striking metaphors, and phrases that stand out because of repeated sounds and rhythms.

For suggestions about editing and proofreading, see the appendix.

## STUDENT SAMPLE: *An Essay Arguing to Mediate*

The following mediatory essay was written by Angi Grellhesl, a first-year student at Southern Methodist University. Her essay examines opposing written views on the institution of speech codes at various U.S. colleges and its effect on freedom of speech.

### MEDIATING THE SPEECH CODE CONTROVERSY
#### Angi Grellhesl

The right to free speech has raised many controversies over the years. Explicit lyrics in rap music and marches by the Ku Klux Klan are just some examples that test the power of the First Amendment. Now, students and administrators are questioning if, in fact, free speech ought to be limited on university campuses. Many schools have instituted speech codes to protect specified groups from harassing speech.

Both sides in the debate, the speech code advocates and the free speech advocates, have presented their cases in recent books and articles. Columnist Nat Hentoff argues strongly against the speech codes, his main reason being that the codes violate students' First Amendment rights. Hentoff links the right to free speech with the values of higher education. In support, he quotes Yale president Benno Schmidt, who says, "Freedom of thought must be Yale's central commitment . . . [U]niversities cannot censor or suppress speech, no matter how obnoxious in content, without violating their justification for existence . . ." (qtd. in Hentoff 223). Another reason Hentoff offers against speech codes is that universities must teach students to defend themselves in preparation for the real world, where such codes cannot shield them. Finally, he suggests that most codes are too vaguely worded; students may not even know they are violating the codes (216).

Two writers in favor of speech codes are Richard Perry and Patricia Williams. They see speech codes as a necessary and fair limitation on free speech. Perry and Williams argue that speech codes promote multicultural awareness, making students more sensitive to the differences that are out there in the real world. These authors do not think that the codes violate First Amendment rights, and they are suspicious of the motives of those who say they do. As Perry and Williams put it, those who feel free speech rights are being threatened "are apparently unable to distinguish between a liberty interest on the one hand and, on the other, a quite specific interest in being able to spout racist, sexist, and homophobic epithets completely unchallenged—without, in other words, the terrible inconvenience of feeling bad about it" (228).

Perhaps if both sides trusted each other a little more, they could see that their goals are not contradictory. Everyone agrees that students' rights should be protected. Hentoff wishes to ensure that students have the right to speak their minds. He and others on his side are concerned about freedom. Defenders of the codes argue that students have the right not to be harassed, especially while they are getting an education. They are concerned about opportunity. Would either side really deny that the other's goal had value?

Also, both sides want to create the best possible educational environment. Here the difference rests on the interpretation of what benefits the students. Is the best environment one most like the real world, where prejudice and harassment occur? Or does the university have an obligation to provide an atmosphere where potential victims can thrive and participate freely without intimidation?

I think it is possible to reach a solution that everyone can agree on. Most citizens want to protect constitutional rights; but they also agree that those rights have limitations, the ultimate limit being when one person infringes on the rights of others to live in peace. All sides should agree that a person ought to be able to speak out about his or her convictions, values, and beliefs. And most people can see a difference between that protected speech and the kind that is intended to harass and intimidate. For example, there is a clear difference between expressing one's view that Jews are mistaken in not accepting Christ as the son of God, on the one hand, and yelling anti-Jewish threats at a particular person in the middle of the night, on the other. Could a code not be worded in such a way as to distinguish between these two kinds of speech?

Also, I don't believe either side would want the university to be an artificial world. Codes should not attempt to ensure that no one is criticized or even offended. Students should not be afraid to say controversial things. But universities do help to shape the future of the real world, so shouldn't they at least take a stand against harassment? Can a code be worded that would protect free speech and prevent harassment?

The current speech code at Southern Methodist University is a compromise that ought to satisfy free speech advocates and speech code advocates. It prohibits hate speech at the same time that it protects an individual's First Amendment rights.

First, it upholds the First Amendment by including a section that reads, "due to the University's commitment to freedom of speech and expression, harassment is more than mere insensitivity or offensive conduct which creates an uncomfortable situation for certain members of the community" (*Peruna* 92). The code therefore should satisfy those, like Hentoff, who place a high value on the basic rights our nation was built upon. Secondly, whether or not there is a need for protection, the current code protects potential victims from hate speech or "any words or acts deliberately designed to disregard the safety or rights of another, and which intimidate, degrade, demean, threaten, haze, or otherwise interfere with another person's rightful action" (*Peruna* 92). This part of the code should satisfy those who recognize that some hurts cannot be overcome. Finally, the current code outlines specific acts that constitute harassment: "Physical, psychological, verbal and/or written acts directed toward an individual or group of individuals which rise to the level of 'fighting words' are prohibited" (*Peruna* 92).

The SMU code protects our citizens from hurt and from unconstitutional censorship. Those merely taking a position can express it, even if it hurts. On the other hand, those who are spreading hatred will be limited as to what harm they may inflict. Therefore, all sides should respect the code as a safeguard for those who use free speech but a limitation for those who abuse it.

## Works Cited

Hentoff, Nat. "Speech Codes on the Campus and Problems of Free Speech." <u>Debating P.C.</u> Ed. Paul Berman. New York: Bantam, 1992. 215–24.

Perry, Richard, and Patricia Williams. "Freedom of Speech." <u>Debating P.C.</u> Ed. Paul Berman. New York: Bantam, 1992. 225–30.

<u>Peruna Express 1993–1994</u>. Dallas: Southern Methodist U, 1993.

# Part Three Two Casebooks for Argument

**Part Three** Two Casebooks for Argument

# Chapter 10

# Casebook on 9/11/01 and After: Coping with Terrorism

## SECTION 3: ASSESSING AND RESPONDING TO INTERPRETATIONS AND ARGUMENTS   422

## GETTING ORIENTED

September 11, 2001, is one of a very few dates in American history most of us cannot forget. The temptation is to compare it (as some did on that frightening Tuesday) to Sunday, December 7, 1941, when the Japanese attacked Pearl Harbor. In almost all respects, however, the two days are alike only in that they are memorable. There was, of course, no television in 1941, so only Americans who happened to be at Pearl Harbor witnessed the attack firsthand. In contrast, many of us saw the second airliner hit the World Trade Center as we watched news coverage of the damage the first plane had inflicted. We sat stunned as first one and then the other great skyscraper collapsed. We didn't see the third and fourth planes crash into the Pentagon and into a field in Pennsylvania, but we saw the jagged, ugly, black holes they had made. Bounced back and forth between scenes in New York and Washington, we recall only too well other vivid images: twisted steel, smoke and dust, sirens and fire hoses, the scrambling of emergency personnel — all in "real time." And if we didn't see the horror as it unfolded, no matter — it would be replayed over and over on news broadcasts that day and for many days after. September 11, 2001, then, is not like December 7, 1941.

Furthermore, the Japanese attack on Pearl Harbor was a conventional military assault on a conventional military target. Soldiers taught, and it was mostly soldiers who died. The enemy had a national identity and purposes of the kind that nations often have. The attack on Pearl Harbor was certainly shocking to many Americans, but it was neither hard to understand nor difficult to imagine what the consequences would be. It meant war, full-scale American participation in a global conflict that had been raging for more than three years before Pearl Harbor.

Terrorist attacks are far more difficult to grasp. Most of terrorism's targets and victims are deliberately chosen because they are civilian. Is terrorism war, or is it crime on a vast scale? The small band of conspirators who carried out the attacks of September 11 were not professional soldiers. What are they exactly? Insane? Sane but misguided? Do they have good reason to take us as the enemy? To what terrorist groups do they belong? Evidence indicates they are somehow connected with the loosely knit international terrorist organization headed by Osama bin Laden. If so, exactly how are they connected? In a sense, we know who the enemy was; we've seen the faces of the conspirators matched with names on TV and in newspapers. But we don't *know* them at all. We struggle to imagine the motives and morality of people who embrace suicide and who understand the murder of innocent Americans as a holy mission sanctioned by God. Nor can we identify "the enemy" as those few who died with their many victims. "The enemy" is bigger than this and frustratingly vague; they won't confront us, as the enemy did sixty years ago, clad in military uniforms. We could walk right past them and not know it. Nor can we easily say what aims and aspirations the terrorists have or how crashing hijacked commercial airliners into buildings contributes to their ends. And what might the consequences be? There are no army, navy, and air force of a foreign nation against which to pit our own military forces. It's not at all clear that the military action in Afghanistan will reduce the terrorist threat in the long run. On the contrary, for all we know, it could increase it.

Amid the justifiable fear, then, we have doubt, a sense of not standing on firm ground. We hope that the following readings and the further research they suggest will help you understand terrorism better, the first step in coping with it intelligently. But part of coping with terrorism is learning to live with doubt. If we can't do that, the terrorists will have accomplished one of their purposes—to unsettle us, to reduce our confidence in ourselves, our institutions, our ways of life.

A warning before you begin reading—terrorism has many faces. The one we saw on September 11 is only one of them. To gain a fuller view, consult the books by Wilkinson and Harmon listed in "For Further Reading and Research" on page 465.

Some assurances as well—most important, terrorism can be understood. It is not as alien as it might seem. To some degree, it can be effectively countered so that attacks will be less likely and, when they do occur, less destructive. Terrorism also can be resisted in many ways. One way is to know a lot about it and to carefully think through the threat it poses and the motives behind it. In this way, we rob it of its mystery and therefore of much of its power to terrorize.

Finally, there are many issues connected with terrorism. Rather than list them all here, we raise them as they emerge in the readings. In this way, our understanding can evolve, as it must with a subject far too complex to take in all at once.

## SECTION 1: RECALLING THE ATTACK

Material devoted to recalling the attack may seem unnecessary. How could anyone forget? Yet the mind has a way of pushing away such painful things, and in our media-saturated world nothing remains sharp and centered for very long. We want to move on, and as the years pass, we surely will, going back to it only to explain what happened to those born since the disaster and those too young to remember it. What matters for them and for us is not so much *that* we remember it but rather *how*, in what way. Even now, many people recall it primarily as a spectacle of destruction, almost surreal because it so closely resembled the special effects of disaster movies. What's lost is the human scale, the level of experience missed by the distant panorama of the camera. And so we concentrate here not on the spectacle but on the human face of the attack, which we think the images and essays capture well if only partially.

We depend on journalism for our first understanding of anything that happens on the world's stage. Probably no other event in human history was covered so intensively as 9/11. Details of that day are still coming out and probably will for some time. But for now, at least, nearly a year after the attack, one source stands out as by far the best we've seen: a special issue of *Rolling Stone* called simply *9.11.01*. Many of the photos and all three of the essays in this first section come from this issue. You may want to buy or borrow your own copy of it. It's well worth careful reading and study.

As you look over the photos, pause to consider what each one "says" to you. Each offers something distinctive. Then, when you get to the essays, remember they were selected and presented in the order they're in for good reasons. The first is a ground-zero view, "up close and personal," as the media like to say, one man's memory from a perspective perilously close to the more than 3,000 people who didn't live to tell their stories. The second is quite far away, about as far from New York as one can get and still be in the continental United States, Ken Kesey's view from his farm in Oregon. How the author of *One Flew over the Cuckoo's Nest* (a celebrated novel made into a movie about distinguishing the sane from the insane) understood the madness of 9/11 has special interest and offers maximum contrast with Timothy Townsend's blow-by-blow account. The last is neither close up nor far away and deals with the distress of Americans who look and sound too much to other Americans like the terrorists themselves. For them, as Reshma Memon Yaqub explains, there was a double-edged pain: "Even as we buckled under the same grief that every American was feeling that day, American

Muslims had to endure the additional burden of worrying for our own safety. . . ." They had to endure accusations such as "'you people' did this."

The essays provide much of what we need most—a fuller appreciation of the human response that no camera can capture, an ability to reflect on the meaning of the tragedy, and a warning about scapegoats and taking anything and anyone at face value. It's a good place to begin our quest to cope better with terrorism.

---

## At Ground Zero: The First Hours
### Timothy Townsend

The first thing I saw in the parking lot across Liberty Street from the South Tower was luggage. Burned luggage. A couple of cars were on fire. Half a block east, a man who'd been working out in a South Tower fitness club was walking barefoot over shards of glass, wearing only a white towel around his waist; he still had shaving cream on the left side of his face. Bits of glass were falling to the ground like hail. I ventured a block south, away from the towers, and that's when I started seeing body parts. At first, just scattered lumps of mangled flesh dotting the road and its sidewalks, then a leg near the gutter. Someone mentioned a severed head over by a fire hydrant. Hunks of metal—some silver and the size of a fist, others green and as big as toasters—were strewn for blocks south of the buildings. Shoes were everywhere.

"Oh, Jesus," I heard someone say. "They're jumping." Every few moments a body would fall from the North Tower, from about ninety floors up. The jumpers all seemed to come from the floors that were engulfed in flames. Sometimes they jumped in pairs—one just after the other. They were up so high, it took ten to twelve seconds for each of them to hit the ground. I counted.

What must have been going through their minds, to choose certain death? Was it a decision between one death and another? Or maybe it wasn't a decision at all, their bodies involuntarily recoiling from the heat, the way you pull your hand off a hot stove.

Moments later, a low metallic whine, quickly followed by a high-pitched *whoosh*, came out of the south. I looked up to see the white belly of an airplane much closer than it should have been. The South Tower of the Trade Center seemed to suck the plane into itself. For an instant it looked like there would be no trauma to the building—it was as if the plane just slipped through a mail slot in the side of the tower, or simply vanished. But then a fireball ballooned out of the top of the building just five blocks from where we stood.

People were running south down the West Side Highway toward Battery Park—the southern tip, the end, of Manhattan—and west toward the          5

Hudson River. I ran with the crowd that veered toward the river, looking back over my shoulder at the new gash in the Trade Center. Once relatively safe among the tree-lined avenues of Battery Park City, people hugged each other and some cried.

After about ten minutes, a wave of calm returned to the streets. Police were trying to get the thousands of people south of the World Trade Center off the West Side Highway, east to the FDR Drive, over the Brooklyn Bridge. And still people were throwing themselves out of the North Tower: You could see suit jackets fluttering in the wind and women's dresses billowing like failed parachutes.

But about five minutes later, a sharp cracking sound momentarily re-placed the shrill squeal of sirens, and the top half of the South Tower im-ploded, bringing the entire thing down. It was the most frightened I've ever been. Screaming and sprinting south toward Battery Park, we all flew from the dark cloud that was slowly funneling toward us. At that moment, I be-lieved two things about this cloud. One, that it was made not just of ash and soot, but of metal, glass and concrete; and two, that soon this shrapnel would be whizzing by—and perhaps through—my head. A woman next to me turned to run. Her black bag came off her shoulder and a CD holder went flying, sending bright silver discs clattering across the ground. An older man to my right tripped and took a face-first dive across the pave-ment, glasses flying off his face.

In the seconds, minutes and hours following the World Trade Center attacks, hundreds—maybe thousands—of ordinary people would find their best selves and become heroes. And then there were the rest of us, running hard, wanting only to live and to talk to someone we loved, even if it meant leaving an old guy lying in the street, glasses gone, a cloud of death and destruction creeping up on him.

I'd always wondered what I'd do in a life-or-death situation. Until that moment, I'd believed I'd do the right thing, would always help the helpless, most likely without regard for my own well-being. All across lower Manhattan at that moment, people were making similar decisions, so many of them so much more critical than mine. September 11th, 2001, at 9:45 A.M. was not my finest moment. As I turned back to help, I saw two younger guys scoop the fallen man up, and we all continued running south.

After about three blocks, I hid for a moment behind a large Dumpster on the west side of the street. But when I looked back toward the towers, I could see that my Dumpster was no match for the cloud, and I took off again. I ran the last few blocks into Battery Park, where the cloud finally did catch up with the thousands of us fleeing it. I could see only a few feet in front of me, and so I followed the silhouettes I could make out. Because Battery Park is the tip of the island, it wasn't much of a surprise that the crowd would wind up dead-ending at the water. When it happened, the people in the front panicked. So they turned around, screamed, and ran back toward us in a stampede. We had nowhere to go—there were thousands of people behind us and hundreds coming back the other way.

As the crowd doubled back on itself, I jumped over a wrought-iron fence and landed in a flower bed. I stayed down for a second, thinking I'd wait out the panic low to the ground. But then I felt other people jumping the fence and landing near me. Thinking I was about to be trampled, I got up and ran behind a nearby tree. In a minute or two the panic subdued, and I hopped back over the fence and onto a park path. But now the air was heavier with debris and there was no clear path out of the park. I took off my tie and wrapped it around my face. People were coughing and stumbling. Some were crying, others screaming. It was difficult to breathe or even keep my eyes open.

Soon, there was another wave of calm and quiet, and the ash that fell from the sky and settled on the grass and trees gave the park the peaceful feel of a light evening snowfall. Eventually, I found a path that led me out to the east side of the Battery area, and I followed a crowd to the FDR. Thousands participated in the exodus up the highway and into Brooklyn. It was now just past ten, and we looked like refugees. In a way, we were. My tie wasn't doing much good against the ash, so I took off my shirt and tied it around my head. We walked in the falling gray dust for fifteen minutes, still hacking, and rubbing our eyes. Then the cloud broke, and, covered in soot, we were in the sunlight again. There wasn't a lot of talking. Some walked in groups, desperately trying to stay together. Others walked alone, crying out the names of friends, co-workers or loved ones from whom they'd been separated.

At 10:25, as I [was] getting ready to cross the bridge, another cracking sound came out of the west. We looked behind us and to the left to see the remaining tower collapse. Soon, that ash reached the Manhattan foot of the Brooklyn Bridge, and the bridge was closed. Three hours later, I was finally back in my apartment in Brooklyn. It was nearly one o'clock. There was a thin layer of ash all over my kitchen from the blast. I made my phone calls and cried with my fiancée. Then I called some friends who'd left messages, checking on me. I called my friend Sully in Boston, and we went through the list of names of our friends who worked in the financial district. I was one of the last to be accounted for. When we'd gotten through most of the names—Sims, Kane, T-Bone, Molloy—Sully said, "It's not all good news. Beazo called his wife from high up in the second building to say he was OK, but she hasn't heard from him since it fell." Beazo—Tom Brennan to those he didn't go to high school or college with—still hasn't been heard from.

As it turns out, when I was watching that tower fall, I was watching my friend die. His wife was at home, in their brand-new house in Westchester County, amid their still boxed-up life. She'd already turned off the TV when Beazo's building collapsed. Their seventeen-month-old daughter is too young to have seen the images of her father's death, but someday—maybe on a distant anniversary of September 11th when each network commemorates the tragedy—I'm sure she'll be able to see it, along with her little brother or sister who is due in two months.

I hung up with Sully and turned on the television to see what I had seen. Places where I once ate lunch or shopped for a sweater or bought stamps were now buried under piles of concrete and metal, as were thousands of people—some of whom I probably rode the subway with every day. One of whom was my friend.

15

Since then, I've been freakishly fine, given what I'd seen. Maybe it's because I realize how lucky I was—my experience was like Christmas morning compared to what other people went through. Maybe it's because I lack the imagination, or the will, to realize the scope of what I'd seen. But sadness works in bizarre ways. The second night after the attack, I sat in front of the news, alone with my eighth or ninth beer, and I listened to a report about NFL officials considering a postponement of the second week of games. I thought about what a nice gesture that would be, and I cried and cried.

## The Real War

### Ken Kesey

I could have written this better on 9-11-01, the day it was happening—if I could have written. Everything was so clear that day, so unencumbered by theories and opinions, by thought, even. It just *was*. All just newborn images, ripped fresh from that monstrous pair of thighs thrust smoking into the morning sunshine. All just amateur cameras allowing us to witness the developing drama in sweeping hand-held seizures. All just muffled mikes recording murmured gasps . . .

Now, more than a week has passed. The cameras are in the grips of professionals, and the microphones are in the hands of the media. Bush has just finished his big talk to Congress and the men in suits are telling us what the men in uniforms are going to do to the men in turbans if they don't turn over the men in hiding. The talk was planned to prepare us for war. It's going to get messy, everyone agrees. It's going to last for years and probably decades, everybody ruefully concedes. Nothing will ever be the same, everybody eventually declares.

Then why does it all sound so familiar? So cozy and comfortable? Was it the row after row of dark-blue suits, broken only by grim clusters of high-ranking uniforms all drizzling ribbons and medals? If everything has changed (as we all knew that it had on that first day), why does it all wear the same old outfits and say the same old words?

Because we are talking not just about war this time, but about the war above the war: the Real War. This war has already been waged, and it's not between the United States and the Taliban, or between the Muslims and the Israelis or any of the familiar forces, but between the ancient, gut-wrenching,

bone-breaking, flesh-slashing way things have always been and the timor-
ous and fragile way things might begin to be. Could begin to be. Must begin to be, if our lives and our children's lives are ever, someday, in the up-
heaving future, to know honest peace.

True, the warriors on our side of this Real War seem few and flimsy,                    5
but we have a secret advantage: We don't fight our battle out of Hate. Anger, yes, if we have to, but anger is enough. Hate is the flag the other side
battles beneath. It is the ancient flag of fire and blood and agony, and it
waves over the graves of millions and millions.

Our side's flag is a thin air-light-blue, drifting almost unseen against
the sky. Our military march is a meadowlark's song among the dandelions.
And our Real War rally isn't given any space at the U.S. Congress. Where can
you hear it? Lots of places, if you listen. Across Dairy Queen counters. In
the careful post-office talk. The e-mail is where I've been hearing it, for days
now, and the entries are getting clearer and more numerous. At first only
ten or fifteen. Then fifty or sixty. And this morning more than 300! Here are
a few chunks and pieces that I printed out:

This is a bit from Charlie Daniels' e-mail; it came on the first day: "I'm
still in a state of shock to see the Trade Towers fall and the Pentagon, the
very symbol of military power in this nation, on fire. It's like watching a
science-fiction movie."

MICHAEL MOORE: "Will we ever get to the point that we realize we will
be more secure when the rest of the world isn't living in poverty so we can
have nice running shoes? Let's mourn, let's grieve, and when it's appropriate
let's examine our contribution to the unsafe world we live in. It doesn't
have to be like this."

VALERIE STEVENSON: "Of late, I've tried to adopt a philosophy of loving
everyone unconditionally. Tuesday morning that went out the window as
feelings of outrage, revenge and retribution flooded my soul. Then I realized just how easy it is for these terrorists to control my feelings."

DEEPAK CHOPRA: "Isn't something terribly wrong when jihads and wars          10
develop in the name of God? Isn't God invoked with hatred in Ireland, Sri
Lanka, India, Pakistan, Israel, Palestine? Is there not a deep wound at the
heart of humanity?"

USMAN FARMAN: "I was on my back. This massive cloud was approaching. I normally wear a pendant around my neck, inscribed with an Arabic
prayer for safety, similar to the cross. A Hasidic Jewish man came up to me
and held the pendant in his hand and looked at it. He read the Arabic out
loud and what he said next I will never forget: 'Brother, if you don't mind,
there's a cloud of glass coming at us. Grab my hand and let's get the hell
out of here!'"

RADIO HABANA CUBA: "There is no joy here in Cuba at the events of Tuesday. There is, instead, a profound feeling of shock, revulsion and compassion—and very real apprehension about the cries for vengeance that em-
anate from every corner of the White House and the U.S. Congress. . . .

Even if Osama bin Laden is found to be responsible, the people of the U.S. should know that he was previously trained and used by the CIA in its war against the former government of Afghanistan. No solution will be forthcoming in the destruction of those deemed responsible. The enemy will still be there because the enemy comes from within."

THE DALAI LAMA, TO PRESIDENT GEORGE BUSH: "On behalf of the Tibetan people I would like to convey our deepest condolence and solidarity with the American people during this painful time. . . . It may seem presumptuous on my part, but I personally believe we need to think seriously whether a violent action is the right thing to do and in the greater interest of the nation and people in the long run. I believe violence will only increase the cycle of violence."

CAROLYN ADAMS GARCIA: "If the Islamic peoples of the world are pushed into coalescing and cooperating against a common enemy that has no respect for them and their culture, we will be in a war with a world of over a billion people. People we have been training and selling weapons to, so that our warplanes, guns and missiles will be used against us."

TAMIN ANSARY: "I am from Afghanistan, and even though I've lived here      15
for 35 years I've never lost track of what's been going on over there. . . . Some say, why don't the Afghans rise up and overthrow the Taliban? The answer is they're starved, exhausted, damaged and incapacitated. A few years ago, the United Nations estimated that there are 500,000 disabled orphans in Afghanistan—a country with no economy, no food. Millions of Afghans are widows of the approximately 2 million men killed during the war with the Soviets. . . . We come to the question of bombing Afghanistan back to the stone age. It's already been done. The Soviets took care of that. Make the Afghans suffer? They're already suffering. Level their houses? Done. Turn their schools into piles of rubble? Done. Eradicate their hospitals? Done. Destroy their infrastructure? There is no infrastructure. Cut them off from medicine and health care? Too late."

LAMA ZOPA RINPOCHE: "May all the people's hearts be filled with loving kindness and the thought to only benefit and not harm. May the sun of peace and happiness arise and may any wars that are happening stop immediately."

CHRIS: "Hate, huh? A real downer."

LAUREN RICK: "As I was passing the firehouse, this guy stuck his hand out to my dog's nose and she licked his hand and he said, 'Thanks, I really needed that,' and I looked up and there stood a man crying gently."

There's a bunch more, but you get the idea. All openhearted e-mail. And all certainly slanted, because these people know who we are and what we believe in, and it can't help but make you a little proud as well as a little humble. But it's more than that. It's . . . Well, I can remember Pearl Harbor. I was only six, but that morning is forever smashed into my memory like a bomb into a metal deck. Hate for the Japanese nation still smolders occasionally from the hole. This 9-11 nastiness is different. There is no nation to blame. There are no diving Zeros, no island-grabbing armies, no seas filled with battleships and carriers. Just a couple dozen batty guys with box knives and absolute purpose. Dead now. Vaporized. Of course we want their leaders, but I'll be damned if I can see how we're gonna get those leaders by deploying our aircraft carriers and launching our mighty air power so we can begin bombing the crippled orphans in the rocky, leafless, already-bombed-out rubble of Afghanistan.

---

## "You People Did This"
### Reshma Memon Yaqub

As I ran through my neighborhood on the morning of September 11th, in search of my son, who had gone to the park with his baby sitter, I wasn't just afraid of another hijacked plane crashing into us. I was also afraid that someone else would get to my son first, someone wanting revenge against anyone who looks like they're from "that part of the world." Even if he is just one and a half years old.

I know I wasn't just afraid that the building where my husband works, a D.C. landmark, might fall on him. I was also afraid that another American might stop him on the street and harass him, or hurt him, demanding to know why "you people" did this. As soon as we heard the news, 7 million American Muslims wondered in terror, "Will America blame me?"

When our country is terrorized, American Muslims are victimized twice. First, as Americans, by the madmen who strike at our nation, at our physical, mental and emotional core. Then we're victimized again, as Muslims, by those Americans who believe that all Muslims are somehow accountable for the acts of some madmen, that our faith—that our God, the same peace-loving God worshipped by Jews and Christians—sanctions it.

It didn't matter when the federal building in Oklahoma City blew up that a Muslim didn't do it. That a Christian man was responsible for the devastation in Oklahoma City certainly didn't matter to the thugs who terrorized a Muslim woman there, nearly seven months pregnant, by attacking her home, breaking her windows, screaming religious slurs. It didn't matter to them that Sahar Al-Muwsawi, 26, would, as a result, miscarry her baby. That she would bury him in the cold ground, alongside other victims of the Oklahoma City bombing, after naming him Salaam, the Arabic word for "peace."

But that travesty and hundreds like it certainly were on my mind that Tuesday morning. And they were reinforced every time a friend called to check on my family and to sadly remind me, "It's over for us. Muslims are done for."

Even as we buckled under the same grief that every American was feeling that day, American Muslims had to endure the additional burden of

5

worrying for our own safety, in our own hometowns, far from hijackers and skyscrapers. Shots would be fired into the Islamic Center of Irving, Texas; an Islamic bookstore in Virginia would have bricks thrown through its windows; a bag of pig's blood would be left on the doorstep of an Islamic community center in San Francisco; a mosque near Chicago would be marched on by 300 people shouting racist epithets. A Muslim of Pakistani origin would be gunned down in Dallas; a Sikh man would be shot and killed in Mesa, Arizona (possibly by the same assailant who would go on to spray bullets into the home of a local Afghani family).

And those were just the cases that were reported. I know I didn't report it when a ten-year-old neighborhood boy walked by and muttered, "Terrorist," as I got into my car. My neurosurgeon friend didn't report that a nurse at the prominent Washington hospital where they both work had announced in front of him that all Muslims and Arabs should be rounded up and put into camps, as Japanese were in World War II. My family didn't report that we're sick with worry about my mother-in-law, another sister-in-law and my niece, who are visiting Pakistan, with their return uncertain.

In the days to come, in the midst of the darkness, there is some light. A neighbor stops by to tell me that he doesn't think Muslims are responsible for the acts of madmen. Strangers in Starbucks are unusually friendly to me and my son, reaching out as if to say, "We know it's not your fault." The head of a church told me his congregation wants to come and put its arms around us, and to help in any way possible — by cleaning graffiti off a mosque, by hosting our Friday prayers, whatever we needed. President Bush warns Americans not to scapegoat Muslims and Arabs. He even visits a mosque, in a show of solidarity. Congress swiftly passes a resolution to uphold the civil rights of Muslims and Arabs, urging Americans to remain united. Jewish and Christian leaders publicly decry the violence against Muslims. At a mosque in Seattle, Muslim worshippers are greeted by members of other faiths bringing them flowers.

There's something America needs to understand about Islam. Like Judaism, like Christianity, Islam doesn't condone terrorism. It doesn't allow it. It doesn't accept it. Yet, somehow, the labels *jihad, holy war* and *suicide martyrs* are still thrown around. In fact, jihad doesn't even mean holy war. It's an Arabic word that means "struggle" — struggle to please God. And suicide itself is a forbidden act in Islam. How could anyone believe that Muslims consider it martyrdom when practiced in combination with killing thousands of innocents? Anyone who claims to commit a politically motivated violent act in the name of Islam has committed a hate crime against the world's 1.2 billion Muslims.

It is not jihad to hijack a plane and fly it into a building. But in fact there was jihad done that Tuesday. It was jihad when firemen ran into imploding buildings to rescue people they didn't know. It was jihad when Americans lined up and waited to donate the blood of their own bodies. It was jihad when strangers held and comforted one another in the streets. It was jihad when rescue workers struggled to put America back together, piece by piece.

10

Yes, there were martyrs made that Tuesday. But there were no terrorists among them. There were only Americans, of every race and religion, who, that Tuesday, took death for us.

---

## For Discussion

1. News coverage has emphasized the heroism of some people on 9/11/01, especially the New York firefighters and police and the ordinary citizens aboard the fourth plane who rushed the hijackers and died preventing the plane's use as a weapon of large-scale destruction. Paying careful attention to the details of his narrative, how would you characterize Townsend's behavior? Why have we heard relatively little about responses like his?

2. "I lack the imagination, or the will, to realize the scope of what I'd seen," Townsend admits. Do we? Even now? Why? Would you call this lack of imagination or will a defense mechanism, or is it the case that the human mind simply can't fully grasp events of such magnitude?

3. Kesey contrasts all the pronouncements that everything has changed after the attack to the statements of our government officials, which he says "sound so familiar." What exactly has changed? Would you agree that the official response was predictable? If so, should we be critical of it, as Kesey is?

4. What does Kesey mean by "the Real War"? What point or points is he trying to make by citing excerpts from e-mails? How does this material relate to his concept of the real war?

5. What does Deepak Chopra mean by "a deep wound at the heart of humanity" (paragraph 10). Do we see this wound in Kesey's last paragraph? In what way or ways? What keeps such wounds perpetually open, beyond any complete healing?

6. Note that Yaqub sees the terrorists much as many Americans do—as madmen. Do you agree with her interpretation? Judging from what she says elsewhere in the essay, what falls inside and outside the meaning of the word *sanity* as she understands it?

7. What does *jihad* mean to Yaqub? What sort of behavior does she say justifies application of the word? And what does she mean by *martyr*? How does her understanding differ from common uses of the word? Is it accurate or helpful to characterize as martyrs the innocent Americans who died in the attack?

## For Writing and Research

1. Tell your own story of where you were and what you thought, felt, and did on 9/11 and how you reacted for a few days or weeks thereafter. Do you detect signs that you too were "freakishly fine," as Town-

send phrases it? If not, how do you characterize your general response during and shortly after the attack? How would you describe it now?

2. "I believe violence will only increase the cycle of violence," the Dalai Lama writes to President Bush. (See Kesey, paragraph 13.) Kesey clearly agrees. Do you? Research what our government has done in response to 9/11. Write an essay assessing American action since the attack. What aspects of this action do you consider defensible, constructive? Of what aspects are you critical?

3. As a class, collect as many photographs from 9/11 and its aftermath as you can find. Sort them out using whatever principles and categories your class considers helpful and appropriate. Which ones would you use to tell the story for a history of the events? Working collaboratively in any way the class thinks will work, write an account of 9/11, incorporating the photos in the text. Conceive of your audience as people in the future who would not remember these events. What would you most want them to know and remember?

## SECTION 2: GETTING INFORMED

Because terrorism has been a significant factor in world politics since the late 1960s, a wealth of material published before 9/11 exists. See the extensive bibliographies in the Harmon and Wilkinson volumes mentioned earlier. The attack has already resulted in thousands of articles and news stories, and new books are no doubt in the works. To understate the matter considerably: There's plenty to read on terrorism.

We've offered here hardly more than the "bare bones," what we think everyone must know to talk and write about 9/11 and its aftermath from a reasonably informed point of view. You'll also be able to use the information here to help you assess the more interpretative, analytical, and argumentative essays of Part Three.

We've divided the material into four sections, each with its own exploratory questions and possible writing assignments.

General Information
Impact on the United States
Understanding Terrorism
Conclusion: The Future of Terrorism

The third section "Understanding Terrorism," is the most extensive, with material on the background of the Palestine-Israeli conflict and the U.S. role in it, information about the aims of bin Laden and his allies, their camps for training terrorists, and much else. The conclusion speculates about the future of terrorism, including the threats posed by nuclear, chemical, and biological weapons, possibilities we cannot ignore after anthrax found its way into the U.S. mail. It's hard to imagine the future of anything, but in the case of terrorism there's an obvious and urgent need to do our best.

Let's start to become informed by considering the following definition of terrorism adopted by The Jonathan Institute in Jerusalem at a 1979 conference. It's cited by Harmon in his book, *Terrorism Today*, where he claims it "has never been surpassed for clarity and concision."

> Terrorism is the deliberate and systematic murder, maiming, and menacing of the innocent to inspire fear for political ends. (p. 1)

Harmon goes on to distinguish terrorism from "civil dissidence" and from "forms of civil violence, or revolution." Both, he says, "occur regularly without terrorism."

The first, "civil dissidence," is "nonviolent opposition to injustice" and comes from "Europe's long and venerable democratic tradition." It would encompass, for example, most of the civil rights movement of the 1960s and 1970s.

The second, "civil violence," would take in, presumably, the American Revolution and our Civil War, as well as parts of the French and Russian Revolutions. Harmon insists that we must distinguish terrorism from the two "legitimate methods" of change, even when they are combined, as they sometimes are, with terrorist tactics. That is: In his view, we cannot condemn categorically violence for political ends *in all cases* nor peaceful protests when they are associated with terrorist acts. In any case of political action, we must be prepared to draw a line between the legitimate and the illegitimate. Terrorism is never acceptable because it targets the innocent.

We think the definition Harmon cites is useful. It raises a key issue in the terrorism debate, namely, Is there a clear and bright line between legitimate political struggle and terrorism? In your reading, you'll encounter efforts to defend terrorism, especially as a response to its most common historical form, *state terrorism*—the use of terrorist tactics by national governments. You must decide whether terrorism is ever justified even in the most extreme of circumstances, and this must include thinking about exactly who's innocent and who's not, a distinction not always easy to make.

Because our ethical outlook is implicated in how we define terrorism, we must think carefully about this and all definitions of it. We must be willing to test any definition in the heat of actual instances, concrete cases of political violence. For it will do us no good to have an abstract definition we can't use to sort out the acceptable from the unacceptable. It also won't do to slip into an easy relativism—to say, as some people have, that "one person's terrorist is somebody else's freedom fighter." If we say this, anything goes and all moral bearing is lost.

## General Information

To study any complex subject, we must both *absorb information* and *strive for conceptual clarity.* Lacking the former, we won't know enough to say or write useful things; without the latter, we'll drown in data, unable to make sense out of all we know. The first article in this section, "Ten Things to Know about the Middle East," contributes to our knowledge; the second article, for which we have supplied the title "Types of Terrorism," breaks down terrorism into five basic categories. Combined with the definition of terrorism offered in the previous section, we are beginning to build the concepts we need, the tools to think with.

"Ten Things" was posted on AlterNet (October 1, 2001) by Stephen Zunes, a professor of political science and chair of the Peace and Justice Studies Program at the University of San Francisco. "Types of Terrorism" is an excerpt from Chapter 2 of Paul Wilkinson's *Terrorism versus Democracy: The Liberal State Response,* a book published in 2000. Wilkinson is a professor of international relations and the director of the Centre for the Study of Terrorism and Political Violence at the University of St. Andrews in Scotland.

## Ten Things to Know about the Middle East
### Stephen Zunes

### 1. Who Are the Arabs?

Arab peoples range from the Atlantic coast in northwest Africa to the Arabian peninsula and north to Syria. They are united by a common language and culture. Though the vast majority are Muslim, there are also sizable Christian Arab minorities in Egypt, Lebanon, Iraq, Syria and Palestine. Originally the inhabitants of the Arabian peninsula, the Arabs spread their language and culture to the north and west with the expansion of Islam in the 7th century. There are also Arab minorities in the Sahel and parts of east Africa, as well as in Iran and Israel. The Arabs were responsible for great advances in mathematics, astronomy and other scientific disciplines while Europe was still mired in the Dark Ages.

Though there is great diversity in skin pigmentation, spoken dialect and certain customs, there is a common identity that unites Arab people, which has sometimes been reflected in pan-Arab nationalist movements. Despite substantial political and other differences, many Arabs share a sense that they are one nation, which has been artificially divided through the machinations of Western imperialism and which came to dominate the region with the decline of the Ottoman Empire in the 19th and early 20th century. There is also a growing Arab diaspora in Europe, North America, Latin America, West Africa and Australia.

### 2. Who Are the Muslims?

The Islamic faith originated in the Arabian peninsula, based on what Muslims believe to be divine revelations by God to the prophet Mohammed.

Muslims worship the same God as do Jews and Christians, and share many
of the same prophets and ethical traditions, including respect for innocent
life. Approximately 90 percent of Muslims are of the orthodox or Sunni tradition; most of the remainder are of the Shi'ite tradition, which dominates
Iran but also has substantial numbers in Iraq, Bahrain, Yemen and Lebanon. Sunni Islam is nonhierarchical in structure. There is not a tradition
of separation between the faith and state institutions as there is in the West,
though there is enormous diversity in various Islamic legal traditions and
the degree to which governments of predominantly Muslim countries rely
on religious bases for their rule.

Political movements based on Islam have ranged from left to right,
from nonviolent to violent, from tolerant to chauvinistic. Generally, the
more moderate Islamic movements have developed in countries where there
is a degree of political pluralism in which they could operate openly. There
is a strong tradition of social justice in Islam, which has often led to conflicts with regimes that are seen to be unjust or unethical. The more radical
movements have tended to arise in countries that have suffered great social
dislocation due to war or inappropriate economic policies and/or are under
autocratic rule.

Most of the world's Muslims are not Arabs. The world's largest Muslim     5
country, for example, is Indonesia. Other important non-Arab Muslim
countries include Malaysia, Bangladesh, Pakistan, Afghanistan, Iran, Turkey
and the five former Soviet republics of Central Asia, as well as Nigeria and
several other black African states. Islam is one of the fastest growing religions in the world and scores of countries have substantial Muslim minorities. There are approximately five million Muslims in the United States.

### 3. Why is There so Much Violence and Political Instability in the Middle East?

For most of the past 500 years, the Middle East actually saw less violence
and warfare and more political stability than Europe or most other regions
of the world. It has only been in the last century that the region has seen
such widespread conflict. The roots of the conflict are similar to those elsewhere in the Third World, and have to do with the legacy of colonialism,
such as artificial political boundaries, autocratic regimes, militarization,
economic inequality and economies based on the export of raw materials
for finished goods. Indeed, the Middle East has more autocratic regimes,
militarization, economic inequality and the greatest ratio of exports to domestic consumption than any region in the world.

At the crossroads of three continents and sitting on much of the world's
oil reserves, the region has been subjected to repeated interventions and
conquests by outside powers, resulting in a high level of xenophobia and
suspicion regarding the intentions of Western powers going back as far as

the Crusades. There is nothing in Arab or Islamic culture that promotes violence or discord; indeed, there is a strong cultural preference for stability, order and respect for authority. However, adherence to authority is based on a kind of social contract that assumes a level of justice which—if broken by the ruler—gives the people a right to challenge it. The word *jihad*, often translated as "holy war," actually means "holy struggle," which can sometimes mean an armed struggle (*qital*), but also can mean nonviolent action and political work within the established system. *Jihad* also can mean a struggle for the moral good of the Muslim community, or even a personal spiritual struggle.

Terrorism is not primarily a Middle Eastern phenomenon. In terms of civilian lives lost, Africa has experienced far more terrorism in recent decades than has the Middle East. Similarly, far more suicide bombings in recent years have come from Hindu Tamils in Sri Lanka than from Muslim Arabs in the Middle East. There is also a little-known but impressive tradition of nonviolent resistance and participatory democracy in some Middle Eastern countries.

### 4. Why Has the Middle East Been the Focus of U.S. Concern about International Terrorism?

There has been a long history of terrorism—generally defined as "violence by irregular forces against civilian targets"—in the Middle East. During Israel's independence struggle in the 1940s, Israeli terrorists killed hundreds of Palestinian and British civilians; two of the most notorious terrorist leaders of that period—Menachem Begin and Yitzhak Shamir—later became Israeli prime ministers whose governments received strong financial, diplomatic and military support from the United States. Algeria's independence struggle from France in the 1950s included widespread terrorist attacks against French colonists. Palestine's ongoing struggle for independence has also included widespread terrorism against Israeli civilians, during the 1970s through some of the armed militias of the Palestine Liberation Organization and, more recently, through radical underground Islamic groups. Terrorism has also played a role in Algeria's current civil strife, in Lebanon's civil war and foreign occupations during the 1980s, and for many years in the Kurdish struggle for independence. Some Middle Eastern governments—notably Libya, Syria, Sudan, Iraq and Iran—have in the past had close links with terrorist organizations. In more recent years, the Al Qaeda movement—a decentralized network of terrorist cells supported by Saudi exile Osama bin Laden—has become the major terrorist threat, and is widely believed to be responsible for the September 11 terrorist attacks on the United States. Bin Laden himself has been given sanctuary in Afghanistan, though his personal fortune and widespread network of supporters have allowed him to be independent of direct financial or logistical support from any government.

The vast majority of the people in the Middle East deplore terrorism,    10
yet point out that violence against civilians by governments has generally
surpassed that of terrorists. For example, the Israelis have killed far more
Arab civilians over the decades through using U.S.-supplied equipment and
ordinance than have Arab terrorists killed Israeli civilians. Similarly, the
U.S.-supplied Turkish armed forces have killed far more Kurdish civilians
than have such radical Kurdish groups like the PKK (the Kurdish acronym
for the Kurdistan Workers' Party). Also, in the eyes of many Middle Easterners, U.S. support for terrorist groups like the Nicaraguan contras and various right-wing Cuban exile organizations in recent decades, as well as U.S.
air strikes and the U.S.-led sanctions against Iraq in more recent years, have
made the U.S. an unlikely leader in the war against terrorism.

### 5. What Kind of Political Systems and Alliances Exist in the Middle East?

There are a variety of political systems in the Middle East. Saudi Arabia,
Oman, Bahrain, Kuwait, United Arab Emirates, Qatar, Morocco and Jordan
are all conservative monarchies (in approximate order of absolute rule).
Iraq, Syria and Libya are left-leaning dictatorships, with Iraq being one of
the most totalitarian societies in the world. Egypt and Tunisia are conservative autocratic republics. Iran is an Islamic republic with an uneven trend in
recent years towards greater political openness. Sudan and Algeria are under military rulers facing major insurrections.

Lebanon, Turkey and Yemen are republics with repressive aspects but
some degree of political pluralism. The only Middle Eastern country with a
strong tradition of parliamentary democracy is Israel, though the benefits of
this political freedom [are] largely restricted to its Jewish citizens (the Palestinian Arab minority is generally treated as second-class citizens and Palestinians in the occupied territories are subjected to military rule and human
rights abuses). The largely autocratic Palestinian Authority has been granted
limited autonomy in a series of noncontiguous enclaves in the West Bank
and Gaza Strip surrounded by Israeli occupation forces.

All Arab states, including the Palestinian Authority, belong to the League
of Arab States, which acts as a regional body similar to the Organization of
African Union or the Organization of American States, which work together
on issues of common concern. However, there are enormous political divisions within Arab countries and other Middle Eastern states. Turkey is a
member of the NATO alliance, [which is] closely aligned with the West and
hopes to eventually become part of the European Union. The six conservative monarchies of the Persian Gulf region have formed the Gulf Cooperation Council (GCC), from where they pursue joint strategic and economic
interests and promote close ties with the West, particularly Great Britain

(which dominated the smaller sheikdoms in the late 19th and early 20th centuries) and, more recently, the United States.

Often a country's alliances are not a reflection of its internal politics. For example, Saudi Arabia is often referred [to] in the U.S. media as a "moderate" Arab state, though it is the most oppressive fundamentalist theocracy in the world today outside of Taliban-ruled Afghanistan; "moderate," in this case, simply means that it has close strategic and economic relations with the United States.

Jordan and Egypt are pro-Western, but have been willing to challenge   15
U.S. policy on occasion. Israel identifies most strongly with the West: most of its leaders are European-born or have been of European heritage, and it has diplomatic relations with only a handful of Middle Eastern countries. Iran alienated most of its neighbors with its threat to expand its brand of revolutionary Islam to the Arab world, though its increasingly moderate orientation in recent years has led to some cautious rapprochement. Syria, a former Soviet ally, has been cautiously reaching out to more conservative Arab governments and to the West; it currently exerts enormous political influence over Lebanon. Iraq under Saddam Hussein, Libya under Muammar Qaddafi and Sudan under their military junta remain isolated from most other Middle Eastern countries due to a series of provocative policies, though many of these same countries oppose the punitive sanctions and air strikes the United States has inflicted against these countries in recent years.

### 6. What Is the Impact of Oil in the Middle East?

The major oil producers of the Middle East include Saudi Arabia, Kuwait, United Arab Emirates, Qatar, Bahrain, Iraq, Iran, Libya and Algeria. Egypt, Syria, Oman and Yemen have smaller reserves. Most of the major oil producers of the Middle East are part of the Organization of Petroleum Exporting Countries, or OPEC. (Non-Middle Eastern OPEC members include Indonesia, Venezuela, Nigeria and other countries.) Much of the world's oil wealth exists along the Persian Gulf, with particularly large reserves in Saudi Arabia, Kuwait and the United Arab Emirates. About one-quarter of U.S. oil imports come from the Persian Gulf region; the Gulf supplies European states and Japan with an even higher percentage of those countries' energy needs. The imposition of higher fuel efficiency standards and other conservation measures, along with the increased use of renewable energy resources for which technologies are already available, could eliminate U.S. dependence on Middle Eastern oil in a relatively short period of time.

The Arab members of OPEC instigated a boycott against the United States in the fall of 1973 in protest of U.S. support for Israel during the October Arab-Israeli war, creating the first in a series of energy shortages. The cartel has had periods of high and low costs for oil, resulting in great economic instability. Most governments have historically used their oil wealth to promote social welfare, particularly countries like Algeria, Libya and Iraq, which professed to a more socialist orientation. Yet all countries have squandered their wealth for arms purchases and prestige projects. In general, the influx of petrodollars has created enormous economic inequality both within oil-producing states and between oil-rich and oil-poor states as well as widespread corruption and questionable economic priorities.

### 7. What Is the Israeli-Palestinian Conflict about?

The Israeli-Palestinian conflict is essentially over land, with two peoples claiming historic rights to the geographic Palestine, a small country in the eastern Mediterranean about the size of New Jersey. The creation of modern Israel in 1948 was a fulfillment of the goal of the Jewish nationalist movement, known as Zionism, as large numbers of Jews migrated to their faith's ancestral homeland from Europe, North Africa and elsewhere throughout the 20th century. They came into conflict with the indigenous Palestinian Arab population, which also was struggling for independence. The 1947 partition plan, which divided the country approximately in half, resulted in a war that ended with Israel seizing control of 78 percent of the territory within a year. Most of the Palestinian population became refugees, in some cases through fleeing the fighting and in other cases through being forcibly expelled. The remaining Palestinian areas — the West Bank and Gaza Strip — came under control of the neighboring Arab states of Jordan and Egypt, though these areas were also seized by Israel in the 1967 war.

Israel has been colonizing parts of these occupied territories with Jewish settlers in violation of the Geneva Conventions and UN Security Council resolutions. Historically, both sides have failed to recognize the legitimacy of the others' nationalist aspirations, though the Palestinian leadership finally formally recognized Israel in 1993. The peace process since then has been over the fate of the West Bank (including Arab East Jerusalem) and the Gaza Strip, which is the remaining 22 percent of Palestine, occupied by Israel since 1967. The United States plays the dual role of chief mediator of the conflict as well as the chief financial, military and diplomatic supporter of Israel. The Palestinians want their own independent state in these territories and to allow Palestinian refugees the right to return. Israel, backed by the United States, insists the Palestinians give up large swaths of the West Bank — including most of Arab East Jerusalem — to Israel and to accept the resettlement of most refugees into other Arab countries. Since September 2000, there [have] been widespread rioting by Palestinians against the ongoing Israeli occupation as well as terrorist bombings within Israel by extremist Islamic groups. Israeli occupation forces, meanwhile, have engaged in widespread killings and other human rights abuses in the occupied territories.

Most Arabs feel a strong sense of solidarity with the Palestinian strug-   20
gle, though their governments have tended to manipulate their plight for
their own political gain. Neighboring Arab states have fought several wars
with Israel, though Egypt and Jordan now have peace agreements and full
diplomatic relations with the Jewish state. In addition to much of the West
Bank and Gaza Strip, Israel still occupies a part of southwestern Syria known
as the Golan Heights. The threats and hostility by Arab states towards Israel's very existence has waned over the years. Full peace and diplomatic recognition would likely come following a full Israeli withdrawal from its occupied territories.

### 8. What Has Been the Legacy of the Gulf War?

Virtually every Middle Eastern state opposed the Iraqi invasion and occupation of Kuwait in 1990, though they were badly divided on the appropriateness of the U.S.-led Gulf War that followed. Even among countries that supported the armed liberation of Kuwait, there was widespread opposition to
the deliberate destruction by the United States of much of Iraq's civilian
infrastructure during the war. Even more controversial has been the enormous humanitarian consequences of the U.S.-led international sanctions
against Iraq in place since the war, which have resulted in the deaths of
hundreds of thousands of Iraqis, mostly children, from malnutrition and
preventable diseases.

The periodic U.S. air strikes against Iraq also have been controversial,
as has the ongoing U.S. military presence in Saudi Arabia, other Gulf states
and in the Persian Gulf and Arabian Sea. Since Iraq's offensive military ca-
pability was largely destroyed during the Gulf War and during the subsequent inspections regime, many observers believe that U.S. fears about
Iraq's current military potential are exaggerated, particularly in light of the
quiet U.S. support for Iraq during the 1980s when its military was at its
peak. In many respects, the Gulf War led the oil-rich GCC states into closer
identification with the United States and the West and less with their fellow
Arabs, though there is still some distrust about U.S. motivations and policies in the Middle East.

### 9. How Has the Political Situation in Afghanistan Evolved and How is it Connected to the Middle East?

Afghanistan, an impoverished, landlocked, mountainous country, has traditionally been identified more with Central and South Asia than with the
Middle East. A 1978 coup by communist military officers resulted in a series of radical social reforms, which were imposed in an autocratic matter
and which resulted in a popular rebellion by a number of armed Islamic

movements. The Soviet Union installed a more compliant communist regime at the end of 1979, sending in tens of thousands of troops and instigating a major bombing campaign, resulting in large-scale civilian casualties and refugee flows. The war lasted for much of the next decade. The United States sent arms to the Islamic resistance, known as the *mujahadin*, largely through neighboring Pakistan, then under the rule of an ultra-conservative Islamic military dictatorship. Most of the U.S. aid went to the most radical of the eight different *mujahadin* factions on the belief that they would be least likely to reach a negotiated settlement with the Soviet-backed government and would therefore drag the Soviet forces down. Volunteers from throughout the Islamic world, including the young Saudi businessman Osama bin Laden, joined the struggle. The CIA trained many of these recruits, including bin Laden and many of his followers.

When the Soviets and Afghanistan's communist government were defeated in 1992, a vicious and bloody civil war broke out between the various *mujahadin* factions, war lords and ethnic militias. Out of this chaos emerged the Taliban movement, led by young seminary students from the refugee camps in Pakistan who were educated in ultra-conservative Saudi-funded schools. The Taliban took over 85 percent of the country by 1996 and imposed long-awaited order and stability, but established a brutal totalitarian theocracy based on a virulently reactionary and misogynist interpretation of Islam. The Northern Alliance, consisting of the remnants of various factions from the civil war in the 1990s, control a small part of the northeast corner of the country.

### 10. How Have Most Middle Eastern Governments Reacted to the September 11 Terrorist Attacks and Their Aftermath?

Virtually every government and the vast majority of their populations reacted with the same horror and revulsion as did people in the United States, Europe and elsewhere. Despite scenes shown repeatedly on U.S. television of some Palestinians celebrating the attacks, the vast majority of Palestinians also shared in the world's condemnation. If the United States, in conjunction with local governments, limits its military response to commando-style operations against suspected terrorist cells, the U.S. should receive the cooperation and support of most Middle Eastern countries. If the response is more widespread, based more on retaliation than self-defense, and ends up killing large numbers of Muslim civilians, it could create a major anti-American reaction that would increase support for the terrorists and lessen the likelihood for the needed cooperation to break up the Al Qaeda network, which operates in several Middle Eastern countries. 25

While few Middle Easterners support bin Laden's methods, the principal concerns expressed in his manifestoes—the U.S.'s wrongful support for Israel and for Arab dictatorships, the disruptive presence of U.S. troops in

Saudi Arabia and the humanitarian impact of the sanctions on Iraq—are widely supported. Ultimately, a greater understanding of the Middle East and the concerns of its governments and peoples are necessary before the United States can feel secure from an angry backlash from the region.

# Types of Terrorism
### Paul Wilkinson

. . . It is useful to distinguish *state* from *factional* terror. . . . Historically, states have conducted terror on a far more massive and lethal scale than groups. They have employed terror as a weapon of tyranny and repression and as an instrument of war. Another important distinction can be made between *international* and *domestic* terrorism: the former is terrorist violence involving the citizens of more than one country, while the latter is confined within the borders of one country, sometimes within a particular locality in the country. . . . However, in reality, it is hard to find an example of any significant terrorist campaign that remains purely domestic: any serious terrorist campaign actively seeks political support, weapons, financial assistance and safe haven beyond its own borders.

Once we move beyond these very broad categories it is useful to employ a basic typology of contemporary perpetrators of terrorism based on their underlying cause or political motivation.[1]

### Nationalist Terrorists

These are groups seeking political self-determination. They may wage their struggle entirely in the territory they seek to liberate, or they may be active both in their home area and abroad. In some cases they may be forced by police or military action or by threat of capture, imprisonment or execution to operate entirely from their places of exile. Nationalist groups tend to be more capable of sustaining protracted campaigns and mobilising substantial support than ideological groups. Even those nationalist groups that can only claim the support of a minority of their ethnic constituency [e.g. the IRA (Irish Republican Army), ETA (Basque Homeland and Liberty)] can gain political resonance because of their deep roots in the national culture for which they claim to be the authentic voice.

### Ideological Terrorists

These terrorists seek to change the entire political social and economic system either to an extreme left or extreme right model. In the 1970s and 1980s studies of ideological terrorism focused on the extreme left, because of the preoccupation with groups such as the Red Army Faction in Germany and the Red Brigades in Italy. Yet, as Walter Laqueur (1977) observes in his magisterial general history of terrorism[2] the dominant ideological orientation of European terrorism between the world wars was fascist. And it is neo-Nazi and neo-fascist groups which are behind so much of the racist and anti-immigrant violence in present-day Germany and other European countries. The Red Army groups so active in the 1970s and 1980s have now largely faded away, the victims of their own internal splits, determined law enforcement by their respective police and judicial authorities, and changing political attitudes among young people in the post-Cold War era.

### Religiopolitical Terrorists

The most frequently cited examples of this type of terrorism are groups such          5
as Hezbollah and Harnas. But it is important to bear in mind that militant fundamentalist factions of major religions other than Islam have also frequently spawned their own violent extremist groups. Striking examples can be found among Sikhs, Hindus and Jews, and there is a well-documented link between certain Christian fundamentalist groups and extreme right-wing terrorism in North and Central America.[3]

### Single-Issue Terrorists

These groups are obsessed with the desire to change a specific policy or practice within the target society, rather than with the aim of political revolution. Examples include the violent animal rights and anti-abortion groups.

### State-Sponsored and State-Supported Terrorists

States use this type of terrorism as a tool of both domestic and foreign policy. For example, when the Iranian regime sent hit-squads to murder leading dissidents and exiled political leaders they were doing so for domestic reasons, to intimidate and eradicate opposition to the regime.[4] However, when North Korea sent its agents to mount a bomb attack on the South Korean government delegation on its visit to Rangoon, the communist regime was engaging in an act of covert warfare against its perceived 'enemy' government in the South, an act designed to further their foreign policy aim of undermining the Republic of South Korea. State sponsors may use their own directly recruited and controlled terror squads, or choose to act through client groups and proxies.[5] They almost invariably go to some lengths to disguise their involvement, in order to sustain plausible deniability. The ending of the Cold War and the overthrow of the Eastern European communist one-party regimes and the former Soviet Union certainly removed in one fell swoop the Warsaw Pact's substantial network of sponsorship and support for a whole variety of terrorist groups. But this does not mean that state sponsorship has ceased to be a factor in the international terrorist scene. Countries such as Iraq, Iran, Syria, Libya, and the Taliban regime in Afghanistan, and Sudan are still heavily involved. . . .

### Notes

1. For a useful review of the social science literature on typologies, see Alex P. Schmid, Albert J. Jongman, Stohl and P. A. Fleming, "Terrorism and Related Concepts: Typologies." In Alex P. Schmid and Albert J. Jongman et al, *Political Terrorism: A New Guide to Actors, Authors, Concepts, Databases, Theories, and Literature* (Amsterdam: North Holland Publishing Company, 1988), pp. 39–57.

2. Walter Laqueur, *The Age of Terrorism* (Boston: Little Brown, 1987).

3. On this linkage in North America, see Michael Barkun, *Religion and the Racist Right* (Chapel Hill, NC: North Carolina University Press, 1994).

4. On the other key aspect of Iranian international terrorist activity, the export of Iranian-style Islamic revolutionism, see Richard H. Shultz, Jr, "Iranian Covert Aggression: Support for Radical Political Islamists Conducting Internal Subversion Against States in the Middle East/South West Asia Region," *Terrorism and Political Violence*, 6: 3 (Autumn 1994), pp. 281–302.

5. For a valuable discussion of the spectrum of state sponsorship and support for terrorism, see John F. Murphy, *State Support of International Terrorism* (Boulder, CO: Westview Press, 1989).

---

*For Discussion*

1. Many Americans use the words *Arab* and *Muslim* interchangeably, as if the two words meant the same thing. What do we learn from Zunes that should help us use these concepts more carefully and precisely?

2. According to Zunes, what unifies the Arab world, giving it a recognizable identity? What tends toward disunity, or separation of the Arab world into groups of people with different interests?

3. We speak of "the Middle East" as if it were a single entity, something more than just a geographical location we distinguish by reference to our own "Western world" and from what we call, again from our own perspective, the "Far East." As Zunes depicts it, what differences in politics, religion, and economics distinguish the various nations of the Middle East from each other?

4. We tend to associate the Middle East with terrorism. What evidence does Zunes offer for the inaccuracy of this association?

5. How does Zunes explain the civil unrest, violence, and terrorism in the recent history of the Middle East?

6. According to Zunes, what has the U.S. government done in the Middle East that has been popular with most Arab peoples? What has not? Explain from an Arab point of view (or several Arab points of view) why they view our policies with such mixed reactions.

7. Wilkinson distinguishes "state" from "factional" terror. State the difference in your own words. What examples of both, present or past, can you provide? Is bin Laden's network clearly one or the other?

8. Wilkinson also distinguishes "international" from "domestic" terrorism. What does he say that undermines this distinction to some degree? In your view, is the distinction nevertheless worth making? Why or why not?

9. The current prominence of Islamic extremist groups have us thinking of terrorism as if only "religiopolitical terrorists," one of Wilkinson's five categories, really matter. What's wrong with this point of view?

### For Research and Writing

At least five million Muslims live in the United States. Worldwide Islam is second only to Christianity in number of adherents and is growing faster than any other faith. Yet most Americans know little or nothing about the religion that began on the Arabian peninsula more than thirteen centuries ago. As a class, research the history and present condition of Islam. Share and discuss the information you find. Compose collaboratively, as a class, an article you might call "Ten Things to Know about Islam." Use Zunes's Alternet piece as a model for both format and audience, and consider posting it on an appropriate Web site of your own choosing.

### For Convincing

It's at least arguable that no knowledge of world affairs is more important than an understanding of the Arab and Muslim worlds. Write a brief op-ed piece arguing for a *mandatory* course in Arab-Muslim culture and politics for all undergraduates in American universities. Try to get it published in your local campus or city newspaper.

## Impact on the United States

We might have titled this section "Homeland Security," the new phrase that refers to the urgent business of protecting the United States against further terrorist attacks. We didn't because the impact of 9/11 extends well beyond additional security measures—indeed, well beyond anything federal, state, and local governments might do. We need only contemplate what 9/11 has done to the airline industry to realize that its impact extends to all of us. Everything has not changed since 9/11, but much has, and all of our lives have been touched in some way.

What we need right now most of all is *perspective,* a sense of the place of 9/11 in the total scheme of things. The relative calm of most Americans since the attack indicates that perspective has not been lost altogether, but we face difficult questions we cannot approach as we did before 9/11. For instance, if we didn't know before, we surely know now that airport security is inadequate. But what measures should we take? What's "adequate"—enough but not too much? It's very hard to say. Before 9/11, airport security was entrusted to private companies; now in large part it has been federalized. Will this improve the situation in the short and long terms? No one can say with assurance right now.

The following two articles raise many issues connected with homeland security. "A Clear and Present Danger," the cover story of the October 8, 2001, issue of *Time,* concentrates primarily on new powers granted to law enforcement to combat terrorism and the difficulties Tom Ridge faces in his new position as director of homeland security. The *Newsweek* piece focuses on the potential for countering terrorism with technology, with devices such as Backscatter X-ray and digital face recognition. Both pieces recognize that the measures being taken, even if they prove effective, raise serious problems, such as threats to privacy and other constitutional protections. Both also recognize practical limitations that make any talk of total safety unrealistic. Terrorists will exploit whatever vulnerabilities remain—and there will always be weak points. We have the resources to counter terrorism effectively, but getting all the agencies coordinated and cooperating with each other is a daunting task.

Homeland security gives us much to think about and many opportunities for research and writing. As we think the issues through, do research, and plan writing projects, let's remember that *balance* is the goal. High tech, for example, has a major role to play in countering terrorism. But it is not a cure-all, and even if it were, we can't—or shouldn't—use it in a way that violates fundamental civil liberties. As the Israeli lawyer cited in the *Time* article says, "You're talking about a balance between things that are inherently flawed." We must accept the flaws while striving always for balance, another word for the perspective we need on the threat posed by terrorism.

---

## A Clear and Present Danger
### Matthew Cooper et al.

The phone lines in the office of Sheriff Bruce Bryant, of York County, S.C., started burning up around 8 p.m. on the night of Saturday, Sept. 15. Helicopters had been seen heading up the Catawba River toward a nuclear power station. Soon two F-16 fighter jets arrived on the scene, and Bryant heard a "tremendous, thunderous noise." A little later, choppers were spotted near the Oconee nuclear plant near Clemson, 90 miles away. Then, shortly after midnight, several more were reported flying over the Savannah River Site, a Department of Energy facility that occupies more than 360 sq. mi. along the border of South Carolina and Georgia. Nuclear waste is disposed of there, and weapons are restocked with tritium. Authorities closed down a highway that runs through the base, until the FBI gave the all clear. But Bryant and his frightened neighbors still don't know what happened that night. Utility-industry analysts say Catawba was subject to a security test, but the feds won't confirm anything. "It's like it never happened," says John Paolucci of the South Carolina Emergency Preparedness Service. "But it did."

If people in York County are nervous, they've got a huge support group. America has become a jittery nation since the attacks on the World Trade Center and the Pentagon, and with good reason. Attorney General John Ashcroft appeared before the Senate Judiciary Committee and declared that "terrorism is a clear and present danger to Americans today." Information available to the FBI, Ashcroft continued, "indicates a potential for additional terrorist incidents." He didn't bother to add what everyone knew: the next incidents could be even more ghastly than those of Sept. 11. A terrorist group prepared to murder more than 6,000 civilians would feel no compunction about killing 60,000 — or 600,000 — if it could deploy the necessary weapons of mass destruction. And so the fear of such an attack — and the government's hasty efforts to contain the threat — became the nation's No. 1 item of business.

From coast to coast, Americans experienced things for which they were quite unprepared. State troopers patrolled airports. "It was like traveling through a combat zone," said Marcia Brier, from Needham, Mass., of a trip from Boston's Logan Airport. At Reagan National Airport in Washington, the gleaming, airy terminal that opened in 1997 remained closed. A tanker carrying 33 million gallons of liquefied natural gas was diverted from highly populated Boston Harbor to Louisiana, just as a precaution. In Idaho and Maryland, there were panicky rumors of missing crop dusters. The Los Angeles subway was shut down for the first time in its history, as passengers complained of dizziness and itchy eyes. No chemical agents were found.

All the while, law-enforcement officers were continuing the greatest dragnet the world had ever seen. FBI sources downplayed the possibility of a second wave of attacks. But less than three weeks after the catastrophe, Ashcroft said that a total of 480 people had already been arrested or detained. Hundreds more had been picked up around the globe, with authorities paying particular attention to possible terrorist support networks in Germany and Britain. Those scooped up included a few who appeared to have links to the hijackers, and some who just had the wrong sort of look at the wrong sort of time. In DeFuniak Springs, a small town in the Florida Panhandle, a local librarian remembered that the hijackers had used library computers to book flight reservations, saw a man from the Middle East seated at a keyboard and called the police. (The man was guilty of nothing.) Those driving into Manhattan were stuck in lines of the sort usually seen only in Bangkok or Mexico City, as authorities made carpools compulsory and searched every van and truck, especially those licensed to carry hazardous materials. "This is how it is because this is how it has to be," said a law-enforcement official, according to the *New York Post.* "This is a police state now."

It's not. But there was a pervasive sense that things weren't as they had been. How could they be, when the President gave the Pentagon the authority to shoot down any hijacked civilian airliner? Pundits quickly learned to trot out the phrase "homeland security," with its faintly Orwellian overtones. And, as often happens in national emergencies, the desire of law enforcement for a free hand bumped into the rights and protections set down by men in wigs in the late 18th century.

In one sense, that's surprising, because in recent years the police have pretty much got what they asked for. As recently as 1998, the year that terrorists bombed two American embassies in Africa, President Clinton granted law-enforcement officials a wish list of extra investigative powers. "Any one of these extremely valuable tools," said a senior FBI official at the time, "could be the keystone" to a successful operation against terrorists. For the bureau, it seems, no kit ever has enough tools. Three years later, it is back for more. In the Anti-Terrorism Act of 2001, Ashcroft seeks to give cops and the FBI yet more powers, including a provision that would allow the Justice Department to detain immigrants suspected of terrorism indefinitely, in contrast to the current time limit of 48 hours. A coalition of civil libertarians and conservatives suspicious of big government has slowed the bill's progress through Congress. Senate Judiciary Committee chairman Patrick Leahy told *Time* that "the biggest danger is that [terrorists] unravel the constitutional protections we've spent 200 years as a democracy to build." By last Thursday, however, Leahy was on the phone to Ashcroft, suggesting that staff members work through the weekend to iron out the remaining points of disagreement.

If fear can erode constitutional protections, it can also eat the soul. Few objects speak to numbing, nameless dread so much as the gas mask, which not long ago seemed an artifact of World War I battlefields. Now there is a run on them. The Army Surplus Warehouse in Idaho Falls sold 180 masks through its website in two hours. A man in New York placed an order for 500 masks for his employees; they work in an office building near ground zero. A book on germ warfare became an unexpected best seller.

Across the country, people changed their behavior—Come to think of it, why shouldn't my teenage girl have a cell phone?—and redefined their lives. *New York Times* columnist Maureen Dowd reported that her chums were debating the finer points of gas masks and antibiotics. St. Petersburg and Pinellas County, Fla., are among the few localities in the country that, under the auspices of the military, have held practice drills to respond to chemical and biological disasters. Says Lieutenant Scott Stiener of the

Pinellas County sheriff's office: "We're going to have to be a lot more suspicious." Stiener wonders if we'll be able to trust the guy who comes to spray our house or office for bugs; he may have something dangerous in his can. Life has already changed for Bryan McCraw, police chief of the small town of Guin, Ala. McCraw ticketed a Saudi driver for running a red light on Labor Day but didn't search the car. On Sept. 11, cops stopped the same man for driving with a flat tire near Washington's Dulles Airport and found flight manuals in the vehicle. "I'm looking for drugs. I'm not looking for flight manuals," said McCraw. "Somebody is going to have to train us on what to do."

Somebody is going to have to train us all. As Governor Tom Ridge of Pennsylvania prepares to step into his new job as Director of Homeland Security, Americans want to know how real these threats are. You don't buy gas masks unless you expect an unspeakable horror. So people are asking: What are the chances that the clear and present danger will manifest as attacks using biological agents like anthrax or smallpox, or chemical compounds like sarin? Will they be sprayed from a crop duster or dumped in the water supply? What is the likelihood that the next attack would be marked not by smoke drifting from lower Manhattan to Brooklyn but by a mushroom cloud?

Officials cannot afford to be sanguine, but when it comes to biological,   10
chemical or nuclear weapons, they try to be realistic. There have been reports that Osama bin Laden's al-Qaeda network has tried to buy fissile material and has experimented with chemical agents. But "it's very difficult for terrorists to manufacture, transport and dispense these types of weapons," says a counterterrorism official. (The spray nozzles on your garden-variety crop duster, for example, are not ideal for the dispersal of deadly germs.) In the Pentagon, officials take the same view: weapons of mass destruction, they think, are beyond the range of "nonstate" actors. Terrorists have so far not been able to acquire an assembled nuclear weapon. Nor do they have the expertise to build and deliver one.

But that's no reason not to make their job as difficult as we possibly can. In 1991, Congress passed a wide-ranging law—named for its principal sponsors, Senators Sam Nunn and Richard Lugar—to reduce the threat of nuclear proliferation. Nunn-Lugar and other programs spend $872 million a year to safeguard the former Soviet Union's weapons of mass destruction. Washington has had some spectacular successes in this field; in 1994, more than 1,300 lbs. of fissile material were airlifted from Kazakhstan to the U.S. But critics contend that Nunn-Lugar is underfunded. The Bush Administration has proposed cutting its budget $100 million this year, a sum that took $20 million out of a program designed to find jobs for unemployed Russian nuclear scientists. Now we must hope they haven't gone to work for bin Laden.

But even if Nunn-Lugar were goldplated, it wouldn't obviate the great lesson of Sept. 11: you don't need so-called weapons of mass destruction to devastate a society. A few airplanes will do. "That's why it was so brilliant," says a Pentagon official. A senior aide to Vice President Dick Cheney falls back on football metaphors. The Administration remains worried about the need to defend against "the long bomb"—a chemical, biological or nuclear attack. But just as crucial, this aide argues, is to protect against "short yardage"—attacks on bridges, tunnels, power plants, chemical-storage facilities and refineries. "There are hundreds of these targets," says a Pentagon official, "and attacking them with conventional means—a truck full of explosives—is a heck of a lot easier than building an atom bomb or a chemical weapon."

That's why, among those paid to think about the ultimate horror, the phrase of the moment is not "weapons of mass destruction" but "weapons of mass effect." The planes that flew into the World Trade Center were just such weapons. They were "conventional," in a sense, but designed to cause great loss of life and spread chaos and despair. The hijackers didn't need sophisticated technology. Nor may their successors. The East Coast power grid, for example, has less than half a dozen key switching points. Six truck bombs, packed with nothing more sophisticated than the fertilizer that blew up the Alfred P. Murrah Federal Building in Oklahoma City six years ago, could disrupt the economy of half the nation.

That's precisely what the bad guys had in mind the last time the U.S. faced a serious threat to homeland security. In 1942, two German submarines landed teams of four people each at Amagansett, N.Y., and Ponte Vedra, Fla. The Germans were supposed to blow up hydroelectric plants [and] key railroad junctions and spread terror in New York by bombing railroad stations and Jewish-owned department stores. The operation was a fiasco; within two weeks, all eight men were caught (six were later executed), but the threat was, and is, real.

All of which helps explain the attention now being paid to hazardous-material licenses. From July 1999 to January 2000, authorities say, an examiner in the Pennsylvania Department of Transportation issued commercial driver's licenses to 20 men without requiring them to take mandatory tests. All but two of the licenses covered haz-mat transport. By the end of last week, all 20 men were in custody. The FBI said that they did not appear to have a connection to the Sept. 11 attacks. But that was scant comfort; they might have had their own scary plans. At the least, the scam exposed gaping holes in the haz-mat licensing process—there are 2.5 million of the licenses nationwide, and in some states they're a notorious source of kickbacks.

It was another reminder that guarding against weapons of mass destruction may miss the real threat. When 100 Florida law-enforcement officials, utility executives and emergency-response officials met in Tallahassee last week, it wasn't a nuclear or biological threat that was most on their mind. It was a conventional attack on the Port of Miami, on the Sunshine Skyway that spans Tampa Bay, or on that most American of symbols, Walt Disney World.

Tom Ridge has the square-jawed profile and can-do resume — blue-collar background, Harvard, staff sergeant in Vietnam — to reassure even the most jittery parent contemplating a family vacation in Orlando. Ridge will need all that and more. He has not yet assumed his new post, which does not require a Senate vote. Officials have "red tagged" his security clearance, hoping he can get the O.K. in two weeks, not the eight months that some Administration officials have been waiting. In a series of White House meetings this week, Ridge started to divide his responsibilities into three baskets. The first will concentrate on emergency response, building on the work of the existing Federal Emergency Management Agency. A second will look at "hardening" targets now so soft that they may tempt terrorists. In the third basket, working with Bush's National Security Council (of which Ridge will be a member), the new office will seek to coordinate intelligence and law-enforcement activities against terrorism.

Senior Administration officials have promised that Ridge will be given budget "pass-back" authority, which means that he will be able to direct the agencies under his purview, like the border patrol, to reorder their spending priorities. His staff is expected to be about 100 strong, many detailed from other agencies. Ridge has already picked Mark Holman, his oldest and most trusted political associate, to run the operation as chief of staff, and is eyeing Admiral Steve Abbott, who has been the military voice on the home-land-security staff currently housed in the Vice President's office. White House officials say Ridge will have as much access to the President as Condoleezza Rice, the National Security Adviser. In the currency of Washington, that's saying a lot, for nobody has more. Ridge, White House officials say, will probably soon have an office in the West Wing.

It had better be a big one, with copious bookshelves and an acre of bare wall. The shelves can hold the reports, of which there have been depressingly many, on the nation's lack of preparedness for homeland security. (The three most recent ones total more than 500 dire pages. And the new General Accounting Office report says that federal bioterrorism defense is so chaotic the agencies can't even agree on which threats to worry about.) The wall space is needed for Ridge's organizational chart, for he will have to coordinate the activities of more than 40 federal agencies — and an unknown but much larger number in state and local governments. On Capitol Hill, if Ridge is ever foolish enough to stray into the building where he served 12 years as a member of the House, 26 full committees of Congress and 17 subcommittees deal with homeland-security matters.

Coordinate is the key word here. Against the recommendations of the recent commission on national security chaired by former Senators Gary Hart and Warren Rudman, Ridge will not be in charge of a superagency into which have been folded operational arms of the Federal Government like FEMA. That may be a mistake. If there is one thing more depressing than the number of reports on homeland security, it is the unanimity of their conclusions. At present, coordination simply doesn't happen; homeland defense is a patchwork quilt made by an inept seamstress. Some stories

20

would be funny if they weren't being told against a backdrop of tragedy. There was the recent joint exercise of the FBI and the Bureau of Alcohol, Tobacco and Firearms, during which agents argued for an hour over who was in charge, while actors playing the dead and dying got hypothermia. There is the sad tale of the Center for Defense Preparedness run by the Department of Justice, which "trains trainers" to respond to toxic emergencies — and whose current budget allows it to operate at 25% of capacity. There is the rivalry — or is it hatred? — between the Immigration and Naturalization Service and the Customs Service, neither of which seems ever to have willingly shared a piece of information with the other.

For old hands, though, one rivalry dwarfs all the others. A senior adviser to President George H. W. Bush says that the historic tension between G-men and spooks at times seem insurmountable. "One of the things we need," says Senator Harry Reid, "is someone with the authority to force the CIA and the FBI to cooperate."

The incompatibilities run deep. The bureau's job is to find evidence that will stand up in a criminal court, while the agency just wants intelligence. But some observers think the old enmities have abated. The deputy director of each agency's counterterrorism division comes from the other one, and joint FBI-CIA operations have had a few notable successes. The real problem, says Representative Saxby Chambliss, a Republican who chairs the House Subcommittee on International Terrorism and Homeland Security, is that the heroes of Langley and the Hoover building won't share information with agencies like the INS and the Federal Aviation Administration — both vital to Ridge's mission. "The dialogue between federal agencies," says Chambliss, "is not at the level that it should be."

And the dialogue between federal and state officials? Ask governors that question, then duck. Governor Dirk Kempthorne of Idaho says that the adjutant-general of his state National Guard is not allowed to share intelligence with him. Governor Frank Keating of Oklahoma, a former FBI agent who took part this summer in a disastrous war game of a smallpox attack, says he was "stunned" at the level of ignorance displayed by the feds about what goes on at a state and local level. And Philadelphia police chief John Timoney says, "The feds actually think that the locals, you can't trust them, they're corrupt, they'll sell information." When working with federal agencies as a senior officer in New York, he says, "there was always a sense that you were not fully briefed on everything that was going on." This isn't just whining. If homeland security has shock troops, they work for state and city governments. "The best response is local," says Keating. "You have to have doctors and nurses and emergency services and police and National Guard who are trained to respond." At present, there are huge holes in that training. Keating freely admits that "doctors and nurses in my state know nothing about anthrax and smallpox."

Can Ridge bring order to this chaos and make an anxious nation believe its government can actually stop — or at least manage — another disaster? The omens aren't good. Without operational authority, successive drug czars have found it extraordinarily difficult to get the relevant agencies to work together. Ridge has an extra problem. If counterterrorism is one of his chief missions, he will have to work closely with the armed forces. Yet not only is the military—properly—barred from performing law-enforcement duties, it also has spent little time figuring out how to discharge any new functions. "I never thought we'd see fighters over our cities defending against a threat that came from inside," Air Force General Richard Myers, the new Chairman of the Joint Chiefs of Staff, has said. "This whole issue of homeland defense needs a lot more thought."

It probably does, not least by those members of the public who, in    25
an understandable reaction to Sept. 11, are loading up on antibiotics and salves. That mood may not last. In the 1950s and '60s, the Federal Civil Defense Administration—remember duck and cover?—distributed 400 million pieces of literature to Americans. But civil defense never really caught on. By 1963, only 1 person in 50 had access to even a rudimentary shelter.

The great difference, of course, is visible in lower Manhattan; Moscow never did drop the Big One. But one day, after they've scoured the Web for a gas mask, and told one another that they're quite comfortable with the idea that airports need to look like armed camps, Americans might heed Daniel Seidemann's wise words. Seidemann is an Israeli lawyer, and hence a man for whom homeland security is an existential matter. "Society needs a balance between Athens and Sparta," he says. "If you're Athens, there's no security. If you're Sparta, you have security, but nobody wants to live there. You're talking about a balance between things that are inherently flawed." As America defends against terror, may it find a balance it can live with.

—Reported by Matthew Cooper, John F. Dickerson, Viveca Novak, Mark Thompson, Karen Tumulty and Douglas Waller/Washington, Alison Jones/Durham and Timothy Roche/Atlanta.

---

## Technology: A High-Tech Home Front
### Steven Levy

At the airports, the much-maligned minimum-wage screeners confiscated nail clippers and corkscrews while cops and soldiers patrolled the corridors. Lines formed at the borders, traffic slowed on the highways, and bridges and tunnel approaches were jammed as agents searched trucks for possible explosives. Even sporting events were transformed. At the Boston College-Naval Academy football game the 12 metal detectors acted as bottlenecks: despite requests to appear two hours before game time, only a third of the 30,064 fans were seated by kickoff. And a tradition of smuggling in noisemakers ended at Mississippi State University when Davis Wade Stadium was declared a strict no-cowbell zone.

Thus began the epic attempt to establish a homeland defense.

Mostly people reacted to delays and inconveniences with patience, or even gratitude. But how long before the grumbling begins — or people stay home to avoid the hassles? That is only one of the many challenges for new homeland security czar Tom Ridge.

Inevitably, in its efforts to stave off terror, America will turn to a familiar friend, one it has long regarded as a panacea: technology. A host of sophisticated devices and software programs are being enlisted in the nation's defense. Some of them will be quite visible, and presumably reassuring to a jittery population. Others will grind away in stealth, at least until someone is pulled into an interrogation room on the basis of an obscure database link. Though adopting many of these schemes will be costly — in cash and, in some cases, privacy — they offer the irresistible promise of higher security without oppressive inconvenience.

The most pressing problem is aviation, as President George W. Bush implicitly acknowledged when he introduced new security measures last Thursday while standing on the tarmac at Chicago's O'Hare airport. They centered on government supervision of checkers and a range of other schemes, including armed marshals on planes and toughened cockpit doors. But new, more sensitive gizmos can also speed and improve the security process. In the foreseeable future, carry-on baggage will be checked with dedicated bomb-detection devices or 3-D scanners. Passengers may also be virtually frisked with the controversial Backscatter X-ray, which is "almost like Superman's X-ray vision, where you can look through the person's clothes and see what they're carrying," says Harry Martz, of the Lawrence Livermore Laboratory. Airports have been reluctant to adopt the system because of a sensitive issue: as Martz puts it, "it is anatomically correct, and pretty revealing." But after the tragedy, Ralph Sheridan, CEO of the company that makes the Backscatter-based BodySearch machine, found himself speaking to a newly receptive government audience in Washington.

New machines will also be sniffing our highways and borders. Ancore, a Santa Clara, Calif., company, uses a technology called Pulsed Fast Neutron Analysis to enable handlers to inspect marine cargo containers, trucks, freight trains and autos. Vehicles pass through the inspection device as if they were going through a carwash and are scanned for all known commercial and military explosives. Cost? Up to $1.5 million a pop.

On streets and throughout indoor public spaces, expect even more ubiquitous security cameras. Techno-optimists believe they can merge these with face-recognition technology that was used in the 2001 Super Bowl to scan fans for the kissers of known disrupters — and was also used by Tampa, Fla., police to see whether they could cut the crime rate in the city's entertainment district by spotting known criminals among pedestrians. "It scans 10 to 15 faces a second and matches them against a [database of] a million people in less than a second," boasts Dr. Joseph Atick of his Visionics system, which he calls "human ID at a distance." But some scientists think the technology is overhyped. "It's easily fooled," says Steven Block, a Stanford professor who consults with the Defense Department. "Faces change all the time."

More reliable biometric indications include retina scans, DNA and good old fingerprints. These markers will be essential in preventing identity fraud by terrorists. They will commonly be implemented on smart cards, plastic badges with chips and hard-to-forge information that authenticates the holder. Before the attack, the smart-card movement "was already on fast-forward," says Paul Beverly, VP of smart cards at SchlumbergerSema. Now smart-card systems are in demand to make sure airline employees and sky-scraper workers are who they say they are.

The ultimate smart card would be a mandatory national ID, a long-debated concept that popped back into the news last week when Oracle CEO Larry Ellison offered to provide free software for such a system. What would be on it? At a minimum, a photo of the bearer (digitally "signed" so it could not be replaced) and a biometric identifier like a fingerprint. An onboard chip would carry information about the cardholder, a concept that disturbs privacy advocates, who fear that the cards would feed massive databases that could be used to track any transaction that involved a swipe of the card.

In any case, computer databases are destined to become a prime component of homeland defense. Some longtime advocates of pooling information residing in various government computers — another concept that gives *agita* to privacy minders — see the hijackings as the trigger for such action. "Ideally we can combine the information of the INS, CIA, FBI and other agencies and get answers in real time," says Mark Hurd, president of NCR.

Once databases merge, the really interesting software kicks in: "data-mining" programs that can dig up needles in gargantuan data haystacks. The same technology now used commercially to spot credit-card fraud has already been converted to locate money launderers and, one hopes, will unearth the digital tracks of terrorists. If Attorney General John Ashcroft gets his way and is permitted to perform warrantless scans of e-mail headers and other evidence of people's Internet activities, such information may be mined as well. Companies like HNC—which makes software that "learns" how to spot money launderers and bioterror microbes—have shifted into overdrive since the terrorist attack. HNC's programs are an example of "neural nets," an emergent learning technique that operates like an organic brain; through the use of feedback, the software makes connections that enable it to discover otherwise imperceptible patterns. "We hope we will be able to save lives with this," says HNC exec Joseph Sirosh.

Finally, some in the tech community are suggesting that the best homeland defense of all would involve decentralizing population centers in order to deny terrorists "soft targets" where massive casualties can come from a single strike. Though digital teleconferencing rose dramatically after the Twin Towers fell, the technology still can't provide the benefits of physical proximity. But some believe that eventually we'll have the tools to replace

10

not only long trips but the experience of working together in a central location. "Before this event we were already moving toward full emergent virtual reality," says author and computer scientist Ray Kurzweil. "Images will be sent directly to our glasses or contact lenses, straight to our retinas. We'll be online all the time." Kurzweil believes that as this technology gets even better, mapping fake reality directly onto our neurons so our brains can't tell the difference, we'll be able to get all the benefits of living in dense population centers from our nests in exburbs or beyond. "The need for cities will dissipate," he says.

Even that will not assure total safety. If we've learned anything from the horrible events of Sept. 11, it's that we are facing an enemy that compensates for its relative lack of power by identifying our vulnerabilities—and adjusting for them. Well-prepared evildoers will take the measure of our most sophisticated technologies and try to route their attacks around them. "Yes, we've sent a man to the moon," says Edward Tenner, author of *Why Things Bite Back: Technology and the Revenge of Unintended Consequences.* "But the moon did not take evasive action."

---

*For Discussion*

1. The opening narrative in the article from *Time* raises a serious issue—the secrecy surrounding antiterrorist activity. How much do you want to know? What information should the government release to the public? For example, several times since 9/11 we've been told that another terrorist attack could occur in this or that location. Is this useful information for the general public to have?

2. Has your behavior changed since 9/11? If so, in what ways? How do you justify the changes? If many or most people altered their behavior in similar ways, what effect, good and bad, would it have on the country?

3. Attorney General Ashcroft's talk of "a clear and present danger" *after* 9/11 raises at least two questions. Given the bombing of the Federal Building in Oklahoma City in 1995 and other attacks, why wasn't the threat a higher priority *before* 9/11? After 9/11, is the threat actually greater or less?

4. One of the many ironies of 9/11 is that the terrorists used the very technology we are so proud of against us: The same equipment that can take us from New York to Seattle in a few hours can be turned into the conventional equivalent of a guided missile. Now, as the *Newsweek* piece indicates, many people think part of the cure for terrorism is still more technology. How might this technology be manipulated by terrorists? How much faith in technological solutions do you think is warranted?

5. The so-called smart card, or national ID, has long been on the table. Do you favor such a measure? Why or why not?

*For Research and Persuasion*

Conduct research into the detaining of immigrants and foreign nationals since 9/11. Note that authorities now can hold such people more or less indefinitely without charging them with a crime or initiating deportation procedures, a clear violation of civil rights. You'll find in your research that many people were being held without recourse for long periods of time *before* 9/11. Write an essay condemning this practice as a whole or in part. Address it to your congressional representative or senator.

*For Inquiry and Collaboration*

Make a list of high-tech devices mentioned in the *Newsweek* article and any others your class knows about. Find out all you can about each device—a good way would be to have small groups assigned to research each one. After careful pondering of the research results, each group should report its assessment, including how useful the device could be, what its limitations are, how it could be circumvented, and how much it invades the right to privacy or threatens other civil liberties. The class as a whole could then compose a more comprehensive view of the promise of high-tech counterterrorism. Which technologies do you think ought to have the highest priority? The next highest? And so on. Be sure to explain and justify your choices.

*For Negotiation*

It's perfectly understandable that Americans should be preoccupied with the terrorist threat and that our government should be taking action on the home front and abroad to reduce the threat. At the same time, if we look into statistical assessments of the likelihood of dying from or being seriously injured by a terrorist attack, we'll find that the threat is not nearly so great as the threat of dying from or being incapacitated by a heart attack or an auto accident, to mention only two more common and permanent threats. In devoting so much of our national resources to combating terrorism, we risk ignoring or reducing support for measures designed to reduce other threats to life and health. How would you negotiate these conflicting imperatives? How much money and other resources, for example, would you devote to counterterrorism as against measures to reduce drunk driving? Write an essay making a case for how much attention and resources terrorism ought to receive as balanced against other risks we face daily.

## Understanding Terrorism

Terrorism, especially in relation to the Middle East, is an enormous and extremely complicated topic. For your special attention, we have isolated writings on three dominant themes connected with this topic:

1. The Palestinian-Israeli conflict and the history of U.S. involvement in maintaining Israel while attempting to broker peace (Landers,

"The Roots of Conflict," with graphic, "Israel through the Years," published 10/28/01)
2. The aims of the fundamentalist Islamic terrorist groups, with special attention to bin Laden and al-Qaeda (Landers, "Bin Laden Allies Want Islamic Unity," published 10/21/01; includes graphic, "Havens for Terrorists, published 9/14/01)
3. The training camps for terrorists run by al-Qaeda and affiliated groups (Jones, "Cradle of a Holy War," published 10/21/01)

As we write this introduction, American military forces and the Northern Alliance in Afghanistan appear on the verge of toppling the Taliban and perhaps killing or capturing bin Laden and his top lieutenants. As the previously mentioned articles both say and imply, even if the Taliban and the present al-Qaeda leadership are eliminated, the story won't be over. Islamic unrest is too deep-seated and has too many long-term sources. Whatever happens in Afghanistan will only be an episode in a long history, just as bin Laden, for all his money and organizational talent, is only one of many leaders of the fundamentalist Islamic cause extending back to the founding of the Muslim Brotherhood in 1928.

Furthermore, if Jerrold M. Post's analysis of "terrorist psycho-logic" is sound, we have still more reason to doubt that terrorism will lose its appeal. This section's fourth and last article, taken from *The Origins of Terrorism*, a book published by Cambridge University Press in 1990, helps us understand terrorism in a way that goes well beyond contemporary events to motives rooted in human psychology and group dynamics.

You'll note that the first three articles are examples of what is called *investigative journalism*, efforts to explain what's behind the news rather than just reporting it. They all come from the *Dallas Morning News*, our local paper. Look into other major dailies for similar articles written around the same time (September through November, 2001). Often they are rich in basic information—not nearly as rich, of course, as scholarly books, but more accessible and timely. Be alert for more such pieces as the so-called war on terrorism unfolds. In this way, your understanding can grow as events transform our current perspectives and concerns.

---

# The Roots of Conflict
## Jim Landers

Every Passover, in every practicing Jewish household, a toast is raised: "Next year in Jerusalem." The ritual has carried national aspirations since Rome expelled the Jews from Palestine in the years after 70 A.D.

For most of the centuries since then, Palestine was a colony of Islamic empires. Its people were largely Arabic-speaking Muslims and Christians who also had national aspirations.

The creation of Israel in 1948 left one people elated, and another in despair.

"Simply put, the problem in Palestine is that Israel is and Palestine is no longer," said Khalil Jahshan, a Palestinian-American who is vice president of the Arab-American Anti-Discrimination Committee.

American presidents have long searched for a settlement that satisfies the national aspirations of both Israelis and Palestinians.                            5

It's been a thankless task, as President Bush has found as he tries to maintain a coalition in the fight against terrorism.

Hundreds of Americans have died because of U.S. involvement in the Arab-Israeli conflict. Israeli warplanes repeatedly strafed the U.S. Navy spy ship *Liberty* in 1967. Several U.S. diplomats were assassinated by the Palestine Liberation Organization in the 1970s. Car bombings by Islamic extremists killed hundreds of Marines and U.S. embassy employees in Lebanon in the wake of Israel's invasion of that country.

Arab oil producers pushed the United States into its most severe economic slump since the Great Depression with their oil embargo during the 1973 Arab-Israeli war.

This month, Prime Minister Ariel Sharon has taxed the patience of Mr. Bush by invading cities ceded to the Palestinians. When Mr. Bush said a Middle East settlement should include creation of a Palestinian state, Mr. Sharon declared Israel would not be victimized by U.S. appeasement.

Arabs and Muslims, even those who reject terrorism, resent the United          10
States for not intervening when Palestinians are shot for throwing stones and when Palestinian homes are dynamited.

"It is a sense of helplessness that causes people to hate, a sense of impotence, like sheep being led to the slaughter," said Mr. Jahshan. "The U.S. protects Israel when it does things that need to be condemned."

Osama bin Laden has vowed no American will sleep in peace until peace comes to Palestine.

Yet no one but the United States can bring the two sides to a political settlement, said Henry Siegman, director of the U.S.-Middle East project of the Council on Foreign Relations and former executive director of the American Jewish Congress.

"On its face, the United States is mediating a conflict between two parties who, at this point, are existential enemies. Neither recognizes the national claims of the other," he said.

"The U.S. comes in with a very clear commitment to Israel. We are stra-          15
tegic allies. We don't pretend to be even-handed. Oddly enough, it is precisely because we have this relationship that we are the most logical mediator. Only a good friend has the leverage to persuade Israel to make the necessary compromise."

Mr. Jahshan agreed.

"Left to their own devices, I think the Palestinians and the Israelis will never find peace," he said. "They will need nudging. This is a high-maintenance conflict."

The United States came late to this role.

The modern idea of a Jewish homeland began in Europe, where Jews had never known a time without persecution. Anti-semitism was so embedded that even the emergence of democracy offered little hope that Jews would be welcomed into society as equals.

With London and Constantinople on opposite sides in World War I, British ministers considered the Ottoman Empire up for grabs. They were particularly interested in securing the land passage to India through Palestine and Mesopotamia (present-day Iraq).

Prime Minister David Lloyd George felt a Jewish homeland would make British control of Palestine easier to manage.

T. E. Lawrence, the adventurer-soldier known as Lawrence of Arabia, championed Arab independence within the Ottoman Empire. He nurtured the ambitions in Palestine of the Hashemite royal family.

The British endorsed the Zionist ideal in 1917 in a formal letter written by Mr. Lloyd George's foreign minister, Arthur Balfour.

When World War I ended and the Ottoman Empire collapsed, the carving-up of the Middle East that followed was aptly summarized by author David Fromkin in the title of his 1989 book, *A Peace to End All Peace.*

France took Syria and Lebanon. Britain took Palestine and Mesopotamia. Britain put Hashemite princes on the thrones of Iraq and Transjordan (a state fashioned out of the eastern boundaries of Palestine known today as the Hashemite Kingdom of Jordan).

The hostility of the Palestinian Arabs and their sympathizers in the British army limited Zionist settlement, and in the 1930s Britain repudiated the Balfour Declaration.

When Adolf Hitler launched World War II, European Jewry was trapped by British resistance to Zionism, and by the hostility of Americans and others who opposed Jewish immigration. More than 6 million Jews perished in the Nazi Holocaust, and Zionism gained force as a moral imperative.

The United Nations approved a partition of Palestine between Zionists and Arab nationalists. Israel declared itself an independent state in 1948 as war broke out with its Arab neighbors.

More than 700,000 Palestinian Arabs became refugees.

In 1956, Israel, Britain and France seized the Suez Canal and the Sinai Peninsula from Egyptian President Gamal Abdel Nasser. President Dwight Eisenhower forced them to return both properties, and American popularity in the Arab world soared. But when the Soviets agreed to build Egypt's Aswan Dam across the Nile River, Cold War rivalry drove America and Israel closer together.

Mr. Nasser regarded Israel as a foreign presence in his vision of a united Arab nation. He urged annihilation, not coexistence. Military maneuvers by

Egypt and Syria led Israel to strike first on June 6, 1967. Syria lost the Golan Heights. Egypt lost the Gaza Strip and the Sinai.

Jordan's King Hussein joined the war and quickly lost East Jerusalem and the West Bank. With Jerusalem now united, Israel vowed it would never again be divided.

After the war, Palestinians under the leadership of Mr. Arafat formed radical political groups and terrorist cells to fight for the right to represent the Palestinian people.

Egyptian President Anwar Sadat led Egypt and Syria to war in 1973 and caught Israel by surprise. President Richard Nixon ordered an emergency arms airlift, the Soviets threatened to reinforce the Egyptian army, and the superpowers came closer to nuclear war than at any point since the Cuban missile crisis.

"It was at that point that the idea began to evolve that the security and 35 well-being of Israel was an American national interest," said Mr. Siegman. "It was the supply of U.S. arms on an urgent basis that made the difference in 1973."

The war also demonstrated the need for the United States to find a solution to the conflict.

Mr. Sadat seemed to lead the way when he flew to Israel in 1977. President Jimmy Carter built on that overture to bring Mr. Sadat and Israeli Prime Minister Menachem Begin to Camp David, Md., for an agreement that included Israel's first peace treaty with an Arab state.

The other Arab nations denounced Egypt, and Muslim extremists assassinated Mr. Sadat in 1981.

The PLO, after violently rejecting the Camp David accords, built an army in Lebanon that Israel destroyed in 1982 with an invasion led by Mr. Sharon.

U.S. intervention allowed the PLO leadership to retreat to Tunisia, but 40 Lebanese Christian militias operating with Israel massacred hundreds of Palestinians in Beirut refugee camps. After the Marines arrived to offer protection, a Muslim extremist drove a truck bomb into their barracks at the Beirut airport and killed 241 U.S. servicemen.

The PLO brought itself back into the picture in 1988 by accepting Israel's right to exist, a concession that led to its first open meetings with U.S. diplomats.

Iraq's invasion of Kuwait again made urgent the need for a settlement that would allow the United States to work with Arab allies in the region on broader strategic interests.

"President Bush said in 1991 that to succeed the United States would have to cater to the legitimate political rights of the Palestinians and the legitimate security interests of the Israelis," Mr. Jahshan said. "Both. That was a first for the United States. A sense of parity did not exist before that."

The Norwegians finally brought the Israelis and the PLO together to negotiate peace. The 1993 Oslo accords described a process for Israel to cede political and police control over the occupied territories to a Palestinian Authority in exchange for security guarantees.

The hardest issues—the status of Palestinian refugees, final boundaries, creation of a Palestinian state and the status of Jerusalem—were left to later negotiations. 45

Prime Minister Yitzak Rabin and Mr. Arafat shook hands at the White House. Jordan's King Hussein signed a peace treaty with Israel. Yet in 1995, a Jewish extremist assassinated Mr. Rabin.

Through the years, Jewish and Muslim extremists have threatened to transform a political conflict in the Middle East into a religious one. Jewish religious groups have pressed into the West Bank to build settlements aimed at fulfilling biblical prophecy. Hamas, the violent offspring of the Muslim Brotherhood of Palestine, has sent suicide bombers into Israel to kill for an Islamic state.

"Once God is brought into the formula, and particularly once He is brought into the formula as a real-estate agent, that limits, if not ends, the prospects for a peaceful settlement," said Mr. Jahshan.

The dangers of fundamentalism helped motivate President Bill Clinton when he brought Israeli Prime Minister Ehud Barak and Mr. Arafat to Camp David last summer. Mr. Arafat was losing support to Hamas and wanted to declare a Palestinian state.

Mr. Barak offered the Palestinians statehood on nearly all of the West 50 Bank and Gaza Strip while leaving in place many Israeli settlements. He offered to discuss shared responsibility for Jerusalem. Mr. Arafat did not take the deal.

Mr. Sharon, an opponent of Mr. Barak's concessions, defied Israeli convention (though not Israeli law) and went to Jerusalem's Temple Mount. Muslims believe this religious apex of Jerusalem is where the Prophet Muhammad ascended into Heaven. Palestinians considered Mr. Sharon's visit provocative.

In the ensuing uprising, more than 650 Palestinians and more than 175 Israelis have been killed.

Israelis and Palestinians seem divided over where to go next. Mr. Sharon has the support of more than 60 percent of Israelis. After Tourism Minister Rehavan Zeevi was assassinated this month, Israelis split down the middle on whether to resume negotiations with the Palestinians.

Mr. Arafat, meanwhile, has seen his popularity among Palestinians slump. Only 20 percent view him favorably, Mr. Jahshan said.

Mr. bin Laden is trying to fill the void with Islamic extremism by com- 55 bining his *jihad* against "crusaders and Jews" with the Palestinian cause.

"That's the great danger, and it's precisely for that reason that Arafat's decision to support the war on terrorism is so critical to us," said Mr. Siegman. "The danger of seeing this conflict in religious terms is a very real one. It's difficult enough as it is. But if it is seen in purely religious terms, it becomes absolutely unsolvable."

# ISRAEL THROUGH THE YEARS

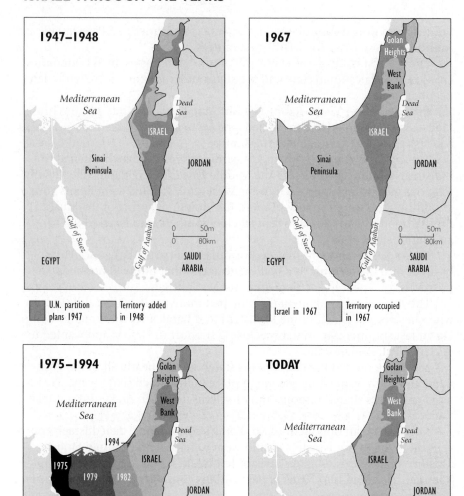

**1947–1948**

Mediterranean Sea

Dead Sea

ISRAEL

Sinai Peninsula

JORDAN

Gulf of Suez

Gulf of Aqabah

0   50m
0   80km

EGYPT

SAUDI ARABIA

U.N. partition plans 1947
Territory added in 1948

**1967**

Golan Heights

West Bank

Mediterranean Sea

Dead Sea

ISRAEL

Sinai Peninsula

JORDAN

Gulf of Suez

Gulf of Aqabah

0   50m
0   80km

EGYPT

SAUDI ARABIA

Israel in 1967
Territory occupied in 1967

**1975–1994**

Golan Heights

West Bank

Mediterranean Sea

1994

Dead Sea

1975

1979   1982

ISRAEL

JORDAN

Gulf of Suez

Gulf of Aqabah

0   50m
0   80km

EGYPT

SAUDI ARABIA

Israeli occupied
Years of withdrawal

**TODAY**

Golan Heights

West Bank

Mediterranean Sea

Dead Sea

ISRAEL

JORDAN

EGYPT

Gulf of Suez

Gulf of Aqabah

0   50m
0   80km

SAUDI ARABIA

**1917**—Britain issues the Balfour Declaration, expressing its support for a Jewish homeland in Palestine.

**1920**—The League of Nations grants Britain a mandate to govern Palestine.

**1947**—The United Nations divides Palestine into a Jewish state and an Arab state.

**1948–1949**—David Ben-Gurion and other Jewish leaders proclaim the establishment of the state of Israel on May 14. Egypt, Syria, Lebanon, Iraq and Jordan attack Israel the next day. Israel wins the war, gaining about half the territory the U.N. had set aside for a new Arab state.

1967—Israel defeats Egypt, Jordan and Syria in the Six-Day War, gaining control of the Gaza Strip, Sinai Peninsula, West Bank and Golan Heights, as well as the rest—the eastern part—of Jerusalem.

1973—Egyptian president Anwar Sadat leads Egypt and Syria in another war against Israel. Arab gains are neutralized by U.S. support of Israel, and Arab oil producers put an embargo on sales to the United States.

1978—Israel and Egypt, with U.S. mediation, reach the Camp David Accords, which would end their dispute and restore the Sinai to its pre-1967 borders.

1981—Islamic extremists assassinate Sadat, largely because he made peace.

1982—Israel invades Lebanon in an attempt to crush the Palestine Liberation Organization.

U.S. intervention allows the PLO to retreat to Tunisia.

1988—The PLO recognizes Israel's right to exist, making the United States willing to negotiate.

1993—Israeli Prime Minister Yitzak Rabin leads Israel into negotiations with the PLO under the auspices of Norway, and then of the United States. He and PLO leader Yasser Arafat shake hands at the White House. The Palestinian Authority is created to provide limited rule over Gaza and growing portions of the West Bank.

1995—A Jewish extremist assassinates Rabin because of the Oslo accords.

2000—Mr. Arafat, Israeli prime minister Ehud Barak and President Bill Clinton fail in an attempt to negotiate a peace agreement.

Sources: *Dallas Morning News* research; World Book Encyclopedia; *New York Times*; Associated Press

---

# Bin Laden Allies Want Islamic Unity

## Jim Landers

Mustafa Kemal Attaturk, the founder of modern Turkey, abolished the caliphate of the Islamic world in 1924 in a deliberate turn toward Western law and politics.

Osama bin Laden is among the Muslim fundamentalists who say this was the biggest calamity of the modern era and the start of a continuing war on Islam.

The caliph—commander of the faithful—was the unifying figure of mosque and palace, the leader who could give spiritual as well as political direction to Muslims worldwide.

It has been the life mission of men such as Mr. bin Laden to bring that unity back, to drive off colonial and occupying powers, to restore *sharia*— divinely inspired Islamic law—and to maintain Islamic cultural identity.

Mr. bin Laden's ideas and organizing methods owe much to the Muslim Brotherhood, a disciplined political force begun in Egypt in 1928 to restore Islamic lands, law, and values.

His method—"death to all Americans"—is widely condemned by Islamic clerics and laity. The few who embrace it can wreak terrifying violence. U.S. officials say the suicide hijackers who killed more than 5,000 Americans on Sept. 11 were part of Mr. bin Laden's al-Qaeda network. Others with al-Qaeda or another fundamentalist terrorist group, or those simply goaded by fiery sermons have raged against "infidels and nonbelievers" from Southeast Asia to West Africa.

Nigerian and Sudanese Muslims war with Christians to assert religious and political dominance. Filipino Muslim terrorists decapitate hostages when their demands for Islamic self-rule go unanswered. Kashmiri militants trained in Afghanistan kill Hindus and tourists to liberate the Muslim majority from Indian rule.

Mr. bin Laden and other al-Qaeda leaders justify all of these groups with the argument that the restoration of the Islamic nation makes their actions righteous.

Terrorism is the choice of only a few. Thousands of others sympathize with Mr. bin Laden's message, if not his methods.

"I don't think theologically he has a leg to stand on," said Michael Hudson, director of contemporary Arab studies at Georgetown University. "But I must say he's very effective. He's going over the heads of the Islamic establishment to say, 'We have an enemy in our midst called the United States of America, invading our space, corrupting our values and killing our people, and we have to do a jihad against it.'    10

"What should be very worrying to the U.S. government is this message seems to be surprisingly widely accepted," Dr. Hudson said.

So far, the anti-American rioting in response to attacks on Mr. bin Laden's supporters in Afghanistan has attracted no more than a few thousand people in Pakistan, Indonesia, Nigeria, Egypt, and the Palestinian Gaza Strip.

This has to be disappointing to al-Qaeda, some analysts say. The dream of restoring the caliphate might have moved from Afghanistan to Pakistan had the U.S. bombing campaign led to an uprising.

Mr. bin Laden's appeal for war against America is not working, said Mark Juergensmeyer, an expert on religious terrorism at the University of California at Santa Barbara.

"The Muslim world is not taking up the cause, so I think it's a big disaster from his point of view," he said. "I think it's a desperate situation for him. My sense is it could be the end of bin Laden."    15

It is early in the war on terrorism, however. Even if hundreds of millions of Muslims reject Mr. bin Laden, his message resonates with thousands of others filled with rage and despair.

### Americans as Targets

Religious radicals have made Americans their targets since at least 1979, when scores of U.S. diplomats and embassy workers were held hostage for more than a year by Iranian revolutionaries.

Hundreds of American soldiers and diplomats died at the hands of Islamic extremists in the 1980s. Those suicide assaults came from Shiite Muslims inspired by Iran's revolutionary guard who formed Hezbollah, or Party of God.

The 1979 Iranian revolution restored a Shiite vision of religion and politics united in the Ayatollah Ruhollah Khomeini. Shiites split from the dominant Sunni branch of Islam more than 1,300 years ago over their belief in hereditary rule through the family of the Prophet Muhammad. Shiite mullahs have more titles and authority than Sunni imams.

Iran's revolutionaries hated America out of a belief that it was coloniz-   20
ing the Islamic world. U.S. support for Israel made America synonymous with the Jewish state. The United States was accused of creating puppet regimes in Iran, then in Iraq, Egypt, and Saudi Arabia, to protect its access to oil.

Dissenters against these regimes were intimidated into silence, imprisoned, or exiled. The popular media were encouraged to voice outrage against Israel and the United States but censored for any criticisms of the government at home.

The anger of being voiceless was often matched by the despair of poverty. Despite the fabled wealth of a few oil producers, the Middle East is poorer than all regions of the world except sub-Saharan Africa. Average annual incomes in Latin American ($1,880 per person) are almost three times as large as incomes in the Middle East ($640).

Politically mute and poor, much of the Muslim world is also young. Most are disappointed when opportunities for education, jobs, or advancement are scarce.

The Arab world has gone through a decade-long population explosion. Thirty-five percent of Egyptians are under 15, as are 40 percent of Saudis. More than half the Palestinians in the West Bank and Gaza Strip are younger than 15.

Islamic countries such as Indonesia and Malaysia have educated their   25
people to the point that more than 85 percent can read and write. But other Muslim countries have suffered in the provision of education. The literacy rate in Bangladesh is 39 percent. In Pakistan it is 41 percent, and it is less than 53 percent in Egypt.

Poverty, disappointment, and youth form a potent mix for revolt.
So it was a shock to some analysts that the suicide hijackers who slammed planes into the World Trade Center and the Pentagon had middle-class origins. Many were college graduates.

## Western Culture

"These are people trying to make sense of a complicated world out there," said Ahmet Karamustafa, a professor of Islamic history at Washington University in St. Louis. "They had a moment to pause and ponder and come up with an explanation, and, tragically, that tends to be an extremely dangerous and faulty scheme.

"No single Muslim should presume the power and authority to turn into almost divine judges of the human condition."

The middle-class, educated backgrounds of the hijackers are much like that of their ancestors in the Muslim Brotherhood, however, said Joseph Kechichian, a Los Angeles consultant and author of two books on Saudi Arabia.

Another aspect of this anti-Americanism is cultural. U.S. culture has 30 spread the allure of change around the world. Anthony Giddens, director of the London School of Economics, writes that "fundamentalism is beleaguered tradition." It seems an apt description of much of Islam's anti-Americanism.

"Muslims the world over are asking, can Islam have a rapprochement with the American-led modern world?" Dr. Hudson said. "It's a world of everything from McDonald's to blue jeans to the notion that religion has no place in the political sphere."

Islamic intellectuals connect globalization with Americanization — and colonization. Egypt's foreign minister and Iraq's deputy prime minister both complained about U.S. cultural hegemony at last year's millennium summit of the United Nations.

The Muslim Brotherhood's founder, Hasan al-Banna, was a devout Egyptian teacher. British journalist Edward Mortimer wrote that Mr. al-Banna began the Brotherhood in 1928 as a reaction against "political turmoil and disunity, increasing moral laxity, widespread enthusiasm for Western secular culture among the upper and middle classes, nominal independence made a mockery by continued British occupation and foreign domination of the economy."

Mahathir Mohamad, Malaysia's prime minister, is a longtime critic of what he sees as the arrogance of Western culture. That critique, however, may no longer be enough to assure his party's hold on power, which is now threatened by Islamists angered by his intolerance of dissident.

## Role of Women

As Dr. Giddens writes in *Runaway World*, nowhere is the clash of ideas more 35 explosive than in family relations and the role of women. Western values are a direct threat to the sexual apartheid practiced in Saudi Arabia and Afghanistan, and to a lesser extent in Iran.

"Equality of the sexes, and the sexual freedom of women, which are incompatible with the traditional family, are anathema to fundamentalist groups," Dr. Giddens wrote. "Opposition to them, indeed, is one of the defining features of religious fundamentalism across the world."

## Muslim Brotherhood

Secular Egyptian governments have fought radical Islamic militants since the Muslim Brotherhood was banned in 1949. Today the militants are with al-

Gama'a al-Islamiyya, or the Islamic Group; and Egyptian Islamic Jihad. Both owe much of their teachings and discipline to the Muslim Brotherhood.

Al-Gama'a and Islamic Jihad merged with Mr. bin Laden's al-Qaeda in the mid-1990s.

Al-Qaeda has cells spread through as many as 60 countries. The Muslim Brotherhood overlaps with al-Qaeda in many of those same countries.

Al-Qaeda "has structural parallels with the Muslim Brotherhood, but    40
what's new is they have been released from nationalism and have created for themselves a transnational type of force, thanks to direct nurturing by Saudi Arabia and Pakistan," said Dr. Karamustafa. "It is no longer dissidents against a particular nation state."

The Brotherhood started with an emphasis on rigorous scholarship, physical fitness, and an ascetic lifestyle honed in desert camps. Soon it was overtly political. Members were indoctrinated within a "family" or five-man cell.

After World War II, the Brotherhood spread widely in the Muslim world. Volunteers fought in Palestine in 1948 against the creation of Israel. Yasser Arafat and other founding members of the Palestine Liberation Organization were once members of the Muslim Brotherhood.

Persecution in Egypt sent many Muslim Brothers to Saudi Arabia and other countries of the Gulf in the 1960s, where some became teachers. The Brotherhood started Medina University, which was the wellspring of the 1979 attempted coup in Saudi Arabia by university students who seized the Grand Mosque in Mecca and proclaimed one of their members the Mahdi, or messiah.

The Muslim Brotherhood in Syria staged a war against the secular regime of President Hafez al-Assad from 1980 to 1982, but Mr. Assad crushed the revolt by destroying Hamas, a Syrian strong-hold of the Brotherhood, killing more than 10,000 people in the process.

The war against the Soviet Union brought thousands of Muslim Broth-    45
erhood volunteers from throughout the Islamic world together in Afghanistan, where the brotherhood's discipline and teachings were bonded with Mr. bin Laden's personal wealth and connections to other rich Saudis.

Muslim Brotherhood leaders in Pakistan and Sudan inspired and tutored Mr. bin Laden, and helped shape his philosophies.

**Bin Laden's Mentor**

Abdullah Azzam, a Palestinian professor of Islamic law, was Mr. bin Laden's mentor in Pakistan. He was fired from his teaching position at Amman University in Jordan in 1980 for criticizing the government. He went to Pakistan to organize a recruiting campaign for Muslim volunteers to fight the Soviet occupation of Afghanistan.

Dr. Azzam, who was killed in a Peshawar car bombing in 1989, also played a leading role in transforming the Muslim Brotherhood of

Palestinians into Hamas, which has conducted many suicide bombings against Israelis.

Mr. bin Laden offered to organize an army of Afghan war veterans to repel Iraq's 1990 invasion of Kuwait. But the Saudi royal family turned to the United States for help instead, and in the process made an enemy of Mr. bin Laden.

Mr. bin Laden went to Sudan at the invitation of Hasan al-Turabi, for-    50
mer dean of the law school at Khartoum University and another of the leading thinkers of the Muslim Brotherhood. Mr. al-Turabi is considered

(article continues on page 400)

## HAVENS FOR TERRORISTS

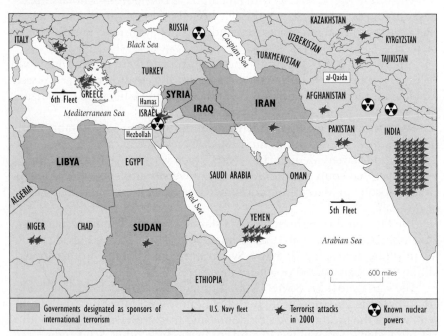

The Middle East has traditionally been a hot spot for terrorism. So much so that five nations—Libya, Sudan, Syria, Iraq and Iran—are on a government-recognized list of states that sponsor terrorism to attain political goals. The terror doesn't stop with the Middle East, as chemical, biological and nuclear weapons from the former Soviet Union must be factored into the equation.

A LOOK AT SOME OF THE GROUPS

**AL-QAIDA:** Established in 1990 by Osama bin Laden, it was originally formed in an attempt to drive the invading Russian army out of Afghanistan. The organization helped finance, support and train Sunni Islamic extremists for the Afghan resistance. Their professed goal is the creation of a Muslim state throughout the world and to work with Islamic extremist groups to overthrow regimes it deems overly influenced by Western values. Al-Qaida issued a statement under the banner of "The World

Islamic Front for Jihad Against The Jews and Crusaders" in February 1998, saying it was the duty of all Muslims to kill U.S. citizens, civilian or military, and their allies everywhere.

**Members:** Hundreds, possibly thousands. Based in Afghanistan.

**Support:** Mr. bin Laden, son of a billionaire Saudi family, is said to have inherited around $300 million that he uses to finance the group. They also maintain moneymaking businesses, collect donations from supporters and illicitly siphon funds from donations to Muslim charitable organizations.

**DEMOCRATIC FRONT FOR THE LIBERATION OF PALESTINE (DFLP):** Originally thought to have claimed responsibility for the World Trade Center explosion, the DFLP, however, has denied the claim. In the 1970s it carried out numerous small bombings and minor assaults in Israel and the occupied territories, concentrating on Israeli targets. It was recently involved in an assault on an Israeli military post that ended with three Israelis dead.

**Members:** Unknown

**Support:** Syria and Libya

**HAMAS:** It was formed in 1987 to establish an Islamic Palestinian state in place of Israel. It conducted many attacks — including large-scale suicide bombings — against Israeli civilian and military targets. It has claimed several attacks during the unrest in late 2000. Hamas' strength is concentrated in the Gaza Strip and a few areas of the West Bank.

**Members:** It has unknown number of hardcore members; tens of thousands of supporters and sympathizers.

**Support:** It receives funding from Iran, and private benefactors in Saudi Arabia and other moderate Arab states. Some fundraising and propaganda activity take place in Western Europe and North America.

**HEZBOLLAH:** It is strongly anti-West and anti-Israel and is closely allied with, and often directed by, Iran but may have conducted operations that were not approved by Tehran. It was known or suspected to have been involved in numerous anti-U.S. terrorist attacks, including the suicide truck bombing of the U.S. Embassy and U.S. Marine barracks in

Beirut in October 1983 and the U.S. Embassy annex in Beirut in September 1984.

**Members:** Thousands of supporters and hundreds of operatives.

**Support:** Receives substantial amounts of support from Iran and Syria.

**MUJAHEDEEN KHALQ (MEK):** Has developed into the largest and most active Iranian dissident group. During the 1970s the MEK staged terrorist attacks inside Iran and killed several U.S. military personnel and civilians in Tehran. It supported the takeover in 1979 of the U.S. Embassy in Tehran.

**Members:** Several thousand based in Iraq.

**Support:** Iraq, front groups

STATE-SPONSORED TERRORISM

The State Department maintains a list of countries that are known to sponsor or support international terrorists. The current list of seven countries (five are mapped):

**IRAN:** Iran has recently been the most active in supporting terrorists. It has supported Hezbollah, Hamas and the Palestinian Islamic Jihad in their attempts to undermine the peace process.

**IRAQ:** It has a reputation for providing support and haven to a number of Palestinian rejectionist groups and terrorists operating against Iran.

**SYRIA:** It also offers support and haven to terrorists opposed to the peace process.

**LIBYA:** While its ties to terrorism have subsided since the late 1980s, Libya has yet to comply with U.N. resolutions regarding the downing of Pan Am Flight 103 over Lockerbie, Scotland.

**SUDAN:** It continues to serve as meeting place, haven and training hub for Osama bin Laden's al-Qaida, Hezbollah, al-Jihad, al-Gama'at, PIJ, Hamas, and the Abu Nidal Organization.

**NORTH KOREA (not shown):** Harboring hijackers. It has links to Osama bin Laden.

**CUBA (not shown):** It harbors terrorists as well as sponsoring Latin American Insurgents.

Sources: Federation of American Scientists; U.S. Navy; U.S. Department of State

the intellectual author of the 1989 coup that brought an Islamic government to power in Khartoum. He is under house arrest for criticizing the
government of Gen. Omar al-Bashir, who has been trying to repair relations
with the United States.

Mr. bin Laden set about organizing al-Qaeda while living in Sudan,
U.S. officials say. There, he worked with veterans of the war in Afghanistan
to organize an effort to free Islam from the corrupting influences of the outside world.

Egyptian Islamic Jihad, al-Gama'a al-Islamiyya, and Kashmiri, Uzbek,
and Filipino radicals endorsed his call to *jihad.*

**Saudi Arabia Issues**

Mr. bin Laden's greatest complaint is close to home. One of the traditions
of Islamic fundamentalism is a supposed deathbed statement from the
Prophet Muhammad: "Do not let the unbelievers live in the land of
Arabia."

Tens of thousands of non-Muslims have worked and lived in Saudi Arabia since the oil price spike of 1973 set the kingdom on the road to riches.
Mr. bin Laden, however, is most disturbed by the presence of U.S. military
forces.

The Saudi government bars non-Muslims from the city limits of Mecca      55
and from entering the Prophet's Mosque in Medina, where Muhammad is
buried.

Mr. bin Laden wants them out of Saudi Arabia entirely. But that won't
be the end of it, said Dr. Karamustafa.

"I think his task clearly would be incomplete from his perspective if the
current Saudi Arabian regime were to stay in power," he said.

To Mr. bin Laden, much of the Saudi royal family is corrupt and apos-
tate. To restore the caliphate, such rulers must be overthrown.

---

# Cradle of a Holy War
### Gregg Jones

*"We are training to save our country, our nation, our religion."*

—MOHAMMED MIRZA

Murree, Pakistan—Yes, there was a time when he wasn't a model Muslim,
Rashid Hussain earnestly admits. He prayed infrequently. He drank alcohol. He gambled on cricket matches. He even lusted after women.

That all changed last year, after 40 days in Afghanistan at a military
training camp run by the ruling Taliban militia and Osama bin Laden's al-
Qaeda group, he says.

"Whether it's the Pakistani army, the U.S. Army, whatever army—
the training they do in six years, we do in 40 days," said Mr. Hussain, 24.
"God is with us."

The camp near Kabul where Mr. Hussain trained with thousands of
other Muslim "holy warriors" last year, and as many as 54 others like it
around Afghanistan, are primary targets of an ongoing U.S. military campaign against the Taliban and the al-Qaeda organization.

But Mr. Hussain and other graduates of the Afghanistan camps say the          5
U.S. campaign comes too late to contain the Islamic militancy that is exploding around the world in terrifying acts such as the Sept. 11 terrorist attacks
on the United States.

It is too late, they say, because thousands of angry young men from
across the Islamic world have already come to the camps to learn how to
kill their non-Muslim enemies with their bare hands, fire automatic weapons, build bombs, hijack airplanes, and survive the sort of high-tech military onslaught a U.S.-led coalition is directing at Afghanistan.

The men trained in these camps are part of a shadowy, international
Islamic army that has taken shape over the last decade—holy warriors
trained to attack and resist what they view as U.S. and Western oppression,
sent home to spread their militant ideology in places such as Pakistan,
Saudi Arabia, and the Philippines, and now poised to return to fight U.S.
and allied forces in a ground war in Afghanistan, camp graduates say.

The accounts of Mr. Hussain and another Pakistani militant who trained
in these camps in the early 1990s offer a look inside what one bin Laden
associate called the "jihad camp for the world," a place where at least three
of the men who participated in the attacks on the United States trained, investigators say.

Their stories provide insights into the ideological motivation—as
well as the furious sense of aggrievement—that is driving a growing number of young men across the Islamic world to embrace terrorism as the preferred weapon against the United States and other perceived oppressors of
Muslims.

The militants interviewed for this report have been identified with pseu-        10
donyms because they fear possible punishment for discussing the inner
workings of the camps.

The Taliban, al-Qaeda, and Mr. bin Laden, who is described by U.S.
officials as the prime suspect in the Sept. 11 attacks, lie at the heart of the
global effort to build a radical, pan-Islamic army, according to graduates
of the Afghanistan camps, foreign experts, and U.S. court testimony.

But while the root of this effort lies in Afghanistan, its branches reach
around the world in a vast network of Islamic religious schools, militant organizations, radical political parties, and even military training camps—all
tied to, funded, and loosely directed by al-Qaeda and the Taliban, Pakistani
militants and Western experts say.

In Pakistan, for example, the militant Islamic organizations "have different names, just to cover their operations," said Mohammed Mirza, 28,

who trained in the Afghanistan camps in 1992 and remains active in a leadership role in Harkat-ul-Jihad, also known as Harkat-ul-Mujahedeen, one of the dozens of Pakistani organizations under the al-Qaeda umbrella.

"If one particular organization is banned and branded as a terrorist organization, the others can operate," he said.

But when members of these organizations go for training in Afghanistan, he said, "they are one."                                                                    15

Mr. bin Laden's organization, al-Qaeda, plays a central role in the operations of the network, raising and dispensing funds, providing logistical support, giving ideological and operational guidance "to many different organizations, by different names, in different countries," Mr. Mirza said.

"Al-Qaeda funds us. Al-Qaeda is the base," he said, using the literal Arabic translation of the name. "There are many people. They are masters of their fields. They have been given different duties, and they are doing them. Al-Qaeda is providing them financial aid and things like that, whatever is needed."

### Far-Reaching Influence

U.S. officials say that in addition to the Sept. 11 attacks, al-Qaeda is responsible for the 1998 attacks on U.S. embassies in Kenya and Tanzania that killed 224 people and the attack on the USS Cole in Yemen last year in which 17 people died.

Russia has given the U.N. Security Council a list of 55 facilities used by Mr. bin Laden and al-Qaeda. U.S. court testimony this year by two graduates of the camps detailed the broad range of military and terrorist training offered by the facilities, ranging from small-arms instruction to courses in how to destroy a country's infrastructure.

Mohamed Atta and at least two other al-Qaeda operatives involved in       20
the Sept. 11 attacks are believed to have undergone training at one of the specialty camps, U.S. authorities allege.

The testimony of Jamal Ahmed al-Fadl, a former bin Laden lieutenant, supports Mr. Mirza's description of al-Qaeda and its network of training camps.

Mr. al-Fadl's testimony in a New York City trial resulted in the May conviction of four bin Laden followers for their role in a plot to kill Americans worldwide, including the embassy bombings. The four, including Arlington [Texas] resident Wadih el Hage, were sentenced Thursday to life in prison without parole.

As described by Mr. Mirza and Mr. Hussain, interviewed separately for more than eight hours, the network directed by al-Qaeda and the Taliban exerts influence even down to the village level in Pakistan, Afghanistan's eastern neighbor and the world's second most populous Muslim nation.

### Not Terrorism, They Say

A key link in the chain of radicalization of Muslim youths are the Islamic schools, known here as *madrassas,* where militant clerics steer young men into the organizations that are supplying the recruits for the Islamic army trained in the Afghan camps, they say.

Last summer, Mr. Mirza's 21-year-old brother disappeared from the family home, leaving a note under his pillow saying that he was going for jihad training. The young man said a local cleric had issued a religious ruling that allowed students to go against their parents' will to undergo such training, said Hafeez Mirza, his father.

"My son and my nephew (who recently completed training in Afghanistan) told me that they don't have to listen to me anymore, only the cleric," the elder Mr. Mirza said.

The global Islamic army grew out of a holy war against the Soviet Union in Afghanistan in the 1980s—a war that was organized, funded, and directed by the CIA, say U.S. and Pakistani officials and members of the militant groups. Some of the camps used by the Taliban and al-Qaeda were built by the CIA to train *mujahedeen,* or holy warriors, to fight the Soviets.

Camp graduates say they are not terrorists but are merely trying to prevent what they describe as the terrorism being committed against Muslims in places such as Indian-controlled Kashmir and the Israeli-occupied territories of the Middle East.

"We are training to save our country, our nation, our religion," Mohammed Mirza said. "This is a stupid statement to say this is terrorism."

Mr. Hussain, who went to Afghanistan last year with nine other young men from his village in northern Pakistan, said he was persuaded to undergo training at one of the al-Qaeda camps by a cousin who had lost a leg fighting the Soviets in Afghanistan during the 1980s. The cousin still maintains contacts with old comrades working with al-Qaeda and the Taliban in Afghanistan, he said.

Many of the veterans of the 1980s CIA proxy war—from Afghanistan, Pakistan, Saudi Arabia, Kuwait, Yemen, and elsewhere—are instructors in the training camps, said Mr. Hussain and Mr. Mirza.

### Levels of Training

The training is broken into stages, beginning with a basic training course that lasts 40 days, they said. Some young men—including Mr. Mirza's younger brother—complete the basic-training course at camps in Pakistan run by militant organizations such as Jaish-i-Mohammad, Lashkar-e-Taiba, and Harkat-ul-Mujahedeen, said Mr. Mirza, Mr. Hussain, and other people familiar with the training.

The second level of training lasts three months at one of the Afghanistan camps and involves courses in more advanced weaponry and tactics, in addition to rigorous religious indoctrination, according to several people familiar with the training. There is also a 60-day course for men who first complete a training course in Pakistan, said Mr. Mirza.

Mr. Mirza said his younger brother, cousin, and three other village youths went to Afghanistan last summer to take the second course. All five of these young men declined to be interviewed, saying they had sworn an oath on the Quran to not discuss their training with outsiders.

Graduates of the second-level course can apply for even more special- 35 ized training that can last from three years to eight years, Mr. Mirza said. This training includes martial arts, intelligence gathering, proficiency in a range of weapons and explosives, and paratrooper capabilities.

"Those instructors who are training the guys, all of them can fight without enough food to eat for weeks," he said. "They can survive in snow-fall. They can go through rivers. It is such a hard training that if you would wake them and not let them sleep for a week, it would make no difference to them."

In at least one of the training camps in Pakistan, run by Lashkar-e-Taiba, students are taught how to hijack an airplane. The instruction is given in a full-sized, fiberglass dummy airplane, said Haroon Asif, a law student who said he witnessed the class during a visit to a Lashkar camp in northern Pakistan.

**Students From All Over**

Mr. Mirza and Mr. Hussain describe their experience in Afghanistan as a cross between a Boy Scout summer camp, a religious retreat, and U.S. Army basic training. Prospective holy warriors are whipped into peak physical condition and fired with religious zeal, they said.

Mr. Mirza said there were 2,500 to 3,000 students in the camp where he trained. Mr. Hussain said there were about 10,000 in his camp, about five or six miles south of Kabul, the capital of Afghanistan.

Many of the instructors were so-called Arab Afghans, Arab veterans 40 of the war against the Soviets and associates of Osama bin Laden. The students represented virtually every Islamic country, including Pakistan, Saudi Arabia, Indonesia, Malaysia, Sudan, and Bangladesh, said Mr. Mirza and Mr. Hussain.

The camp where Mr. Hussain received his training "was huge," built on a mountain, he said. The students slept in tents, but there was also a vast complex of man-made caves that offered security in case of air attack—like the 1998 U.S. cruise missile attack on several training camps after the embassy bombings in Africa.

At Mr. Hussain's camp, the emir — a veteran of holy wars in Chechnya, Bosnia, Afghanistan, India, and Indian-controlled Kashmir — boasted that their arch-enemies, the United States and India, knew about their camp, "but they cannot do anything."

### Strict Daily Schedules

In the first week of training, daily life revolved around religious instruction emphasizing strict adherence to their fundamentalist Islamic faith and the religious basis of their armed struggle, said Mr. Mirza and Mr. Hussain.

The day began at 4 a.m. with prayers and Quran recitations, followed by calisthenics and sprints up and down the mountainsides. After breakfast and a short rest, the students reported for two hours of religious instruction at 9 a.m., followed by 1 1/2 hours of stick fighting and hand-to-hand combat.

Most of the afternoon was devoted to prayers and recitations of the   45
Quran. After dinner and evening prayers, the emir presided over a general assembly at which guard assignments and other security arrangements for the night were announced, the men said.

Living on a diet of only rice three times a day, "the first few days we were very weak, but then after a few days we grew stronger and our stamina grew," Mr. Hussain said. Military training began in earnest in the second week, when the morning religious instruction was replaced by three hours of weapons training. The students learned to fire various types of assault rifles, pistols, mortars, rockets, and small artillery, Mr. Hussain said.

As the days went on, they learned to climb trees and rappel from mountains, how to sneak up on their enemy by crawling stealthily, how to swim across icy cold rivers. The students were pushed to their limits, running up and down mountainsides without water, deprived of food and sleep.

"They were training us in such a hard way to make sure that we'll not run when we'll be actually fighting, we'll be aware of every problem, and we'll be in a position to handle anything," Mr. Mirza said.

Every Thursday evening, instructors would regale the students with war stories about *mujahedeen* who had been martyred in the cause of Islam.

"The circumstances of when they fought, how they died, what they did,   50
what they learned, what they ate — all those stories are told to the new guys, just to build their morale," Mr. Mirza said.

### Motivational Tales

Mr. Hussain recalled one of his favorite stories, told by an instructor who went by the nom de guerre Commander R. K. The setting of the story was a village called Lanjot, in Indian-controlled Kashmir.

"The Indian army went in, claiming there were some *mujahedeen* within that village," said Mr. Hussain, recounting the story told by Commander R. K. "They beheaded 20 innocent civilians, picked up their heads, put them on their guns and put their heads on display to the Pakistani side.

"Commander R. K., who saw all this, said that the Pakistani army is not doing anything, so within 48 hours I'll take revenge," Mr. Hussain said. "He, with his fellow commandos, crossed into Indian-occupied Kashmir. There were three Indian soldiers drinking water. They beheaded them, took their uniforms, and went to one of the Indian army camps.

"When they went in the Indian army camps, first they shot the soldiers in their feet and legs," continued Mr. Hussain. "When all the soldiers fainted, then they beheaded them, put their heads on their guns, and brought their heads back to Pakistan."

Mr. Hussain said the story drove home to the students the importance    55
of learning how to defend their fellow Muslims—and how to punish their oppressors.

Another instructor who made a lasting impression on Mr. Hussain went by the nom de guerre of Sheikh Osama. He is a legendary figure among the Islamic militants in Pakistan and Afghanistan for his role in the December 1999 hijacking of an Indian commercial jetliner. The jet and its passengers were flown to Kandahar, the Taliban spiritual capital. To end the standoff, India agreed to release a jailed militant cleric named Masood Azhar.

As Sheikh Osama told the story, he and five friends flew to Nepal to put their plan into action, Mr. Hussain said.

"They had five Kalashnikov automatic assault rifles in their bag, and they prayed to God that if God is with them, these guns should not be detected," Mr. Hussain said. "They went through the security check, God was with them, and the guns were not detected. They boarded the plane and in midair they took over the plane."

After his release, Maulana Masood returned to Pakistan and formed a militant group known as Jaish-i-Mohammad. This month, after Jaish claimed credit for a car bomb attack in Indian-controlled Kashmir that killed 38 people, the U.S. State Department added the group to its list of terrorist organizations. A Jaish spokesman has since disavowed responsibility for the attack.


**'God Willing, So Will I'**

These days, like many men trained in the camps of Afghanistan and Paki-    60
stan, Mr. Hussain talks of going to Afghanistan to join the holy war against the United States. He went to Pakistani-controlled Kashmir on Sept. 30 with seven friends for another week of military training at a camp run by Harkat-ul-Mujahedeen—another group listed as a terrorist organization by the U.S. State Department.

"We knew that America would attack Afghanistan, and so we went to prepare to retaliate against that attack," Mr. Hussain said.

Seven of his friends have already gone to Afghanistan to fight against U.S. forces, and four more friends are planning to go, he said.

"God willing, so will I," Mr. Hussain said—although he also said he would like to become a rich software tycoon and "support the jihad financially," as Mr. bin Laden does.

Mr. Mirza said there are tens of thousands of trained militants in Pakistan alone who are awaiting orders from their superiors to cross the border and fight U.S. forces in Afghanistan.

Thousands of recently trained al-Qaeda soldiers were sent to Pakistan before the U.S. bombing began "to avoid the casualties of trained persons," he said. "But when the Americans arrive, they will go back to fight. It could be me, too."

Some of the men have been specially trained as commandos and guerrillas, "and they will try their best to capture [American soldiers] alive," he said.

"If I could speak to a reasonable person from the allied forces, I would like to advise him to go back," he said. "In the history of the United States, this would be the most major mistake they are going to commit."

When the call goes out, as it will soon, he said, tens of thousands of men will begin moving toward Afghanistan, working their way through an

65

underground network of safehouses and secret contacts. Others, he said, will move into place to launch attacks on the Pakistani air bases being used by U.S. forces.

The chain of command is secret and strictly compartmentalized, "but we are in contact, all of us," Mr. Mirza said. "We are organized from the very base. We are in touch with Kabul, we are in touch with the Taliban. There are many ways for the trained persons, the warriors, the *mujahedeen*, to get to Afghanistan."

---

## Terrorist Psycho-Logic: Terrorist Behavior as a Product of Psychological Forces
### Jerrold M. Post

. . . [T]he principal argument of this essay is that *individuals are drawn to the path of terrorism in order to commit acts of violence*, and their special logic, which is grounded in their psychology and reflected in their rhetoric, becomes the justification for their violent acts.

Considering the diversity of causes to which terrorists are committed, the uniformity of their rhetoric is striking. Polarizing and absolutist, it is a rhetoric of "us versus them." It is a rhetoric without nuance, without shades of gray. "They," the establishment, are the source of all evil, in vivid contrast to "us," the freedom fighters, consumed by righteous rage. And if "they" are the source of our problems, it follows ineluctably, in the special psycho-logic of the terrorist, that "they" must be destroyed. It is the only just and moral thing to do. Once the basic premises are accepted, the logical reasoning is flawless. . . .

. . . [W]hat accounts for the uniformity of the terrorists' polarizing absolutist rhetoric? The author's own comparative research[1] on the psychology of terrorists does not reveal major psychopathology, and is in substantial agreement with the finding of Crenshaw[2] that "the outstanding common characteristic of terrorists is their normality." Her studies of the National Liberation Front (FLN) in Algeria in the 1950s found the members to be basically normal. Nor did Heskin[3] find members of the Irish Republican Army (IRA) to be emotionally disturbed. In a review of the social psychology of terrorist groups, McCauley and Segal[4] conclude that "the best documented generalization is negative; terrorists do not show any striking psychopathology."

Nor does a comparative study reveal a particular psychological type, a particular personality constellation, a uniform terrorist mind. But although diverse personalities are attracted to the path of terrorism, an examination of memoirs, court records, and rare interviews suggests that people with particular personality traits and tendencies are drawn disproportionately to terrorist careers.

What are these traits, these personality characteristics? Several au- [5] thors[5,6] have characterized terrorists as action-oriented, aggressive people who are stimulus-hungry and seek excitement. Particularly striking is the reliance placed on the psychological mechanisms of "externalization" and "splitting," psychological mechanisms found in individuals with narcissistic and borderline personality disturbances.[7] It is not my intent to suggest that all terrorists suffer from borderline or narcissistic personality disorders or that the psychological mechanisms of externalization and splitting are used by every terrorist. It is my distinct impression, however, that these mecha- nisms are found with extremely high frequency in the population of terror- ists, and contribute significantly to the uniformity of terrorists' rhetorical style and their special psycho-logic.

In this regard, it is particularly important to understand the mechanism of "splitting." This is believed to be characteristic of people whose personal- ity development is shaped by a particular type of psychological damage dur- ing childhood which produces what clinicians have characterized as narcis- sistic wounds. This leads to the development of what Kohut[8] has termed "the injured self."

Individuals with a damaged self-concept have never fully integrated the good and bad parts of the self. These aspects of the self are "split" into the "me" and the "not me." An individual with this personality constellation idealizes his grandiose self and *splits out* and *projects* onto others all the hated and devalued weakness within. Individuals who place high reliance on the mechanisms of splitting and externalization look outward for the source of difficulties. They need an outside enemy to blame. This is a domi- nant mechanism of the destructive charismatic,[9] such as Hitler, who proj- ects the devalued part of himself onto the interpersonal environment and then attacks and scapegoats the enemy without. Unable to face his own inadequacies, the individual with this personality style needs a target to blame and attack for his own inner weakness and inadequacies. Such peo- ple find the polarizing absolutist rhetoric of terrorism extremely attractive. The statement, "It's not us — it's them; they are the cause of our problems," provides a psychologically satisfying explanation for what has gone wrong in their lives. . . .

**Pressures to Conform**

Given the intensity of the need to belong, the strength of the affiliative needs, and, for many members, the as-yet incomplete sense of individual identity, terrorists have a tendency to submerge their own identities into the group, so that a kind of "group mind" emerges.[10] The group cohesion that emerges is magnified by the external danger, which tends to reduce internal divisiveness in unity against the outside enemy. "The group was born under the pressure of pursuit" according to members of the Red Army Faction,[11] and group solidarity was "compelled exclusively by the illegal situation, fashioned into a common destiny." Another Red Army Faction member went so far as to consider this pressure "the sole link holding the group together." [12]

Doubts concerning the legitimacy of the goals and actions of the group are intolerable to such a group. The person who questions a group decision risks the wrath of the group and possible expulsion. Indeed, the fear is even more profound, for, as Baumann [13] has stated, withdrawal was impossible "except by way of the graveyard." *The way to get rid of doubt is to get rid of the doubters.* Extreme pressure to conform has been reported by all who have discussed the atmosphere within the group. Baeyer-Kaette [14] has described the first meeting of a new recruit to the Heidelberg cell of the Red Army Faction. The group, which previously had targeted only identified representatives of the establishment such as magistrates and policemen, was discussing a plan to firebomb a major department store. Horrified, the new recruit blurted out, "But that will lead to loss of innocent lives!" A chill fell over the room, and the new recruit quickly realized that to question the group consensus was to risk losing his membership in the group. What an interesting paradox, that these groups, whose ideology is intensely against the dominance of authority, should be so authoritarian and should so insist on conformity and unquestioning obedience.

The group ideology plays an important role in supporting this conformity-inducing group environment. When questions are raised, the absolutist ideology becomes the intellectual justification. Indeed, the ideology becomes, in effect, the scripture for the group's morality. In the incident just described, the leader of the cell patiently explained to the new recruit that anyone who would shop in such an opulent store was no innocent victim, but was indeed a capitalist consumer. 10

Questions have often been raised as to how people socialized to a particular moral code could commit such violent antisocial acts. Insofar as an individual submerges his own identity into the group, the group's moral code becomes each individual's moral code. As Crenshaw [15] has observed, "The group, as selector and interpreter of ideology, is central." What the group, through its interpretation of its ideology, defines as moral becomes moral — and becomes the authority for the compliant members. And if the ideology indicates that "they are responsible for our problems," to destroy "them" is not only viewed as justified but can be seen to be a moral imperative. . . .

Consider a youth seeking an external target to attack. Before joining the group, he was alone, not particularly successful. Now he is engaged in a life-and-death struggle with the establishment, his picture on the "most wanted" posters. He sees his leaders as internationally prominent media personalities. Within certain circles, he is lionized as a hero. He travels first class, and his family is provided for should his acts of heroism lead to his death as a martyr to the cause. Heady stuff that; surely this is the good life, a role and position not easily relinquished.

Now if authenticity is defined as "revolutionary heroism," then this definition has important implications for the outcomes of debates and personal rivalries within the group. A leader who advocates prudence and moderation is likely to lose his position quickly to a bolder person committed to the continuation of the struggle. Indeed, on the basis of his observations of underground resistance groups during World War II, Zawodny[16] has concluded that the primary determinant of underground group decision making is not the external reality but the psychological climate within the group. He has described the unbearable tension that builds when a resistance group is compelled to go underground. For these action-oriented people, forced inaction is extremely stressful. What, after all, are freedom fighters if they do not fight? *A terrorist group needs to commit acts of terrorism in order to justify its existence.* The wise leader, sensing the building tension, will plan an action so that the group's members can reaffirm their identity and discharge their aggressive energy. Better to have the group attack the outside enemy, no matter how high the risk, than turn on itself — and him.

This suggests a dynamic within the group pressing for the perpetuation of violence and leading toward ever-riskier decisions. Indeed, the terrorist group displays, in extreme degree, the characteristics of "group think" as described by Janis.[17] Among the characteristics he ascribes to groups demonstrating "groupthink" are the following:

1. Illusions of invulnerability leading to excessive optimism and excessive risk taking
2. Presumptions of the group's morality
3. One-dimensional perceptions of the enemy as evil
4. Intolerance of challenges by a group member to shared key beliefs.

This research on "groupthink" relates to another important body of research bearing on risky decision making by groups. Using U.S. military officers as subjects, Semel and Minix[18] found that groups regularly opted for riskier choices than those that would have been preferred by individuals.

This momentum toward ever-riskier choices has important implications for mass-casualty terrorism. Analysis conducted for the International Task Force for the Prevention of Nuclear Terrorism[19] leads me to conclude that the internal constraints against the unthinkable prospect of nuclear terrorism are weakening, that although it is still in the realm of "low probability-high consequences," the prospects are increasing, and a major contribution to that increase are the risk-increasing group dynamics of the terrorist group. . . .

### Policy Implications

If the foregoing conclusions concerning the individual, group, and organizational psychology of political terrorism are valid, what are the implications for antiterrorist policy?

*Terrorists whose only sense of significance comes from being terrorists cannot be forced to give up terrorism, for to do so would be to lose their very reason for being.* Indeed, for such persons, violent societal counterreactions reaffirm their core belief that "it's us against them and they are out to destroy us." . . .

. . . *There is no short-range solution to the problem of terrorism.* Once an individual is in the pressure cooker of the terrorist group, it is extremely difficult to influence him. In the long run, the most effective antiterrorist policy is one that inhibits potential recruits from joining in the first place.

Political terrorism is not simply a *product* of psychological forces; its central *strategy* is psychological, for *political terrorism, is, at base, a particularly vicious species of psychological warfare.* Until now, the terrorists have had a virtual monopoly on the weapon of the television camera, as they manipulate their target audiences through the media. Terrorists perpetuate their organizations by shaping the perceptions of future generations of terrorists. Manipulating a reactive media, they demonstrate their power and significance and define the legitimacy of their cause. Countering the terrorists' highly effective media-oriented strategy through more effective dissemination of information and public education—deromanticizing the terrorists and portraying them for what they are—must be key elements of a proactive policy.

As important as it is to inhibit potential terrorists from joining terrorist groups, it is equally important to facilitate their leaving those groups. The powerful hold of the group has been detailed. By creating pathways out of terrorism, we can loosen that grip. Amnesty programs modeled after the highly effective program of the Italian government can contribute to that goal. Reducing support for the group—both in its immediate societal surroundings and in the nation at large—are further long-range programs worth fostering. In the long run, the most effective way of countering terrorism is to reduce external support, to facilitate pathways out of terrorism, and, most important, to reduce the attractiveness of the terrorist path for alienated youth.

20

### Notes

1. J. Post, "Notes on a Psychodynamic Theory of Terrorist Behavior," *Terrorism* 7, no. 3 (1984): 241–56.

2. M. Crenshaw, "The Causes of Terrorism," *Comparative Politics* 13 (1981): 379–99.

3. K. Heskin, "The Psychology of Terrorism in Ireland," in *Terrorism in Ireland*, edited by Y. Alexander and A. O'Day (New York: St. Martin's Press, 1984).

4. C. R. McCauley and M. E. Segal, "Social Psychology of Terrorist Groups," in *Group Processes and Intergroup Relations*, vol. 9 of *Annual Review of Social and Personality Psychology*, edited by C. Hendrick (Beverly Hills: Sage, 1987).

5. W. Laqueur, *The Age of Terrorism* (Boston: Little, Brown, 1987).

6. See L. Süllwold, in *Analysen Zum Terrorismus 2: Lebenslauf-Analysen*, edited by H. Jäger, G. Schmidtchen, and L. Süllwold (Darmstadt: Westdeutscher Verlag, 1981).

7. O. Kernberg, *Borderline Conditions and Pathological Narcissism* (New York: Jacob Aronson, 1975).

8. H. Kohut, *The Analysis of the Self* (New York: International University Press, 1983).

9. J. Post, "Narcissism and the Charismatic Leader-Follower Relationship," *Political Psychology* 7, no. 5 (1986): 675–88.

10. Post, "'Hostilité,' 'Conformité,' 'Fraternité.'"

11. B. Sturm, *Der Spiegel* 7 (1972): 57.

12. V. Spietel, *Der Spiegel* 33 (1980): 35.

13. See Baumann, in Baeyer-Kaette et al., *Analysen Zum Terrorismus.*

14. W. Baeyer-Kaette, "A Left-Wing Terrorist Indoctrination Group," paper presented to the 6th Annual Meeting of the International Society of Political Psychology, Oxford, England, July 1983.

15. M. Crenshaw, "An Organizational Approach to the Analysis of Political Terrorism," *Orbis* 29 (1985): 465–89.

16. J. K. Zawodny, "Internal Organizational Problems and the Sources of Tensions of Terrorist Movements as Catalysts of Violence," *Terrorism* 1, no. 3/4 (1978): 277–85.

17. I. Janis, *Victims of Groupthink* (Boston: Houghton-Mifflin, 1972).

18. See A. K. Semel and D. A. Minix, in *Psychological Models and International Politics,* edited by L. S. Falkowski (Boulder, Colo.: Westview Press, 1979).

19. J. Post, "Prospects for Nuclear Terrorism: Psychological Motivations and Constraints," in *Preventing Nuclear Terrorism,* edited by P. Leventhal and Y. Alexander (Lexington, Mass.: Lexington Books, 1987).

*For Discussion*

1. Regarding the Palestinian-Israeli conflict, what makes the U.S. role unique? How do bin Laden and his allies see this role? Would a peaceful settlement of the conflict reduce the likelihood of further terrorism against Americans here and abroad?

2. In "The Roots of Conflict," a distinction is made between merely *political* aims and the far more highly charged *religious* motivations that drive some Palestinians and Israelis. Is this a meaningful distinction for either side in the conflict, or just the way Western observers see it within a tradition of church-state separation? One expert cited at the end of "Roots" claims that "if it [the Palestinian-Israeli conflict] is seen in purely religious terms, it becomes absolutely unsolvable." Is that why, despite repeated efforts, no resolution has been found?

3. Using both "Roots" and "Bin Laden Allies Want Islamic Unity," summarize the Islamic fundamentalist goals. Which of these might be realized? Which seem at least highly unlikely? Without sacrificing our allies in the region or ignoring our own strategic interests, what

can the U.S. do to lessen the appeal of Islamic extremists among the
general Muslim population?
4. How is the appeal of Islamic fundamentalism, especially among
Arab young men, explained in the second article? If the explanation
is adequate, what, if anything, can be done to reduce the attraction
to terrorism?
5. How does Jerrold M. Post explain the appeal of terrorism? Are there
connections between his psychological-rhetorical view and the more
economic-demographic explanations given in "Bin Laden's Allies"?
6. In "Cradle of a Holy War," what goes on in al-Qaeda's training camps
for terrorists is described and to some extent explained. Do the
methods used accord with Post's theory of terrorist psycho-logic?
If so, in what ways?

## For Further Discussion

Nothing is more crucial to resisting terrorism than understanding it. If we
think, for example, that terrorists in general and suicidal terrorists in particular are insane, then our attitudes and policies will certainly be misguided.
How would you describe the outlook of Islamic fundamentalism after reading the articles in this section? Do they resemble the stances of radical religious groups, past and present, in Europe and America? In your view, will the
ongoing westernization of the Middle East defuse the explosive tensions over
time? Or is neocolonialism, the domination of other people economically,
politically, and culturally, part of the problem rather than part of the solution?

## For Further Research and Convincing

Our military power in the Middle East has at present no serious rival, nor
is there much prospect of one developing. But there's evidence that we are
losing the propaganda war, the struggle to win the hearts and minds of the
Arab population — so much evidence, in fact, that Washington is clearly concerned by it. Find out what you can about the propaganda war. Write an essay advocating whatever measures you think we ought to take to enhance
U.S. appeal among both Arabs and Muslims. Be sure to assess our current efforts as part of your own proposals. Address your paper to an audience that
would know most of the information contained in the first three articles of
this section.

## For Informal Research and Dialogue

If there is an Arab or Islamic community within or near your college or the
neighborhood where you reside, attempt to establish contact with them, perhaps by inviting a representative to class. Listen carefully to their points of
view and ask questions designed to clarify from an attitude of sympathy for
the plight of fellow human beings and Americans. What did you learn that
all Americans should know? Consider posting what you've learned to an appropriate Web site.

## Conclusion: The Future of Terrorism

Yet another indication that everything hasn't changed after 9/11 is the following excerpt from Paul Wilkinson's *Terrorism versus Democracy,* the same source from which we took "Types of Terrorism" (pages 371–373). Written before 9/11, his analysis of the threats posed by nuclear, chemical, biological, and conventional weapons apply now as well. Sadly, little has changed.

In essence, we face a range of possibilities defined at one end by "low probability, high consequences" and at the other by "high probability, low consequences." The use of a nuclear weapon is an example of the former, the use of a surface-to-air missile (SAM) to bring down a commercial airliner an example of the latter. The difficulty, of course, is that we must fear the former more because the consequences would be so drastic, dwarfing the impact of 9/11, and yet we are far more vulnerable to the latter, whose smaller-scale consequences we can't ignore.

As Wilkinson properly insists, the key to countering all terrorist activity, regardless of tactics, is better intelligence-gathering, which requires both more cooperation among U.S. agencies and more cooperation with foreign governments. It's been said that "eternal vigilance is the price of freedom"; if so, then good intelligence is the cornerstone of vigilance. We may hope that at least one thing has changed since 9/11: We now realize that intelligence gathering must improve.

---

## Analysis of Terrorist Weapons and the Liberal State Response
### Paul Wilkinson

### Nuclear Terrorism

Many analysts have endorsed the somewhat sanguine assessment of an American writer that "the threat of nuclear action by terrorists appears to be exaggerated."[1] In support of this optimistic view it has been argued that terrorists are not really interested in mass murder, but in gaining publicity and using propaganda to influence people. Of course publicity and propaganda are generally key tactical objectives. But in many cases the terrorists' cardinal aim is to create a climate of fear and collapse, essentially by terrifying and demoralising their targets into capitulation. And what more potent weapon of psychological coercion can be conceived in the modern age than the threat to explode a nuclear device or to release lethal levels of radioactivity into the atmosphere, perhaps rendering an entire area of a city uninhabitable.

It would be extraordinarily foolish to assume that all terrorist groups shared the same perceptions of rationality, humanity and prudence that inform the consciences of most of humanity. In the strange transcendental logic of the fanatical political terrorist, as I have earlier observed, the end is held to justify any means. If any individual life is expendable in the cause of "revolutionary justice" or "liberation" so many hundreds, even thousands, of lives may have to be "sacrificed." One has only to turn to the hysterical writings of Johannes Most, Pierre Vallières or the Weathermen to find mass slaughter of "bourgeois vermin" not only commended but proudly and enthusiastically advocated.[2] Justifications for mass killing are not confined to religious and ethnic fanatics. As for international terrorists, who may be operating in the heart of the territory of their hated enemy, there has been a similar readiness on their part to regard the "enemy" civil population as expendable. Hence, although still a low probability, nuclear terrorism is potentially so high a consequence that we must have contingency plans to prevent such an attack and to deal with the possible consequences should it happen, in order to minimise loss of life. . . .

## Vulnerable Targets

There are extremely grave dangers involved in the diffusion of civil nuclear facilities and technologies in many states. These processes involve the use of substances which could be employed to make a nuclear explosive device. Plutonium, which is used for incorporation into reactor fuel, has to be shipped and in some cases transported by road. It is clearly vulnerable to theft by terrorists while it is in transit. Still more dangerous is the practice which has developed in the nuclear power industry of transporting plutonium nitrate in liquid form by road. This is a hazardous process. Plutonium transported as a pure compound, even in small quantities, is a particularly tempting target for terrorist theft or hijack because of the material's obvious value in constructing a nuclear weapon. And, because of its extreme toxicity, it could also be used by terrorists as a weapon of radiological extortion. Reports by scientific experts have underlined both these dangers, but this does not appear to have influenced the policy of the EU member states' authorities regarding the transportation of nuclear fuels. Plutonium is also present in spent reactor fuel. It then has to be stored because there is to date no commercially viable system for reprocessing it. And in the special case of the liquid metal fast-breeder reactor, more plutonium is produced than is actually consumed, so that the problem of disposal is especially acute.

Terrorists, therefore, might seek by various means, including infiltration of the nuclear industry workforce, to obtain regular small supplies of nuclear materials. The particularly vulnerable points for nuclear theft include storage facilities for spent fuel, fuel reprocessing plants, and fabrication and uranium enrichment plants. There is little doubt that sufficient quantities of enriched uranium and plutonium could be obtained to make possible the manufacture of a primitive device. Recent firm evidence of the smuggling of nuclear materials from Russian installations underlines the growing seriousness of this threat. Even more worrying is the strong possibility that disaffected scientists and engineers from the Former Soviet Union's nuclear weapons programme have been lured into the employ of rogue states or terrorist groups. It is certainly credible that a group of competent and qualified scientists and engineers could be recruited for the special purpose of building an atomic weapon or advising the group on techniques of nuclear sabotage and extortion. A team of five or six could probably accomplish this within the space of five or six weeks without incurring any serious risk to their personal health or safety. Estimates of the financial costs involved vary. . . .

It is sometimes argued that terrorists would be effectively discouraged from sabotage of nuclear installations because of the risks involved to their own safety, lack of knowledge of safety precautions and ignorance of nuclear technology. We have already noted that these weaknesses could be overcome by certain terrorist groups through the employment of their own "expert" advisers on nuclear technology, or alternatively by the use of employees in the installation as agents and collaborators, and that some fanatical groups include individuals willing to martyr themselves for their cause.

Governments and security forces would be wise to plan for the "worst possible" terrorist contingencies. Much as they may like to reassure themselves that anarchist fringe groups or "crazy state" terrorists are a tiny minority, they cannot afford to discount the possibility of a small number of fanatics launching into nuclear terrorism. It is the duty of the authorities to do all they can to prevent any such attacks from succeeding. There is no shortage of evidence that individuals and groups have been tempted into attacks and threats against nuclear installations. It is noteworthy that the Japanese police discovered documents showing that the Aum cult was very interested in nuclear technology, and they believe that they were actively seeking to purchase a nuclear weapon and to obtain a supply of uranium.[3]

### Chemical and Biological Weapons

Most specialists in the study of terrorism have been as sceptical about the possibility of terrorists using chemical or biological weapons as they have about the prospect of nuclear terrorism. Dr Richard Clutterbuck in his *Terrorism in an Unstable World* concluded:

> Clearly we should not be complacent about nuclear, biological and chemical weapons, both because of the need to evaluate hoax calls . . . and because all of them would be feasible for a group which was both desperate and suicidal. But the threat is far less, and would in many ways be easier to handle because of its lack of credibility, than the terrorist actions to which we are accustomed.[4]

The tragic attack on the Tokyo underground system with the nerve gas Sarin, which killed 12 and injured many more, has made it vital to reconsider the conventional wisdom. It is unlikely that there are more than a tiny number of groups willing to commit such acts. It is still a low-probability threat. But the fact that it has been attempted and that it clearly could have caused a large number of deaths if the Sarin had been used in a purer form, may tempt another group to emulate the Aum group's action.

The methods for making nerve gases and biological pathogens have been known for decades. The formula for making Sarin is on the Internet. The materials and equipment for making crude chemical and biological weapons are cheap and easily obtained and the weapons could be made by a person with only basic scientific training.[5] . . .

### Terrorist Tactics and the Use of Conventional Weapons

In a recently published symposium edited by myself, a number of experts   10
rightly stressed that the most likely trend in terrorist weaponry and tactics was further refinement and adaptation, and deployment of what is already widely available and affordable. Why go to the trouble of acquiring more hazardous and costly weapons when so much death and destruction can be achieved by traditional means? It is worth bearing in mind that the bomb used in the most lethal terrorist attack ever carried out in the United States, in Oklahoma, which killed 169, comprised ammonium nitrate and fuel oil; the same bomb is also one of the most effective conventional weapons used by the IRA. The IRA provides us with the outstanding example of an experienced terrorist group improvising and adapting traditional weaponry, for example in its development of the drogue grenade, home-made mortars and booby-trap devices. There are reports that they have recently been developing a remote control device to guide a driverless car containing a bomb to its target. When terrorist groups are able to achieve "successes" using such improvisations, they are less likely to feel the need to experiment with entirely new weapons that carry a high risk of death or injury to their own operatives. We are likely to see more developments of this kind in a constant battle to keep ahead of the technology available to the counter-terrorist agencies.[6]

One important source of innovations or switches in tactics and weaponry is the introduction by the authorities of more effective countermeasures against certain types of attack. For example, as the civil aviation system's measures to improve protection against the sabotage bombing of airliners become more efficient, we are likely to see a greater use of alternative means of terrorist attack against aviation, such as surface-to-air missiles. There are clear signs that this was already happening in the 1990s. There have been at least 25 attacks using man-portable SAMs since November 1990, and in 15 of these incidents an aircraft was shot down causing an estimated 300 deaths. So far most of the aircraft involved have been military. However, in view of the clear evidence that terrorist groups in many parts of the world have managed to obtain SAMs, the security authorities in the European democracies should be urgently concerting efforts to combat this growing threat.[7]

### Countering International Terrorism: The Democratic Response

In countering international terrorism, the democratic state confronts an inescapable dilemma. It has to deal effectively with the terrorist threat to citizens and to vulnerable potential targets, such as civil aviation, diplomatic and commercial premises, without at the same time destroying basic civil rights, the democratic process and the rule of law. On the one hand, the democratic government and its agencies of law enforcement must avoid the heavy handed overreaction which many terrorist groups deliberately seek to provoke: such a response would only help to alienate the public from the government and could ultimately destroy democracy more swiftly and completely than any small terrorist group ever could. On the other hand, if government, judiciary and police prove incapable of upholding the law and protecting life and property, then their whole credibility and authority will be undermined.

If this balance is to be maintained, the liberal state should seek at all times to combat terrorism using its criminal justice and law-enforcement mechanisms. However, it is clearly the case that some terrorist groups attain a level of fire-power that outstrips even the capabilities of elite squads of armed police. It has been proven time and again that in certain circumstances of high emergency, such as the hijacking to Entebbe in 1976 and the Iranian embassy siege of 1980, it may be essential to deploy a highly trained military rescue commando force to save hostages. Military, naval or air forces may be invaluable in interdicting a major terrorist assault, as has been seen in the case of Israel's measures against terrorist groups attacking its borders from land and sea. But in the more normal conditions enjoyed by the democratic states in Western Europe, the occasions when military deployment to tackle international terrorists is required will be very rare.

A number of dangers need to be constantly borne in mind when deploying the army in a major internal terrorist emergency role. First, an unnecessarily high military profile may serve to escalate the level of violence by polarising pro- and anti-government elements in the community. Second, there is a constant risk that a repressive overreaction or a minor error in judgment by the military may trigger further civil violence. Internal security duties inevitably impose considerable strains on the soldiers, who are made well aware of the hostility of certain sections of the community towards them. Third, anti-terrorist and internal security duties absorb considerable manpower and involve diverting highly trained military technicians from their primary NATO and external defence roles. Fourth, there is a risk that the civil power may become overdependent on the army's presence and there may be a consequent lack of urgency in preparing the civil police for gradually reassuming the internal security responsibility. Finally, in the event of an international terrorist attack, a military operation to punish a state sponsor or to strike at alleged terrorist bases may trigger an international conflict worse than the act of terrorism one is seeking to oppose.

High-quality intelligence is at the heart of the proactive counter-terrorism strategy. It has been used with notable success against many terrorist groups. By gaining advanced warning of terrorists' planned operations, their weaponry, personnel, financial assets and fund-raising, tactics, communications systems and so on, it becomes feasible to preempt terrorist attacks, and ultimately to crack open the terrorist cell structure and bring its members to trial. Impressive examples of this proactive intelligence-led counter-terrorism strategy are frequently ignored or forgotten by the public, but this should not deceive us into underestimating their value. At the international level, the most impressive example has been the brilliant intelligence cooperation among the Allies to thwart Saddam Hussein's much-vaunted campaign of "holy terror" during operations Desert Shield and Desert Storm. Sadly, such high levels of international cooperation against terrorism are hard to find. Just as the lack of intelligence sharing between uniformed and nonuniformed security agencies often damages national counter-terrorism responses, so international mistrust and reluctance to share information often vitiates an effective international response. The most useful enhancements of policy to combat terrorism at the international level need to be made in intelligence gathering, by every means available, intelligence sharing, intelligence analysis and threat assessment. This is my key recommendation, and it is my hope that there will be a fuller debate on refining a better proactive strategy for America and G8 and EU friends and allies, and the newly democratised states of Eastern Europe. . . .

It would be a grave error to assume that even the most sophisticated intelligence and security measures are going to be sufficient to eradicate or even contain the most dangerous forms of international terrorism. In situations where there is a deep-seated ethnic or ethnoreligious conflict involved, as in the case of the relationship between Israel and the Palestinians, much will depend on the will and ability of the political leaders involved to address the underlying causes of the conflict by imaginative political and socioeconomic measures and a generous spirit of compromise. If the efforts to rejuvenate the Middle East peace process do not succeed the consequences will almost certainly involve a fresh wave of terrorism, including international terrorism, and the eruption of further Middle East wars. It would be dangerous complacency to assume that the course of the Israeli–Palestinian peace process is inevitably going to lead to a peaceful resolution of their bitter conflict.[8] Only a combination of dedication and hard work on political and security aspects by both sides is likely to bring eventual success. Terrorism has demonstrated its potential for disrupting the peace process. It could destroy the peace efforts completely if there is an inadequate will on the part of the parties to the Oslo accords and the wider international community to sustain them.

## Notes

1. Brian Jenkins, "International Terrorism: Trends and Potentialities: A Summary of Conclusions," unpublished mimeographed paper, March 1976, p. 3.

2. See for example, Pierre Vallières, *White Niggers of America* (New York: Monthly Review Press, 1970).

3. For a detailed account see James K. Campbell, "Weapons of Mass Destruction and Terrorism," *Terrorism and Political Violence*, 9: 2 (summer 1997).

4. Richard Clutterbuck, *Terrorism in an Unstable World* (London: Macmillan, 1994), p. 54.

5. The threat is discussed by R. H. Kupperman and D. M. Trent in their pioneering study of potential terrorist weaponry, tactics and targets, *Terrorism, Threat, Reality, Response* (Stanford, CA: Hoover Institute Press, 1979).

6. This is a recurrent theme in the contributions to Paul Wilkinson (ed.), *Technology and Terrorism* (London: Frank Cass, 1993).

7. See Thomas B. Hunter, "The Proliferation of Manportable SAMs," *Counter-Terrorism and Security Report*, Vol. 6, No. 2, July/August 1997, pp. 2–5.

8. See Paul Wilkinson, "Politics, Diplomacy and Peace Processes: Pathways out of Terrorism" in Max Taylor and John Horgan (eds), *The Future of Terrorism* (London: Frank Cass, 2000), pp. 66–82.

## For Discussion

1. According to Wilkinson, what factors make the nuclear threat more likely despite its low probability by comparison to conventional attacks?

2. What factors make the biological-chemical threat a realistic possibility? What lessons can be drawn from the anthrax episode?

3. Variations on the use of conventional weapons, 9/11 being a prime example, constitute the most likely continuing threat. What variations can you imagine that haven't been used at all or not against Americans so far? Which of these do you think are the most probable?

4. Should the United States resort *regularly, as a standard policy* to "pre-emptive strikes" such as commando raids on terrorist cells suspected of plotting terrorist attacks? Israel, whose vulnerability is far greater than ours, has used such strikes often. Should we?
5. According to Wilkinson, what are the dangers in using the military for counterterrorism? Are any of the dangers evident in the deployment of our forces in Afghanistan?

*For Further Research and Collaborative Writing*

Divide the class into three groups corresponding to the sources of possible nonconventional attack: nuclear, biological, chemical. Have each group research the threat posed by each kind more deeply. The results should be presented orally or in writing to the class. Then, working together in whatever way seems best, put together a report about the nonconventional threat, recommending whatever course of action seems most promising to counter it within the limitations imposed by our open, democratic system. Consider posting your report to an appropriate Web site.

## SECTION 3: ASSESSING AND RESPONDING TO INTERPRETATIONS AND ARGUMENTS

We have arranged the thirteen selections comprising this third and last part of our terrorism source book into four groupings:

Initial Readings of 9/11
Arguments: Right and Left
A Conflict of Cultures?
Conclusion: Two Philosophical Interpretations

A few comments about this section and its divisions should help orient you for reading.

In general, the selections range in time from those written soon after the event to those written a month or more later. The events of 9/11 were so shattering to most Americans that the initial struggle was simply to grasp it somehow, to work through the emotions of the moment toward a measure of intellectual control. That is, amid the shock and grief, we tried to *interpret* 9/11—to decide what it meant to us individually and to our country. For the most part, these first interpretations were only asserted, not argued, partly because the views were deeply personal, not intended primarily to convince or persuade, and partly because the spontaneous feeling of solidarity following the attack temporarily made argument seem inappropriate. The Initial Readings section offers five such interpretations, all from within two weeks after 9/11. Although much in these pieces is asserted without argument, almost everything asserted is arguable, as we shall see.

It was not long, of course, before interpretation of the event and its consequences became the familiar struggle between the politics of left and right, liberal and conservative. We can see politics in the initial, groping readings of the event, but the second phase was more consciously political and more inclined toward argument as divisions over how to interpret the attack began to crystallize. The selections in the second section, "Arguments, Right and Left," are four representative examples.

Implicit and explicit in these arguments is the question of how to understand the clash of cultures that seems to define current antagonisms, friends and foes. No one doubts that there are profound differences between what we call "the West" and what we call "the Muslim world." The question is whether these differences explain the current conflict. We have one essay that says they do, another that says they don't.

We conclude with two essays that are more philosophical than political, that some might see as "longer" or "deeper" views. Whether they really are is disputable, but as we return to "politics as usual" we surely need challenges to the comfortable ways of thinking we categorize as liberal and conservative, West and East. In quite different ways, these essays try to do that. If they lead us to think in ways that aren't so automatic and familiar, they will have served a useful purpose.

## Initial Readings of 9/11

On September 24, 2001, two weeks after the attacks on the World Trade Center and the Pentagon, a now-famous issue of *The New Yorker* appeared, its cover a funereal black. Four of the five commentaries that follow come from this edition, two by social and political critics (Hertzberg and Sontag), two by creative writers (Updike and Appelfeld). To these we have added one more, by a professor of Latin American history at Duke University, John D. French. His contribution is the text of a paper delivered at a Duke University forum entitled "The New War on Terrorism: Initial Assessment." None of these responses can be said to represent "the American response," if we can speak at all of a general public outlook; all certainly cut deeper than the "facile punditry" French singles out for criticism. As you'll discover in reading the other selections, Sontag's is the best known and has drawn the most fire, for reasons you'll have no trouble supplying when you read it.

Taken together, the readings raise many fundamental issues, among them perhaps the most important of all: What metaphors are we using to talk about 9/11? There's no neutral, objective way to discuss it; we have to use analogies of some kind. Implicit in these analogies are whole points of view, including the actions we should take in response to the attack. In other words, it's not too much to say that the future is in the language we use, so we had better ponder our metaphors carefully.

# From "The Talk of The Town"
## The New Yorker

Hendrik Hertzberg*

The catastrophe that turned the foot of Manhattan into the mouth of Hell on the morning of September 11, 2001, unfolded in four paroxysms. At a little before nine, a smoldering scar on the face of the north tower of the World Trade Center (an awful accident, like the collision of a B-25 bomber with the Empire State Building on July 28, 1945?); eighteen minutes later, the orange and gray blossoming of the second explosion, in the south tower; finally, at a minute before ten and then at not quite ten-thirty, the sickening slide of the two towers, collapsing one after the other. For those in the immediate vicinity, the horror was of course immediate and unmistakable; it occurred in what we have learned to call real time, and in real space. For those farther away—whether a few dozen blocks or halfway around the world—who were made witnesses by the long lens of television, the events were seen as through a glass, brightly. Their reality was visible but not palpable. It took hours to begin to comprehend their magnitude; it is taking days for the defensive numbness they induced to wear off; it will take months—or years—to measure their impact and meaning.

New York is a city where, however much strangers meet and mix on the streets and in the subways, circles of friends are usually demarcated by work and family. The missing and presumed dead—their number is in the thousands—come primarily from the finance, international trade, and government service workers in the doomed buildings, and from the ranks of firefighters and police officers drawn there by duty and courage. The umbra of personal grief already encompasses scores or even hundreds of thousands of people; a week or two from now, when the word has spread from friend to colleague to relative to acquaintance, the penumbra will cover millions. The city has never suffered a more shocking calamity from any act of God or man.

The calamity, of course, goes well beyond the damage to our city and to its similarly bereaved rival and brother Washington. It is national; it is international; it is civilizational. In the decade since the end of the Cold War, the human race has become, with increasing rapidity, a single organism. Every kind of barrier to the free and rapid movement of goods, information, and people has been lowered. The organism relies increasingly on a kind of trust—the unsentimental expectation that people, individually and collectively, will behave more or less in their rational self-interest. (Even the anti-globalizers of the West mostly embrace the underlying premises of the new dispensation; their demand is for global democratic institutions to mitigate the cruelties of the global market.) The terrorists made use of that trust. They rode the flow of the world's aerial circulatory system like lethal viruses.

With growing ferocity, officials from the President on down have described the bloody deeds as acts of war. But, unless a foreign government turns out to have directed the operation (or, at least, to have known and approved its scope in detail and in advance), that is a category mistake. The metaphor of war—and it is more metaphor than description—ascribes to the perpetrators a dignity they do not merit, a status they cannot claim, and a strength they do not possess. Worse, it points toward a set of responses that could prove futile or counterproductive. Though the death and destruction these acts caused were on the scale of war, the acts themselves were acts of terrorism, albeit on a wholly unprecedented level. From 1983 until last week, according to the *Times*, ten outrages had each claimed the lives of more than a hundred people. The worst—the destruction of an Air-India 747 in 1985—killed three hundred and twenty-nine people; the Oklahoma City bombing, which killed a hundred and sixty-eight, was the seventh worst. Last week's carnage surpassed that of any of these by an order of magnitude. It was also the largest violent taking of life on American soil on any day since the Civil War, including December 7, 1941. And in New York and Washington, unlike at Pearl Harbor, the killed and maimed were overwhelmingly civilians.

The tactics of the terrorists were as brilliant as they were depraved. The    5
nature of those tactics and their success—and there is no use denying that what they did was, on its own terms, successful—points up the weakness of the war metaphor. Authorities estimated last week that "as many as" fifty people may have been involved. The terrorists brought with them nothing but knives and the ability to fly a jumbo jet already in the air. How do you take "massive military action" against the infrastructure of a stateless, compartmentalized "army" of fifty, or ten times fifty, whose weapons are rental cars, credit cards, and airline tickets?

The scale of the damage notwithstanding, a more useful metaphor than war is crime. The terrorists of September 11th are outlaws within a global polity. They may enjoy the corrupt protection of a state (and corruption, like crime, can be ideological or spiritual as well as pecuniary in motive). But they do not constitute or control a state and do not even appear to aspire to control one. Their status and numbers are such that the task of dealing with them should be viewed as a police matter, of the most urgent kind. As with all criminal fugitives, the essential job is to find out who and where they are. The goal of foreign and military policy must be to induce recalcitrant governments to coöperate, a goal whose attainment may or may not entail the use of force but cannot usefully entail making general war on the peoples such governments rule and in some cases (that of Afghanistan, for example) oppress. Just four months ago, at a time when the whole world was aware both of the general intentions of the terrorist Osama bin Laden and of the fact that the Afghan government was harboring him, the United

States gave the Taliban a forty-three-million-dollar grant for banning poppy cultivation. The United States understands that on September 11th the line between the permissible and the impermissible shifted. The Taliban must be made to understand that, too.

As for America's friends, they have rallied around us with alacrity. On Wednesday, the NATO allies, for the first time ever, invoked the mutual-defense clause of the alliance's founding treaty, formally declaring that "an armed attack" against one—and what happened on September 11th, whether you call it terrorism or war, was certainly an armed attack—constitutes an attack against all. This gesture of solidarity puts to shame the contempt the Bush Administration has consistently shown for international treaties and instruments, including those in areas relevant to the fight against terrorism, such as small-arms control, criminal justice, and nuclear proliferation. By now, it ought to be clear to even the most committed ideologues of the Bush Administration that the unilateralist approach it was pursuing as of last Tuesday is in urgent need of reëvaluation. The world will be policed collectively or it will not be policed at all.

### John Updike

Suddenly summoned to witness something great and horrendous, we keep fighting not to reduce it to our own smallness. From the viewpoint of a tenth-floor apartment in Brooklyn Heights, where I happened to be visiting some kin, the destruction of the World Trade Center twin towers had the false intimacy of television, on a day of perfect reception. A four-year-old girl and her babysitter called from the library, and pointed out through the window the smoking top of the north tower, not a mile away. It seemed, at that first glance, more curious than horrendous: smoke speckled with bits of paper curled into the cloudless sky, and strange inky rivulets ran down the giant structure's vertically corrugated surface. The W.T.C. had formed a pale background to our Brooklyn view of lower Manhattan, not beloved, like the stony, spired midtown thirties skyscrapers it had displaced as the city's tallest, but, with its pre-postmodern combination of unignorable immensity and architectural reticence, in some lights beautiful. As we watched the second tower burst into ballooning flame (an intervening building had hidden the approach of the second airplane), there persisted the notion that, as on television, this was not quite real; it could be fixed; the technocracy the towers symbolized would find a way to put out the fire and reverse the damage.

And then, within an hour, as my wife and I watched from the Brooklyn building's roof, the south tower dropped from the screen of our viewing; it fell straight down like an elevator, with a tinkling shiver and a groan of concussion distinct across the mile of air. We knew we had just witnessed thousands of deaths; we clung to each other as if we ourselves were falling. Amid the glittering impassivity of the many buildings across the East River, an empty spot had appeared, as if by electronic command, beneath the sky that, but for the sulfurous cloud streaming south toward the ocean, was pure blue, rendered uncannily pristine by the absence of jet trails. A swiftly expanding burst of smoke and dust hid the rest of lower Manhattan; we saw the collapse of the second tower only on television, where the footage of hell-bent airplane, exploding jet fuel, and imploding tower was played and replayed, much rehearsed moments from a nightmare ballet.

The nightmare is still on. The bodies are beneath the rubble, the last-minute cell-phone calls—remarkably calm and loving, many of them—are still being reported, the sound of an airplane overhead still bears an unfamiliar menace, the thought of boarding an airplane with our old blasé blitheness keeps receding into the past. Determined men who have transposed their own lives to a martyr's afterlife can still inflict an amount of destruction that defies belief. War is conducted with a fury that requires abstraction—that turns a planeful of peaceful passengers, children included, into a missile the faceless enemy deserves. The other side has the abstractions; we have only the mundane duties of survivors—to pick up the pieces, to bury the dead, to take more precautions, to go on living.

American freedom of motion, one of our prides, has taken a hit. Can we afford the openness that lets future kamikaze pilots, say, enroll in Florida flying schools? A Florida neighbor of one of the suspects remembers him saying he didn't like the United States: "He said it was too lax. He said, 'I can go anywhere I want to, and they can't stop me.'" It is a weird complaint, a begging perhaps to be stopped. Weird, too, the silence of the heavens these days, as flying has ceased across America. But fly again we must; risk is a price of freedom, and walking around Brooklyn Heights that afternoon, as ash drifted in the air and cars were few and open-air lunches continued as usual on Montague Street, renewed the impression that, with all its failings, this is a country worth fighting for. Freedom, reflected in the street's diversity and daily ease, felt palpable. It is mankind's elixir, even if a few turn it to poison.

The next morning, I went back to the open vantage from which we had    5
watched the tower so dreadfully slip from sight. The fresh sun shone on the eastward façades, a few boats tentatively moved in the river, the ruins were still sending out smoke, but New York looked glorious.

**Aharon Appelfeld**\*
**(Translated from the Hebrew by Dina Fein.)**

For almost a year now, Jerusalem has been under siege. Not a day goes by without something terrible happening: a man stabbed in a quiet street, a bomb exploding from a watermelon, a booby-trapped car. Just weeks ago, a suicide bomber blew himself up in the center of town, injuring dozens of innocent people. Shrewd enemies, hidden from sight, are fighting in this city of stone.

Every day, I go to Ticho, my coffee shop, which is in a garden in an old house in the heart of the city. Despite the threat of danger, everyone seems to go out. Often, it seems as if life is able to continue because of the shared illusion that "this won't happen to me." At Ticho, I read a newspaper or a book, or work on a manuscript. In the past, people who recognized me didn't interfere with my privacy. But recently they have stopped to inquire after my health and to ask my opinion of the stressful situation.

I am a writer, not a prophet or a political analyst. Like everyone else, I am groping in this darkness. From a writer, people expect a wise word or a joke. But what can one say when what is happening blunts the few thoughts that one has? I try to overcome the uncertainty by working every day. I am in the middle of a novel, progressing sluggishly, writing and erasing. It seems that the daily disturbances are stronger than internal motivation. It is hard to be with oneself when everything around is burning.

I used to feel that those of us who had suffered in the Holocaust were immune to fear. I was wrong. We are more sensitive to danger. We can smell it. A few days ago, a Holocaust survivor came over to my table and enumerated the dangers ahead of us. During the war, he had been in three death camps. He was a master of dangers. There wasn't a danger that he didn't know in the most minute detail.

The daily disasters evoke images of the Holocaust. Fifty-six years have     5
passed, and the images don't go away. Last night, a man approached me and said that he reads all my books with great diligence. Like me, he was an orphaned child during the war, roaming the forests and taking refuge with farmers. He, too, arrived in Israel. He is an engineer, and he is worried about Jewish destiny. Why do the Jews arouse such hatred? he asked. We had naïvely thought that all the anger and hatred toward us would disappear once we had our own state. I didn't know what to say. I have never dealt in abstract questions—I try to see the world in pictures. And so I kept quiet while he, dismayed, also kept quiet.

After the attack on America, I stayed up all night watching television. It had been a long time since I'd felt such identification with events that were happening so far away. The next day, when I arrived at Ticho, it occurred to me that all of us here were feeling this blow in our flesh. In modern Jewish mythology, America is the father figure who saved many Jews from the cruel Bolsheviks and Nazis by granting us a home. Now the loving father is united with his sons in a Jerusalem coffee shop, in grief over the evil that refuses to disappear from the world.

**Susan Sontag**

The disconnect between last Tuesday's monstrous dose of reality and the self-righteous drivel and outright deceptions being peddled by public figures and TV commentators is startling, depressing. The voices licensed to follow the event seem to have joined together in a campaign to infantilize the public. Where is the acknowledgment that this was not a "cowardly" attack on "civilization" or "liberty" or "humanity" or "the free world" but an attack on the world's self-proclaimed superpower, undertaken as a consequence of specific American alliances and actions? How many citizens are aware of the ongoing American bombing of Iraq? And if the word "cowardly" is to be used, it might be more aptly applied to those who kill from beyond the range of retaliation, high in the sky, than to those willing to die themselves in order to kill others. In the matter of courage (a morally neutral virtue): whatever may be said of the perpetrators of Tuesday's slaughter, they were not cowards.

Our leaders are bent on convincing us that everything is O.K. America is not afraid. Our spirit is unbroken, although this was a day that will live in infamy and America is now at war. But everything is not O.K. And this was not Pearl Harbor. We have a robotic President who assures us that America still stands tall. A wide spectrum of public figures, in and out of office, who are strongly opposed to the policies being pursued abroad by this Administration apparently feel free to say nothing more than that they stand united behind President Bush. A lot of thinking needs to be done, and perhaps is being done in Washington and elsewhere, about the ineptitude of American intelligence and counter-intelligence, about options available to American foreign policy, particularly in the Middle East, and about what constitutes a smart program of military defense. But the public is not being asked to bear much of the burden of reality. The unanimously applauded, self-congratulatory bromides of a Soviet Party Congress seemed contemptible. The unanimity of the sanctimonious, reality-concealing rhetoric spouted by American officials and media commentators in recent days seems, well, unworthy of a mature democracy.

Those in public office have let us know that they consider their task to be a manipulative one: confidence-building and grief management. Politics, the politics of a democracy—which entails disagreement, which promotes candor—has been replaced by psychotherapy. Let's by all means grieve together. But let's not be stupid together. A few shreds of historical awareness might help us understand what has just happened, and what may continue to happen. "Our country is strong," we are told again and again. I for one don't find this entirely consoling. Who doubts that America is strong? But that's not all America has to be.

---

# Beyond Words, without Words, and Finding Words: Responding to the Catastrophe
### John D. French

The catastrophe of September 11th has left us without the words to adequately capture our feelings of shock, anger, and frustration. Yet with each passing day, we are more and more tempted to fill this void through a cheap and easy resort to empty fist shaking and ill-considered words. The current rhetoric of war, vengeance, and retribution, I would suggest, is entirely inadequate to the task of finding ways to express the loss, mourning, and grief in which we find ourselves. Words such as "attack," "war," or the ubiquitous invocation of "Pearl Harbor," now fading, do not plumb the depths of a catastrophe so sudden, unexpected, and ruinous that it can only be experienced as a calamitous fate.

Yet how *are* we to come to terms with what has happened? Daily we are subject to a barrage of images and rhetoric from a media that has done far too little to prepare us for the world in which we live. The proliferation of facile punditry and self-interested posturing has worked to reinforce our collective ignorance rather than help us understand and thus more effectively combat the passions that have so grievously wounded us. We are, after all, only a small part of a world of six billion people that is profoundly divided by power, wealth, culture, and ideology. And we have been betrayed in the last decade by self-satisfied cheerleaders who have suggested that the world is becoming ever more like us — the myth of globalization — or that each and everyone of "them" envies us because they are not like "us." As has often been said, the citizens of the United States are a generous people who will do anything for the rest of the world, except learn about them.

Self-centered flights of fantasy — among which I would count the "new war on terrorism" — are all the more dangerous now because they feed off the anger, confusion, and helplessness that we have all experienced. There are simple truths that have remained unsaid: this is *not* Pearl Harbor, would that it were. And there are no winners to be had, only losers, if we buy into the simplistic imagery and rhetoric of war. I can understand, to a degree, why our political leaders like George W. Bush have been so quick to "reassure" us by emphasizing our supreme military might when wielded with decisiveness and unity.

The truth, however, is that *this* catastrophe speaks to the limits of our power, to the vulnerability we are exposed to *despite* our wealth, our awesome technology, and our status as the world's unchallenged superpower. The deaths of thousands of our fellow citizens and residents stem from the unthinkable. Illusions of invulnerability have collapsed from a deadly combination of the lowest of low-tech weapons wielded with perverse ingenuity by ruthlessly single-minded religious fanatics, a small group of men intoxicated with the desire to punish rather than to convince or convert.

The "terrorism" with a capital "T" that appears on our TV screens tells us much too little of what we need to know about the world, while threatening to morph into an all-encompassing conglomeration of our society's fears and weaknesses, its wounded vanity and pride. The anger that tempts us to embrace the false words we are offered is even more dangerous when it is linked to an older self-righteous colonialist rhetoric pitting "civilization" against "barbarism." Would that the moral lessons of history were so clear and unambiguous.

5

In truth, responsibility for the two greatest global catastrophes of the twentieth century lay neither with the world's "backward" peoples nor with Islam, but rather with the very countries that offered themselves up as "teachers" of civilization and Christianity. After all, it was the self-proclaimed center of western civilization that devastated itself in a paroxysm of violence and destruction twice in a little over a quarter century. The massive slaughter of World War I, which cost 20 million lives, was followed with the 50 million lives lost in World War II, one half of them civilians, and these massacres were made possible only by the very advances in scientific and technological knowledge and industrial organization that are still the source of our inordinate pride today. In view of this history, it should surprise no one that exaggerated claims for "modern civilization" rang and ring so falsely to the world's "backward" peoples and "barbaric" nations. Asked by an English reporter in 1930 his opinion about western civilization, Mahatma Gandhi paused for a moment's reflection, and replied, "That would be a good idea."

We have now lost our illusions that we are immune from the world's passions. Yet the loss of that feeling of untouchability should not be replaced with an even more dangerous illusion: that it is possible to remake the world in order to extinguish its passions. It would be especially tragic if we chose the path of teaching "civilization," once again through soldiers and bombs—a course of action unworthy of those who have died.

Personally, I believe that we should not embrace a rhetoric that gives grandeur to a group of criminals and their conspiracy; it makes him/them our equal and fails completely to understand that even if you killed all of those who made this possible, and all who knowingly financed them, and acted in their support (all 200–300 or so), the truth is that they would still have won on their own terms. These are knowingly and consciously "dead men" and the threat of death—whether in a bombing or a proposed assassination—would in no way constrain or restrain them. Nor would such actions—even if entirely "surgical" with limited "collateral damage" (our favored euphemisms)—eliminate the anxieties, anger and megalomania that create and inspire such groups of religious fanatics.

Theirs is not a political struggle, in a fundamental sense, and they are in this way quite different [from] others who are called "terrorists," which is also why they neither care to minimize civilian deaths nor make even a pretense that they do. They are acting, in their minds, under God's orders, at his command, and for his grandeur and majesty. Moreover, they are not a state and thus can act and calculate without attention to their citizens or subjects.

Although not an absolute pacifist, I strongly agree with my colleague Stanley Hauerwas when he recently suggested that the US should respond to the events of 11 September with a police action whose goal is to identify, arrest, and punish the perpetrators of these crimes. I also strongly believe that it is ill-advised for us to write a blank check to our government, the

10

military, and its associated interests. Rather than embarking on an ill-defined and open-ended "war on terrorism," it would be best to treat the catastrophe as a law enforcement problem of striking international dimension and global reach. They are murderers, not terrorists, and should be treated as such.

In the last few days, I have carefully studied our President's speech to the nation and have found some high points. Unfortunately, it is also characterized by far too much self-righteous bombast and dangerous ambiguities. As a student of many speeches by presidents, prime ministers, and statesman, I found it especially worrisome that President Bush was so careless in his definition of the objectives that we are pursuing. This speech could be a declaration in favor of arresting someone or a blueprint for conquering the world; and I wish that the evidence did not point so strongly towards the more ambitious unilateralist possibility.

Some have said that history is bunk while others have insisted, like Santayana, that those who do not know history are condemned to repeat it. I worry that we are using the wrong words in embarking on a "crusade" in pursuit of "infinite justice." We need to ask the hard questions now, at the outset of this course of action, rather than tumbling forward into an ill-considered adventure. I may be wrong, and I hope that I am, but I do have confidence in the people of the United States who are characterized, above all else, by a pragmatic common sense in their weighing of alternatives. If we speak up, I believe that we can help to guide our leaders away from the dangers involved with the adventure they have proposed in our name. Rather than style my contribution as talking "truth to power," I would suggest that we all must talk "common sense to those with less."

---

## For Discussion

1. "The human race has become . . . a single organism," Hertzberg claims, and the terrorists are like "lethal viruses" loose in that organism's blood stream. Assess his metaphor: Are we becoming "a single organism"? What does the comparison to viruses imply?

2. Both Hertzberg and French resist the rhetoric of war and distrust calling our government's actions "the war on terrorism." What reasons do they give for their resistance? Are you convinced by their arguments? Why or why not? If we call the terrorists "criminals," do we have a better metaphor than, say, "warriors"? Why or why not?

3. Hertzberg, Sontag, and French are all critical of our government's response to 9/11 and critical of the Bush administration's actions before and after it. What do they single out for criticism? What's your assessment of their critiques?

4. Pointing to "an amount of destruction that defies belief," Updike claims that "war is conducted with a fury that requires abstraction." What does he mean? Does war *always* require abstraction on both

sides? Updike says we are left with the concrete, "the mundane duties of survivors," such as burying the dead. Is this true?

5. Understandably, given his own experience, Appelfeld compares 9/11 to the Holocaust. Is this comparison illuminating, more helpful, say, than the analogy to Pearl Harbor?

6. Sontag attributes the attack to "specific American alliances and actions." Based on what you learned in the section "Getting Informed," is there anything to her claim?

7. Sontag claims not to be comforted by assurances that America is strong. "That's not all America has to be," she says. What do you think she has in mind? What else do you think the U.S. should be to handle our present circumstances well?

### For Collaborative Inquiry and Convincing

As a class project, collect as many responses to 9/11 as you can find—from scholars and critics, creative writers, newspaper columnists, politicians, and so on. Isolate their metaphors; that is, discuss the words they are using to characterize 9/11 and events after it. Assess these metaphors in class discussion; consider how they represent and misrepresent reality as your class understands it. Then write a paper defending the language you think best guides our thinking about the event and any actions that might be taken in response to it.

### For Assessing Persuasive Tactics

To say the least, Sontag's statement is provocative. Write an essay assessing it *as persuasion*, using our chapter on "appealing to the whole person." Are there ways that she might have made her points that would have greater appeal? If you think there are, illustrate by rewriting a paragraph or two, making the same point or points but in language that is less deliberately designed to draw fire.

## Arguments: Right and Left

The first two essays in this section are the work of prominent conservative voices; these are balanced against two equally prominent liberal ones. We have the *National Review,* perhaps the best-known organ of the right, pitted against *The Nation,* for a long time a standard-bearer of the left. If we gain nothing else, then, we should at least know what the dividing lines of intellectual conflict are.

What's at stake? Most important, what's at issue is how the United States understands itself. Were we attacked because, as Bennett claims, "we are good," because we "support . . . human rights and democracy" against an evil "militant Islam"? Or were we attacked because of "blowback," the unintended consequences of foreign policies that have nothing to do with our ideals and everything to do with naked self-interest and temporary expediency? Throughout American history we have tended to see ourselves as something special, as better than other nations, as sometimes even the only hope of humankind. But this very assumption of high virtue and of moral and political world leadership has always had its critics, and there is a counter-tradition, also very American, that constantly exposes the dark underside of U.S. policies both domestic and foreign. In other words, our self-concept is conflicted, at once idealistic and skeptical, inclined both to self-glorification and self-hatred.

Closely related to this struggle over what we are is the issue of how we should think. For Bennett and most conservatives, 9/11 should lead to "a moment of moral clarity," in which we can be confident that what we think is good, right, and true really is. There are absolute standards for all three, in-dependent of anyone's interpretation of them. Against this view we have what Fish calls "postmodern relativism," which takes our convictions as rela-tive to our culture, our way of life. We cannot hope, Fish maintains, to jus-tify "our response to the attacks in universal terms that would be persuasive to everyone." We can't claim "justice and truth" because "our adversaries lay claim" to the same virtues. On the one hand, then, we want to say that what we think is *not* just my opinion but also *the* truth; on the other hand, we live in a nation and a world of many cultures and many perspectives within these cultures, and we know that any claim to *the* truth (or good or right) will not go uncontested. Our thinking is as conflicted as our self-concept, full of con-tradiction and opposing impulses.

We hope you will see that there's no easy way out of these contradictions and opposing impulses, that simply flopping to one side or the other, right or left, is not the way to go. Let's listen carefully to all the arguments. Let's take them apart and think them through. Let's be patient with complexity and our own contradictory desires. We won't reason our way to universal agreement about 9/11 and what its consequences should be, but perhaps we can come closer to an intelligent consensus, positions that have the power to convince most thoughtful and well-informed people. That should be our goal even if our arguments fall short of it.

---

## Their Amerika:
## The Song of the "Counter-Tribalists"
### John O'Sullivan

"Who is responsible for the attack on the World Trade Center?" I was asked on *Counterspin*, Canada's version of *Crossfire*.

"The men who hijacked the planes and flew them into the buildings, and those who financed and assisted them," I replied.

It was the wrong answer.

Another guest swiftly explained that though the terrorists were indeed partly to blame, we must understand that they were themselves responding to deeper causes—the general poverty and hopelessness of Afghanistan and

many other Muslim countries, of course, but also America's interventions
in Afghanistan and the Persian Gulf. By joining Pakistan in supporting the
more fundamentalist mujahedin in the 1980s and then leaving postwar Afghanistan to fend for itself, the U.S. had helped to create the Taliban. And
by basing infidel American troops in Saudi Arabia near the Muslim holy
places during the Gulf War, the U.S. drove Osama bin Laden to transform
himself into the Ford Foundation of terrorism. Americans themselves must
therefore accept some of the blame for the terrorist attacks of September 11.

Now, there are reasonable criticisms of U.S. foreign policy embedded         5
in that argument, for my fellow guests on *Counterspin* were in the main reasonable. Even so, that particular mixture of arguments does not even begin
to establish some remote American responsibility for the acts of terrorism.
It slyly implies that the U.S. spontaneously erupted into Afghanistan and
the Gulf, when in fact the U.S. involved itself in Afghanistan in response to
the Soviet occupation of that country, and placed troops in the Gulf to reverse the invasion of Kuwait — acting in both cases at the request of Muslim
and Arab powers. It glosses over the fact that the U.S. was following Pakistan's lead in supporting Afghan fundamentalists for the practical reason
that the U.S., which is not omnipotent, needed Pakistan's help in assisting
the Afghan resistance. And it generally exaggerates America's capacity for either harm or good, by blaming the U.S. for the poverty and backwardness
of Arab and Muslim countries, including Afghanistan, when those evils very
largely stem from the failure of such societies to generate civil institutions,
sensible economic policies, or free democratic governments (or, in the case
of Afghanistan, any kind of stable government at all). In the light of such
persistent systemic failures, it is perverse to blame America for not imposing political and economic enlightenment on these societies — the more so
when we all know that America would instantly be denounced for cultural
imperialism if it tried to do so.

But the Canadian audience did not really want to hear such an excul-
pation. It did not want to place the blame for over 6,000 violent deaths on
the shoulders of the terrorists alone. Nor was this because it was composed
of Muslims or anti-Americans (though there were probably some of both
present). You would have had a very similar reaction from almost any Ivy
League audience. Or from the League of Women Voters. Or from a session
of Americans for Democratic Action. Or from a town meeting in almost any
college town or gentrified urban area in the U.S. For in the Western world
today there is a substantial audience — well short of a majority but still
large — for arguments that combine two factors: a tendency to self-blame
and a taste for complex causal explanations, preferably made still more
complex by social-science jargon.

Examine some of the "anti-American" remarks made since September 11. Here, for instance, is a columnist in the student newspaper at the
University of Michigan. Its author is a young man, of course, but his reflec-
tions mirror more senior academic opinion, as well as the opinions of

Susan Sontag, Michael Moore, and the rest of the usual suspects. If it seems harsh to single him out for criticism here, remember that he will be extravagantly praised by those suspects for his idealism in penning these thoughts:

> If the leadership of this country has its way, a dangerous cycle will be allowed to continue. It is one in which America makes enemies abroad, via broken treaties, unattended summits, and tyrannical international policing. Terrorism follows, allowing leaders to call for appropriations to "fix" our national defense. The cycle needs to end, and it ends at the beginning. Funding the military at this point is a band-aid solution to a more complex problem.

Ah yes, as the English critic John Gross has remarked: "Complexity is the *first* refuge of the scoundrel." If indeed the World Trade Center was attacked because the U.S. withdrew from the Kyoto treaty, then the primary suspects are presumably the German and French "Green" parties, which were the bodies most enthusiastic about it. The Muslim countries were either indifferent to it, or nervously skeptical (some oil-producing countries), or outspokenly hostile (Malaysia). But our student strategist does not wish to place even partial or subsidiary blame for the attack on anyone but America. In his formulation, no one actually *does* the terrorism; it merely "follows" from some prior American beastliness, such as withdrawing from an international conference booming with anti-Semitic rhetoric. The terrorists themselves were not active protagonists in this scenario; they merely went through certain motions that American diplomacy had set in train, like billiard balls clicking over the green baize. But the U.S., when it retaliates, will enjoy no such excuse: Any response to the World Trade Center attack will be seen as a free and premeditated act of "tyrannical international policing."

In the immediate aftermath of the murder of more than 6,000 Americans, such comments have been relatively rare and muted in the U.S. They have been more common abroad: Fintan O'Toole in the *Irish Times* describing the U.S. as "merciless and arrogant"; the British *New Statesman* explaining that the Americans deserved to be bombed because they had voted for Bush, and even Gore, rather than for Ralph Nader; Edward Said in the London *Observer* unmasking the naïve American concepts of "freedom and terrorism" as "large abstractions [that] have mostly hidden sordid material interests, the influence of the oil, defense and Zionist lobbies now consolidating their hold on the entire Middle East, and an age-old religious hostility to (and ignorance of) 'Islam' that takes new forms every day"; an entire stable of *Guardian* writers all piously hoping that Americans will now take the trouble to learn from this painful episode why they are "hated"; and almost all of this vile nonsense written in falsely neutral or sympathetic tones behind which a passionate hostility is barely held in check, like a Freudian psychoanalyst explaining to a patient of whom he is secretly and viciously jealous the valid reasons why no one likes him.

When such comments appear, we are reasonably inclined to describe them as uncomplicatedly "anti-American." But it would be mistaken to

10

see them as exhibiting a foreign nationalist rejection of American influence. Such feelings do exist, of course: sometimes in diplomatic or European bureaucracies, sometimes in intellectual coteries like the High Tory historians who blame the U.S. for the decline of the British Empire. But these are minority reactions. Most anti-American diatribes of the kind quoted above come from people who dislike their own country almost as much as they dislike America. Indeed, their dislike of the U.S. is partly rooted in their perception that America is an obstacle to their hopes of transforming their own societies in a statist, regulated, and bureaucratic direction. By its example, America gives hope to both the organic traditionalist and the spontaneous modernizing elements in their own societies. And, of course, many Americans share the sentiments of those who would reject these American influences—which is why anti-Americanism has been a popular import in certain parts of the U.S. in recent years.

Self-blame and a taste for complexity go very comfortably together to form something I call "counter-tribalism." This is a form of intellectual snobbery. A person in its grip has imbibed the notion that the patriotism of ordinary people is something simplistic, vulgar, and shameful, and thus to be avoided. He has been told that a genuinely sophisticated person—a university professor, say—has thrown off patriotic prejudice to become a citizen of the world. Now, of course, genuine cosmopolitanism is an admirable thing, drawing upon wide cultural sympathies but perfectly compatible with a simple love of country, as the work of any number of poets demonstrates. It is accordingly very rare. So what the counter-tribalist mistakes for cosmopolitanism is an inverted jingoism—an instinctive preference for other nations and a marked prejudice that in any conflict the enemy of America is in the right.

Hence the extraordinary convolutions whereby feminists and multiculturalists find themselves taking the side of medieval Islamists against the common American enemy. They feel more comfortable in such superior company than alongside a hard-hat construction worker or a suburban golfer in plaid pants. But such preferences take some explaining. Hence not merely the taste for—but the absolute necessity of—complex explanations.

And all of this is in service of the notion of separating oneself from one's fellow citizens who are not sophisticated enough to rise above simple loyalties. A wonderful example of such self-infatuation comes from Barbara Kingsolver, commenting on patriotism:

> Patriotism threatens free speech with death. It is infuriated by thoughtful hesitation, constructive criticism of our leaders, and pleas for peace. It despises people of foreign birth who've spent years learning our culture and contributing their talents to our economy . . . In other words, the American flag stands for intimidation, censorship, violence, bigotry, sexism, homophobia and shoving the Constitution through a paper-shredder.

Despite its obvious intellectual deficiencies, counter-tribalism has advanced considerably in recent years. Many of America's troubles stem in part from the fact that it is the first nation with a dissident ruling class. Our elites in government, cultural institutions, the courts, the media, and even business have increasingly adopted the view that the American people are racist, sexist, and homophobic, and that it is therefore a prime duty of government to protect other people from them. In the current crisis, commentators have been predicting a vast national pogrom against American Muslims and have had desperately to exaggerate the relatively few (if shameful) incidents that have occurred to avoid disappointing their readers. In foreign policy, the first instinct of diplomatic elites when faced with a hostile attack is not to "overreact." What makes the situation worse is that the elites have had some success in inculcating counter-tribalism into a large lumpenintelligentsia of teachers, librarians, researchers, small-town-newspaper "liberals," clergymen, and assorted ancillary brainworkers. As journalist Mark Steyn has pointed out, in his own district the local teachers and clergymen were primarily concerned not to allow the reactions of the local people to degenerate into patriotic national sentiment. Twenty years of inculcating multiculturalist clichés into people has made the old expressions of patriotic sentiment seem taboo and even racist to some ears.

Will the terrorist attack change all this? Will it provoke a cultural change    15
in America that will make patriotism seem more natural to the elites? Will it, indeed, mean that a different America will develop a wider and more inclusive patriotism, one more likely to defeat the multicultural platitudes in vogue until recently? All these things are possible. But they will not happen by themselves. In particular, they will not happen without intellectual and moral effort on the part of people who know that patriotism is a virtue perfectly compatible with other virtues such as a genuine easygoing tolerance. Indeed, an American patriotism (and, I would add, a British one) would be among other things a celebration of tolerance. A first step in present circumstances, however, is to reveal the arguments of the counter-tribalists for the shallow, silly, self-regarding snobbery they undoubtedly are.

---

## America Was Attacked Because It Is Good
### William Bennett

In the aftermath of the attacks on the World Trade Center and the Pentagon, the United States will be changed culturally, militarily, politically and psychologically. It is too close to the events of Sept. 11 to understand their full impact. But one certain result is that they have forced us to clarify and answer again universal questions that have been muddled during the past four decades.

Speaking about World War II, C. S. Lewis put it this way: "The war creates no absolutely new situation. It simply aggravates the permanent human situation so that we no longer can ignore it. Human life always has been lived on the edge of a precipice."

For too long, we have ignored the hostility shown toward the United States and democratic principles by *some* Muslims who adhere to a militant and radical interpretation of the Koran. We have created a moral equivalence between Israel and the Palestinians who seek to eradicate Israel. We have ignored Islamic clarion calls for our destruction and the bombings of our embassies and the U.S. destroyer Cole. This situation hasn't changed, but we now realize what the situation is.

This is a moment of moral clarity in the United States. For almost 40 years, we have been a nation that has questioned whether good and evil, right and wrong, true and false really exist. Some—particularly those in our institutions of higher learning and even some inside our own government—have wondered whether the United States really is better than its enemies around the world. After the events of Sept. 11, we no longer should be unsure of such things, even in the academy. We have seen the face and felt the hand of evil. Moral clarity should bring with it moral confidence, and we must be reassured of some things.

Good and evil never have gone away; we merely had the luxury to question their existence. At the beginning of Allan Bloom's classic *The Closing of the American Mind*, he says, "There is one thing a professor can be absolutely certain of: Almost every student entering the university believes, or says he believes, that truth is relative." Can one culture, it was asked, really presume to say what should be the case in other cultures? Are there any cross-cultural values?

Yes. The use of commercial airplanes as missiles, guided into buildings where civilians work, is evil. The goal of the hijackers was the intentional destruction of innocent life so as to strike fear into the hearts of Americans. And what they did was simply wrong.

It has been said that the attacks of Sept. 11 were the inevitable reaction to modern-day U.S. imperialism. They are retribution, it is claimed, for our support of Israel, our attacks on Saddam Hussein or cruise missiles launched at Afghanistan and Sudan.

That is nonsense. The United States' support for human rights and democracy is our noblest export to the world. And when we act in accord with those principles, time after time after time, we act well and honorably. We aren't hated because we support Israel; we are hated because liberal democracy is incompatible with militant Islam.

Despite what Saddam Hussein, Osama bin Laden and, shamefully, some American clerics have said, the United States wasn't punished because we are bad but because we are good.

Therefore, it is past time for what novelist Tom Wolfe has called the "great relearning." We have engaged in a frivolous dalliance with dangerous theories—relativism, historicism and values clarification. Now, when faced with evil on such a grand scale, we should see such theories for what they are: empty. We must begin to have the courage of our convictions, to believe that some actions are good and some evil and to act on those beliefs to prevent evil.

And so we must respond to the attacks of Sept. 11 and prevent future attacks. We do that to protect our own citizens and our own way of life. We do that to protect the idea that good and evil exist and that man is capable of soaring to great heights and sinking to terrible lows. We do that, in the end, to prevent the world from becoming the prisoner of terrorists.

The recognition that some things are right and some things are wrong has come at a terrible cost of thousands of lives lost.

The only comparable tragedy in American history, I believe, was the Civil War. And so we must join in the hopes of our 16th president and pray "that these dead shall not have died in vain, that this nation under God shall have a new birth of freedom and that government of the people, by the people, for the people shall not perish from the Earth."

---

## Condemnation without Absolutes
### Stanley Fish

During the interval between the terrorist attacks and the United States response, a reporter called to ask me if the events of Sept. 11 meant the end of postmodernist relativism. It seemed bizarre that events so serious would be linked causally with a rarefied form of academic talk. But in the days that followed, a growing number of commentators played serious variations on the same theme: that the ideas foisted upon us by postmodern intellectuals have weakened the country's resolve. The problem, according to the critics, is that since postmodernists deny the possibility of describing matters of fact objectively, they leave us with no firm basis for either condemning the terrorist attacks or fighting back.

Not so. Postmodernism maintains only that there can be no independent standard for determining which of many rival interpretations of an event is the true one. The only thing postmodern thought argues against is the hope of justifying our response to the attacks in universal terms that would be persuasive to everyone, including our enemies. Invoking the abstract notions of justice and truth to support our cause wouldn't be effective anyway because our adversaries lay claim to the same language. (No one declares himself to be an apostle of injustice.)

Instead, we can and should invoke the particular lived values that unite us and inform the institutions we cherish and wish to defend.

At times like these, the nation rightly falls back on the record of aspiration and accomplishment that makes up our collective understanding

of what we live for. That understanding is sufficient, and far from undermining its sufficiency, postmodern thought tells us that we have grounds
enough for action and justified condemnation in the democratic ideals we
embrace, without grasping for the empty rhetoric of universal absolutes to
which all subscribe but which all define differently.

But of course it's not really postmodernism that people are bothered
by. It's the idea that our adversaries have emerged not from some primor-
dial darkness, but from a history that has equipped them with reasons and
motives and even with a perverted version of some virtues. Bill Maher, Dinesh D'Souza and Susan Sontag have gotten into trouble by pointing out
that "cowardly" is not the word to describe men who sacrifice themselves
for a cause they believe in.

Ms. Sontag grants them courage, which she is careful to say is a "morally neutral" term, a quality someone can display in the performance of a
bad act. (Milton's Satan is the best literary example.) You don't condone
that act because you describe it accurately. In fact, you put yourself in a better position to respond to it by taking its true measure. Making the enemy
smaller than he is blinds us to the danger he presents and gives him the
advantage that comes along with having been underestimated.

That is why what Edward Said has called "false universals" should be
rejected: they stand in the way of useful thinking. How many times have
we heard these new mantras: "We have seen the face of evil"; "these are irrational madmen"; "we are at war against international terrorism." Each is at
once inaccurate and unhelpful. We have not seen the face of evil; we have
seen the face of an enemy who comes at us with a full roster of grievances,
goals and strategies. If we reduce that enemy to "evil," we conjure up a
shape-shifting demon, a wild-card moral anarchist beyond our comprehension and therefore beyond the reach of any counterstrategies.

The same reduction occurs when we imagine the enemy as "irrational."
Irrational actors are by definition without rhyme or reason, and there's no
point in reasoning about them on the way to fighting them. The better
course is to think of these men as bearers of a rationality we reject because
its goal is our destruction. If we take the trouble to understand that rationality, we might have a better chance of figuring out what its adherents will
do next and preventing it.

And "international terrorism" does not adequately describe what we
are up against. Terrorism is the name of a style of warfare in service of a
cause. It is the cause, and the passions informing it, that confront us. Focusing on something called international terrorism — detached from any specific purposeful agenda — only confuses matters. This should have been evident when President Vladimir Putin of Russia insisted that any war against
international terrorism must have as one of its objectives victory against
the rebels in Chechnya.

When Reuters decided to be careful about using the word "terrorism"
because, according to its news director, one man's terrorist is another man's

freedom fighter, Martin Kaplan, associate dean of the Annenberg School for Communication at the University of Southern California, castigated what he saw as one more instance of cultural relativism. But Reuters is simply recognizing how unhelpful the word is, because it prevents us from making distinctions that would allow us to get a better picture of where we are and what we might do. If you think of yourself as the target of terrorism with a capital T, your opponent is everywhere and nowhere. But if you think of yourself as the target of a terrorist who comes from somewhere, even if he operates internationally, you can at least try to anticipate his future assaults.

Is this the end of relativism? If by relativism one means a cast of mind that renders you unable to prefer your own convictions to those of your adversary, then relativism could hardly end because it never began. Our convictions are by definition preferred; that's what makes them *our* convictions. Relativizing them is neither an option nor a danger.

But if by relativism one means the practice of putting yourself in your adversary's shoes, not in order to wear them as your own but in order to have some understanding (far short of approval) of why someone else might want to wear them, then relativism will not and should not end, because it is simply another name for serious thought.

---

# Blowback

### Chalmers Johnson

For Americans who can bear to think about it, those tragic pictures from New York of women holding up photos of their husbands, sons and daughters and asking if anyone knows anything about them look familiar. They are similar to scenes we have seen from Buenos Aires and Santiago. There, too, starting in the 1970s, women held up photos of their loved ones, asking for information. Since it was far too dangerous then to say aloud what they thought had happened to them—that they had been tortured and murdered by US-backed military juntas—the women coined a new word for them, los *desaparecidos*—"the disappeareds." Our government has never been honest about its own role in the 1973 overthrow of the elected government of Salvador Allende in Chile or its backing, through "Operation Condor," of what the State Department has recently called "extrajudicial killings" in Argentina, Paraguay, Brazil and elsewhere in Latin America. But we now have several thousand of our own disappeareds, and we are badly mistaken if we think that we in the United States are entirely blameless for what happened to them.

The suicidal assassins of September 11, 2001, did not "attack America," as our political leaders and the news media like to maintain; they attacked American foreign policy. Employing the strategy of the weak, they killed innocent bystanders who then became enemies only because they had already become victims. Terrorism by definition strikes at the innocent in order to draw attention to the sins of the invulnerable. The United States deploys such overwhelming military force globally that for its militarized opponents only an "asymmetric strategy," in the jargon of the Pentagon, has any chance of success. When it does succeed, as it did spectacularly on September 11, it renders our massive military machine worthless: The terrorists offer it no targets. On the day of the disaster, President George W. Bush told the American people that we were attacked because we are "a beacon for freedom" and because the attackers were "evil." In his address to Congress on September 20, he said, "This is civilization's fight." This attempt to define difficult-to-grasp events as only a conflict over abstract values—as a "clash of civilizations," in current post-cold war American jargon—is not only disingenuous but also a way of evading responsibility for the "blowback" that America's imperial projects have generated.

"Blowback" is a CIA term first used in March 1954 in a recently declassified report on the 1953 operation to overthrow the government of Mohammed Mossadegh in Iran. It is a metaphor for the unintended consequences of the US government's international activities that have been kept secret from the American people. The CIA's fears that there might ultimately be some blowback from its egregious interference in the affairs of Iran were well founded. Installing the Shah in power brought twenty-five years of tyranny and repression to the Iranian people and elicited the Ayatollah Khomeini's revolution. The staff of the American embassy in Teheran was held hostage for more than a year. This misguided "covert operation" of the US government helped convince many capable people throughout the Islamic world that the United States was an implacable enemy.

The pattern has become all too familiar. Osama bin Laden, the leading suspect as mastermind behind the carnage of September 11, is no more (or less) "evil" than his fellow creations of our CIA: Manuel Noriega, former commander of the Panama Defense Forces until George Bush pere in late 1989 invaded his country and kidnapped him, or Iraq's Saddam Hussein, whom we armed and backed so long as he was at war with Khomeini's Iran and whose people we have bombed and starved for a decade in an incompetent effort to get rid of him. These men were once listed as "assets" of our clandestine services organization.

Osama bin Laden joined our call for resistance to the Soviet Union's           5
1979 invasion of Afghanistan and accepted our military training and equipment along with countless other mujahedeen "freedom fighters." It was only after the Russians bombed Afghanistan back into the stone age and suffered a Vietnam-like defeat, and we turned our backs on the death and destruction we had helped cause, that he turned against us. The last straw as far as bin Laden was concerned was that, after the Gulf War, we based "infidel" American troops in Saudi Arabia to prop up its decadent, fiercely authoritarian regime. Ever since, bin Laden has been attempting to bring the

things the CIA taught him home to the teachers. On September 11, he appears to have returned to his deadly project with a vengeance.

There are today, ten years after the demise of the Soviet Union, some 800 Defense Department installations located in other countries. The people of the United States make up perhaps 4 percent of the world's population but consume 40 percent of its resources. They exercise hegemony over the world directly through overwhelming military might and indirectly through secretive organizations like the World Bank, the International Monetary Fund and the World Trade Organization. Though largely dominated by the US government, these are formally international organizations and therefore beyond Congressional oversight.

As the American-inspired process of "globalization" inexorably enlarges the gap between the rich and the poor, a popular movement against it has gained strength, advancing from its first demonstrations in Seattle in 1999 through protests in Washington, DC; Melbourne; Prague; Seoul; Nice; Barcelona; Quebec City; Goteborg; and on to its violent confrontations in Genoa earlier this year. Ironically, though American leaders are deaf to the desires of the protesters, the Defense Department has actually adopted the movement's main premise—that current global economic arrangements mean more wealth for the "West" and more misery for the "rest"—as a reason why the United States should place weapons in space. The US Space Command's pamphlet "Vision for 2020" argues that "the globalization of the world economy will also continue, with a widening between the 'haves' and the 'have-nots,'" and that we have a mission to "dominate the space dimension of military operations to protect US interests and investments" in an increasingly dangerous and implicitly anti-American world. Unfortunately, while the eyes of military planners were firmly focused on the "control and domination" of space and "denying other countries access to space," a very different kind of space was suddenly occupied.

On the day after the September 11 attack, Democratic Senator Zell Miller of Georgia declared, "I say, bomb the hell out of them. If there's collateral damage, so be it." "Collateral damage" is another of those hateful euphemisms invented by our military to prettify its killing of the defenseless. It is the term Pentagon spokesmen use to refer to the Serb and Iraqi civilians who were killed or maimed by bombs from high-flying American warplanes in our campaigns against Slobodan Milosevic and Saddam Hussein. It is the kind of word our new ambassador to the United Nations, John Negroponte, might have used in the 1980s to explain the slaughter of peasants, Indians and church workers by American-backed right-wing death squads in E1 Salvador, Guatemala, Honduras and Nicaragua while he was ambassador to Honduras. These activities made the Reagan years the worst decade for Central America since the Spanish conquest.

Massive military retaliation with its inevitable "collateral damage" will, of course, create more desperate and embittered childless parents and parentless children, and so recruit more maddened people to the terrorists' cause. In fact, mindless bombing is surely one of the responses their grisly strategy hopes to elicit. Moreover, a major crisis in the Middle East will inescapably cause a rise in global oil prices, with, from the assassins' point of view, desirable destabilizing effects on all the economies of the advanced industrial nations.

What should we do? The following is a start on what, in a better world,    10
we might modestly think about doing. But let me concede at the outset that none of this is going to happen. The people in Washington who run our government believe that they can now get all the things they wanted before the trade towers came down: more money for the military, ballistic missile defenses, more freedom for the intelligence services and removal of the last modest restrictions (no assassinations, less domestic snooping, fewer lists given to "friendly" foreign police of people we want executed) that the Vietnam era placed on our leaders. An inevitable consequence of big "blowback" events like this one is that, the causes having been largely kept from American eyes (if not Islamic or Latin American ones), people cannot make the necessary connections for an explanation. Popular support for Washington is thus, at least for a while, staggeringly high.

Nonetheless, what we should do is to make a serious analytical effort to determine what overseas military commitments make sense and where we should pull in our horns. Although we intend to continue supporting Israel, our new policy should be to urge the dismantling of West Bank Israeli settlements as fast as possible. In Saudi Arabia, we should withdraw our troops, since they do nothing for our oil security, which we can maintain by other means. Beyond the Middle East, in Okinawa, where we have thirty-eight US military bases in the midst of 1.3 million civilians, we should start by bringing home the Third Marine Division and demobilizing it. It is understrength, has no armor and is not up to the standards of the domestically based First and Second Marine Divisions. It has no deterrent value but is, without question, an unwanted burden we force the people of this unlucky island to bear.

A particular obscenity crying out for elimination is the US Army's School of the Americas, founded in Panama in 1946 and moved to Fort Benning, Georgia, in 1984 after Panamanian President Jorge Illueca called it "the biggest base for destabilization in Latin America" and evicted it. Its curriculum includes counterinsurgency, military intelligence, interrogation techniques, sniper fire, infantry and commando tactics, psychological warfare and jungle operations. Although a few members of Congress have long tried to shut it down, the Pentagon and the White House have always found ways to keep it in the budget. In May 2000 the Clinton Administration sought to provide new camouflage for the school by renaming it the "Defense Institute for Hemispheric Security Cooperation" and transferring authority over it from the Army Department to the Defense Department.

The school has trained more than 60,000 military and police officers from Latin American and Caribbean countries. Among SOA's most illustrious graduates are the dictators Manuel Noriega (now serving a forty-year sentence in an American jail for drug trafficking) and Omar Torrijos of Panama; Guillermo Rodrigues of Ecuador; Juan Velasco Alvarado of Peru; Leopoldo Galtieri, former head of Argentina's junta; and Hugo Banzer Suarez of Bolivia. More recently, Peru's Vladimiro Montesinos, SOA class of 1965, surfaced as a CIA asset and former President Alberto Fujimori's closest adviser.

More difficult than these fairly simple reforms would be to bring our rampant militarism under control. From George Washington's "farewell address" to Dwight Eisenhower's invention of the phrase "military-industrial complex," American leaders have warned about the dangers of a bloated, permanent, expensive military establishment that has lost its relationship to the country because service in it is no longer an obligation of citizenship. Our military operates the biggest arms sales operation on earth; it rapes girls, women and schoolchildren in Okinawa; it cuts ski-lift cables in Italy, killing twenty vacationers, and dismisses what its insubordinate pilots have done as a "training accident"; it allows its nuclear attack submarines to be used for joy rides for wealthy civilian supporters and then covers up the negligence that caused the sinking of a Japanese high school training ship; it propagandizes the nation with Hollywood films glorifying military service (Pearl Harbor); and it manipulates the political process to get more carrier task forces, antimissile missiles, nuclear weapons, stealth bombers and other expensive gadgets for which we have no conceivable use. Two of the most influential federal institutions are not in Washington but on the south side of the Potomac River—the Defense Department and the Central Intelligence Agency. Given their influence today, one must conclude that [what] the government outlined in the Constitution of 1787 no longer bears much relationship to the government that actually rules from Washington. Until that is corrected, we should probably stop talking about "democracy" and "human rights."

Once we have done the analysis, brought home most of our "forward deployed" troops, refurbished our diplomatic capabilities, reassured the world that we are not unilateralists who walk away from treaty commitments and reintroduced into government the kinds of idealistic policies we once pioneered (e.g., the Marshall Plan), then we might assess what we can do against "terrorism." We could reduce our transportation and information vulnerabilities by building into our systems more of what engineers call redundancy: different ways of doing the same things—airlines and railroads, wireless and optical fiber communications, automatic computer backup programs, land routes around bridges. It is absurd that our railroads do not even begin to compare with those in Western Europe or Japan, and their inadequacies have made us overly dependent on aviation in travel between US cities. It may well be that some public utilities should be nationalized, just as safety aboard airliners should become a federal function. Flight decks need to be made genuinely inaccessible from the passenger compartments, as they are on El Al. In what might seem a radical change, we could even hire intelligence analysts at the CIA who can read the languages of the countries they are assigned to and have actually visited the places they write about (neither of these conditions is even slightly usual at the present time).

If we do these things, the crisis will recede. If we play into the hands of the terrorists, we will see more collateral damage among our own citizens. Ten years ago, the other so-called superpower, the former Soviet Union, disappeared almost overnight because of internal contradictions, imperial overstretch and an inability to reform. We have always been richer, so it might well take longer for similar contradictions to afflict our society. But it is nowhere written that the United States, in its guise as an empire dominating the world, must go on forever.

---

## For Discussion

1. In your own words, explain what O'Sullivan means by "counter-tribalism." Do you detect any evidence of it at your university? When 9/11 and ifs aftermath was discussed, did you detect in either students or instructors "an instinctive preference for other nations and a marked prejudice" in favor of the views of Islamic extremists?

2. Feminists and multiculturalists, apparently, are prime examples of counter-tribalist sentiment in O'Sullivan's view. What is a feminist? What has the feminist attitude been toward the treatment of women under fundamentalist Muslim rule? What is a multiculturalist? Is multiculturalism incompatible with patriotism?

3. Bennett contends that the 9/11 attack was "simply wrong." Have you heard any serious argument that it was right, that is, morally justified? Is there a difference between *explaining the motivations* that led to the terrorist attack and *claiming that it was morally correct*? Is Bennett confusing the two?

4. What is "relativism"? "Historicism"? "Values clarification"? Bennett claims they are "dangerous theories." What or whom do they endanger? Do you see any connection between Bennett's opposition to them and O'Sullivan's opposition to what he called "counter-tribalism"?

5. "At times like these," Fish claims, "the nation rightly falls back on the record of aspiration and accomplishment that makes up our collective understanding of what we live for." How, according to Fish, is this different from what he calls "the empty rhetoric of universal absolutes"? In your view, is it different? If we "fall back on" our aspirations and accomplishments, can we also claim relativism in the sense Fish endorses, that is, "putting yourself in your adversary's shoes," which he says is "another name for serious thought"?

6. What, according to Fish, is inadequate about the concept of "international terrorism"? When people use this term do they usually "detach [it] from any specific purposeful agenda" and therefore

contribute to confusion and mystification? Is there any harm is using the term simply in contrast to domestic terrorism?

7. "Blowback" is yet another of many metaphors used to characterize 9/11. What evidence does Chalmers Johnson offer that the attack was one of the many "unintended consequences of the U.S. government's international activities"? Is his evidence convincing? Why or why not?

8. Describe in your own words what Johnson thinks would be an appropriate response to 9/11. If carried out, would the threat of terrorism diminish?

## For Collaboration and Inquiry

As a class, collect as much foreign commentary on 9/11 and its aftermath as you can find. Classify the commentary in some useful way: perhaps "clearly anti-American," "pro-American but critical," and "clearly pro-American" will do, but create as many categories as you seem to need.

After thorough class discussion, write an essay exploring those views you consider most helpful for Americans to know. That is, *explore those views that offer insight into how other countries and people understand the United States and Americans.* Whether you agree or not with the views expressed is not the point. The point is "to see ourselves as others see us," to gain self-understanding by reflecting on viewpoints not our own.

Conclude your essay by saying what, if anything, we or our government should do to respond intelligently to foreign criticism. Be sure to distinguish between perceptions you consider valid and those you consider mistaken or the result of ill will or jealousy.

## For Persuasion

By now you should be ready to state and defend your own view of 9/11, including how you think our government and citizens should respond to it. Explain and defend your interpretation of the attack. In accord with your interpretation, recommend a course or courses of action. Make a clear case and support it with sufficient evidence. Also employ the other means of persuasion discussed in Chapter 8. Address your essay to a readership that will not agree or not agree fully with your interpretation and recommended action.

## A Conflict of Cultures?

In this section and the following one, we move beyond 9/11 and its aftermath to related but broader concerns. The question here is: What is the world situation? Are we facing, as Samuel Huntington argues, a "West against the rest" alignment, a new world order that has replaced the Cold War struggle between the U.S. and its allies and the now defunct USSR and its allies? Or do we have what Edward Said argues for in direct and clear opposition to Huntington, a world of intermingling cultures and "bewildering interdependence"?

There are ways to think about the world situation other than the two views represented here. But most recent argument coalesces around one or the other of these two visions. Even if we agree with neither or only parts of both, then, we need to understand them and ponder their consequences.

Huntington is the Eaton Professor of the Science of Government and Director of the John M. Olin Institute for Strategic Studies at Harvard University. We offer here an excerpt from his influential article. "The Clash of Civilizations?" published in *Foreign Affairs* (Summer 1993). Said is University Professor of English and Comparative Literature at Columbia University. His critique of Huntington appeared in *The Nation* (October 22, 2001).

---

## The Clash of Civilizations?
### Samuel P. Huntington

### The Next Pattern of Conflict

World politics is entering a new phase, and intellectuals have not hesitated to proliferate visions of what it will be—the end of history, the return of traditional rivalries between nation states, and the decline of the nation state from the conflicting pulls of tribalism and globalism, among others. Each of these visions catches aspects of the emerging reality. Yet they all miss a crucial, indeed a central, aspect of what global politics is likely to be in the coming years.

It is my hypothesis that the fundamental source of conflict in this new world will not be primarily ideological or primarily economic. The great divisions among humankind and the dominating source of conflict will be cultural. Nation states will remain the most powerful actors in world affairs, but the principal conflicts of global politics will occur between nations and groups of different civilizations. The clash of civilizations will dominate global politics. The fault lines between civilizations will be the battle lines of the future. . . .

### The Nature of Civilizations

During the Cold War the world was divided into the First, Second and Third Worlds. Those divisions are no longer relevant. It is far more meaningful now to group countries not in terms of their political or economic systems or in terms of their level of economic development but rather in terms of their culture and civilization.

What do we mean when we talk of a civilization? A civilization is a cultural entity. Villages, regions, ethnic groups, nationalities, religious groups, all have distinct cultures at different levels of cultural heterogeneity. The culture of a village in southern Italy may be different from that of a village in northern Italy, but both will share in a common Italian culture that distinguishes them from German villages. European communities, in turn, will share cultural features that distinguish them from Arab or Chinese communities. Arabs, Chinese and Westerners, however, are not part of any broader cultural entity. They constitute civilizations. A civilization is thus the highest cultural grouping of people and the broadest level of cultural identity people have short of that which distinguishes humans from other species. It is defined both by common objective elements, such as language, history, religion, customs, institutions, and by the subjective self-identification of people. People have levels of identity: a resident of Rome may define himself with varying degrees of intensity as a Roman, an Italian, a Catholic, a Christian, a European, a Westerner. The civilization to which he belongs is the broadest level of identification with which he intensely identifies. People can and do redefine their identities and, as a result, the composition and boundaries of civilizations change. . . .

### Why Civilizations Will Clash

Civilization identity will be increasingly important in the future, and the    5
world will be shaped in large measure by the interactions among seven or eight major civilizations. These include Western, Confucian, Japanese, Islamic, Hindu, Slavic-Orthodox, Latin American and possibly African civilization. The most important conflicts of the future will occur along the cultural fault lines separating these civilizations from one another.

Why will this be the case?

First, differences among civilizations are not only real; they are basic. Civilizations are differentiated from each other by history, language, culture, tradition and, most important, religion. The people of different civilizations have different views on the relations between God and man, the individual and the group, the citizen and the state, parents and children, husband and wife, as well as differing views of the relative importance of rights and responsibilities, liberty and authority, equality and hierarchy. These differences are the product of centuries. They will not soon disappear. They are far more fundamental than differences among political ideologies and political regimes. Differences do not necessarily mean conflict, and conflict does not necessarily mean violence. Over the centuries, however, differences among civilizations have generated the most prolonged and the most violent conflicts.

Second, the world is becoming a smaller place. The interactions between peoples of different civilizations are increasing; these increasing interactions intensify civilization consciousness and awareness of differences between civilizations and commonalities within civilizations. North African immigration to France generates hostility among Frenchmen and at the same time increased receptivity to immigration by "good" European Catholic Poles. Americans react far more negatively to Japanese investment than to larger investments from Canada and European countries. Similarly, as Donald Horowitz has pointed out, "An Ibo may be . . . an Owerri Ibo or an Onitsha Ibo in what was the Eastern region of Nigeria. In Lagos, he is simply an Ibo. In London, he is a Nigerian. In New York, he is an African." The interactions among peoples of different civilizations enhance the civilization-consciousness of people that, in turn, invigorates differences and animosities stretching or thought to stretch back deep into history.

Third, the processes of economic modernization and social change throughout the world are separating people from longstanding local identities. They also weaken the nation state as a source of identity. In much of the world religion has moved in to fill this gap, often in the form of movements that are labeled "fundamentalist." Such movements are found in Western Christianity, Judaism, Buddhism and Hinduism, as well as in Islam. In most countries and most religions the people active in fundamentalist movements are young, college-educated, middle-class technicians, professionals and business persons. The "unsecularization of the world," George Weigel has remarked, "is one of the dominant social facts of life in the late twentieth century." The revival of religion, "la revanche de Dieu," as Gilles Kepel labeled it, provides a basis for identity and commitment that transcends national boundaries and unites civilizations.

Fourth, the growth of civilization-consciousness is enhanced by the dual role of the West. On the one hand, the West is at a peak of power. At the same time, however, and perhaps as a result, a return to the roots phenomenon is occurring among non-Western civilizations. Increasingly one hears references to trends toward a turning inward and "Asianization" in Japan, the end of the Nehru legacy and the "Hinduization" of India, the failure of Western ideas of socialism and nationalism and hence "re-Islamization" of the Middle East, and now a debate over Westernization versus Russianization in Boris Yeltsin's country. A West at the peak of its power confronts non-Wests that increasingly have the desire, the will and the resources to shape the world in non-Western ways.

In the past, the elites of non-Western societies were usually the people who were most involved with the West, had been educated at Oxford, the Sorbonne or Sandhurst, and had absorbed Western attitudes and values. At the same time, the populace in non-Western countries often remained deeply imbued with the indigenous culture. Now, however, these relationships are being reversed. A de-Westernization and indigenization of elites is occurring in many non-Western countries at the same time that Western, usually American, cultures, styles and habits become more popular among the mass of the people.

Fifth, cultural characteristics and differences are less mutable and hence less easily compromised and resolved than political and economic ones. In the former Soviet Union, communists can become democrats, the rich can become poor and the poor rich, but Russians cannot become Estonians and

10

Azeris cannot become Armenians. In class and ideological conflicts, the key question was "Which side are you on?" and people could and did choose sides and change sides. In conflicts between civilizations, the question is "What are you?" That is a given that cannot be changed. And as we know, from Bosnia to the Caucasus to the Sudan, the wrong answer to that question can mean a bullet in the head. Even more than ethnicity, religion discriminates sharply and exclusively among people. A person can be half-French and half-Arab and simultaneously even a citizen of two countries. It is more difficult to be half-Catholic and half-Muslim. . . .

## The Fault Lines Between Civilizations

The fault lines between civilizations are replacing the political and ideological boundaries of the Cold War as the flash points for crisis and bloodshed. The Cold War began when the Iron Curtain divided Europe politically and ideologically. The Cold War ended with the end of the Iron Curtain. As the ideological division of Europe has disappeared, the cultural division of Europe between Western Christianity, on the one hand, and Orthodox Christianity and Islam, on the other, has reemerged. . . .

Conflict along the fault line between Western and Islamic civilizations has been going on for 1,300 years. After the founding of Islam, the Arab and Moorish surge west and north only ended at Tours in 732. From the eleventh to the thirteenth century the Crusaders attempted with temporary success to bring Christianity and Christian rule to the Holy Land. From the fourteenth to the seventeenth century, the Ottoman Turks reversed the balance, extended their sway over the Middle East and the Balkans, captured Constantinople, and twice laid siege to Vienna. In the nineteenth and early twentieth centuries as Ottoman power declined Britain, France, and Italy established Western control over most of North Africa and the Middle East.

After World War II, the West, in turn, began to retreat; the colonial empires disappeared; first Arab nationalism and then Islamic fundamentalism manifested themselves; the West became heavily dependent on the Persian Gulf countries for its energy; the oil-rich Muslim countries became money-rich and, when they wished to, weapons-rich. Several wars occurred between Arabs and Israel (created by the West). France fought a bloody and ruthless war in Algeria for most of the 1950s; British and French forces invaded Egypt in 1956; American forces went into Lebanon in 1958; subsequently American forces returned to Lebanon, attacked Libya, and engaged in various military encounters with Iran; Arab and Islamic terrorists, supported by at least three Middle Eastern governments, employed the weapon of the weak and bombed Western planes and installations and seized Western hostages. This warfare between Arabs and the West culminated in 1990, when the United States sent a massive army to the Persian Gulf to defend some Arab countries against aggression by another. In its aftermath NATO planning is increasingly directed to potential threats and instability along its "southern tier." 15

This centuries-old military interaction between the West and Islam is unlikely to decline. It could become more virulent. The Gulf War left some Arabs feeling proud that Saddam Hussein had attacked Israel and stood up to the West. It also left many feeling humiliated and resentful of the West's military presence in the Persian Gulf, the West's overwhelming military dominance, and their apparent inability to shape their own destiny. Many Arab countries, in addition to the oil exporters, are reaching levels of economic and social development where autocratic forms of government become inappropriate and efforts to introduce democracy become stronger. Some openings in Arab political systems have already occurred. The principal beneficiaries of these openings have been Islamist movements. In the Arab world, in short, Western democracy strengthens anti-Western political forces. This may be a passing phenomenon, but it surely complicates relations between Islamic countries and the West.

Those relations are also complicated by demography. The spectacular population growth in Arab countries, particularly in North Africa, has led to increased migration to Western Europe. The movement within Western Europe toward minimizing internal boundaries has sharpened political sensitivities with respect to this development. In Italy, France and Germany, racism is increasingly open, and political reactions and violence against Arab and Turkish migrants have become more intense and more widespread since 1990.

On both sides the interaction between Islam and the West is seen as a clash of civilizations. The West's "next confrontation," observes M. J. Akbar, an Indian Muslim author, "is definitely going to come from the Muslim world. It is in the sweep of the Islamic nations from the Maghreb to Pakistan that the struggle for a new world order will begin." Bernard Lewis comes to a similar conclusion:

> We are facing a mood and a movement far transcending the level of issues and policies and the governments that pursue them. This is no less than a clash of civilizations—the perhaps irrational but surely historic reaction of an ancient rival against our Judeo-Christian heritage, our secular present, and the world wide expansion of both.[1] . . .

# The Clash of Ignorance
## Edward W. Said

Samuel Huntington's article. "The Clash of Civilizations?" appeared in the Summer 1993 issue of *Foreign Affairs*, where it immediately attracted a surprising amount of attention and reaction. Because the article was

---

[1] Bernard Lewis, "The Roots of Muslim Rage," *The Atlantic Monthly,* vol. 266, September 1990, p. 60; *Time,* June 15, 1992, pp. 24–28.

intended to supply Americans with an original thesis about "a new phase" in world politics after the end of the cold war, Huntington's terms of argument seemed compellingly large, bold, even visionary. He very clearly had his eye on rivals in the policy-making ranks, theorists such as Francis Fukuyama and his "end of history" ideas, as well as the legions who had celebrated the onset of globalism, tribalism and the dissipation of the state. But they, he allowed, had understood only some aspects of this new period. He was about to announce the "crucial, indeed a central, aspect" of what "global politics is likely to be in the coming years." Unhesitatingly he pressed on:

"It is my hypothesis that the fundamental source of conflict in this new world will not be primarily ideological or primarily economic. The great divisions among humankind and the dominating source of conflict will be cultural. Nation states will remain the most powerful actors in world affairs, but the principal conflicts of global politics will occur between nations and groups of different civilizations. The clash of civilizations will dominate global politics. The fault lines between civilizations will be the battle lines of the future."

Most of the argument in the pages that followed relied on a vague notion of something Huntington called "civilization identity" and "the interactions among seven or eight [sic] major civilizations," of which the conflict between two of them, Islam and the West, gets the lion's share of his attention. In this belligerent kind of thought, he relies heavily on a 1990 article by the veteran Orientalist Bernard Lewis, whose ideological colors are manifest in its title, "The Roots of Muslim Rage." In both articles, the personification of enormous entities called "the West" and "Islam" is recklessly affirmed, as if hugely complicated matters like identity and culture existed in a cartoonlike world where Popeye and Bluto bash each other mercilessly, with one always more virtuous pugilist getting the upper hand over his adversary. Certainly neither Huntington nor Lewis has much time to spare for the internal dynamics and plurality of every civilization, or for the fact that the major contest in most modern cultures concerns the definition or interpretation of each culture, or for the unattractive possibility that a great deal of demagogy and downright ignorance is involved in presuming to speak for a whole religion or civilization. No, the West is the West, and Islam Islam.

The challenge for Western policy-makers, says Huntington, is to make sure that the West gets stronger and fends off all the others, Islam in particular. More troubling is Huntington's assumption that his perspective, which is to survey the entire world from a perch outside all ordinary attachments and hidden loyalties, is the correct one, as if everyone else were scurrying around looking for the answers that he has already found. In fact, Huntington is an ideologist, someone who wants to make "civilizations" and "identities" into what they are not: shut-down, sealed-off entities that have been purged of the myriad currents and countercurrents that animate human history, and that over centuries have made it possible for that history not only to contain wars of religion and imperial conquest but also to be one of exchange, cross-fertilization and sharing. This far less visible history is ignored in the rush to highlight the ludicrously compressed and constricted warfare that "the clash of civilizations" argues is the reality. When he published his book by the same title in 1996, Huntington tried to give his argument a little more subtlety and many, many more footnotes; all he did, however, was confuse himself and demonstrate what a clumsy writer and inelegant thinker he was.

The basic paradigm of West versus the rest (the cold war opposition reformulated) remained untouched, and this is what has persisted, often insidiously and implicitly, in discussion since the terrible events of September 11. The carefully planned and horrendous, pathologically motivated suicide attack and mass slaughter by a small group of deranged militants has been turned into proof of Huntington's thesis. Instead of seeing it for what it is—the capture of big ideas (I use the word loosely) by a tiny band of crazed fanatics for criminal purposes—international luminaries from former Pakistani Prime Minister Benazir Bhutto to Italian Prime Minister Silvio Berlusconi have pontificated about Islam's troubles, and in the latter's case have used Huntington's ideas to rant on about the West's superiority, how "we" have Mozart and Michelangelo and they don't. (Berlusconi has since made a half-hearted apology for his insult to "Islam.")

But why not instead see parallels, admittedly less spectacular in their destructiveness, for Osama bin Laden and his followers in cults like the Branch Davidians or the disciples of the Rev. Jim Jones at Guyana or the Japanese Aum Shinrikyo? Even the normally sober British weekly *The Economist*, in its issue of September 22–28, can't resist reaching for the vast generalization, praising Huntington extravagantly for his "cruel and sweeping, but nonetheless acute" observations about Islam. "Today," the journal says with unseemly solemnity, Huntington writes that "the world's billion or so Muslims are 'convinced of the superiority of their culture, and obsessed with the inferiority of their power.'" Did he canvas 100 Indonesians, 200 Moroccans, 500 Egyptians and fifty Bosnians? Even if he did, what sort of sample is that?

Uncountable are the editorials in every American and European newspaper and magazine of note adding to this vocabulary of gigantism and apocalypse, each use of which is plainly designed not to edify but to inflame the reader's indignant passion as a member of the "West," and what we need to do. Churchillian rhetoric is used inappropriately by self-appointed combatants in the West's, and especially America's, war against its haters, despoilers, destroyers, with scant attention to complex histories that defy such reductiveness and have seeped from one territory into another, in the process overriding the boundaries that are supposed to separate us all into divided armed camps.

This is the problem with unedifying labels like Islam and the West: They mislead and confuse the mind, which is trying to make sense of a disorderly reality that won't be pigeonholed or strapped down as easily as all that. I remember interrupting a man who, after a lecture I had given at a West Bank university in 1994, rose from the audience and started to attack my ideas as "Western," as opposed to the strict Islamic ones he espoused. "Why are you wearing a suit and tie?" was the first retort that came to mind. "They're Western too." He sat down with an embarrassed smile on his face, but I recalled the incident when information on the September 11 terrorists started to come in: how they had mastered all the technical details required to inflict their homicidal evil on the World Trade Center, the Pentagon and the aircraft they had commandeered. Where does one draw the line between "Western" technology and, as Berlusconi declared, "Islam's" inability to be a part of "modernity"?

One cannot easily do so, of course. How finally inadequate are the labels, generalizations and cultural assertions. At some level, for instance, primitive passions and sophisticated know-how converge in ways that give the lie to a fortified boundary not only between "West" and "Islam" but also between past and present, us and them, to say nothing of the very concepts of identity and nationality about which there is unending disagreement and debate. A unilateral decision made to draw lines in the sand, to undertake crusades, to oppose their evil with our good, to extirpate terrorism and, in Paul Wolfowitz's nihilistic vocabulary, to end nations entirely, doesn't make the supposed entities any easier to see; rather, it speaks to how much simpler it is to make bellicose statements for the purpose of mobilizing collective passions than to reflect, examine, sort out what it is we are dealing with in reality, the interconnectedness of innumerable lives, "ours" as well as "theirs."

In a remarkable series of three articles published between January and March 1999 in *Dawn*, Pakistan's most respected weekly, the late Eqbal Ahmad, writing for a Muslim audience, analyzed what he called the roots of the religious right, coming down very harshly on the mutilations of Islam by absolutists and fanatical tyrants whose obsession with regulating personal behavior promotes "an Islamic order reduced to a penal code, stripped of its humanism, aesthetics, intellectual quests, and spiritual devotion." And this "entails an absolute assertion of one, generally de-contextualized, aspect of religion and a total disregard of another. The phenomenon distorts religion, debases tradition, and twists the political process wherever it unfolds." As a timely instance of this debasement, Ahmad proceeds first to present the rich, complex, pluralist meaning of the word *jihad* and then goes on to show that in the word's current confinement to indiscriminate war against presumed enemies, it is impossible "to recognize the Islamic — religion, society, culture, history or politics — as lived and experienced by Muslims through the ages." The modern Islamists, Ahmad concludes, are "concerned with power, not with the soul; with the mobilization of people for political purposes rather than with sharing and alleviating their sufferings and aspirations. Theirs is a very limited and time-bound political

10

agenda." What has made matters worse is that similar distortions and zealotry occur in the "Jewish" and "Christian" universes of discourse.

It was Conrad, more powerfully than any of his readers at the end of the nineteenth century could have imagined, who understood that the distinctions between civilized London and "the heart of darkness" quickly collapsed in extreme situations, and that the heights of European civilization could instantaneously fall into the most barbarous practices without preparation or transition. And it was Conrad also, in *The Secret Agent* (1907), who described terrorism's affinity for abstractions like "pure science" (and by extension for "Islam" or "the West"), as well as the terrorist's ultimate moral degradation.

For there are closer ties between apparently warring civilizations than most of us would like to believe; both Freud and Nietzsche showed how the traffic across carefully maintained, even policed boundaries moves with often terrifying ease. But then such fluid ideas, full of ambiguity and skepticism about notions that we hold on to, scarcely furnish us with suitable, practical guidelines for situations such as the one we face now. Hence the altogether more reassuring battle orders (a crusade, good versus evil, freedom against fear, etc.) drawn out of Huntington's alleged opposition between Islam and the West, from which official discourse drew its vocabulary in the first days after the September 11 attacks. There's since been a noticeable de-escalation in that discourse, but to judge from the steady amount of hate speech and actions, plus reports of law enforcement efforts directed against Arabs, Muslims and Indians all over the country, the paradigm stays on.

One further reason for its persistence is the increased presence of Muslims all over Europe and the United States. Think of the populations today of France, Italy, Germany, Spain, Britain, America, even Sweden, and you must concede that Islam is no longer on the fringes of the West but at its center. But what is so threatening about that presence? Buried in the collective culture are memories of the first great Arab-Islamic conquests, which began in the seventh century and which, as the celebrated Belgian historian Henri Pirenne wrote in his landmark book *Mohammed and Charlemagne* (1939), shattered once and for all the ancient unity of the Mediterranean, destroyed the Christian-Roman synthesis and gave rise to a new civilization dominated by northern powers (Germany and Carolingian France) whose mission, he seemed to be saying, is to resume defense of the "West" against its historical-cultural enemies. What Pirenne left out, alas, is that in the creation of this new line of defense the West drew on the humanism, science, philosophy, sociology and historiography of Islam, which had already interposed itself between Charlemagne's world and classical antiquity. Islam is inside from the start, as even Dante, great enemy of Mohammed, had to concede when he placed the Prophet at the very heart of his *Inferno*.

Then there is the persisting legacy of monotheism itself, the Abrahamic religions, as Louis Massignon aptly called them. Beginning with Judaism and

Christianity, each is a successor haunted by what came before; for Muslims, Islam fulfills and ends the line of prophecy. There is still no decent history or demystification of the many-sided contest among these three follow-ers—not one of them by any means a monolithic, unified camp—of the most jealous of all gods, even though the bloody modern convergence on Palestine furnishes a rich secular instance of what has been so tragically ir-reconcilable about them. Not surprisingly, then, Muslims and Christians speak readily of crusades and *jihads*, both of them eliding the Judaic pres-ence with often sublime insouciance. Such an agenda, says Eqbal Ahmad, is "very reassuring to the men and women who are stranded in the middle of the ford, between the deep waters of tradition and modernity."

But we are all swimming in those waters, Westerners and Muslims and     15 others alike. And since the waters are part of the ocean of history, trying to plow or divide them with barriers is futile. These are tense times, but it is better to think in terms of powerful and powerless communities, the secu-lar politics of reason and ignorance, and universal principles of justice and injustice, than to wander off in search of vast abstractions that may give momentary satisfaction but little self-knowledge or informed analysis. "The Clash of Civilizations" thesis is a gimmick like "The War of the Worlds," better for reinforcing defensive self-pride than for critical understanding of the bewildering interdependence of our time.

---

## For Discussion

1. According to Huntington, what is a civilization? Is a civilization the same thing as a culture?

2. On the one hand, Huntington says that "people can and do redefine their identities," so that "the composition and boundaries of civiliza-tion change." On the other hand, he also says that "cultural charac-teristics and differences are less mutable . . . than political and eco-nomic ones," that "in the former Soviet Union, communists can become democrats . . . but Russians cannot become Estonians." Are these statements contradictory? Are some aspects of our identity more resistant to change than others? If so, why?

3. What does Huntington mean by "fault lines" between civilizations? What mental image does this geological metaphor create? What does it imply? Does 9/11 call this metaphor into question, since the at-tack took place in New York and Washington and not near the "fault zones" in the Middle and Far East?

4. At the very end of our excerpt from Huntington's article, he cites Ber-nard Lewis, who refers to "the *perhaps irrational* but surely historic re-action of an ancient rival [that is, Islam] against our Judeo-Christian heritage" (our emphasis). This raises the uncomfortable possibility that the forces of history might be quite counter to reason and there-fore unapproachable by reason. That is, "the West" and "the Muslim

world" cannot resolve or reduce their differences by rational negotiation but only by some form of force. What do you think? Are the
differences irrational, basically ancient animosities, or are they rational and capable of being mediated?

5. What does Said mean by the "pluralism of civilizations"? How plu-
ralistic is the U.S.? Has our governmental response to 9/11 showed
our pluralism? Does Huntington show any awareness of the pluralism Said points to?

6. Without evidence, Said claims that Huntington in his 1996 book is
"a clumsy writer and inelegant thinker." How would you explain this
personal attack? That is, what is it about Said's viewpoint that makes
him openly hostile to Huntington's theory? Is the hostility based on
political differences, Said being influential on the liberal side, Huntington on the conservative side? Or is it more than that?

7. Said claims that "there are closer ties between apparently warring
civilizations than most of us would like to believe." What evidence
does he cite for these "closer ties"?

8. "We are all swimming in these waters," Said claims in his last paragraph, giving us yet another metaphor for our situation, one quite
different from "fault lines." Which metaphor do you find the more
attractive? Why?

## For Collaboration and Group Inquiry

Huntington's "clash of civilizations" theory has led to a wealth of commentary, positive, negative, and mixed. As a class, collect a dozen or so responses
and sort them out, first by quality, preserving the best, and then by the stance
each takes toward Huntington. Then, in class discussion, attempt to isolate
the best points made by each writer, and ponder these carefully. Do you see
a class consensus forming about the value of Huntington's theory? If not,
what are the lines of disagreement? That is, why do some favor Huntington
while others do not?

## Conclusion: Two Philosophical Interpretations

The following essays offer answers to two key questions: Who is the enemy?
and, How should we think about the fate of civilizations, including our own?
The well-known conservative columnist, Charles Krauthammer, contends
that the enemy is *nihilism*, which the *Scribner Dictionary* defines as "total rejection of all existing political and social institutions and traditional religious
and moral values." Behind nihilism with a small *n* is Nihilism with a capital *N*,
which the same dictionary glosses as "a revolutionary movement in Russia in
the late nineteenth century that opposed existing institutions and advocated
the use of assassination and terrorism." Historically, then, nihilism and terrorist tactics are connected, and it's not hard to see how: If we reject *all* existing structures, then, in the words of the *Bhagavad Gita*, we "are become death,
the destroyer of worlds." What else could a committed nihilist be and do?

So far as the fate of civilizations is concerned, history offers an unambiguous answer: They are mortal; they are born, flourish, and die, just as individual human beings do but over a longer span of time. James Atlas, writing in the *New York Times* (October 7, 2001), wants us to ponder not just our own individual deaths, which nearly everyone did after 9/11, but also the deaths of our country and our civilization. Why? Somewhat paradoxically because "acknowledging the inevitable transience and brevity of our own historical epoch could be the key to ensuring its long duration." If we realize the fragility of all that seems so permanent, we lose our blinding arrogance and can approach the challenges of the moment with deeper care.

These are somber thoughts for the conclusion of a somber topic. What they tell us, beyond their own particular viewpoints, is that we should not get too caught up in the flow of events, thinking only in terms of the latest headlines and theories. We need perspectives beyond the details of the moment, ways of thinking that provide a place for everything, including the horror of 9/11 and all the unforeseeable events that flow from it.

---

## The Enemy Is Not Islam: It Is Nihilism
### Charles Krauthammer

Europe's great religious wars ended in 1648. Three and a half centuries is a long time, too long for us in the West to truly believe that people still slaughter others to vindicate the faith.

Thus in the face of radical Islamic terrorism that murders 6,000 innocents in a day, we find it almost impossible to accept at face value the reason offered by the murderers. Yet Osama bin Laden could not be clearer. Jihad has been declared against the infidel, whose power and influence thwart the triumph of Islam, and whose success and example—indeed, whose very existence—are an affront to the true faith. As a leader of Hamas declared at a rally three days after the World Trade Center attack, "the only solution is for Bush to convert to Islam."

To Americans, who are taught religious tolerance from the cradle, who visit each other's churches for interdenominational succor and solidarity, this seems simply bizarre. On September 25, bin Laden issues a warning to his people that Bush is coming "under the banner of the cross." Two weeks later, in his pre-taped post-attack video, he scorns Bush as "head of the infidels."

Can he be serious? This idea is so alien that our learned commentators, Western and secular, have gone rummaging through their ideological attics to find more familiar terms to explain why we were so savagely attacked: poverty and destitution in the Islamic world; grievances against the West, America, Israel; the "wretched of the earth"—Frantz Fanon's 1960s apotheosis of anti-colonialism—rising against their oppressors.

Reading conventional notions of class struggle and anti-colonialism into bin Laden, the Taliban, and radical Islam is not just solipsistic. It is nonsense. If poverty and destitution, colonialism and capitalism are animating radical Islam, explain this: In March, the Taliban went to the Afghan desert where stood great monuments of human culture, two massive Buddhas carved out of a cliff. At first, Taliban soldiers tried artillery. The 1,500-year-old masterpieces proved too hardy. The Taliban had to resort to dynamite. They blew the statues to bits, then slaughtered 100 cows in atonement—for having taken so long to finish the job.

Buddhism is hardly a representative of the West. It is hardly a cause of poverty and destitution. It is hardly a symbol of colonialism. No. The statues represented two things: an alternative faith and a great work of civilization. To the Taliban, the presence of both was intolerable.

The distinguished Indian writer and now Nobel Prize winner V. S. Naipaul, who has chronicled the Islamic world in two books (*Among the Believers* and *Beyond Belief*), recently warned (in a public talk in Melbourne before the World Trade Center attack), "We are within reach of great nihilistic forces that have undone civilization." In places like Afghanistan, "religion has been turned by some into a kind of nihilism, where people wish to destroy themselves and destroy their past and their culture . . . to be pure. They are enraged about the world and they wish to pull it down." This kind of fury and fanaticism is unappeasable. It knows no social, economic, or political solution. "You cannot converge with this [position] because it holds that your life is worthless and your beliefs are criminal and should be extirpated."

This insight offers a needed window on the new enemy. It turns out that the enemy does have recognizable analogues in the Western experience. He is, as President Bush averred in his address to the nation, heir to the malignant ideologies of the 20th century. In its nihilism, its will to power, its celebration of blood and death, its craving for the cleansing purity that comes only from eradicating life and culture, radical Islam is heir, above all, to Nazism. The destruction of the World Trade Center was meant not only to wreak terror. Like the smashing of the Bamiyan Buddhas, it was meant to obliterate greatness and beauty, elegance and grace. These artifacts represented civilization embodied in stone or steel. They had to be destroyed.

This worship of death and destruction is a nihilism of a ferocity unlike any since the Nazis burned books, then art, then whole peoples. Goebbels would have marvelled at the recruitment tape for al Qaeda, a two-hour orgy of blood and death: image after image of brutalized Muslims shown in various poses of victimization, followed by glorious images of desecration of the infidel—mutilated American soldiers in Somalia, the destruction of the USS *Cole*, mangled bodies at the American embassies in Kenya and Tanzania. Throughout, the soundtrack endlessly repeats the refrain "with blood, with blood, with blood." Bin Laden appears on the tape to counsel that "the love of this world is wrong. You should love the other world . . . die in the right cause and go to the other world." In his October 9 taped message, al Qaeda spokesman Sulaiman abu Ghaith gloried in the "thousands of young people who look forward to death, like the Americans look forward to living."

Once again, the world is faced with a transcendent conflict between those who love life and those who love death both for themselves and their enemies. Which is why we tremble. Upon witnessing the first atomic bomb explode at the Trinity site at Alamogordo, J. Robert Oppenheimer recited a verse from the Hindu scripture *Bhagavad Gita:* "Now I am become death, the destroyer of worlds." We tremble because for the first time in history, nihilism will soon be armed with the ultimate weapons of annihilation. For the first time in history, the nihilist will have the means to match his ends. Which is why the war declared upon us on September 11 is the most urgent not only of our lives, but in the life of civilization itself.

10

---

## Among the Lost: Illusions of Immortality

### James Atlas

On Sept. 11, as innumerable commentators have noted, the death toll in the World Trade Center bombing was greater than at the Battle of Antietam; it exceeded, by several thousand, the casualties inflicted on Pearl Harbor. In our efforts to grasp the number, and the scale of destruction, we've been forced to conjure up comparisons from beyond our borders: to the Somme, or even Hiroshima, the first Ground Zero. The wreckage has no American precedent. As in every other sphere, only a global perspective will now serve.

Analogy is a basic tool of teaching. By saying that something is like something else, we find a way to talk about what otherwise has no identity or name. But part of what troubles us about this event is its novelty. From a local perspective, there is no analogue. That the United States managed to live through 225 turbulent years without experiencing mass murder on such a scale has prompted us to reach for comparisons that in fact dwarf the magnitude of what happened here. The loss of life in the financial heart of New York was heart-rending, unfathomable, nearly beyond our capacity to tolerate, but—if you take the long view, the very long view—nothing out of the ordinary. We're so spoiled by our good fortune, material and geographic, that we've never even needed a sense of scale.

The history of mankind is a history of anonymous and random slaughter—civilizations we think of as "civilized" were no exception. When Caesar marched on Rome, writes Plutarch, "the city was filled with uproar, consternation and terror such as had never been known before." Attacking the Numidians, "in a small part of a single day he killed 50,000 of the enemy." The world of antiquity was a vast killing field.

Nor did the bloodletting abate after that world vanished into history. Europe over the last millennium was as violent as in any period. George Steiner, in his eloquent essay "In Bluebeard's Castle," provides a corrective to our belief that the end of the Middle Ages, with its plagues and social anarchy, meant the end of barbarism. "The material realities of the inhuman are detailed, endlessly, in Western iconography, from the mosaics at Torcello to the panels of Bosch," Steiner observed. "It is in the fantasies of the infernal, as they literally haunt Western sensibility, that we find the technology of pain without meaning, of bestiality without end, of gratuitous terror."

What these images represent is a knowledge of the perishability of all          5
civilizations. It's a lesson to which the familiar lore of American history has been notably oblivious. Our national habit of optimism resonates in our triumphal phrases: the City on the Hill, Manifest Destiny, the New Deal. In this almost touchingly hopeful narrative, history is a progressive continuum from barbarism to liberation, a passage on our mission from darkness into light. What it fails to grapple with is the darker reality that civilizations, like all else, have a beginning and an end.

The highest civilizations are eventually brought low: The Persians destroyed the Acropolis; the Visigoths sacked Rome; the Vikings plundered Europe. They all go into the dark, and never peacefully. Our great American empire seems bound to crumble at some point. It used to be a point beyond the horizon of our imagining. But since Sept. 11, the end of Western civilization has become a possibility against which the need to fight terrorism is being framed, as Roosevelt and Churchill framed the need to fight Hitler.

Only a nation shielded from the possibility of its own demise could have produced a theory as cheerful as the one put forth by the political philosopher Francis Fukuyama a few years ago, that we had come to "the end of history." Mr. Fukuyama's argument was that the forces of totalitarianism had been conquered once and for all by the United States and the West, "the end point of mankind's ideological evolution." Freedom had prevailed. Non-Western cultures were irrelevant. "For our purposes," Mr. Fukuyama wrote in a widely quoted—and widely derided—passage, "it matters very little what strange thoughts occur to people in Albania or Burkina Faso." Apparently it does.

Terror is the downside of globalization. Like AIDS and other deadly viruses that traverse international borders aboard jet aircraft, terrorism thrives on mobility. Our secure geographical fortress has at last been breached. Images of America transmitted on CNN that can rouse a foreign religious sect to rage; porous borders that enable terrorists to easily penetrate our defenses; clandestine information that can be exchanged via cellphone or satellite: the same technology that drives the West drives those who would threaten its survival.

Sept. 11 was, among other things, an education: It brought us closer to the proximity to death that has been a feature of daily life everywhere else on the globe at virtually every moment in its history. "The artifacts of death are embedded in the texture of European life," the writer Francine du Plessix Gray observes. "Cemeteries and burial grounds are common features of the landscape; town squares are crowded with plaques and monuments to the dead." (Jewish refugees from Europe often refer to their homeland as a graveyard.)

Now we, too, have a cemetery in our midst. Perhaps it will serve as a lesson in how to decipher the motives and intentions of those death-haunted, death-worshipping societies that have so suddenly come to occupy a central place in our consciousness. 10

Before they struck, we could think we had conquered the mortality of civilizations, just as we seem bent on conquering our own mortality. Heart transplants, a cure for Alzheimer's, unlocking the cellular secrets of aging would enable us to double our Biblical span: in the same way, our global isolation would protect us from the wholesale violence convulsing the rest of the globe. Like so many other rapidly discarded notions—war can be conducted without casualties; terrorism is confined to Europe—our exemption from the rules of history is a myth that it's getting harder and harder to sustain.

Edward Gibbon, upon completing *The Decline and Fall of the Roman Empire,* reflected on his own mortality and on the mortality of civilizations: "The present is always a fleeting moment, the past is no more; and our prospect of futurity is dark and doubtful." It has always been thus. That we belong to the cycle of history—not, as Mr. Fukuyama would have us believe, to its "endpoint," but caught within its motion of rise and fall—is a profoundly disquieting thought; who really believes that nothing is eternal?

But that thought can also be comforting. In its seemingly limitless power and prosperity, the United States has increasingly come to see itself as unique. To join the procession of states stretching backward and forward through time is to dispel the illusion that we stand alone in history, aloof from its wrack and turmoil. Acknowledging the inevitable transience and brevity of our own historical epoch could be the key to ensuring its long duration.

---

*For Discussion*

1. Krauthammer provides much support for William Bennett's contention (pages 438–440) that liberal democracy and militant, fundamentalist Islam are fundamentally incompatible. What support does he provide? Then, if we find merit in Huntington's theory about the clash of civilizations determining lines of future conflict and combine it with Bennett's contention, toward what course of action are we led? Is the destruction of militant Islam our only real option?

2. "The world is faced," Krauthammer contends, "with a transcendent conflict between those who love life and those who love death both for themselves and their enemies." What does *transcendent* mean? In your view, does this life-death contrast hold up?
3. James Atlas is also concerned with nihilism. In what way? How does his view of nihilism differ from Krauthammer's?
4. "Who really believes that nothing is eternal?" Atlas asks. To live a meaningful life, must we believe that *something* is eternal? Are "illusions of immortality" a necessity for meaning and value?

*For Analysis and Convincing*

Find out more about nihilism both as a concept and an historical phenomenon. A good place to start is the *Encyclopedia of Philosophy.*

Then, based on what you know about fundamentalist Islam, assess Krauthammer's identification of it with nihilism. Write an essay making a case either in favor of or against the identification. That is, argue that fundamentalist Islam either is or is not nihilistic *according to your understanding of nihilism as developed through research and your analysis of it as applied to the beliefs of people like Osama bin Laden.*

## FOR FURTHER READING AND RESEARCH

Harmon, Christopher C. *Terrorism Today.* London: Frank Cass, 2000.

Huntington, Samuel P. *The Clash of Civilizations and the Remaking of World Order.* New York: Simon and Schuster, 1996.

Hussain, Asaf. *Political Terrorism and the State in the Middle East.* London: Mansell, 1988.

Miller, Judith. *God Has Ninety-Nine Names: Reporting from a Militant Middle East.* New York: Simon and Schuster, 1996.

Reich, Walter, ed. *Origins of Terrorism: Psychologies, Ideologies, Theologies, States of Mind.* Cambridge: Cambridge UP, 1990.

Seale, Patrick. *Abu Nidal: A Gun for Hire: The Secret Life of the Most Notorious Arab Terrorist.* New York: Random House, 1992.

Wilkinson, Paul. *Terrorism versus Democracy: The Liberal State Response.* London: Frank Cass, 2000.

# Chapter 11

# Casebook on Marriage and Family: Responding to a Changing Institution

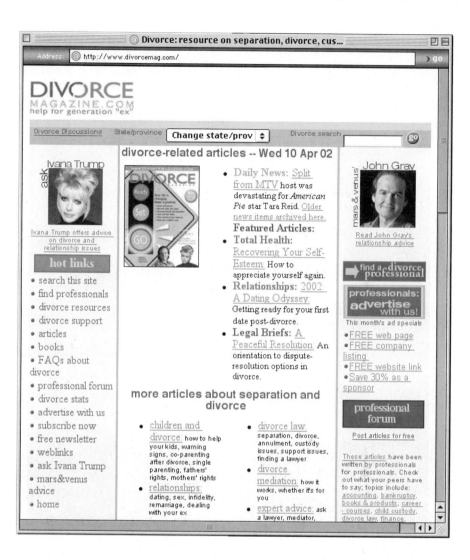

## Now that her life partner is gone...

**HOSPITAL VISITATION**
– right up to the end, she had to fight her way into the room every time.

**TAXATION**
– they could never file jointly and she couldn't claim her daughter by law.

**INHERITANCE**
– her partner's estate will be taxed by the federal government from dollar one.

**IMMIGRATION**
– if her loved one was from a foreign land, their years of commitment would have provided no basis to live on U.S. soil.

**SOCIAL SECURITY**
– she can't collect survivor benefits, even though her partner worked her whole life.

**HEALTH BENEFITS (COBRA)**
– her employer had domestic partner health benefits, but they don't extend under COBRA.

**MILITARY & EMPLOYER PENSIONS**
– her partner served in the Gulf War, but she has no right to her partner's pension benefits.

**MARRIAGE**
– they never had the right to marry — not in any state. After more than twenty years and a child together, they had fewer protections than a couple married for one hour.

Through professional and passionate advocacy, and educational programs like HRC FamilyNet and HRC WorkNet, the Human Rights Campaign, the nation's largest gay and lesbian advocacy organization, is working to bring about equal benefits and protections for every GLBT family. Please support these efforts. To learn more, visit the websites below.

### Call 1.800.727.4723

www.hrc.org  |  www.hrc.org/familynet  |  www.hrc.org/worknet

**HUMAN RIGHTS CAMPAIGN®**

## MORE NONTRADITIONAL FAMILY UNITS

Guy, Chair, Three-Way Lamp

A Woman, Her Daughter, Forty-four My Little Ponies

The Troy Triplets and Their Personal Trainer

Two Guys, Two Gals, Two Phones, a Fax, and a Blender

R. Chast

## GETTING ORIENTED: THEN AND NOW, IDEAL AND REAL

In 1823, a young Frenchman toured the United States to learn what factors contributed to the success of a democratic society. In his book, *Democracy in America,* Alexis de Tocqueville identified one of these factors as the American family, which he described as superior to the European family in contributing to the nation's stability and social order. As opposed to Europe, where family life was "tumultuous," family life for the American was

> a perfect picture of order and peace. There all [man's] pleasures are simple and natural and his joys innocent and quiet, and . . . the regularity of life brings him happiness. . . . Whereas the European tries to escape his sorrows at home by troubling society, the American derives from his home that love of order which he carries over into the affairs of state. (291–92)

Had Tocqueville actually lived in a nineteenth-century American family, he might not have painted such a rosy picture. However, his interviews and observations revealed that Americans held a strong ideal of the happy family as the foundation for a strong and healthy society. In spite of the vast changes in America since Tocqueville's visit, Americans continue to hold on to that ideal. Family is still source of emotional and moral sustenance in our collective imagination. It is still "a haven in a heartless world" (Skolnik, paragraph 21). Many of the readings in this chapter argue about how realistic, or even desirable, it is for families today to resemble Tocqueville's ideal model.

When Tocqueville talked about family, he described what we would call the *nuclear family.* The traditional nuclear family is an intimate circle consisting of a man and a woman bound by marriage and children born to them or adopted. In some parts of the world, when people think of *family,* it is a very large unit, including past generations and many relatives—uncles, great-aunts, second cousins. But for Americans, our primary definition of family remains focused on this small household unit. But how the unit has changed! Our idea of family now includes childless couples, committed couples of the same sex, unwed mothers or divorced parents and their children, blended families of multiple marriages or partnerships, and even a child with five parents. Writers in this chapter debate the wisdom and consequences of these departures from tradition.

Tocqueville also noted the importance of marriage in America. He described America as the one country in all the world in which "the marriage tie is most respected and where the highest and truest conception of conjugal happiness has been conceived." He saw this exulted idea of marriage as the product of life in a democratic society, where men and women were free to choose their life partners, unlike couples in aristocratic Europe, where marriages were often arranged and families defined in terms of blood lines. American expectations for happiness in marriage have always been high. For the Puritans, marriage was based on "friendship and esteem," but by the nineteenth century, "love, based on strong and mystical personal attraction, came to be viewed as the only legitimate reason for marriage" (Berend). Many New England women chose never to marry rather than settle for less-than-perfect emotional "oneness" with a man. This view still finds expression today as individuals seek a "soul mate" and postpone marriage until that right partner comes along. Or people marry and then divorce their spouses when passion ebbs and the marriage no longer provides emotional satisfaction. In the section entitled "Love and Marriage," we will present arguments about how realistic it is to expect romantic love to provide a lasting basis for marriage.

The well-ordered life of the American family, at the time of Tocqueville's visit, also depended upon the husband and wife performing distinct roles. Tocqueville observed America just at the time when business and industry were on the rise, moving families from farm to city and fathers from work at home to work in factories and offices. Married women became the keepers of the domestic sphere, and Tocqueville observed that their efforts to instill morals in both their children and their husbands was the source of America's greatness (603). Arguments in this chapter show that such distinct roles were not the case in early American families, and the writers debate whether distinct gender roles are important in families today.

As many of the essays and arguments in this chapter claim, the ideal nuclear family may always have been more myth than reality. If it ever existed, it has been challenged by all the great engines of social change in the United

States: the ideologies of equality, democracy, individualism, and materialism. The family also has had to respond to industrialization, technological advancement, and higher education.

With all these departures from the stereotypical model, many people today claim that the family is in crisis. They argue that we should support policies that would return us to the age before no-fault divorce, fifty-year marriages, and more distinct parental roles. Others argue that the family is not in crisis at all but simply responding to broad social and economic forces that would be hard to turn back. They argue that what needs to change are the social policies that serve the old model rather than the reality of what families have become. No one denies that the family is one of the most important institutions in American society. Our casebook on marriage and the family is intended to help you explore these important issues in depth.

Works Cited

Berend, Zsuzsa. "'The Best or None!' Spinsterhood in Nineteenth-Century New England." *Journal of Social History.* Summer, 2000: 935–1000.

Tocqueville, Alexis de. *Democracy in America.* Ed. J. P. Mayer. New York: Harper Collins Perrennial Classics, 2000.

## SECTION 1: FACTS ABOUT FAMILIES

The two readings in this section provide background information. They will help you put the later readings into the larger perspective.

"American Families" reproduces most of the December 2000 issue of *Population Bulletin,* a periodical published by the Population Reference Bureau. The Bureau is a good source of data, as it is a "nonprofit, nonadvocacy" group whose goal since 1929 has been to "provide timely, objective information on U.S. and international population trends to policymakers, educators, the media, and concerned citizens." The authors of "American Families" are Suzanne M. Bianchi and Lynne M. Casper. Bianchi is a professor of sociology at the Center on Population, Gender, and Social Inequality at the University of Maryland, College Park. Casper is health science administrator and demographer at the Demographic and Behavioral Sciences Branch of the National Institute of Child Health and Human Development. Their overview of American families at the beginning of the twenty-first century is thorough and well documented but also highly readable. Subdivisions address particular issues such as cohabitation, household chores, and fathering.

The second reading, Arlene Skolnik's "The Paradox of Perfection," is more an argument. Skolnik holds that Americans have gathered from the media and other mass-produced images of the family some unrealistic "ideal" of what family should be like, an ideal which they "project back into the past" so that they think families used to be perfect and have now gone astray. Skolnik, a psychologist from the University of California at Berkeley, uses historical evidence to show that the ideal was a myth. She extends her argument to suggest that subscribing to the myth is harmful to families today. This essay was originally published in the *Wilson Quarterly* in 1980, but it continues to be reprinted because it offers a history of the American family prior to World War II that is both concise and interestingly detailed. Because the "ideal" family image is highly sentimental, this essay is good preparation for the essays on romantic love as the basis for marriage and family.

---

## American Families

### Suzanne M. Bianchi and Lynne M. Casper

If there is one "mantra" about family life in the last half century, it is that the family has undergone tremendous change. No other institution elicits as contentious debate as the American family. Many argue that family life has been seriously degraded by the movement away from marriage and traditional gender roles. Others view family life as amazingly diverse, resilient, and adaptive to new circumstances.[1]

Any assessment of the general "health" of family life in the United States and the well-being of family members, especially children, requires a look at what we know about demographic and socioeconomic trends that affect families. The latter half of the 20th century was characterized by tumultuous change in the economy, in civil rights, and in sexual freedom, and by dramatic improvements in health and longevity. Marriage and family life felt the reverberations of these societal changes.

At the beginning of the 21st century, as we reassess where we have come from and where we are, one thing stands out. Our rhetoric about the dramatically changing family may be a step behind the reality. Recent trends suggest a quieting of changes in the family, or at least of the pace of change. There was little change in the proportion of two-parent or single-mother families during the 1990s. The living arrangements of children stabilized, as did the living arrangements of young adults and the elderly. The divorce rate had been in decline for more than two decades. The rapid growth in cohabitation among unmarried adults has also slowed.

Yet family life is still evolving. Age at first marriage rose as more young adults postponed marriage and children to complete college and settle into a labor market increasingly inhospitable to poorly educated workers. Accompanying this delay in marriage was the continued increase in births to unmarried women, though here, too, the pace of change slowed in the 1990s.[2]

Within marriage or marriage-like relationships, the appropriate roles    5
for each partner are shifting as American society accepts and values more
equal roles for men and women. The widening role of fathers has become a
major agent of change in the family. There are an increasing number of father-only families, a shift toward shared custody of children by fathers and
mothers after divorce, and increased father involvement with children in
two-parent families.

Whether the slowing, and in some cases cessation, of change in family
living arrangements is a temporary lull or part of a new, more sustained
equilibrium will only be revealed in the first decades of the 21st century.
New norms may be emerging about the desirability of marriage, the optimal timing of children, and the involvement of fathers in childrearing and
of mothers in breadwinning. . . .

## A Changing Economy and Society

Consider the life of a young woman reaching adulthood in the 1950s or
early 1960s. Such a woman was likely to marry straight out of high school
or to take a clerical or retail sales job until she married. She would have
moved out of her parents' home only after she married, to form a new
household with her husband. This young woman was likely to marry by
age 20 and begin a family soon after. If she was working when she became
pregnant, she would probably have quit her job and stayed home to care
for her children while her husband had a steady job that paid enough to
support the entire family.

Fast forward to the last few years of the 20th century. A young woman
reaching adulthood in the late 1990s is not likely to marry before her 25th
birthday. She will probably attend college and is likely to live by herself,
with a boyfriend, or with roommates before marrying. She may move in
and out of her parents' house several times before she gets married. Like her
counterpart reaching adulthood in the 1950s, she is likely to marry and
have at least one child, but the sequence of those events may well be reversed. She probably will not drop out of the labor force after she has children, although she may curtail the number of hours she is employed to balance work and family. She is also much more likely to divorce and possibly
even to remarry compared with a young woman in the 1950s or 1960s.

Many of the changes in when women (and men) marry, have children,
and enter the labor force reflect changed economic circumstances since the
1950s. After World War II, the United States enjoyed an economic boom
characterized by rapid economic growth, full employment, rising productivity, higher wages, low inflation, and increasing earnings. A man with a
high school education in the 1950s and 1960s could secure a job that paid

enough to allow him to purchase a house, support a family, and join the swelling ranks of the middle class.

The economic realities of the 1970s and 1980s were quite different. The two decades following the oil crisis in 1973 were decades of economic change and uncertainty marked by a shift away from manufacturing and toward services, stagnating or declining wages (especially for less-educated workers), high inflation, and a slowdown in productivity growth. The 1990s were just as remarkable for the turnaround: sustained prosperity, low unemployment, albeit with increased inequality in wages, but with economic growth that seems to have reached many in the poorest segments of society.[3]

When the economy is on such a roller coaster, family life often takes a similar ride. Marriage was early and nearly universal in the decades after World War II; mothers remained in the home to rear children, and the baby-boom generation was born and nurtured. When baby boomers hit working age in the 1970s, the economy was not as hospitable as it had been for their parents. They postponed entry into marriage, delayed having children, and found it difficult to establish themselves in the labor market. . . .

Both men and women are remaining single longer, and are more likely to leave home to pursue a college education, to live with a partner, and to launch a career before taking on the responsibility of a family of their own. After a period of "no family" living, these young adults will increasingly form "new families."[4] Many of these new families have increasingly egalitarian roles for men and women. The traditional, gender-based organization of home life (in which mothers have primary responsibility for care of the home and children, and fathers provide financial support) has not disappeared, but young women today can expect to be employed while raising children, and young men will likely be called upon to share in childrearing and household tasks.

### CHANGING FAMILY NORMS

In 1950, there was one dominant and socially acceptable way for adults to live their lives. Those who deviated could expect to be censured and stigmatized. The idealized family was composed of a homemaker-wife, a breadwinner-father, and two or more children. Americans shared a common image of what a family should look like and how mothers, fathers, and children should behave. These shared values reinforced the importance of the family and the institution of marriage.[5] This vision of family life showed amazing staying power, even as its economic underpinnings were eroding.

For this 1950s-style family to exist, Americans had to support distinct gender roles and the economy had to be vibrant enough for a man to financially support a family on his own. Government policies and business practices perpetuated this family type by reserving the best jobs for men and

10

discriminating against working women when they married or had a baby. After 1960, with the civil rights movement and an energetic women's liberation movement, women and minorities gained legal protections in the workplace and discriminatory practices began to recede.

A transformation in attitudes toward family behaviors also occurred. 15 People became more accepting of divorce, cohabitation, and sex outside marriage; less sure about the universality and permanence of marriage; and more tolerant of blurred gender roles and of mother's working outside the home.[6] Society became more open-minded about a variety of living arrangements, family configurations, and lifestyles.

While the transformation of many of these attitudes occurred throughout the 20th century, the pace of change accelerated in the 1960s and 1970s. These years brought many political, social, and medical developments, including the highly publicized, although unsuccessful, attempt to pass the Equal Rights Amendment (ERA);[7] the development of new, effective contraception; the legalization of abortion; and the dawn of the sexual revolution and an era of "free love."

A new ideology was emerging during these years that stressed personal freedom, self-fulfillment, and individual choice in living arrangements and family commitments. People began to expect more out of marriage and to leave bad marriages if their expectations were not fulfilled. These changes in norms and expectations about marriage may have followed rather than preceded increases in divorce and delays in marriage; however, such cultural changes have important feedback effects, leading to later marriage and more divorce. . . .

### Family Structure and Living Arrangements

The term "family" carries rich social and cultural meanings, and it has deep personal significance for most people—but for statistical purposes a family is defined as two or more people living together who are related by blood, marriage, or adoption. Most households—which are defined by the U.S. Census Bureau as one or more people who occupy a house, apartment, or other residential unit (but not "group quarters" such as dormitories)—are maintained by families. But the social and economic transformation of the family in recent decades means that the family share of U.S. households has been declining, as shown in Figure 1. In 1960, 85 percent of households were family households; by 2000, just 69 percent were family households. At the same time, nonfamily households, which consist primarily of people who live alone or who share a residence with roommates or with a partner, have been on the rise. The fastest growth was among persons living alone. The proportion of households with just one person doubled from 13 percent to 26 percent between 1960 and 2000.

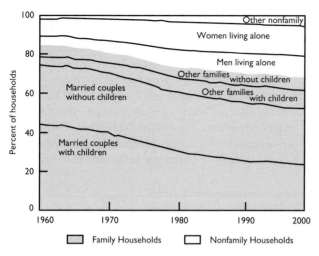

*Figure 1    Trends in U.S. Households, 1960 to 2000*

*Source: U.S. Census Bureau, March supplements of the Current Population Surveys, 1960 to 2000.*

Most of the decline in family households reflects the decrease in the share of married-couple households with children. Declines in fertility within marriage between 1960 and 1975, . . . later marriage, and frequent divorce help explain the shrinking proportion of households consisting of married couples with children. The divorce rate rose sharply between 1960 and 1980, and then eased, while the rate of first marriages declined steadily after 1970 (see Figure 2). Two-parent family households with children dropped from 44 percent to 24 percent of all households between 1960 and 2000.

Change in household composition began slowly in the 1960s, just as society was embarking on some of the most radical social changes in our nation's history (see Box 1, page 484), and the leading edge of the huge baby-boom generation was reaching adulthood. The steepest decline in the share of family households was in the 1970s when the first baby boomers entered their 20s. By the 1980s, change was still occurring, but at a much less rapid pace. By the mid-1990s, household composition reached relative equilibrium, where it has been since. . . .

**YOUNG ADULTS**

In 1890, one-half of American women had married by age 22 and one-half of American men had married by age 26. The ages of entry into marriage dipped to an all-time low during the post-World War II baby-boom years, when median age at first marriage reached 20 years for women and nearly 23 years for men in 1956. Age at first marriage then began to rise and reached

20

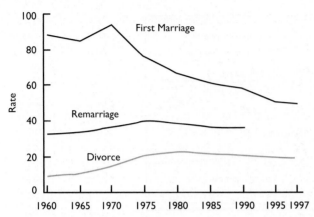

*Figure 2    Rates of First Marriage, Remarriage, and Divorce, 1960 to 1997*
*Note: First marriage rate is the number of first marriages per 1,000 women ages 15 and older (ages 14 and older in 1960 and 1965); Remarriage rate is remarriages per 1,000 divorced and widowed women ages 15 and older (ages 14 and older in 1960 and 1965); Divorce rate is the number of divorces per 1,000 married women ages 15 and older. Remarriage rates are not available after 1990.*

*Source: National Center for Health Statistics,* National Vital Statistics Reports.

25 years for women and 27 years for men by the end of the 1990s.[8] In 1960, it was unusual for a woman to reach age 25 without marrying: Only 10 percent of women ages 25 to 29 had never married. In 2000, a woman in her late 20s who had never been married was not typical, but she had many more friends like herself because two-fifths of women ages 25 to 29 had not been married. And, in 2000, the majority (52 percent) of men were still unmarried at these ages.[9]

This delay in marriage has shifted the family behaviors in young adulthood in three important ways. First, it lengthens the period of time young adults have to settle into adult roles and stable relationships. Consequently, later marriage coincides with a greater diversity and fluidity in living arrangements in young adulthood. Secondly, delaying marriage has accompanied an increased likelihood of entering a cohabiting union before marriage. Third, the trend to later marriage affects fertility in two important ways. It tends to delay entry into parenthood and, at the same time, increases the chances that a birth (sometimes planned but more often unintended) may happen before marriage.

The young adult years have been referred to as "demographically dense" because these years involve many interrelated life-altering transitions.[10] Between the ages of 18 and 30, young adults usually finish their formal schooling, leave home, develop careers, marry, and begin families; but these events do not always occur in this order. Delayed marriage extends the period young adults can experiment with alternative living arrangements before they adopt family roles. Young adults may experience any number of independent living arrangements before they marry, as they change jobs, pursue education, and move into and out of intimate relationships. They may also return home during school breaks, if money becomes tight, or if a relationship breaks up.

Many demographic, social, and economic factors influence young adults' decisions about where and with whom to live.[11] Family and work transitions are influenced greatly by fluctuations in the economy as well as by changing ideas about appropriate family life and roles for men and women. Since the 1980s, the transition to adulthood has been hampered by recurring recessions, tight job markets, slow wage growth, and soaring housing costs, in addition to the confusion over roles and behavior sparked by the gender revolution.[12] Even though young adults today may prefer to live independently, they may not be able to afford to do so. Many entry-level jobs today offer low wages yet housing costs have soared, which has put independent living out of reach for many young adults. Higher education, increasingly necessary in today's labor market, is expensive, and living at home may be a way for families to curb college expenses. Even when young adults attend school away from home, they still frequently depend on their parents for financial help and may return home after graduation if they can't find a suitable job.

Annual data from the Current Population Survey (CPS) chronicle how the living arrangements of young American adults have changed over the decades. Married living declined dramatically between 1970 and 2000, among both young men and young women. . . . Thirty-one percent of men ages 18 to 24 lived with their spouses in 1970, for example, while only 9 percent lived with a spouse in 2000. A similar drop occurred for women— from 45 percent in 1970 to 16 percent in 2000.

As a declining share of young adults chose married life, a greater share lived with parents or on their own. The percentage of young men living in their parents' homes was 57 percent in 2000, about the same as in 1970, while the percentage increased for young women from 39 percent to 47 percent. . . .

**UNMARRIED COUPLES**

One of the most significant changes in the second half of the 20th century was the increase in men and women living together without marrying. The rise of cohabitation outside marriage appeared to counterbalance the delay of marriage among young adults and the general increase in divorce.

Most adults in the United States eventually marry. In 2000, 91 percent of women ages 45 to 54 had been married at least once.[13] An estimated 88 percent of U.S. women born in the 1960s will eventually marry.[14] But the meaning and permanence of marriage may be changing. Marriage used to be the primary demographic event that marked the formation of new households, the beginning of sexual relations, and the birth of a child. Marriage also implied that an individual had one sexual partner, and it

## Box I
## Gay and Lesbian Families*

Demographic statistics can inform policy debates and provide sound information on which to base policies and develop social programs. One area in desperate need of accurate information is the demographics of gay men and lesbian
women in the United States. Issues surrounding gay and lesbian family rights
and responsibilities have emerged as one of the most hotly contested social and
political debates of the past five years. Topics of discussion include policies concerning the extension of family benefits such as health insurance, life insurance,
and family leave to gay and lesbian couples; the parental rights of gays and lesbians and their suitability as adoptive parents; and the legalization of same-sex
marriage. The importance of these issues and the need to inform policy have
prompted demographers and social scientists to develop national estimates for
the gay and lesbian population.

Accurate measurement of cohabitation among the gay and lesbian population is even more difficult than among heterosexual couples. . . . Great strides
have been made toward societal acceptance of opposite-sex couples living together without being married, yet people are much less accepting of homosexual
relationships in general, and *cohabiting* same-sex relationships in particular. This
stigma may lead more gay and lesbian couples to misreport their relationship status in surveys. Most nationally based surveys with questions regarding sexual orientation are not large enough to provide reliable estimates. Quality estimates are
even difficult to make using the nation's largest dataset—the decennial census.

A recently published report constructed the first real portrait of gay and lesbian families in the United States.[1] The report, based on 1990 Census data, finds
that gay and lesbian families are highly urban: About 60 percent of gay families
and 45 percent of lesbian families were concentrated in only 20 cities in the
United States in 1990. The greatest proportions resided in San Francisco, Wash
ington, D.C., Los Angeles, Atlanta, and New York City. In contrast, about 26 percent of the total U.S. population resided in these same 20 cities.

*We refer to gay and lesbian cohabiting couples as families. They are not considered families ac-
cording to official definitions because they are not legally married, although some gay and lesbian couples would marry if they could.

theoretically identified the two individuals who would parent any child born
of the union. The increasing social acceptance of cohabitation outside marriage has meant that these linkages could no longer be assumed. Unmarried
couples began to set up households that might include the couple's children
as well as children from previous marriages or other relationships. Similarly,
what it meant to be single was no longer always clear, as the personal lives
of unmarried couples began to resemble those of their married counterparts.

A number of gay and lesbian families include children: 22 percent of lesbian families and 5 percent of gay families, compared with 59 percent of married-couple families. Many of the children in same-sex families were probably born of previous marriages: 17 percent of gays and 29 percent of lesbians had previously been in a heterosexual marriage.

Gays and lesbians who live with partners have higher educational attainment than men and women in heterosexual marriages. In 1990, 13 percent of cohabiting gay men ages 25 to 34 had a postgraduate education, compared with 7 percent of married men. The differences are even greater for women in this age group: 16 percent of lesbians living with a partner had some postgraduate education compared with 5 percent of married women.

Gay men who live with a partner generally earn less than other men, however, while cohabiting lesbians generally earn more than other women, even when taking into account differences in age and education. The rate of homeownership is lower for gay and lesbian families than for married-couple families. Among those who own a home, however, gay and lesbian families tend to own more expensive homes than married couples, although this may reflect the large proportion of gays and lesbians who live in cities with extremely high housing costs. About 67 percent of gay families and 55 percent of lesbian families who owned homes had homes valued at $100,000 or more compared with only 15 percent for married-couple families.

Gay and lesbian families share many of the same lifestyle choices as families of heterosexual couples: Many pursue higher education, have children, hold down well-paying jobs, and own homes. But they also differ from heterosexual families in some important ways — gay men earn less than other men with similar education, for example. Do these differences reflect personal preferences, discrimination, or other factors? We do not know, but the emerging information about how gay and lesbian families resemble and differ from other families should help to answer some of these questions and to guide social research and family policy.

**Reference**
1. Dan Black, Gary Gates, Seth Sanders, and Lowell Taylor, "Demographics of the Gay and Lesbian Population in the United States: Evidence from Available Systematic Data Sources," *Demography* 37 (May 2000): 139–54.

Cohabiting and marital relationships have much in common — shared living space; emotional, psychological, and sexual intimacy; and some degree of economic interdependence. But the two relationships differ in important ways. Marriage is a relationship between two people of the opposite sex that adheres to legal, moral, and social rules. It is a social institution that rests upon common values and shared expectations for appropriate behavior. Society upholds and enforces appropriate marital behavior both formally and informally. In contrast, there is no widely recognized social blueprint to guide appropriate behavior between men and women who live together, or for the behavior of their friends, family, and the other institutions with whom they interact.

Because there is no legal bond, and because fear of social disapproval       30
might discourage people from stating publicly that they live together, measuring trends in cohabitation has been tricky. . . . There is little disagreement, however, that cohabitation has increased in U.S. society. Unmarried-couple households made up less than 1 percent of U.S. households in 1960 and 1970.[15] This share rose to 2.2 percent by 1980, to 3.6 percent in 1990, and to nearly 5 percent by 1998. Unmarried-couple households also are increasingly likely to include children. In 1978, 29 percent of unmarried-couple households included children under age 18; by 1998, 43 percent included children.

The number of unmarried-couple households surged from 1.3 million in 1978 to 3.0 million in 1988, and to 4.9 million in 1998. These figures suggest that the growth in cohabitation from 1978 to 1998 could account for 38 percent of the decline in marriage over the period, assuming that all the cohabitors would have married.

Although a relatively small percentage of U.S. households consists of an unmarried couple—one in 20 households in 1998—many Americans have lived with a partner outside marriage at some point, which means that cohabitation is a large and growing component of U.S. family life. The 1987–1988 National Survey of Families and Households found that 25 percent of all adults and 45 percent of adults in their early 30s had lived with a partner outside marriage. More than one-half of the couples who married in the mid-1990s had lived together before marriage, up slightly from 49 percent in 1985–1986, and a big jump from just 8 percent of first marriages in the late 1960s.[16]

Why has cohabitation increased so much since the 1970s? Researchers have offered several explanations, including increased uncertainty about the stability of marriage, the erosion of norms against cohabitation and sexual relations outside of marriage, the wider availability of reliable birth control, and increased individualism and secularization. Youth reaching adulthood in the past two decades are much more likely to have witnessed divorce than any generation before them. Some have argued that cohabitation allows a couple to experience the benefits of an intimate relationship without committing to marriage. If a cohabiting relationship isn't successful, one can simply move out; if a marriage isn't successful, one suffers through a sometimes lengthy and messy divorce.

The increase in unmarried-couple households is slowing from the frantic pace of the 1970s and 1980s. The CPS estimates show the number of households with unmarried couples increasing 67 percent in the five years between 1978 and 1983, but just 23 percent in the five years between 1993 and 1998. . . .

*Table 1*

Unmarried Couples by Relationship Type in 1987–1988, and after Five to Seven Years

| Type of relationship in 1987–1988 | All couples Percent | Outcome of relationship after 5 to 7 years | | |
|---|---|---|---|---|
| | | Still live together[1] | Married[2] | Separated[3] |
| All unmarried couples | 100 | 21 | 40 | 39 |
| | | | | |
| Substitute for marriage | 10 | 39 | 25 | 35 |
| Precursor to marriage | 46 | 17 | 52 | 31 |
| Trial marriage | 15 | 21 | 28 | 51 |
| Coresidential dating | 29 | 21 | 33 | 46 |

Note: Couples were interviewed between 1987 and 1988 and again from 1992 to 1994.

1 Couple was still cohabiting at the time of the second survey.
2 Got married some time between the two surveys (may or may not be currently married).
3 No longer cohabiting.

Source: L. M. Casper and L. C. Sayer, "Cohabitation Transitions: Different Attitudes and Purposes, Different Paths." (Paper presented at the annual meeting of the Population Association of America, Los Angeles, March 2000.)

Cohabitation serves different purposes for different couples. It may be a precursor to marriage, a trial marriage, a substitute for marriage, or simply a serious boyfriend-girlfriend relationship.[17] In a 1987–1988 survey, 46 percent of cohabitors characterized their living arrangement as a precursor to marriage (see Table 1). Another 15 percent of these relationships were classified as a trial marriage and 10 percent as a substitute for marriage. Nearly 30 percent of the relationships were characterized as coresidential dating.

Some researchers believe that cohabitation closely resembles marriage. If so, family life as we know it is not likely to be altered much as a consequence of cohabitation because these cohabitors will either eventually marry (precursor) or are already in a relationship which functions like a marriage (substitute).

Other researchers maintain that cohabitation is more like being single. Cohabitation is seen as an enjoyable relationship of convenience that provides intimacy without the long-term commitment of marriage. This interpretation worries many people because it suggests that the increase in cohabitation signals a retreat from marriage. It allows for an intimate, but temporary, relationship without commitment or responsibility.

Still others argue that living together before marriage is somewhere between marriage and singlehood and that cohabitation provides a couple the opportunity to assess their compatibility before getting married. In this trial period, incompatible mates can easily end their relationship and presumably escape an unsuitable marriage. Thus, cohabitation might strengthen marriage and family life because some unsuited couples are weeded out before they marry. . . .

35

How do unmarried couples compare with married couples? Although many cohabiting couples eventually marry, men and women who choose to live together outside marriage differ from married couples in some very interesting ways. In general, cohabiting couples tend to be more egalitarian and less traditional than married couples. Compared with a woman who is part of a married couple, for example, a woman in a cohabiting relationship is more likely to be older than the man, to be of a different race or ethnic group than the man, to contribute a greater percentage to the couple's income, and to have more education than the man.

American women tend to marry men a few years older than themselves    40
and relatively few marry a much younger man. Yet nearly one-fourth of women in cohabiting couples were two or more years older than their male partner, compared with one-eighth of women in married couples. . . . Cohabiting couples were also more than twice as likely to be of different races than married couples — 13 percent compared with 5 percent. About one-half of the interracial unmarried couples consisted of a white woman and a man who was African American, Hispanic, or of some other racial or ethnic group.

In many married couples, the husband has a higher educational level than the wife. Women had a higher education level in 21 percent of cohabiting couples, compared with 16 percent of married couples. In almost four of five cohabiting couples, both partners were working in 1997, compared with only three in five married couples. Women in cohabiting couples contributed 41 percent of the couple's annual income in 1997, while married women contributed 37 percent. In addition, men earned at least $30,000 more than their partners in just 11 percent of cohabiting couples compared with 27 percent of married couples.

### Parenting

Even with the rise in divorce and cohabitation, postponement of marriage, and decline in fertility, most Americans have children and most children live with two parents. In 2000, 73 percent of families with children were two-parent families. But the changes in marriage, cohabitation, and nonmarital childbearing over the past few decades have had a profound effect on American families with children and are changing our images of parenthood.

Changes in marriage and cohabitation tend to blur the distinction between one-parent and two-parent families. The increasing acceptance of cohabitation as a substitute for marriage, for example, may reduce the chance that a premarital pregnancy will lead to marriage before the birth.[18] A greater share of children today are born to a mother who is not currently married than in previous decades, but some of those children are born to cohabiting parents and begin life in a household that includes both their parents. Cohabitation has also become a widely accepted pathway into remarriage. It may effectively bring "stepfathers" into the picture before there is a formal remarriage.

Demographers Larry Bumpass and R. Kelly Raley show that the increase in cohabitation among Americans may be reducing the time children spend in a single-parent household. Bumpass and Raley found that the number of years a white mother spent as a single parent declined by one-fourth when they took into account the time she and her children shared a home with a partner.[19] Black women with children spent half as many years as a single parent after adjusting for the years they lived with an unmarried partner.

Many single-father families may also effectively be two-parent families because the father is living with his children and another woman. Demographers Steven Garasky and Daniel Meyer used census data from 1960 through 1990 to track the increase in the percentage of families that are father-only families. When they ignored the increase in cohabitation, Garasky and Meyer estimated that father-only families rose from 1.5 percent to 5.0 percent of families with children between 1960 and 1990. When they remove fathers who are likely to be cohabiting, the 1990 figure falls to 3.2 percent of all families with children.[20]

The percentage of unmarried mothers who were cohabiting grew from 5 percent to 13 percent between 1978 and 1998, according to the CPS (see Table 2). Cohabitation increased for unmarried mothers in all race and ethnic groups but especially among whites. Cohabiting couples account for up to 16 percent of the white mothers classified as unmarried mothers in 1998, compared with 8 percent of black and 10 percent of Hispanic mothers.

Unmarried fathers living with children are much more likely than unmarried mothers to be living with a partner: 33 percent of the 2.1 million "single" fathers lived with a partner in 1998, more than twice the percentage for single mothers. About 1.4 million American men were raising their children on their own, without a wife or partner, in 1998.

### SINGLE MOTHERS

Single mothers with children at home face a multitude of challenges: they usually are the primary breadwinner, disciplinarian, playmate, and caregiver for their children. They must manage the financial and practical aspects of a household, and plan for their children's and their own futures. Most mothers cope remarkably well, and many benefit from financial support and help from relatives and from their children's fathers.

Most single mothers are not poor, but they tend to be younger, earn lower incomes, and be less educated than married mothers. Women earn less than men, on average, and because single mothers are younger and less educated than other women, they are often at the lower end of the income curve. Single mothers often must curtail their work hours to care for their children. Many do not receive regular child support from their children's fathers. . . .

*Table 2*

Living Arrangements of Unmarried Fathers and Mothers
with Children under Age 18: 1978, 1988, and 1998

| Living arrangement | 1978 | 1988 | 1998 | Change, 1978–1998 |
|---|---|---|---|---|
| Unmarried fathers (percent) | 100 | 100 | 100 | |
|   Only adult in household | 42 | 47 | 38 | -4.2 |
|   Cohabiting[1] | 14 | 27 | 33 | 19.8 |
|   Living with parent(s) | 18 | 10 | 10 | -7.1 |
|   Living with other adults[2] | 26 | 16 | 18 | -8.5 |
| Unmarried mothers (percent) | 100 | 100 | 100 | |
|   Only adult in household | 60 | 56 | 54 | -5.8 |
|   Cohabiting[1] | 5 | 10 | 13 | 8.0 |
|   Living with parent(s) | 14 | 15 | 17 | 2.4 |
|   Living with other adults[2] | 21 | 19 | 17 | -4.6 |

1 Includes a partner of the opposite sex who is not married to the parent.
2 Other adults include nonrelatives other than a cohabiting partner and relatives other
than parents.

Source: Authors' tabulations of the March supplements of the Current Population
Surveys of 1978, 1988, and 1998.

In the early years of the 20th century, it was not uncommon for chil-     50
dren to live with only one parent because of high mortality.[21] As falling
death rates reduced the number of widowed single parents, there was a
counterbalancing increase in single-parent families because of divorce. Still,
at the time of the 1960 Census, almost one-third of single mothers living
with children under age 18 were widows.[22] As divorce rates rose precipi-
tously in the 1960s and 1970s, most single-parent families were created
through divorce or separation. By the end of the 1970s, only 11 percent of
single mothers were widowed and two-thirds were divorced or separated.
During the past two decades, the path to single motherhood has increasingly bypassed marriage. In 1978, about one-fifth of single mothers had
never married, but had a child and was raising that child on their own.
By 2000, two-fifths of single mothers had never married.

The remarkable increase in the number of single-mother households
with women who have never married was driven by a dramatic shift to childbearing outside marriage. The number of births to unmarried women grew
from less than 90,000 per year in 1940 to more than 1.3 million per year in
1999. Less than 4 percent of all births in 1940 were to unmarried mothers
compared with 33 percent in 1999. The rate of nonmarital births—the
number of births per 1,000 unmarried women—increased from 7.1 in
1940 to 43.9 in 1999. The nonmarital birth rate peaked in 1994 at 46.9
and leveled out in the latter 1990s (see Figure 3). A similar plateau in the
early 1970s proved to be temporary, so demographers cannot predict
whether the stability of nonmarital birth rates in the late 1990s is a temporary lull or an end to one of the most pronounced trends in the latter half
of the 20th century.[23]

*Table 3*

Trends in Single-Parent and Two-Parent Families with
Children under Age 18, 1950 to 2000

| Year | Percentage distribution of families | | |
|------|---------------|---------------|-------------|
|      | Single mother | Single father | Two parents |
| 1950 | 6  | 1 | 93 |
| 1960 | 8  | 1 | 91 |
| 1970 | 10 | 1 | 89 |
| 1980 | 18 | 2 | 80 |
| 1990 | 20 | 4 | 76 |
| 2000 | 22 | 5 | 73 |

Note: Includes only families who maintain their own households.

Source: U.S. Census Bureau, "Families, by Presence of Own Children Under 18:
1950 to Present." Accessed online at: www.census.gov/population/socdemo/
hh-fam/htabFM-1.txt, on October 13, 2000; and PRB analysis of the March 2000
Current Population Survey.

Trends in nonmarital fertility are connected to broad trends in marriage
and fertility. The delay in marriage, for example, can lead to an increase in
the number of births outside marriage even if the birth rate for unmarried
women remains the same. When women remain single longer, they spend
more years at risk of becoming pregnant and having a child outside marriage. At the same time, married women are having fewer children, which
means that children born to unmarried women make up a greater share of
all births.

In the 1960s and 1970s, the delay in marriage and decline in fertility
within marriage were the major factors contributing to the increase in the
proportion of births outside marriage. During the past two decades, the increase in the birth rates of unmarried women has been a much more important factor and, indeed, has raised concerns about the move away from
marriage and a breakdown of social sanctions against out-of-wedlock childbearing.[24] . . .

**FATHERING**

A new view of fatherhood emerged out of the feminist movement of the
late 1960s and early 1970s. The new ideal father was a co-parent who was
responsible for and involved in all aspects of his children's care. The ideal
has been widely accepted throughout U.S. society; people today, compared
with those in earlier times, believe that fathers should be highly involved in
caregiving.[25] Fathers do spend more time with their children and are doing
more housework than in earlier decades. In 1998, married fathers in the
United States reported spending an average of 4.0 hours per day with their
children compared with 2.7 hours in 1965.[26] Parallel findings emerge from
data collected on children and who they spend time with. Studies of fathers' time with their children in other industrialized countries, including

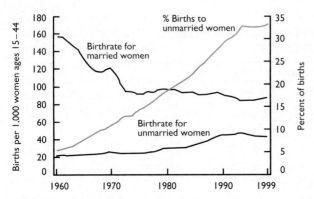

*Figure 3   Birth Rates for Married and Unmarried Women, and Percent of Births to Unmarried Women, 1960 to 1999*

*Source: National Center for Health Statistics,* National Vital Statistics Reports 48, *no. 16 (Oct. 18, 2000): table 1.*

Great Britain and Australia, also indicate that fathers are becoming more involved in parenting.[27]

At the same time, other trends increasingly remove fathers from their children's lives. When the mother and father are not married, for example, ties between fathers and their children often are tenuous. Family demographer Frank Furstenberg uses the label "good dads, bad dads" to describe the parallel trends of increased commitment to children and childrearing on the part of some fathers at the same time that there seems to be less connection to and responsibility for children on the part of other fathers.[28] . . .

55

### Father-Only Families

One of the new aspects of the American family in the last 50 years has been an increase in the number of families maintained by the father without the mother present. Between 1950 and 2000, the number of households with children that were maintained by an unmarried father increased from 229,000 to nearly 1.8 million. An additional 250,000 unmarried fathers lived with their children in someone else's household, bringing the total count of single fathers to about 2 million for 2000.

While mothers generally get custody of children after divorce, shared physical custody—in which children alternate between their mother's and father's households—has become more common in recent years. While divorced fathers still rarely are granted sole custody of their children, shared custody promotes close involvement in all aspects of their children's lives.[29]

In one of the few analyses of child custody trends, researchers Maria Cancian and Daniel Meyer examined the custody outcomes of divorce cases in Wisconsin between 1986 and 1994.[30] Their study found little change in the percentage of cases in which fathers were awarded sole custody of children; fathers got sole custody in about 10 percent of divorce cases throughout the period. The percentage of cases in which mothers were awarded sole custody declined, however, from 80 percent to 74 percent, and the percentage of cases with shared physical custody between the mother and father rose from 7 percent to 14 percent over the period. If trends in other states are similar to Wisconsin's, fathers are becoming more involved in the lives of their children after divorce, not as sole custodians but as increased participants in legal decisions (joint legal custody) and in shared physical custody arrangements. . . .

### Income and Poverty

The amount of income available to each American depends on the type of family in which he or she lives, and how many people in the family earn incomes. For families with children, the income differences can be stark. Families with two parents who both work earn the highest family incomes, and their family members have the highest per capita incomes. Two-parent families in which just one parent works produce less income, and they have been losing ground to the two-earner families since the 1970s. For every $1 of per capita income in the two-earner family, the one-earner family — the traditional working dad and stay-at-home mom family — had just 82 cents in 1977, and just 66 cents in 1997 (see Figure 4). Perhaps because they tend to have fewer family members, father-only families supported by the father's income had higher per capita incomes than married-couple families supported by one employed parent. But they too have lost ground to families in which both the mother and father are employed.

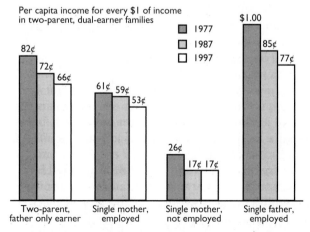

*Figure 4    Per Capita Income of Selected Family Types Relative to Two-Parent, Dual-Earner Families, 1977, 1987, and 1997*

*Source: L. Casper and S. Bianchi,* Trends in the American Family *(forthcoming).*

Families with two working parents also have higher living expenses than    60
families with a parent who is not employed outside the home, and many
question whether the extra income really covers these expenses. Many dual-
earner families pay dearly for child care that a parent would provide in a
traditional one-earner family. They often spend more on convenience
foods, household help, restaurant meals, and clothing than families with a
parent at home. Nevertheless, an increasing proportion of two-parent families have both parents in the labor force, and the income-advantage of having two working parents has increased in recent decades. A single-parent
family that relies on the mother's income had just 53 cents for every dollar
of per capita income in the two-earner families in 1997. The children of
single-mother families in which the mother is unemployed face especially
bleak economic circumstances: they have just 17 cents for every $1 of in-
come in the dual-earner families, down from 26 cents in 1977. . . .

### INCREASE IN FAMILY INCOME INEQUALITY

In 1949, 15 percent of children lived in the poorest 20 percent of families,
but by 1996, 28 percent of children were in the poorest 20 percent. The percentage of children in families at the bottom of the income distribution almost doubled over a 50-year period. This widening gap in income for families with and without children paralleled a notable shift in family structure.
More children lived in mother-only families, which are more likely to have
extremely low incomes: 15 percent of families in the bottom fifth of the
income distribution had a female householder in 1949, but this rose to
42 percent by 1996. Reflecting this shift toward mother-child families, in
1949, 75 percent of the poorest families had at least one employed person
in the household, while in 1996, 62 percent of these families had at least
one person working.[31]

At the other end of the income distribution — in the top 20 percent of
families — another revolution was underway. The likelihood that married-
couple families had earnings from both husband and wife grew tremen-
dously. The likelihood of a wife being employed outside the home rose for
married-couple families at all income levels. In 1949, for example, 32 percent of married-couple families in the richest 20 percent of families had an
employed wife; this rose to 81 percent in 1996.[32]

By any measure, income inequality has grown in the United States in
recent decades. In 1970, the bottom 20 percent of households controlled
only 4.1 percent of all household income, whereas the top 20 percent of
households controlled 43.3 percent of income. By 1999, the gap had widened — the income share of the poorest 20 percent of families dropped to
3.6 percent, while it expanded to 49.4 percent for the families in the top
20 percent.

Why has the gap between the poorest and wealthiest families increased? The answer is complex and involves a mix of factors having to do with how well certain types of workers are doing in the labor force and with marriage and living arrangements. Inequality in the earnings distribution increased as the earnings of less-educated workers fell behind those of college-educated workers. Families relying on earnings from high school-educated (or less educated) householders are increasingly disadvantaged. The increase in single-parent households during this same period only amplified the income inequality.[33]

### ECONOMICS AND CHANGES IN FAMILY LIFE

Changing family structure and changing economic opportunities of men and women interweave in complex ways to widen the gap in family and household income. Shifts in family structure and economic change interact and affect each other. A relatively large body of theory and empirical research assesses the ways in which economic changes may have promoted such changes in the family as later marriage, more cohabitation, less marriage (especially among the African American population), and more divorce and marital separation.

65

There have been two main thrusts in the literature on the economic causes of changes in marriage timing and divorce. First are theories that place major emphasis on male economic opportunities as determinants of when couples marry, whether couples marry at all, and whether marriages are disrupted. The second set of theories emphasizes the role of women's enhanced labor market opportunities in the delay in first marriage and the increase in marital disruption. Some argue that women's labor market opportunities should encourage marriage because women's high earnings may make them more "attractive" as a marital partner. Others assert that women's employment inhibits marriage and erodes marital stability to the extent that women's increased opportunities for employment and enhanced earnings make them more independent and less inclined toward marriage.

Men's breadwinning ability speeds the transition from cohabitation to marriage. Men with higher earnings are more likely to marry and less likely to divorce.[34] Married men earn more than unmarried men, whether because higher-earning men are more likely to marry or because marriage changes the behaviors of men in ways that enhance labor market productivity. Men's unemployment is associated with an increased likelihood of divorce.[35] All this is evidence for the importance of men's employment and earnings in facilitating marriage and enhancing marital stability.

The alternative hypothesis, that women's employment destabilizes marriage, is prominent in both sociological and economic theories of marital instability. Under this hypothesis, women's decreased specialization in child-rearing and household maintenance, coupled with their increased labor force participation, reduce the benefits from marriage for men and women.[36] The effect of a wife's increased economic resources on marital disruption has been termed the "independence effect." Because of this effect, women who can support themselves and their children, either through their own earnings or via welfare payments, would have less incentive to marry and find it easier to exit unsatisfactory marriages.

The independence effect may delay marriage as men and women take longer to search for a good match when the job market is unstable, but there is little evidence that men or women are rejecting marriage because of women's increased economic opportunities.[37] The relationship among employment, earnings, and marriage is quite similar for men and women: Higher earnings and better job prospects enhance the likelihood of marriage, although the effects are larger and more consistent for men's than for women's employment and earnings.[38] Evidence relating a wife's greater economic independence to an increased likelihood of divorce is mixed. Studies that find that the wife's relative contribution to family income or her wages are positively associated with increased risks of marital disruption are counterbalanced by studies that find no relationship between a wife's economic independence and marital disruption.[39]

Just as economic conditions affect who marries and divorces, decisions about whether to marry or remain married have economic consequences. The wide gap in economic conditions of husband and wife after divorce or separation has garnered considerable attention among the American public, and may affect the decision to separate, especially if dependent children are involved. When a couple with children separates, the children usually live with their mother. The mother is likely to have a lower salary than her husband, but much higher living expenses, especially if she must pay for child care. Many mothers do not receive regular child support. Fathers, however, may reduce their living costs when they separate from their family, while maintaining the same salary.

For couples who had children and who separated in the late 1980s or early 1990s, economic well-being declined for mothers by 36 percent, while the financial status of fathers improved by 28 percent. One-fifth of mothers improved their standard of living, but two-thirds of fathers benefited financially from the separation. In poor families, fathers are significantly more likely than mothers to rise out of poverty after marital separation. Only one-quarter of fathers who were poor when they separated remained in poverty, compared with almost three-quarters of mothers. Similarly, among couples whose income was above the poverty line before the separation, 19 percent of mothers compared with 3 percent of fathers fell below poverty as a result of the separation.[40]

In sum, a complex set of interconnections among changes in family structure, decisions adults make about employment, and conditions in the labor market and the larger economy constrain, or at least set the context, for how well families do economically.

### Blending Work and Family

A little over two decades ago, sociologist Rosabeth Kanter pointed out that, despite the "myth of separate worlds" of work and family, there were a myriad of ways in which work "spilled" over into family life.[41] The influence of work on family continues to be strong, probably stronger than the influence of family on work. Financial rewards from work define the opportunities families have and, hence, men, women, and children are called upon to adapt home life to the work schedules of the adults within the home. The dramatic increase in mother's labor force participation, particularly married mothers, has meant that more married couples commit more than 40 hours a week to market work because now both husband and wife are working for pay. A sizable reallocation of time is underway in American households with children.

Perhaps the most striking aspect of women's labor force participation over the past 20 years is how steadily the trends have moved upward.[42] In 1978, almost 66 percent of women in the prime "work and family" ages (25 to 54 years) worked during the year; this increased to 79 percent in 1998. . . . The percentage of women in these ages who worked full-time year-round increased from 32 percent to 50 percent between 1978 and 1998. The average annual hours of paid employment for all women increased 40 percent over the period, from 1,002 hours to 1,415 hours. Most of the increase occurred because more women were working in 1998 rather than because working women dramatically increased the number of hours they worked during the year.

In recent decades, the most dramatic increases in labor force participation have been among married women, particularly those with young children. In 1998, 71 percent of married mothers of children under age 6 did some work for pay during the year. But just 35 percent worked full-time year-round, which means that nearly two-thirds of married mothers of preschoolers did not work full time in 1998. Most married mothers have not traded raising their own children for paid work. Although U.S. mothers of young children are much more likely to work in the 1990s than they were in the 1970s, which implies an increasing attachment of women to market work, married mothers tend to scale back their hours during their children's preschool years.

#### HOUSEWORK

How have American men and women fulfilled their childrearing and job responsibilities, given women's increased hours in the labor market? One strategy has been to do less housework—or to do it faster. In 1965, women spent about 30 hours weekly doing unpaid household work, which included such core tasks as cooking meals, meal clean-up, housecleaning, and laundry, as well as more discretionary or less time-consuming tasks such as outdoor chores and repairs, gardening, animal care, and bill paying. By 1995,

*Table 4*

Average Hours Spent on Housework by Women and Men,
Ages 25 to 64, in 1965 and 1995

| | Hours per week | | | | Ratio of women's hours to men's | |
| | Women | | Men | | | |
| Household task | 1965 | 1995 | 1965 | 1995 | 1965 | 1995 |
| --- | --- | --- | --- | --- | --- | --- |
| Total housework | 30.0 | 17.5 | 4.9 | 10.0 | 6.1 | 1.8 |
| Core housework | 26.9 | 13.9 | 2.3 | 3.8 | 11.9 | 3.7 |
| Cooking meals | 9.3 | 4.6 | 1.1 | 1.6 | 8.8 | 2.8 |
| Meal clean-up | 4.5 | 0.7 | 0.5 | 0.1 | 9.9 | 5.4 |
| Housecleaning | 7.2 | 6.7 | 0.5 | 1.7 | 15.5 | 3.8 |
| Laundry, ironing | 5.8 | 1.9 | 0.3 | 0.3 | 22.1 | 6.9 |
| Other housework | 3.1 | 3.6 | 2.6 | 6.2 | 1.2 | 0.6 |
| Outdoor chores | 0.3 | 0.8 | 0.4 | 1.9 | 0.7 | 0.4 |
| Repairs, maintenance | 0.4 | 0.7 | 1.0 | 1.9 | 0.4 | 0.4 |
| Garden, animal care | 0.6 | 0.8 | 0.2 | 1.0 | 2.4 | 0.8 |
| Bills, other | 1.8 | 1.3 | 0.9 | 1.5 | 2.0 | 0.9 |
| Number of women/men | 579 | 493 | 469 | 359 | | |

Source: S. Bianchi, J. Robinson, L. Sayer, and M. Milkie, *Social Forces* 79
(September 2000): 192–228.

women spent just 17.5 hours per week on these tasks (see Table 4). While
U.S. men spent much more time on household tasks in the 1990s than in
the 1960s, they did not make up for the decline in women's time on housework. Women averaged 6.1 times more hours of housework than men in
1965, but this ratio fell to 1.8 in 1995 primarily because women spent so
much less time on these chores. Men increased their time on weekly household chores from 4.9 hours to 10.0 hours between 1965 and 1995.

About half of the 12-hour decline in women's average weekly hours of
housework could be attributed to the fact that more women were employed
and fewer were married and living with children in the household in 1995
than in 1965. More specifically, if women in 1995 had the same characteristics as those in 1965 — the same low rates of labor force participation and
higher rates of marriage and greater numbers of children — the decline in
hours would be about six hours per week, not 12 hours.[43]

### CHILD CARE

Another change that has accompanied women's movement into the workplace is the type of child-care arrangements mothers and fathers use. Between 1965 and 1994, the use of center care for preschool-age children increased, with a corresponding decline in mothers caring for their children
while they worked, and care by other relatives and babysitters. . . . In 1965,
just 7 percent of preschoolers of employed mothers were in center care as
their primary arrangement; by 1994, 29 percent were in center care. The
proportion of preschoolers who were in family day care — usually cared for
by a nonrelative in a private home — increased until the mid-1980s and

then declined sharply. . . . Care by fathers increased from 14 percent to 19 percent.

### ATTITUDES ABOUT WOMEN'S WORK AND FAMILY

Attitudinal data suggest that Americans have become much more support-ive of paid work for mothers but that they are still concerned about the consequences for children of combining paid work and childrearing. Re-sponses to the General Social Survey between 1977 and 1994 show that the percentage of Americans, men or women, who disapprove of a married woman working even if her husband can support her has declined from one-third to less than one-fifth. In 1977, more women than men (61 per-cent and 53 percent, respectively) agreed with the statement: "It is more im-portant for a wife to help her husband's career than to have one herself." In 1994, only a little more than 20 percent of both men and women agreed with that statement. Americans were much less likely to agree with the tra-ditional division of labor in the home in 1994 than they were in 1977, but 38 percent of men and 33 percent of women still agreed in 1994 that it is better if a man achieves outside the home and a woman cares for home and family.[44]

Questions about children also show a dramatic change over time, with a smaller percentage of respondents thinking children will suffer if a mother is employed outside the home. But Americans still display a sur-prisingly large gender difference and express considerable ambivalence when asked about the wisdom of combining mothering and paid work. In 1994, almost 40 percent of men but about one-quarter of women felt that a working mother cannot have as warm and secure a relationship with a child as a mother who is not employed. And one-half of men and more than one-third of women still feel that a preschool child is likely to suffer if a mother works for pay.

Families use several strategies to balance paid work and childrearing. First, as women increase their market work, they seem to be shedding un-paid housework at a rapid rate. Second, despite the increase in women's employment, many mothers still do not work full-time year-round when their children are preschool-age. And, although there has been a substantial shift in attitudes toward more acceptance of working women and mothers, many Americans are uncertain about the effect of women's paid work on children's well-being.

Many individuals feel they have struck a reasonable balance between paid work and family, and interestingly, men and women are equally likely to report success in their balancing act. Yet there continue to be large gen-der differences in work-family balance. Men are more likely to take on ad-ditional work if they feel the need for additional income for their families, and more likely to miss a family event to fulfill work obligations. Women are far more likely than men to reduce their hours of market work to give

80

## Box 2
## How Involved Are Fathers?
## It Depends on Whom You Ask . . .

Most of the research on parenting has surveyed mothers, but not fathers. The recent surge of interest in the father's role has promoted surveys of both parents, which have, incidentally, documented substantial discrepancies between men's and women's reports about their relative involvement in raising their children. A 1999 University of Maryland study explored these discrepancies by asking a sample of mothers and fathers about five domains of parenting: discipline, play, emotional support, monitoring of activities and playmates, and basic care.

Parents were asked: "Ideally, who should discipline children, mainly the mother, mainly the father, or both equally?" Similarly, respondents were also asked: "In parenting your children, who disciplines the children, mainly you, mainly the child's father/mother, or both parents equally?" Questions were repeated for each domain of childrearing and were asked both of parents who currently had children in the home as well as of parents who had adult children.

There is overwhelming consensus between men and women that parenting should be shared equally across most domains, as shown in the figure on the left. For four of the areas—disciplining children, playing with children, providing emotional support, and monitoring activities and friends—at least 90 percent of men and women say these parenting domains should be shared equally. More than two-thirds of men and women say that caring for children's needs should be shared equally by mothers and fathers.

Parents' reports of actual involvement, however, do not agree (figure on the right). Mothers are far more likely than fathers to report that the mother is the main disciplinarian of children (47 percent, compared with 17 percent), and that it is mainly the mother who plays with children (37 percent, compared with

more time to childrearing.[45] The implications these gendered responses to work-family balance have—for men's "caring" selves, for women's labor market success, and for children's lives—are the major issues and challenges ahead (see Box 2, above).

Finally, with the aging of the population, meeting needs of parents as well as children will challenge more of tomorrow's working families. The increase in the number of elderly also is important for the public policy debates that will take place in the coming years. Work-family initiatives may not be enacted without support from those who no longer juggle work and family as intensely as in the past, that is, support from grandparents as well as parents.

14 percent). Similarly, mothers are far more likely than fathers to report that the mother provides most of the emotional support of children (45 percent compared with 24 percent) and that the mother is the one who mainly monitors their children's activities (51 percent compared with 27 percent). More mothers than fathers believe that mothers are the main caretakers of children (70 percent vs. 58 percent). Overall, fathers are much more likely to hold the view that domains are shared equally with their partners, while mothers are much more likely to report that they are primarily the ones involved in rearing their children.

**Reference**
Melissa Milkie, Suzanne M. Bianchi, Marybeth Mattingly, and John Robinson, "Fathers' Involvement in Childrearing: Ideals, Realities, and Their Relationship to Parental Well-Being." (Revised version of a paper presented at the annual meeting of the American Association for Public Opinion Research, Portland, OR, May 18–21, 2000.)

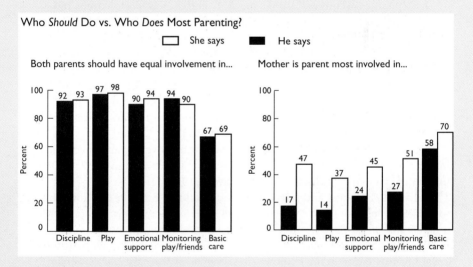

**Conclusion**

Families change in response to economic conditions, cultural change, and demographics such as the aging of the population. The United States may have gone through a particularly tumultuous period in the last few decades, resulting in rapid change in family behaviors. Families have emerged more diverse, with boundaries among family types more blurred than in the past. Whether U.S. families have now adjusted to the dramatic social changes that occurred in the latter half of the 20th century and have reached a new equilibrium, only time will tell.

Economic fortunes and family relationships remain interwined. Issues      85
growing in importance are how families will balance paid work with childrearing, what income inequality will do to the fortunes of the next generation, whether fathers will increasingly play a nurturing role given the
growing similarity in mothers' and fathers' breadwinning roles, and how relationships between the generations will be altered by the increase in life
expectancy. Families have been amazingly adaptive and resilient in the past;
one would expect them to be so in the future.

## Notes

1. David Popenoe, "American Family Decline, 1960–1990: A Review and Appraisal," *Journal of Marriage and the Family* 55 (August 1993): 527–55; and Judith
Stacey, "Good Riddance to 'The Family': A Response to David Popenoe," *Journal
of Marriage and the Family* 55, no. 3 (August 1993): 545–47.

2. Stephanie J. Ventura, C. A. Bachrach, L. Hill, K. Kay, P. Holcomb, and
E. Koff, "The Demography of Out-of-Wedlock Childbearing," in *Report to Congress
on Out-of-Wedlock Childbearing*, ed. National Center for Health Statistics (Washington, DC: U.S. Department of Health and Human Services, 1995): 1–133.

3. Reynolds Farley, *The New American Reality: Who We Are, How We Got Here,
Where We Are Going* (New York: Russell Sage Foundation, 1996); and Frank Levy,
*The New Dollars and Dreams* (New York: Russell Sage Foundation, 1998).

4. Frances K. Goldscheider and Linda J. Waite, *New Families, No Families?*
(Berkeley, CA: University of California Press, 1991).

5. Sara McLanahan and Lynne Casper, "Growing Diversity and Inequality in
the American Family," in *State of the Union: America in the 1990s*, Vol. 2, ed. Reynolds Farley (New York: Russell Sage Foundation, 1995): 1–46.

6. Larry L. Bumpass and James A. Sweet, "National Estimates of Cohabitation," *Demography* 26, no. 4 (November 1989): 615–25; Andrew J. Cherlin, *Marriage, Divorce, Remarriage* (Cambridge, MA: Harvard University Press, 1992); Farley, *The New American Reality*, Chapter 2; Arland Thornton, "Changing Attitudes
Toward Family Issues in the United States," *Journal of Marriage and the Family* 51,
no. 4 (November 1989): 873–93.

7. The ERA was first introduced in Congress in 1923. It stated that "equality
or rights under the law shall not be denied or abridged by the United States or
by any State on account of sex." After nearly a half century, the amendment was
passed by Congress in 1972. The first campaign to ratify the proposed 27th
Amendment to the U.S. Constitution—the Federal Equal Rights Amendment—
ended on June 30, 1982, three states shy of the 38 required for ratification. National Women's Conference Committee, *National Plan of Action Update* (Washington, DC: 1986).

8. U.S. Census Bureau, "Estimated Median Age at First Marriage, by Sex: 1890
to the Present." Accessed online at www.census.gov/population/socdemo/ms-la/
tabms-2.txt, on Oct. 11, 2000.

9. Casper and Bianchi, *Trends in the American Family* (forthcoming): table 1.4;
and PRB analysis of the March 2000 Current Population Survey.

10. Ronald R. Rindfuss, "The Young Adult Years: Diversity, Structural Change, and Fertility," *Demography* 28, no. 4 (November 1991): 493–512.

11. These trends are discussed in detail in Casper and Bianchi, *Trends in the American Family:* Chapter 1.

12. Frances Goldscheider and Calvin Goldscheider, "Leaving and Returning Home in 20th Century America," *Population Bulletin* 48, no. 4 (Washington, DC: Population Reference Bureau, March 1994).

13. U.S. Census Bureau, "Marital Status and Living Arrangements: March 1998"; and PRB analysis of the March 2000 Current Population Survey.

14. R. Kelly Raley, "Recent Trends and Differentials in Marriage and Cohabitation," in *Ties That Bind: Perspectives on Marriage and Cohabitation,* ed. Linda Waite (New York: Aldine de Gruyter, 2000): 19–39.

15. Lynne M. Casper and Philip Cohen, "How Does POSSLQ Measure Up? Historical Estimates of Cohabitation," *Demography* 37, no. 2 (May 2000): 237–45.

16. Larry Bumpass, "What's Happening to the Family? Interactions Between Demographic and Institutional Change," *Demography* 27, no. 4 (November 1990): 483–93; Larry L. Bumpass and James A. Sweet, "National Estimates of Cohabitation," *Demography* 26, no. 4 (November 1989): 615–25; Larry Bumpass and Hsien-Hen Lu, "Trends in Cohabitation and Implications for Children's Family Contexts in the United States," *Population Studies* 54, no. 1 (March 2000): 29–41.

17. Bumpass, "What's Happening to the Family?"; Lynne M. Casper and Liana C. Sayer, "Cohabitation Transitions: Different Attitudes and Purposes, Different Paths." (Paper presented at the annual meeting of the Population Association of America, Los Angeles, March 2000); Wendy D. Manning, "Marriage and Cohabitation Following Premarital Conception," *Journal of Marriage and the Family* 55 (November 1993): 839–50; McLanahan and Casper, "Growing Diversity and Inequality in the American Family," in *State of the Union: America in the 1990s,* Vol. 2; and Ronald Rindfuss and Audrey VandenHuevel, "Cohabitation: A Precursor to Marriage or an Alternative to Being Single?" *Population and Development Review* 16. no. 4 (September 1990): 703–26.

18. R. Kelly Raley, "Then Comes Marriage? Recent Changes in Women's Response to a Non-Marital Pregnancy." (Paper presented at the annual meeting of the Population Association of America, New York, March 1999.)

19. Larry Bumpass and R. Kelly Raley, "Redefining Single-Parent Families: Cohabitation and Changing Family Reality," *Demography* 32, no. 1 (February 1995): 97–109.

20. Steven Garasky and Daniel R. Meyer, "Reconsidering the Increase in Father-Only Families," *Demography* 33, no. 3 (August 1996): 385–93.

21. Peter Uhlenberg, "Death and the Family," *Journal of Family History* (Fall 1980): 313–20.

22. Suzanne M. Bianchi, "The Changing Demographic and Socioeconomic Characteristics of Single-Parent Families," *Marriage and Family Review* 20, no. 1–2 (1995): 71–97.

23. National Center for Health Statistics, "Births: Final Data for 1998," by Stephanie Ventura, J. A. Martin, S. C. Curtin, T. J. Mathews, and M. M. Park,

*National Vital Statistics Report* 48, no. 3 (March 2000): table C; and Ventura, Bachrach, Hill, Kay, Holcomb, and Koff, "The Demography of Out-of-Wedlock Childbearing," in *Report to Congress on Out-of-Wedlock Childbearing.*

24. S. Philip Morgan, "Characteristic Features of Modern American Fertility," in *Fertility in the United States: New Patterns, New Theories,* ed. John B. Casterline, Ronald D. Lee, and Karen A. Foote (New York: The Population Council, 1996): 19–66.

25. Elizabeth H. Pleck and Joseph H. Pleck, "Fatherhood Ideals in the United States: Historical Dimensions," in *The Role of the Father in Child Development,* 3d ed., ed. Michael E. Lamb (New York: Wiley and Sons, 1997): 33–48.

26. Suzanne M. Bianchi, "Maternal Employment and Time With Children: Dramatic Change or Surprising Continuity?" *Demography* 37, no. 4 (November 2000): 401–14.

27. Michael Bittman, "Recent Changes in Unpaid Work." (Occasional paper from the Social Policy Research Centre, University of New South Wales, Sydney, Australia, 1999); Kimberly Fischer, Andrew McCulloch, and Jonathan Gershuny, "British Fathers and Children." (Working Paper, Institute for Social and Economic Research, University of Essex, England, December 1999); John F. Sandberg and Sandra L. Hofferth, "Changes in Parental Time with Children, U.S. 1981–1997." (Paper presented at the annual meeting of the International Association of Time Use Research, University of Essex, Colchester, England, October 6–8, 1999.)

28. Frank Furstenberg Jr., "Good Dads–Bad Dads: Two Faces of Fatherhood," in *The Changing American Family and Public Policy,* ed. A. J. Cherlin (Washington, DC: The Urban Institute, 1998): 193–218.

29. Maria Cancian and Daniel R. Meyer, "Who Gets Custody?" *Demography* 35 (May 1998): 147–58; and Steven Garasky and Daniel R. Meyer, "Reconsidering the Increase in Father-Only Families," *Demography* 33, no. 3 (August 1996): 385–93.

30. Cancian and Meyer, "Who Gets Custody?"

31. Levy, *The New Dollars and Dreams.*

32. Ibid.

33. Maria Cancian and Deborah Reed, "The Impact of Wives' Earnings on Income Inequality: Issues and Estimates," *Demography* 36, no. 2 (May 1999): 173–84; Lynn A. Karoly and Gary Burtless, "Demographic Change, Rising Earnings Inequality, and the Distribution of Personal Well-Being," *Demography* 32, no. 3 (August 1995): 379–406; Levy, *The New Dollars and Dreams;* and Paul Ryscavage, "A Surge in Growing Income Inequality?" *Monthly Labor Review* 118, no. 8 (August 1995): 51–61.

34. Saul D. Hoffman and Greg J. Duncan, "The Effect of Income, Wages, and AFDC Benefits on Marital Disruption," *The Journal of Human Resources* 30 (1995): 19–41; K. M. Lloyd and S. J. South, "Contextual Influences on Young Men's Transitions to First Marriages," *Social Forces* 74 (1996): 1097–119; Pamela J. Smock and Wendy D. Manning, "Cohabiting Partners' Economic Circumstances and Marriage," *Demography* 34 (August 1997): 331–41; and S. J. South and K. M. Lloyd, "Spousal Alternatives and Marital Dissolution," *American Sociological Review* 60, no. 1 (February 1995): 21–35.

35. L. L. Bumpass, T. C. Martin, and J. A. Sweet, "The Impact of Family Background and Early Marital Factors on Marital Disruption," *Journal of Family Issues* 12 (1991): 22–42; Jeffrey S. Gray, "The Fall in Men's Return to Marriage: Declining Productivity Effects or Changing Selection?" *The Journal of Human Resources* 32, no. 3 (1997): 481–504; Robert Kaestner, "Recent Changes in the Labor Supply Behavior of Married Couples," *Eastern Economic Journal* 19, no. 2 (1993): 185–208; Sanders Korenman and David Neumark, "Does Marriage Really Make Men More Productive?" *The Journal of Human Resources* 26, no. 2 (1991): 282–307; and Steven L. Nock, *Marriage in Men's Lives* (New York: Oxford University Press, 1998).

36. Gary Becker, "A Theory of Marriage," in *Economics of the Family: Marriage, Children, and Human Capita,* ed. T. W. Schultz (Chicago: University of Chicago Press, 1974): 299–344; Gary Becker, *A Treatise on the Family* (Cambridge, MA: Harvard University Press, 1981); Gary Becker, Elizabeth M. Landes, and Robert T. Michael, "An Economic Analysis of Marital Instability," *Journal of Political Economy* 85 (December 1977): 1141–87; and Thomas Espenshade, "Marriage Trends in America: Estimates, Implications, and Underlying Causes," *Population and Development Review* 11, no. 2 (June 1985): 193–245.

37. Valerie Kinkade Oppenheimer, "A Theory of Marriage Timing," *American Journal of Sociology* 94, no. 3 (November 1988): 563–91; and Valerie Kinkade Oppenheimer, "Women's Employment and the Gain to Marriage: The Specialization and Trading Model," *Annual Review of Sociology* 23 (1997): 431–53.

38. Lynn White and Stacy Rogers, "Economic Circumstances and Family Outcomes: A Review of the 90s," *Journal of Marriage and the Family* 62 (November 2000).

39. Liana Sayer and Suzanne M. Bianchi, "Women's Economic Independence and the Probability of Divorce: A Review and Reexamination," *Journal of Family Issues* 21 (October 2000), 906–43.

40. Suzanne M. Bianchi, Lekha Subaiya, and Joan R. Kahn, "The Gender Gap in the Economic Well-Being of Nonresident Fathers and Custodial Mothers," *Demography* 36, no. 2 (May 1999): 195–203.

41. Rosabeth Moss Kanter, *Work and Family in the United States: A Critical Review and Agenda for Research and Policy* (New York: Russell Sage Foundation, 1977).

42. Philip N. Cohen and Suzanne M. Bianchi, "Marriage, Children, and Women's Employment: What Do We Know?" *Monthly Labor Review* 122 (December 1999): 22–31.

43. Suzanne M. Bianchi, Melissa Milkie, Liana Sayer, and John Robinson, "Is Anyone Doing the Housework?" *Social Forces* 79 (September 2000): 191–228.

44. Suzanne M. Bianchi and Jane Lawler Dye. "Women's Labor Force Participation in the U.S.: Trends and Future Prospects," in *Gender Stratification: Social Construction and Structural Accounts,* ed. Dana Vannoy (Los Angeles: Roxbury, forthcoming).

45. Melissa Milkie and Pia Peltola, "Playing All the Roles: Gender and the Work-Family Balancing Act," *Journal of Marriage and the Family* 61, no. 2 (May 1999): 476–90.

# The Paradox of Perfection
## Arlene Skolnick

The American Family, as even readers of *Popular Mechanics* must know by now, is in what Sean O'Casey would have called "a terrible state of chassis." Yet, there are certain ironies about the much-publicized crisis that give one pause.

True, the statistics seem alarming. The U.S. divorce rate, though it has reached something of a plateau in recent years, remains the highest in American history. The number of births out-of-wedlock among all races and ethnic groups continues to climb. The plight of many elderly Americans subsisting on low fixed incomes is well known.

What puzzles me is an ambiguity, not in the facts, but in what we are asked to make of them. A series of opinion polls conducted in 1978 by Yankelovich, Skelley, and White, for example, found that 38 percent of those surveyed had recently witnessed one or more "destructive activities" (e.g., a divorce, a separation, a custody battle) within their own families or those of their parents or siblings. At the same time, 92 percent of the respondents said the family was highly important to them as a "personal value."

Can the family be at once a cherished "value" and a troubled institution? I am inclined to think, in fact, that they go hand in hand. A recent "Talk of the Town" report in *The New Yorker* illustrates what I mean:

> A few months ago word was heard from Billy Gray, who used to play brother Bud in "Father Knows Best," the 1950s television show about the nice Anderson family who lived in the white frame house on a side street in some mythical Springfield—the house at which the father arrived each night swinging open the front door and singing out "Margaret, I'm home!" Gray said he felt "ashamed" that he had ever had anything to do with the show. It was all "totally false," he said, and had caused many Americans to feel inadequate, because they thought that was the way life was supposed to be and that their own lives failed to measure up.

As Susan Sontag has noted in *On Photography,* mass-produced images have "extraordinary powers to determine our demands upon reality." The family is especially vulnerable to confusion between truth and illusion. What, after all, is "normal"? All of us have a backstairs view of our own families, but we know The Family, in the aggregate, only vicariously.

Like politics or athletics, the family has become a media event. Television offers nightly portrayals of lump-in-the-throat family "normalcy" ("The Waltons," "Little House on the Prairie") and, nowadays, even humorous "deviance" ("One Day at a Time," "The Odd Couple"). Family advisers sally forth in syndicated newspaper columns to uphold standards, mend re-

5

lationships, suggest counseling, and otherwise lead their readers back to the True Path. For commercial purposes, advertisers spend millions of dollars to create stirring vignettes of glamorous-but-ordinary families, the kind of family most 11-year-olds wish they had.

All Americans do not, of course, live in such a family, but most share an intuitive sense of what the "ideal" family should be—reflected in the precepts of religion, the conventions of etiquette, and the assumptions of law. And, characteristically, Americans tend to project the ideal back into the past, the time when virtues of all sorts are thought to have flourished.

We do not come off well by comparison with that golden age, nor could we, for it is as elusive and mythical as Brigadoon. If Billy Gray shames too easily, he has a valid point: While Americans view the family as the proper context for their own lives—9 out of 10 people live in one— they have no realistic context in which to view the family. Family history, until recently, was as neglected in academe as it still is in the press. The familiar, depressing charts of "leading family indicators"—marriage, divorce, illegitimacy—in newspapers and newsmagazines rarely survey the trends before World War II. The discussion, in short, lacks ballast.

Let us go back to before the American Revolution.

Perhaps what distinguishes the modern family most from its colonial counterpart is its newfound privacy. Throughout the 17th and 18th centuries, well over 90 percent of the American population lived in small rural communities. Unusual behavior rarely went unnoticed, and neighbors often intervened directly in a family's affairs, to help or to chastise.

10

The most dramatic example was the rural "charivari," prevalent in both Europe and the United States until the early 19th century. The purpose of these noisy gatherings was to censure community members for familial transgressions—unusual sexual behavior, marriages between persons of grossly discrepant ages, or "household disorder," to name but a few. As historian Edward Shorter describes it in *The Making of the Modern Family:*

> Sometimes the demonstration would consist of masked individuals circling somebody's house at night, screaming, beating on pans, and blowing cow horns . . . on other occasions, the offender would be seized and marched through the streets, seated perhaps backwards on a donkey or forced to wear a placard describing his sins.

The state itself had no qualms about intruding into a family's affairs by statute, if necessary. Consider 17th-century New England's "stubborn child" laws that, though never actually enforced, sanctioned the death penalty for chronic disobedience to one's parents.

If the boundaries between home and society seem blurred during the colonial era, it is because they were. People were neither very emotional nor very self-conscious about family life, and, as historian John Demos points out, family and community were "joined in a relation of profound reciprocity." In his *Of Domesticall Duties*, William Gouge, a 17th-century Puritan preacher, called the family "a little community." The home, like the larger community, was as much an economic as a social unit; all members of the family worked, be it on the farm, or in a shop, or in the home.

There was not much to idealize. Love was not considered the basis for marriage but one possible result of it. According to historian Carl Degler, it was easier to obtain a divorce in colonial New England than anywhere else in the Western world, and the divorce rate climbed steadily throughout the 18th century, though it remained low by contemporary standards. Romantic images to the contrary, it was rare for more than two generations (parents and children) to share a household, for the simple reason that very few people lived beyond the age of 60. It is ironic that our nostalgia for the extended family—including grandparents and grandchildren—comes at a time when, thanks to improvements in health care, its existence is less threatened than ever before.

Infant mortality was high in colonial days, though not as high as we are accustomed to believe, since food was plentiful and epidemics, owing to generally low population density, were few. In the mid-1700s, the average age of marriage was about 24 for men, 21 for women—not much different from what it is now. Households, on average, were larger, but not startlingly so: A typical household in 1790 included about 5.6 members, versus about 3.5 today. Illegitimacy was widespread. Premarital pregnancies reached a high in 18th-century America (10 percent of all first births) that was not equalled until the 1950s.

In simple demographic terms, then, the differences between the American family in colonial times and today are not all that stark; the similarities are sometimes striking.

The chief contrast is psychological. While Western societies have always idealized the family to some degree, the *most vivid* literary portrayals of family life before the 19th century were negative or, at best, ambivalent. In what might be called the "high tragic" tradition—including Sophocles, Shakespeare, and the Bible, as well as fairy tales and novels—the family was portrayed as a high-voltage emotional setting, laden with dark passions, sibling rivalries, and violence. There was also the "low comic" tradition—the world of hen-pecked husbands and tyrannical mothers-in-law.

It is unlikely that our 18th-century ancestors ever left the book of Genesis or *Tom Jones* with the feeling that their own family lives were seriously flawed.

By the time of the Civil War, however, American attitudes toward the family had changed profoundly. The early decades of the 19th century marked the beginnings of America's gradual transformation into an urban, industrial society. In 1820, less than 8 percent of the U.S. population lived in cities; by 1860, the urban concentration approached 20 percent, and by 1900 that proportion had doubled.

15

Structurally, the American family did not immediately undergo a comparable transformation. Despite the large families of many immigrants and farmers, the size of the *average* family declined — slowly but steadily — as it had been doing since the 17th century. Infant mortality remained about the same, and may even have increased somewhat, owing to poor sanitation in crowded cities. Legal divorces were easier to obtain than they had been in colonial times. Indeed, the rise in the divorce rate was a matter of some concern during the 19th century, though death, not divorce, was the prime cause of one-parent families, as it was up to 1965.

Functionally, however, America's industrial revolution had a lasting effect on the family. No longer was the household typically a group of interdependent workers. Now, men went to offices and factories and became breadwinners; wives stayed home to mind the hearth; children went off to the new public schools. The home was set apart from the dog-eat-dog arena of economic life; it came to be viewed as a utopian retreat or, in historian Christopher Lasch's phrase, a "haven in a heartless world." Marriage was now valued primarily for its emotional attractions. Above all, the family became something to worry about.

The earliest and most saccharine "sentimental model" of the family appeared in the new mass media that proliferated during the second quarter of the 19th century. Novels, tracts, newspaper articles, and ladies' magazines — there were variations for each class of society — elaborated a "Cult of True Womanhood" in which piety, submissiveness, and domesticity dominated the pantheon of desirable feminine qualities. This quotation from *The Ladies Book* (1830) is typical:

> See, she sits, she walks, she speaks, she looks — unutterable things! Inspiration springs up in her very paths — it follows her footsteps. A halo of glory encircles her, and illuminates her whole orbit. With her, man not only feels safe, but actually renovated.

In the late 1800s, science came into the picture. The "professionalization" of the housewife took two different forms. One involved motherhood and childrearing, according to the latest scientific understanding of children's special physical and emotional needs. (It is no accident that the publishing of children's books became a major industry during this period.) The other was the domestic science movement — "home economics," basically — which focused on the woman as full-time homemaker, applying "scientific" and "industrial" rationality to shopping, making meals, and housework.

The new ideal of the family prompted a cultural split that has endured, one that Tocqueville had glimpsed (and rather liked) in 1835. Society was divided more sharply into man's sphere and woman's sphere. Toughness, competition, and practicality were the masculine values that ruled the outside world. The softer values — affection, tranquility, piety — were worshiped in the home and the church. In contrast to the colonial view, the ideology of the "modern" family implied a critique of everything beyond the front door.

What is striking as one looks at the writings of the 19th-century "experts"—the physicians, clergymen, phrenologists, and "scribbling ladies"— is how little their essential message differs from that of the sociologists, psychiatrists, pediatricians, and women's magazine writers of the 20th century, particularly since World War II.

Instead of men's and women's spheres, of course, sociologists speak of "instrumental" and "expressive" roles. The notion of the family as a retreat from the harsh realities of the outside world crops up as "functional differentiation." And, like the 19th-century utopians who believed society could be regenerated through the perfection of family life, 20th-century social scientists have looked at the failed family as the source of most American social problems.

None of those who promoted the sentimental model of the family— neither the popular writers nor the academics—considered the paradox of perfectionism: the ironic possibility that it would lead to trouble. Yet it has. The image of the perfect, happy family makes ordinary families seem like failures. Small problems loom as big problems if the "normal" family is thought to be one where there are no real problems at all.

One sees this phenomenon at work on the generation of Americans born and reared during the late 19th century, the first generation reared on the mother's milk of sentimental imagery. Between 1900 and 1920, the U.S. divorce rate doubled, from four to eight divorces annually per 1,000 married couples. The jump—comparable to the 100 percent increase in the divorce rate between 1960 and 1980—is not attributable to changes in divorce laws, which were not greatly liberalized. Rather, it would appear that, as historian Thomas O'Neill believes, Americans were simply more willing to dissolve marriages that did not conform to their ideal of domestic bliss—and perhaps try again.

If anything, family standards became even more demanding as the 20th century progressed. The new fields of psychology and sociology opened up whole new definitions of familial perfection. "Feelings"—fun, love, warmth, good orgasm—acquired heightened popular significance as the invisible glue of successful families.

Psychologist Martha Wolfenstein, in an analysis of several decades of government-sponsored infant care manuals, has documented the emergence of a "fun morality." In former days, being a good parent meant carrying out certain tasks with punctilio; if your child was clean and reasonably obedient, you had no cause to probe his psyche. Now, we are told, parents must commune with their own feelings and those of their children—an edict which has seeped into the ethos of education as well. The distinction is rather like that between religions of deed and religions of faith. It is one thing to make your child brush his teeth; it is quite another to transform the whole process into a joyous "learning experience."

The task of 20th-century parents has been further complicated by the advice offered them. The experts disagree with each other and often contradict themselves. The kindly Dr. Benjamin Spock, for example, is full of contradictions. In a detailed analysis of *Baby and Child Care,* historian Michael Zuckerman observes that Spock tells mothers to relax ("trust yourself") yet warns them that they have an "ominous power" to destroy their children's innocence and make them discontented "for years" or even "forever."

Since the mid-1960s, there has been a youth rebellion of sorts, a new "sexual revolution," a revival of feminism, and the emergence of the two-worker family. The huge postwar Baby-Boom generation is pairing off, accounting in part for the upsurge in the divorce rate (half of all divorces occur within seven years of a first marriage). Media images of the family have become more "realistic," reflecting new patterns of family life that are emerging (and old patterns that are re-emerging).

Among social scientists, "realism" is becoming something of an ideal in itself. For some of them, realism translates as pluralism: All forms of the family, by virtue of the fact that they happen to exist, are equally acceptable — from communes and cohabitation to one-parent households, homosexual marriages, and, come to think of it, the nuclear family. What was once labeled "deviant" is now merely "variant." In some college texts, "the family" has been replaced by "family systems." Yet, this new approach does not seem to have squelched perfectionist standards. Indeed, a palpable strain of perfectionism runs through the pop literature on "alternative" family lifestyles.

For the majority of scholars, realism means a more down-to-earth view of the American household. Rather than seeing the family as a haven of peace and tranquility, they have begun to recognize that even "normal" families are less than ideal, that intimate relations of any sort inevitably involve antagonism as well as love. Conflict and change are inherent in social life. If the family is now in a state of flux, such is the nature of resilient institutions; if it is beset by problems, so is life. The family will survive.

*For Discussion*

1. Skolnik refers to the power of the photograph to cause us to see illusion as reality. Look at some magazines aimed at parents or grandparents. What models of family life do they portray? What do the images suggest the family is like today? In what ways are these depicted families "ideal"? What is the size of the family? Are members outside the nuclear family often depicted? What gender roles do the parents play in these images?

2. Bianchi and Casper describe the "idealized" family in paragraph 13 of their article and explain that "[t]his vision of family life showed

amazing staying power, even as its economic underpinnings were eroding." After reading the entire article, what are some of the economic forces that have undermined this version of family life? What other forces have worked to keep the traditional image alive in spite of these changes?

3. Look at the Human Rights Campaign ad on page 472. What arguments does this ad, which appeared in major publications as *The New York Times* and *Time*, make about gay and lesbian families? What in general does this ad say about families in America today?

4. In paragraph 51, Bianchi and Casper tell us that out-of-wedlock births per 1,000 women increased from 7.1 in 1940 to 46.9 in 1994. Since then, there has been a slight decline, to 43.9 in the late 1990s. Has public opinion begun to change regarding births outside of marriage? What social or economic factors may be influencing public opinion? What image of single motherhood do we get from the media and popular culture today?

5. Bianchi and Casper report that even with all the factors that have reduced the percentage of married-with-children households, in the year 2000 "73 percent of families with children were two-parent families" (paragraph 42). Compare this fact with the findings of a University of Chicago researcher who found that "In 1972, 73 percent of children lived with their original two parents, who were married. By 1998, 51.7 lived in such households." What has changed? What do Bianchi and Casper's findings indicate about the relationship between women's employment outside the home and the rate of divorce? Compare what this article has to say with Stephanie Coontz's section on "Working Women, Singlehood, and Divorce," on pages 550–551 in her essay, "The Future of Marriage."

6. In her essay "The Madness of the American Family," (see pages 574–584) Midge Decter argues that the family is in "profound disorder" because differentiation of sex roles has blurred. Read the box on pages 500–501 about fathers' involvement in parenting. What do the surveys show about actual American attitudes and practices? What do you think explains the different responses of the males and females in the tables about who should do what kind of parenting, and who actually does that type of parenting?

## For Research and Convincing

The traditional nuclear family, the "haven in a heartless world," developed along with the Industrial Revolution, mass communication, and advertising. Look at images of the ideal family in film, advertising, and TV. Is this model one way that we keep a healthy economy running by stimulating demand for goods and services? Or does the "ideal family" in our culture promote nonmaterial values? If you find that images suggest that "perfect" family happiness can be bought, write an argument to convince your readers of the harm these images might do.

## For Persuading

Skolnick looks only at the evolution of white, middle-class ideas of the family. Look into the history of the family in another cultural tradition, such as African American or Native American or one of the many immigrant cultures. What differences in family models do you find? If you find that these cultures have different values and practices, argue for or against preserving them rather than assimilating to the dominant model of the "typical/ideal" American family. What conflicts might arise for family members as they negotiate between competing models of "family"?


## SECTION 2: LOVE AND MARRIAGE

The readings in this section all have to do with marriage in America today. Married couples, while still the majority of households, have declined in percentage of the total picture of American households (see Figure 1 on page 481). Some explanations are that longer life spans have resulted in more elderly people living alone, while later marriage and the frequency of divorce have also contributed to single-person households. According to Bianchi and Casper, the "proportion of households with just one person doubled from 13 percent to 26 percent between 1960 and 2000" (paragraph 18). There has also been an increase in the number of people living with roommates or unmarried partners.

Why have so many young people delayed getting married and starting families? Some of the readings in this section attempt to answer these questions. The essay "Happily Ever After?" comes from a book entitled *The Case for Marriage*. Its authors, Linda Waite and Maggie Gallagher, see a strong connection between doubt about the value of marriage and Americans' desire to fulfill their individual human potentials. For people who put "autonomy, independence, growth, and creativity" high on their list of needs, marriage can be an impediment. Waite and Gallagher are concerned that myths about the oppressive nature of the marriage bond are turning America into a "post-marriage culture," a culture "in which marriage is viewed as unnecessary, or strictly speaking, optional—a private taste rather than a matter of urgent shared concern" (3). Another reason marriage is in trouble is that Americans expect too much of it in terms of personal emotional fulfillment. Laura Kipnis (*New York Times Magazine*, October 14, 2001) argues that Americans are unrealistic in their expectations that "romance and sexual attraction can last a lifetime" (paragraph 3). Kipnis's essay responds directly to the question raised by the sentimental idea of nineteenth-century marriage: How important is it that marriage be based on romantic rather than rational feelings?

Should we marry the good friend or the one who sweeps us off our feet? No-rah Vincent, in her essay for the gay-lesbian journal *The Advocate* (December 2000), has one answer: Marriage is in trouble because our culture defines love in illusory, romantic terms. She offers a less romantic but more durable definition. However, Ethan Watters, writing in the same *New York Times Magazine* as Kipnis, says the romantic definition is rising in popularity. Describing his generation's view as *"über-romantic,"* he argues that it will be good for the institution of marriage.

Despite all the doubts about marriage, Waite and Gallagher report that in a recent survey, ninety-three percent of Americans said that "having a happy marriage" was one of their chief goals. Some researchers who questioned college students on the subject concluded, "They are desperate to have only one marriage, and they want it to be happy. They just don't know whether this is possible anymore" (qtd. in Waite 3).

Works Cited

Waite, Linda and Maggie Gallagher. <u>The Case for Marriage: Why Married People Are Happier, Healthier, and Better Off Financially</u>. New York: Broadway Books. 2000.

---

## Happily Ever After?
### Linda Waite and Maggie Gallagher

In most cultures, marriage marks the end of carefree adolescence and the beginning of serious adult responsibility. Marriage is both the end point of romantic longing but perhaps also, we fear, the end of romantic love.

Most of us carry within us, unresolved, both images of marriage: a source of happiness, satisfaction, and gratification and a source of restriction, frustration, and curtailment.

Thus, in his study of successful men, Robert Weiss reports, "When men who have been married fifteen or twenty years are asked how marriage changed their lives, their first thought is apt to be lost freedom."

"If I weren't married I'd probably have one hell of a time" is Mr. Brewer's first, immediate response. "I'd probably spend my summers in Newport and my winters on the Caribbean." In the next breath, Mr. Brewer offers a different vision of life without the burdens of marriage: "Much as I wouldn't want to admit it, I'd probably be lonesome with life. Because I know quite a few guys that got divorced and what it really comes down to, a lot of them go home at night to a cold home."[1]

Now that women have the same sexual license as men do and more economic opportunity, they, too, voice a similar ambivalence about the relationship between marriage and happiness. Today's young women live with both the fairy tale and its negation, the old yearning for a happily-ever-after and the modern disillusioned "knowledge" that pinning one's hopes for happiness on a husband is a recipe for disaster. Women, experts warn, may be "casualties of a marital subculture that crushes their emerging identities."[2]

These two competing visions of marriage—the wedding as a doorway to happiness and the wedding as an obstacle to individual growth—subsist side by side in contemporary American culture. Each has resonance; each perhaps reflects some hard-won bits of personal truth.

Is there any objective way to sort out the probabilities of these competing points of view? Is marriage generally good for one's mental and emotional health, or is living with one person for the rest of your life enough to drive a sane person bonkers? When people consider getting or staying married, the question often at the forefront of their minds is, Will getting married (or getting a divorce) make me happy?

### A Measure of Happiness?

For a social scientist, the first step to answering such a question is defining the terms. For one thing, the line between physical and mental health is nowhere near as sharp and bright as people commonly assume. Emotional distress . . . often leads to physical illness, while chronic physical illness frequently results in mental distress, including depression. Moreover, mental disorders such as anxiety or depression often manifest themselves in a series of physical symptoms, such as sleeplessness, fatigue, sweaty palms, racing heartbeats, or a loss of appetite. Separating the mind from the body is not so easy.

And mental health and happiness, though intimately related, are not exactly the same thing either. Researchers have developed various measures to help capture subjective well-being. Psychological well-being consists of feeling hopeful, happy, and good about oneself. Those in good emotional health feel energetic, eager to get going, and connected to others.

Psychological distress, by contrast, comes in a variety of forms, including depression, or feelings of sadness, loneliness, and hopelessness. Psychological distress may also appear as anxiety, tenseness, or restlessness. Anxiety can also produce other physical symptoms such as acid stomach, sweaty palms, shortness of breath, and hard, rapid beating of the heart in the absence of exercise.[3]

Like physical health, emotional well-being is both a good in itself and a means to other goods, the necessary precondition to functioning effectively in our various roles and fulfilling our diverse ambitions.

How does marriage influence our odds of achieving a sense of emotional well-being or avoiding psychological distress? Does marriage more often make us happy or frustrate our desire for emotional growth? Overall, perhaps surprisingly, the evidence gathered by social science points more in

10

the direction of an older, rosier view than the bleaker modern suspicion. Marriage appears to be an important pathway toward better emotional and mental health.

*[handwritten note: What about those who have never married!]*

### Escaping the Abyss

When it comes to avoiding misery, a wedding band helps. Married men and women report less depression, less anxiety, and lower levels of other types of psychological distress than do those who are single, divorced, or widowed.[4]

As one researcher summarized the international data on marriage and mental health, "Numerous studies have shown that the previously married tend to be considerably less happy and more distressed than the married."[5]

*[handwritten margin note: statistics]*

One study of the more than eighty thousand suicides in the United States between 1979 and 1981 found that overall, both widowed and divorced persons were about three times as likely to commit suicide as the married were.[6] Although more men than women kill themselves, marriage protects wives as well as husbands. Divorced women are the most likely to commit suicide, following by widowed, never-married, and married (in that order).[7]

When it comes to happiness, the married have a similarly powerful advantage. One survey of fourteen thousand adults over a ten-year period, for example, found that marital status was one of the most important predictors of happiness.[8] According to the latest data, 40 percent of the married said they are very happy with their life in general, compared to just under a quarter of those who were single or who were cohabiting. The separated (15 percent very happy) and the divorced (18 percent very happy) were the least happy groups. The widowed were, perhaps surprisingly, just about as likely to say they are very happy as singles or as cohabitors—22 percent.[9]

On the other end of the scale, married people were also about half as likely as singles or cohabitors to say they are unhappy with their lives. The divorced were two and a half times more likely, and the widowed were almost three times more likely than spouses to confess they are "not too happy." The most miserable were the separated, who at 27 percent were almost four times more likely than the married to say they are "not too happy with life."[10]

### Does Marriage Make You Happy or Do Happy People Get Married?

Why are married people so much healthier mentally and happier emotionally than those who are not married? One possibility is that happy, healthy people find it easier to get (and keep) mates. Divorced and widowed people may be unhappier, because the gay divorcées and merry widows disproportionately remarry. The happiness boost from marriage may be more apparent than real, a function of the selection of individuals into and out of the married state.

In recent years social scientists have extensively investigated this theory, tracking people into and out of the married state to see if marriage really is a cause of mental health and happiness. This powerful new body of research clearly comes down against the cynics: The selection of happy and healthy people into marriage cannot explain the big advantage in mental and emotional health husbands and wives enjoy.

Certainly happily married people do not doubt that the love of their spouses helps them weather the storms and shocks of life. "Before my father died, we went on a vacation together where we talked and talked. We told each other how much we loved each other. . . . Matt was there with me and for me, always, to get through these terrible things, as I was with him when his parents died," said Sara, a slim woman in her early fifties.[11] "[S]he shares and defends my interests," her husband, Matt, an environmental policy analyst, chimes in. "She understands what I do. None of what I do now would have happened without her active support. She encourages me all the time."[12]

Economists write a great deal about the economic specialization that takes place in marriage; spouses just as often spontaneously offer stories of emotional specialization, a balancing act that leaves both partners better off. "I've learned I need balance, to be cautious. Otherwise I'll get into a lot of trouble," notes Helen, the livelier and less emotionally inhibited member of her marriage. "And [Keith] provides that. [He] is not a risk taker. I add spice to his life. I want quick solutions and I tend to jump ahead. He's slower to act and react."[13]

Tina acknowledges the role her tumultuous marriage played even in providing the support she needed to resolve her childhood traumas: "As crazy as he [her husband] was—and he was crazy—I never had to wonder if I was alone," she said. "Sometimes I felt alone, but I knew I wasn't alone. Because I wasn't alone, I could feel how lonely I used to be. I felt safe and protected and loved. And by my midthirties I could finally begin to face that I had been unsafe, unprotected, and unloved throughout my whole childhood. . . ."[14]

When Nicholas, a very successful executive, went to the hospital with an anxiety attack, he credits his wife with knowing just what he needed to help him recover: "During that entire frightening time, she was wonderful. She was calm, sympathetic, reassuring, but never intrusive and certainly never hysterical. Whatever she suffered—and I'm sure she did, we both did—she protected me. She gave me the support and the space that I needed."[15]

Spouses can help in these times of crisis in a way that a friend or lover cannot precisely because of what marriage means: someone who will be there for you, in sickness or in health. Living with someone "until death do us part" provides a particular kind of intimacy—a spouse comforts partly because he or she has the knowledge that comes from long, emotional acquaintance but also because only a spouse can offer the peculiar reassurance that whatever life tosses at you, as Tina put it, at least you won't face it alone.

The most convincing evidence that marriage causes better emotional health comes from studies that follow people's life changes over a number of years, as some marry and stay married, some marry and divorce, and some remain divorced or never marry.                                                    25

Nadine Marks and James Lambert did precisely this kind of work, looking at changes in the psychological health of men and women from the late 1980s to the mid-1990s. They took into account the psychological health of each individual in the year the monitoring began and watched what happened to him or her over the next five years. They measured psychological well-being in amazing detail, along eleven separate dimensions, including many measures that psychologists have used for years, such as depression, happiness with life in general, and self-esteem, as well as other, newer measures: personal mastery (which reflects the feeling that one has control over his or her life and can reach the goals set for oneself); hostility (feeling angry, irritable, or likely to argue); autonomy (being independent of influence by others); positive relations with others (having close personal relations, being a giving person); having a purpose in life (which reflects one's aims in life); self-acceptance (liking oneself); environmental mastery (being able to meet the demands of everyday life); and personal growth, which reflects one's learning, changing, and growing.[16]

When people married, their mental health improved — consistently and substantially. Meanwhile, over the same period, when people separated and divorced, they suffered substantial deterioration in mental and emotional well-being, including increases in depression and declines in reported happiness, compared to the married — even after Marks and Lambert took into account their subjects' mental health at the start of the study. Those who dissolved a marriage also reported less personal mastery, less positive relations with others, less purpose in life, and less self-acceptance than their married peers did.

Divorce, Marks and Lambert found, was especially damaging to women's mental health; divorcing women reported more of an increase in depression, more hostility, more of a decline in self-esteem, less personal growth, and less self-acceptance and environmental mastery than divorcing men.[17]

Because they had measures of people's mental health both before and after marriage, Marks and Lambert were able to rule out selection as the explanation for the mental-health advantage of married people. Instead, they found the act of getting married actually makes people happier and healthier; conversely, getting a divorce reverses these gains — even when we take into account prior measures of mental and emotional health.

In a similarly powerful study aptly titled "Becoming Married and Mental Health," researchers Allan Horwitz, Helen Raskin White, and Sandra      30

Howell-White examined changes in psychological well-being among young adults over a seven-year period. They paid particular attention to those men and women who got married during the study period. The researchers measured the emotional health of each person at the beginning of the study, using that data as their starting point, and looked for changes when certain events occurred, especially marriage. They compared the mental health of those who got married with that of people who stayed single over the entire study. They used two measures of mental health: depression and problems with alcohol.

Once again, marriage made a big difference: Young adults who got married experience sharper drops in levels of both depression and problem drinking than did young adults who stay single. Interestingly, although more of the men than the women were problem drinkers, getting married led to bigger declines in problem drinking for women.[18] By the same token, more of the women were depressed than the men, but getting married reduced depression for the men but not for the women.[19] Horwitz and his colleagues concluded that "adequate statements about the relative advantages of marriage for men and women cannot be based on single mental health outcomes." They also concluded that marriage advantages both men and women, but does it through different mechanisms.[20]

Selection played a surprisingly small role in who marries, at least with regard to depression and alcohol abuse. Horwitz, White, and Howell-White found that alcohol use has no impact on entry into marriage; problem drinkers were just as likely as abstainers to find someone to marry. The same was true of depression, at least for the men; relatively high levels of depression do not preclude marriage or even reduce a person's chances of marrying. More of the depressed women did face increased chances of remaining single. But the strong positive impact of getting married remained even when the researchers took into account initial levels of depression and alcohol abuse for the individuals. Their conclusion? "Selection effects do not account for the lower rates of depression among people who become married, compared to those who remain single."[21]

### The Lonely Heart?

Researchers who first noticed this correlation between mental health and marital status speculated that simply living with other persons—which almost all married persons do—was the source of the emotional-health advantages of the married. Living alone, they theorized, causes distress, and those single men and women who live with others probably are as psychologically healthy as the married.

But social scientists who have tested the idea found, to their surprise, that living arrangements cannot explain the emotional advantages of marriage. Walter R. Gove and Michael Hughes compared mental-health measurements of married adults and unmarried adults who lived alone with those of people who lived with someone else. Even single adults who lived with others were more depressed than the married.[22]

The latest studies confirm these findings. In their joint research, Linda     35
Waite and Mary Elizabeth Hughes examined two different measures of emotional health among adults in their fifties and early sixties. They found that all the single adults, whether living alone, with children, or with others, described their emotional health more negatively than did the married people. Just 17 percent of older wives characterized their emotional health as either fair or poor, compared to 28 percent of the older single women. Similarly, just 14 percent of the husbands versus 27 percent of the single men described their emotional health as fair or poor. At the other end of the happiness spectrum, 50 percent of the wives versus only 38 percent of the unmarried women described their emotional health as either very good or excellent. Meanwhile, 53 percent of the husbands but only 42 percent of the older unmarried guys rated their emotional health so high.

The husbands and wives also reported substantially fewer symptoms of depression than the single adults did, who were more depressed, on average, than the married even when they were living with their children or other people.[23]

To married couples, these results must not have been so surprising. For marriage changes not just people's outward physical arrangement but their inner relation to one another. The tendency among social scientists has been to conceptualize marriage as an external, structural category and to look beneath the piece of paper for the "real" reasons married people appear happier and healthier. But in American society, marriage is not just a label, it remains a transformative act — marriage not only names a relationship but it creates a relationship between two people, one that is acknowledged, not just by the couple itself, but by the couples' kin, friends, religious community, and larger society.

Almost by definition, married people share their lives with each other to a much greater extent than single adults do. Roommates, parents, adult children, friends, even live-in lovers, all have separate lives from those of the people they live with and expect more independence and autonomy from each other than spouses do.

### The Limits of Cohabitation

Indeed, researchers have found that a desire to retain one's autonomy — to keep a life apart — is one of the prime factors that drives individuals toward cohabitation over marriage. Cohabitors, for example, are far more likely to spend leisure time apart from their lovers than spouses are. Cohabitors also place a higher value than do the married on having time for one's own individual leisure activities.[24]

In the short term, cohabitors may gain some (though not nearly all) of the emotional benefits of marriage. But over the long haul, it appears cohabitors may be no better off than singles. Another large study, this time of more than 100,000 Norwegians, found that for both the men and women, "the married have the highest level of subjective well-being, followed by the widowed."   40

Even the divorced or separated people who cohabited did not seem to be much better off than those who lived alone, with one important exception: Those who moved in with a new partner within one year after divorce or separation reported very high rates of happiness, higher even than those of the married.

This phenomenon may reflect, as the study suggests, a buffering effect that protects an ex-spouse during the strains of divorce. But it may also reflect the likelihood that those who move in with a partner immediately following a divorce began the relationship before the end of the marriage. The glow of happiness these couples report may reflect the underlying social reality: It is far more pleasant to be the one who dumps one's spouse for a new love than to be traded in for a different model. But this newfound happiness of live-in lovers appears to be short-lived (at least among those who do not quickly remarry). "[A]mong those who have remained divorced for three years or more the level of well-being is much lower and very similar for the single and cohabiting," the study concludes.[25]

Cohabitation provides some—but not all—of the same emotional benefits of marriage, yet only for a short time and at a high price. Breaking up with a live-in lover carries many of the same emotional costs as divorce but happens far more frequently. People who are cohabiting are less happy generally than the married and are less satisfied with their sex lives. In America, long-term cohabiting relationships are far rarer than successful marriages.[26]

Of course, marriage can be a source of stress as well as comfort. The strong emotional benefits of marriage come only from relationships that spouses rate as "very happy."[27] Those who describe their marriages as "pretty happy" are somewhat better off than singles, but not as well off as those in "very happy" relationships.[28]

Not surprisingly, the men and women in the relatively small number of "not too happy" marriages show more psychological distress than do singles. Horwitz and his colleagues find that the quality of the marriage is the most consistent determinant of both depression and problem drinking; both husbands and wives who say they have a good relationship with their spouses also report lower levels of depression and fewer problems with alcohol.[29] People who say their relationships are unhappy, that they would like to change many aspects of their relationship and that they often consider leaving their spouses or partners have higher distress levels than people without partners at all.[30]   45

Fortunately for the mental health of the country, most married people describe their marriages as "very happy." Among the nearly twenty thousand married men and women questioned over the last several decades as part of the General Social Survey, 66 percent of the husbands and 62 percent of the wives give their marriage the highest possible happiness rating. Almost no one—2 percent of the married men and 4 percent of the married women—described their marriage as "not too happy."[31] So the emotional damage from an unhappy marriage is quite a rare occurrence, and the vast majority of married men and women get emotional benefits—usually very large ones—from being married.

Nor do unhappy marriages necessarily stay that way: 86 percent of those who rated their marriage as unhappy in the late eighties and who were still married five years later said their marriages had become happier.[32]

### The Marital Transformation

New marriage partners together create a shared sense of social reality and meaning—their own little separate world, populated by only the two of them. This shared sense of meaning can be an important foundation for emotional health.[33]

Ordinary, good-enough marriages provide the partners with a sense that what they do matters, that someone cares for, esteems, needs, loves, and values them as a person. No matter what else happens in life, this knowledge makes problems easier to bear.

Over a century ago, sociologist Émile Durkheim found that people who were integrated into society were much less likely to commit suicide than people who were more socially marginal. Life is uncertain and often hard, he argued, but being part of a larger group one loves gives people the strength and will to cling to life in the face of difficulties.[34]

Marriage and family provide the sense of belonging that Durkheim had in mind, the sense of loving and being loved, of being absolutely essential to the life and happiness of others. Believing that one has a purpose in life and a reason for continued existence, that life is worth the effort because one's activities and challenges are worthy comes from having other people depending on you, counting on you, caring about you. Married people have a starring role in the lives of their spouses; their shared universe would cease to exist if something happened to one of them. When the shared universe includes children, the sense of being essential, of having a purpose and a full life expands as well. Marriage improves emotional well-being in part by giving people a sense that their life has meaning and purpose.[35]

The enhanced sense of meaning and purpose that marriage provides protects each spouse's psychological health. Russell Burton examined reports of psychological distress for a national sample of adults. As other sociologists have, Burton found that multiple social roles seem to protect people's mental health. Men who were employed, married, and parents, for example, were less distressed than other men.[36] Men who were employed and married or married and a parent but not employed also felt that their lives had more meaning and purpose than other men did. Burton found a similar picture for women: Employed single women, employed wives, employed single mothers, married mothers, and employed married mothers *duh !* were less distressed than women who were single, childless, and not employed. But while having more than one social role can boost one's health, marriage appears to be the key role. Married women — regardless of whether they worked or had children — reported greater purpose and meaning in life, and neither work nor children, in the absence of marriage, increased women's feelings of purpose and meaning. The sense of meaning and purpose marriage creates, concluded Burton, seems to be in itself responsible for the better psychological health of husbands and wives.[37]

Oddly, contemporary experts have often failed to notice the immense transformative power of the marriage act. Perhaps because, in the age of divorce, sensible people naturally place a great deal of emphasis on finding the right partner, experts tend to talk as if a marriage license were only a "piece of paper," as if the relationship were everything and the marriage ceremony merely a public certification of a preexisting condition.

The ideas that happiness is a purely individual rather than an interpersonal achievement, that marriage is simply a sum of the characteristics of the individuals that enter into it, that getting married cannot change an individual's outlook, behavior, or internal feelings is surprisingly influential in contemporary America. Noting that married people say they are lonely less often than do singles, a recent college textbook on marriage and family concludes, "It would be ludicrous to suggest that young adults who experience loneliness and stress should marry to alleviate their problems. Obviously, the same personal characteristics that resulted in their distressful state in singleness would also be reflected in marriage."[38]

As Professor Norval Glenn stated in a critique of textbooks, "[M]ost social scientists who have studied the data believe that marriage itself accounts for a great deal of the difference in average well-being between married and unmarried persons. Indeed, loneliness is probably the negative feeling most likely to be alleviated simply by being married."[39]

The latest research shows the skeptics are wrong: In real life, the public legal commitment represented by that "piece of paper" makes a big difference. The married really are emotionally healthier than their single counterparts because they've chosen to live in this particular type of committed relationship. The commitment married people make to each other is reinforced and supported not only by their own private efforts and emotions, but by the wider community — by the expectations and support of friends, families, bosses, and colleagues who share basic notions about how married people behave.

The emotional support and monitoring of a spouse encourages healthy behavior that in turn affects emotional as well as physical well-being: regular sleep, a healthy diet, moderate drinking. But the key seems to be the marriage bond itself: Having a partner who is committed for better or for worse, in sickness and in health, makes people happier and healthier. The knowledge that someone cares for you and that you have someone who depends on you helps give life meaning and provides a buffer against the inevitable troubles of life.

In contemporary folklore, marriage may represent the end of the period of happy, carefree youth. But science tends to confirm Grandma's wisdom: On the whole, man was not meant to live alone, and neither was woman. Marriage makes people happier.

### Notes

1. Robert S. Weiss, *Staying the Course: The Emotional and Social Lives of Men Who Do Well at Work* (New York: Fawcett Columbine, 1990), 113.

2. Christopher Hayes, Deborah Anderson, and Melina Blau, *Our Turn: Women Who Triumph in the Face of Divorce* (New York: Pocket Books, 1993), 70, quoted in Barbara Dafoe Whitehead, *The Divorce Culture: How Divorce Became an Entitlement and How It Is Blighting the Lives of Our Children* (New York: Alfred A. Knopf, 1997), 60.

3. John Mirowsky and Catherine E. Ross, *Social Causes of Psychological Distress* (New York: Aldine De Gruyter, 1989).

4. Ibid., 90–92.

5. Arne Mastekaasa, "The Subjective Well-being of the Previously Married: The Importance of Unmarried Cohabitation and Time Since Widowhood or Divorce," *Social Forces* 73 (1994): 665.

6. Jack C. Smith, Mercy, and Conn, "Marital Status and the Risk," 78–80.

7. Ibid.

8. James A. Davis, "New Money, an Old Man/Lady, and 'Two's Company': Subjective Welfare in the NORC General Social Surveys, 1972–1982," *Social Indicators Research* 15 (1984): 319–50. Davis also found that race and recent financial change predicted happiness.

9. Seven percent of spouses versus 13 percent of singles said they were "not too happy." Twenty percent of the widowed were "not too happy," as were 18 percent of the divorced and 27 percent of the separated. Tabulations by Linda J. Waite from the General Social Survey, 1990–1996 waves.

10. Tabulations by Linda J. Waite from the General Social Survey, 1990–1996 waves.

11. Judith S. Wallerstein and Sandra Blakeslee, *The Good Marriage: How and Why Love Lasts* (Boston: Houghton Mifflin, 1995), 85.

12. Ibid., 45.

13. Ibid., 115.

14. Ibid., 139.

15. Ibid., 219.

16. For a detailed discussion of these measures, see Carol D. Ryff and Corey Lee M. Keyes, "The Structure of Psychological Well-being Revisited," *Journal of Personality and Social Psychology* 69 (1995): 719–27.

17. Nadine F. Marks and James D. Lambert, "Martial Status Continuity and Change among Young and Midlife Adults: Longitudinal Effects on Psychological Well-being." *Journal of Family Issues* 19 (1998): 652–86.

18. Allan V. Horwitz, Helene Raskin White, and Sandra Howell-White, "Becoming Married and Mental Health: A Longitudinal Study of a Cohort of Young Adults," *Journal of Marriage and the Family* 58 (1996): 895–907. Once the authors take into account age, income, and social support, the impact of marriage on problem drinking becomes statistically insignificant for men but remains significant for women.

19. For women, Horwitz et al. ("Becoming Married and Mental Health," 895–907) find that depression in the later year depends *only* on depression at the beginning of the study.

20. Horwitz et al., "Becoming Married and Mental Health," 904.

21. Ibid., 901. See also Marks and Lambert, "Marital Status Continuity," 652–86.

22. Walter R. Gove and Michael Hughes, "Possible Causes of the Apparent Sex Differences in Physical Health: An Empirical Investigation," *American Sociological Review* 44 (1979): 126–46.

23. Tabulations done for this book by Linda J. Waite from the Health and Retirement Survey. See Juster, Thomas F., and Richard Suzman, "An Overview of the Health and Retirement Survey," *Journal of Human Resources* 30 (1995): S7–S56. See also Linda J. Waite and Mary Elizabeth Hughes, "At Risk on the Cusp of Old Age: Living Arrangements and Functional Status among Black, White, and Hispanic Adults in the Health and Retirement Survey," *Journal of Gerontology: Social Sciences* 54B (1998): S136–S144.

24. Blumstein and Schwartz, *American Couples*, 186–87; Clarkberg, Stolzenberg, and Waite, "Attitudes, Values and Entrance," 609–34.

25. Mastekaasa, "Subjective Well-being," 682.

26. Bumpass and Sweet, "National Estimates of Cohabitation," 615–25.

27. Horwitz et al., "Becoming Married and Mental Health," 903.

28. Ross, "Reconceptualizing Marital Status," 129–40.

29. Horwitz et al., "Becoming Married and Mental Health," 903.

30. Ross, "Reconceptualizing Marital Status," 137.

31. Linda J. Waite's tabulations from the 1972–1994 General Social Survey. Although we might suspect that many more people are unhappy in their marriage than will admit this to a survey interviewer, responses on marital happiness are closely related to reports of overall happiness. We might also suspect that in an era of easy divorce, unhappily married people divorce, leaving only the happily married. In fact, we see no evidence that this has occurred. See Norval D. Glenn, "Values, Attitudes," 15–33.

32. Linda J. Waite's tabulations from the National Survey of Families and Households, 1987/88 and 1992/94.

33. Peter Berger and Hansfried Kellner, "Marriage and the Construction of Reality: An Exercise in the Microsociology of Knowledge," *Diogenes* 46 (1964): 1–25.

34. Émile Durkheim, *Suicide* (1897; reprint, New York: Free Press, 1951).

35. Russell P. D. Burton, "Global Integrative Meaning as a Mediating Factor in the Relationship between Social Roles and Psychological Distress," *Journal of Health and Social Behavior* 39 (1998): 201–15. See also Mirowsky and Ross, *Social Causes*, 25.

36. Ibid., 209. Burton also found that men who were employed but neither married nor parents were less distressed than the comparison group—men who were unemployed, single, and not parents.

37. Ibid, 210–13.

38. J. Kenneth Davidson Sr., and Nelwyn B. Moore, *Marriage and Family: Change and Continuity* (Boston: Allyn and Bacon, 1996) 322.

39. Norval Glenn, *Closed Hearts, Closed Minds: The Textbook Story of Marriage* (New York: Institute for American Values 1997), 11.

---

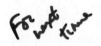

# Against Love
### Laura Kipnis

Love is, as we know, a mysterious and controlling force. It has vast power over our thoughts and life decisions. It demands our loyalty, and we, in turn, freely comply. Saying no to love isn't simply heresy; it is tragedy—the failure to achieve what is most essentially human. So deeply internalized is our obedience to this most capricious despot that artists create passionate odes to its cruelty, and audiences seem never to tire of the most deeply unoriginal mass spectacles devoted to rehearsing the litany of its torments, fixating their very beings on the narrowest glimmer of its fleeting satisfactions.

Yet despite near total compliance, a buzz of social nervousness attends the subject. If a society's lexicon of romantic pathologies reveals its particular anxieties, high on our own list would be diagnoses like "inability to settle down" or "immaturity," leveled at those who stray from the norms of domestic coupledom either by refusing entry in the first place or, once installed, pursuing various escape routes: excess independence, ambivalence, "straying," divorce. For the modern lover, "maturity" isn't a depressing signal of impending decrepitude but a sterling achievement, the sine qua non of a lover's qualifications to love and be loved.

This injunction to achieve maturity—synonymous in contemporary usage with 30-year mortgages, spreading waistlines and monogamy—obviously finds its raison d'être in modern love's central anxiety, that structuring social contradiction the size of the San Andreas Fault: namely, the expectation that romance and sexual attraction can last a lifetime of coupled togetherness despite much hard evidence to the contrary.

Ever optimistic, heady with love's utopianism, most of us eventually pledge ourselves to unions that will, if successful, far outlast the desire that impelled them into being. The prevailing cultural wisdom is that even if sexual desire tends to be a short-lived phenomenon, "mature love" will kick in to save the day when desire flags. The issue that remains unaddressed is whether cutting off other possibilities of romance and sexual attraction for the more muted pleasures of mature love isn't similar to voluntarily amputating a healthy limb: a lot of anesthesia is required and the phantom pain never entirely abates. But if it behooves a society to convince its citizenry that wanting change means personal failure or wanting to start over is shameful or simply wanting more satisfaction than what you have is an illicit thing, clearly grisly acts of self-mutilation will be required.

There hasn't always been quite such optimism about love's longevity. For the Greeks, inventors of democracy and a people not amenable to being pushed around by despots, love was a disordering and thus preferably brief experience. During the reign of courtly love, love was illicit and usually fatal. Passion meant suffering: the happy ending didn't yet exist in the cultural imagination. As far as togetherness as an eternal ideal, the 12th-century advice manual "De Amore et Amor is Remedio" ("On Love and the Remedies of Love") warned that too many opportunities to see or chat with the beloved would certainly decrease love.

5

The innovation of happy love didn't even enter the vocabulary of romance until the 17th century. Before the 18th century—when the family was primarily an economic unit of production rather than a hothouse of Oedipal tensions—marriages were business arrangements between families; participants had little to say on the matter. Some historians consider romantic love a learned behavior that really only took off in the late 18th century along with the new fashion for reading novels, though even then affection between a husband and wife was considered to be in questionable taste.

Historians disagree, of course. Some tell the story of love as an eternal and unchanging essence; others, as a progress narrative over stifling social conventions. (Sometimes both stories are told at once; consistency isn't required.) But has modern love really set us free? Fond as we are of projecting our own emotional quandaries back through history, construing vivid costume dramas featuring medieval peasants or biblical courtesans sharing their feelings with the post-Freudian savvy of lifelong analysands, our amatory predecessors clearly didn't share all our particular aspirations about their romantic lives.

We, by contrast, feel like failures when love dies. We believe it could be otherwise. Since the cultural expectation is that a state of coupled permanence is achievable, uncoupling is experienced as crisis and inadequacy—even though such failures are more the norm than the exception.

As love has increasingly become the center of all emotional expression in the popular imagination, anxiety about obtaining it in sufficient quantities—and for sufficient duration—suffuses the population. Everyone knows that as the demands and expectations on couples escalated, so did divorce rates. And given the current divorce statistics (roughly 50 percent of all marriages end in divorce), all indications are that whomever you love today—your beacon of hope, the center of all your optimism—has a good chance of becoming your worst nightmare tomorrow. (Of course, that 50 percent are those who actually leave their unhappy marriages and not a particularly good indication of the happiness level or nightmare potential of those who remain.) Lawrence Stone, a historian of marriage, suggests—rather jocularly, you can't help thinking—that today's rising divorce rates are just a modern technique for achieving what was once taken care of far more efficiently by early mortality.

Love may or may not be a universal emotion, but clearly the social                    10
forms it takes are infinitely malleable. It is our culture alone that has dedicated itself to allying the turbulence of romance and the rationality of the long-term couple, convinced that both love and sex are obtainable from one person over the course of decades, that desire will manage to sustain itself for 30 or 40 or 50 years and that the supposed fate of social stability is tied to sustaining a fleeting experience beyond its given life span.

Of course, the parties involved must "work" at keeping passion alive (and we all know how much fun that is), the presumption being that even after living in close proximity to someone for a historically unprecedented length of time, you will still muster the requisite desire to achieve sexual congress on a regular basis. (Should passion fizzle out, just give up sex. Lack of desire for a mate is never an adequate rationale for "looking elsewhere.") And it is true, many couples do manage to perform enough psychic retooling to reshape the anarchy of desire to the confines of the marriage bed, plugging away at the task year after year (once a week, same time, same position) like diligent assembly-line workers, aided by the occasional fantasy or two to help get the old motor to turn over, or keep running, or complete the trip. And so we have the erotic life of a nation of workaholics: if sex seems like work, clearly you're not working hard enough at it.

But passion must not be allowed to die! The fear—or knowledge—that it does shapes us into particularly conflicted psychological beings, perpetually in search of prescriptions and professional interventions, regardless of cost or consequence. Which does have its economic upside, at least. Whole new sectors of the economy have been spawned, with massive social investment in new technologies from Viagra to couples' porn: capitalism's Lourdes for dying marriages.

There are assorted low-tech solutions to desire's dilemmas too. Take advice. In fact, take more and more advice. Between print, airwaves and the therapy industry, if there were any way to quantify the G.N.P. in romantic counsel, it would be a staggering number. Desperate to be cured of love's temporality, a love-struck populace has molded itself into an advanced race of advice receptacles, like some new form of miracle sponge that can instantly absorb many times its own body weight in wetness.

Inexplicably, however, a rebellious breakaway faction keeps trying to leap over the wall and emancipate themselves, not from love itself—unthinkable!—but from love's domestic confinements: The escape routes are well trodden—love affairs, midlife crises—though strewn with the left-behind luggage of those who encountered unforeseen obstacles along the way (panic, guilt, self-engineered exposures) and beat self-abashed retreats to their domestic gulags, even after pledging body and soul to newfound loves in the balmy utopias of nondomesticated romances. Will all the adulterers in the audience please stand up? You know who you are. Don't be embarrassed! Adulterers aren't just "playing around." These are our home-grown closet social theorists, because adultery is not just a referendum on the sustainability of monogamy; it is a veiled philosophical discussion about the social contract itself. The question on the table is this: "How much renunciation of desire does society demand of us, versus the degree of gratification it provides?" Clearly, the adulterer's answer, following a long line of venerable social critics, would be, "Too much."

But what exactly is it about the actual lived experience of modern domestic love that would make flight such a compelling option for so many? Let us briefly examine those material daily life conditions. 15

Fundamentally, to achieve love and qualify for entry into that realm of salvation and transcendence known as the couple (the secular equivalent of entering a state of divine grace), you must *be* a lovable person. And what precisely does being lovable entail? According to the tenets of modern love, it requires an advanced working knowledge of the intricacies of *mutuality.*

Mutuality means recognizing that your partner has needs and being prepared to meet them. This presumes, of course, that the majority of those needs can and should be met by one person. (Question this, and you question the very foundations of the institution. So don't.) These needs of ours run deep, a tangled underground morass of ancient, gnarled roots, looking to ensnarl any hapless soul who might accidentally trod upon their outer radices.

Still, meeting those needs is the most effective way to become the object of another's desire, thus attaining intimacy, which is required to achieve the state known as psychological maturity. (Despite how closely it reproduces the affective conditions of our childhoods, since trading compliance for love is the earliest social lesson learned; we learn it in our cribs.)

You, in return, will have your own needs met by your partner in matters large and small. In practice, many of these matters turn out to be quite small. Frequently, it is the tensions and disagreements over the minutiae of daily living that stand between couples and their requisite intimacy. Taking out the garbage, tone of voice, a forgotten errand—these are the rocky shoals upon which intimacy so often founders.

Mutuality requires *communication*, since in order to be met, these needs 20 must be expressed. (No one's a mind reader, which is not to say that many of us don't expect this quality in a mate. Who wants to keep having to tell someone what you need?) What you need is for your mate to understand you—your desires, your contradictions, your unique sensitivities, what irks you. (In practice, that means what about your mate irks you.) You, in turn, must learn to understand the mate's needs. This means being willing to hear what about yourself irks your mate. Hearing is not a simple physiological act performed with the ears, as you will learn. You may think you know how to *hear*, but that doesn't mean that you know how to *listen*.

With two individuals required to coexist in enclosed spaces for extended periods of time, domesticity requires substantial quantities of compromise and adaptation simply to avoid mayhem. Yet with the post-Romantic ideal of unconstrained individuality informing our most fundamental ideas of the self, this can prove a perilous process. Both parties must be willing to jettison whatever aspects of individuality might prove irritating while being simultaneously allowed to retain enough individuality to feel their autonomy is not being sacrificed, even as it is being surgically excised.

Having mastered mutuality, you may now proceed to *advanced intimacy.* Advanced intimacy involves inviting your partner "in" to your most interior self. Whatever and wherever our "inside" is, the widespread—if somewhat metaphysical—belief in its existence (and the related belief that whatever is in there is dying to get out) has assumed a quasi-medical status. Leeches once served a similar purpose. Now we "express our feelings" in lieu of our fluids because everyone knows that those who don't are far more prone to cancer, ulcers or various dire ailments.

With love as our culture's patent medicine, prescribed for every ill (now even touted as a necessary precondition for that other great American obsession, longevity), we willingly subject ourselves to any number of arcane procedures in its quest. "Opening up" is required for relationship health, so lovers fashion themselves after doctors wielding long probes to penetrate the tender regions. Try to think of yourself as one big orifice: now stop clenching and relax. If the procedure proves uncomfortable, it just shows you're not open enough. Psychotherapy may be required before sufficient dilation can be achieved: the world's most expensive lubricant.

Needless to say, this opening-up can leave you feeling quite vulnerable, lying there psychically spread-eagled and shivering on the examining table of your relationship. (A favored suspicion is that your partner, knowing exactly where your vulnerabilities are, deliberately kicks you there—one reason this opening-up business may not always feel as pleasant as advertised.) And as anyone who has spent much time in—or just in earshot of—a typical couple knows, the "expression of needs" is often the Trojan horse of intimate warfare, since expressing needs means, by definition, that one's partner has thus far failed to meet them.

In any long-term couple, this lexicon of needs becomes codified over time into a highly evolved private language with its own rules. Let's call this couple grammar. Close observation reveals this as a language composed of one recurring unit of speech: the interdiction—highly nuanced, mutually imposed commands and strictures extending into the most minute areas of household affairs, social life, finances, speech, hygiene, allowable idiosyncrasies and so on. From bathroom to bedroom, car to kitchen, no aspect of coupled life is not subject to scrutiny, negotiation and codes of conduct.

A sample from an inexhaustible list, culled from interviews with numerous members of couples of various ages, races and sexual orientations:

You can't leave the house without saying where you're going. You can't not say what time you'll return. You can't go out when the other person feels like staying at home. You can't be a slob. You can't do less than 50 percent of the work around the house, even if the other person wants to do 100 percent more cleaning than you find necessary or even reasonable. You can't leave the dishes for later, load them the way that seems best to you, drink straight from the carton or make crumbs. You can't leave the bathroom door open — it's offensive. You can't leave the bathroom door closed — your partner needs to get in. You can't not shave your underarms or legs. You can't gain weight. You can't watch soap operas. You can't watch infomercials or the pregame show or Martha Stewart. You can't eat what you want — goodbye Marshmallow Fluff; hello tofu meatballs. You can't spend too much time on the computer. And stay out of those chat rooms. You can't take risks, unless they are agreed-upon risks, which somewhat limits the concept of "risk." You can't make major purchases alone, or spend money on things the other person considers excesses. You can't blow money just because you're in a bad mood, and you can't be in a bad mood without being required to explain it. You can't begin a sentence with "You always. . . ." You can't begin a sentence with "I never. . . ." You can't be simplistic, even when things are simple. You can't say what you really think of that outfit or color combination or cowboy hat. You can't be cynical about things the other person is sincere about. You can't drink without the other person counting your drinks. You can't have the wrong laugh. You can't bum cigarettes when you're out because it embarrasses your mate, even though you've explained the unspoken fraternity between smokers. You can't tailgate, honk or listen to talk radio in the car. And so on. The specifics don't matter. What matters is that the operative word is "can't."

Thus is love obtained.

Certainly, domesticity offers innumerable rewards: companionship, child-rearing convenience, reassuring predictability and many other benefits too varied to list. But if love has power over us, domesticity is its enforcement wing: the iron dust mop in the velvet glove. The historian Michel Foucault has argued that modern power made its mark on the world by inventing new types of enclosures and institutions, places like factories, schools, barracks, prisons and asylums, where individuals could be located, supervised, processed and subjected to inspection, order and the clock. What current social institution is more enclosed than modern intimacy? What offers greater regulation of movement and time, or more precise surveillance of body and thought, to a greater number of individuals?

Of course, it is your choice — as if any of us could really choose not to desire love or not to feel like hopeless losers should we fail at it. We moderns   30 are beings yearning to be filled, yearning to be overtaken by love's mysterious power. We prostrate ourselves at love's portals, like social strivers waiting at the rope line outside some exclusive club hoping to gain admission and thereby confirm our essential worth. A life without love lacks an organizing narrative. A life without love seems so barren, and it might almost make you consider how empty the rest of the world is, as if love were vital plasma and everything else just tap water.

Exchanging obedience for love comes naturally—after all, we all were once children whose survival depended on the caprices of love. And there you have the template for future intimacies. If you love me, you'll do what I want—or need, or demand—and I'll love you in return. We all become household dictators, petty tyrants of the private sphere, who are, in our turn, dictated to.

And why has modern love developed in such a way as to maximize submission and minimize freedom, with so little argument about it? No doubt a citizenry schooled in renouncing desire instead of imagining there could be something more would be, in many respects, advantageous. After all, wanting more is the basis for utopian thinking, a path toward dangerous social demands, even toward imagining the possibilities for altogether different social arrangements. But if the most elegant forms of social control are those that came packaged in the guise of individual needs and satisfactions, so wedded to the individual psyche that any opposing impulse registers as the anxiety of unlovability, who needs a soldier on every corner? We are more than happy to police ourselves and those we love and call it living happily ever after. Perhaps a secular society needed another metaphysical entity to subjugate itself to after the death of God, and love was available for the job. But isn't it a little depressing to think we are somehow incapable of inventing forms of emotional life based on anything other than subjugation?

---

## Cartoon

### Tom Cheney

*The cartoon on page 533, which appeared in the* New Yorker Magazine, *gets its humor from a revision of the wording of the standard wedding vows—and the expressions of the couple at the altar, who have apparently never thought of their lifelong monogamous commitment exactly as the preacher's words describe it.*

---

### For Discussion

The cartoon invites a discussion of the role of style in persuasion. The standard wedding vows, while solemn, are romantic and poetic. With small

*"And do you, Rebecca, promise to make love only to Richard, month after month, year after year, and decade after decade, until one of you is dead?"*

variations in the wordings, all the standard vows aim to bind the bride and groom to fidelity for a lifetime. What is the effect of the wording in the cartoon?

## What Is This Thing Called Love?
### Norah Vincent

We've all heard the statistic that half of all marriages end in divorce. It's unsurprising, then, that Congress passed and the first so-called gay-friendly president, Bill Clinton, signed the Defense of Marriage Act in 1996. Conservatives think marriage is too loosely conceived and see the encroachments of anathemas like gay marriage, polygamy, and no-fault divorce as the culprits. Meanwhile, committed leftists see marriage as being too strictly conceived and, at bottom, repressive of women. Thus, they're denouncing it (even the same-sex variety) with renewed vigor. Strangely, both sides seem to agree: Marriage, as we define it, is the problem.

Nonsense. Marriage itself (gay, poly, or otherwise) is not the problem. On the contrary, properly conceived, it may well be the solution. By most measures, like those Linda Waite and Maggie Gallagher marshal in their book *The Case for Marriage*, marriage is good for us. We need it. One might even call it the linchpin of a healthy, thriving culture—the most intimate manifestation, perhaps, of what Francis Fukuyama called "social capital." Married people tend to live longer, healthier lives. When married, criminals are less prone to recidivism.

So, then, if the problem is not marriage itself, what is it? Neither liberals nor conservatives are finding the answer, for the decline of traditional marriage can no more be blamed on groups who don't yet enjoy its benefits (for example, gays and polygamists) than it can on antiquated notions of tribal ownership or sexism. No. More likely the problem is us and our pervasive misunderstanding both of what makes marriage tick and what makes it indispensable: love.

The Western world is suffused with the mythology of romantic love. Its cultural heritage is rife with archetypes: Samson and Delilah, Cupid and Psyche, Tristram and Isolde, Romeo and Juliet, and on and on. Each of us comes of age expectant, inculcated in the baroque masochism of Eros, waiting for that decidedly pagan euphoria to overcome and inhabit us like the flu. And inevitably it does, transforming us utterly and yet most often leaving us crushed in its wake, empty-handed, and, if once married under its spell, now divorced.

How could it be otherwise? Artificial paradises degrade of necessity, said Baudelaire. When people exchange illusions, however strong and pleasurable, the transaction is, of course, empty. Love is giving something you don't possess, wrote Lacan, to someone who doesn't exist. This is the essence of romantic love as our folklore unwittingly purveys it. 5

But there is another kind of love in the Western world, one that, like faith, is not primarily a feeling but an act or a series of acts. It, like faith, is a commandment, not a whim or a virus. Somewhere along the way we've forgotten this.

Interestingly, Westerners misunderstand the Sanskrit term *karma* in the same way, thinking it means "fate" or "destiny"—something passive and imposed—when, in fact, it literally means "action" or "deed." Thus, your karma is what you do. It only becomes your fate because your actions become your fate.

Similarly, true love, even romantic love, is what you do, not what you feel. That is why, when we pledge ourselves to another in marriage, we say "I do," not "I feel." Conceived this way, love is not subject to outrageous fortune. And so marriage is a promise, not a flourish. It is a declaration of personal responsibility for another human being, an act of charity by which we say, "I am my lover's keeper."

There is no sociological evidence that traditional, gay, or consensual polygamous marriages, when dutifully undertaken, erode the social fabric, whereas there is considerable evidence that acts of love, when legally and communally reinforced, become strong and mutually beneficial social bonds. We should overcome our considerable misgivings and learn to practice love. We should, in the interests of forging trust and social capital, be in favor of all marriage—indeed, as much marriage as possible.

*Ethan Watters, center, with his tribe in San Francisco*

## In My Tribe
### Ethan Watters

You may be like me: between the ages of 25 and 39, single, a college-educated city dweller. If so, you may have also had the unpleasant experience of discovering that you have been identified (by the U.S. Census Bureau, no less) as one of the fastest-growing groups in America—the "never marrieds." In less than 30 years, the number of never-marrieds has more than doubled, apparently pushing back the median age of marriage to the oldest it has been in our country's history—about 25 years for women and 27 for men.

As if the connotation of "never married" weren't negative enough, the vilification of our group has been swift and shrill. These statistics prove a "titanic loss of family values," according to *The Washington Times*. An article in *Time* magazine asked whether "picky" women were "denying themselves and society the benefits of marriage" and in the process kicking off "an outbreak of 'Sex and the City' promiscuity." In a study on marriage conducted at Rutgers University, researchers say the "social glue" of the family is at stake, adding ominously that "crime rates . . . are highly correlated with a large percentage of unmarried young males."

Although I never planned it, I can tell you how I became a never-married. Thirteen years ago, I moved to San Francisco for what I assumed was a brief transition period between college and marriage. The problem was, I wasn't just looking for an appropriate spouse. To use the language of the Rutgers researchers, I was "soul-mate searching." Like 94 percent of never-marrieds from 20 to 29, I, too, agree with the statement "When you marry, you want your spouse to be your soul mate first and foremost." This *über*-romantic view is something new. In a 1965 survey, fully three out of four college women said they'd marry a man they didn't love if he fit their criteria in every other way. I discovered along with my friends that finding that soul mate wasn't easy. Girlfriends came and went, as did jobs and apartments. The constant in my life—by default, not by plan—became a loose group of friends. After a few years, that group's membership and routines began to solidify. We met weekly for dinner at a neighborhood restaurant. We traveled together, moved one another's furniture, painted one another's apartments, cheered one another on at sporting events and open-mike nights. One day I discovered that the transition period I thought I was living wasn't a transition period at all. Something real and important had grown there. I belonged to an urban tribe.

I use the word "tribe" quite literally here: this is a tight group, with unspoken roles and hierarchies, whose members think of each other as "us" and the rest of the world as "them." This bond is clearest in times of trouble. After earthquakes (or the recent terrorist strikes), my instinct to huddle with and protect my group is no different from what I'd feel for my family.

Once I identified this in my own life, I began to see tribes everywhere I looked: a house of ex-sorority women in Philadelphia, a team of ultimate-frisbee players in Boston and groups of musicians in Austin, Tex. Cities, I've come to believe, aren't emotional wastelands where fragile individuals with arrested development mope around self-indulgently searching for true love. There are rich landscapes filled with urban tribes. 5

So what does it mean that we've quietly added the tribe years as a developmental stage to adulthood? Because our friends in the tribe hold us responsible for our actions, I doubt it will mean a wild swing toward promiscuity or crime. Tribal behavior does not prove a loss of "family values." It is a fresh expression of them.

It is true, though, that marriage and the tribe are at odds. As many ex-girlfriends will ruefully tell you, loyalty to the tribe can wreak havoc on romantic relationships. Not surprisingly, marriage usually signals the beginning of the end of tribal membership. From inside the group, marriage can seem like a risky gambit. When members of our tribe choose to get married, the rest of us talk about them with grave concern, as if they've joined a religion that requires them to live in a guarded compound.

But we also know that the urban tribe can't exist forever. Those of us who have entered our mid-30's find ourselves feeling vaguely as if we're living in the latter episodes of "Seinfeld" or "Friends," as if the plot lines of our lives have begun to wear thin.

So, although tribe membership may delay marriage, that is where most of us are still heading. And it turns out there may be some good news when we get there. Divorce rates have leveled off. Tim Heaton, a sociologist at Brigham Young University, says he believes he knows why. In a paper to be published next year, he argues that it is because people are getting married later.

Could it be that we who have been biding our time in happy tribes 10 are now actually grown up enough to understand what we need in a mate?

What a fantastic twist—we "never marrieds" may end up revitalizing the very institution we've supposedly been undermining.

And there's another dynamic worth considering. Those of us who find it so hard to leave our tribes will not choose marriage blithely, as if it is the inevitable next step in our lives, the way middle-class high-school kids choose college. When we go to the altar, we will be sacrificing something precious. In that sacrifice, we may begin to learn to treat our marriages with the reverence they need to survive.

## For Discussion

1. "Happily Ever After?" is a chapter from Linda Waite and Maggie Gallagher's book *The Case for Marriage* (Broadway Books, 2000). As such, it's a good example of a case to convince. What evidence do they offer to convince readers who are skeptical about the benefits of marriage that married people really are happier than unmarried people? This argument illustrates the importance of definition, concession (some marriages are not happy), and refuting of an opposing view (that cohabitation is as good as marriage if not better). Discuss how effectively the authors built their argument. Are you convinced?

2. Waite and Gallagher report that of 20,000 married men and women surveyed, most married people are "very happy," with over 60 percent giving their marriages the "highest possible happiness rating" (paragraph 46). They report that "[a]lmost no one—2 percent of the married men and 4 percent of the married women—described their marriage as 'not too happy'"; however, Stephanie Coontz reports in 2001 that "40 percent of all marriages will end in divorce before a couple's 40th anniversary." Americans have the highest divorce rate in the world. Discuss the possible connections between the high divorce rate and the self-reported happiness of those in the survey cited above.

3. Laura Kipnis argues against "love," by which she means the "tyranny" of mature love. How does she define "mature love"? Paraphrase her argument against mature love. Is she against romantic love? She says that although love may be a universal emotion, "It is our culture alone that has dedicated itself [to the idea] that both love and sex are obtainable from one person over the course of decades. . . ." How do these messages come to us? Does she convince you that this idea is completely "utopian," as she calls it?

4. Compare the various definitions of love quoted in Vincent's essay with Vincent's own definition of love. How does her definition of love compare with Kipnis's idea of "mature love"?

5. Kipnis offers many metaphors (such as the leeches and other medical procedures in paragraphs 21–23) and personal observations

(paragraph 27) to support her point. Is her lack of interviews and scholarly research a fatal flaw in her argument? Why or why not?

6. Both Kipnis and Waite/Gallagher use social theories to support their arguments about committed domestic relationships. Kipnis, in explaining the social demand for "the tyranny of love," cites Michel Foucault (paragraph 29) on the rise of institutions in the modern world that keep the population under social control. Reread her conclusion to see how she applies this theory to modern love. Waite and Gallagher cite Émile Durkheim (paragraphs 50–51) on the need of individuals to be integrated into a social unit to help them face up to the uncertainties and hardships of life. Discuss the usefulness of these theories and their effects on each author's interpretation of domestic love.

7. Ethan Watters offers an inside perspective on the statistical fact that young people are postponing marriage. How does his discussion of the benefits and shortcomings of tribal life compare with Kipnis's and Waite/Gallagher's discussions of life without a spouse? What do you think Kipnis would say in response to this argument?

8. What have scientists found about biological and physiological aspects of what we call "love"? What are the various chemical changes that occur in the "infatuation" stage? Look into findings that suggest this stage has a limited term — something like seven years. Do you think Americans have unrealistic expectations about passionate love as the basis for marriage? Would a less romantic view of the basis of marriage better suit the biological reality of long-term partnerships?

Works Cited

Coontz, Stephanie. "The American Family: New Research about An Old Institution." *Life.* Nov. 1, 1999: 79+.

*For Inquiry*

Write an imaginary dialogue between Laura Kipnis, Linda Waite, and Ethan Watters on the value of postponing marriage rather than marrying earlier or not marrying at all. Put yourself in the conversation, using any of the "Questions for Inquiry" (pages 177–178) to probe the thinking of these writers.

*For Convincing*

Write an argument for or against lifelong married monogamy as the norm or ideal for American couples today. Use evidence from the essays in this chapter, other sources found through research, and your own observations and interviews of friends and family.

## SECTION 3: THE DIVORCE DEBATE

Lifelong marriage is still the goal of most Americans, but a goal that is hard to achieve. Although it has leveled off, the divorce rate still claims roughly half of all marriages. Why are Americans the most divorcing people in the world?

One answer is that Americans have always valued individualism and self-fulfillment. As Arlene Skolnik points out, in the last two centuries the family has been expected increasingly to fulfill one's emotional needs: "The new fields of psychology and sociology opened up whole new definitions of familial perfection. 'Feelings'—fun, love, warmth, good orgasm—acquired heightened popular significance as the invisible glue of successful families" (paragraph 29). Paradoxically, the search for perfect happiness may be one explanation for our high rate of divorce. Whether realistic or not, people hope to find greater fulfillment in a new relationship. Eighty percent of those who divorce remarry.

In exploring the causes of divorce, authors with a conservative perspective see divorce as a consequence of selfishness. Barbara Dafoe Whitehead, in a chapter from her 1997 book *The Divorce Culture,* argues that the family has lost its "distinctive identity as the realm of duty, service, and sacrifice" (paragraph 6). She describes what she calls "expressive divorce," divorce seen as part of the one's right to a "satisfying inner life." Stephanie Coontz, a historian at Evergreen State College, argues from a more liberal perspective; the high divorce rate is not the result of individual failure to commit but rather "the product of long-term social and economic changes, not of a breakdown in values" (paragraph 33).

The most debated question concerns the effects of divorce on the couple's children and on the society as a whole. Writing for the conservative Heritage Foundation, Patrick F. Fagan and Robert Rector enumerate the ways children are hurt but also go on to argue that divorce also harms the institutions that keep a society healthy: "family, church, school, marketplace, and government itself" (paragraph 50). Responding to what she calls the "antidivorce movement," Barbara Ehrenreich challenges some of the studies showing harm to children and claims that putting the stigma and blame back into divorce would only hurt children more. In a personal narrative, William Cobb shows how divorce hurts fathers, as he describes his losing struggle to maintain his fatherly relationship with his ex-wife's little girl.

Finally, we show one legislative attempt to restore the permanence of marriage vows. A news article explains the "covenant marriages" that are legal options in three states and gives perspectives on all sides about their usefulness and legality. How realistic is it that any laws can make lifelong marriage the norm in the United States today? The most we may hope for is what we have right now—lifelong marriage as the ideal to which all newlyweds aspire.

# The Making of a Divorce Culture
### Barbara Dafoe Whitehead

Divorce is now part of everyday American life. It is embedded in our laws and institutions, our manners and mores, our movies and television shows, our novels and children's storybooks, and our closest and most important relationships. Indeed, divorce has become so pervasive that many people naturally assume it has seeped into the social and cultural mainstream over a long period of time. Yet this is not the case. Divorce has become an American way of life only as the result of recent and revolutionary change.

The entire history of American divorce can be divided into two periods, one evolutionary and the other revolutionary. For most of the nation's history, divorce was a rare occurrence and an insignificant feature of family and social relationships. In the first sixty years of the twentieth century, divorce became more common, but it was hardly commonplace. In 1960, the divorce rate stood at a still relatively modest level of nine per one thousand married couples. After 1960, however, the rate accelerated at a dazzling pace. It doubled in roughly a decade and continued its upward climb until the early 1980s, when it stabilized at the highest level among advanced Western societies. As a consequence of this sharp and sustained rise, divorce moved from the margins to the mainstream of American life in the space of three decades.

Ideas are important in revolutions, yet surprisingly little attention has been devoted to the ideas that gave impetus to the divorce revolution. Of the scores of books on divorce published in recent decades, most focus on its legal, demographic, economic, or (especially) psychological dimensions. Few, if any, deal fully with its intellectual origins. Yet trying to comprehend the divorce revolution and its consequences without some sense of its ideological origins is like trying to understand the American Revolution without taking into account the thinking of John Locke, Thomas Jefferson, or Thomas Paine. This more recent revolution, like the revolution of our nation's founding, has its roots in a distinctive set of ideas and claims.

. . . The making of a divorce culture has involved three overlapping changes: first, the emergence and widespread diffusion of a historically new and distinctive set of ideas about divorce in the last third of the twentieth century; second, the migration of divorce from a minor place within a system governed by marriage to a freestanding place as a major institution governing family relationships; and third, a widespread shift in thinking about the obligations of marriage and parenthood.

Beginning in the late 1950s, Americans began to change their ideas                    5
about the individual's obligations to family and society. Broadly described, this change was away from an ethic of obligation to others and toward an obligation to self. I do not mean that people suddenly abandoned all re-

sponsibilities to others, but rather that they became more acutely conscious of their responsibility to attend to their own individual needs and interests. At least as important as the moral obligation to look after others, the new thinking suggested, was the moral obligation to look after oneself.

This ethical shift had a profound impact on ideas about the nature and purpose of the family. In the American tradition, the marketplace and the public square have represented the realms of life devoted to the pursuit of individual interest, choice, and freedom, while the family has been the realm defined by voluntary commitment, duty, and self-sacrifice. With the greater emphasis on individual satisfaction in family relationships, however, family well-being became subject to a new metric. More than in the past, satisfaction in this sphere came to be based on subjective judgments about the content and quality of individual happiness rather than on such objective measures as level of income, material nurture and support, or boosting children onto a higher rung on the socioeconomic ladder. People began to judge the strength and "health" of family bonds according to their capacity to promote individual fulfillment and personal growth. As a result, the conception of the family's role and place in the society began to change. The family began to lose its separate place and distinctive identity as the realm of duty, service, and sacrifice. Once the domain of the obligated self, the family was increasingly viewed as yet another domain for the expression of the unfettered self.

These broad changes figured centrally in creating a new conception of divorce which gained influential adherents and spread broadly and swiftly throughout the society—a conception that represented a radical departure from earlier notions. Once regarded mainly as a social, legal, and family event in which there were other stakeholders, divorce now became an event closely linked to the pursuit of individual satisfactions, opportunities, and growth.

The new conception of divorce drew upon some of the oldest, and most resonant, themes in the American political tradition. The nation, after all, was founded as the result of a political divorce, and revolutionary thinkers explicitly adduced a parallel between the dissolution of marital bonds and the dissolution of political bonds. In political as well as marital relationships, they argued, bonds of obligation were established voluntarily on the basis of mutual affection and regard. Once such bonds turned cold and oppressive, peoples, like individuals, had the right to dissolve them and to form more perfect unions.

In the new conception of divorce, this strain of eighteenth-century political thought mingled with a strain of twentieth-century psycho-therapeutic thought. Divorce was not only an individual right but also a psychological resource. The dissolution of marriage offered the chance to make oneself over from the inside out, to refurbish and express the inner self, and to acquire certain valuable psychological assets and competencies, such as initiative, assertiveness, and a stronger and better self-image.

The conception of divorce as both an individual right and an inner ex-    10
perience merged with and reinforced the new ethic of obligation to the self.
In family relationships, one had an obligation to be attentive to one's own
feelings and to work toward improving the quality of one's inner life. This
ethical imperative completed the rationale for a sense of individual entitlement to divorce. Increasingly, mainstream America saw the legal dissolution of marriage as a matter of individual choice, in which there were no
other stakeholders or larger social interests. This conception of divorce
strongly argued for removing the social, legal, and moral impediments
to the free exercise of the individual right to divorce. . . .

. . . The divorce ethic radically changed established ideas about the social and moral obligations associated with divorce. In the past Americans
assumed that there were multiple stakeholders in the unhappy business of
marital dissolution: the other spouse, the children, relatives, and the larger
society. All these stakeholders held an interest in the marital partnership
as the source of certain goods, goods that were put at risk each time a marriage dissolved. At particular risk were children, who were the most likely to
experience severe losses as a consequence of divorce, especially the loss of
the steady support and sponsorship of a father. In divorcing, spouses also
jeopardized their own relationships with their children and put at risk
the children's relationships with grandparents, relatives, and even family
friends. Moreover, since married parents had the central social responsibility for preparing the next generation for useful lives as citizens, workers,
and future family members, the dissolution of a marriage was an event
in which the society claimed an interest.

However, the notion of divorce as the working out of an inner life experience cast it in far more individualistic terms than in the past. Because divorce originated in an inner sense of dissatisfaction, it acknowledged no
other stakeholders. Leaving a marriage was a personal decision, prompted
by a set of needs and feelings that were not subject to external interests or
claims. Expressive divorce reduced the number of legitimate stakeholders in
divorce to one, the individual adult.

If expressive divorce excluded the idea that there are other parties at
interest in the "divorce experience," it also overturned earlier notions about
one's moral responsibilities to others. An individual's right to divorce was
rooted in the individual's right to have a satisfying inner life to fulfill his/
her needs and desires. The entitlement to divorce was based on the individual entitlement to pursue inner happiness.

Like all entitlements, the psychological entitlement to divorce was jeal-
ously guarded and protected. No one, including the divorcing individual's
children, had a "right" to intervene in this intensely private experience or to
try to disrupt the course of an emotionally healthy journey toward divorce.
Nor were there morally compelling arguments for considering the interests
and claims of others in the marriage. If divorce was an entirely subjective
and individual experience, rooted in a particular set of needs, values, and

preferences, then there was no basis for making judgments about the decision to divorce. The new ethic of divorce was morally relativistic: There could be no right or wrong reasons for divorce; there were only reasons, which it was the task of therapy to elicit and affirm.

Taken together, the conception of divorce as an inner journey of the self  15 and the ethical imperative to put one's interests and needs first had one far-reaching consequence: It weakened the rationale for the legal or social regulation of divorce. If the divorce experience was an inner journey of the sovereign self, what right had anyone to place impediments in the way? . . .

The shift to a system of no-fault divorce both reflected and contributed to the new conception of divorce. For a couple who had come to a mutual decision to end a marriage, the traditional practice of finding and assigning fault to one spouse often required fabricating some offense like adultery and thereby tainting the reputation of one partner. No-fault divorce was designed to eliminate this legal playacting and thereby to make divorce more honest. California enacted the nation's first no-fault statute in 1970, and other states soon followed; by 1980, all but two states had no-fault divorce laws on the books. Fault no longer sullied divorce or tarnished reputations; in this sense, the legal dissolution of marriage had become a "cleaner" as well as an easier process.

However, no-fault divorce fully supported the single-stakeholder theory of expressive divorce. It established a disaffected spouse's right unilaterally to dissolve a marriage simply by declaring that the relationship was over. Characterizing standard legal practice in the states, legal scholar Mary Ann Glendon has observed: ". . . the virtually universal understanding . . . is that the breakdown of a marriage is irretrievable if one spouse says it is." Even more consequentially, no-fault gave one parent the unilateral power to disrupt at will and without cause the other parent's affective relationship with his or her child. . . .

. . . By the 1970s the elimination of fault in most of the states' divorce laws made the sorting out of responsibility for marital breakup a psychological rather than a legal endeavor. Considerations of fault did not disappear so much as change venue; fault was not assigned by the courts but worked out in therapy. Achieving a constructive "emotional" divorce became a dominant goal of marriage therapy.

Nonetheless, according to therapeutic precepts, the fault for marital breakup must be shared, even when one spouse unilaterally seeks a divorce. In essence, counseling established a joint-fault system aimed at persuading each individual to accept responsibility for the breakup. As one study of therapeutic opinion notes, "the strategy which most clearly differentiates divorce therapy from marital or family therapy is what we have labelled orchestrating the motivation to divorce." This may include "openly arguing for the advantages of the divorce as opposed to continuing marital unhappiness and trial separation." The goal here was to accept responsibility for the failure of the marriage and thereby to achieve a new level of self-understanding.

"To view oneself as innocent victim is thus to engage in fundamental distortion," the study goes on, "the consequence of which is a high probability for an equally bad remarriage."

Such therapeutic reasoning defied a more commonsense view of right 20 and wrong, however. Many husbands and wives who did not seek or want divorce were stunned to learn from their therapists that they were equally "at fault" in the dissolution of their marriages. The notion of fault apparently had a moral basis which endured even after the notion of fault had been eradicated in law and mores. . . .

One consequence of this individualistic approach was its neglect of marriage as the domain of obligation and commitment, particularly to children. Not only did marriage counseling ignore the spousal relationship, it also excluded children as stakeholders in the marital partnership. Intentionally or not, it relieved divorcing couples of their responsibilities for considering their children's well-being. . . .

. . . [D]ivorce has indeed hurt children. It has created economic insecurity and disadvantage for many children who would not otherwise be economically vulnerable. It has led to more fragile and unstable family households. It has caused a mass exodus of fathers from children's households and, all too often, from their lives. It has reduced the levels of parental time and money invested in children. In sum, it has changed the very nature of American childhood. Just as no patient would have designed today's system of health care, so no child would have chosen today's culture of divorce.

Divorce figures prominently in the altered economic fortunes of middle-class families. Although the economic crisis of the middle class is usually described as a problem caused by global economic changes, changing patterns in education and earnings, and ruthless corporate downsizing, it owes more to divorce than is commonly acknowledged. Indeed, recent data suggest that marriage may be a more important economic resource than a college degree. According to an analysis of 1994 income patterns, the median income of married-parent households whose heads have only a high school diploma is ten percent higher than the median income of college-educated single-parent households. Parents who are college graduates *and* married form the new economic elite among families with children. Consequently, those who are concerned about what the downsizing of corporations is doing to workers should also be concerned about what the downsizing of families through divorce is doing to parents and children.

Widespread divorce depletes social capital as well. Scholars tell us that strong and durable family and social bonds generate certain "goods" and services, including money, mutual assistance, information, caregiving, protection, and sponsorship. Because such bonds endure over time, they accumulate and form a pool of social capital which can be drawn down upon, when needed, over the entire course of a life. An elderly couple, married for fifty years, is likely to enjoy a substantial body of social and emotional capital, generated through their long-lasting marriage, which they can draw upon in caring for each other and for themselves as they age. Similarly, children who grow up in stable, two-parent married households are the beneficiaries of the social and emotional capital accumulated over time as a result of an enduring marriage bond. As many parents know, children continue to depend on these resources well into young adulthood. But as family bonds become increasingly fragile and vulnerable to disruption, they become less permanent and thus less capable of generating such forms of help, financial resources, and mutual support. In short, divorce consumes social capital and weakens the social fabric. At the very time that sweeping socioeconomic changes are mandating greater investment of social capital in children, widespread divorce is reducing the pool of social capital. As the new economic and social conditions raise the hurdles of child-rearing higher, divorce digs potholes in the tracks.

. . . The media routinely portray the debate over the family as one be-   25
tween nostalgists and realists, between those who want to turn back the clock to the fifties and those who want to march bravely and resolutely forward into the new century. But this is a lazy and misguided approach, driven more by the easy availability of archival photos and footage from 1950s television sitcoms than by careful consideration of the substance of competing arguments.

More fundamentally, this approach overlooks the key issue. And that issue is not how today's families might stack up against those of an earlier era; indeed, no reliable empirical data for such a comparison exist. In an age of diverse family structures, the heart of the matter is what kinds of contemporary family arrangements have the greatest capacity to promote children's well-being, and how we can ensure that more children have the advantages of growing up in such families.

In the past year or so, there has been growing recognition of the personal and social costs of three decades of widespread divorce. A public debate has finally emerged. Within this debate, there are two separate and overlapping discussions.

The first centers on a set of specific proposals that are intended to lessen the harmful impact of divorce on children: a federal system of child-support collection, tougher child-support enforcement, mandatory counseling for divorcing parents, and reform of no-fault divorce laws in the states. What is striking about this discussion is its narrow focus on public policy, particularly on changes in the system of no-fault divorce. In this, as in so many other crucial discussions involving social and moral questions, the most vocal and visible participants come from the world of government policy, electoral politics, and issue advocacy. The media, which are tongue-tied unless they can speak in the language of left-right politics, reinforce this situation. And the public is offered needlessly polarized arguments that hang on a flat yes-or-no response to this or that individual policy measure. All too often, this discussion of divorce poses what *Washington Post* columnist E. J. Dionne aptly describes as false choices.

Notably missing is a serious consideration of the broader moral assumptions and empirical claims that define our divorce culture. Divorce touches on classic questions in American public philosophy — on the nature of our most important human and social bonds, the duties and obligations imposed by bonds we voluntarily elect, the "just causes" for the dissolution of those bonds, and the differences between obligations volunteered and those that must be coerced. Without consideration of such questions, the effort to change behavior by changing a few public policies is likely to founder.

The second and complementary discussion does try to place divorce    30 within a larger philosophical framework. Its proponents have looked at the decline in the well-being of the nation's children as the occasion to call for a collective sense of commitment by all Americans to all of America's children. They pose the challenging question: "What are Americans willing to do 'for the sake of *all* children'?" But while this is surely an important question, it addresses only half of the problem of declining commitment. The other half has to do with how we answer the question: "What are individual parents obliged to do 'for the sake of their own children'?"

Renewing a *social* ethic of commitment to children is an urgent goal, but it cannot be detached from the goal of strengthening the *individual* ethic of commitment to children. The state of one affects the standing of the other. A society that protects the rights of parents to easy, unilateral divorce, and flatly rejects the idea that parents should strive to preserve a marriage "for the sake of the children," faces a problem when it comes to the question of public sacrifice "for the sake of the children." To put it plainly, many of the ideas we have come to believe and vigorously defend about adult prerogatives and freedoms in family life are undermining the foundations of altruism and support for children.

With each passing year, the culture of divorce becomes more deeply entrenched. American children are routinely schooled in divorce. Mr. Rogers teaches toddlers about divorce. An entire children's literature is devoted to divorce. Family movies and videos for children feature divorced families. *Mrs. Doubtfire*, originally a children's book about divorce and then a hit movie, is aggressively marketed as a holiday video for kids. Of course, these books and movies are designed to help children deal with the social reality and psychological trauma of divorce. But they also carry an unmistakable message about the impermanence and unreliability of family bonds. Like romantic love, the children's storybooks say, family love comes and goes. Daddies disappear. Mommies find new boyfriends. Mommies' boyfriends leave. Grandparents go away. Even pets must be left behind.

More significantly, in a society where nearly half of all children are likely to experience parental divorce, family breakup becomes a defining event of American childhood itself. Many children today know nothing but divorce in their family lives. And although children from divorced families often say they want to avoid divorce if they marry, young adults whose parents divorced are more likely to get divorced themselves and to bear children outside of marriage than young adults from stable married-parent families. . . .

. . . Divorce has spread throughout advanced Western societies at roughly the same pace and over roughly the same period of time. Yet nowhere else has divorce been so deeply imbued with the larger themes of a nation's political traditions. Nowhere has divorce so fully reflected the spirit and susceptibilities of a people who share an extravagant faith in the power of the individual and in the power of positive thinking. Divorce in America is not unique, but what we have made of divorce is uniquely American. . . .

---

# The Future of Marriage
## Stephanie Coontz

Most Americans support the emergence of alternative ways of organizing parenthood and marriage. They don't want to reestablish the supremacy of the male breadwinner model or to define masculine and feminine roles in any monolithic way. Many people worry, however, about the growth of alternatives to marriage itself. They fear that in some of today's new families parents may not be devoting enough time and resources to their children. The rise of divorce and unwed motherhood is particularly worrisome, because people correctly recognize that children need more than one adult involved in their lives.

As a result, many people who object to the "modified male breadwinner" program of the "new consensus" crusaders are still willing to sign on to the other general goals of that movement: "to increase the proportion of children who grow up with two married parents," to "reclaim the ideal of marital permanence," to keep men "involved in family life," and to establish the principle "that every child deserves a father."[1]

Who could disagree? When we appear on panels together, leaders of "traditional values" groups often ask me if I accept the notion that, on the whole, two parents are better than one. If they would add an adjective such as two *good* parents, or even two *adequate* ones, I'd certainly agree. And of course it's better to try to make a marriage work than to walk away at the firt sign of trouble.

As a historian, however, I've learned that when truisms are touted as stunning new research, when aphorisms everyone agrees with are presented as a courageous political program, and when exceptions or complications are ignored for the sake of establishing the basic principles, it's worth taking a close look for a hidden agenda behind the clichés. And, in fact, the new consensus crowd's program for supporting the two-parent family turns out to be far more radical than the feel-good slogans might lead you to believe.

Members of groups such as the Council on Families in America claim they are simply expressing a new consensus when they talk about "reinstitutionalizing enduring marriage," but in the very next breath they declare that it "is time to raise the stakes." They want nothing less than to make lifelong marriage the "primary institutional expression of commitment and obligation to others," the main mechanism for regulating sexuality, male–female relations, economic redistribution, and child rearing. Charles Murray says that the goal is "restoration of marriage as an utterly distinct, legal relationship." Since marriage must be "privileged," other family forms or child-rearing arrangements should not receive tax breaks, insurance benefits, or access to public housing and federal programs. Any reform that would make it easier for divorced parents, singles, unmarried partners, or stepfamilies to function is suspect because it removes "incentives" for people to get and stay married. Thus, these groups argue, adoption and foster care policies should "reinforce marriage as the child-rearing norm." Married couples, and only married couples, should be given special tax relief to raise their children. Some leaders of the Institute for American Values propose that we encourage both private parties and government bodies "to distinguish between married and unmarried *couples* in housing, credit, zoning, and other areas." Divorce and illegitimacy should be stigmatized.[2]

We've come quite a way from the original innocuous statements about the value of two-parent families and the importance of fathers to children. Now we find out that we must make marriage the only socially sanctioned method for organizing male–female roles and fulfilling adult obligations to the young. "There is no realistic alternative to the one we propose," claims the Council on Families in America. To assess this claim, we need to take a close look at what the consensus crusaders mean when they talk about the need to reverse the "deinstitutionalizing" of marriage.[3]

Normally, social scientists have something very specific in mind when they say that a custom or behavior is "institutionalized." They mean it comes "with a well-understood set of obligations and rights," all of which are backed up by law, customs, rituals, and social expectations. In this sense, marriage is still one of America's most important and valued institutions.[4]

But it is true that marriage has lost its former monopoly over the organization of people's major life transitions. Alongside a continuing commitment to marriage, other arrangements for regulating sexual behavior, channeling relations between men and women, and raising children now exist. Marriage was once the primary way of organizing work along lines of age and sex. It determined the roles that men and women played at home and in public. It was the main vehicle for redistributing resources to old and young, and it served as the most important marker of adulthood and respectable status.

All this is no longer the case. Marriage has become an option rather than a necessity for men and women, even during the child-raising years.

5

Today only half of American children live in nuclear families with both biological parents present. One child in five lives in a stepfamily and one in four lives in a "single-parent" home. The number of single parents increased from 3.8 million in 1970 to 6.9 million in 1980, a rate that averages out to a truly unprecedented 6 percent increase each year. In the 1980s, the rate of increase slowed and from 1990 to 1995 it leveled off, but the total numbers have continued to mount, reaching 12.2 million by 1996.[5]

These figures understate how many children actually have two parents     10
in the home, because they confuse marital status with living arrangements. Approximately a quarter of all births to unmarried mothers occur in households where the father is present, so those children have two parents at home in fact if not in law. Focusing solely on the marriage license distorts our understanding of trends in children's living arrangements. For example, the rise in cohabitation between 1970 and 1984 led to more children being classified as living in single-parent families. But when researchers counted unmarried couples living together as two-parent families, they found that children were spending *more* time, not less, with both parents in 1984 than in 1970. Still, this simply confirms the fact that formal marriage no longer organizes as many life decisions and transitions as it did in the past.[6]

Divorce, cohabitation, remarriage, and single motherhood are not the only factors responsible for the eclipse of marriage as the primary institution for organizing sex roles and interpersonal obligations in America today. More people are living on their own before marriage, so that more young adults live outside a family environment than in earlier times. And the dramatic extension of life spans means that more people live alone after the death of a spouse.[7]

The growing number of people living on their own ensures that there are proportionately fewer families of *any* kind than there used to be. The Census Bureau defines families as residences with more than one householder related by blood, marriage, or adoption. In 1940, under this definition, families accounted for 90 percent of all households in the country. By 1970, they represented just 81 percent of all households, and by 1990 they represented 71 percent. The relative weight of marriage in society has decreased. Social institutions and values have adapted to the needs, buying decisions, and lifestyle choices of singles. Arrangements other than nuclear family transactions have developed to meet people's economic and interpersonal needs. Elders, for example, increasingly depend on Social Security and private pension plans, rather than the family, for their care.[8]

Part of the deinstitutionalization of marriage, then, comes from factors that few people would want to change even if they could. Who wants to shorten the life spans of the elderly, even though that means many more people are living outside the institution of marriage than formerly? Should we lower the age of marriage, even though marrying young makes people more likely to divorce?[9] Or should young people be forced to live at home until they do marry? Do we really want to try to make marriage, once again, the only path for living a productive and fulfilling adult life?

### Working Women, Singlehood, and Divorce

If the family values crusaders believe they are the only people interested in preserving marriages, especially where children's well-being is involved, self-righteousness has blinded them to reality. I've watched people of every political persuasion struggle to keep their families together, and I've met very few divorced parents who hadn't tried to make their marriages work. Even the most ardent proponents of reinstitutionalizing marriage recognize that they cannot and should not force everyone to get and stay married. They do not propose outlawing divorce, and they take pains to say that single parents who were not at fault should not be blamed. Yet they still claim that moral exhortations to take marriage more seriously will reduce divorce enough to "revive a culture of enduring marriage."

This is where the radical right wing of the family values movement is    15 far more realistic than most moderates: So long as women continue to make long-term commitments to the workforce, marriage is unlikely to again become the lifelong norm for the vast majority of individuals unless draconian measures are adopted to make people get and stay married. Paid work gives women the option to leave an unsatisfactory marriage. In certain instances, much as liberals may hate to admit it, wives' employment increases dissatisfaction with marriage, sometimes on the part of women, sometimes on the part of their husbands. When a wife spends long hours at work or holds a nontraditional job, the chance of divorce increases.[10]

I'm not saying we can't slow down the divorce rate, lessen emotional and economic disincentives for marriage, and foster longer-lasting commitments. But there is clearly a limit to how many people can be convinced to marry and how many marriages can be made to last when women have the option to be economically self-supporting. In this sense, the right-wing suspicion that women's work destabilizes marriage has a certain logic.

There is, however, a big problem with the conclusion that the radical right draws from this observation. To say that women's employment has *allowed* divorce and singlehood to rise in society as a whole does not mean that women's work *causes* divorce and singlehood at the level of the individual family, or that convincing women to reduce their work hours and career aspirations would reestablish more stable marriages.[11]

Trying to reverse a historical trend by asking individuals to make personal decisions opposing that trend is usually futile. When individuals try to conduct their personal lives as if broader social forces were not in play, they often end up worse off than if they adapted to the changing times. What traditional values spokesman in his right mind would counsel his own daughter not to prepare herself for higher-paid, nontraditional jobs because these might lead to marital instability down the road?

After all, even if a woman *prefers* to have a male breadwinner provide for her, the fact that people can now readily buy substitutes for what used to require a housewife's labor changes marriage dynamics in decisive ways. Most individuals and families can now survive quite easily without a full-time domestic worker. If this frees women to work outside the home, it also frees men from the necessity of supporting a full-time homemaker.

Before the advent of washing machines, frozen foods, wrinkle-resistant fabrics, and 24-hour one-stop shopping, Barbara Ehrenreich has remarked, "the single life was far too strenuous for the average male." Today, though, a man does not really need a woman to take care of cooking, cleaning, decorating, and making life comfortable. Many men still choose marriage for love and companionship. But as Ehrenreich notes, short of outlawing TV dinners and drip-dry shirts, it's hard to see how we can make marriage as indispensable for men as it used to be. And short of reversing laws against job discrimination, there's no way we can force women into more dependence on marriage. Neither men nor women need marriage as much as they used to. Asking people to behave as if they do just sets them up for trouble.[12]

Wives who don't work outside the home, for instance, are at much higher economic and emotional risk if they *do* get deserted or divorced than women who have maintained jobs. They are far more likely to be impoverished by divorce, even if they are awarded child support, and they eventually recover a far lower proportion of the family income that they had during marriage than women who had been working prior to the divorce.[13]

Women who refrain from working during marriage, quit work to raise their children, or keep their career aspirations low to demonstrate that "family comes first" are taking a big gamble, because there are many factors other than female independence that produce divorce. Some of them are associated with women's decisions or expectations *not* to work or *not* to aspire to higher education. For example, couples who marry in their teens are twice as likely to divorce as those who marry in their twenties. Women who marry for the first time at age 30 or more have exceptionally low divorce rates, despite their higher likelihood of commitment to paid work. Women who don't complete high school have higher divorce rates than women who do, and high school graduates have higher divorce rates than women who go on to college. With further higher education, divorce rates go up again, but should we advise a woman to abandon any aspirations she may have developed in college because her statistical chance of staying married will rise if she quits her education now? . . .

Highly educated and high-paid women may have a greater chance of divorcing, but women with low earnings and education have lower prospects of getting married in the first place. Men increasingly choose to marry women who have good jobs and strong educational backgrounds. In the 1980s, reversing the pattern of the 1920s, "women with the most economic resources were the most likely to marry." But of course these are also the women most able to leave a bad marriage.[14]

20

## The Issue of No-Fault Divorce

Some people believe we could stabilize families, and protect homemakers who sacrifice economic independence, by making divorce harder to get, especially in families with children. This sounds reasonable at first hearing. Divorce tends to disadvantage women economically, and to set children back in several ways. It is hardest of all on women who committed themselves and their children to the bargain implied by the 1950s marriage ideal—forgoing personal economic and educational advancement in order to raise a family, and expecting lifetime financial support from a husband in return. A 47-year-old divorced mother describes what happened to her: "Instead of starting a career for myself, I helped my husband get his business started. I had four children. I made the beds. I cooked the meals. I cleaned the house. I kept my marriage vows. Now I find myself divorced in midlife with no career. My husband makes $100,000 a year, and we're struggling to get by on a quarter of that."[15]

We could avoid such inequities, say the family values crusaders, if today's marriage contract was not "considerably less binding than, for example, a contract to sell a car or a cow." "The first step is to end unilateral divorce," says Maggie Gallagher of the Institute for American Values. She advocates imposing a five- to seven-year waiting period for contested divorces.[16]

The argument that "we ought to enforce marriage just like any other contract" sounds reasonable until you take a historical and sociological perspective on the evolution of divorce law. Then a number of problems become clear. First, requiring people to stay together has nothing to do with enforcing contract law. When someone breaks a contract, the courts don't normally force the violator to go back and provide the services; they merely assign payment of money damages. If an entertainer refuses to perform a concert, for example, no matter how irresponsibly, the promoter cannot call the police to haul the performer into the theater and stand over him while he sings, or even impose a cooling-off period so he can rethink whether he wants to honor the contract. Instead, the promoter is awarded damages. The contract analogy may make a case for seeking damages, but it has no relevance to the issue of making divorce harder to get.

A woman who has sacrificed economic opportunities to do the bulk of child raising ought to get compensation for that when a marriage breaks up, no matter whose "fault" the failure is. Even full-time working wives often give up higher-paying jobs or education in order to take the lion's share of responsibility for family life. The tendency of many courts during the 1970s to reduce alimony and maintenance allowances for wives was based on the mistaken assumption that because more women were working, male–female equality had already been achieved. Maintenance awards need to be rethought, as well as separated from child support payments, a process now occurring in many states. But improving maintenance provi-

25

sions for the spouse who did family caregiving is a separate question from forcing someone to remain in a marriage against his or her will—or to do *without* support for a protracted period of time while the courts sort through who was "at fault."[17]

Second, making divorces harder to get would often exacerbate the bitterness and conflict that are associated with the *worst* outcomes of divorce for kids. One of the hot new concepts of the consensus school is that we need to preserve the good-enough marriage—where there is not abuse or neglect but merely an "acceptable" amount of adult unhappiness or discontent in comparison to the benefits for children in keeping the family together. But what government agency or private morals committee will decide if a marriage is "good enough"?

One author suggests we might require parents with children under 18 to "demonstrate that the *family* was better off broken than intact. Unhappiness with one's spouse would not then be a compelling argument for divorce. Domestic violence would be." Yet what would prevent the person who wanted out of the marriage from upping the ante—for example, from threatening domestic violence to get his or her way?[18]

Furthermore, it is *women* more than men who have historically needed   30
the protection of divorce. And yes, I mean protection. Because of men's greater economic and personal power, one divorce historian points out, husbands traditionally handled marital dissatisfaction by intimidating or coercing their wives into doing what the men wanted, such as accepting an extramarital affair or living with abuse. Alternatively, the man simply walked away, taking no legal action. Women, with less social and domestic power, "turned to an external agency, the law, for assistance." Women were the majority of petitioners for divorce and legal separation in English and American history long before the emergence of a feminist movement. Access to divorce remains a critical option for women.[19]

Finally, sociological research finds little evidence that no-fault laws have been the main cause of rising divorce rates, or that, on average, women do worse with no-fault than they did in the days when spouses had to hire detectives or perjurers to prove fault. While more than half the states enacted some form of no-fault divorce legislation in the 1970s, the rates of marital dissolution in most of these states were no higher in the 1970s than would be expected from trends in states that did *not* change their laws. Researcher Larry Bumpass suggests that, in some instances, no-fault has speeded up "cases that were already coming down the pipeline," but the rise in divorce seems to be independent of any particular legal or social policy. And, of course, making divorce harder to get does nothing to prevent separation or desertion.[20]

Work on preventing unnecessary divorces, separations, and desertions needs to happen *before* a marriage gets to the point of rupture. We can experiment with numerous ways to do that, from marriage education to moral persuasion to parenting classes to counseling. We can educate young people about the dangers of our society's throwaway mentality, pointing out that it creates emotional as well as material waste. We should certainly warn people that divorce is never easy for the partners or for their children. Still, history suggests that no amount of classes, counseling, or crusades will reinstitutionalize marriage in the sense that the family values crusaders desire.

Divorce rates are the product of long-term social and economic changes, not of a breakdown in values. Individual belief systems are a comparatively minor factor in predicting divorce. Despite the Catholic Church's strong opposition to divorce, for example, practicing Catholics are as likely to divorce as non-Catholics. Studies have shown that prior disapproval of divorce has little bearing on a person's later chance of divorce, although people who do divorce are likely to modify their previous disapproval. Once again, we have a situation where many intricately related factors are involved. Neither legal compulsions nor moral exhortations are likely to wipe out historical transformations that have been building for so long. . . .[21]

### Reality Bites

It makes little sense to whip up hysteria about an issue if you don't have any concrete solutions. Yet for people who believe we're on the verge of "cultural suicide," the measures proposed by the family values crusaders are curiously halfhearted. Amitai Etzioni urges individuals to make "super-vows," voluntary premarriage contracts indicating "that they take their marriage more seriously than the law requires." One of the few concrete reforms David Blankenhorn proposes to ensure "a father for every child" is that we forbid unmarried women access to sperm banks and artificial insemination. In addition, he asks men to take pledges that "marriage is the pathway to effective fatherhood," wants the president to issue an annual report on the "state of fatherhood," and thinks Congress should designate "Safe Zones" for male responsibility. Can anyone who looks at the historical trends in divorce, unwed motherhood, and reproductive technology seriously think such measures will bring back the married-couple–biological-parent monopoly over child rearing?[22]

Barbara Dafoe Whitehead of the Institute for American Values advocates    35
"restigmatization" of divorce and unwed motherhood; "stigmatization," she argues, "is a powerful means of regulating behavior, as any smoker or overeater will testify." But while overeaters may now feel "a stronger sense of shame than in the past," this has hardly wiped out the problem of obesity. Indeed, the proportion of overweight Americans has increased steadily since the 1950s. As for curbing smoking, the progress here has come from stringent public regulations against smoking, combined with intensive (and expensive) interventions to help people quit. The pretended "consensus" of the new family values crusaders would quickly evaporate if they attempted to institute an equally severe campaign against single parents. After all, 90 percent of the people in a 1995 Harris poll believe society "should value all types of families."[23]

Besides, stigmatization is a blunt instrument that does not distinguish between the innocent and the guilty any better than no-fault divorce. Dan Quayle's latest book, for example, includes a divorced family among five examples he gives of the "strong" families that still exist in America. He puts a divorced single mother into a book intended to prove that "intact" families are ideal because, "Though Kathy experienced divorce, she did not foresee or want it." It was not this woman's intent, Quayle explains, to pursue "a fast-track career." She "expected to play the traditional role, to raise her children and create a home for a husband of whom she was proud." Such distinctions put the consensus brokers in the tricky business of examining people's motives to decide which divorced or single parents had good intentions and therefore should be exempt from stigmatization.[24]

It would be easy to dismiss the flimsy reforms proposed by the "new consensus" proponents as fuzzy-headed wishful thinking were it not for the fact that their approach opens such a dangerous gap between practice and theory. At best, affirming lifelong marriage as a principle while issuing exceptions for people whose *intentions* were good encourages a hypocrisy that is already far too common in today's political and cultural debates. Consider Congressman Newt Gingrich, who was born into a single-parent family, made his ex-wife a single mom by divorcing her, and has a half-sister who is gay. "I'm not sitting here as someone who is unfamiliar with the late twentieth century," he has said. "I know life can be complicated." Yet that didn't stop him from blaming Susan Smith's murder of her two children in 1994 on lack of family values. . . .[25]

At worst, this approach offers right-wing extremists moderate-sounding cover for attempts to penalize or coerce families and individuals that such groups find offensive. Insisting that everyone give lip service to lifelong marriage as an ideal while recognizing in practice that life is complicated is like having a law on the books that *everyone* breaks at one time or another. Authorities can use it selectively to discipline the poor, the powerless, or the unpopular, while letting everyone else off the hook.

The family values crusade may sound appealing in the abstract. But it offers families no constructive way to resolve the new dilemmas of family life. Forbidding unmarried women access to sperm banks, for instance, is hardly going to put the package of child rearing and marriage back together. It would take a lot more repression than that to reinstitutionalize lifelong marriage in today's society.

As Katha Pollitt argues, "we'd have to bring back the whole nineteenth century: Restore the cult of virginity and the double standard, ban birth control, restrict divorce, kick women out of decent jobs, force unwed pregnant women to put their babies up for adoption on pain of social death, make out-of-wedlock children legal nonpersons. That's not going to happen."[26] If it did happen, American families would be worse off, not better, than they are right now.

40

Notes

1. "Marriage in America: A Report to the Nation" (New York: Council on Families in America, Mar. 1995) 10–11, 13.

2. David Popenoe, "Modern Marriage: Revising the Cultural Script," in David Popenoe, Jean Bethke Elshtain, and David Blankenhorn, eds., *Promises to Keep: Decline and Renewal of Marriage in America,* (Lanham: Rowman, 1996) 254; "Marriage in America" 4; David Popenoe, *Life without Father: Compelling New Evidence That Fatherhood and Marriage Are Indispensable for the Good of Children and Society* (New York: Free Press, 1996) 222; David Blankenhorn, *Fatherless America: Confronting Our Most Urgent Social Problem* (New York: Basic, 1995) 229; Charles Murray, "Keep It in the Family," *Times of London* 14 Nov. 1993; Maggie Gallagher, *The Abolition of Marriage: How We Destroy Lasting Love* (Washington: Regnery, 1996) 250–57; Barbara Dafoe Whitehead, "Dan Quayle Was Right," *Atlantic Monthly* 271 (April 1993): 49.

3. "Marriage in America" 4. The "deinstitutionalizing" phrase comes from Blankenhorn 224.

4. William Goode, *World Changes in Divorce Patterns* (New Haven: Yale UP, 1993) 330.

5. On the leveling off of family change, see Peter Kilborn, "Shifts in Families Reach a Plateau," *New York Times* 27 Nov. 1996. Other information in this and the following three paragraphs, unless otherwise noted, come from Steven Rawlings and Arlene Saluter, *Household and Family Characteristics: March 1994,* Current Population Reports Series P20-483 (Washington: Bureau of the Census, U.S. Department of Commerce, Sept. 1995) xviii–ix; Michael Haines, "Long-term Marriage Patterns in the United States from Colonial Times to the Present," *History of the Family* 1 (1996); Arthur Norton and Louisa Miller, *Marriage, Divorce, and Remarriage in the 1990s,* Current Population Reports Series P23-180 (Washington: Bureau of the Census, Oct. 1992); Richard Gelles, *Contemporary Families: A Sociological View* (Thousand Oaks: Sage, 1995) 116–20, 176; Shirley Zimmerman, "Family Trends: What Implications for Family Policy?" *Family Relations* 41 (1992): 424; Margaret Usdansky, "Single Motherhood: Stereotypes vs. Statistics," *New York Times* 11 Feb. 1996: 4; *New York Times* 30 Aug. 1994: A9; *New York Times* 10 Mar. 1996: A11, and 17 Mar. 1996: A8; U.S. Bureau of the Census, *Statistical Abstracts of the United States* (Washington: 1992); Sara McLanahan and Lynne Casper, "Growing Diversity and Inequality in the American Family," in Reynolds Farley, ed., *State of the Union: America in the 1990s,* vol. 1 (New York: Russell Sage, 1995).

6. Larry Bumpass, "Patterns, Causes, and Consequences of Out-of-Wedlock Childbearing: What Can Government Do?" *Focus* 17 (U of Wisconsin–Madison Institute for Research on Poverty, 1995): 42; Larry Bumpass and R. Kelly Raley, "Redefining Single-Parent Families: Cohabitation and Changing Family Reality," *Demography* 32 (1995): 98.

7. *Olympian* 26 Feb. 1996: D6.

8. Susan Watkins, Jane Menken, and John Bongaarts, "Demographic Foundations of Family Change," *American Sociological Review* 52 (1987): 346–58.

9. Barbara Wilson and Sally Clarke, "Remarriages: A Demographic Profile," *Journal of Family Issues* 13 (1992).

10. Gelles 344–45; Alan Booth, David Johnson, Lynn White, and John Edwards, "Women, Outside Employment, and Marital Instability," *American Journal of Sociology* 90 (1989): 567–83.

11. Saul Hoffman and Greg Duncan, "The Effect of Incomes, Wages, and AFDC Benefits on Marital Disruption," *Journal of Human Resources* 30 (1993): 1–41.

12. Barbara Ehrenreich, "On the Family," *Z Magazine* Nov. 1995: 10; Ailsa Burns and Cath Scott, *Mother-Headed Families and Why They Have Increased* (Hillsdale: Erlbaum, 1994) 183.

13. Terry Arendell, "Women and the Economics of Divorce in the Contemporary United States," *Signs* 13 (1987): 125.

14. Valerie Oppenheimer and Vivian Lew, "American Marriage Formation in the Eighties: How Important Was Women's Economic Independence?" in K. O. Mason and A. Jensen, eds., *Gender and Family Change in Industrialized Countries* (Oxford: Oxford UP, 1994); Aimee Dechter and Pamela Smock, "The Fading Breadwinner Role and the Economic Implications for Young Couples," Institute for Research on Poverty, Discussion Paper 1051–94, Dec. 1994: 2; Marian Wright Edelman, *Families in Peril: An Agenda for Social Change* (Cambridge: Harvard UP, 1987) 55; Lawrence Lynn and Michael McGeary, eds., *Inner-City Poverty in the United States* (Washington: National Academy Press, 1990) 163–67; University of Michigan researcher Greg Duncan, testimony before the House Select Committee on Children, Youth and Families, 19 Feb. 1992; *New York Times* 4 Sept. 1992: A1; Daniel Lichter, Diane McLaughlin, George Kephart, and David Landry, "Race and the Retreat from Marriage: A Shortage of Marriageable Men?" *American Sociological Review* 57 (1992): 797; Kristin Luker, "Dubious Conceptions–The Controversy over Teen Pregnancy," *American Prospect* Spring 1991.

15. Dirk Johnson, "Attacking No-Fault Notion, Conservatives Try to Put Blame Back in Divorce," *New York Times* 12 Feb. 1996: A8.

16. Maggie Gallagher, "Why Make Divorce Easy?" *New York Times* 20 Feb. 1996; "Welfare Reform and Tax Incentives Can Reverse the Anti-Marriage Tilt," *Insight* 15 Apr. 1996: 24; Suzanne Fields, "The Fault-Lines of Today's Divorce Policies," *Washington Times* 22 Apr. 1996. See also Maggie Gallagher, *The Abolition of Marriage: How We Destroy Lasting Love* (Washington: Regnery, 1996).

17. Stephen Sugarman and Herma Hill Kay, eds., *Divorce Reform at the Crossroads* (New Haven: Yale UP, 1990); Cynthia Stearns, "Divorce and the Displaced Homemaker: A Discourse on Playing with Dolls, Partnership Buyouts and Dissociation under No-Fault," *University of Chicago Law Review* 60 (1993): 128–39; Ann Luquer Estin, "Maintenance, Alimony, and the Rehabilitation of Family Care," *North Carolina Law Review* 71 (1993). For my understanding of recent legal trends, I am greatly indebted to conversations with Olympia attorney Christina Meserve.

18. Maggie Gallagher, "Recreating Marriage," in Popenoe, Elshtain, and Blankenhorn 237.

19. Roderick Phillips, *Untying the Knot: A Short History of Divorce* (Cambridge: Cambridge UP, 1991) 232. The one exception to this occurs in countries where men, but not women, have the right to divorce. High divorce rates in these countries tend to be associated with low status for women; in other situations, high

divorce rates are associated with women's higher status and greater amount of economic and personal autonomy. See Burns and Scott 182.

20. Larry Bumpass, "What's Happening to the Family? Interactions between Demographic and Institutional Change," *Demography* 27 (1990) 485.

21. Andrew Cherlin, *Marriage, Divorce, Remarriage* (Cambridge: Harvard UP, 1981) 49; Johnson; William Goode, *World Changes in Divorce Patterns* (New Haven: Yale UP, 1993) 318; Shirley Zimmerman, "The Welfare State and Family Breakup: The Mythical Connection," *Family Relations* 40 (1991): 141.

22. Ruth Shalit, "Family Mongers," *New Republic* 16 Aug. 1993: 13; Popenoe 194; David Popenoe, "American Family Decline, 1960–1990," *Journal of Marriage and the Family* 55 (1993): 539; Blankenhorn 220–33; and quoted in *Newsweek* 6 Feb. 1995: 43; "Marriage in America: A Report to the Nation," Council on Families in America, March 1995: 4.

23. Whitehead 49; Carole Sugarman, "Jack Sprat Should Eat Some Fat," *Washington Post National Weekly Edition* 2–8 May 1994; *Olympian* 5 Feb. 1996: A8; Janet Giele, "Decline of the Family: Conservative, Liberal, and Feminist Views," in Popenoe, Elshtain, and Blankenhorn 104.

24. Dan Quayle and Diane Medved, *The American Family: Discovering the Values That Make Us Strong* (New York: Harper, 1996) 2, 87, 114.

25. Katharine Seelye, "The Complications and Ideals," *New York Times* 24 Nov. 1994.

26. Katha Pollitt, "Bothered and Bewildered," *New York Times* 22 July 1993.

---

# The Effects of Divorce on America
## Patrick F. Fagan and Robert Rector

American society may have erased the stigma that once accompanied divorce, but it can no longer ignore divorce's massive effects. As social scientists track successive generations of American children whose parents have ended their marriages, the data are leading even some once-staunch supporters to conclude that divorce is hurting American society and devastating children's lives. Its effects are obvious in family life, educational attainment, job stability, income potential, physical and emotional health, drug use, and crime.

Each year, over one million American children suffer as their parents divorce. Moreover, half of all children born in wedlock this year will see their parents divorce before reaching [the children's] eighteenth birthday. This fact alone should give policymakers and those whose careers focus on children reason for pause.

Social science research is showing that the effects of divorce continue into adulthood and affect the next generation of children as well. If the effects are indeed demonstrable, grave, and long-lasting, then something must be done to protect children and the nation from these consequences. Reversing the effects of divorce will entail nothing less than a cultural shift in attitude, if not a cultural revolution, because society still embraces divorce in its laws and popular culture, sending out myriad messages that "it's okay."

It is not. Mounting evidence in the annals of scientific journals details the plight of the children of divorce. It clearly indicates that divorce has lasting effects which spill over into every aspect of life. For example:

Children whose parents have divorced are increasingly the victims of abuse and neglect.                                                                                          5

They exhibit more health, behavioral, and emotional problems, are involved more frequently in crime and drug abuse, and have higher suicide rates.

Children of divorced parents more frequently demonstrate a diminished learning capacity, performing more poorly than their peers from intact two-parent families in reading, spelling, and math. They have higher dropout rates and lower rates of college graduation.

Divorce generally reduces the income of the child's primary household and seriously diminishes the potential of every household member to accumulate wealth. For families that were not poor before the divorce, the drop in income can be as much as 50 percent.

Religious worship, which has been linked to health and happiness as well as longer marriages and better family life, is less prevalent in divorced families.

Such evidence should give all Americans reason to speak out on this problem. If nothing is done, America will continue the downward spiral into social decay.                                                                                              10

The effects of divorce are immense. The research shows that it permanently weakens the relationship between a child and his parents and leads to destructive ways of handling conflict and a poorer self-image. Children of divorce demonstrate an earlier loss of virginity, more cohabitation, higher expectations of divorce, higher divorce rates later in life, and less desire to have children. These effects on future family life perpetuate the downward spiral of family breakdown.

Policymakers at the federal and state levels have ample evidence to lend weight to efforts to change the culture of divorce. Even the legal system seriously neglects children's interests.

State officials should greatly expand effective marriage-education and divorce-prevention programs. They also should end the legal status of "no fault" divorce for parents who have children under the age of 18.

Federal officials can assist them by establishing the importance of marriage in federal policies and programs. For example, Washington could require the states to collect and provide accurate data on marriages and divorces, noting in each case the ages of the children involved.

Congress could create demonstration grants, by diverting existing funding, to enable local community groups to provide marriage-education and divorce-prevention programs. Finally, Congress could establish a onetime                   15 tax credit for married parents who keep their marriage intact at least until their youngest child reaches age 18.

American society, through its institutions, must teach core principles: marriage is the best environment in which to raise healthy, happy children who can achieve their potential, and the family is the most important institution for social well-being.

## Crime and Education

To understand the significant relationship between a community's crime rate and family background, one need only look at the evidence. For example, Robert Sampson, professor of sociology at the University of Chicago, found that the divorce rate predicted the rate of robbery in any given area, regardless of economic and racial composition. Sampson studied 171 U.S. cities with populations of more than 100,000. In these communities, he found that the lower the rates of divorce, the higher the formal and informal social controls (such as supervision of children) and the lower the crime rates.

Child abuse is closely related to delinquency and violent crime, and divorce is a relevant factor in an abused child's background. Not only do higher levels of divorce accompany higher levels of child abuse, remarriage does not reduce the level of child abuse and may even add to it.

After a divorce, mothers may marry again or acquire new boyfriends, but the presence of a stepfather or boyfriend increases the risk of abuse, though at significantly different rates.

When parents divorce, most children suffer. For some, this suffering turns into long-lasting psychological damage. Neglect of children, which can be psychologically more damaging than physical abuse, is twice as high among separated and divorced parents.

Children who use drugs and abuse alcohol are more likely to come from family backgrounds characterized by parental conflict and rejection. Because divorce increases these factors, it increases the likelihood that children will abuse alcohol and begin using drugs. Comparing all family structures, drug use in children is lowest in the intact married family.

Throughout a child's educational experience, divorce hinders learning and achievement.

Divorce impedes learning by disrupting productive study patterns, as children are forced to move between domiciles, and by increasing anxiety and depression in both parents and children. Because of its impact on stable home life, divorce can diminish the capacity to learn—a principle demonstrated by the fact that children whose parents divorce have lower rates of graduation from high school and college and also complete fewer college courses.

## Economy and Personality

According to data reported in 1994 by Mary Corcoran, professor of political science at the University of Michigan, "During the years children lived with two parents, their family incomes averaged $43,600, and when these same children lived with one parent, their family incomes averaged $25,300."

Divorce has significant negative economic consequences for families. The breakup of families leaves one parent trying to do the work of two people — and one person cannot support a family as well as two can. The result is decreased household income and a higher risk of poverty.

25

Almost 50 percent of households with children undergoing divorce move into poverty following the divorce. Some 40 percent of families on AFDC are divorced or separated single-parent households.

Divorce also wreaks havoc with children's psychological stability. When their families break up, they experience reactions ranging from anger, fear, and sadness to yearning, worry, rejection, conflicting loyalties, lowered self-confidence, heightened anxiety and loneliness, depression, suicidal thoughts, and even suicide attempts.

Divorce affects all of society's major institutions, but none more than the family itself and the child's capacity to sustain family life as an adult. The severing of the relationship between mother and father rends the hearts of most children, making their own capacity to have deep and trusting relationships more tenuous.

Indeed, divorce seems to perpetuate itself across successive generations. The impact on home life is so strong that children of divorced parents struggle as adults to create a positive, healthy family environment for their own children. Adults who experienced divorce as children prove less capable of breaking the cycle and instead pass on a legacy of tragedy to their children and grandchildren.

## Weakened Relationships

Parents not only divorce each other, they in effect divorce or partially divorce their children.

30

The primary result of divorce is the deterioration of the relationship between the child and at least one parent. Divorced mothers, despite their best intentions, are less able than married mothers to give the same level of emotional support to their children. Divorced fathers are less likely to have a close relationship with their children; and the younger the children are at the time of the divorce, the more likely the father is to drift away from regular contact with them.

Divorce diminishes children's capacity to handle conflict. One important difference between marriages that stay intact and those that end in divorce is the couple's ability to handle conflict and move toward agreement. Children of divorced parents can acquire the same incapacity to work through conflict from their parents.

Many teenagers struggle with feelings of inadequacy and frequently turn these feelings into erroneous judgments of peer rejection. Daughters of divorce find it more difficult to value their femininity or believe that they are genuinely lovable. Sons of divorced parents frequently demonstrate less confidence in their ability to relate with women, either at work or romantically.

When a family breaks apart, the rhythm of family life is deeply affected, and this often means that religious practice is disrupted. The diminished practice of religion, in turn, can have negative consequences. The data clearly show that parents and children in intact families are much more likely to worship than are members of divorced families or stepfamilies. Moreover, following a divorce, children are more likely to stop practicing their faith. Even when they enter a new stepfamily, their frequency of religious worship does not return to its prior level.

This drop-off in worship has serious consequences because religious 35 practice has been found to have beneficial effects on such factors as physical and mental health, education level, income, virginity, marital stability, crime, addiction, and general happiness. Church attendance is the most significant predictor of marital stability; it is closely related to sexual restraint in adolescence. Regular worship, more than religious attitudes or affiliation, is associated with lower crime rates and lower rates of use and abuse of alcohol and illicit drugs. Religious worship is associated with better health and longevity, reducing the risk of suicide, both in America and abroad.

**Reversing These Trends**

As the available evidence shows, divorce is bad for society and very harmful for children. It weakens relationships, communities, cities, states, and the nation. The increased rates of child abuse and neglect, crime, behavioral and emotional problems, health problems, cohabitation, future divorce, and out-of-wedlock births as well as the decrease in religious worship, educational attainment, and income potential should alarm every policymaker and community leader. The effects of divorce transcend generations and contribute to the all-too-evident cycle of social decay.

Sen. Daniel Patrick Moynihan (D-New York) was right when he said that "Congress cannot legislate useful attitudes," but this does not mean that politicians cannot work to change attitudes that undermine families and society. Many great politicians, from Augustus through Ronald Reagan, have used the podium and gavel to do exactly that. But changing attitudes toward divorce will require politicians and civic leaders at the federal, state, and local levels to make this one of their most important future tasks if America is to protect tomorrow's children from the effects of divorce.

Moreover, restoration of marriage will require a modest commitment of resources to pro-marriage programs. While fiscal conservatives may balk at this recommendation, they should consider that federal and state governments currently spend $150 billion per year to subsidize and sustain single-parent families.

By contrast, only $150 million is spent to strengthen marriage. Thus, for every $1,000 spent to deal with the effects of family disintegration, only $1 is spent to prevent that disintegration.

The folly of such misplaced priorities should be evident to all.                    40

Refocusing funds to preserve marriage by reducing divorce and illegitimacy will be good for children and society and will save money in the long run as well.


**What Congress Should Do**

Congress should take the following steps to combat the problem:

First, establish, by resolution, a national goal of reducing divorce among families with children by one-third over the next decade. Setting such a goal would immediately focus national attention on the severe problems related to divorce. Setting a national goal would help channel resources into divorce prevention and foster new approaches to strengthening marriage.

Reducing the divorce rate by one-third would roll it back to roughly the level that existed in the early 1970s.

Second, establish pro-marriage demonstration programs. The federal                    45
government should divert sufficient funds from existing social programs to establish a wide range of demonstration programs to provide training in marriage skills. Such programs should give young people, dating couples, and married couples the information and tools necessary to help them build and maintain a strong marriage, including an understanding of the major reasons why marriages break up. The programs also should seek to develop skills for handling conflict, dealing with change, and enhancing the marital relationship.

Third, rebuild the federal-state system for gathering statistics on marriage and divorce. Since 1993, the gathering of accurate data on divorce has stopped; in 1995, the Clinton administration ended federal support for this system. Half the states no longer compile data from marriage registries and divorce courts. Without such information, the nation cannot assess the true impact of marriage or divorce on families, schools, communities, and taxpayers.

Fourth, host a National Marriage Summit in conjunction with governors who are leading in this area. Govs. Frank Keating of Oklahoma, Mike

Leavitt of Utah, Bill Owens of Colorado, Mike Huckabee of Arkansas, Jeb Bush of Florida, and Mike Foster of Louisiana have publicly voiced their interest in reforming marriage policy. The summit's focus should be what must be done to restore marriage to its rightful place as this society's center beam.

Fifth, give a onetime tax credit to always-married couples when their youngest children reach age 18. Giving a onetime tax credit of, for example, $500 to always-married parents would signal to Americans that an intact marriage is important and fundamental to the well-being of children and the nation. This would represent a small reward for those who commit their marriages to nurturing the next generation into adulthood, and it would begin to help offset the marriage penalty in the current tax code.

### What States Can Do

Marriage and divorce are governed by state law. States should change their laws to reduce the impact of divorce on children. Specifically, they should:

- Establish a goal within each state to reduce the divorce rate among parents with children by one-third over the next decade.
- Set up pro-marriage education and mentoring programs. State governments should establish programs to provide young people, dating couples, and married couples with the information and tools necessary to build and maintain strong marriages.
- Require married couples with minor children to complete divorce education and a mediated copartnering plan before filing for divorce. Education can help couples resolve problems and save their marriage; however, it is most effective when undertaken in the initial stages of the divorce process.
- End "no-fault" divorce for parents with children under age 18. No-fault divorce is a meaningless term for children because of the damage divorce does.
- Make the covenant marriage option available to couples who seek to marry. In a covenant marriage, couples are bound by force of law to a marriage contract that lengthens the process for obtaining a divorce by two years, thus applying a brake on the divorce. Louisiana and Arizona have enacted covenant marriage laws. In approximately 25 states, such legislation has been introduced but has not progressed through the legislative process.
- Take a page from the educational outreach strategy embodied in Florida's 1998 Marriage Preservation and Preparation Act. This bill requires marriage education classes for all high school students and offers a marriage license fee reduction to couples who take a minimum four-hour marriage education course.

Divorce has pervasive ill effects on children and the five major institu- 50
tions of society: the family, church, school, marketplace, and government
itself. If the family is the building block of society, then marriage is the
foundation. This foundation is growing weaker, however, with fewer adults
entering into marriage, more adults leaving it in divorce, and more and
more adults eschewing it altogether for single parenthood or cohabitation.

Given the prevalence of divorce, American children are becoming
weaker educationally, emotionally, and physically. Yet few are willing to
point to divorce as a major contributor to these problems. Few policymakers like to dwell on its effects, but ignoring the problems will do little to
change the culture of divorce.

To set about rebuilding a culture of family based on marriage and providing it with all the protections and supports necessary to make intact
marriages commonplace again, federal, state, and local officials must begin
to talk about the problem and experiment to find sound strategies. America's forefathers had to rebuff threats from outside the nation. Today's generations are called to counter threats from within. What is required is the
will to act.

---

## In Defense of Splitting Up:
## The Growing Antidivorce Movement
## Is Blind to the Costs of Bad Marriages
### Barbara Ehrenreich

No one seems much concerned about children when the subject is welfare
or Medicaid cuts, but mention divorce, and tears flow for their tender psy-
ches. Legislators in half a dozen states are planning to restrict divorce on
the grounds that it may cause teen suicide, an inability to "form lasting
attachments" and possibly also the piercing of nipples and noses.

But if divorce itself hasn't reduced America's youth to emotional crip-
ples, then the efforts to restrict it undoubtedly will. First, there's the effect
all this antidivorce rhetoric is bound to have on the children of people already divorced—and we're not talking about some offbeat minority. At
least 37% of American children live with divorced parents, and these children already face enough tricky interpersonal situations without having to
cope with the public perception that they're damaged goods.

Fortunately for the future of the republic, the alleged psyche-scarring
effects of divorce have been grossly exaggerated. The most frequently
cited study, by California therapist Judith Wallerstein, found that 41%
of the children of divorced couples are "doing poorly, worried, under-
achieving, deprecating and often angry" years after their parents' divorce.
But this study has been faulted for including only 60 couples, two-thirds of
whom were deemed to lack "adequate psychological functioning" even before they split, and all of whom were self-selected seekers of family therapy.

Furthermore, there was no control group of, say, miserable couples who stayed together.

As for some of the wilder claims, such as "teen suicide has tripled as divorces have tripled": well, roller-blading has probably tripled in the same time period too, and that's hardly a reason to ban in-line skates.

In fact, the current antidivorce rhetoric slanders millions of perfectly     5
wonderful, high-functioning young people, my own children and most of their friends included. Studies that attempt to distinguish between the effects of divorce and those of the income decline so often experienced by divorced mothers have found no lasting psychological damage attributable to divorce per se. Check out a typical college dorm, and you'll find people enthusiastically achieving and forming attachments until late into the night. Ask about family, and you'll hear about Mom and Dad . . . and Stepmom and Stepdad.

The real problems for kids will begin when the antidivorce movement starts getting its way. For one thing, the more militant among its members want to "re-stigmatize" divorce with the cultural equivalent of a scarlet D. Sadly though, divorce is already stigmatized in ways that are harmful to children. Studies show that teachers consistently interpret children's behavior more negatively when they are told that the children are from "broken" homes — and, as we know, teachers' expectations have an effect on children's performance. If the idea is to help the children of divorce, then the goal should be to de-stigmatize divorce among all who interact with them — teachers, neighbors, playmates.

Then there are the likely effects on children of the proposed restrictions themselves. Antidivorce legislators want to repeal no-fault divorce laws and return to the system in which one parent has to prove the other guilty of adultery, addiction or worse. True, the divorce rate rose after the introduction of no-fault divorce in the late '60s and '70s. But the divorce rate was already rising at a healthy clip before that, so there's no guarantee that the repeal of no-fault laws will reduce the divorce rate now. In fact, one certain effect will be to generate more divorces of the rancorous, potentially child-harming variety. If you think "Mommy and Daddy aren't getting along" sounds a little too blithe, would you rather "Daddy (or Mommy) has been sleeping around"?

Not that divorce is an enviable experience for any of the parties involved. But just as there are bad marriages, there are, as sociologist Constance Ahrons argues, "good divorces," in which both parents maintain their financial and emotional responsibility for the kids. Maybe the reformers should concentrate on improving the quality of divorces — by, for example, requiring prenuptial agreements specifying how the children will be cared for in the event of a split.

The antidivorce movement's interest in the emotional status of children would be more convincing if it were linked to some concern for their physical survival. The most destructive feature of divorce, many experts argue, is the poverty that typically ensues when the children are left with a low-earning mother, and the way out of this would be to toughen child-support collection and strengthen the safety net of supportive services for low-income families—including childcare, Medicaid and welfare.

Too difficult? Too costly? Too ideologically distasteful compared with denouncing divorce and, by implication, the divorced and their children? Perhaps. But sometimes grownups have to do difficult and costly things, whether they feel like doing them or not. For the sake of the children, that is.

10

---

## Alone

### William Jelani Cobb

I wake up each morning and think about Aiesha, first thing. I haven't spoken to her in a month, but all her messages are still saved on my answering machine. There is a T-shirt in the exact spot she left it on her last visit three months ago. I still tell her that she is my favorite person. Aiesha is 8, spoiling for 9. She is my daughter, once removed.

In my wide-eyed youth I subscribed to such naive notions as love makes one a parent, and "23 chromosomes don't make you Daddy." I believed that fatherhood is created every morning at 6:00 A.M., when you creak out of bed to crack eggs, rattle pans and let yourself be hustled into granting your kid ten more minutes of sleep. I still believe that genes don't make the parent, but now I ask, what does a voided wedding vow make me?

If you listen to the running dialogue on talk radio, in barbershops and from pulpits, the American father has been dispatched, part of some planned obsolescence, done in by feminism and sperm banks. The old Dad model has been discontinued in favor of a newer, sleeker, single-parent alternative. I don't subscribe to that theory, but I do think we're in danger of becoming a society of temporary families. We're full of books and how-to guides that make it easier for people to survive the end of a marriage, but as a consequence, we run the risk of making *divorce* a cure-all for marital woe.

I know Aiesha because her mother, Shana, was my college girlfriend, and I broke up with her and then years later found myself wishing for her again. She was wild and beautiful, the opposite of my self-conscious, bookish ways. We were done in less than six months but stayed in touch with each other. Five years later I moved to New York for graduate school. When we threw a surprise party for my mother's fiftieth birthday, I invited Shana, and she showed up with a buoyant 2-year-old who had impossibly round cheeks and whose favorite word was no! As in "You are adorable." "No!"

Soon Shana and I were hanging out again, back to our old routines. When I occasionally spent the night, I slept on the couch so that Aiesha wouldn't get the wrong idea. The first night we slept together again, Shana told me that she wasn't looking for another short-term relationship.

5

I understood; neither was I. At some point in those first months of being reunited, I realized that I loved Shana again and that Aiesha had already chosen me as her father. Shana and I got married.

I think men secretly want to raise their daughters to be the kind of women who were out of their league when they were young. And so it was with Aiesha. But really, it was about the words, teaching her the words to old classics like "Ain't No Sunshine" and giggling through the part where Bill Withers sings, "And I know, I know, I know, I know, I know . . ." Kids dig repetition. She turned out volumes of poems, plays, songs and stories that were duly typed up and E-mailed to all my friends, coworkers and distant relatives as evidence of her burgeoning literary genius.

There were signs early on, now that I think of it, that the marriage was headed south. I saw in gradual degrees that my wife was less and less interested in our relationship and knew that I was at the point where many a man would've bailed. I chose to work harder. When the newspapers ranked Aiesha's public school in the bottom half of those in the city, I reduced my grad classes and worked part-time to send her to a private school. When Shana was stuck at work a few hours before her women's-group meeting was to be held in our apartment, I came home early and surprised her by cleaning up and preparing the food. I was like an outfielder who knows that the ball is headed for the bleachers, but smashes face first into the wall trying to catch it anyway. In my world, there was no such thing as a warning track.

A marital cliché: You're in the kitchen cooking dinner when your spouse returns home from a hard day at the office and announces that it's over. Just like that. It's a scenario that any writing instructor worth his salt would trash, but that's really how it went down. The exact words: "I don't love you the way a wife should love a husband, and I would like you to move out." Then silence. I was broken for a long time afterward. Shana had married me because I was the proverbial good catch, not out of a desire to build a lifelong connection. When Shana asked me to leave, I stared at her blankly for about five minutes. When she told Aiesha that I was leaving, Aiesha asked, "Does this mean I don't have a father anymore?"

There are easy answers. Friends (mainly female) tell me once a father, always a father. But experience tells me differently—that I could just as easily be evicted again, that Shana could remarry and leave me a parental second-string player. Experience has taught me that ex-stepfather does not exist as a census category. That I no longer qualify for a Father's Day card.

Looking at it now, I know that I deeply and profoundly love that little     10
girl. I understand the weight of the bond between parent and child. I also know that I was trying to single-handedly undo the mythology directed at Black men, that I wanted a family that would laugh past the bleak statistics and damning indictments of Black-male irresponsibility. When I married Shana, Aiesha had not seen her biological father in more than a year. As far as I know, she has not seen him since. I saw tragedy in her growing up as

yet another fatherless Black girl, another child whose father abandoned her in favor of emptier pursuits. I wanted to be like my old man, quietly heroic in raising my brother and sister and never once letting on that they were not his biological kin. I wanted to be a keeper.

These days, I know that my relationship with Aeisha is unwieldy, that it is sagging under the weight of its own ambiguity. Fatherhood is all about watching the daily changes, the new word learned or noticing that now she doesn't have to stand on a stool to reach her toothbrush. But I know that in a year or two my work may require that I move to Texas or California or Alaska, and it's possible that I'll fade from her preadolescent memory.

Christmas is a hard, bright day, and I wake up alone with my head heavy from the previous night's bender. Aiesha has left me a message saying that she has a gift for me and could I please come today so she can give it to me. Her mother and I have lived apart for six months, and I don't know Aiesha as well as I did in June. In another six months, she'll be a different child altogether.

When I see her outside, riding her bike in the parking lot of her building, I think how she has grown tall and slender as a reed. I bought her a watch, yellow and red, but with no cartoon characters because Aiesha fancies herself a sophisticate. The note says, "Dear Aiesha: My father once told me that keeping track of time is the first step to becoming an adult. I hope you think of me when you wear this." She gives me a gift card, and written in her best 8-year-old scrawl it says simply, "I love you." She's telling me the plot points to her latest story, the one she wants to publish when she's 12. A moment later she wants me to toss her into the air and pleads "one more time" until my deltoids are burning. She still remembers most of the words to "Ain't No Sunshine." Today, she's my daughter. Today.

---

# In Covenant Marriage, Forging Ties That Bind
## Diana Jean Schemo

North Little Rock, Ark.—By the time Dewaldon and Rita Frazier found each other at Gloryland Baptist Church, they had both learned a thing or two about the heart's capacity to falter and rise again. He had left the Army in disgrace, living with a prostitute and mainlining heroin. She had had a daughter out of wedlock and divorced a faithless husband.

So before they married in September, their pastor, Cedric Hayes, urged covenant marriage, a form of matrimony that makes divorce harder. They did not have to think long.

"Covenant," Mrs. Frazier said at the couple's home here. "Just the word tells you it's serious."

Rooted in biblical teachings about the sanctity of marriage, covenant marriages bar divorce except under extreme circumstances like adultery,

*In January 2001, in Baton Rouge, Louisiana, Kelly and Michael Johnson posed for this portrait. The couple was married under Louisiana's covenant-marriage law in 1999. Less than four percent of couples in Louisiana choose this legal option, which requires pre-marital counseling and includes conditions that make obtaining a divorce more difficult than under the state's standard marriage laws.*

abandonment or, in the words of the Arkansas law, "cruel and barbarous treatment." Such unions require counseling before taking marital vows or breaking them through divorce. And for cases that would correspond to current no-fault divorces, they extend the waiting time to up to two and a half years.

In August, Arkansas became the third state to adopt a covenant mar-    5
riage law, after Arizona in 1999 and Louisiana two years earlier. Fewer than 3 percent of couples who marry in Louisiana and Arizona take on the extra restrictions of marriage by covenant. But supporters believe that such marriages will take off in Arkansas, where Gov. Mike Huckabee, a former pastor and president of the state's chapter of the Southern Baptist Convention, has thrown the weight of his office behind the law.

James D. Wright, a sociologist at the University of Central Florida, contends that covenant marriage bills, which have been proposed in more than 20 states and are under consideration in the Michigan and Iowa Legislatures, reflect a shift away from individual liberties toward "a resurrection of traditional values: family, community and patriotism."

Steven Knock, author of *Marriage in Men's Lives* (1998), said interest in covenant marriage laws grew after federal welfare reform, which put a five-year limit on federal aid to poor families. States moved to tackle the two biggest determinants of poverty: divorce and births out of wedlock, Mr. Knock said.

Research has shown that about 33 percent to 45 percent of couples on the brink of divorce may reconcile if they are legally prevented from divorcing within six months, said Dr. Knock, who—with Dr. Wright and another sociologist, Laura Sanchez—is conducting a five-year study comparing relationships in covenant and standard marriages.

States are also offering incentives for premarital counseling and marriage education courses in an effort to reduce divorce, which soared in the

1970's. In 1968, the year before California adopted the nation's first no-fault divorce law, there were 584,000 divorces in the country, a rate of 2.9 divorces per 1,000 Americans. By 1998, the number of divorces had reached 1,135,000, or 4.2 per 1,000. (The divorce rate is highest in Southern states—roughly 50 percent higher than in the rest of the country—and lowest in New York, New Jersey and Connecticut.)

While the law's largely evangelical Christian supporters hoped that churches would require covenant marriage as a condition for performing wedding ceremonies, most religious leaders balked. The Roman Catholic Church, which represents the largest religious group in Louisiana, objected to discussions of divorce under any circumstances. 10

"Doesn't that tell you something about the advisability of this?" said Jeanne Carriere, a professor at Tulane Law School in New Orleans.

Professor Carriere said she doubted the ability of the courts to enforce covenant marriage vows, particularly inasmuch as the Supreme Court ruled more than half a century ago that the state of residence at the time of divorce, not marriage, determined which laws governed the divorce.

The states that have passed the laws have created little infrastructure to sustain or dissolve covenant marriages. While the law requires counseling to overcome discord, Louisiana's Legislature took no steps to provide low-cost counselors to the needy. The laws require counseling even in cases of abuse—an approach that alarms those running shelters for battered women.

So far, the Knock-Wright-Sanchez research has found that couples who choose covenant marriages have higher incomes and more education than other couples. They are deeply connected to their churches, and approached courtship and marriage very seriously.

These couples, the researchers say, also tend to bring fewer unresolved problems to the marriage: fewer bridegrooms are in debt, and the brides, at least, appear to be more skilled at communicating. Only a third of standard couples discussed children before they married; virtually all of the covenant couples did. And though the research is still early, so far, four times more standard couples in the study have divorced, Dr. Knock said. 15

One recently wed covenant couple—Christian Lesher, 27, and Samantha Myers, 24—began seeing each other six years ago and were engaged for over a year. They spent hours in counseling discussing their experiences, foibles and attitudes, but say they never allowed themselves physical intimacy.

Taking a break from decorating the First Baptist Church in Little Rock the day before their wedding the couple said they liked the signal that covenant marriage sent.

"This was right for us, 100 percent," Ms. Myers said.

"This is insurance that we're not going to make a decision that we're going to regret because we hit a valley in our marriage," [she] said.

*For Discussion*

1. What does Whitehead mean by "expressive divorce"? How does she see marriage counseling and therapy as contributing to the problem of widespread divorce?

2. In paragraph 28, Coontz summarizes her opponents' views about staying in marriages that are "good enough." Do you think her opponents are arguing that adults should simply accept a certain amount of unhappiness or discontent for the sake of the children? Is this what Whitehead means by "the idea that parents should strive to preserve a marriage 'for the sake of the children'"?

3. Does Barbara Dafoe Whitehead advocate any measures to turn around the values of the "divorce culture"? Compare hers with the solutions offered in the conclusion of Fagan and Rector's essay on "The Effects of Divorce on America." Which, if any, seem to hold some promise? (Note that Fagan and Rector give Ronald Reagan as an example of a politician whose policies influenced American attitudes about family. Yet Reagan himself was divorced from his first wife). How else do you think marriage could become a stronger institution in our society today? What would have to change?

4. In Coontz's essay, paragraphs 24–33 offer a case for maintaining no-fault divorce laws. Outline the case and assess its strength.

5. After reading William Jelani Cobb's description of his changing relationship with Aiesha, discuss possible reasons for a father to lose touch with children after a divorce even if he would prefer to stay close.

6. One thing everyone agrees on is that divorce does cause problems. Compare Ehrenreich's descriptions of these problems (paragraphs 2, 6, and 9) with Whitehead's (paragraphs 19–24). Then compare the solutions each offers, Ehrenreich's in paragraphs 6 and 9 and Whitehead's in paragraphs 30–31. Is it hypocritical to expect Americans to vote for legislation to reduce child poverty at the same time that they allow no-fault divorce?

7. Do you think that the covenant marriage movement is a good idea? Would you consider such a marriage for yourself? Why or why not?

*For Inquiry and Convincing*

1. Research the introduction of "no-fault" divorce laws and the reasons for their creation. Could "no-fault" be eliminated or modified in a way that would not bring back the circumstances that led to this reform in divorce law? Make an argument either for retaining the laws as they are or for modifying them.

2. The themes Whitehead finds in American culture are similar to those discussed in Robert Bellah's best-seller *Habits of the Heart: Individualism and Commitment in American Life*. Bellah is a sociologist

of religion at University of California, Berkeley, and his book has become a classic in sociology. Read the chapter "Love and Marriage," which offers many examples from his research about how American couples talk in expressive and therapeutic terms about their marriages. Compare Bellah's perspective with Whitehead's, and do further research to determine if expressive individualism could be a factor in our nation's high rate of divorce. Is it fair to say that the prevalence of divorce has as much to do with values as it does with economic and social forces? Write an argument in support of your conclusions.

### For Inquiry and Persuasion

Research the success of premarital marriage counseling in preventing divorce. In addition to finding written articles on the subject, you may be able to interview some ministers who perform such counseling for their church members before marrying them. If you are convinced that such counseling makes a difference, write an essay to persuade couples to undergo such counseling. If you are not convinced, simply write up the experience of inquiring as an exploratory essay, showing how you arrived at the conclusion you did.

## SECTION 4: THE CHANGING FAMILY

In this final section of our unit on marriage and the family, we look at arguments about where current trends are taking the family. One of the main issues addressed is the blurring of traditional gender roles. In her historical essay, Arlene Skolnik describes the development of a "cultural split" after the industrial revolution that assigned the world of work to the men and the increasingly "professional" job of homemaking to the women. Skolnik sees these gender roles as a product of economic forces. In this section, Midge Decter disagrees, saying that these roles are biological, not cultural: Part of the "madness" of today's American family is the refusal to accept the "limits of human existence," in this case the "natural differences between the sexes" (paragraph 26). Decter's essay was originally a speech she presented to the Heritage Foundation, a research institute aimed at promoting conservative public policies. Betty Holcomb, author of *Not Guilty! The Good News about Working Mothers*, argues that new divisions of labor among today's couples are improving marital relations and allowing men to discover the pleasures of deep involvement with their children.

Related to the gender-role debate is the question of how important it is for a child to have a mother and a father to provide the complementary parenting styles associated with each sex. For Decter, the two-parent, opposite-sex family is essential. David Popenoe, a sociology professor at Rutgers University, New Brunswick, New Jersey, agrees. In "A World without Fathers," he argues that fathers' parenting is unique and vital to children's development.

However, a contrasting view is offered by Louise Silverstein and Carl Auerbach, psychology professors at Yeshiva University. They describe alternative forms of family, in which the father is absent or in which the parents are gay or lesbian, to show that children can be healthier in these homes than in ones that "attempt to conform to idealized myths" (paragraph 28).

Another myth that American families hold to is that even if couples divorce, blood relatives are forever—families forgive everything and stay close through life's stresses and strains. But the truth is that blood relationships do not ensure closeness. As Arlene Skolnik reminds us, in the best literature, the "most vivid" pictures of family life were "negative or, at best, ambivalent," a "high-voltage emotional setting, laden with dark passions, sibling rivalries, and violence" (paragraph 17). In one of the most famous lines in literature, Leo Tolstoy wrote, "All happy families resemble one another; each unhappy family is unhappy in its own way." There are many reasons for families to break apart, and in this section, Barbara Lebey, an attorney and author of a book on family estrangements, explains four societal changes that have caused American families to drift apart. But unhappiness can run in families; children in unhappy homes can grow up like Pam Houston, feeling unsure of their abilities to raise children. In her personal essay "Creating Your Own," Houston describes how she and her husband share their home and lives with a "rotating" family of students and friends.

The institution of family is one of the foundations of a society, but it cannot avoid being influenced by changes that occur in that society. This has been the case with the American family; it reflects all the things Americans are today—for good and for ill. We are individualistic, materialistic, ambitious, and mobile. We are democratic and free. We have moved toward greater openness about our problems at the same time that we remain optimistic about solving them. As Arlene Skolnik concludes, "Conflict and change are inherent in social life. . . . The family will survive."

---

## The Madness of the American Family
### Midge Decter

The idea of talking about the subject called "family" always puts me in mind of a line from the ancient Greek playwright Euripides. "Whom the Gods would destroy," he said, "they first make mad." Now, to be sure, there are no gods—there is only God—and even if there were, you would have to think that, far from destroying us, they are busily arranging things very nicely for us. Nor do I think that American society has gone mad, exactly. Look around you at this magnificent country: You would have to say that somebody is surely doing something right.

Nevertheless, the ghost of that ancient Greek keeps whispering his words of ageless experience in my ear. If we Americans cannot be said to have gone mad, we have certainly been getting nuttier by the day.

Take one example of our nuttiness. We are healthier than people have ever been in all of human history. Just to list the possibly debilitating diseases that American children need never again experience—measles, whooping cough, diphtheria, smallpox, scarlet fever, polio—is to understand why we have begun to confront the issue of how to provide proper amenities to the fast-growing number of people who are being blessed with a vigorous old age.

And yet, as it seems, from morning until night we think of nothing but our health and all the potential threats to it. We measure and count and think about everything we put into our mouths. While we are speculating about which of the many beautiful places there will be for us to retire to, we are at the same time obsessed with all the substances and foodstuffs that are lying in wait to kill us, and try out each new magical prescription for the diet that will keep us ever young and beautiful. This has gone so far that, for example, not long ago a group of pediatricians had to issue a warning to new mothers that, far from beneficial, a low-fat diet was in fact quite injurious to infants and toddlers.

And as if an obsession with nutrition were not enough, every day millions upon millions of us whom life has seen fit to save from hard labor find ourselves instead, like so many blinded horses of olden times, daily enchained to our exercise treadmills. 5

So we treat our health as if it were a disease and the benign conditions of our lives as if they were so many obstacles to our well-being.

And if that is nutty, what shall we say about finding ourselves engaged in discussing something called the family? How on earth, if the gods are not out to destroy us, have we got ourselves into *this* fix? Talking about the family should be like talking about the earth itself: interesting to observe in all its various details—after all, what else are many if not most great novels about?—but hardly up for debate. And yet people just like you and me nowadays find themselves doing precisely that: Is it good for you? Is it necessary, especially for children? And—craziest of all—what is it?

In our everyday private lives, of course, we drive around in, or fly around in, and otherwise make household use of the products of various technologies of a complexity that is positively mind-boggling without giving it a second thought. Yet at the same time, millions among us who have attended, or who now attend, universities find it useful to take formal courses in something called "family relations," as if this were a subject requiring the most expert kind of technical training. And in our lives as a national community we call conferences, engage in public programs, create new organizations, and beyond that publish and read several libraries of books devoted entirely to questions about the family—not to speak of the fact that here I am as well this evening, offering you some further conversation on the subject.

I look around this room and wonder, how on earth have we come to this place, you and I? How did the wealthiest, healthiest, and luckiest people who have ever lived get to such a point? It is as if, in payment for our good fortune, we had been struck by some kind of slow-acting but in the long run lethal plague. This plague is a malady we must diagnose and put a name to if we are ever as a nation to return to our God-given senses.

Where did the idea that the family might somehow be an object of debate and choice come from? It is never easy, as epidemiologists will tell you, to trace the exact origin of a plague. Who exactly is our Typhoid Mary?                                                      10

I can't say I know, precisely, but I knew we were in trouble back in the late 1950s when I picked up *Esquire* magazine one day and read an essay about his generation written by a young man still in university. The writer concluded with the impassioned assertion that if he thought he might end up some day like his own father, working hard every day to make a nice home for the wife and kids, he would slit his throat. *Slit his throat.* Those were his exact words.

Now, I might not have paid close attention to the sentiment expressed by this obviously spoiled and objectionable brat were it not for two things: First, we were in those days hearing a lot from their teachers about just how brilliant and marvelous was the new generation of students in the universities, and second, *Esquire* was in those days known for its claim to have its finger on the cultural pulse. Thus, this was a young man whose mountainous ingratitude was worth paying a little attention to.

And sure enough, not too much later, what we know as the 1960s began to happen. Enough said. Should it, then, have come as a surprise that in short order that young author's female counterparts began in their own way to declare that throat-cutting would be the proper response to the prospect of ending up like their mothers? Well, surprise or no, the plague was now upon us for fair.


### The End of Responsibility

Am I trying to suggest that the only course of social health is to live exactly as one's parents did? Of course not. The United States is a country whose character and achievements have depended precisely on people's striking out for new territories — actual territories and territories of the mind as well. We have not lived as our parents did, and we do not expect our children — or, anyway, our grandchildren — to live as we do.

Several years ago I was privileged to attend my grandfather's hundredth      15
birthday party. When we asked him what, looking back, was the most important thing that had ever happened to him, without a moment's hesitation he astonished us by answering that the most important thing that ever happened to him was being privileged to witness the introduction of the use of electricity into people's homes. And now I see my own grandchildren, even the youngest of them, sitting hunched over their keyboards, fingers flying, communing with unseen new-found friends in far-flung places and giving this new possibility not a second thought.

So of course we do not live as our parents lived, but that young man writing in *Esquire* was saying something else: Underneath the posturing, he was saying that he did not wish ever to become a husband and father. And the raging young women who came along soon after him were saying they, for their part, would be all too happy to be getting along without him.

And what, finally, when the dust of all these newfound declarations of independence began to settle, was the result of this new turmoil? The young men began to cut out—cut out of responsibility, cut out of service to their country, and cut out of the terms of everyday, ordinary life. They said they were against something they called "the system." But what, in the end, did they mean by that? Insofar as the system was represented by business and professional life, most of them after a brief fling as make-believe outcasts cut back into that aspect of the system very nicely; but insofar as it meant accepting the terms of ordinary daily life, of building and supporting a home and family, they may no longer have been prepared to slit their throats, but they would for a long time prove to be at best pretty skittish about this last act of becoming grown men.

And their girlfriends and lovers? They, on their side, were falling under the influence of a movement that was equating marriage and motherhood with chattel slavery. "We want," said Gloria Steinem, one of this movement's most celebrated spokeswomen ("a saint" is what *Newsweek* magazine once called her), "to be the husbands we used to marry."

Let us ponder that remark for a moment: "We want to be the husbands we used to marry." Underlying the real ideology of the women's movement, sometimes couched in softer language and sometimes in uglier, is the proposition that the differences between men and women are merely culturally imposed—culturally imposed, moreover, for nefarious purposes. That single proposition underlies what claims to be no more than the movement's demands for equal treatment, and it constitutes the gravamen of the teaching of women's studies in all our universities.

And need I say that it has been consequential throughout our society? I don't, I think, have to go through the whole litany of the women's complaints. Nor do I have to go into detail about their huge political success in convincing the powers that be that they represented half the country's population, and thus obtaining many truly disruptive legislative remedies for their would-be sorrows. 20

Among the remedies that follow from the proposition that the differences between men and women are merely culturally imposed has been that of letting women in on the strong-man action. Why, it was successfully argued, should they not be firemen, policemen, coal miners, sports reporters—in many ways most significant of all—combat soldiers?

**The Soldier and the Baby-Tender**

At the outset of the Gulf War, early in that first phase of it called Desert Shield, the *New York Post* carried on its front page a newsphoto—it may have appeared in many papers, or at least it should have—illustrating a story about the departure for Saudi Arabia of a group of reservists. The picture was of a young woman in full military regalia, including helmet, planting a farewell kiss on the brow of an infant at most three months old being held in the arms of its father. The photo spoke volumes about where this society has allowed itself to get dragged to and was in its way as obscene as anything that has appeared in that cesspool known as *Hustler* magazine. It should have been framed and placed on the desk of the president, the secretary of defense, the chairman of the Joint Chiefs, and every liberal senator in the United States Congress.

That photo was not about the achievement of women's equality; it was about the nuttiness—in this case, perhaps the proper word *is* madness—that has overtaken all too many American families. For the household in which—let's use the social scientists' pompous term for it—"the sexual differentiation of roles" has grown so blurry that you can't tell the soldier from the baby-tender without a scorecard is a place of profound disorder. No wonder we are a country with a low birthrate and a high divorce rate.

We see milder forms of this disorder all over the place, especially in cases where young mothers have decreed that mothers and fathers are to be indistinguishable as to their—my favorite word—roles. Again, you cannot tell—or rather, you are not supposed to be able to tell—the mommy from the daddy. The child, of course, knows who is what. No baby or little kid who is hungry or frightened or hurting ever calls for his daddy in the middle of the night. He might *get* his daddy, but it is unlikely that that would have been his intention.

Everybody has always known such things: What is a husband, what is a wife; what is a mother, what is a father. How have we come to the place where they are open for debate? "Untune that string," says Shakespeare, "and hark what discord follows."  25

It is not all that remarkable, for instance, that there should have been the kind of women's movement that sprang up among us. There have from time to time throughout recorded history been little explosions of radicalism, of refusal to accept the limits of human existence, and what could be a more radical idea than that there is no natural difference between the sexes? Just to say the words is to recognize that what we have here is a rebellion not against a government or a society, but against the very constitution of our beings, we men and women.

The question is, what caused such an idea to reverberate as it did among two generations of the most fortunate women who ever lived? As for their men, what idea lay at the bottom of their response to all this we do not quite know, for they giggled nervously and for the most part remained silent. But it is not difficult to see that if the movement's ideas represented an assault on the age-old definition of their manhood, it also relieved them of a great burden of responsibility: Seeing that their services as protectors and defenders and breadwinners had been declared no longer essential, they were now free — in some cases literally, in some cases merely emotionally — to head for the hills.

Since the condition of families depends to a considerable degree on the condition of marriages, small wonder, then, that the subject of family has been put up for debate.

Most recently, we are being asked to consider whether two lesbians or two male homosexuals should not also be recognized as a family. Oftentimes the ostensible issue centers on money; that is, spousal benefits for one's homosexual mate. But actually, as we know, what is being demanded is about far more than money.

Money is easy to think about; that's why the homosexual-rights movement has placed such emphasis on this particular legislative campaign. But what is really being sought is that society should confer upon homosexual unions the same legitimacy as has always been conferred upon heterosexual ones. 30

What comes next, of course, is the legal adoption of children. Why not a family with two daddies? After all, some unfortunates among us don't even have one. (Lesbians, of course, suffer no such complications. All their babies require for a daddy is a syringe. Thus, we have that little classic of children's literature, to be found in the libraries of the nation's public schools, entitled *Heather Has Two Mommies.*)

In other words, when it comes to families, any arrangement is considered as good as any other.

People don't pick their professions that way; they don't decide where to live that way; they don't furnish their lives or their houses that way; they don't even dress themselves that way . . . but families? Why not? Aren't they, after all, no more than the result of voluntary agreements between two private individuals? And anyway, don't people have rights? Who are their fellow citizens to tell them how to live and decide that one thing is good and another is bad?

Such questions explain why it was that in the 1970s a famous White House Conference on the Family, called primarily to discuss the crisis in the inner cities and packed full of so-called family experts and advocates from all over the country, could not even begin to mount a discussion, let alone provide a report, because from the very first day they could not even reach agreement on the definition of the word "family."

### You Can't Fool Mother Nature

The question is, how did we as a society ever come to this disordered place? For one thing, what has encouraged us to imagine that anything is possible if we merely will it to be? And for another, how have we strayed this far from the wisdom so painfully earned by all those who came before us and prepared the earth to receive us? I ask these questions in no polemical spirit, 35 because few of us have not in one way or another been touched by them, if not in our own households, then in the lives of some of those near and dear to us.

What is it, in short, that so many Americans have forgotten, or have never learned, about the nature of human existence?

One thing they have forgotten — or perhaps never learned — is that you can't fool Mother Nature. If you try to do so, you sicken and die, spiritually speaking — like those little painted turtles that used to be a tourist novelty for children and, because their shells were covered in paint, could never live beyond a few days.

Well, we do not, like those novelty turtles, literally die: On the contrary, as I have said, we have been granted the possibility of adding years to our lives; but far too many of us, especially the young people among us, live what are at bottom unnatural lives. Too many young women, having recovered from their seizure of believing that they were required to become Masters of the Universe, cannot find men to marry them, while the men on their side cannot seem to find women to marry. Both grope around, first bewildered and then made sour by what is happening to them. And there is nothing in the culture around them — that nutty, nutty culture — to offer medicine for their distemper.

What is it Mother Nature knows that so many of us no longer do? It is that marriage and family are not a choice like, say, deciding where to go and whom to befriend and how to make a living. Together, marriage and parenthood are the rock on which human existence stands.

Different societies may organize their families differently — or so, at least, the anthropologists used to take great pleasure in telling us (I myself have my doubts) — and they may have this or that kinship system or live beneath this or that kind of roof. But consider: In societies, whether primitive or advanced, that have no doubt about how to define the word "family," every child is born to two people, one of his own sex and one of the other, to whom his life is as important as their own and who undertake to instruct him in the ways of the world around him.

Consider this again for a moment: *Every child is born to two people, one of his own sex and one of the other, to whom his life is as important as their own and who undertake to instruct him in the ways of the world around him.* Can you name the social reformer who could dream of a better arrangement than that?

40

### The Swamp of Self

Are there, then, no violations of this arrangement? Among the nature-driven families I am talking about are there no cruel fathers or selfish and uncaring mothers? Of course there are. I have said that family is a rock, not the Garden of Eden; and a rock, as we know, can sometimes be a far from comfortable place to be. Off the coast of San Francisco there used to be a prison they called "the rock," and that is not inapt imagery for some families I can think of.

But even in benign families there are, of course, stresses and strains. To cite only one example, it takes a long time, if not forever, for, say, a late-blooming child, or a child troubled or troublesome in some other way, to live down his past with his own family, even should he become the world's greatest living brain surgeon. Families are always, and often quite unforgivingly, the people Who Knew You When. So, as I said, the rock of family can sometimes have a pretty scratchy surface.

But there is one thing that living on a rock does for you: It keeps you out of the swamps. The most dangerous of these swamps is a place of limitless and willfully defined individual freedom.

The land of limitless freedom, as so many among us are now beginning to discover, turns out to be nothing other than the deep muck and mire of Self. And there is no place more airless, more sunk in black boredom, than the land of Self, and no place more difficult to be extricated from. How many among us these days are stuck there, seeking for phony excitements and emotions, flailing their way from therapy to therapy, from pounding pillows to primal screaming to ingesting drugs to God knows what else, changing their faces and bodies, following the dictates first of this guru and then of that, and all the while sinking deeper and deeper into a depressing feeling of disconnection they cannot give a name to?

The only escape from the swamp of Self is the instinctual and lifelong engagement in the fate of others. Now, busying oneself with politics or charity—both of which are immensely worthy communal undertakings involving the needs and desires of others—cannot provide the escape I am talking about. For both, however outwardly directed, are voluntary. The kind of engagement I mean is the involuntary discovery that there are lives that mean as much to you as your own, and in some cases—I am referring, of course, to your children and their children and their children after them—there are lives that mean more to you than your own. In short, the discovery that comes with being an essential member of a family.

I do not think it is an exaggeration to use the word "discovery." No matter how ardently a young man and woman believe they wish to spend their lives with one another, and no matter how enthusiastically they greet the knowledge that they are to have a baby, they do not undertake either of these things in full knowledge of the commitment they are undertaking. They nod gravely at the words "for richer or poorer, in sickness and in health," but they do not know—not really, not deep down—that they are embarked upon a long, long, and sometimes arduous and even unpleasant journey.

I think this may be truer of women than of men. A woman holding her first-born in her arms, for instance, is someone who for the first time can truly understand her own mother and the meaning of the fact that she

45

herself had been given life. This is not necessarily an easy experience, especially if her relations with her mother have been in some way painful to her; but even if they have not, this simple recognition can sometimes be quite overwhelming. That, in my opinion, is why so many first-time mothers become temporarily unbalanced.

I cannot, of course, speak for the inner life of her husband; his experience is bound to be a different one. But the panic that so often and so famously overtakes a first-time expectant father is surely related to it. To become a family is to lose some part of one's private existence and to be joined in what was so brilliantly called "the great chain of being."

In short, being the member of a family does not make you happy; it     50
makes you human.

### One Choice among Many?

All this should be a very simple matter; God knows, it's been going on long enough. So why have we fallen into such a state of confusion?

The answer, I think, lies in the question. By which I mean that we Americans living in the second half of the 20th century are living as none others have lived before. Even the poor among us enjoy amenities that were once not available to kings. We live with the expectation that the babies born to us will survive. The death of an infant or a child is an unbearable experience. Yet go visit a colonial graveyard and read the gravestones: Our forefathers upon this land lived with the experience, year after year after year, of burying an infant—lived two weeks, lived four months, lived a year. How many burials did it take to be granted a surviving offspring?

I am not speaking of prehistoric times, but of 200 years ago. Two hundred years, my friends, is but a blink of history's eye. Could any of us survive such an experience? I doubt it.

Even a hundred years ago—*half* a blink of history's eye—people lived with kinds of hardship only rarely known among us now. Read the letters of the Victorians (fortunately for our instruction in life, people used to write a lot of letters; those who come after us, with our phone calls and e-mail, will know so little about us). They were sick *all the time.* Or take a more pleasant example, provided by my husband, the music nut: We can sit down in the comfort of home every afternoon and listen to works of music their own composers may never have heard performed and that not so long ago people would travel across Europe to hear a single performance of.

So we live as no others who came before us were privileged to do. We     55
live with the bounties of the universe that have been unlocked by the scientists and engineers and then put to use by those old swashbucklers with names like Carnegie and Edison and Ford—and, yes, Gates—who were seeking their own fortunes and in the process made ours as well. Moreover, not long from now, we are told, there will be nearly one million Americans one hundred years old or more.

We live, too—and should not permit ourselves to forget it—with another kind of bounty: We are the heirs of a political system that, despite a number of threatened losses of poise and balance, has remained the most benign and just, and even the most stable, in the world.

The truth is that precisely because we are living under an endless shower of goodies, we are as a people having a profoundly difficult time staying in touch with the sources of our being. That is why so many young women were so easily hoodwinked into believing that marriage and motherhood were what they liked to call "options," just one choice among many. That is why so many young men were so easily convinced to settle for the sudden attack of distemper afflicting the women whom fate intended for them. That is why so many people of good will find it difficult to argue with the idea that homosexual mating is no different from their own—everybody to his own taste, and who's to say, especially when it comes to sex, that anything is truer, or better, or more natural than anything else?

In short, because God has permitted us to unlock so many secrets of His universe, we are in constant danger of fancying that any limits upon us are purely arbitrary and we have the power to lift them. In the past half-century, what has not been tried out, by at least some group or other in our midst, in the way of belief and ritual or—horrible word—lifestyle? We have watched the unfolding of catalogues-full of ancient and newly made-up superstitions, the spread of fad medicines and "designer" drugs (each year, it seems, produces a new one of these). Lately we have seen beautiful young children, children living in the most advanced civilization on earth, painfully and hideously mutilating their bodies in the name, they will tell you, of fashion.

All this, I believe, stems from the same profound muddle that has left us as a society groping for a definition of the word "family." Maybe people are just not constituted to be able to live with the ease and wealth and health that have been granted to us.

But this would be a terrible thing to have to believe, and I do not believe it, and neither do you, or you would not be here this evening. As Albert Einstein once said, the Lord God can be subtle, but He is not malicious. What does seem to be a fair proposition, however, is that given the whole preceding history of mankind, to live as we do takes more than a bit of getting used to. It takes, indeed, some serious spiritual discipline.

**Wisdom and Gratitude**

I believe that two things will help us to be restored from our current nuttiness. The first is for us, as a people and a culture, to recapture our respect for the wisdom of our forbears. That wisdom was earned in suffering and trial; we throw it away—and many of us have thrown it away—at their and our very great peril. The second is a strong and unending dose of gratitude: the kind of gratitude that people ought to feel for the experience of living in

60

freedom; the kind of gratitude the mother of a newborn feels as she counts the fingers and toes of the tiny creature who has been handed to her; the kind of gratitude we feel when someone we care about has passed through some danger; the kind of gratitude we experience as we walk out into the sunshine of a beautiful day, which is in fact none other than gratitude for the gift of being alive.

All around us these days, especially and most fatefully among the young women in our midst, there are signs of a surrender to nature and the common sense that goes with it. The famous anthropologist Margaret Mead—a woman who in her own time managed to do quite a good deal of damage to the national ethos—did once say something very wise and prophetic. She said that the real crimp in a woman's plans for the future came not from the cries but from the smiles of her baby.

How many young women lawyers and executives have been surprised to discover, first, that they could not bear to remain childless, and second, that they actually preferred hanging around with their babies to preparing a brief or attending a high-level meeting? One could weep for the difficulty they had in discovering the true longings of their hearts. Next—who knows—they may even begin to discover that having a real husband and being a real wife in return may help to wash away all that bogus posturing rage that has been making them so miserable to themselves and others.

When that happens, we may be through debating and discussing and defining and redefining the term "family" and begin to relearn the very, very old lesson that life has limits and that only by escaping Self and becoming part of the onrushing tide of generations can we ordinary humans give our lives their intended full meaning. We have been endowed by our Creator not only with unalienable rights but with the knowledge that is etched into our very bones.

All we have to do is listen. And say thank you. And pray.                    65

---

## Families Are Changing—For the Better
### Betty Holcomb

When Laura Koenig arrives home from work in Stoughton, Wisconsin, she often finds dinner on the table, the dishwasher empty and waiting for a new load of dishes. There may even be a load of clothes already in the wash. All of this is done by her husband, Kurt, who gets home a couple hours ahead of her. "It's awesome, isn't it?" Laura says. "My marriage is better than it's ever been. I couldn't be happier."

Koenig, an occupational therapist and mother of two, still sounds a little surprised in early 1997 as she recounts this homecoming scene. "It sure beats the heck out of being angry all the time," she says, laughing. Five years ago, she thought their marriage was over, largely because Kurt did so little child care and housework. "All I used to think about was how could I screw him over. Now I look for things to make him feel good. It's so different."

Her husband, Kurt, sounds equally awed by the change in their marriage. He now uses the same words as Laura to describe it. "It's better than it's ever been," he says. "We couldn't be happier."

Not only that, but Kurt says he's much closer to his children. "It's been a gradual evolution. Taking part in the day-to-day rigors of life has helped my relationship with the kids." That means the children now turn to him for solace and support. "The kids don't go to Mom for everything now; they have confidence that I can meet their needs. My daughter will ask to do things with me, to read and draw with her. It's much more comfortable now."

But the road to this marital bliss was a remarkably bumpy one. It was not so long ago that Laura issued Kurt an ultimatum: "Either come to marriage counseling or move out." The issue? As for so many dual-earner couples, his lack of participation in child care and domestic chores. Kurt's new engagement at home grew directly from the insights he gained in counseling as a way to save his marriage. Both he and Laura learned that it can be far more dangerous to resist change than to embrace it.

Indeed, the Koenigs show just how much family life in America has changed over the past two decades—all in response to the growing numbers of mothers who now have jobs outside the home. Between 1975 and 1993, the number of two-paycheck families in America swelled from 43 to 63 percent of all families, making them the solid majority today. As that happens, life inside the average household is shifting, with Americans reinventing what it means to be a husband or wife, mom or dad, son or daughter.

"Having women work after having children changes everything. We now have a new family form," says Rosalind Barnett, scholar at the Murray Research Center at Radcliffe College and coauthor, with Caryl Rivers, of *She Works, He Works: How Two Income Families Are Happier, Healthier, and Better Off.* And contrary to the handwringing from social conservatives, this new kind of family turns out to be quite a vibrant one, with benefits for men, women, and children. Women's new earning power offers both men and women more flexibility about the way they pursue their careers and family life. With two incomes, families are more secure economically and better able to weather a recession or downsizing at work, which has had savage effects on family life in the past. There is also plenty of evidence that women's new economic clout has the effect of encouraging a new intimacy between men and their children, as Kurt is discovering.

To be sure, the mere fact that a woman has a job outside the home does not automatically guarantee a happy life. Marriage is one of the most complicated human relationships; so is the one between parents and children. The effects of women's employment on a marriage and family life are as various as the jobs they hold, the husbands they marry, the children they bear. Nor is the fallout from a job on family life some static phenomenon. Rather, the effects vary over time, as circumstances change both at work and at home. And there is a growing body of research that shows that the attitudes a woman or man has about male and female roles matter as much as anything.

Sociologists and psychologists also report that the best marriages today are those forged between equals, much like the one Kurt and Laura have achieved, where responsibilities for home, children, and breadwinning are shared. Such a union breeds a sense of reciprocity, empathy, and affirmation for both mates that deepens intimacy, trust, and respect in a marriage. "People are more willing to be direct, to reveal themselves and be themselves when they feel like equals," says Janice Steil, professor of psychology at Adelphi University's Derner Institute of Advanced Psychological Studies and author of *His and Her Marriage from the 1970's to the 1990's.*

That this message is still a faint one in American culture, that there is    10
still a deep ambivalence about mothers working, is not surprising to researchers, however. The truth is that American families are caught in the cross fire of change as society moves ever so slowly to accept the new family roles. Today men and women live in what sociologists call a "transitional" phase; that is, the daily realities of individual families have changed, but the nation's institutions and social expectations lag behind. Most still follow rules created for families of another era. "We're in the middle of an evolution," says James Levine, head of the Fatherhood Project at the Families and Work Institute. "These patterns just don't change overnight, because gender roles are so overdetermined. The scripts that women and men have internalized growing up, the economic realities, the continuing differential between men's and women's earning power, all conspire to keep men and women in the old roles."

Nonetheless, there is a louder call than ever from social conservatives for a return to old-fashioned "family values," when men earned a living and women stayed home with the kids. "One Breadwinner Should Be Enough," conservative economist Jude Wanniski headlined in the *Wall Street Journal* in early 1996. "When both husband and wife must work full-time to make ends meet," he insisted, "children are more likely to become unruly, communication between the spouses breaks down . . . the divorce rate increases and so does abortion." At about the same time, the right-wing Rockford Institute featured a picture of the 1950s Cleaver family, from the sitcom *Leave It to Beaver,* under the headline "Ward and June Were Right" on the cover of one of its 1996 monthly newsletters. Social conservative David Blankenhorn at the Institute for American Values asserts that "marriage is the most fragile institution in society today," and calls for a return to the old ways. "Feminists are constantly talking about wanting to reengineer sex roles, that men should do more nurturing. But it would be better to accept the premise that fathers are different from mothers. Men still see their primary responsibility as breadwinning and protection. And both men and women like it that way."

Certainly, there are some men and women who prefer those roles. But the evidence shows that many families are thriving today as they adapt to a changing way of life. Men want more expansive roles, more involvement with kids. And what Blankenhorn and other social conservatives miss is that the core problem in many marriages today is not that men's and women's roles are changing. Rather, the real threat to marriage and family life often lies in the inability or resistance to change those roles. Further, it is not some feminist plot or liberal ideology that inspires men and women to reinvent their family life. Rather, it is the day-to-day realities of home life today, transformed by women's new earning power, that drives couples to alter the terms of marriage and parenthood.

For Laura Koenig, it took a full five years after the birth of her first child, Danny, for the tension in her marriage to build to a crisis. By then, she had had a second child, Alexandra, who was eight months old. And by then, fights over housework and child care had become the stuff of daily life. "I felt such a lack of support and appreciation. I began to feel it would be easier to be with my children by myself. It would mean one less person to clean up after."

That truth came hard to her. "I went into marriage thinking I'd be married for the rest of my life," she says. When she found herself pregnant at twenty-two, she knew raising a child would be demanding. But she trusted that she and Kurt could do a good job. She never expected to be overwhelmed by the duties of raising the kids and keeping the house running.

But at twenty-six, with a job and two kids, housework and child care were foremost on her mind. Because of their different work schedules, Kurt generally arrived home a few hours ahead of her, with the two children. Back then, she recalls, "I'd typically arrive home and the kids' stuff would be all over the floor in front of the door. The kids would be hollering for something to eat. And Kurt was there reading the paper, hanging out and watching TV. I always wondered how he could do that," she recalls.

After dinner, the scenario was no less frustrating to Laura. Kurt would again retreat into his own world with a newspaper or watching television, while she cleaned the kitchen, gave the kids a bath, and got them into bed. "Kurt never used to take responsibility for the kids. He saw it as my job and only helped if I asked him to. If he gave them a bath, he'd tell me it was for me. If he put on their pajamas, he'd say he did it for me."

His attitude infuriated her. "I blew up. I asked him, 'Why is it always my job? Don't you enjoy these children? Aren't they your children, too?'"

At the time, this was hardly a new question in the Koenig household. Over the years since the birth of their first child and then their second, she had tried to get Kurt to take more responsibility for the kids. "We went through stages of trying to negotiate this. I remember sitting down and saying, 'These are all the things that need to get done around the house above and beyond my job. We have to get meals, clean up, give the kids baths,' and so on," she recalls. "I'd ask him, 'Which items will you do, will I do? Which do you never want to do?' These talks would change things for a while." But, she recalls, "it was never a sustained effort. It would work for a couple of weeks or a couple of months. Then it reverted back to the old scenario. He always paid the bills and took care of the cars. But otherwise, I did everything else. It was like I had two full-time jobs."

And this, she came to see, was corrosive to the marriage. "My anger was biting his head off. I'd swear and stomp my feet," she says, to prompt the talks about chores. Otherwise, she retreated into her anger, withdrawing from Kurt. "The anger went into every depth of our life. I remember feeling he didn't do this and didn't do that, then I'd be damned if I'd cuddle with him. I would just be cold," she says. "If he was watching TV, I'd just find anything to do besides go down and watch TV with him."

Such a situation is a familiar one to psychologists who deal with two-career couples. While the external trappings of their lives are dramatically different from those of earlier generations, many still inhabit the psychic landscape of the past. Kurt, for example, says that he didn't sense there was a truly serious problem in the marriage, even after the repeated talks about housework and child care. He'd grown up as an only child; his mom took care of all the household chores. The stress that Laura was experiencing was invisible to him. "I was off in my little world, assuming things were fine," he says. That is, until Laura gave him the ultimatum to get out or go into marriage counseling.                                                                    20

Such a situation is also a common one to family counselors. With few role models and no real system for assigning duties in the marriage, many couples wage war over the minutiae of daily life. "It's a new structure for marriage, so questions arise all the time about the extent to which expectations match in the marriage. Who's going to stay home with a sick child? Who's going to do the housework?" says Lisa Silberstein, a clinical psychologist in New Haven, Connecticut, and author of *Dual-Career Marriage: A System in Transition.* "The success in the marriage and marital satisfaction depend on how much a couple can keep those issues on the table and talking about them."

The conversations the Koenigs had in marriage counseling over the course of a year helped them arrive at new roles at home. Kurt began to take more initiative with the children and household chores. Not only that, but Kurt says he now views his wife as his true equal. "It was never an issue what my wife earns. I've never been the type to have a wife who sits home and takes care of the nest. I just never felt real strongly about that, that I needed a stay-at-home wife taking care of my kids," he says. On the other hand, he adds that "there maybe was a time when I was working and Laura was still in school, when I didn't see her as equal. But now we split everything fifty-fifty and there are a lot of benefits from that."

And that is exactly what the research on marriage shows. Dual-career couples who manage to share child care and housework tend to describe their marriages as far more satisfying than others. Such give-and-take in all aspects of family life makes both men and women feel valued and supported, and allows an intimacy that is otherwise hard to achieve, according to sociologist Pepper Schwartz, who has conducted broad surveys of marriage in America. The "mutual friendship"—the shared values and shared sense of responsibility for all aspects of family life—is the most gratifying aspect of their lives, Schwartz asserted in her book *Peer Marriage.* . . .

Still, marriage counselors and sociologists who study dual-career couples concede that such easygoing acceptance of the new expectations, roles, and responsibilities in marriage is far from a simple task for many couples. The questions that Laura Koenig put to her husband, Kurt, at the flash point in their marriage—Why was child care always her job? Didn't he enjoy their children? Weren't they his children, too?—reverberate through American culture. "Who Takes Care of the House and the Kids?" asked the headline of the *Newark Star-Ledger* in February 1997. That story covered a survey by *American Baby* magazine that found a majority of moms wished their spouses would do more around the house. By now, no one has to explain what is meant by the term "second shift." Survey after survey shows that women still put in far more hours than men do at home. Women managers at the nation's major corporations put in thirty-three hours a week on housework and child care, compared with eighteen hours a week for men, according to a study by Rodgers and Associates, the research arm of Work/Family Directions. That means the average woman manager puts in a total of eighty hours a week between duties at home and on the job, compared with sixty-seven hours for a man. It also means that a man is typically putting in a couple extra hours a week on the job, a powerful reinforcement of traditional roles for men and women. Strategies for getting men to share housework and child care are now regular topics for women's and parenting magazines.

Why, then, is it so hard to arrive at equity on the home front, given the benefits for both men and women? More than anything, the answer seems to lie in a deep-rooted cultural allegiance to old-fashioned gender roles. Although family life is clearly changing, the cultural attachment to the old ways is deeply internalized and hard to shake. 25

When Ellen Galinsky and Dana Friedman, then copresidents of the Families and Work Institute, released their research in mid-1995 showing that married women were now true breadwinners, bringing in half or more of the income in the majority of American families, their research made news for weeks, reaching millions of Americans.

But even before the findings were released, there was one inconsistency in the raw data that intrigued Friedman. While the new numbers left no doubt that women were now true providers, women still insisted that men's careers were more important than women's. Almost two-thirds of the married women polled said their husbands' jobs provided more financial security for their families. "Their opinions just didn't jibe with reality; they didn't reflect what women were bringing into the family," Friedman recalls.

Unfortunately, neither she nor Galinsky had anticipated the response, so they had no way to explain the inconsistency. Still curious, Friedman decided to pursue the issue in small focus groups. What she found was illuminating. "Women are in a sort of collusion with men in making men feel that their work is more important than women's."

Women confided, for example, that they understood the need to "preserve the natural order" between the sexes. "Women told me men would just be too threatened if women said their careers were as important as men's," says Friedman. "They said maybe women devalue what they do to make men feel more important."

This finding comes as no surprise to Janice Steil, professor of psychology at Adelphi University, who has devoted her career to exploring how men and women work out equality in the context of intimate relationships. And increasingly, she has come to see that the psychic reality of men and women, the way they define what it means to be a good husband and father or a good wife and mother, is key in predicting marital happiness. "The more I looked at the research, the more it led me to think about the importance of the way men and women internalize their gender roles," says Steil. Indeed, many social scientists now describe "sex role ideology" as a key factor in predicting how well or how poorly people will fare in modern marriage. Such beliefs are among the most powerful and most deeply held ideas people have, since gender is such an important part of a person's sense of self. And the notion of femaleness, of what it means to be a woman, is very closely bound up with being a mother. "When you listen to the stereotypes of what you say a mother is and what a woman is, they're very, very similar," says psychologist Kay Deaux, who pioneered research on gender stereotypes. Words such as "nurturing," "warm," "sensitive," "caring," for example. And those ideas are so powerful because they are instilled and reinforced from birth. "Gender is something that is part of nearly every interaction we have in life, and the stereotypes are reinforced over and over again." Such ideas can be comforting in that they maintain the status quo. "Part of gender identification has to do with power issues," says Susan Fiske, the social psychologist who took her arguments about stereotypes all the way to the U.S. Supreme Court. Although Fiske has focused primarily on how gender identity plays out in the workplace, her ideas about the interplay of gender and power certainly have relevance for marriage. "People do understand the function that maintaining a certain identity has in maintaining power. It can happen without it being conscious. It's not intentional, but it's comfortable to hold a set of beliefs because it maintains things as they are." . . .

. . . [W]hile women may "collude" in saying that men's jobs are more   30
important in public survey data, economists and other social scientists note a very different phenomenon playing itself out in the privacy of American households. A woman's paycheck does play a very pivotal role in the bargaining that goes on between husbands and wives. Indeed, in the past five

years, a new body of economic research has come to illuminate — and even quantify — the way a woman's paycheck, or lack of one, impacts family life. "Economists used to treat the family as a little factory run by one person," says Joan Lundberg, professor of economics at the University of Washington and a leading expert on the economics of family life. Under that model, economists assumed the "factory" was run by the male breadwinner, and family members simply pooled resources and acted in the common interest of the group. The idea that women stayed home was perceived as a simple choice, for example, based on women's lower earning power outside the home. "But we came to realize [that] that really trivialized the way family life works, especially since couples now have to contemplate the fact that they may be divorced," Lundberg says. "We have had to look at how individuals operate within the family, not just the family as a unit."

Indeed, women's economic stake in marriage is profoundly changed by their relatively new ability to earn a good living — and that changes the terms of marriage. Not only that, but most will have fewer children and live longer, and so work will play a larger role in their lives than it did in previous generations. "No young woman in her right mind today would think she could specialize in the profession of homemaking as women did in previous generations," says Lundberg. "They can't count on that as a reasonable lifetime possibility anymore."

Nor is it one that particularly appeals to most women, even after they have children. "I believe more women are working today not just because they 'have' to, but because they are choosing economic autonomy," says Heidi Hartmann, economist at the Women's Policy Institute in Washington, D.C. "Work does change power within the family. It means that if a woman finds herself in a bad situation, it's easier to get out of it. Basically, I think it's great that women are moving toward economic self-determination. It's empowering for them." . . .

Having that sense of control is certainly one reason why women generally fare better in marriages when they earn a paycheck. But, of course, the formula for women's well-being is not quite so simple as all that. It's not the mere existence of a paycheck that empowers women. Were that the case, Americans would have reached marital bliss by now. "If chores in the home were divided on a *purely* rational basis, husbands and wives who were employed equal numbers of hours would do equal amounts of housework," wrote sociologist Catherine Ross in one of the earliest and most important studies of how couples divvy up the chores.

What she found in 1987, and other researchers have confirmed since then, was that relative earning power is often at the heart of domestic relations. It is the difference between a husband's and wife's income that is often the deciding factor in how a couple divvies up child care and housework. The larger the difference between the two paychecks, the wider the disparity between the spouses. "The more money the wife contributes to the family, the greater leverage in getting her husband to help around the house," wrote Ross. Part of the reason is related to the way that housework and child care are valued in America, of course. Ross noted that "if housework is devalued, unrewarded, onerous and menial, the spouse with more power should be able to delegate it to the other." Which is precisely the conclusion that Steil finds in a review of the literature in the mid-1990s. The economics, combined with the power of gender roles, make for a potent mix in marriage, setting the terms of work and intimacy, of power and dependency, and, most of all, of who owns which work. Once again, it is the association of certain types of work with gender that takes center stage in the relationship. "There is a sense that men shouldn't have to get stuck doing female tasks, that it's somehow denigrating to men, that doing 'women's work' will hurt their self-esteem," she says.

Conversely, some women feel driven to do "women's work" to prove        35
they are "real women," that is, good mothers. That urge can be especially acute when they earn more than their husbands, a situation that obviously upsets the usual assumptions of power between men and women. Their career success calls into question their femininity, their ability to fulfill the traditional expectations of women. One female executive and mother of two children in Fort Worth, Texas, vividly recalls the days not so long ago when she hurried home from her job to cook dinner, supervise her son's piano practice, clean up after the meal, and get him to bed. "I rushed home to make dinner, set the table. Then we'd eat, and I'd drag my son to the piano to practice. We'd spend a half hour at the piano. It was excruciating pain for both my son and me. And I was exhausted by trying to do all this after work," she says. She says she felt compelled to keep this grueling evening schedule to maintain her own esteem. "I had to prove I was a good mother, and cooking dinner every night was part of that."

As she grew more confident in her abilities as a mother, she gave up the routine. "I can't believe I did that to myself," she says, laughing. Now that her children are nine and fourteen, she no longer needs or wants to keep up the grueling schedule. And unlike many women, she can afford to buy her way out of this situation if her husband doesn't pick up the slack. Both are professionals and live a comfortable lifestyle, and these days, she is just as likely to order takeout at a local restaurant or go to a restaurant. They also have a cleaning service to lighten the load of housework. Interestingly, the services she buys to keep her life on track also incorporate assumptions about gender. Both the housework and child care have always been done by women. . . .

. . . [However,] women's growing economic clout can only enlarge the possibilities for men, women, and their children. Freed from the shackles of old gender roles, they can explore their options in life as they see them.

Most notably, there is a new cultural expectation that men will be more involved fathers. "The idea that men will be active participants in raising children is still relatively new. But it's so evident; when you walk around any major city, you see young men carrying their babies and pushing baby carriages," says Lois Hoffman, professor of psychology at the University of Michigan and one of the nation's leading experts on how women's employment affects today's families. "You just wouldn't have seen that even a decade ago." Indeed, psychologist Faye Crosby notes that it's not so long ago that men were derided as "henpecked" when they did household chores. Now, she and others note, the men who are actively involved with their children are "heroes," making a distinct change in the culture. "Of course, we all know that women still do more than men at home," Crosby adds. "But the point is that the public dialogue is changing, and men's resistance to participating at home is less than it once was." . . .

There is also evidence the "new male," the one driven by his own desire to be a deeply involved father, does indeed exist and his ranks are growing. "Men are still as concerned as ever about providing for their families, but they are also concerned about having a close emotional relationship with their kids," Levine from the Fatherhood Project says. "They see the old role of father as provider as just too narrow. They understand that that role meant that women took care of the emotional lives of families. And that's not what they want."

Such a view is not yet sanctioned in the culture, he quickly adds, and what he hears most from men working in corporations is that they need a "safe place" to talk about what it means to be a father today. "Their emotional conflicts are different from women's because they don't feel as comfortable about their conflicts. They don't feel they have permission until they hear another guy talking about it," he says. "And they have a great fear that they're going to be considered uncommitted to the company if they talk about their families and explore how to be an involved father."

When men do break through the constraints of their traditional roles, studies show, they achieve an intimacy with their children—even with tiny babies—that is very similar to what moms describe. In one breakthrough study, Kyle Pruett, a psychiatrist at Yale University, looked at the dynamics in seventeen families in which the fathers were the primary caregivers for their children. The family situations varied widely: Some of the men were unemployed; the incomes of the rest ranged from $7,000 to $125,000. Some were at home full-time for quite an extended period; in other cases, the men returned to work after a paternity leave. Yet despite all these different circumstances, virtually every one of them reported feelings that paralleled those of new moms—including a reluctance to leave their new babies in anyone else's care, even their wives'. In one case, for example, a father called home repeatedly his first day back on the job—just to make sure that his wife knew how to properly care for their infant.

Men's attachment to their children grows from those same rewards that women have always known come from caring for a child. The drudgery of diapers and whining is worth enduring once a close bond is forged with a child. Indeed, Mike Downey sounds very much like the stereotype of a proud

40

mother as he describes his eight-month-old son. "Davis smiles with his whole face and body. His little legs kick. Nothing could be more exciting," he croons. "Right now, he's just this lump of happiness."

Downey, a technical writer at the University of Texas A&M, insists that "nothing is better or more important than being a dad." And he is true to his word. He took a six-week paternity leave after the birth of their first child, Chelsea. He remembers the days after Chelsea was born as the most special. "I had a reclining chair, and I'd sit in it with Chelsea resting on my cheek and both of us sleeping." After Davis was born, he took a three-week paternity leave. If he had his druthers, he'd cut back to part-time work to be with the kids even more. He is not overly romantic. "I don't think I could do this full-time. I think everyone needs a balance." He's had to learn how to deal with temper tantrums and days that just get plain wearing. Still, he insists, "There's no other job like this. The rewards are instant. You always know when you're doing well, and when you're not. It's hard when you're not. But there's this instant gratification when you do it right. There's nothing else like it, having your child in love with you," he says. "It definitely keeps you wanting to come back the next day."

Rebecca Downey delights in her husband's involvement with the kids. "I think he was sorry he couldn't breast-feed Chelsea," she says, laughing. "But he shared everything else. I think he changed more diapers than I did, took her to half the doctor's appointments, and knows everything about the kids that I do." Part of Mike's devotion, she concedes, is that this is his second marriage. "I think he thought a lot about what it takes to make relationships work," she says.

She believes both her children benefit from the two of them sharing the care. "We both feel that it's good for the kids to have two involved parents, instead of only one or one and a half. We want them to grow up to have a good sense of themselves, that both parents care about them." 45

At home, the Downeys also divvy up the household chores. "He does his share of the housekeeping, his share of the laundry, and he cleans up after big meals," says Rebecca, a human resources manager. This is a conscious decision, worked out in advance of having children. "He and I chose to share it all, so I have the luxury of pursuing a career and not neglecting my children. I love going to work and coming home."

There is an important lesson in this for their children, Rebecca adds. These kids are growing up seeing that men and women need not be constrained by their gender. Many women feel especially strongly about the expanded options for their daughters. "Chelsea is bright. I want her to believe she can do anything she wants, whatever she's good at," says Rebecca. "She sees Mike doing the chores and assumes men do that. I want her to have that expectation when she gets married someday."

Thousands of miles away, in Kent, Washington, Barbara Brazil, the assistant to the chief counsel in her local school district, echoes similar hopes for her children. With two boys, however, her hopes are to instill a sense of equity on the domestic front. "In our house, our kids know both of us work. They see Dad do the wash and the cooking. I think that's very important. I want them to see men and women sharing the work and treating each other with respect," she says.

Some research bears out Brazil's belief. Kids raised in dual-earner households do tend to be more flexible about men's and women's roles when they become adults. But there are still few wide-ranging, long-term studies of how children turn out when they grow up in such new-style families. The truth is, of course, that most families are still wrestling with the practical and psychological fallout of the changing terms of marriage, making it hard to gauge just how today's kids will react to their parents as role models. Open conflict over the household chores could, for example, turn a girl off from wanting to fight for equity at home. A cultural pessimism, fanned by the conservative backlash, can undermine young women's confidence that men can and will change. As the article "The Death of Supermom" in the widely circulated Long Island newspaper *Newsday*, for example, quoted [elsewhere], shows, young women may be fearful of pressing for equality. "Young women find that after they get married, they don't want to 'poison' the atmosphere with their husbands by an 'overinsistence on equality,'" according to Teri Apter, a social psychologist.

One can only hope that such pessimism won't be allowed to take root  50
in the hearts and minds of today's children. Equality in both work and home life is clearly a winning proposition for everyone. "Women tell me that their kids are proud of them. They feel that one of the gifts they're giving their children is a new model for a different type of life, one where women can do anything they like," says therapist Lisa Silberstein. For that to happen, Americans need to broaden their idea of possibilities for both men and women.

---

# A World without Fathers

## David Popenoe

The decline of fatherhood is one of the most basic, unexpected, and extraordinary social trends of our time. Its dimensions can be captured in a single statistic: in just three decades, between 1960 and 1990, the percentage of children living apart from their biological fathers more than doubled, from 17 percent to 36 percent. By the turn of the century, nearly 50 percent of American children may be going to sleep each evening without being able to say good night to their dads.

No one predicted this trend, few researchers or government agencies have monitored it, and it is not widely discussed, even today. But the decline of fatherhood is a major force behind many of the most disturbing problems that plague American society: crime and delinquency; premature sexuality and out-of-wedlock births to teenagers; deteriorating educational achievement; depression, substance abuse, and alienation among adolescents; and the growing number of women and children in poverty.

The current generation of children and youth may be the first in our nation's history to be less well off—psychologically, socially, economically, and morally—than their parents were at the same age. The United States, observes Senator Daniel Patrick Moynihan (D.-NY), "may be the first society in history in which children are distinctly worse off than adults."

Even as this calamity unfolds, our cultural view of fatherhood itself is changing. Few people doubt the fundamental importance of mothers. But fathers? More and more, the question of whether fathers are really necessary is being raised. Many would answer no, or maybe not. And to the degree that fathers are still thought necessary, fatherhood is said by many to be merely a social role that others can play: mothers, partners, stepfathers, uncles and aunts, grandparents. Perhaps the script can even be rewritten and the role changed—or dropped.

There was a time in the past when fatherlessness was far more common     5
than it is today, but death was to blame, not divorce, desertion, and out-of-wedlock births. In early-17th-century Virginia, only an estimated 31 percent of white children reached age 18 with both parents still alive. That percentage climbed to 50 percent by the early 18th century, to 72 percent by the turn of the present century, and close to its current level by 1940. Today, well over 90 percent of America's youngsters reach 18 with two living parents. Almost all of today's fatherless children have fathers who are alive, well, and perfectly capable of shouldering the responsibilities of fatherhood. Who would ever have thought that so many men would choose to relinquish them?

Not so long ago, the change in the cause of fatherlessness was dismissed as irrelevant in many quarters, including among social scientists. Children, it was said, are merely losing their parents in a different way than they used to. You don't hear that very much anymore. A surprising finding of recent social science research is that it is decidedly worse for a child to lose a father in the modern, voluntary way than through death. The children of divorced and never-married mothers are less successful in life by almost every measure than the children of widowed mothers. The replacement of death by divorce as the prime cause of fatherlessness, then, is a monumental setback in the history of childhood.

Until the 1960s, the falling death rate and the rising divorce rate neutralized each other. In 1900, the percentage of all American children living in single-parent families was 8.5 percent. By 1960, it had increased to just 9.1 percent. Virtually no one during those years was writing or thinking about family breakdown, disintegration, or decline.

Indeed, what is most significant about the changing family demography of the first six decades of the 20th century is this: because the death rate was dropping faster than the divorce rate was rising, by 1960 more children were living with both of their natural parents than at any other time in world history. The figure was close to 80 percent for the generation born in the late 1940s and early 1950s.

But then the decline in the death rate slowed, and the divorce rate sky-rocketed. "The scale of marital breakdowns in the West since 1960 has no historical precedent that I know of, and seems unique," says Lawrence Stone, the noted Princeton University family historian. "There has been nothing like it for the last 2,000 years, and probably longer."

Consider what has happened to children. Most estimates are that only about 50 percent of the children born during the 1970–84 "baby bust" period will still live with their natural parents by age 17—a staggering drop from nearly 80 percent.                                                              10

One estimate paints the current scene in even starker terms and also points up the enormous difference that exists between whites and blacks. By age 17, white children born between 1950 and 1954 had spent eight percent of their lives with only one parent; black children had spent 22 percent. But among those born in 1980, by one estimate, white children will spend 31 percent of their childhood years with one parent and black children 59 percent.

In theory, divorce need not mean disconnection. In reality, it often does. One large survey in the late 1980s found that about one in five divorced fathers had not seen his children in the past year, and less than half of divorced fathers saw their children more than several times a year. A 1981 survey of adolescents who were living apart from their fathers found that 52 percent had not seen them at all in more than a year; only 16 percent saw their fathers as often as once a week. Moreover, the survey showed fathers' contact with their children dropping off sharply with the passage of time after the marital breakup.

The picture grows worse. Just as divorce has overtaken death as the leading cause of fatherlessness, out-of-wedlock births are expected to surpass divorce later in the 1990s. They accounted for 30 percent of all births by 1991; by the turn of the century they may account for 40 percent of the total (and 80 percent of minority births). And there is substantial evidence that having an unmarried father is even worse for a child than having a divorced father.

Across time and cultures, fathers have always been considered essential—and not just for their sperm. Indeed, until today, no known society ever thought of fathers as potentially unnecessary. Marriage and the nuclear family—mother, father, and children—are the most universal social institutions in existence. In no society has the birth of children out of wedlock been the cultural norm. To the contrary, a concern for the legitimacy of children is nearly universal.

At the same time, being a father is universally problematic for men.      15
While mothers the world over bear and nurture their young with an intrinsic acknowledgment and, most commonly, acceptance of their role, the

process of taking on the role of father is often filled with conflict and doubt. The source of this sex-role difference can be plainly stated. Men are not biologically as attuned to being committed fathers as women are to being committed mothers. The evolutionary logic is clear. Women, who can bear only a limited number of children, have a great incentive to invest their energy in rearing children, while men, who can father many offspring, do not. Left culturally unregulated, men's sexual behavior can be promiscuous, their paternity casual, their commitment to families weak. This is not to say that the role of father is foreign to male nature. Far from it. Evolutionary scientists tell us that the development of the fathering capacity and high paternal investments in offspring—features not common among our primate relatives—have been sources of enormous evolutionary advantage for human beings.

In recognition of the fatherhood problem, human cultures have used sanctions to bind men to their children, and of course the institution of marriage has been culture's chief vehicle. Marriage is society's way of signaling that the community approves and encourages sexual intercourse and the birth of children, and that the long-term relationship of the parents is socially important. Margaret Mead once said, with the fatherhood problem very much in mind, that there is no society in the world where men will stay married for very long unless culturally required to do so. Our experience in late-20th-century America shows how right she was. The results for children have been devastating.

In my many years as a sociologist, I have found few other bodies of evidence that lean so much in one direction as this one: on the whole, two parents—a father and a mother—are better for a child than one parent. There are, to be sure, many factors that complicate this simple proposition. We all know of a two-parent family that is truly dysfunctional—the proverbial family from hell. A child can certainly be raised to a fulfilling adulthood by one loving parent who is wholly devoted to the child's well-being. But such exceptions do not invalidate the rule any more than the fact that some three-pack-a-day smokers live to a ripe old age casts doubt on the dangers of cigarettes.

The collapse of children's well-being in the United States has reached breathtaking proportions. Juvenile violent crime has increased sixfold, from 16,000 arrests in 1960 to 96,000 in 1992, a period in which the total number of young people in the population remained relatively stable. Reports of child neglect and abuse have quintupled since 1976, when data were first collected. Eating disorders and rates of depression have soared among adolescent girls. Teen suicide has tripled. Alcohol and drug abuse among teenagers, although it has leveled off in recent years, continues at a very high rate. Scholastic Aptitude Test scores have declined nearly 80 points, and most of the decline cannot be accounted for by the increased academic diversity of students taking the test. Poverty has shifted from the elderly to the young. Of all the nation's poor today, 38 percent are children.

One can think of many explanations for these unhappy developments: the growth of commercialism and consumerism, the influence of television and the mass media, the decline of religion, the widespread availability of guns and addictive drugs, and the decay of social order and neighborhood relationships. None of these causes should be dismissed. But the evidence is now strong that the absence of fathers from the lives of children is one of the most important causes.

The most tangible and immediate consequence of fatherlessness for children is the loss of economic resources. By the best recent estimates, the income of the household in which a child remains after a divorce instantly declines by about 21 percent per capita on average, while expenses tend to go up. Over time, the economic situation for the child often deteriorates further. The mother usually earns considerably less than the father, and children cannot rely on their fathers to pay much in the way of child support. About half of previously married mothers receive no child support, and for those who do receive it, both the reliability and the amount of the payment drop over time.

20

Child poverty, once endemic in America, reached a historic low point of 14 percent in 1969 and remained relatively stable through the 1970s. Since then, it has been inching back up. Today more than 20 percent of the nation's children (and 25 percent of infants and toddlers) are growing up in poverty.

The loss of fathers' income is the most important cause of this alarming change. By one estimate, 51 percent of the increase in child poverty observed during the 1980s (65 percent for blacks) can be attributed to changes in family structure. Indeed, much of the income differential between whites and blacks today, perhaps as much as two-thirds, can be attributed to the differences in family structure. Not for nothing is it said that marriage is the best antipoverty program of all. . . .

What [else] do fathers do? Much of what they contribute to the growth of their children, of course, is simply the result of being a second adult in the home. Bringing up children is demanding, stressful, and often exhausting. Two adults can not only support and spell each other; they can offset each other's deficiencies and build on each other's strengths.

Beyond being merely a second adult or third party, fathers — men — bring an array of unique and irreplaceable qualities that women do not ordinarily bring. Some of these are familiar, if sometimes overlooked or taken for granted. The father as protector, for example, has by no means outlived his usefulness. His importance as a role model has become a familiar idea. Teenage boys without fathers are notoriously prone to trouble. The pathway to adulthood for daughters is somewhat easier, but they still must learn from their fathers, as they cannot from their mothers, how to relate to men. They learn from their fathers about heterosexual trust, intimacy, and difference. They learn to appreciate their own femininity from the one male who is most special in their lives (assuming that they love and respect their fathers). Most important, through loving and being loved by their fathers, they learn that they are love-worthy.

Recent research has given us much deeper—and more surprising—insights into the father's role in child rearing. It shows that in almost all of their interactions with children, fathers do things a little differently from mothers. What fathers do—their special parenting style—is not only highly complementary to what mothers do but is by all indications important in its own right for optimum child rearing.

For example, an often-overlooked dimension of fathering is play. From their children's birth through adolescence, fathers tend to emphasize play more than caretaking. This may be troubling to egalitarian feminists, and it would indeed be wise for most fathers to spend more time in caretaking. Yet the father's style of play seems to have unusual significance. It is likely to be both physically stimulating and exciting. With older children it involves more physical games and teamwork requiring the competitive testing of physical and mental skills. It frequently resembles an apprenticeship or teaching relationship: come on, let me show you how.

Mothers tend to spend more time playing with their children, but theirs is a different kind of play. Mothers' play tends to take place more at the child's level. Mothers provide the child with the opportunity to direct the play, to be in charge, to proceed at the child's own pace. Kids, at least in the early years, seem to prefer to play with daddy. In one study of $2^1/_2$-year-olds who were given a choice, more than two-thirds chose to play with their father.

The way fathers play has effects on everything from the management of emotions to intelligence and academic achievement. It is particularly important in promoting the essential virtue of self-control. According to one expert, "children who roughhouse with their fathers . . . usually quickly learn that biting, kicking, and other forms of physical violence are not acceptable." They learn when enough is enough and when to "shut it down." . . .

At play and in other realms, fathers tend to stress competition, challenge, initiative, risk taking, and independence. Mothers, as caretakers, stress emotional security and personal safety. On the playground, fathers will try to get the child to swing ever higher, higher than the person on the next swing, while mothers will be cautious, worrying about an accident. It's sometimes said that fathers express more concern for the child's longer-term development, while mothers focus on the child's immediate well-being (which, of course, in its own way has everything to do with a child's long-term well-being). What is clear is that children have dual needs that must be met. Becoming a mature and competent adult involves the integration of two often-contradictory human desires: for communion, or the feeling of being included, connected, and related, and for agency, which entails independence, individuality, and self-fulfillment. One without the other is a denuded and impaired humanity, an incomplete realization of human potential.

For many couples, to be sure, these functions are not rigidly divided       30
along standard female–male lines. There may even be a role reversal in some
cases, with men largely assuming the female style and women the male style.
But these are exceptions that prove the rule. Gender-differentiated parenting is of such importance that in child rearing by homosexual couples, either gay or lesbian, one partner commonly fills the male-instrumental role
while the other fills the female-expressive role. . . .

We know, however, that fathers—and fatherlessness—have surprising
impacts on children. Fathers' involvement seems to be linked to improved
quantitative and verbal skills, improved problem-solving ability, and higher
academic achievement. Several studies have found that the presence of the
father is one of the determinants of girls' proficiency in mathematics. And
one pioneering study found that the amount of time fathers spent reading
was a strong predictor of their daughters' verbal ability.

For sons, who can more directly follow their fathers' example, the results have been even more striking. A number of studies have uncovered a
strong relationship between father involvement and the quantitative and
mathematical abilities of their sons. Other studies have found a relationship between paternal nurturing and boys' verbal intelligence.

How fathers produce these intellectual benefits is not yet clear. No
doubt it is partly a matter of the time and money a man brings to his family. But it is probably also related to the unique mental and behavioral
qualities of men; the male sense of play, reasoning, challenge, and problem
solving, and the traditional male association with achievement and occupational advancement.

Men also have a vital role to play in promoting cooperation and other
"soft" virtues. We don't often think of fathers in connection with the teaching of empathy, but involved fathers, it turns out, may be of special importance for the development of this important character trait, essential to an
ordered society of law-abiding, cooperative, and compassionate adults.
Examining the results of a 26-year longitudinal study, a trio of researchers
reached a "quite astonishing" conclusion: the most important childhood
factor of all in developing empathy is paternal involvement in child care. Fathers who spent time alone with their children more than twice a week, giving meals, baths, and other basic care, reared the most compassionate adults.

Again, it is not yet clear why fathers are so important in instilling this       35
quality. Perhaps merely by being with their children they provide a model
for compassion. Perhaps it has to do with their style of play or mode of reasoning. Perhaps it is somehow related to the fact that fathers typically are
the family's main arbiter with the outside world. Or perhaps it is because
mothers who receive help from their mates have more time and energy to
cultivate the soft virtues. Whatever the reason, it is hard to think of a more
important contribution that fathers can make to their children.

Fatherlessness is directly implicated in many of our most grievous social ills. Of all the negative consequences, juvenile delinquency and violence probably loom largest in the public mind. Reported violent crime has

soared 550 percent since 1960, and juveniles have the fastest-growing crime rate. Arrests of juveniles for murder, for example, rose 128 percent between 1983 and 1992.

Many people intuitively believe that fatherlessness is related to delinquency and violence, and the weight of research evidence supports this belief. Having a father at home is no guarantee that a youngster won't commit a crime, but it appears to be an excellent form of prevention. Sixty percent of America's rapists, 72 percent of its adolescent murderers, and 70 percent of its long-term prison inmates come from fatherless homes. Fathers are important to their sons as role models. They are important for maintaining authority and discipline. And they are important in helping their sons to develop both self-control and feelings of empathy toward others. . . .

Another group that has suffered in the new age of fatherlessness is, perhaps unexpectedly, women. In this new era, Gloria Steinem's oft-quoted quip that a woman without a man is like a fish without a bicycle no longer seems quite so funny. There is no doubt that many women get along very well without men in their lives and that having the wrong men in their lives can be disastrous. But just as it increases assaults on children, fatherlessness appears to generate more violence against women. . . .

[. . . M]arriage appears to be a strong safety factor for women. A satisfactory marriage between sexually faithful partners, especially when they are raising their own biological children, engenders fewer risks for violence than probably any other circumstance in which a woman could find herself. Recent surveys of violent-crime victimization have found that only 12.6 of every 1,000 married women fall victim to violence, compared with 43.9 of every 1,000 never-married women and 66.5 of every 1,000 divorced or separated women.

Men, too, suffer grievously from the growth of fatherlessness. The world over, young and unattached males have always been a cause for social concern. They can be a danger to themselves and to society. Young unattached men tend to be more aggressive, violent, promiscuous, and prone to substance abuse; they are also more likely to die prematurely through disease, accidents, or self-neglect. They make up the majority of deviants, delinquents, criminals, killers, drug users, vice lords, and miscreants of every kind. Senator Moynihan put it succinctly when he warned that a society full of unattached males "asks for and gets chaos."

Family life—marriage and child rearing—is an extremely important civilizing force for men. It encourages them to develop those habits of character, including prudence, cooperativeness, honesty, trust, and self-sacrifice, that can lead to achievement as an economic provider. Marriage also focuses male sexual energy. Having children typically impresses on men the importance of setting a good example. Who hasn't heard at least one man personally testify that he gave up certain deviant or socially irresponsible patterns of life only when he married and had children? . . .

Marriage by itself, even without the presence of children, is also a major civilizing force for men. No other institution save religion (and perhaps the military) places such moral demands on men. To be sure, there is a selection factor in marriage. Those men whom women would care to marry already have some of the civilized virtues. And those men who are morally beyond the pale have difficulty finding mates. Yet epidemiological studies and social surveys have shown that marriage has a civilizing effect independent of the selection factor. Marriage actually promotes health, competence, virtue, and personal well-being. With the continued growth of fatherlessness, we can expect to see a nation of men who are at worst morally out of control and at best unhappy, unhealthy, and unfulfilled.

Just as cultural forms can be discarded, dismantled, and declared obsolete, so can they be reinvented. In order to restore marriage and reinstate fathers in the lives of their children, we are somehow going to have to undo the cultural shift of the last few decades toward radical individualism. We are going to have to re-embrace some cultural propositions or understandings that throughout history have been universally accepted but which today are unpopular, if not rejected outright.

Marriage must be re-established as a strong social institution. The father's role must also be redefined in a way that neglects neither historical models nor the unique attributes of modern societies, the new roles for women, and the special qualities that men bring to child rearing.

Such changes are by no means impossible. Witness the transformations wrought by the civil rights, women's, and environmental movements, and even the campaigns to reduce smoking and drunk driving. What is necessary is for large numbers of adults, and especially our cultural and intellectual leaders, to agree on the importance of change. . . .

. . . Current laws send the message that marriage is not a socially important relationship that involves a legally binding commitment. We should consider a two-tier system of divorce law: marriages without minor children would be relatively easy to dissolve, but marriages with such children would be dissolvable only by mutual agreement or on grounds that clearly involve a wrong by one party against the other, such as desertion or physical abuse. Longer waiting periods for divorcing couples with children might also be called for, combined with some form of mandatory marriage counseling or marital education. . . .

Today in America the social order is fraying badly. We seem, despite notable accomplishments in some areas, to be on a path of decline. The past three decades have seen steeply rising rates of crime, declining political and interpersonal trust, growing personal and corporate greed, deteriorating communities, and increasing confusion over moral issues. For most Americans, life has become more anxious, unsettled, and insecure.

In large part, this represents a failure of social values. People can no longer be counted on to conduct themselves according to the virtues of honesty, self-sacrifice, and personal responsibility. In our ever-growing pursuit of the self—self-expression, self-development, self-actualization, and self-fulfillment—we seem to have slipped off many of our larger social obligations.

At the heart of our discontent lies an erosion of personal relationships. People no longer trust others as they once did; they no longer feel the same sense of commitment and obligation to others. In part, this may be an unavoidable product of the modern condition. But it has gone much deeper than that. Some children across America now go to bed each night worrying about whether their father will be there the next morning. Some wonder whatever happened to their father. And some wonder who he is. What are these children learning at this most basic of all levels about honesty, self-sacrifice, personal responsibility, and trust?

What the decline of fatherhood and marriage in America really means, then, is that slowly, insidiously, and relentlessly our society has been moving in an ominous direction. If we are to make progress toward a more just and humane society, we must reverse the tide that is pulling fathers apart from their families. Nothing is more important for our children or for our future as a nation.   50

---

## The Myth of the "Normal" Family
### Louise B. Silverstein and Carl F. Auerbach

Our Cultural Mythology about parenting is that there is "one right way" to raise children. Most people believe that the best way to raise children is with both a stay-at-home mother (at least while the kids are young) and a breadwinner father in a long-term marriage that lasts "till death do us part." We have been told that any family that is different from this norm short-changes youngsters.

This point of view has become known as the family values perspective. However, the majority of families do not fit this model. Most mothers have to, or want to, be part of the paid workforce; about half of all marriages will end in divorce; and many more people than ever before will choose to have children without getting married.

New scientific information has emerged in the last ten years that contradicts the idea that there is one right way. We now know that children can thrive in many different family forms. The scientific evidence shows conclusively that what is important for them is the quality of the relationships they have with the people who care for them, rather than the number, sex, or marital status of their caregivers.

Nevertheless, perfectly normal families that do not fit into the traditional mold feel abnormal and berate themselves for providing their offspring with an inferior version of family life. For these parents, trying to conform to the Myth of the Normal Family often generates guilt, anxiety, power struggles, and other stress.

The Myth of Father Absence maintains that most social problems—like juvenile violence, crime, and teen pregnancy—are caused by the lack of a   5 father. If every child had a father, these social problems would disappear, argue the advocates of this viewpoint.

Susan and John, a middle-class African-American couple, had two boys aged six and ten when Susan came into therapy asking for help to work out her marital problems. John attended one or two sessions, but then refused to come to therapy. John was a devoted father in terms of spending time with the boys. The marital problems were caused because he was often out of work. He had difficulty getting along with bosses and had recently begun to smoke marijuana.

John was a bright man, but always had difficulty in school. He had graduated from high school with a great deal of tutoring and had gone to junior college briefly. From his description of his struggles in school, he probably had an undiagnosed learning disability. Because these problems had not been understood, John had not gotten the help he needed, and he felt stupid. This sense of inadequacy about his intelligence was probably at the root of his difficulty in getting along with superiors and his retreat into drugs.

Susan, in contrast, had always done well in school. She had become a licensed practical nurse and was going to night school to become a registered nurse. She often worked additional hours on the weekends in a nursing home so that the boys could attend parochial school. She was exhausted from this difficult work schedule and the responsibility for all of the cooking and housework. Her stress was exacerbated by the fact that, in the last year, she was frequently the only breadwinner, as John had been fired from several jobs.

Over the next eight years, John's drug problems became much worse. He began using and selling cocaine. When he was using, he often became physically violent with Susan. Although he continued to share responsibility for child care, John was mostly out of work.

Susan stated that she wanted to leave John, but just could not bring herself to do it. She knew that their fights were frightening to the children and that seeing their father in bad shape was not helpful to them. Still, she could not convince herself to separate from her husband. Despite the fact that she was functioning as both caregiver and breadwinner, she believed that her boys needed their father. She worded that leaving John would mean that she was the stereotypical "black matriarch" who emasculated her man. Most important, she feared that, if John left, the boys would become involved with gangs, drop out of school, and generally get into trouble.

Did it make sense for Susan to stay in a marriage that was not working for her, for John, or for her children? If she did decide to raise the boys on her own, would they really be more likely to get into trouble than if she stayed in a marriage with a husband who was abusing her and cocaine?

The Myth of the Male Role Model is based on the premise that boys have a special need for fathers because only a male role model can teach a boy how to become a man.

Sharon is a physician. She is a very bright, no-nonsense kind of woman who feels more comfortable in the operating room than in a dating situation. She has always liked men and gotten along well with them, but had difficulty establishing and maintaining a romantic relationship. She had one very serious boyfriend in medical school, but they broke up after four years because of his drinking. After that, she had brief affairs with several other doctors throughout internship and residency training, but none of those relationships ever developed. The men she was involved with always ended up marrying nurses or secretaries, never a doctor.

In her late 30s, she began a relationship with an investment banker who recently had been divorced. He was determined never to get married again and certainly never to have children. He and Sharon were very compatible. However, she really wanted children. When she celebrated her 40th birthday, she decided that she would have to contemplate having children without a man or lose the opportunity to have kids altogether. She contacted a sperm bank and became pregnant through artificial insemination. Her boyfriend decided he did not want to remain in the relationship. Sharon had a relatively easy pregnancy and delivery, and with her new baby boy, she embarked on the adventure of single motherhood. Sharon has felt a great deal of anxiety that she will not be able to teach her son how to be a man. Although her son is now four years old and doing fine, she still worries constantly that he may be permanently scarred by not having a father.

Myths about Gay Families. A major component of the myth of the idealized father is that he cannot be gay.                                                            15

Many of the gay fathers in our research study forced themselves to deny the fact that they were gay because they wanted to be fathers. As one of them put it, "Being gay and being a father seemed mutually exclusive." These men desperately wanted to be "normal," which was defined as being married and having children. They tried to fit themselves into the mold of a married man, hoping against hope that getting married would save them from being gay.

Tom is one of these men. He met Sheri, his wife, in college, and she became a good friend. He admired her and liked her a lot. Tom is very religious, so he prayed that marriage would turn friendship into love. "If Christ could raise the dead, I thought that he could surely cure a homosexual," he reasoned.

Although he and Sheri developed a relationship of mutual respect, they were not in love. Yet, when they had children, they were both so pleased with becoming parents that the kids provided a sort of glue that kept the marriage together. Tom recalled that he felt so happy bonding with his offspring that he was able to avoid the loneliness he felt in his relationship with Sheri.

However, when their second child was six years old, the pleasure of being a father was no longer enough to compensate for an empty marriage. Tom remembered "the moment my life fell apart" — the day he no longer could deny his homosexuality to himself. He then spent several years in torment, feeling torn between his desire to live with his children and his desire to be true to himself. When he finally got enough courage to leave his marriage, he still did not feel brave enough to admit his homosexuality to his wife or his children. He was terrified that he would lose visitation rights with his kids if the court discovered that he was gay.

To his surprise and sorrow, many of his gay friends were not a source      20
of support on this issue. They were interested in living a single gay lifestyle that did not include children. Thus, he could not admit his identity as a gay man to his family, and his gay friends did not support his identity as a father. He expressed his isolation by saying, "I felt I was the only man on the planet who was a father and was gay."

Did Tom have to feel tortured about being a gay father? Can only straight men be good fathers?

In reviewing the scientific research, we found that there is not a single study showing that a male role model is necessary for boys to become well-adjusted men. We now know that both boys and girls use same-sex and opposite-sex role models: parents, grandparents, and other extended family members; teachers; and cultural heroes. In our own research, many of our subjects stated, "My mother taught me how to be a good father."

In terms of "fatherless" families, it is important to point out that the research has been done primarily with poor, ethnic minority families. Because more single-mother families are poor, it is difficult to differentiate the effects of father absence from the effects of poverty. When we look at the research on middle-class lesbian-mother families, we find that the children being raised in these fatherless families are doing just fine. These youngsters score within the normal range on measures of intelligence, social behavior, and emotional well-being. This finding suggests that the studies focusing on poor, mother-headed families are actually studying the effect of poverty, rather than the absence of a father.

Studies on children being raised by gay fathers have also shown that children raised in these families are growing up healthy. They do not become gay any more frequently than children raised by heterosexual parents.

The people cited above were able to establish a sense of psychological      25
security only after they stopped trying to live up to a family values ideal that simply did not fit their realities. Susan's story is a dramatic example of trying to live up to the cultural mythology about fathers and families, even when it flies in the face of one's better judgment. Susan's decision to stay with John was not helpful to herself, her sons, or John. When she left him, he finally sought help for his drug addiction. He ultimately got and kept a good job, remarried, and became a financially responsible father to his sons and stepdaughter.

Sharon's story is another example of how the family values point of view generates unnecessary stress. Although Sharon worries about raising her son without a father, she is not raising him without a man. In fact, he has close relationships with several men.

Her first cousin is his godfather and spends every Sunday with him. One of his usual babysitters is another cousin of hers, a male student who loves kids and needs spending money. Moreover, Sharon's father comes to stay with her for several weeks three times a year. The presence of men in the life of a single mother is not unusual. Most women have men in their lives.

Finally, Tom is the same father as an openly gay male that he was as a married man. His relationship with his teenage children did not deteriorate when he told them he was gay; rather, their relationship deepened. The kids' immediate reaction was, "Oh, Dad, we've known that for a long time! Tell us something we don't know." Tom reported that he felt so reassured by their acceptance of him that he has since been able to establish a much deeper sense of closeness with them. We are not saying that everything will be easy or will work out fine if only people give up the family values perspective. Instead, we are suggesting that there is no general solution to the complex challenges of family life. Trying to conform to a single version of family life is not just doomed to failure, but unnecessary. Intimate relationships and good-enough parenting are always difficult to achieve. However, if people attempt to conform to idealized myths, they are making the difficult challenge of raising healthy children even more difficult. Rather than trying to find the "one right way," parents need to be flexible and creative in seeking strategies that work for their particular family.

## American Families Are Drifting Apart
### Barbara Lebey

A variety of reasons—from petty grievances to deep-seated prejudices, misunderstandings to all-out conflicts, jealousies, sibling rivalry, inheritance feuds, family business disputes, and homosexual outings—are cause for families to grow apart. Family estrangements are becoming more numerous, more intense, and more hurtful. When I speak to groups on the subject, I always ask: Who has or had an estrangement or knows someone who does? Almost every hand in the room goes up. Sisters aren't speaking to each other since one of them took the silver when Mom died. Two brothers rarely visit because their wives don't like each other.

A son alienates himself from his family when he marries a woman who wants to believe that he sprang from the earth. Because Mom is the travel agent for guilt trips, her daughter avoids contact with her. A family banishes a daughter for marrying outside her race or religion. A son eradicates a divorced father when he reveals his homosexuality. And so it goes.

The nation is facing a rapidly changing family relationship landscape. Every assumption made about the family structure has been challenged, from the outer boundaries of single mothers raising out-of-wedlock children to gay couples having or adopting children to grandparents raising their grandchildren. If the so-called traditional family is having trouble maintaining harmony, imagine what problems can and do arise in less conventional situations. Fault lines in Americans' family structure were widening throughout the last 40 years of the 20th century. The cracks became evident in the mid 1970s when the divorce rate doubled. According to a 1999 Rutgers University study, divorce has risen 30% since 1970; the marriage rate has fallen faster; and just 38% of Americans consider themselves happy in their married state, a drop from 53% 25 years ago. Today, 51% of all marriages end in divorce.

How Americans managed to alter their concept of marriage and family so profoundly during those four decades is the subject of much scholarly investigation and academic debate. In a May 2000 *New York Times Magazine* article titled "The Pursuit of Autonomy" the writer maintains that "the family is no longer a haven; all too often a center of dysfunction, it has become one with the heartless world that surrounds it." Unlike the past, the job that fits you in your 20s is not the job or career you'll likely have in your 40s. This is now true of marriage as well—the spouse you had in your 20s may not be the one you will have after you've gone through your midlife crisis.

In the 1960s, four main societal changes occurred that have had an enormous impact on the traditional family structure. The sexual revolution, women's liberation movement, states' relaxation of divorce laws, and mobility of American families have converged to foster family alienation, exacerbate old family rifts, and create new ones. It must be emphasized, however, that many of these changes had positive outcomes. The nation experienced a strengthened social conscience, women's rights, constraints on going to war, and a growing tolerance for diversity, but society also paid a price.

The 1960s perpetuated the notion that we are first and foremost entitled to happiness and fulfillment. It's positively un-American not to seek it! This idea goes back to that early period of our history when Thomas Jefferson dropped the final term from British philosopher John Locke's definition of human rights—"life, liberty, and . . . property"—and replaced it with what would become the slogan of our new nation: "the pursuit of happiness." In the words of author Gail Sheehy, the 1960s generation "expressed their collective personality as idealistic, narcissistic, anti-establishment, hairy, horny and preferably high."

Any relationship that was failing to deliver happiness was being tossed out like an empty beer can, including spousal ones. For at least 20 years, the pharmaceutical industry has learned how to cash in on the American obsession with feeling good by hyping mood drugs to rewire the brain circuitry for happiness through the elimination of sadness and depression.

Young people fled from the confines of family, whose members were frantic, worrying about exactly where their adult children were and what they were doing. There were probably more estrangements between parents and adult children during the 1960s and early 1970s than ever before.

In the wake of the civil rights movement and Pres. Lyndon Johnson's Great Society came the women's liberation movement, and what a flashy role it played in changing perceptions about the family structure. Women who graduated from college in the late 1960s and early 1970s were living in a time when they could establish and assert their independent identities. In Atlanta, Emory Law School's 1968 graduating class had six women in it, the largest number ever to that point, and all six were in the top 10%, including the number-one graduate. In that same period, many all-male colleges opened their doors to women for the first time. No one could doubt the message singer Helen Reddy proclaimed: "I am woman, hear me roar." For all the self-indulgence of the "hippie" generation, there was an intense awakening in young people of a recognition that civil rights must mean equal rights for everyone in our society, and that has to include women.

Full equality was the battle cry of every minority, a status that women claimed despite their majority position. As they had once marched for the right to vote, women began marching for sexual equality and the same broad range of career and job opportunities that were always available to men. Financial independence gave women the freedom to walk away from unhappy marriages. This was a dramatic departure from the puritanical sense of duty that had been woven into the American fabric since the birth of this nation.

For all the good that came out of this movement, though, it also changed forever traditional notions of marriage, motherhood, and family unity, as well as that overwhelming sense of children first. Even in the most-conservative young families, wives were letting their husbands know that they were going back to work or back to school. Many women had to return to work either because there was a need for two incomes to maintain a moderate standard of living or because they were divorced and forced to support their offspring on their own. "Don't ask, don't tell" day-care centers proliferated where overworked, undertrained staff, and two-income yuppie parents, ignored the children's emotional needs—all in the name of equality and to enable women to reclaim their identifies. Some might say these were the parents who ran away from home.

Many states began to approve legislation that allowed no-fault divorce, eliminating the need to lay blame on spouses or stage adulterous scenes in sleazy motels to provide evidence for states that demanded such evidence for divorces. The legal system established procedures for easily dissolving marriages, dividing property, and sharing responsibility for the children. There were even do-it-yourself divorce manuals on bookstore shelves. Marriage had become a choice rather than a necessity, a one-dimensional status sustained almost exclusively by emotional satisfaction and not worth maintaining in its absence. Attitudes about divorce were becoming more lenient, so much so that the nation finally elected its first divorced president in 1980—Ronald Reagan.

With divorced fathers always running the risk of estrangement from their children, this growing divorce statistic has had the predictable impact of increasing the number of those estrangements. Grandparents also experienced undeserved fallout from divorce, since, almost invariably, they are alienated from their grandchildren.

The fourth change, and certainly one of the most pivotal, was the increased mobility of families that occurred during those four decades. Family members were no longer living in close proximity to one another. The organization man moved to wherever he could advance more quickly up the corporate ladder. College graduates took the best job offer, even if it was 3,000 miles away from where they grew up and where their family still lived.

Some were getting out of small towns for new vistas, new adventures, and new job opportunities. Others were fleeing the overcrowded dirty cities in search of cleaner air, a more reasonable cost of living, and retirement communities in snow-free, warmer, more-scenic locations. Moving from company to company had begun, reaching what is now a crescendo of job-hopping. Many young people chose to marry someone who lived in a different location, so family ties were geographically severed for indeterminate periods of time, sometimes forever.

According to Lynn H. Dennis' "Corporate Relocation Takes Its Toll on Society," during the 10 years from 1989 to 1999, more than 5,000,000 families were relocated one or more times by their employers. In addition to employer-directed moves, one out of five Americans relocated at least once, not for exciting adventure, but for economic advancement and/or a safer place to raise children. From March 1996 to March 1997, 42,000,000 Americans, or 16% of the population, packed up and moved from where they were living to another location. That is a striking statistic. Six million of these people moved from one region of the country to another, and young adults aged 20 to 29 were the most mobile, making up 32% of the moves during that year. This disbursement of nuclear families throughout the country disconnected them from parents, brothers, sisters, grandparents, aunts, uncles, and cousins—the extended family and all its adhesive qualities.

Today, with cell phones, computers, faxes, and the Internet, the office can be anywhere, including in the home. Therefore, we can live anywhere we want to. If that is the case, why aren't more people choosing to live in the cities or towns where they grew up? There's no definitive answer. Except for the praise heaped on "family values," staying close to family no longer plays a meaningful role in choosing where we reside.

These relocations require individuals to invest an enormous amount of time to reestablish their lives without help from family or old friends. Although nothing can compare to the experience of immigrants who left their countries knowing they probably would never see their families again, the phenomenon of Americans continually relocating makes family relationships difficult to sustain.

Our culture tends to focus on the individual, or, at most, on the nuclear family, downplaying the benefits of extended families, though their role is vital in shaping our lives. The notion of "moving on" whenever problems arise has been a time-honored American concept. Too many people would rather cast aside some family member than iron out the situation and keep the relationship alive. If we don't get along with our father or if our mother doesn't like our choice of mate or our way of life, we just move away and see the family once or twice a year. After we're married, with children in school, and with both parents working, visits become even more difficult. If the family visits are that infrequent, why bother at all? Some children grow up barely knowing any of their relatives. Contact ceases; rifts don't resolve; and divisiveness often germinates into a full-blown estrangement.

In an odd sort of way, the more financially independent people become, the more families scatter and grow apart. It's not a cause, but it is a facilitator. Tolerance levels decrease as financial means increase. Just think how much more we tolerate from our families when they are providing financial support. Look at the divorced wife who depends on her family for money to supplement alimony and child support, the student whose parents are paying all college expenses, or the brother who borrows family money to save his business.

Recently, a well-known actress being interviewed in a popular magazine was asked, if there was one thing she could change in her family, what would it be? Her answer was simple: "That we could all live in the same city." She understood the importance of being near loved ones and how, even in a harmonious family, geographical distance often leads to emotional disconnectedness. When relatives are regularly in each other's company, they will usually make a greater effort to get along. Even when there is dissension among family members, they are more likely to work it out, either on their own or because another relative has intervened to calm the troubled waters. When rifts occur, relatives often need a real jolt to perform an act of forgiveness. Forgiving a family member can be the hardest thing to do, probably because the emotional bonds are so much deeper and usually go all the way back to childhood. Could it be that blood is a thicker medium in which to hold a grudge?

With today's families scattered all over the country, the matriarch or patriarch of the extended family is far less able to keep his or her kin united, caring, and supportive of one another. In these disconnected nuclear families, certain trends—workaholism, alcoholism, depression, severe stress, isolation, escapism, and a push toward continuous supervised activity for children—are routinely observed. What happened to that family day of rest and togetherness? We should mourn its absence.

For the widely dispersed baby boomers with more financial means than any prior generation, commitment, intimacy, and family togetherness have never been high on their list of priorities. How many times have you heard of family members trying to maintain a relationship with a relative

20

via e-mail and answering machines? One young man now sends his Mother's Day greeting by leaving a message for his mom on his answering machine. When she calls to scold him for forgetting to call her, she'll get a few sweet words wishing her a happy Mother's Day and his apology for being too busy to call or send a card! His sister can expect the same kind of greeting for her birthday, but only if she bothers to call to find out why her brother hadn't contacted her.

Right now, and probably for the foreseeable future, we will be searching for answers to the burgeoning problems we unwittingly created by these societal changes, but don't be unduly pessimistic. Those who have studied and understood the American psyche are far more optimistic. The 19th-century French historian and philosopher Alexis de Tocqueville once said of Americans, "No natural boundary seems to be set to the effort of Americans, and in their eyes what is not yet done, is only what they have not yet attempted to do." Some day, I hope this mindset will apply not to political rhetoric on family values, but to bringing families back together again.

---

## Creating Your Own
### Pam Houston

When I was 14 years old, I spent a year in Wales as an exchange student. I stayed with a family called the Couches, one of the wealthiest families in the tiny village of Pontnewynydd. Ron and Ceinwen were my host parents; they owned a lovely stone house with a half-acre garden and they had two sons, Gary, 21, and Paul, 19. Gary lived with his wife in a cottage in one corner of his parents' garden. Paul would be married the next summer and would live with his wife in the cottage in the opposite corner. The seven of us sat down to dinner every night as a family, sometimes for breakfast and lunch, too. We all went on weekend outings—to visit a castle or to see a play at Stratford-upon-Avon or to compete in a kind of road rally/treasure hunt that was particularly exciting given the narrow country lanes. In the summertime we went together to their cottage in Tenby on the coast, and the rest of the year both boys worked for their father in the tiling business that his father had started. They all seemed to love one another very much, including the current and future daughters-in-law.

Stepping from my family into this one felt not so much like crossing from North America to Great Britain as it did from, say, Earth to Alpha Centauri. My year there was by far the happiest of my childhood, though even at the time an aura of, if not impossibility, at least fantasy surrounded it. Now as I write this, I keep double-checking my memory to make sure I'm not making up that family, that year, and the entire Rotary Club exchange program that made it possible. I cried all the way back across the Atlantic.

Short of being raised in a 19th-century orphanage or by a nomadic pack of wolves, I can't imagine a less family-focused lineage than my own. My father was an only child; his mother died more than 30 years before I was born, his father, more than 40. My mother's mother died in childbirth with my mother, and my mother's father abandoned my newborn mother and her 1½-year-old sister the very next day. My mother and her sister, Jean, were raised by their aunt and uncle, but they ran away to Broadway (with a little encouragement from starstruck Aunt Ermie) when they were 12 and 14. My mother adored New York, beginning her career as a singing/dancing comedian and not missing her Spiceland, Indiana, junior high school one bit. But Jean found New York corrupt and distasteful, eventually returning to Indiana and blaming the aging aunt for sullying her reputation and ruining their lives. Jean's ingratitude toward Ermie infuriated my mother so much it caused a rift between the sisters. Or at least this is the side of the story I heard—my mother's side; the silence between the sisters was so deep and long-lasting, I never met my aunt Jean.

My mother's father called her for the first time ever from his deathbed and asked if she would come shake his hand. I was in my early twenties, she in her early sixties, though it was such a nonevent in our household I can't remember the exact year. The day after he called, she flew to Florida, and when she returned and I asked her what happened, she said, "I walked in the room, shook his hand, and walked back out again. That's what he asked for, so that's what I did."

It probably goes without saying that since neither of my parents had much     5
in the way of family, they weren't that great at making one of their own. As a childless only child, I am apparently not so hot at it either.

In a recent visit to my father, I smiled to hear him explain to my new husband, Martin, "Pam had a lot of personal freedom as a child," which may be one of the great understatements of the century. My parents lived in pursuit of a relatively few pleasures: sun, sand, alcohol, European cities, and great Italian food. Because of one or another of these pursuits, I was often left to "babysit myself" for days at a time. Today I suppose they would have been put in jail, though I was such a pinnacle of responsibility that it's very likely they would never have been found out.

I suppose it was all that "personal freedom" that has led me to spend a good part of my life searching for substitutes, a family, as my friend Karla would say, of re-creation versus procreation.

My ranch high in the Colorado mountains—which everyone tells me (some of them pointedly) would be so perfect for kids—has become my substitute family headquarters, especially in summer. My house has only two bedrooms, but I have a couple of old cabins down by the river and 120 acres for tents. It's rare that on a given summer night I'm cooking dinner for fewer than six people, and if I made a list of all my favorite things on earth, cooking for a kitchen full of friends would definitely make the top ten.

In the fall I invite 12 writing students here for two weeks of intensive work. The students sleep in town, but I cook all their meals and we eat together at my big kitchen table. There is always somebody living here besides me and, now, Martin: a student, a dog sitter, a friend who's in the middle of a divorce or a job change or a nervous breakdown. This land I live on is healing land—even the biggest skeptic can't deny it—and no one who comes for even a few days leaves unchanged. I do a lot of talking about my responsibility to share this ground with others, but I am well aware that the revolving-door policy at this place gives me what I need: a fairly stable, if constantly rotating, family.

In the beginning it was always parents I was looking for. Father figures 10 above all, since my father was even less parental than my mother, and then mother figures after her death in 1992. What I wished for most when I was a little girl was a big brother, though lately I find myself in a big-sister role with at least one male friend. I also seem to be sliding gradually from the role of child with my much older friends to the role of parent with my much younger friends. I find myself writing $100 checks and slipping them into letters to my young friend Jo, who's in massage school in Salt Lake City. I have been able to help three young men I met in Bolivia, Laos, and Tibet pay for college. I hear questions coming out of my mouth as my younger friends are about to pull out of my driveway, "Do you have enough gas money?" "Are you eating any vegetables at all these days?"

I was the only keeper of the rituals in my family of origin. I was the one who put the photos into albums, starting at the age of 5. I was the one who put my foot down about turkey dinner for Thanksgiving, cooking it myself as soon as I was tall enough to stand over the stove. I was the one who insisted on buying a tree even though I knew that come Christmas Eve we'd be hurtling down I-95 from Bethlehem, Pennsylvania, to Boca Raton without a hotel reservation, listening to Casey Kasem's Christmas dedications— *Silver Bells* going out from Mary Lou in Toledo to Jerry in Duluth—my parents focused, almost rabidly, on a couple of days in the sun.

These days for Thanksgiving I normally round up all the full-grown (though not necessarily grown-up) orphans I can find in my mountain town—a place where full-grown orphans tend to congregate—and we drive to the desert of southern Utah in a car full of turkey and stuffing, camping gear and Coleman stoves. We go to a beautiful spot called Fisher Towers, claim one of the three campsites, dig a big hole in the ground, fill it with charcoal, and spend every bit of daylight cooking our turkey in the hole, our mashed potatoes, green beans, and pearl onions on the white gas Coleman stoves, and our pumpkin and pecan pies in cast-iron Dutch ovens. Instead of watching the Lions play the Bears after dinner, we watch Orion and the Pleiades on the rise and take turns saying out loud what we are thankful for.

Christmas as a grown-up has always been a little trickier for me. I either spend hundreds of dollars on handmade ornaments and stockings for all my horses, cats, and dogs, which makes me feel pathetic and desperate, or I plan to be somewhere like Laos or Tibet where I'm surrounded by non-Christian strangers, which makes me feel lonely and sad.

It has not escaped me that another person with my history would likely have gotten married at 16 and had a gaggle of children by 21. It has also not escaped me that something in me seems to prefer these "not quite real families" to an actual one. A simple failure of courage maybe, but perhaps it's only in the natural scheme of things for me to live out my parents' legacy of independence. My substitute families allow me to experience some of the best parts of familial intimacy without the immense responsibility of actual parenthood or the intricate web of expectation and demand that siblings and parents seem to put on one another. I love the freedom my life gives me to write books and see the world. At the same time I don't doubt that by having no real family to speak of, I am missing out on one of the richest patterns in the tapestry of life. My parents never let the fact that they had a child keep them from any of their professional or recreational pursuits. It is with bemusement (rather than disappointment or joy) that I realize I am living much as they did.

I got a call a few years ago from my only living relative besides my father: my cousin Jeff, Jean's son, who lives near Anchorage with his wife. The call woke me up, literally, and in my groggy confusion I tried to pretend I knew who he was, pretend this was just a normal, pleasant call between family members.

"Pam," he said, "I know how screwed up our family is. Why do you think I live in Alaska? I'd probably live in Siberia if they had better food."

A voice out of the wilderness. Was it possible that another renegade from my lonely clan existed? Jeff and I have exchanged Christmas cards every year since that call. One of these days, I always write, I'll make it up to Alaska, and he sometimes threatens to come to Colorado. But we are our mothers' children after all, and neither of us so far has done any rushing to the ticket counter, proving we have more confidence in our families of re-creation than the blood that runs in our veins.

Tonight my friends Leo and Tim from New York are coming to dinner. Tim is a playwright and Leo is just finishing NYU film school. They'll likely bring Bill, an acting teacher from L.A., and his friend Wendy. I'll be making grouper with a lime-and-chili sauce, and my signature garlic mashed potatoes, which Bill says are the best in the world. Tomorrow my friend Amanda is flying in from Seattle, Gail is driving up from Denver, and Doug is driving down from Steamboat Springs. I'll make organic prime rib, steamed turnips, spinach salad. After dinner we'll be doing the last of our packing for the Grand Canyon, where the five of us will join six other people we don't know as well, and the 11 of us will spend nearly three weeks on four rubber rafts riding the rapids of the Colorado. I'm in charge of rowing one of the boats and of the first six dinners. After 18 days of risking our lives together, of absorbing the mind-bending colors and shapes and shadows in the canyon, of making temporary homes along the riverbank, of eating and laughing and singing and most likely yelling and crying together, we will have become maybe not quite the Welsh Couches, but something it will be impossible not to call a family. As far as I can figure, that's the very best reason to go.

---

## For Discussion

1. Decter, in paragraphs 22–27, argues that the blurring of gender roles in the family is unnatural and even "nutty." What are some of the problems she sees as a result of this loss of distinct responsibilities for each sex? How does Holcomb's essay contrast with Decter's speech? How does Holcomb attempt to persuade her readers that there is a "natural order" between the sexes? In evaluating these two readings, which stands up to the tests of inquiry? Explain, using the "Questions for Inquiry" on pages 177–178 of this text. You might want also to consult paragraphs 73–83 of Bianchi and Casper's article and Box 2 of the same article to see what the latest surveys show about how the sexes are handling the duties of child raising and housework.

2. Popenoe argues that fathers have a distinct and necessary role in the raising of children. What is it that he claims they can do that mothers cannot do? What evidence does he offer? Do you find his argument convincing? Why or why not? Compare his argument with the argument in the essay by Silverstein and Auerbach. Are these essays addressing the same issue? What are the myths Silverstein and Auerbach seek to overturn? How effective is their evidence in making this case?

3. Lebey claims in paragraph 3 that only 38 percent of Americans are happy in their marriages. However, in our excerpt from *The Case for Marriage*, Waite and Gallagher report a much higher percentage of marital happiness, 66 percent for husbands and 62 percent for wives (paragraph 46). How would you evaluate these conflicting sources to determine which is more likely to be accurate?

4. Both Lebey and Decter discuss the impact on the family of the social changes that took place during the 1960s. What do they agree upon? How do their analyses of this decade's influence differ?

5. One factor Lebey discusses as impacting the family, not mentioned by the other writers, is the rising mobility of the American population. Americans have always believed in setting out to make a life of one's own, whether for individual expression or to improve material well-being. Even grandparents seem to prefer their freedom over family closeness, as evidenced by the popularity of retirement

communities far from children and grandchildren. Is it fair to say that as Americans increase their ability to choose, they will opt for greater freedom rather than accept limits and make sacrifices?

6. Houston says her created family allows her to "experience some of the best parts of familial intimacy without the immense responsibility of actual parenthood or the intricate web of expectation and demand that siblings and parents seem to put on one another" (paragraph 14). Compare Houston's life with what Decter has to say about "the land of limitless freedom" (paragraph 45). Is Houston escaping the "swamp of self" or wallowing in it, in your estimate? Does her "rotating" family allow her to engage herself in other people's lives? What would be Decter's opinion of Houston's "family"?

7. Decter seems to define parenting in terms of birth parents. What would she say about couples who choose to adopt rather than to give birth to a child of their own, assuming that they can? What do you think about the motivations for adopting a child and the responsibilities of adoptive parents as opposed to birth parents?

## For Convincing

Decter sees an important difference between accepting parental obligations on the one hand and doing charity work or community service on the other. Explain what that difference is, in terms of self-sacrifice, and use evidence of your own, from your experiences and observations and from library research, to support or refute her position.

## For Research and Convincing

Decter argues that life has meaning only when one becomes part of "the unrushing tide of generations," in other words, by having children. Yet many women, and men, choose to remain childless. For couples, and especially for women, voluntary childlessness is often stigmatized as selfish. Look into studies of the reasons people choose to remain childless. Is it a refusal to accept limits and make sacrifices? Support or refute Decter's charge that choosing not to be a parent is a way of ducking responsibility. Or support or refute Decter's claim that parenting is an escape from "the swamp of self." Are there selfish reasons for choosing to have a baby?

## FOR FURTHER READING AND RESEARCH

Carter, Elizabeth A. *The Expanded Family Life Cycle: Individual, Family, and Social Perspectives.* 3d ed. Boston: Allyn & Bacon, 1998.

Coontz, Stephanie. *The Way We Never Were: American Families and the Nostalgia Trap.* New York: Basic Books, 2000.

Coontz, Stephanie. *The Way We Really Are: Coming to Terms with America's Changing Families.* Reprint ed. New York: Basic Books, 1998.

Hetherington, E. Mavis, and John Kelly. *For Better or for Worse: Divorce Reconsidered.* New York: W. W. Norton & Company, 2002.

Paul, Pamela. *The Starter Marriage and the Future of Matrimony.* New York: Villard Books, 2002.

Stacey, Judith. *Brave New Families: Stories of Domestic Upheaval in Late-Twentieth-Century America.* Berkeley: University of California Press, 1998.

Willson, James Q. *The Marriage Problem: How Our Culture Has Weakened Families.* New York: HarperCollins, 2002.

# Part 4 Readings: Issues and Arguments

# Chapter 12

# Feminism: Evaluating the Effects of Gender Roles

I n the United States, the women's rights movement dates back to the nineteenth century, when the main issues were full rights of citizenship and access to higher education. The women's movement was highly visible during the early part of the twentieth century, leading up to the achievement of voting rights in 1920. By that time, some women and men had realized that the fight for particular rights must be part of a larger revolution in society's attitudes toward the relationship between the sexes. Those who wanted to eliminate the long-standing, oppressive, and patriarchal attitudes that held women subordinate to men became known as feminists. The classic definition of feminism is simply the doctrine that women should enjoy all the rights—political, social, and economic—that men enjoy.

What became known as the "second wave" of feminism began in the 1960s and received its greatest impetus from the success of Betty Friedan's 1963 book *The Feminine Mystique*. Friedan argued that a myth prevailed in American society that told women they could be happy and fulfilled only by accepting their "feminine" role as sexually passive, nurturing homemakers, content to live under male protection and domination. Second-wave feminism therefore advocated independence from men, liberation from the sexual double standard, and achievement in the world outside the home.

As the twentieth century moved to a close and the twenty-first century opened, debate increased about the nature of feminism. Some argue that feminism is dead, that it is no longer needed, that we have entered the "postfeminist" era and the battles are over. In a 2001 study of young women ages thirteen through twenty, only 34 percent said they would call themselves feminists. Yet 97 percent said women should receive the same pay as men for the same work, and 92 percent agreed that "a woman's lifestyle choices should not be limited by her gender." In this same study, only 25 percent of these young women believe "there are still many inequalities between the sexes, and women need to continue to fight for their rights." However, in the year 2000, women made up only 13 percent of the U.S. Congress and 10 percent of the Senate, and a study by the AFL-CIO in 2001 found women still earn, on average, 79 cents to every dollar earned by men (Infante). Because of statistics like these, Gloria Steinem, Betty Friedan, and other second-wave feminists say that women need to keep fighting for policies and projects that will give them greater equality in the twenty-first century: restructuring the workplace with child care, parental leaves, and flexible hours so that work and parenting are possible for both men and women; instituting a national program of child care as most other industrialized nations have; passing legislation to ensure shelter, adequate nutrition, and health care for children; and changing stereotypical gender roles to make men and women more equal inside the home.

We begin with an overview of the history of the American feminist movement and then turn to a series of arguments about equality and gender roles. We present a chapter from Friedan's landmark book on women's frustration in the 1950s with confinement to the "feminine" roles of homemaker and mother. Suzanne Fields's essay is a direct response to Friedan's description of the "problem that has no name"—the *ennui* and depression of women whose ambitions were confined to the home. Fields describes women who have gone into the workforce and found that it did not offer them the fulfillment they expected. Similarly, Katie Roiphe argues that many "liberated" young women of her generation nevertheless have the deeply held fantasy of finding a man with good prospects to take care of them. This "dark truth" is part of "girl culture" that keeps the traditional gender roles alive. Motherhood is the gender role most problematic for women who aspire to greatness in their careers. As a writer, Anne Roiphe, mother of Katie, wonders how much more successful she would have been had she not had children.

All these arguments address the problems of how women can have what they want from both gender roles: the same political power and professional opportunities that men have and the deeply satisfying role that traditionally belonged to a woman—caring for children and keeping a home. But in a recent book, *Unbending Gender*, Joan Williams suggests that this dilemma may result from the wrong assumptions about the goals of feminism. In a chapter from this book, she argues for a "reconstructive" feminism that would change not just women's roles but men's as well in both the home and the workplace.

We also include a classic argument about cultural impairment of opportunity for women in Western culture. Naomi Wolfe's introduction to her 1991 book *The Beauty Myth: How Images of Beauty Are Used against Women* argues that despite gains in equality, women continue to be oppressed by traditional images of feminine beauty that undermine their mental and physical health. But such Western concerns need to find their place in a larger context. In recent years, violations of human rights and women's rights in particular have been noted around the globe. In countries affected by war and economic collapse, millions of women and girls have been forced into prostitution, sex slavery, and domestic servitude in foreign lands. In the concluding essay, Katha Pollitt cites these and other abuses such as genital mutilation, forced marriage, AIDS, denial of education, and legalized wife murder as evidence of the need for an international feminist movement. In light of the abuses Pollitt discusses, it is difficult to say that we live in a "postfeminist" world.

# What Is Feminism?

### Cassandra L. Langer

*This selection comes from the first chapter of Cassandra Langer's* A Feminist Critique: How Feminism Has Changed American Society, Culture and How We Live *from the 1940s to the Present. Here, Langer attempts to define feminism by showing how events since colonial times have influenced the evolution of the concept. Her purpose, however, is not merely to present a historical narrative from a feminist perspective. She believes that reminders of the movement's historical accomplishments will help modern feminists get beyond the current polarizations that are weakening the movement.*

Today we are still grappling with Sigmund Freud's question, "What do women want?" This is a fascinating, poorly understood, time-consuming, and often disheartening topic to explore.[1] It's hard to make sense of the ever-shifting points of view and developments within a social movement, as well as the many academic controversies found in the popular presentations of it. The interests of feminism are varied, and the balancing of rights against responsibilities still challenges us. The feminist critique is a way of asking questions and searching for answers based on women's experience. Although not all women want the same things, feminism has had an unparalleled influence on American life and culture. . . .

The central goal of feminism is to reorganize the world on the basis of equality between the sexes in all human relations. To advance their cause, feminists have focused on a variety of problems, including patriarchy, gender modeling, individual freedom, social justice, equal educational opportunity, equal pay for equal work, sexual harassment, and human rights. Unfortunately, woman's power in shaping governmental policy to her own needs has been severely limited by the politics of gender. The revolutionary fathers did not heed Abigail Adams's advice to her husband, John (who was sitting as a delegate to the Continental Congress in Philadelphia in 1777), when she wrote:

> In the new code of laws which I suppose will be necessary for you to make, I desire you would remember the ladies and be more generous and favorable to them than your ancestors. Do not put such unlimited power into the hands of the husbands. Remember, all men would be tyrants if they could. If particular care and attention is not paid to the ladies, we are determined to foment a rebellion, and will not hold ourselves bound by any laws in which we have no voice or representation.[2]

Among the mothers of the American Revolution, Abigail Adams is particularly prominent. Her strength of character and her patriotism stood the severest test, and she realized that she could not simply surrender to the legislative process created by her husband and the Sons of Liberty. Unfortunately, she could not enforce her womanly sentiments, so they went unheeded.

Higher education for women became a primary goal of the reform movement. In the United States change came at a snail's pace. Only as women emerged from the home as public speakers and abolitionists could they effect any meaningful change in their conditions. Only by breaking the bondage of the home and the handicap of silence imposed on them by patriarchy did women begin to transcend their condition. The term *patriarchy* means a system of male authority that oppresses women through its social, political, and economic institutions. In all the historical forms that patriarchal society takes, whether feudal, capitalist, or socialist, a sex-gender system and a system of economic discrimination operate simultaneously. Patriarchy results from men's greater access to, and control of, the resources and rewards of the social system. Furthermore, specifically male values are expressed through a system of sanctions that reward the upholders and punish the transgressors.[3] In the socioeconomic sphere, women are disadvantaged by a system that favors men through legal rights, religion, education, business, and access to sex.

This imbalance led analytic feminists to coin the word *sexism*, a social situation in which men exert a dominant role over women and express in a variety of ways, both private and institutional, the notion that women are inferior to men. The terms *patriarchy* and *sexism* reflect women's rising awareness of the oppression women suffer under this system.[4] The British writer Virginia Woolf showed that she understood the circumstances that gave rise to these terms (long before the 1970s) when she argued that a woman needs financial independence and "a room of her own" to become herself. Woolf's 1929 essay "A Room of One's Own" is applicable today.[5] For the vast majority of women workers, finding a way to obtain better wages and working conditions is still a priority. Although the number of women who were "gainfully employed" increased rapidly during the nineteenth century, they were unable to control their own wages, legally manage their own property, or sign legal papers. The American writer Lydia Maria Child was outraged when she was not allowed to sign her own will; her husband, David, had to do it for her.

For these and other reasons, most feminists agree that poverty is not gender neutral. During the nineteenth century, inequities were worse for working-class women who could be forced to hand over all their earnings to an irresponsible husband, even if they were left with nothing for their own survival or the maintenance of their children. If a woman tried to divorce such a husband, he was legally entitled to sole guardianship of the children. In this system, a woman had no right to her own children, and male lawmakers customarily gave custody of the babies even to an alcoholic father. Women were subordinate to men on the basis of discriminatory legislation, as well as men's exclusive ability to participate in public life.

Many men, as well as women, rebelled against this unjust system, considering the marriage laws unfair and iniquitous because they gave men control over the rights of women. Between 1839 and 1850, most states passed some kind of legislation recognizing the right of married women to own property. Women continued to struggle against the perception that they were unfit to participate in government because of their physical circumstances. Since the founding of our nation, the politics of reproduction has dominated social and economic relations between the sexes. Because of gender manipulations, it becomes very difficult to see and understand the realities of women's experience and how it affected them. . . .

Organized feminism . . . began with the Seneca Falls Convention of 1848, an event that articulated what some American women wanted in the mid-nineteenth century.[6] On July 19 and 20 of that year, five women decided to call a Women's Rights Convention at Seneca Falls, New York, to discuss the social, civil, and religious rights of women. During this period, Elizabeth Cady Stanton and Lucretia Mott reviewed the Declaration of Independence in light of their own experiences and those of other women. Their Declaration of Principles, which fueled generations of women in their bid for equality, declared: "The history of mankind is a history of repeated injuries and usurpations on the part of man toward woman, having in direct object the establishment of an absolute tyranny over her. To prove this, let facts be submitted to a candid world."[7]

In a manner similar to the current presentation of facts offered by the contemporary women's movement, these foremothers and others introduced a range of issues that implicated men and showed how their self-serving acts affected woman's status in society. These reforming women had no illusions about the gender system and knew that their views would be distorted. The declaration asserted, "In entering upon the great work before us, we anticipate no small amount of misconception, misrepresentation, and ridicule; but we shall use every instrumentality within our power to effect our object."[8]

The struggle was on. Margaret Fuller's brave book, *Woman in the Nineteenth Century,* put it bluntly:

> We would have every arbitrary barrier thrown down. We would have every path
> laid open to Woman as freely as Man . . . then and then only will mankind
> be ripe for this, when inward and outward freedom for Women as much as for
> Man shall be acknowledged as a *right,* not yielded as a concession. As the friend
> of the Negro assumes that one man cannot by right hold another in bondage,
> so would the friend of Woman assume that Man cannot by right lay even well-
> meant restrictions on Woman.[9]

Indeed, women have been answering Freud's question for a long time. The main problem is that they still are not being heard.

The Civil War of 1861 helped bring women into national politics. After    10
the victory, the intersection of the women's liberation movement and the

emancipation of the slaves underscored the issue of enlarging the electorate. Since the blacks were now free citizens, they were entitled to the suffrage rights of citizens. Women saw this development as one that might bring them the vote as well. They were totally unprepared for the opposition of the Republican politicians and the desertion of their cause by the abolitionists, who had been their staunch allies. Appalled at the appearance of the word *male* in the proposed Fourteenth Amendment to the Constitution, Elizabeth Cady Stanton, Susan B. Anthony, and Lucy Stone, leaders of the liberation movement, raised the issue of whether women were actually citizens of the United States. The advocacy of "manhood" suffrage, as Stanton warned, "creates an antagonism between black men and all women that will culminate in fearful outrages on womanhood." [10] Men, including large numbers of white men, were concerned with ensuring the vote for black men, but they were little interested in how such a measure would affect women.

From a historical vantage point, Stanton's misgivings seem prophetic. Racism and the condition of women have continued to be explosive national issues since the Civil War. These twin injustices ignited the revolution of the 1960s and sparked the heated debates surrounding the Anita Hill and Clarence Thomas Senate hearings of the 1990s. [11]

The growing chasm between men and women, regardless of race, was thrown into sharp relief by the Fourteenth Amendment, which was passed in July 1868. Although Senator Cowan of Pennsylvania offered to strike the word *male* from the legislation, and Senator Williams of Oregon argued that the interests of men and women were one, their views were ignored. Williams understood that putting women in an adversarial, rather than a complementary, position in relation to men would eventually create a state of war and "make every home a hell on earth."

On the other side of the divide, Senator Frelinghuysen of New Jersey argued that women had a "holier mission" in the home, which was to assuage the passions of men as "they come in from the battles of life." When all was said and done, the hand that rocked the cradle still had no say in the process.

The beginning of the twentieth century saw American women still fighting for the right to vote. Inequities continued in education, marriage, property rights, legal rights, religion, and the realm of divorce. The years between 1910 and 1915 were a period of confusion and growth, during which a growing number of female workers were providing fresh arguments for women's suffrage. The foundation of the Women's Party in 1916 brought new energy into the political sphere. Twelve states had finally given women the vote, so that women now constituted a new force in the presidential election.

By this time, it was clear to all parties that the group that opposed national suffrage for women would lose women's support in twelve states that controlled nearly a hundred electoral votes. Even though the female vote

15

did not sway the election of 1916, women were able to win presidential support and reorganize their party. By 1918, after years of dogged effort, the suffrage amendment passed by a vote of 274 to 136, exactly the two-thirds majority required to accomplish it. After fifty-three years of progressive effort, women finally had won the right to vote. This was the wedge women would need in the coming years to force their way past what Carrie Chapman Catt warned suffragists would be "locked doors."

Women's greatest challenge, however, was not to gain the vote, but to change patriarchal values. Their efforts were based on two assumptions: (1) that a man claiming to be sensitive to what women want must first recognize, as Fuller pointed out, that "Man cannot by right lay even well-meant restrictions on Woman" and (2) that men who are humanists can be persuaded to give up their unfair advantages voluntarily. These assumptions bring forth an underlying assumption that feminism is both a movement that strives for equal rights for women and an ideology of social transformation whose aim is to create a better world for women beyond simple social equity. In fact, feminism urges such men to question the whole idea that an unfair advantage is really an "advantage." . . .

There are many different views and factions within feminism. The movement encompasses major differences of opinion about how its goals can best be achieved and how they should be defined. This situation is not unusual, since in all the major movements in the history of ideas and social reform, the participants have had such differences. What unites all feminists, what they all have in common that makes them "feminists," is the belief that they must question and challenge sexual stereotypes and that opportunity should not be denied to either men or women on the grounds of gender. Friedan, who is often called the mother of contemporary feminism, defined it as a conviction "that women are people in the fullest sense of the word, who must be free to move in society with all the privileges and opportunities and responsibilities that are their human and American right." [12] This is a major aspect of "classical feminism." Its mission is to achieve full equality for women of every race, religion, ethnic group, age, and sexual orientation. . . .

A major premise of feminist theory is that sexual politics supports patriarchy in its politicization of personal life. [13] In such a system, the majority of men view women first and foremost as child bearers. So the female body and how it is represented is continually and inevitably caught up in any discussion of women's liberation. Most men imagine that women's chief concerns, because of their reproductive biology, center on home and family. Thus, a patriarchal system locks women into roles that are based on their bodies' capacity to reproduce. Most men think of the home as the physical space in which women do their work: housekeeping, cooking, serving, taking care of the children, and other tasks associated with the domestic sphere. It is in this frame of reference that feminist theorists work.

The "myth of motherhood" and the cult of the nineteenth-century "true woman" persist. They categorize all women as mothers and caregivers even when they do not wish to perform these roles, or as Mary Wollstonecraft put it, "All women are to be levelled, by meekness and docility, into one character of yielding softness and gentle compliance." Under patriarchy, differences between men's and women's "true" natures have been based on a conviction that women have softer emotions than do men and that their job is to marry, produce children, and strengthen family life. According to this implied contract, as long as a woman sticks to the program, she is entitled to certain compensations and privileges. Thus, traditional marriage ensures a wedded woman's use of her husband's name and his protection and financial support. . . .

Although the 1950s were seen as a golden age of marriage and domesticity by many, Friedan's groundbreaking study of "The Happy Housewife Heroine" in *The Feminine Mystique* (1963) exposed the frustration of the unhappy, educated, middle-class, mostly white housewives between what they were supposed to feel and what they actually felt. Each one believed that "the problem that has no name" was hers alone—such was women's isolation from each other. At home, these women tried to make themselves beautiful, cultured, and respectable, but they were never really away from their children; they went marketing with their children, changed their children's diapers, talked about their children, and played mahjong or bridge.

"Raising three small children in suburbia," artist and writer Phyllis Rosser explained, "was the most depressing work I've ever done." Surrounded by baby bottles, cereal boxes, and dirty dishes, married women found that child rearing consumed most of their day. This was the "American Dream" that Rosser and millions of other intelligent American women were living, and for many it was a nightmare. Friedan's comparison of housewives' lives to conditions in Nazi concentration camps may seem extreme to many women (although many women viewed their mothers' lives this way), but during the 1960s, it struck a resounding chord for a generation of middle-class white women whose self-respect had been systematically destroyed by their inferior status as unpaid home workers and consumers.

The "mystique of feminine fulfillment" that Friedan chronicled emerged after World War II, when suburban housewives like my mother became the "dream image" of women all over the world. Behind it, as Friedan demonstrated, was anger and mental anguish—even insanity, brought about by the fact that they had no public careers. The loss of identity that came from being relegated to and isolated in the home created the psychic distress that many of these women experienced—"the problem with no name." It contributed to the depression and rage that many middle-class women of that generation felt because their contributions to society were belittled and child rearing was not considered intellectually challenging. Friedan rejected the biological determinism of Freudian theory. Her view of women as a weaker social group led her to argue for a massive self-help program to help women reenter the labor market.

Inspired by Friedan's book, women began to form consciousness-raising groups. In the absence of psychological experts, women's own thoughts and feelings about marriage, motherhood, and their bodies began to emerge. They discovered that women were treated like children. In essence, they felt they had no identity of their own, which led them to sail boldly into the unknown in search of themselves. . . .

From the late 1960s to the mid-1980s, feminism was a clear force for progress and against alienation. Feminism's effects on gender issues, business, government, the military, education, religion, families, and dating and sexuality—in short, all aspects of life—was felt throughout the society and culture. But Friedan's book established a framework that was hostile to the traditional nuclear family and conventional female roles, and it seemed to exclude the homemaker from feminism's brave new world. The idea of staying home, raising a family, and doing housework was so negatively portrayed that it left no place for many women who wanted to do so.

During this stage, Kate Millett's *Sexual Politics* became a best-seller, and it was by far the most demanding feminist book of the 1970s. The author charged that throughout history, the interaction between men and women was one of domination and subordination. On the basis of this premise, Millett isolated "patriarchy," a pattern of male domination based on gender, as the chief institution of women's oppression. From this vantage point, it was reasonable to see the nuclear family as a "feudal institution that reduces women to chattel status." In such a system, there is no possibility of an honest disagreement among equals. In Millett's view, patriarchy authorizes the relative dominance of male domains over female ones. This dominance disadvantages women and puts them at the mercy of those who control the resources. In fact, women themselves are resources, like water or pastureland, to be traded among men. If a woman belongs to a man, she is like a slave; for example, a father may marry a daughter off against her will to further his own ambitions. The woman has no rights, and her offspring are her husband's property to do with as he likes. Millett's appraisal simply reiterated the judgments of nineteenth-century feminists, who saw a connection between the sexual division of labor in the home and in the workplace and women's oppression in modern industrial society.

According to Millett's reasoning, marriage is a financial arrangement—an exchange of goods and services in which men benefit and women lose. In this pooling of resources and sharing of responsibilities, one party, the man, retains everything he came into the marriage with, whereas in many cases, the woman brings a dowry with her, contributes free domestic and child care services, and serves her husband and his career. If she has an education and aspirations of her own, they are sacrificed to the needs of her husband and family. . . .

Coming out of the first stage of the contemporary women's movement, Millett believed that her main concern was to find an explanatory theory for the subordination of women to men. In the United States, an alliance

25

of conservative women and clergymen insists that woman's role is to be a homemaker and caretaker. Modernism and sexism view gender in terms of occupational specialties: Man is the hardworking provider who has liberated his woman from the burdens of production. Contrary to this model, Millett and many socialist feminists of the period believed that most women would be better off if they did not have to choose between their offspring and meaningful work. They argued for professional care of the young because it would allow women to . . . choose both. In short, they were attempting to change the prevailing idea that the domestic sphere was the sole appropriate domain of women. . . .

The 1960s and 1970s saw the emergence of many spokespersons for feminism, which led to the establishment of courses that introduced women into history. It was not surprising that with a discipline as new, as unusual, and as speculative as contemporary women's studies, dissension soon emerged. I think dissension arose for two reasons. First, some of the major feminist thinkers, such as Friedan, Millett, and Gloria Steinem, were inflexible about their initial theories—Steinem's notion of women's moral superiority, for example. Many people were put off, especially, by these women's views on the nature of men and women and on women's oppression in marriage, home, and bed. Second, and, in the long run, more important, was the natural growth and continuing outreach of the liberation movement itself. Changes in occupations, day care centers, dual earning capacity, and family leave have all contributed to a more egalitarian and less conventional contemporary lifestyle in the United States.

Despite these factional disputes about the actual conditions of women's lives, despite the hardships that the antifeminist backlash of the 1980s, with its attempts to scare women back into the home, imposed on those struggling for women's liberation, feminism has impelled all types of people to construct and reconstruct their respective roles in this society and culture. The current unrest and mood of apprehension that seems to pervade the women's movement arose from the fact that many people don't really understand the double bind that women are in. Moreover, women generally fail to see their own position within the private and public domains. Caught between their own lives and political ideologies, they are only beginning to gain some insight into how policy decisions are directed at them. The ongoing debates about welfare, for example, demonstrate how laws manage women and children. "Each time we talk about things that can be experienced only in privacy or intimacy," explained political scientist Hannah Arendt, "we bring them out into a sphere where they will assume a kind of reality, which, their intensity notwithstanding, they never could have had before."[13]

Nowhere is this situation more evident than in attempts to deal with     30
women's experience in the world. Foes of feminism argue that contrary to what Friedan said, what happens in the home has an impact on society and the public sphere. Their relatively recent attempts to police the womb in

order to protect the life of the unborn have collapsed the private into the public. The medical control of birth has given new meaning to the expression "the personal is the political." But what does this phrase really mean? As author Mary Gordon explained, "We have to examine the definition of the personal. . . . The personal and the private have long been the hiding place of scandals. As long as the personal is defined by men, and until men listen to what women consider the personal, neither side knows what the other is talking about." [14] So it is imperative to examine individual women's experiences to provide a framework of meaning: to understand women's experiences from the standpoint of how we actually live our lives, rather than through theoretical investigations. It is crucial to ask how we arrived at where we are now. This is far more important than knowing the political cataclysms that occurred along the way. Only by striving to transcend the unproductive polarization that has grown out of questions of private and public, identity and value, masculine and feminine, can we move beyond the play of politics and get closer to the true meaning of the movement to liberate women. . . .

. . . Between 1963 and the present, ideas stemming from the movement to liberate women have permeated psychology, sociology, anthropology, literature, art, and politics, and gained measurable influence over educational theory. Many people now recognize that inequality limits women's participation in public life and perpetuates the social emphasis on male values.

Feminism, for all its faults, has given birth to one of the few compelling visions of our era. It is a vision that attempts to deal compassionately not only with women's inequality, but with the pressing problems in the world.

The struggle for knowledge, for training, and for opportunity was first articulated by American women because of their discontent with women's status. This discontent gave birth to a reform movement on behalf of women. It was women's general belief that they were treated as mere chattel, having no rights whatsoever, existing merely to serve a father, husband, brother, or some other man. Such a picture contains partial truths. The stories of feminist networks, individual courageous acts, and collective pioneering exploits offer touchstones on the long road to answering Freud's question, "What do women want?"

### Notes

1. For instance, Gloria Steinem's books make the best-seller list; Susan Faludi's blockbuster *Backlash* exposed an undeclared war against American women; Naomi Wolf's *Fire with Fire* urged women to seize the day; and in *Who Stole Feminism?* Christina Hoff Sommers accused feminist extremists of promoting a dangerous new agenda.

2. *Familiar Letters of John Adams and His Wife Abigail Adams during the Revolution* (New York, 1876) 286–87, letter dated March 31, 1776.

3. Maggie Humm, ed., *Modern Feminisms: Political Literary Cultural* (New York: Columbia UP, 1992) 408.

4. Marilyn French, *The War against Women* (New York: Summit, 1992).

5. Virginia Woolf, *A Room of One's Own* (New York: Harcourt, 1929).

6. For an excellent overview of these women and the events that shaped the women's rights movement, see Eleanor Flexner, *Century of Struggle: The Woman's Rights Movement in the United States* (New York: Atheneum, 1970).

7. Flexner 75.

8. Flexner 75.

9. Flexner 67.

10. Flexner 144.

11. Anna Quindlen, "Apologies to Anita" in the *New York Times* Nov. 1994: Op-Ed 5. See Jane Mayer and Jill Abramson, *Strange Justice* (New York: Hougton, 1994) regarding the many confusions about this historic case of sexual harassment and sexual politics.

12. Betty Friedan, *It Changed My Life: Writings on the Women's Movement* (New York: Random, 1976) 127.

13. Hannah Arendt, *The Human Condition* (Chicago: U of Chicago P, 1958) 50.

14. See "Mary Gordon and Robert Stone Talk about Sexual Harassment," in *Pen Newsletter* 85 (Fall 1994): 27.

---

*For Discussion*

1. To what extent were you already familiar with some of the people and events described in this reading? Did you know about the property laws, the contributions of women to the Seneca Falls Convention, or the attitudes of Abigail Adams? If you have been taught about the women's movement, was it part of a women's studies course or part of a course in U.S. history? If you have had little exposure to the subject, can you explain why that might be?

2. From this account, what seems to be the explanation of why black males were able to achieve voting rights before any women did, even though white women had more money and more education?

3. Langer states in paragraph 16 that feminists assume that "men who are humanists can be persuaded to give up their unfair advantages voluntarily." Is this what happened in the case of women gaining the right to vote, to be paid the same as men, or to serve alongside men in the military? Substitute "people" for "men" in this sentence, and discuss whether it holds true in general. Do problems come from the word "unfair"?

4. In paragraph 27, Langer presents Millett's argument that state-supported, professional child care would enable women to choose both raising children and engaging in "meaningful work." Does such language suggest that child rearing is not meaningful work? Does

our society as a whole regard it as meaningful work? How does our society reward those in occupations that we respect?

## For Research and Analysis

As examples of persuasion, some of the writings and speeches from female abolitionists are outstanding. Angeline Grimke's speech "Bearing Witness Against Slavery" is particularly moving. Find one of these speeches or writings, and assess its rhetorical context: speaker, audience, occasion, purpose. Write an essay in which you describe the key persuasive strategies, such as identification, emotional appeals, and stylistic devices.

## For Inquiry and Persuasion

Look at two or three contemporary U.S. history textbooks, for either high school or college, and compare their treatment of the women's movement. (Even high school texts are often found in your college library.) You might consider the amount of space allotted to the topic, the types of evidence included (for example, are there primary texts such as the portion of the letter from Abigail Adams?), and the perspective of the authors. Write an essay persuading an audience of teachers to adopt the textbook you think provides the best treatment of the issue, being very clear about what "best" means to you.

# Cartoon
## Kirk Anderson

*The following cartoon appeared in* Ms. *magazine in 1993. How commonly do your friends and acquaintances share the attitudes expressed by these characters?*

THE INCREDIBLE SHRINKING WOMAN

*For Discussion*

What is the point of the cartoon's title? What definition of "feminism" is being expressed? Evaluate the effectiveness of the cartoon as persuasion.

# The Problem That Has No Name
## Betty Friedan

*It is no exaggeration to say that Betty Friedan started a revolution when she published* The Feminine Mystique *in 1963. She showed American women that they had been living since the end of World War II with an identity imposed upon them by women's magazines and advertising, a set of ideas she called "the feminine mystique." Friedan argued that earlier decades of educated women from 1900 through the 1940s had aspired to careers outside of the home and development of their full human potential. She used evidence from literature and advertisements aimed at women from the past and present to show how messages about gender roles had changed to limit women's prospects and make them feel guilty and unwomanly if they did not accept the mystique's dictum that women "can find fulfillment only in sexual passivity, male domination, and nurturing maternal love." This selection is the first chapter from the book, which sets out to establish that there was indeed a problem in the picture-perfect life of the American housewife.*

The problem lay buried, unspoken, for many years in the minds of American women. It was a strange stirring, a sense of dissatisfaction, a yearning that women suffered in the middle of the twentieth century in the United States. Each suburban wife struggled with it alone. As she made the beds, shopped for groceries, matched slipcover material, ate peanut butter sandwiches with her children, chauffeured Cub Scouts and Brownies, lay beside her husband at night—she was afraid to ask even of herself the silent question—"Is this all?"

For over fifteen years there was no word of this yearning in the millions of words written about women, for women, in all the columns, books and articles by experts telling women their role was to seek fulfillment as wives and mothers. Over and over women heard in voices of tradition and of Freudian sophistication that they could desire no greater destiny than to glory in their own femininity. Experts told them how to catch a man and keep him, how to breastfeed children and handle their toilet training, how to cope with sibling rivalry and adolescent rebellion; how to buy a dishwasher, bake bread, cook gourmet meals, and build a swimming pool with their own hands; how to dress, look, and act more feminine and make marriage more exciting; how to keep their husbands from dying young and their sons from growing into delinquents. They were taught to pity the neurotic, unfeminine, unhappy women who wanted to be poets or physicists or presidents. They learned that truly feminine women do not want careers, higher education, political rights—the independence and the opportunities that the old-fashioned feminists fought for. Some women, in their forties and fifties, still remembered painfully giving up those dreams, but most of the younger women no longer even thought about them. A thousand expert voices applauded their femininity, their adjustment, their new maturity. All they had to do was devote their lives from earliest girlhood to finding a husband and bearing children.

By the end of the nineteen-fifties, the average marriage age of women in America dropped to 20, and was still dropping, into the teens. Fourteen million girls were engaged by 17. The proportion of women attending college in comparison with men dropped from 47 per cent in 1920 to 35 per cent in 1958. A century earlier, women had fought for higher education; now girls went to college to get a husband. By the mid-fifties, 60 per cent dropped out of college to marry, or because they were afraid too much education would be a marriage bar. Colleges built dormitories for "married students," but the students were almost always the husbands. A new degree was instituted for the wives—"Ph.T." (Putting Husband Through).

Then American girls began getting married in high school. And the women's magazines, deploring the unhappy statistics about these young marriages, urged that courses on marriage, and marriage counselors, be installed in the high schools. Girls started going steady at twelve and thirteen, in junior high. Manufacturers put out brassieres with false bosoms of foam rubber for little girls of ten. And an advertisement for a child's dress, sizes 3–6x, in the *New York Times* in the fall of 1960, said: "She Too Can Join the Man-Trap Set."

By the end of the fifties, the United States birthrate was overtaking India's. The birth-control movement, renamed Planned Parenthood, was asked to find a method whereby women who had been advised that a third or fourth baby would be born dead or defective might have it anyhow. Statisticians were especially astounded at the fantastic increase in the number of babies among college women. Where once they had two children, now they had four, five, six. Women who had once wanted careers were now making careers out of having babies. So rejoiced *Life* magazine in a 1956 paean to the movement of American women back to the home.

In a New York hospital, a woman had a nervous breakdown when she found she could not breastfeed her baby. In other hospitals, women dying of cancer refused a drug which research had proved might save their lives: its side effects were said to be unfeminine. "If I have only one life, let me live it as a blonde," a larger-than-life-sized picture of a pretty, vacuous woman proclaimed from newspaper, magazine, and drugstore ads. And across America, three out of every ten women dyed their hair blonde. They ate a chalk called Metrecal, instead of food, to shrink to the size of the thin young models. Department-store buyers reported that American women, since 1939, had become three and four sizes smaller. "Women are out to fit the clothes, instead of vice-versa," one buyer said.

Interior decorators were designing kitchens with mosaic murals and original paintings, for kitchens were once again the center of women's lives. Home sewing became a million-dollar industry. Many women no longer left their homes, except to shop, chauffeur their children, or attend a social engagement with their husbands. Girls were growing up in America without ever having jobs outside the home. In the late fifties, a sociological phenomenon was suddenly remarked: a third of American women now worked, but most were no longer young and very few were pursuing careers. They were married women who held part-time jobs, selling or secretarial, to put their husbands through school, their sons through college, or to help pay the mortgage. Or they were widows supporting families. Fewer and fewer women were entering professional work. The shortages in the nursing, social work, and teaching professions caused crises in almost every American city. Concerned over the Soviet Union's lead in the space race, scientists noted that America's greatest source of unused brain-power was women. But girls would not study physics: it was "unfeminine." A girl refused a science fellowship at Johns Hopkins to take a job in a real-estate office. All she wanted, she said, was what every other American girl wanted—to get married, have four children and live in a nice house in a nice suburb.

The suburban housewife—she was the dream image of the young American women and the envy, it was said, of women all over the world. The American housewife—freed by science and labor-saving appliances from the drudgery, the dangers of childbirth and the illnesses of her grandmother. She was healthy, beautiful, educated, concerned only about her husband, her children, her home. She had found true feminine fulfillment. As a housewife and mother, she was respected as a full and equal partner to man in his world. She was free to choose automobiles, clothes, appliances, supermarkets; she had everything that women ever dreamed of.

In the fifteen years after World War II, this mystique of feminine fulfillment became the cherished and self-perpetuating core of contemporary American culture. Millions of women lived their lives in the image of those pretty pictures of the American suburban housewife, kissing their husbands goodbye in front of the picture window, depositing their stationwagonsful of children at school, and smiling as they ran the new electric waxer over the spotless kitchen floor. They baked their own bread, sewed their own and their children's clothes, kept their new washing machines and dryers running all day. They changed the sheets on the beds twice a week instead of once, took the rug-hooking class in adult education, and pitied their poor frustrated mothers, who had dreamed of having a career. Their only dream was to be perfect wives and mothers; their highest ambition to have five children and a beautiful house, their only fight to get and keep their husbands. They had no thought for the unfeminine problems of the world outside the home; they wanted the men to make the major decisions. They gloried in their role as women, and wrote proudly on the census blank: "Occupation: housewife."

For over fifteen years, the words written for women, and the words women used when they talked to each other, while their husbands sat on the other side of the room and talked shop or politics or septic tanks, were about problems with their children, or how to keep their husbands happy, or improve their children's school, or cook chicken or make slipcovers. No-

10

body argued whether women were inferior or superior to men; they were simply different. Words like "emancipation" and "career" sounded strange and embarrassing; no one had used them for years. When a Frenchwoman named Simone de Beauvoir wrote a book called *The Second Sex,* an American critic commented that she obviously "didn't know what life was all about," and besides, she was talking about French women. The "woman problem" in America no longer existed.

If a woman had a problem in the 1950's and 1960's, she knew that something must be wrong with her marriage, or with herself. Other women were satisfied with their lives, she thought. What kind of a woman was she if she did not feel this mysterious fulfillment waxing the kitchen floor? She was so ashamed to admit her dissatisfaction that she never knew how many other women shared it. If she tried to tell her husband, he didn't understand what she was talking about. She did not really understand it herself. For over fifteen years women in America found it harder to talk about this problem than about sex. Even the psychoanalysts had no name for it. When a woman went to a psychiatrist for help, as many women did, she would say, "I'm so ashamed," or "I must be hopelessly neurotic." "I don't know what's wrong with women today," a suburban psychiatrist said uneasily. "I only know something is wrong because most of my patients happen to be women. And their problem isn't sexual." Most women with this problem did not go to see a psychoanalyst, however. "There's nothing wrong really," they kept telling themselves. "There isn't any problem."

But on an April morning in 1959, I heard a mother of four, having coffee with four other mothers in a suburban development fifteen miles from New York, say in a tone of quiet desperation, "the problem." And the others knew, without words, that she was not talking about a problem with her husband, or her children, or her home. Suddenly they realized they all shared the same problem, the problem that has no name. They began, hesitantly, to talk about it. Later, after they had picked up their children at nursery school and taken them home to nap, two of the women cried, in sheer relief, just to know they were not alone.

Gradually I came to realize that the problem that has no name was shared by countless women in America. As a magazine writer I often interviewed women about problems with their children, or their marriages, or their houses, or their communities. But after a while I began to recognize the telltale signs of this other problem. I saw the same signs in suburban ranch houses and split-levels on Long Island and in New Jersey and Westchester County; in colonial houses in a small Massachusetts town; on patios in Memphis; in suburban and city apartments; in living rooms in the Midwest. Sometimes I sensed the problem, not as a reporter, but as a suburban housewife, for during this time I was also bringing up my own three children in Rockland County, New York. I heard echoes of the problem in college dormitories and semi-private maternity wards, at PTA meetings and luncheons of the League of Women Voters, at suburban cocktail parties, in

station wagons waiting for trains, and in snatches of conversation over-
heard at Schrafft's. The groping words I heard from other women, on quiet
afternoons when children were at school or on quiet evenings when husbands worked late, I think I understood first as a woman long before I understood their larger social and psychological implications.

Just what was this problem that has no name? What were the words
women used when they tried to express it? Sometimes a woman would say
"I feel empty somehow . . . incomplete." Or she would say, "I feel as if I
don't exist." Sometimes she blotted out the feeling with a tranquilizer.
Sometimes she thought the problem was with her husband, or her children, or that what she really needed was to redecorate her house, or move
to a better neighborhood, or have an affair, or another baby. Sometimes,
she went to a doctor with symptoms she could hardly describe: "A tired
feeling . . . I get so angry with the children it scares me . . . I feel like crying
without any reason." (A Cleveland doctor called it "the housewife's syndrome.") A number of women told me about great bleeding blisters that
break out on their hands and arms. "I call it the housewife's blight," said a
family doctor in Pennsylvania. "I see it so often lately in these young women
with four, five and six children who bury themselves in their dishpans. But
it isn't caused by detergent and it isn't cured by cortisone."

Sometimes a woman would tell me that the feeling gets so strong she       15
runs out of the house and walks through the streets. Or she stays inside her
house and cries. Or her children tell her a joke, and she doesn't laugh because she doesn't hear it. I talked to women who had spent years on the analyst's couch, working out their "adjustment to the feminine role," their
blocks to "fulfillment as a wife and mother." But the desperate tone in these
women's voices, and the look in their eyes, was the same as the tone and the
look of other women, who were sure they had no problem, even though
they did have a strange feeling of desperation.

A mother of four who left college at nineteen to get married told me:

> I've tried everything women are supposed to do — hobbies, gardening, pick-
> ling, canning, being very social with my neighbors, joining committees, run-
> ning PTA teas. I can do it all, and I like it, but it doesn't leave you anything to
> think about — any feeling of who you are. I never had any career ambitions.
> All I wanted was to get married and have four children. I love the kids and Bob
> and my home. There's no problem you can even put a name to. But I'm des-
> perate. I begin to feel I have no personality. I'm a server of food and a putter-
> on of pants and a bedmaker, somebody who can be called on when you want
> something. But who am I?

A twenty-three-year-old mother in blue jeans said:

> I ask myself why I'm so dissatisfied. I've got my health, fine children, a
> lovely new home, enough money. My husband has a real future as an electron-
> ics engineer. He doesn't have any of these feelings. He says maybe I need a va-
> cation, let's go to New York for a weekend. But that isn't it. I always had this

idea we should do everything together. I can't sit down and read a book alone. If the children are napping and I have one hour to myself I just walk through the house waiting for them to wake up. I don't make a move until I know where the rest of the crowd is going. It's as if ever since you were a little girl, there's always been somebody or something that will take care of your life: your parents, or college, or falling in love, or having a child, or moving to a new house. Then you wake up one morning and there's nothing to look forward to.

A young wife in a Long Island development said:

> I seem to sleep so much. I don't know why I should be so tired. This house isn't nearly so hard to clean as the cold-water flat we had when I was working. The children are at school all day. It's not the work. I just don't feel alive.

In 1960, the problem that has no name burst like a boil through the image of the happy American housewife. In the television commercials the pretty housewives still beamed over their foaming dishpans and *Time's* cover story on "The Suburban Wife, an American Phenomenon" protested: "Having too good a time . . . to believe that they should be unhappy." But the actual unhappiness of the American housewife was suddenly being reported—from the *New York Times* and *Newsweek* to *Good Housekeeping* and CBS Television ("The Trapped Housewife"), although almost everybody who talked about it found some superficial reason to dismiss it. It was attributed to incompetent appliance repairmen (*New York Times*), or the distances children must be chauffeured in the suburbs (*Time*), or too much PTA (*Redbook*). Some said it was the old problem—education: more and more women had education, which naturally made them unhappy in their role as housewives. "The road from Freud to Frigidaire, from Sophocles to Spock, has turned out to be a bumpy one," reported the *New York Times* (June 28, 1960). "Many young women—certainly not all—whose education plunged them into a world of ideas feel stifled in their homes. They find their routine lives out of joint with their training. Like shut-ins, they feel left out. In the last year, the problem of the educated housewife has provided the meat of dozens of speeches made by troubled presidents of women's colleges who maintain, in the face of complaints, that sixteen years of academic training is realistic preparation for wifehood and motherhood."

There was much sympathy for the educated housewife. ("Like a two-headed schizophrenic . . . once she wrote a paper on the Graveyard poets; now she writes notes to the milkman. Once she determined the boiling point of sulphuric acid; now she determines her boiling point with the overdue repairman. . . . The housewife often is reduced to screams and tears. . . . No one, it seems, is appreciative, least of all herself, of the kind of person she becomes in the process of turning from poetess into shrew.")  20

Home economists suggested more realistic preparation for housewives, such as high-school workshops in home appliances. College educators suggested more discussion groups on home management and the family, to prepare women for the adjustment to domestic life. A spate of articles appeared in the mass magazines offering "Fifty-eight Ways to Make Your Marriage More Exciting." No month went by without a new book by a psychiatrist or sexologist offering technical advice on finding greater fulfillment through sex.

A male humorist joked in *Harper's Bazaar* (July, 1960) that the problem could be solved by taking away woman's right to vote. ("In the pre-19th Amendment era, the American woman was placid, sheltered and sure of her role in American society. She left all the political decisions to her husband and he, in turn, left all the family decisions to her. Today a woman has to make both the family *and* the political decisions, and it's too much for her.")

A number of educators suggested seriously that women no longer be admitted to the four-year colleges and universities: in the growing college crisis, the education which girls could not use as housewives was more urgently needed than ever by boys to do the work of the atomic age.

The problem was also dismissed with drastic solutions no one could take seriously. (A woman writer proposed in *Harper's* that women be drafted for compulsory service as nurses' aides and baby-sitters.) And it was smoothed over with the age-old panaceas: "love is their answer," "the only answer is inner help," "the secret of completeness—children," "a private means of intellectual fulfillment," "to cure this toothache of the spirit—the simple formula of handing one's self and one's will over to God."

The problem was dismissed by telling the housewife she doesn't realize    25
how lucky she is—her own boss, no time clock, no junior executive gunning for her job. What if she isn't happy—does she think men are happy in this world? Does she really, secretly, still want to be a man? Doesn't she know yet how lucky she is to be a woman?

The problem was also, and finally, dismissed by shrugging that there are no solutions: this is what being a woman means, and what is wrong with American women that they can't accept their role gracefully? As *Newsweek* put it (March 7, 1960):

> She is dissatisfied with a lot that women of other lands can only dream of. Her discontent is deep, pervasive, and impervious to the superficial remedies which are offered at every hand. . . . An army of professional explorers have already charted the major sources of trouble. . . . From the beginning of time, the female cycle has defined and confined woman's role. As Freud was credited with saying: "Anatomy is destiny." Though no group of women has ever pushed these natural restrictions as far as the American wife, it seems that she still cannot accept them with good grace. . . . A young mother with a beautiful family, charm, talent and brains is apt to dismiss her role apologetically. "What do I do?" you hear her say. "Why nothing. I'm just a housewife." A good education, it seems, has given this paragon among women an understanding of the value of everything except her own worth. . . .

And so she must accept the fact that "American women's unhappiness is merely the most recently won of women's rights," and adjust and say with the happy housewife found by *Newsweek:* "We ought to salute the wonderful freedom we all have and be proud of our lives today. I have had college and I've worked, but being a housewife is the most rewarding and satisfying role. . . . My mother was never included in my father's business affairs . . . she couldn't get out of the house and away from us children. But I am an equal to my husband; I can go along with him on business trips and to social business affairs."

The alternative offered was a choice that few women would contemplate. In the sympathetic words of the *New York Times:* "All admit to being deeply frustrated at times by the lack of privacy, the physical burden, the routine of family life, the confinement of it. However, none would give up her home and family if she had the choice to make again." *Redbook* commented: "Few women would want to thumb their noses at husbands, children and community and go off on their own. Those who do may be talented individuals, but they rarely are successful women."

The year American women's discontent boiled over, it was also reported (*Look*) that the more than 21,000,000 American women who are single, widowed, or divorced do not cease even after fifty their frenzied, desperate search for a man. And the search begins early—for seventy per cent of all American women now marry before they are twenty-four. A pretty twenty-five-year-old secretary took thirty-five different jobs in six months in the futile hope of finding a husband. Women were moving from one political club to another, taking evening courses in accounting or sailing, learning to play golf or ski, joining a number of churches in succession, going to bars alone, in their ceaseless search for a man.

Of the growing thousands of women currently getting private psychiatric help in the United States, the married ones were reported dissatisfied with their marriages, the unmarried ones suffering from anxiety and, finally, depression. Strangely, a number of psychiatrists stated that, in their experience, unmarried women patients were happier than married ones. So the door of all those pretty suburban houses opened a crack to permit a glimpse of uncounted thousands of American housewives who suffered alone from a problem that suddenly everyone was talking about, and beginning to take for granted, as one of those unreal problems in American life that can never be solved—like the hydrogen bomb. By 1962 the plight of the trapped American housewife had become a national parlor game. Whole issues of magazines, newspaper columns, books learned and frivolous, educational conferences and television panels were devoted to the problem.

Even so, most men, and some women, still did not know that this problem was real. But those who had faced it honestly knew that all the superficial remedies, the sympathetic advice, the scolding words and the cheering words were somehow drowning the problem in unreality.

A bitter laugh was beginning to be heard from American women. They were admired, envied, pitied, theorized over until they were sick of it, offered drastic solutions or silly choices that no one could take seriously. They got all kinds of advice from the growing armies of marriage and child-guidance counselors, psychotherapists, and armchair psychologists, on how to adjust to their role as housewives. No other road to fulfillment was offered to American women in the middle of the twentieth century. Most adjusted to their role and suffered or ignored the problem that has no name. It can be less painful, for a woman, not to hear the strange, dissatisfied voice stirring within her.

It is no longer possible to ignore that voice, to dismiss the desperation of so many American women. This is not what being a woman means, no matter what the experts say. For human suffering there is a reason; perhaps the reason has not been found because the right questions have not been asked, or pressed far enough. I do not accept the answer that there is no problem because American women have luxuries that women in other times and lands never dreamed of; part of the strange newness of the problem is that it cannot be understood in terms of the age-old material problems of man: poverty, sickness, hunger, cold. The women who suffer this problem have a hunger that food cannot fill. It persists in women whose husbands are struggling internes and law clerks, or prosperous doctors and lawyers; in wives of workers and executives who make $5,000 a year or $50,000. It is not caused by lack of material advantages; it may not even be felt by women preoccupied with desperate problems of hunger, poverty or illness. And women who think it will be solved by more money, a bigger house, a second car, moving to a better suburb, often discover it gets worse.

It is no longer possible today to blame the problem on loss of femininity: to say that education and independence and equality with men have made American women unfeminine. I have heard so many women try to deny this dissatisfied voice within themselves because it does not fit the pretty picture of femininity the experts have given them. I think, in fact, that this is the first clue to the mystery: the problem cannot be understood in the generally accepted terms by which scientists have studied women, doctors have treated them, counselors have advised them, and writers have written about them. Women who suffer this problem, in whom this voice is stirring, have lived their whole lives in the pursuit of feminine fulfillment. They are not career women (although career women may have other problems); they are women whose greatest ambition has been marriage and children. For the oldest of these women, these daughters of the American middle class, no other dream was possible. The ones in their forties and fifties who once had other dreams gave them up and threw themselves joyously into life as housewives. For the youngest, the new wives and mothers, this was the only dream. They are the ones who quit high school and college to marry, or marked time in some job in which they had no real interest until they married. These women are very "feminine" in the usual sense, and yet they still suffer the problem. . . .

The fact is that no one today is muttering angrily about "women's rights," even though more and more women have gone to college. In a recent study of all the classes that have graduated from Barnard College, a significant minority of earlier graduates blamed their education for making them want "rights," later classes blamed their education for giving them career dreams, but recent graduates blamed the college for making them feel it was not enough simply to be a housewife and mother; they did not want to feel guilty if they did not read books or take part in community activities. But if education is not the cause of the problem, the fact that education somehow festers in these women may be a clue.

If the secret of feminine fulfillment is having children, never have 35 so many women, with the freedom to choose, had so many children, in so few years, so willingly. If the answer is love, never have women searched for love with such determination. And yet there is a growing suspicion that the problem may not be sexual, though it must somehow be related to sex. I have heard from many doctors evidence of new sexual problems between man and wife—sexual hunger in wives so great their husbands cannot satisfy it. "We have made woman a sex creature," said a psychiatrist at the Margaret Sanger marriage counseling clinic. "She has no identity except as a wife and mother. She does not know who she is herself. She waits all day for her husband to come home at night to make her feel alive. And now it is the husband who is not interested. It is terrible for the women, to lie there, night after night, waiting for her husband to make her feel alive." Why is there such a market for books and articles offering sexual advice? The kind of sexual orgasm which Kinsey found in statistical plenitude in the recent generations of American women does not seem to make this problem go away.

On the contrary, new neuroses are being seen among women—and problems as yet unnamed as neuroses—which Freud and his followers did not predict, with physical symptoms, anxieties, and defense mechanisms equal to those caused by sexual repression. And strange new problems are being reported in the growing generations of children whose mothers were always there, driving them around, helping them with their homework— an inability to endure pain or discipline or pursue any self-sustained goal of any sort, a devastating boredom with life. Educators are increasingly uneasy about the dependence, the lack of self-reliance, of the boys and girls who are entering college today. "We fight a continual battle to make our students assume manhood," said a Columbia dean.

A White House conference was held on the physical and muscular deterioration of American children: were they being over-nurtured? Sociologists noted the astounding organization of suburban children's lives: the lessons, parties, entertainments, play and study groups organized for them. A suburban housewife in Portland, Oregon, wondered why the children "need" Brownies and Boy Scouts out here. "This is not the slums. The kids out here have the great outdoors. I think people are so bored, they organize the children, and then try to hook everyone else on it. And the poor kids have no time left just to lie on their beds and daydream."

Can the problem that has no name be somehow related to the domestic routine of the housewife? When a woman tries to put the problem into words, she often merely describes the daily life she leads. What is there in this recital of comfortable domestic detail that could possibly cause such a feeling of desperation? Is she trapped simply by the enormous demands of her role as modern housewife: wife, mistress, mother, nurse, consumer, cook, chauffeur; expert on interior decoration, child care, appliance repair, furniture refinishing, nutrition, and education? Her day is fragmented as she rushes from dishwasher to washing machine to telephone to dryer to station wagon to supermarket, and delivers Johnny to the Little League field, takes Janey to dancing class, gets the lawnmower fixed and meets the 6:45. She can never spend more than 15 minutes on any one thing; she has no time to read books, only magazines; even if she had time, she has lost the power to concentrate. At the end of the day, she is so terribly tired that sometimes her husband has to take over and put the children to bed.

This terrible tiredness took so many women to doctors in the 1950's that one decided to investigate it. He found, surprisingly, that his patients suffering from "housewife's fatigue" slept more than an adult needed to sleep—as much as ten hours a day—and that the actual energy they expended on housework did not tax their capacity. The real problem must be something else, he decided—perhaps boredom. Some doctors told their women patients they must get out of the house for a day, treat themselves to a movie in town. Others prescribed tranquilizers. Many suburban housewives were taking tranquilizers like cough drops. "You wake up in the morning, and you feel as if there's no point in going on another day like this. So you take a tranquilizer because it makes you not care so much that it's pointless."

It is easy to see the concrete details that trap the suburban housewife, the continual demands on her time. But the chains that bind her in her trap are chains in her own mind and spirit. They are chains made up of mistaken ideas and misinterpreted facts, of incomplete truths and unreal choices. They are not easily seen and not easily shaken off. 40

How can any woman see the whole truth within the bounds of her own life? How can she believe that voice inside herself, when it denies the conventional, accepted truths by which she has been living? And yet the women I have talked to, who are finally listening to that inner voice, seem in some incredible way to be groping through to a truth that has defied the experts.

I think the experts in a great many fields have been holding pieces of that truth under their microscopes for a long time without realizing it. I found pieces of it in certain new research and theoretical developments in psychological, social and biological science whose implications for women seem never to have been examined. I found many clues by talking to suburban doctors, gynecologists, obstetricians, child-guidance clinicians, pediatricians, high-school guidance counselors, college professors, marriage counselors, psychiatrists and ministers—questioning them not on their theories, but on their actual experience in treating American women. I became aware of a growing body of evidence, much of which has not been reported publicly because it does not fit current modes of thought about women—evidence which throws into question the standards of feminine normality, feminine adjustment, feminine fulfillment, and feminine maturity by which most women are still trying to live.

I began to see in a strange new light the American return to early marriage and the large families that are causing the population explosion; the recent movement to natural childbirth and breastfeeding; suburban conformity, and the new neuroses, character pathologies and sexual problems being reported by the doctors. I began to see new dimensions to old problems that have long been taken for granted among women: menstrual difficulties, sexual frigidity, promiscuity, pregnancy fears, childbirth depression, the high incidence of emotional breakdown and suicide among women in their twenties and thirties, the menopause crises, the so-called passivity and immaturity of American men, the discrepancy between women's tested intellectual abilities in childhood and their adult achievement, the changing incidence of adult sexual orgasm in American women, and persistent problems in psychotherapy and in women's education.

If I am right, the problem that has no name stirring in the minds of so many American women today is not a matter of loss of femininity or too much education, or the demands of domesticity. It is far more important than anyone recognizes. It is the key to these other new and old problems which have been torturing women and their husbands and children, and puzzling their doctors and educators for years. It may well be the key to our future as a nation and a culture. We can no longer ignore that voice within women that says: "I want something more than my husband and my children and my home."

## For Discussion

1. Discuss the statistics in paragraphs 3 through 6. Friedan is talking about the decade immediately following the end of World War II. Do you think that the returning soldiers' entry into colleges and workplace could have been a factor in any of the changes in women's lives as reflected by these statistics?

2. Examine women's magazines today. To what extent do they advise women to do the things Friedan lists in paragraph 2? People today joke about Martha Stewart's advice on the domestic arts. How has the advice in women's magazines changed?

3. Discuss the reasoning in Friedan's argument. Does she have sufficient evidence to convince you that the problem with no name was a real problem?

4. In our chapter on marriage and family, Arlene Skolnik writes in "The Paradox of Perfection" about the post-industrial-revolution establishment of distinct gender roles for men and women and about the increasing emphasis on the home as the feminine sphere. Read her essay, paying particular attention to paragraphs 21 through 25. How does the ideal nineteenth-century woman as described by Skolnik compare to the woman of the "mystique" Friedan describes?

5. In paragraphs 36 and 37, Friedan describes the effects that some claim maternal over-attentiveness had on children of the 1950s. With more mothers working today, do children have fewer problems of the sort described here?

6. Friedan's work had impact in part because of the persuasive quality of Friedan's prose. Her primary audience was educated homemakers. What do you notice about Friedan's style, arrangement, and voice that would have made her book effective as persuasion? Be ready to discuss features of specific passages.

## For Inquiry

In *The Feminine Mystique,* the chapter reproduced here and the one following it describe the kinds of articles and fiction women's magazines contained in the 1950s. Get a copy of the book and read the second chapter, titled "The Happy Housewife Heroine." Friedan claims that this genre of popular culture had an enormous persuasive impact on women, in effect constructing their identities for them. Do a similar, if smaller, survey of women's magazines and best-selling books today. You may limit yourself to literature and periodicals aimed at a particular generation, such as *Seventeen* or *Redbook.* What images of successful and happy women do you find? Do you feel that these images could be constructing an identity for women today? What possible effects do you find?

## For Inquiry and Convincing

The women who subscribed to the "feminine mystique" were living a materially comfortable life. The mystique persuaded them to assume an identity as consumers, buying more appliances, furniture, decorations for the home, as well as nice clothes and beauty products for themselves. To what extent today does popular culture persuade us to an identity as consumers? What rewards does this persuasion offer? Does it promise success and fulfillment as "feminine" or "masculine" people? If you find evidence that women, men, or both are being led toward an identity based in material goods, make an argument to prove that point. Use illustrations from popular culture to support your case.

## Mission No Longer Impossible—Or Is It?
### Suzanne Fields

*Suzanne Fields is a syndicated columnist who comments here on the appearance in the late 1990s of several books by women who decided work outside the home was not as fulfilling as they had believed it would be. Notice that Fields is not actually reviewing these books in any depth but simply informing her readers about this new set of complaints. As you read, decide what her own position is on the issues raised by these books.*

Four decades ago Betty Friedan, in her groundbreaking book, *The Feminine Mystique,* wrote about women who suffer "a problem that had no name." They were sick and tired of being sick and tired of having no identity to call their own: "The problem is always being the children's mommy, or the minister's wife, and never being myself." One woman described her situation as living in a "comfortable concentration camp."

There's a new problem without a name now and it's a mare of another color. Women are complaining about work and writing about it. Elizabeth Perle McKenna left a high-powered position in publishing to search for the neglected parts of her life. In writing *When Work Doesn't Work Anymore,* she found lots of baby boomers like herself who had bought into what they call the New Oppression—hard-earned success. The symptoms include burnout, boredom and lack of balance.

The boomers are the polar opposites of Friedan's suburban housewives. Typical then was the mother of four who complained that she'd tried everything—hobbies, gardening, pickling, canning, socializing with neighbors, joining committees, running PTA teas. I love the kids and Bob and my home," she said. "There's no problem you can even put a name to. But I'm desperate. I begin to feel I have no personality."

How spoiled this woman can sound to a young mother today, who has to work to support her family and who would be thrilled to have the time to garden and can fruits and vegetables. But she sounds no more spoiled than the new whiners who complain that they're undervalued by their bosses, unfulfilled by their careers and enraged by workaholic lives where they must always hide their inner feelings. Who ever said work would be easy? (Certainly not a man.)

"I became the title on my business card," says one woman. "And while it was never a totally comfortable fit, I gauged it to be an essential part of my wardrobe, like panty hose or a brief case." She learned not to protest having to work on Saturday when there was a strategic-planning meeting, instead of taking the kids to a matinee, and never to refuse to work late. She learned to stay cool in the face of office politics and backstabbing.

With the hindsight that comes from living with half a loaf, rather than talking about what women want, even Gloria Steinem chastises these boomer women. "If I had a dollar for every time we said you couldn't do it all, I'd be rich," she says. "Look at me, I don't have it all; I never had or wanted children. And I know I couldn't have done what I have with my life if I'd had them." (So that's what she meant when she said "a woman needs a man like a fish needs a bicycle.")

Iris Krasnow, formerly a feature writer for United Press International, who interviewed the rich and the famous and gave it all up to raise a family, tells a different tale. In *Surrendering to Motherhood* (to raise four sons), she writes that she found spiritual fulfillment and deep satisfaction in newly acquired domesticity. As a full-time mother she enjoys "the liberation that comes from the sheer act of living itself."

Friedan has discovered a new "paradigm," too. In her book, *Beyond Gender,* she calls for moving beyond identity politics to reframe family values in the interest of putting children first.

Two boomer ladies, Barbara McFarland and Virginia Watson-Rouslin, agree. They've rediscovered their mothers' wisdom, written about it in a new book called simply, *My Mother Was Right,* and offer this insight: "It is now occurring to us that the person we rebelled against, whom we used as a role model of how we would not like to lead our lives and who upheld outmoded ideas on the place a woman should take in society and how she would behave . . . may not have been entirely wrong."

What goes around comes around.                                                    10

When columnist Hall Lancaster asked his *Wall Street Journal* readers to help him craft a mission statement, referring to ends and goals in life, love and work, more than 200 readers wrote about what sounds like a mission impossible. The tsunami of advice ranged from "obtaining eternal bliss to losing 20 pounds by Christmas" to "the astral projection route." For some readers it was all a matter of business procedures. Others emphasized dreams, visions, values, instincts and purpose. Some suggested he write his own obituary and still others told him to return to the pleasures of childhood.

He finally settled on the two aspects that are most important to him— his writing and his family: "My mission is to enlighten and entertain people through my writing and to help provide a life for my family that is emotionally and financially secure, loving, learning and fun."

So true. Doesn't that sound just like a woman?

---

*For Discussion*

1. How does Fields present Friedan's book *The Feminine Mystique?* What seems to be her attitude toward it in paragraphs 1, 3, and 4?
2. What is the "mission" that Fields suggests is no longer "impossible"? Does she actually conclude that women as well as men can have it all? Does the man's "mission" statement in paragraph 11 sound like

a real possibility for either sex? Does it sound "just like a woman," as Fields claims in paragraph 12?

3. How can you explain the happiness these women claim to have found in domesticity when the women Friedan interviewed in the 1950s felt so confined by domestic life?

4. A survey conducted for *American Demographics* magazine of young women aged 13–20 found that 56 percent had mothers who worked full-time outside the home throughout the girls' childhood, and 57 percent of the young women expect to do the same. Only nine percent of these young women believed "a woman's place is in the home" ("Granddaughters"). Consider the advice of Barbara McFarland and Virginia Watson-Rouslin in paragraph 9 of Fields's essay. Discuss how different generations may have different ideas of gender roles depending upon the role models they know as they grow up.

5. Of the Fortune 500 companies, only five percent are headed by women. There is still a glass ceiling in the business world. And women still make 79 cents for every dollar earned by men. Are women more likely than men to find the kind of workplace complaints listed in paragraph 4 of Fields's essay?

## For Inquiry

Read one of the books Fields describes here, or a portion of it, and explore its argument. Compare the description of domesticity with Friedan's in "The Problem That Has No Name." You might also interview some women who are full-time homemakers about how satisfying they find life.

## For Persuasion

Do research about men who have chosen to switch traditional gender roles with their wives and stay at home to take care of the home and children. How do they describe their motivations for doing this? Make an argument to persuade other men who might have considered domesticity to go ahead and take the plunge.

## For Inquiry and Convincing

Do research about women who have tried to "do it all." Make a case that it is or is not possible. Be sure to define what you mean by "it." Does "it" include success in a competitive and well-paying job? A successful marriage? A close relationship with their children? Does "it" mean living the exact same life as a family man? You might conclude that doing it all is possible provided that certain conditions exist. (Anne Roiphe's essay on pages 681–687 gives one answer to this question from the perspective of a mother and writer.)

Works Cited

"Granddaughters of Feminism." *American Demographics.* April 1, 2000, 43.

# Cartoon
## B. Smaller

*"Sex brought us together, but gender drove us apart."*

## For Discussion

The speaker is describing a relationship that broke up. Have cultural definitions of gender caused conflict in your own romantic relationships?

# Reconstructive Feminism
## Joan Williams

*Knowing the difference between sex and gender is important in understanding this essay, which is an excerpt from Joan Williams's book* Unbending Gender: Why Family and Work Conflict and What to Do About It *(Oxford, 2000). Sex refers to biological difference, whereas* gender *and* gender roles *refer to the behavior that is typical for each sex within a culture. Williams, a professor at American University Law School, argues that a gender role system that she calls "domesticity" emerged in the United States around the beginning of the nineteenth century, assigning the role of breadwinner to the male sex and the role of homemaker to the females. (For more on this historical development, see pages 467– 619 in our casebook on marriage and family.) Domesticity meant that the worker outside the home was freed from household responsibilities, and that is how the workplace has come to define its ideal workers: people who work at least forty-hour weeks, put in long overtime, travel when the job demands it, and never take personal time off for the demands of family. Williams's argument is that feminism, rather than seeking to change women's roles and lives so that they can participate in this system in a way equal to men, needs to redefine its mission to mean nothing less than changing the system itself. In this excerpt, she describes how Betty Friedan's feminism put women into the impossible predicament of trying to "have it all" as she defines a more family-friendly brand of feminism.*

The traditional feminist strategy for women's equality is for women to work full time, with child care delegated to the market. Economist Barbara Bergmann has christened this the "full-commodification strategy." Its most influential exposition was in Betty Friedan's 1962 book, *The Feminine Mystique.*[1]

This strategy proved extraordinarily effective in starting what Friedan called a "sex-role revolution": Whereas few mothers of young children were in the labor force in the 1960s, most are today. But what is required to start a revolution is often different from what is required to complete it. . . .

Friedan defended the full-commodification model by depicting housewifery as virtually a human rights violation, culminating in her famous analogy to a concentration camp.[2] In the popular imagination, feminism still is linked with the glorification of market work and the devaluation of family work. This leaves many women confused once they have children. When they feel the lure and importance of family work, they are left with the sense that feminism has abandoned them.[3] Mothers who frame their lives around caregiving may feel that feminism contributes to their defensiveness at being a part-time real estate agent or "just a housewife."

Another challenge for feminism is the sense that "all feminism ever got us was more work."[4] This reflects the situation that has resulted because the full-commodification model did not go far enough in deconstructing domesticity. This model glossed over the fact that men's market work always has been, and still is, supported by a flow of family work from women. Because women do not enjoy the same flow of family work from men, allowing women to perform as ideal workers means that most must do so without the flow of family work that permits men to be ideal workers. The result is that most women go off to work only to return home to the second shift, leaving many feeling distinctly overburdened and skeptical of feminism.

These forces have exacerbated the unpopularity of feminism among many Americans. "Don't use the word," warned a publisher, "you'll lose half your audience." A 1998 *Time*/CNN survey found that only about one-quarter of U.S. women self-identify as feminists, down from one-third in 1989; just 28 percent of those surveyed saw feminism as relevant to them personally. A common rejoinder is that a "feminist majority" supports programs such as equal pay for equal work. But the sharp disparity between support for feminist programs and support for "feminism" reinforces the sense that feminism is not a beckoning rhetoric.[5]

In part feminism's unpopularity reflects only that it is, inevitably and appropriately, inconsistent with femininity's demands for compliant and reassuring women rather than "strident" and "ball-busting" ones. But the high levels of unpopularity are tied as well to the specific inheritance of the full-commodification model. This chapter explains how and argues for a mid-course correction. Feminists need to abandon the full-commodification model in favor of a reconstructive feminism that pins hopes for women's equality on a restructuring of market work and family entitlements. Instead of defining equality as allowing women into market work on the terms traditionally available to men, we need to redefine equality as changing the relationship of market and family work so that all adults—men as well as women—can meet both family and work ideals. This new strategy holds far greater potential for raising support for feminism by building effective coalitions between women and men, as well as with unions, the "time movement," and children's rights advocates. . . .

. . . Access to market work was not a key agenda for women's rights advocates in the first half of the nineteenth century. They focused instead on gaining entitlements for women based on their family roles.[6] It was only after the Civil War that feminists began to focus on equal access to market work as the key to women's equality. Indeed, feminists from other countries often have a hard time understanding U.S. feminists' obsession with market work.[7] Why did it take on such profound importance?

Feminists' emphasis on market work reflects the freighted quality of work roles in the twentieth century. In prior eras, privileged women did not need market work to maintain their social position. In the eighteenth century status was tied not to work roles but to class: Privileged women enjoyed high levels of deference and respected social roles by virtue of their membership in the elite. This tradition of social deference gradually ended in the nineteenth century, but by then privileged women had begun to transform their accepted role as the moral beacons of the home into leadership roles within their communities. Women joined clubs, societies, and associations that took active leadership roles in many communities, and engaged in activities that subsequently have turned into consumer, welfare, and environmental activism and social work. Through the female moral reform and temperance movements, women began to challenge traditional male privileges, notably the sexual double standard and the traditional right of a man to "correct" his wife. The "age of association" offered huge numbers of women interesting work and a respected role in their communities.[8]

As the twentieth century progressed, the work formerly performed by married women in associations gradually was professionalized and taken over by men, and the Woman's Christian Temperance Union and like organizations ceased to be sources of status and became objects of derision. People began to place in work the hopes for vocation and self-fulfillment that earlier eras had reserved for religion. With increases in mobility and new patterns of social isolation, work often represented people's chief social role and the center of social life. By midcentury, for all but a tiny group of the very rich, social status was determined by work roles. Arlie Hochschild argues in her most recent book, *The Time Bind,* that today work has become the center of workers' social and emotional as well as their economic lives.[9] Work also provides the key to most social roles involving authority and responsibility even when those roles do not stem directly from the market.

Friedan's emphasis on market work reflects not only the end of the era of women's associations but also the withering of respect for women's domestic role. *The Feminine Mystique* reflects housewives' lack of status by the 1960s. "What do I do? . . . Why nothing. I'm just a housewife," quotes Friedan. In a world where adult "success" was defined by work, housewives lost a sense of self. "I begin to feel I have no personality. I'm a server of food and a putter-on of pants and a bedmaker, somebody who can be called on when you want something. But who am I?" said one. And another: "I just don't feel alive." Friedan concludes: "A woman who has no purpose of her own in society, a woman who cannot let herself think about the future because she is doing nothing to give herself a real identity in it, will continue to feel a desperation in the present. . . . You can't just deny your intelligent mind; you need to be part of the social scheme." To a nineteenth-century "moral mother," the notion that she played no part in the social scheme would have seemed bizarre.[10]

Meanwhile, increasingly misogynist attacks on housewives at midcentury were linked with the anxiety produced by the changing roles of men. Books such as David Reisman's 1950 *The Lonely Crowd* and William Whyte's 1956 *The Organization Man* reflected widespread fears that men, formerly manly and inner-directed, were becoming feminized and outer-directed by the lockstep of corporate life. Said Reisman, "Some of the occupational and cultural boundaries have broken down which help men rest assured that they are men." Whyte and Reisman painted a picture of "outer-directed" men eager for approval. They reflected men's sense of an imagined past

10

where they had independence and autonomy. Men's sense of loss was exacerbated by their loss of patriarchal authority over children, as a result of the growing importance of peer influence attributable to the rise of mass consumer culture and the spread of secondary schools. Cartoons, films, and studies abounded with imagery of henpecked men unable to stand up to domineering wives.[11] The "moral mother" had become the domineering housewife.

Friedan's belittlement of housewives was an ingenious use of misogynist stereotyping in the cause of women's liberation. She deployed misogynist images of women as evidence that the breadwinner/housewife model hurt not only women but their families as well. She skillfully turned the literature attacking housewives into evidence in favor of the need to eliminate the housewife role. She argued, first, that housewifery frustrated women so much that they made their husbands' lives a misery. To these arguments Friedan added a deadpan public health perspective: "The problem that has no name . . . is taking a far greater toll on the physical and mental health of our country than any known disease."[12]

In summary, the full-commodification strategy arose in a social context where work roles determined social status and personal fulfillment to an extent they never had before. Access to market work seemed particularly important because the only accepted alternative, the housewife role, had lost the cultural power it had enjoyed during the nineteenth century, and had become the object of misogynist attack. Ironically, the cultural devaluation of housewives ultimately came to be associated not with misogyny but with feminism. As we will see later, this stemmed in part from events that occurred after Friedan had ceased to dominate the feminist scene.

Friedan's goal was to start a "sex-role revolution." To accomplish this, she had to downplay the changes necessary to incorporate mothers into market work. First, she minimized the difficulty of finding a responsible job after a period out of the workforce. She pointed to the suburban housewife who found "an excellent job in her old field after only two trips to the city." "In Westchester, on Long Island, in the Philadelphia suburbs," she continued breezily, "women have started mental-health clinics, art centers, day camps. In big cities and small towns, women all the way from New England to California have pioneered new movements in politics and education. Even if this work was not thought of as a 'job' or 'career,' it was often so important that professionals are now being paid for doing it." "Over and over," she continued, "women told me that the crucial step for them was simply to take the first trip to the alumnae employment agency, or to send for the application for teacher certification, or to make appointments with former job contacts in the city." The only thing women had to fear, Friedan implied, was fear itself.[13]

She also minimized the question of who would take care of the children. "There are, of course, a number of practical problems involved in

15

making a serious career commitment. But somehow those problems only seem insurmountable when a woman is still half-submerged in the false dilemmas and guilts of the feminine mystique." Friedan criticized one woman willing to accept only volunteer jobs without deadlines "because she could not count on a cleaning woman. Actually," Friedan tells us, "if she had hired a cleaning woman, which many of her neighbors were doing for much less reason, she would have had to commit herself to the kind of assignments that would have been a real test of her ability." Would a "cleaning woman" really have solved this family's child care problems? Typically they come only once a week.[14]

This was one of the rare moments where Friedan mentioned household help. Her erasure of women's household work was strategic, for she knew full well what was required for a wife and mother to go back to work. When she returned to work in 1955, she hired "a really good mother-substitute— a housekeeper-nurse." But she carefully evaded this threatening issue in *The Feminine Mystique.* It soon returned to haunt women.[15]

Friedan's evasion of these difficult issues was understandable, and probably necessary, at the time she wrote *The Feminine Mystique.* If she had demanded that husbands give up their traditional entitlement to their wives' services, husbands simply would have forbidden their wives to work. If she had admitted the difficult obstacles mothers would face in a work world designed for men, her revolution never would have gotten off the ground. To give Friedan her due, she did reopen each of these questions as soon as she felt she could. By 1973 she was demanding that men share equally in family work, a theme she had mentioned but downplayed eleven years earlier. She also argued that it was "necessary to change the rules of the game to restructure professions, marriage, the family, the home." Finally, in 1981, Friedan picked up a theme she had not stressed twenty years before: that our society devalues work traditionally associated with women. In her controversial *The Second Stage,* Friedan bent over backward to send the message that she was no longer belittling family work, and demanded that work be restructured around its requirements.[16]

But by this time Friedan was no longer in control of the conversation she had helped create. Popular feminism fossilized into the full-commodification strategy and stayed there. Some feminists engaged in frontal attacks on homemaking, as in Jessie Bernard's statement that "being a housewife makes women sick." That statement was repeated almost verbatim a quarter century later in Rosalind C. Barnett and Caryl Rivers' *She Works/He Works,* which asserted in 1996 that "[t]he mommy track can be bad for your health." *She works/He Works* dramatizes the extent to which popular feminism remains stuck in the full-commodification model. It reports that women are now happy and healthy in the workforce, men are helping at home, and children are better off than ever in day care. It glosses over the pervasive marginalization of mothers, the widespread sense of strain among parents of both sexes, and the central fact that mothers' entrance into the labor force has not been accompanied by fathers' equal participation in family work.[17]

In fact, the drawbacks of the full-commodification model became evident as early as the 1970s. Some drawbacks concern its hidden racial and class dynamics. . . . Other dynamics became apparent much earlier. One way to trace the dawning recognition of these drawbacks is through stories in women's magazines in the 1970s through the 1990s. *Glamour* and *Mc-Call's* are most useful for this purpose.

Articles in the 1970s showed great excitement about the prospect of go-      20
ing to work and remind us what a big step it was to take even a part-time job for little money. "I got the check from *GLAMOUR* and bought some schoolmarm clothes. For the first time since we'd been married, I didn't feel guilty spending money on myself," recounted one woman. Another article on the same topic commented, "A very striking conclusion to come out of the questionnaire is that six out of ten women who work believe that what suffers most . . . is the quality of their housekeeping, but their letters are eloquent testimony that their most frequent reaction is, 'So what!'" This article discussed the excitement of market work and the challenges of combining this new role with their existing workload: "I don't think you have to make a choice. I never felt I had to compromise my femininity to continue to work. . . . It makes perfect sense to me to move from one area to another (i.e. home to office). In one day, I pick a fabric for a chair, arrange a party, sign a business deal, pay bills and give rich attention to my husband and children." Other articles are more realistic but still upbeat: "There is a whole generation of liberated young women who are quietly putting the ideals of revolution into practice, combining marriage, motherhood, and a master's degree, cooking and career. . . . Combining the two is far from an easy task. It is not an impossible dream but it takes hard work. The trick is in learning how; the art is in doing it well." This was the era of the Enjoli perfume ad: "I can bring home the bacon, fry it up in a pan. And never, never, never let you forget you're a man." A TV jingle declared:

> I can put the wash on the line,
> feed the kids, get dressed, pass out the kisses
> And get to work by five to nine
> 'Cause I'm a woman.[18]

By 1975 one begins to hear of "casualties." "For more than two years, Ms. Chechik ran her own interior design boutique. Being mother, wife, homemaker and career woman had . . . exhausted her physically and mentally. . . . She explained that by the time she finished all her housework, it was one or two in the morning 'and I was so hyper I couldn't sleep.' When she began breaking out in hives, [she] decided that something had to go: it was the boutique." Men also awoke to the implications of the new trends: "My husband doesn't *mind* my working, but he won't help me. He says when I can't do my own work then I'll have to quit. So naturally I don't ask him to do anything for me." Said one husband, "Now it's all very fine to agree that today's women should have more rights, but whom do they think they are going to get them from? From me, that's who. Well, I don't have enough rights as it is."[19]

Articles in the 1980s show the dawning recognition that entering the workforce without changing the conditions of work resulted in longer working hours for women. The term superwoman was coined in the early 1980s, implicitly blaming the situation on women themselves. The term deflected attention away from the fact that women were forced to do it all because men would not give up their traditional entitlement to women's household work. . . .

In the popular imagination, feminism came to be associated with careerists whose model of equality married them to money rather than to caregiving. Thus, to Deborah Fallows, "the feminist movement seemed mainly to celebrate those heroines who had made their mark in business, politics, or the arts; and magazines like *Working Mother* tried to say it was all pointless anyway, since working makes for better mothers and stronger children." Fallows bristled when she heard Gloria Steinem on the radio decrying the "narrow and stifled" lives of women at home. "The feminists may officially say that 'choice' is at the top of their agenda for women. But there are too many hints and innuendos that suggest that this talk comes fairly cheap."[20]

If the first liability of the full-commodification model is its devaluation of family work, the second is its denial that structural changes are necessary in order for women to reach equality. Women's entrance into the workforce without changes to either the structure of market work or the gendered allocation of family work means that women with full-time jobs work much longer hours than women at home. Although it made perfect sense for Friedan to argue in 1962 that women should join the workforce without waiting for changes from their husbands, their employers, or the government, it quickly became apparent that "having it all" under these circumstances often leads to exhausted women doing it all.[21] . . .

In "The Superwoman Squeeze" in 1980, *Newsweek* spotted the syndrome Arlie Hochschild named the "second shift" nine years later.[22] That article painted a picture of "an eighteen-hour mother" who works incessantly from sunup to midnight, while her husband "occasionally helps clean up or puts the boys to bed. But for the most part, Jim reads in the living room while Sue vacuums, does late-night grocery shopping, grades papers from 9 P.M. to 11 P.M. and collapses." *Newsweek* documents the "guilt, the goals, and the go-it-alone grind [that] have become achingly familiar to millions of American women." "Now we get the jobs all right," said one woman, "all the jobs: at home, with the kids, and at work."[23]

In her brilliant 1989 book *The Second Shift*, Arlie Hochschild sought to transform work/family conflict from being evidence against feminism into proof of the need for more of it. She argued that men were enjoying the

25

benefits of wives' salaries but refused to share equally in household work. Through carefully constructed narratives, she communicated the message that women's failure to perform as ideal workers was attributable in significant part to their husbands' failure to shoulder their fair share of family work.[24]

Hochschild crystallized an important change. Once husbands lost their felt entitlement to have women do all the housework, the revised standard version of the full-commodification model stressed the need to reallocate household work. This was a shift in focus away from early feminists' reliance on the government, as they envisioned day care centers as being as common, and as free, as public libraries. Thus the solution Hochschild highlighted in the first edition of her bestseller was a redistribution of family work between fathers and mothers (a shift from her path-breaking call nearly twenty years earlier for restructuring of "the clockwork of male careers").[25]

Another element of the full-commodification model was its focus on relatively privileged women. This emphasis was reflected both in the assumption that market work meant high-status, high-paying careers, and in the assumption that child care should be delegated to the market, often without much consideration of what this would mean for women who cannot afford quality child care.[26]

The final assumption of full-commodification feminism was that women should be ready, willing, and able to delegate child care to the same extent male ideal workers do. This proved the most problematic assumption of all.

### The Norm of Parental Care

> Every day I leave my kids at day care, I think to myself: *What kind of a mother am I?* It's like I'm not raising my own children.[27]

> The biggest problem as I see it for both men and women [lawyers] is how to balance children in a large-firm environment. I plan to go part-time when I have a child, and I *hate* the idea. If the firm had a 24-hour day care or nursery, I would not work part-time—I would stay full-time. Obviously, even this is no solution: kids can't grow up in a day care center.[28]

A central assumption of the full-commodification model was that women    30
would feel comfortable delegating family work to the market to the same extent traditional fathers had. Many don't. . . .

Lillian Rubin comments, "The notion that mom should be there for the children always and without fall, that her primary job is to tend and nurture them, that without her constant ministrations their future is in jeopardy, is deeply embedded in our national psyche." Mothers who do not stay home often find themselves wondering, as did the woman quoted earlier, "What kind of a mother am I?" Sometimes this manifests as explicit gender policing; an extreme example is the hate mail received by the Boston family whose nanny killed their son. "It seems the parents didn't really want a kid," said one caller to a talk show host. "Now they don't have one." Note that the mother "at fault" worked only part time.[29]

. . . [T]wo-thirds of Americans believe it would be best for women to stay home and care for family and children. In significant part, this reflects the paucity of attractive alternatives.[30] In European countries, the shift of mothers into the workforce was supported through government benefits. In Russia and Eastern Europe, programs included maternity leave with guaranteed reemployment, sick leave, and paid time off for child care and housework. In Western Europe, high-quality child care is provided or subsidized by the government. In France, an extensive system of neighborhood child-care centers exists throughout the country, staffed by trained teachers and psychologists, with ready access to medical personnel, so that children's illnesses are both spotted and treated at the center. Parents fight to get their children in, with the sense that being in child care helps children develop social skills. In Belgium and France an estimated 95 percent of nursery-school-age children are in publicly funded child care. Sweden also has a comprehensive system of quality child care.[31]

In the United States, feminists' dream that day care facilities would be as common as public libraries never came true. In 1971, when Congress passed the Comprehensive Child Development Act, President Nixon vetoed it under pressure from an intense lobbying campaign that decried the proposal as "a radical piece of social legislation" designed to deliver children to "communal approaches to child-rearing over and against the family-centered approach." A 1975 proposal was also defeated, decried as an effort to "sovietize the family." As a result, the United States offers less governmental support for child care than does any other industrialized nation. The successful efforts to defeat the kinds of proposals implemented in Europe dramatizes how profoundly U.S. women have been affected by Americans' distinctive lack of solidarity.[32]

As a result, the imagery and the reality of day care are different here than elsewhere. Where child care is prevalent and government-sponsored, it is seen as an expression of social solidarity and national investment in the next generation. In sharp contrast, in the United States, day care is seen as an expression of the market. These perceptions are accurate in part. In countries with significant government support for child care, notably France, child-care workers are well-paid civil servants with steady and respected employment. Child care in the United States, in sharp contrast, suffers from very low wages and very high turnover. One child-care worker of my acquaintance works for Head Start; after fourteen years and several promotions, she now earns about $14,000 a year. At these pay rates, high rates of turnover are not surprising. Nor is it surprising that many Americans have a negative image of day care centers. While many centers are excellent, market realities militate against quality child care.[33]

Day care in the United States also suffers from imagery and symbolism    35
derived from domesticity. Recall the insistent split between home and market. [. . . D]omesticity from the beginning provided very negative images of
the market. If economics encapsulates our positive imagery of the market
as the benign deliverer of quality goods to satisfied customers, domesticity
embeds very different imagery of the market as a selfish and calculating
world out of touch with people's needs for genuine intimacy. Throwing
child care into this metaphoric maelstrom in a society without a third
realm of social solidarity results in a predictable revulsion against market
solutions. Some people preserve the negative market imagery for day care
centers and contrast it with their chosen form of care. Despite the shift of
child care into the market, today most Americans choose child care that is
as homelike as they can manage. Keep in mind that one-third of married
mothers, and a slightly higher percentage of single ones, are home full-
time. Most children not cared for by their mothers are cared for by another
relative — care by relatives (typically fathers or grandmothers) accounts for
nearly 50 percent of all children in child care. Another 22 percent are cared
for by nannies in their own homes, or in the homes of their sitters. All in
all, in one-half to one-third of families, mothers are at home. In the remaining families, about 70 percent of children are in care associated with
home or family. Only about 30 percent of children in child care are in day
care centers.[34] . . .

A second major force feeding the resistance to day care as a solution is
the sharp increase in the number of hours in the workweek. Juliet Schor, in
*The Overworked American*, documented that Americans' average workweek
has lengthened in recent years. Increases are concentrated in "good" jobs
with a high benefits "load," which include high-paying blue-collar jobs as
well as many high-status white-collar jobs. Factory workers in 1994 put in
the highest levels of overtime ever registered. Nearly one-fourth of office
workers now work forty-nine or more hours a week. A survey of Fortune
500 corporations in the 1970s found that many managers worked sixty
hours a week or more, excluding business travel: "They'd leave home at
7:30 A.M. and return home about the same time that evening. They'd also
bring home a few hours of work each day." This has not changed much.
. . . [O]ne-third of fathers work forty-nine or more hours a week; in high-
status white-collar jobs it is closer to 50 percent. Said one forty-one-year-
old public relations officer in a major corporation: "I can't imagine having
a baby, which I want to do, and still keeping this job. All corporate jobs are
like this — you're valued according to the long hours you are willing to put
in, and the schedule is so rigid that anyone who wants to do it differently
has to leave." Schor notes, "The 5:00 Dads of the 1950s and 1960s (those
who were home for dinner and an evening with the family) are becoming
an endangered species." The increase in hours means that an ideal worker
with a half-hour commute to a "good" job often will be away from home
from 8:00 A.M. to 7 P.M. Very few people would consider this an ideal sched-

ule for both parents in a family with children. The result is often that, among people with access to "good" jobs, fathers work overtime while mothers work part-time or on the no-overtime mommy track. Families see little choice.[35]

The forces named thus far—the lack of social solidarity and the sharp increase in working hours—are peculiar to the United States. However, data from Sweden raise intriguing questions about whether the full-commodification model is viable even where these peculiarly American conditions do not exist.

Sweden has implemented the full-commodification model with a level of commitment higher than anyplace else in the world. As a result of a severe labor shortage in a country with no self-consciousness about crafting governmental solutions to social problems, Sweden encouraged workforce participation by mothers by providing child care as well as generous parental leaves available to either parent, accompanied by government efforts to increase men's participation in family work.

The result has not been equality for women. Swedish mothers still suffer marginalization in order to care for children. As of 1986, 43 percent of working women were employed part time. Women continued to do a disproportionate share of family work and took fifty-two days of leave for every day taken by a man. Industrial workers were much less likely to take parental leave than were professional and public employees. Sweden's level of sex segregation is *higher* than even our own very high level: One study concluded that 70 percent of all women would have to change occupations for women to achieve the same occupational distribution as men. Swedish women earn only 37 percent of the country's total wages.[36]

These findings place the full-commodification strategy in a somber light. The Swedish example suggests that many people in advanced industrialized countries feel that having both parents working the ideal-worker schedule is inconsistent with the level and type of parental attention children need. This reflects the fact that children's success in these middle-class societies depends in part on parents' ability to instill the discipline, motivation, and independence necessary to do well in middle-class life.

To say this in a less clinical way, one key to success in life is having your children turn out well: healthy, well-adjusted, secure, successful (in widely varying senses of the word). We are willing to give up a lot to achieve this; often we do. In the face of our dreams for our children, marginalization at work often seems a price worth paying even if it may lead to disappointments or to economic vulnerability later on in life.

All this suggests that it is time to acknowledge the *norm of parental care.* Let me say loud and clear that this is not the same as saying that children need full-time mothercare. Domesticity's mother-as-sole-source ideal is not ideal at all. Its most important drawback is that it links caregiving with disempowerment. Not only does this make children vulnerable to impoverishment if their parents divorce; it also means that the adults who know our children best and are most invested in meeting their needs have relatively little power within the household and outside of it. Sociological studies since the 1960s have documented that power within the family generally tracks power outside it.[37] . . .

While Friedan was right to reject that model, the time has come to abandon the fiction that both mothers and fathers can perform as ideal workers in a system designed for men supported by a flow of family work from women. We need to open a debate on how much parental care children truly need given the trade-offs between providing money and providing care. A good place to start is with the consensus that children are not best served if both parents are away from home eleven hours a day. This means that the jobs that require fifty-hour workweeks are designed in a way that conflicts with the norm of parental care.

Beyond the fifty-hour week, little consensus exists about how much child care is delegable. However, once feminists name and acknowledge the norm of parental care, discussions of how much delegation is too much will replace conversations in which mothers protest that they "chose" to cut back or quit when further investigation reveals that they did so because they could not find quality child care, or because the father works such long hours that without a marginalized mother the children would rarely see a parent awake.

A formal acknowledgment of the norm of parental care will serve a sec-    45
ond important purpose as well: to empower mothers in situations where their partners meet demands for equal contributions to family work by claiming that virtually all child care is delegable. This dynamic does not emerge when mothers marginalize without a fuss; in such cases the conclusion that not all child care is delegable typically is treated as a matter of consensus. But when mothers refuse to follow docilely in domesticity's caregiver role, a game of chicken emerges in which fathers advocate higher levels of delegation than mothers consider appropriate. The classic example is of the high-status father who advocates hiring two sets of nannies to give sixteen hours of coverage so that no one's career is hurt. Or the father who suggested that his wife hire a babysitter to care for the children during a weekend when he had promised to be available so that she could take a long-planned trip. One ambitious father expressed it this way: "Over-involvement with children may operate to discourage many fathers from fully sharing because they do not accept the ideology of close attention to children."[38] Until this "ideology" is formally stated and publicly defended, mothers will have their decision to marginalize cited as evidence of their own personal priorities (for which they should naturally be willing to make trade-offs) rather than as an expression of a societal ideal (for which parents share equal responsibility).

Naming and acknowledging the norm of parental care can help poor women as well as more privileged ones. One central difficulty in the welfare reform debate is the lack of a language in which to defend the right of poor women to stay home with their children, in a society where the child care available to them is often not only unstimulating but downright unsafe. . . . [I]t is hard to defend poor women's right to stay home in a society where a much higher percentage of poor women than of working-class women are homemakers: about 33 percent of poor women are at home, but only about 20 percent of working-class ones. This situation is bound to generate working-class anger. Naming the norm of parental care is not enough to change the dynamics of the welfare debate; that will require a social system where working-class as well as poor children are seen as being entitled to a certain amount of parental care. But acknowledging the existence of a norm of parental care is an important first step.[39]

Defining the norm of parental care starts from an assessment of children's needs, and then splits the resulting responsibilities down the middle. In such a world, mothers' work patterns would look much more similar to fathers'. Consider the following example. Say the parents of elementary-school children decide that one parent needs to be home two days a week, to drive the children to doctor and dentist appointments, to enable them to take lessons not available in the after-school program, to help with homework, to allow for play dates. Then the father and the mother would both work four days each week, and half a day or not at all the fifth. This would be much easier for an employer to accommodate than if the mother comes in alone demanding a three-day week. "They are so unreasonable," a top manager complained to me recently. "A woman came in demanding a three-day schedule. We told her she could either work four days a week and keep her [middle-level] management position, or three days a week in which case she would have to give it up, because things around here just won't run with a three-day-a-week manager. She got angry and quit." If fathers were truly sharing in family work, mothers' demands would be much easier to accommodate. This would end the situation where the only viable alternative a family sees is to have the mother quit or go part-time (making, on average, 40 percent less per hour than a full-time worker), in which case the father has to work overtime to make up for the loss in income. A more equal sharing of market and family work would also avoid the situation where, if the parents divorce, the children are impoverished along with their marginalized mother. We have much to gain from shifting to a strategy of reconstructing both the ideal-worker and marginalized-caregiver roles we have inherited from domesticity. The time has come to abandon the full-commodification strategy in favor of ending the system of providing for children's care by marginalizing their caregivers. This is the agenda of reconstructive feminism.

. . . In my view feminism has never been anti-family, but the time has come to point out that feminism is pro-family, in that it advocates changes that will help children as well as women. The system of providing care by marginalizing the caregivers hurts not only children but also the sick and the elderly. The current system rests on the assumption that all people at all times are the full-grown, healthy adults of liberal theory, making the social compact and pursuing citizenship and self-interest within it. This is a very unrealistic view of human life. The time has come to recognize that humanity does not consist only of healthy adults. We have changed from a society that formally delegates to women the care of children, the sick, and the elderly to a society that pretends those groups do not exist. The result, to women's credit, is that women still do the caregiving. But they pay a stiff price for doing so. . . .

. . . The early feminist vision of two parents working forty-hour weeks did not come to pass; neither did the vision of child-care centers being as common and as respected as public libraries. What we have instead [. . .] is an economy of mothers and others, where many fathers work overtime and a majority of mothers are not ideal workers. This chapter proposes that we abandon the full-commodification strategy in favor of transforming domesticity's norm of mothercare into a template for restructuring the relationship of market work and family work.

If we as a society take seriously children's need for parental care, it is     50
time to stop marginalizing the adults who provide it. The current structure of work is not immutable: it was invented at a particular point in time to suit particular circumstances. Those circumstances have changed. [. . .]

Notes

1. Betty Friedan, *The Feminine Mystique* (1962; 1983). Barbara Bergmann, *The Only Ticket to Equality*, 9 J. Contemp. L. Issues 75 (1998).

2. Friedan, *supra* note 4, at 282 *et seq.* (concentration camp).

3. Anna Quindlen, *Let's Anita Hill This*, N.Y. Times, Feb. 28, 1993, at 15 ("At a meeting I attended, one of the women said that the women's movement had been the guiding force in her life until she had children, and then she felt abandoned by feminist rhetoric and concerns.")

4. Steven A. Holmes, *Is This What Women Want?*, N.Y. Times, Dec. 15, 1996, at 1 (quoting Heidi Hartman: "That may be feeding some of the backlash against feminism among some women. People are saying that all feminism ever got us was more work").

5. *See* Ginia Bellafante, *Feminism: It's All About Me!*, Time, June 29, 1998, at 54. The "feminist majority" argument is associated with the Fund for a Feminist Majority, now called the Feminist Majority Foundation. *See* <http://www.feminist.org>. *See also* Nancy Levit, *The Gender Line* 123–67 (1998).

6. Reva Siegel *Home as Work*, 103 Yale L. J. 1073.

7. *See, e.g.*, Paolo Wright-Carozza, *Organic Goods: Legal Understandings of Work, Parenthood, and Gender Equality in Comparative Perspective*, 81 Cal. L. Rev. 531 (1993).

8. *See* Barbara L. Epstein, *The Politics of Domesticity: Women, Evangelism, and Temperance in Nineteenth Century America* (1981). *See generally* Sara Evans, *Born for Liberty: A History of Women in America* 67–143 (1989) (discussing emergence of

women's associational activity); *see also* Epstein, *supra* note 10, at 115–51 (1981) (describing growth of Woman's Christian Temperance Union), Evelyn Brooks Higginbotham, *Righteous Discontent: The Women's Movement in the Black Baptist Church, 1880–1920* (1993).

9. Arlie R. Hochschild, *The Time Bind: When Work Becomes Home and Home Becomes Work* (1997).

10. Friedan, *supra* note 1, at 24 (first quote), 21 (second), 22 (third), 343–44 (fourth).

11. *See* Wini Breines, *Young, White, and Miserable: Growing Up Female in the Fifties* 28–29. (1992); *id.* at 32–33 (quoting Reisman).

12. *Id.* at 364. *See* Glenna Matthews, *"Just a Housewife"* 197–200 (1987) (misogynist stereotyping); Friedan, *supra* note 1, at 350, 364.

13. Friedan, *supra* note 1, at 384 (sex-role revolution), 349 (only two trips), 345 ("now being paid"), 349 (last quote).

14. *Id.*

15. Daniel Horowitz, *Rethinking Betty Friedan and* The Feminine Mystique: *Labor Union Radicalism and Feminism in Cold War America*, 48 Am. Q. 1, 20 (1996) (Friedan quote).

16. *See* Friedan, *supra* note 1, at 350, 354, 385; Betty Friedan, *The Second stage* (1981).

17. Breines, *supra* note 14, at 32–33 (first quote: quoting Jessie Bernard); Rosalind C. Barnett & Carl Rivers, *She Works, He Works: How Two-Income Families Are Happier, Healthier, and Better off* 32 (1996) (second). *See also* Jessie Bernard, *The Future of Marriage* (1972, reprint 1973).

18. Rivvy Berkman, *The Funny, Searching, Scary, Devastatingly Honest Diary of A Young Woman's Decision to Return to Work*, Glamour, Sept. 1971, at 280 (schoolmarm clothes); Vivian Cadden, *How Women Really Feel About Working*, McCall's, June 1974, at 125 (So what!); Roberta Brandes Gratz & Elizabeth Pochoda, *Women's Lib: So Where Do Men Fit In*, Glamour, July 1970, at 138 (rich attention; not an impossible dream); Claudia Wallis, *Onward, Women: The Superwoman Is Weary, the Young Are Complacent but Feminism Is Not Dead, and Baby. There's Still a Long Way to Go*, Time, Dec. 4, 1989, at 80, 81 ("fry it up in a pan"); Lynn Langway, *The Superwoman Squeeze*, Newsweek, May 19, 1980, at 256 (TV jingle).

19. Shirley G. Streshin, *The Guilt of the Working Mother*, Glamour, Sept. 1975, at 256 (Mrs. Chechik); Gratz & Pochoda, *supra* note 21, at 138 (not enough rights).

20. Deborah Fallows, *A Mother's Work* 28, 214 (1985) (all three quotes).

21. *See* Joan C. Williams, *Gender Wars: Selfless Women in the Republic of Choice*, 66 N.Y.U.L. Rev. 1559, 1612 (1991).

22. *See* Langway, *supra* note 21. Arlie Hochschild found that, after adding together the time it takes to do home and child care with the time it takes to do a paying job, women work about fifteen hours longer per week than do men. *See* Hochschild, *supra* note 12, at 3.

23. Langway, *supra* note 21, at 72 (all other quotes).

24. *See generally* Hochschild, *supra* note 12, at 110–27.

25. *See id.* at 257–78, Arlie Hochschild, Inside the Clockwork of Male Careers, in *Women and the Power to Change* (Florence Howe ed., 1971).

26. *See id.* at 266–70.

27. Lillian Rubin, *Families on the Fault Line* 79 (1994).

28. Emily Couric, *Women in Large Firms: A Higher Price of Admission?*, Nat. L. J., Dec. 11, 1989, at S2, S12.

29. Rubin, *supra* note 32, at 79 (national psyche); Peggy Orenstein, *Almost Equal*, N.Y. Times, Apr. 5, 1998, § 6 (Magazine), at 45 (Boston nanny).

30. *See* Richard Morin & Megan Rosenfeld, *With More Equity, More Sweat; Poll Shows Sexes Agree on Pros and Cons of New Roles*, Wash. Post, Mar. 22, 1998, at A1 (two-thirds).

31. *See* Joan C. Williams, *Privatization as a Gender Issue*, in *A Fourth Way? Privatization, Property, and the Emergence of the New Market Economics* 215 (Gregory S. Alexander & Grazyna Skapka eds., 1994) (Russia and East-Central Europe); Barbara Bergmann, *Saying Our Children from Poverty: What the United States Can Learn from France* (1996). (data on France and Belgium); Marlise Simons, *Child Care Sacred as France Cuts Back the Welfare State*, N.Y. Times, Dec. 31, 1997, at A1 (Fench parents fight to get children in); Marguerite G. Rosenthal, *Sweden: Promise and Paradox*, in *The Feminization of Poverty: Only in America?* (Gertrude Schaffuel Goldberg & Eleanor Kremen eds., 1990) 129, 137, 144, 147–49 (Sweden).

32. Mary Frances Berry. *The Politics of Parenthood* 137–38, 142 (1993) (Nixon quote; 1975 quote); Jane Rigler, *Analysis and Understanding of the Family and Medical Leave Act of 1993*, 45 Case W. Res. L. Rev. 457 (1995) (less governmental support in United States).

33. *See* Gina C. Adams & Nicole Oxendine Poersch, Children's Defense. Fund, Key Facts About Child Care and Early Education: A Briefing Book, at B-7 (1997) (low pay and high turnover).

34. Press Release from University of Tennessee News Center, by Dr. Jan Allen, at <http://www.utenn.edu/uwa/vpps/ur/news/may96/kidcare.htm>.

35. *See* Juliet B. Schor, *The Overworked American* 30 tbl. 2.2 (1992) (Hours per Week, Labor Force Participants) (only those fully employed) (workweek); Peter T. Kilborn, *The Work Week Grows; Tales from the Digital Treadmill*, N.Y. Times, June 3, 1990, § 4 (Week in Review), at 1 (24 percent; managers' hours; first quote); Peter T. Kilborn, *It's Too Much of a Good Thing, G.M. Workers Say in Protesting Overtime*, N.Y. Times, Nov. 22, 1994, at A16 (production workers); Schor, *supra*, at 41 (5:00 dad); Ureta Census Data, *see* note 4 in the introduction (one-third of fathers).

36. *See* Rosenthal, *supra* note 36, at 137, 144, 147–49; Janeen Baxter & Emily W. Kane, *Dependence and Independence: A Cross-National Analysis of Gender Inequality and Gender Attitudes*, 9 Gender & Soc'y 193, 195 (1995) (level of sex segregation).

37. For power studies, see Robert O. Blood & Donald M. Wolfe, *Husbands and Wives: The Dynamics of Married Living* (1960); Phyllis N. Hallenbeck, *An Analysis of Power Dynamic in Marriage*, 28 J. Marriage & Family 200 (1966); Gerald W. McDonald, *Family Power: The Assessment of a Decade of Theory and Research, 1970–1979*, J. Marriage & Family 841 (1980); Paula England & Barbara Stanek Kil-

bourne, *Markets, Marriages, and Other Mates: The Problem of Power,* in *Beyond the Market Place: Rethinking Economy and Society* (Roger Friedland & A. F. Robertson eds., 1990).

38. *See* S. M. Miller, *The Making of a Confused, Middle-Aged Husband,* in *Men and Masculinity* 44, 50 (Joseph H. Pleck & Jack Sawyer eds., 1974); Rosenthal, *supra* note 36, at 137, 144, 147–49.

39. Bureau of Labor Statistics, U.S. Department of Labor, Unpublished Marital and Family Tabulations from the Current Population Survey, tbl. 28A (1996) ("Unemployed Persons Not at Work and Persons at Work in Nonagricultural Industries by Actual Hours of Work at All Jobs During Reference Week, Marital Status, Sex, and Age, Annual Average 1995").

---

## For Discussion

1. What is the "full-commodification strategy" version of women's equality with men? What happens to housekeeping and child rearing under the full-commodification strategy?
2. Why does Williams feel that a nationwide, state-supported system of day care is not a solution to the problems of raising children in a society where men and women are equal in the workplace? What reasons and evidence does she offer to show that day care is not a viable solution?
3. In contrast to the commodification strategy and day care, Williams offers the norm of parental care. Explain what she means by this and how it could be achieved.
4. In the preface to her book, Williams cites that working mothers earn 60 cents to every dollar earned by working fathers. Compare this to the average of all women to all men, which was 79 cents to every dollar as we went to press with this book. What can explain why mothers' salaries are so much lower than fathers'? Look at paragraph 36, which talks about the time commitments of ideal workers in "good" jobs. Do you believe that Williams has made a good case to show that workplace and parenting are in conflict?
5. What evidence does Williams give that in spite of our proclaimed interest in children, our society has put business interests ahead of family interests? What evidence do you observe that corroborates her view? If you feel that you were raised in the "full-commodification" type of household, do you agree or disagree that it hurts children?

## For Inquiry

Williams depicts the nationalized day care system in Sweden as ineffective in helping to bring about equality of the sexes. Look into the results in other countries, such France, that are known for providing high-quality, state-funded day care to determine if they also stop short of helping women achieve equality with men in the workplace.

*For Inquiry and Convincing*

In the second chapter of her book, Williams suggests some options for management to change the workplace from its traditional "male" norms, which assume a worker has no responsibilities at home. Do further research into businesses that have tried to install more family-friendly policies. Do you find many that truly meet Williams's objections to the model of "domesticity" with its devaluation of all work connected to child rearing and homemaking? What policies encourage a norm of parental involvement? Write an argument to convince your readers that such policies are possible and useful, or if you decide that they are unrealistic and bad for the economy, make a case against changing the status quo.

*For Persuasion*

If you believe that creating a "norm of parental involvement" would be a good thing for men, women, and children, imagine a society in which such a norm existed, and write a description of this parental "utopia" that would encourage your readers to bring it about.

# Cartoon

## Garry Trudeau

### Doonesbury

BY GARRY TRUDEAU

*For Discussion*

In the cartoon, two working parents are talking about raising their son. Why is the mother angry with her husband? What comment does the cartoon make about the difficulty of escaping from the gender roles our parents model for us?

# The Independent Woman (and Other Lies)
## Katie Roiphe

*Katie Roiphe is a controversial figure among feminists. Her well-known book* The Morning After: Sex, Fear, and Feminism on Campus *(1993) attempted to prove that concern over "date rape" on college campuses was inflated, the result of women's refusal to take responsibility for their own sexual behavior. In this reading, which was originally printed in a men's magazine,* Esquire, *in 1997, she reflects on a recurring fantasy that she knows is politically incorrect in "our liberated, postfeminist world."*

I was out to drinks with a man I'd recently met. "I'll take care of that," he said, sweeping up the check, and as he said it, I felt a warm glow of security, as if everything in my life was suddenly going to be taken care of. As the pink cosmopolitans glided smoothly across the bar, I thought for a moment of how nice it would be to live in an era when men always took care of the cosmopolitans. I pictured a lawyer with a creamy leather briefcase going off to work in the mornings and coming back home in the evenings to the townhouse he has bought for me, where I have been ordering flowers, soaking in the bath, reading a nineteenth-century novel, and working idly on my next book. This fantasy of a Man in a Gray Flannel Suit is one that independent, strong-minded women of the nineties are distinctly not supposed to have, but I find myself having it all the same. And many of the women I know are having it also.

Seen from the outside, my life is the model of modern female independence. I live alone, pay my own bills, and fix my stereo when it breaks down. But it sometimes seems like my independence is in part an elaborately constructed facade that hides a more traditional feminine desire to be protected and provided for. I admitted this once to my mother, an ardent seventies feminist, over Caesar salads at lunch, and she was shocked. I saw it on her face: How could a daughter of mine say something like this? I rushed to reassure her that I wouldn't dream of giving up my career, and it's true that I wouldn't. But when I think about marriage, somewhere deep in the irrational layers of my psyche, I still think of the man as the breadwinner. I feel as though I am working for "fulfillment," for "reward," for the richness of life promised by feminism, and that mundane things such as rent and mortgages and college tuitions are, ultimately, the man's responsibility—even though I know that they shouldn't be. "I just don't want to have to think about money," one of my most competent female friends said to me recently, and I knew exactly what she meant. Our liberated, postfeminist world seems to be filled with women who don't want to think about money and men who feel that they have to.

There are plenty of well-adjusted, independent women who never fantasize about the Man in the Gray Flannel suit, but there are also a surprising number who do. Of course, there is a well-established tradition of women looking for men to provide for them that spans from Edith Wharton's *The House of Mirth* to Helen Gurley Brown's *Sex and the Single Girl* to Mona Simpson's *A Regular Guy.* You could almost say that this is the American dream for women: Find a man who can lift you out of your circumstances, whisk you away to Venice, and give you a new life.

In my mother's generation, a woman felt she had to marry a man with a successful career, whereas today she is supposed to focus on her own. Consider that in 1990, women received 42 percent of law degrees (up from 2.5 percent in 1960) and that as of 1992, women held 47 percent of lucrative jobs in the professions and management. And now that American women are more economically independent than ever before, now that we don't need to attach ourselves to successful men, many of us still seem to want to. I don't think, in the end, that this attraction is about bank accounts or trips to Paris or hundred dollar haircuts, I think it's about the reassuring feeling of being protected and provided for, a feeling that mingles with love and attraction on the deepest level. It's strange to think of professional women in the nineties drinking cafe lattes and talking about men in the same way as characters in Jane Austen novels, appraising their prospects and fortunes, but many of us actually do.

A friend of mine, an editor at a women's magazine, said about a recent breakup, "I just hated having to say, 'My boyfriend is a dog walker.' I hated the fact that he didn't have a real job." And then immediately afterward, she said, "I feel really awful admitting all of this." It was as if she had just told me something shameful, as if she had confessed to some terrible perversion. And I understand why she felt guilty. She was admitting to a sort of 1950s worldview that seemed as odd and unfashionable as walking down the street in a poodle skirt. But she is struggling with what defines masculinity and femininity in a supposedly equal society, with what draws us to men, what attracts us, what keeps us interested. She has no more reason to feel guilty than a man who says he likes tall blonds.

I've heard many women say that they wouldn't want to go out with a man who is much less successful than they are because "he would feel uncomfortable." But, of course, he's not the only one who would feel uncomfortable. What most of these women are really saying is that they themselves would feel uncomfortable. But why? Why can't the magazine editor be happy with the dog walker? Why does the woman at Salomon Brothers feel unhappy with the banker who isn't doing as well as she is? Part of it may have to do with the way we were raised. Even though I grew up in a liberal household in the seventies, I perceived early on that my father was the one who actually paid for things. As a little girl, I watched my father put his credit card down in restaurants and write checks and go to work every morning in a suit and tie, and it may be that this model of masculinity is still imprinted in my mind. It may be that there is a picture of our fathers that many of us carry like silver lockets around our necks: Why shouldn't we find a man who will take care of us the way our fathers did?

I've seen the various destructive ways in which this expectation can affect people's lives. Sam and Anna met at Brown. After they graduated, Anna went to Hollywood and started making nearly a million dollars a year in television production, and Sam became an aspiring novelist who has never even filed a tax return. At first, the disparity in their styles of life manifested itself in trivial ways. "She would want to go to an expensive bistro," Sam, who is now twenty-seven, remembers, "and I would want to get a burrito for $4.25. We would go to the bistro, and either she'd pay, which was bad, or I'd just eat salad and lots of bread, which was also bad." In college, they had been the kind of couple who stayed up until three in the morning talking about art and beauty and *The Brothers Karamazov,* but now they seemed to be spending a lot of time arguing about money and burritos. One night, when they went out with some of Anna's Hollywood friends, she slipped him eighty dollars under the table so that he could pretend to pay for dinner. Anna felt guilty. Sam was confused. He had grown up with a feminist mother who'd drummed the ideal of strong, independent women into his head, but now that he'd fallen in love with Anna, probably the strongest and most independent woman he'd ever met, she wanted him to pay for her dinner so badly she gave him money to do it. Anna, I should say, is not a particularly materialistic person, she is not someone who cares about Chanel suits and Prada bags. It's just that to her, money had become a luminous symbol of functionality and power.

The five-year relationship began to fall apart. Sam was not fulfilling the role of romantic lead in the script Anna had in her head. In a moment of desperation, Sam blurted out that he had made a lot of money on the stock market. He hadn't. Shortly afterward, they broke up. Anna started dating her boss, and she and Sam had agonizing long-distance phone calls about what had happened. "She kept telling me that she wanted me to be more of a man," Sam says. "She kept saying that she wanted to be taken care of." There was a certain irony to this situation, to this woman who was making almost a million dollars a year, sitting in her Santa Monica house, looking out at the ocean, saying that she just wanted a man who could take care of her.

There is also something appalling in this story, something cruel and hard and infinitely understandable. The strain of Anna's success and Sam's as of yet unrewarded talent was too much for the relationship. When Anna told Sam that she wanted him to be more masculine, part of what she was saying was that she wanted to feel more feminine. It's like the plight of the too-tall teenage girl who's anxiously scanning the dance floor for a fifteen-year-old boy who is taller than she is. A romantic might say, What about love? Love isn't supposed to be about dollars and cents and who puts their Visa card down at an expensive Beverly Hills restaurant. But this is a story about love in its more tarnished, worldly forms, it's about the balance of power, what men and women really want from one another, and the hidden mechanics of romance and attraction. In a way, what happened between my friends Sam and Anna is a parable of the times, of a generation of strong women who are looking for even stronger men.

I've said the same thing as Anna — "I need a man who can take care of   10
me" — to more than one boyfriend, and I hear how it sounds. I recognize how shallow and unreasonable it seems. But I say it anyway. And, even worse, I actually feel it.

The mood passes. I realize that I can take care of myself. The relationship returns to normal, the boyfriend jokes that I should go to the bar at the plaza to meet bankers, and we both laugh because we know that I don't really want to, but there is an undercurrent of resentment, eddies of tension and disappointment that remain between us. This is a secret refrain that runs through conversations in bedrooms late at night, through phone wires, and in restaurants over drinks. One has to wonder, why, at a moment in history when women can so patently take care of themselves, do so many of us want so much to be taken care of?

The fantasy of a man who pays the bills, who works when you want to take time off to be with your kids or read *War and Peace,* who is in the end responsible, is one that many women have but fairly few admit to. It is one of those fantasies, like rape fantasies, that have been forbidden to us by our politics. But it's also deeply ingrained in our imaginations. All of girl culture tells us to find a man who will provide for us, a Prince Charming, a Mr. Rochester, a Mr. Darcy, a Rhett Butler. These are the objects of our earliest romantic yearnings, the private desires of a whole country of little girls, the fairy tales that actually end up affecting our real lives. As the feminist film critic Molly Haskell says, "We never really escape the old-fashioned roles. They get inside our heads. Dependence has always been eroticized."

Many of the men I know seem understandably bewildered by the fact that women want to be independent only sometimes, only sort of, and only selectively. The same women who give eloquent speeches at dinner parties on the subject of "glass ceilings" still want men to pay for first dates, and this can be sort of perplexing for the men around them who are still trying to fit into the puzzle that the feminism of the seventies has created for them. For a long time, women have been saying that we don't want a double standard, but it sometimes seems that what many women want is simply a more subtle and refined version of a double standard: We want men to be the providers and to regard us as equals. This slightly unreasonable expectation is not exactly new. In 1963, a reporter asked Mary McCarthy what women really wanted, and she answered, "They want everything. That's the trouble — they can't have everything. They can't possibly have all the prerogatives of being a woman and the privileges of being a man at the same time."

"We're spoiled," says Helen Gurley Brown, one of the world's foremost theorists on dating. "We just don't want to give up any of the good stuff." And she may have a point. In a world in which women compete with men, in which all of us are feeling the same drive to succeed, there is something reassuring about falling—if only for the length of a dinner—into traditional sex roles. You can just relax. You can take a rest from yourself. You can let the pressures and ambitions melt away and give in to the archaic fantasy: For just half an hour, you are just a pretty girl smiling at a man over a drink. I think that old-fashioned rituals, such as men paying for dates, endure precisely because of how much has actually changed; they cover up the fact that men and women are equal and that equality is not always, in all contexts and situations, comfortable or even desirable.

This may explain why I have been so ungratefully day-dreaming about 15 the Man in the Gray Flannel Suit thirty years after Betty Friedan published *The Feminine Mystique.* The truth is, the knowledge that I can take care of myself, that I don't really need a man, is not without its own accompanying terrors. The idea that I could make myself into a sleek, self-sufficient androgyne is not all that appealing. Now that we have all of the rooms of our own that we need, we begin to look for that shared and crowded space. And it is this fear of independence, this fear of not needing a man, that explains the voices of more competent, accomplished corporate types than me saying to the men around them, "Provide for me, protect me." It may be one of the bad jokes that history occasionally plays on us: that the independence my mother's generation wanted so much for their daughters was something we could not entirely appreciate or want. It was like a birthday present from a distant relative—wrong size, wrong color, wrong style. And so women are left struggling with the desire to submit and not submit, to be dependent and independent, to take care of ourselves and be taken care of, and it's in the confusion of this struggle that most of us love and are loved.

For myself, I continue to go out with poets and novelists and writers, with men who don't pay for dates or buy me dresses at Bergdorf's or go off to their offices in the morning, but the Man in the Gray Flannel Suit lives on in my imagination, perplexing, irrational, revealing of some dark and unsettling truth.

---

*For Discussion*

1. Do you agree with Roiphe that "marrying up" is the woman's version of the American Dream? What is the man's version? Are the genders blurring in their views of achieving success? Are men likely to aspire to "marry up"—or does that violate social definitions of masculinity?

2. While this seems to be a personal essay, Roiphe is making an argument here. What is her claim? What is her evidence? What are some key terms—for example, what does she mean by "need" when she speaks of her fear of "not needing a man" (paragraphs 10 and 15)? What assumptions is she making about men? What assumptions about working women? (You might consider what she means by "androgyne" in paragraph 15.) What are the implications of her argument? Is it realistic, given today's economy? today's divorce rates? Finally, do you think she is serious about this argument, or is she merely sharing an escapist daydream?

3. In paragraphs 4 and 9, Roiphe says that women's attraction to successful men is not just about financial security. What else is it about, as you interpret these paragraphs?

### For Convincing

Roiphe quotes Molly Haskell as saying, "We never really escape the old-fashioned roles. They get inside our heads. Dependence has always been eroticized" (paragraph 12). Roiphe gives examples of how our culture romanticizes female dependence in works like *Gone with the Wind* and characters like Prince Charming. She does not complain that such messages harm women, but rather she complains that women must now reject these, along with rape fantasies, as politically incorrect. What do you think? Do you agree that our culture sends girls and women messages that associate women's sexuality with domination by men? Consider film, fiction, fashion promotions, and music. What conclusions do you draw? Are these messages harmful to women? Decide on an appropriate audience, and write to convince them of your conclusions.

### For Exploration

Roiphe seems to think that women have a choice: either be dependent on a man or be a modern liberated woman, meaning an independent, "sleek, self-sufficient androgyne" (paragraph 15). In other words, she sees women as having to choose between the traditional feminine gender role of dependence on a male breadwinner and the unfeminine role of competing with men in the workplace. Roiphe quotes Mary McCarthy as saying pretty much the same thing: Women can't expect to have "all the prerogatives of being a woman and the privileges of being a man at the same time" (paragraph 13). Evaluate the truth of this argument. You may want to look into Joan Williams's essay, pages 655–671, in which Williams blames seventies feminism for urging women to adopt the traditional male gender roles rather than question the entire set of gender roles for both men and women.

### For Persuasion

Roiphe says the traditional role of dependent woman means "You can just relax. You can take a rest from yourself. You can let the pressures and ambitions melt away . . ." (paragraph 14). The traditional male gender role of the "Man in the Gray Flannel Suit" does not permit men to have similar desires to let up on their ambitions and efforts at their careers. Why should women be the only sex that can admit to feeling this need to duck out of responsibility? Is it unmasculine to express such desires? What happens when men feel they must conform to the image of "the Man in the Gray Flannel Suit" in order to be real men? Explore the effects on men's career choices and health. Write an essay to persuade Roiphe that the image of the "Man in the Gray Flannel Suit" may have harmful implications for men.

# A Real Mother in the Modern World
## Anne Roiphe

*The following essay is excerpted from a chapter in Anne Roiphe's book* Fruitful *(Houghton Mifflin, 1996). Roiphe, who has written seven novels and three works of nonfiction, undertakes to explore the provocative question, "Does having children strain or drain the creative force; does it weaken ambition?" In this personal essay she asks, "If I'd had no children, would I have written better books . . . ?"*

. . . The point of feminist politics was always to give women fuller, better lives, a chance for equality with men and an opportunity to use all of their human potential. It's all very well in the abstract to speak of the virtues of motherhood like the flowers sent from across the country on Mother's Day, but up close, in the thick of it, we have to consider, is it worth it, what does it do to us, how exactly does it make us feel. Because the emotions good and bad of the common mother are the building blocks of our next political direction. Feminism, which was all about self-fulfillment, forgot that giving up some of the self, which is necessary for motherhood, is part of most women's self-fulfillment, another one of God's not so funny jokes.

Not have a child, not ever to have a child, the idea echoes down the corridors of my mind as if I were playing with fire, arsonist of my life. To conceive and bear a child alters, reframes, collapses the old self and sets all kinds of limits on the new. I can never know who I would have been had I not had my first, second, third child, or for that matter what would have become of me if I had not been a stepmother. If I'd had no children would I have written better books, would I have had a more adventurous life, would I have traveled to Tibet or seen the giraffes run on the African veldt, seen the sun set on the Parthenon? Would I be a better friend to my friends, would my love life have taken more curves, who would I know, what would I say or think? Would I be a politician, a talk show host, a lady with dogs or cats or clean upholstery? This is not a question that has an answer.

Some days it seems to me that I might have been more than I am if I had not become a self divided among others, one ear listening for a cry, one eye following the fate of another, one heart divided in many pieces, many times more vulnerable to fortune's turn, the sound of an ambulance five blocks away, the bad breaks and steep falls of a being that is as dear to you as yourself but is not yourself. Some days it certainly seems to me that I might have remembered to put lotion on my face, exercised daily, put money away in the bank if I had not had children. Other days I have no interest in those things and I think that without my children, whatever I might be, I would be less, diminished, reduced, imprisoned inside my own skin, a person who will not leave a forward trace, the trail would only wind back. Some days I think if I had not had my children I would surely have gone mad, paced the inside of my mind till I knew every cranny and crack and, like a flower plucked by its roots, thirst for the ground, dream of the soil, wilt in the sun. Sometimes I think that if I had not had children I would never have grown up, that I would always be watching my own bubbles as if I were a goldfish swimming in a bowl. It is true that having children is a sanding of the ego, a rubbing down of pride, a kind of placing in proportion one's ambitions, defusing the grandiose, cutting back the unreal. However, it may not always be a positive thing to grow up, to regard oneself as light on the way to being extinguished rather than as a comet shooting across the applauding night sky. Just because psychiatrists make such a fuss about maturity that does not mean that immaturity might not be, after all, the preferable condition. The truth is that I am not sure if having children is good or bad for one's happiness, good or bad for one's creativity, all I know is that conception brought to term or not is never forgotten, and congratulations to a new mother is something of an oversimplification.

. . . Of course, just because you can have your own child doesn't mean you should. How does motherhood affect our creativity? Is there some devil's bargain here, give me a child and I will stop drawing, composing, writing? Is the fact that all the great women writers of the nineteenth century abstained from childbearing a mere coincidence or a significant clue? Certainly Jane Austen, George Eliot, the Brontës, America's Emily Dickinson and Edith Wharton were not weighed down with offspring. Virginia Woolf, the only writer in the twentieth century whose reputation stands up to James Joyce and Marcel Proust, did not have children either. Kate Chopin's heroine Daisy in *The Awakening* begins to draw, to respond to music, color, as she sends her sons away and decides that she has no interest in mothering them. The great Southern female literary voices that appeared in the postwar era included Eudora Welty, Carson McCullers, and Flannery O'Connor, all of them women without children. Mary McCarthy had a child but barely raised him. She declared openly her unmaternal nature.

Ellen Glasgow reports in her autobiography that when she consulted a 5 doctor on some minor physical complaint he said, "The best advice I can give you is to stop writing and go back to the South and have some babies. The greatest woman is not the woman who has written the finest book, but the woman who has had the finest babies." Sexist, old-fashioned, and probably ridiculous as this remark now seems, the thought hangs around in our heads. It takes the form of either/or. It assumes that women are the ones most involved with the baby. No one would ever have said this to a man. It is assumed that his reproductive life history is irrelevant to his creative work and no comparisons are needed or expected. It would be easy to ignore this as the prattle of dismissed generations. But women do pick up the prejudices against them in their culture and repeat them like so many performing parrots. I stopped working when my children were ill, not so much because I was needed every second by the bedside but because my concentration was gone, anxiety held me captive. At those times my work seemed unimportant. I know that when I dried my children with a towel, feeling their round limbs in my hands, I felt waves of contentment that no paragraph well done could bring me. As they got older I began to browse in bookstores, would they like this one or that one. I began to check the theater listings, this or that. I watched *Peter Pan* with them at my side. Wonder returned to me through their wonder. Better than writing, better than anything.

Isadora Duncan, a dancer who broke a few molds, had this to say about the first flames of feminism that were flickering across America's avant-garde. "Oh, women, what is the good of us learning to become lawyers, painters or sculptors, when this miracle [of birth] exists? Now I know this tremendous love, surpassing the love of men. I was stretched and bleeding, torn and helpless while the little being sucked and howled, life, life, life! Give me life. Oh where was my art, my art or any art? But what did I care for art! I felt I was a god, superior to any artist." Poor always overwrought Isadora Duncan whose children were drowned as the car they were riding in sank into the Seine, who herself was always larger than truth, emotions blown up with intensity if not purity. Isadora who did nothing because it was conventional uttered those conventional words when she gave birth.

An entire feminist movement has come to pass since Isadora wore her last toga, got into a sports car in Nice with an Italian boyfriend, and flipped her long scarf over her shoulder only to have it wind itself around the wheels and snap her neck as the car began to move. Some sixty years later in 1985 Mary Gordon writes in the *New York Times Book Review* as she is about to give birth to her second child, "It is impossible for me to believe that anything I write could have a fraction of the importance of this child growing inside of me or of the child who lies now her head on my belly with the sweet yet offhand stoicism of a sick child." No one asked Mary Gordon to measure her children against her books. It is a habit women come to naturally. Men don't.

This whole discussion makes me squirm. I know where the argument is leading. Either I should not have had children and made my books the object of my affections or I should have paid more attention to my children, had a few more of them, and let my work wait. Either way I feel coerced, not happy. Like Mary Gordon and Isadora Duncan I hold my children more important to me than any work I might accomplish. I know this is not the correct feminist position. And yet it seems so universal, so prevalent that I can't help believe that its truth lies in some biological force that won't be reasoned with, that has no agenda other than its own (species) survival, and there's no use fighting it because it comes back at you again and again if you try to avoid it. Even a feminist scholar at the University of Chicago, Virginia Held, has said, "Creating new human persons and new human personalities with new thoughts and attitudes is as creative an activity as humans are involved in anywhere."

Of course it may be that great art requires a kind of monomania, an absorption so intense that children would be interferences, beside the point. It may be that great art is made by men and women who are exempt from the pull of ordinariness. The artists we admire may all be half mad. I doubt they have any choice in the matter. Who would choose to be an artist when they could be just a man or a woman living an ordinary life? Most of us would prefer ordinary satisfactions along with ordinary pain. Possibly I say that because I'm a woman lacking in ambition. Possibly I say that because I have seen so many lives consumed in the pursuit of great art. That passion is not unconnected to alcoholism and madness and while great art comforts us all its creators are frequently moral freaks. Ambition is certainly not an exclusively male characteristic but in its extreme, a desire to challenge the gods, it may be a condition incompatible with child care.

This is why the "I'm just a mom" answer ("What do you do?") is so grating. I can answer that question with a proper professional I.D. but I know that in ways that really count I too am "just a mom." So is Mary Gordon and most of the other women I know. Even after our children are grown, even when we have grandchildren (I will show you the pictures of my step-grandchildren just the way the ladies around my mother's canasta table showed theirs), this sense of identity, of meaning, lies with our children. 10

However, it isn't a full-time occupation. It certainly doesn't fill all one's hours or days. It doesn't prevent all the other work one does. It never has. That child rearing may be the center of the soul does not mean that there isn't room for other things. There is time enough in one life to find many different kinds of satisfactions and satisfy many different kinds of necessities. It has done us no service to have work opposed to our child rearing. It has done us no service to make child rearing the mother's thing like some compensation, a bone tossed to keep the distaff side content, to keep the generations coming.

How nice if men would feel this child necessity too. How nice if they would experience some jarring of their most ambitious grandiose dreams with their desire to reproduce. They don't have swelling bellies or lactating breasts. They don't carry the fetus or expel the baby into the world. Nevertheless, the creation is theirs too. I resent work vs. child arguments because both are possible, both are necessary to most of us, both make the world turn round. Both gratify our always thirsty egos. Both require the most individual personal stamp of our souls. Having said that, having children is more important than anything else we humans do, primary even. Then we can go back to our nondomestic work.

Still, a voice inside keeps on asking: Does having children strain or drain the creative force, does it weaken ambition? . . .

Tillie Olsen, who wrote one extraordinary book of stories including the classic "Tell Me a Riddle," then wrote a book called *Silences* in which she explained how her artistic drive, her needs had been chased away by the voices of her children, by the demands, and they are never minor, of domestic life. Many of us in the seventies thought that motherhood was probably not the way to artistic success. Men had always been fathers and artists too. They did not carry the primary responsibility for their offspring. They were never the primary psychological parent so their responsibility, financial and worldly, barely claimed their attention. The male writers of the fifties and sixties were with some exceptions always divorcing wives, leaving their progeny behind while they went on to the next woman, who would ofttimes both bear their next child and appear in their next novel. Unfair.

After my writer husband left I decided to try my own gift and write a   15
novel. It doesn't take much courage to begin a novel when no one is looking at you. It's rather like testing out a recipe for a soufflé in your kitchen at midnight, no guests expected. I bought a notebook and began. I wrote when my baby was taking a nap. I wrote in the playground looking up from time to time to be sure she was still there and hadn't fallen off anything. I wrote waiting in line in the supermarket. I wrote at night with her sleeping in the bed beside me. She was afraid of the dark so we kept all the lights on all night. I was able to write despite having a child. However, that covers only the mechanics of the matter. How well I was able to write is another story. Would my first novel have been better if I had not had a child? That's one of those questions that can't be answered. What can be said is that many mothers have written books, poems, scripts. Women's voices are now participating in all forms of cultural dialogue and many of those women are mothers. What has to be admitted is that American writers of the fifties, sixties, seventies, eighties, and nineties, with the exception of black women, have not achieved as a group, even as individuals, the same level of genius as the men. Or does it just seem so? The males, Updike, Walker Percy, Cheever, Malamud, Roth, Bellow, Mailer, Heller, Barth, Styron, Doctorow, dominate the scene, as did the men in the generation before them, Fitzgerald, Hemingway, Steinbeck, Dos Passos, Faulkner, Saroyan, Sinclair Lewis.

Of course these fellows got all the awards and all the attention. Perhaps the appearance of male genius as weightier on the whole than the female's is an artifice, a result of the way we view things, not a reality at all. Perhaps the trouble with female genius is not that it is diverted to the womb but that it is overlooked when it appears. I prefer to think of women's creativity as a continuum. It starts with biology, it can result in a child, it can result in a book, or both. Women's literary work tends to be slimmer, plotted less like a Napoleonic campaign and more like a dinner party at which everyone drank too much or talked too much, more domestic in focus, but nonetheless electric. It hits like a lightning bolt when carefully aimed. Women's fiction may in fact be more suited to the modern novel, which finds its subject right under the ordinary, beneath the surface of spoken thought, in the resonances of our common condition. Think of Toni Morrison, Alice Munro, Margaret Atwood, Grace Paley, Jane Smiley, E. Annie Proulx, Pat Barker, A. S. Byatt.

Feminists looking on the art of other generations could say that the best women writers were like men, unencumbered by children. Their babies were sublimated and transformed into work on the printed page. Feminists who felt unfriendly toward motherhood could say that raising a child was an obstacle to achievement, an apron string that tied the spirit to the mundane and prevented imagination from finding its own way to Mount Olympus. If we knew this to be true we'd have to decide if it was the conditions of women in other times that made this so or if it was something in the biological condition of pregnancy, lactating, caring for a child that drained the female resources and would limit women's artistic gifts no matter how feminist the society around them.

Optimism brings us to the conclusion that once women and men participate equally in child care we will have women who become as extraordinary as Shakespeare and Dickens who are also mothers increasing our pool of genius, resources for us all. My anxious soul tells me otherwise. It may be true that the female biological story in some way limits the woman artist with children. It is not a matter of finding quiet time to do the work. That, difficult as it is, can be managed. The more serious problem is that she cannot close herself off. She cannot stop her heart from beating with her child's. Her attention is divided and her emotional energy, the soil of creation, is constantly depleted. Perhaps this puts an outer limit on her creation. Time will tell.

The only thing I know for sure is that I would rather have a child than a book. I would rather have a warm-blooded body to carry my message to the world than the most perfect of artistic creations issued in my name. I do not think this makes me anti-feminist or opposed to female achievement, it is just a statement of priorities, one that I have found rings true in every corner of my being. I know that no male writer would say that, at least not yet. Does that make their books better or worse? It could be my view because I was a child in the forties. It could be my view because I brought the fifties along with me into the rest of my life and consciousness rises only as high as the arms of the individual can lift it. It could be I am typical of most men and women who are destined not to change the cultural currents but simply to swim awkwardly in them.

Women writers are hardly the only ones who wonder if their creativity, if their drive to excel, will be weakened by child care. We all want to stay in the race whatever our worldly ambitions might be. Children should not be a limitation on half of us if they carry forward the humanity of all of us. But what if they truly are? 20

In the nineteen fifties the short story turned to the handwriting on the wall of suburban marriage. Again and again we read the story about the wandering man, the woman who fell in love with the tennis pro, the martini drinkers who pined away after each other's wives, dancing with them at the club. If one begins at the beginning of the fifties and reads through every issue of the *New Yorker* until yesterday, some forty-five years' worth, one's head would be full of the disappointment man causes woman and woman causes man. It is rare indeed to find fictional reports of that disappointment which is at least as common: child disappoints parent, in particular the mother. But surely writers know this tale well enough. The best writing seems to have it the other way around. Parent disappoints child. That we have in first novels. Again and again the sensitive kid watches parents create havoc, ruin marriages, drift off, abandon love, in Salinger and Roth, in Cormac McCarthy and Alice Walker. The pernicious footfall of the adults going about their business haunts our literary experiences. To see from the parent's point of view children fouling things up is rare. Which isn't to say that outside of fiction it doesn't happen all the time.

Surveys have been done that report that children are bad for marriage. Adolescent children present great obstacles to the parents' marriage. The sociological surveys seem to indicate that childless marriages that do survive produce more partners satisfied with themselves. Whatever questions were asked we know that this kind of survey is not a subtle instrument and cannot measure the inner experience of people who may be angry at a child one day and delighted the next, and the sum total of their emotional relationship cannot be given a number or quantified by a stranger. However, it seems reasonable to me that childless marriages would be steadier, less caught in panics, upheavals, reproaches, fears. Whether or not that amounts to a happier marriage is a more complicated question. By those standards happiest of all perhaps is the person who never marries, never leaves home, is without ambition in the outside world, and passes his or her days like the family dog, sleeping contentedly on the porch, flicking flies away with its tail.

There are things one learns through being a mother, things one has by being a mother that are not measurable on the charts. Here is Mary Gordon writing about nursing an infant: "Perfectly still, almost without volition, I nourish. A film of moisture covers my flesh and my son's. Both of us drift in and out of sleep. I could be any woman lying there. There is nothing original about me. I am ancient, repetitive. In a life devoted to originality I adore the animal's predictability. The pleasures of instinct are more real than any I would ever have known." This last sentence is not quite accurate because there are instincts that women know without bearing children. Sex, sleeping when tired, eating when hungry, screaming when mad, crying when sad are a few of them. What I think she means primarily is the melting of ego, the closeness to human process, the fact of being unoriginal, animal-like, is experienced as having entered a sacred spot and becomes one of those revelations that leaves behind altering perspectives. The bond of woman to child carries with it the potential bond of woman to humanity, of earthlings to space, of dust to dust. It has a hint of death in it. It is holy knowledge.

---

## For Discussion

1. Roiphe's essay is a good example of exploratory argumentation. She seems to be posing to herself and her sympathetic readers a series of

questions on the same theme beginning with "Is motherhood worth it?" (paragraph 1). Note and mark how the question reappears and how it changes as she moves through her inquiry.

2. What is Roiphe's answer to the question, "Does having children strain or drain the creative force?" What are the reasons for her answer? What about her evidence? Is it convincing? Do you have any evidence about women writers who were also mothers that would argue against her case?

3. Roiphe says that "giving up some of the self . . . is part of most women's self-fulfillment" (paragraph 1). Track this idea through her essay. Does she tie this need to biological differences between the sexes, or does she suggest that it is part of the gender role for women in the cultures she is examining?

4. Does she offer evidence to convince you that fathers do not find that having children jars "their most ambitious grandiose dreams" (paragraph 12)?

5. Read Joan Williams's essay "Reconstructive Feminism" (pages 655–671), which argues for a more "family-friendly" version of gender roles and workplace structure. Do you think that if men and women were equally involved in child rearing, the issues Roiphe raises here about the difference between motherhood and fatherhood would disappear? Make a case for your conclusion.

# The Beauty Myth
## Naomi Wolf

*Feminist writer Naomi Wolf, a 1984 graduate of Yale, sees a backlash against femi-
nism in our culture's promotion of female beauty. Her controversial book* The Beauty
Myth: How Images of Beauty Are Used against Women *(1991) charges that as
women's material opportunities have expanded, an insidious psychological force has
begun to undermine their sense of self-worth. Constantly dissatisfied with their real
faces and bodies, women devote inordinate attention, time, and money to pursuing the
slender, youthful, unchanging female image dictated by our society as the ideal, some
even risking their health to do so through surgery or starvation. Wolf argues that the
beauty myth is political, not aesthetic; it is imposed by a society threatened by women's
rise in power. The following excerpt is Wolf's introduction to her book. As you read, decide to what extent Wolf seems to be anti-beauty: Does she seem to oppose all efforts to
"look good"?*

At last, after a long silence, women took to the streets. In the two decades
of radical action that followed the rebirth of feminism in the early 1970s,
Western women gained legal and reproductive rights, pursued higher education, entered the trades and the professions, and overturned ancient and
revered beliefs about their social role. A generation on, do women feel free?

The affluent, educated, liberated women of the First World, who can enjoy freedoms unavailable to any women ever before, do not feel as free as
they want to. And they can no longer restrict to the subconscious their
sense that this lack of freedom has something to do with—with apparently
frivolous issues, things that really should not matter. Many are ashamed to
admit that such trivial concerns—to do with physical appearance, bodies,
faces, hair, clothes—matter so much. But in spite of shame, guilt, and denial, more and more women are wondering if it isn't that they are entirely
neurotic and alone but rather that something important is indeed at stake
that has to do with the relationship between female liberation and female
beauty.

The more legal and material hindrances women have broken through,
the more strictly and heavily and cruelly images of female beauty have
come to weigh upon us. Many women sense that women's collective progress has stalled; compared with the heady momentum of earlier days, there
is a dispiriting climate of confusion, division, cynicism, and above all, ex-
haustion. After years of much struggle and little recognition, many older
women feel burned out; after years of taking its light for granted, many
younger women show little interest in touching new fire to the torch.

During the past decade, women breached the power structure; meanwhile, eating disorders rose exponentially and cosmetic surgery became the
fastest-growing medical specialty. During the past five years, consumer

spending doubled, pornography became the main media category, ahead of legitimate films and records combined, and thirty-three thousand American women told researchers that they would rather lose ten to fifteen pounds than achieve any other goal (Wooley and Wooley). More women have more money and power and scope and legal recognition than we have ever had before; but in terms of how we feel about ourselves *physically,* we may actually be worse off than our unliberated grandmothers. Recent research consistently shows that inside the majority of the West's controlled, attractive, successful working women, there is a secret "underlife" poisoning our freedom; infused with notions of beauty, it is a dark vein of self-hatred, physical obsessions, terror of aging, and dread of lost control (Cash et al.).[1]

It is no accident that so many potentially powerful women feel this way.        5
We are in the midst of a violent backlash against feminism that uses images of female beauty as a political weapon against women's advancement: the beauty myth. It is the modern version of a social reflex that has been in force since the Industrial Revolution. As women released themselves from the feminine mystique of domesticity, the beauty myth took over its lost ground, expanding as it waned to carry on its work of social control.

The contemporary backlash is so violent because the ideology of beauty is the last one remaining of the old feminine ideologies that still has the power to control those women whom second wave feminism would have otherwise made relatively uncontrollable: It has grown stronger to take over the work of social coercion that myths about motherhood, domesticity, chastity, and passivity, no longer can manage. It is seeking right now to undo psychologically and covertly all the good things that feminism did for women materially and overtly.

This counterforce is operating to checkmate the inheritance of feminism on every level in the lives of Western women. Feminism gave us laws against job discrimination based on gender; immediately case law evolved in Britain and the United States that institutionalized job discrimination based on women's appearances. Patriarchal religion declined; new religious dogma, using some of the mind-altering techniques of older cults and sects, arose around age and weight to functionally supplant traditional ritual. Feminists, inspired by Friedan, broke the stranglehold on the women's popular press of advertisers for household products, who were promoting the feminine mystique; at once, the diet and skin care industries became the new cultural censors of women's intellectual space, and because of their pressure, the gaunt, youthful model supplanted the happy housewife as the arbiter of successful womanhood. The sexual revolution promoted the discovery of female sexuality; "beauty pornography"—which for the first time

---

[1] Dr. Cash's research shows very little connection between "how attractive women are" and "how attractive they feel themselves to be." All the women he treated were, in his terms, "extremely attractive," but his patients compare themselves only to models, not to other women. [Author's note]

in women's history artificially links a commodified "beauty" directly and explicitly to sexuality—invaded the mainstream to undermine women's new and vulnerable sense of sexual self-worth. Reproductive rights gave Western women control over our own bodies; the weight of fashion models plummeted to 23 percent below that of ordinary women, eating disorders rose exponentially, and a mass neurosis was promoted that used food and weight to strip women of that sense of control. Women insisted on politicizing health; new technologies of invasive, potentially deadly "cosmetic" surgeries developed apace to re-exert old forms of medical control of women.

Every generation since about 1830 has had to fight its version of the beauty myth. "It is very little to me," said the suffragist Lucy Stone in 1855, "to have the right to vote, to own property, etcetera, if I may not keep my body, and its uses, in my absolute right" (qtd. in Dworkin 11). Eighty years later, after women had won the vote, and the first wave of the organized women's movement had subsided, Virginia Woolf wrote that it would still be decades before women could tell the truth about their bodies. In 1962, Betty Friedan quoted a young woman trapped in the Feminine Mystique: "Lately, I look in the mirror, and I'm so afraid I'm going to look like my mother." Eight years after that, heralding the cataclysmic second wave of feminism, Germaine Greer described "the Stereotype": "To her belongs all that is beautiful, even the very word beauty itself . . . she is a doll . . . I'm sick of the masquerade" (55, 60). In spite of the great revolution of the second wave, we are not exempt. Now we can look out over ruined barricades: A revolution has come upon us and changed everything in its path, enough time has passed since then for babies to have grown into women, but there still remains a final right not fully claimed.

The beauty myth tells a story: The quality called "beauty" objectively and universally exists. Women must want to embody it and men must want to possess women who embody it. This embodiment is an imperative for women and not for men, which situation is necessary and natural because it is biological, sexual, and evolutionary: Strong men battle for beautiful women, and beautiful women are more reproductively successful. Women's beauty must correlate to their fertility, and since this system is based on sexual selection, it is inevitable and changeless.

None of this is true. "Beauty" is a currency system like the gold standard. Like any economy, it is determined by politics, and in the modern age in the West it is the last, best belief system that keeps male dominance intact. In assigning value to women in a vertical hierarchy according to a culturally imposed physical standard, it is an expression of power relations in which women must unnaturally compete for resources that men have appropriated for themselves.

"Beauty" is not universal or changeless, though the West pretends that all ideals of female beauty stem from one Platonic Ideal Woman; the Maori

10

admire a fat vulva, and the Padung, droopy breasts. Nor is "beauty" a function of evolution: Its ideals change at a pace far more rapid than that of the evolution of species, and Charles Darwin was himself unconvinced by his own explanation that "beauty" resulted from a "sexual selection" that deviated from the rule of natural selection; for women to compete with women through "beauty" is a reversal of the way in which natural selection affects all other mammals.[1] Anthropology has overturned the notion that females must be "beautiful" to be selected to mate: Evelyn Reed, Elaine Morgan, and others have dismissed sociobiological assertions of innate male polygamy and female monogamy. Female higher primates are the sexual initiators; not only do they seek out and enjoy sex with many partners, but "every nonpregnant female takes her turn at being the most desirable of all her troop. And that cycle keeps turning as long as she lives." The inflamed pink sexual organs of primates are often cited by male sociobiologists as analogous to human arrangements relating to female "beauty," when in fact that is a universal, nonhierarchical female primate characteristic.

Nor has the beauty myth always been this way. Though the pairing of the older rich men with young, "beautiful" women is taken to be somehow inevitable, in the matriarchal Goddess religions that dominated the Mediterranean from about 25,000 B.C.E. to about 700 B.C.E., the situation was reversed: "In every culture, the Goddess has many lovers. . . . The clear pattern is of an older woman with a beautiful but expendable youth—Ishtar and Tammuz, Venus and Adonis, Cybele and Attis, Isis and Osiris . . . their only function the service of the divine 'womb'" (Miles 43). Nor is it something only women do and only men watch: Among the Nigerian Wodaabes, the women hold economic power and the tribe is obsessed with male beauty; Wodaabe men spend hours together in elaborate makeup sessions, and compete—provocatively painted and dressed, with swaying hips and seductive expressions—in beauty contests judged by women (Woodhead). There is no legitimate historical or biological justification for the beauty

---

[1] See Cynthia Eagle Russett, "Hairy Men and Beautiful Women," *Sexual Science: The Victorian Construction of Womanhood* (Cambridge: Harvard UP, 1989) 78–103.

On page 84 Russett quotes Darwin: "Man is more powerful in body and mind than woman, and in the savage state he keeps her in a much more abject state of bondage, than does the male of any other animal; therefore it is not surprising that he should have gained the power of selection. . . . As women have long been selected for beauty, it is not surprising that some of their successive variations should have been transmitted exclusively to the same sex; consequently that they should have transmitted beauty in a somewhat higher degree to their female than to their male offspring, and thus have become more beautiful, according to general opinion, than men." Darwin himself noticed the evolutionary inconsistency of this idea that, as Russett puts it, "a funny thing happened on the way up the ladder: Among humans, the female no longer chose but was chosen." This theory "implied an awkward break in evolutionary continuity," she observes: "In Darwin's own terms it marked a rather startling reversal in the trend of evolution."

See also Natalie Angier, "Hard-to-Please Females May Be Neglected Evolutionary Force," *New York Times* 8 May 1990, and Natalie Angier, "Mating for Life? It's Not for the Birds or the Bees," *New York Times* 21 Aug. 1990. [Author's note]

myth; what it is doing to women today is a result of nothing more exalted than the need of today's power structure, economy, and culture to mount a counteroffensive against women.

If the beauty myth is not based on evolution, sex, gender, aesthetics, or God, on what is it based? It claims to be about intimacy and sex and life, a celebration of women. It is actually composed of emotional distance, politics, finance, and sexual repression. The beauty myth is not about women at all. It is about men's institutions and institutional power.

The qualities that a given period calls beautiful in women are merely symbols of the female behavior that that period considers desirable: *The beauty myth is always actually prescribing behavior and not appearance.* Competition between women has been made part of the myth so that women will be divided from one another. Youth and (until recently) virginity have been "beautiful" in women since they stand for experiential and sexual ignorance. Aging in women is "unbeautiful" since women grow more powerful with time, and since the links between generations of women must always be newly broken: Older women fear young ones, young women fear old, and the beauty myth truncates for all the female life span. Most urgently, women's identity must be premised upon our "beauty" so that we will remain vulnerable to outside approval, carrying the vital sensitive organ of self-esteem exposed to the air.

Though there has, of course, been a beauty myth in some form for as long as there has been patriarchy, the beauty myth in its modern form is a fairly recent invention. The myth flourishes when material constraints on women are dangerously loosened. Before the Industrial Revolution, the average woman could not have had the same feelings about "beauty" that modern women do who experience the myth as continual comparison to a mass-disseminated physical ideal. Before the development of technologies of mass production—daguerreotypes, photographs, etc.—an ordinary woman was exposed to few such images outside the Church. Since the family was a productive unit and women's work complemented men's, the value of women who were not aristocrats or prostitutes lay in their work skills, economic shrewdness, physical strength, and fertility. Physical attraction, obviously, played its part; but "beauty" as we understand it was not, for ordinary women, a serious issue in the marriage marketplace. The beauty myth in its modern form gained ground after the upheavals of industrialization, as the work unit of the family was destroyed, and urbanization and the emerging factory system demanded what social engineers of the time termed the "separate sphere" of domesticity, which supported the new labor category of the "breadwinner" who left home for the workplace during the day. The middle class expanded, the standards of living and of literacy rose, the size of families shrank; a new class of literate, idle women developed, on whose submission to enforced domesticity the evolving system of industrial capitalism depended. Most of our assumptions about the way women have always thought about "beauty" date from no earlier than

15

the 1830s, when the cult of domesticity was first consolidated and the beauty index invented.

For the first time new technologies could reproduce — in fashion plates, daguerreotypes, tintypes, and rotogravures — images of how women should look. In the 1840s the first nude photographs of prostitutes were taken; advertisements using images of "beautiful" women first appeared in mid-century. Copies of classical artworks, postcards of society beauties and royal mistresses, Currier and Ives prints, and porcelain figurines flooded the separate sphere to which middle-class women were confined.

Since the Industrial Revolution, middle-class Western women have been controlled by ideals and stereotypes as much as by material constraints. This situation, unique to this group, means that analyses that trace "cultural conspiracies" are uniquely plausible in relation to them. The rise of the beauty myth was just one of several emerging social fictions that masqueraded as natural components of the feminine sphere, the better to enclose those women inside it. Other such fictions arose contemporaneously: a version of childhood that required continual maternal supervision; a concept of female biology that required middle-class women to act out the roles of hysterics and hypochondriacs; a conviction that respectable women were sexually anesthetic; and a definition of women's work that occupied them with repetitive, time-consuming, and painstaking tasks such as needlepoint and lacemaking. All such Victorian inventions as these served a double function — that is, though they were encouraged as a means to expend female energy and intelligence in harmless ways, women often used them to express genuine creativity and passion.

But in spite of middle-class women's creativity with fashion and embroidery and child rearing, and, a century later, with the role of the suburban housewife that devolved from these social fictions, the fictions' main purpose was served: During a century and a half of unprecedented feminist agitation, they effectively counteracted middle-class women's dangerous new leisure, literacy, and relative freedom from material constraints.

Though these time- and mind-consuming fictions about women's natural role adapted themselves to resurface in the post-war Feminine Mystique, when the second wave of the women's movement took apart what women's magazines had portrayed as the "romance," "science," and "adventure" of homemaking and suburban family life, they temporarily failed. The cloying domestic fiction of "togetherness" lost its meaning and middle-class women walked out of their front doors in masses.

So the fictions simply transformed themselves once more: Since the     20
women's movement had successfully taken apart most other necessary fictions of femininity, all the work of social control once spread out over the whole network of these fictions had to be reassigned to the only strand left intact, which action consequently strengthened it a hundredfold. This reimposed onto liberated women's faces and bodies all the limitations, taboos, and punishments of the repressive laws, religious injunctions, and repro-

ductive enslavement that no longer carried sufficient force. Inexhaustible but ephemeral beauty work took over from inexhaustible but ephemeral housework. As the economy, law, religion, sexual mores, education, and culture were forcibly opened up to include women more fairly, a private reality colonized female consciousness. By using ideas about "beauty," it reconstructed an alternative female world with its own laws, economy, religion, sexuality, education, and culture, each element as repressive as any that had gone before.

Since middle-class Western women can best be weakened psychologically now that we are stronger materially, the beauty myth, as it has resurfaced in the last generation, has had to draw on more technological sophistication and reactionary fervor than ever before. The modern arsenal of the myth is a dissemination of millions of images of the current ideal; although this barrage is generally seen as a collective sexual fantasy, there is in fact little that is sexual about it. It is summoned out of political fear on the part of male-dominated institutions threatened by women's freedom, and it exploits female guilt and apprehension about our own liberation—latent fears that we might be going too far. This frantic aggregation of imagery is a collective reactionary hallucination willed into being by both men and women stunned and disoriented by the rapidity with which gender relations have been transformed: a bulwark of reassurance against the flood of change. The mass depiction of the modern woman as a "beauty" is a contradiction: Where modern women are growing, moving, and expressing their individuality, as the myth has it, "beauty" is by definition inert, timeless, and generic. That this hallucination is necessary and deliberate is evident in the way "beauty" so directly contradicts women's real situation.

And the unconscious hallucination grows ever more influential and pervasive because of what is now conscious market manipulation: powerful industries—the $33-billion-a-year diet industry (O'Neill), the $20-billion cosmetics industry, the $300-million cosmetic surgery industry (*Standard and Poor's*), and the $7-billion pornography industry ("Crackdown")—have arisen from the capital made out of unconscious anxieties, and are in turn able, through their influence on mass culture, to use, stimulate, and reinforce the hallucination in a rising economic spiral.

This is not a conspiracy theory; it doesn't have to be. Societies tell themselves necessary fictions in the same way that individuals and families do. Henrik Ibsen called them "vital lies," and psychologist Daniel Goleman describes them working the same way on the social level that they do within families: "The collusion is maintained by directing attention away from the fearsome fact, or by repackaging its meaning in an acceptable format" (16–17). The costs of these social blind spots, he writes, are destructive communal illusions. Possibilities for women have become so open-ended that they threaten to destabilize the institutions on which a male-dominated culture has depended, and a collective panic reaction on the part of both sexes has forced a demand for counterimages.

The resulting hallucination materializes, for women, as something all too real. No longer just an idea, it becomes three-dimensional, incorporating within itself how women live and how they do not live: It becomes the Iron Maiden. The original Iron Maiden was a medieval German instrument of torture, a body-shaped casket painted with the limbs and features of a lovely, smiling young woman. The unlucky victim was slowly enclosed inside her; the lid fell shut to immobilize the victim, who died either of starvation or, less cruelly, of the metal spikes embedded in her interior. The modern hallucination in which women are trapped or trap themselves is similarly rigid, cruel, and euphemistically painted. Contemporary culture directs attention to imagery of the Iron Maiden, while censoring real women's faces and bodies.

Why does the social order feel the need to defend itself by evading the fact of real women, our faces and voices and bodies, and reducing the meaning of women to these formulaic and endlessly reproduced "beautiful" images? Though unconscious personal anxieties can be a powerful force in the creation of a vital lie, economic necessity practically guarantees it. An economy that depends on slavery needs to promote images of slaves that "justify" the institution of slavery. Western economies are absolutely dependent now on the continued underpayment of women. An ideology that makes women feel "worth less" was urgently needed to counteract the way feminism had begun to make us feel worth more. This does not require a conspiracy; merely an atmosphere. The contemporary economy depends right now on the representation of women within the beauty myth. Economist John Kenneth Galbraith offers an economic explanation for "the persistence of the view of homemaking as a 'higher calling'": the concept of women as naturally trapped within the Feminine Mystique, he feels, "has been forced on us by popular sociology, by magazines, and by fiction to disguise the fact that woman in her role of consumer has been essential to the development of our industrial society. . . . Behavior that is essential for economic reasons is transformed into a social virtue" (qtd. in Minton). As soon as a woman's primary social value could no longer be defined as the attainment of virtuous domesticity, the beauty myth redefined it as the attainment of virtuous beauty. It did so to substitute both a new consumer imperative and a new justification for economic unfairness in the workplace where the old ones had lost their hold over newly liberated women.

Another hallucination arose to accompany that of the Iron Maiden: The caricature of the Ugly Feminist was resurrected to dog the steps of the women's movement. The caricature is unoriginal; it was coined to ridicule the feminists of the nineteenth century. Lucy Stone herself, whom supporters saw as "a prototype of womanly grace . . . fresh and fair as the morning," was derided by detractors with "the usual report" about Victorian feminists: "a big masculine woman, wearing boots, smoking a cigar, swearing like a trooper" (qtd. in Friedan 79). As Betty Friedan put it presciently in 1960, even before the savage revamping of that old caricature: "The unpleasant

25

image of feminists today resembles less the feminists themselves than the image fostered by the interests who so bitterly opposed the vote for women in state after state" (87). Thirty years on, her conclusion is more true than ever: That resurrected caricature, which sought to punish women for their public acts by going after their private sense of self, became the paradigm for new limits placed on aspiring women everywhere. After the success of the women's movement's second wave, the beauty myth was perfected to check-mate power at every level in individual women's lives. The modern neuroses of life in the female body spread to woman after woman at epidemic rates. The myth is undermining—slowly, imperceptibly, without our being aware of the real forces of erosion—the ground women have gained through long, hard, honorable struggle.

The beauty myth of the present is more insidious than any mystique of femininity yet: A century ago, Nora slammed the door of the doll's house; a generation ago, women turned their backs on the consumer heaven of the isolated multiapplianced home; but where women are trapped today, there is no door to slam. The contemporary ravages of the beauty backlash are destroying women physically and depleting us psychologically. If we are to free ourselves from the dead weight that has once again been made out of femaleness, it is not ballots or lobbyists or placards that women will need first; it is a new way to see.

### Works Cited

"Crackdown on Pornography: A No-Win Battle." *U.S. News & World Report* 4 June 1984.

Cash, Thomas, Diane Cash, and Jonathan Butters. "Mirror-Mirror on the Wall: Contrast Effects and Self-Evaluation of Physical Attractiveness." *Personality and Social Psychology Bulletin* 9.3 (1983).

Dworkin, Andrea. *Pornography: Men Possessing Women.* New York: Putnam, 1981.

Friedan, Betty. *The Feminine Mystique.* 1963. London: Penguin, 1982.

Goleman, Daniel. *Vital Lies, Simple Truths: The Psychology of Self-Deception.* New York: Simon, 1983.

Greer, Germaine. *The Female Eunuch.* London: Paladin Grafton, 1970.

Miles, Rosalind. *The Women's History of the World.* London: Paladin Grafton, 1988.

Minton, Michael H., with Jean Libman Block. *What Is a Life Worth?* New York: McGraw, 1984.

Morgan, Elaine. *The Descent of Woman.* New York: Bantam, 1979.

O'Neill, Mollie. "Congress Looking into the Diet Business." *New York Times* 25 July 1988.

*Standard and Poor's Industry Survey.* New York: Standard and Poor's, 1988.

Reed, Evelyn. *Woman's Evolution: From Matriarchal Clan to Patriarchal Family.* New York: Pathfinder, 1986.

Woodhead, Linda. "Desert Dandies." *The Guardian* July 1988.

Wooley, S. C., and O. W. Wooley. "Obesity and Women: A Closer Look at the Facts." *Women's Studies International Quarterly* 2 (1979): 69–79.

*For Discussion*

1. Wolf seeks to convince her readers that the beauty myth is just that—a myth. What reasons and evidence does she offer to make them see that beauty is not an aesthetic absolute? Do you find her case convincing?

2. What reasons and evidence does Wolf offer to convince her readers that in creating the beauty myth, society is motivated by politics and economics? (To be sure you understand this part of her argument, write a paraphrase of paragraph 25.) Explain her analogy between the beauty myth and the medieval Iron Maiden (paragraph 24). How does this analogy reinforce Wolf's argument that the myth is politically motivated?

3. Wolf says in paragraph 14, "The qualities that a given period calls beautiful in women are merely symbols of the female behavior that that period considers desirable: *The beauty myth is always actually prescribing behavior and not appearance.*" For example, the quality of thinness might symbolize that our society wants women to deny themselves the pleasures of food, even to exist on the daily calorie rations of a person in the Third World or in a prison camp. What other behavior might the beauty myth prescribe?

4. In a preface to a later edition of *The Beauty Myth,* Wolf wrote that she was misunderstood by many critics as being anti-beauty and that she would like to make clear to readers that women should be free to adorn and show off their bodies if they want, celebrating their real beauty. She says it is fine to wear lipstick but not to feel guilty about not conforming to the ideal image of beauty. Do you find any evidence in the excerpt to suggest that Wolf is not against makeup and fashion? Do you find any evidence to suggest that she is against them? Could you write a new first paragraph to introduce Wolf's argument more clearly?

*For Convincing*

Women know that achieving "beauty" is often painful and expensive, in terms of both time and money. Wolf charges that entire industries have formed to profit from women's anxieties about their appearance. However, a glance at men's magazines in most newsstands shows a proliferation of reading material devoted to men's fashion, grooming, and physique—the "masculine" term for "figure." The advertisements here suggest that a similar industry exists for men. Do men have their own masculine version of the "beauty myth" that causes them to suffer, to spend time and money for the sake of their appearance? If so, how widely is it subscribed to? Do you think any motives other than simple vanity underlie it? Write an argument, perhaps addressed to Naomi Wolf, to make the case that excessive concern for one's appearance is not limited to the female sex. If you don't think this is a significant concern for men, write an argument addressed to women, to convince them that they should or should not be more like men in this respect.

## For Research and Persuasion

In "Sex," a later chapter of *The Beauty Myth*, Wolf attempts to persuade her readers that men would prefer women to accept themselves as they are. She writes, "At least one major study proves that men are as exasperated with the beauty myth as women are. 'Preoccupation with her appearance, concern about face and hair' ranked among the top four qualities that most annoyed men about women" (171). However, she does admit that "some men get a sexual charge from a woman's objective beauty," an attraction that is often a form of "exhibitionism" as a man "[imagines] his buddies imagining him doing what he is doing while he does it" (175). You may want to look at the entire chapter in which Wolf discusses love and the beauty myth. Do additional research, both in the field and in the library, to draw some conclusions of your own about how images of "ideal" beauty affect sexual relationships. Depending upon your conclusions, write an essay in which you attempt to change the behavior of men, women, or both sexes.

## Women's Rights: As the World Turns
### Katha Pollitt

*Violations of women's rights in countries around the world have drawn increasing at-
tention. Western feminism may not suit all countries and cultures, but an international feminism is developing to address many of the problems Katha Pollitt cites in
the reprinted column below. Pollitt writes a regular column for the liberal periodical*
The Nation; *a collection of her writings, a book titled* Subject to Debate, *was published in 2001 (Modern Library). This column appeared before the fall of the Taliban
in Afghanistan, but the other abuses of women's rights continue with little change.
Pollitt concludes her argument with a list of excellent Web sites where interested readers can update their knowledge about international women's issues.*

. . . The struggle [for women's rights] in the United States may seem
stymied — as if the big shakeup of the seventies were settling into a new,
improved, but still sexist, status quo — but abroad all sorts of things are
happening, awful and hopeful. We tend to hear more about the former:
You probably know about the Italian judge who ruled that women wearing
blue jeans can't be raped because it takes two to pull them off — sparking a
protest by jeans-wearing female MPs. But did you know that in India the
Supreme Court ruled for the first time that mothers, not just fathers, are
the legal guardians of their children? Besides rectifying a major insult to
women, this ruling has important implications for divorcing women seeking custody and child support. The same court ruled in January that sexual
harassment violates women's rights and need not involve actual touching — a particularly interesting verdict, given that sexual harassment,
along with legal abortion, is often seen as the obsession of a handful
of U.S. feminists.

And speaking of abortion, recently two countries, Poland and El Salvador, made abortion harder to get. El Salvador, indeed, is now one of the
only countries to enact in law the official position of the Catholic Church
and the platform of the U.S. Republican Party, both of which reject abortion even to save the mother's life. But eight countries — Albania, South
Africa, Seychelles, Guyana, Germany, Portugal, Cambodia and Burkina
Faso — liberalized their abortion laws. And before you write those letters
pointing out that Cambodian and Salvadoran women have bigger problems than abortion, consider that in Nepal, a desperately poor country
where abortion is illegal, there are women, including rape victims, serving twenty years in prison for having abortions. Poor women have always
needed liberal abortion laws the most, because they are the ones who seek
the back alleys or who self-abort, and they are also the ones targeted by the
police.

These positive changes—Senegal, Togo and three other African countries have banned clitoridectomy; Spain's Basque region pays battered women a "salary" to encourage them to leave their abusers—flicker like candles in a darkening room. Islamic fanaticism is sending women back to the Middle Ages. In the Taliban's Afghanistan, women are banned from schooling, jobs, healthcare and public life, and are subject to beatings and stonings. The new world disorder of the global economy has thrown millions of women and girls into prostitution, sex slavery and, well, slavery as housebound servants in foreign lands. The Asian economic collapse has caused millions of families to stop their daughters' schooling. War, refugee camps, AIDS, poverty, illiteracy, maternal mortality (one in thirty-eight women in Pakistan) are everyday realities for vast numbers of women. Culturally sanctioned coercion and violence persist—"honor killings," genital mutilation, forced marriage, wife murder (half the murders in India)—sometimes with a weird postmodern twist. In famine-stricken North Korea, women are being sold across the border to Chinese farmers unable to find wives because sex-selective abortion, female infanticide and neglect have produced a demographic disaster: 122 males for every 100 females.

Against these terrible tides, set the movement for women's human rights. Only a decade ago the idea that women's rights are human rights was dismissed as sentimental Western cant: Human rights pertained to state action, not to family, marriage or community norms, however cruel and oppressive. Today, academics—and they usually are academics—who compare clitoridectomy to male circumcision or footbinding to high heels are the ones who seem indifferent to reality. And slowly, as the result of immense effort on the part of millions of women and men, a new set of social and moral paradigms is being articulated.

On International Women's Day, the United Nations opened its first-ever session on violence against women with a teleconference broadcast around the world. "It was something to see," said a friend who attended, "all those heads of state having to listen to women tell them about the harm their laws had done to them." 5

I don't want to make too much of what is at least in part political theater. Behind all the talk about "empowering women" how much really changes? The Cairo conference in 1994 was supposed to overturn the population-control approach to family planning in favor of one that placed women's "empowerment" at the center, but how many clinics in Asia (or the United States) have shifted course? It will take a decade, Barbara Becker of the Center for Reproductive Law and Policy told me, or maybe even two, for practices to change. But little by little a language is developing that did not exist before, one in which new hopes can be voiced and new demands made. It's a language we could learn to speak in the United States as well.

## Background and Related Information

*The Feminist Majority*
<http://www.feminist.org>

The Feminist Majority Foundation online offers a Feminist Internet Gateway, Feminist University Network, Breast Cancer Center and Career Center. Among other topics, they have information on global feminism, current news and events and women's sports. There is a special feature called "Take Action," which helps to advance women's rights through enabling quick response on key issues of the day.

*Feminist.com*
<http://www.feminist.com>

This site offers a Q&A with Gloria Steinem, the ability to search for women's services by location, weekly news updates, links to pro-feminist men's groups and personal stories of affirmative action. They have an amazing volume of links to other organizations.

*Aviva*
<http://www.aviva.org>

A huge site for information on international women's issues and current news, including abortion. They have an action alert and a books section.

*The United Nations*                                                          10
<http://www.un.org>

The U.N. site can be searched for information on and documents from UNIFEM (United Nations International Development Fund for Women) and UNDP (United Nations Development Program).

---

*For Discussion*

1. In paragraph 4, Pollitt describes a change of perspective on women's rights as human rights. What have human rights organizations begun to look at that they had considered off limits before? Which of the abuses described by Pollitt in paragraph 3 are state actions, and which are family and community (cultural) norms?
2. Pollitt names three countries that recently banned clitoridectomy—the cutting of young girls' genitals. By the end of 2001, Kenya had also banned this practice. Pollitt mentions that in the United States, some people, especially academics, have defended the practice as

part of some cultures' traditions and beliefs. What are the debatable issues on this topic?

3. Pollitt mentions that women's rights abuses often increase in hard economic times. In what countries has economic disorder affected women's rights?

## For Exploration and Convincing

Pollitt's column is a brief introduction to the topic of international abuses of women's rights. She is not specific or detailed about the problems she lists. Get specific. Research a particular problem mentioned by Pollitt, for example, the sexual harassment of women workers in Russia or other formerly Communist countries. Or you may be aware of news reports about abuses Pollitt does not mention. In South Africa, rape is not treated as a serious crime, and women who are raped are not given medication to fight possible exposure to AIDS. If your exploration indicates that a violation of human rights exists, write a paper to convince others of the seriousness of the problem.

## For Persuasion

Do research to find what organizations are working internationally to fight for women's rights. Write an argument to persuade skeptical Americans who may think that Americans are powerless to correct problems beyond our borders. Or argue that these problems must be addressed by the citizens of the countries in which the abuses occur.

## For Further Research and Discussion

1. Research Elizabeth Cady Stanton's nineteenth-century arguments for communal living and child-rearing arrangements. What were her objections to traditional marriage and family?

2. One factor that makes it difficult for American women to have a career and a family is that the United States is one of the few countries that does not have some type of government-supported day care. Look into the arrangements that other countries have made that assist working mothers.

3. Cassandra Langer's account stresses the feminist assertion that "the personal is political," but she has omitted from her history a discussion of women's struggle to acquire knowledge and means of birth control. Reread paragraphs 18 and 19. Look into Margaret Sanger's efforts to win this right for women and the resistance she met from men of her day. How might Langer have used this information in her explanation of sexual politics?

4. Since writing *The Beauty Myth,* Naomi Wolf has published another book, *Fire with Fire* (1993), in which she argues for a version of feminism that would make women the equals of men but would not deny them their sexuality. Read both Friedan's *The Second Stage* and Wolf's *Fire with Fire,* and compare their suggested revisions to feminism.

## Additional Suggestions for Writing

1. *Convincing.* Those who support same-sex education for girls argue that females achieve more when males are not in the academic environment. Look into the arguments for and against sexually segregated education for women. One argument in favor is that women have different learning styles from men; for example, some proponents say that women learn better in less competitive, more collaborative environments. Recent studies have shown that girls' sense of identity and self-confidence is as strong as that of boys until they reach the age of twelve or thirteen. Do girls become less self-assured as they enter puberty? What theories explain this change? Could anxieties about their femininity be behind the problem? You probably have experiences and observations of your own pertaining to these questions. After you have inquired into the subject, make a case for your position on sexually segregated education.
2. *Persuasion.* After considering the goals of feminism and the possible definitions of "femininity," decide if it is possible to be feminine and a feminist. As you inquire, think about who decides what is feminine—men or women or both sexes? Research the biographies of some leading feminists: Would they serve as examples to support your position? Why do so many people have an image (Naomi Wolf calls it a "hallucination") of the Ugly Feminist? Write a persuasive argument aimed at college women, taking either the position that they can be feminists without losing their femininity *or* the position that, at least in our society today, being a feminist necessarily makes a woman appear less feminine.
3. *Analysis-persuasion.* The consumer culture is very persuasive—toward men, women, and children. Inquire into how advertising might be contributing to some common form of behavior in American society today. Is this behavior in the self-interest of the group targeted by the advertising? Is it in the best interest of society as a whole? Or is it merely in the interest of the business or organization sponsoring the advertisement? Consider how visual images contribute to the persuasion. You might want to look at student Kelly Williams's essay

on pages 100–102 to see how one student looked at one advertisement that she believes aimed to make mothers conform to a stereotyped image. Write an essay, with or without graphic support, aimed at persuading the target audience to resist the arguments you have selected.

# Chapter 13

# Gay and Lesbian Rights: Responding to Homophobia

Homosexuality may not have increased in recent decades, but society's awareness of it certainly has, largely because many gay men and women have become more open about their sexual orientation. Their "coming out" has brought many issues to the public's attention, most notably whether gay people should be protected against discrimination in employment, housing, and insurance and in custody cases and adoption. Indeed, many ask, Why should gay people not be able to marry? In some communities, "domestic partnerships"—both homosexual and heterosexual—have recently been legally recognized as unions similar to marriage, and a small but growing number of employers extend benefits to the partners of homosexual employees.

While many homosexual men and women have decided to become activists, publicly pressing for protection against discrimination, others prefer to stay "in the closet," largely out of fear. According to the National Gay and Lesbian Task Force, over ninety percent of gay men and lesbians have been victims of some type of violence or harassment. One issue we take up here is *why* some heterosexuals react so strongly to homosexuality and the issues surrounding it. Homophobia is often referred to as "the last acceptable prejudice," because so many heterosexuals think that discriminating against gay people—even exhibiting open hostility toward them—is defensible on moral grounds. Those who call homosexuality immoral usually turn to religion for support. But how strong are these religious arguments? And if homosexuality is judged immoral, what bearing does that judgment have on an individual's constitutional rights?

The causes of homosexuality have been much debated, and so far researchers have yet to agree on an explanation. From the nineteenth century until 1973, the medical community regarded homosexuality as a disease or pathology, something that could be cured using treatments such as aversion and electroshock therapy and neurosurgery—none of which succeeded. Although many still agree with former Vice President Dan Quayle that homosexuality is a choice, current biological research increasingly suggests that it is not. Recent work points to the role of hormones, especially hormones to which the fetus is exposed while in the womb. Research on twins reinforces the view that genetics plays a significant role in sexual orientation.

Why and how people become homosexual, however, is not the primary concern of the public debate over attitudes and policies regarding homosexuals and their rights. Five to ten percent of the American population is gay and lesbian, and because of their minority status, they face discrimination and harassment of one sort or another. The arguments in this chapter address these questions:

Why do many heterosexual people react so strongly to homosexuality?
How does homophobia affect American society as a whole? Should people who disapprove of homosexuality be able to discriminate against homosexuals?
What might both gay and straight people do about homophobia?
Should sexual orientation be protected by civil rights legislation as race, gender, and religion now are?

The issues raised in these readings are central to the debates about more specific gay rights issues such as the role of homosexuals in the military, the right of homosexuals to marry, and the need for antidiscrimination laws.

# Everybody's Threatened by Homophobia
### Jeffrey Nickel

Homophobia *is a term often used to describe the attitude of those who express hostility toward homosexuals; it suggests a prejudice that is actually rooted in fear. Whatever the cause, the prejudice too often results in acts of violence against gay men and lesbian women. The following argument appeared originally in* Christopher Street, *a literary magazine whose writers and readers are primarily homosexual. In his essay, Jeffrey Nickel wants to show his readers that they can make a case against homophobia that will appeal to the interests of heterosexuals.*

*Do I hate my brother because he reminds me of myself, or do I hate my brother because he reminds me of someone who is "not" myself? Whom do I hate; the one who is me, or the one who is anything but me?*

—ELIE WIESEL

The answer is both. But knowing that would seem to be of little help. Our brothers *are* hated; sisters, too. We're right to tell America of the horrors that hatred visits upon us; of the humiliation, the isolation, and even the killings perpetuated, all in the name of heterosexual hegemony. These should be enough to convince this country that it's been terribly wrong about who we are. But there's more to the story. We can also tell about what homophobia—perhaps surprisingly—does to *others*; those who are perceived to be gay, those who are afraid they *might* be, and everyone else who clearly isn't but is nevertheless forced to feel bigotry's nasty bite. This is a lot of people—close to everyone, really. If only they could understand *these* things, too; maybe they would see.

As Allen Ginsberg wrote, "They can! They can! They can!" Practically every school child in America knows that a "faggot" is the worst thing they could be. How many wonder to themselves, is that *me*? Kids do have the vague perception that there are people in the world called homosexuals, though that's about all they know. How many boys who don't yet "like" girls think homosexuality is the explanation, when in fact for them, it's not? If gay weren't "bad" in their minds, they would feel no more anguish than that experienced by a child who discovers she's left-handed. But gay *is* bad in the country's consciousness, so children *do* worry a hell of a lot about being it. The "late-bloomer" thinks constantly of what might be "wrong" with him. Because the mere *possibility* that some of our children will be gay isn't even entertained, children who, in a freer society, would be relieved by that plausible conclusion are instead shut off from even *thinking* (much less talking) about it. It is awful that so many young gay people attempt, and often succeed in, killing themselves because of who they are. It's just as awful that so many straight kids try and die for what they mistakenly *think.* How refreshing it would be for young people to be able to discover their sexuality without fear. But right now, that's only a fantasy. Kids in this country must not only be straight; they must make absolutely sure that they are *not* gay. They shouldn't *have* to make sure.

A straight friend of mine whom I came out to when I was seventeen confided in me that he occasionally had gay thoughts and dreams. I told him there was no cause to worry; that virtually all people have same-sex (and other-sex) fantasies to some degree or another. But as enlightened as he truly was about homosexuality, these thoughts *still* bothered him deeply. What would it be like for someone who believed the worst things about homosexuality? I know what it is to be gay and feel the guilt, but I have a hard time imagining what it's like to really be straight and feel it. As a gay person I've had the "coming out process" to sort out all the meanings, but what do straight people have? It doesn't lessen the pain of the gay person's coming-to-terms to admit that these feelings are probably excruciating for many heterosexuals as well. And as is true in our case too, it's all for nothing.

I remember, especially in boyhood, the amazing level of paranoia that surrounded any form of male-to-male physical contact—aside perhaps from sports—as well as any kind of inter-male emotional experience. Males can hardly touch each other in this culture, except, as always, by lashing out. Susan Trausch of the *Boston Globe* put it well when she said that many men (and boys too) are fighting desperately to continue breathing what she called "100 percent pure macho air." They wish to be super-men; super-aggressive, super-obnoxious, and super-ignorant. Their mentality has the dual disadvantage of making automatons of men, and figurines of women. A lot of this mentality is attributable to self- and other-directed homophobia. Men practically have to go to counseling just to be able to talk to each other in real ways. What a pointless chasm we've created, just to make sure that closeness isn't "misconstrued."

I've told before the awful story of what happened to a friend of mine while we were in grade school. This boy hung around another boy so much and so ardently that it seemed he had a crush on him. He probably did. The other kids teased him for it a great deal, as I vaguely recall. But the teacher believed this was so intolerable that she had to do something about it, immediately. It really is unbelievable, but here's what she did: A "trial" was held in the classroom, with all members of the class present, at which this boy had to "defend" his feelings toward the other boy. The teacher herself served as the prosecutor. (He had no real defense.) My understanding is that this boy (now a man) really *isn't* gay. Yet he was totally humiliated in front of all of his peers, in such a way that it took him several years to once again build up any semblance of his lost self-esteem. Dating was impos-

5

sible for him for quite a long time. Some day, I would like to confront this teacher—whom theretofore I'd adored—and ask her what the hell she thought she was doing. It was child abuse of the worst kind, perpetuated against someone who didn't even possess the "demons" she most loathed.

Although I don't presume to know all of what this anxiety does to women, I imagine that it heightens an already well-inculcated sense that women are supposed to have no sexuality whatsoever. Women are taught to please men. Though they are, in a way, given more latitude to express affection for other women than men are for other men. Because women's sexuality is trivialized, they're often prevented from knowing just what would constitute lesbianism and what would not. If there were no stigma to homosexuality, this stultifying paranoia just wouldn't exist. Prejudice against homosexuality sharply limits how all men and women may acceptably behave, among themselves and with each other.

I hadn't thought much about how homophobia hurts heterosexuals until I saw a piece on the TV show *20/20* about two or three years ago. They had fascinating stories about several straight people who were actually attacked—physically—because others thought they were gay. One heterosexual couple holding hands walking down the street was beaten repeatedly. It seems the woman's short hair made it seem from the back that they were two men. What an awful education in bigotry it must have been for these poor people. It's interesting to contemplate how these bigots reacted to the knowledge that they were pummeling a wife and her husband: "Oh—we're very sorry to have broken your bones, but we mistook you for someone else."

A similar event took place in Lewes, Delaware, just last year. A man walking down the street with his arm around the shoulder of his (male) friend was struck and seriously injured by a pickup truck, after the driver yelled "faggot" at him. A second man in the truck then hit him in the head with a beer bottle. Then, the driver backed the truck over a curb and onto the sidewalk where the man was standing, crushing the man's legs between the rear of the truck and three metal mailboxes. He then put the truck in reverse once again in order to run over this man a second time, apparently in order to finish him off. He was prevented from doing so only because he couldn't gain the necessary momentum in the space available to jump the curb. The man's legs were so severely injured that the doctors had to graft muscles, tendons, and skin from other parts of his body in order to repair them. During the entire incident the men on the sidewalk were pleading with their attackers: "We're just buddies; we're not gay." One of the men attacked was a married, heterosexual father. But it didn't matter.

And this year, three Pensacola teenagers who said they were out to beat up a gay person in order to get beer money, did so with a lead pipe, fatally, to a man named John Braun, who was a married (straight) father of four. It's incredible: Heterosexuals have actually *died* because of homophobia.

For John Braun and many others, it's too late to understand their      10
stake in eliminating prejudice against gay people. It's too late for him to
join P-FLAG[1] and march on Gay Pride Day. But for most people, it isn't
too late. Before their children kill themselves far from home; before they lie
bleeding, mistaken, and prone; before their brothers die slowly alone; if we
talk about it, they can understand. They can! They can! They can!

---

### For Discussion

1. Nickel divides his argument into three main sections, each focusing
   on a different segment of the heterosexual population hurt by homophobia: young people whose sexuality is just developing (paragraphs 2–3), children and adults who do not feel comfortable expressing affection for friends of their own sex (paragraphs 4–6),
   and men and women who are attacked because they are mistaken
   for homosexuals (paragraphs 7–9). Which section provides Nickel's
   strongest reason? Comment on his strategy for arranging and supporting these three reasons.
2. Do you agree that "[p]ractically every school child in America knows
   that a 'faggot' is the worst thing they could be" (paragraph 2)? If you
   agree, can you say how our society conveys this idea?
3. What do you think Nickel means when he says that in our society
   "women's sexuality is trivialized" (paragraph 6)? Do you agree that
   society gives women "more latitude to express affection" for each
   other? Could this be related to the idea that their sexuality is not
   as powerful as that of men?
4. Notice that Nickel wants his readers to feel sympathetic to the problems of heterosexuals. How can you tell that his own sympathies are
   genuine?
5. What persuasive devices does Nickel use to urge his readers on to
   action?

### For Inquiry

In your writer's notebook, assess the truth of Nickel's argument, based on
your own experiences and observations.

---

[1] P-FLAG is an acronym for the national organization Parents–Friends of Lesbians and Gays.

# Confessions of a Heterosexual
## Pete Hamill

*Responding to acts of discrimination and violence, some gay rights activists make a point of displaying their pride and their anger through marches, demonstrations, and civil disobedience. In this selection,* Esquire *columnist Pete Hamill argues that some of the protesters have gone too far and are in fact creating a backlash among people who thought they had overcome their prejudices against gay people. As you read, consider whether Hamill is writing to militant homosexuals or to other heterosexuals — and what his purpose is.*

Early one evening in the spring, I left my apartment in Greenwich Village and went out to get a few things from the grocery store. The air was mild, the leaves were bursting from the trees. I paused for a moment on a corner, waiting for a light to change and the kamikaze traffic to come to a halt. Waiting beside me was a gray-haired man with a face the color of boiled ham and the thick, boxy body of an old dockwalloper. Before the light turned green, we heard distant chants, tramping feet, and suddenly, like a scene from a Chaplin movie, a small army of the night turned the corner. They came marching directly at us.

"Bash back!" they chanted. "Bash back!"

One of them looked at me and the other man and screamed: "You're fuckin' *killing* us! And we're not gonna *take it* anymore!"

Most of the members of this particular mob were young. A few were joking around, enjoying the fraternity of the march. But the faces of most of the demonstrators were contorted in fury as they raised clenched fists at the sky. While drivers leaned on auto horns and people came to their windows to watch, one wide-eyed kid spat in our direction and shouted, "Breeder shit!"

"What the hell *is* this?" the man beside me said. "Who *are* they?"   5

One marcher peeled off and explained. They were protesting gay-bashing and its most recent local manifestation, the planting of a bomb inside Uncle Charlie's, one of the more popular homosexual hangouts in the city. The marchers paraded off, and the man beside me said: "Tell ya the truth, I'd like to bash a few of these bastards myself."

With that brutal parting line, he stormed off. But as I watched him go, I felt an odd, uncomfortable solidarity with the man. He was my age, born in the Depression, raised in the '40s and '50s, and though we had probably led different lives, we almost surely came from the same roots. We were both out of the New York working class, children of immigrants, shaped by codes, geographies, and institutions now lost. We had thought the neighborhood triumvirate of church, saloon, and Tammany Hall would last forever; it didn't. We learned from our fathers and the older men (and not from television) what a man was supposed to do if he was to call himself a man: put money on the kitchen table, defend wife and children, pay his debts, refuse to inform, serve his country when called, honor picket lines, and never quit in a fight. Sexuality was crude and uncomplicated: Men fucked women. Period. So when my accidental companion had strangers curse him and spit at him, and above all, when he understood that they were gay, he reacted out of that virtually forgotten matrix. He wanted to give them a whack in the head.

But I was alarmed that a milder version of the same dark impulse rose in me. After all, I know that gay-bashing is real; homosexuals are routinely injured or murdered every day, all over the world, by people who fear or hate their version of human sexuality.

Yet what rose in me that night wasn't an instinct to hurt anyone in some homophobic spasm. It was more than simple irritation, and it was not new. In some fundamental way, I was bored by the exhibition of theatrical rage from the gay movement. I am tired of listening to people who identify themselves exclusively by what they do with their cocks. And I don't think I'm alone. Discuss the subject long enough with even the most liberal straight males of my generation, and you discover that twenty years of education, lobbying, journalism, and demonstrating by gays have had only a superficial effect; in some deep, dark pool of the psyche, homosexuals are still seen with a mixture of uneasiness and contempt.

Gay activists, of course, would laugh darkly at the above and think: *This is not news.* But most of them won't even listen to the reasons for these prejudices. Sadly, the folklore of the old neighborhood is not the only cause. Much of this persistent distaste is based on personal experience. Most males of my generation first encountered homosexuals during adolescence, and those men were not exactly splendid representatives of the gay community. When I was growing up, there were four known homosexuals in the neighborhood. All were in their forties. All singled out boys in the low teens. Two paid for sex, and in a neighborhood where poverty was common, a few dollars was a lot of money.

By all accounts, gay men, in those darkest years of The Closet, lived more dangerous and vulnerable lives than they do now. They were subject to blackmail, murder, beatings, and exposure on a more ferocious scale than today. But nothing so melodramatic seemed to happen in our neighborhood. Though everybody on the street knew about three of the four gay men, I don't remember any incidents of gay-bashing. Only one suffered public disgrace. One day, the police came to his door and took him off. A few days later his weeping wife and baffled children moved away, never to be seen again.

When I understood what these men actually *did*, I was horrified. For an Irish Catholic kid in those years, sex itself was terrifying enough; the homosexual variety seemed proof of the existence of Satan. Through all my years of adolescence, I believed that homosexuals were people who preyed exclusively on the very young, a belief strengthened by later experiences on subways, in men's rooms, and in the high school that I attended (where I met one of those tortured priests of the Catholic literary tradition). That belief was shared by most of the boys I grew up with, and when we left the neighborhood for the service (the working-class version of going off to college), we saw more of the same.

In the sailor joints of Norfolk or Pensacola, homosexuals were constantly on the prowl, looking for kids who were drunk, lonesome, naive, or broken-hearted over some Dear John letter shoved in their hip pockets. Again, older men taught us the code, demonstrating how Real Men were supposed to react. It was never very pretty: There was often violence, some gay man smashed and battered into the mud outside a tough joint after midnight. There was a lot of swaggering machismo, a triumphant conviction that by stomping such people we were striking a mighty blow against predators and corrupters. I'm still ashamed of some of the things I saw and did in those years.

It never occurred to us that some of these older gay men were actually looking for—and finding—other homosexuals, as driven in their search for love and connection as we were in our pursuit of lush young women. We were all so young that we arrogantly assumed that all of us were straight and they were bent; *we* were healthy, *they* were carriers of some sickness. It took me a while to understand that the world was more complicated than it was in the *Bluejackets' Manual.*[1]

The years passed. I grew up. I worked with homosexuals. I read novels    15
and saw plays written by homosexuals about the specifics of their lives. Gradually, the stereotypes I carried were broken by experience and knowledge. At the same time, I was roaming around as a reporter, seeing riots and wars, too much poverty and too many dead bodies. The ambiguities, masks, and games of human sexuality seemed a minor issue compared with the horrors of the wider world. Even after the gay-liberation movement began, in the wake of the 1969 Stonewall Riot, in New York, the private lives of homosexuals seldom entered my imagination. I didn't care what people did in bed, as long as they didn't wake up in the morning and napalm villages, starve children, or harm the innocent.

Some of my friends "came out" in the years after Stonewall. The process was more difficult for them than it was for me. On more than a few evenings, I found myself listening to a painful account of the dreadful angst that accompanied living in The Closet, and the delirious joy that came with kicking down its door forever. I apologized for any crudities I might have uttered while they were in The Closet; they forgave me. We remained friends.

In the years after Stonewall, I met gay men living in monogamous relationships, gay men of austere moral codes, gay men with great courage. I read interviews with gay cops, soldiers, and football players. I knew that

---

[1] A bluejacket is an enlisted member of the U.S. Navy.

there were thousands of gay men living lives of bourgeois respectability. There were even right-wing gay Republicans. Like many men my age, I thought, What the hell, there's room for everybody.

Then came AIDS.

And for people like me, everything about homosexuals changed once more. Thousands have died from this terrible disease, but for people my age, the gulf between straight and gay seems to be widening instead of closing. I find myself deploring homophobia, like any good liberal, and simultaneously understanding why it seems to be spreading among otherwise decent people. A phobia, after all, is a fear. And AIDS terrifies.

Under the combined pressures of fear and pity, I've been forced to confront my own tangled notions about gays. I cherish my gay friends, and want them to live long and productive lives. But while AIDS has made many millions even more sympathetic to and understanding of gay lives, I find myself struggling with the powerful undertow of the primitive code of my youth. I've lost all patience with much of the paranoid oratory of gay radicals. I can't abide the self-pitying aura of victimhood that permeates so much of their discussion. Their leaders irritate me with their insistence on seeing AIDS as if it were some tragic medieval plague of unknown origin instead of the result of personal behavior. 20

I know that AIDS cases are increasing among heterosexuals, and the virus is spreading wildly among intravenous drug users. For me, this knowledge is not abstract. I know one sweet young woman who died of the disease, picked up from her junkie husband; I was at her christening, and I'm still furious that she's dead. I also know that the rate of infection among homosexuals is down, the result of "safe sex" campaigns, education, and abstinence.

But when the gay militants in ACT UP go to St. Patrick's Cathedral and one of them crushes a Communion Host on the floor as a protest against the Church's traditional policies, I'm revolted. This is cheap blasphemy and even worse politics. I'm angered when the homosexual bedroom police force gays out of The Closet against their will while simultaneously opposing the tracing of AIDS carriers. When gay activists harass doctors, disrupt public meetings, and scream self-righteously about their "rage," my heart hardens.

I'm sure the government isn't doing enough to find a cure for AIDS. But it's also not doing enough to cure lung cancer, which kills 130,000 people every year, or acute alcoholism (57,000 every year), or to avert the ravages of cocaine addiction. Like AIDS (which has killed 81,000 Americans in a decade), these afflictions are spread, or controlled, by personal behavior. I've had more friends die of smoking, drinking, or doing dope than I have friends who died of AIDS. But I don't ever hear about the "rage" of the cigarette addict or the stone drunk or the crackhead, even though none of my stricken friends went gently into that good night. If anything, most current social rage is directed *against* such people, while the diseases continue to kill. And yet in most American cities, if you measured inches of type in newspapers, you might believe that all of the old diseases have been conquered and only AIDS remains.

I'm not among those who believe there is some all-powerful "Homintern" that manipulates the media while filling the museums with Robert Mapplethorpe photographs. But I don't feel I'm lining up with the unspeakable Jesse Helms when I say that I'm also fed up with the ranting of those gays who believe that all straights are part of some Monstrous Conspiracy to end homosexual life. One lie is not countered with another.

Certainly, as gay rhetoric becomes more apocalyptic, the entire public     25
discussion is being reduced to a lurid cartoon, devoid of criticism, irony, nuance, and even common sense. Certainly, there is less room for tolerance. I know a few gay people who resent being told that if they don't follow the party line they are mere "self-hating gays." And as someone outside the group, I don't like being told that I must agree with the latest edition of the established creed or be dismissed as a homophobe. More than anything else, I'm angry with myself when some of the old specters come rising out of the psychic mists of my own generation.

In the face of the AIDS plague, gays and straights should be forging a union by cool reason. Instead, we are presented with cheap pity, romantic bullshit, or the irrational, snarling faces of haters. As in so many areas of our society, divisions are drawn in black and white; there are no shades of gray. Homophobia is countered by heterophobia; the empty answer to gay-bashing is a vow to bash back. There are sadder developments in American life, I suppose, but for the moment, I can't think of one.

---

*For Discussion*

1. Using the "folklore" and experiences of his own working-class background, Hamill suggests that there was a connection between homophobia and socioeconomic class when he was growing up in the 1940s and 1950s. Do you think such a connection still exists?

2. Hamill refers to the 1940s and 1950s as "those darkest years of The Closet" (paragraph 11). Can you make any connection between homosexuals' staying in the closet and the experiences Hamill describes in paragraphs 10–13?

3. What made it possible for Hamill to overcome his prejudices? Have you had a similar experience in overcoming any form of prejudice?

4. Hamill defends his own recurring homophobia as a reaction to AIDS and the "ranting" of gay activists. What evidence does he offer to justify his new attitude? Is it all related to AIDS? How does Hamill use language as a tool to persuade readers to see the militant activity as he does?

5. In paragraph 9, Hamill says that "twenty years of education, lobbying, journalism, and demonstrating by gays have had only a superficial effect" on public perceptions. What solution is he proposing to the problem of homophobia?

*For Inquiry and Persuasion*

Research any recent demonstrations by gay rights activists, such as those in ACT UP. What are these groups protesting, and what methods are they using? How confrontational are their protests? How often is civil disobedience involved? Why have they taken such a militant approach? Look also at what they are saying, at what kind of language they are using. You might have to turn to periodicals aimed at the gay community, such as *The Advocate* and *Christopher Street*, which are indexed in *InfoTrac*. Your campus may have an organization for gay and lesbian students, which might also be a source for gay rights literature.

After inquiring thoroughly, if you feel Hamill's criticisms are justified, write persuasively to the militants, suggesting a cooler approach. If you think their approach is justified, write to Hamill and others like him who have lost patience with the demonstrations; try to generate understanding and sympathy.

*For Mediation*

After inquiring into gay rights demonstrations, write a mediatory essay aimed at both militant gays and an audience of men and women who feel as Hamill does. Before you write, create a brief of each side's position and reasons. In your mediatory essay, attempt to get each side to understand the other's emotions and interests. How might militant gays and straights work together to eliminate homophobia?

# Cartoon
## Garry Trudeau

*In one segment of Garry Trudeau's comic strip* Doonesbury, *Mike Doonesbury's good friend Mark realizes that he is homosexual.*

### Doonesbury

BY GARRY TRUDEAU

*For Discussion*

The cartoon makes us laugh at Mike's attitude, a stereotype of heterosexual males' discomfort around homosexuals. But in spite of its humor, the strip raises many issues. Does it suggest that homosexuality is or is not a choice? If sexual preference is innate, not a choice, how could a young man or woman grow up not recognizing gay or lesbian attractions, as happened in the case of the character Mark? Is it possible that American culture, in which heterosexual eroticism pervades our advertising and entertainment, and even the literature that young people read, could lead most everyone to assume that he or she is heterosexual?

# Homophobic? Reread Your Bible

### Peter J. Gomes

*Those who contend that homosexuality is immoral often cite the Bible for support. Although nonbelievers would find these arguments weak, the weight of biblical authority is unquestionable among many Christian audiences. During the crucial election year of 1992, fundamentalist Christians and others called upon Scripture to make their case that homosexuality is immoral and gay rights a threat to "traditional family values"; several gay rights measures were defeated in the process. In the following argument, Peter J. Gomes, a minister and professor of Christian morals at Harvard University, challenges the fundamentalists' interpretation of the Bible.*

Opposition to gays' civil rights has become one of the most visible symbols of American civic conflict this year, and religion has become the weapon of choice. The army of the discontented, eager for clear villains and simple solutions and ready for a crusade in which political self-interest and social anxiety can be cloaked in morality, has found hatred of homosexuality to be the last respectable prejudice of the century.

Ballot initiatives in Oregon and Maine would deny homosexuals the protection of civil rights laws. The Pentagon has steadfastly refused to allow gays into the armed forces. Vice President Dan Quayle is crusading for "traditional family values." And Pat Buchanan, who is scheduled to speak at the Republican National Convention this evening, regards homosexuality as a litmus test of moral purity.

Nothing has illuminated this crusade more effectively than a work of fiction, *The Drowning of Stephan Jones*, by Bette Greene. Preparing for her novel, Ms. Greene interviewed more than 400 young men incarcerated for gay-bashing, and scrutinized their case studies. In an interview published in *The Boston Globe* this spring, she said she found that the gay-bashers generally saw nothing wrong in what they did, and, more often than not, said their religious leaders and traditions sanctioned their behavior. One convicted teen-age gay-basher told her that the pastor of his church had said, "Homosexuals represent the devil, Satan," and that the Rev. Jerry Falwell had echoed that charge.

Christians opposed to political and social equality for homosexuals nearly always appeal to the moral injunctions of the Bible, claiming that Scripture is very clear on the matter and citing verses that support their opinion. They accuse others of perverting and distorting texts contrary to their "clear" meaning. They do not, however, necessarily see quite as clear a meaning in biblical passages on economic conduct, the burdens of wealth, and the sin of greed.

Nine biblical citations are customarily invoked as relating to homosexuality. Four (Deuteronomy 23:17, I Kings 14:24, I Kings 22:46, and II Kings 23:7) simply forbid prostitution, by men and women.

Two others (Leviticus 18:19–23 and Leviticus 20:10–16) are part of what biblical scholars call the Holiness Code. The code explicitly bans homosexual acts. But it also prohibits eating raw meat, planting two different kinds of seed in the same field, and wearing garments with two different kinds of yarn. Tattoos, adultery, and sexual intercourse during a woman's menstrual period are similarly outlawed.

There is no mention of homosexuality in the four Gospels of the New Testament. The moral teachings of Jesus are not concerned with the subject.

Three references from St. Paul are frequently cited (Romans 1:26–2:1, I Corinthians 6:9–11, and I Timothy 1:10). But St. Paul was concerned with homosexuality only because in Greco-Roman culture it represented a secular sensuality that was contrary to his Jewish-Christian spiritual idealism. He was against lust and sensuality in anyone, including heterosexuals. To say that homosexuality is bad because homosexuals are tempted to do morally doubtful things is to say that heterosexuality is bad because heterosexuals are likewise tempted. For St. Paul, anyone who puts his or her interest ahead of God's is condemned, a verdict that falls equally upon everyone.

And lest we forget Sodom and Gomorrah, recall that the story is not about sexual perversion and homosexual practice. It is about inhospitality, according to Luke 10:10–13, and failure to care for the poor, according to Ezekiel 16:49–50: "Behold, this was the iniquity of thy sister Sodom, pride, fullness of bread, and abundance of idleness was in her and in her daughters, neither did she strengthen the hand of the poor and needy." To suggest that Sodom and Gomorrah is about homosexual sex is an analysis of about as much worth as suggesting that the story of Jonah and the whale is a treatise on fishing.

Part of the problem is a question of interpretation. Fundamentalists and literalists, the storm troopers of the religious right, are terrified that Scripture, "wrongly interpreted," may separate them from their values. That fear stems from their own recognition that their "values" are not derived from Scripture, as they publicly claim.

10

Indeed, it is through the lens of their own prejudices and personal values that they "read" Scripture and cloak their own views in its authority. We all interpret Scripture: Make no mistake. And no one truly is a literalist, despite the pious temptation. The questions are, By what principle of interpretation do we proceed, and by what means do we reconcile "what it meant then" to "what it means now"?

These matters are far too important to be left to scholars and seminarians alone. Our ability to judge ourselves and others rests on our ability to interpret Scripture intelligently. The right use of the Bible, an exercise as old as the church itself, means that we confront our prejudices rather than merely confirm them.

For Christians, the principle by which Scripture is read is nothing less than an appreciation of the work and will of God as revealed in that of Jesus. To recover a liberating and inclusive Christ is to be freed from the semantic bondage that makes us curators of a dead culture rather than creatures of a new creation.

Religious fundamentalism is dangerous because it cannot accept ambiguity and diversity and is therefore inherently intolerant. Such intolerance, in the name of virtue, is ruthless and uses political power to destroy what it cannot convert.

It is dangerous, especially in America, because it is anti-democratic and is suspicious of "the other," in whatever form that "other" might appear. To maintain itself, fundamentalism must always define "the other" as deviant.    15

But the chief reason that fundamentalism is dangerous is that, at the hands of the Rev. Pat Robertson, the Rev. Jerry Falwell, and hundreds of lesser-known but equally worrisome clerics, preachers, and pundits, it uses Scripture and the Christian practice to encourage ordinarily good people to act upon their fears rather than their virtues.

Fortunately, those who speak for the religious right do not speak for all American Christians, and the Bible is not theirs alone to interpret. The same Bible that the advocates of slavery used to protect their wicked self-interests is the Bible that inspired slaves to revolt and their liberators to action.

The same Bible that the predecessors of Mr. Falwell and Mr. Robertson used to keep white churches white is the source of the inspiration of the Rev. Martin Luther King, Jr., and the social reformation of the 1960's.

The same Bible that antifeminists use to keep women silent in the churches is the Bible that preaches liberation to captives and says that in Christ there is neither male nor female, slave nor free.

And the same Bible that on the basis of an archaic social code of ancient Israel and a tortured reading of Paul is used to condemn all homosexuals and homosexual behavior includes metaphors of redemption, renewal, inclusion, and love—principles that invite homosexuals to accept their freedom and responsibility in Christ and demands that their fellow Christians accept them as well.    20

The political piety of the fundamentalist religious right must not be exercised at the expense of our precious freedoms. And in this summer of our discontent, one of the most precious freedoms for which we must all fight is freedom from this last prejudice.

---

*For Discussion*

1. In paragraphs 5–9 Gomes offers his interpretations of the biblical passages usually cited as showing God's condemnation of homosexuality. How well does Gomes deflate the arguments from Leviticus and from the letters written by St. Paul? To what extent does Gomes's own authority as a minister and Harvard theologian lend force to his view of these passages? (You may want to consult the biblical passages yourself before you respond.)

2. Gomes argues that all reading of Scripture involves interpretation (paragraph 11). What, for him, is the difference between right and wrong interpretation? How is "right" interpretation similar to inquiry, as we describe it on pages 161–163? Must a "right" interpretation be apolitical—that is, influenced by no political viewpoint?

3. What argumentative and stylistic techniques does Gomes use in paragraphs 17–20 to support his point about right and wrong interpretations of the Bible?

4. In his criticism of the rhetorical, or persuasive, strategy of the religious right, Gomes says their use of the Bible "encourage[s] ordinarily good people to act upon their fears rather than their virtues" (paragraph 16). Do you agree? Is it always bad to use fear as an emotional appeal in persuasive argumentation?

5. What other issues can you think of in which people commonly call upon the authority of the Bible for support? Do you think Gomes would argue that any of these misuse Scripture in the way he describes here?

*For Analysis and Persuasion*

A classic example of persuasive argumentation that calls upon the Bible as a source of authority is "Letter from Birmingham Jail" by Martin Luther King, Jr. (pages 258–271). After you have read King's "Letter" and our analysis of King's audience and purpose (pages 271–280), go back and locate all of King's references to the Bible. Write a paper in which you discuss King's use of the Bible, noting the specific fears or virtues of his audience to which he is appealing.

# Degrees of Discomfort
## Jonathan Alter

*A person who has no tolerance for others of a particular race is a racist. The following argument, originally published in* Newsweek, *asks whether homophobia, or prejudice against homosexuals, is equivalent to racism. The question is important because defenders of homosexual rights argue that the two forms of discrimination are comparable, while those who oppose gay rights claim their own right to disapprove of people whose behavior is repugnant or even sinful according to their own moral standards. Note how Jonathan Alter's argument makes the case for civil rights for gay people but not for universal tolerance of homosexuality. Note, too, that Alter wrote his essay in response to an incident in which Martin Luther King's son first made and then retracted a statement critical of homosexuals.*

When Andy Rooney got in trouble last month, gay activists complained he was being publicly rebuked for his allegedly racist remarks and not for his gay-bashing.[1] They wanted to know why homophobia was viewed as less serious than racism. The case of Martin Luther King III last week brought the comparison into even sharper relief. After a speech in Poughkeepsie, NY, in which he said "something must be wrong" with homosexuals, the young Atlanta politician met with angry gay leaders and quickly apologized. His father's legacy, King said, was "the struggle to free this country of bigotry and discrimination." In that light, he added, he needed to examine his own attitudes toward homosexuals.

King will need to ask himself this question: Is homophobia the moral equivalent of racism? To answer yes sounds right; it conforms to commendable ideals of tolerance. But it doesn't take account of valid distinctions between the two forms of prejudice. On the other hand, to answer no — to say, homophobia is not like racism for this reason or that — risks rationalizing anti-gay bias.

Discrimination against homosexuals is not the same as personal distaste for homosexuality. The former is clearly akin to racism. There is no way to explain away the prejudice in this country against gays. People lose jobs, promotions, homes, and friends because of it. Incidents of violence against gays are up sharply in some areas. Hundreds of anti-sodomy laws remain on the books, and gays are shamelessly discriminated against in insurance and inheritance. The fact is, a lot of people are pigheaded enough to judge a person entirely on the basis of his or her sexuality. Rooney's mail — and that of practically everyone else commenting publicly on this issue — is full of ugly anti-gay invective.

---

[1] Rooney, a commentator on *60 Minutes,* was briefly suspended by CBS in 1990 for making remarks that offended blacks but not for comments critical of homosexuality.

But does that mean that anyone who considers the homosexual sex act sinful or repulsive is the equivalent of a racist? The answer is no. Objecting to it may be narrow-minded and invasive of privacy, but it does not convey the same complete moral vacuity as, say, arguing that blacks are born inferior. There is a defensible middle position. Recall Mario Cuomo's carefully articulated view of abortion: personally opposed, but deeply supportive of a woman's right to choose. That tracks quite closely to polls that show how the majority of Americans approach the subject of homosexuality.

Like all straddles, this one offends people on both sides: straights who consider all homosexuality sinful, and gays who consider a hate-the-sin-but-not-the-sinner argument merely another form of homophobia. Moreover, the "personal opposition" idea rings more hollow on homosexuality than on abortion; after all, there is no third-party fetus—just consenting adults whose private behavior should not be judged by outsiders. Of course there are times when squeamishness is understandable. In coming of age, many gays have made a point of flaunting their sexuality, moving, as one joke puts it, from "the love that dare not speak its name" to "the love that won't shut up." Exhibitionism and promiscuity (less common in the age of AIDS) are behavioral choices that, unlike innate sexual preference, can be controlled. It's perfectly legitimate to condemn such behavior—assuming heterosexuals are held to the same standard.

Simply put, identity and behavior are not synonymous. A bigot hates blacks for what they *are*; a reasonable person can justifiably object to some things homosexuals *do*. The distinction between objecting to who someone is (unfair) and objecting to what someone does (less unfair) must be maintained. The worst comment about gays allegedly made by Rooney was that he would not like to be locked in a room with them. That would be a tolerable sentiment only if the homosexuals were *having sex* in the room. Otherwise it's a form of bigotry. Who would object to being locked in a room with cigarette smokers if they weren't smoking?

"Acting gay" often involves more than sexual behavior itself. Much of the dislike for homosexuals centers not on who they are or what they do in private, but on so-called affectations—"swishiness" in men, the "butch" look for women—not directly related to the more private sex act. Heterosexuals tend to argue that gays can downplay these characteristics and "pass" more easily in the straight world than blacks can in a white world.

This may be true, but it's also irrelevant. For many gays those traits aren't affectations but part of their identities; attacking the swishiness is the same as attacking *them*. Why the visceral vehemence, particularly among straight men? Richard Isay, a psychiatrist and author of the 1989 book *Being Homosexual*, suggests that homophobia actually has little to do with the sex act itself. "This hatred of homosexuals appears to be secondary in our society to the fear and hatred of what is perceived as being 'feminine' in other men and in oneself."

Such fears, buried deep, are reminiscent of the emotional charge of racial feelings. At its most virulent, this emotion leads to blaming the victim — for AIDS, for instance, or for poverty. In its more modest form, the fear, when recognized, can be helpful in understanding the complexities of both homosexuality and race.

That consciousness is sometimes about language — avoiding "fag" and 10 "nigger." But the interest groups that expend energy insisting that one use "African-American" instead of "black" or "gay and lesbian" instead of "homosexual" are missing the point. Likewise, the distinctions between racism and homophobia eventually shrivel before the larger task at hand, which is simply to look harder at ourselves.

---

*For Discussion*

1. In your own words explain what Alter sees as "a defensible middle position" on the issue of discrimination against homosexuals (paragraph 4). How does he support and defend that position?
2. Evaluate Alter's argument in paragraph 6, which compares homosexuals to cigarette smokers. In context, how valid is this analogy?
3. In paragraphs 7–8, Alter points out that what many straight people call "affected" behavior in gay people is actually part of their identities, something that they may not be able to hide even if they wanted to. Is one's sexual orientation something everyone should try to downplay in public? Should, for example, heterosexual couples be expected to avoid romantic physical contact in public, as most homosexual couples feel they must do?
4. Alter seems to conclude that homophobia, or "personal distaste for homosexuality," is not as severe a character flaw as racism (paragraphs 3–4). How does he support this point? Do you agree with him?
5. Alter quotes psychiatrist Richard Isay on a possible cause for homophobia (paragraph 8). What do you think of Isay's theory? Look at Pete Hamill's description of how "Real Men were supposed to react" if approached by a homosexual (paragraph 13 in his essay earlier in this chapter). Do you think Isay's theory might help explain some of the violence committed against gay men?

*For Inquiry*

Alter acknowledges that his middle position would offend "people on both sides" (paragraph 5). Write a dialogue with Alter in which you examine the truth of his position, posing questions that would represent the viewpoints of both sides. See pages 177–178 for suggestions about what to ask.

# Beyond Oppression
## Jonathan Rauch

*Some writers have claimed that gay men and lesbians are an oppressed class. Jonathan Rauch sets forth what he sees as criteria for claiming oppression, and he argues that gay men and lesbians in the United States do not meet these criteria. What is Rauch's purpose in denying victim status to gay people?*

At 10:30 on a weeknight in the spring of 1991, Glenn Cashmore was walking to his car on San Diego's University Avenue. He had just left the Soho coffee house in Hillcrest, a heavily gay neighborhood. He turned down Fourth Street and paused to look at the display in an optician's window. Someone shouted, "Hey, faggot!" He felt pain in his shoulder and turned in time to see a white Nissan speeding away. Someone had shot him, luckily only with a pellet gun. The pellet tore through the shirt and penetrated the skin. He went home and treated the wound with peroxide.

Later that year, on the night of December 13, a 17-year-old named John Wear and two other boys were headed to the Soho on University Avenue when a pair of young men set upon them, calling them "faggots." One boy escaped, another's face was gashed and Wear (who, his family said, was not gay) was stabbed. Cashmore went to the hospital to see him but, on arriving, was met with the news that Wear was dead.

This is life—not all of life, but an aspect of life—for gay people in today's America. Homosexuals are objects of scorn for teenagers and of sympathy or moral fear or hatred for adults. They grow up in confusion and bewilderment as children, then often pass into denial as young adults and sometimes remain frightened even into old age. They are persecuted by the military, are denied the sanctuary of publicly recognized marriage, occasionally are prosecuted outright for making love. If closeted, they live with fear of revelation; if open, they must daily negotiate a hundred delicate tactical issues. (Should I bring it up? Tell my boss? My co-workers? Wear a wedding band? Display my lover's picture?)

There is also AIDS and the stigma attached to it, though AIDS is not uniquely a problem of gay people. And there is the violence. One of my high school friends—an honors student at Brophy Prep, a prestigious Catholic high school in Phoenix—used to boast about his late-night exploits with a baseball bat at the "fag Denny's." I'm sure he was lying, but imagine the horror of being spoken to, and about, in that way.

If you ask gay people in America today whether homosexuals are oppressed, I think most would say yes. If you ask why, they would point to the sorts of facts that I just mentioned. The facts are not blinkable. Yet the oppression diagnosis is, for the most part, wrong.

5

Not wrong in the sense that life for American homosexuals is hunky-dory. It is not. But life is not terrible for most gay people, either, and it is becoming less terrible every year. The experience of gayness and the social status of homosexuals have changed rapidly in the last twenty years, largely owing to the courage of thousands who decided that they had had enough abuse and who demanded better. With change has come the time for a reassessment.

The standard political model sees homosexuals as an oppressed minority who must fight for their liberation through political action. But that model's usefulness is drawing to a close. It is ceasing to serve the interests of ordinary gay people, who ought to begin disengaging from it, even drop it. Otherwise, they will misread their position and lose their way, as too many minority groups have done already.

"Oppression" has become every minority's word for practically everything, a one-size-fits-all political designation used by anyone who feels unequal, aggrieved, or even uncomfortable. I propose a start toward restoring meaning to the notion of oppression by insisting on *objective* evidence. A sense of grievance or discomfort, however real, is not enough.

By now, human beings know a thing or two about oppression. Though it may, indeed, take many forms and work in different ways, there are objective signs you can look for. My own list would emphasize five main items. First, direct legal or governmental discrimination. Second, denial of political franchise—specifically, denial of the right to vote, organize, speak, or lobby. Third—and here we move beyond the strictly political—the systematic denial of education. Fourth, impoverishment relative to the non-oppressed population. And, fifth, a pattern of human rights violations, without recourse.

Any one or two of those five signposts may appear for reasons other than oppression. There are a lot of reasons why a people may be poor, for instance. But where you see a minority that is legally barred from businesses and neighborhoods and jobs, that cannot vote, that is poor and poorly educated, and that lives in physical fear, you are looking at, for instance, the blacks of South Africa, or blacks of the American South until the 1960s; the Jews and homosexuals of Nazi Germany and Vichy France; the untouchable castes of India, the Kurds of Iraq, the women of Saudi Arabia, the women of America 100 years ago; for that matter, the entire population of the former Soviet Union and many Arab and African and Asian countries.

And gay people in America today? Criterion one—direct legal or governmental discrimination—is resoundingly met. Homosexual relations are illegal in twenty-three states, at least seven of which specifically single out acts between persons of the same sex. Gay marriage is not legally recognized anywhere. And the government hounds gay people from the military, not for what they do but for what they are.

Criterion two—denial of political franchise—is resoundingly not met. Not only do gay people vote, they are turning themselves into a constituency to be reckoned with and fought for. Otherwise, the Patrick Buchanans of the world would have sounded contemptuous of gay people at the Republican convention last year, rather than panicked by them. If gay votes didn't count, Bill Clinton would not have stuck his neck out on the military issue during the primary season (one of the bravest things any living politician has done).

Criterion three—denial of education—is also resoundingly not met. Overlooked Opinions Inc., a Chicago market-research company, has built a diverse national base of 35,000 gay men and lesbians, two-thirds of whom are either not out of the closet or are only marginally out, and has then randomly sampled them in surveys. It found that homosexuals had an average of 15.7 years of education, as against 12.7 years for the population as a whole. Obviously, the findings may be skewed if college-educated gay people are likelier to take part in surveys (though Overlooked Opinions said that results didn't follow degree of closetedness). Still, any claim that gay people are denied education appears ludicrous.

Criterion four—relative impoverishment—is also not met. In Overlooked Opinions' sample, gay men had an average household income of $51,624 and lesbians $42,755, compared with the national average of $36,800. Again, yuppie homosexuals may be more likely to answer survey questions than blue-collar ones. But, again, to call homosexuals an impoverished class would be silly.

Criterion five—human rights violations without recourse—is also, in the end, not met, though here it's worth taking a moment to see why it is not. The number of gay bashings has probably increased in recent years (though it's hard to know, what with reporting vagaries), and, of course, many gay-bashers either aren't caught or aren't jailed. What too many gay people forget, though, is that these are problems that homosexuals have in common with non-gay Americans. Though many gay-bashers go free, so do many murderers. In the District of Columbia last year, the police identified suspects in fewer than half of all murders, to say nothing of assault cases.

And the fact is that anti-gay violence is just one part of a much broader pattern. Probably not coincidentally, the killing of John Wear happened in the context of a year, 1991, that broke San Diego's all-time homicide record (1992 was runner-up). Since 1965 the homicide rate in America has doubled, the violent crime arrest rate for juveniles has more than tripled; people now kill you to get your car, they kill you to get your shoes or your potato chips, they kill you because they can do it. A particularly ghastly fact is that homicide due to gunshot is now the second leading cause of death in high school–age kids, after car crashes. No surprise, then, that gay people are afraid. So is everyone else.

Chances are, indeed, that gay people's social class makes them safer, on average, than other urban minorities. Certainly their problem is small compared with what blacks face in inner-city Los Angeles or Chicago, where young black males are likelier to be killed than a U.S. soldier was in a tour of duty in Vietnam.

15

If any problem unites gay people with non-gay people, it is crime. If any issue does not call for special-interest pleading, this is it. Minority advocates, including gay ones, have blundered insensitively by trying to carve out hate-crime statutes and other special-interest crime laws instead of focusing on tougher measures against violence of all kinds. In trying to sensitize people to crimes aimed specifically at minorities, they are inadvertently desensitizing them to the vastly greater threat of crime against everyone. They contribute to the routinization of murder, which has now reached the point where news of a black girl spray-painted white makes the front pages, but news of a black girl murdered runs in a round-up on page D-6 ("Oh, another killing"). Yes, gay-bashing is a problem. But, no, it isn't oppression. It is, rather, an obscenely ordinary feature of the American experience.

Of course, homosexuals face unhappiness, discrimination, and hatred. But for everyone with a horror story to tell, there are others like an academic I know, a tenured professor who is married to his lover of fourteen years in every way but legally, who owns a split-level condo in Los Angeles, drives a Miata, enjoys prestige and success and love that would be the envy of millions of straight Americans. These things did not fall in his lap. He fought personal and professional battles, was passed over for jobs and left the closet when that was much riskier than it is today. Asked if he is oppressed, he says, "You're damn straight." But a mark of oppression is that most of its victims are not allowed to succeed; they are allowed only to fail. And this man is no mere token. He is one of a growing multitude of openly gay people who have overcome the past and, in doing so, changed the present.

"I'm a gay person, so I don't live in a free country," one highly success-    20
ful gay writer said recently, "and I don't think most straight people really sit down and realize that for gay people this is basically a totalitarian society in which we're barely tolerated." The reason straight people don't realize this is because it obviously isn't true. As more and more homosexuals come out of hiding, the reality of gay economic and political and educational achievement becomes more evident. And as that happens, gay people who insist they are oppressed will increasingly, and not always unfairly, come off as yuppie whiners, "victims" with $50,000 incomes and vacations in Europe. They may feel they are oppressed, but they will have a harder and harder time convincing the public.

They will distort their politics, too, twisting it into strained and impotent shapes. Scouring for oppressions with which to identify, activists are driven further and further afield. They grab fistfuls of random political demands and stuff them in their pockets. The original platform for April's March on Washington [1] called for, among other things, enforced bilingual education, "an end to genocide of all the indigenous peoples and their cultures," defense budget cuts, universal health care, a national needle exchange

[1] A major gay rights demonstration was held in Washington, D.C., on April 25, 1993.

program, free substance-abuse treatment on demand, safe and affordable abortion, more money for breast cancer "and other cancers particular to women," "unrestricted, safe and affordable alternative insemination," health care for the "differently-abled and physically challenged," and "an end to poverty." Here was the oppression-entitlement mentality gone haywire.

Worst of all, oppression politics distorts the face of gay America itself. It encourages people to forget that homosexuality isn't hell. As the AIDS crisis has so movingly shown, gay people have built the kind of community that evaporated for many non-gay Americans decades ago. You don't see straight volunteers queuing up to change cancer patients' bedpans and deliver their groceries. Gay people—and unmarried people generally—are at a disadvantage in the top echelons of corporate America, but, on the other hand, they have achieved dazzlingly in culture and business and much else. They lead lives of richness and competence and infinite variety, lives that are not miserable or squashed.

The insistence that gay people are oppressed is most damaging, in the end, because it implies that to be gay is to suffer. It affirms what so many straight people, even sympathetic ones, believe in their hearts: that homosexuals are pitiable. That alone is reason to junk the oppression model, preferably sooner instead of later.

If the oppression model is failing, what is the right model? Not that of an oppressed people seeking redemption through political action; rather, that of an ostracized people seeking redemption through personal action. What do you do about misguided ostracism? The most important thing is what Glenn Cashmore did. After John Wear's murder, he came out of the closet. He wrote an article in the *Los Angeles Times* denouncing his own years of silence. He stepped into the circle of people who are what used to be called known homosexuals.

This makes a difference. *The New York Times* conducted a poll on homosexuals this year and found that people who had a gay family member or close friend "were much more tolerant and accepting." Whereas oppression politics fails because it denies reality, positive personal example works because it demonstrates reality. "We're here, we're queer, get used to it," Queer Nation's chant,[1] is not only a brilliant slogan. It is a strategy. It is, in some ways, *the* strategy. To move away from oppression politics is not to sit quietly. It is often to hold hands in public or take a lover to the company Christmas party, sometimes to stage kiss-ins, always to be unashamed. It is to make of honesty a kind of activism.

Gay Americans should emulate Jewish Americans, who have it about right. Jews recognize that to many Americans we will always seem different (and we are, in some ways, different). We grow up being fed "their" culture

25

---

[1] Queer Nation is a gay political organization—many members of which are in their twenties— that advocates a highly visible gay presence in society.

in school, in daily life, even in the calendar. It never stops. For a full month of every year, every radio program and shop window reminds you that this is, culturally, a Christian nation (no, not Judeo-Christian). Jews could resent this, but most of us choose not to, because, by way of compensation, we think hard, we work hard, we are cohesive, we are interesting. We recognize that minorities will always face special burdens of adjustment, but we also understand that with those burdens come rewards of community and spirit and struggle. We recognize that there will always be a minority of Americans who hate us, but we also understand that, so long as we stay watchful, this hateful minority is more pathetic than threatening. We watch it; we fight it when it lashes out; but we do not organize our personal and political lives around it.

Gay people's main weapons are ones we already possess. In America, our main enemies are superstition and hate. Superstition is extinguished by public criticism and by the power of moral example. Political activists always underestimate the power of criticism and moral example to change people's minds, and they always overestimate the power of law and force. As for hate, the way to fight it is with love. And that we have in abundance.

---

*For Discussion*

1. Rauch acknowledges the opposition's arguments in paragraphs 1–4, but he denies that any of the examples constitute "*objective* evidence" of oppression (paragraph 8). Would you agree?
2. Does Rauch offer enough evidence to show that homosexuals meet only one of his criteria for claiming oppression? Could you raise any questions about the five criteria he sets up? Can you think of additional criteria?
3. In paragraph 24, Rauch argues that gay people work on the model that they are ostracized, not oppressed. What is the difference?
4. Rauch suggests that gay people can improve their situation through personal rather than political action. What is he advocating? Do you think his plan will work?

*For Convincing*

Many of the arguments in this chapter suggest or deny that parallels exist between racism and discrimination against homosexuals. Make your own case for or against such parallels, using some of the readings here as well as additional sources and evidence.

# In or Out in the Classroom
## Toni A. H. McNaron

*Toni A. H. McNaron is professor of English and women's studies at the University of Minnesota. Over the course of her more than thirty years of college teaching, she initially hid her identity as a lesbian but eventually decided to acknowledge it openly in her classroom. The dilemma of whether to teach from inside or outside the closet intrigued her enough to survey other gay and lesbian professors. The result of her research is her book* Poisoned Ivy: Lesbian and Gay Academics Confronting Homophobia *(1997), from which this selection is excerpted.*

If I as faculty member have a secret pertaining to my personal life, being in so public a venue as a classroom will be dangerous. On any given day, a student might ask a question that relates to the secret and threatens its exposure. My response will have to be in the nature of a cover-up or escape unless I am prepared to blow my carefully constructed cover.

During my years in the pedagogical closet, in the late 1960s and early 1970s, I routinely taught an advanced course in Shakespeare that was made up almost entirely of graduate students. Each time we discussed the sonnets, a bright male student asked if I saw something more than friendship going on between the poet and the young man to whom the first 127 poems are dedicated. My response was immediate and forceful: "Oh, no, but I can see what's happened here. You've misunderstood the poems in question because you are reading as a twentieth-century person. During the Renaissance, a revival of Platonic ideals was taking place; hence, platonic friendship was being practiced by many English noblemen. Within such a framework, the bond between two friends was actually superior to a sexual liaison because such relationships were susceptible to suspicion, jealousy, and anger, whereas friendships were more permanent and highly valued. The poet in the sonnets, then, is extolling the difference between the trust and harmony he can feel with his fair-haired young male friend and the consuming, destructive passion awakened by the dark-haired lady of the last twenty-seven sonnets."

My response was a flat denial of the text, because the poems to the young man describe jealousy over his youth, beauty, and the possibility that he is seeing other people. More importantly, I was misusing esoteric knowledge to protect my own identity. If I had admitted the possibilities behind the student's question, I risked saying "we" when I spoke of same-sex relationships. The danger of outing myself prevented me from being of any intellectual or potentially personal assistance to the student who had most likely taken a risk in asking such a question. Similarly, I discouraged serious discussion of the relationships between Romeo and Mercutio, Hamlet and

Horatio, Bassanio and Antonio, Rosalind and Celia, Othello and Iago or Cassio, and Hermione and Paulina. I broke into a sweat even when students expressed interest in the sixteenth-century stage practice of having young men play women's parts and the cross-dressing involved in this practice or the use of gender disguise in the comedies. Lecturing about such instances of sexual ambiguity and fluidity frightened me.

Thinking about these once so-frightening moments and the impact of being closeted on pedagogical effectiveness, I am reminded of a jack-in-the-box. Once presented with this toy, a child is prompted by curiosity to unlatch the brightly decorated box. A painted face springs up and the unsuspecting child often reacts with terror before feeling pleasure or enjoyment. Once out of the box, the jack is much harder to fold back into its hiding place. The springing out is sudden, whereas the replacement is slow and tricky. Often the jack pops back up rather than settling back into its container, and the toy is not enjoyable unless someone can put the coiled figure back in place.

My immediate impulse to lecture my student about arcane matters     5
seemed at the time nothing more than a serious Renaissance scholar's intent to correct a reading of the text before us. What I see today is an attempt to fold the entire issue of homosexuality as well as my own secret life back into an academic container.

Ironically, by stuffing the issue back into what I prayed was safety, I practically ensured that students would continue to ask questions. My only real protection would have been to laugh back in the jack's face, to acknowledge the legitimate basis of this curiosity about same-sex relationships as they figured in Shakespeare's work. A second irony turns around my flying in the face of my own pedagogical philosophy. I held that by encouraging spontaneity in general, I could facilitate inquiry into the more complex and contested aspects of the Renaissance. I spoke about the pervasiveness of paradox and ambiguity during this period of English history and letters, and about the uneasiness with such ambiguity in our own culture. Yet on the subject of one of the most fundamental ambiguities of the period, sexual and gender identity, I did not allow discussion.

A gay professor of linguistics for 17 years, currently teaching on the West Coast, remarks as follows: "In the closet, I was always aware of 'neutralizing' any language marked for sexual orientation. I also felt that while straight colleagues could, in class, make reference to their personal lives to 'put a human touch' on what they were teaching and thereby develop greater rapport with their students, I could not." Similarly, a lesbian philosophy professor recalls teaching an introductory course before she was out. A student commented in a derogatory tone that if John Stuart Mill's liberty principle were "used to defend homosexuality, someone might suspect Mill of being homosexual." The professor countered by saying that such a suspicion could also lead its thinker to develop a better opinion of homosexuality, since Mill was clearly a respected thinker of his era. Once out, this same professor received several student complaints referring to her "exhibition-ism" and saying they would never "advertise" their sexual orientation and wished she would have the "good taste" to keep hers to herself. She reflects on these circumstances as follows: "If I had been out, I doubt the first situation would have occurred at all; if I hadn't been, there would have been no occasion for the second."

There is no agreement among the respondents to my questionnaire about what constitutes outness, but they all speak about what it means in their own academic lives to teach and conduct research from inside or outside their own particular definitions of a closet. I myself define teaching as an out professor as being willing and even eager to integrate my lesbian perspective into my literary studies. Furthermore, I practice this willingness by introducing theoretical and interpretive remarks with a phrase like "as a lesbian-feminist scholar." For many respondents, such a stance is either not possible because of their subject matter or not preferred because of personal styles. I make no claims for my own definition. Rather I offer it to clarify my own academic perspective and to open up the whole question of what the concept means to each person involved.

Teaching as a publicly declared lesbian scholar has allowed me tremendous opportunities to challenge lesbian or gay and also heterosexual students in my classes. I no longer worry about being surprised by student questions regarding possibly coded homoerotic energy in literary works. If anything, I now must be alert to the students who find it disquieting if not annoying for me to announce that Walt Whitman and Stephen Crane or Willa Cather and Emily Dickinson were among the American writers who felt and expressed love and passion for members of their own sex. In responding to them, I try to remember how terrified I was in the past so that I do not repress whatever it may be that motivates their discomfort.

However, I also am unwilling to stop telling students the truth. Since I teach literature written in England and the United States, and since many of the finest writers in and out of the canons of literary study were and are gay or lesbian, to bury this central biographical fact is to commit an injustice. To colleagues who argue that they never include biographical information of any kind, I can only point out that students, like the general population, assume heterosexuality unless invited or even forced to do otherwise. Silence about any biographical detail that has a bearing on plot, character development, tone, and language could prevent a full understanding of a text.

I have found that most students welcome the truth, even when it disturbs them. It seems only sensible to espouse a pedagogy built on the hypothesis that the more a student knows about the environment from which culture springs and within which knowledge and ideas are generated, the fuller that student's learning and understanding will be. Therefore, a fundamental principle of higher education is served if faculty of all persuasions tell students the truth about the men and women studied in courses, including their sexuality.

Many heterosexual faculty may well omit such information out of ignorance. We tend to teach what we ourselves have been taught. Others may withhold information out of anxiety over perhaps being thought to be gay or lesbian themselves. Those who are convinced that their sexual orientation is the only "normal" or "decent" one might lie about their subject matter when it comes into direct conflict with their moral beliefs or might fear that they will encourage their students to see erotic and sexual energy toward members of one's own sex as a viable option for human beings.

### Gains and Risks

Lesbian and gay faculty who do choose to come out in their classrooms note both the gains and risks involved. A lesbian teaching at a midwestern graduate school describes her coming out as a process: "For years I stewed on whether I could be out in class—finally did it in one class, now do it regularly. I think it has a profound impact on my relationships with my students. I have become de facto counselor for many lesbian and gay students."

This faculty member also faced one of the more complex risks of being out, i.e., being unwilling to collude in any effort to continue burying gay or lesbian truths within their subject fields. She resigned from a lesbian graduate student's Ph.D. committee because that student was writing on secrets in Willa Cather's novels without dealing with the author's lesbianism as perhaps the most significant "secret" of all.

The lesbian professor mentions her relationship with the student's primary advisor, a heterosexual colleague with whom she had a mutually supportive history and who insisted that it was valid for the graduate student to ignore the author's sexual identity. The lesbian professor's response was emotional: "Young people are still dying regularly, literally dying, because they have nothing in their lives to let them know that being lesbian or gay is OK, that there are successful, healthy lesbian and gay people in the world." 15

This lesbian professor recalls another awkward conversation with the same colleague in which the appropriateness of her decision to come out in all her classes was questioned. Her colleague asked why she had to be a "lesbian" to her students rather than a "person." When the professor shared a letter she routinely sends to prospective students, her colleague grew more accepting. Reading a description of a person who loves the outdoors, comes from New Jersey, and is an avid gardener lessened the colleague's anxiety over the inclusion of lesbianism as a defining marker. The lesbian professor hoped through this exercise to convince her colleague of the possibility of being both a lesbian and a person.

Years of painful personal experience have taught me that a reductionistic view of sexual identity as total selfhood is entirely too prevalent among academics. These same academics would be appalled if I were to assume that their mentioning a spouse or children in class meant that they gave students only information tied to their sexual orientation. . . .

In some instances, respondents report a certain flattening of discussion of gay and lesbian issues as a result of their coming out:

> For a couple years when I was closeted I used an exercise in a sophomore level class that I really liked. When discussing Amy Lowell's love poems, identified in the text as being written to another woman, I asked the class in small groups to assume they were an editorial board of *The World's Greatest Love Poems.* Having already decided to use her poems, they now must decide if they will include information that they were written to another woman. . . . This exercise had generated good discussion on a complex topic. However, one of the first times I used it after I had come out early in the semester, there was little good discussion. I suspected then, and still do, that their knowing I was a lesbian inhibited them.

In other cases, faculty feel marked conflicts between their attempts at objectivity and their own responses to students' negative comments, as one lesbian professor who has taught for 15 years in the midAtlantic region writes:

> The semester the classroom became an unsafe place for me, I decided to go back into the closet.

While teaching a first-year writing course on "Race, Class, and Sexuality," which included work by people of color, gays, and lesbians, writers from different social classes, and heterosexuals, the professor was surprised to learn that some students thought the course was "about" lesbianism. Of her 68 texts, only 4 were written by lesbians. However, the teacher realized that for at least one male student, her identification as a lesbian had become part of the course content. When asked by him if he might write on why lesbians should not be allowed to parent, she responded professionally: Of course he had a right to argue his beliefs.

The student's initial argument turned on these points: children of gay and lesbian parents would be subjected to homophobia; and lesbian and gay parenting, because subject to more planning and/or technological intervention, was a sign of selfishness rather than "natural" desire. [20]

The class and the professor responded by pointing out that there is racism in the world but no one thinks of arguing that people of color stop having children. She continues as follows:

> We convinced him. He would have to come up with a better argument and evidence. He did. When he next presented, he had carefully researched Civil

Rights law. He used the lack of civil rights to argue that legally gays and lesbians should not be allowed to parent since they were not protected. At the
end of the semester, I asked myself what he had learned: to challenge his professor; to use effective argumentation as a means of voicing bigotry; he even
earned an A− on the paper.

Later this professor asked herself what she had learned, and her answer
is sobering: If she is to continue believing that by making students better
thinkers, she helps make them better people, she cannot teach that course
again. She used these words:

> Now I hide behind a text [that] is my closet. I peek out behind its pages to de-
> nounce the editors who remark that Kate O'Flaherty married Oscar Chopin
> while failing to mention anything about Langston Hughes' or E. M. Forster's
> sexual orientation. I inform my students "according to your editors, unless you
> are married, you have no sexuality." But I no longer teach many works I admire,
> enjoy, and have an investment in.

Faculty teaching in conservative areas or teaching the sciences, and some
working in church-related or community colleges, often said they would
lose too much of their students' respect to make it worthwhile to be out in
classes. A lesbian who has worked at a community college in the Midwest
for 26 years commented on the loss of credibility: "During the years I was
more out in [first-year] English classes, one of my colleagues (lesbian) suggested I was trying to teach with both hands tied behind my back. She was
likely correct; it's difficult to have credibility with many of our students."
Whatever personal loss she may have experienced from a decision to be
less out in the classroom, this faculty member has chosen to do so to teach
more effectively. This dilemma was caused by a homophobic climate too
deeply rooted for one teacher to combat.

Campus homophobia was often noted by faculty in this study. A gay
faculty member who has been teaching for 16 years in a Catholic university
reports: "Since the student body is so homophobic, I can never be a popular teacher. I can't hope for advancement based on my record with students.
Only closeted gays can advance this way, so 90% stay closeted. It's a horrible set-up." This faculty member understands the pressures on his colleagues and describes a context over which neither he nor they has much
control. His own decision to remain out even at the expense of his student
evaluations must be taken seriously. He reflected that change is unlikely at
his large private institution. "I'm really convinced of little improvement in
16 years teaching. A handful of people who are the official gay scholars
can capitalize on being gay, which is OK, but it's of no help to anyone else."
This context might be compared with England during the reign of Queen
Elizabeth I. Though a woman was on the throne, education and opportunities for the average woman did not change. It seems that, for many, benefits
do not trickle down from those enjoying advantages. . . .

For me, coming out in class took a very long time. Years after I had tenure and could no longer attribute remaining closeted to any fear of losing my job, I nonetheless held back from making this information public to students. More than one respondent notes that he or she lost a position offer or a promotion or advancement because of being openly gay or lesbian. Telling myself my heterosexual colleagues were not "ready" for my big announcement, I led a double life for several years. I was out in the local community but remained tightly closeted at the university. In the summer of 1975 I was teaching Introduction to Women's Studies. Knowing that I wanted to have a couple of class meetings focus on lesbianism, I found myself in a quandary. Finally I decided I would lecture one day about the history of lesbianism in the twentieth century; the second day I would invite a panel of women from the community to speak about being lesbians.

I got through the lecture, though my palms were sweating by the end and my heartbeat racing to the finish line. The people I had asked to participate in the panel had all agreed to come, accepting my inability to speak out myself and seeming to bear me no grudge for what could easily be construed as cowardice attached to privilege. Driving to campus on the fateful morning, I rehearsed my introductory speech: "Today we are fortunate to have a panel of local lesbians who are going to talk with us about their lives and about the levels of oppression lesbians suffer." The slight awkwardness caused by my having to repeat "lesbians" twice in the same sentence was more than compensated for by my relief at finding a way to avoid using the disassociative "they."

Class assembled, the panel members seated themselves around a table on the lecture podium, and the bell rang. Nothing else stood between me and the anxiety-ridden introduction. In the back of the room were two friends with whom I was currently working at a rural feminist center for women and young children. I had asked them to come because this panel was the first time a formal class at the university had included out lesbians.

I called the class to order, reminded them of our topic, and began my introduction. Soon I was appalled and excited to hear coming from my mouth, "They are going to talk with us about their lives as lesbians and the levels of oppression we suffer." My friends stood up for a moment at the back of the room, wide grins on their faces; the panel members exchanged surprised but pleased glances; I sat down. I have no idea what the generous women who spoke to those undergraduates actually said. All I could hear were my words, which may well have gone unnoticed by most students in the room, but which echoed loudly and triumphantly in my own head. I knew change had come for me for good. . . .

**Teaching out of the Closet**

In the excitement and empowerment that flowed from my tiny announcement on a summer morning in the late 1970s, I did what converts usually do: I swung the pendulum to the farthest extreme from where it had been originally. On the first day of every class, after asking students to fill out index cards on which they told me such demographic facts as name, majors, and progress toward graduation, and such narrative data as why they were taking my course, what hobbies and talents they possessed, and the last movie or book they had seen or read, I told them about myself. Always included was the fact that my major interests were lesbian literature and culture.

I have no idea how most students responded, but several vivid incidents remain in my memory. In a class on Shakespeare in which I made my stock comments on the first day, I noticed that on the second day one student sat with two books open on her desk: Shakespeare's *As You Like It* and the *Holy Bible*. Initially I thought perhaps she had found some line in the play that echoed something she knew from the Bible, but this did not seem to be the case. When she continued to bring the Bible to class, often choosing to sit right beside my own desk in the circle, I began to ponder what was going on. On a late afternoon walk, a thought came to me: Perhaps the student brought her Bible to defend herself against me as the sinning soul she undoubtedly thought me. I flashed to scenes from novels and films in which people held crosses in front of their faces to ward off some attacking vampire.

Rather than becoming angry or defensive as a result of this epiphany, I felt genuinely amused and then sympathetic toward the student. How difficult her position must be. She needed my course and so had to stay in it. I went to the next class determined to make the effort less frightening for her. By then we were studying *Romeo and Juliet*, so I decided to give a short talk about the place of religion in Shakespeare's day and of Christianity in particular in the plot of that play. While some of what I said was critical of the character of the Friar, that criticism came not from his practicing his Christian faith but rather from his dangerous failure to do so.

My tactic seemed to succeed. The student in question returned the next class period still in possession of her Bible but relaxed enough to leave it closed and under the text of the play. By midterm, she had stopped bringing it altogether, had begun to contribute positively to discussions, and even visited me during office hours to ask whether Shakespeare was a Christian since she kept finding veiled references to Christian beliefs. Without fudging the truth (i.e., no hard evidence can be found to label him in this way), I managed to show her that some basic Christian tenets such as forgiveness and fidelity are central to any moral or ethical system. At the end of the term, I received a course evaluation from a female student who commented that she had learned about more than Shakespeare during the term and that the instructor had heard and respected her religious views. I felt certain this had come from the student who started out so frightened of who I was and what I had to say.

If I ask myself why this story has stuck in my mind for so long, I know the answer has to do with teaching out of the closet. It is absolutely my right to come out to students; it is equally my responsibility to consider their well-being and perhaps to take some unusual measures to ensure that my desire to create a safer context for myself and the gays or lesbians in my classes does not create a dangerous or frightening context for the heterosexual students. It doesn't matter that no heterosexual teachers of mine ever seemed to have given any thought to the likes of me when they taught. I want to act more inclusively than others whom I find ignorant at best, bigoted at worst.

Many students find it empowering to study in such an open setting. This is true not only for gay and lesbian students, who naturally appreciate my public openness about my own sexual orientation, but also for many heterosexual students. In about 1980 I offered a graduate seminar on the nineteenth-century American poet Emily Dickinson. Since a great many of her poems reflect homoerotic feelings for several close women friends, I encouraged students to read for coded lesbian content. While explaining the process of reading for various codes in earlier literatures, I mentioned my own schemes for recognizing lesbian references. These approaches depend upon an erotics and aesthetics based on physical and emotional likeness, constructs that have evolved at least in part from my personal experience of lesbianism.

My frankness in the seminar opened up space for the students to discuss their own sense of the relationship between sexual expression and linguistic or poetic practice. This became apparent from in-class discussions, from students' reading journals, and in their final evaluations of the course. I was wrong in assuming that such space was presumed by heterosexual students. Several of them wrote long, eloquent comments about how emancipating the seminar had been; they said they were able for the first time to incorporate body knowledge into an intellectual setting. I was moved by this and became even more committed to coming out in classes, seeing that the benefits spread to a much larger group than I had imagined.

In 1989 I taught a course on black women writers. One of our texts was Audre Lorde's *Zami*, an account of her childhood and young adulthood. Since Lorde remains one of the most outspoken African-American lesbians, much of her story concerns her early awareness of her attraction to women. Most students in my class were white undergraduates who had given relatively little serious thought to how or why they were heterosexual, though they were part of the campus feminist community and so had considered matters related to gender. In many cases, Lorde's book was their first unequivocal exposure to lesbian material in a college course.

Even though *Zami* is about nonsexual aspects of Lorde's coming of age, the lesbian scenes stuck in students' minds. Each session devoted to

35

the book was punctuated with comments about matters such as "why" she became a lesbian.

Since the previously studied books had all been written by heterosexual black women, I had not made any reference to lesbianism. However, I did assume that everyone in class knew that I was a lesbian, and I was surprised when students began making overtly homophobic comments: "She probably became a lesbian because of her close relationship with her mother"; "I like the book except for the scenes about her being lesbian—they make me feel ishy"; "Why does she have to write so much about her sex life—the other books we've read have all sorts of other things going on in them"; "I can't relate to this book at all—not only is she black but since she's a lesbian nothing about her personal life makes any sense to me at all." During the second discussion period I felt compelled to come out directly in an effort not to squelch such remarks but to open up the discussion for me and any students who wanted to argue for a different emphasis.

Some heterosexual students felt immediately embarrassed, rushing to assure me that they were "just fine" with the subject, that some of their best friends were lesbian, that they had not meant anything negative or critical of Lorde even though they had voiced obviously negative and critical reactions to one of the central facts in Lorde's self-definition. One or two lesbian students came out, making clear to their classmates just how silenced and invisible they felt when judgmental remarks are made without any apparent concern for live lesbians who might be sitting next to the speakers.

Though the classroom atmosphere was decidedly tense for a time, the overall effect was productive. Not only was the remainder of our work on Audre Lorde truer to her text, but subsequent discussion of all books and issues was marked by a more rigorous analysis and a higher degree of self-reflection on most students' parts about their own sexual development and the ideas of the erotic in the works of such major figures as Toni Morrison and Alice Walker. On a broader scale, my intervention, together with the admission of invisibility on the part of lesbian students, encouraged many of the heterosexual women to acknowledge the limiting effects of unexamined heterosexism. They began to grasp how that system had kept them even from realizing there might be lesbians in the same room with them.

In their evaluations, students wrote movingly about the course's having 40 prompted them to begin a serious consideration of their journeys into heterosexuality. Some spoke of being inspired by Audre Lorde's brave example to begin writing their own sexual autobiographies, a process that was obviously affording them new insights into their private choices and the way in which heterosexist hegemony continues to flourish. Lorde herself said that what she wanted most from all sisters, black or white, lesbian or heterosexual, was for us to live a conscious life; these comments seemed integral to the course.

Many students thanked me for interrupting the usual class discussion to come out, telling me that everything about the class had seemed to deepen from that point. Since then, I have continued to acknowledge my lesbianism at some point during the term, no matter what the subject matter. However, I realize that my being in literature gives me an advantage; coming out in science or math or engineering classes surely depends upon a determined stance about the need to be open with one's students about this particular aspect of one's life. In such fields, a professor must make a decision about when and how to incorporate the fact of being gay or lesbian into her or his pedagogical approach. While, as one respondent told me, "Molecules aren't sexed," the learning situation is. Furthermore, at some point in almost every discipline, we are obligated to offer examples to our students. A professor who values being out in class surely has an opportunity to make lesbian or gay reality a part of his or her discourse. . . .

Some faculty feel no need to come out to students, even if their campuses are accepting of diversity. A lesbian professor of comparative literature makes no effort to hide her identity from individual students when asked direct questions. She includes lesbian and gay texts in her courses, but she has never come out in the classroom. She does not ascribe to the notion that being lesbian allows her to read differently from those who are not. Were she to teach lesbian or gay studies, she would see her identity as directly relevant and would consider it productive to come out.

However clear this individual is about not revealing her lesbianism in classroom settings, she nonetheless remembers two moments in her teaching career when she felt a need, "not acted upon in either case, to announce [her] sexuality to a class as a pertinent part of discussion." The first was in the early 1980s, when she and several other women faculty were invited to a class taught by an African-American colleague. The topic was feminism in Alice Walker's *The Color Purple.* "In the discussion, the instructor deplored the lesbianism in the novel as denigrating to ideas about black life in America in a way that I found offensive and bigoted. I challenged prescribing content because of what we 'want' from texts." The professor did not make a personal statement because doing so would have distracted from the main point of the discussion. She was highly unsatisfied with the experience.

The second instance came in 1994 during the final class meeting of a course on forms of discrimination related to the history of infectious diseases. The lesbian professor reports "less dynamic discussion and less controversy than we had hoped, less lively debate than had occurred the last time we taught the course." The class was nearly half students of color, a far higher percentage than that on campus as a whole. Several of those students commented that discussions had "walked right up to issues of race but then skirted around them," an accusation the professor felt was justified. She asked whether beginning the semester with some discussion of overlapping identities would have improved the climate so that students might have taken more risks:

> This elicited a productive conversation in which students identified aspects of their identities that complicated their classroom lives. I did not come out, largely because the students were talking about themselves in important ways and I did not want to shift attention. However, as I think about my pedagogical strategies, next time I teach [this course], I will handle the issue differently.

• • •

For me, pedagogical strength seems to be attendant upon my coming out early in the term. In most undergraduate classes, I tell a favorite story on my "coming out day": 45

> Let's say I get to know, like, and respect someone through shared social or political activities or aims. At some point in our process, I learn that they occupy some category previously off my scale of acceptability. It's as if I had built a picture frame around what is "normal" or "good," which I assume includes the individual, who suddenly I find possesses characteristics that force me to exclude him or her from my picture. I can leave my friend or colleague outside the frame or I can revisit my lumberyard to purchase more wood to enlarge my frame.

This story usually works in getting students to think about the limitations inherent in prejudice against whole groups of people. On several occasions, the story has prompted notes from students who want to thank me for giving them a way to understand what happens when they find out something surprising about a friend or family member. One person wrote the following: "I just want to thank you, Toni, for your story about your picture frame. After class, I went right over to my lumberyard and bought more wood!" . . .

As more becomes known about the rich diversity of approaches to teaching as gay or lesbian faculty, I need to remember that circumstances vary widely and each individual must make his or her own decisions. I remind myself constantly that none of us ever knows the innermost processes any lesbian or gay faculty member goes through in finding the best solution. For many gay and lesbian colleagues in this country, there is no genuine solution at all. People simply must do what they can to keep body and soul intact, and this is perhaps the saddest reality shared with me during this research. I want to carry that reality close to my heart and mind as I continue to argue for the highest degree of openness possible in a given context.

---

*For Discussion*

1. What are some of the pros and cons that McNaron and her colleagues have had to face following their decision to come out? Do

you think that the subject matter of McNaron's teaching made her sexuality more relevant to class discussions and her students' education than if she had been teaching a course in which questions of sexual relationships would not arise? Has she convinced you that, at least in her case, coming out was a reasonable decision?

2. How did you react to the narrative about McNaron's own experience of coming out in class for the first time? Have you ever been in a class in which a professor spoke openly about his or her homosexuality? If so, what was the reaction? How would you feel as a student in that situation?

3. Paragraphs 19–21 should be of interest to students in a course emphasizing argument. If you have read the chapters in this text on arguing to inquire and arguing to convince, what do you think of the student's argument discussed here? How did he revise his thinking after the class inquired into his original argument? From what is given about his second argument, do you feel it would have been convincing? to which readers? What assumptions and values does it imply?

4. Should teachers avoid teaching texts that might bring out students' prejudices in class discussion? If students express intolerance, should their views go unchallenged?

5. What is McNaron's reasoning on the fact that some students might be profoundly uncomfortable with her announcement? Do you agree?

6. Do you think that it would be more difficult for homosexual faculty or for homosexual students to be open about their sexuality in class discussions, assuming that such discussion was relevant to the subject matter?

## For Persuasion

1. Do you believe becoming a better thinker makes you a better person? Can you use examples from your own education to show that any projects, especially writing projects in which you had to reason about an issue, made you a better person? Be sure to explain what you mean by "better," and be specific about the research, thinking, and lasting influence of the experience.

2. As a student, what is your perspective on having a professor be open about his or her sexuality in the classroom, in particular in a first-year writing program? Suppose a class was reading the essays in this chapter, and the teacher was gay or lesbian. Do you feel he or she should come out as part of the inquiry into issues surrounding gay and lesbian rights? Consider some of the issues that gay and lesbian faculty have to confront and the purpose of using current issues as topics for writing, and make a case directed to the teacher from a writing student's point of view.

*For Further Research and Discussion*

1. One large area of debate related to homosexual rights involves marriage, or the legal benefits of marriage: tax breaks, employer-sponsored insurance coverage for spouses, inheritance rights, even the right not to be forced to testify in court against one's mate. There is, further, the symbolic statement that marriage makes about a couple's commitment to each other. In 1967, the Supreme Court called marriage "one of the basic civil rights of man," yet no state recognizes marriages between members of the same sex. Inquire into this issue, and be ready to report to the class on the range of opinions about marriage and domestic partnerships. (Gay people themselves are divided on the question.)

2. Inquire into the latest research on the causes of homosexuality. What interpretation do most gay people seem to accept on this matter? If a clear case could be made for biological causation, your class might want to discuss how such a conclusion would influence any of the arguments about homophobia and gay rights.

*Additional Suggestions for Writing*

1. *Inquiry and convincing.* Based on your inquiry into the views on gay marriage, write an exploratory essay in which you discuss areas of agreement and disagreement. Conclude with a statement of your own position on this issue, indicating which reasons uncovered in your research best support your position. Then go on to draft and revise a case for an opposing audience.

2. *Persuasion.* In this chapter's first selection, Jeffrey Nickel points out that homophobia is something children learn at an early age in our society. Some school districts have devised curriculums aimed at encouraging greater tolerance of homosexuals through, for example, the use of storybooks that depict children who have "two mommies" or "two daddies." This aspect of New York City's "Rainbow Curriculum" was quite controversial.

   Do research into educational curriculums that deal with homosexuality. Find out where such curriculums have been tried and what the pro and con arguments are. If you decide such curriculums would not be effective in reducing homophobia or that reducing homophobia should not be a function of the schools, write a persuasive argument against instituting such curriculums. If you decide that they are a good idea, make a persuasive argument for some specific course of action.

3. *Mediation.* The AIDS epidemic has focused public attention on questions of rights and responsibilities. Some gay advocates argue that it is the responsibility of the government and the medical community to find a vaccine to prevent AIDS so that people need not live in ter-

ror if they fail to follow all the guidelines for safe sex. At the other extreme, people argue that because AIDS is a preventable disease, it is the responsibility of each adult to see that he or she is not exposed through risky behavior and that the government and medical community ought to give their full attention to life-threatening diseases that strike at random. Investigate these arguments about AIDS research and spending and the range of viewpoints in between. Write a mediatory essay that suggests a position all sides could find reasonable.

# Chapter 14

# The News and Ethics: Reading Journalism Today

Probably no other institution is more controversial or subject to more conflicting pressures than "the press," a term we casually use to refer to all the media that give us our sense of what's going on in the world. Once the press really was *the press*, wholly a print medium; but first radio, then television, and now the Internet compete successfully with the daily newspaper for the public's loyalties. Indeed, the electronic media, especially television, compete so well that there are serious doubts about whether newspapers can survive. Those who think they won't point to the demise of many newspapers and the scramble of many others to maintain a circulation large enough to secure the advertising revenue that sustains all organized news operations.

A basic premise of this chapter is that our open, democratic society has a high stake not merely in the survival but in the long-term health of high-quality print journalism, especially in newspapers. As important and influential as the electronic media are, they typically do not and probably cannot offer the depth and detail, the analysis and reflection that can make news more than sound bites, sensationalism, and disconnected stories. Knowing what is happening is one thing, understanding another. And even knowing can be problematic if television is our only source for news. The more complex the issue and the less superficially "interesting" it is, the more we must depend on print journalism. That which doesn't "play" well on television gets little or no attention.

Recognizing the importance of newspapers, however, does not mean we should be uncritical of them. On the contrary, to varying degrees and in different ways, all the selections in this chapter are critical of current journalistic practices. Indeed, it is difficult to find spirited defenses of the current system, even among journalists themselves, who in the past have often proudly defended their profession against detractors. Almost everyone agrees that the daily newspaper is in crisis and that part of this crisis is ethical, concerned with norms governing how news is gathered and disseminated.

Especially when an institution is in crisis, it is always a good idea to return to fundamental questions. Nothing could be more fundamental than the question Jack Fuller poses in the first selection: What is news? Any honest answer will reveal how constrained even a "free" press is and how descriptive questions tend to merge with normative ones, for we cannot ask what the news is without at least implying what it *should* be. And, of course, both questions are worth thinking and arguing about.

We move in the next two selections deeper into what Fuller calls "news values." Everyone agrees that the news should be fair. But what is "fair"? Is fairness more important than accuracy or intellectual honesty? What exactly are the values involved in responsible journalism? Are some values more important than others? If so, why?

In the second reading Michael Schudson offers a historical perspective on fairness. What was fair in colonial America is not necessarily fair now or fair a century ago. Norms change. But Schudson clearly advocates "modern analytical and procedural fairness" as an enduring value, whereas the next writer, Jim Squires, thinks that fairness is impossible given the largely unconscious biases of reporters and the corruption of contemporary news by the demand that it be entertaining. Do any of the traditional journalistic values have much of a chance when news media are judged entirely by the numbers, TV ratings, and circulation?

Clearly, if we agree with Squires that "real news" has lost out in an "entertainment culture with no moral compass and no concern for fairness — or taste," then we must also ask, How can the news be reformed? It won't do to conclude that the press is hopelessly corrupt and the news untrustworthy and leave it at that. We simply can't afford to "write off" the news, for we depend on it for most of our knowledge about the world and for information to guide important decisions. If the news isn't doing its job, then it must be reformed. But how? in what ways exactly? and by whom? Some avenues of reform have been tried already, such as the experiments in so-called public or civic journalism, which our last author, James Fallows, finds promising. Is this the way to go? Or should we try something else?

Of course, we need not judge the press as harshly as some of its severest critics do; we could hold that the case against the press is overstated and that news coverage is actually more extensive than ever and on the whole reasonably reliable and even-handed. Perhaps only modest reforms are needed, or even none at all—and we can also question the motives of the reformers, motives that may not be as purely altruistic or as public-spirited as they are given out to be. Just as the current system has "winners" and "losers," so any reform of it will as well.

Regardless of how we assess current journalism, we need to evolve our own critical strategies for "reading"—that is, interpreting—the news. Some people are naive and believe everything they read. Others opt for extreme skepticism, avowing that they believe "only half of what they see and nothing that they read." Neither attitude—all or nothing—will do. The first approach lacks sophistication, the second discrimination. Perhaps, then, the fourth reading, by W. Lance Bennett, is the most important, for it suggests ways to take the news in without being "taken in," ways to think critically about the news without rejecting it wholesale.

The press has never been uncontroversial, and in our society it can't and shouldn't be. Precisely because it matters so much, because a free society cannot exist without a free press, we must return again and again to "news values." If the values must change, if they must be refined and redefined, the issue endures. It is something we must care about if we want informed citizens making intelligent choices.

# What Is News?

## Jack Fuller

*A novelist, winner of the prestigious Pulitzer Prize, and publisher of the* Chicago Tribune, *Jack Fuller's view of news and ethics carries special weight, the authority of an accomplished and experienced journalist. In this excerpt from his 1996 book* News Values: Ideas for an Information Age, *he advances a modest view of what "truth" in news reporting should mean, what biases the news cannot escape, and what values should inform the telling of news stories. Perhaps most interesting is his examination of the concept of fairness and his valuing of other intellectual virtues over it.*

*As you read, bear in mind that certain newspapers, because of their age, prestige, and financial backing, enjoy special status as "national institutions." The* Tribune *is one of these, as are the* New York Times, *the* Wall Street Journal, *and a handful of other papers. Views of journalism from such sources merit respect, but they may not be representative of "news values" found in less well-established papers.*

What is the proper standard of truth for the news? To answer that, one must first come to some clear understanding of what news is. Even at its most presumptuous, the news does not claim to be timeless or universal. It represents at most a provisional kind of truth, the best that can be said quickly. Its ascription is modest, so modest that some of the most restless and interesting journalists have had trouble making any claim of truth at all.

In *Let Us Now Praise Famous Men*, James Agee, then a writer for *Fortune* magazine, savaged the whole idea of journalistic truth:

> Who, what, where, when and why (or how) is the primal cliché and complacency of journalism: but I do not wish to appear to speak favorably of journalism. I have never yet seen a piece of journalism which conveyed more than the slightest fraction of what any even moderately reflective and sensitive person would mean and intend by those inachievable words, and that fraction itself I have never seen clean of one or another degree of patent, to say nothing of essential falsehood. Journalism is true in the sense that everything is true to the state of being and to what conditioned and produced it (which is also, but less so perhaps, a limitation of art and science): but that is about as far as its value goes. . . . [J]ournalism is not to be blamed for this; no more than a cow is to be blamed for not being a horse.

Even accepting that news is not the kind of truth that would meet the rigors of science or the clarity of revealed religious insight, there is still too little agreement on how to define it. Though journalists might agree the beast is a cow, they will debate what breed and how much milk it can produce. Look at one day's newspapers from a dozen cities and you will find, even correcting for local factors, no consensus.

One might be tempted to say that news is anything that news organizations report. In fact, this definition has adherents among a few journalists whose fascination with power leads them to overestimate their own. It also appeals to certain outsiders, such as those who encourage the media to do more uplifting stories in the expectation that they might revise grim reality as easily as they revise a sentence.

But the definition of news does not have to be so empty in order to explain most variations in coverage. Most respectable journalists on American newspapers would, I think, roughly agree with this statement: News is a report of what a news organization has recently learned about matters of some significance or interest to the specific community that news organization serves.

This narrows the debate over the news value of any particular item but does not lead to unanimity. The *New York Times* may consider a vote in Congress on free trade to be the most important story of the day while the *New York Daily News* leads with a deadly fire in the Bronx. This is because of each newspaper's understanding of the community of readers it serves and, perhaps, because of differing judgments about what is significant.

There are some papers, to be sure, that do not seem to be concerned with the element of significance at all. Such a paper would always go with a sex scandal over a coup attempt in the Soviet Union. Most contemporary journalists would scoff at this as pandering, but the honest ones have to say that they, too, take account of the pull of basic (even base) human curiosity; the difference is whether any consideration of larger interests comes into play.

What is significant will always be a matter of debate, but in general the evaluation should turn on the foreseeable consequences. Significance and interest provide separate bases for calling an event or piece of information news, and either may be sufficient. No matter how few people were interested in reading about strategic arms limitation talks, the enormous importance of these negotiations to the future of the planet made them extremely newsworthy. And no matter how insignificant Michael Jordan's performance in minor-league baseball may have been to the history of the United States, the deep popular interest in it justified extensive coverage.

**The Fundamental Biases**

My proposed definition of news includes several elements that are not wholly subjective (though this does not mean they are unambiguous): timeliness, interest for a given community, significance. These look beyond the journalists' personal preferences outward to phenomena in the world that can be discussed, if not measured.

The elements of the definition also suggest some ways in which the journalist's report of reality is likely to be fundamentally biased.

First, journalism emphasizes the recent event or the recently discovered fact at the expense of that which occurred before or had already been known. Journalists recognize this bias and talk about the need to put "background" information into their pieces. But commonly the internal logic of reporting puts "background" information very much in the background and tolerates little more of it than is absolutely necessary to permit the reader to make some sense of the new material. From time to time a newspaper may go back and attempt to tell about an event or issue comprehensively, but this is very special treatment. The bias of immediacy is the rule.

Second, the journalist has a bias in favor of information that interests his audience. This helps explain the favorite complaint about news—that it accentuates the negative. People's curiosity shows a tropism for misfortune. Disaster always becomes the talk of a community in a way that good fortune less commonly does. Trouble touches some people's empathy and others' sense of doom. Fear and anger operate strongly at greater distances than love, so bad news travels farther. One might delight to hear that the daughter of someone he knew had just received a prestigious scholarship, but he would shudder at the brutal murder of a stranger's child a continent away.

The bias of interest also means that the audience's blind spots will tend to be blind spots in the news. If people are generally indifferent about a particular subject—say international trade talks such as GATT—the journalist knows that it will be very difficult to make them pay attention to it, regardless of how important it may be in their lives. Whole areas of inquiry go years, decades without attention in the news until they become involved in an event that captures people's imagination. The engineering of bridges receives scant notice until a large span collapses. Human retrovirology meant nothing to the general population until the scourge of AIDS. Even disciplines that find themselves more commonly in the news—economics, law, medicine—are lit up piecemeal, depending on the fascination of the day. The Phillips curve in economics reaches public print when in defiance of it inflation and unemployment both begin to run high. Even an obscure field of law such as admiralty might get an examination in the news when something of sufficient drama happens upon the high seas. We learn everything we never wanted to know about the human colon when a president has part of his removed.

Walter Lippmann described the press as a searchlight that restlessly prowls across the expanses, never staying on any feature for very long. Actually, human curiosity is the searchlight. We journalists just go where it points.

Finally, there is a bias toward what occurs close to the audience's     15
community. Often this manifests itself as a simple matter of geography.
A *National Lampoon* parody of a hometown newspaper called the *Dacron Republican-Democrat* some years back had a page one headline that read: "Two Dacron Women Feared Missing in Volcanic Disaster." The drop head read: "Japan Destroyed."

Community is not always defined by physical proximity. Communities of interest have newspapers, too, and the list of publications includes more than the trade press. Consider, for example, the *Wall Street Journal* and the *New York Times*. Both have specialized audiences and are edited to satisfy their interests. *USA Today* also appeals to a distinct public—the business traveler away from home—and this explains many of the editing choices it makes, which would be foolish for a metropolitan daily newspaper with an audience that has a much different set of shared interests.

The bias of community provides an answer to a snobbish question one often hears: Why don't other newspapers pay as much attention to international affairs as the *New York Times* does? The *Times* recognizes that for much of its audience the world is the pertinent community of interest. A disproportionate part of its readership engages directly in international business and public policy. Since it is circulated nationally, the *Times* becomes a kind of local newspaper for this community (and can be as provincial about matters outside its territory as any other paper; just try to get guidance from the *Times* about the best easy-listening CDs or religious TV shows). There are not enough people in most cities who are deeply engaged in international affairs to command strong international coverage in their metropolitan dailies, though in certain centers such as Los Angeles, Washington, DC, and Chicago the audience is large enough to support a substantial foreign-news commitment by the local papers, and in others such as Miami there is enough interest in one part of the world to require the newspaper to make a large commitment of space and attention to it.

The element of significance in the definition of news does not necessarily introduce a bias. Rather it might be said to be the heading under which to group all other biases. These may arise out of the social circumstances of journalists, the imperatives of the economic market on their news organizations, the culture from which a journalist comes, or the larger intellectual currents of the times: interesting issues, but [. . .] they do not distinguish observational bias among journalists from the bias of any other observer. . . .

### Intellectual Honesty and the Golden Rule

. . .

Intellectual honesty means that in presenting a news report a journalist may draw certain conclusions and make certain predictions about the consequences of a particular event, but it also imposes a duty to do justice to the areas of legitimate debate. This is what separates news from polemical writing. The former must attempt to represent a matter of public concern in its fullness. A polemic aims to persuade the audience that one view of the matter is undoubtedly correct.

The Golden Rule has endured through the centuries as an ethical proposition of enormous force because it offers a subjective method for determining the moral direction one's behavior should take. It asks that an individual treat others the way he would like to be treated, to turn the tables, to

20

empathize. This is a useful way to look at the requirement of intellectual honesty. In reporting a matter of legitimate debate (How big should the Pentagon budget be? Did Alderman X take a bribe?), the journalist will surely reach some conclusions. And, with some constraints described later, he should feel free to share his conclusions with his readers. But in doing so, the Golden Rule suggests that the reporter must try to put the case against his conclusions as forcefully as he would want an opponent to put the reporter's own arguments.

This, like many moral propositions, sets an extraordinarily high aspiration. If you deeply believe your own position, you will find it very difficult to express the opposite point of view with the same enthusiasm and force. But the Golden Rule is a corrective; it points the right direction. And, with discipline, it is not too much to expect reporters (freed of the impossible requirement of objectivity and the nonfunctional requirement of neutral expression) to play square with others' arguments, stating them honestly and presenting the facts and logic supporting them. The Golden Rule is a perfectionist goal, toward which to stumble in our imperfect, human way.

Even the unalloyed gold standard does not require a journalist to report every view of a subject, only those that could be held by informed, reasonable people. Of course, a journalist's bias may unduly restrict what he considers the range of reasonable, informed opinion. And illegitimate claims may need to be reported as important facts in their own right—such as the racist, antisemitic, and xenophobic views that mar the political landscape from time to time. A reporter also needs to operate within the constraints of time, space, and reader attention span that limit everything a newspaper does. But these must not become excuses for lapsing into the one-sided, polemical approach in the news columns. A journalist's reputation should turn in large part upon the quality of his judgment in wisely sorting through these difficult issues so as to produce work of genuine intellectual integrity. . . .

### Fairness

Journalists often use the concept of fairness to describe their discipline. Unfortunately, the idea of fairness has a rich philosophical history. This gives it implications that may be inimical to the truth discipline. Even as journalistic cliché, the idea of fairness leads in odd directions.

"Journalism," one saying goes, "should comfort the afflicted and afflict the comfortable." Taken loosely as a call for journalists to concern themselves with the suffering of the weakest members of society and to have the courage to tell unpleasant truths about the powerful, the statement makes sense. But it also can be an invitation to bias, and journalists too often accept the call. Should journalists *always* afflict the comfortable, even when the comfortable are doing no harm? Should they afflict them simply *because* of their comfort? And what about the afflicted? What if telling the truth to and about them would cause them discomfort? Should the truth be shaded or withheld in order to give them comfort instead? What if truth were the painful antidote that in the long run would cure the affliction?

Any deep consideration of the idea of fairness leads eventually to questions of distributive justice of the very sort raised by these tidings of comfort and affliction. In its simplest terms, the issue is whether fairness means letting everyone compete on the same terms, regardless of the advantages and disadvantages they bring to the competition, or whether fairness requires that players carry a handicap. Is it fair to say that a poor child from the urban projects and the child of wealth and privilege should be judged by the same standard when evaluating them for admission to college? What about when trying to understand the moral quality of their behavior?

John Rawls's *Theory of Justice* provides an excellent contemporary example of the idea of distributive justice. Rawls has the courage to face the whole range of social advantages and disadvantages, as well as natural abilities and disabilities (with which one may be born and for which one thus may be said to have no personal responsibility)—not only physical strength and intellectual acumen, but also creativity, ambition and indolence, beauty and ugliness. He boldly calls on people's sense of distributive fairness to compensate for them, as if to repair God's injustice. This leads him a long way from the idea of fairness as equality of opportunity.

What might fairness in its Rawlsian, distributive sense mean in journalism? Some participants in the public debate come better equipped for it than others. Distributive fairness would have to involve some form of compensation by the journalist for this disparity. He might, for example, call all close factual issues for the weaker party or shade the way he put both sides' arguments in order to give the weaker side a chance of persuading the audience. In more extreme cases, he might have to withhold information helpful to the advantaged side in order to keep the game even. All of these compensatory strategies sharply conflict with a journalist's primary duty of simple candor, and this is why fairness is a poor choice of words to describe a journalist's discipline.

The ideal of intellectual honesty, tested by the Golden Rule, offers a much surer guide. But this requires a degree of self-restraint that is not natural in people who become immersed in a subject and develop strong feelings about it. The Golden Rule must be taught, and that has been difficult in journalism because of the lack of clarity and consensus about just what the proper discipline should be.

One problem has been the shift in weight between fact and value in news reports. No journalist I know would favor lying to give the weaker party a more even chance of prevailing in the debate. Far more likely would a journalist shade his report of a valuative debate to favor an individual suffering under a disadvantage. Somebody, he might say, has to speak up for the flood victims, or the physically handicapped, or the urban underclass, or the Vietnam veteran, or the AIDS victim. And he might even overlook some strong counterarguments on the assumption that the secure, well-financed majority interests can look out for their side of the argument very well by themselves, thank you very much. This helps account, I think, for the populist streak in American journalism as well as for journalists' reputation for being more liberal than their audience. It also may be one reason journalists have seemed to many people to be getting more liberal over time. As self-restraint against expressing opinion in news reports has fallen, the compensatory impulse becomes more marked. . . .

### The Limit of Opinion

But this is not the end of the requirements of journalism's basic disciplines.      30
Beyond intellectual honesty, journalists reporting the news need to restrain the expression of their opinions, showing modesty in their judgments about facts and always withholding ultimate judgment on matters of value. A political writer should not include in his report on a presidential campaign his view about whom people should vote for. Nor should he write his story in a way that would lead a reasonable reader to infer his preference. A reporter covering a trial should not reveal his conclusions about who is lying or whether the defendant is guilty or innocent. In an article about the abortion controversy, the writer should not come out for or against *Roe v. Wade.* . . .

 This . . . stricter approach is necessary in order to uphold the traditional distinction between news reporting and editorializing. (Editorials are polemical. They make their opinion about ultimate issues plain. And they need not recite all contrary arguments, though taking them into account makes for more persuasive editorials.) Preserving this distinction makes good sense for a number of reasons. People have grown used to it. Withholding ultimate judgment communicates the reporter's commitment to neutrality in his approach to reporting a story even as he departs from strict neutrality of expression. (It is hard to read the comments of an explicit supporter of a candidate and avoid the thought that he will not give the candidate's opponent an even break.) Modesty of opinion and holding back ultimate judgments of value produce a report that invites the audience to weigh information for itself and at the same time offer the audience some help in getting through the ambiguities and complexities. These disciplines make it easier for journalists to put all reasonable positions forcefully. (It is one thing to give all arguments their due when one does not choose between them explicitly. It is another to take an ultimate position and then have to give everyone the benefit of the Golden Rule.) Finally, withholding ultimate judgments makes pluralism in the reporting staff easier to manage.

 It is hard enough under the discipline of modesty of opinion to permit writers latitude and still produce a newspaper with a sense of coherence. This would be virtually impossible if reporters were freed to express ultimate judgments. To make all the judgments in the paper consistent, editors and publishers would have to impose a political view, story by story, or else choose only those reporters whose views were essentially consistent with the paper's editorial positions. The result would be a coherent publication, on the model of the European press, but not one that reflects a large, geographic community the way American audiences have come to expect their newspapers to do. . . .

*For Discussion*

1. In his definition of the news and his discussion of "the fundamental biases" of news coverage, Fuller stresses "the specific community [a] news organization serves"—that is, its readership. Obviously, no paper can ignore its readers and survive. But what is the difference between "writing for" one's specific community and "writing down" to it? Should newspapers both challenge their readers and accommodate them? In what ways?

2. According to Fuller, what kind of truth does responsible journalism seek? To what does he compare journalistic truth? What truth are you looking for when you read a paper? Would you describe "newspaper truth" as Fuller does? Why or why not?

3. Fuller points to an obvious tension when an editor must decide whether to print a story and how much emphasis to give it—the sometimes sharp contrast between significance and interest. No one faults a paper for covering a significant story that may not captivate the average reader. Problems arise when papers "play up" stories that interest people too much but have no real, long-term significance. Fuller justifies the latter as dictated by reader interest. But to what extent does the news *create* interest in a story by giving it more space and prominence than it deserves? Do we need more rules and norms especially for reducing the scandal-mongering so dominant in today's press?

*For Discussion and Analysis*

Most readers would say that Fuller's view of the news is balanced, honest, and reasonable. But to what extent does his view represent current practice?

Address this question by bringing to class several editions of a local paper or papers. As a class or in groups, assess the news according to Fuller's definition. Do you find the biases Fuller discusses? Do you find the intellectual virtues Fuller espouses? Do you like the way your paper or papers covered the news for a particular day? What changes, if any, would you like to see?

After full class discussion, assess some aspect of the coverage—say, political or international news—or some feature story at length and in detail, applying Fuller's analysis. Share your insights with other class members, and assess what they have to say. In further class discussion, address this question: On balance, how good a job is the paper doing?

---

## In All Fairness
### Michael Schudson

*We tend to think of ethics as something unchanging and universal. But notions of right and wrong always have a history, and norms change as the economic and social conditions of ordinary life change. Lending money at interest, for example, was once considered unnatural and sinful, whereas now we condemn only loan-sharking, the taking of excessive interest by force or the threat of force.*

*Clearly, then, we need historical perspective to understand and assess current news ethics. We must be willing to examine whatever norms we invoke. And we cannot talk intelligently about right and wrong in news coverage without seeing the news in the general context of contemporary life. Michael Schudson's article, published in the Me-dia Studies Journal (Spring/Summer 1998), offers this needed historical perspective. Schudson is a professor in the communication department at the University of California, San Diego, and author of an important book relevant to our topic,* The Power of News.

Everybody's a media critic in a democracy. The news media are the chief institutions for making our public life visible, and a lot rides on how they present us to ourselves. As citizens, we have a stake in trying to make our standards theirs. So people complain that the news media are too liberal—or too conservative. The media overplay violence—or they sanitize it. They are the lapdogs of their corporate owners—or they bite the economic system that feeds them. They are insufferably prurient—or they are rigidly puritanical. They are insidiously partisan—or they are boringly neutral. And on and on. Where have you been, Monica Lewinsky?

American journalists, buffeted by critics from every corner and wracked by self-criticism too, have long insisted that they try to be fair. But what's fair? That has changed from one era to the next.

In colonial journalism, printers proclaimed their concern for fairness in order to shed responsibility for what appeared in their pages. Benjamin Franklin insisted in his "Apology for Printers," published in 1731, that the printer was just that—one who prints, not one who edits, exercises judgment or agrees with each opinion in his pages. "Printers are educated in the Belief that when Men differ in Opinion, both Sides ought equally to have the Advantage of being heard by the Publick; and that when Truth and Error have fair Play, the former is always an overmatch for the latter: Hence they chearfully serve all contending Writers that pay them well, without regarding on which side they are of the Question in Dispute."

At first, colonial printers did not imagine their newspapers to be either political instruments or professional agencies of news gathering. None of the early papers reached out to collect news; they printed what came to them. Colonial printers, more than their London brethren, were public figures — running the post office, serving as clerks for the government and printing the laws. But they were also small businessmen who were careful not to offend their customers.

In the first half-century of American journalism, little indicated that the    5
newspaper would become a central forum for political discourse. Colonial printers avoided controversy when they could, preached the printer's neutrality when they had to and printed primarily foreign news because it afforded local readers and local authorities no grounds for grumbling. Out of a sample of 1,900 items Franklin's weekly *Pennsylvania Gazette* printed from 1728 to 1765, only 34 touched on politics in Philadelphia or Pennsylvania.

As conflict with England heated up after 1765, politics entered the press and printerly "fairness" went by the board. In a time when nearly everyone felt compelled to take sides, printers found neutrality harder to maintain than partisanship. The newspaper began its long career as the mouthpiece of political parties and factions. Patriots had no tolerance for the pro-British press, and the new states passed and enforced treason and sedition statutes.

American victory in the war for independence did not bring immediate freedom for the press. During the state-by-state debates over ratification of the Constitution in 1787 and 1788, Federalists dominated the press and squeezed Antifederalists out of public debate. In Pennsylvania, leading papers tended not to report Antifederalist speeches at the ratification convention. When unusual newspapers in Philadelphia, New York and Boston sought to report views on both sides, Federalists stopped their subscriptions and forced the papers to end their attempt at evenhandedness.

Some of the nation's founders supported outspoken political criticism so long as they were fighting a monarchy for their independence but held that open critique of a duly elected republican government could be legitimately curtailed. Sam Adams, the famed Boston agitator during the struggle for independence, changed his views on political action once republican government was established. This great advocate of open talk, committees of correspondence, an outspoken press and voluntary associations of citizens now opposed all hint of public associations and public criticism that operated outside the regular channels of government. As one contemporary of Adams observed, it did no harm for writers to mislead the people when the people were powerless, but "To mislead the judgement of the people, where they have all power, must produce the greatest possible mischief."

The Sedition Act of 1798 forbade criticism of the Federalist government and as many as one in four editors of oppositional papers were brought up on charges under this law. But this went one step further than many Americans of the day could stomach. Federalist propaganda notwithstanding, Thomas Jefferson won the presidency in 1800. The Sedition Act expired, party opposition began to be grudgingly accepted and a more libertarian theory of the press gained ground.

In 19th-century journalism, editors came to take great pride in the    10
speed and accuracy of the news they provided. With the introduction in the
1830s of the rotary press and soon the steam-powered press, amidst an expanding urban economy on the Eastern seaboard and the rush of enthusiasm for Jacksonian democracy, commercial competition heated up among
city newspapers. A new breed of "penny papers" hired newsboys to hawk
copies on the street; penny-press editors competed for wider readership and
increasingly sought out local news — of politics, crime and high society.

While this newly aggressive commercialism in journalism was an important precondition for modern notions of objectivity, at first it fostered
only a narrow concept of stenographic fairness. Newspapers boasted more
and more about the speed and accuracy of their news gathering, but editors
found this perfectly consistent with political partisanship and choosing to
cover only the speeches or rallies of their favorite party. It was equally consistent, in their eyes, for reporters to go over speeches with sympathetic
politicians they had covered to improve, in printed form, on the oral presentation. Into the 1870s and 1880s, Washington correspondents routinely
supplemented their newspaper income by clerking for the very congressional committees they wrote about.

As late as the 1890s, when a standard Republican paper covered a presidential election, it not only deplored and derided Democratic candidates in
editorials but often neglected to mention them in the news. In the days before public-opinion polling, the size of partisan rallies was taken as a proxy
for likely electoral results. Republican rallies would be described as "monster meetings" while Democratic rallies were often not covered at all. In the
Democratic papers, of course, it was just the reverse.

While partisanship endured, reporters came to enjoy a culture of their
own independent of political parties. They developed their own mytholo-
gies (reveling in their intimacy with the urban underworld), their own
clubs and watering holes and their own professional practices. Interviewing, for instance, became a common activity for reporters only in the 1870s
and 1880s. No president submitted to an interview before Andrew Johnson
in 1868, but by the 1880s the interview was a well-accepted and institutionalized "media event," an occasion created by journalists from which
they could then craft a story. This new journalistic practice did not erase
partisanship. It did, however, foreshadow reporters' emerging dedication
to a sense of craft. Journalists began to locate themselves in a new occupational culture with its own rules, its own rewards and its own *esprit*.

Interviewing was a practice oriented more to pleasing an audience of
news consumers than to parroting or promoting a party line. By the 1880s,
newspapers had become big business. They erected towering downtown
buildings, employed scores of reporters, sponsored splashy civic festivals
and ran pages of advertising from the newly burgeoning department stores.
The papers vastly expanded their readership in this growing marketplace.
Accordingly, reporters writing news came to focus less on promoting parties
and more on making stories.

Yet not until the 1920s was American journalism characterized by what    15
we might call modern analytical and procedural fairness. Analytical fairness
had no secure place until journalists as an occupational group developed
loyalties more to their audiences and to themselves as an occupational
community than to their publishers or their publishers' favored political
parties. At this point journalists also came to articulate rules of the journalistic road more often and more consistently. As an Associated Press executive declared in 1925, "If you do not remember anything else that I have
said, I beg of you to remember this, for it is fundamental: The Associated
Press never comments on the news."

This newly articulated fairness doctrine was related to the sheer growth
in news gathering: Rules of objectivity enabled editors to keep lowly reporters in check, although they had less control over high-flying foreign correspondents. Objectivity as ideology was a kind of industrial discipline. At
the same time, it seemed a natural and progressive ideology for an aspiring
occupational group at a moment when science was god, efficiency was cherished, and increasingly prominent elites judged partisanship a vestige of the
tribal 19th century. First Mugwump reformers, led by the Anglo-Saxon pa-
tricians of the Northeast during the late 19th century, and then the Progres-
sives, who pursued a broader reform movement in the early 20th century,
argued that politics itself should be beyond partisanship. No wonder journalists picked up on their appeal.

Yet at the very moment that journalists embraced "objectivity," they
also recognized its limits. In the 1930s, there was a vogue for what contemporaries called "interpretive journalism." Leading journalists and journalism educators insisted that the world had grown increasingly complex
and needed not only to be reported but explained. Political columnists,
like Walter Lippmann, David Lawrence, Frank Kent and Mark Sullivan,
came into their own. Journalists insisted that their task was to help readers not only to know but to understand. At the same time, they now took
it for granted that understanding had nothing to do with party or partisan
sentiment.

Was this progress? Was a professional press taking over from party
hacks? Not everyone was sure. If the change brought a new dispassionate
tone to news coverage, it also opened the way to making entertainment
rather than political coherence a chief criterion of journalism.

Speaker of the House "Uncle" Joe Cannon objected in 1927: "I believe
we had better publicity when the party press was the rule and the so-called
independent press the exception, than we have now," he said in his autobiography, *Uncle Joe Cannon.* "The correspondents in the press gallery then
felt their responsibility for reporting the proceedings of Congress. Then
men representing papers in sympathy with the party in power were alert to
present the record their party was making so that the people would know
its accomplishments, and those representing the opposition party were
eager to expose any failures on the part of the Administration." In the independent press, in contrast, serious discussion of legislation gave way to

entertainment: "The cut of a Congressman's whiskers or his clothes is a better subject for a human interest story than what he says in debate."

News, Cannon mourned, had replaced legislative publicity. What had 20 really happened was that journalists had become their own interpretive community, writing to one another and not to parties or partisans.

The triumph of an ethic of analytical and procedural fairness (or "objectivity" as it has presumptuously been called) was never complete. Even journalism's leaders took it for granted that fairness in journalism could be combined with active partisanship in politics. Claude Bowers proudly recalled in his autobiography, *My Life*, that, while an editorial writer for the New York *World*, he wrote speeches for Democratic senatorial candidate Robert Wagner while running daily editorials in Wagner's support. As Ronald Steel recounts in his biography *Walter Lippmann and the American Century*, Lippmann and James Reston in 1945 helped write a speech for Republican Sen. Arthur Vandenberg in which he broke from his isolationism. Lippmann then praised the turnabout in his column. Reston wrote a front page story on the speech in *The New York Times*, noting the "unusual interest" it attracted and observing that Sen. Vandenberg presented his theme "with force." President-elect John F. Kennedy shared with Lippmann a draft of his inaugural address. Lippmann proposed some modest changes that Kennedy accepted. After the new president delivered his speech, Lippmann praised it in his column as a "remarkably successful piece of self-expression." When George Will helped Ronald Reagan prepare for his television debates with Jimmy Carter in 1980 and then as an ABC commentator discussed Reagan's performance, he acted in a well-developed tradition.

With such intimate political involvement from leading lights of the journalism establishment, it is difficult to accept journalists' claims of political innocence — even the claims of journalists, like *Washington Post* editor Leonard Downie, who forswear voting for fear it could taint their scrupulous neutrality. But scrupulous accuracy and fairness are indeed the watchwords of journalistic competence today, even though the work of editorial writers, columnists and sports reporters (who are obliged to write from the viewpoint of the home team) offers countercurrents to professional ideals of detachment.

In the 1960s and again in the 1990s, some journalists have rebelled at the voicelessness of objective reporting and seek to write with an edge or an attitude that calls attention to the story as a piece of writing, not just a neutral vessel for transporting purportedly raw reality to audiences. Cutthroat competition encourages this. So does a postmodern relativism that spits at pretensions to objectivity.

At the same time, journalists, when criticized, invariably return to the old standbys. They assert their accuracy, their impartiality and their intrepid willingness to pursue the truth without fear or favor. There is safety in this. There is also honor: honor in the abnegation rather than the aggrandizement of self, and honor in the ordinary ambition to pursue a craft well rather than pursue art or influence badly. . . .

Is modern professional fairness better for democracy, on balance, than the partisan press? So far as I know, no one has ever seriously studied this question. There are few studies that compare, say, party-oriented European journalism with objectivity-oriented American journalism, and none that successfully answer the tricky question of which serves democracy better. Do citizens know more about politics and vote more often where there is a party press or an independent press? In most European democracies, there is higher voter turnout and higher scores on tests of political knowledge than in the United States. But in Europe there are also stronger political parties and very different electoral institutions. What their effect might be on the values that direct the news media is simply unknown.

There is something enduring about the desire to be fair in journalism—both the writer's quest to be believed and the news institution's strong interest in maintaining its own credibility. But there is nothing at all stable across history or across national cultures about the actual rules and practices that pass for fairness. Today's journalistic fairness in the United States is a blend of high hopes, historic traditions, contemporary political culture and the expediencies journalists face in keeping audiences, owners and sources at bay. It is a shifting set of principles and practices that will be tested and reformulated by a changing informational environment whose shape will not hold still.

*For Discussion*

1. What are the most important phases in the history of the press as Schudson tells the story? How does he explain the changes? Probably the most important recent innovation is news via the Internet—newspapers themselves now often update their own stories on Web sites. What long-term effect might Internet news have on newspapers?
2. What exactly is "modern analytical and procedural fairness"? How does Schudson explain it? Read or reread the Fuller selection in this chapter. Does Fuller shed any light on it? If so, how? Watch the evening news on one of the major networks and/or examine headline stories in your local paper. Do you detect this notion of fairness in how the stories are told? In what specific ways?
3. What is your reaction to Schudson's exposure of the double role that some journalists play—that is, on the one hand, writing speeches for politicians, and on the other, writing favorably in the news about these politicians and their speeches? Should this practice be banned or at least discouraged by news agencies and newspapers?

*For Inquiry and Convincing*

In the United States, mainstream news journalism now strives to be nonpartisan, reporting the news without apparent political bias. But this was not the case in the nineteenth century in our own papers, nor is it common practice in Europe today. Schudson asks, "Is modern professional fairness better for democracy, on balance, than the partisan press?" Another, more pointed way to phrase this question is to say: Many Americans profess to be bored by the news and alienated from politics. Would they be less bored and alienated if the press was openly partisan?

We can investigate this question in at least two ways: by comparing our papers with European ones or, more easily, by comparing papers with well-known partisan news magazines published in the United States, such as the *National Review* (conservative) or *The Nation* (liberal). Choose one or both routes, and study the coverage of one or two major stories. Write a paper that either defends current newspaper practice or argues for a more partisan press. Remember that the issue is not excitement as such, but rather *what is better for democracy.*

*For Inquiry*

We tend to think about news in terms of contrasting opposites—partisan versus neutral, news stories versus editorials. But Schudson mentions a third possibility, interpretive journalism, which attempts to provide more background for a story and a more extensive context or contexts for understanding and evaluating it. We can find examples of interpretive journalism in most daily newspapers, especially in efforts to cover unusually complex and confusing issues such as genetic engineering. Some papers are heavily committed to interpretive journalism; the *Christian Science Monitor* is a distinguished example.

Locate several instances of interpretive journalism from two or three different papers. Compare it to routine news reporting and to partisan writing. Are they really different? How? Write a paper exploring the differences and the role played by interpretive journalism in news coverage. Conclude by offering a tentative position on the following question: Is an interpretive press preferable to a neutral or partisan one for developing well-informed citizens?

# The Impossibility of Fairness
## Jim Squires

*"The news is subordinated to entertainment" is the gist of Jim Squires's argument, and, he claims, it is so subordinated because too many news sources are owned by huge entertainment conglomerates like Time Warner. The result is not merely distortion of the news, he contends, but much more seriously "outright corruption of journalism." This article appeared in the same issue of* Media Studies Journal *as the previous selection by Michael Schudson and represents a traditional perspective sharply critical of current journalism. Squires was once editor of the* Chicago Tribune *and a media adviser to Ross Perot. His book* Read All about It!: The Corporate Takeover of America's Newspapers *develops his case in more detail.*

Establishing parameters of fairness in the age of cyberspace is no different from trying to set them 50 years ago at the Chicago *Tribune* or *The New York Times*. Each case is unique, and the debate always ends the way it did in the Victorian England of author Thomas Hughes.

"He never wants anything but what's right and fair;" Hughes wrote of a character in *Tom Brown's Schooldays*, "only when you come to settle what's right and fair, it's everything that he wants, and nothing that you want."

Recollection of my own record starts with my treatment of a Nashville used-car salesman who committed suicide in the 1960s following my story of his pending indictment. *The* (Nashville) *Tennessean*, though entirely accurate, was unfair to the car dealer by singling him out for front-page notoriety. Not all those expected to be indicted by the grand jury that day were treated the same way.

I also wrote countless stories based on anonymous sources, and I was not once concerned about the racial, ethnic and gender balance of the sources I quoted. A great deal of my unfairness was rooted in my unavoidable personal profile as a Southern white male. In the broad sense that fairness by news media is now being debated in the public mind, it is possible that none of the zillion stories I wrote was fair.

Yet even the worst individual case of unfairness does not approach the level of injustice being perpetrated by the information industry as a whole. What could be more unfair to citizens than the outright corruption of journalism, which takes place daily in all quarters of the so-called news media?

With the exception of a few fine and committed newspapers and magazines, the professional standards and values of journalism have gone to hell in a hand-basket, cast out in favor of an entertainment culture with no moral compass and no concern for fairness — or taste.

Even at its worst and most unfair, the American brand of journalism once had as its goal a quest for accuracy and perspective that would eventually produce truth. News, which is the product of real journalism, was best defined by the Hutchins Commission on freedom of the press in 1947 as a "truthful, comprehensive, and intelligent account of the day's events in a context which gives them meaning."

Ostensibly, information was gathered, evaluated and eventually disseminated in the interest of enlightenment and education. Conversely, the consumers of journalism had good reason to believe that the purveyors of news existed to provide them a fair deal and a fair account. Journalism's value in the marketplace was its quality, of which fairness is a vital part. Like all the great products of American capitalism, brand-name integrity was its greatest asset. Shoddy, inferior news coverage invariably failed in the competitive marketplace. This is no longer true.

The broadcast industry is an entertainment industry to which news is purely incidental. It is primarily television's shoddy attempts at journalism, such as its injurious handling of the identification of the Atlanta Olympics bombing suspect, that have fueled the fairness controversy and spawned cries for press regulation. Print journalism used to routinely withhold the names of suspects until they had been charged. Even when one publication felt it necessary, others often restrained themselves, minimizing the damage. This is no longer possible when TV has a breathless correspondent, dressed like a cat burglar, camped outside the suspect's apartment, endlessly speculating live on camera about everything but the color of the man's underwear. "The bigger the lie, the louder the cry" has taken on new meaning in light of the instant global impact of a CNN bulletin or a report on the Internet.

Today television and movie producers, networks, cable operators and information providers of all stripes value "news" not for its importance, quality or public service contributions but for its ability to attract an audience and turn a profit. Thus, for today's press, the best story is a sex scandal such as the "bimbo eruptions" that have plagued President Clinton. 10

In a speech last year Harold Evans, the distinguished English author, editor and former president and publisher of Random House, quoted William S. Paley, founder of CBS, as saying that the day news becomes a profit center will be lamentable. "Well, the day has come," Evans said. "It's about dusk."

With the passing of time, the standards of journalism have been relaxed to the point of nonexistence. Yet news remains the favorite subject of the entertainment business to such an extent that the lines between news and entertainment have been forever obliterated. News provides a steady stream of programming free of creative and promotion costs. From the ABC and CNN coverage of the Iranian hostage crisis to television's obsession with O. J. Simpson nearly 20 years later, true stories have proven to be a sure ticket to ratings and profits.

Movies, television specials and even sitcoms are built around "news" situations and actual events. Celebrity personalities are most often substituted for genuine newsmakers, but sometimes the newsmakers end up getting hired by the news media and become celebrities themselves. Accuracy in the retelling of their stories is, quite naturally, less important to scripts than excitement and audience appeal. People walk out of movies like *JFK,* which purported to chronicle the conspiracy behind the assassination of President Kennedy, or last year's fictional extravaganza on the Titanic, and say in all seriousness, "I didn't know that." Guess not, it never happened.

For today's press the "best news" combines sex and crime and prominent people, like O. J. Simpson and President Clinton. The actual events become great television entertainment. Then they spawn books, which are turned into movies, which attempt to make them even more entertaining than they were originally.

News events spawn new celebrities, who show up at a later event with a microphone, pretending to practice the craft of journalism. Actors, comedians, politicians, lawyers, infamous criminals—and some who fit all five categories—now regularly masquerade as reporters on newscasts and talk shows. Watergate burglar G. Gordon Liddy and Clinton White House political adviser George Stephanopoulos are both now widely considered to be journalists. Former Nixon speechwriter Patrick Buchanan and civil rights activist Jesse Jackson go from being story subject one month to storyteller the next. Lawyer Johnnie Cochran may be on television standing beside a famous defendant one day and on another interviewing the same defendant from behind an anchor desk.    15

Worse, many of the people signing the paychecks of these pretenders and making the programming decisions can't see any difference between real news and celebrity news programming. They think that having been celebrated in one news event qualifies someone to cover another. It never crosses their minds that their position in charge of news organizations carries with it a responsibility to protect and preserve the values of real journalism.

Sadly, through acquisition and merger much of the real journalism establishment has been swallowed up by the entertainment industry. Some of the biggest, most important and powerful news organizations in the world today are owned by companies whose main business is make believe. The Cable News Network and *Time* magazine, for example, are controlled by the entertainment giant Time Warner, cable owner, maker of HBO movies and producer of sleazy rap songs.

To grasp the implications of this for journalism and democracy, what would happen if a strong grass-roots movement for media censorship were ever mounted in this country? Its most just and likely targets would be cable television pornography, the violence-profanity-sex formula movies of HBO and Time Warner's abhorrent rap lyrics—all of which trumpet the legally obscene F-word.

It is easy to imagine that Time Warner would raise its First Amendment shield and march behind it to Washington to oppose this assault on its profit centers. So would many other major media companies with whom Time Warner has significant financial dealings and mutual interests.

But would this be fair to the watchers of CNN, the readers of *Time* and the customers of other journalism organizations with ties to Time Warner? How much fairness could censorship proponents and their political leaders expect from *Time* and CNN, or from any journalist assigned to the story?    20

No matter how ethical, scrupulous and professional these journalists might be, their freedom from the appearance of conflict of interest would be gone. How fair is that to citizens who expect and depend on a free press to educate them on matters of public policy? . . .

Throughout our history, the free press has enjoyed a right to a special place in the democracy with special privileges under law because it was a special business with a unique goal of serving the public interest.

Journalism can't make that claim anymore. Except for a few newspaper companies, news organizations have become indistinguishable from other media. Journalists' paychecks come from the same payroll as those of the movie moguls, TV execs, radio personalities and record producers; from the same corporate bank accounts as the cash for independent movies and freelance magazine pieces.

These same coffers are the source of virtually all the big book contracts that are handed out not to real authors but to tabloid journalists, kiss-and-tell gold diggers, toe-sucking, secret-spilling presidential political advisers and tattooed, rule-breaking, in-your-face athletes whose stock in trade is incivility. . . .

A favorite phrase in the "lexicon" of the new entertainment/journalism . . . is "the smoking gun," meaning, of course, irrefutable evidence. For "the smoking gun" on what happened to the free press in America, look no further than its embarrassing performance on the most perfect of all television "news stories"—the Monica Lewinsky scandal. When two newspapers as serious and respected as *The Dallas Morning News* and *The Wall Street Journal* get so carried away with tabloidism that they both rush into print leaked phony stories using anonymous sources and then have to apologize, there's only one conclusion. With all due respect to my admired friend Harry Evans, it's past dusk. It is midnight in the garden and far too late to worry about fairness.

---

*For Discussion*

1. Early in his article Squires calls attention to one source of bias in his own news reporting: his "unavoidable personal profile as a Southern white male." He concedes that, as we now understand fairness, "it is possible that none of the zillion stories I wrote was fair." Do we expect fairness in the sense Squires describes it? Is it realistic or desirable to expect reporters to become aware of their personal backgrounds and to adjust to some degree for them?

2. Squires contends that news has fallen prey to "an entertainment culture with no moral compass and no concern for fairness—or taste." How does he back up this assertion? Do you find this central contention convincing? Why or why not? To what extent would you say his rejection of current journalism stems from a distaste for mass or popular culture generally?

3. Squires paints a very bleak picture and offers no hope for improvement, much less reform. In other words, he depicts a problem we all
recognize but offers no solution. Suppose that his basic contention
about the press is correct—that the news is merely entertainment—
and that the root of the problem is corporate takeovers. How might
the industry be reformed or the conditions conducive to what he
calls "real news" be enhanced?

## For Research and Persuasion

We should not be surprised when older, traditional journalists see their
craft as in decline and blame it on the electronic media, especially television.
Journalism *has* changed a great deal in the past three or four decades—and
changed in ways that many journalists themselves find unacceptable. People
who remember when television didn't exist or didn't have nearly the impact
it has now will certainly tend to make it the culprit.

But before we rush to support this condemnation of TV journalism, we
should at least study it. As a class, make a list of as many TV news programs
as you can think of. Be sure to include both new and long-running ones, as
well as a broad spectrum of programs ranging from the stodgy to the sensa-
tional. Divide the list among class members, and have each watch several segments, taking careful notes about what is covered and how. Then discuss
what you've found. Are the news media as hopelessly bad as Squires claims?

Write an essay in response to Squires but addressed to your peers, who
have always lived in a TV-saturated world. Advocate some sort of responsible, personal approach to TV news watching, and attempt to persuade your
readers to at least try your approach.

## For Inquiry and Mediation

How we judge the news depends almost entirely on what we think it is or
ought to be. In this chapter's first selection, Jack Fuller offers a modest and realistic view of the news—"a report of what a news organization has recently
learned about matters of some significance or interest to the specific community [it] serves." In contrast, Squires cites a definition that makes strong,
idealistic claims for what the news should be—a "truthful, comprehensive,
and intelligent account of the day's events in a context which gives them
meaning."

Inquire into both definitions, paying close attention to the words used
and their implications. As you consider them, bear in mind the tension in
any profession between what is and what ought to be, and the difficulty of
balancing standards that challenge the profession to improve against standards that demoralize, that are too high to reach and thus foster cynicism.

Then write a paper attempting to combine the best of Fuller with the best
of Squires, together with your own notions of what the news is and should
be. Address your paper to other students, whose expectations for the news
need to be *both* demanding *and* realistic, neither too low nor too high.

# Cartoon
## Mike Twohy

*In the previous essay, "The Impossibility of Fairness," Jim Squires argues that standards of honesty and accuracy erode as the news becomes more and more an entertainment industry, with each paper and news team competing for the public's attention. This cartoon from the* New Yorker *magazine comments on the media obsession to be first with a story—or even the possibility of a story.*

### For Discussion

Are you aware of recent examples of false reporting or news stories that have proven to be inaccurate? Do you think public perception of the media is as bad as this cartoon suggests? If, as Squires points out, "[j]ournalism's value in the marketplace was its quality," what will be the future of journalism if the public sees it as this cartoon does?

## Escaping the News Prison:
## How People See beyond the Walls
### W. Lance Bennett

*It is fashionable to be critical of the press, but rarely do we hear critiques of the con-
sumer, the person who reads the paper and listens to the evening news. If we simply
"absorb" the news, W. Lance Bennett suggests, taking it in passively, without any critical thinking, we are doomed never to see beyond the "news prison walls," beyond what
might be called the "official construction" of reality, for newspapers generally report
what officials say with little or no analysis. But how can we interpret the news intelligently? This is the question Bennett, a specialist in mass communication and professor
at the University of Washington, tries to answer. This selection is taken from his 1988
book,* News: The Politics of Illusion.

A small percentage of people stand in sharp contrast to the majority who
absorb and expel news information as though they were contestants in a
lifelong trivia match. Some people seem to have an inside line on the politics behind news reports. . . .

Consider two facts that help explain who becomes liberated from the
political confines of the news. First, we already know that the news consists
overwhelmingly of "objective" (or at least "fair") "documentary" reports
that pass along, with little analysis, the political messages of official spokespersons. Less than 1 percent of mass media coverage contains any sort of
independent analysis from the reporter's perspective, while around 90 percent of the news originates from circumstances that give officials substantial
control over political content. Second, consider the fact that most Americans who are politically active, system-supporting citizens have been socialized in environments (family, school, workplace) that discourage analytical
or ideological political thinking. This combination of nonanalytical news
with nonanalytical people does not bode well for much analytical thinking
in response to political messages in the news.

A third factor further undermines the critical thinking of the public. Political actors tend to construct simplistic political messages that appeal to
myths and unquestioned beliefs held by large segments of the public. Such
messages are seldom brought into focus because of the absence of analysis
in the news and the lack of analytical dispositions in the audience. As a result, most news messages appeal directly to unconscious myths and unquestioned beliefs. In short, the propagandistic, nonanalytical qualities of
mass news mesh smoothly with the well-conditioned, nonanalytical orientation of the citizenry.

This profile of the news prisoner contains an obvious clue about those
who escape. *In order to escape the news prison, people must develop some independent, analytical perspective from which to interpret the news.* So much for
the obvious. More difficult is to identify the sort of perspective that helps

people understand the news more clearly. There are actually several orientations that would enable people to break through the layers of subtle persuasion in the news and think sensibly about what might be going on behind the stories. For example, *a grasp of American history would provide a perspective on the patterns of myth and rhetoric in political events.* A common technique of political propaganda is to blur the relationship between past and present. When historic disasters like foreign involvements or economic collapses seem to be on the verge of recurring, public officials can be expected to persuade the public that important differences distinguish present circumstances from the past. At other times, when the signs of change seem entirely clear, threatened elites may try to persuade the public to avoid the fearsome future and step back into the comforting shadow of the past. The repeated and successful use of these communication patterns suggests that the American people can be led easily to see differences where none exist and to ignore distinctions where they are apparent.

A firm grasp of political history would provide people with a more secure foundation than they now have from which to resist political pressures and with which to develop alternative understandings. Unfortunately, most school boards look with disfavor on history curricula that offer coherent interpretations of American politics. As a result, the majority of American children suffer through several years of the same history course—a course that emphasizes disconnected facts and events, reinforces basic myths that leave people vulnerable to political rhetoric, discourages people from developing a secure understanding of power and politics in American society, and, above all, emphasizes the deeds of great national heroes. This "hero history" not only brings myths to life but also encourages people to trust contemporary hero-leaders to do their thinking and acting for them. There are, to put it bluntly, few Americans with an adequate grasp of their country's history.

*Another possible frame of reference for the news would be the sort provided in this book, namely, a theoretical grasp of how politicians and journalists act together to make the news.* Such a perspective would help people to locate and interpret the gaps and biases in mass media coverage. When diplomatic talks are called "cordial and productive," people could assume immediately that nothing had happened and that the leaders involved had some other political reason to hold the conference. Flags would go up cautioning people to discount unverified rumors spread by "unidentified" officials. Similar skepticism would apply to "doublespeak" statements like this one in the news: "'We've made no secret of our views,' said a U.S. official who insisted on anonymity." People could recognize political manipulation in the news through the use of leaks, pseudo-events, and various image-making techniques. After hearing "both sides of an issue," people might even begin to wonder what the third side looked like and why it was not reported.

Unfortunately, people are not required to take courses on how to interpret the news. To the contrary, most people are encouraged by every trusted authority, particularly parents and teachers, to take the news seriously and at face value. The majority of us are taught to ingest large quantities of news and wait for an objective understanding of events to strike as if by revelation. Waiting for objective revelations from the news may be more satisfying than waiting for Godot, but it is surely as pointless. Children are quizzed in school on the content of classroom news supplements as though they represented the most accurate and comprehensive coverage of the known world. By memorizing the "right answers" to news quizzes, these children grow up thinking that knowing the facts in the news is equivalent to understanding something about the real world.

The news worship that begins in childhood is continued in adult life by the widespread support for the ideal of objective reporting. The notion that events can and should be presented without values or interpretation feeds the image of the good citizen as a concerned seeker of truth. At the same time, the widespread belief in objective reporting obscures the possibility that most "truths" that emerge from the news are likely to be the result of subtle political messages that appeal to subconscious beliefs and prejudices. People can hardly be blamed for thinking that they have found truth under such circumstances. After all, few things seem as objectively true as having one's deepest prejudices confirmed by respected authorities. Presenting two sides of every story with no critical "bridge" to transcend the differences between the sides only invites people to choose the version closest to their existing beliefs. Studies of newspaper readers (presumably the most critical information-seekers) have shown that newspapers primarily reinforce preexisting political attitudes.

*In the absence of a grasp of newsmaking theory or political history, the only other obvious source of independent news judgment is political ideology.* Ideologies are formal systems of belief about the nature, origins, and means of promoting values that people regard as important. Not only do ideologies provide people with a clear sense of life's purpose, but they provide a logic for interpreting the world by giving rules for translating real-world events into illustrations of how those values are promoted or damaged. Thus, people who view the news through the lens of an ideology are likely to spot hidden political messages and translate them into independent political statements. The trouble with ideologies is that they can become rigid and limiting frames of reference, leading people to select only the information that fits them while rejecting all other input. For example, many people in the United States continue to hold a "cold war" ideology that views the appearance of socialism or communism anywhere in the world as inherently threatening to democracy, freedom, and the American way of life. For those who cling rigidly to the "cold war" belief system, many important distinctions about world politics may be lost. The emergence of Socialist governments in Europe may seem to be a threatening step along the road to world totalitarianism. Socialism in the Western hemisphere ("our backyard") seems intolerable. Lost in this ideological view is the understanding

that all Socialist and Communist governments are not alike, and that most
of them do not pose threats to democracy, freedom, or the American way.

Since the news seldom explains how other political systems work from          10
the standpoint of the people who live in them, we tend to hear mostly U.S.
official and expert opinion about other systems. And when it comes to Communist or Socialist systems, the chances are pretty good that equal time will
be given some venerable "cold warrior" quick to predict the end of democracy and communism on our doorstep. News consumers with kindred and
rigid ideological views can use these familiar pronouncements to reinforce
existing beliefs rather than learn something new about the world from another viewpoint.

If people recognized this vicious circle of news and popular belief, they
might be more inclined to build an imperative for learning into their belief
systems, turning ideology into a dynamic rather than a static outlook. *If
used constructively, ideologies could create challenging understandings of the
world by enabling people to find the inconsistencies, puzzles, and paradoxes in
events.* Thinking through the puzzles in political events can broaden an
ideology by adapting it to resolve the puzzles. This process of adaptation
simultaneously creates new ways of seeing the world. For example, Richard Nixon and Henry Kissinger were able to see beyond ideology to recognize the advantages of opening political and economic relations with
once-dreaded "Communist" China. After high political authorities had
pronounced China safe to think about, journalists began to cover Chinese events from a less rigid ideological viewpoint. If it is possible to do
business with a one-party Communist state like China, why not a multi-
party Socialist country like Nicaragua? The answer depends largely on
whether one's ideology is open or closed to learning new things about
the world.

In a perfect world, people would supplement their ideologies with a
command of history and a theoretical grasp of news politics. Such a combination of perspectives would enable people to combat news propaganda
with their own conclusions. This is not, as you probably guessed, a perfect
world. It is unlikely that more than a tiny fraction of the public has an understanding of American history or news politics, and by even the most
generous estimates, few people can be called self-reflective ideologues.

Even those few people who manage to construct a political worldview
may find it a mixed blessing. On the one hand, they are able to understand
political communication in comprehensive and personally satisfying ways.
On the other hand, their ideological insights are likely to be discredited
by the majority of their fellow citizens, who have been taught to wait for
"objective" revelations to emerge from the news. Hence, another paradox:
People who espouse a stance of objectivity toward the news are likely to
accept blindly the institutional bias of the news media (if, indeed, they are
able to form any political conclusions at all), while those, who manage to

form clear political perspectives are likely to be condemned for being "opinionated." . . .

---

## For Discussion

1. "The Associated Press never comments on the news," an executive of that organization claimed in 1925 (quoted by Michael Schudson; see the second reading in this chapter). In other words, official news sources don't, in a strong sense, *interpret* the news but rather claim "neutral" or "objective" ground. According to Bennett, this claim is suspect. Why? In what ways do reporters interpret the news even when they don't offer commentary? In what sense does the news come to reporters already interpreted, shaped for public consumption by the very sources consulted?

2. Bennett claims that most Americans are socialized to "absorb and expel news information as though they were contestants in a life-long trivia match." Is this an accurate description of your experience? Do you attach high value to knowing factual details about current events? Were you taught in school or at home to question the news or subject it to analysis?

3. According to Bennett, *"people must develop some independent, analytical perspective from which to interpret the news"* (his emphasis). What does "independent" mean? Independent from what or from whom? Is this independence total? That is, mustn't we be dependent on *something* to have an "independent" view of anything?

4. Bennett says that waiting for "an objective understanding of events" to arise from the news is like "waiting for Godot," an illusion to a play by Samuel Beckett in which several characters stand around talking, anticipating the arrival of a character who never comes. There are some things we can understand more or less, as we say, scientifically, like the structure of an atom. Why is the news not like this? What exactly must we be able to do to *understand* human events, as opposed to merely reciting so-called facts about them?

## For Analysis

Probably Bennett's most important point is that "news messages appeal directly to unconscious myths and unquestioned beliefs." In class discussion develop a list of some of these myths and beliefs, and question their basis and history. In other words, make them conscious and subject to question.

Then secure the latest edition of a daily paper, and study it with your list in mind. Write an essay analyzing the myths and beliefs appealed to in one or two news stories. Conclude your essay by addressing this question: Is there an alternative to myths and beliefs? That is, can the news work at all without appealing to myths or beliefs of some kind?

*For Research and Convincing*

Bennett suggests several ways to "see beyond the prison walls." With his ideas in mind, do some research into other sources that purport to help us read the news more critically. Then, taking what seems best from Bennett and your other sources and combining it with your own ideas, write an essay for your peers to convince them, first, that the news should be read critically and, second, that you have a good way of doing it. For the second part, bear in mind that people usually read papers quickly and that a too-elaborate approach won't be practical.

# "Public Journalism":
# An Attempt to Connect the Media with the Public
## James Fallows

*Attempts to reform the media are motivated primarily by two closely related perceptions: that increasingly the public is indifferent to and/or cynical about traditional news coverage and that the gap between politicians and ordinary citizens, especially between Washington and most of the rest of the country, is threatening to become unbridgeable. Both are obviously dangerous for the health of a democracy and are reflected in declining circulations for some papers and low voter turnout even in major election years.*

*One such reform is so-called public or civic journalism. It is designed to overcome the problem Bennett describes in the previous selection—that "around 90 percent of the news originates from circumstances that give officials substantial control over political content." Instead of going to politicians or "spin doctors" for the news, public journalism goes to the public first, asking them what they care about and want discussed, and then offers the politicians a chance to respond. The goal is to get a dialogue going between politicians and the public, with the former less in control of the agenda. James Fallows, a distinguished journalist and editor of the* New Republic, *explores public journalism in the following excerpt from his important recent book,* Breaking the News: How the Media Undermine American Democracy.

During the U.S. military's darkest moments just after the Vietnam War, a group of officers and analysts undertook a "military reform" movement. Rather than papering over the deep problems that the Vietnam years had revealed, and rather than searching for external sources of blame, this group attempted to locate the internal problems that had weakened the military so that the problems could be faced and solved. The "military reformers'" record of success was not perfect, but at their instigation the U.S. military coped with more of its fundamental difficulties than any other American institution has.

Since the early 1990s, a group of journalistic reformers has launched a similar attempt to cope with the basic weaknesses of their institution. As was the case with the military reformers, their efforts have been scorned by some of the most powerful leaders of the current establishment. As with the military reformers, they do not have the complete or satisfying answer to all of today's journalistic problems. But, like the military reformers, they are more right than wrong. At a minimum their ideas point the way to a media establishment that is less intensely scorned than today's is.

Those involved in the "public journalism" (sometimes called "civic journalism") movement stress its cooperative, collaborative nature. But several people have played large roles in developing its ideas.

One is Davis Merritt, a man in his late fifties, who since the mid-1970s has been editor of the *Wichita Eagle* in Kansas. The cover of his 1995 book

*Public Journalism and Public Life* says "by Davis 'Buzz' Merritt," and he has
the laconic, unrushable bearing one would associate with a test pilot or as-
tronaut named "Buzz." . . .

People involved in the public journalism movement often talk of                    5
"epiphanies" or transforming experiences that convinced them that a different course was necessary. Merritt says that his came just after the 1988
presidential election campaign. His paper was carrying the predictable wire
stories: about the Dukakis campaign's response to the Bush campaign's attacks, about Gary Hart and his girl friends, about what Willie Horton did or
did not do, about what Michael Dukakis would or would not do if his wife
was raped.

Merritt says that as he put these stories into his paper each day, he
found himself asking, Why are we publishing this? What are we doing? The
accepted style of political coverage, he thought, was bringing out the worst
in every participant in public life. It drove out serious candidates. It rewarded gutter-fighting. It disgusted most of the public. It embarrassed even
the reporters. It trivialized the election—and it made everyone feel dirty
when it was done. With the election experience fresh in his mind, Merritt
began thinking about how journalists could use all their traditional tools
of investigation, explanation, fair-mindedness, and so on in a way that
was less destructive to the society in which journalists and readers alike
had to live . . .

In 1991 the fledgling [public journalism] movement got an important boost when David Broder of the *Washington Post*, probably the best-
respected political reporter of his time, gave a lecture in California implicitly endorsing their approach. His statement was seen as significant not
simply because of his personal stature but also because he had had contact
with the public-journalism advocates and had come to a conclusion like
theirs on his own.

In a speech sponsored by the Riverside, California, *Press-Enterprise* and
the University of California at Riverside, Broder said that coverage of public
affairs had become a cynical and pointless insiders' game. Political consultants—rather than candidates—had come to have a dominant role in politics, Broder said. And these hired guns, "these new political bosses, have become for those of us in political journalism not only our best sources but,
in many cases, our best friends."

The two groups got along because they both loved the operating details
of politics, Broder said. They felt a distance from the slightly comic, sweating candidates who had to give speeches and raise money and submit themselves to the voters' will. For these poor candidates, Broder said, election
day really was a judgment day. But for the reporters and consultants, no
matter what the results of the election, they could play the game over and
over again.

There was a more disturbing similarity between the groups, Broder said.    10
"We both disclaim any responsibility for the consequences of elections."

> Let me say again, for emphasis: We disclaim ANY responsibility for the conse-
> quences of elections. Consultants will tell you they are hired to produce victory
> on Election Day. Reporters will tell you that we are hired to cover campaigns. . . .
> I've often said to our White House reporters, "My job is to deliver these turkeys;
> after they're in office, they're your responsibility."
>
> What this means in less facetious terms is that a very large percentage of the
> information that the American people get about politics comes from people
> who disclaim any responsibility for the consequences of our politics.

After spending nearly four decades in this activity, Broder said, he felt
uneasy about the consequences of his life's work. By concentrating on the
operations of politics and disdaining the results, reporters "have colluded
with the campaign consultants to produce the kind of politics which is
turning off the American people." By the early 1970s—the time of movies
like *The Candidate* and books like *The Selling of the President*—journalists
began to realize that the most important part of a political campaign was
the ads a candidate put on radio and television:

> So we began to focus on the ads, and we began to write about them. We began
> to write about the people who made the ads, the campaign consultants and
> media advisers and pollsters. We wrote about them so often that I think we
> have turned some of them into political celebrities in their own right. We have
> helped to make them both famous and rich.
>
> In all of this, we forgot about the people who were the consumers of these
> ads, those who had the message pushed at them, willingly or not, every time
> they turned on their radio or television set. We forgot our obligation as journal-
> ists to help them cope with this mass of political propaganda coming their way.

The line Broder had drawn—between accepting and ignoring the consequences of what reporters wrote—was to be the main dividing line between the public journalism movement and the "mainstream" press. Even
before this speech, Broder had written a column issuing a similar challenge
to journalists. "It is time for us in the world's freest press to become activists," he wrote in 1990, "not on behalf of a particular party or politician,
but on behalf of the process of self-government."

Toward the end of advancing this kind of "activism," Broder laid out in
his speech recommendations for future campaign coverage that would pay
less attention to tactical maneuvers and more to the connection between
the campaign and real national problems. One specific suggestion, which
seems obvious now but had rarely been done before Broder proposed it,
was that reporters cover campaign ads not from the candidates' point of
view but from the voters'. That is, instead of emphasizing what each campaign was trying to accomplish with the ads—how they were exploiting
their opponents' vulnerabilities, which interest groups they were trying
to peel off, and how—the reporters should examine how truthful and
realistic the advertisements were. One immediate effect of Broder's

recommendation was the rapid spread of "Ad Watch"–type coverage in campaign coverage, in which correspondents examined political ads for smears and misrepresentations.

### Public Journalism in Practice

Through meetings coordinated by Jay Rosen's Project on Public Life and the Press (which is based at New York University and funded by the Knight Foundation), public journalism became a "movement" by 1993. Its main base of support was in regional newspapers and some broadcast stations, usually working in partnership with the papers. . . .

The best-known project in public journalism's short history is probably    15
the *Charlotte Observer*'s approach to covering the North Carolina elections in 1992. The paper's editors, who had carefully studied Broder's proposals [. . .] didn't want their coverage to be driven by the issues that each candidate thought would be tactically useful in the election. Instead, they began an elaborate effort to determine what issues the state's people believed were most important, and what other issues might have the greatest impact on the state's future welfare even though the public was not yet fully aware of them. The paper commissioned a poll of more than a thousand area residents (not merely subscribers) to ask their views about the public issues that concerned them most. The poll was not a yes-or-no survey but involved extensive discussions to explore the reasons behind the respondents' views. After the initial polling, the *Observer* arranged for five hundred residents to serve as an ongoing citizens' advisory panel to the paper through the election season.

Based on the issues that emerged from the polls and panel discussions, as well as from efforts by the paper's reporters and editors to judge the trends that would affect the state, the paper drew up lists of topics about which the public expected answers from the candidates. These citizen-generated issues were not the same as the ones on which many of the candidates had planned to run. For instance, the citizen panels showed a widespread concern about environmental problems caused by Charlotte's rapid growth. Politicians had not planned to emphasize this theme, but the paper decided to push for statements on this and the other issues the citizen panels had recommended. At the same time, it ran fewer stories about advertising strategies, about horse-race-style opinion polls, and about other traditional campaign techniques.

The moment of truth for this new approach came early in the campaign season, and it involved a question that a newspaper did *not* ask. After the citizens' panel had stressed its interest in environmental issues (among other concerns), the *Observer* prepared a big grid to run in the newspaper, showing each candidate's position on the questions the panel had raised. At the time, the long-time Democratic officeholder Terry Sanford was running for the Senate. The *Observer's* editor, Rich Opel, has described what happened next:

> Voters are intensely interested in the environment. . . . So our reporters went out to senatorial candidates and said, "Here are the voters' questions." Terry Sanford, the incumbent senator, called me up from Washington and said, "Rich, I have these questions from your reporter and I'm not going to talk about the environment until the general election." This was the primary. I said, "Well, the voters want to know about the environment now, Terry." He said, "Well, that's not the way I have my campaign structured." I said, "Fine, I will run the questions and I will leave a space under it for you to answer. If you choose not to, we will just say, 'Would not respond' or we will leave it blank." We ended the conversation. In about ten days he sent the answers down.

Most political reporters for most newspapers know how they would instinctively respond when a candidate told them he was delaying discussion of an issue. "That's interesting," they would say. "What's the thinking behind that?" Like a campaign consultant, the reporter would be instantly engaged in figuring out why the issue would be useless against other Democrats in the primaries but would be useful against Republicans in the general election. By responding as proxies for the public rather than as consultants manqués, the reporters evoked the discussion their readers wanted to hear.

"This is not a way of being 'tough' on a candidate for its own sake, but of using toughness in service of certain public values," Jay Rosen has said of the Charlotte project. "It is also a way of adding some civility, since there are rewards to balance the penalties that dominate today's campaigns. In normal campaign coverage, candidates get praised and criticized, but on the basis of what values? In this case the paper said: *here* are the issues the public wants to hear about. We'll judge you on whether you respond to these views." Most newspapers, he said, also judge candidates by a set of values—but never lay out clearly for the reader or the candidate exactly what those values are. . . .

### Complaints from the Media Establishment

There has, however, been one important source of backlash against the public-journalism approach. It has come from the editors of the country's largest and most influential newspapers. Leonard Downie, executive editor of the *Washington Post,* has said the movement's basic premise is "completely wrong." Max Frankel, the former executive editor of the *New York Times,* has expressed a similar hostility—as have others, including William F. Woo, editor of the *St. Louis Post-Dispatch.*

The crux of their unhappiness lies with the concept of "objectivity." One of public journalism's basic claims is that journalists should stop kidding themselves about their ability to remain detached from and objective about

20

public life. Journalists are not like scientists, observing the behavior of fruit flies but not influencing what the flies might do. They inescapably change the reality of whatever they are observing by whether and how they choose to write about it.

From the nearly infinite array of events, dramas, tragedies, and successes occurring in the world each day, newspaper editors and broadcast producers must define a tiny sample as "the news." The conventions of choosing "the news" are so familiar, and so much of the process happens by learned and ingrained habits, that it is easy for journalists to forget that the result reflects *decisions,* rather than some kind of neutral scientific truth.

At the national level, the daily public-affairs news concentrates heavily on what the president said and did that day; how well- or badly organized his staff seems to be; whether he is moving ahead or falling behind in his struggle against opponents from the other party; and who is using what tactics to get ready for the next presidential race. Each time the chairman of the Federal Reserve opens his mouth, he usually gets on the front page of the newspaper and on the evening network news. Each month, when the government releases its report on unemployment rates and consumer-price increases, papers and networks treat this as a genuine news event. Each summer when the leaders of industrialized nations hold their G-7 meeting, the news gives us a few minutes of prime ministers and presidents discussing their latest economic disputes. When the local school board selects a new superintendent of schools, that announcement, and the comments of the new superintendent, are played prominently in the local news.

A case could be made that some or all of these events are really the most important "news" that a broad readership needs each day. But you could just as easily make a case that most of these official, often ceremonial events should be overlooked and that a whole different category of human activity deserves coverage as "news." Instead of telling us what Newt Gingrich will do to block Bill Clinton's spending plans for education, the "news" might involve the way parochial schools work and ask whether their standard of discipline is possible in public schools. Instead of describing rivalries on the White House staff, the "news" could treat the presidency the way it does the scientific establishment, judging it mainly by public pronouncements and not looking too far behind the veil. The simplest daily reminder that the news is the result of countless judgment calls, rather than some abstract truth, is a comparison of the front page of the *Wall Street Journal* with that of almost any other major newspaper. The "news" that dominates four-fifths of most front pages is confined, in the *Journal,* to two little columns of news summary. (Here is an alarming fact: Those two columns represent more words than a half-hour TV news show would, if written out.) The rest of the front page represents the *Journal's* attempt to explain what is interesting and important about the world, though it may not be at the top of the breaking "news." The two great journalistic organizations that illustrate how creatively the "news" could be defined are in fact the *Journal's* news (not editorial) sections and National Public Radio's news staff. Each of them covers the breaking news but does so in a summary fashion, so it can put its energy, space, and professional pride into reports that are not driven by the latest official pronouncement.

"It's absolutely correct to say that there are objectively occurring events," 25 says Cole Campbell, of the *Virginian-Pilot*. "Speeches are made, volcanoes erupt, trees fall. But *news* is not a scientifically observable event. News is a choice, an extraction process, saying that one event is more meaningful than another event. The very act of saying that means making judgments that are based on values and based on frames."

It might seem that in making this point, Campbell and his colleagues had "discovered" a principle that most people figure out when they are in high school. There is no such thing as "just the news," and that's why editors are both necessary and powerful. But the public-journalism advocates have pushed this obvious-seeming point toward a conclusion that has angered many other editors. They have argued that the way modern journalists *choose* to present the news increases the chance that citizens will feel unhappy, powerless, betrayed by, and angry about their political system. And because the most powerful journalistic organs are unwilling to admit that they've made this choice, Rosen says, it is almost impossible for them to change.

"I couldn't disagree more with that view of newspaper journalism," Leonard Downie of the *Washington Post* has said in discussing the public-journalism theory that reporters should be actively biased in favor of encouraging the community to be involved in politics:

> I think our job is to report the news. To come as near as we can to giving people the truth, recognizing that the truth is multifaceted and that it changes from time to time as we learn more. I know that is what we do at the *Washington Post*. I know there are times when individual feelings among reporters and editors may cause them to want to take a side. We work very hard here to try to drive that out of our work.

Downie says that this approach is hard on his reporters, who in an attempt to suppress their personal feelings about an issue must "pretend to be less fully human than they really are." (Downie himself takes this belief to such an extreme that he *refuses to vote* in elections, feeling that this would make him too involved in the political process.) He admits that the newspaper's claim of "objectivity" is not convincing to many readers, who believe that the paper has its own angle on many stories. But he says that wavering even for a moment from the pursuit of "objectivity" would be disastrous.

> Where I am most bothered is when a newspaper uses its news columns—not its editorial page or its publisher—to achieve specific outcomes in the community. That is what I think is wrong, and very wrong. That line is very bright, and

very sharp, and extremely dangerous. It is being manipulated by academics who are risking the terrible prostitution of our profession. Telling political candidates that they must come to a newspaper's forum, or that they must discuss certain issues—that is very dangerous stuff. That is not our role. There are plenty of institutions in every community to do this sort of thing. If newspapers are lax in covering these activities—if we are guilty only of covering crime and horse-race politics, then we should do our job better. We shouldn't change our job.

This defense of pure, detached "objectivity" drives many public-journalism advocates crazy. Rosen, Merritt, Campbell, and others say that when papers and TV stations have taken a more "engaged," less "objective" approach, they virtually never receive complaints from their readers or viewers. "*All* of the resistance to public journalism has come from other journalists, not from the public or politicians," Jay Rosen has said. "The resistance is always in the name of the community, but it is hard to find anyone in the community who objects." In its several years of public-journalism projects, the *Virginian-Pilot* has received one hostile letter to the editor, claiming that its new approach to the community's problems meant abandoning the old standard of objectivity. But that letter came from a retired newspaper editor; the paper says it has received no similar complaints from readers without a professional axe to grind.

"I think Len Downie is right when he says that public journalism is an 30 'ideology,'" says Cole Campbell. "There are *two* ideologies, and he is unself-conscious about the ideology that drives his kind of journalism.

> The ideology of mainstream journalism is, When there is conflict, there is news. When there is no conflict, there's no news. That is ideological. It is out of touch with how people experience life.

Buzz Merritt elaborated on this point in *Public Journalism and Public Life*: "It is interesting that journalism's binding axiom of objectivity allows, even requires, unlimited toughness as a tool as well as a credo, yet it rejects *purposefulness*—having a motivation beyond mere exposure—as unprofessional. Without purposefulness, toughness is mere self-indulgence."

### The Hidden Consensus

Beneath the apparent gulf that separates the public-journalism advocates from their elite critics is a broader ground of hopeful consensus. Although Leonard Downie objects vehemently to public journalism in theory, he has said that he respects most of the actual journalistic projects that have been done in its name. "The notion that in political campaigns you should shift some of your resources away from covering consultants and toward reporting the issues voters are primarily interested in—that is simply an evolution of good political journalism," he said.

These are not new ways of reporting. Using public opinion surveys to find out what people think about their own communities, doing solutions reporting to see what things are working in solving societal problems—this is all part of what I would see as normal newspaper reporting.

But why, Downie asks, call this "public journalism"? Why not just call it "good journalism" and try to do more of it?

Other editors who have been on the warpath against the public-journalism concept, including William Woo of the *St. Louis Post-Dispatch* and Howard Schneider of *Newsday,* have also said there is "nothing new" in the concept of public-spirited reporting. It's what papers should have been doing all along.

The public-journalism advocates might take this as a sign that they are winning the battle. In the 1970s and early 1980s, the military reformers in the Pentagon knew that the tide had turned their way when their opponents began saying that there was "nothing new" in the reformers' analysis. After all, its principles had been in circulation since the time of Douglas MacArthur, or Robert E. Lee, or for that matter Genghis Khan.    35

The rancor surrounding the public-journalism debate actually seems to arise from two misunderstandings. One concerns the nature of journalism's "involvement" in public life. When Leonard Downie and Max Frankel hear that term, they seem to imagine drumbeating campaigns by a newspaper on behalf of a particular candidate or a specific action-plan for a community. What the editors who have put public journalism into effect mean is "just good journalism"—that is, making people care about the issues that affect their lives, and helping them see how they can play a part in resolving those issues.

And when big-paper editors hear that the public journalists want to "listen" to the public and be "guided" by its concerns, the editors imagine something that they dread. This sounds all too similar to pure "user-driven" journalism, in which the marketing department surveys readers to find out what they're interested in, and the editors give them only that. This version of public journalism sounds like an invitation to abandon all critical judgment and turn the paper into a pure "feel good" advertising sheet. It misrepresents the best conception of public journalism, which is that editors and reporters will continue to exercise their judgment about issues, as they claim to now, but will pay more attention than today's elite journalists do to the impact of their work on the health of democracy.

"I think the people who make this criticism have not looked closely enough at what public interest journalism is doing," William Kovach, of the Nieman Foundation, said in 1995. "Papers are using surveys, but they are very careful surveys; they're doing a lot of work in neighborhoods. It's not a politically designed opinion poll to take a snap judgment." The editors who have undertaken public-journalism projects say they are using their best reportorial skills to determine not what people want to hear but what issues concern them most, and then applying that knowledge in their coverage.

Leonard Downie is right: This approach is "just good journalism." The real questions it raises are not hair-splitting quarrels about what it should be called but the practical work of implementation. . . .

*For Discussion*

1. What exactly is the point of David Broder's speech — in his own words, as Fallows cites them, and according to Fallow's interpretation? In what sense and to what degree can reporters be held "responsible" for what they write?

2. Most thoughtful people respond positively to the notion that politics in general and political campaigns in particular ought to connect more vitally with genuine national problems. But how do we know when we are dealing with genuine national problems? How does public journalism go about determining what they are? Do you find this approach satisfactory?

3. Recent surveys of the attitudes of current college students and recent college graduates conclude that the vast majority are alienated from politics. Suppose that the goals and methods of public journalism became more common — would that make a difference? Would you take a greater interest in politics if the politicians and their "hired guns" had less control over the news? Or does the alienation from politics have deeper sources than news coverage?

4. In criticizing public journalism, Leonard Downie of the *Washington Post* contends that "[t]elling political candidates that they must come to a newspaper's forum . . . is very dangerous . . . [and] not our role. There are plenty of institutions in every community to do this sort of thing." What institutions does he have in mind? Are they doing "this sort of thing" well? How do newspapers cover, for instance, debates between political candidates sponsored by the League of Women Voters?

*For Convincing*

Fallows contends that there is really a "hidden consensus" on the values, goals, and methods of public journalism — that even what he calls its "elitist critics" are moving in the direction of this reform movement. Look at political coverage in several newspapers and on reputable television news sources. Can you detect the alleged hidden consensus?

Write a paper affirming, denying, or partly affirming and denying Fallows's contention.

*For Research and Inquiry*

Since 1993 especially, much has been written about civic or public journalism. Thus far, as Fallows indicates, the experiment has been mostly restricted to "small time" papers, not the big national ones. As a class project, find out everything you can about the movement, and discuss the results of your research in class. Write a paper exploring this apparent limitation and suggesting ways that it might be overcome.

*Additional Suggestions for Writing*

Many journalists first practice their craft as college students working for campus newspapers more or less run by students. Study several editions of your campus paper (or, if there isn't one, of a paper from a campus close to yours). Compare it, if possible, to other campus papers, and consult with students working for the paper. Discuss the results of your research as a class.

Then write an essay assessing the campus newspaper. Does it represent its community? all of it? How does it represent its community? What sources do the reporters use? To what extent and in what ways do the stories interpret campus events? Could the coverage be improved? How?

# Chapter 15

# Liberal Education and Contemporary Culture: What Should Undergraduates Learn?

N o institution in the United States receives more attention than our educational system. Studies of it abound, and new ones seem to appear almost weekly. It is rare not to hear or read something about education in the news every day, while scholarly articles and books about it proliferate beyond anyone's ability to read them all.

Why are we so obsessed with this topic? Most Americans believe that education is the route to a better life, the foundation of democracy, and the key to a strong economy, a competitive work force, and social and moral progress. "Better education" becomes the magic solution to so many questions concerning the nation's problems. We are obsessed with it, then, because our perceived stake in it is so high. That's why the press covers it extensively and why politicians push the issue toward the top of their campaigns for office and their legislative agendas.

With ideals and expectations so high, we should not be surprised that the educational system often disappoints enough to be called "failing" or "a failure." Until the past decade or so, however, almost all the criticism was directed at the public schools, especially high schools, while our universities and colleges were extolled as among the best in the world. Now higher education comes in for as much criticism as the public schools. As the cost of a college education continues to soar, rising much faster than the rate of inflation, more and more people wonder whether we are getting our money's worth, especially when a degree may no longer lead as often as it once did to a desired first job. Industry spends millions educating their employees after college, in part because many lack even basic communication skills, and businesses increasingly resort to hiring people whose degrees were earned in other countries. There is much talk that we are losing our competitive edge and that college graduates are no longer well-informed citizens, able to provide moral and intellectual leadership. In short, whereas once it was always the public schools that were failing, now many also apply the label to higher education, public and private.

The focus of concern is undergraduate education, especially the first two years, when students traditionally receive broad exposure to the liberal arts (literature, history, philosophy, and so on) prior to concentrating on their majors. The notion of "liberal arts" comes to us from ancient Athens and Rome, where *liberal* meant "free" in the sense of not being a slave: male citizens were educated in the liberal arts, slaves in the manual or practical arts. Liberal arts education still has strong identifications with social class: Virtually all of our most prestigious (that is, selective and usually expensive) universities claim to offer a liberal arts education, as contrasted with technical and vocational schools, which supposedly do not. One problem the liberal arts face in the United States is the association with privilege in a democratic culture uneasy with class distinctions. We want to say the liberal arts are for everyone. But are they?

Another problem is that university faculties cannot agree about what an "educated person" should know and therefore what a liberal arts education should be. The typical result is a laundry list of courses that satisfy what we call "basic requirements" but that do not constitute either a coherent course of study or a shared body of knowledge required for all students. Perhaps we should resign ourselves to such disagreements in a diverse culture with universities offering courses in virtually all fields of knowledge. Who's to say what an "educated person" should know? But if we can't answer this question, does the ideal of a liberal arts education have any substance, any meaning? Or is it merely an empty ideal we cling to out of habit?

Liberal arts education faces many other problems, none of which have easy solutions. For example, the traditional liberal arts education is limited to the West, primarily to the heritage of Greece and Rome as transmitted through later European culture to those parts of the world colonized by European powers. We live, however, in a world of global commerce, communication, and politics, where knowledge of the West alone is insufficient and can foster a destructive cultural arrogance. How inclusive can a liberal arts education become without losing focus and character? Can an essentially Western educational ideal function in a global context?

No matter how we answer the questions posed thus far—and even if we think, as many critics do, that liberal arts education is dead—we should ponder this: fundamentally, the liberal arts are the study of human achievements, cultures, and institutions. Because nothing human can be created or studied without language, the liberal arts also include English, foreign languages, and mathematics. Clearly, education wouldn't amount to much without humanistic study and couldn't go on at all without knowledge of the various symbol systems that enable all study. As long as we invest in education, we'll be investing in the liberal arts.

But if there is something permanent about the liberal arts, dealing as they do with human culture, they must be responsive to the times, to cultural change and pressures. All the selections in this chapter deal with contemporary American culture. "Collegiate Life: An Obituary" offers a sketch of the undergraduate student and college life based on extensive empirical research. The two articles "on the uses of a liberal education" offer sharply contrasting personal narratives, one by a professor at the University of Virginia, whose students are relatively privileged, and the other by a researcher into poverty, who created a liberal arts course for ghetto students in New York City. For the first writer, a liberal arts education is too often "lite entertainment for bored college students," and for the second, "a weapon in the hands of the restless poor"—a forceful reminder that the cultural situation in which liberal arts are taught has everything to do with what they are and how they function.

No inquiry into liberal education and contemporary culture can afford to ignore university culture itself, exclusive of students—in other words, the institutional structure. Our final reading, John Tagg's "The Decline of the Knowledge Factory," exposes this structure well en route to explaining why reforming liberal arts education is so difficult.

Above all, as we think about liberal arts education and contemporary culture, we must always remember how closely tied together they are. Physics may be physics regardless of where it's taught and to whom, but literature and philosophy, to mention only two important liberal arts, assuredly are not. No curriculum will work if it is out of touch with its culture, and a culture divorced from the liberal arts will be thin and puerile. Getting them to dance together more or less harmoniously while preserving the rigor and discipline of higher education is probably the major challenge we face.

# Collegiate Life: An Obituary
## Arthur Levine and Jeanette S. Cureton

*Arthur Levine is president of Teacher's College at Columbia University; Jeanette Cureton was an educational researcher at Harvard during their collaboration. Their book,* When Hopes and Fears Collide: A Portrait of Today's College Student *(1998), presents the results of five years (1992–1997) of research involving many universities and colleges and including extensive conversations with students and student affairs officers. This article from the journal* Change *summarizes their conclusions.*

*Our institutions of higher education are almost unimaginably diverse, each having its own unique history, character, and student profile. Any discussion of general trends or treatment of the "typical" or "average" student, therefore, may only imperfectly reflect your own experience. Yet we think you will recognize the portrait and find it helpful in understanding and articulating what's happening on college campuses today.*

In 1858, John Henry Cardinal Newman wrote *The Idea of a University.* His ideal was a residential community of students and teachers devoted to the intellect. To him, a college was "an alma mater, knowing her children one by one, not a foundry, or a mint, or a treadmill." Given a choice between an institution that dispensed with "residence and tutorial superintendence and gave its degrees to any person who passed an examination in a wide range of subjects" or "a university which . . . merely brought a number of young men together for three or four years," he chose the latter.

Newman's ideal was so appealing that it has been embraced regularly over the years by higher education luminaries from Robert Hutchins and Paul Goodman to Alexander Meiklejohn and Mortimer Adler. Belief in it remains a staple of nearly every college curriculum committee in the country.

But that ideal is moribund today. Except for a relatively small number of residential liberal arts colleges, institutions of higher education and their students are moving away from it at an accelerating pace. The notion of a living-learning community is dead or dying on most campuses today.

This is a principal finding of several studies we conducted between 1992 and 1997, which involved our surveying a representative sample of 9,100 undergraduate students and 270 chief student affairs officers, as well as holding focus groups on 28 campuses. . . .

### Demographics

A major reason for the changes we describe is simply demographic. In comparison with their counterparts of the 1960s and 1970s, undergraduates today are more racially diverse and, on average, considerably older. In fact, since 1980, the lion's share of college enrollment growth has come from students who might be described as nontraditional. By 1993, 24 percent of all college students were working full-time, according to our Undergraduate Survey; at two-year colleges, this figure had reached 39 percent.

By 1995, 44 percent of all college students were over 25 years old; 54 percent were working; 56 percent were female; and 43 percent were attending part-time. Currently, fewer than one in six of all undergraduates fit the traditional stereotype of the American college student attending full-time, being 18 to 22 years of age, and living on campus (see U.S. Department of Education, in Resources).

What this means is that higher education is not as central to the lives of today's undergraduates as it was to previous generations. Increasingly, college is just one of a multiplicity of activities in which they are engaged every day. For many, it is not even the most important of these activities; work and family often overshadow it.

As a consequence, older, part-time, and working students — especially those with children — often told us in our surveys that they wanted a different type of relationship with their colleges from the one undergraduates historically have had. They preferred a relationship like those they already enjoyed with their bank, the telephone company, and the supermarket.

**What Students Want**

Think about what you want from your bank. We know what we want: an ATM on every corner. And when we get to the ATM, we want there to be no line. We also would like a parking spot right in front of the ATM, and to have our checks deposited the moment they arrive at the bank, or perhaps the day before! And we want no mistakes in processing — unless they are in our favor. We also know what we do not want from our banks. We do not want them to provide us with softball leagues, religious counseling, or health services. We can arrange all of these things for ourselves and don't wish to pay extra fees for the bank to offer them.

Students are asking roughly the same thing from their colleges. They want their colleges to be nearby and to operate at the hours most useful to them — preferably around the clock. They want convenience: easy, accessible parking (at the classroom door would not be bad); no lines; and a polite, helpful, efficient staff. They also want high-quality education but are eager for low costs. For the most part, they are willing to comparison shop, and they place a premium on time and money. They do not want to pay for activities and programs they do not use.

In short, students increasingly are bringing to higher education exactly the same consumer expectations they have for every other commercial establishment with which they deal. Their focus is on convenience, quality, service, and cost.

They believe that since they are paying for their education, faculty should give them the education they want; they make larger demands on faculty than past students ever have. They are also the target audience for alternatives to traditional higher education. They are likely to be drawn to distance education, which offers the convenience of instruction at home or the office.

They are prime candidates for stripped-down versions of college, located in the suburbs and business districts of our cities, that offer low-cost instruction made possible by heavy faculty teaching loads, mostly part-time faculties, limited selections of majors, and few electives. Proprietary institutions of this type are springing up around the country.

On campus, students are behaving like consumers, too. More than nine out of 10 chief student affairs officers told us in last year's Student Affairs Survey that student power in college governance has increased during the 1990s (or at least has remained the same), but that undergraduates are less interested in being involved in campus governance than in the past.

A small minority of undergraduates continue to want voting power or 15 control over admissions decisions, faculty appointments, bachelor's degree requirements, and the content of courses; however, a decreasing percentage desire similar roles in residential regulations and undergraduate discipline, areas in which students would seem most likely to want control. Overall, the proportion of students who want voting or controlling roles in institutional governance is at its lowest level in a quarter century, according to comparisons between our 1993 Undergraduate Survey and the 1969 and 1976 Carnegie Council surveys.

This is precisely the same attitude most of us hold with regard to the commercial enterprises we patronize. We don't want to be bothered with running the bank or the supermarket; we simply want them to do their jobs and do them well—to give us what we need without hassles or headaches. That is, help the consumers and don't get in their way. Students today are saying precisely the same things about their colleges.

### Social Life

From a personal perspective, students are coming to college overwhelmed and more damaged than in the past. Chief student affairs officers in 1997 reported rises in eating disorders (on 58 percent of campuses), classroom disruption (on 44 percent), drug abuse (on 42 percent), alcohol abuse (on 35 percent), gambling (on 25 percent), and suicide attempts (on 23 percent).

As a consequence, academic institutions are being forced to expand their psychological counseling services. Three out of five colleges and universities reported last year that the use of counseling services had increased. Not only are counselors seeing students in record numbers, but the severity of the students' problems and the length of time needed to treat them are greater than in the past.

Students tell us they are frightened. They're afraid of deteriorating social and environmental conditions, international conflicts and terrorism, multiculturalism and their personal relationships, financing their education and getting jobs, and the future they will face. Nearly one-third of all college freshmen (30 percent) grew up with one or no parent (see Sax et al., in Resources). As one dean of students we talked with concluded, "Students expect the [college] community to respond to their needs—to make right their personal problems and those of society at large."

The effect of these accumulated fears and hurts is to divide students and isolate them from one another. Students also fear intimacy in relationships; withdrawal is easier and less dangerous than engagement. 20

Traditional dating is largely dead on college campuses. At institutions all over the country, students told us, in the words of a University of Colorado undergraduate, "There is no such thing as dating here." Two-person dating has been replaced by group dating, in which men and women travel in unpartnered packs. It's a practice that provides protection from deeper involvement and intimacy for a generation that regularly told us in focus group interviews that they had never witnessed a successful adult romantic relationship.

Romantic relationships are seen as a burden, as a drag or potential anchor in a difficult world. Yet sexual relationships have not declined, even in the age of AIDS. Student descriptions of sexual activity are devoid of emotional content; they use words such as "scoping," "clocking," "hooking," "scamming," "scrumping," "mashing," and "shacking" to describe intimate relations.

In general, with increasing pressures on students, collegiate social life occupies a smaller part of their lives. In the words of an undergraduate at the University of the District of Columbia, "Life is just work, school, and home." In fact, one-fifth of those queried on our campus site visits (21 percent) defined their social lives in terms of studying; for another 11 percent, sleeping was all they cared about. When we asked students at the University of Colorado for the best adjective to describe this generation, the most common choice was "tired."

But not all of the retreat from social life is time-based. Chief student affairs officers describe students as loners more often now than in the past. Requests for single rooms in residence halls have skyrocketed. The thought of having a roommate is less appealing than it once was.

Similarly, group activities that once connected students on college campuses are losing their appeal and are becoming more individualized. For instance, the venue for television watching has moved from the lounge to the dorm room. Film viewing has shifted from the theater to the home VCR. With student rooms a virtual menagerie of electronic and food-preparation equipment, students are living their lives in ways that allow them to avoid venturing out if they so choose. 25

### Student Organizational Mitosis

None of this is to say that collegiate social life is dead, but its profile and location have changed. On campus, there is probably a greater diversity of activities available than ever before, but each activity—in the words of the chief student affairs officer of the University of Southern Mississippi—"appeals to smaller pockets of students."

This is, in many respects, the consequence of student organizational mitosis and the proliferation of the divides between undergraduates. For instance, the business club on one college campus divided into more than a dozen groups—including women's; black; Hispanic; gay, lesbian, and bisexual; and Asian and Filipino business clubs.

Deans of students regularly told us last year that "there is less larger-group socializing" and that "more people are doing things individually and in separate groups than campus-wide." In contrast to the Carnegie Council's 1979 study, current students describe themselves in terms of their differences, not their commonalities. Increasingly, they say they associate with people who are like themselves rather than different.

In the main, when students do take time to have fun, they are leaving campus to do so. Our Campus Site Visits study indicated that drinking is the primary form of recreation for 63 percent of students, followed closely by going to clubs and bars (59 percent) and simply getting off campus (52 percent). By contrast, the latter two activities were not mentioned in the Carnegie Council's 1979 study.

Drinking was not a surprise. It was the first choice in our earlier study, but there is more binge drinking today. Drinking to get drunk has become the great escape for undergraduates.

Escaping from campus is a trend that goes hand in hand with the high numbers of students living in off-campus housing—more than triple the percentage in the late 1960s. Only 30 percent of students we surveyed reported living on campus. Add to this the fact that students are also spending less time on campus because of jobs and part-time attendance, and the result is that increasingly campuses are places in which instruction is the principal activity. Living and social life occur elsewhere.

### Multiculturalism

Campuses are more deeply divided along lines of race, gender, ethnicity, sexuality, and other differences today than in the past. A majority of deans at four-year colleges told us last year that the climate on campus can be described as politically correct (60 percent), civility has declined (57 percent), students of different racial and ethnic groups often do not socialize together (56 percent), reports of sexual harassment have increased (55 percent), and students feel uncomfortable expressing unpopular or controversial opinions (54 percent).

Multiculturalism is a painful topic for many students. The dirty words on college campuses now are no longer four letters: they are six-letter words like "racist" and "sexist"—and "homophobic," which is even longer. Students don't want to discuss the topic. In focus group interviews, students were more willing to tell us intimate details of their sex lives than to discuss diversity on campus.

Tension regarding diversity and difference runs high all across college life. Students talked about friction in the classroom; in the residence halls; in reactions to posters placed on campus or to visiting speakers; in campus activities and the social pursuits of the day; in hiring practices; in testing; in the dining room, library, bookstore, and sports facilities; in every aspect of their campus lives. In this sense, the campus in the 1990s is a less hospitable place for all undergraduates, regardless of background, than it once was.

### Academics

Although instruction remains the principal on-campus activity that brings undergraduates together, the academic arena is experiencing its own form of student disengagement. Pursuit of academic goals is clearly utilitarian. It's as if students have struck a bargain with their colleges. They're going to class all right, but they're going by the book: they're doing what's necessary to fulfill degree requirements and gain skills for a job, but then they're out the door. They're focused and career-oriented, and see college as instrumental in leading to a lucrative career. "Task-oriented students who focus on jobs" is how a Georgia Tech student affairs official labeled them.

Although students do not believe that a college education provides a money-back guarantee of future success, they feel that without one, a good job—much less a lucrative or prestigious job—is impossible to obtain. At the very least, it's a kind of insurance policy to hedge bets against the future. As a student at Portland (Oregon) Community College put it, "College is the difference between white-collar and blue-collar work." Fifty-seven percent of undergraduates we surveyed in 1993 believed that the chief benefit of a college education is increasing one's earning power—an 11 percentage-point increase since 1976.

By contrast, the value placed on nonmaterial goals (that is, learning to get along with people and formulating the values and goals of one's life) has plummeted since the late 1960s, dropping from 71 and 76 percent respectively to 50 and 47 percent. Whereas in 1969 these personal and philosophic goals were cited by students as the primary reasons for attending college, in 1993, students placed them at the bottom of the list.

Although a great number of students are focused and intent on pursuing career goals, many also face a variety of academic hurdles. They are coming to college less well prepared academically. Nearly three-fourths (73 percent) of deans in 1997 reported an increase within the last decade in the proportion of students requiring remedial or developmental education at two-year (81 percent) and four-year (64 percent) colleges.

Nearly one-third (32 percent) of all undergraduates surveyed reported having taken a basic skills or remedial course in reading, writing, or math,

35

up from 29 percent in 1976. Despite high aspirations, a rising percentage of students simply are not prepared for the rigors of academe.

Another academic hurdle for students is a growing gap between how students learn best and how faculty teach. According to research by Charles Schroeder of the University of Missouri – Columbia, published in the September/October 1993 *Change,* more than half of today's students perform best in a learning situation characterized by "direct, concrete experience, moderate-to-high degrees of structure, and a linear approach to learning. They value the practical and the immediate, and the focus of their perception is primarily on the physical world." According to Schroeder, three-quarters of faculty, on the other hand, "prefer the global to the particular; are stimulated by the realm of concepts, ideas, and abstractions; and assume that students, like themselves, need a high degree of autonomy in their work."

Small wonder, then, that frustration results and that every year faculty believe students are less well prepared, while students increasingly think their classes are incomprehensible. On the faculty side, this is certainly the case. The 1997 Student Affairs Survey revealed that at 74 percent of campuses, faculty complaints about students are on the rise. One result is that students and faculty are spending less time on campus together. With work and part-time attendance, students increasingly are coming to campus just for their classes.

This explains, in part, why students are taking longer to complete college. Fewer than two out of five are able to graduate in four years (see Astin et al., in Resources). Twenty-eight percent now require a fifth year to earn a baccalaureate, according to U.S. Department of Education statistics from 1996. In reality, obtaining the baccalaureate degree in four years is an anomaly today, particularly at public and less selective institutions.

### The Future

The overwhelming majority of college students believe they will be successful. But their fears about relationships, romance, and their future happiness were continuing themes in every focus group. Their concerns about finances were overwhelming. There was not one focus group in which students did not ask whether they would be able to repay their student loans, afford to complete college, get a good job, or avoid moving home with Mom and Dad.

The college graduate driving a cab or working at the Gap was a universal anecdote. There was more mythology here than there were concrete examples, however. College graduates being forced to drive taxis is one of the great American legends, rivaled only by the tale of George Washington and the cherry tree.

Finances were a constant topic of discussion. Students told us of the need to drop out, stop out, and attend college part-time because of tuition costs. They told us of the lengths they had to go to pay tuition—even giving blood. More than one in five (21 percent) who participated in the Undergraduate Survey said that someone who helped pay their tuition had been out of work while they attended college.

At heart, undergraduates are worried about whether we can make it as a society, and whether they can actually make it personally. In our surveys, the majority did say they expected to do better than their parents. But in our focus groups, students regularly told us, "We're going to be the first generation that doesn't surpass our parents in making more money." "How will I buy a house?" "How will I send my kids to college?"

This is a generation of students desperately clinging to the American Dream. Nearly nine out of 10 (88 percent) students are optimistic about their personal futures, but their hope, though broadly professed, is fragile and gossamer-like. Their lives are being challenged at every turn: in their families, their communities, their nation, and their world. This is a generation where hope and fear collide.

### Conclusion

In sum, these changes in America's undergraduates add up to a requiem for historic notions of collegiate life—the ivory tower, the living-learning community, the residential college, and all the rest. But the changes are not sudden; they began even before Cardinal Newman wrote his classic. Most are a natural consequence of the democratization of higher education. This is what happens when 65 percent of all high school graduates go on to college and higher education is open to the nation's population across the lifespan. Four years of living in residence becomes a luxury few can afford.

So how should higher education respond? Dismissing the present or recalling a golden era lost are not particularly helpful—for the most part the changes are permanent. But there are a few things colleges can do.

The first is to focus. Most colleges have less time with their students on campus than in the past. They need to be very clear about what they want to accomplish with students and dramatically reduce the laundry lists of values and goals that constitute the typical mission statement. 50

The second is to use all opportunities available to educate students. Required events, such as orientation, should be used to educate rather than to deal with logistics. The awards a college gives should represent the values it most wants to teach. The same is true for speakers. The in-house newsletter can be used to educate. And of course, maybe the best advice is that almost any event can be used for educational purposes if the food and music are good enough.

Third, build on the strengths unique to every generation of students. For instance, current undergraduates, as part of their off-campus activities, are involved in public service—an astounding 64 percent of them, according to the Undergraduate Survey. Service learning, then, becomes an excellent vehicle to build into the curriculum and cocurriculum of most colleges.

Fourth, work to eliminate the forces that push students off campus unnecessarily. For example, most colleges talk a great deal about multiculturalism, but in general have not translated the rhetoric into a climate that will make the campus more hospitable to current students.

In like manner, using financial aid more to meet need than to reward merit would lessen the necessity for students to work while attending college. These are steps any college with the will and commitment can take. Both campus life and our students would benefit greatly.

Resources

Astin, A. W., L. Tsui, and J. Avalos. *Degree Attainment Rates at American Colleges and Universities: Effects of Race, Gender, and Institutional Type.* Los Angeles: Higher Education Research Institute, UCLA, 1996.

Sax, L. J., A. W. Astin, W. S. Korn, and K. M. Mahoney. *The American Freshman: National Norms for Fall 1997.* Los Angeles: Higher Education Research Institute, UCLA, 1997.

U.S. Department of Education. National Center for Education Statistics. *Condition of Education, 1996* (NCES 96304). Washington: GPO, 1996.

---. National Center for Education Statistics. *Digest of Education Statistics, 1997* (NCES 98–015). Washington: GPO, 1997.

*For Discussion*

1. The article opens by recalling Newman's 144-year-old *Idea of a University,* an ideal grounded in "a residential community of students and teachers devoted to the intellect." By definition, ideals do not correspond to realities, but do you find the ideal of *alma mater* (Latin, "bountiful mother") appealing? If so, in what ways exactly? Why?

2. Which of the demographic trends delineated in paragraphs 4–6 seem most incompatible with the survival and vitality of the residential college?

3. As the subtitle of the article, "an obituary," would suggest, its view of student culture is gloomy and largely negative: Students are said to be afraid and tired, anxious about money, burdened with personal problems, inclined toward escapism, overly demanding of teachers and college services, socially alienated and fragmented, and so on. Would you say the sketch is accurate? fair? balanced? How much do the attitudes and behaviors described reflect American culture in general rather than student culture in particular? How different are they from the attitudes and behaviors of your parents and their parents?

4. Current college students are described routinely as taking an instrumental view of college, seeing it as only a means to an end, not as

an end in itself. That is, "task-oriented students who focus on jobs" *is* the common view "we" take of "you." What intrinsic value might college have? How could it be an end in itself? Have your classes so far helped you detect and appreciate the intrinsic value of learning and the overall college experience?

## For Analysis and Convincing

If we are feeling charitable, we might describe the authors' suggestions at the end of the article as too general and obvious; if we are feeling less charitable, as vague and unhelpful. Can we do better?

Write an essay offering your own portrait of your generation of students or an essay that assesses the image offered here. Your portrait should reflect the demographics and other characteristics of your school. Then, working from the situation as you depict it, offer more concrete and detailed suggestions for coping with student problems and for improving campus life at your school. Address your essay to your school's student governing body.

## For Inquiry and Dialogue

If the residential college is dying or dead, as these authors claim and as a good deal of independent evidence supports, what model might replace it? Could we, for example, build a sense of student community and interaction between students and teachers via the electronic media, especially computers, as some have suggested? If student groups are fragmenting into smaller and smaller communities, how can we get these groups back together and engaged in useful dialogue? In short, a key question to think about and discuss is, How can we recapture something of the values represented by the residential college in an environment that does not lend itself to a closely knit community of students and teachers?

# Photograph
## Lois Bernstein

*When the University of Chicago was founded in the late nineteenth century, its trustees chose for its original buildings the English Gothic architectural style of Oxford University rather than a more contemporary design. The photograph below accompanied a recent* New York Times *article about the University's refusal to soften its rigorous academic standards and requirements in order to attract more applicants. The students are sitting in Hutchinson Commons, the main dining hall, which was constructed in 1901.*

## For Discussion

Architecture is a form of visual rhetoric, similar to public sculpture. The style of the buildings at a college or university makes an argument about the education offered there: its purpose, origins, and values. How do you read the argument implied by the interior of this college dining hall? Discuss the architecture of your own school's campus. Is it all in one style? A mix of styles and periods? Do different buildings seem to make different arguments? Consider these arguments in the context of changing ideas about liberal arts education, as discussed in the readings in this chapter.

# On the Uses of Liberal Education:
# As Lite Entertainment for Bored College Students
## Mark Edmundson

*This essay and the next one by Earl Shorris appeared together in the September 1997 issue of* Harper's Magazine. *Each can stand alone as an argument about the liberal arts and culture, but they are far more interesting read together as contrasting perspectives. Mark Edmundson is a professor at the prestigious University of Virginia and thus teaches relatively privileged students of traditional college age, while Shorris, a poverty researcher, discusses an experimental liberal arts program he developed for older, disadvantaged students in New York City. As one might expect, the view from "the top" is radically different from the view at "the bottom." Yet, at a deeper level, the essays connect and illuminate each other in provocative ways.*

*Edmundson wrote for people of his age, the sixties generation, not for college students. If you wonder about how professors see you, this essay may enlighten and perhaps irritate. Of course, his view does not represent all professors, nor do University of Virginia students typify the current population. But we think most professors and students will see something of themselves and their institutions in what Edmundson has to say. Furthermore, the issues he raises surely relate to higher education generally.*

Today is evaluation day in my Freud class, and everything has changed. The class meets twice a week, late in the afternoon, and the clientele, about fifty undergraduates, tends to drag in and slump, looking disconsolate and a little lost, waiting for a jump start. To get the discussion moving, they usually require a joke, an anecdote, an off-the-wall question—When you were a kid, were your Halloween getups ego costumes, id costumes, or superego costumes? That sort of thing. But today, as soon as I flourish the forms, a buzz rises in the room. Today they write their assessments of the course, their assessments of me, and they are without a doubt wide-awake. "What is your evaluation of the instructor?" asks question number eight, entreating them to circle a number between five (excellent) and one (poor, poor). Whatever interpretive subtlety they've acquired during the term is now out the window. Edmundson: one to five, stand and shoot.

And they do. As I retreat through the door—I never stay around for this phase of the ritual—I look over my shoulder and see them toiling away like the devil's auditors. They're pitched into high writing gear, even the ones who struggle to squeeze out their journal entries word by word, stoked on a procedure they have by now supremely mastered. They're playing the informed consumer, letting the provider know where he's come through and where he's not quite up to snuff.

But why am I so distressed, bolting like a refugee out of my own classroom, where I usually hold easy sway? Chances are the evaluations will be much like what they've been in the past—they'll be just fine. It's likely that

I'll be commended for being "interesting" (and I am commended, many times over), that I'll be cited for my relaxed and tolerant ways (that happens, too), that my sense of humor and capacity to connect the arcana of the subject matter with current culture will come in for some praise (yup). I've been hassled this term, finishing a manuscript, and so haven't given their journals the attention I should have, and for that I'm called — quite civilly, though — to account. Overall, I get off pretty well.

Yet I have to admit that I do not much like the image of myself that emerges from these forms, the image of knowledgeable, humorous detachment and bland tolerance. I do not like the forms themselves, with their number ratings, reminiscent of the sheets circulated after the TV pilot has just played to its sample audience in Burbank. Most of all I dislike the attitude of calm consumer expertise that pervades the responses. I'm disturbed by the serene belief that my function — and, more important, Freud's, or Shakespeare's, or Blake's — is to divert, entertain, and interest. Observes one respondent, not at all unrepresentative: "Edmundson has done a fantastic job of presenting this difficult, important & controversial material in an enjoyable and approachable way."

Thanks but no thanks. I don't teach to amuse, to divert, or even, for    5
that matter, to be merely interesting. When someone says she "enjoyed" the course — and that word crops up again and again in my evaluations — somewhere at the edge of my immediate complacency I feel encroaching self-dislike. That is not at all what I had in mind. The off-the-wall questions and the sidebar jokes are meant as lead-ins to stronger stuff — in the case of the Freud course, to a complexly tragic view of life. But the affability and the one-liners often seem to be all that land with the students; their journals and evaluations leave me little doubt.

I want some of them to say that they've been changed by the course. I want them to measure themselves against what they've read. It's said that some time ago a Columbia University instructor used to issue a harsh two-part question. One: What book did you most dislike in the course? Two: What intellectual or characterological flaws in you does that dislike point to? The hand that framed that question was surely heavy. But at least it compels one to see intellectual work as a confrontation between two people, student and author, where the stakes matter. Those Columbia students were being asked to relate the quality of an encounter, not rate the action as though it had unfolded on the big screen.

Why are my students describing the Oedipus complex and the death drive as being interesting and enjoyable to contemplate? And why am I coming across as an urbane, mildly ironic, endlessly affable guide to this intellectual territory, operating without intensity, generous, funny, and loose?

Because that's what works. On evaluation day, I reap the rewards of my partial compliance with the culture of my students and, too, with the culture of the university as it now operates. It's a culture that's gotten little exploration. Current critics tend to think that liberal-arts education is in crisis because universities have been invaded by professors with peculiar ideas: deconstruction, Lacanianism, feminism, queer theory. They believe that genius and tradition are out and that P.C., multiculturalism, and identity politics are in because of an invasion by tribes of tenured radicals, the late millennial equivalents of the Visigoth hordes that cracked Rome's walls.

But mulling over my evaluations and then trying to take a hard, extended look at campus life both here at the University of Virginia and around the country eventually led me to some different conclusions. To me, liberal-arts education is as ineffective as it is now not chiefly because there are a lot of strange theories in the air. (Used well, those theories can be illuminating.) Rather, it's that university culture, like American culture writ large, is, to put it crudely, ever more devoted to consumption and entertainment, to the using and using up of goods and images. For someone growing up in America now, there are few available alternatives to the cool consumer worldview. My students didn't ask for that view, much less create it, but they bring a consumer [worldview] to school, where it exerts a powerful, and largely unacknowledged, influence. If we want to understand current universities, with their multiple woes, we might try leaving the realms of expert debate and fine ideas and turning to the classrooms and campuses, where a new kind of weather is gathering.

From time to time I bump into a colleague in the corridor and we have   10
what I've come to think of as a Joon Lee fest. Joon Lee is one of the best students I've taught. He's endlessly curious, has read a small library's worth, seen every movie, and knows all about showbiz and entertainment. For a class of mine he wrote an essay using Nietzsche's Apollo and Dionysus to analyze the pop group The Supremes. A trite, cultural-studies bonbon? Not at all. He said striking things about conceptions of race in America and about how they shape our ideas of beauty. When I talk with one of his other teachers, we run on about the general splendors of his work and presence. But what inevitably follows a JL fest is a mournful reprise about the divide that separates him and a few other remarkable students from their contemporaries. It's not that some aren't nearly as bright — in terms of intellectual ability, my students are all that I could ask for. Instead, it's that Joon Lee has decided to follow his interests and let them make him into a singular and rather eccentric man; in his charming way, he doesn't mind being at odds with most anyone.

It's his capacity for enthusiasm that sets Joon apart from what I've come to think of as the reigning generational style. Whether the students are sorority/fraternity types, grunge aficionados, piercer/tattooers, black or white, rich or middle class (alas, I teach almost no students from truly poor backgrounds), they are, nearly across the board, very, very self-contained. On good days they display a light, appealing glow; on bad days, shuffling disgruntlement. But there's little fire, little passion to be found. . . .

How did my students reach this peculiar state in which all passion seems to be spent? I think that many of them have imbibed their sense of self from consumer culture in general and from the tube in particular. They're the progeny of 100 cable channels and omnipresent Blockbuster outlets. TV, Marshall McLuhan famously said, is a cool medium. Those who play best on it are low-key and nonassertive; they blend in. Enthusiasm, à la Joon Lee, quickly looks absurd. The form of character that's most appealing on TV is calmly self-interested though never greedy, attuned to the conventions, and ironic. Judicious timing is preferred to sudden self-assertion. The TV medium is inhospitable to inspiration, improvisation, failures, slipups. All must run perfectly.

Naturally, a cool youth culture is a marketing bonanza for producers of the right products, who do all they can to enlarge that culture and keep it grinding. The Internet, TV, and magazines now teem with what I call persona ads, ads for Nikes and Reeboks and jeeps and Blazers that don't so much endorse the capacities of the product per se as show you what sort of person you will be once you've acquired it. The jeep ad that features hip, outdoorsy kids whipping a Frisbee from mountaintop to mountaintop isn't so much about what jeeps can do as it is about the kind of people who own them. Buy a Jeep and be one with them. The ad is of little consequence in itself, but expand its message exponentially and you have the central thrust of current consumer culture—buy in order to be.

Most of my students seem desperate to blend in, to look right, not to make a spectacle of themselves. . . . The specter of the uncool creates a subtle tyranny. It's apparently an easy standard to subscribe to, this Letterman-like, Tarantino-like cool, but once committed to it, you discover that matters are rather different. You're inhibited, except on ordained occasions, from showing emotion, stifled from trying to achieve anything original. You're made to feel that even the slightest departure from the reigning code will get you genially ostracized. This is a culture tensely committed to a laid-back norm.

Am I coming off like something of a crank here? Maybe. Oscar Wilde,    15
who is almost never wrong, suggested that it is perilous to promiscuously contradict people who are much younger than yourself. Point taken. But one of the lessons that consumer hype tries to insinuate is that we must never rebel against the new, never even question it. If it's new—a new need, a new product, a new show, a new style, a new generation—it must be good. So maybe, even at the risk of winning the withered, brown laurels of crankdom, it pays to resist newness-worship and cast a colder eye.

Praise for my students? I have some of that too. What my students are, at their best, is decent. They are potent believers in equality. They help out at the soup kitchen and volunteer to tutor poor kids to get a stripe on their resumes, sure. But they also want other people to have a fair shot. And in their commitment to fairness they are discerning; there you see them at their intellectual best. If I were on trial and innocent, I'd want them on the jury.

What they will not generally do, though, is indict the current system. They won't talk about how the exigencies of capitalism lead to a reserve army of the unemployed and nearly inevitable misery. That would be getting too loud, too brash. For the pervading view is the cool consumer perspective, where passion and strong admiration are forbidden. "To stand in awe of nothing, Numicus, is perhaps the one and only thing that can make a man happy and keep him so," says Horace in the Epistles, and I fear that his lines ought to hang as a motto over the university in this era of high consumer capitalism.

It's easy to mount one's high horse and blame the students for this state of affairs. But they didn't create the present culture of consumption. (It was largely my own generation, that of the Sixties, that let the counterculture search for pleasure devolve into a quest for commodities.) And they weren't the ones responsible, when they were six and seven and eight years old, for unplugging the TV set from time to time or for hauling off and kicking a hole through it. It's my generation of parents who sheltered these students, kept them away from the hard knocks of everyday life, making them cautious and overfragile, who demanded that their teachers, from grade school on, flatter them endlessly so that the kids are shocked if their college profs don't reflexively suck up to them.

Of course, the current generational style isn't simply derived from culture and environment. It's also about dollars. Students worry that taking too many chances with their educations will sabotage their future prospects. They're aware of the fact that a drop that looks more and more like one wall of the Grand Canyon separates the top economic tenth from the rest of the population. There's a sentiment currently abroad that if you step aside for a moment, to write, to travel, to fall too hard in love, you might lose position permanently. We may be on a conveyor belt, but it's worse down there on the filth-strewn floor. So don't sound off, don't blow your chance. . . .

From the start, the contemporary university's relationship with students has a solicitous, nearly servile tone. As soon as someone enters his junior year in high school, and especially if he's living in a prosperous zip code, the informational material—the advertising—comes flooding in. Pictures, testimonials, videocassettes, and CD ROMs (some bidden, some not) arrive at the door from colleges across the country, all trying to capture the student and his tuition cash. The freshman-to-be sees photos of well-appointed dorm rooms; of elaborate phys-ed facilities; of fine dining rooms; of expertly kept sports fields; of orchestras and drama troupes; of students working alone (no overbearing grown-ups in range), peering with high seriousness into computers and microscopes; or of students arrayed outdoors in attractive conversational garlands.

Occasionally—but only occasionally, for we usually photograph rather badly; in appearance we tend at best to be styleless—there's a professor teaching a class. (The college catalogues I received, by my request only, in the late Sixties were austere affairs full of professors' credentials and course descriptions; it was clear on whose terms the enterprise was going to unfold.) A college financial officer recently put matters to me in concise, if slightly melodramatic, terms: "Colleges don't have admissions offices anymore, they have marketing departments." Is it surprising that someone who has been approached with photos and tapes, bells and whistles, might come in thinking that the Freud and Shakespeare she had signed up to study were also going to be agreeable treats?

How did we reach this point? In part the answer is a matter of demographics and (surprise) of money. Aided by the G.I. bill, the college-going population in America dramatically increased after the Second World War. Then came the baby boomers, and to accommodate them, schools continued to grow. Universities expand easily enough, but with tenure locking faculty in for lifetime jobs, and with the general reluctance of administrators to eliminate their own slots, it's not easy for a university to contract. So after the baby boomers had passed through—like a fat meal digested by a boa constrictor—the colleges turned to energetic promotional strategies to fill the empty chairs. And suddenly college became a buyer's market. What students and their parents wanted had to be taken more and more into account. That usually meant creating more comfortable, less challenging environments, places where almost no one failed, everything was enjoyable, and everyone was nice.

Just as universities must compete with one another for students, so must the individual departments. At a time of rank economic anxiety, the English and history majors have to contend for students against the more success-insuring branches, such as the sciences and the commerce school. In 1968, more than 21 percent of all the bachelor's degrees conferred in America were in the humanities; by 1993, that number had fallen to about 13 percent. The humanities now must struggle to attract students, many of whose parents devoutly wish they would study something else.

One of the ways we've tried to stay attractive is by loosening up. We grade much more softly than our colleagues in science. In English, we don't give many Ds, or Cs for that matter. (The rigors of Chem 101 create almost as many English majors per year as do the splendors of Shakespeare.) A professor at Stanford recently explained grade inflation in the humanities by observing that the undergraduates were getting smarter every year; the higher grades simply recorded how much better they were than their predecessors. Sure.

Along with softening the grades, many humanities departments have     25
relaxed major requirements. There are some good reasons for introducing more choice into curricula and requiring fewer standard courses. But the move, like many others in the university now, jibes with a tendency to serve—and not challenge—the students. Students can also float in and out of classes during the first two weeks of each term without making any commitment. The common name for this time span—shopping period—speaks volumes about the consumer mentality that's now in play. Usually, too, the kids can drop courses up until the last month with only an innocuous "W" on their transcripts. Does a course look too challenging? No problem. Take it pass-fail. A happy consumer is, by definition, one with multiple

options, one who can always have what he wants. And since a course is something the students and their parents have bought and paid for, why can't they do with it pretty much as they please?

A sure result of the university's widening elective leeway is to give students more power over their teachers. Those who don't like you can simply avoid you. If the clientele dislikes you en masse, you can be left without students, period. My first term teaching I walked into my introduction to poetry course and found it inhabited by one student, the gloriously named Bambi Lynn Dean. Bambi and I chatted amiably awhile, but for all that she and the pleasure of her name could offer, I was fast on the way to meltdown. It was all a mistake, luckily, a problem with the scheduling book. Everyone was waiting for me next door. But in a dozen years of teaching I haven't forgotten that feeling of being ignominiously marooned. For it happens to others, and not always because of scheduling glitches. I've seen older colleagues go through hot embarrassment at not having enough students sign up for their courses: they graded too hard, demanded too much, had beliefs too far out of keeping with the existing disposition. It takes only a few such instances to draw other members of the professoriat further into line. . . .

How does one prosper with the present clientele? Many of the most successful professors now are the ones who have "decentered" their classrooms. There's a new emphasis on group projects and on computer-generated exchanges among the students. What they seem to want most is to talk to one another. A classroom now is frequently an "environment," a place highly conducive to the exchange of existing ideas, the students' ideas. Listening to one another, students sometimes change their opinions. But what they generally can't do is acquire a new vocabulary, a new perspective, that will cast issues in a fresh light.

The Socratic method—the animated, sometimes impolite give-and-take between student and teacher—seems too jagged for current sensibilities. Students frequently come to my office to tell me how intimidated they feel in class; the thought of being embarrassed in front of the group fills them with dread. I remember a student telling me how humiliating it was to be corrected by the teacher, by me. So I asked the logical question: "Should I let a major factual error go by so as to save discomfort?" The student—a good student, smart and earnest—said that was a tough question. He'd need to think about it.

Disturbing? Sure. But I wonder, are we really getting students ready for Socratic exchange with professors when we push them off into vast lecture rooms, two and three hundred to a class, sometimes face them with only grad students until their third year, and signal in our myriad professorial ways that we often have much better things to do than sit in our offices and talk with them? How bad will the student–faculty ratios have to become, how teeming the lecture courses, before we hear students righteously complaining, as they did thirty years ago, about the impersonality of their schools, about their decline into knowledge factories? "This is a firm," said Mario Savio at Berkeley during the Free Speech protests of the Sixties, "and

if the Board of Regents are the board of directors, . . . then . . . the faculty
are a bunch of employees and we're the raw material. But we're a bunch of
raw material that don't mean . . . to be made into any product."

Teachers who really do confront students, who provide significant chal-    30
lenges to what they believe, can be very successful, granted. But sometimes
such professors generate more than a little trouble for themselves. A controversial teacher can send students hurrying to the deans and the counselors,
claiming to have been offended. ("Offensive" is the preferred term of re-
pugnance today, just as "enjoyable" is the summit of praise.) Colleges have
brought in hordes of counselors and deans to make sure that everything is
smooth, serene, unflustered, that everyone has a good time. To the counselor, to the dean, and to the university legal squad, that which is normal,
healthy, and prudent is best. . . .

Then how do those who at least occasionally promote genius and high
literary ideals look to current students? How do we appear, those of us who
take teaching to be something of a performance art and who imagine that
if you give yourself over completely to your subject you'll be rewarded with
insight beyond what you individually command?

I'm reminded of an old piece of newsreel footage I saw once. The speaker
(perhaps it was Lenin, maybe Trotsky) was haranguing a large crowd. He
was expostulating, arm waving, carrying on. Whether it was flawed technology or the man himself, I'm not sure, but the orator looked like an intricate
mechanical device that had sprung into fast-forward. To my students, who
mistrust enthusiasm in every form, that's me when I start riffing about
Freud or Blake. But more and more, as my evaluations showed, I've been
replacing enthusiasm and intellectual animation with stand-up routines,
keeping it all at arm's length, praising under the cover of irony.

It's too bad that the idea of genius has been denigrated so far, because it
actually offers a live alternative to the demoralizing culture of hip in which
most of my students are mired. By embracing the works and lives of extraordinary people, you can adapt new ideals to revise those that came courtesy
of your parents, your neighborhood, your clan — or the tube. The aim of
a good liberal-arts education was once, to adapt an observation by the
scholar Walter Jackson Bate, to see that "we need not be the passive victims of what we deterministically call 'circumstances' (social, cultural, or
reductively psychological-personal), but that by linking ourselves through
what Keats calls an 'immortal free-masonry' with the great we can become
freer — freer to be ourselves, to be what we most want and value."

But genius isn't just a personal standard; genius can also have political
effect. To me, one of the best things about democratic thinking is the conviction that genius can spring up anywhere. Walt Whitman is born into the
working class and thirty-six years later we have a poetic image of America
that gives a passionate dimension to the legalistic brilliance of the Constitution. A democracy needs to constantly develop, and to do so it requires the
most powerful visionary minds to interpret the present and to propose pos-

sible shapes for the future. By continuing to notice and praise genius, we create a culture in which the kind of poetic gamble that Whitman made—a gamble in which failure would have entailed rank humiliation, depression, maybe suicide—still takes place. By rebelling against established ways of seeing and saying things, genius helps us to apprehend how malleable the present is and how promising and fraught with danger is the future. If we teachers do not endorse genius and self-overcoming, can we be surprised when our students find their ideal images in TV's latest persona ads?

A world uninterested in genius is a despondent place, whose sad denizens drift from coffee bar to Prozac dispensary, unfired by ideals, by the glowing image of the self that one might become. As Northrop Frye says in a beautiful and now dramatically unfashionable sentence, "The artist who uses the same energy and genius that Homer and Isaiah had will find that he not only lives in the same palace of art as Homer and Isaiah, but lives in it at the same time." We ought not to deny the existence of such a place simply because we, or those we care for, find the demands it makes intimidating, the rent too high.

What happens if we keep trudging along this bleak course? What happens if our most intelligent students never learn to strive to overcome what they are? What if genius, and the imitation of genius, become silly, outmoded ideas? What you're likely to get are more and more one-dimensional men and women. These will be people who live for easy pleasures, for comfort and prosperity, who think of money first, then second, and third, who hug the status quo; people who believe in God as a sort of insurance policy (cover your bets); people who are never surprised. They will be people so pleased with themselves (when they're not in despair at the general pointlessness of their lives) that they cannot imagine humanity could do better. They'll think it their highest duty to clone themselves as frequently as possible. They'll claim to be happy, and they'll live a long time.

It is probably time now to offer a spate of inspiring solutions. Here ought to come a list of reforms, with due notations about a core curriculum and various requirements. What the traditionalists who offer such solutions miss is that no matter what our current students are given to read, many of them will simply translate it into melodrama, with flat characters and predictable morals. (The unabated capitalist culture that conservative critics so often endorse has put students in a position to do little else.) One can't simply wave a curricular wand and reverse acculturation.

Perhaps it would be a good idea to try firing the counselors and sending half the deans back into their classrooms, dismantling the football team and making the stadium into a playground for local kids, emptying the fraternities, and boarding up the student-activities office. Such measures would convey the message that American colleges are not northern outposts of Club Med. A willingness on the part of the faculty to defy student conviction and affront them occasionally—to be usefully offensive—also might not be a bad thing. We professors talk a lot about subversion, which generally means subverting the views of people who never hear us talk or read

35

our work. But to subvert the views of our students, our customers, that would be something else again.

Ultimately, though, it is up to individuals—and individual students in particular—to make their own way against the current sludgy tide. There's still the library, still the museum, there's still the occasional teacher who lives to find things greater than herself to admire. There are still fellow students who have not been cowed. Universities are inefficient, cluttered, archaic places, with many unguarded corners where one can open a book or gaze out onto the larger world and construe it freely. Those who do as much, trusting themselves against the weight of current opinion, will have contributed something to bringing this sad dispensation to an end. As for myself, I'm canning my low-key one-liners; when the kids' TV-based tastes come to the fore, I'll aim and shoot. And when it's time to praise genius, I'll try to do it in the right style, full-out, with faith that finer artistic spirits (maybe not Homer and Isaiah quite, but close, close), still alive somewhere in the ether, will help me out when my invention flags, the students doze, or the dean mutters into the phone. I'm getting back to a more exuberant style; I'll be expostulating and arm waving straight into the millennium, yes I will.

---

*For Discussion*

1. This essay links with the previous one in at least one important way: both see a "consumer mentality" in contemporary students and both are critical of it. But to what extent is it *appropriate* to view colleges and universities as vendors, selling a service in demand, much like any other business? To what extent is this economic understanding limited?

2. The sixties generation is often described as anticommercial and antibusiness, an attitude clearly present in this essay's negative comments on capitalism. To what extent is Edmundson's view a continuation of the rebellions of the sixties or perhaps guilt-ridden compensation for his obviously becoming part of "the system"? If we "read" him this way, must we also dismiss what he has to say? Is his critique any less valid?

3. The more or less conscious cultivation of "cool" or "laid back" extends beyond the sixties to at least "the beats" of the fifties, and arguably further, and thus provides some common ground for half a century or more of young adult experience. Such an attitude has always been vulnerable to Edmundson's charge of lacking "passion and strong admiration." To what extent is "cool" an appropriate and functional way of coping with modern society? Is passion necessary for a meaningful life? If we should have "strong admirations," for what or whom should we have them? Should these commitments be unqualified and uncritical—that is, total?

4. In a part of his essay not printed here, Edmundson contends that "some measure of self-dislike, or self-discontent . . . [is] a prerequisite for getting an education that matters" and that "my students . . . usually lack the confidence to acknowledge . . . their ignorance." What is "an education that matters"? What does self-discontent have to do with it? Is his charge true? Are you and your friends too content with yourselves and too insecure to admit ignorance?

## For Analysis and Persuasion

Edmundson claims to want his students to be "changed by [his] course," to "measure themselves against what they've read." As he goes on to explain, "intellectual work [should be] a *confrontation* between two people, student and author, where the stakes matter" (our emphasis).

If he is right, most education is wrong, for very little of it changes us, takes our measure, or confronts us with anything whose stakes are higher than meeting a requirement. But there are exceptions. In an essay, describe a course, a work, or a teacher (or all three) that did ignite the fire Edmundson admires, that did change you. Then analyze the experience: What was it, exactly, that made the difference?

In the second part of your essay, which you can think of as an "open letter" to college teachers, advocate whatever it was that made the difference so that professors themselves might be moved to alter their attitudes and approaches. Be tactful—don't make your essay merely an indictment of teachers. And be thoughtful—perhaps what worked for you won't work all the time or in all classes or subjects.

## For Inquiry

The unifying theme of Edmundson's essay is power—the power of money and of economic forces generally, the power of the media to shape culture, the power of students over professors, and so on. The last he may exaggerate, because student evaluations alone almost never make or break a professor's career. But in any case, professors must be evaluated as teachers somehow, and part of this process nearly everywhere are student evaluations.

Secure a copy of the current instrument or instruments used at your school. Consider it/them carefully. Are they as blunt and unsubtle as Edmundson depicts them? Do they encourage professors to entertain rather than instruct? Based on your analysis, explore ways to improve teacher evaluations. If you know or can find out what committees charged with designing evaluations have considered, ponder their ideas and approaches as well. Then consider how the evaluations are used. Can they be applied more constructively? If so, what are the options? What are the "up" and "down" sides of each?

Design your inquiry as an independent report to whatever committee or committees are charged with creating and assessing student evaluations.

# On the Uses of Liberal Education:
# As a Weapon in the Hands of the Restless Poor
### Earl Shorris

*Earl Shorris was several years into research for a book on poverty and thought he had heard it all—until he met a remarkable young woman, a prison inmate, who gave him the idea for an experimental curriculum in the liberal arts for poor people. The lengthy story of how he developed his idea and found modest financial support for it we have left out, the better to highlight what counts most—attitudes, course content, the students, teaching methods, and results, all of which he reports with disarming honesty, in an account of genuine power.*

*We agree with Shorris that his course of study cannot reach everyone nor solve by itself the massive and complicated problem of poverty in the United States. But its success is worth pondering, especially when we consider the billions we spend on poverty every year, money that brings relief but no solution. Perhaps the big question implicit in this essay is one we need to address: Do Americans really want to empower the poor, give them weapons to resist their condition, make them more personally and socially effective? If so, what role can a liberal arts education play?*

Next month I will publish a book about poverty in America, but not the book I intended. The world took me by surprise—not once, but again and again. The poor themselves led me in directions I could not have imagined, especially the one that came out of a conversation in a maximum-security prison for women that is set, incongruously, in a lush Westchester suburb fifty miles north of New York City.

I had been working on the book for about three years when I went to the Bedford Hills Correctional Facility for the first time. The staff and inmates had developed a program to deal with family violence, and I wanted to see how their ideas fit with what I had learned about poverty.

Numerous forces—hunger, isolation, illness, landlords, police, abuse, neighbors, drugs, criminals, and racism, among many others—exert themselves on the poor at all times and enclose them, making up a "surround of force" from which, it seems, they cannot escape. I had come to understand that this was what kept the poor from being political and that the absence of politics in their lives was what kept them poor. I don't mean "political" in the sense of voting in an election but in the way Thucydides used the word: to mean activity with other people at every level, from the family to the neighborhood to the broader community to the city-state.

By the time I got to Bedford Hills, I had listened to more than six hundred people, some of them over the course of two or three years. Although my method is that of the bricoleur, the tinkerer who assembles a thesis of the bric-a-brac he finds in the world, I did not think there would be any more surprises. But I had not counted on what Viniece Walker was to say.

[. . .] Viniece Walker came to Bedford Hills when she was twenty years    5
old, a high school dropout who read at the level of a college sophomore,
a graduate of crackhouses, the streets of Harlem, and a long alliance with
a brutal man. On the surface Viniece has remained as tough as she was
on the street. She speaks bluntly, and even though she is HIV positive and
the virus has progressed during her time in prison, she still swaggers as she
walks down the long prison corridors. While in prison, Niecie, as she is
known to her friends, completed her high school requirements and began
to pursue a college degree (psychology is the only major offered at Bedford
Hills, but Niecie also took a special interest in philosophy). She became a
counselor to women with a history of family violence and a comforter to
those with AIDS.

Only the deaths of other women cause her to stumble in the midst
of her swaggering step, to spend days alone with the remorse that drives
her to seek redemption. She goes through life as if she had been imagined
by Dostoevsky, but even more complex than his fictions, alive, a person, a
fair-skinned and freckled African-American woman, and in prison. It was
she who responded to my sudden question, "Why do you think people
are poor?"

We had never met before. The conversation around us focused on the
abuse of women. Niecie's eyes were perfectly opaque—hostile, prison eyes.
Her mouth was set in the beginning of a sneer.

"You got to begin with the children," she said, speaking rapidly, clipping
out the street sounds as they came into her speech.

She paused long enough to let the change of direction take effect, then
resumed the rapid, rhythmless speech. "You've got to teach the moral life of
downtown to the children. And the way you do that, Earl, is by taking them
downtown to plays, museums, concerts, lectures, where they can learn the
moral life of downtown."

I smiled at her, misunderstanding, thinking I was indulging her. "And    10
then they won't be poor anymore?"

She read every nuance of my response, and answered angrily, "And they
won't be poor no more.

"What you mean is—"

"What I mean is what I said—a moral alternative to the street."

She didn't speak of jobs or money. In that, she was like the others I had
listened to. No one had spoken of jobs or money. But how could the "moral
life of downtown" lead anyone out from the surround of force? How could
a museum push poverty away? Who can dress in statues or eat the past?
And what of the political life? Had Niecie skipped a step or failed to take a
step? The way out of poverty was politics, not the "moral life of downtown." But to enter the public world, to practice the political life, the poor
had first to learn to reflect. That was what Niecie meant by the "moral life
of downtown." She did not make the error of divorcing ethics from politics.
Niecie had simply said, in a kind of shorthand, that no one could step out
of the panicking circumstance of poverty directly into the public world.

Although she did not say so, I was sure that when she spoke of the                    15
"moral life of downtown" she meant something that had happened to her.
With no job and no money, a prisoner, she had undergone a radical transformation. She had followed the same path that led to the invention of politics in ancient Greece. She had learned to reflect. In further conversation
it became clear that when she spoke of "the moral life of downtown" she
meant the humanities, the study of human constructs and concerns, which
has been the source of reflection for the secular world since the Greeks first
stepped back from nature to experience wonder at what they beheld. If the
political life was the way out of poverty, the humanities provided an entrance to reflection and the political life. The poor did not need anyone to
release them; an escape route existed. But to open this avenue to reflection
and politics a major distinction between the preparation for the life of the
rich and the life of the poor had to be eliminated.

Once Niecie had challenged me with her theory, the comforts of tinkering came to an end; I could no longer make an homage to the happen-
stance world and rest. To test Niecie's theory, students, faculty, and facilities were required. Quantitative measures would have to be developed; an-
ecdotal information would also be useful. And the ethics of the experiment
had to be considered: I resolved to do no harm. There was no need for the
course to have a "sink or swim" character; it could aim to keep as many
afloat as possible. . . .

On an early evening that same week, about twenty prospective students
were scheduled to meet in a classroom. . . . Most of them came late. Those
who arrived first slumped in their chairs, staring at the floor or greeting me
with sullen glances. A few ate candy or what appeared to be the remnants
of a meal. The students were mostly black and Latino, one was Asian, and
five were white; two of the whites were immigrants who had severe problems with English. When I introduced myself, several of the students would
not shake my hand, two or three refused even to look at me, one girl giggled, and the last person to volunteer his name, a young man dressed in a
Tommy Hilfiger sweatshirt and wearing a cap turned sideways, drawled,
"Henry Jones, but they call me Sleepy, because I got these sleepy eyes — ".

"In our class, we'll call you Mr. Jones."

He smiled and slid down in his chair so that his back was parallel to
the floor.

Before I finished attempting to shake hands with the prospective stu-                    20
dents, a waiflike Asian girl with her mouth half-full of cake said, "Can we get
on with it? I'm bored."

I liked the group immediately.

. . . "You've been cheated," I said. "Rich people learn the humanities;
you didn't. The humanities are a foundation for getting along in the world,
for thinking, for learning to reflect on the world instead of just reacting to
whatever force is turned against you. I think the humanities are one of the

ways to become political, and I don't mean political in the sense of voting in an election but in the broad sense." I told them Thucydides' definition of politics.

"Rich people know politics in that sense. They know how to negotiate instead of using force. They know how to use politics to get along, to get power. It doesn't mean that rich people are good and poor people are bad. It simply means that rich people know a more effective method for living in this society.

"Do all rich people, or people who are in the middle, know the humanities? Not a chance. But some do. And it helps. It helps to live better and enjoy life more. Will the humanities make you rich? Yes. Absolutely. But not in terms of money. In terms of life.

"Rich people learn the humanities in private schools and expensive            25
universities. And that's one of the ways in which they learn the political life. I think that is the real difference between the haves and have-nots in this country. If you want real power, legitimate power, the kind that comes from the people and belongs to the people, you must understand politics. The humanities will help.

"Here's how it works: We'll pay your subway fare; take care of your children, if you have them; give you a snack or a sandwich; provide you with books and any other materials you need. But we'll make you think harder, use your mind more fully, than you ever have before. You'll have to read and think about the same kinds of ideas you would encounter in a first-year course at Harvard or Yale or Oxford.

"You'll have to come to class in the snow and the rain and the cold and the dark. No one will coddle you, no one will slow down for you. There will be tests to take, papers to write. And I can't promise you anything but a certificate of completion at the end of the course. I'll be talking to colleges about giving credit for the course, but I can't promise anything. [. . .] You must do it because you want to study the humanities, because you want a certain kind of life, a richness of mind and spirit. That's all I offer you: philosophy, poetry, art history, logic, rhetoric, and American history.

"Your teachers will all be people of accomplishment in their fields," I said, and I spoke a little about each teacher. "That's the course. October through May, with a two-week break at Christmas. It is generally accepted in America that the liberal arts and the humanities in particular belong to the elites. I think you're the elites."

The young Asian woman said, "What are you getting out of this?"

"This is a demonstration project. I'm writing a book. This will be proof,            30
I hope, of my idea about the humanities. Whether it succeeds or fails will be up to the teachers and you."

All but one of the prospective students applied for admission to the course. . . .

Of the fifty prospective students who showed up . . . for personal interviews [to gain admission to the course], a few were too rich (a postal supervisor's son, a fellow who claimed his father owned a factory in Nigeria that employed sixty people) and more than a few could not read. Two home-care workers from Local 1199 could not arrange their hours to enable them to take the course. Some of the applicants were too young: a thirteen-year-old and two who had just turned sixteen. . . .

Some of those who came for interviews were too poor. I did not think that was possible when we began, and I would like not to believe it now, but it was true. There is a point at which the level of forces that surround the poor can become insurmountable, when there is no time or energy left to be anything but poor. Most often I could not recruit such people for the course; when I did, they soon dropped out.

Over the days of interviewing, a class slowly assembled. I could not then imagine who would last the year and who would not. One young woman submitted a neatly typed essay that said, "I was homeless once, then I lived for some time in a shelter. Right now, I have got my own space granted by the Partnership for the Homeless. Right now, I am living alone, with very limited means. Financially I am overwhelmed by debts. I cannot afford all the food I need . . ."

A brother and sister, refugees from Tashkent, lived with their parents in    35
the farthest reaches of Queens, far beyond the end of the subway line. They had no money, and they had been refused admission by every school to which they had applied. I had not intended to accept immigrants or people who had difficulty with the English language, but I took them into the class.

I also took four who had been in prison, three who were homeless, three who were pregnant, one who lived in a drugged dream-state in which she was abused, and one whom I had known for a long time and who was dying of AIDS. As I listened to them, I wondered how the course would affect them. They had no public life, no place; they lived within the surround of force, moving as fast as they could, driven by necessity, without a moment to reflect. Why should they care about fourteenth-century Italian painting or truth tables or the death of Socrates?

Between the end of recruiting and the orientation session that would open the course, I made a visit to Bedford Hills to talk with Niecie Walker. It was hot, and the drive up from the city had been unpleasant. I didn't yet know Niecie very well. She didn't trust me, and I didn't know what to make of her. While we talked, she held a huge white pill in her hand. "For AIDS," she said.

"Are you sick?"

"My T-cell count is down. But that's neither here nor there. Tell me about the course, Earl. What are you going to teach?"

"Moral philosophy."    40

"And what does that include?"

She had turned the visit into an interrogation. I didn't mind. At the end of the conversation I would be going out into "the free world"; if she wanted our meeting to be an interrogation, I was not about to argue. I said, "We'll begin with Plato: the *Apology,* a little of the *Crito,* a few pages of the *Phaedo* so that they'll know what happened to Socrates. Then we'll read Aristotle's *Nicomachean Ethics.* I also want them to read Thucydides, particularly Pericles' Funeral Oration in order to make the connection between ethics and politics, to lead them in the direction I hope the course will take them. Then we'll end with *Antigone,* but read as moral and political philosophy as well as drama."

"There's something missing," she said, leaning back in her chair, taking on an air of superiority.

The drive had been long, the day was hot, the air in the room was dead and damp. "Oh, yeah," I said, "and what's that?"

"Plato's Allegory of the Cave. How can you teach philosophy to poor    45
people without the Allegory of the Cave? The ghetto is the cave. Education is the light. Poor people can understand that."

At the beginning of the orientation at the Clemente Center a week later, each teacher spoke for a minute or two. Dr. Inclan and his research assistant, Patricia Vargas, administered the questionnaire he had devised to measure, as best he could, the role of force and the amount of reflection in the lives of the students. I explained that each class was going to be videotaped as another way of documenting the project. Then I gave out the first assignment: "In preparation for our next meeting, I would like you to read a brief selection from Plato's *Republic:* the Allegory of the Cave."

I tried to guess how many students would return for the first class. I hoped for twenty, expected fifteen, and feared ten. [My wife] Sylvia, who had agreed to share the administrative tasks of the course, and I prepared coffee and cookies for twenty-five. We had a plastic container filled with subway tokens. Thanks to Starling Lawrence, we had thirty copies of Bernard Knox's *Norton Book of Classical Literature,* which contained all of the texts for the philosophy section except the *Republic* and the *Nicomachean Ethics.*

At six o'clock there were only ten students seated around the long table, but by six-fifteen the number had doubled, and a few minutes later two more straggled in out of the dusk. I had written a time line on the blackboard, showing them the temporal progress of thinking—from the role of myth in Neolithic societies to The Gilgamesh Epic and forward to the Old Testament, Confucius, the Greeks, the New Testament, the Koran, the Epic of Son-Jara, and ending with Nahuatl and Maya poems, which took us up to the contact between Europe and America, where the history course began. The time line served as context and geography as well as history: no race, no major culture was ignored. "Let's agree," I told them, "that we are all human, whatever our origins. And now let's go into Plato's cave."

I told them that there would be no lectures in the philosophy section of the course; we would use the Socratic method, which is called maieutic dialogue. "'Maieutic' comes from the Greek word for midwifery. I'll take the role of midwife in our dialogue. Now, what do I mean by that? What does a midwife do?"

It was the beginning of a love affair, the first moment of their infatuation    50
with Socrates. Later, Abel Lomas would characterize that moment in his no-nonsense fashion, saying that it was the first time anyone had ever paid attention to their opinions.

Grace Glueck began the art history class in a darkened room lit with slides of the Lascaux caves and next turned the students' attention to Egypt, arranging for them to visit the Metropolitan Museum of Art to see the Temple of Dendur and the Egyptian Galleries. They arrived at the museum on a Friday evening. Darlene Codd brought her two-year-old son. Pearl Lau was late, as usual. One of the students, who had told me how much he was looking forward to the museum visit, didn't show up, which surprised me. Later I learned that he had been arrested for jumping a turnstile in a subway station on his way to the museum and was being held in a prison cell under the Brooklyn criminal courthouse. In the Temple of Dendur, Samantha Smoot asked questions of Felicia Blum, a museum lecturer. Samantha was the student who had burst out with the news, in one of the first sessions of the course, that people in her neighborhood believed it "wasn't no use goin' to school because the white man wouldn't let you up no matter what." But in a hall where the statuary was of half-human, half-animal female figures, it was Samantha who asked what the glyphs meant, encouraging Felicia Blum to read them aloud, to translate them into English. Toward the end of the evening, Grace led the students out of the halls of antiquities into the Rockefeller Wing, where she told them of the connections of culture and art in Mali, Benin, and the Pacific Islands. When the students had collected their coats and stood together near the entrance to the museum, preparing to leave, Samantha stood apart, a tall, slim young woman, dressed in a deerstalker cap and a dark blue peacoat. She made an exaggerated farewell wave at us and returned to Egypt—her ancient mirror.

Charles Simmons began the poetry class with poems as puzzles and laughs. His plan was to surprise the class, and he did. At first he read the poems aloud to them, interrupting himself with footnotes to bring them along. He showed them poems of love and of seduction, and satiric commentaries on those poems by later poets. "Let us read," the students demanded, but Charles refused. He tantalized them with the opportunity to read poems aloud. A tug-of-war began between him and the students, and the standoff was ended not by Charles directly but by Hector Anderson. When Charles asked if anyone in the class wrote poetry, Hector raised his hand.

"Can you recite one of your poems for us?" Charles said.

Until that moment, Hector had never volunteered a comment, though he had spoken well and intelligently when asked. He preferred to slouch in his chair, dressed in full camouflage gear, wearing a nylon stocking over his hair and eating slices of fresh cantaloupe or honeydew melon.

In response to Charles's question, Hector slid up to a sitting position. "If you turn that camera off," he said. "I don't want anybody using my lyrics." When he was sure the red light of the video camera was off, Hector stood and recited verse after verse of a poem that belonged somewhere in the triangle formed by Ginsberg's *Howl*, the Book of Lamentations, and hip-hop. When Charles and the students finished applauding, they asked Hector to say the poem again, and he did. Later Charles told me, "That kid is the real thing." Hector's discomfort with Sylvia and me turned to ease. He came to our house for a small Christmas party and at other times. We talked on the telephone about a scholarship program and about what steps he should take next in his education. I came to know his parents. As a student, he began quietly, almost secretly, to surpass many of his classmates.

Timothy Koranda was the most professorial of the professors. He arrived precisely on time, wearing a hat of many styles — part fedora, part Borsalino, part Stetson, and at least one-half World War I campaign hat. He taught logic during class hours, filling the blackboard from floor to ceiling, wall to wall, drawing the intersections of sets here and truth tables there and a great square of oppositions in the middle of it all. After class, he walked with students to the subway, chatting about Zen or logic or Heisenberg.

On one of the coldest nights of the winter, he introduced the students to logic problems stated in ordinary language that they could solve by reducing the phrases to symbols. He passed out copies of a problem, two pages long, then wrote out some of the key phrases on the blackboard. "Take this home with you," he said, "and at our next meeting we shall see who has solved it. I shall also attempt to find the answer."

By the time he finished writing out the key phrases, however, David Iskhakov raised his hand. Although they listened attentively, neither David nor his sister Susana spoke often in class. She was shy, and he was embarrassed at his inability to speak perfect English.

"May I go to blackboard?" David said. "And will see if I have found correct answer to zis problem."

Together Tim and David erased the blackboard, then David began covering it with signs and symbols. "If first man is earning this money, and second man is closer to this town . . . ," he said, carefully laying out the conditions. After five minutes or so, he said, "And the answer is: B will get first to Cleveland!"

Samantha Smoot shouted, "That's not the answer. The mistake you made is in the first part there, where it says who earns more money."

Tim folded his arms across his chest, happy. "I shall let you all take the problem home," he said.

When Sylvia and I left the Clemente Center that night, a knot of students was gathered outside, huddled against the wind. Snow had begun to fall, a slippery powder on the gray ice that covered all but a narrow space down the center of the sidewalk. Samantha and David stood in the middle of the group, still arguing over the answer to the problem. I leaned in for a moment to catch the character of the argument. It was even more polite than it had been in the classroom, because now they govern themselves.

One Saturday morning in January, David Howell telephoned me at home. "Mr. Shores," he said, Anglicizing my name, as many of the students did.

"Mr. Howell," I responded, recognizing his voice.                                                              65

"How you doin', Mr. Shores?"

"I'm fine. How are you?"

"I had a little problem at work."

Uh-oh, I thought, bad news was coming. David is a big man, generally good-humored but with a quick temper. According to his mother, he had a history of violent behavior. In the classroom he had been one of the best students, a steady man, twenty-four years old, who always did the reading assignments and who often made interesting connections between the humanities and daily life. "What happened?"

"Mr. Shores, there's a woman at my job, she said some things to me          70
and I said some things to her. And she told my supervisor I had said things to her, and he called me in about it. She's forty years old and she don't have no social life, and I have a good social life, and she's jealous of me."

"And then what happened?" The tone of his voice and the timing of the call did not portend good news.

"Mr. Shores, she made me so mad, I wanted to smack her up against the wall. I tried to talk to some friends to calm myself down a little, but nobody was around."

"And what did you do?" I asked, fearing this was his one telephone call from the city jail.

"Mr. Shores, I asked myself, 'What would Socrates do?'"

David Howell had reasoned that his co-worker's envy was not his prob-          75
lem after all, and he had dropped his rage.

One evening, in the American history section, I was telling the students about Gordon Wood's ideas in *The Radicalism of the American Revolution.* We were talking about the revolt by some intellectuals against classical learning at the turn of the eighteenth century, including Benjamin Franklin's late-life change of heart, when Henry Jones raised his hand.

"If the Founders loved the humanities so much, how come they treated the natives so badly?"

I didn't know how to answer this question. There were confounding explanations to offer about changing attitudes toward Native Americans, vaguely useful references to views of Rousseau and James Fenimore Cooper. For a moment I wondered if I should tell them about Heidegger's Nazi past. Then I saw Abel Lomas's raised hand at the far end of the table.

"Mr. Lomas," I said.

Abel said, "That's what Aristotle means by incontinence, when you know what's morally right but you don't do it, because you're overcome by your passions."

The other students nodded. They were all inheritors of wounds caused by the incontinence of educated men; now they had an ally in Aristotle, who had given them a way to analyze the actions of their antagonists.

Those who appreciate ancient history understand the radical character of the humanities. They know that politics did not begin in a perfect world but in a society even more flawed than ours: one that embraced slavery, denied the rights of women, practiced a form of homosexuality that verged on pedophilia, and endured the intrigues and corruption of its leaders. The genius of that society originated in man's re-creation of himself through the recognition of his humanness as expressed in art, literature, rhetoric, philosophy, and the unique notion of freedom. At that moment, the isolation of the private life ended and politics began.

The winners in the game of modern society, and even those whose fortune falls in the middle, have other means to power: they are included at birth. They know this. And they know exactly what to do to protect their place in the economic and social hierarchy. As Allan Bloom, author of the nationally best-selling tract in defense of elitism, *The Closing of the American Mind,* put it, they direct the study of the humanities exclusively at those young people who "have been raised in comfort and with the expectation of ever increasing comfort."

In the last meeting before graduation, the Clemente students answered the same set of questions they'd answered at orientation. Between October and May, students had fallen to AIDS, pregnancy, job opportunities, pernicious anemia, clinical depression, a schizophrenic child, and other forces, but of the thirty students admitted to the course, sixteen had completed it, and fourteen had earned credit from Bard College. Dr. Inclan found that the students' self-esteem and their abilities to divine and solve problems had significantly increased; their use of verbal aggression as a tactic for resolving conflicts had significantly decreased. And they all had notably more appreciation for the concepts of benevolence, spirituality, universalism, and collectivism.

It cost about $2,000 for a student to attend the Clemente Course. Compared with unemployment, welfare, or prison, the humanities are a bargain. But coming into possession of the faculty of reflection and the skills of politics leads to a choice for the poor—and whatever they choose, they will be dangerous: they may use politics to get along in a society based on the game, to escape from the surround of force into a gentler life, to behave as citizens, and nothing more; or they may choose to oppose the game itself. No one can predict the effect of politics, although we all would like to think that wisdom goes our way. That is why the poor are so often mobilized and so rarely politicized. The possibility that they will adopt a moral

view other than that of their mentors can never be discounted. And who
wants to run that risk? . . .

On May 14, 1997, Viniece Walker came up for parole for the second
time. She had served more than ten years of her sentence, and she had
been the best of prisoners. In a version of the Clemente Course held at the
prison, she had been my teaching assistant. After a brief hearing, her request for parole was denied. She will serve two more years before the parole board will reconsider her case.

A year after graduation, ten of the first sixteen Clemente Course graduates were attending four-year colleges or going to nursing school; four of
them had received full scholarships to Bard College. The other graduates
were attending community college or working full-time. Except for one:
she had been fired from her job in a fast-food restaurant for trying to start
a union.

---

## For Discussion

1.  This essay requires us to think about familiar terms in unfamiliar
    ways. What does Shorris mean by "the political"? How does this re-
    late to the "moral life of downtown," also called the "moral alterna-
    tive to the street"? How do most college students know about the
    political in Shorris's sense? What prevents most poor people from
    knowing?
2.  "You've been cheated," Shorris tells his prospective students, denied
    an education in the humanities, and therefore "a foundation . . . for
    learning to reflect on the world instead of just reacting to whatever
    force is turned against you." What does "reflect" mean here? What
    sort of practical consequences can it have? To what extent has your
    education encouraged reflection?
3.  One interesting feature of Shorris's course on moral philosophy is
    his concentration on classical Greece, on major works by Plato, Aris-
    totle, the historian Thucydides, and the playwright Sophocles. Does
    this focus surprise you? What might justify it? Should the classics be
    part of your curriculum?
4.  How would you characterize the attitudes, approaches, and methods
    used by the professors? How important a role did they play in the suc-
    cess of the courses? Compare them to your high school instruction
    and what you've encountered so far in college. Are they comparable?
    If so, in what ways? If not, how do you explain the differences?
5.  Near the end of the essay, Shorris reports how the class handled a
    thorny question: "If the Founders [of the United States] loved the
    humanities so much, how come they treated the natives so badly?"
    Is Abel's answer adequate? What's the point of Shorris's commentary

on the culture in which ancient Greek thought and art arose? How do you respond to what he says?

6. Read carefully the last four paragraphs and note the details about what happened to the students. How successful would you say the curriculum was? What are its limitations? On what does its long-term impact depend? What measures might be taken to improve the odds of more students completing the course?

## For Inquiry and Persuasion

It is not hard to imagine what Shorris's critics will say. In teaching his students how to "get along" with European white culture, some will say, he is only encouraging acquiescence to the system, trying to make white people out of people of color, and devaluing by neglect the cultures to which his students belong. Others will say that most poor people do not need a liberal education but rather basic literacy skills, the ability to read and write, coupled with training in some marketable skill, such as data processing.

List on the board these and any other criticisms that occur to you. After extensive class discussion, write an essay either supporting Shorris's program as part of what poor people need for self-improvement or advocating something else. Direct your essay to public school systems whose student populations include people from backgrounds similar to Shorris's group. As preparation for your paper, you may wish to visit such schools and/or talk to members of the faculty.

## For Inquiry

As a class select one or two of the works Shorris had his students study in his moral philosophy course. Read them and, paying special attention to their moral and political "lessons," discuss what we can learn from them about how to live better.

Do they have the virtues Shorris believes they have? Understanding them is more difficult than works written closer to our place and time, works that are not necessarily less insightful or profound. Is the struggle with the classics worth it? Did you gain as much from them as some of Shorris's students apparently did? Why or why not?

## For Inquiry and Convincing

Anyone who reads Shorris's essay together with the previous one by Edmundson is likely to detect an apparent paradox, which can be expressed in at least two ways. The liberal arts were created by the privileged classes and largely taught to the privileged for the past 2,500 years. So why do they serve now as at best only "lite entertainment" for the very class of student who belongs to the tradition of privilege? Put another way, both Edmundson and Shorris want their courses to change their students, transforming how they understand the world and how they behave in it, but only Shorris believes that change has actually occurred. Edmundson should have the easier time. Why doesn't he?

Write an essay in which you render this paradox less paradoxical. Tie your explanation to your own experiences with the liberal arts, to your background, to the way your classes have been taught. At the end make a case for how the liberal arts might be taught better. Or, if you believe the paradox has little or nothing to do with teaching, make a case for what must change to reenergize the liberal arts.

# The Decline of the Knowledge Factory: Why Our Colleges Must Change
## John Tagg

*In the 1960s, "the system" was often a topic of discussion. Many of the conversations were not especially helpful, but implicit in all of them was an insight we must not forget: Often, what's wrong with society has little to do with particular individuals or the roles they play, with philosophies, or with cultural gaps between generations; rather, the problems may be traced to the way a society is structured in general and to an institution's organization in particular. Individuals may or may not like "the system," but they are caught up in it anyway and realize the powerful forces invested in maintaining the status quo. Understandably, they turn to the practical business of getting the system to pay off for them rather than trying to change it. And so change itself becomes difficult and for many people beyond imagining. It's just "the way things are."*

*In this article from the journal* World and I *(June 1998), John Tagg depicts "the system" at most of our colleges and universities well. We must understand it to grasp why things are as they are and what impedes all proposals for change that go beyond mere tinkering. Whether Tagg's own proposals amount to tinkering or represent meaningful change to "the system" is a question we should keep in mind as we read.*

## Do Colleges Work?

. . . In 1991, Ernest Pascarella of the University of Illinois, Chicago, and Patrick Terenzini of the Center for the Study of Higher Education at Pennsylvania State University published a massive volume, *How College Affects Students: Findings and Insights from Twenty Years of Research.* Their assessments are carefully weighted and qualified, and they find, not surprisingly, that college students learn a good deal while in college and change in many ways. College does make a difference. But perhaps their most striking conclusion is that while attending college makes a difference, the particular college one attends makes hardly any predictable difference at all.

One of the foundational assumptions that guides parents, students, alumni, and taxpayers in thinking about colleges is that a greater investment in human and economic resources produces a better product in terms of educational outcome. Conventional thinking holds that those who run these institutions have some coherent conception of quality, and that this conception of quality is embodied in the best colleges, which others seek to emulate. Parents pay the breathtaking tuition charged by Ivy League institutions, and legislators invest public money in enormous state universities, because they believe quality is worth paying for—and because they believe that while they may not be able to define just what that quality consists of, those professionals who govern higher education can define it and, given adequate resources, create it.

But Pascarella and Terenzini found that there is little consistent evidence to indicate that college selectivity, prestige, or educational resources have any important net impact on students in such areas as learning, cognitive and intellectual development, other psychosocial changes, the development of principled moral reasoning, or shifts in other attitudes and values. Nearly all of the variance in learning and cognitive outcomes is attributable to individual aptitude differences among students attending different colleges. Only a small and perhaps trivial part is uniquely due to the quality of the college attended.

In other words, if colleges know what quality is in undergraduate education, they apparently do not know how to produce it.

In 1993 Alexander Astin, director of the Higher Education Research Institute at UCLA, published a new study: *What Matters in College: Four Critical Years Revisited.* Astin attempted to assess the effects of college using longitudinal studies of students at many varied institutions and finding correlations between the institutions' characteristics and selected student outcomes. His research, like Pascarella and Terenzini's, leaves us with a disappointing picture, a picture of colleges that attend least to what matters most and often act in ways that seem almost designed to assure they fail at their avowed mission.

Astin's research reveals that what colleges actually do bears little resemblance to what we would be likely to extract from college catalogs or commencement speeches. This probably should not surprise us. Harvard organizational theorist Chris Argyris has demonstrated that the way people say they act in business organizations—their "espoused theory," Argyris calls it—has little relationship with their "theory-in-use," which governs how they actually behave. Astin has discovered essentially the same thing in American colleges:

> Institutions espouse high-sounding values, of course, in their mission statements, college catalogues, and public pronouncements by institutional leaders. The problem is that the explicitly stated values—which always include a strong commitment to undergraduate education—are often at variance with the actual values that drive our decisions and policies.

For an outsider—and for not a few insiders—the first barrier to realistically assessing baccalaureate education is simply finding it in the morass of muddled missions that make up the contemporary multiversity. Astin quotes "one of our leading higher education scholars" as dismissing research about undergraduate learning with the remark, "The modern American university is not a residential liberal arts college." Indeed. Astin responds that

> all types of institutions claim to be engaged in the same enterprise: the liberal education of the undergraduate student. While it is true that certain kinds of institutions also do other things—research, vocational education, and graduate education, to name just a few—does having multiple functions "give permission" to an institution to offer baccalaureate education programs that are

second-rate? Does engaging in research and graduate education justify short-changing undergraduate education? Does engaging in vocational education justify offering mediocre transfer education?

The answer to that question today is, for all practical purposes, "yes." A multiplicity of functions does justify mediocrity and incoherence in undergraduate education, at least to the not very exacting standards of most of our colleges.

### What Happened?

Why are our colleges failing? Because they have substituted standardized processes for educational substance. They have become bureaucratized assembly lines for academic credit and have largely ceased, at the institutional level, to know or care what their students learn.

If we look at higher education as it exists today, what we see is counterintuitive. In a nation with over thirty-five hundred colleges serving more than fourteen million students, we find an amazing homogeneity. Despite the vast number of colleges, they display more sameness than difference. Why?

Today's system of higher education is a product of the postwar world. With the impetus of the GI Bill of Rights, rapid economic growth, and the baby boom, the college population surged after World War II. Between 1950 and 1970 college enrollment more than tripled. The percentage of Americans over twenty-five who completed a bachelor's degree doubled between the end of the war and 1970 and nearly doubled again by 1993. And the most dramatic growth has taken place in public colleges. In 1947 less than half of the nation's college students attended public institutions. By 1993 nearly 80 percent did.

Today's colleges have developed as part of a nationwide system of higher education, and hence they have become nearly interchangeable. In such a system, colleges, especially public colleges, have been able to thrive only by growing. Thus their operations have become standardized and focused on providing more of their product to more students. The mission of colleges in this system is to offer classes. My colleague Robert Barr has labeled the governing set of assumptions, attitudes, and rules that define colleges in this system—the theory-in-use of most colleges—the Instruction Paradigm. In the Instruction Paradigm, the product of colleges is classes; colleges exist for the purpose of offering more instruction to more students in more classes.

In this system, the "atom" of the educational universe is the one-hour block of lecture and the "molecule" is the three-unit course. The parts of the educational experience have transferrable value only in the form of completed credit hours. For almost any student at nearly any college today, the essential meaning of "being a student" is accumulating credit hours. 10

A credit hour is a measurement of time spent in class. I do not mean to suggest that credit is automatic for students who merely show up. They must, of course, pass the course. But the amount of credit, the weight of the course in the transcript, is based on the length of time the student sits in a room. What the student does in the room, what the teacher does in the room, what they think after they leave the room—these things are irrelevant to academic credit. The qualifications and experience and attitudes of the teacher are irrelevant to academic credit—three units from a creative scholar passionately interested in her subject and her students are equal to three units from a bored grad student who finds teaching a largely avoidable irritation. The attitude and involvement of the student are irrelevant to academic credit—three units earned by a committed and involved student who finds a whole new way of thinking and a life-changing body of ideas in a course are equal to three units earned by a student who thinks about the course only long enough to fake temporary knowledge with borrowed notes.

Public funding mechanisms in most states reward colleges for offering courses, credit hours. Not for grades, not for course completion, and certainly not for learning. States pay colleges for students sitting in classrooms. You get what you pay for.

### The Knowledge Factory

The Instruction Paradigm college of the postwar period is a knowledge factory: The student passes through an assembly line of courses. As the students pass by, each faculty member affixes a specialized part of knowledge. Then the students move on down the assembly line to the next instructor, who bolts on another fragment of knowledge. The assembly line moves at a steady pace. Each instructor has exactly one semester or quarter to do the same job for every student, who is assumed to be as like every other as the chassis of a given model of car. The workers on this line tend to view their jobs narrowly, as defined by the part of knowledge that it is their business to affix. No one has the job of quality control for the finished product.

In the college as knowledge factory, students learn that the only value recognized by the system, the only fungible good that counts toward success, is the grade on the transcript. It is a fractured system dedicated to the production of parts, of three-unit classes. The reason colleges fail is that the parts don't fit together. They don't add up to a coherent whole. They add up to a transcript but not an education.

Most of the lower division, the first two years of college, is dominated 15 by general education requirements. These requirements at most colleges consist of lists of classes—in a variety of categories such as the humanities, social science, and physical science—from which the student may choose. William Schaefer, emeritus professor of English and former executive vice chancellor at UCLA, describes general education as "a conglomeration of unrelated courses dedicated to the proposition that one's reach should never exceed one's grasp."

The incoherence of the curriculum flows from the internal organizational dynamic of the knowledge factory. Required classes are shaped by the dominant organizational unit of college faculties: academic departments. At nearly all colleges, the fundamental duty and allegiance of the faculty is to their home departments. Most academic departments hire their own faculty. Most faculty members literally owe their jobs not to the college as an institution but to their departments. Most of the crucial decisions about a faculty member's workload and duties are primarily departmental decisions. As Schaefer notes, "Departments have a life of their own — insular, defensive, self-governing, compelled to protect their interests because the faculty positions as well as the courses that justify funding those positions are located therein."

Departments become large by bolting more of their distinctive parts onto more student chassis in the educational assembly line, by offering those bread-and-butter required general education courses that garner large guaranteed enrollments. But these are often just the kinds of innocuous survey courses that faculty prefer not to teach. And the highest rewards in most universities are reserved not for those who teach undergraduates but for those who are recognized for their research contributions to their academic disciplines. Academic departments have achieved the "best" of both worlds by hiring large numbers of graduate students or part-time instructors, at low salaries and often with no benefits, to teach undergraduate courses, while freeing up senior faculty for research activities.

Our great research universities have for many years subsidized their research programs and graduate schools at the expense of undergraduate programs. They have, in effect, pawned their undergraduate colleges to buy faculty the jewel of research time. There is no penalty to pay for this transaction, because undergraduate programs are funded based on seat time; learning doesn't count; the failure of students to learn exacts no cost to the department or the institution.

Academic departments are ostensibly organized in the service of "disciplines" — coherent and discrete bodies of knowledge or methods of study. While many of the academic disciplines that make up the sciences and humanities are of ancient and proud lineage, their configuration in the modern university is largely a product of academic politics. And their trajectory in the development and deployment of general education courses is almost entirely a product of competition between departments for campus resources. On the academic assembly line of the knowledge factory, each part must be different, so the incentive is to emphasize what makes a discipline unlike others and to shape all knowledge into these highly differentiated disciplines.

Even skills of universal relevance to virtually everything we do in life  20
have become the property of one department or another. Thus, writing in

the student's native language becomes the concern of the Department of English; speaking the student's native language is relegated to the Department of Communication. Quantitative reasoning belongs to the Department of Mathematics. The atomized curriculum has taken an increasingly conspicuous toll: the inability of students to think globally or to transfer methods of analysis from one subject or problem to another. The evidence mounts that what students learn in one course they do not retain and transfer to their experience in other courses or to their lives and their work. The fragments never fit together. This has led to a growing demand for the teaching of "critical thinking." But even the subject of thought itself becomes in the knowledge factory an object of competitive bidding among academic departments. Adam Sweeting, director of the Writing Program at the Massachusetts School of Law at Andover, warns that "if we are not careful, the teaching of critical thinking skills will become the responsibility of one university department, a prospect that is at odds with the very idea of a university."

But then much about the modern university is at odds with the very idea of a university. The competition between "academic disciplines" for institutional turf generates a bundle of fragments, a mass of shards, and no coherent whole at all. It lacks precisely that quality of discipline that provided the rationale for the enterprise from the beginning. It creates a metacurriculum in which students learn that college is a sequence of disconnected parts, valuable only as credits earned. And what comes off the assembly line of the knowledge factory in the end is an "education" that might have been designed by Rube Goldberg, with marketing advice from the Edsel team.

The result is an institution that satisfies nobody. College faculties complain bitterly, often about the administration, but most often about the students. History and philosophy professors complain that students can't write. English professors complain that students know little about history and culture. Science professors complain that students have only a rudimentary grasp of mathematics. And everyone complains that students can't think. Yet grades have never been higher. The mean grade point average of all college graduates in 1994 was 3.0 on a scale of 4. It seems unfair to penalize students with poor grades for deficiencies that really fall outside the scope of the course, deficiencies that could not possibly be addressed in a three-unit, one-semester class. So the professors blame the students or the administration and fight pitched battles in the faculty senate. Yet nothing seems to work, because the deficiencies that plague students are almost by definition problems that cannot be addressed in any three-unit class. But three-unit classes are all there are; they are what the college is made of.

Perhaps least satisfied with the knowledge factory are the students. Those students who come to college from high school today come hoping for something better, but with no framework of educational value to bring to the experience themselves. For many of them, the defining experience of college becomes drunkenness. While some colleges have begun belatedly to recognize the costs of the culture of irresponsibility that has grown up on many campuses, it remains the case that substance abuse is one of the few measurable outcomes of a college education. A commission chaired by former Health, Education, and Welfare Secretary Joseph Califano Jr. reported in 1994 that a third of college students are binge drinkers and that the number of college women who reported that they drink in order to get drunk had tripled since 1973, now matching the rate for men.

William Willimon, dean of the chapel at Duke University, and Thomas Naylor, emeritus professor of economics at Duke, have characterized the chaos and aimlessness that college is for many students in their book *The Abandoned Generation: Rethinking Higher Education.* They offer an especially telling statement of the experience of the knowledge factory from a University of Michigan senior:

> So you get here and they start asking you, "What do you think you want to major in?" "Have you thought about what courses you want to take?" And you get the impression that that's what it's all about—courses, majors. So you take the courses. You get your card punched. You try a little this and a little that. Then comes GRADUATION. And you wake up and you look at this bunch of courses and then it hits you: They don't add up to anything. It's just a bunch of courses. It doesn't mean a thing.

### Do Colleges Have a Future?

The knowledge factory is breaking down as we approach the twenty-first century. The transformation to the knowledge society means that the demand for higher education will increase both in quantity and quality: More students will require more sophisticated knowledge and skills. But this transformation has also brought into existence something new on the higher education landscape: competition.   25

Competition has emerged for two reasons. First, private employers who need skilled employees have found that the graduates of conventional colleges are poorly prepared to do the work they need to do. Many corporations have either established their own "universities" or sought the support of outside vendors to provide educational services. The second reason competition has burgeoned is that contemporary information technology has made possible immediate access to educational services from anywhere. Education is no longer bound to the campus. Hence many providers can compete to serve students who were formerly too distant. The competition is real. Stan Davis and Jim Botkin—in *The Monster under the Bed,* their book about the growing imperative for corporate education—offer little hope to the conventional college: "Employee education is not growing 100 percent faster than academe, but 100 times—or 10,000 percent—faster."

In the face of such competition, if conventional colleges hold fast to the Instruction Paradigm and continue to grant degrees on seat time, many of those colleges will wither and die—going down, we can hardly doubt, in a blaze of acrimony as the nation's great minds fulminate in faculty senates across the land. If colleges are to thrive, and in some cases if they are even to survive, they must change.

Colleges need to make a paradigm shift, to set aside a whole body of assumptions and implicit rules and adopt a fundamentally different perspective, a new theory-in-use. They must recognize that the Instruction Paradigm mistakes a means for an end, confuses offering classes with producing learning. To put that end in its proper place would be to embrace what Barr calls "the Learning Paradigm." From the perspective of the Learning Paradigm, the central defining functions of the knowledge factory are trivial. What counts is what students learn. That the mission of colleges is to produce learning should be fairly noncontroversial, since it is consistent with what nearly all college faculty and administrators already say in public.

The problem is that most colleges do not assess in any meaningful way what students have learned. They can tell you what classes their students have taken but not what their graduates know or what they can do. The shift to the Learning Paradigm would require that colleges begin to take learning seriously, to assess and measure it, and to take responsibility for producing it.

A large and growing number of faculty and administrators have seen                30
that major changes in the way colleges do business are both desirable and inevitable. The prestigious California Higher Education Policy Center, in a 1996 report, urged that "colleges and universities . . . begin a transition toward making student learning, not the time spent on courses taken, the principal basis on which degrees and certificates are rewarded."

Excellent models of such colleges exist. Alverno College in Milwaukee has for decades been developing "assessment-as-learning," an approach that seeks to both monitor and guide students' development toward the mastery of a set of core competencies that define a liberal education. The new Western Governors' University will reward students with credit only when they have established through rigorous assessment that they have mastered the required skills. According to Alan Guskin, chancellor of Antioch University, more than two hundred colleges across the country are seriously discussing major restructuring.

Nonetheless, if we contrast the glacial rate at which colleges and universities seem inclined to change with the lightning speed with which the society they serve is transforming itself, we must be disturbed by the contrast. Many believe that undergraduate colleges cannot meet the challenge of the knowledge society. Davis and Botkin, for example, foresee that "corporations will continue to need traditional universities to carry out basic education and research. Nevertheless they will increasingly take on teaching themselves." Drucker predicts: "Thirty years from now the big university campuses will be relics. Universities won't survive. . . . Such totally uncontrollable expenditures, without any visible improvement in either the content or the quality of education, means that the system is rapidly becoming untenable. Higher education is in deep crisis."

Should we, after all, care? What matter if many of our colleges pass away or diminish into support institutions for market-driven forces that can adapt more flexibly to the needs of a changing world? What would be lost? Perhaps not much. Perhaps a great deal. For colleges hold a place in American society that no other institution is likely to fill. They hold the place of liberal education, of education for liberty, of the kind of experience through which children grow into citizens, through which men and women learn the exercise of the freedom that is tempered by choosing responsibility. I say that colleges "hold the place" of liberal education today because I cannot say that they serve the function. But they remain the institutional focus of the ideal, which survives as an ideal. . . .

Changing the governing paradigm, becoming learning-driven institutions, may seem a daunting task for today's knowledge factories. It seems a little like asking the post office to become a church. Yet the reason that the ideal of liberal education survives in our cultural imagination is that it addresses an ongoing need, the need to nurture in the young the development of both heart and mind, the need to set young people on a course that offers not just facility but maturity, not just cleverness but wisdom. . . .

---

*For Discussion*

1. The first article in this chapter strongly supports the remark that Tagg quotes with evident disapproval—that "the modern American university is not a residential liberal arts college." The cold facts—demographic data—back up this contention so that how we *feel* about the diminishing role of the traditional college is one thing and well-documented trends another. Read or reread the first article. How does it "speak to" Tagg's argument? What considerations does it raise for his proposals he does not address?

2. Tagg is right, of course, to say that "the 'atom' of the educational universe is the one-hour block of lecture and the 'molecule' is the three-unit course" and that therefore "the essential meaning of 'being a student' is accumulating credit hours." But would his proposed shift from the Instructional Paradigm to the Learning Paradigm necessarily change this? Why or why not?

3. "The evidence mounts," Tagg alleges, "that what students learn in one course they do not retain and transfer to their experience in other courses or to their lives and work." Is this true? Do you see connections among the courses you're taking? Do you see applications to your life and work? Tagg blames this problem on the "atomized

curriculum." Do you agree? That is, would a more coherent curriculum *necessarily* result in more connection and application? Is the problem structural, or does it somehow involve more than how "the system" is organized?

4. What is the relation between knowledge and learning? Is knowing a lot about some subject the same thing as understanding it? If not, what's the difference? What sort of educational structure and approach to teaching would best promote both?

## For Research, Inquiry, and Convincing

All shrewd people know the difference between an organization's "espoused theory" and its "theory-in-use"—the difference between public relations and reality, between what we say we are doing and what we are actually doing. There's always a gap because we want to present ourselves to the world in the best possible light while also coping with realities within the organization that may be known only to insiders and that may be discomforting or embarrassing.

Problems arise when the gap becomes too great—when the official rhetoric no longer represents merely a favorable spin but rather becomes an outright lie. The result is cynicism and eventual loss of organizational cohesion, pride, and spirit.

Investigate the distinction by examining the official rhetoric of your school. Collect a representative body of it and, as a class, analyze what it says, implies, and promises, paying special attention to the image or character of the school it tries to project. Compare the image with the reality—what you have experienced, what your classmates think is going on—and, if possible, with the impressions of older students, your professors, and the administration.

Then write a paper addressed to your fellow students or prospective students assessing some aspect of the official rhetoric. How honest is it? Is there a tolerably good match between the said and the done? If not, how could it change and still present your school positively?

## Additional Suggestions for Writing

1. *Persuasion.* With the exception of Shorris's, all the selections in this chapter have a negative view of present practices in higher education and of current college students. In this sense they tend to be one-sided, mainly "gloom and doom," as we say. But matters are rarely this simple. For example, the decline of the residential college is matched by greater educational opportunity for more students, who can live at home more cheaply and attend school part-time while holding down a job. Loss of coherence in the curriculum has produced fewer required courses and more options to meet requirements—more freedom of choice. Consumerism has forced colleges to listen more to their students and respond to their needs better, including greater regard for how well professors "reach" students. And

so on. We do not have to be Pollyannas, "all sunshine and light," to see that what is bad from one perspective can be good, or at least not so bad, from another.

Write a response to any one of the negative articles or to some significant part of one. Conceive of it in the genre of a letter to the editor of a journal, but direct it to the readership the essay tried to reach. Argue for the "up" side of the negative points the author raised, and try to persuade your readers that things are not as bad as the author contends.

2. *Exploration.* One of the best remedies for confusion is to return again and again to basic questions. So far as higher education and the college experience are concerned, perhaps the basic question is what *you* want from it—not what the college or some "expert" says you should want or what your parents say they want or even what you think you should want, but rather what you are actually here for.

Over a period of perhaps a week or two, take time to record in your writer's notebook everything you have done, and ponder it from the standpoint of both apparent motives and deeper or hidden ones. Why are you doing what you're doing? What do your choices say about your real motivations?

Write an essay exploring your genuine motives. Good, bad, or indifferent, what are they exactly? Where do they come from? What motives do you admire that you wish you had? Compare your thoughts with those of your classmates. In class discussion, address this question: Will our motives likely change over the next few years? In what specific ways? Why?

# Chapter 16

# Race and Class: Examining Social Inequality

*P*rejudice—in its root meaning "prejudge, to evaluate someone or something before knowing the facts, in advance of a particular encounter with the individual thing or person that provokes judgment"—is a more subtle and difficult concept than most people realize. We want to say that prejudice is simply wrong and shameful—for instance, the history of black people in the United States certainly proves that prejudice can be wrong and shameful. We could point also to the treatment of Native Americans, Chinese and Japanese immigrants, Hispanics, and many others whose skin color and cultures marked them as different from the white majority. Hence, we hope to end prejudice and overcome prejudice in ourselves and our institutions. "You're prejudiced" becomes one of the worst of accusations, something that we fear as much as past generations feared steps to undo prejudice, such as integration.

We fear the accusation because most of us know we're guilty. When we encounter anyone for the first time, we don't see that person as an individual. Rather, we see classes of attributes: the person is male or female; is young, middle-aged, or old; dresses this way or that; speaks with a certain accent; and so on, through a host of categories through which we *discriminate*—that is, perceive—*all* people we meet. The problem is that each of the categories carries certain cultural expectations. If the person is female, for example, we expect her to be more or less conventionally feminine, and we are likely to judge her negatively to the degree she doesn't act the part. Of course, not all prejudices result in negative evaluations. When Americans hear a cultivated, upper-class British accent, for example, many will associate the speaker with high intelligence and sophistication, investing that person with all sorts of "positives" he or she may not actually have.

The point is that prejudice and the tendency to discriminate are as inevitable as breathing. We can and should eliminate or reduce some kinds of prejudice, but we can't cease to prejudge things and people and remain human. Simply by living in a society and speaking a language whose words carry positive and negative associations, we will necessarily have prejudices and discriminate. Nor is discrimination always bad. For instance, as a juror in a criminal case, we may be asked to decide whether the accused is legally sane. We can and should make such judgments—indeed, the law says we must.

This chapter is about prejudice in the wrong and shameful sense. What exactly makes some kinds of prejudice wrong and shameful? We would not criticize a home loan company for denying the application of a person whose financial condition should exclude them from moving into an exclusive neighborhood he or she can't afford. But if a person can qualify and is denied simply because he or she is black and the neighborhood is "exclusive" in the sense of all white, that would be not only wrong but also actionable, justification for a lawsuit. The difference is clear: a person's finances are relevant to a loan application; skin color is not. Accordingly, prejudice is justified in the first case and entirely without justification in the second.

Similarly, colleges discriminate among applicants routinely, and no one blames a school for rejecting a student because grades and test scores don't measure up. But sometimes, of course, students get in because, say, a parent has "pull"—there is money in the family and significant contributions have been made or promised. This is wrong, as is favoring students who come from prosperous neighborhoods, because just as race should have nothing to do with loan qualifications, so wealth should have no bearing on qualifications for college admission.

The preceding are examples of racism and classism, prejudice based on skin color and socioeconomic background or standing. The articles in this chapter are about both—as well as about how one can merge with or substitute for the other and how both tend to overlap with other kinds of unwarranted bias, such as ethnic or cultural favoritism. Inevitably, the articles emphasize the black-white division, which has plagued us for about 400 years now, since the beginning of the slave trade and long before there was a United States. We cannot forget this dreadful history, but here we focus on what many have called the "new racism," subtler kinds of discrimination and animosity that progress in civil rights and integration have not as yet touched. We also wanted to bring class issues into the picture because Americans generally resist acknowledging the harsh realities of class-based prejudices. We need to recognize, confront, and understand them better.

Among the issues raised by the readings in this chapter are the following: First, what is the future of race and race-oriented prejudice? Are we headed toward a society of "beige and brown," in which skin color differences are less discernible and may well cease to matter? Second, what is "equal opportunity," the core value of most American thinking on issues of social justice and equity? To what extent does equal opportunity exist? Is it an adequate response to the dehumanizing effects of present and past discrimination? Finally, is there a new racism? If so, what forms does it take? How exactly does it differ from older practices? What strategies will reduce prejudice and help victims cope better?

These and other key questions must concern us as we struggle with an old problem that now often takes unfamiliar, confusing, and complicated routes in (and out) of our awareness. One thing we can be sure of as we explore the territory: We have not and will not escape prejudging everything and everybody we encounter. And so we must examine our prejudices carefully and honestly, discarding those that hurt and harm and cultivating those that promote tolerance and understanding.

# Photograph
## Bruce Roberts

*Before the civil rights era of the 1960s, it was common to see blatant discrimination, especially in the South. This photograph of segregated restrooms reveals a great deal about the prejudices of an earlier time. The photograph was taken in South Carolina in 1965.*

## For Discussion

Rhetorically, the doors are an argument, made by the white majority to members of both white and black races. Discuss the argument in terms of rhetorical context as described on pages 26–27.

# Second Thoughts about America's Racial Paradise
## Ryszard Kapuscinski

*The following two-part article appeared in the* New Perspectives Quarterly *(1991), published by the Center for the Study of Democratic Institutions. We include the head-note written by the editors of* NPQ, *which explains the unusual circumstances of its composition.*

*The article provides a European's perspective on racism in the United States. The author is clearly a prophet of sorts, focusing more on what might be or could be than on what is. And yet if we recognize that his vision is, as even he admits, "perhaps . . . overly naive and idealistic," we must yet grant its appeal—and its challenge. What do we see when we consider race in the United States? What perspective will allow us to understand best what is unfolding before our eyes?*

Author most recently of *The Soccer War,* Ryszard Kapuscinski has spent the last several decades reporting on the Third World for the Eastern European press.

In 1988, *NPQ* invited the acclaimed writer to Los Angeles to comment on a city that had become dubbed the "capital of the Third World." We reproduce a portion of his ode to LA's multiculturalism below.

After the beating of Rodney King by white cops, we asked Kapuscinski for his second thoughts, which he sent to us from Warsaw.

How is it, we asked him to ponder, that the same city celebrated for its inter-ethnic peace and remarkable cultural diversity—a city which attracts immigrants of color from all over the world seeking a new chance—was also the setting of the brutal beating of a black man by white police worthy of South Africa?

Is the multicultural paradise beginning to fray as the American economy falters? At the outset of the 1990s, LA's two major economic pillars—real estate and aerospace—have begun to crumble. Is violent inter-ethnic conflict on the horizon without the social glue of economic growth?

In such an eventuality, will Los Angeles remain, as Kapuscinski has postulated, a premonition of the future?

1988—traditional history has been a history of nations. But for the first time since the Roman Empire, there is the possibility of creating the history of a civilization. Now is the first chance, on a new basis with new technologies, to create a civilization of unprecedented openness and pluralism. A civilization of the polycentric mind. A civilization that leaves behind forever the ethnocentric, tribal mentality. The mentality of destruction.

Los Angeles is a premonition of this new civilization. Linked more to the Third World and Asia than to the Europe of America's racial and cultural roots, Los Angeles and Southern California will enter the 21st century as a multi-racial and multicultural society. This is absolutely new. There is no previous example of a civilization that is being simultaneously created by so many races, nationalities, and cultures. This new type of cultural pluralism is completely unknown in the history of mankind.

America is becoming more plural every day because of the unbelievable facility of the new Third World immigrants to put a piece of their original culture inside of American culture. The notion of a "dominant" American culture is changing every moment. It is incredible coming to America to find you are somewhere else—in Seoul, in Taipei, in Mexico City. You can travel inside Korean culture right on the streets of Los Angeles. Inhabitants of this vast city are veritable tourists in the place of their own residence.

There are large communities of Laotians, Vietnamese, Cambodians, Mexicans, Salvadorans, Guatemalans, Iranians, Japanese, Koreans, Armenians, Chinese. We find here Little Taipei, Little Saigon, Little Tokyo, Koreatown, Little Central America, the Iranian neighborhood in Westwood, the Armenian community in Glendale or Hollywood, and the vast Mexican-American areas of East Los Angeles. Eighty-one languages, few of them European, are spoken in the elementary school system of the city of Los Angeles.

This transformation of American culture anticipates the general trend    5
in the composition of mankind. Ninety percent of the immigrants to this city are from the Third World. At the beginning of the 21st century, nearly 90 percent of the world's population will be dark-skinned; the white race will be no more than 11 percent of all human beings living on our planet.

Usually, the contact between developed and underdeveloped worlds has the character of exploitation—just taking people's labor and resources and giving them nothing. And the border between races has usually been a border of tension, of crisis.

But this Pacific Rim civilization being created is a new relationship between development and underdevelopment. Here, there is openness. There is hope. And a future. There is a multicultural crowd. But it is not fighting. It is cooperating, peacefully competing, building. For the first time in 400 years of relations between the nonwhite Western world and the white Western world, the general character of the relationship is cooperation and construction, not exploitation or destruction.

Unlike any other place on the planet, Los Angeles shows us the potential of development once the Third World mentality merges with an open sense of possibility, a culture of organization, a Western conception of time.

In 1924, the Mexican philosopher Jose Vasconcellos wrote a book entitled *La Raza Cosmica*. He dreamt of the possibility that, in the future, mankind would create one human race, a mestizo race.[1] All races on the planet would merge into one type of man. *La Raza Cosmica* is being born in Los Angeles, in the cultural sense if not the anthropological sense. A vast mo-

---

[1] *Mestizo* refers specifically to a person of mixed European and Native-American blood; Vasconcellos's *La Raza Cosmica* (*The Cosmic Race*) envisions a world in which all races are blended.

saic of different races, cultures, religions and moral habits are working toward one common aim. From the perspective of a world submerged in religious, ethnic, and racial conflict, this harmonious cooperation is something unbelievable. It is truly striking.

For the destructive, paralyzed "Third World" where I have spent most of my life, it is important, simply, that such a possibility as Los Angeles exists.

10

1991 — Several thoughts crossed my mind almost simultaneously when I learned that white policemen in Los Angeles had beaten up a black man named Rodney G. King. The first thought — or, rather, feeling — was of surprise. Perhaps I have an overly naive and idealistic view of Los Angeles. My visit there left me with the impression of a city that, despite its indisputable problems with traffic jams, excessive pollution, and drugs, is nevertheless a model of the harmonious coexistence of people of various races, languages, and religions. I have widely voiced this positive assessment. Meantime, in my exemplar of racial harmony, white cops had beaten up a black man!

Because the whole unpleasant incident came to light through the sole fact that someone had recorded it on a videocamera, my second thought was of the revolution brought about in the world (a revolution that continues and develops) by this small, practically pocket-size object. Beware! Your every gesture can from now on be observed and registered without your knowledge or consent!

The vigilant eye of the meddlesome camera watches us from a thousand places — from windows, from balconies, from rooftops, from stationary or moving cars, from behind bushes. We can be filmed by someone who is standing at a bus stop, or sitting at a table in a bar. We can be filmed at all times, almost everywhere, and, potentially, by everyone. This is precisely what happened to the policemen who beat up Rodney King. They fell into the net of that ubiquitous lens, which has itself become a kind of weapon that is virtually universally accessible.

Next, as my attention was drawn to the enormous publicity given the deplorable incident by the American mass media, I thought — fortunate Americans! It is a fortunate country, a fortunate nation, that is able to call forth such a storm of anger and protests because somebody beat up somebody else.

After all, Los Angeles lies on the same planet on which on the very day, at the very instant, that the policemen were beating up Rodney King, there perished in various wars or from hunger thousands upon thousands of people, in Ethiopia, in Mozambique, in Afghanistan, in Iraq; and it didn't occur to anyone to raise a voice of indignation and protest against these massive and cruel deaths. I thought — although it is an absurd thought — that it is fortunate to be one of the beaten in America, for afterwards one can demand a million dollars for every blow (as Rodney King has cleverly done), while the wretches in Africa and the Middle East, although they are harmed by fate in a truly horrible way, can't even count on a handful of rice

15

and a few drops of water. (At that moment I found myself on slippery ground—for one cannot use a greater wrong to excuse a lesser one.)

Nevertheless, I decided to read once again what the American press had written about the incident. And upon rereading, one thing struck me—that the indignation did not result only from the fact of someone having been so badly beaten, but from the fact that *white* policemen had beaten up a *black* citizen. Whites beat up a black—that was the real cause of the press's anger and disapproval. While at first I was inclined to belittle and make light of the entire Rodney King incident, as I began to appreciate all its racial implications, the outrage of American public opinion started to seem understandable and justified. For today humanity is threatened by three powder kegs, variously dispersed around our planet: One keg is nationalism, the second, racism, and the third, religious fundamentalism.

The point is not to allow one of these kegs to explode in our own house, in our own country; for such an explosion would demolish our present order in its entirety. It would bring about its ruin. And the best way to prevent such an explosion is to snuff out even the smallest incident while it is still but a flicker.

For our increasingly irrational and unpredictable world, even something of seemingly little importance can serve as the catalyst of a larger and devastating conflict. That is why I understand the voice of criticism and censure raised against the Los Angeles policemen: They were playing with dangerous, easily spreading fire.

---

*For Discussion*

1. What meanings would you attach to the terms "openness," "pluralism," and "the polycentric mind" (paragraph 1)? Are these "good" terms to you—that is, do they have positive connotations? How do you react to the extreme racial and ethnic diversity of cities like Los Angeles and New York? How do you account for your reaction?

2. Kapuscinski is attracted to Los Angeles because, in his view, it represents "[a] civilization that leaves behind forever the ethnocentric, tribal mentality. The mentality of destruction" (paragraph 1). How do you understand the notion of ethnocentricity? In your view, is the author justified in condemning the tribal mentality so completely? Is it "the mentality of destruction"?

3. With what is the author comparing the "racial paradise" of the United States? What can we learn from seeing our own racial problems in the context of, say, conflicts in the Middle East or the former Yugoslavia? How do you react to the label "fortunate Americans" (paragraph 14)?

4. In paragraph 16 Kapuscinski refers to "three powder kegs"—nationalism, racism, and religious fundamentalism. How would you define

each of these "isms"? How do they figure in world problems? How do they figure in tensions and conflicts within the United States?

*For Inquiry and Convincing*

Find out all you can about the Rodney King episode, including the subsequent rioting, the trials of both the police officers involved and rioters arrested in other acts of brutality, and the aftermath for Los Angeles residents generally. Write an essay that agrees or disagrees (or does some of both) with Kapuscinski's evaluation of this event.

# The Beige and the Black
## Michael Lind

*We may hope for mutual understanding among the races and toleration of racial differences, but nothing indicates the actual breakdown of old racial tensions more clearly and profoundly than large numbers of racially mixed couples. Hence, many respond favorably to* The Cosmic Race, *Jose Vasconcellos's 1924 book, which predicted the end of race through interracial marriage. In the previous selection, Ryszard Kapuscinski refers to this possibility as part of his vision of Los Angeles as a new civilization free of racial and ethnic hostilities.*

*Perhaps the cosmic race will eventually emerge; however, as this article argues, the next fifty years will likely see only part of the vision realized. Americans of European, Hispanic, Asian, and Native American ancestry are intermarrying at significant and increasing rates. African Americans intermarry as well but at much lower percentages. Thus, even as the old racial divide between white and black weakens, a new line may form separating "the beige"—"a white-Asian-Hispanic . . . majority"—from "the black," especially from impoverished African Americans segregated in our inner cities.*

*Michael Lind is the Washington editor of* Harper's. *This article appeared originally in the* New York Times Magazine *(August 16, 1998).*

Just when you think you're ready for 21st-century America, it changes on you yet again. A few years ago, predictions that whites would eventually become a minority group in the United States galvanized the multicultural left—and horrified the nativist right. More recently, news of the growing number of mixed-race Americans has inspired the political center with a vision of a true racial melting pot, one in which white and black alike will blend into a universal brown. But a closer look at demographic trends suggests that neither of these futures—a nonwhite majority, a uniformly "beige" society—will very likely come to pass. Instead, shifting patterns of racial intermarriage suggest that the next century may see the replacement of the historic white-black dichotomy in America with a troubling new division, one between beige and black.

Racial intermarriage has long been a source of anxiety in America. After World War II, Senator Theodore G. Bilbo of Mississippi defended white supremacy in a book titled *Take Your Choice: Separation or Mongrelization*. Like other racists of his era, Bilbo believed that an inevitable result of dismantling segregation would be the amalgamation of the races through intermarriage. He was right: since the U.S. Supreme Court, in *Loving v. Virginia* (1967), struck down the last antimiscegenation laws of the states, marriage across racial lines has grown at a remarkable rate.

Between 1960 and 1990, interracial marriages in this country skyrocketed by more than 800 percent. Roughly 1 in 25 American married couples today are interracial. In fact, there are at least three million children of mixed-race parentage in the United States—and this figure doesn't even include the millions of Hispanic mestizos and black Americans who have European and Indian ancestors. Perhaps the best-known multiracial American is Tiger Woods, who has described himself as "Cablinasian": a mix of Caucasian, black, Native American and Asian.

Oddly, the U.S. Census Bureau has yet to account properly for the presence of mixed-race Americans. As a result, many of its projections are off target. For example, the bureau has famously predicted that in 2050, whites will make up 52.7 percent of the U.S. population. (In 1990, it was 75.7 percent.) Hispanics will account for 21.1 percent of the population; blacks, 15 percent, and Asians, 10.1 percent. Presumably, 2050 will be white America's last stand. But this projection is dubious, because it assumes that for the next half-century there will be absolutely no intermarriage among the four major conventionally defined racial groups in the United States: whites, blacks, Hispanics and Asians. Each group is supposed to somehow expand—or decline—in hermetic isolation.

But according to an analysis of the 1990 U.S. Census data for persons       5
ages 25–34 by Reynolds Farley, a demographer with the Russell Sage Foundation, 31.6 percent of native-born Hispanic husbands and 31.4 percent of native-born Hispanic wives had white spouses. The figures were even higher for Asians: 36 percent for native-born Asian husbands and 45.2 percent for native-born Asian wives. (In fact, Asian wives were as likely to marry white Americans as they were to marry Asian-Americans.) The highest intermarriage rates are those of American Indians. Majorities of American Indian men (52.9 percent) and American Indian women (53.9 percent) married whites rather than American Indians (40.3 percent and 37.2 percent, respectively). And these figures, which themselves document the creolization of America, undoubtedly understate the extent of racial intermarriage that the 2000 Census will reveal.

Of course intermarriage rates vary by region. White men in California in 1990 were more than six times as likely as Midwestern white men to marry outside their race. Overall, interracial marriages are more than twice as common in California (1 in 10 new couples) as in the rest of the country (1 in 25). According to the magazine *Interrace*, San Jose, San Diego and Oakland are among the Top 10 cities for interracial couples. America's racial complexion, then, will change more quickly on the coasts than in the heartland.

Nevertheless, the overall increase in intermarriage means that both multicultural liberals and nativist conservatives have misunderstood the major demographic trends in this country. There is not going to be a nonwhite majority in the 21st century. Rather, there is going to be a mostly white mixed-race majority. The only way to stop this is to force all Hispanic and Asian-Americans from now on to marry within their officially defined groups. And that is not going to happen.

Thus, the old duality between whites and nonwhites is finally breaking down. But don't cheer just yet. For what seems to be emerging in the United

States is a new dichotomy between blacks and nonblacks. Increasingly, whites, Asians and Hispanics are creating a broad community from which black Americans may be excluded.

Disparities in interracial marriages underline this problem. Black-white marriages have risen from a reported 51,000 in 1960 (when they were still illegal in many states) to 311,000 in 1997. Marriages between white men and black women, though still uncommon, rose from 27,000 in 1980 to 122,000 in 1995. Although black out-marriage rates have risen, they remain much lower than out-marriage rates for Hispanics, Asians and American Indians. For the 25–34 age group, only 8 percent of black men marry outside their race. Less than 4 percent of black women do so.

While many blacks frown upon marriage by blacks to members of other groups—such relationships are viewed by some as disloyal—it seems very unlikely that such conservative attitudes are more pronounced among black Americans than among whites or Hispanic or Asian immigrants. The major cause of low black out-marriage rates may well be antiblack prejudice—the most enduring feature of the eroding American caste system. Furthermore, antiblack prejudice is often picked up by immigrants, when it is not brought with them from their countries of origin.

In the past, the existence of an "untouchable" caste of blacks may have made it easier for Anglo-Americans to fuse with more recent European immigrants in an all-encompassing "white" community. Without blacks as a common "other," the differences between Anglo-Americans, German-Americans, Irish-Americans and Italian-Americans might have seemed much more important. Could this be occurring again? A Knight-Ridder poll taken in May 1997 showed that while respondents were generally comfortable with intermarriage, a full 3 in 10 respondents opposed marriage between blacks and whites.

In the 21st century, then, the U.S. population is not likely to be crisply divided among whites, blacks, Hispanics, Asians and American Indians. Nor is it likely to be split two ways, between whites and nonwhites. Rather, we are most likely to see something more complicated: a white-Asian-Hispanic melting-pot majority—a hard-to-differentiate group of beige Americans—offset by a minority consisting of blacks who have been left out of the melting pot once again.

The political implications of this new racial landscape have not yet been considered. On the positive side, the melting away of racial barriers between Asians, Latinos and whites will prevent a complete Balkanization of American society into tiny ethnic groups. On the negative side, the division between an enormous, mixed-race majority and a black minority might be equally unhealthy. The new mixed-race majority, even if it were predominantly European in ancestry, probably would not be moved by appeals to white guilt. Some of the new multiracial Americans might disingenuously invoke an Asian or Hispanic grandparent to include themselves among the victims rather than the victimizers. Nor would black Americans find many partners for a "rainbow coalition" politics, except perhaps among recent immigrants.

One political response to a beige-and-black America might be a movement to institutionalize binationalism. In Canada, Anglophones and Francophones have been declared the country's two "founding nations." Blacks, as a quasi-permanent minority, might insist upon a status different from that of voluntary immigrants who merge with the majority in a few generations. Such compromises, however, are difficult to maintain. If most immigrants blend into one of the two founding nations—the Anglophone majority in Canada, the mixed-race majority in the U.S.—then working out a stable modus vivendi between the expanding community and the shrinking community becomes almost impossible.

The other possibility is that black Americans will, in time, participate in the melting pot at rates comparable with other groups. Such a result cannot and should not be the aim of public policy—how can you legislate romance?—but it may be an incidental result of greater social mobility and economic equality. The evidence suggests that the association of people as equals erodes even the oldest and deepest prejudice in American life.

According to the 1990 census, white men 25–34 in the U.S. military were 2.3 times as likely to marry nonwhite women as civilians. And white women in the same age group who served in the military in the 1980's were seven times as likely as their civilian counterparts to have black husbands. Indeed, for all groups except for Asian men, military service makes outmarriage much more likely. The reason for this is clear: the U.S. military is the most integrated institution in American society because it is the most egalitarian and meritocratic. It is also—not coincidentally—the least libertarian and least tolerant of subcultural diversity. It may be that in the nation as a whole, as in the military, the integration of individuals can be achieved only at the price of the sacrifice of lesser differences to a powerful common identity.

In the end, racial intermarriage is a result, not a cause, of racial integration. Racial integration, in turn, is a result of social equality. The civil rights revolution abolished racial segregation by law, but not racial segregation by class. Ending racial segregation by class might—just might—bring about an end to race itself in America. It is certainly worth a try.

---

## For Discussion

1. "Intermarriage rates vary by region," Lind notes. There are far more mixed-race couples on both U.S. coasts than in the heartland, the interior regions of the country. Does this matter? If so, in what ways?
2. Intermarriage is also more common in big cities than in small towns or rural communities. Does this matter? If so, in what ways?

3. How do you explain the lower rate of out-marriage for black women as opposed to black men?
4. According to a 1997 Knight-Ridder poll Lind cites, thirty percent of Americans continue to oppose marriage between whites and blacks. How do you account for the opposition?
5. In the next-to-last paragraph, Lind discusses the military and intermarriage. How does he interpret the data? What implications do you see for American society in general?

*For Inquiry*

"[R]acial intermarriage is a result, not a cause, of racial integration. Racial integration, in turn, is a result of social equality." So Lind claims, and his logic seems compelling.

Investigate his assertions in the context of interracial dating. If you have had experience with it, examine your relationship(s). Talk with classmates and/or with friends who also have had experience with it. If you feel comfortable approaching interracial couples on campus you don't know or don't know well, get their input, too.

How much does integration have to do with interracial dating? Are the people involved always social equals—that is, do they come from the same socioeconomic class and share other similarities in background? Are such factors as important in dating as they are in marriage? Why or why not?

In a short essay, discuss the conclusions you've reached, and compare them with those of other class members.

# Black Progress: How Far We've Come— And How Far We Have to Go
## Abigail and Stephan Thernstrom

*A persistent problem in assessing race relations is how to characterize current conditions. In their controversial 1997 book* Americans in Black and White: One Nation Indivisible, *Abigail and Stephan Thernstrom argue that blacks have made extraordinary gains over the past half-century and that most of the advance had little to do with government programs. Further progress, they contend, depends on narrowing the "skills gap" between black and white—that is, on effective education—not on affirmative action, which they see as contributing little to the total picture. They urge optimism about the future of race relations.*

   *Abigail Thernstrom is a senior fellow at the Manhattan Institute in New York; Stephan Thernstrom the Winthrop Professor of History at Harvard. The following article, which appeared in the* Brookings Review *(Spring 1998), summarizes their book's argument.*

Let's start with a few contrasting numbers. Sixty and 2.2. In 1940, 60 percent of employed black women worked as domestic servants; today the number is down to 2.2 percent, while 60 percent hold white-collar jobs. Forty-four and 1. In 1958, 44 percent of whites said they would move if a black family became their next door neighbor; today the figure is 1 percent. Eighteen and 86. In 1964, the year the Great Civil Rights act was passed, only 18 percent of whites claimed to have a friend who was black; today 86 percent say they do, while 87 percent of blacks assert they have white friends.

Progress is the largely suppressed story of race and race relations over the past half-century. And thus it's news that more than 40 percent of African Americans now consider themselves members of the middle class. Forty-two percent own their own homes, a figure that rises to 75 percent if we look just at black married couples. Black two-parent families earn only 13 percent less than those who are white. Almost a third of the black population lives in suburbia.

Because these are facts the media seldom report, the black underclass continues to define black America in the view of much of the public. Many assume blacks live in ghettos, often in high-rise public housing projects. Crime and the welfare check are seen as their main source of income. The stereotype crosses racial lines. Blacks are even more prone than whites to exaggerate the extent to which African Americans are trapped in inner-city poverty. In a 1991 Gallup poll, about one-fifth of all whites, but almost half of black respondents, said that at least three out of four African Americans were impoverished urban residents. And yet, in reality, blacks who consider themselves to be middle class outnumber those with incomes below the poverty line by a wide margin.

## A Fifty-Year March Out of Poverty

Fifty years ago most blacks were indeed trapped in poverty, although they did not reside in inner cities. When Gunnar Myrdal published *An American Dilemma* in 1944, most blacks lived in the South and on the land as laborers and sharecroppers. (Only one in eight owned the land on which he worked.) A trivial 5 percent of black men nationally were engaged in nonmanual, white-collar work of any kind; the vast majority held ill-paid, insecure, manual jobs—jobs that few whites would take. As already noted, six out of ten African-American women were household servants who, driven by economic desperation, often worked 12-hour days for pathetically low wages. Segregation in the South and discrimination in the North did create a sheltered market for some black businesses (funeral homes, beauty parlors, and the like) that served a black community barred from patronizing "white" establishments. But the number was minuscule.

Beginning in the 1940s, however, deep demographic and economic change, accompanied by a marked shift in white racial attitudes, started blacks down the road to much greater equality. New Deal legislation, which set minimum wages and hours and eliminated the incentive of southern employers to hire low-wage black workers, put a damper on further industrial development in the region. In addition, the trend toward mechanized agriculture and a diminished demand for American cotton in the face of international competition combined to displace blacks from the land.

As a consequence, with the shortage of workers in northern manufacturing plants following the outbreak of World War II, southern blacks in search of jobs boarded trains and buses in a Great Migration that lasted through the mid-1960s. They found what they were looking for: wages so strikingly high that in 1953 the average income for a black family in the North was almost twice that of those who remained in the South. And through much of the 1950s wages rose steadily and unemployment was low.

Thus by 1960 only one out of seven black men still labored on the land, and almost a quarter were in white-collar or skilled manual occupations. Another 24 percent had semiskilled factory jobs that meant membership in the stable working class, while the proportion of black women working as servants had been cut in half. Even those who did not move up into higher-ranking jobs were doing much better.

A decade later, the gains were even more striking. From 1940 to 1970, black men cut the income gap by about a third, and by 1970 they were earning (on average) roughly 60 percent of what white men took in. The advancement of black women was even more impressive. Black life expectancy went up dramatically, as did black homeownership rates. Black college enrollment also rose—by 1970 to about 10 percent of the total, three times the prewar figure.

In subsequent years these trends continued, although at a more leisurely pace. For instance, today more than 30 percent of black men and nearly

60 percent of black women hold white-collar jobs. Whereas in 1970 only 2.2 percent of American physicians were black, the figure is now 4.5 percent. But while the fraction of black families with middle-class incomes rose almost 40 percentage points between 1940 and 1970, it has inched up only another 10 points since then.

### Affirmative Action Doesn't Work

Rapid change in the status of blacks for several decades followed by a definite slowdown that begins just when affirmative action policies get their start: that story certainly seems to suggest that racial preferences have enjoyed an inflated reputation. "There's one simple reason to support affirmative action," an op-ed writer in the *New York Times* argued in 1995. "It works." That is the voice of conventional wisdom.

In fact, not only did significant advances predate the affirmative action era, but the benefits of race-conscious politics are not clear. Important differences (a slower overall rate of economic growth, most notably) separate the pre-1970 and post-1970 periods, making comparison difficult.

We know only this: some gains are probably attributable to race-conscious educational and employment policies. The number of black college and university professors more than doubled between 1970 and 1990; the number of physicians tripled; the number of engineers almost quadrupled; and the number of attorneys increased more than six-fold. Those numbers undoubtedly do reflect the fact that the nation's professional schools changed their admissions criteria for black applicants, accepting and often providing financial aid to African-American students whose academic records were much weaker than those of many white and Asian-American applicants whom these schools were turning down. Preferences "worked" for these beneficiaries, in that they were given seats in the classroom that they would not have won in the absence of racial double standards.

On the other hand, these professionals make up a small fraction of the total black middle class. And their numbers would have grown without preferences, the historical record strongly suggests. In addition, the greatest economic gains for African Americans since the early 1960s were in the years 1965 to 1975 and occurred mainly in the South, as economists John J. Donahue III and James Heckman have found. In fact, Donahue and Heckman discovered "virtually no improvement" in the wages of black men relative to those of white men outside of the South over the entire period from 1963 to 1987, and southern gains, they concluded, were mainly due to the powerful antidiscrimination provisions in the 1964 Civil Rights Act.

With respect to federal, state, and municipal set-asides, as well, the jury is still out. In 1994 the state of Maryland decided that at least 10 percent of the contracts it awarded would go to minority- and female-owned firms. It more than met its goal. The program therefore "worked" if the goal was merely the narrow one of dispensing cash to a particular, designated group. But how well do these sheltered businesses survive long-term without extraordinary protection from free-market competition? And with almost 30 percent of black families still living in poverty, what is their trickle-down effect? On neither score is the picture reassuring. Programs are often fraudulent, with white contractors offering minority firms 15 percent of the profit with no obligation to do any of the work. Alternatively, set-asides enrich those with the right connections. In Richmond, Virginia, for instance, the main effect of the ordinance was a marriage of political convenience—a working alliance between the economically privileged of both races. The white business elite signed on to a piece-of-the-pie for blacks in order to polish its image as socially conscious and secure support for the downtown revitalization it wanted. Black politicians used the bargain to suggest their own importance to low-income constituents for whom the set-asides actually did little. Neither cared whether the policy in fact provided real economic benefits—which it didn't.

### Why Has the Engine of Progress Stalled?

In the decades since affirmative action policies were first instituted, the poverty rate has remained basically unchanged. Despite black gains by numerous other measures, close to 30 percent of black families still live below the poverty line. "There are those who say, my fellow Americans, that even good affirmative action programs are no longer needed," President Clinton said in July 1995. But "let us consider," he went on, that "the unemployment rate for African Americans remains about twice that of whites." Racial preferences are the president's answer to persistent inequality, although a quarter-century of affirmative action has done nothing whatever to close the unemployment gap.

15

Persistent inequality is obviously serious, and if discrimination were the primary problem, then race-conscious remedies might be appropriate. But while white racism was central to the story in 1964, today the picture is much more complicated. Thus while blacks and whites now graduate at the same rate from high school today and are almost equally likely to attend college, on average they are not equally educated. That is, looking at years of schooling in assessing the racial gap in family income tells us little about the cognitive skills whites and blacks bring to the job market. And cognitive skills obviously affect earnings.

The National Assessment of Educational Progress (NAEP) is the nation's report card on what American students attending elementary and secondary schools know. Those tests show that African-American students, on average, are alarmingly far behind whites in math, science, reading, and writing. For instance, black students at the end of their high school career are almost four years behind white students in reading; the gap is comparable in other subjects. A study of 26- to 33-year-old men who held full-time jobs in 1991 thus found that when education was measured by years of school completed, blacks earned 19 percent less than comparably educated whites. But when word knowledge, paragraph comprehension, arithmetical reasoning, and mathematical knowledge became the yardstick, the results were reversed. Black men earned 9 percent more than white men with the same education—that is, the same performance on basic tests.

Other research suggests much the same point. For instance, the work of economists Richard J. Murnane and Frank Levy has demonstrated the increasing importance of cognitive skills in our changing economy. Employers in firms like Honda now require employees who can read and do math problems at the ninth-grade level at a minimum. And yet the 1992 NAEP math tests, for example, revealed that only 22 percent of African-American high school seniors but 58 percent of their white classmates were numerate enough for such firms to consider hiring them. And in reading, 47 percent of whites in 1992 but just 18 percent of African Americans could handle the printed word well enough to be employable in a modern automobile plant. Murnane and Levy found a clear impact on income. Not years spent in school but strong skills made for high long-term earnings.

### The Widening Skills Gap

Why is there such a glaring racial gap in levels of educational attainment? It is not easy to say. The gap, in itself, is very bad news, but even more alarming is the fact that it has been widening in recent years. In 1971, the average African-American 17-year-old could read no better than the typical white child who was six years younger. The racial gap in math in 1973 was 4.3 years; in science it was 4.7 years in 1970. By the late 1980s, however, the picture was notably brighter. Black students in their final year of high school were only 2.5 years behind whites in both reading and math and 2.1 years behind on tests of writing skills.

Had the trends of those years continued, by today black pupils would   20
be performing about as well as their white classmates. Instead, black progress came to a halt, and serious backsliding began. Between 1988 and 1994, the racial gap in reading grew from 2.5 to 3.9 years; between 1990 and 1994, the racial gap in math increased from 2.5 to 3.4 years. In both science and writing, the racial gap has widened by a full year.

There is no obvious explanation for this alarming turnaround. The early gains doubtless had much to do with the growth of the black middle class, but the black middle class did not suddenly begin to shrink in the late 1980s. The poverty rate was not dropping significantly when educational progress was occurring, nor was it on the increase when the racial gap began once again to widen. The huge rise in out-of-wedlock births and the steep and steady decline in the proportion of black children growing up with two parents do not explain the fluctuating educational performance of African-American children. It is well established that children raised in single-parent families do less well in school than others, even when all other variables, including income, are controlled. But the disintegration of the black nuclear family—presciently noted by Daniel Patrick Moynihan as early as 1965—was occurring rapidly in the period in which black scores were rising, so it cannot be invoked as the main explanation as to why scores began to fall many years later.

Some would argue that the initial educational gains were the result of increased racial integration and the growth of such federal compensatory education programs as Head Start. But neither desegregation nor compensatory education seems to have increased the cognitive skills of the black children exposed to them. In any case, the racial mix in the typical school has not changed in recent years, and the number of students in compensatory programs and the dollars spent on them have kept going up.

What about changes in the curriculum and patterns of course selection by students? The educational reform movement that began in the late 1970s did succeed in pushing students into a "New Basics" core curriculum that included more English, science, math, and social studies courses. And there is good reason to believe that taking tougher courses contributed to the temporary rise in black test scores. But this explanation, too, nicely fits the facts for the period before the late 1980s but not the very different picture thereafter. The number of black students going through "New Basics" courses did not decline after 1988, pulling down their NAEP scores.

We are left with three tentative suggestions. First, the increased violence and disorder of inner-city lives that came with the introduction of crack cocaine and the drug-related gang wars in the mid-1980s most likely had something to do with the reversal of black educational progress. Chaos in the streets and within schools affects learning inside and outside the classroom.

In addition, an educational culture that has increasingly turned teachers into guides who help children explore whatever interests them may have affected black academic performance as well. As educational critic E. D. Hirsch, Jr., has pointed out, the "deep aversion to and contempt for factual knowledge that pervade the thinking of American educators" means that students fail to build the "intellectual capital" that is the foundation of all further learning. That will be particularly true of those students who come to school most academically disadvantaged—those whose homes are not, in effect, an additional school. The deficiencies of American education hit hardest those most in need of education.

25

And yet in the name of racial sensitivity, advocates for minority students too often dismiss both common academic standards and standardized tests as culturally biased and judgmental. Such advocates have plenty of company. Christopher Edley, Jr., professor of law at Harvard and President Clinton's point man on affirmative action, for instance, has allied himself with testing critics, labeling preferences the tool colleges are forced to use "to correct the problems we've inflicted on ourselves with our testing standards." Such tests can be abolished—or standards lowered—but once the disparity in cognitive skills becomes less evident, it is harder to correct.

Closing that skills gap is obviously the first task if black advancement is to continue at its once-fast pace. On the map of racial progress, education is the name of almost every road. Raise the level of black educational performance, and the gap in college graduation rates, in attendance at selective professional schools, and in earnings is likely to close as well. Moreover, with educational parity, the whole issue of racial preferences disappears.

### The Road to True Equality

Black progress over the past half-century has been impressive, conventional wisdom to the contrary notwithstanding. And yet the nation has many miles to go on the road to true racial equality. "I wish I could say that racism and prejudice were only distant memories, but as I look around I see that even educated whites and African Americans . . . have lost hope in equality," Thurgood Marshall said in 1992. A year earlier *The Economist* magazine had reported the problem of race as one of "shattered dreams." In fact, all hope has not been "lost," and "shattered" was much too strong a word, but certainly in the 1960s the civil rights community failed to anticipate just how tough the voyage would be. (Thurgood Marshall had envisioned an end to all school segregation within five years of the Supreme Court's decision in *Brown v. Board of Education*.) Many blacks, particularly, are now discouraged. A 1997 Gallup poll found a sharp decline in optimism since 1980; only 33 percent of blacks (versus 58 percent of whites) thought both the quality of life for blacks and race relations had gotten better.

Thus, progress—by many measures seemingly so clear—is viewed as an illusion, the sort of fantasy to which intellectuals are particularly prone. But the ahistorical sense of nothing gained is in itself bad news. Pessimism is a self-fulfilling prophecy. If all our efforts as a nation to resolve the "American dilemma" have been in vain—if we've been spinning our wheels in the rut of ubiquitous and permanent racism, as Derrick Bell, Andrew Hacker, and others argue—then racial equality is a hopeless task, an unattainable ideal. If both blacks and whites understand and celebrate the gains of the past, however, we will move forward with the optimism, insight, and energy that further progress surely demands.

---

*For Discussion*

1. The Thernstroms contend that "the black underclass continues to define black America in the view of much of the public." Is this true?

What do you think of when "black America" is mentioned? How do you explain your image of it?

2. To what forces do the Thernstroms attribute most of the economic and social gains of black Americans since World War II? Do you agree with their analysis? Why or why not?

3. What is your attitude toward the future of race relations? On what do you base your stance? How did you acquire your attitude?

# Photograph

## A. Ramey

*In 1998, when California's Proposition 209 went into effect, ending affirmative action programs in public employment and at public colleges and universities, students on many California campuses demonstrated against the law and their schools' compliance with it. The intense moment captured in the photograph below shows police barring the doors of a building on UCLA's campus as students attempted to occupy it.*

## For Discussion

The photograph raises many issues for discussion. Most obviously, the policy of affirmative action is still under debate, as voters in other states have attempted to introduce legislation similar to California's. Look into the effects of Proposition 209 and the Hopwood court decision in Texas. What has been the effect on minority enrollment at schools there? The essays in this chapter by Linda Darling-Hammond and Abigail and Stephan Thernstrom address the question of whether equal education opportunity already exists. Discuss their opposing views on the need for affirmative action.

# Unequal Opportunity: Race and Education
## Linda Darling-Hammond

*The key principle of social justice in the thinking of most Americans is equal opportunity, as contrasted with equal results. That is, we favor a fair chance for all but believe that outcomes should be different based on individual talent and drive. This article argues that, so far as funding for our school systems is concerned, there is no equity and therefore no genuinely fair chance for all children to get a good education.*

*Linda Darling-Hammond is an educational researcher at Columbia University Teacher's College and author of* The Right to Learn *(1997). This essay appeared in the same issue of the* Brookings Review *as the previous selection.*

W. E. B. Du Bois was right about the problem of the 21st century. The color line divides us still. In recent years, the most visible evidence of this in the public policy arena has been the persistent attack on affirmative action in higher education and employment. From the perspective of many Americans who believe that the vestiges of discrimination have disappeared, affirmative action now provides an unfair advantage to minorities. From the perspective of others who daily experience the consequences of ongoing discrimination, affirmative action is needed to protect opportunities likely to evaporate if an affirmative obligation to act fairly does not exist. And for Americans of all backgrounds, the allocation of opportunity in a society that is becoming ever more dependent on knowledge and education is a source of great anxiety and concern.

At the center of these debates are interpretations of the gaps in educational achievement between white and non-Asian minority students as measured by standardized test scores. The presumption that guides much of the conversation is that equal opportunity now exists; therefore, continued low levels of achievement on the part of minority students must be a function of genes, culture, or a lack of effort and will (see, for example, Richard Herrnstein and Charles Murray's *The Bell Curve* and Stephan and Abigail Thernstrom's *America in Black and White*).

The assumptions that undergird this debate miss an important reality: educational outcomes for minority children are much more a function of their unequal access to key educational resources, including skilled teachers and quality curriculum, than they are a function of race. In fact, the U.S. educational system is one of the most unequal in the industrialized world, and students routinely receive dramatically different learning opportunities based on their social status. In contrast to European and Asian nations that fund schools centrally and equally, the wealthiest 10 percent of U.S. school districts spend nearly 10 times more than the poorest 10 percent, and spending ratios of 3 to 1 are common within states. Despite stark differences in funding, teacher quality, curriculum, and class sizes, the prevailing view is that if students do not achieve, it is their own fault. If we are ever to get beyond the problem of the color line, we must confront and address these inequalities.

## The Nature of Educational Inequality

Americans often forget that as late as the 1960s most African-American, Latino, and Native American students were educated in wholly segregated schools funded at rates many times lower than those serving whites and were excluded from many higher education institutions entirely. The end of legal segregation followed by efforts to equalize spending since 1970 has made a substantial difference for student achievement. On every major national test, including the National Assessment of Educational Progress, the gap in minority and white students' test scores narrowed substantially between 1970 and 1990, especially for elementary school students. On the Scholastic Aptitude Test (SAT), the scores of African-American students climbed 54 points between 1976 and 1994, while those of white students remained stable.

Even so, educational experiences for minority students have continued     5
to be substantially separate and unequal. Two-thirds of minority students still attend schools that are predominantly minority, most of them located in central cities and funded well below those in neighboring suburban districts. Recent analyses of data prepared for school finance cases in Alabama, New Jersey, New York, Louisiana, and Texas have found that on every tangible measure—from qualified teachers to curriculum offering—schools serving greater numbers of students of color had significantly fewer resources than schools serving mostly white students. As William L. Taylor and Dianne Piche noted in a 1991 report to Congress:

> Inequitable systems of school finance inflict disproportionate harm on minority and economically disadvantaged students. On an inter-state basis, such students are concentrated in states, primarily in the South, that have the lowest capacities to finance public education. On an intra-state basis, many of the states with the widest disparities in educational expenditures are large industrial states. In these states, many minorities and economically disadvantaged students are located in property-poor urban districts which fare the worst in educational expenditures . . . (or) in rural districts which suffer from fiscal inequity.

Jonathan Kozol's 1991 *Savage Inequalities* described the striking differences between public schools serving students of color in urban settings and their suburban counterparts, which typically spend twice as much per student for populations with many fewer special needs. Contrast MacKenzie High School in Detroit, where word processing courses are taught without word processors because the school cannot afford them, or East St. Louis Senior High School, whose biology lab has no laboratory tables or usable dissecting kits, with nearby suburban schools where children enjoy a computer hookup to Dow Jones to study stock transactions and science laboratories that rival those in some industries. Or contrast Paterson, New Jersey, which could not afford the qualified teachers needed to offer foreign language courses to most high school students, with Princeton, where foreign languages begin in elementary school.

Even within urban school districts, schools with high concentrations of low-income and minority students receive fewer instructional resources than others. And tracking systems exacerbate these inequalities by segregating many low-income and minority students within schools. In combination, these policies leave minority students with fewer and lower-quality books, curriculum materials, laboratories, and computers; significantly larger class sizes; less qualified and experienced teachers; and less access to high-quality curriculum. Many schools serving low-income and minority students do not even offer the math and science courses needed for college, and they provide lower-quality teaching in the classes they do offer. It all adds up.

### What Difference Does It Make?

Since the 1966 Coleman report, *Equality of Educational Opportunity,* another debate has raged as to whether money makes a difference to educational outcomes. It is certainly possible to spend money ineffectively; however, studies that have developed more sophisticated measures of schooling show how money, properly spent, makes a difference. Over the past 30 years, a large body of research has shown that four factors consistently influence student achievement: all else equal, students perform better if they are educated in smaller schools where they are well known (300 to 500 students is optimal), have smaller class sizes (especially at the elementary level), receive a challenging curriculum, and have more highly qualified teachers.

Minority students are much less likely than white children to have any of these resources. In predominantly minority schools, which most students of color attend, schools are large (on average, more than twice as large as predominantly white schools and reaching 3,000 students or more in most cities); on average, class sizes are 15 percent larger overall (80 percent larger for non-special education classes); curriculum offerings and materials are lower in quality; and teachers are much less qualified in terms of levels of education, certification, and training in the fields they teach. And in integrated schools, as UCLA professor Jeannie Oakes described in the 1980s and Harvard professor Gary Orfield's research has recently confirmed, most minority students are segregated in lower-track classes with larger class sizes, less qualified teachers, and lower-quality curriculum.

Research shows that teachers' preparation makes a tremendous difference to children's learning. In an analysis of 900 Texas school districts, Harvard economist Ronald Ferguson found that teachers' expertise—as measured by scores on a licensing examination, master's degrees, and experience—was the single most important determinant of student achievement, accounting for roughly 40 percent of the measured variance

10

in students' reading and math achievement gains in grades 1–12. After controlling for socioeconomic status, the large disparities in achievement between black and white students were almost entirely due to differences in the qualifications of their teachers. In combination, differences in teacher expertise and class sizes accounted for as much of the measured variance in achievement as did student and family background.

Ferguson and Duke economist Helen Ladd repeated this analysis in Alabama and again found sizable influences of teacher qualifications and smaller class sizes on achievement gains in math and reading. They found that more of the difference between the high- and low-scoring districts was explained by teacher qualifications and class sizes than by poverty, race, and parent education.

Meanwhile, a Tennessee study found that elementary school students who are assigned to ineffective teachers for three years in a row score nearly 50 percentile points lower on achievement tests than those assigned to highly effective teachers over the same period. Strikingly, minority students are about half as likely to be assigned to the most effective teachers and twice as likely to be assigned to the least effective.

Minority students are put at greatest risk by the American tradition of allowing enormous variation in the qualifications of teachers. The National Commission on Teaching and America's Future found that new teachers hired without meeting certification standards (25 percent of all new teachers) are usually assigned to teach the most disadvantaged students in low-income and high-minority schools, while the most highly educated new teachers are hired largely by wealthier schools. Students in poor or predominantly minority schools are much less likely to have teachers who are fully qualified or hold higher-level degrees. In schools with the highest minority enrollments, for example, students have less than a 50 percent chance of getting a math or science teacher with a license and a degree in the field. In 1994, fully one-third of teachers in high-poverty schools taught without a minor in their main field and nearly 70 percent taught without a minor in their secondary teaching field.

Studies of underprepared teachers consistently find that they are less effective with students and that they have difficulty with curriculum development, classroom management, student motivation, and teaching strategies. With little knowledge about how children grow, learn, and develop, or about what to do to support their learning, these teachers are less likely to understand students' learning styles and differences, to anticipate students' knowledge and potential difficulties, or to plan and redirect instruction to meet students' needs. Nor are they likely to see it as their job to do so, often blaming the students if their teaching is not successful.

Teacher expertise and curriculum quality are interrelated, because a challenging curriculum requires an expert teacher. Research has found that both students and teachers are tracked: that is, the most expert teachers teach the most demanding courses to the most advantaged students, while lower-track students assigned to less able teachers receive lower-quality

15

teaching and less demanding material. Assignment to tracks is also related to race: even when grades and test scores are comparable, black students are more likely to be assigned to lower-track, nonacademic classes.

### When Opportunity Is More Equal

What happens when students of color do get access to more equal opportunities? Studies find that curriculum quality and teacher skill make more difference to educational outcomes than the initial test scores or racial backgrounds of students. Analyses of national data from both the High School and Beyond Surveys and the National Educational Longitudinal Surveys have demonstrated that, while there are dramatic differences among students of various racial and ethnic groups in course-taking in such areas as math, science, and foreign language, for students with similar course-taking records, achievement test score differences by race or ethnicity narrow substantially.

Robert Dreeben and colleagues at the University of Chicago conducted a long line of studies documenting both the relationship between educational opportunities and student performance and minority students' access to those opportunities. In a comparative study of 300 Chicago first graders, for example, Dreeben found that African-American and white students who had comparable instruction achieved comparable levels of reading skill. But he also found that the quality of instruction given African-American students was, on average, much lower than that given white students, thus creating a racial gap in aggregate achievement at the end of first grade. In fact, the highest-ability group in Dreeben's sample was in a school in a low-income African-American neighborhood. These children, though, learned less during first grade than their white counterparts because their teacher was unable to provide the challenging instruction they deserved.

When schools have radically different teaching forces, the effects can be profound. For example, when Eleanor Armour-Thomas and colleagues compared a group of exceptionally effective elementary schools with a group of low-achieving schools with similar demographic characteristics in New York City, roughly 90 percent of the variance in student reading and mathematics scores at grades 3, 6, and 8 was a function of differences in teacher qualifications. The schools with highly qualified teachers serving large numbers of minority and low-income students performed as well as much more advantaged schools.

Most studies have estimated effects statistically. However, an experiment that randomly assigned seventh grade "at-risk" students to remedial, average, and honors mathematics classes found that the at-risk students who took the honors class offering a pre-algebra curriculum ultimately outperformed all other students of similar backgrounds. Another study compared African-American high school youth randomly placed in public housing in the Chicago suburbs with city-placed peers of equivalent income and initial academic attainment and found that the suburban students, who attended largely white and better-funded schools, were substantially more likely to take challenging courses, perform well academically, graduate on time, attend college, and find good jobs.

## What Can Be Done?

. . . Last year the National Commission on Teaching and America's Future     20
issued a blueprint for a comprehensive set of policies to ensure a "caring, competent, and qualified teacher for every child," as well as schools organized to support student success. Twelve states are now working directly with the commission on this agenda, and others are set to join this year. Several pending bills to overhaul the federal Higher Education Act would ensure that highly qualified teachers are recruited and prepared for students in all schools. Federal policymakers can develop incentives, as they have in medicine, to guarantee well-prepared teachers in shortage fields and high-need locations. States can equalize education spending, enforce higher teaching standards, and reduce teacher shortages, as Connecticut, Kentucky, Minnesota, and North Carolina have already done. School districts can reallocate resources from administrative superstructures and special add-on programs to support better-educated teachers who offer a challenging curriculum in smaller schools and classes, as restructured schools as far apart as New York and San Diego have done. These schools, in communities where children are normally written off to lives of poverty, welfare dependency, or incarceration, already produce much higher levels of achievement for students of color, sending more than 90 percent of their students to college. Focusing on what matters most can make a real difference in what children have the opportunity to learn. This, in turn, makes a difference in what communities can accomplish.

## An Entitlement to Good Teaching

The common presumption about educational inequality—that it resides primarily in those students who come to school with inadequate capacities to benefit from what the school has to offer—continues to hold wide currency because the extent of inequality in opportunities to learn is largely unknown. We do not currently operate schools on the presumption that students might be entitled to decent teaching and schooling as a matter of course. In fact, some state and local defendants have countered school finance and desegregation cases with assertions that such remedies are not required unless it can be proven that they will produce equal outcomes. Such arguments against equalizing opportunities to learn have made good on Du Bois's prediction that the problem of the 20th century would be the problem of the color line.

But education resources do make a difference, particularly when funds are used to purchase well-qualified teachers and high-quality curriculum and to create personalized learning communities in which children are well known. In all of the current sturm und drang about affirmative action, "special treatment," and the other high-volatility buzzwords for race and class politics in this nation, I would offer a simple starting point for the next century's efforts: no special programs, just equal educational opportunity.

---

## For Discussion

1. Darling-Hammond provides much evidence of funding inequities in our school systems. How does the funding system work? What social and political forces operate to keep it in place?
2. Darling-Hammond mentions that many modern, industrialized nations fund their schools centrally — that is, by the equivalent of our federal government. How do you respond to the idea of Washington handling the funding of our schools? Would such an approach work in the United States?
3. According to Darling-Hammond, what makes the greatest difference in student learning and achievement? How exactly is the level of funding related to this difference?
4. How would you define a "prepared teacher"? Is preparation the same thing as effectiveness?

## For Research and Convincing

Investigate school funding in the city and state where your university is located or in a neighboring city or state. Are there inequities? How great are they? Do the inequities correlate with educational achievement? By what measures?

Write a paper assessing the school system's (or systems') success in providing equal opportunity. If reform is needed, indicate what should be done. Address your essay to an appropriate authority, such as a state legislator or education agency.

## For Inquiry

Inquire into the positions of Darling-Hammond and the Thernstroms on the question of the education gap between whites and minorities. How does each define the gap — or example, what do the Thernstroms mean by a "skills gap," and how is that different from an education gap? Does Darling-Hammond recognize a difference between a skills gap and an education gap? How do the two essays differ in their assessment of how the educational system itself fails to correct the gap? What problems does each essay identify? Evaluate the two arguments, and do some additional research to determine what you think is the best explanation of the gap.

# The Recoloring of Campus Life
## Shelby Steele

*The following personal and reflective essay centers on what the author calls "concentrated microsocieties," our college campuses. In recent years, there has been much discussion of a "new racism" on campuses across the country. Shelby Steele, a professor of English at San Jose State University who attended college in the 1960s, argues that today's campus racism is indeed new; he tries to explain why it exists and how it works. His essay appeared originally in 1989 in* Harper's, *an eclectic monthly magazine offering essays on various current topics. Much discussed and often reprinted, "The Recoloring of Campus Life" may well be a contemporary classic.*

In the past few years, we have witnessed what the National Institute Against Prejudice and Violence calls a "proliferation" of racial incidents on college campuses around the country. Incidents of on-campus "intergroup conflict" have occurred at more than 160 colleges in the last three years, according to the institute. The nature of these incidents has ranged from open racial violence — most notoriously, the October 1986 beating of a black student at the University of Massachusetts at Amherst after an argument about the World Series turned into a racial bashing, with a crowd of up to 3,000 whites chasing twenty blacks — to the harassment of minority students, to acts of racial or ethnic insensitivity, with by far the greatest number falling in the last two categories. At Dartmouth College, three editors of the *Dartmouth Review,* the off-campus right-wing student weekly, were suspended last winter for harassing a black professor in his lecture hall. At Yale University last year a swastika and the words "white power" were painted on the school's Afro-American cultural center. Racist jokes were aired not long ago on a campus radio station at the University of Michigan. And at the University of Wisconsin at Madison, members of the Zeta Beta Tau fraternity held a mock slave auction in which pledges painted their faces black and wore Afro wigs. Two weeks after the president of Stanford University informed the incoming freshman class last fall that "bigotry is out, and I mean it," two freshmen defaced a poster of Beethoven — gave the image thick lips — and hung it on a black student's door.

In response, black students around the country have rediscovered the militant protest strategies of the Sixties. At the University of Massachusetts at Amherst, Williams College, Penn State University, UC Berkeley, UCLA, Stanford, and countless other campuses, black students have sat in, marched, and rallied. But much of what they were marching and rallying about seemed less a response to specific racial incidents than a call for broader action on the part of the colleges and universities they were attending. Black students have demanded everything from more black faculty members and new courses on racism to the addition of "ethnic" foods in the cafeteria. There is the sense in these demands that racism runs deep.

Of course, universities are not where racial problems tend to arise. When I went to college in the mid-Sixties, colleges were oases of calm and understanding in a racially tense society; campus life—with its traditions of tolerance and fairness, its very distance from the "real" world—imposed a degree of broadmindedness on even the most provincial students. If I met whites who were not anxious to be friends with blacks, most were at least vaguely friendly to the cause of our freedom. In any case, there was no guerrilla activity against our presence, no "mine field of racism" (as one black student at Berkeley recently put it) to negotiate. I wouldn't say that the phrase "campus racism" is a contradiction in terms, but until recently it certainly seemed an incongruence.

But a greater incongruence is the generational timing of this new problem on the campuses. Today's undergraduates were born after the passage of the 1964 Civil Rights Act. They grew up in an age when racial equality was for the first time enforceable by law. This too was a time when blacks suddenly appeared on television, as mayors of big cities, as icons of popular culture, as teachers, and in some cases even as neighbors. Today's black and white college students, veterans of *Sesame Street* and often of integrated grammar and high schools, have had more opportunities to know each other—whites and blacks—than any previous generation in American history. Not enough opportunities, perhaps, but enough to make the notion of racial tension on campus something of a mystery, at least to me.

To try to unravel this mystery I left my own campus, where there have been few signs of racial tension, and talked with black and white students at California schools where racial incidents had occurred: Stanford, UCLA, Berkeley. I spoke with black and white students—and not with Asians and Hispanics—because, as always, blacks and whites represent the deepest lines of division, and because I hesitate to wander onto the complex territory of other minority groups. A phrase by William H. Gass—"the hidden internality of things"—describes with maybe a little too much grandeur what I hoped to find. But it *is* what I wanted to find, for this is the kind of problem that makes a black person nervous, which is not to say that it doesn't unnerve whites as well. Once every six months or so someone yells "nigger" at me from a passing car. I don't like to think that these solo artists might soon make up a chorus or, worse, that this chorus might one day soon sing to me from the paths of my own campus.

I have long believed that trouble between the races is seldom what it appears to be. It was not hard to see after my first talks with students that racial tension on campus is a problem that misrepresents itself. It has the same look, the archetypal pattern, of America's timeless racial conflict— white racism and black protest. And I think part of our concern over it comes from the fact that it has the feel of a relapse, illness gone and come again. But if we are seeing the same symptoms, I don't believe we are dealing with the same illness. For one thing, I think racial tension on campus is the result more of racial equality than inequality.

How to live with racial difference has been America's profound social problem. For the first 100 years or so following emancipation it was controlled by a legally sanctioned inequality that acted as a buffer between the races. No longer is this the case. On campuses today, as throughout society, blacks enjoy equality under the law—a profound social advancement. No student may be kept out of a class or a dormitory or an extracurricular activity because of his or her race. But there is a paradox here: On a campus where members of all races are gathered, mixed together in the classroom as well as socially, differences are more exposed than ever. And this is where the trouble starts. For members of each race—young adults coming into their own, often away from home for the first time—bring to this site of freedom, exploration, and now, today, equality very deep fears and anxieties, inchoate feelings of racial shame, anger, and guilt. These feelings could lie dormant in the home, in familiar neighborhoods, in simpler days of childhood. But the college campus, with its structures of interaction and adult-level competition—the big exam, the dorm, the "mixer"—is another matter. I think campus racism is born of the rub between racial difference and a setting, the campus itself, devoted to interaction and equality. On our campuses, such concentrated micro-societies, all that remains unresolved between blacks and whites, all the old wounds and shames that have never been addressed, present themselves for attention—and present our youth with pressures they cannot always handle.

I have mentioned one paradox: racial fears and anxieties among blacks and whites bubbling up in an era of racial equality under the law, in settings that are among the freest and fairest in society. And there is another, related paradox, stemming from the notion of—and practice of—affirmative action. Under the provisions of the Equal Employment Opportunity Act of 1972, all state governments and institutions (including universities) were forced to initiate plans to increase the proportion of minority and women employees—in the case of universities, of students too. Affirmative action plans that establish racial quotas were ruled unconstitutional more than ten years ago in *University of California Regents v. Bakke.*[1] But quotas are only the most controversial aspect of affirmative action; the principle of affirmative action is reflected in various university programs aimed at redressing and overcoming past patterns of discrimination. Of course, to be conscious of patterns of discrimination—the fact, say, that public schools in the black inner cities are more crowded and employ fewer top-notch teachers than white suburban public schools, and that this is a factor in student

---

[1] Allan Bakke, a white applicant turned down for admission by a California State University medical school, sued the California system, claiming discrimination because the school's policy of maintaining a sixteen percent minority enrollment meant that minority applicants with lower grade point averages were admitted instead of him. The case was settled in 1978, when a divided U.S. Supreme Court ruled that specific quotas such as those in effect in the California system were not permissible; Bakke was subsequently admitted to the program. However, the Court ruling also stated that race could be considered by college administrators in an effort to achieve a diverse student body. The full legal implications of the ruling have thus been ambiguous.

performance—is only reasonable. However, in doing this we also call attention quite obviously to difference: in the case of blacks and whites, racial difference. What has emerged on campus in recent years—as a result of the new equality and affirmative action, in a sense, as a result of progress—is a *politics of difference,* a troubling, volatile politics in which each group justifies itself, its sense of worth and its pursuit of power, through difference alone.

In this context, racial, ethnic, and gender differences become forms of sovereignty, campuses become balkanized, and each group fights with whatever means are available. No doubt there are many factors that have contributed to the rise of racial tension on campus: What has been the role of fraternities, which have returned to campus with their inclusions and exclusions? What role has the heightened notion of college as some first step to personal, financial success played in increasing competition, and thus tension? Mostly what I sense, though, is that in interactive settings, while fighting the fights of "difference," old ghosts are stirred, and haunt again. Black and white Americans simply have the power to make each other feel shame and guilt. In the "real" world, we may be able to deny these feelings, keep them at bay. But these feelings are likely to surface on college campuses, where young people are groping for identity and power, and where difference is made to matter so greatly. In a way, racial tension on campus in the Eighties might have been inevitable.

I would like, first, to discuss black students, their anxieties and vulnerabilities. The accusation that black Americans have always lived with is that they are inferior—inferior simply because they are black. And this accusation has been too uniform, too ingrained in cultural imagery, too enforced by law, custom, and every form of power not to have left a mark. Black inferiority was a precept accepted by the founders of this nation; it was a principle of social organization that relegated blacks to the sidelines of American life. So when today's young black students find themselves on white campuses, surrounded by those who historically have claimed superiority, they are also surrounded by the myth of their inferiority.

Of course it is true that many young people come to college with some anxiety about not being good enough. But only blacks come wearing a color that is still, in the minds of some, a sign of inferiority. Poles, Jews, Hispanics, and other groups also endure degrading stereotypes. But two things make the myth of black inferiority a far heavier burden—the broadness of its scope and its incarnation in color. There are not only more stereotypes of blacks than of other groups, but these stereotypes are also more dehumanizing, more focused on the most despised of human traits—stupidity, laziness, sexual immorality, dirtiness, and so on. In America's racial and ethnic hierarchy, blacks have clearly been relegated to the lowest level— have been burdened with an ambiguous, animalistic humanity. Moreover, this is made unavoidable for blacks by the sheer visibility of black skin, a skin that evokes the myth of inferiority on sight. And today this myth is sadly reinforced for many black students by affirmative action programs, under which blacks may often enter college with lower test scores and high-school grade point averages than whites. "They see me as an affirmative action case," one black student told me at UCLA.

So when a black student enters college, the myth of inferiority compounds the normal anxiousness over whether he or she will be good enough. This anxiety is not only personal but also racial. The families of these students will have pounded into them the fact that blacks are not inferior. And probably more than anything, it is this pounding that finally leaves a mark. If I am not inferior, why the need to say so?

This myth of inferiority constitutes a very sharp and ongoing anxiety for young blacks, the nature of which is very precise: It is the terror that somehow, through one's actions or by virtue of some "proof" (a poor grade, a flubbed response in class), one's fear of inferiority—inculcated in ways large and small by society—will be confirmed as real. On a university campus, where intelligence itself is the ultimate measure, this anxiety is bound to be triggered.

A black student I met at UCLA was disturbed a little when I asked him if he ever felt vulnerable—anxious about "black inferiority"—as a black student. But after a long pause, he finally said, "I think I do." The example he gave was of a large lecture class he'd taken with more than 300 students. Fifty or so black students sat in the back of the lecture hall and "acted out every stereotype in the book." They were loud, ate food, came in late—and generally got lower grades than the whites in the class. "I knew I would be seen like them, and I didn't like it. I never sat by them." Seen like what? I asked, though we both knew the answer. "As lazy, ignorant, and stupid," he said sadly.

Had the group at the back been white fraternity brothers, they would not have been seen as dumb *whites*, of course. And a frat brother who worried about his grades would not worry that he would be seen "like them." The terror in this situation for the student I spoke with was that his own deeply buried anxiety would be given credence, that the myth would be verified, and that he would feel shame and humiliation not because of who he was but simply because he was black. In this lecture hall his race, quite apart from his performance, might subject him to four unendurable feelings—diminishment, accountability to the preconceptions of whites, a powerlessness to change those preconceptions, and, finally, shame. These are the feelings that make up his racial anxiety, and that of all blacks on any campus. On a white campus a black is never far from these feelings, and even his unconscious knowledge that he is subject to them can undermine his self-esteem. There are blacks on every campus who are not up to doing good college-level work. Certain black students may not be happy or motivated or in the appropriate field of study—*just like whites*. (Let us not forget that many white students get poor grades, fail, drop out.) Moreover, many more blacks than whites are not quite prepared for college, may have to catch up, owing to factors beyond their control: poor previous schooling, for example. But the white who has to catch up will not be anxious that his being behind is a matter of his whiteness, of his being *racially* inferior. The black student may well have such a fear.

This, I believe, is one reason why black colleges in America turn out 34 percent of all black college graduates, though they enroll only 17 percent of black college students. Without whites around on campus the myth of inferiority is in abeyance and, along with it, a great reservoir of culturally imposed self-doubt. On black campuses feelings of inferiority are personal; on campuses with a white majority, a black's problems have a way of becoming a "black" problem.

But this feeling of vulnerability a black may feel in itself is not as serious a problem as what he or she does with it. To admit that one is made anxious in integrated situations about the myth of racial inferiority is difficult for young blacks. It seems like admitting that one *is* racially inferior. And so, most often, the student will deny harboring those feelings. This is where some of the pangs of racial tension begin, because denial always involves distortion.

In order to deny a problem we must tell ourselves that the problem is something different than what it really is. A black student at Berkeley told me that he felt defensive every time he walked into a class and saw mostly white faces. When I asked why, he said, "Because I know they're all racists. They think blacks are stupid." Of course it may be true that some whites feel this way, but the singular focus on white racism allows this student to obscure his own underlying racial anxiety. He can now say that his problem—facing a class full of white faces, *fearing* that they think he is dumb—is entirely the result of certifiable white racism and has nothing to do with his own anxieties, or even that this particular academic subject may not be his best. Now all the terror of his anxiety, its powerful energy, is devoted to simply *seeing* racism. Whatever evidence of racism he finds—and looking this hard, he will no doubt find some—can be brought in to buttress his distorted view of the problem, while his actual deep-seated anxiety goes unseen.

Denial, and the distortion that results, places the problem *outside* the self and in the world. It is not that I have any inferiority anxiety because of my race; it is that I am going to school with people who don't like blacks. This is the shift in thinking that allows black students to reenact the protest pattern of the Sixties. Denied racial anxiety-distortion-reenactment is the process by which feelings of inferiority are transformed into an exaggerated white menace—which is then protested against with the techniques of the past. Under the sway of this process, black students believe that history is repeating itself, that it's just like the Sixties, or Fifties. In fact, it is the not yet healed wounds from the past, rather than the inequality that created the wounds, that is the real problem.

This process generates an unconscious need to exaggerate the level of racism on campus—to make it a matter of the system, not just a handful of    20 students. Racism is the avenue away from the true inner anxiety. How many students demonstrating for a black "theme house"—demonstrating in the style of the Sixties, when the battle was to win for blacks a place on campus—might be better off spending their time reading and studying? Black students have the highest dropout rate and lowest grade point average of any group in American universities. This need not be so. And it is not the result of not having black theme houses.

It was my very good fortune to go to college in 1964, when the question of black "inferiority" was openly talked about among blacks. The summer before I left for college I heard Martin Luther King, Jr., speak in Chicago, and he laid it on the line for black students everywhere. "When you are behind in a footrace, the only way to get ahead is to run faster than the man in front of you. So when your white roommate says he's tired and goes to sleep, you stay up and burn the midnight oil." His statement that we were "behind in a footrace" acknowledged that because of history, of few opportunities, of racism, we were, in a sense, "inferior." But this had to do with what had been done to our parents and their parents, not with inherent inferiority. And because it was acknowledged, it was presented to us as a challenge rather than a mark of shame.

Of the eighteen black students (in a student body of 1,000) who were on campus in my freshman year, all graduated, though a number of us were not from the middle class. At the university where I currently teach, the dropout rate for black students is 72 percent, despite the presence of several academic-support programs; a counseling center with black counselors; an Afro-American studies department; black faculty, administrators, and staff; a general education curriculum that emphasizes "cultural pluralism"; an Educational Opportunities Program; a mentor program; a black faculty and staff association; and an administration and faculty that often announce the need to do more for black students.

It may be unfair to compare my generation with the current one. Parents do this compulsively and to little end but self-congratulation. But I don't congratulate my generation. I think we were advantaged. We came along at a time when racial integration was held in high esteem. And integration was a very challenging social concept for both blacks and whites. We were remaking ourselves—that's what one did at college—and making history. We had something to prove. This was a profound advantage; it gave us clarity and a challenge. Achievement in the American mainstream was the goal of integration, and the best thing about this challenge was its secondary message—that we *could* achieve.

There is much irony in the fact that black power would come along in the late Sixties and change all this. Black power was a movement of uplift and pride, and yet it also delivered the weight of pride—a weight that would burden black students from then on. Black power "nationalized" the black identity, made blackness itself an object of celebration and allegiance. But if it transformed a mark of shame into a mark of pride, it also, in the name of

pride, required the denial of racial anxiety. Without a frank account of one's
anxieties, there is no clear direction, no concrete challenge. Black students
today do not get as clear a message from their racial identity as my generation got. They are not filled with the same urgency to prove themselves, because black pride has said, You're already proven, already equal, as good as
anybody.

The "black identity" shaped by black power most powerfully contrib-    25
utes to racial tensions on campuses by basing entitlement more on race
than on constitutional rights and standards of merit. With integration,
black entitlement was derived from constitutional principles of fairness.
Black power changed this by skewing the formula from rights to color—if
you were black, you were entitled. Thus, the United Coalition Against Racism (UCAR) at the University of Michigan could "demand" two years ago
that all black professors be given immediate tenure, that there be special
pay incentives for black professors, and that money be provided for an all-
black student union. In this formula, black becomes the very color of entitlement, an extra right in itself, and a very dangerous grandiosity is promoted in which blackness amounts to specialness.

Race is, by any standard, an unprincipled source of power. And on
campuses the use of racial power by one group makes racial or ethnic or
gender *difference* a currency of power for all groups. When I make my difference into power, other groups must seize upon their difference to contain
my power and maintain their position relative to me. Very quickly a kind of
politics of difference emerges in which racial, ethnic, and gender groups are
forced to assert their entitlement and vie for power based on the single
quality that makes them different from one another.

On many campuses today academic departments and programs are established on the basis of difference—black studies, women's studies, Asian
studies, and so on—despite the fact that there is nothing in these "difference" departments that cannot be studied within traditional academic
disciplines. If their rationale truly is past exclusion from the mainstream
curriculum, shouldn't the goal now be complete inclusion rather than sepa-
rateness? I think this logic is overlooked because these groups are too interested in the power their difference can bring, and they insist on separate departments and programs as a tribute to that power.

This politics of difference makes everyone on campus a member of a
minority group. It also makes racial tensions inevitable. To highlight one's
difference as a source of advantage is also, indirectly, to inspire the enemies
of that difference. When blackness (and femaleness) becomes power, then
white maleness is also sanctioned as power. A white male student at Stanford
told me, "One of my friends said the other day that we should get together
and start up a white student union and come up with a list of demands."

It is certainly true that white maleness has long been an unfair source
of power. But the sin of white male power is precisely its use of race and
gender as a source of entitlement. When minorities and women use their

race, ethnicity, and gender in the same way, they not only commit the same sin but also, indirectly, sanction the very form of power that oppressed them in the first place. The politics of difference is based on a tit-for-tat sort of logic in which every victory only calls one's enemies to arms.

This elevation of difference undermines the communal impulse by making each group foreign and inaccessible to others. When difference is celebrated rather than remarked, people must think in terms of difference, they must find meaning in difference, and this meaning comes from an end-less process of contrasting one's group with other groups. Blacks use whites to define themselves as different, women use men, Hispanics use whites and blacks, and on it goes. And in the process each group mythologizes and mystifies its difference, puts it beyond the full comprehension of outsiders. Difference becomes an inaccessible preciousness toward which outsiders are expected to be simply and uncomprehendingly reverential. But beware: In this world, even the insulated world of the college campus, preciousness is a balloon asking for a needle. At Smith College, graffiti appears: "Niggers, Spics, and Chinks quit complaining or get out." 30

Most of the white students I talked with spoke as if from under a faint cloud of accusation. There was always a ring of defensiveness in their com-plaints about blacks. A white student I spoke with at UCLA told me: "Most white students on this campus think the black student leadership here is made up of oversensitive crybabies who spend all their time looking for things to kick up a ruckus about." A white student at Stanford said: "Blacks do nothing but complain and ask for sympathy when everyone really knows they don't do well because they don't try. If they worked harder, they could do as well as everyone else."

That these students felt accused was most obvious in their compulsion to assure me that they were not racists. Oblique versions of some-of-my-best-friends-are stories came ritualistically before or after critiques of black students. Some said flatly, "I am not a racist, but. . . ." Of course, we all deny being racists, but we only do this compulsively, I think, when we are work-ing against an accusation of bias. I think it was the color of my skin, itself, that accused them.

This was the meta-message that surrounded these conversations like an aura, and in it, I believe, is the core of white American racial anxiety. My skin not only accused them, it judged them. And this judgment was a sad gift of history that brought them to account whether they deserved such an accounting or not. It said that wherever and whenever blacks were con-cerned, they had reason to feel guilt. And whether it was earned or un-earned, I think it was guilt that set off the compulsion in these students to disclaim. I believe it is true that in America black people make white people feel guilty.

Guilt is the essence of white anxiety, just as inferiority is the essence of black anxiety. And the terror that it carries for whites is the terror of discovering that one has reason to feel guilt where blacks are concerned — not so much because of what blacks might think but because of what guilt can say about oneself. If the darkest fear of blacks is inferiority, the darkest fear of whites is that their better lot in life is at least partially the result of their capacity for evil — their capacity to dehumanize an entire people for their own benefit, and then to be indifferent to the devastation their dehumanization has wrought on successive generations of their victims. This is the terror that whites are vulnerable to regarding blacks. And the mere fact of being white is sufficient to feel it, since even whites with hearts clean of racism benefit from being white — benefit at the expense of blacks. This is a conditional guilt having nothing to do with individual intentions or actions. And it makes for a very powerful anxiety because it threatens whites with a view of themselves as inhuman, just as inferiority threatens blacks with a similar view of themselves. At the dark core of both anxieties is a suspicion of incomplete humanity.

So the white students I met were not just meeting me; they were also    35
meeting the possibility of their own inhumanity. And this, I think, is what explains how some young white college students in the late Eighties can so frankly take part in racially insensitive and outright racist acts. They were expected to be cleaner of racism than any previous generation — they were born into the Great Society. But this expectation overlooks the fact that, for them, color is still an accusation and judgment. In black faces there is a discomforting reflection of white collective shame. Blacks remind them that their racial innocence is questionable, that they are the beneficiaries of past and present racism, and that the sins of the father may well have been visited on the children.

And yet young whites tell themselves that they had nothing to do with the oppression of black people. They have a stronger belief in their racial innocence than any previous generation of whites, and a natural hostility toward anyone who would challenge that innocence. So (with a great deal of individual variation) they can end up in the paradoxical position of being hostile to blacks as a way of defending their own racial innocence.

I think this is what the young white editors of the *Dartmouth Review* were doing when they shamelessly harassed William Cole, a black music professor. Weren't they saying, in effect, I am so free of racial guilt that I can afford to ruthlessly attack blacks and still be racially innocent? The ruthlessness of that attack was a form of denial, a badge of innocence. The more they were charged with racism, the more ugly and confrontational their harassment became. Racism became a means of rejecting racial guilt, a way of showing that they were not ultimately racists.

The politics of difference sets up a struggle for innocence among all groups. When difference is the currency of power, each group must fight for the innocence that entitles it to power. Blacks sting whites with guilt, remind them of their racist past, accuse them of new and more subtle forms of racism. One way whites retrieve their innocence is to discredit blacks and deny their difficulties, for in this denial is the denial of their own guilt. To blacks this denial looks like racism, a racism that feeds black innocence and encourages them to throw more guilt at whites. And so the cycle continues. The politics of difference leads each group to pick at the sore spots of the other.

Men and women who run universities—whites, mostly—also participate in the politics of difference, although they handle their guilt differently than many of their students. They don't deny it, but still they don't want to *feel* it. And to avoid this *feeling* of guilt they have tended to go along with whatever blacks put on the table rather than work with them to assess their real needs. University administrators have too often been afraid of their own guilt and have relied on negotiation and capitulation more to appease that guilt than to help blacks and other minorities. Administrators would never give white students a racial theme house where they could be "more comfortable with people of their own kind," yet more and more universities are doing this for black students, thus fostering a kind of voluntary segregation. To avoid the anxieties of integrated situations, blacks ask for theme houses; to avoid guilt, white administrators give them theme houses.

When everyone is on the run from his anxieties about race, race relations on campus can be reduced to the negotiation of avoidances. A pattern of demand and concession develops in which each side uses the other to escape itself. Black studies departments, black deans of student affairs, black counseling programs, Afro houses, black theme houses, black homecoming dances and graduation ceremonies—black students and white administrators have slowly engineered a machinery of separatism that, in the name of sacred difference, redraws the ugly lines of segregation.   40

Black students have not sufficiently helped themselves, and universities, despite all their concessions, have not really done much for blacks. If both faced their anxieties, I think they would see the same thing: Academic parity with all other groups should be the overriding mission of black students, and it should also be the first goal that universities have for their black students. Blacks can only *know* they are as good as others when they are, in fact, as good—when their grades are higher and their dropout rate lower. Nothing under the sun will substitute for this, and no amount of concessions will bring it about.

Universities and colleges can never be free of guilt until they truly help black students, which means leading and challenging them rather than negotiating and capitulating. It means inspiring them to achieve academic parity, nothing less, and helping them see their own weaknesses as their greatest challenge. It also means dismantling the machinery of separatism, breaking the link between difference and power, and skewing the formula for entitlement away from race and gender and back to constitutional rights.

As for the young white students who have rediscovered swastikas and the word "nigger," I think they suffer from an exaggerated sense of their own innocence, as if they were incapable of evil and beyond the reach of guilt. But it is also true that the politics of difference creates an environment which threatens their innocence and makes them defensive. White students are not invited to the negotiating table from which they see blacks and others walk away with concessions. The presumption is that they do not deserve to be there because they are white. So they can only be defensive, and the less mature among them will be aggressive. Guerrilla activity will ensue. Of course this is wrong, but it is also a reflection of an environment where difference carries power and where whites have the wrong "difference."

I think universities should emphasize commonality as a higher value than "diversity" and "pluralism"—buzzwords for the politics of difference. Difference that does not rest on a clearly delineated foundation of commonality not only is inaccessible to those who are not part of the ethnic or racial group but is antagonistic to them. Difference can enrich only the common ground.

Integration has become an abstract term today, having to do with little    45
more than numbers and racial balances. But it once stood for a high and admirable set of values. It made difference second to commonality, and it asked members of all races to face whatever fears they inspired in each other. I doubt the word will have a new vogue, but the values, under whatever name, are worth working for.

---

*For Discussion*

1. Steele claims that "racial tension on campus [now] is the result more of racial equality than inequality" (paragraph 6). How does he support this contention? Do you find it convincing? Why or why not? Test his assertion against what you see around you. Are blacks and other minorities treated equally on your campus?

2. Steele has much to say about what he calls a "politics of difference" (paragraph 8) on college campuses. How exactly does he depict it? In paragraphs 26–30, he presents an argument against it. What reasons make up the case? Judging from what you know of American history, is this politics of difference new? Is it restricted to college campuses?

3. How does Steele view the influence of black power? Do you find it persuasive? Why or why not?

4. How does Steele explain the anxieties of black and white students? Do you agree that "[a]t the dark core of both anxieties is a suspicion of incomplete humanity" (paragraph 34)? How might this diagnosis apply to women on campus? to gay men and lesbians? to minority races other than blacks?

*For Research, Discussion, and Convincing*

Conduct research as Steele did—by interviewing students. (Chapter 5 provides guidelines for conducting interviews.) Talk to members of all races and significant ethnic groups on your campus. Pose the kind of questions Steele did, along with any questions his conclusions suggest to you. Record or take careful notes about what your interviewees say. Then meet as a class and discuss how to interpret and explain the responses.

Finally, write an essay about some aspect of difference on your campus—it need not be black versus white. Attempt, as Steele does, to get to "the hidden internality of things" (paragraph 5), the deeper sources of tension and anxiety. Propose ways to cope better with the aspect of difference you isolate for analysis.

---

# The Distribution of Distress
### Patricia J. Williams

*The previous selection explored the "new racism" on campus; this one takes us from the campus to society at large and explores prejudice of several kinds, some of it masked so well that we do not recognize it as prejudice. Chief among these is classism, prejudice based not on skin color or ethnic origin but on socioeconomic differences. If, as the American social critic H. L. Mencken contended, class is the "dirty little secret" of American life, this author tells it eloquently and memorably.*

*Patricia Williams is a law professor, columnist for* The Nation, *and author of* Seeing a Color-Blind Future: The Paradox of Race *(1997), from which the following selection comes.*

Many years ago, I was standing in a so-called juice bar in Berkeley, California. A young man came in whom I had often seen begging in the neighborhood. A more bruised-looking human one could not imagine: he was missing several teeth, his clothes were in rags, his blond hair was matted, his eyes red-rimmed, his nails long and black and broken. On this particular morning he came into the juice bar and ordered some sort of protein drink from the well-scrubbed, patchouli-scented young woman behind the counter. It was obvious that his presence disturbed her, and when he took his drink and mumbled, "Thanks, little lady," she exploded.

"Don't you dare call me 'little lady'!" she snarled with a ferocity that turned heads. "I'm a *woman* and you'd better learn the difference!"

"Sorry," he whispered with his head bowed, like a dog that had been kicked, and he quite literally limped out of the store.

"Good riddance," the woman called after him.

This took place some fifteen years ago, but I have always remembered    5
the interchange because it taught me a lot about the not so subliminal messages that can be wrapped in the expression of Virtue Aggrieved, in which antibias of one sort is used to further the agenda of bias of another kind.

In an abstract sense, I understood the resentment for girlish diminutives. Too often as a lawyer I have been in courtroom situations where coy terms of endearment were employed in such a way that "the little lady, God-bless-her" became a marginalizing condescension, a precise condensation of "She thinks she's a lawyer, poor thing." Yet in this instance, gender power was clearly not the issue, but rather the emotional venting of a revulsion at this man's dirty and bedraggled presence. It wasn't just that he had called her a little lady; she seemed angry that he had dared address her at all.

If, upon occasion, the ploughshare of feminism can be beaten into a sword of class prejudice, no less can there be other examples of what I call battling biases, in which the impulse to antidiscrimination is defeated by the intrusion or substitution of a different object of enmity. This revolving door of revulsions is one of the trickiest mechanisms contributing to the enduring nature of prejudice; it is at heart, I suppose, a kind of traumatic reiteration of injurious encounters, preserving even as it transforms the overall history of rage.

I was in England several years ago when a young Asian man was severely beaten in East London by a young white man. I was gratified to see the immediate renunciation of racism that ensued in the media. It was a somewhat more sophisticated and heartfelt collective self-examination than sometimes occurs in the United States in the wake of such incidents, where, I fear, we are much more jaded about all forms of violence. Nevertheless, what intrigued me most about the media coverage of this assault was the unfortunate way in which class bias became a tool for the denunciation of racism.

"Racial, Ethnic, or Religious Prejudice Is Repugnant," screamed the headlines.

Hooray, I thought.                                                                                  10

And then the full text: "It is repugnant, *particularly*"—and I'm embellishing here—"when committed by a miserable low-class cockney whose bestial nature knows no plummeted depth, etc. etc."

Oh dear, I thought.

In other words, the media not only defined anti-Asian and anti-immigrant animus as ignorance, as surely it is, but went on to define that ignorance as the property of a class, of "the" lower classes, implying even that a good Oxbridge education inevitably lifts one above that sort of thing. As surely it does not.

And therein lies a problem, I think. If race or ethnicity is not a synonym for either ignorance or foreignness, then neither should class be an explanatory trashbin for racial prejudice, domestic incivility, and a host of other social ills. If the last fifty years have taught us nothing else, it is that our "isms" are no less insidious when beautifully polished and terribly refined.

None of us is beyond some such pitfalls, and in certain contexts type-         15
casting can even be a necessary and helpful way of explaining the social world. The hard task is to untangle the instances where the categoric helps us predict and prepare for the world from those instances where it verges on scapegoating, projection, and prejudice.

To restate the problem, I think that the persistence of racism, ethnic and religious intolerance, as well as gender and class bias, is dependent upon recirculating images in which the general and the particular duel each other endlessly.

"*En garde*, you heathenish son of an inferior category!"

"Brute!" comes the response. "I am inalienably endowed with the unique luminosity of my rational individualism; it is you who are the guttural eruption of an unspeakable subclassification . . ."

Thrust and parry, on and on, the play of race versus ethnicity versus class versus blood feud. One sword may be sharper or quicker, but neither's wound is ever healed.

Too often these tensions are resolved simply by concluding that stereo-    20
typing is just our lot as humans so let the consequences fall where they
may. But stereotyping operates as habit not immutable trait, a fluid project
that rather too easily flows across the shifting ecology of human relations.
And racism is a very old, very bad habit.

This malleability of prejudice is underscored by a little cultural comparison. If class bias has skewed discussions of racism in the British examples I
have just described, it is rather more common in the United States for race
to consume discussions of class altogether. While I don't want to overstate
the cultural differences between the United States and the United Kingdom—there is enough similarity to conclude that race and class present a
generally interlocking set of problems in both nations—the United States
does deem itself classless with almost the same degree of self-congratulation
that the United Kingdom prides itself on being largely free of a history of
racial bias. Certainly these are good impulses and desirable civic sentiments, but I am always one to look closely at what is deemed beyond the
pale. *It will never happen here* . . . The noblest denials are at least as interesting study as the highest ideals.

Consider: for a supposedly classless society, the United States nevertheless suffers the greatest gap of any industrialized nation between its richest
and poorest citizens. And there can be no more dramatic and ironic class
consciousness than the Dickensian characteristics ascribed to those in the
so-called underclass, as opposed to the rest—what are we to call them, the
*over*class? Those who are deemed to have class versus those who are so far
beneath the usual indicia of even lower class that they are deemed to have
no class at all.

If this is not viewed by most Americans as a problem of class stasis, it
is perhaps because class denominations are so uniformly understood to
be stand-ins for race. The very term *underclass* is a *euphemism* for blackness,
class operating as euphemism in that we Americans are an upbeat kind of
people and class is usually thought to be an easier problem than race.

Middle-classness, on the other hand, is so persistently a euphemism for
whiteness, that middle-class black people are sometimes described as "hon-
orary whites" or as those who have been deracinated in some vaguely political sense. More often than I like to remember, I have been told that my
opinion about this or that couldn't possibly be relevant to "real," "authentic" black people. Why? Simply because I don't sound like a Hollywood
stereotype of the way black people are "supposed" to talk. "Speaking white"
or "Talking black." No in-between. Speaking as a black person while sounding like a white person has, I have found, engendered some complicated
sense of betrayal. *"You're* not black! You're not *white!"* No one seems particularly interested in the substantive ideas being expressed; but everyone is
caught up with the question of whether anyone should have to listen to a
white-voiced black person.

It is in this way that we often talk about class and race such that we    25
sometimes end up talking about neither, because we insist on talking about

race as though it were class and class as though it were race, and it's hard to see very clearly when the waters are so muddied with all that simile and metaphor.

By the same token, America is usually deemed a society in which the accent with which one speaks Does Not Matter. That is largely true, but it is not so where black accents are concerned. While there is much made of regional variations—New Yorkers, Minnesotans, and Southerners are the butts of a certain level of cheap satire—an accent deemed "black" is the one with some substantial risk of evoking outright discrimination. In fact, the speech of real black people ranges from true dialects to myriad patois, to regional accents, to specific syntactical twists or usages of vocabulary. Yet language identified as black is habitually flattened into some singularized entity that in turn becomes synonymous with ignorance, slang, big lips and sloppy tongues, incoherent ideas, and very bad—terribly unruly!—linguistic acts. Black speech becomes a cipher for all the other stereotypes associated with racial discrimination; the refusal to understand becomes rationalized by the assumption of incomprehensibility.

My colleague Professor Mari Matsuda has studied cases involving accent discrimination. She writes of lawsuits whose transcripts revealed an interesting paradox. One case featured a speaker whose accent had been declared incomprehensible by his employer. Nevertheless, his recorded testimony, copied down with no difficulty by the court reporter, revealed a parlance more grammatically accurate, substantively coherent, and syntactically graceful than any other speaker in the courtroom, including the judge. This paradox has always been the subject of some interest among linguists and sociolinguists, the degree to which language is understood in a way that is intimately linked to relations among speakers.

"Good day," I say to you. Do you see me as a genial neighbor, as part of your day? If so, you may be generously disposed to return the geniality with a hearty "Hale fellow, well met."

"Good day," I say. Do you see me as an impudent upstart the very sound of whose voice is an unwelcome intrusion upon your good day? If so, the greeting becomes an act of aggression; woe betide the cheerful, innocent upstart.

"Shall we consider race?" I say to you. If you are disposed to like me, 30 you might hear this as an invitation to a kind of conversation we have not shared before, a leap of faith into knowing more about each other.

"Shall we consider race?" I say. *Not* "Shall I batter you with guilt before we riot in the streets?" But only: "Shall we *consider* race?" Yet if I am that same upstart, the blood will have boiled up in your ears by now, and very shortly you will start to have tremors from the unreasonable audacity of my meddlesome presumption. Nothing I actually say will matter, for what matters is that I am out of place . . .

This dynamic, this vital ingredient of the willingness to hear, is apparent in the contradiction of lower-status speech being simultaneously understood yet not understood. Why is the sound of black voices, the shape of black bodies so overwhelmingly agreeable, so colorfully comprehensible in some contexts, particularly in the sports and entertainment industries, yet deemed so utterly incapable of effective communication or acceptable presence when it comes to finding a job as a construction worker?

This is an odd conundrum, to find the sight and the sound of oneself a red flag. And it is a kind of banner, one's face and one's tongue, a banner of family and affiliation—that rhythm and stress, the buoyance of one's mother's tongue; that plane of jaw, that prominence of brow, the property of one's father's face. What to make of those social pressures that would push the region of the body underground in order to allow the purity of one's inner soul to be more fully seen? When Martin Luther King, Jr., urged that we be judged by the content of our character, surely he meant that what we looked like should not matter. Yet just as surely that enterprise did not involve having to deny the entirely complicated symbolic character of one's physical manifestation. This is a hard point, I confess, and one fraught with risk of misunderstanding. The color of one's skin is a part of ourselves. It does not matter. It is precious, and yet it should not matter; it is important and yet it must not matter. It is simultaneously our greatest vanity and anxiety, and I am of the opinion, like Martin Luther King, that none of this should matter.

Yet let me consider the question of self-erasure. I've written elsewhere about my concern that various forms of biotechnological engineering have been turned to such purposes—from skin lighteners to cosmetic surgery to the market for sperm with blond hair and eggs with high IQs. Consider the boy I read about who had started some sort of computer magazine for children. A young man of eleven, celebrated as a computer whiz, whose family had emigrated from Puerto Rico, now living in New York. The article recounted how much he loved computers because, he said, nobody judged him for what he looked like, and he could speak without an accent. What to make of this freedom as disembodiment, this technologically purified mental communion as escape from the society of others, as neutralized social space. What a delicate project, this looking at each other, seeing yet not staring. Would we look so hard, judge so hard, be so hard—what would we look like?—if we existed unself-consciously in our bodies—sagging, gray-haired, young, old, black, white, balding and content?

Let me offer a more layered illustration of the way in which these issues of race and class interact, the markers of class distinction and bias in the United Kingdom emerging also in the United States as overlapping substantially with the category of race. A few years ago, I purchased a house. Because the house was in a different state than where I was located at the time, I obtained my mortgage by telephone. I am a prudent little squirrel when it comes to things financial, always tucking away sufficient stores of nuts for the winter, and so I meet all the criteria of a quite good credit risk. My loan was approved almost immediately.

A short time after, the contract came in the mail. Among the papers the bank forwarded were forms documenting compliance with what is called the Fair Housing Act. It is against the law to discriminate against black people in the housing market, and one of the pieces of legislation to that effect is the Fair Housing Act, a law that monitors lending practices to prevent banks from doing what is called "red-lining." Red-lining is a phenomenon whereby banks circle certain neighborhoods on the map and refuse to lend in those areas for reasons based on race. There are a number of variations on the theme. Black people cannot get loans to purchase homes in white areas; or black people cannot get start-up money for small businesses in black areas. The Fair Housing Act thus tracks the race of all banking customers to prevent such discrimination. Unfortunately, some banks also use the racial information disclosed on the Fair Housing forms to engage in precisely the discrimination the law seeks to prevent.

I should repeat that to this point my entire mortgage transaction had been conducted by telephone. I should also say that I speak what is considered in the States a very Received-Standard-English, regionally northeastern perhaps, but not marked as black. With my credit history, with my job as a law professor, and no doubt with my accent, I am not only middle-class but match the cultural stereotype of a good white person. It is thus perhaps that the loan officer of this bank, whom I had never met in person, had checked off a box on the Fair Housing form indicating that I *was* "white."

Race shouldn't matter, I suppose, but it seemed to in this case, and so I took a deep breath, crossed out "white," checked the box marked "black," and sent the contract back to the bank. That will teach them to presume too much, I thought. A done deal, I assumed.

Suddenly said deal came to a screeching halt. The bank wanted more money as a down payment, they wanted me to pay more points, they wanted to raise the rate of interest. Suddenly I found myself facing great resistance and much more debt.

What was most interesting about all this was that the reason the bank gave for its newfound recalcitrance was not race, heaven forbid — racism doesn't exist anymore, hadn't I heard? No, the reason they gave was that property values in that neighborhood were suddenly falling. They wanted more money to cover the increased risk.

40

Initially, I was surprised, confused. The house was in a neighborhood that was extremely stable; prices in the area had not gone down since World War II, only slowly, steadily up. I am an extremely careful shopper and I had uncovered absolutely no indication that prices were falling at all.

It took my real estate agent to make me see the light. "Don't you get it," he sighed. "This is what they always do."

And even though I work with this sort of thing all the time, I really hadn't gotten it: for of course, *I* was the reason the prices were in peril.

The bank was proceeding according to demographic data that show any time black people move into a neighborhood in the States, whites are overwhelmingly likely to move out. In droves. In panic. In concert. Pulling every imaginable resource with them, from school funding to garbage collection to social workers who don't want to work in black neighborhoods to police whose too frequent relation to black communities is a corrupted one of containment rather than protection.

It's called a tipping point, this thing that happens when black people     45
move into white neighborhoods. The imagery is awfully catchy you must admit: the neighborhood just tipping right on over like a terrible accident, whoops! Like a pitcher I suppose. All that nice fresh wholesome milk spilling out, running away . . . leaving the dark, echoing, upended urn of the inner city.

This immense fear of "the black" next door is one reason the United States is so densely segregated. Only two percent of white people have a black neighbor, even though black people constitute approximately thirteen percent of the population. White people fear black people in big ways, in small ways, in financial ways, in utterly incomprehensible ways.

As for my mortgage, I threatened to sue and eventually procured the loan on the original terms. But what was fascinating to me about this whole incident was the way in which it so exemplified the new problems of the new rhetoric of racism. For starters, the new rhetoric of racism never mentions race. It wasn't race but risk with which the bank was concerned. Second, since financial risk is all about economics, my exclusion got reclassified as just a consideration of class, and there's no law against class discrimination, after all, for that would present a restraint on one of our most precious liberties, the freedom to contract or not. If public schools, trains, buses, swimming pools, and neighborhoods remain segregated, it's no longer a racial problem if someone who just happens to be white keeps hiking the price for someone who just accidentally and purely by the way happens to be black. White people set higher prices for the "right," the "choice" of self-segregation. If black people don't move in, it's just that they can't *afford* to. Black people pay higher prices for the attempt to integrate, even as the integration of oneself is a threat to one's investment by lowering its value.

By this measure of mortgage worthiness, the ingredient of blackness is cast not just as a social toll but as an actual tax. A fee, an extra contribution at the door, an admission charge for the higher costs of handling my dangerous propensities, my inherently unsavory properties. I was not judged based on my independent attributes or individual financial worth as a client; nor even was I judged by statistical profiles of what my group actually do. (For, in fact, anxiety-stricken, middle-class black people make grovelingly good cake-baking neighbors when not made to feel defensive by the unfortunate, historical welcome strategies of bombs, burnings, or abandon.)

Rather, I was being evaluated based on what an abstraction of White Society writ large thinks we — or I — do, and that imagined "doing" was treated and thus established as a self-fulfilling prophecy.

However rationalized, this form of discrimination is a burden: one's     50
very existence becomes a lonely vacuum when so many in society not only

devalue *me*, but devalue *themselves* and their homes for having me as part of the landscaped view from the quiet of their breakfast nook.

I know, I know, I exist in the world on my own terms surely. I am an individual and all that. But if I carry the bank's logic out with my individuality rather than my collectively imagined effect on property values as the subject of this type of irrational economic computation, then *I*, the charming and delightful Patricia J. Williams, become a bit like a car wash in your backyard. Only much worse in real price terms. I am more than a mere violation of the nice residential comfort zone in question; my blackness can rezone altogether by the mere fortuity of my relocation.

"Dumping district," cringes the nice, clean actuarial family next door; "there goes the neighborhood . . ." as whole geographic tracts slide into the chasm of impecuniousness and disgust. I am the economic equivalent of a medical waste disposal site, a toxic heap-o'-home.

In my brand-new house, I hover behind my brand-new kitchen curtains, wondering whether the very appearance of my self will endanger my collateral yet further. When Benetton ran an advertisement that darkened Queen Elizabeth II's skin to a nice rich brown, the *Sun* newspaper ran an article observing that this "obviously cheapens the monarchy." Will the presentation of my self so disperse the value of my own, my ownership, my property?

This is madness, I am sure, as I draw the curtain like a veil across my nose. In what order of things is it *rational* to thus hide and skulk?

It is an intolerable logic. An investment in my property compels a selling of myself.                                                                                   55

I grew up in a white neighborhood where my mother's family had been the only black people for about fifty years. In the 1960s, Boston began to feel the effects of the great migration of Southern blacks to the north that came about as a result of the Civil Rights Movement. Two more black families moved into the neighborhood. There was a sudden churning, a chemical response, a collective roiling with streams of froth and jets of steam. We children heard all about it on the playground. The neighborhood was under siege. The blacks were coming. My schoolmates' parents were moving out *en masse*.

It was remarkable. The neighborhood was entirely black within about a year.

I am a risk pool. I am a car wash.

I was affected, I suppose, growing up with those children who frightened themselves by imagining what it would be like to touch black bodies, to kiss those wide unkissable lips, to draw the pure breath of life through that crude and forbidden expanse of nose; is it really possible that a gentle God—their God, dear God—would let a *human* heart reside within the wet charred thickness of black skin?

I am, they told me, a jumble of discarded parts: low-browed monkey bones and infected, softly pungent flesh.                                                         60

In fact, my price on the market is a variable affair. If I were crushed and sorted into common elements, my salt and juice and calcinated bits are worth approximately five English pounds. Fresh from the kill, in contrast, my body parts, my lungs and liver, heart and healthy arteries, would fetch some forty thousand. There is no demand for the fruit of my womb, however; eggs fresh from their warm dark sanctuary are worthless on the open market. "Irish Egg Donor Sought," reads an ad in the little weekly newspaper that serves New York City's parent population. And in the weird economy of bloodlines, and with the insidious variability of prejudice, "Irish eggs" command a price of upwards of five thousand pounds.

This silent market in black worth is pervasive. When a certain brand of hiking boots became popular among young people in Harlem, the manufacturer pulled the product from inner-city stores, fearing that such a trend would "ruin" the image of their boot among the larger market of whites.

It's funny . . . even shoes.

Last year I had a funny experience in a shoe store. The salesman would bring me only one shoe, not two.

"I can't try on a pair?" I asked in disbelief.                                                65

"When you pay for a pair," he retorted. "What if there were a hundred of you," he continued. "How would we keep track?"

I was the only customer in the store, but there were a hundred of me in his head.

In our Anglo-American jurisprudence there is a general constraint limiting the right to sue to cases and controversies affecting the individual. As an individual, I could go to the great and ridiculous effort of suing for the minuscule amount at stake in waiting for the other shoe to drop from his hand; but as for the real claim, the group claim, the larger defamation to all those other hundreds of me . . . well, that will be a considerably tougher row to hoe.

I am one, I am many.

I am amiable, orderly, extremely honest, and a very good neighbor indeed. I am suspect profile, market cluster, actuarial monster, statistical being.     70

My particulars battle the generals.

"Typecasting!" I protest.

"Predictive indicator," assert the keepers of the gate.

"Prejudice!" I say.

"Precaution," they reply.                                                            75

Hundreds, even thousands, of me hover in the breach.

---

*For Discussion*

1. Williams opens her essay with two examples of what she calls "battling biases," one kind of enmity substituting for another. Have you witnessed "this revolving door of revulsions" yourself? When? Un-

der what circumstances? Did you recognize the prejudice of the person resisting prejudice or not?

2. "[I]n certain contexts," Williams says, "typecasting can be a necessary and helpful way of explaining the social world." What contexts? Can you offer examples of when typecasting was necessary and useful? When does typecasting verge "on scapegoating, projection, and prejudice"?

3. Williams alleges that, in contrast to Britain, a very class-conscious society, in the United States "it is rather more common . . . for race to consume discussions of class altogether." Do you see her point in your own experience? Why might class prejudice mask itself as race prejudice in the United States?

4. Williams says that accent prejudice — judging people based on their speech, which often reveals regional and class origins — is more a problem for blacks than for other races. Can you think of examples of stereotyping based on speech differences involving other races? How did the stereotypes affect your behavior?

## For Research and Inquiry

Much has been written in recent years about the problems of the black middle class, the forty percent or so of African Americans whom most would say are relatively well off. Williams gives us some insight into the tensions and conflicts of black middle-class life, but let's find out more by reading some of the literature and discussing these problems openly with students from all racial and social backgrounds.

What does the literature identify as sources of problems? Are the difficulties serious? Are they essentially different from the struggles of the white majority or from other minorities? If so, how exactly? Are the problems temporary, or are they likely to remain problems for many years to come? What strategies do blacks use to cope with their situation? Does the rest of middle-class America need to be aware of the resentments of black members of their class? Would awareness by itself be helpful?

Compare what the literature says with your own experience or the experiences of classmates whose backgrounds might provide special insight into the issue and questions.

After full class discussion, write an essay offering a tentative "reading" — that is, interpretation — of black middle-class consciousness. Consider especially the future: Will race/class problems be different from those faced by your parents?

## For Further Research and Discussion

1. For most of U.S. history, racial conflict stemmed from the unequal balance of power between white Europeans on the one hand and Native Americans, blacks, and Hispanics on the other. But more recently, racial tensions have been complicated by the influx of many

new racial and ethnic minorities. Who are they? What do you know about them?

Divide the class into groups, and with your group do intensive research on one of the United States' new minorities; summarize the results of your group research to the rest of the class. Then ask, How do the background and conditions of these new minorities resemble those of the older ones? How are they unique?

2. Much has been written about the breakdown of the American family—especially the black family. Find out as much as you can about what is happening to the black family and why. How much of our present racial problems can be traced to the virtual disappearance of the traditional family, especially in urban ghettos?

## Additional Suggestions for Writing

1. *Persuading.* Much has been written about so-called voluntary segregation, such as the black theme houses Steele mentions. Write an essay for your school paper or some other suitable publication arguing for or against such theme houses.

2. *Inquiry.* Examine yourself for traces of racism, new or old. In what ways and to what degree are you guilty of race stereotyping, avoiding people of other races, and so forth? Do you sometimes feel the "racial anxiety" that Steele found in both black and white students? Where did you acquire whatever residual racism you have? What can you do to overcome it? What should universities do to help students and professors recognize and cope with latent racism?

3. *Research and Convincing.* The Thernstroms contend that affirmative action is at most responsible for increasing the size of the black professional class, a small percentage of the black middle class. Is this true? Conduct research into affirmative action in an effort to confirm or disconfirm their contention.

Write a letter to the editor of the *Brookings Review* that takes a definite stance on the Thernstroms's view of the impact of affirmative action. Support your stance with recent and authoritative information on the program.

# Appendix

# A Short Guide to Editing and Proofreading

Editing and proofreading are the final steps in creating a finished piece of writing. Too often, however, these steps are rushed as writers race to meet a deadline. Ideally, you should distinguish between the acts of revising, editing, and proofreading. Because each step requires that you pay attention to something different, you cannot reasonably expect to do them well if you try to do them all at once.

Our suggestions for revising appear in each of Chapters 6–9 on the aims of argument. Revising means shaping and developing the whole argument with an eye to audience and purpose; when you revise, you are ensuring that you have accomplished your aim. Editing, on the other hand, means making smaller changes within paragraphs and sentences. When you edit, you are thinking about whether your prose will be a pleasure to read. Editing improves the sound and rhythm of your voice. It makes complicated ideas more accessible to readers and usually makes your writing more concise. Finally, proofreading means eliminating errors. When you proofread, you correct everything you find that will annoy readers, such as misspellings, punctuation mistakes, and faulty grammar.

In this appendix, we offer some basic advice on what to look for when editing and proofreading. For more detailed help, consult a handbook on grammar and punctuation and a good book on style, such as Joseph Williams's *Ten Lessons in Clarity and Grace* or Richard Lanham's *Revising Prose*. Both of these texts guided our thinking in the advice that follows.

## EDITING

Most ideas can be phrased in a number of ways, each of which gives the idea a slightly distinctive twist. Consider the following examples:

In New York City, about 74,000 people die each year.

In New York City, death comes to one in a hundred people each year.

Death comes to one in a hundred New Yorkers each year.

To begin an article on what becomes of the unknown and unclaimed dead in New York, Edward Conlon wrote the final of these three sentences. We can only speculate about the possible variations he considered, but because openings are so crucial, he almost certainly cast these words quite deliberately.

For most writers, such deliberation over matters of style occurs during editing. In this late stage of the writing process, writers examine choices made earlier, perhaps unconsciously, while drafting and revising. They listen to how sentences sound, to patterns of rhythm both within and among sentences. Editing is like an art or craft; it can provide you the satisfaction of knowing you've said something gracefully and effectively. To focus on language this closely, you will need to set aside enough time following the revision step.

In this section, we discuss some things to look for when editing your own writing. Don't forget, though, that editing does not always mean looking for weaknesses. You should also recognize passages that work well just as you wrote them, that you can leave alone or play up more by editing passages that surround them.

## Editing for Clarity and Conciseness

Even drafts revised several times may have wordy and awkward passages; these are often places where a writer struggled with uncertainty or felt less than confident about the point being made. Introductions often contain such passages. In editing, you have one more opportunity to clarify and sharpen your ideas.

### Express Main Ideas Forcefully

Emphasize the main idea of a sentence by stating it as directly as possible, using the two key sentence parts (*subject* and *verb*) to convey the two key parts of the idea (*agent* and *act*).

As you edit, first look for sentences that state ideas indirectly rather than directly; such sentences may include (1) overuse of the verb *to be* in its various forms (*is, was, will have been,* and so forth), (2) the opening words "There is . . ." or "It is . . . ," (3) strings of prepositional phrases, or (4) many vague nouns. Then ask, "What is my true subject here, and what is that subject's action?" Here is an example of a weak, indirect sentence:

> It is a fact that the effects of pollution are more evident in lower-class neighborhoods than in middle-class ones.

The writer's subject is pollution. What is the pollution's action? Limply, the sentence tells us its "effects" are "evident." The following edited version makes pollution the agent that performs the action of a livelier verb, "fouls." The edited sentence is more specific—without being longer.

> *Pollution* more frequently *fouls* the air, soil, and water of lower-class neighborhoods than of middle-class ones.

*Editing Practice*

The following passage about a plan for creating low-income housing contains two weak sentences. In this case, the weakness results from wordiness. (Note the overuse of vague nouns and prepositional phrases.) Decide what the true subject is for each sentence, and make that word the subject of the verb. Your edited version should be much shorter.

> As in every program, there will be the presence of a few who abuse the system. However, as in other social programs, the numbers would not be sufficient to justify the rejection of the program on the basis that one person in a thousand will try to cheat.

*Choose Carefully between Active and Passive Voice*

Active voice and passive voice indicate different relationships between subjects and verbs. As we have noted, ideas are usually clearest when the writer's true subject is also the subject of the verb in the sentence—that is, when it is the agent of the action. In the passive voice, however, the agent of the action appears in the predicate or not at all. Rather than acting as agent, the subject of the sentence *receives* the action of the verb.

The following sentence is in the passive voice:

> The air of poor neighborhoods is often fouled by pollution.

There is nothing incorrect about the use of the passive voice in this sentence, and in the context of a whole paragraph, passive voice can be the most emphatic way to make a point. (Here, for example, it allows the word *pollution* to fall at the end of the sentence, a strong position.) But, often, use of the passive voice is not a deliberate choice at all but rather a vague and unspecific way of stating a point.

Consider the following sentences, in which the main verbs have no agents:

> It *is believed* that dumping garbage at sea is not as harmful to the environment as *was* once *thought*.
>
> Ronald Reagan *was considered* the "Great Communicator."

Who thinks such dumping is not so harmful? environmental scientists? industrial producers? Who considered former president Reagan a great communicator? speech professors? news commentators? Such sentences are clearer when they are written in the active voice:

> Some environmentalists believe that dumping garbage at sea is not as harmful to the environment as they used to think.
>
> Media commentators considered Ronald Reagan the "Great Communicator."

In editing for the passive voice, look over your verbs. Passive voice is easily recognized because it always contains (1) some form of *to be* as a helping verb and (2) the main verb in its past participle form (which ends in *-ed, -d, -t, -en,* or *-n,* or in some cases may be irregular: *drunk, sung, lain,* and so on).

When you find a sentence phrased in the passive voice, decide who or what is performing the action; the agent may appear after the verb or not at all. Then decide if changing the sentence to the active voice will improve the sentence as well as the surrounding passage.

*Editing Practice*

1. The following paragraph from a student's argument needs to be edited for emphasis. It is choking with excess nouns and forms of the verb *to be,* some as part of passive constructions. You need not eliminate all passive voice, but do look for wording that is vague and ineffective. Your edited version should be not only stronger but shorter.

   > Although emergency shelters are needed in some cases (for example, a mother fleeing domestic violence), they are an inefficient means of dealing with the massive numbers of people they are bombarded with each day. The members of a homeless family are in need of a home, not a temporary shelter into which they and others like them are herded, only to be shuffled out when their thirty-day stay is over to make room for the next incoming herd. Emergency shelters would be sufficient if we did not have a low-income housing shortage, but what is needed most at present is an increase in availability of affordable housing for the poor.

2. Select a paragraph of your own writing to edit; focus on using strong verbs and subjects to carry the main idea of your sentences.

## Editing for Emphasis

When you edit for emphasis, you make sure that your main ideas stand out so that your reader will take notice. Following are some suggestions to help.

### Emphasize Main Ideas by Subordinating Less Important Ones

*Subordination* refers to distinctions in rank or order of importance. Think of the chain of command at an office: the boss is at the top of the ladder, the middle management is on a lower (subordinate) rung, the support staff is at an even lower rung, and so on.

In writing, subordination means placing less important ideas in less important positions in sentences in order to emphasize the main ideas that should stand out. Writing that lacks subordination treats all ideas equally; each idea may consist of a sentence of its own or may be joined to another idea by a coordinator (*and, but,* and *or*). Such a passage follows with its sentences numbered for reference purposes.

> (1) It has been over a century since slavery was abolished and a few decades since lawful, systematic segregation came to an unwilling halt. (2) Truly, blacks

have come a long way from the darker days that lasted for more than three centuries. (3) Many blacks have entered the mainstream, and there is a proportionately large contingent of middle-class blacks. (4) Yet an even greater percentage of blacks are immersed in truly pathetic conditions. (5) The inner-city black poor are enmeshed in devastating socioeconomic problems. (6) Unemployment among inner-city black youths has become much worse than it was even five years ago.

Three main ideas are important here — that blacks have been free for some time, that some have made economic progress, and that others are trapped in poverty — and of these three, the last is probably intended to be the most important. Yet, as we read the passage, these key ideas do not stand out. In fact, each point receives equal emphasis and sounds about the same, with the repeated subject-verb-object syntax. The result seems monotonous, even apathetic, though the writer is probably truly disturbed about the subject. The following edited version, which subordinates some of the points, is more emphatic. We have italicized the main points.

> *Blacks have come a long way* in the century since slavery was abolished and in the decades since lawful, systematic segregation came to an unwilling halt. Yet, although many blacks have entered the mainstream and the middle class, *an even greater percentage is immersed in truly pathetic conditions.* To give just one example of these devastating socioeconomic problems, *unemployment among inner-city black youths is much worse now than it was even five years ago.*

Although different editing choices are possible, this version plays down sentences 1, 3, and 5 in the original so that sentences 2, 4, and 6 stand out.

As you edit, look for passages that sound wordy and flat because all the ideas are expressed with equal weight in the same subject-verb-object pattern. Then single out your most important points, and try out some options for subordinating the less important ones. The key is to put main ideas in main clauses and modifying ideas in modifying clauses or phrases.

*Modifying Clauses*   Like simple sentences, modifying clauses contain a subject and verb. They are formed in two ways: (1) with relative pronouns and (2) with subordinating conjunctions.

*Relative pronouns* introduce clauses that modify nouns, with the relative pronoun relating the clause to the noun it modifies. There are five relative pronouns: *that, which, who, whose,* and *whom.* The following sentence contains a relative clause:

> Alcohol advertisers are trying to sell a product *that is by its very nature harmful to users.*
>
> —JASON RATH (student)

Relative pronouns may also be implied:

> I have returned the library book [that] *you loaned me.*

Relative pronouns may also be preceded by prepositions, such as *on, in, to,* or *during:*

> Drug hysteria has created an atmosphere *in which civil rights are disregarded.*

*Subordinating conjunctions* show relationships among ideas. It is impossible to provide a complete list of subordinating conjunctions in this short space, but here are the most common and the kinds of modifying roles they perform:

> To show time: *after, as, before, since, until, when, while*
> To show place: *where, wherever*
> To show contrast: *although, though, whereas, while*
> To show cause and effect: *because, since, so that*
> To show condition: *if, unless, whether, provided that*
> To show manner: *how, as though*

By introducing it with a subordinating conjunction, you can convert one sentence into a dependent clause that can modify another sentence. Consider the following two versions of the same idea:

> Pain is a state of consciousness, a "mental event." It can never be directly observed.

> *Since pain is a state of consciousness, a "mental event,"* it can never be directly observed.
>
> —PETER SINGER, "Animal Liberation"

*Modifying Phrases*   Unlike clauses, phrases do not have a subject and a verb. Prepositional phrases and infinitive phrases are most likely already in your repertoire of modifiers. (Consult a handbook if you need to review these.) Here, we remind you of two other useful types of phrases: (1) participial phrases and (2) appositives.

*Participial phrases* modify nouns. Participles are created from verbs, so it is not surprising that the two varieties represent two verb tenses. The first is present participles ending in *-ing:*

> *Hoping to eliminate harassment on campus,* many universities have tried to institute codes for speech and behavior.

> The desperate Haitians fled here in boats, *risking all.*
>
> —CARMEN HAZAN-COHEN (student)

The second is past participles ending in *-ed, -en, -d, -t,* or *-n:*

> Women themselves became a resource, *acquired by men much as the land was acquired by men.*
>
> —GERDA LERNER

> *Linked more to the Third World and Asia than to the Europe of America's racial and cultural roots,* Los Angeles and Southern California will enter the 21st century as a multi-racial and multicultural society.
>
> —RYSZARD KAPUSCINSKI

Notice that modifying phrases should immediately precede the nouns they modify.

An *appositive* is a noun or noun phrase that restates another noun, usually in a more specific way. Appositives can be highly emphatic, but more often they are tucked into the middle of a sentence or added to the end, allowing a subordinate idea to be slipped in. When used like this, appositives are usually set off with commas:

> Rick Halperin, *a professor at Southern Methodist University,* noted that Ted Bundy's execution cost Florida taxpayers over six million dollars.
>
> —DIANE MILLER (student)

### Editing Practice

1. Edit the following passage as needed for emphasis, clarity, and conciseness, using subordinate clauses, relative clauses, participial phrases, appositives, and any other options that occur to you. If some parts are effective as they are, leave them alone.

   > The monetary implications of drug legalization are not the only reason it is worth consideration. There is reason to believe that the United States would be a safer place to live if drugs were legalized. A large amount of what the media has named "drug-related" violence is really prohibition-related violence. Included in this are random shootings and murders associated with black-market transactions. Estimates indicate that at least 40 percent of all property crime in the United States is committed by drug users so they can maintain their habits. That amounts to a total of 4 million crimes per year and $7.5 billion in stolen property. Legalizing drugs would be a step toward reducing this wave of crime.

2. Edit a paragraph of your own writing with an eye to subordinating less important ideas through the use of modifying phrases and clauses.

### Vary Sentence Length and Pattern

Even when read silently, your writing has a sound. If your sentences are all about the same length (typically fifteen to twenty words) and all structured according to a subject-verb-object pattern, they will roll along with the monotonous rhythm of an assembly line. Obviously, one solution to this problem is to open some of your sentences with modifying phrases and clauses, as we discuss in the previous section. Here we offer some other strategies, all of which add emphasis by introducing something unexpected.

1. Use a short sentence after several long ones.

   > [A] population's general mortality is affected by a great many factors over which doctors and hospitals have little influence. For those diseases and injuries for which modern medicine can affect the outcome, however, which country the patient lives in really matters. Life expectancy is not the same among developed countries for premature babies, for children

> born with spina bifida, or for people who have cancer, a brain tumor, heart disease, or chronic renal failure. *Their chances of survival are best in the United States.*
>
> —JOHN GOODMAN

2. Interrupt a sentence.

> The position of women in that hippie counterculture was, *as a young black male leader preached succinctly,* "prone."
>
> —BETTY FRIEDAN

> Symbols and myths—*when emerging uncorrupted from human experience*—are precious. Then it is the poetic voice and vision that informs and in-fuses—*the poet-warrior's, the prophet-seer's, the dreamer's*—reassuring us that truth is as real as falsehood. And ultimately stronger.
>
> —OSSIE DAVIS

3. Use an intentional sentence fragment. The concluding fragment in the previous passage by Ossie Davis is a good example.
4. Invert the order of subject-verb-object.

> Further complicating negotiations is the difficulty of obtaining relevant financial statements.
>
> —REGINA HERZLINGER

> This creature, with scarcely two thirds of man's cranial capacity, was a fire user. Of what it meant to him beyond warmth and shelter, we know nothing; with what rites, ghastly or benighted, it was struck or main-tained, no word remains.
>
> —LOREN EISELY

## Use Special Effects for Emphasis

Especially in persuasive argumentation, you will want to make some of your points in deliberately dramatic ways. Remember that just as the crescendos stand out in music because the surrounding passages are less intense, so the special effects work best in rhetoric when you use them sparingly.

*Repetition*   Deliberately repeating words, phrases, or sentence patterns has the effect of building up to a climactic point. In Chapter 8, we noted how Martin Luther King, Jr., in the emotional high point of his "Letter from Bir-mingham Jail," used repeated subordinate clauses beginning with the phrase "when you" to build up to his main point: ". . . then you will understand why we find it difficult to wait" (paragraph 14, pages 261–262). Here is another example, from the conclusion of an argument linking women's rights with environmental reforms:

> Environmental justice goes much further than environmental protection, a pas-sive and paternalistic phrase. *Justice requires that* industrial nations pay back the environmental debt incurred in building their wealth by using less of nature's resources. *Justice prescribes that* governments stop siting hazardous waste facili-

ties in cash-poor rural and urban neighborhoods and now in the developing world. *Justice insists that* the subordination of women and nature by men is not only a hazard; it is a crime. *Justice reminds us that* the Earth does not belong to us; even when we "own" a piece of it, we belong to the Earth.

—H. PATRICIA HYNES

***Paired Coordinators***   Coordinators are conjunctions that pair words, word groups, and sentences in a way that gives them equal emphasis and that also shows a relationship between them, such as contrast, consequence, or addition. In grade school, you may have learned the coordinators through the mnemonic *FANBOYS*, standing for *for, and, nor, but, or, yet, so.*

Paired coordinators emphasize the relationship between coordinated elements; the first coordinator signals that a corresponding coordinator will follow. Some paired coordinators are:

both _____ and _____

not _____ but _____

not only _____ but also _____

either _____ or _____

neither _____ nor _____

The key to effective paired coordination is to keep the words that follow the marker words as grammatically similar as possible. Pair nouns with nouns, verbs with verbs, prepositional phrases with prepositional phrases, and whole sentences with whole sentences. (Think of paired coordination as a variation on repetition.) Here are some examples:

Feminist anger, or any form of social outrage, is dismissed breezily—*not* because it lacks substance *but* because it lacks "style."

—SUSAN FALUDI

Alcohol ads that emphasize "success" in the business and social worlds are useful examples *not only* of how advertisers appeal to people's envy *but also* of how ads perpetuate gender stereotypes.

—JASON RATH (student)

***Emphatic Appositives***   While an appositive (a noun or noun phrase that restates another noun) can subordinate an idea, it can also emphasize an idea if it is placed at the beginning or the end of a sentence, where it will command attention. Here are some examples:

*The poorest nation in the Western hemisphere,* Haiti is populated by six million people, many of whom cannot obtain adequate food, water, or shelter.

—SNEED B. COLLARD III

[Feminists] made a simple, though serious, ideological error when they applied the same political rhetoric to their own situation as women versus men: *too literal an analogy with class warfare, racial oppression.*

—BETTY FRIEDAN

Note that at the end of a sentence, an appositive may be set off with a colon or a dash.

*Emphatic Word Order* The opening and closing positions of a sentence are high-profile spots, not to be wasted on weak words. The following sentence, for example, begins weakly with the filler phrase "there are":

> *There are* several distinctions, all of them false, that are commonly made between rape and date rape.

A better version would read:

> My opponents make several distinctions between rape and date rape; all of these are false.

Even more important are the final words of every paragraph and the opening and closing of the entire argument.

*Editing Practice*

1. Select one or two paragraphs from a piece of published writing you have recently read and admired. Be ready to share it with the class, explaining how the writer has crafted the passage to make it work.
2. Take a paragraph or two from one of your previous essays, perhaps even an essay from another course, and edit it to improve clarity, conciseness, and emphasis.

## Editing for Coherence

Coherence refers to what some people call the "flow" of writing; writing flows when the ideas connect smoothly, one to the next. In contrast, when writing is incoherent, the reader must work to see how ideas connect and must infer points that the writer, for whatever reason, has left unstated.

Incoherence is a particular problem with writing that contains an abundance of direct or indirect quotations. In using sources, be careful always to lead into the quotation with some words of your own, showing clearly how this new idea connects with what has come before.

Because finding incoherent passages in your own writing can be difficult, ask a friend to read your draft to look for gaps in the presentation of ideas. Here are some additional suggestions for improving coherence.

*Move from Old Information to New Information*

Coherent writing is easy to follow because the connections between old information and new information are clear. Sentences refer back to previously introduced information and set up reader expectations for new information to come. Notice how every sentence fulfills your expectations in the following excerpts from an argument on animal rights by Steven Zak.

> The credibility of the animal-rights viewpoint . . . need not stand or fall with the "marginal human beings" argument.

Next, you would expect to hear why animals do not have to be classed as "marginal human beings"—and you do:

> Lives don't have to be qualitatively the same to be worthy of equal respect.

At this point you might ask upon what else we should base our respect. Zak answers this question in the next sentence:

> One's perception that another life has value comes as much from an appreciation of its uniqueness as from the recognition that it has characteristics that are shared by one's own life.

Not only do these sentences fulfill reader expectations, but each also makes a clear connection by referring specifically to the key idea in the sentence before it, forming an unbroken chain of thought. We have italicized the words that accomplish this linkage and connected them with arrows.

> The credibility of the animal rights viewpoint . . . need not stand or fall with the *"marginal human beings"* argument.

> Lives don't have to be *qualitatively the same* to be worthy of *equal respect.*

> One's perception that *another life has value* comes as much from an *appreciation of its uniqueness* as from the recognition that it has characteristics that are shared by one's own life.

> One can imagine that the lives of various kinds of animals *differ radically.* . . .

In the following paragraph, reader expectations are not so well fulfilled:

> We are presently witness to the greatest number of homeless families since the Great Depression of the 1930s. The cause of this phenomenon is a shortage of low-income housing. Mothers with children as young as two weeks are forced to live on the street because there is no room for them in homeless shelters.

While these sentences are all on the subject of homelessness, the second leads us to expect that the third will take up the topic of shortages of low-income housing. Instead, it takes us back to the subject of the first sentence and offers a different cause—no room in the shelters.

Looking for ways to link old information with new information will help you find problems of coherence in your own writing.

### Editing Practice

1. In the following paragraph, underline the words or phrases that make the connections back to the previous sentence and forward to the next, as we did earlier with the passage from Zak.

The affluent, educated, liberated women of the First World, who can enjoy freedoms unavailable to any women ever before, do not feel as free as they want to. And they can no longer restrict to the subconscious their sense that this lack of freedom has something to do with—with apparently frivolous issues, things that really should not matter. Many are ashamed to admit that such trivial concerns—to do with physical appearance, bodies, faces, hair, clothes—matter so much. But in spite of shame, guilt, and denial, more and more women are wondering if it isn't that they are entirely neurotic alone but rather that something important is indeed at stake that has to do with the relationship between female liberation and female beauty.

—NAOMI WOLF

2. The following student paragraph lacks coherence. Read through it, and put a slash (/) between sentences expressing unconnected ideas. You may try to rewrite the paragraph, rearranging sentences and adding ideas to make the connections tighter.

Students may know what AIDS is and how it is transmitted, but most are not concerned about AIDS and do not perceive themselves to be at risk. But college-age heterosexuals are the number-one high-risk group for this disease (Gray and Sacarino 258). "Students already know about AIDS. Condom distribution, public or not, is not going to help. It just butts into my personal life," said one student surveyed. College is a time for exploration and that includes the discovery of sexual freedom. Students, away from home and free to make their own decisions for maybe the first time in their lives, have a "bigger than life" attitude. The thought of dying is the farthest from their minds. Yet at this point in their lives, they are most in need of this information.

## Use Transitions to Show Relationships between Ideas

Coherence has to be built into a piece of writing; as we discussed earlier, the ideas between sentences must first cohere. However, sometimes readers need help in making the transition from one idea to the next, so you must provide signposts to help them see the connections more readily. For example, a transitional word like *however* can prepare readers for an idea in contrast to the one before it, as in the second sentence in this paragraph. Transitional words can also highlight the structure of an argument ("These data will show three things: first . . . , second . . . , and third . . ."), almost forming a verbal path for the reader to follow. Following are examples of transitional words and phrases and their purposes:

To show order: *first, second, next, then, last, finally*
To show contrast: *however, yet, but, nevertheless*
To show cause and effect: *therefore, consequently, as a result, then*
To show importance: *moreover, significantly*

To show an added point: *as well, also, too*
To show an example: *for example, for instance*
To show concession: *admittedly*
To show conclusion: *in sum, in conclusion*

The key to using transitional words is similar to the key to using special effects for emphasis: Don't overdo it. To avoid choking your writing with these words, anticipate where your reader will genuinely need them, and limit their use to these instances.

### Editing Practice

Underline the transitional words and phrases in the following passage of published writing:

> When people believe that their problems can be solved, they tend to get busy solving them.
>
> On the other hand, when people believe that their problems are beyond solution, they tend to position themselves so as to avoid blame. Take the woeful inadequacy of education in the predominantly black central cities. Does the black leadership see the ascendancy of black teachers, school administrators, and politicians as an asset to be used in improving those dreadful schools? Rarely. You are more likely to hear charges of white abandonment, white resistance to integration, conspiracies to isolate black children, even when the schools are officially desegregated. In short, white people are accused of being responsible for the problem. But if the youngsters manage to survive those awful school systems and achieve success, leaders want to claim credit. They don't hesitate to attribute that success to the glorious Civil Rights movement.
>
> —WILLIAM RASPBERRY

## PROOFREADING

Proofreading is truly the final step in writing a paper. After proofreading, you ought to be able to print your paper out one more time; but if you do not have time, most instructors will be perfectly happy to see the necessary corrections done neatly in ink on the final draft.

Following are some suggestions for proofreading.

### Spelling Errors

If you have used a word processor, you may have a program that will check your spelling. If not, you will have to check your spelling by reading through again carefully with a dictionary at hand. Consult the dictionary whenever you feel uncertain. You might consider devoting a special part of your writer's notebook to your habitual spelling errors: some students always misspell *athlete*, for example, whereas others leave the second *n* out of *environment*.

## Omissions and Jumbled Passages

Read your paper out loud. Physically shaping your lips around the words can help locate missing words, typos (*saw* instead of *was*), or the remnants of some earlier version of a sentence that did not get fully deleted. Place a caret (∧) in the sentence and write the correction or addition above the line, or draw a line through unnecessary text.

## Punctuation Problems

Apostrophes and commas give writers the most trouble. If you have habitual problems with these, you should record your errors in your writer's notebook.

### Apostrophes

Apostrophe problems usually occur in forming possessives, not contractions, so here we discuss only the former. If you have problems with possessives, you may also want to consult a good handbook or seek a private tutorial with your instructor or your school's writing center.

Here are the basic principles to remember.

1. Possessive pronouns—*his, hers, yours, theirs, its*—never take an apostrophe.
2. Singular nouns become possessive by adding -'s.

   A single parent's life is hard.

   A society's values change.

   Do you like Mr. Voss's new car?

3. Plural nouns ending in -s become possessive by simply adding an apostrophe.

   Her parents' marriage is faltering.

   Many cities' air is badly polluted.

   The Joneses' house is up for sale.

4. Plural nouns that do not end in -s become possessive by adding -'s.

   Show me the women's (men's) room.

   The people's voice was heard.

If you err by using apostrophes where they don't belong in nonpossessive words ending in -s, remember that a possessive will always have a noun after it, not some other part of speech such as a verb or a preposition. You may even need to read each line of print with a ruler under it to help you focus more intently on each word.

### Commas

Because commas indicate a pause, reading your paper aloud is a good way to decide where to add or delete them. A good handbook will elaborate on the following basic principles. The example sentences have been adapted from an argument by Mary Meehan, who opposes abortion.

1. Use a comma when you join two or more main clauses with a coordinating conjunction.

   *Main clause, conjunction* (and, but, or, nor, so, yet) *main clause.*

   Feminists want to have men participate more in the care of children, but abortion allows a man to shift total responsibility to the woman.

2. Use a comma after an introductory phrase or dependent clause.

   *Introductory phrase or clause, main clause.*

   To save the smallest children, the Left should speak out against abortion.

3. Use commas around modifiers such as relative clauses and appositives unless they are essential to the noun's meaning. Be sure to put the comma at both ends of the modifier.

   _____, *appositive,* _____

   _____, *relative clause,* _____

   One member of the 1972 Presidential commission on population growth was Graciela Olivarez, a Chicana who was active in civil rights and anti-poverty work. Olivarez, who later was named to head the Federal Government's Community Services Administration, had known poverty in her youth in the Southwest.

4. Use commas with a series.

   ___x___ , ___y___ , and ___z___ ,

   The traditional mark of the Left has been its protection of the underdog, the weak, and the poor.

## Semicolons

Think of a semicolon as a strong comma. It has two main uses.

1. Use a semicolon to join two main clauses when you choose not to use a conjunction. This works well when the two main clauses are closely related or parallel in structure.

   *Main clause; main clause.*

   Pro-life activists did not want abortion to be a class issue; they wanted to end abortion everywhere, for all classes.

   As a variation, you may wish to add a transitional adverb to the second main clause. The adverb indicates the relationship between the main clauses, but it is not a conjunction, so a comma preceding it would not be correct.

*Main clause; transitional adverb* (however, therefore, thus, moreover, consequently), *main clause.*

When speaking with counselors at the abortion clinic, many women change their minds and decide against abortion; however, a woman who is accompanied by a husband or boyfriend often does not feel free to talk with the counselor.

2. Use semicolons between items in a series if any of the items themselves contain commas.

\_\_\_\_\_,\_\_\_\_; \_\_\_\_,\_\_\_\_; \_\_\_\_,\_\_\_\_

A few liberals who have spoken out against abortion are Jesse Jackson, a Civil Rights leader; Richard Neuhaus, a theologian; the comedian Dick Gregory; and politicians Mark Hatfield and Mary Rose Oakar.

*Colons*

The colon has two common uses.

1. Use a colon to introduce a quotation when both your own lead-in and the words quoted are complete sentences that can stand alone. (See the section in Chapter 5 entitled "Incorporating and Documenting Source Material in the Text of Your Argument" for more on introducing quotations.)

*Main clause in your words: "Quoted sentence(s)."*

Mary Meehan criticizes liberals who have been silent on abortion: "If much of the leadership of the pro-life movement is right-wing, that is due largely to the default of the Left."

2. Use a colon before an appositive that comes dramatically at the end of a sentence, especially if the appositive contains more than one item.

*Main clause: appositive, appositive, and appositive.*

Meehan argues that many pro-choice advocates see abortion as a way to hold down the population of certain minorities: blacks, Puerto Ricans, and other Latins.

## Grammatical Errors

Grammatical mistakes can be hard to find, but once again we suggest reading aloud as one method of proofing for them; grammatical errors tend not to "sound right" even if they look like good prose. Another suggestion is to recognize your habitual errors and then look for particular grammatical structures that lead you into error.

## *Introductory Participial Phrases*

Constructions such as these often lead writers to create dangling modifiers. To avoid this pitfall, see the discussion of participial phrases earlier in this appendix. Remember that an introductory phrase dangles if it is not immediately followed by the noun it modifies.

> *Incorrect:* Using her conscience as a guide, our society has granted each woman the right to decide if a fetus is truly a "person" with rights equal to her own.

(Notice that the implied subject of the participial phrase is "each woman," when in fact the subject of the main clause is "our society"; thus, the participial phrase does not modify the subject.)

> *Corrected:* Using her conscience as a guide, each woman in our society has the right to decide if a fetus is truly a "person" with rights equal to her own.

## *Paired Coordinators*

If the words that follow each of the coordinators are not of the same grammatical structure, then an error known as nonparallelism has occurred. To correct this error, line up the paired items one over the other. You will see that the correction often involves simply adding a word or two to, or deleting some words from, one side of the paired coordinators.

> not only _____ but also _____
>
> *Incorrect:* Legal abortion not only protects women's lives, but also their health.
>
> *Corrected:* Legal abortion protects not only women's lives but also their health.

## *Split Subjects and Verbs*

If the subject of a sentence contains long modifying phrases or clauses, by the time you get to the verb you may make an error in agreement (using a plural verb, for example, when the subject is singular) or even in logic (for example, having a subject that is not capable of being the agent that performs the action of the verb). Following are some typical errors:

> The *goal* of the courses grouped under the rubric of "Encountering Non-Western Cultures" *are* . . .

Here the writer forgot that *goal*, the subject, is singular.

> During 1992, *the Refugee Act of 1980*, with the help of President Bush and Congress, *accepted* 114,000 immigrants into our nation.

The writer here should have realized that the agent doing the accepting would have to be the Bush administration, not the Refugee Act. A better version would read:

During 1992, the Bush administration accepted 114,000 immigrants into our nation under the terms of the Refugee Act of 1980.

## Proofreading Practice

Proofread the following passage for errors of grammar and punctuation.

The citizens of Zurich, Switzerland tired of problems associated with drug abuse, experimented with legalization. The plan was to open a central park, Platzspitz, where drugs and drug use would be permitted. Many European experts felt, that it was the illegal drug business rather than the actual use of drugs that had caused many of the cities problems. While the citizens had hoped to isolate the drug problem, foster rehabilitation, and curb the AIDS epidemic, the actual outcome of the Platzspitz experiment did not create the desired results. Instead, violence increased. Drug-related deaths doubled. And drug users were drawn from not only all over Switzerland, but from all over Europe as well. With thousands of discarded syringe packets lying around, one can only speculate as to whether the spread of AIDS was curbed. The park itself was ruined and finally on February 10, 1992, it was barred up and closed. After studying the Swiss peoples' experience with Platzspitz, it is hard to believe that some advocates of drug legalization in the United States are urging us to participate in the same kind of experiment.

# Glossary

**agent-action:** Technical term for a sentence in "who-does-what" form.

**alliteration:** The repetition of consonant sounds.

**annotation:** A brief critical commentary on a text or section of text.

**apologia:** An effort to explain and justify what one has done, or chosen not to do, in the face of condemnation or at least widespread disapproval or misunderstanding.

**argument:** Mature reasoning; a considered opinion backed by a reason or reasons.

**bibliography:** A list of works on a particular topic.

**case strategy:** The moves a writer makes to shape a particular argument, including selecting reasons, ordering them, developing evidence, and linking the sections of the argument for maximum impact.

**case structure:** A flexible plan for making any argument to any audience; it consists of one or more theses, each of which is supported by one or more reasons, each of which is supported by evidence.

**claim:** In argument, what the author wants the audience to believe or to do.

**connotation:** What a word implies or what we associate it with; see also *denotation*.

**conviction:** An earned opinion achieved through careful thought, research, and discussion.

**convincing:** One of the four aims of argument; to use reasoning to secure the assent of people who do not share the author's conviction.

**critical reading:** A close reading involving analyzing and evaluating a text.

**denotation:** A word's literal meaning; see also *connotation*.

**dialectic:** Dialogue or serious conversation; the ancient Greeks' term for argument as inquiry.

**graphics:** Visual supplements to a longer text such as an essay, article, or manual.

**identification:** A strong linking of the readers' interests and values with an image, which represents something desired or potentially desirable.

**implied question:** A question that is inherent in an argument but not explicitly stated; all statements of opinion are answers to questions, usually implied ones.

**inquiry:** One of the four aims of argument; to use reasoning to determine the best position on an issue.

**issue:** An aspect of a topic that presents a problem, the solution to which people disagree about.

**middle style:** A style of persuasive writing that is neither stiff and formal nor chatty and familiar.

**negotiation:** One of the four aims of argument; using reason and understanding to bring about consensus among disagreeing parties or positions.

**paraphrase:** To restate someone else's writing or speech in one's own words.

**persuasion:** One of the four aims of argument; persuasion uses both rational and emotional appeals to influence not just thinking but also behavior.

**plagiarism:** The act of presenting someone else's words and/or ideas as one's own, without acknowledging the source.

**position:** An overall, summarizing attitude or judgment about some issue.

**rhetoric:** The art of argument as mature reasoning.

**rhetorical context:** The circumstances surrounding the text as an act of communication: the time and place in which it was written; its place of publication; its author and his or her values; the ongoing, historical debate to which it contributes.

**rhetorical prospectus:** A plan for proposed writing that includes a statement of the thesis, aim, audience, speaker's persona, subject matter, and organizational plan.

**sampling:** A fast, superficial, not necessarily sequential reading of a text, not to learn all that a text has to say but to get a feeling for the territory it covers.

**thesis:** In argumentation, a very specific position statement that is strategically designed to appeal to readers and to be consistent with available evidence.

**topic:** A subject or aspect of a subject; see also *issue.*

**visual rhetoric:** The use of images, sometimes coupled with sound or appeals to the other senses, to make an argument or persuade one's audience to act as the image-maker would have them act.

# Credits

## Text Credits

CHARLES KRAUTHAMMER, "The Enemy Is Not Islam: It Is Nihilism" by Charles Krautham-mer who is a contributing editor of *The Weekly Standard* magazine, where this article originally appeared (October 22, 2001). It is reprinted with Dr. Krauthammer's permission.

JIM LANDERS, "The Roots of Conflict" from *The Dallas Morning News*, October 28, 2001, sec-tion J, p. 5 and "Bin Laden Allies Want Islamic Unity" from *The Dallas Morning News*, October 21, 2001, page 1 A. Reprinted with permission.

CASSANDRA LANGER, "What is Feminism?" from *A Feminist Critique* by Cassandra Langer. Copyright © 1996 by Westview Press. Reprinted by permission of Westview Press, a member of Perseus Books, L.L.C.

BARBARA LEBEY, "American Families Are Drifting Apart". Copyright © September 2001 by the Society for the Advancement of Education Inc. Reprinted by permission from *USA To-day* magazine.

ARTHUR LEVINE AND JEANNETTE S. CURETON, "Collegiate Life: An Obituary." *Change*, May–June 1998, 30, pp. 12–19. Reprinted with permission of the Helen Dwight Reid Edu-cational Foundation. Copyright © 1998 Heldref Publications. Published by Heldref Publications, 1319 Eighteenth St., NW, Washington, DC 20036-1802.

STEVEN LEVY, "Technology: A High-Tech Homefront" from *Newsweek*, October 8, 2001. Copyright © 2001 Newsweek, Inc. All rights reserved. Reprinted by permission.

MICHAEL LIND, "The Beige and the Black." Copyright © 1998 Michael Lind. Reprinted by per-mission of International Creative Management, Inc.

ANDRES MARTIN, "On Teenagers and Tattoos." *Journal of Child and Adolescent Psychiatry*, 1997, 36(6), pp. 860–861. Copyright © 1997 by the American Academy of Child and Ado-lescent Psychiatry. Reprinted by permission of Lippincott, Williams & Wilkins.

WILLIAM F. MAY, "Rising to the Occasion of our Death." Copyright © 1993 Christian Century Foundation. Reprinted with permission from the July 11, 1993, issue of the *Christian Century*. Subscriptions: $49/yr. from P. O. Box 378, Mt. Morris, IL 61054.

MARGARET LIU MCCONNELL, "Living with *Roe v. Wade.*" *Commentary*, November 1990. Used by permission of the author.

TONI A. H. MCNARON, from "In or Out in the Classroom," which appears in *Poisoned Ivy: Les-bian and Gay Academics Confronting Homophobia*, by Toni A. H. McNaron, pages 31–41 and 52–60. Reprinted by permission of Temple University Press. © 1997 by Temple University. All Rights Reserved.

JEFFREY NICKEL, "Everybody's Threatened by Homophobia." *Christopher Street*, Issue 185, Au-gust 17, 1992. Reprinted with permission.

JOHN O'SULLIVAN, "Their Amerika; The Song of the 'Counter-Tribalists'" from *National Re-view*, October 15, 2001. Copyright © 2001 by National Review, Inc., 215 Lexington Avenue, New York, NY 10016. Reprinted by permission.

JOSEPH PICKETT et al, definition of "mature," "critical" and "agent." Copyright © 2000 by Houghton Mifflin Company. Reproduced by permission from *The American Heritage Dictionary of the English Language, Fourth Edition*.

LEONARD PITTS, JR., "You Also Have the Right to Tell a Bigot What You Think" from *Miami Herald*, March 1, 2001. Copyright © 2002 by Miami Herald. Reproduced with permis-sion of Miami Herald in the format Textbook via Copyright Clearance Center.

KATHA POLITT, "Women's Rights: As the World Turns" originally published in *The Nation*, March 29, 1999. Reprinted by permission.

DAVID POPENOE, "A World Without Fathers" from *Life Without Father*, NY: The Free Press, 1996. Reprinted by permission of the author.

JERROLD M. POST, "Terrorist Psycho-Logic: Terrorist Behavior as a Product of Psychological Forces" from *Origins of Terrorism*, edited by Walter Reich, 1990. Reprinted with the per-mission of Cambridge University Press and Woodrow Wilson Center Press.

JAMES RACHELS, "The End of Life" by James Rachels. Copyright © 1986 James Rachels. Re-printed from *The End of Life: Euthanasia and Morality* by James Rachels (1986) by per-mission of Oxford University Press.

BARBARA DAFOE WHITEHEAD, "The Making of a Divorce Culture" from *The Divorce Culture* by Barbara Dafoe Whitehead. Copyright © 1996 by Barbara Dafoe Whitehead. Used by permission of Alfred A. Knopf, a division of Random House, Inc.

PAUL WILKINSON, "Analysis of Terrorist Weapons and the Liberal State Response" and "The Emergence of Modern Terrorism" from *Terrorism Versus Democracy.* Copyright © 2001 Frank Cass Publishers. Reprinted by permission.

PATRICIA J. WILLIAMS, "The Distribution of Distress" from *Seeing A Color-Blind Future: The Paradox of Race* by Patricia J. Williams. Copyright © 1997 by Patricia J. Williams. Reprinted by permission of Farrar, Straus and Giroux, LLC.

JOAN WILLIAMS, "Reconstructive Feminism" from *Unbending Gender* by Joan Williams. Copyright © 1999 by Oxford University Press, Inc. Used by permission of Oxford University Press, Inc.

ELLEN WILLIS, "Putting Women Back into the Abortion Debate." Copyright © Ellen Willis. Reprinted by permission of Charlotte Sheedy Literary Agency.

NAOMI WOLF, "The Beauty Myth" from *The Beauty Myth* by Naomi Wolf. Copyright © 1991 by Naomi Wolf. Reprinted by permission of HarperCollins Publishers Inc. (William Morrow).

RESHMA MEMON YAQUB, "'You People Did This.'" *Rolling Stone,* October 25, 2001, p. 81. Reprinted by permission of Reshma Memon Yaqub, Reshmay@aol.com.

STEPHEN ZUNES, "10 Things to Know about the Middle East" as appeared on Alternet.org, October 1, 2001. Used by permission of Stephen Zunes.

## *Photo Credits*

**Page 6** The J. Paul Getty Museum, Malibu, California. **Page 24** © The New Yorker Collection 1998 Roz Chast from cartoonbank.com. Reprinted by permisssion. **Page 29** Bill Aron/PhotoEdit. **Page 77** dePIXion studios. Reprinted by permission. **Page 78** (top) *The News Leader,* Staunton Virginia. Reprinted by permission; (bottom) Courtesy of Creators Syndicate. **Page 79** Courtesy of Creators Syndicate. **Page 80** Courtesy, Department of Defense. **Page 82** (top) © Barbara Alper/Stock Boston, Inc.; (bottom) © Richard Pasley/ Stock Boston, Inc. **Page 83** © Bruce Young/Corbis-Bettmann. **Page 87** By permission of Yan Nascimbene. **Page 91** © 1998 Terese Winslow. **Page 95** Stephen Rose/Liaison Agency. **Page 114** Courtesy, Library of Congress. **Page 114** Internet Explorer frame reprinted by permission from Microsoft Corporation. **Page 213** AP Photo/Kathy Willens. **Page 256** AP Photo/Gene Herrick. **Page 297** Paul Conklin/PhotoEdit. **Page 345** AP Photo/Patrick Sison. **Page 346** © AFP/Corbis. **Page 347** (top) AP Photo/Ernesto Mora; (bottom) AP Photo/Shawn Baldwin. **Page 348** (top) © AFP/Corbis; (bottom) © AFP/Corbis. **Page 349** AP Photo/Ed Betz. **Page 407** © AFP/Corbis. **Page 469** AP Photo/file. **Page 470** © Gary Kufner/Corbis. **Page 471** Courtesy of <www.divorcemag.com>. **Page 471** Internet Explorer frame reprinted by permission from Microsoft Corporation.**Page 472** Courtesy of the Human Resource Campaign. **Page 473** © The New Yorker Collection 1992 Roz Chast from cartoonbank.com. Reprinted by permisssion. **Page 474** © Pamela Strauss/Corbis. **Page 533** © The New Yorker Collection 1997 Tom Cheney from cartoonbank.com. Reprinted by permisssion. **Page 535** © Jim Goldberg. **Page 570** AP Photo/Bill Feig. **Page 622** AP Photo/Susan Ragan. **Page 637** Reprinted by permission of Kirk Anderson. **Page 654** © The New Yorker Collection 2001 Barbara Smaller from cartoonbank.com. Reprinted by permission. **Page 673** Doonesbury © 1987 G. B. Trudeau. Reprinted with permission of Universal Press Syndicate. All rights reserved. **Page 706** © Larry Kolvoord/The Image Works. **Page 719** Doonesbury © 1993 G. B. Trudeau. Reprinted with permission of Universal Press Syndicate. All rights reserved. **Page 749** AP Photo/Marty Lederhandler. **Page 772** © The New Yorker Collection 1998 Mike Twohy from cartoonbank.com. Reprinted by permission. **Page 790** © Steve Raymer/Corbis. **Page 804** © Lois Bernstein. **Page 840** (top) © Robert Crandall/The Image Works; (bottom) © Kathy McLaughlin/The Image Works. **Page 844** © Bruce Roberts/Photos Researchers, Inc. **Page 863** © A. Ramey/PhotoEdit.

# Index